AMOS

VOLUME 24A

THE ANCHOR BIBLE is a fresh approach to the world's greatest classic. Its object is to make the Bible accessible to the modern reader; its method is to arrive at the meaning of biblical literature through exact translation and extended exposition, and to reconstruct the ancient setting of the biblical story, as well as the circumstances of its transcription and the characteristics of its transcribers.

THE ANCHOR BIBLE is a project of international and interfaith scope. Protestant, Catholic, and Jewish scholars from many countries contribute individual volumes. The project is not sponsored by any ecclesiastical organization and is not intended to reflect any particular theological doctrine. Prepared under our joint supervision, THE ANCHOR BIBLE is an effort to make available all the significant historical and linguistic knowledge which bears on the interpretation of the biblical record.

THE ANCHOR BIBLE is aimed at the general reader with no special formal training in biblical studies; yet it is written with the most exacting standards of scholarship, reflecting the highest technical accomplishment.

This project marks the beginning of a new era of cooperation among scholars in biblical research, thus forming a common body of knowledge to be shared by all.

William Foxwell Albright
David Noel Freedman
GENERAL EDITORS

THE ANCHOR BIBLE

AMOS

A New Translation
with
Introduction and Commentary

Francis I. Andersen
and
David Noel Freedman

THE ANCHOR BIBLE
DOUBLEDAY
NEW YORK LONDON TORONTO SYDNEY AUCKLAND

The Anchor Bible
Published by Doubleday, a division of Bantam Doubleday
Dell Publishing Group, Inc., 666 Fifth Avenue, New York,
N.Y. 10103. **The Anchor Bible, Doubleday,** and the portrayal
of an anchor with the letters AB are trademarks of
Doubleday, a division of Bantam Doubleday Dell Publishing
Group, Inc.

Library of Congress
Library of Congress Cataloging-in-Publication Data

Bible. O.T. Amos. English. Andersen-Freedman. 1989.
Amos / a new translation with notes and commentary by
Francis I. Andersen and David Noel Freedman. — 1st ed.
p.   cm. — (The Anchor Bible ; v. 24A)
Bibliography: p.
Includes indexes.
ISBN 0-385-00773-6
1. Bible. O.T. Amos—Commentaries.   I. Andersen,
Francis   I., 1925–   .
II. Freedman, David Noel, 1922–   . III. Title.
IV. Series: Bible. English. Anchor Bible. 1964 ; v. 24A.
BS192.2.A1   1964.G3 vol. 24A
[BS1583]
220.7'7 s—dc19
[224'.8007]   87-34494
                                                               CIP

PREFACE

It is almost obligatory these days, especially in prefaces or prefatory remarks to quote Ecclesiastes 12:12:

> Book learning is an endless occupation,
> and much study is exhausting.

as part of an atavistic apotropaic rite or prophylactic procedure to justify yet one more bulky commentary on a thin book of Scripture—to exorcise the demons lying in wait at the door of the Temple of Learning or, more prosaically, to disarm and defuse the critics and reviewers ready to pounce.

In the case of the Anchor Bible commentary on Amos, however, a slight paraphrase or adaptation of the familiar bicolon would be more appropriate: of the making of this massive work there was, is, and would seem to be no end, and as to the weariness of the flesh, we could write even more if we had any energy left.

When we began our work on the eighth-century prophets of Israel (Hosea, Amos, Micah, Isaiah), we thought it best to deal with the books separately and together, because the prophets and their books exhibit a variety of links and connectors as well as striking differences. Such a procedure could and, we hoped, would produce both a sharper delineation of the distinctive features of each prophet, when examined in the light and against the background of the others, and a better understanding and synthesis of common elements or motifs. That way, also, successive volumes would express and reflect a more complete picture of the prophets and their work in the eighth century, and when the series was concluded, a group portrait might emerge that would fill the canvas or tapestry with all the rich detail of each of the books woven together.

Results do not always match expectations, and ends often outrun means or even intentions. As far as the general plan is concerned, we are right on target, only the progression seems to be veering from the arithmetic to the geometric. The second work is about twice as long as the first, and we have been able to expand the study of Amos on the basis of the work on Hosea. We also believe that we learned something from doing the earlier commentary and especially from the reviewers who went to great trouble to read the tome placed before them and to comment realistically and helpfully on the palpable shortcomings. While we hope that there are fewer of the latter in the new work, we can also say that there is more material on which to work. We make no predictions about the future but can promise that the work on the next of these prophets, Micah, is already well advanced and that it will incorporate what we learned from our previous works: how large the third undertaking will be and how long it will take are matters of urgent concern but beyond our power to predict. We need more help from our mentors, the prophets, than we have been able to get so far.

From the start we have focused our attention and concentrated our efforts on the text of the prophetic book.* In the contexts of the Bible, ancient Near Eastern literature, archaeology, and history, we have read it over and over, studied it, analyzed and interpreted it. We have made the rounds several times, and now it is time to stop and step off the carrousel. While we will never be finished with such work, we must present our findings to date and submit to the necessary, arduous, and immensely helpful responses of our colleagues, as well as of the reading public. The intention first and last is to explain the ancient literature and mediate the message of these extraordinary human beings, whose words still speak, whose thoughts still have currency.

After twenty years of hard labor, we, like Jacob, are worn out and ready to take leave of this phase of the enterprise and go on to the next work in the series. But before we do so, we must happily and gratefully acknowledge the vast contribution made to the completion of this work by many, many others—a list that includes many names from many places over many years. We fear that through some oversight, we may omit some or overlook others, but we nevertheless wish to set down the names of those who have helped us and without whose efforts the work would never have been brought to the present stage:

Colleagues, for insights and observations, for recommendations and material assistance (maps and pictures): Philip J. King and Shalom Paul.

Graduate assistants, especially with regard to the Bibliography, but in other ways as well: David Seely, Tim LaVallee, Belinda Bicknell, Lyn Fyfe, Gary Herion, and John David Pleins.

Secretarial help: Diane Feikema, Lynette Lowey, Gloria Reinhold, and Teresa Nehra.

A special and particular vote of thanks is owed to Dr. Astrid Beck for masterminding and coordinating the production of the final manuscript: this is the first of the Anchor Bible volumes to be produced through the computer and to be stored on diskettes as well as on paper.

DAVID NOEL FREEDMAN
Ann Arbor, Michigan
July 27, 1987

---

* Unless specifically noted, Bible translations are the authors' own.

CONTENTS

LIST OF ILLUSTRATIONS

PHOTOGRAPHS
following page 470

1. General view of Samaria.
2. Israelite masonry from Samaria.
3. Israelite masonry—"houses of hewn stone."
4. Israelite masonry—"a plastered wall."
5. "Mesad Hashavyahu" Letter.
6. Bronze copy of seal of "Shema, servant of Jeroboam."
7. "Woman in the window" ivory.
8. Altars from the high place (Holy of Holies)

MAPS

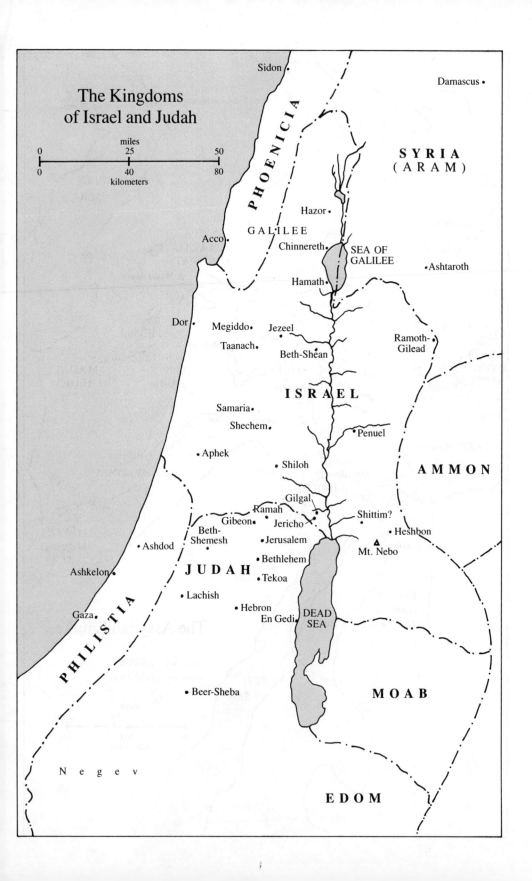

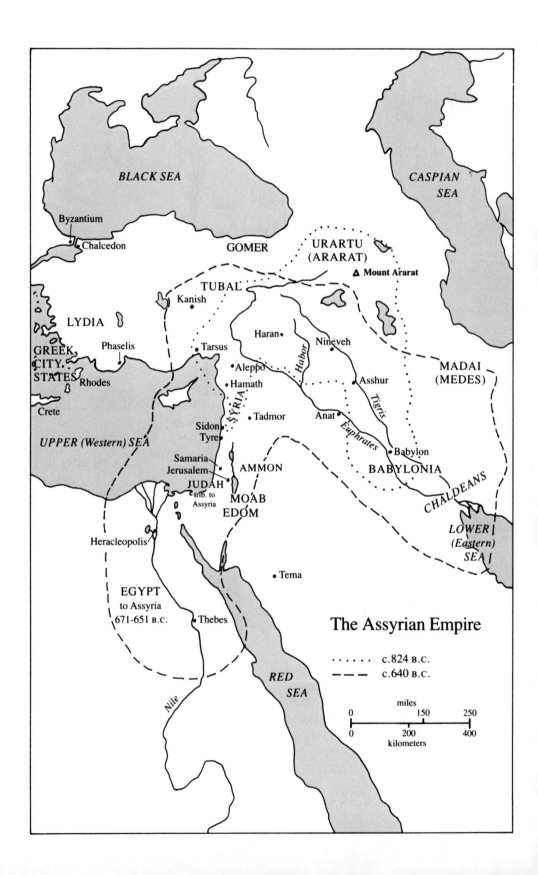

BLACK SEA

Byzantium
Chalcedon

GOMER

URARTU
(ARARAT)

△ Mount Ararat

CASPIAN
SEA

TUBAL

Kanish

LYDIA

Haran

Nineveh

MADAI
(MEDES)

GREEK
CITY
STATES

Phaselis

Tarsus

Aleppo

Habor

Rhodes

Hamath

Asshur

Crete

SYRIA

Tadmor

Anat

Tigris

UPPER (Western) SEA

Sidon
Tyre

Euphrates

Babylon

Samaria
Jerusalem

AMMON

BABYLONIA

JUDAH
trib. to
Assyria

MOAB
EDOM

CHALDEANS

Heracleopolis

LOWER
(Eastern)
SEA

Tema

EGYPT
to Assyria
671-651 B.C.

Thebes

The Assyrian Empire

Nile

RED
SEA

· · · · · ·   c.824 B.C.
– – –   c.640 B.C.

miles

0   150   250

0   200   400

kilometers

v(v)   verse(s)
VT   *Vetus Testamentum*
VTS   *Vetus Testamentum Supplements*
ZAW   *Zeitschrift für die alttestamentliche Wissenschaft*
ZDPV   *Zeitschrift des deutschen Palästina-Vereins*

LXX   Septuagint
  LXX^L   Lucianic recension
  LXX^B   Vaticanus
m.   masculine gender
MQR   *Michigan Quarterly Review*
MT   Masoretic Text
n.   note
NAB   New American Bible
NASB   New American Standard Bible
NEB   New English Bible
neg.   negative
NIV   New International Version
NJPS   The New Jewish Publication Society of America translations of the Holy Scriptures: *The Torah,* 2d ed., Philadelphia, 1967; *The Prophets: Nevi'im,* Philadelphia, 1978; *The Writings: Kethubim,* Philadelphia, 1978
NT   New Testament
OT   Old Testament
OTS   *Oudtestamentische Studiën*
P   Priestly Source
PEQ   *Palestine Exploration Quarterly*
pl.   plural
Q   Qumran
RHPR   *Revue d'histoire et de philosophie réligieuses*
RQ   *Revue de Qumrân*
RSV   Revised Standard Version
RTR   *Reformed Theological Review*
RV   Revised Version
s.   singular
SBL   Society of Biblical Literature
TB   Babylonian Talmud
TDOT   *Theological Dictionary of the Old Testament,* 5 vols., ed. G. J. Botterweck and H. Ringgren. Grand Rapids: Eerdmans, 1974–86
TEV   Today's English Version
Tg   Targum
TWAT   *Theologisches Wörterbuch zum Alten Testament,* 6 vols., ed. G. J. Botterweck, H. Ringgren, and H. J. Fabry. Stuttgart: Kohlhammer, 1970–88
TZ   *Theologische Zeitschrift*
UF   *Ugarit-Forschungen*
UT   C. H. Gordon, *Ugaritic Textbook.* Rome, 1965; Supplement, 1967

EAEHL	*Encyclopedia of Archaeological Excavations in the Holy Land.* 4 vols. Jerusalem: Massada Press, 1975–78.
EI	*Eretz Israel*
Enc Jud	*Encyclopaedia Judaica* (1971)
ExpT	*Expository Times*
f.	feminine gender
GKC	*Gesenius' Hebrew Grammar* (2d ed.), ed. E. Kautzsch, trans. A. E. Cowley. Oxford: Clarendon Press, 1910
H	Holiness code
HAT	Handbuch zum Alten Testament
Heb	Hebrew language
HTR	*Harvard Theological Review*
HUCA	*Hebrew Union College Annual*
IB	*Interpreter's Bible.* Nashville: Abingdon Press, 1951–57
IDB	*Interpreter's Dictionary of the Bible,* ed. G. A. Buttrick et al. Nashville: Abingdon Press, 1962
IDBSup	*Interpreter's Dictionary of the Bible: Supplementary Volume.* Nashville: Abingdon Press, 1976
IEJ	*Israel Exploration Journal*
inf.	infinitive
J	Yahwist
JAOS	*Journal of the American Oriental Society*
JB	Jerusalem Bible
JBL	*Journal of Biblical Literature*
JNES	*Journal of Near Eastern Studies*
JSOT	*Journal for the Study of the Old Testament*
JSS	*Journal of Semitic Studies*
JTS	*Journal of Theological Studies*
KAI	*Kanaanäische und aramäische Inschriften*
KAT	*Kommentar zum alten Testament,* ed. E. Sellin, cont. J. Herrmann
KB	L. Koehler and W. Baumgartner. *Lexicon in Veteris Testamenti Libros.* Leiden: Brill, 1958.
KJV	Authorized Version (= King James Version). *The Holy Bible Containing the Old and New Testaments.* New York: American Bible Society, n.d.
Krt	*Keret*
KTU	*Die keilalphabetischen Texte aus Ugarit.* M. Dietrich, O. Loretz, and J. Sanmartin. AOAT Neukirchen-Vluyn, Neukirchener Verlag, 1976.
L	*Codex Leningradensis*
LAR	D. D. Luckenbill. *Ancient Records of Assyria and Babylonia.* 2 vols. Chicago: University of Chicago Press, 1926

PRINCIPAL ABBREVIATIONS

A	Aramaic language
AB	Anchor Bible
AHw	W. von Soden, *Akkadisches Handwörterbuch.* 3 vols. Wiesbaden: Harrassowitz, 1965–81
Akk	Akkadian (the language of ancient Mesopotamia)
ANEP	*The Ancient Near East in Pictures Relating to the Old Testament,* ed. J. B. Pritchard. 2d ed. with suppl. Princeton: Princeton University Press, 1954, 1969
ANET	*Ancient Near Eastern Texts Relating to the Old Testament,* ed. J. B. Pritchard. 3d ed. with suppl. Princeton: Princeton University Press, 1955, 1969
ASV	American Standard Version
B.C.E.	Before the Common Era
BA	*Biblical Archaeologist*
BASOR	*Bulletin of the American Schools of Oriental Research*
BDB	F. Brown, S. R. Driver, and C. A. Briggs, *Hebrew and English Lexicon of the Old Testament.* Oxford University Press, 1907, 1955
BH³	Biblia Hebraica, 3d ed.
BHS	Biblia Hebraica Stuttgartensia
Bib	*Biblica*
BJ	Bible de Jérusalem
BJRL	*Bulletin of the John Rylands University Library of Manchester*
BZAW	Beihefte zur Zeitschrift für die alttestamentliche Wissenschaft
CAD	*The Assyrian Dictionary of the University of Chicago,* ed. L. Oppenheim. et al. University of Chicago Press, 1956
CBQ	*Catholic Biblical Quarterly*
C.E.	Common Era
c.g.	common gender
chap(s).	chapter(s)
conj.	conjunction
D	Deuteronomist
DJD 3	*Discoveries in the Judean Desert of Jordan,* M. Baillet, J. T. Milik, and R. de Vaux. Oxford: Clarendon Press, 1962.
E	Elohist

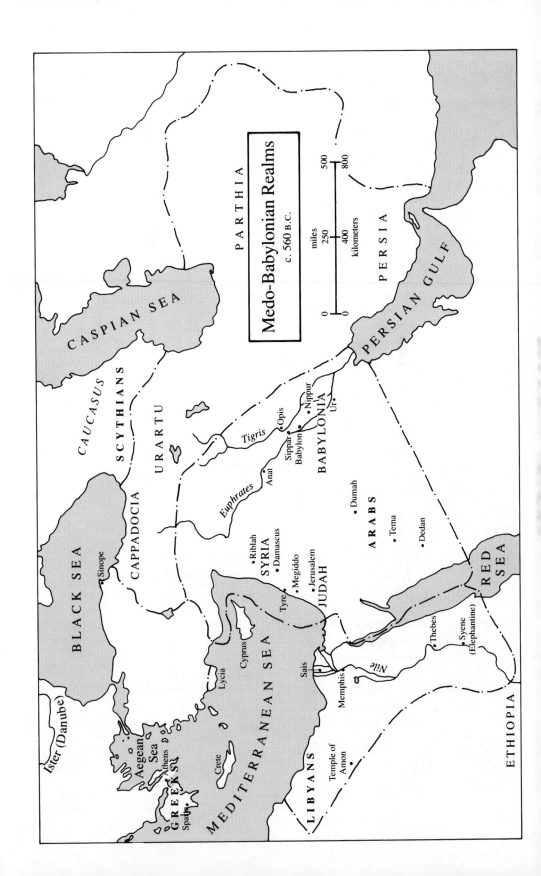

Medo-Babylonian Realms
c. 560 B.C.

miles
0 250 500
kilometers
0 400 800

PARTHIA

PERSIA

PERSIAN GULF

CASPIAN SEA

CAUCASUS

SCYTHIANS

URARTU

CAPPADOCIA

BLACK SEA

Sinope

Tigris

Opis

Nippur

Ur

Sippar

Babylon

BABYLONIA

Anat

Euphrates

Dumah

ARABS

Tema

Dedan

Riblah

SYRIA

Damascus

Megiddo

Jerusalem

JUDAH

Tyre

Cyprus

Lycia

MEDITERRANEAN SEA

Sais

Memphis

Nile

RED SEA

Thebes

Syene
(Elephantine)

ETHIOPIA

LIBYANS

Temple of
Amon

Ister (Danube)

Aegean
Sea

Athens

GREEKS

Sparta

Crete

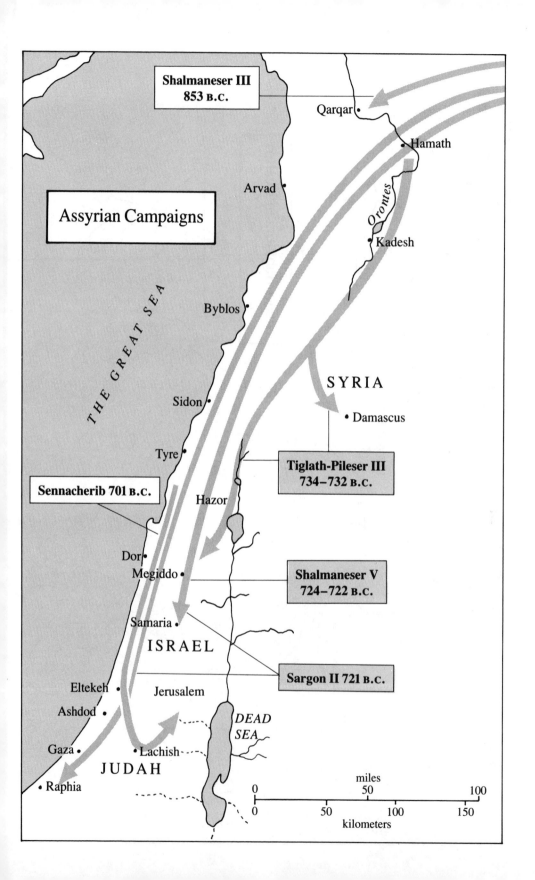

**Shalmaneser III
853 B.C.**

Qarqar

Hamath

Arvad

Orontes

Assyrian Campaigns

Kadesh

Byblos

THE GREAT SEA

SYRIA

Sidon

Damascus

Tyre

**Tiglath-Pileser III
734–732 B.C.**

Sennacherib 701 B.C.

Hazor

Dor

Megiddo

**Shalmaneser V
724–722 B.C.**

Samaria

ISRAEL

Sargon II 721 B.C.

Eltekeh

Jerusalem

Ashdod

*DEAD
SEA*

Gaza

Lachish

JUDAH

Raphia

miles

0   50   100

0   50   100   150

kilometers

AMOS:
OUTLINE AND TRANSLATION

PART I. THE BOOK OF DOOM (1:1–4:13)

Heading (1:1)

1 ¹The words of Amos—who was one of the sheep raisers from Tekoa—who had visions concerning Israel in the days of Uzziah the king of Judah, and in the days of Jeroboam ben-Joash the king of Israel, two years before the earthquake.

I.A. Oracles Against the Nations (1:2–2:8)

I.A.1. Yahweh Roars from Zion//Jerusalem (1:2)

1:2a And he said:

> Yahweh—from Zion has roared,
> > and from Jerusalem has given forth his voice;

2b and the pastures of the shepherds are in mourning,
> and the peak of Carmel is withered.

I.A.2. The Eight Nations (1:3–2:8)
I.A.2.a. Six Neighbors (1:3–2:3)
I.A.2.a.i. Aram (1:3–5)

1:3a Thus Yahweh said:

> For three violations by Damascus,
> > and for four,
> > > I will not reverse it:

3b Because they threshed Gilead with iron sledges.

4a So I will send Fire against the house of Hazael,

4b and She will consume the citadels of Ben-Hadad.

5a And I will break the bar of Damascus,
> and I will cut off the sovereign from Biqʿat-Awen,
> > and the scepter wielder from Beth-Eden—

5b and the Aramaean people will go into exile to Qir.

> **Yahweh has spoken!**

I.A.2.a.ii. Philistia (1:6–8)

1:6a   Thus Yahweh said:

    For three violations by Gaza,
      and for four,
      I will not reverse it:

6b   Because they took into captivity an entire captivity,
      to hand (them) over to Edom.

7a   And I will send Fire against the wall of Gaza,
7b   and She will consume its citadels.

8a   And I will cut off the sovereign from Ashdod,
      and the scepter wielder from Ashkelon;

8b   and I will bring back my hand against Ekron,
    and the Philistines will perish, even to the remnant.
          My Lord Yahweh has spoken!

I.A.2.a.iii. Tyre (1:9–10)

1:9a   Thus Yahweh said:

    For three violations by Tyre,
      and for four,
      I will not reverse it:

9b   Because they handed over an entire captivity to Edom,
      and did not remember the covenant of brothers.

10a   And I will send Fire against the wall of Tyre,
10b   and She will consume its citadels.

I.A.2.a.iv. Edom (1:11–12)

1:11a   Thus Yahweh said:

    For three violations by Edom,
      and for four,
      I will not reverse it:

11b   Because he pursued his brother with the sword,
      and he destroyed his allies;
    and his anger tore perpetually,
      and his rage persisted always.

12a   And I will send Fire against Teman,
12b   and She will consume the citadels of Bozrah.

I.A.2.a.v. Ammon (1:13–15)

1:13a   Thus Yahweh said:

    For three violations by the Ammonites,
      and for four,
      I will not reverse it:

13b   Because they ripped open the pregnant women of Gilead, in order to enlarge their territory.

14a   And I will kindle Fire upon the wall of Rabbah,
           and She will consume its citadels;
14b   with shouting on the day of battle,
           with a tempest on the day of windstorm.
15a   And their king will go into exile,
15b   he and his princes together.

                                    Yahweh has spoken!

I.A.2.a.vi. Moab (2:1–3)

2:1a   Thus Yahweh said:
           For three violations by Moab,
               and for four,
               I will not reverse it:
1b   Because he burned the bones of the king of Edom to lime.
2a   And I will send Fire against Moab,
           and She will consume the citadels of Kerioth.
2b   And Moab will die in tumult,
               with battle shout,
               with trumpet blast.
3a   And I will cut down the judge from its midst,
3b   and all its princes I will slay with him.
                                    Yahweh has spoken!

I.A.2.b. Judah and Israel Separately (2:4–8)
I.A.2.b.vii. Judah (2:4–5)

2:4a   Thus Yahweh said:
           For three violations by Judah,
               and for four,
               I will not reverse it:
4b   Because they rejected the instruction of Yahweh,
               and his statutes they failed to observe;
           and their falsehoods led them astray,
               after which their fathers went.
5a   And I will send Fire against Judah,
5b   and She will consume the citadels of Jerusalem.

I.A.2.b.viii. Israel (2:6–8)

2:6a   Thus Yahweh said:
           For three violations by Israel,
               and for four,
               I will not reverse it:
6b   Because they sell for money the righteous,

and the poor for the sake of a pair of sandals—

7a   those who trample upon the dust of the earth
            the head of the destitute,
       and they push the humble out of the way—

7b   and a man and his father go to the Girl,
            so as to desecrate my holy name.

8a   And because they spread out garments pledged for debt be-
                                                    side every altar,

8b   and drink the wine
       of those who have been fined,
       in the house of their God.

I.B. Oracles Against the Whole of Israel (2:9–3:8)

I.B.1. Historical Recital and Threat (2:9–16)
I.B.1.a. Yahweh's Gracious Acts (2:9–11)

2:9a   As for me, I destroyed the Amorite before them,
            whose height was like the height of cedars,
            and he was as powerful as oak trees;

9b   and I destroyed his fruit from above,
            and his roots from beneath.

10a   And as for me, I brought you up from the land of Egypt,

10b   and I led you in the wilderness for forty years,
            so that you could take possession of the land of the
                                                    Amorite.

11a   And I raised up some of your sons to be prophets,
            and some of your choice young men to be nazirites.

11b   Isn't that actually so, you Israelites?
                        The solemn declaration of Yahweh!

I.B.1.b. The Present Situation (2:12)

2   12aAnd you made the nazirites drink wine, 12band against the prophets
you gave commands, saying, "You shall not prophesy!"

I.B.1.c. A Transitional Statement (2:13)

2   13aIndeed, I am creaking underneath you, 13bjust as the cart that is full of
sheaves creaks.

I.B.1.d. The Threatened Calamity (2:14–16)

2:14a Then flight will fail the swift,
            and the mighty will not prevail through his strength,

14b   and the warrior will not save his life;

15a   The archer will not survive,

	and the swift of foot will not save himself,
15b	and the charioteer will not save his life.
16a	Even the most stout-hearted among the warriors
16b	will run away naked in that day—

The solemn declaration of Yahweh!

I.B.2. Oracle and Riddles (3:1–8)
I.B.2.a. The Whole "Family" (3:1–2)

3 [1a]Hear this word that Yahweh has spoken about you, O Israelites, [1b]about the whole family that I brought up from the land of Egypt: [2a]"Only you have I known of all the families of the earth; [2b]therefore I will punish you for all your iniquities."

I.B.2.b. Some Riddles (3:3–8)

3:3a	Do two go together,
3b	unless they have arranged to meet?
4a	Does a lion roar in the forest,
	if it has no prey?
4b	Does a young lion thunder from its lair,
	unless it has seized [a victim]?
5a	Does a bird alight upon a ground trap,
	if there is no lure for it?
5b	Does a trap spring up from the ground,
	except to make a capture?
6a	If a trumpet is sounded in a city,
	will not the people be disturbed?
6b	If disaster befalls a city,
	is it not Yahweh's doing?
7a	For my Lord Yahweh does nothing,
7b	unless he has disclosed his plan to his servants, the prophets.
8a	The lion has roared;
	who is not frightened?
8b	My Lord Yahweh has spoken;
	who could not prophesy?

I.C. Messages for Israel//Samaria (3:9–4:3)

I.C.1. The International Setting (3:9–12)

3:9a	Proclaim upon the ramparts of Assyria [MT: Ashdod],
	and upon the ramparts of the land of Egypt.
9b	Say:

"Assemble on the mountains of Samaria,
and observe the great tumults in its midst,

the acts of oppression within it.
10a   They have no interest in doing right—
                            Oracle of Yahweh—
10b   those who store away the rewards of lawless behavior in
                            their strongholds."

11a   Therefore thus my Lord Yahweh has said:
        "The foe indeed surrounds your land,
11b   and will pull down your fortresses in your midst,
            and your strongholds will be sacked."
12a   Thus Yahweh has said:
        "Just as a shepherd rescues from the mouth of a lion
            two legs or a piece of an ear,
12b   in the same way shall the Israelites be rescued—
            those who dwell in Samaria—
            only the corner of a bed—
            only the *dmšq* of a couch—"

I.C.2. Israel (North)—Bethel (3:13–15)

3:13a   Confirm what you have heard about Jacob's family—
13b   Oracle of my Lord Yahweh, God of the hosts—
14a   When I punish Israel for its acts of rebellion,
14b   I will also punish the altars of Bethel;
                the horns of the altar will be cut down,
                and will fall to the ground.
15a   I will smash the winter palace
                as well as the summer palace;
15b   the ivory palaces will be destroyed,
                and the magnates' palaces will be swept
                                    away—
                            Oracle of Yahweh!

I.C.3. Mount Samaria (4:1–3)

4   ¹ªHear this word, you cows of Bashan who are in Mount Samaria,
oppressing the poor, crushing the needy, ¹ᵇsaying to their lords, "Bring,
that we may drink!"
2a   My Lord Yahweh has sworn by his holiness:
        "Indeed, behold, days are coming upon you,
2b   when they will take you away with grappling hooks,
            and your rear guard with fishhooks.
3a   Through the breaches you will go out,
            each one through the gap in front of her,
3b   and you will be cast away beyond Harmon—"
                            Oracle of Yahweh!

I.D. Messages for All Israel (4:4–13)

I.D.1. Condemnation of the Cult (4:4–5)

4:4a   Come to Bethel
           and rebel at Gilgal
           —rebel repeatedly!

   4b   Bring your sacrifices for the morning,
           and tithes for the third day;

   5a   Burn sacrifices without leaven,
       Thank offerings—and announce
       freewill offerings—proclaim.

   5b   For that's what you love, O Israelites—
                   Oracle of my Lord Yahweh!

I.D.2. Plagues (4:6–11)

4:6a   Indeed it was I who decreed cleanness of teeth in all your cities,
           and shortage of bread in all your districts;

   6b   yet you did not return to me—
                   Oracle of Yahweh!

   7a   And I also withheld the rain from you,
           although there were still three months before harvest;
       and I would make it rain upon one city,
           and upon another city I would not make it rain:

   7b   one section would receive rain,
               while the section upon which it did not rain would dry
                                                                   up.

   8a   And two or three cities would take refuge in one city,
                   to drink its water;
                       but there would not be enough to satisfy them;

   8b   yet you did not return to me—
                           Oracle of Yahweh!

   9a   I smote you with blight and with mildew repeatedly,
           your gardens,
           and your vineyards,
           and your fig trees,
               and your olive trees the locust devoured;
                   yet you did not return to me—
                                       Oracle of Yahweh!

  10a   I sent against you Pestilence in the way of Egypt;
               I killed with the sword your choice young men [soldiers],
               along with your horsemen;

  10b   and I made the stench of your camps rise up,

even into your nostrils;
  yet you did not return to me—
          Oracle of Yahweh!

11a I overturned a number of you,
   as God overturned Sodom and Gomorrah,
  and you were like a brand plucked from what was burned;
11b yet you did not return to me—
        Oracle of Yahweh!

I.D.3. Threat to Israel (4:12)

4:12a Therefore thus have I done to you, O Israel!
 12b Because I have done this to you:
    prepare to confront your God, O Israel!

I.D.4. Cosmic Hymn (4:13)

4:13a For behold!
   The Shaper of the mountains,
   and the Creator of the wind,
   and the One who declared his secret thought to Adam;
   the Maker of dawn out of darkness,
   and the One who treads upon the mountains of earth—
 13b Yahweh, God of hosts, is his name!

PART II. THE BOOK OF WOES (5:1–6:14)

II.A. Exhortations for Israel and Judah, Separately and Together (5:1–27)

II.A.1. Exhortation to the House of Israel (5:1–6)
II.A.1.a. The Fallen Virgin: Introduction and Qinah (5:1–2)

5 ¹Hear this message that I am going to utter about you, a dirge, O house of Israel:

 2a "The virgin Israel has fallen,
    she will never stand up again;
 2b she has been left lying on her land,
    and no one raises her up."

II.A.1.b. Decimation (5:3)

5:3a For thus my Lord Yahweh has said:
   "The city that marches forth a thousand strong

shall have only a hundred left;
3b   and the one that marches forth a hundred strong
      shall have only ten left—
        O house of Israel!"

II.A.1.c. The Sanctuaries (5:4–6)
II.A.1.c.i. "Seek Me and Live" (5:4–5)

5:4a   For thus Yahweh has said:
      "O house of Israel,
4b   seek me and live!
5a   But don't seek [me] at Bethel,
      and to Gilgal do not come,
      and to Beer-sheba do not cross over;
5b   because Gilgal will certainly go into exile,
      and Bethel will become nothing."

II.A.1.c.ii. Threat Against Bethel (5:6)

5:6a   Seek Yahweh and live,
6b   lest he rush [upon you] like a flame,
      O house of Joseph,
      and it consume [you] with none to quench [it],
      O house of God!

II.A.2. First Woe (5:7–13), Including the Second Hymn (5:8–9)
II.A.2.a. First Woe (5:7, 10–12)

5:7a   [Woe to] those who turn justice into wormwood,
7b   and equity in the earth they bury.

II.A.2.b. Second Hymn (5:8–9)

5:8a   The One who fashioned the Pleiades and Orion,
      who transforms pitch darkness into daylight,
      who darkens the day into night;
8b   the One who summoned the waters of the sea,
      and poured them out on the surface of the earth—
          Yahweh is his name!
9a   The One who makes destruction burst upon the stronghold,
9b   and destruction upon the fortress when he comes.

II.A.2.a. (continued). First Woe (5:10–12)

5:10a   They hate the reprover in the gate,
10b   and the one who speaks truth they abhor.
11a   Therefore, because you trample upon the needy,
        and extract levies of grain from them,

the houses of hewn stone that you built—
you shall not dwell in them;
11b the prized vineyards that you planted—
you shall not drink their wine.
12a I am aware that your rebellions are many
and your sinful acts are numerous—
12b Those who harass the upright,
those who hold them for ransom,
and the poor from the gate they thrust.

II.A.2.c. The Wise Man (5:13)

5 ¹³ᵃTherefore the wise man remains silent at such a time, ¹³ᵇfor it is an evil time.

II.A.3. Exhortation and Lamentation (5:14–17)
II.A.3.a. Repentance (5:14–15)

5:14a Seek Good and not Evil,
so that you may live!
14b And let it happen so—
let Yahweh, the God of hosts, be with you as you have
claimed!
15a Hate Evil and love Good,
and establish justice in the gate.
15b Perhaps Yahweh the God of hosts will treat [you] kindly,
O remnant of Joseph.

II.A.3.b. Lamentation (5:16–17)

5:16a Therefore, thus has said Yahweh the God of hosts, my Lord:
"In all the squares let there be lamentation,
and in all the streets
Let them say, 'Alas! Alas!'—
16b and let them summon the field hands
to mourning and lamentation—
to those trained in wailing.
17a And in all the vineyards let there be lamentation,
17b when I pass through, in the midst of you."
Yahweh has spoken.

II.A.4. Warning and Woe (5:18–27)
II.A.4.a. The Day of Yahweh (5:18–20)

5 ¹⁸ᵃWoe to you who long for Yahweh's Day! ¹⁸ᵇWhat does it mean to you? Yahweh's Day will be darkness rather than light. ¹⁹ᵃIt will be as though a man were to escape from the lion, only to have the bear meet him; ¹⁹ᵇor, having reached his house, to rest his hand on the wall, and have the snake

bite him. [20a]Is not Yahweh's Day darkness rather than light, [20b]pitch darkness without a glimmer of light?

II.A.4.b. Justice (5:21–24)

5:21a I detest, I loathe your festivals,
21b   I have no satisfaction in your solemn gatherings.
22a   Whatever you sacrifice to me
                —your burnt offerings and gifts—
                I cannot accept
22b   —your peace offerings and fat cattle—
                I cannot approve.
23a   Take your loud songs away from me!
23b   I won't listen to your instrumental music.
24a   But let justice roll on like the ocean,
24b   and equity like a perennial stream.

II.A.4.c. Threat of Exile (5:25–27)

5 [25]Did you bring me sacrifices and gifts for forty years in the desert, O house of Israel? [26a]But you shall carry Sakkuth your king, and Kaiwan your star-god, [26b]your images, which you made for yourselves, [27a]when I drive you into exile beyond Damascus, [27b]said he, whose name is Yahweh, God of hosts.

II.B. Woes and Warnings (6:1–14)

II.B.1. Woes (6:1–7)
II.B.1.a. The Seven Woes (6:1–6)

6:1a Woe to you who luxuriate in Zion,
        and [woe] to you who feel secure in Mount Samaria;
1b   the notables of the foremost of the nations,
            who have come for themselves to the house of Israel!
2a   Cross over to Calneh, and see;
            proceed from there to Greater Hamath,
2b   and go down to Gath of the Philistines:
                Are you better than these kingdoms?
                Or is their territory greater than yours?
3a   [Woe] to you who rush along toward the day of calamity,
3b   who draw ever nearer to the reign of lawlessness!
4a   [Woe] to those who lie on beds of ivory,
            who sprawl upon their couches;
4b   and [woe] to those who devour lambs from the flock,
            and calves from the stall.
5a   [Woe] to those who improvise on the lyre

5b   —like David—
            who compose for their pleasure on musical instruments!
6a   [Woe] to those who drink from basins of wine,
                who anoint themselves with the best oils!
6b   They are not distressed at Joseph's crash.

II.B.1.b. The Exiles (6:7)

6:7a   Now indeed they shall go at the head of those who go into exile,
   7b   they shall depart,
                these sprawling "mourners."

II.B.2. The Oath and Woes (6:8–14)
II.B.2.a. The Oath (6:8–10)

6:8a   My Lord Yahweh has sworn by his life
                —Oracle of Yahweh, God of hosts—
            "I abhor the pride of Jacob,
            its citadels I reject;
   8b   so I will hand over the city in its entirety."
   9   So it will be,
            that, if ten men are left in a single house, they shall die.
   10a Then the nearest relative and his *msrp*
            will arrive to remove the corpse from the house.
            One will say to the other in the remote corners of the house,
            "Is anyone still with you?"
        He will reply,
            "No one."
   10b Then the former will say,
            "Silence! For we must not invoke Yahweh's name."

II.B.2.b. Last Woes (6:11–13)

6:11a For behold, Yahweh is commanding;
            he will smash the largest house into pieces,
   11b   and the smallest house into bits.
   12a "Do horses run upon the rocks?
        Or does one plow the sea with oxen?
   12b   But you have turned justice into poison,
                and the fruit of righteousness into wormwood.
   13a [Woe to] you who are delighted over Lo-Dabar;
   13b [woe to] you who say,
            'Have we not captured Qarnaim for ourselves by our
        might?' "

II.B.2.c. The Final Threat (6:14)

6:14a For soon I will raise against you,
      O house of Israel
          —Oracle of Yahweh, God of the hosts—
      a nation

14b   that will overpower you from the gateway of Hamath
          as far as the Wadi Arabah.

PART III. THE BOOK OF VISIONS
(7:1–9:6)

III.A. The First Four Visions (7:1–8:3)

III.A.1. The First Pair of Visions (7:1–6)
III.A.1.a. The First Vision (Locusts) (7:1–3)

7 ¹Thus my Lord Yahweh showed me:

Indeed he was forming locusts, just when the latter growth was beginning to appear, that is, the latter growth after the king's mowings. ²When they were about to devour the vegetation of the land entirely, I said, "My Lord Yahweh, please forgive! How can Jacob survive, as he is so small?"

³Yahweh repented of this. "It shall not happen," Yahweh said.

III.A.1.b. The Second Vision (Fire) (7:4–6)

7 ⁴Thus my Lord Yahweh showed me:

Indeed my Lord Yahweh was summoning showers of fire. When it had consumed the Great Deep, and was consuming the allotted land, ⁵I said, "My Lord Yahweh, please desist! How can Jacob survive, as he is so small?"

⁶Yahweh repented of this. "This also shall not happen," my Lord Yahweh said.

III.A.2. The Second Pair of Visions and Insertion (7:7–8:3)
III.A.2.a. The Third Vision (7:7–9)

7 ⁷Thus he showed me:

Indeed my Lord was standing beside a plastered wall [wall of *'ănāk*], with a lump of tin (*'ănāk*) in his hand. ⁸Yahweh said to me, "What do you see, Amos?" I said, "A lump of tin (*'ănāk*)." My Lord said, "Soon I will put grief (*'ănāk*) in the midst of my people Israel. I shall not spare them again."

7:9a   "The high places of Isaac will be devastated,
          and Israel's sanctuaries will be laid waste;
⁹ᵇand I shall attack the house of Jeroboam with my sword."

III.A.2.b. First Insertion: The Confrontation (7:10–17)

¹⁰Then Amaziah the priest of Bethel sent word to Jeroboam, the king of Israel: "Amos has conspired against you inside the house of Israel; the land cannot endure all his words.

11a   For Amos has said the following:
          'By the sword shall Jeroboam die,
11b   and Israel shall surely go into exile from its land.' "

¹²Then Amaziah said to Amos: "O seer, go, run away to the land of Judah. ¹³Eat your food there, and there do your prophesying. But at Bethel never prophesy again, because it is the king's chapel, it is a royal temple."

¹⁴Then Amos answered Amaziah: "I was no prophet, nor was I trained as a prophet, but I am a cattleman and a dresser of sycamores. ¹⁵And Yahweh took me from following the flock. And Yahweh said to me: 'Go prophesy to my people Israel.' ¹⁶ᵃNow hear Yahweh's word! You say,
   "Don't prophesy against Israel,
   and don't preach against Isaac's domain!"

17a   Yahweh, on the contrary, has said the following:
          'Your wife shall become a prostitute in the city,
          and your sons and your daughters shall fall by the sword;
          and your land shall be parceled out by the measuring line;
17b   and you yourself shall die in a polluted land;
          and Israel shall surely go into exile from its land.' "

III.A.2.c. The Fourth Vision (Ripe Fruit) (8:1–3)

8   ¹ᵃThus my Lord Yahweh showed me:
   ¹ᵇIndeed there was a basket of summer fruit (qāyīṣ). ²ᵃHe said, "What do you see, Amos?" I said, "A basket of summer fruit (qāyiṣ)." ²ᵇYahweh said to me, "The end (qēṣ) is coming for my people Israel; I shall never spare them again."

8:3a   The palace singers shall howl in that day
          —Oracle of my Lord Yahweh!—
   3b   many are the corpses that will be cast away everywhere.
          Silence!

III.B. The Fifth Vision (8:4–9:6)

III.B.1. Second Insertion: Woes (8:4–14)
III.B.1.a. Woes (8:4–6)

8:4a   Hear this, you who trample upon the poor,

4b   and put an end to the wretched of the land;
5a   who say:
          "When will the new moon pass,
              so that we may sell our grain;
              and the sabbath,
              so that we may open our stores of grain?"—
5b   who reduce the quantity (*ephah*),
          while raising the price (*shekel*);
      and cheat with crooked scales;
6a   who buy the needy for money,
          and the poor for a pair of sandals
6b   —"and that we may sell the husks of the grain."

III.B.1.b. Oath (8:7–8)

8:7a Yahweh has sworn by the pride of Jacob:
7b   "I will never forget any of their misdeeds."
8a For this reason, should not the earth tremble,
8b   and everyone who dwells in it mourn?
    Shall it not all rise like the Nile,
      and be tossed about,
        then sink like the Nile of Egypt?

III.B.1.c. Lamentation (8:9–10)

8:9a And it shall happen on that day
      —Oracle of my Lord Yahweh—
    that I shall make the sun set at noon
9b   and I shall make the earth dark in broad daylight.
10a   I will turn your festivals into mourning,
      and all your songs into a dirge.
    I will put sackcloth on every pair of thighs,
      and baldness on every head.
10b   I will make it like the mourning for an only son,
      and its climax like the bitter day.

III.B.1.d. Famine of the Words (8:11–12)

8:11a   Behold! The time is coming
      —Oracle of my Lord Yahweh—
    when I will send famine throughout the earth:
11b   not a hunger for food,
      nor a thirst for water,
    but a famine of hearing Yahweh's words.
12a   They shall wander from sea to sea,
      and from north to east,

12b   they will run back and forth,
     seeking the word of Yahweh—
      but they shall not find it.

    III.B.1.e. Woes (8:13–14)

8:13   On that day
     the loveliest virgins will faint,
     and the choicest youths from thirst.

 14a   [Woe to] those who swear by the Guilt of Samaria,
     who say:
       "By the life of your god!"
       [from] Dan—
     and:
       "By the life of your pantheon!"
       —[to] Beer-sheba.

 14b   They shall fall
     and never rise again.

    III.B.2. The Fifth Vision (9:1–6)
    III.B.2.a. Temple and Earthquake (9:1–4)

9:1a I saw my Lord standing beside the altar.
   He said:
     "Strike the capitals
      so that the thresholds shake!
     and smite them on the head—all of them;
     and their remainder I shall slay with the sword;

 1b   no fugitive among them shall make good his flight,
      no survivor among them shall escape.

 2a   If they dig down to Sheol,
     from there my hand shall fetch them.

 2b   If they climb up to Heaven,
     from there I will bring them down.

 3a   If they hide themselves on the top of Carmel,
     I will seek them out from there at once, and seize them.

 3b   If they conceal themselves from my eyes on the bottom of the
                  Sea,
     I will command the Serpent from there at once,
      and He shall bite them.

 4a   If they go into captivity before their enemies,
     I will command the Sword from there at once,
      and She shall slay them.

 4b   For I shall set my eye upon them
      to do them harm and not good."

III.B.2.b. Third Hymn (9:5–6)

9:5a My Lord Yahweh of hosts:
> who strikes the earth so that it melts,
> > and all who dwell in it mourn;

5b   it all rises like the Nile,
> > and subsides like the Nile of Egypt;

6a   who built its upper stories in the sky,
> > and its supports he founded upon the earth;

6b   who summoned the waters of the sea,
> > and poured them over the surface of the earth—
> > > His name is Yahweh!

PART IV. EPILOGUE (9:7–15)

IV.A. The End of the Nation (9:7–10)

IV.A.1. The Wicked Nation (9:7–8)

9   [7a]Aren't you like Cushites to me, O Israelites?—Oracle of Yahweh—[7b]Didn't I bring Israel up from the land of Egypt, the Philistines from Caphtor, and Aram from Qir? [8a]Indeed, the eyes of my Lord Yahweh are upon the sinful kingdom; I shall destroy it from the surface of the earth. [8b]Nevertheless, I shall not utterly destroy the house of Jacob—Oracle of Yahweh!

IV.A.2. The Sieve (9:9–10)

[9a]Indeed I will command:
> I will shake the house of Israel among all the nations [9b]just as the grain is shaken in a sieve, but no kernel falls to the ground.

10a   All the sinners of my people shall die by the sword,
10b   those who say:
> > "Calamity shall not even come close,
> > > much less confront us, during our lifetime."

IV.B. The Restoration (9:11–15)

IV.B.1. The Booth of David (9:11–12)

11a On that day I will set up David's booth that has fallen,
11b   and I will repair their breaches,

and I will restore his ruins;
I will rebuild it as in the days of old—
12a   so that they may dispossess the remnant of Edom,
even all the nations over whom my name was
pronounced—
12b   Oracle of Yahweh, who will do this.

IV.B.2. *The Calendar: Superabundance (9:13–15)*

9:13a   Indeed the time is at hand
—Oracle of Yahweh!—
when the plowman will overtake the reaper,
and the treader of grapes the sower of seed;
13b   the mountains will drip with sweet wine,
and all the hills will flow with it.
14a   Then I will restore the fortunes of my people Israel;
they shall build the ruined cities, and inhabit them;
they shall plant vineyards, and drink their wine;
14b   they shall cultivate gardens, and eat their fruit.
15a   I will plant them upon their land,
15b   and they shall never be rooted out of the land
that I have given them—
Yahweh your God has spoken!

INTRODUCTION

THE STUDY OF AMOS

This is a study of the book of Amos. There are many ways of investigating and interpreting such a book. Good work already done by others does not need to be repeated here. Scholars in the nineteenth century took up the task in their own way. One of their concerns was to discover the "real" Amos and to recover his "original" words (Löhr 1901:2), which meant identifying genuine sayings and restoring corrupted readings. The brilliant emendations of J. Wellhausen (1893) and others have now become part of the common stock. The sifting of primary from secondary components required criteria for form and for content. The results of all of this labor were gathered together by W. R. Harper and other commentators at the turn of the century.

The literary analysis of the text prepared the way for more delicate detection of the genres of the pieces used, an enterprise brought to a high pitch of skill and precision in form criticism. Such analysis was a prime concern of research in the middle decades of this century. The rich results have been sufficiently harvested and presented in the exemplary commentaries of H. W. Wolff and W. Rudolph.

We admire and appreciate this work, but we concentrate now on the text itself. By this we mean the traditional Masoretic text, not a revised form of the text produced by modern scholars, which is more commonly used in contemporary translations. One has only to compare current translations of Amos 2:13 with the original Hebrew to realize how much things have changed. We are interested in looking once more at the available text of the book of Amos. We are more concerned with its literary form as a finished, though not necessarily perfect, product than with the forms of the numerous and very diverse ingredients that were used in the making of it.

We are more reluctant to emend the text than scholars of a previous generation. It is not because we have secret knowledge that the text is immaculate. That cannot possibly be the case for anyone. Our diffidence toward conjectural emendations, which can be a lot of fun, does not betray some preconceived notions about the supernatural properties of the text. Rather, our caution arises from concern for sound empirical method. The textual evidence we have, in manuscripts and versions, always has a better claim on our attention than readings that have been made up in order to solve a problem. In particular, we are unwilling to proceed to comment on an emended text, or to develop further arguments or inferences from a reconstructed text. We prefer to leave some problems unsolved rather than attempt to explain the unknown by the unknown. We are not, however, so naïve as to apply that good rule *proclivi scriptioni praestat ardua* uncritically. Our approach in this matter should not be misconstrued as doctrinaire conservatism. If a "conservative" result emerges from the work, so be it. That will be neither good nor bad in itself, but only as good or bad as the methods and arguments used to arrive at that outcome. And the assessment must be made in the process, not in the product. We are reluctant to emend the MT, but we are quite prepared to do so, and actually do make changes when a good case can be made. The MT enjoys prestige but not privilege. It needs to be subjected to all of the critical procedures that may be applied to any ancient text. It is hardly likely that the text is immaculate; indeed, we are certain that it is not. There is no call to defend it at all costs. It is self-defeating to save a bad reading by resorting to farfetched explanations, however cleverly they may be defended by arguments from paleography, epigraphy, orthography, comparative philology, and all of the other things that the modern scholar has in his bag of tricks. *Lectio difficilior potior* is only a rule of thumb, and it can reasonably be invoked only when there are arguments, specific for each case, that this difficult reading is not impossible.

So we are prepared to be patient with textual difficulties, to bring to bear on them the many new insights and methods—textual, philological, literary —that have been developed in recent years to supplement and improve the research techniques of previous generations. Our aim is to make as much sense as we can of the text as it now stands; and to the degree that we can interpret the given text without changing it, to that extent it is probable that the text is in good shape. If the textual difficulties, which previous scholars identified as errors and which prompted them to make corrections, are now discovered to be the result of subtlety and sophistication in the creation of the book, rather than the result of damage inflicted on it in its transmission, then instead of a low estimate of the text we have a high estimate of the author. We also have confidence that the text has been preserved with a high degree of fidelity to its original, or at least early, state.

We are similarly cautious in our treatment of literary questions. We do not wish to deny the validity and value of the results of modern criticism, but we can no longer display those results with the confidence and finality that are found in many old handbooks; for example, we cannot assert that the book is mainly the work of postexilic editors, a theory that is often repeated but seldom defended in detail. The major discipline of form criticism now seems to have reached its limits without solving its problems, and it has become so preoccupied with the parts that it misses—or even denies the existence of—the whole. A valid observation can lead to an invalid result, as has been the case with the three hymns in Amos (4:13; 5:8–9;

9:5–6). These hymns belong to a familiar genre used widely throughout the Bible and found in other ancient religious texts as well. The achievements of the deity are recited as a list of actions, with a participle frequently used as a kind of title. The recitation has the effect of an invocation of the many names of God (it could be done with theurgical intent), in crescendo to the supreme name—"Yahweh!"—at the very end (9:6). If that name and that form are mandatory, then the variations in Amos point to deficiencies in the text we now have. The three pieces are often viewed as fragments of one original composition, of which three strophes have survived, so that we might hope to recover all or at least some of the original source (Watts 1958:51–68). Numerous attempts have been made to retrieve and reconstruct the original piece. Whether there ever was one original composition as the source of the quotations in Amos, and whether it can be recovered with a measure of certainty that would make the exercise worthwhile, are debatable questions. The observations above about the form of the cosmic hymn passages are sound, but the inferences are shaky; and when all of that work has been done to the best of our ability, the fact remains that these hymns (or hymn fragments) now exist in the book of Amos. The question then remains—it is quite a distinct one, to be handled on its own terms—*not* what did such hymns do when they were sung in the cult, but what are these pieces now doing in the book of Amos?

To the degree that we can demonstrate the structural unity of the completed book we have confirmation on another level that the text is in good shape. Such a discovery is all the more impressive in the case of a book like Amos when the work turns out to be coherent in spite of the great diversity of the materials that were used to make it.

Insofar as we can speak about the *book* of Amos, we can recognize one master hand. If not Amos himself, then at least an editor unified the text who must have been very close to his teacher and whose contribution was to arrange and integrate the prophecies that Amos himself produced.

Earlier scholars gained the impression that the whole book could not have come from Amos. Besides the formal diversity in literary expression, the book presents several quite different points of view. It has a number of contradictory "messages." Announcements of unqualified, irreversible doom are found side by side with declarations that seem to hold out some hope. Amos has always been one of the most popular prophets, and criticisms that his thinking was muddled and that his composition was confused have been softened by blaming the inconsistencies we now find in the book on editors and scribes.

We advance a different explanation. We relate the changes in posture and policy to dynamic developments in the prophet's career. It is possible to distinguish the points of view that we encounter in the book.

1. There are passages that celebrate the faithfulness of God in the past

and appeal to the people to honor that experience, repeating the old promise:

> Seek Good and not Evil,
> . . . .
> Hate Evil and love Good. (5:14–15)

These exhortations, at the center of the book, are hopeful. The situation is open for remedy and redemption, and even without amendment by the people it is possible at this stage for the prophet to make successful intervention to secure a stay in the divine retribution (Visions 1 and 2 [7:1–6]).

2. More serious, but still not hopeless, is the situation represented by the series of plagues (4:6–11). These disasters were intended to be disciplinary, minatory. If, as we shall suggest when the time comes, they are associated with the first two visions (notionally, if not historically), then the double assurance—"It shall not happen . . . This also shall not happen" (7:3, 6) —was not absolute. Amos' intercessions bought time during which Israel had further opportunities to return to Yahweh.

These situations represent the early stages in Amos' career. He heads into double failure—failure to persuade the people to repent, and failure to secure more time for repentance from the Lord. Amos' minimal contribution to the dialogue in Visions 3 and 4 (7:7–8:2) shows that he is no longer able to speak effectively to God; and Amaziah's prohibition makes him no longer able to speak to the people. The voice of prophecy falls silent (8:11–12—a worse famine than the one of bread [4:6]).

There is, then, a great turning point in Amos' life, and the differences within the book can be connected with the occurrence of any particular item before or after that crisis. Two developments brought the time of probation to an end: first, the repeated refusals to repent (4:6–11); and second, and quite decisively, Amaziah's attempt to silence and expel Amos (7:10–17). Amaziah claimed in 7:10 that "the land cannot endure all his words," as in 2:12. At this point Yahweh says, "I shall never spare them again" (7:8; 8:2b). Punishment is now inevitable.

3. There are two sides to that punishment. On the one side there are warnings of cosmic convulsions, of an earthquake of unusual severity (Vision 5 [9:1–4]). On the other side are defeat and destruction by military means (see the full list in the INTRODUCTION to 2:14–16, below). It is in this context that Yahweh's judgment against all of the nations, including Israel, is declared to be irreversible (1:3–2:8), and these oracles contain the same blend of the mythic and the historical. The now inevitable doom has two aspects. First there is defeat and exile. Then, even for many of the survivors and exiles, there is no escape; every sinner will be killed (9:10a).

4. In some places, and quite clearly toward the end of the book, Amos

sounds a positive note. Judgment, even when severe, even when total, is not the end. In spite of everything, Yahweh and his people still have a future.

Many scholars have found the true voice of Amos in the messages of doom, but not in the idea of survivors, remnant, return, or recovery. The text has to suffer considerable surgery to reach this result. But the assumption that for Amos the future beyond the doom was empty and blank is not self-evident. If that were so, the Epilogue (9:11–15) could not have come from him. But more is involved here than simply a critical decision about the authenticity of this passage or of any other. Each such case must be judged on its own merits, and such questions are open, but they should not be prejudged by assertions that Amos was only a prophet of doom. Neither can they be judged by the formal contradiction between those passages that insist that there will be no survivors (9:1; "All" in 9:10), and those that anticipate a continuation of Yahweh's activities in "coming days." Amos' criticism is directed mainly at the leadership. It is they, not necessarily all mankind, who will perish. The broken (6:6) and fallen (5:2) nation will be raised up again. The book of Amos, if not Amos himself (and why not Amos?), speaks about the End Time in strongly eschatological terms.

The book is far from uniform in focus and emphasis. It will be one of our aims in the following study to relate the changes in presentation to developments in Amos' career. That career is not unfolded step by step from the beginning of the book to the end; the main emphases are found throughout, though one strong note is dominant in each major section. In effect, everything is presented twice, so that we might speak about two books—a "Book of Oracles" (chaps. 1–6) and a "Book of Visions" (7:1–9:6). The latter is organized so that the three sets of visions—2 + 2 + 1—represent the turning points in Amos' life, the phases of his message. The order of these phases is inverted in The Book of Oracles. The woe oracles (chaps. 5–6) come first in time, then the plagues (chap. 4), and finally the oracles of doom (chaps. 1–3). From the very beginning, prophetic vision gives cosmic depth to the matching plagues of locusts (7:1 = 4:9) and fire (7:4 = 4:11). The proclamation begins with the Woes of chaps. 5–6, along with exhortations (in the very center of the book) that spell out what it means to repent (5:14–15). The failure of these messages is marked by the dramatic shift from the first two to the second two visions, with a deterioration of the situation to the point that no remedy, no respite, is possible anymore. It is too late for repentance, too late for intercession. The double "never again" (7:8, 8:2) of Visions 3 and 4 matches the repeated "I will not reverse it" of the opening oracles. The more severe and hopeless message of chaps. 1 and 2 thus corresponds to a climax that follows the more open situation of Visions 1 and 2 and the exhortations of chaps. 5 and 6.

It would be unwise to force such identifications into too tight a scheme. There is a parallel movement through the series of visions and through the series of oracles, in contrary motion. But this fact does not mean that we should insist on a one-to-one correspondence between the two sets, linking all the oracles with the visions. The plagues reported in chap. 4 serve as a bridge from the still hopeful situation in chaps. 5 and 6 to the now hopeless situation in chaps. 1 and 2, working backward.

Amaziah's ban on Amos was another factor in the collapse of the situation, but it is harder to locate it, except to connect it very closely with Visions 3 and 4. Perhaps the most likely chain of events is as follows:

1. Amos was called; he received Visions 1 and 2; he interceded successfully; he delivered exhortations to repentance (chaps. 5 and 6). They were not heeded. Even the plagues (chap. 4) did not bring repentance.

2. Amos received two more visions (3 and 4) and proclaimed their consequences in oracles of doom on all of the nations (chaps. 1–3).

3. These prophecies provoked Amaziah; Vision 5 followed, and resulted in threats of even more complete destruction (9:1–10).

4. The hope of salvation in the near future was given up completely, but not all hope for the future. The hope was reframed in vaguer terms and set in a more remote and indeterminate future. The beginnings of prophetic eschatology are already present (9:11–15).

The main uncertainty in this scheme is the connection between the confrontation with Amaziah (7:10–17) and the visions. By embedding this incident in the second set of visions, the editor makes it clear that all of these things go together. Because the two visions in the first pair are in direct sequence, the insertion of this unique piece of biography into the second set (equally a pair) must have been deliberate. In fact, as we shall see, this report has been woven into the visions. But we cannot tell whether God's double "never again" is the response to Amaziah's ban, or Amaziah's accusations are a denunciation as sedition of the oracles that come from these visions. It is likely that we have only a small fraction of Amos' messages. Amaziah accuses him of prophesying Jeroboam's death (7:11). Such an oracle, in so many words, is not recorded, but we do not need to infer that Amaziah is fabricating the charge. Such a threat is implied in 7:9, which supplies the judgment otherwise lacking in the oracle against Israel in chap. 2, bringing it in line with the judgments against the other nations. In other words, Amaziah's reaction suggests that messages like those in chaps. 1 and 2 had already been delivered. Amaziah's ban then follows Visions 3 and 4 and the ensuing oracles and leads directly to Vision 5. But, as we freely admit, reconstruction in such detail is more than the extant evidence will permit, if we are hoping for certainty. At least it makes sense and supplies a useful working hypothesis. The present arrangement is literary, not chronological. It presents an artistic schema, not a chain of cause and effect.

This provisional outline of Amos' career will be discussed and developed in more detail below. This preliminary sketch is intended simply to announce and illustrate our attitude and approach to the general problem of the present arrangement of the variegated materials in the completed book.

THE BOOK OF AMOS

The Process

The book of the prophet Amos, on first reading, seems to be a miscellaneous collection of various prophetic materials. It does not seem to have much system or order. It is more like an accidentally gathered or badly edited assemblage of speeches made by the prophet or traditionally assigned to him than a well-planned and well-wrought book.

The untidiness (to modern literary taste) of the text that we now have could be due to either of two quite opposite circumstances in its origin and history. Either it is owing to the raw state of the material, coming immediately from the prophet's life situation, largely untouched and unpolished by those who collected it, wrote it down, and transmitted it. The occasional, specific character of many of the utterances and their great intensity attest spontaneous, inspired urgency, undamped by subsequent reflection and moderation. Or else the roughness, the discontinuity, and the obscurity we now find as we read could be due to a complicated process of editorial development or to injuries sustained by the text (which might have been in much better shape when it came from Amos or his editors) during its long transmission and frequent copying in the centuries that followed.

Which of these two explanations we prefer will make a considerable difference in our treatment of the text. We do not have to go to extremes, choosing between a pristine text, immaculately preserved, or a badly mangled remote copy. In the first case we would make every effort to understand the text as it is, hesitant to suspect textual errors and reluctant to emend them. In the second case we would feel much more at liberty to blame the difficulties we now experience, not on Amos or on his early editors, but on later editors and scribes; we would feel free to correct such errors, claiming even to have recovered the original reading by such means.

The truth probably lies somewhere between these two extremes. It is hardly likely that a text of such antiquity has survived unscathed the long and perilous journey from copy to copy to copy. We cannot assume that its sanctity guaranteed miraculous preservation, even though, in due time if not from the beginning, its status as a canonical writing would commit the scholars who handled it to reverence and vigilance. There is no reason to believe, however, that divine Providence would render scribes incapable of error. Neither is it evident that the text has been badly corrupted in transmission. Yet who can now tell just where between the extremes of perfect preservation and extensive deterioration it should be placed? Only the recovery of the original, or of very ancient copies close to the original, could answer that question. A blank period of hundreds of years lies between Amos and the first available evidence of his book, and who knows what might have happened during that time?

What we have just said about the textual criticism of particular readings found in the book applies to the book as a whole. Again two extremes are possible. One exaggerates the wholeness and integrity of the complete composition and finds continuity and connection among all the parts. It finds consistency in the prophet's point of view, his "message"; it finds the argument logical. The other points out the inconsistencies in the point of view, the contradictions in the messages, the great variety of styles and literary forms, the difficulties in relating one part to another.

Once again we take the middle ground. It would be perverse to place the worst assessment on the obscurities and formal contradictions; it would be artificial to try to clear up all of the obscurities and resolve all of the inconsistencies by means of farfetched harmonizations. The work done in preparing this commentary has, however, convinced us with ever increasing force that the text is in better shape than has been generally supposed in modern criticism, and that the contents are not as variegated as is often asserted.

The unity of the book is not found in uniformity, either of literary expression or of ideas. The range of ideas and the variety of forms are remarkable. The integrity of the book is to be found rather in "the words of Amos" (1:1), that is, in his life and ministry. His career moved through several phases, which we hope to analyze and relate to the content of the book. The materials derived from that career consist almost entirely of the prophet's spoken words, with only one brief biographical incident. The preservation of this material is in the form of a literary composition, which has more structure than a mere anthology of Amos' oracles but less symmetry than a completely fresh literary work.

Like all critical scholars, we are naturally interested in the forms of prophetic speech and in the original oral declarations of the prophets. But these are not what we now have. By the gathering and organizing of them into a book, with undetermined amounts of modification and adaptation, they have been given a new kind of literary identity. They are no longer complete and brief messages for some occasion. They are now related to one another as a memorial for Amos and as a monument for posterity. The spoken oracles have become a written prophecy. It is a legitimate exercise to attempt to recover the original speeches that were given out during the prophet's lifetime, and which supplied the material for the book, although we do not believe that much certainty can be achieved in such a venture, and we do not think that it should be the scholar's prime task. Attention remains rather on the book we now have, and the more so if, as we contend, the book itself (or something very close to it) comes from Amos himself, representing a comprehensive synthesis and testament prepared either by him or by an immediate disciple.

We cannot now recover the editorial processes through which spoken oracles became a written book. For all we know, some quite extensive portions of the book might have already been worked up into sustained discourses for public declaration. Organization of similar materials into sets (the eight oracles against the nations in chaps. 1 and 2, the visions in chaps. 7, 8, and 9) would have supplied the prophet with substantial speeches, more powerful than their ingredients taken separately. Even if each of the five visions was received separately, or if the five visions came in three installments, each batch having its own validity at the time of its reception, the accumulation, the movement from the first pair to the second pair to the fifth and last one gives to the completed set a higher unity in which each contributing part acquires additional meaning for itself from the others.

Before the full development of form criticism gave the researcher better tools for analyzing and classifying the literary components of a book such as Amos, thematic and prosodic features suggested that the present disorder in the text was not due to half-completed editorial harmonization of original small fragments, but rather to too much editorial interference with speeches of considerable length that originally were consistent in their content and regular in their poetic form. M. Löhr (1901), for instance, recovered five such speeches, as well as two narrative portions. The latter, in chaps. 7:1–8:3, are straightforward, but the former require extensive adjustment—gathering scattered materials and trimming away superfluous words —in order to achieve more regularity in both scansion and strophic structure. Even after all of that effort, the "original" speeches, as reconstituted by Löhr, are not very regular. In other words, the assumption of formal regularity as an aid to reconstruction of source materials did not prove very beneficial. One gain in Löhr's work was his recognition that 8:4–9:4 contains numerous echoes of material in chaps. 1–6. But it is quite a different exercise to recover an originally well-made speech from these now scattered materials. E. Baumann (1903), building on Löhr's 1901 work, did not include material from chap. 9 with similar material in the first speech he recovered. Löhr and Baumann also disagreed substantially over the content of the other speeches. The criteria used are so soft that the impression remains that a reconstruction could have been done in other ways, each equally plausible.

In contrast to scholars who found in the book not much more than a miscellaneous assemblage of small oracles, each for a different occasion, J. Morgenstern (1941) went to the opposite extreme. He concluded from the precise date in 1:1 and from the single incident reported in chap. 7 that Amos delivered but one address. He thought it possible that Amos' single prophecy would have been proclaimed at the Bethel shrine, and there are plenty of analogies for such an event. Even if it comprised most of the present book, it need have taken no more than half an hour. The trouble with this theory is that, in order to recover this original address, Morgenstern subjected the present text to heavy revision, with deletions and rearrangements on a scale unsurpassed in the history of Amos studies. The only difference between him and a scholar like H. Gressmann (1921), who found as many as thirty distinct oracles in the book, is that Morgenstern puts all of these pieces together. Unlike scholars who explain any apparent order and system in the book as it now stands as the work of later redactors, Morgenstern allows that Amos himself produced a "sermon" of considerable length. If it was given extempore under the stimulus of the situation, as is sometimes done by preachers, no auditor could have remembered it exactly after one hearing, not even Amos as its author. Even if it settled into a stock address, after many subsequent renditions, in due time it would have to be recorded by Amos himself, or be lost. By contrast, numerous short oracles could be remembered well enough within a band of followers so that most of them could be salvaged from the combined recollections of the group. But putting them all together would be a different matter.

Appropriate literary interpretation of the final result needs to attend simultaneously to the diversity of the constituents and to the structural relationships that work all of the ingredients up into a total statement.

The Ingredients

Considered in a general and purely formal way, the book of Amos contains dozens of distinct pieces. There is a title and an opening thematic statement (1:1–2); there are eight oracles against the nations (1:3–2:16), each with the same format; there are five exhortations (3:1–12, 3:13–15, 4:1–5, 5:1–7 and 10–17, 8:4–6), to which might be added two threatening speeches (4:12, 5:25–27); there are five statements about disasters, though more than five agencies are at work (4:6–11); there are three hymns (4:13, 5:8–9, 9:5–6); there are three declarations of "Woe!" (5:18–24, 6:1–3, 6:4–7 [the word hôy does not actually occur in this one]), though some other participial passages might be included in this series; there are two oaths (6:8–14, 8:7–8); five visions (7:1–3, 7:4–6, 7:7–9, 8:1–3, 9:1–4); four or five eschatological predictions using the catchphrase "that day" (8:9–10, 8:13–14, 9:11–12) or "the time is coming" (8:11–12, 9:13–15); there is one anecdote (7:10–17). Finer analysis and more delicate classification would yield as well several passages of a "wisdom" genre scattered throughout these materials (Wolff 1964, 1973).

The judgment oracles against the eight nations make up a single block, as do the linked disasters. This gathering together has not been done for the other related sets. The fourth and fifth "Hear this!" messages are detached from the others. The three woes come together, but the complete inventory of persons denounced has to be gathered from other places. The five visions come together as a pair, a pair, and a single; but a story is inserted between the third and fourth that spoils the symmetry, and several short oracular pieces intervene between the fourth and the fifth. The eschatological passages congregate toward the end, but the oaths and the hymns are interspersed throughout, and it is not at all obvious why they are placed where they are.

It now seems to us that the arrangement would be neater if each of the distinctive sets had been gathered together, if the editor had done with the exhortations, the visions, the oaths, and the hymns what he has done with the judgment oracles and the disaster oracles. If we assume that the original editor did just this in the first place, then we must infer that the text was later reorganized, that materials were added at places that are puzzling to us, but that presumably made sense for the person who did it. Or we can assume that an originally continuous speech was broken up into small pieces, which were then used at various places near statements to which they did not originally belong. Thus Löhr (1901), attempting to reverse this supposed process, reconstructed an original speech out of 3:1b, 2–4a, 5a, 6, 8–15; 4:1–3; 8:4–14; and 9:1 (*wᵉhrytm*), 4a. The common theme is the *Untergang* (destruction) of Israel. Strophic organization as well as thematic content supported the result (Löhr 1901:8). The words *nišbaᶜ* (4:2, 8:7) and *ʾaḥărît* (4:2, 8:10, 9:1) are identified as links. Appealing to logic, Löhr did not think that 8:4 could follow 8:1–3; rather, 8:4–10 supplies the threat needed to complete the accusation in 4:1–3. We acknowledge such thematic links, but we recognize them as long-range, and intentionally so.

There is no reason, however, to believe that items that break up otherwise continuous series are later additions, of dubious authenticity as Amos traditions. The truth of this point is conspicuous with the story of Amos and Amaziah (7:10–17), the originality and authenticity of which have seldom been questioned. We are therefore obliged to ask with the greatest seriousness if its placement at this point was deliberate and a vital part of the total presentation. We are obliged to search for the mutual connections between this story and the vision reports in which it is now embedded. We hope to show, in fact, that it is not just an insertion; the whole has been

The following chart shows the location of the several sets of diverse ingredients in the book of Amos.

Title and theme (1:1–2)

JUDGMENT ORACLES
Against nations (1:3–2:16)
Aram (1:3–5)
Philistia (1:6–8)
Tyre (1:9–10)
Edom (1:11–12)
Ammon (1:13–15)
Moab (2:1–3)
   Judah (2:4–5)
   Israel (2:6–16)

EXHORTATIONS
Hear this (3:1–12)
Confirm (3:13–15)
Hear this (4:1–5)

PLAGUES
Famine (4:6)
Drought (4:7–8)
Blight and locusts (4:9)
Plague and war (4:10)
Fire (4:11)
Threat (4:12)

HYMNS
1 (4:13)

2 (5:8–9)

Hear this (5:1–7)

Warning (5:10–17)

Warning (5:25–27)

Final threat (6:14)

Hear this (8:4–6)

3 (9:5–6)

Threat (9:7–10)

This chart is little more than a broad classification. Many of the pieces placed under different headings have important connections among themselves that cross the lines set out in the chart. Here are just two striking examples. The vital theme of *judgment//righteousness* is enunciated in 5:7 (in what we have called a woe), in 5:24 (in an exhortation), and in 6:12 (in an oath). Woes are declared against persons described by means of participles. Other participles, serving a similar purpose, occur in passages that do not use the term "woe," but which almost certainly add up to a single series. These include 5:7 (in an exhortation) and 8:14 (in the eschatological material).

WOES
Day of Yahweh (5:18–24)

Complacency (6:1–3)
Luxury (6:4–7)

          OATHS
          1 (6:8–14)
          The Oath (6:8–10)

Last Woes (6:11–13)

                               VISIONS
                               Locusts (7:1–3)
                               Fire (7:4–6)
                               Lump of tin (7:7–9)

Anecdote (7:10–17)   Summer fruit (8:1–3)

                    2 (8:7–8)

                                                      ESCHATOLOGY
                                                        That day (8:9–10)
                                                        Time coming (8:11–12)
                                                      That day (8:13–14)

                                   Altar (9:1–4)

                                                          That day (9:11–12)
                                                        Time at hand (9:13–15)

When the book is read continuously, it falls into three main parts, finished off by an Epilogue. Each part is dominated by one or two prominent themes or forms, found less clearly, or not at all, in the other parts. A running analysis of these major divisions, yields the following description. Some of the decisions, reflected in the analysis and the headings used, anticipate the results of research that will be presented in due course, notably in the essay on Amos' political terminology.

woven tightly together. Similar considerations apply to the oaths and the hymns. We consider that the decision to excise the hymns as nonprophetic, fragmentary, and out of place has been made too hastily in the past. In arguing for their authenticity, we do not claim that Amos composed them; they obviously derive from cult traditions. But we do raise seriously the question of their use by the prophet or compiler and their placement at strategic positions that contribute to the total presentation and to the integral structure of the whole. In other words, we would rather give the benefit of the doubt to the literary character of the book in questions of this kind.

We have divided the whole book into three major parts (or books) with an Epilogue. The Book of Visions (7:1–9:6) is clearly delimited, also organized. At least the vision reports follow a plan. How the additional materials are arranged around the visions and attached to them is more problematical. There is a set of oracles against eight nations in chaps. 1 and 2, unified by repeated formulas. But the lack of the complete formula for the eighth oracle makes it difficult to decide where this set ends. A set of plague oracles in chap. 4 (vv 6–11) has similar repetitions. Unlike the oracles and the plague reports, which all come right after one another, the five visions are not presented in a single block. They come in three installments—a pair, a pair, a single. There are formulaic repetitions in each of the pairs, but even the second pair is divided by a narrative piece. These details highlight the question of the integral (or intrusive) character of this story and the other nonvisionary material in The Book of Visions. The woes are less formulaic and are partly gathered, partly spread out. The series is unified by the repeated call to "Hear!" (3:1, 4:1, 5:1, 8:4; cf. 3:9), and by the set of participial constructions that identify the persons against whom the woes are directed.

We have called chaps. 5–6 The Book of Woes, because woes dominate this section; but they are not confined to it. They begin at 2:7 (at least the participle series begins there) and reappear in chap. 8 (vv 4, 14). We have called chaps. 1–4 The Book of Doom; but its limits and its integrity as a major unit on a par with the other two are not so clearly marked by the use of similar forms or formulas throughout. If the eight oracles (assuming that we could be sure where the eighth one ends) are separated from the material that follows them, then the new beginning at 3:1 is an obvious break. But there are continuities as well, and it could be that the eighth oracle (against Israel) goes right through to the end of chap. 4, so that the use of the name "Israel" in 4:12 is a long-range inclusion with 2:6. The language used in 3:1 shows that all of Israel is in view; in fact we suggest that everything from 2:9 to 3:8 and from 4:4 to 4:11 is addressed to the whole nation of two kingdoms, while recognizing that the spotlight is on Samaria.

The closing section (9:7–15) can be called an Epilogue, but these verses have important organic connections with the rest of the book. The whole book exhibits the same compositional technique; there are assemblages of similar material, and sometimes clear transitions from one part to the next. But there are also continuities across these breaks. The exact number of constituent sections to be recognized does not matter. The ones we employ are essentially descriptive and are presented simply for convenient reference. We do not think that they necessarily exhibit the compositional or editorial history of the complete work. We have found it increasingly difficult to distinguish original from redactional components. In terms of the methodology of redaction criticism, this means that the more difficult it becomes to separate the redactors' work from the material that came into their hands, the more difficult it becomes to talk about redactors at all. A thoroughly creative rewriting of available material becomes indistinguishable from original creative writing.

When the intricate arrangement of the book as a whole is examined more closely, it reveals a number of devices—verbal, structural, thematic—which serve as long-range connections linking and unifying the whole. These bonds are all the more impressive when there is chiasmus (which is often the case) between the two widely separated corresponding parts, and they will be discussed in full detail in the NOTES and COMMENTS. A few specimens will serve to introduce the general idea at this point:

1. A topic already announced or dealt with at some length may be picked up again later by way of echo or inclusion. Thus 3:8 returns to the theme of 1:2, an inclusion that rounds off 1:2–3:8 as a major unit. The nations listed in 9:7 correspond to three of those mentioned in 1:3–2:8, but in reverse order—another inclusion. The plagues described in 4:6–11 find an echo in 6:9–10. The disaster described in 2:14–16 has a matching piece in 9:2–4. The riddle in 6:12a reminds one of the larger set in 3:3–6. And so on.

2. A theme may be declared but not fully developed until later. A major indictment of Israel is its suppression of prophecy (2:12); but only in 7:10–17 is its significance drawn out.

3. Contrastive material is inserted at key locations, often to serve a structural purpose. The three hymns come at strategic points in the three bodies of oracles, which correspond in turn to the three sets of visions. The first Hymn (4:13) comes at the end of the first book. The third (9:5–6) comes at the beginning of the Epilogue (or at the end of The Book of Visions). The middle one is near the beginning of The Book of Woes. A similar pattern in the placement of hymns may be seen in the book of Isaiah (cf. chaps. 12, 26).

4. The first set of oracles contains a numerical formula $x \mathbin{/\!/} x + 1$, familiar in the Bible and in Canaanite poetry generally. In this oracle it is $3 \mathbin{/\!/} 4$. The oracles themselves contain no indication of why these particu-

lar numerals are used. The indictment sets forth only one crime, perhaps the last and worst (the fourth after three bad ones, or perhaps the seventh). Seven is a common climactic number. Other numerals in the book (3:3; 4:4, 7, 8; 5:3; 6:9) do not seem to have similar symbolic significance. The sequence that begins in 5:3 is not completed until 6:9. Yet even where numerals are not used, we may suspect that numerical groupings are part of the plan. Seven plus one nations are condemned in the Oracles Against Nations (1:2–2:8). There are two oaths, three hymns, five visions (in three sets), five plagues (4:6–11, although as many as eight distinct disasters can be counted in the series). There are five elements in each of the apostrophes.

Although a one-to-one correlation cannot be worked out, we suspect that there is a connection between the five plagues and the five visions. If there was a historical connection in the first place, it has not been preserved in the final written version. If the editor was striving for a literary effect, he did not force the available material into artificial schemes.

The call to hear is given five times (3:1, 13; 4:1; 5:1; 8:4), but it is possible that the two messages that contain *lākēn* ("therefore," 4:12, 5:11) should be added to them to make seven. Two oracles are introduced by "Woe!" (5:18, 6:1), but the participles that are found in other places without the word "woe" are probably blanketed by this term, sometimes at a considerable distance. There could be as many as nineteen of them, some in parallel pairs. How many of them belong to the complete "woe" series? Some that would qualify quite well, such as the trio in 4:1, come in a "Hear!" oracle; and the same is true for the participle in 8:4. The others are located at nine places throughout the book (2:7; 3:10; 5:7, 12, 18; 6:1–6, 13; 8:14; 9:10). Whether there is a core of seven "woes" in this list will be discussed in the NOTES. The only point that needs to be made here is that participial descriptions of miscreants are found in nearly every chapter (infinitives are used in the oracles against the nations in chaps. 1–2, with a change to a participle at 2:7, which inaugurates the long catalog of accusations against Israel). The one in 9:10 seems to form an inclusion with 6:13, and the construct forms in 5:12 could be excluded from those with articles, leaving seven distinct woes. The point need not be pressed. At least the great woe oracle in 6:1–7, which serves as a centerpiece for all of the others, has seven participles.

THE HISTORY OF AMOS' TIMES

The title of the book of Amos (1:1) states that he had his visions in the days of Uzziah of Judah and Jeroboam (II) of Israel. These two kings enjoyed very long reigns, exceptional for those times: Uzziah ruled for fifty-two years and Jeroboam for forty-one, each setting a record for his kingdom up to that time. Coregencies may have been involved at the beginning of both their reigns and at the end of Uzziah's, and the figures could be regarded as including such overlap periods. It says in 2 Kgs 14:23 that Jeroboam became king in the fifteenth year of Amaziah and in 2 Kgs 15:1–2 that Uzziah (Azariah) became king (aged sixteen years) in the twenty-seventh year of Jeroboam II's reign. E. R. Thiele (1965:77–89) has made the most successful bid to bring all of the available data together into a consistent picture. Absolute dates cannot be determined, but for purposes of this study it will be enough to say that Uzziah's fifty-two years probably extended from about 792 B.C.E. to about 740 B.C.E., the first twenty-four years or so as his father's coregent, and the last decade or so with his son Jotham as regent. His period of sole reign could then have been little more than eighteen years (767–750). Jeroboam II's reign ran from 793/2 to 753/2 (Thiele) or 786–746 (Albright), the first eleven years as his father's coregent. Accordingly, we may look first at the decade during which these two monarchs were both in full power as the best location for the activities of Amos, say 765–755. It could have been earlier, but it could not have been much later, for we must find the best fit for the historical situation as it can be reconstructed from all of the indications within the book of Amos and what can be determined from additional contemporary records, biblical and otherwise.

In view of the extraordinary lengths of their reigns, the reports of their doings and achievements by biblical historians are astonishingly brief. Jeroboam II received only seven verses (2 Kgs 14:23–29), Uzziah (Azariah) only nine (2 Kgs 14:21–22, 15:1–7) in the Primary History. It is true that the Chronicler devotes a whole chapter to Uzziah (2 Chr 26), but the overlay of legend and exaggeration that characterizes the work of that historian restrains us from using his data with complete confidence. There is no need, however, to go to the other extreme and ignore his notices altogether. The Chronicler's report of Uzziah's military achievements enlarges on the brief notices in 2 Kings 15, and both fit in with what Amos says, especially in chaps. 5 and 6.

Comparison of these three sources brings out the basic differences in the way the events of those years were read by the various schools of thought in Israel. The royal archives were compiled by officers of the establishment who put a positive construction on the kings' military successes. Uzziah regained and rebuilt Elath (2 Kgs 14:22; 2 Chr 26:2) and, if we are to believe the Chronicler, enjoyed remarkable triumphs against old enemies to both east and west (26:6–8). Jeroboam II likewise was able to restore the territory of Israel to its old and greatest extent (2 Kgs 14:25). Amos supplies a few more details (e.g., 6:13) not found in these other histories, and his comment in 6:14 is in line with 2 Kgs 14:25, even though it strikes an opposite note. The Deuteronomistic and Priestly historians present the kings approvingly as working in collaboration with prophetic advisers— Jonah in the case of Jeroboam (2 Kgs 14:25) and Zechariah in the case of Uzziah (2 Chr 26:5). Their endorsement is not unqualified, however. The usual adverse comment is made about the northern king (2 Kgs 14:24), but it is so stereotyped as to add nothing concrete to our knowledge. The comments of the Chronicler about Uzziah's downfall are more sensational and pious. It may sound timid to say that we have no grounds for contradicting him except, perhaps, modern distrust of that kind of reportage. But, for what they are worth, and within their narrow range of Priestly vision, they provide a partial explanation of the rapid decline that took place in both kingdoms after the reigns of these two kings, developments more in line with Amos' analysis of the situation. Compared with Amos' diagnosis of the spiritual condition of both nations, the comments of the biblical historians are superficial. Just as national successes are attributed to the religiosity of the kings, so national failures are blamed on the kings' impiety. In each case there is a connection with the cult: Jeroboam's maintenance of the idolatrous shrines of Jeroboam (I) the son of Nebat (2 Kgs 14:24), and Uzziah's presumptuous intrusion into the sacred precincts (2 Chr 26:16). It is an irony that the hero on this occasion was a priest who ejected the unwanted intruder from the shrine, whereas the priest who does the same to Amos at Bethel is the villain of that piece.

In contrast to the historian whose almost exclusive interest is in the leadership role of the kings as determining national weal or woe, Amos says practically nothing about the monarchs of his day. True, Amos was accused of uttering seditious words against Jeroboam (7:11), and we do not think that Amaziah was just making that up. But all of the oracles that are preserved and presented in his book are concerned with oppression and corruption in commerce and courtroom. Crimes against humanity, not deviations from the proprieties of the cult, are his main target. As far as Amos is concerned, their high-handed attitude toward Yahweh is shown (besides these social injustices) not in neglect or distortion of the traditional institutions of national religion (which seem, as a matter of fact, to be thriving) but in prohibiting the prophets and neutralizing the nazirites. The official historians give us the view from above, Amos the view from ground level. The complacency with which the people were able to rejoice in their prosperity (6:4–6) and military victories (6:13), thronging the temples at the great festivals of thanksgiving, was to Amos (or rather, to Yahweh) proof of abhorrent pride (6:8). One can hardly imagine points of view more opposite. And one can understand why Amos failed completely, at least at the time, to put his point across except perhaps to a few like-minded supporters and converts.

The freedom with which Jeroboam and Uzziah were able to embark on such successful military enterprises was doubtless made possible because there was a lull in the wars against Aram that had taken up so much of Israel's attention in the preceding reigns. And Assyria was quiet—for the time being. It was not until the accession of Tiglath-pileser III (745 B.C.E.) that this "unnatural" state of affairs ended. Amos never mentions Assyria (in the existing MT—but see NOTES on 3:9), even as a distant menace, though there are a few hints that he is aware of danger in the wings (6:14). It is only in retrospect, after it was all over, that we can see how some of his threats were fulfilled by the Assyrian conquests. Amos' prophecies, especially his oracles of woe and judgment, can thus be connected with the special and peculiar circumstances of the military and political activities of the first half of the eighth century, certainly in the heyday of Jeroboam II (aided and abetted by Jonah ben-Amittai) and Uzziah, who may well have had his own prophetic assistants (cf. 2 Chr 26:5—Zechariah "who instructed him in the fear of God").

We must be dealing therefore with the period of both kingdoms' triumphant expansion and of a series of military successes by both kings. As Jeroboam is said to have recaptured the whole territory of Transjordan from Lebo-Hamath to the Sea of the Arabah in the area of the Dead Sea, it is difficult to imagine this happening without the acquiescence and probably the support of Judah, especially in the territory of Moab adjoining Edom, the latter being within Judah's sphere of influence. Thus we are told in 2 Chr 26:2 that Uzziah rebuilt Eloth, showing that both kings were operating in neighboring areas at roughly the same time and without noticeable friction. Normally one would think of Israel as the dominant party in any cooperative relationship; but in this situation and during the lifetimes and reigns of these two kings, the arrangement may have been more of an equal one than otherwise, at least in principle.

In addition, both Meunites and Ammonites are mentioned in vv 7–8 of 2 Chr 26, indicating that Uzziah's operations were extensive all around the borders of Judah and beyond. Whatever the difficulties with individual readings, there can be little doubt that Uzziah was a man and force to be reckoned with, as we know from his later entanglements in Syria during the reign of Tiglath-pileser III. We should therefore suppose that Jeroboam and Uzziah acted in concert in their separate but associated enterprises. Whether there was a formal alliance and whether they plotted their strategy together may remain uncertain, but it seems clear that they intended together to restore the classic boundaries of the united kingdom of David and Solomon. Jeroboam devoted his considerable energies to recapturing the east-bank territories that had been part of Israel according to tradition from the time of Moses, and we hear of the traditional boundary of Lebo-Hamath on the northeast in the account of his conquests. The fact that the borders extended down to the Wadi Arabah shows that Judahite interests must have been consulted, and if Judah did not actually cooperate in this part of the enterprise, certainly it was approved by the chancellery in Jerusalem. It is likely that their activities dovetailed, with Jeroboam regaining control over Moab while Uzziah restored Judah's suzerainty over Edom.

Similarly, Uzziah concentrated his efforts on the southwestern quadrant, attacking the Philistine cities successfully and either annexing them or subjecting them to tribute. Clearly his other borders were secure enough to allow him to focus his fighting forces on the Philistines. The reason for this security was that his partner Jeroboam controlled the other border territories. Because they were both at peace and in league there was nothing to fear on either side from the other, which allowed both to prosecute winning battles on their other fronts. Each may have been involved more directly in the campaigns of the other, in terms of logistics or troops, but the record is too spotty and fragmentary to hazard more than a guess. There seems to be a little evidence of Uzziah's involvement east of the Jordan if the reference to the Ammonites can be sustained, and Jeroboam may have had a hand in Uzziah's southern operations.

In any event both kings were enormously successful, at least for a period, and the strategy seems to have worked well. Some further observations may be in order:

1. Both kings had spiritual advisers who apparently encouraged them in their military-political exploits and undertakings. This is explicitly stated of the prophet Jonah in the case of Jeroboam, and in a more general way of Zechariah the wise man (*mēbîn*) in the case of Uzziah. Therefore the kings could feel secure in the theological implications and applications, undertones and overtones of their policies, which would most likely make them very resistant to any criticism offered by other but effectively unlicensed prophets. We have good evidence for this cavalier resistance to and dismissal of prophets such as Amos and Hosea in the case of Jeroboam, but we know less about the reign of Uzziah, even though both Amos and Hosea were active in Judah in the lifetime of Uzziah, according to the headings of their books. As we know from Isaiah 6, that prophet's ministry apparently began in the year that King Uzziah died.

2. Another important point is that in the period of which we are speaking, roughly from 785/780 to 755/750, Israel and Judah had few if any worries about the great powers to the northeast and southwest, Assyria and Egypt. Even for the later period of the book of Hosea, while both nations are repeatedly referred to, there is little sense on the part of the military-political establishment of any serious threat to the existence or integrity of the two small nations coming from either or both of the superpowers. The concern and the activities are therefore confined for the most part to the territory occupied by the eight small nations listed in Amos' opening diatribe. Certainly this interval of passivity on the part of the great powers

allowed both Israel and Judah to operate much more freely in those territories than would otherwise have been the case. After the rise of Tiglath-pileser III and the movement of the Assyrian armies west, with the corresponding increment in Egyptian military moves, though the latter were never quite as vigorous or violent, conditions would never be the same again. Already with Hosea the two great nations figure prominently in all of the small nations' calculations or decisions, and by the time of Isaiah and Micah, the definitive and irresistible tide of events has been set into motion, specifying Assyria as the divine agent of destruction and domination, while Egypt is to serve largely as a foil and to be reduced by ridicule to a symbol of impotence. Amos alone seems to reflect conditions of the earlier time, before the serious intervention of the great powers, and therefore deserves to be studied all the more carefully for descriptive clues to the historical situation in his day and for the association of oracles with events and circumstances during the reigns of the two contemporary and overlapping monarchs.

THE CONTENTS OF THE BOOK OF AMOS

The book of Amos is quite short. It consists of 9 chapters, 146 verses (according to the Masorah at the end of the text in the Hebrew manuscripts, so it is a traditional number), and about 2,053 words (Even-Shoshan 1985:xxxviii). There is no tradition about the word count, which is open to uncertainty due to vague definitions of "word" or due to differing orthographic conventions concerning word boundaries. Our count (2,042) agrees with that of Weil (1980:34). Amos covers about eight pages in an ordinary edition of the Bible and can be read easily in fifteen or twenty minutes. It can also be studied profitably, though not completely, for fifteen or twenty years by scholars and students alike. The communities that acknowledge its authority have preserved and revered it as part of the collection of twelve prophets for well over two thousand years, while its history as a literary work may go back much farther.

Its central message and meaning are not difficult to discern, and most of those who have read it come away with a vivid and often indelible impression of the words and the man who uttered them. At the same time the book is not transparent, and numerous difficulties have been encountered by careful and conscientious readers. Details of language and intent often elude us. Features, background, and setting remain stubbornly obscure and opaque. We often wish that Amos and his editors had been less rigorous and concise and more generous with explanations and elaborations, more merciful to generations far removed from their own and without essential

items of information and understanding. For the truth is that the man and
prophet is unknown outside of this small book. He is not mentioned elsewhere in the Bible, and there is no information about him from any other
contemporary source.

The Lives of the Prophets, a late apocryphal work, supplies meager details: "He was from Tekoa. Amaziah (the priest of Bethel) had often beaten
him, and at last Amaziah's son killed him with a cudgel, striking him on
the temple. While still living he made his way to his land, and after some
days died and was buried there" (Torrey 1946:40, cf. Hare 1985:391). Notices of this kind, of which the earliest known attestation is so long after the
event, do not normally inspire confidence. Yet such traditions are often
quite tenacious in oral transmission and, in spite of being vulnerable to
corruption and contamination, may preserve authentic data. The information given is plausible, but could be no more than an imaginative elaboration of possibilities suggested by the original text. Some of the details seem
to be of independent origin (the involvement of Amaziah's son and the
circumstances of his death, including the cudgel and the head wounds), and
such a development can be accepted as a plausible outcome of the confrontation described in chap. 7. Amos could hardly have carried on as usual
after such a crisis, and it is hard to believe that he simply took Amaziah's
advice and went back home. At the same time the assertion that he died in
Judah may have been intended to link up with some tradition about his
grave. In our view, which can be stated fully only after we have presented
the results of our investigations in more detail, Amos himself had a major
hand in the selection and organization of his messages into something fairly
close to the book we now have. If the argument with Amaziah was followed
promptly by Amos' execution, we must suppose either that the text of the
book was already in an advanced state of preparation, and could well have
been used as a great address to the worshipers assembled at Bethel, provok-
ing Amaziah's attack; or that its essential substance was already in the
custody (in writing or in memory) of faithful friends who subsequently
completed the editorial task. The account in *The Lives of the Prophets*
includes a short interval during which Amos could have supervised the
preparation of his memoirs. It also explains why only one incident is reported in the final form of the book, when so much else must have been
known and could have been included. His rejection by the priest of Bethel
provided both the occasion and the initial reason for securing his message
in written form.

While on this point we might mention that the existence of a coherent
work properly called "The Words of Amos," as attested by the title, does
not necessarily imply that the present form of the book corresponds, more
or less closely, to the actual form of a prophetic speech. Morgenstern is
unusual among modern scholars for having claimed "that the entire active

career of Amos as a prophet, his complete functioning before the people in his prophetic role, consisted only of the single moment of his appearance at Bethel, and that there he delivered his entire, closely unified address" (1936:27). The weakness of this hypothesis is betrayed by the need Morgenstern has in his lengthy study for achieving "a rearrangement of the at present disorganized text into what will seem after careful analysis to have been approximately the original sequence of thoughts in the single address" (ibid.). We do not think that all of the prophecies in the present collection could have been proclaimed originally on one occasion; rather, they come from several stages or phases in the development of Amos' ministry, and we hope to trace this movement by relating the visions to the oracles. The present arrangement is neither chronological nor logical; but it has its own literary character, the result of a purely literary presentation of materials gathered from the decisive stages of Amos' career. The most appropriate time for gathering these materials was either shortly before Amos' death by Amos himself, or shortly after his death by a close follower. We suggest that "two years before the earthquake" (1:1) is when this was achieved. Inevitably the title itself was attached or expanded after the earthquake that was the occasion for the book's publication in substantially its present form.

Our acknowledgment of the almost complete lack of information about Amos himself does not negate in any way the immense value of the other books of the Bible in supplying information of all kinds—historical, literary, socioeconomic, and cultural—that bears on the analysis and interpretation of the book of Amos. Similarly, help can be derived from other ancient sources, including inscriptions and other results of archaeological research. We only wish to emphasize the unique importance of the book of Amos itself and the necessity for examining it very carefully if we are to recover essential data about the prophet. In what follows, we shall be guided by the book and attempt to reconstruct as much of the history and the meaning of Amos' message as possible.

We begin with the heading (1:1), which has a number of unusual features but essentially tells us that it is a chronicle, an account of Amos, who was a shepherd and farmer, and became a prophet; who had visions in the days of Uzziah, king of Judah, and his older contemporary Jeroboam, king of Israel; and whose career apparently ended two years before the earthquake. The latter mode of dating is unusual in headings, and we are justified in supposing that the earthquake was a major tremor and a memorable one, as it is evidently referred to in the book of Zechariah (14:5), compiled about 250 years later, as causing widespread panic.

Apart from the heading, the book can be subdivided into four sections of varying size, or else three major parts and a concluding unit or Epilogue:

I. The Book of Doom: oracles against the nations and Israel (chaps. 1–4)
  A. Oracles against the nations (chaps. 1:3–2:8)
  B. The charge against Israel (chaps. 2:9–4:13)
II. Woes and Lamentations (chaps. 5–6)
III. The Book of Visions (chaps. 7:1–9:6)
IV. Epilogue (chap. 9:7–15)

A more detailed outline has been supplied in the Table of Contents, but for the purposes of an initial presentation here, this skeletal structure will suffice.

Part I. The Book of Doom (1:1–4:13)

I.A. ORACLES AGAINST THE NATIONS (1:2–2:8)

Chapters 1 and 2 comprise Amos' central message as formulated in a speech that we will call the Great Set Speech. We shall not at this point attempt to analyze the speech in detail or to discuss the many questions relating to specific elements in each of the oracles; rather we shall discuss its major features and place in the general outline.

The speech itself is formally organized and uses formulaic repetitions in all of its parts. This pattern of repetitions establishes the common and central themes of the whole speech. The precise orderliness breaks down with the eighth and final entry—Israel, the northern kingdom—but this change may have been deliberate because it seems clear that the last entry on the list received special and added attention.

The first thing to note is that the same basic charge is leveled at all eight nations, namely, that they have revolted against divine rule. The root $p\check{s}^c$ is used of rebellion against higher authority, and specifically of nations and their rulers revolting against their suzerains. In this case, however, the rebellion is against the rule of Yahweh (cf. Ps 2:1–3). Because of the accumulation of these transgressions, an irrevocable decision has been made by Yahweh ("I will not reverse it") to destroy each of the eight nations. The eight repetitions establish that they all have equal standing before God, are equally guilty, and will suffer equivalent fates. In seven cases the doom is specified as resulting from a fire sent by God, which will devour the capital city, tantamount to or symbolic of destruction of the national entity. In some cases (four in all) further details are given, which reflect the actual circumstances and consequences of siege and invasion, resulting in death and captivity. In three others nothing further is said, while in the case of Israel a different treatment and development of the message take place. The threat pronounced against all of the others is not repeated for Israel, though the consequences are spelled out in greater detail in other places in this and in subsequent units.

The second point to be noted is that the eight nations or states occupy substantially the whole territory between Egypt to the southwest and Assyria to the northeast. The term "nation" is sometimes more appropriate than state, because the oracle embraces more than one city-state, as in the case of the Philistines and, apparently, the Aramaeans. Certainly it is appropriate for the Philistines, four of whose chief cities are mentioned, with the fifth turning up elsewhere in the book (6:2). In the case of the Aramaeans, Damascus is the chief state mentioned, but the other cities included in the threat of punishment may have been autonomous. Hamath also is mentioned in 6:2, and historically it was a separate state. In the case of the people of Israel, however, we have one people in two nations, each given a distinct oracle. The different presentation of the Phoenicians raises a slight question, whether the entire territory between Assyria and Egypt is intended; Tyre is listed, but no other Phoenician city. Are they meant to be included? If Amos mentions the several Philistine cities rather than only one, would he not have listed additional Phoenician cities if he had meant them to be included? The conclusion, or at least the impression, is that the whole area will be overrun and all of the city-states destroyed in a single divinely organized and executed campaign, though in practice it will be a matter of invasion, defeat, destruction, and either wholesale slaughter or large-scale captivity, or to some extent both.

The judgment on the nations is limited, but it is final. It does not embrace the whole world, only the eight nations; and no other nation is indicted and condemned in the book of Amos. Only the nations in the area that was occupied at one time largely by the Davidic and Solomonic kingdoms are involved. All nations in that area will be destroyed by Yahweh, to whom they owed allegiance but against whom they rebelled.

The third point is that when we look at the crimes charged against the nations, only the last two, Judah and Israel, are accused of specifically religious offenses, which amount to rejecting the covenant and not giving Yahweh due worship and service. The language about Judah is fairly stereotyped (but nevertheless there are unusual features). In Israel's case more detail is given, and the charges cover a spectrum of unacceptable practices; but the critical element seems to be the worship of other gods, or the corruption of the worship of Yahweh. With regard to the other nations, their crimes are civil rather than religious, and they seem to be violations of a kind of "natural law." None of them is condemned for worshiping other gods, which they assuredly do; but apparently they are not expected to do otherwise, at least not now and not yet. If Amos, who clearly recognizes the jurisdiction of Yahweh over all of these peoples, whatever the basis for that claim might have been (creation or past history), cannot be imagined as condoning—let alone endorsing—their religions, at least in the context of these oracles the crimes exposed loom larger than polytheism or idolatry as causes of the divine anger. By and large the nations are charged with crimes that most people would agree were reprehensible; in any case, no catalog is given for any nation but Israel. So the listing of essentially a single item for each nation must be taken as typical, symbolic, and representative rather than as the only crime or even the main one.

Fourth, the order and arrangement of the nations probably defy rational analysis except for one point, on which all interpreters seem to be agreed, that Israel should come last. The oracle for Judah has attracted more suspicion than any of the others; but, granted its authenticity, the reversal of the usual sequence is understandable to secure the final position for Israel. The others are not in any order that could reflect the progress of an actual invasion, whether from the Assyrians in the northeast or from the Egyptians in the southwest or even simultaneously from both ends. The present order boxes the compass, as though Yahweh were going to attack all of them at once; and the vantage point from which he would be able to do so would be his heavenly headquarters. This perspective, and the obscure and artificial character of much of the language, implies that this text is the transcript of a vision rather than the declaration or description of an actual military program. It requires considerable interpretation to obtain the rather commonplace result that Amos is describing the natural course of historical events. Thus Löhr (1901:2) says that chaps. 1 and 2 threaten Assyrian invasion under the picture of a tempest. The effect is certainly dramatic, and it may or may not reflect the prophet's thought about how the judgment would be carried out in reality. The fact that there is an order, however, in no way implies a sequential fulfillment, a temporal order of events. If Amos intended such a thing, no one has succeeded in discovering the significance of the arrangement. The seemingly random order does, indeed, reflect the impossibility of expressing simultaneity either orally or in writing without explaining that the purpose is to transcend the limitations of each medium. The impression made by Amos' statement is that one great conflagration will wipe out all of the nations mentioned. Alternatively, separate and simultaneous campaigns seem to be carried out against each of them. Otherwise one would have to abandon the search for meaning in the present arrangement by viewing chaps. 1 and 2 not as a single speech but as no more than a collection of independent oracles—composed along the same lines, it is conceded, and put all together simply because of their formal similarity but not otherwise connected with one another. Our more detailed study that follows will show that this negative conclusion creates more problems than it solves. Removal of one or more of the separate oracles on various grounds, mainly historical, disturbs the symmetry now displayed by the total assemblage; and the climactic position of the last oracle (for Israel) has its maximum strength when it is finally placed in the center of the ring that is completed by the other seven.

Needless to say, the historical outcome showed little resemblance to what is threatened here. It took centuries before all eight nations were actually obliterated, and at no time were all destroyed together. So the Great Set Speech is not to be understood or explained as a later reflex of historical developments, rather as the articulation of a vision and a message received from God, which was intended to have and would have historical consequences. But that is quite different from saying that the oracles were precise predictions of the future or, more importantly, descriptions of a historical past. They are, in a word, genuine prophecy, neither a mechanical nor a cynical game played by professional deluders of the public, past or present.

Fifth, the simplest analysis of the list sees in it a series of pairs, with adjoining oracles sharing characteristic features. Thus the first pair, Aram and Philistia (cf. 9:7, where they are paired again, but in reverse order; cf. also Hamath and Gath in 6:2), follows the same pattern with brief charges and extended presentation of punishments—Aram will go into exile and Philistia will perish. The second pair, Tyre and Edom, consists of shorter oracles with slightly extended charges but with no further specification of punishment beyond the formula already mentioned. The third pair, Ammon and Moab, is extended in fashion similar to the first pair. The charges are brief but the punishments are expanded; again, curiously, the first (Ammon) goes into exile while the second (Moab) will have its rulers killed. Of the three pairs, Ammon and Moab are the only couple linked by tradition in a close ethnic relationship.

When we reach Judah and Israel we expect expanded charges and reduced sentences, following the pattern of the second pair, and that is true of Judah. With Israel the charges are greatly expanded (2:6–8), but the oracle then breaks off. The following material is dramatically different in content and form and represents a considerable change from the standard format. It is difficult to explain why the punishment is lacking altogether where we expect it, after the charges are completed in v 8; we do not even have the standard formula. Instead there is an expansion to the end of the chapter, which relates to the two kingdoms of Israel and Judah together rather than to the other nations. At the proper place we shall take up the more nuanced question of whether the punishment threatened in 2:14–16 is meant for the whole region.

We must now deal with this expanded oracle for Israel and the reasons for it. If we are right in claiming that the message in Amos 1–2 constituted a "first"—namely, that before Amos and his time no prophet had threatened, in the name and words of Yahweh, the very existence of the nation, or at least not since its founding in the wilderness—then Amos and we could expect a rather strong and skeptical reaction.

As we gather from the extraordinary statement in 3:1–2, people would naturally react by saying that the idea was unthinkable and impossible because they were Yahweh's people and he was their God—while they were bound to him, he was also bound to them. Further, if they were required to worship and serve him (which they would protest they were doing all the time) he was also bound to support their welfare and well-being. They were tied together indissolubly in a mutual assistance pact. In drawing his conclusion Amos could not be more wrong; hence he could not be a prophet at all, and certainly not a true one.

Either Amos or his editor must be ready with a defense, and one is provided in the distinctive material following 2:8. In this section the relationship of Yahweh with his people is explained in historical terms, and both his right to demand obedience and compliance with his requirements and his right to judge and punish them if they fall short of those requirements are asserted.

I.B. ORACLES AGAINST THE WHOLE OF ISRAEL (2:9–3:8)
I.B.1. HISTORICAL RECITAL AND THREAT (2:9–16)

In the unit beginning with 2:9 and extending at least through 2:12 and possibly to 2:13, we have a classic statement of Yahweh's basic relationship with Israel. Its national history and Yahweh's claim to a unique status, requiring exclusive worship and service, are rooted in the affirmation of 2:10: "And as for me, I brought you up from the land of Egypt, and I led you in the wilderness for forty years, so that you could take possession of the land of the Amorite." The same sentiment is expressed in 3:1 and 9:7. The point is that the decision announced in 2:4 against Judah and in 2:6 against Israel is neither arbitrary nor tyrannical. The claim to jurisdiction arises not merely from Yahweh's general status as sovereign of the universe, but specifically from his act of grace and his mighty deed in rescuing Israel from bondage in Egypt and in establishing it as a nation in the land of the Amorites (Canaan). Here we have the general argument: failure on Israel's part to show its gratitude in appropriate worship and service would result in judgment and punishment, a point made sharply and explicitly in 3:1–2, the next speech. But the specific points to be added in 2:9–13 have to do with Yahweh's continuing concern for his people. The objective was not simply to establish them in the land and let them go their own way but to provide timely warning in the event of their going astray or before such deviation took place, and timely assistance in circumstances of aggression and distress, should they suffer the inevitable consequences of their defection.

Amos mentions two classes of people, chosen by God and appointed by him to be his agents among his people: (1) prophets, to be guardians and messengers of his word, to announce the divine message and counsel, to advise and warn, to threaten and condemn, but also to console and encourage—essentially to tell the people about the current status of the relationship with Yahweh and what it portended for the future—and (2) nazirites, of whom we know much less, but from the meager information provided about Samson we surmise that these heroes, dedicated from birth and bound by vow to their God, were raised up to perform acts of deliverance and salvation, to rescue Israel from oppression and suffering. Here the mighty act is stressed, where with the prophets it is the mighty word. With the prophets it was mainly words of warning, and with the nazirites it was primarily deeds of saving. But these agents of Yahweh, intended to be of benefit to the nation, have been effectively silenced and subverted by the people so that they are unable to carry out their responsibilities. The prophets have been silenced by being commanded not to prophesy, while the nazirites have been forced to violate a vow against drinking wine or strong drink (i.e., with an alcoholic content). If now Israel finds itself in grave jeopardy, it has only itself to blame (reference throughout this material is to the combined nation—historic Israel from its inception—and here the two states of Amos' day are conceived as a unit). Israel has compounded the initial felony of covenant violation by shutting off both the means of communication and the possibilities of reformation and recovery by silencing the prophets on the one hand and forcing the nazirites to break their vows on the other. The reference to their being made to drink wine contrary to the dedicatory vow seems to be exemplary and representative, rather than central. The point is that they are rendered unfit for their calling. It may be, too, that their assigned role was somewhat different from what we had imagined. Instead of being agents of salvation like Samson, they may instead be regarded as models of an ascetic holy-man tradition who were ever before the Israelites as examples of dedication or commitment to Yahweh.

Another possibility is exemplified by Samuel, at once a prophet and a nazirite, combining the exemplary life with the messenger function. Furthermore, as one of the judges of Israel he is also the agent of salvation. Whatever specific interpretation we put on this interesting combination of terms, it is clear that the statements here are intended to support the view that Yahweh, the original redeemer and savior, has continued to look after his people by providing prophets and nazirites, or naziritic prophets or prophetic nazirites. The people, however, are doubly condemned because, first, they have violated the covenant (as spelled out in 2:4–5 and 2:6–8) and, second, they have closed off the channels of communication and the agents of divine action (or their role models in the community) so as to ensure their own condemnation and destruction. Not only are they unable to blame Yahweh for the disaster that threatens, but they must blame themselves for breaking the compact and then compounding this wrong not just by ignoring the prophets, which would be bad enough, but by going farther and preventing the prophets from speaking and the nazirites from being nazirites. By such behavior they have shown themselves to be intransigent sinners and therefore beyond hope of repentance and salvation. Their doom is sure, and it is their own fault.

The last unit of chap. 2 is a stark description of the promised doom. Because the language is military, it sounds like a description of a final battle in which the army is defeated and destroyed, and the survivors scattered in flight. But even they will not escape. The use of the phrase "in that day" (2:16) is indicative of its futuristic and eschatological character, for there are affinities with 9:1-4 (especially the vision in v 1 and the comment about those who try to escape).

What we are left with at the end of the speech in its present form is the assured destruction of all eight kingdoms in this middle area between Africa and Asia and a special statement about the destiny of the two specifically Yahwistic nations, Judah and Israel, including an explanation of policy and a defense of the decision made about them. Presumably if asked by or about the other nations, the prophet would offer a similar argument, explanation, and defense (as we know from the comments about two of them in 9:7).

I.B.2. ORACLE AND RIDDLES (3:1-8)

Turning then to the second main section of Part I, chaps. 3-4, we find not a single great speech but a more heterogeneous grouping. Nevertheless the main themes are the same, and more arguments and reasons are given for the course adopted by Yahweh.

The whole case against Israel (and Judah) is summed up in the apparent paradox of 3:1-2. As already indicated, the status of Yahweh as the suzerain of Israel is affirmed on the basis of his gracious and mighty action in bringing them out of Egypt. Then the judgment is affirmed in equally explicit language: "Only you have I known [loved] of all the families of the earth; therefore I will punish you for all your iniquities." This emphatic assertion, a condensation and crystallization of the essential elements concerning Israel (and Judah) in the Great Set Speech of chaps. 1-2, also serves as the heading and summary of what follows in the next two chapters and is thus a pivotal expression or bridge between the two sections, lying at the center of Part I—a nuclear expression of the whole message and its meaning and tenor. Yahweh has done these things for you in the past, and Yahweh will do this thing to you in the future. You did not deserve the first, but he did them for you anyway; you certainly deserve the second, and in spite of every effort on his part, he finally cannot and will not avert it.

The next part, vv 3–8, is a remarkable discourse, containing riddles and usually described as reflecting or embodying wisdom motifs. That may be true of the examples and instances cited, but the main objective is a defense of the prophet in his role as messenger of Yahweh. The theme already mentioned in 2:11–12 is taken up again. (The total number of items in 3:3–8 seems to be eight, as is the case in chaps. 1–2.) The point made in this section is that the prophet is privy to the counsel of Yahweh, and when a decision is reached, Yahweh speaks; then the prophet has no choice but to bring that message to the attention of the people so that they will know about divine plans and decisions. To refuse to listen—to shut up the prophet—therefore is tantamount to shutting off the deity himself, because he is the established medium of communication between Yahweh and his people. The combination of Yahweh speaking and the prophet prophesying or reporting Yahweh's speech is as firm, certain, and inevitable as a half-dozen other combinations in the world of nature and of humanity. To disrupt an order of things established specifically by Yahweh for the benefit and protection of the people who have now wrecked the system is intolerable and only another irrefutable indication that they are beyond rescue.

Compared with the others, the first question in the riddles section seems bland, a low-key opener, a trivial truism designed to disarm the listeners so that the more disturbing and puzzling questions that follow will also reach them. As far as themes are concerned, the following six questions all deal with harm and danger. They come in three related pairs. In the first pair it is the lion who seizes prey, while in the second pair it is the trapper. In the third pair the trouble comes from Yahweh himself, so we can suspect that he is the person behind the figure of the lion in the first pair (compare the similar images with similar vocabulary in Isa 31:4 and Hos 5:14, especially the detail in the latter that "Ephraim"//"Judah" are the lion's intended victims), and behind the figure of the trapper in the second pair (Isa 24:18 and Jer 48:44 present a similar picture; although Yahweh does not set the trap as such, he does bring his victims into the pit and the snare). There is an ominous note throughout, and the last pair brings fear close to home. In every case the association is harmful, and in the last pair the fear engendered in the first instance is justified in the second.

The imagery implies, it would seem, that in the first four cases (vv 3a–5a) the first thing listed happens, but only because the second thing listed has already happened. The true order is reversed. That is also true of the fifth instance, even though the actions seem to be simultaneous. But with the sixth and seventh the action switches. In v 6a the trumpet sounds and the people tremble. Here the order is clear, for the reverse is not feasible: the

trembling of the people does not cause the trumpet to sound. It is the
sounding of the shofar that signals danger or trouble, and then the people
tremble. But the seventh instance is more enigmatic. The point is that when
harm or calamity befalls a city, there is no doubt that Yahweh has done it;
the actions are simultaneous. All of this seems very threatening, so we can
probably say that the group of seven was a set piece for Amos from any
period or phase of his career, just as it is, with ominous overtones but no
particular application. The point would be that nothing happens without
Yahweh's involvement as prime and sole cause, but the specific case cited is
harm to a city. Such an event is no accident, and people should know it.
There may be a context somewhere that would clarify the point—a particular city or incident that people may have passed off or explained away as an
accident or inadvertence. But Amos argues that there are inseparable and
inevitable connections between events and causes, and the direct cause of
harm to a city—any city—is the action of Yahweh. After the speech in
chaps. 1–2 with its assaults by Yahweh against capital cities all over the
area, this argument would make a point for the hearers.

So much for the original piece with its beautifully symmetrical structure.
What follows in vv 7–8 seems to have very little to do with the preceding,
though the general theme is perhaps still to be seen, namely, that there are
unbreakable associations, and if one thing is true the other will be. Verse 7
may be understood as a different kind of transition in which the speaker or
writer has picked up the statement in v 6b that Yahweh has done something
—he has caused damage in a city—and generalizes the point, adding that
he never does anything at all without first revealing his plan to the
prophets. As a blanket claim this is obviously untrue, even if we take into
account the plural "prophets." We can hardly believe that the only events
to be explained as actions of Yahweh are those for which there was a prior
confidential consultation with one of the prophets. The reference to "his
servants, the prophets" clearly ties back to 2:11–12 and links with the
succession of individual prophets, from Moses onward, each in his turn the
confidant and public agent for Yahweh for notable deeds that he wished to
have publicized as his, whether before or after the happening itself. Amos is
certainly in this succession, identifying and explaining certain events as
actions of God (4:6–11), predicting others as impending. In this setting the
word *dābār* is more likely to mean "decree" than simply "something," so
ʿśh dbr means "carry out a decree."

Verse 7 thus belongs in the context, both the immediate one, notably vv
3–6, and the general one (chaps. 1–4). This integral position is made even
more certain when we notice that the next verse (v 8) has a double function
in the structure, serving as a short-range inclusion for 3:4 and a long-range
inclusion for 1:2. Yet v 7 is quite different in texture from the surrounding
material. It is a long, categorical statement, with no poetic features such as

we find in the neighboring expressions. The verb "to do" is a domino link with v 6, but the title "my Lord Yahweh" betrays the prophet's more personal speech. At the same time, v 7 is necessary in order to understand v 8. The point in v 7 is that an event to be identified as a significant act of God, which in this context probably means *rāʿâ*, "harm" rather than "good," is first revealed to his servants the prophets. It has another connection with the preceding set of questions in the idea of a warning being given (the shofar) of impending calamity. The statement in v 7 bears a resemblance to the preceding questions also in associating two things: the divine decision to do something and the revelation to the prophets. Yet it is rather broad, and one could infer that when something happens it is certain that two things go together, that Yahweh did it and that he told a prophet. But the real purpose is to advise the people that because Yahweh tells the prophets what he is going to do before he does it, it is a good idea to listen to them. In fact they must warn the people of impending danger because that is their obligation. When Yahweh makes a decision, he announces it in the heavenly court where the prophets are present, and then they must report it to the people (v 8b) for whom it is meant.

So transitional v 7 leads to v 8, which is a different pairing too, though it draws some imagery from the earlier list. Even so, the connection of the lion image with 1:2 is closer than the connection with 3:4. The use of the lion image for Yahweh has two distinct elements, capturing prey and roaring. The roaring in 3:8, like that in 1:2, is connected more with speech, corresponding to the utterance of a decision and a message that inspires fear in a possible victim. In 3:4, by contrast, as in Hos 5:14–15, the lion has already made his kill, and his roar in celebration is an indication that a predator is on the loose. It would probably be pressing the imagery beyond the prophet's intention to force the verses apart on the basis of this distinction. The analogy with the divine utterance is only partial. With regard to the lion we are terrified because we know what the animal might do; Yahweh's word induces fear because it announces a deliberated judgment. Connecting 3:8 with 2:12 brings out the absurd and tragic situation. The response to the lion's roar is spontaneous and uncontrollable fear; the response to the prophet's word is to ignore or even suppress it. The details should not be overinterpreted; the general comparison is clear enough, especially because the image of Yahweh as a lion was a traditional one.

The logic of vv 3–6 points to another component as well. Just as anyone and everyone will be frightened by the roaring of a lion, whatever the reason (cf. v 4) or the figure behind the imagery, so there is another equally obvious or certain connection: If a lion's roar makes people afraid (or other animals—it is not necessary to say who the "who" of v 8a is) then Yahweh's speaking causes the prophet to prophesy. His response thus contrasts with that of the people (2:12b). The "who" of v 8b is thus not as general as the "who" of v 8a, in spite of the formal parallelism. It does not mean that anyone or everyone is driven to prophesy. It applies only to the prophet(s) who have been privy to the counsel of Yahweh (v 7a). While theoretically it might be anyone, the speech of Yahweh in the *sôd* shows that only prophets are meant, that the class of human listeners is restricted to prophets. Verse 7b also has an exclusive implication. It is only in the council that Yahweh reveals the "word" (*dābār*) that he intends to do. So the referent of the "who" in v 8b is the prophet, or any prophet, or all of them considered severally.

The point is twofold. First, there is a link, as in the others, to the effect that when Yahweh has spoken, the prophet must prophesy. This piece in its totality carries on the debate or discussion initiated in 2:11–12. The argument is that it is very wrong as well as dangerous to prevent the prophets from speaking, because their word is Yahweh's word. If he is planning something, for example, to attack a city, no one would know about it unless the prophets were able to give warning. If no warning is given because none is allowed, then disaster will strike and people will learn of the truth of Yahweh's decisive action only in the events. Second, there is an additional emphasis that doubtless reflects the severe tension in Israelite society about prophets, as seen, for instance, in the charge against Jeremiah that he did not speak Yahweh's words but was acting on Baruch's premeditated injurious counsel and hence his words were not only worthless, but seditious (Jer 43:3). As prophets regularly assail their opposite numbers, the false prophets, and charge them with speaking falsely their own words and claiming divine authority for themselves, the same must have been true in reverse. In effect, that is what Amaziah says about and to Amos. We see this point dramatically in the confrontation between Jeremiah and Hananiah or in the one between Micaiah and the royal prophets in 1 Kings 22.

There are connections between v 8a and 8b and other nearby passages. Verses 8aA and 4aA show chiasmus and the switch from imperfect to perfect:

3:4a	*hyšᵌg ᵓryh*	Does a lion roar
3:8a	*ᵓryh šᵌg*	The lion has roared

while 3:8b is matched with a chiasmus in 3:1a:

3:1a	*dibber yhwh*	Yahweh has spoken
3:8b	*ᵓdny yhwh dibber*	My Lord Yahweh has spoken

The effect—and probably the intention—is to integrate the unit 3:3–6 into the larger sequence beginning with 3:1 and ending with 3:8.

I.C. Messages for Israel//Samaria (3:9–4:3)
I.C.1. The International Setting (3:9–12)

We can characterize the next section (3:9–12) as an extension of the condemnation of Israel in 2:6–8. Here the punishment to be meted out to Samaria and the rest of the country is outlined. More details are added to both charges and penalties. To be more precise, this material fills the gap between 2:6–8 and 3:13–15, where we have the final battle and destruction in which there are no survivors.

In 3:9–11 there is a description of terrible things going on in Samaria and the consequence, which will be the invasion of the land and the siege and reduction of the fortresses and citadels. It is not clear whether the accusation about oppression and violence in Samaria is actual (historical) or predictive (proleptic); but if the account of the plagues in chap. 4 is historical, then the circumstances in the north may well have been chaotic or approaching anarchy at this time. (Compare the story of famine in the days of Elijah and Elisha and the near collapse of civil authority.)

Verse 12 adds a bitterly ironic picture of the "rescue" of the people of Israel, comparable to what a shepherd rescues from the mouth of the lion—two legs or a piece of an ear. All that will be left of the *bny yśr'l* will be a corner of a bed or a piece (?) of a couch. This is not what the *bny yśr'l* will rescue or salvage in the way of furniture, rather what will be left of all of Israel—a few scraps to show that there used to be a people there, in other words, what an archaeologist might find in the ruins.

I.C.2. Israel (North)—Bethel (3:13–15)

Verses 13–15 make another statement to the same effect, using language very similar to the Great Set Speech of chaps. 1–2. There is a shift of focus here from Samaria to Bethel and an explicit insistence that the horns of the altar will be cut off and will fall to the ground. One is reminded of the fate of the horns of a large altar found in the excavations of Beer-sheba—they were reused later as part of an outer wall of the city. (The reconstructed object is often pictured: e.g., Cornfeld 1976:142.) The destruction of the altar symbolizes the fate of the temple there along with that of the city. While the distinction should not be pressed too far, and while both the leadership and its activity covered the civil and religious aspects of the life of the people, it seems as if Samaria stands for the royal administration and Bethel for the priestly authority. Amos focuses attention on these two cities as the targets of denunciation and judgment. Together they represent the ecclesiastical authority and secular administration of the northern kingdom. In 3:9–15 Amos touches both bases, fulfilling the implications of the original pronouncement against Israel in chap. 2. The closing words of the chapter are aimed at the same elite; and while the immediate antecedent (Bethel) implies that these palaces are in the domain of the priests, it is more likely that Amos has in mind both cities and both sets of leaders with their winter and summer palaces, along with the inlaid ivory decorations, samples of which have turned up in excavations at Samaria, as a matter of fact (Paul and Dever 1973:204–7).

I.C.3. MOUNT SAMARIA (4:1–3)

Here we have another attack on the nobility of Samaria and perhaps a particular condemnation of the women along with their husbands. The syntax and grammar are difficult, but their destiny or, more particularly, destination is clear. In the second of the so-called futurist passages (using the formula *ymym b'ym*) there is a clear allusion to exile and the direction in which the captives are to go, as well as presumably the direction from which the threat will come. With this passage we complete the elaboration of charges and judgments against Israel that began in 2:6–8 (we are speaking only of Part I, of course). With the destruction described in 3:9–15 and the exile announced in 4:3 the same elements are covered as in the punishments stipulated in chaps. 1–2 for other nations. Curiously, there is an alternation in such threats in the case of two pairs of peoples, as previously mentioned: with regard to Aram and the Philistines—the first pair—the punishment specifies, along with the basic and repeated destruction by fire, exile for Aram and death in defeat for the Philistines. Similarly with the third pair, Ammon and Moab, exile is the fate of Ammon, while death is the fate of Moab. In view of the continuation of these components with regard to Israel, we may suppose that the distinctions are somewhat artificial and that the pairs of nations will actually experience similar fates, including both of these basic tragedies: defeat (including destruction and death) and exile for any unhappy survivors.

I.D. MESSAGES FOR ALL ISRAEL (4:4–13)
I.D.1. CONDEMNATION OF THE CULT (4:4–5)

Verses 4–5 constitute a transition to the set piece on the plagues in 4:6–11. In vv 4–5 there is mention of Bethel again and another historic cultic center, Gilgal, the exact location of which is a continuing puzzle, but no doubt it was in the territory of the northern kingdom. The association is repeated in Amos, and later a third city, Beer-sheba, will be added. They were all religious centers with traditional connections with the patriarchs (Bethel and Beer-sheba) and with the Exodus and Settlement (Gilgal and Bethel). Apparently they were pilgrimage centers and attracted travelers from the whole domain of Yahweh, embracing Judah and Israel. Because of their ancient associations, they continued to be regarded as national shrines, though simply out of convenience they would mainly serve the regional population, and in that sense could be regarded as local sanctuaries. No doubt each shrine had its own priesthood; Bethel's distinction was that it was a royal establishment, and it would be a reasonable inference that the presiding priest at that shrine would be regarded as the primate of the whole northern kingdom. There might well be rivals at places like Dan (also a royal chapel) or Samaria, where apparently the chief temple may have been dedicated to other gods besides Yahweh or jointly with him.

As a kind of explanation or comment about the priesthood and services at Bethel and its destiny to be destroyed (but ironically by Josiah, something that may have been far from Amos' expectation), Amos here with savage sarcasm encourages the people to go to these ancient sacred shrines, not to worship, but to transgress; he uses the same root ps^c (twice) as he had used in the denunciation of all nations including Israel in chaps. 1–2. The list of activities is perfectly in order and consistent with proper worship, but to Amos it is exactly the reverse. The root of the problem is precisely in the worship and service that Israel performs in accordance with the dictates and desires of the priesthood and the rest of the northern kingdom's leadership. There are more than a few indications that the Israelites did not put all of their religious eggs in one basket: as a safety measure and perhaps for practical and economic reasons they worshiped other gods, at least one female and one male in addition to or as a substitute for Yahweh. The apostasy and idolatry can be documented for the ninth century from the stories of Elijah and Elisha and Ahab and Jezebel and Jehu. But for the eighth century we also have the somewhat cryptic but nevertheless decisive testimony of Hosea. Amos makes a different point more clearly and more emphatically. That will come in chap. 5, especially vv 21–24; but what is clear here is that the destruction of Bethel will be no tragedy in terms of religious life in the country, and that Bethel was the center of all that was fundamentally wrong with the country in its relationship with Yahweh. Considering just those few passing references to Bethel in the book, we can understand why there was no love lost between Amos and Amaziah, but instead observe the undying and unlimited hostility and totally opposed views on all important issues. It is also no wonder that the culminating confrontation between prophet and priest took place at that sanctuary.

I.D.2. PLAGUES (4:6–11)

This passage is a set piece like the opening oracle against the nations. Refrains and formulas are used regularly and repeatedly in this series. As with the oracles on the nations, so here the grouping of the data gives the whole collection a particular force and achieves a particular objective. The underlying and unifying sense is that the plagues were sent by God to warn his people of an impending judgment and to encourage them to repent, to reverse their direction and be saved from the ultimate disaster implied in each of the plagues and the almost indescribable and inconceivable catastrophe implied by all of them together.

The plagues are presented here, however, from a point in time after all five plagues had already come and perhaps gone, though they have left lasting marks on the country. The point the prophet wishes to bring home to his people is that the whole exercise was a failure. The plagues were sent in order to achieve a constructive purpose beyond the obvious and dreadful damage they did. Looking back on the series of plagues that afflicted, over-ran, and deeply injured the country and its life, the prophet concludes repeatedly in the name of God: "yet you did not return to me." While the material is vitally important for understanding and explaining the earlier phases of Amos' calling and career as a prophet, especially his preaching of repentance, here its function as a set piece is to balance the great oracles of chaps. 1–2 and to offer yet another defense of Yahweh's behavior and attitude toward his own people. We have already remarked that the flat statement that Yahweh would destroy and devastate his people and tear them away from their land, the same God who had created them as a nation and given them the land, was not only new and shocking but probably incomprehensible to his audience. No one had ever said anything quite like it, and if it were to be taken seriously, then serious questions about this God would have to be asked and answered.

We have seen that in 2:9–12 Amos provides one set of answers to one set of questions: By what right does God judge his people and how can you show that he is not being arbitrary or even capricious as well as peremptory and unfeeling? The answer is that Yahweh is the sovereign Lord who brought them from Egypt and gave them the land. He also told them how to live in this land and warned them about the consequences of not living up to the standards he had set for them. He did so by raising up prophets and nazirites to set an example and to bring them timely words about their condition. So the God of Israel has every right to judge, but he especially has the claims of a gracious and loving Lord. Furthermore, there is nothing arbitrary in the decisions, for he has been sending prophets over the centuries to warn and guide them. Because they have silenced the prophets, however, it is clear that such efforts to warn and encourage have been futile; hence judgment will fall.

In the same way, the account of the plagues reinforces the argument about the God who sent prophets to warn and help the people meet the requirements of their God. The plagues were the counterparts of the prophets and were sent with the same intention to serve as a warning, even as a threat of worse to come. We can be sure that the people were not left to make this interpretation of the plagues for themselves. Each would have been accompanied by prophetic commentary identifying the plague as an act of God, both punishment and plea, and exhorting the people to take it as an opportunity to return to Yahweh, rather than intensify their neglect and resentment. The objective was repentance on the part of the people. Yahweh was eager to spare his people and had no desire that they should perish. But just as they resisted his pleading through the prophets, so they resisted his pleading through the plagues. The account here is designed to explain why the judgment of chaps. 2–3 must be imposed. Israel has had every opportunity to repent and return to Yahweh, but it has refused. The refrain here, *wĕlō'-šabtem 'āday,* "yet you did not return to me," is balanced and matched by the refrain in chaps. 1–2, *lō' 'ăšîbennû,* "I will not reverse it [the judgment]." The reason for the harsh judgment pronounced in the great oracle, especially with regard to Judah and Israel, is the persistent and repeated refusal—the equally hard rejection of the messages of both prophets and plagues—to repent and return. So while the plagues came first and this material is chronologically prior to the great speech of chaps. 1–2, the reversal of the order is quite appropriate. The judgment is presented first, in an imposing and impressive way as a part of the general condemnation of the eight nations. Then in follow-up pieces, the natural and serious questions arising from such a condemnation are addressed. Yahweh has every right to judge the people he created and established in their own land (his land). Far from taking any pleasure in it, he has been trying for a long time to reach them through prophets and plagues, and they have persistently refused to listen and to turn. So now there is only one thing left; the ominous warning and potential threat are voiced in one of the closing verses of the unit, "prepare to confront your God" (4:12). The next item on the divine agenda is neither prophecy nor plague: there will be no more calls to repent; there will be devastating judgment.

The plagues themselves follow a fairly conventional routine, which reflects a standard literary category ultimately derived from or parallel to so-called treaty curses. The best and most extensive biblical examples may be found in the curses of Deuteronomy 28–29 and Leviticus 26. Of course the ten plagues in the Exodus story doubtless reflect an old tradition; they reflect a long history of transmission as well, but also the actuality of experience. Plagues tend to multiply and pile up on each other, so there is no reason to suppose they were spread over many years or that they are grouped artificially.

In the list we have, famine is first, having pride of place. It is followed by drought, but it seems likely the first may have been the result of the second. Famine is hardly a plague in the usual sense, rather an effect or result. The third plague combines both blight and mildew, as well as a pest, the all too familiar plague of locusts. These, separately and together, would intensify the famine and interfere seriously with efforts to overcome its effects. In the fourth group we have disease and defeat, the twin products of all too many wars. These elements also go together, for defeat in battle exposes an army to all kinds of other difficulties and problems. At the same time pestilence in various forms is a constant companion of the army camp and battlefield and has often defeated armies before they fought or weakened them so severely as to make them easy prey for their enemies. Such troubles only make things on the home front worse, and the effect of drought and blight and famine hardly helps the military on the battlefront.

The final item on the list is remarkable, because we do not know exactly what is meant by the comparison with Sodom and Gomorrah. That figure was popular with the prophets beginning in the eighth century and symbolized total devastation of great cities. We may point out that the operative word for Sodom and Gomorrah in this passage is destruction by fire. It is true, of course, that fires often follow severe earth tremors, and such an association may be implied in the accounts of the obliteration of the cities on the plain; the principal agent of destruction was "fire from heaven." Any natural side effect of this action must have been the ignition of the bitumen pits and pools mentioned in Genesis 14, but the essential point is that the cities were completely burned. Amos is talking about the same sort of fire in chaps. 1–2 as the established mode of destruction determined by Yahweh. Apparently a combination of seismic disturbance and fire storm of undetermined or heavenly origin did horrendous and almost total damage to one or more of the cities of Israel, and as Amos puts it, "And you were like a brand [a stick] plucked from what was burned [burning]" (4:11). The fire is to be regarded as literal in this situation. The last plague probably was regarded as the worst and the one from which they made the narrowest escape. But even that proved futile, and the experiment with repentance through plagues was abandoned.

I.D.3. THREAT TO ISRAEL (4:12)

The next stage would be the final judgment, and the warning is solemnly given in 4:12. This is not a call to repent—though that is presumably always a possibility even to the last moment—but a summons to the great assize. (Note the inclusion: *yhwh* [1:2] and *'lhyk* [4:12].)

I.D.4. COSMIC HYMN (4:13)

The whole unit of chaps. 1–4 closes with a hymnic fragment or apostrophe in 4:13. There are three such hymns distributed in the text, and this one serves to close the first major section (called The Book of Doom [Part I] in our analysis). While it is not directly connected either with what precedes or with what follows, it enhances the effect of the whole book along with the other similar units as a reminder to all of the identity of Yahweh the God of Israel. In a world filled with deities and surrounded by nations with their own patron gods, Yahweh was not one among many or even *primus inter pares*. He was unique, a nonpareil. Because of his association with Judah and Israel, a deity involved and enmeshed in the affairs of a pair of tiny kingdoms, people might become confused and suppose he was just a minor god of minor peoples who could be listed with the others and ignored with impunity. The eighth-century prophets did not see things this way, and from first to last the theme was held consistently, even stubbornly: the size of Israel had nothing to do with the size of its god. He was the maker and ruler of the universe who alone was worthy of the title, who brooked no rivals, had no consort or progeny, was dependent on no one and nothing, and exercised a full monopoly of power and authority.

Part II. The Book of Woes (5:1–6:14)

The second main part of the book of Amos extends through chaps. 5 and 6. We call it The Book of Woes (and Lamentations) because the dominant theme is grief and the dominant type or genre of literature is the woe oracle. This is a very persistent category in the prophetic books extending from Amos and his contemporaries of the eighth century B.C.E. all the way into the New Testament. There is comparatively little variation. The opening word, "Woe!" (*hôy*) gives the genre its title, though the word itself is often omitted or understood. There follows an address to a group of people (which is identified by a participle or a noun of similar type) denouncing them for actions and attitudes contrary to the covenant or will of God, and then threatening them with appropriate punishment. The main group of Woes is to be found in chap. 6:1–6, but other Woes are scattered through the two chapters (cf. 5:7, 5:18–20, 6:13), so the label is appropriate. We may also designate the section as Amos' call to repentance, because it is only in chap. 5 that such preaching is found. We observed that in the first unit the last substantial section is devoted to an account of the plagues with the somber refrain that in spite of every effort on the part of Yahweh, or in spite of prophets and plagues that were intended to serve the same purpose, there was in fact no repentance. So logically the material containing the call to repentance (chaps. 5–6) must come chronologically before the determination that no repentance has occurred (chap. 4), which in turn leads to the resolution that judgment must proceed and that this time there will be no reversal (chaps. 1–2). So in Amos 5–6 we have his *earlier* preaching, while in chaps. 1–4 we have his subsequent proclamation. We connect the first two visions with the earlier preaching of repentance. We could also connect them with the plagues, so that the woes and exhortations in chaps. 5–6 are delivered during the plagues and serve to interpret the plagues in a characteristically prophetic way. The review in 4:6–11 can then be explained as a final analysis given after the plagues were over and the conclusion had been reached that Israel has not repented and will not.

If, therefore, we conclude that chaps. 5–6 represent Amos' earliest preaching, as a result of the first and second visions and matching plagues, then we can place chaps. 5–6 before the main oracles (1–4) in time, but justify the present literary arrangement by saying that chaps. 5–6 document the earlier phase and thus help to refute any complaint that Yahweh has not been fair or given the people a chance. Here is the evidence that Amos came preaching repentance first, stuck at it through all the plagues, and only changed his course under the pressure of the second pair of visions. We could allow some time for that and give Amos a precedent career of several years while the plagues ran their course. So Amos' preaching came at a time of stress and strain, anxiety and trouble reflected by the plagues (cf. 2 Kgs 14:25–27).

II.A. EXHORTATIONS FOR ISRAEL AND JUDAH, SEPARATELY AND TOGETHER (5:1–27)
II.A.1. EXHORTATION TO THE HOUSE OF ISRAEL (5:1–6)
II.A.1.a. THE FALLEN VIRGIN (5:1–2)

The general heading and the first entry (vv 1–2) constitute a qinah, a well-known prophetic and liturgical type. If this was in fact the first oracle offered by the prophet, it set a suitably solemn and serious tone for the whole of his prophetic career. In our opinion it is addressed to and about all of Israel (*btwlt yśr'l* is a variant for *byt yśr'l*) and sets the tone for what is to follow. Lamentations are the appropriate accompaniment of woes. In this oracle the outcome is portrayed as having already occurred, and the supposition is that there is no change in the situation and will be none.

II.A.1.b. DECIMATION (5:3)

Verse 3 summarizes a military campaign in which a catastrophic defeat is suffered, what we might call reverse decimation in which the army does not suffer 10 percent casualties (a high figure) but has 10 percent survivors. No nation can survive such an experience. Amos makes it even worse, if our analysis is correct. The first campaign or series of engagements results in 90 percent casualties, and then the same thing happens to the 10 percent who survived. When it is over only ten out of a thousand are left—that is, 1 percent—representing a 99 percent destruction. It is difficult even to conceive, so this must be reckoned as annihilation (but cf. Isa 6:12–13, where the same sort of calculation is made: a double decimation is described, resulting in almost total destruction). Curiously, Amos may not have been satisfied even with that, for in 6:9–10 he may have in mind the same ten remaining people—and of them there will be no survivors at all.

II.A.1.c. THE SANCTUARIES (5:4–6)

This is the first of only three or four passages in the whole book in which the prophet urges "the house of Israel," or the equivalent, to seek Yahweh and live. In the context of visions and/or plagues the message is clear enough. If you go on as before you will perish. The only way out, the only recourse, is to seek Yahweh, in short, to repent. We take this to be the basic original message.

The plain statement is accompanied by warnings about how and where to seek Yahweh. The emphasis in 5:5 is on where, but the advice is all negative. The first clause involves the same verb *drš*, and we must suppose that the suffix carries over as well, so the meaning is: "Don't seek *me* at Bethel."

The other two clauses involve more ordinary verbs of motion and can be understood directly with the place-names:

wĕ'al tidrĕšû bêt-'ēl	But don't seek [me] at Bethel,
wĕhaggilgāl lō' tābō'û	and to Gilgal do not come,
ûbĕ'ēr šebaʿ lō' taʿābōrû	and to Beer-sheba do not cross over

Note the chiastic structure in which the first colon is balanced against the other two. The verb comes first in the first line and last in the others. The place-names are bunched in the middle, at the end of the first line and at the beginning of the second and third lines. The point is transparent and disturbing. Repentance, seeking Yahweh, consists first of all in staying away from the cult centers. In view of the earlier statement, 4:4–5, it is hardly surprising. Just going to these places in Amos' judgment is to commit an irreparable breach of covenant (*pšʿ*), so clearly the first step toward rectifying the relationship with God is to avoid the great shrines. This admonition can only be regarded as a direct condemnation of the hierarchy at the shrines. Bethel and Gilgal have been mentioned, and Beer-sheba is added here; but clearly it is regarded as sharing the same characteristics. Amos is nothing if not ecumenical in his judgments: there is really no difference between north and south in this respect, and the warning is surely addressed to the whole house of Israel, the people of both kingdoms.

We are not told yet what constitutes a positive step in the right direction, but that will come. What we have so far is a wholesale rejection of the official cult, of the principles and practices of the hierarchy; and apparently those shrines and their priesthoods are regarded as beyond reform or restoration.

There is no reason to imagine that Amos saw the solution in Deuteronomic terms, that is to say, that Jerusalem was the only proper place to worship. In view of the caustic remarks of Isaiah especially along the same lines about the cult of Jerusalem, one suspects that Amos would share that opinion and find Jerusalem equally objectionable; but it is of interest that Amos never mentions the cult of Jerusalem. Nevertheless, the views of the prophets on the subject of the corrupted worship of the shrines in the hinterland probably gave encouragement to those who wished to centralize the cult and provide central authority with better means to control its practice. In view of the evidence one wonders whether Amos or Isaiah would have regarded such a move sympathetically. They might have agreed about removing the shrines in the outlying areas but could hardly have regarded Jerusalem and its Temple as above reproach. Clearly, too, the solution does not lie in cosmetic changes at those places. It is doubtful whether it is a matter of the ritual, except that much is made of it, while the underlying issues are neglected or obscured. But the fate of the sanctuaries is sealed along with that of the leadership. It is possible for Israel to be saved at this point, but the sanctuaries seem to be beyond redemption. The prophet announces that Gilgal will go into exile and that Bethel will become a place of trouble or misery. In both clauses there are plays on words, the comment on Gilgal employing alliteration while the association of Bethel with Beth-awen is a crux also in Hosea, where the latter name occurs several times. The structure of v 5 is complex or chiastic, but the general meaning is hardly in doubt. The house of Israel is commanded to stay away from all of the major shrines (except perhaps Jerusalem) as the first step in the process of repentance, redemption, and restoration. The fate of the shrines is described symbolically, and we recognize the familiar components: exile for one place, destruction for the other. Integrating the elements means destruction and exile for all.

The specific fate of Bethel is spelled out more clearly in v 6. Here the destruction of the city and sanctuary is described in connection with the house of Joseph. Bethel belonged to Ephraim, so the association is appropriate. Verse 6 may be addressed directly to the "house of Joseph," as vv 4–5 are addressed to the "house of Israel." In our view the latter is the larger entity, while the "house of Joseph" is linked to the north. The distinction here seems appropriate, for it is altogether probable that all of Israel would be involved with the three shrines, with people from both kingdoms frequenting all of them. At the same time there would be an obvious and special connection between Bethel and the house of Joseph; Bethel would be the sacral tribal shrine as well as the national center.

In vv 4–5 we have first-person address by Yahweh to the house of Israel:

"Seek me and live." In v 6 the prophet is speaking: "Seek Yahweh and live." So the verse is in the third person, about Yahweh rather than spoken by him. The expression *pen-yiṣlaḥ kā'ēš* is difficult, and the connections with *byt ywsp* and *byt-'l* are difficult to determine. We suggest the following analysis as a possibility:

> Seek Yahweh and live,
>> lest he rush [upon you] like a flame,
>>> O house of Joseph,
>> and it consume [you] with none to quench [it],
>>> O house of God [Bethel]!

The double vocative secures parallelism. Whether *l-* with "Bethel" is vocative or a preposition is debatable. Normally the verb *ṣlḥ* is used with the prepositions *'el* and *'al,* but it is possible to extend that usage to *l-* as well. So the meaning could be: lest he rush at Bethel like a fire that devours, and which no one can put out—O house of Joseph. This statement expresses the parlous state of things in the period of prophecy and plagues. It is the last opportunity to repent and be saved. Otherwise everything will go up in flames, down in ashes, and away in exile. We are not told the fate of Beersheba, but it can hardly have been different in the mind of the prophet. So the admonition to stay away and the threat to destroy and depopulate apply to all of them and perhaps even more suitably to the land in which they are located, a sure indication that Judah is involved as well as Joseph —which together make up the house of Israel. In v 6, however, the focus is clearly on the northern kingdom, while Bethel and its temple have been singled out for destruction by Yahweh in the figure of a consuming fire symbolic of the rush of Yahweh's spirit and of the divine Fire that destroys with none to quench it.

II.A.2. FIRST WOE (5:7–13), INCLUDING THE SECOND HYMN (5:8–9)
II.A.2.a. FIRST WOE (5:7, 10–12)

Here we have the first of the many Woes in these chapters. This one is directed against those who turn justice (and righteousness) into wormwood, and who bring down some person or group to the earth (cf. Isa 28:2 for the same expression). Just who is brought down is not clear, but presumably it is the recipients of this twisted and reversed version of justice. Just who the perpetrators are is not entirely clear either, but the charge applies to a wide spectrum of people, generally those in a position to administer justice. This group would not be limited to civil administrators, but would also apply to temple personnel, as well as to the merchant class. There may well be an association here with those addressed in vv 4–6, because later we will be told that the way to rectify the terrible situation in the temples, with all of the false feasts and sacrifices, is to do justice and righteousness. The Woe (not expressed) is that these people have been identified as the root and center of evil; they are responsible, and the Woe is more than a warning or even threat: it is an assurance, a promise, even an oath. They are targeted, their days are numbered, and their execution is nigh.

We believe that vv 10–12 further elaborate the behavior of these perverters of justice. They are the main group of woe people in chap. 5, coming up again for attention in vv 21–24 (probably) and certainly in 6:12, where almost identical terminology is used of them. There is, therefore, an intrusion here in the form of vv 8–9, which contribute another hymn like those of 4:13 and 9:5–6. The latter two naturally close major sections, and it would suit our analysis better if 5:8–9 did the same at the end of chap. 6, where it more properly belongs. We will come back to it. Verses 10–12 do not have a clear subject, though it is m. pl. address. Who are these people who do such terrible things and are so broadly condemned, both directly (second person, vv 11–12) and indirectly (v 10, third person)? They seem to belong to the woe complex, and the nearest antecedent is *hhpkym* (5:7). Another possibility are the *š'pym* (the "tramplers") in 2:7 and 8:4, but there is no need to say that one group excludes the other. Certainly those who crush the poor and needy are perverters of justice, and those who pervert justice either condone the oppression of others or practice it themselves. If they are not identical groups, they nevertheless have a great deal in common.

Turning then to 5:10–12, what do we find? Verses 10 and 12b form an envelope in the third person about these miscreants who are guilty of two basic crimes:

1. They hate the one who reproves in the gate—that is, the prophet or any protester against their behavior—but because Amos is on record denouncing their practices publicly this reference seems to be a personal one, though not necessarily an exclusive one. The parallel expressions emphasize the same point: they abhor or condemn or spurn the speaker of truth. There is an elegant chiasm within the line, also one with v 12. This is essentially an example of the practice of silencing the prophets and preventing them from delivering the message, a major problem for Amos and a factor in the ultimate decision. As long as the channels of communication are open between God and people, in particular the one maintained through the prophets, it is possible to entertain hope of a double reversal: the people may repent, and then Yahweh will also repent. Because we already know the negative outcome of that effort from the material in chaps. 1–4, especially the unending repetition of the negative *lō'*, five times with *šabtem*, "you did [not] return [= repent]" (4:6, 8, 9, 10, 11), and eight times with *'ăšîbennû*, "I will [not] reverse it [= turn it around or back]" (1:3, 6, 9, 11,

13; 2:1, 4, 6, but especially 2:4 and 6) with the clear cadence "You didn't turn [toward me]; so I certainly will not reverse my judgment of doom" (4:11–12), we sense an ominous and negative tone here as well. These people in v 10 are not prime prospects for repentance. Not only will they not listen to the word from God, they will not even allow it to be spoken. They are hostile not only to the message but also to the messenger, and the latter they can intimidate and suppress.

2. Their second crime is that they oppress the righteous, take bribes, and shove the poor around either in or outside the gateway. They are the same as those in v 10, and the activity is concentrated in the gateway, where all kinds of community matters, both commercial and legal, were transacted. As already noted, these people, the perverters of justice, have a lot in common with the *š*ᵉ*pym* of 2:6–7 (cf. 8:4–6), and with the priests at the shrines who have turned them into dens of iniquity, partly at least by silencing the prophets who came there to speak. Gradually the picture is being clarified both in detail and in depth; we see who the offenders are who are most in need of repentance, and that this reversal will entail the shift from blatantly criminal practice against the innocent and helpless to behavior in accord with divine principles and requirements of justice and righteousness.

The two components fit together in the following manner:

			SYLLABLES	
5:10*	śānĕʾû	baśśaʿar	môkîaḥ	3 + 2 + 2 = 7
	wĕdōbēr	tāmîm	yĕtāʿēbû	3 + 2 + 4 = 9
12b	ṣorĕrê	ṣaddîq		3 + 2 = 5
	lōqĕḥê	kōper		3 + 1 = 4
	wᵉʾebyônîm	baśśaʿar	hiṭṭû	4 + 2 + 2 = 8

16 (for 5:10) · 9 and 17 (for 12b)

5:10   They hate the reprover in the gate,
            and the one who speaks truth they abhor.

12b   Those who harass the upright,
            those who hold them for ransom,
            and the poor from the gate they thrust.

* Key words in the following verses contain arbitrary markers to indicate various parts of speech (••••• = verbs; ˍˍˍˍ = prepositional phrases; ------ = nouns; ::::::: = participles)

The second unit takes us back to the statement in 2:6, where the two words *ṣdyq//ʾbywn* are also associated, that is to say, the righteous poor. The activity reflected in 5:12b is similar to 2:6 (and 8:6) in which through illegitimate judicial proceedings the righteous, though poor, are deprived of property, rights, even liberty. In this case, unscrupulous judges (another subgroup among the perverters of justice and the oppressors of the poor) take bribes from the rich to decide cases against the poor, who are in the right but are thrust away literally and figuratively from the court and bar of justice.

Turning to 5:11–12a, we have another complex envelope construction with external and internal rings. Following our analysis of the parallel construction in a similar passage (vv 4–6) we suggest here that the third-person material just discussed is the prophet's statement about these people to another audience, perhaps the leadership, while the core of the material is a second-person address to the accused. It may be divided again into an outer ring and an inner circle: 11aA, . . . 12a, and 11aB–b. The outer ring concentrates attention on the transgressions and sins (*pšʿykm* and *ḥṭʾykm*) while also giving a practical example of what these transgressors are doing, namely, despoiling the poor. The inner circle deals with consequences, and using the language of treaty curses (also found in the formulas of Deuteronomy and Leviticus) emphasizes that they will not enjoy the fruits of their criminal behavior. An essential feature of jurisprudence, ancient and modern, is that criminals should not profit from their crimes. From their ill-gotten gains they have built houses of hewn stone, but they will not live to dwell in them, or more precisely they will not be around to dwell in them, thus exactly reversing the experience of their ancestors who came into the land as victors and occupied and lived in houses that others had built. Now others will occupy the houses they have built. As with houses, so also with the luxuriant vineyards that they have planted. They will never drink wine from those grapes, but again reversing the experience of the first Israelites, who drank the fruit of vines they had not planted, others will gain the fruit of this generation's labors. There will be a complete reversal, and for a good cause.

		SYLLABLES	
5:11a	*lākēn yaʿan bôšaskem ʿal-dāl*	$2 + 1 + 3 + 1 + 1 = 8$	$\Big\}17$
	ûmaśʾat-bar tiqḥû mimmennû	$3 + 1 + 2 + 3 \quad = 9$	
	bāttê gāzît běnîtem	$2 + 2 + 3 \quad = 7$	$\Big\}13$
	wělōʾ-tēšěbû bām	$2 + 3 + 1 \quad = 6$	

11b	karmê-ḥemed nĕṭaʿtem	$2 + 1 + 3$	$= 6$	$\Big\}13$
	wĕlōʾ tištû ʾet-yênām	$2 + 2 + 1 + 2$	$= 7$	
12a	kî yādaʿtî rabbîm pišʿêkem	$1 + 3 + 2 + 3$	$= 9$	
				$\Big\}17$
	waʿăṣūmîm ḥaṭṭōʾtêkem	$4 + 4$	$= 8$	

The whole unit can or should be read sequentially, as the connecting
particles show. The structure is concentric and symmetrical, as the syllable
counts show. They also show that the first and fourth units belong together,
as even more clearly the second and third subsections do.

> 5:11a   Therefore, because you trample upon the needy,
> and extract levies of grain from them,
> the houses of hewn stone that you built—
> you shall not dwell in them;
>
> 11b   the prized vineyards which you planted—
> you shall not drink their wine.
>
> 12a   I am aware that your rebellions are many
> and your sinful acts are numerous.

Probably the seizure of the grain is done with court approval and is not a
matter of ordinary robbery. Presumably such goods would be seized under
court order for payment of debts or on some other trumped-up charge. It is
the combination of illegal activity and the power or prestige of authority
reinforcing that activity that produces the effects described in this denunciation and makes the situation so hopeless for those on the receiving end of
such abuse. When the judiciary and the clergy, the heads of each of those
branches of authority, provide no recourse for the poor and downtrodden,
then their only appeal is to heaven—and the prophet has no doubt that the
response will be devastating for all of those who participated in or profited
from such criminal activity.

II.A.2.b. SECOND HYMN (5:8–9)

In v 8 we have the middle one of three hymns about the incomparable
power and majesty of the one true God. While the material seems far
removed from the central issues of the oracles and more like what we find
in the Psalter or Proverbs or even in Job, nevertheless these entries have an
important and distinctive place in the book apart from providing boundaries for the major sections (this one is near the beginning of the middle
one). This example has points in common with both the first and the third
hymns and serves as a transition from one to the other. It is essential to the
book's premises and conclusions that the God of Israel, the one so deeply

involved in the history and affairs of his people, also be identified as the supreme ruler of the universe and the director of the destiny of all nations, including especially those listed in chaps. 1–2 and others mentioned in the book. Without the absolute statement about the unrestricted power and authority of this deity in contrast to all other powers and gods, the prophet is talking in the same way as the prophets of the other nations and the false prophets of his own. For all of them the message is false because they have no contact with the one real, regnant God. For the true prophet two things must also be true: that the message he has heard is an authentic one, that is, from a living God; that this God be the actual God, that is, unique and alone in that status. Anything less is nothing at all. So these hymns simply spell out the necessary truth behind and underlying everything else in the book.

II.A.2.c. THE WISE MAN (5:13)

Verse 13 serves as a fitting conclusion to the first half of the chapter and a pause in the rush to judgment. Whatever the ultimate origin of this statement, and whoever may be responsible for its placement at this point, it serves an important function and is entirely appropriate where it is. Whether it was originally composed in this context or has been drawn from another source for use here, it stands as a useful and sardonic comment on the prophet's predicament. Any wise man would remain silent in the circumstances described in vv 7 and 10–12. Clearly when faced by threats from people who do not hesitate to use the power they have (and there is a lot of it) to crush and strip innocent people not only of possessions (maybe it is the robbing that makes them poor) but of liberty and perhaps of life, and by threats that are anything but veiled, hesitant, or obscure, the practical wise man keeps silent. Why add one more victim to the heap, when speaking out would only provoke these violent men to further violence? The prophet could well say such a thing because clearly it was true. But it could only be said with deep irony, because a wise man's option was not available to a prophet. Hosea speaks of the prophet as a demented man rather than as a wise one (see Hos 9:7–9), and this is the other side of the coin. The prophet is not prudent and cannot be. He cannot be concerned about his safety, his future, or his well-being, only about delivering the words of Yahweh. To be silent in the face of threats and other intimidating circumstances would be to fail in his duty, to be derelict. In other words, the wisdom of the world would be folly toward God, while obedience to God in this situation would be to run counter to the best wisdom and counsel the world could offer. The passage serves as a comment on various statements made in the book.

II.A.3. Exhortation and Lamentation (5:14–17)
II.A.3.a. Repentance (5:14–15)

We now come to the central unit of the whole book of Amos, which is also just past the middle of chap. 5: the center of the chapter comes after v 13, while the center of the book is vv 14–15, almost to the word. Taken together the two verses are a capsule of the book's essential message, but they also have a specific function in the immediate context. The opening verb *diršû* picks up the theme of 5:4–5, while the closing reference to the "remnant of Joseph" evokes v 6 with its reference to the "house of Joseph." There will be one more echo in 6:6 of "Joseph's crash." The sequence is similar to that of 5:4–6, where a general statement addressed to all of Israel is followed by one addressed to the remnant of Joseph (the north only).

Along with 5:4–5 and 5:24, this passage constitutes the essential content of the repentance theme in Amos. Now the positive side of the program or strategy of survival and success is emphasized. In 5:4–5 the stress was on something negative—avoiding the great sanctuaries—while here the emphasis will be on the choice between good and evil, a fairly basic issue, and on establishing justice in the gate, a reversal of the theme of the first major woe (5:7, 10–12). There will be one more opportunity, in 5:21–24, for both sides to be brought together, the rejection of public piety as expressed in the liturgies and rituals of the great shrines, and the turning to Yahweh by the establishment of "justice in the gate." As a whole, then, vv 14–15 constitute the basic speech on repentance that is a prescription for the salvation of Israel in its present perilous condition. The two verses are so tightly and carefully bound together that it is difficult not to regard them as a single self-contained unit. Not only is there a considerable amount of repetition, but there is an impressive chiasm that crosses the verses. They are also complementary. The remaining question, however, is whether there is a shift in subject between v 14 and v 15, and exactly what the "remnant of Joseph" (*š³ryt ywsp*) signifies. It seems to be addressed in the vocative case, just as the *byt ywsp* is in the parallel passage in 5:6. But what of the "remnant"? Normally "remnant" points to what is left after the major disaster or catastrophe, and using it with the Philistines (1:8) and the Edomites (9:12) implies that those countries have already been devastated and that a mopping-up operation is involved. In other words, is the *š³ryt ywsp* the same as the *byt ywsp* or has a change occurred; and is the prophet thinking about the future after the debacle and in terms of 9:9–10? Put another way, does 5:15 stand at the end of the sequence while 5:14 is at the beginning? In that case, 5:14 would be the message to Israel *now* while it is still possible to salvage something, while 5:15 would be the message after the disaster in an effort to salvage the remnant. The fact that the message is the same, essentially unchanged, would not be lost on the attentive hearer or reader. It is always right to seek Good (the Good One), and always right to hate Evil (the Evil One); it is always obligatory to establish justice in the gate, and there is no secret about right relations with God, but he must be sought. It could be that the reference here to the "remnant of Joseph" is like the one to "Joseph's crash," not to the future catastrophe but rather to the present crisis; but then the choice of words does not seem to be appropriate. The "remnant" and the "crash" certainly imply some permanent disabling amputation of territory, such as Tiglath-pileser III inflicted some thirty or forty years later in his first campaign against Galilee and Transjordan. And the "remnant of Joseph" seems clearly to be the subject in 5:15. Logically it could be the subject of the whole complex, but we think it more likely that 5:14 refers to the "house of Israel," as is the case in 5:4, and therefore that both subjects are intended here as in 5:4–6.

> 5:14a **diršû-ṭôb** *we'al-rāʿ*
>   *lĕmaʿan tiḥyû*
> 14b   *wîhî-kēn* **yhwh 'ĕlōhê-ṣĕbā'ôt** *'ittĕkem*
>   *ka'ăšer 'ămartem*

> 15a   **śin'û-rāʿ wĕ'ehĕbû ṭôb**
>   *wĕhaṣṣîgû baššaʿar mišpāṭ*
> 15b   *'ûlay yeḥĕnan* **yhwh 'ĕlōhê-ṣĕbā'ôt**
>   *šĕ'ērît yôsēp*

> 5:14   Seek Good [the Good One] and not Evil [the Evil One],
>   so that you may live!
>   And let it happen so—
>   let Yahweh, the God of hosts, be with you as you have
>   claimed!

> 5:15   Hate Evil [the Evil One] and love Good [the Good One],
>   and establish justice in the gate.
>   Perhaps Yahweh the God of hosts will treat [you] kindly,
>   O remnant of Joseph.

The mood is the same in both parts. Repentance is the only way, and there is still hope for Israel. In 5:14 the hope is expressed that all will yet be well and that Israel will survive and have life. Then the current empty boast about God being with them may become true. This is the basic original message to Israel, already stated in 5:4–6, and the one that was so totally rejected, as the five refrains in 4:6–11 have made clear.

What of 5:15? Here, except for the "remnant of Joseph," the theme is the same. If you repent, in other words, hate Evil and love Good and express or implement the basic change in attitude by doing something fundamental and necessary, establishing justice in the gate, not continuing the sort of pretense and contradiction that prevails there now, then there is a chance that Yahweh will be gracious. Such a response would be essentially equivalent to divine repentance. The verbs *ḥnn* and *nḥm* are not far apart in meaning or sound, and we find them linked in the prophetic version of the credo derived from Exod 34:6–7, but with the addition of *nḥm* (see Joel 2:13–14, and Jonah 3:9 and 4:2). All of this would fit well with the circumstances under which Amos commenced his ministry, and the first messages must have been along these lines. The least clear detail is the "remnant of Joseph." Is the hope of the future still contingent on repentance and the administration of justice? Does the apparent pattern or schema here conform to the expectation in 9:9–15, or does this verse remain anomalous under all conditions? Can we come in at one end and go out the other? As no subject is given for 5:14, does the "remnant of Joseph" extend over both verses, complicating the problem even further? In view of the context and the way in which matters are handled in 5:4–6 or again in 5:21–24, the supposition would be that the reference is contemporary, that as elsewhere throughout these chapters all of Israel is addressed, but there is a specific reference to Joseph (i.e., the northern kingdom) to show that the northern entity is the particular or immediate focus of attention. Perhaps the use of the term *š'ryt* has a futurist reference; it is proleptic, but the primary emphasis of the passage would seem to be contemporary or immediate. Even in the other passages in which it occurs, the term *š'ryt* (Philistines and Edom) may be somewhat ambivalent. Perhaps we can leave the matter partly open.

II.A.3.b. LAMENTATION (5:16–17)

The Lamentation goes with the Woe as a basic prophetic category. Clearly it belongs to the period of consequences, just as the Woe falls earlier in the sequence, belonging to the warnings and threats. The prophet presents the various stages of the message and its effects. Lamentation is the ultimate consequence; when the warnings, the woes, and the call to repentance are disregarded along with the plagues, then comes judgment, disastrous and complete, and along with that the unbroken lamentation of the survivors. There are other references to mourning in the book; we have already had one in this chapter, the dirge over the Virgin Israel. Another, comparable piece is to be found in 8:9–10, which is even more extensive and gloomier, if that is possible. The current passage has some interesting features, discussed elsewhere, but we can examine it here:

> 5:16a   *lākēn kōh-ʾāmar yhwh*
>   *ʾĕlōhê ṣĕbāʾôt ʾădōnāy*
>   *bĕkol-rĕḥōbôt mispēd*
>   *ûbĕkol-ḥûṣôt yōʾmĕrû hô-hô*
> 16b   *wĕqārĕʾû ʾikkār ʾel-ʾēbel*
>   *ûmispēd ʾel-yôdĕʿê nehî*
> 17a   *ûbĕkol-kĕrāmîm mispēd*
> 17b   *kî-ʾeʿĕbōr bĕqirbĕkā*
>   *ʾāmar yhwh*

Apart from the introduction and conclusion, there seem to be six lines forming three bicola. The arrangement is complicated and there are unusual features, but the basic scheme seems to be reasonably clear. In the first bicolon, *bkl-rhbwt* balances *bkl-hwṣwt,* while the mourning is expressed in the words *hw-hw.* The latter serve also for the second unit.

In the second unit there is also only one verb, *wqrʾw.* We note the parallel construction for *ʾl-ʾbl* and *mspd-ʾl,* very unusual but perhaps deliberate, with the preposition after the noun it modifies, in effect a postposition. It is also to be noted that *ywdʿy nhy* is not equivalent or even parallel to *ʾkr;* rather, *ywdʿy nhy* is the subject of the verb *qrʾw,* and *ʾkr* is the object. The whole unit, 5:16–17, would read as follows:

5:16a   Therefore, thus has said Yahweh the God of hosts, my Lord:
        "In all the squares let there be lamentation,
           and in all the streets
        Let them say, 'Alas! Alas!'—
16b   and let them summon the field hands
             to mourning and to lamentation—
      those trained in wailing.
17a   And in all the vineyards let there be lamentation,
17b   when I pass through, in the midst of you."
                          Yahweh has spoken.

Those professional mourners are the ones who say "Alas! Alas!" and in that way they summon the plowmen to the memorial services.

The final statement is ominous—*ʿbr* is used in an opposite sense to its meaning in connection with the third and fourth visions, where we read *lōʾ-ʾôsîp ʿôd ʿăbôr lô* (7:8, 8:2). It is curious to have the same verb used affirmatively and negatively with the same basic meaning. He will pass through in judgment, and he will not excuse the culprit.

II.A.4. WARNING AND WOE (5:18–27)

This substantial unit begins with formal introduction of the Woe by use of the key word itself. In v 18 we have *hôy* followed by the participle with the definite article, which is the standard form (repeated in full only at the beginning of the major sevenfold Woe, 6:1–7). The Woe here is contained in vv 18–20, but because we have no explicit subject of the following material (5:21–24) we may assume that the same subject is carried forward. In addition, because of the reference to *mšpṭ wṣdqh* ("justice and equity") in 5:24 we must look back to the first Woe in this section (5:7, 10–12) to identify the subject more fully. As we have observed previously, the people indicted in the Woes constitute a large group, and the various specified elements in that group overlap and intermingle, so that a reference to one of the units also includes others. Thus we find different people sharing similar features, or the same groups having diverse characteristics or activities. In this case we can assume that the primary target of vv 21–24 is the people mentioned in 5:7 because they above all should establish the justice that they have changed into poison, but there is no reason not to include the self-deluded seekers of the Day of Yahweh.

II.A.4.a. THE DAY OF YAHWEH (5:18–20)

Verses 18–20 are a self-enclosed unit: vv 18 and 20 constitute the envelope and v 19 is an elaborate simile involving a sequence of circumstances designed to provide an analogy to the Day of Yahweh in terms of expectations (or rather delusions). As Amos puts it, the difference between what they expect and what will happen is like the difference between light and dark, night and day. The truth is that the Day of the Lord will be the Night of the Lord. The emphasis on the contrast between light and dark is hardly accidental; the whole framework of creation, beginning with light and day, is involved. What will happen on the Day of the Lord is a return to chaos, such as Jeremiah envisions in chap. 4:23–26 (cf. also Amos 8:9, where the darkening of the day is associated with ultimate mourning).

The simile or parable Amos uses presents a series of disasters to be compared with the Day of Yahweh for these people. There is nothing positive in it at all. It starts with flight and ends with being bitten by "the snake." One is reminded of the penalty imposed on those who attempt to flee from Yahweh's punitive judgment in chap. 9 as part of the closing vision (9:1–4), as they are threatened by the sword that will slay them and/ or the serpent that will bite them.

5:19	*ûnĕšākô hannāḥāš*	and have the snake bite him
9:3	*ʾăṣawweh ʾet-hannāḥāš*	I will command the Serpent at once,
	ûnĕšākām	and he shall bite them

The structure of the whole is as follows:

5:18a *hôy hammitʾawwîm ʾet-yôm yhwh*
18b   *lāmmâ-zzeh lākem*
        yôm yhwh hûʾ-ḥōšek wĕlōʾ-ʾôr
19a   *kaʾăšer yānûs ʾîš mippĕnê hāʾărî*
        ûpĕgāʿô haddōb
19b   *ûbāʾ habbayit wĕsāmak yādô ʿal-haqqîr*
        ûnĕšākô hannāḥāš
20a   *hălōʾ-ḥōšek yôm yhwh wĕlōʾ-ʾôr*
20b   *wĕʾāpēl wĕlōʾ-nōgah lô*

5:    [18a]Woe to you who long for Yahweh's Day! [18b]What does it mean to you? Yahweh's Day will be darkness rather than light. [19a]It will be as though a man were to escape from the lion, only to have the bear meet him; [19b]or, having reached his house, to rest his hand on the wall, and have the snake bite him. [20a]Is not Yahweh's Day darkness rather than light, [20b]pitch darkness without a glimmer of light?

Verses 18 and 20 together are almost precisely the same length as v 19. The division is very clearly marked. The outer ring deals with the Day of Yahweh in terms of darkness against light, while the intervening v 19 deals with the comparison and is restricted to the images of animals, including lion, bear, and snake. The conclusion is the same: just as the adventure mentioned in v 19 describes the worst possible day in any person's life, with one unexpected disaster after another, so will the Day of the Lord be for those who seek it most eagerly. It will be a series of disasters, perhaps like the plagues they have been experiencing lately, only this time they will not escape.

II.A.4.b. JUSTICE (5:21–24)

As indicated earlier, the Woes and the theme of repentance come together in this memorable address. The material interlocks with v 25, so we can recognize the general subject as the "house of Israel." But as it is tied to both woe utterances (in 5:7, 10–12; and in 5:18–20) we are doubtless right in seeing in this material a statement of the choice before Israel, a last chance at repentance and reversal. So again, if the general subject is the "house of Israel," as it has been throughout the chapter, then particular groups in the larger entity are those targeted in the Woes. We have noted elsewhere that vv 22 and 25 are linked by the references to sacrifice (in the wilderness), thus identifying the group in 21–24 with the one in 25–27. The culminating point is reached with the statement on justice and equity (*mšpṭ wṣdqh*) in v 24. This verse has connections with the woe passages in 5:7 (and 10–12) and 6:12–13, where the same pair occurs and where the same point is made about those who turn justice and righteousness into wormwood and gall. The way to repent is to abandon the sanctuaries, with their false worship and elaborate ritual, which sponsor and condone rank injustice and outright criminal behavior, and to institute real justice and equity in the gate like an ever-flowing stream.

The unusual shift from 2d m. pl. to 2d m. s. in v 24 is discussed in the Notes and Comment and there may be a deliberate element in the switch from the group to the individual. Except for the specific references to the king in 7:9–17, the royal house is not mentioned elsewhere directly in the content of the speeches or the book (aside from the heading), but in Amos' view the king must bear heavy responsibility, perhaps the heaviest of all, for the state of the nation. Ultimately the issue of justice and righteousness rests on his shoulders, and the reference may well be to the person at the top of the heap, though without any intention of excluding the others from their share of responsibility.

II.A.4.c. THREAT OF EXILE (5:25–27)

Here we have another of the historic references to ancient times, the Exodus and wilderness experience (cf. 2:10 and in particular the reference to forty years). The specific point here has to do with the sacrifices in the wilderness, if any, and the contrast with the current practice. We suggest that the prophet here and the others are not necessarily against sacrifices altogether but have two important points in mind: (1) the temples are so corrupt that it is better to stay away entirely and have nothing to do with sacrifice at all than to join in worship of that kind; and (2) justice and righteousness and the other virtues and attitudes associated with Yahweh himself are much more important than sacrifices—there is no comparison as far as true religion is concerned. Thus justice without sacrifices is much better than sacrifices without justice. It does not seem likely, in view of the tradition, that Israel failed to sacrifice at all in the desert, but rather that the circumstances were very different. Sacrifices themselves are neutral. It depends on the attitude and behavior of the person making them and those who are supervising.

Verse 26 remains enigmatic, but it seems to refer to the worship of foreign gods in Israel, gods whose images they will carry into exile with them. The gods themselves seem to be at home in the land(s) of exile, thus adding an ironic twist to the situation. Israel will leave its land to go into exile, while the gods they imported from other lands will be returning home. The gods they trusted failed them, and the God they failed to trust and who could have delivered them will abandon them as they deserve. There is an explicit reference to Damascus in v 27, which indicates the direction of the exile (northeastward) and likewise the direction from which the judgment will come.

If we review the chapter briefly we see that the contents converge on a few basic or central themes:

1. Woes—there are severe warnings in the form of judgments against segments of the population;

2. Call to repentance as the only possible way to escape impending judgment;

3. Lamentations—the end result of the series beginning with the Woes; they reflect the disaster imposed by judgment and the resulting endless and unredeemed sorrow and tragedy;

4. The target is all of Israel (*byt yśr'l*), but there is special attention to the house of Joseph, the preferred designation of the northern kingdom;

5. The specific threat is exile "beyond Damascus."

There is still a chance, however, and that requires repentance, which involves both a negative and a positive factor:

1. On the negative side, stay away from the great sanctuaries and their services.

2. On the positive side, seek Yahweh by establishing justice in the gate. Justice is the evidence of true repentance and the abandonment and replacement of the present misrule, which causes great injustice.

II.B. Woes and Warnings (6:1–14)

The major part of chap. 6 is devoted to more Woes, and over the two chapters they are the dominant feature, 5:7, 10–12; 5:18 (with 21–27); 6:1–7; 6:11–14. Along with woes there are judgments (condemnations) and at least one oath of retribution, as well as laments. There is also an important note of repentance, a summons to change while there is yet time. The title used for the people most often is *byt yśr'l*, which we believe applies to the double kingdom (also *btwlt yśr'l* and *g'wn y'qb*). The northern kingdom is singled out for special attention and is designated by the term *ywsp*, which is unique in this section of the book of Amos. There is also a fierce concentration on the corruption and depravity of the great religious centers and an equally fierce denunciation of unjust behavior. The woes are directed at a special class in society, the leadership in both civilian and religious life, in commerce and business as well as in military and diplomatic matters. All is brought to a head in the prescription for salvation: seek Yahweh and live, but avoid the shrines and their services and practice justice instead. The fate of the nation hangs in the balance, and only repentance will help. Then perhaps Yahweh will relent. The mood is gloomy and the odds are steep. The future seems to be defined more by the threat of doom and the accompanying wailing and mourning than by any serious expectation of repentance or reform. The Book of Woes provides a suitable basis for and introduction to the preceding section, chaps. 1–4, in which the judgment is pronounced without qualification. The function of The Book of Woes is to provide further justification and defense of the solemn judgment pronounced against Judah and Israel (that is, the house of Israel) in chaps. 1–4. That judgment did not materialize without warning, but only after a long, agonizing effort to warn and exhort and encourage the people to repentance. Only when all efforts had failed and further attempts were effectively prevented did the gears shift and the period of grace end.

II.B.1. WOES (6:1–7)

This passage contains the main collection of Woes. The word itself is used only once but is intended for all seven groups who are listed and charged with a multiplicity of crimes of commission and omission. Basically they are heartless, callous people who indulge themselves while disaster threatens the whole nation. The negative charge that involves them all is failure to be "distressed at Joseph's crash" (6:6). They are responsible and they do not care—so they are irresponsible. And they will suffer the same certain fate—they will lead the exiles into captivity. It is also to be noted that both Zion and Samaria are explicitly included in the Woes; in fact Judah (Zion) comes first in the list, with Israel (Samaria) second. The double nation is called *byt yśr'l* here as it is regularly in Part II of Amos. Because we will deal with the details of this unit at some length in the COMMENT sections, we will not anticipate that enterprise here. Nonetheless, a few general observations may be in order.

1. The first pair of Woes implies and perhaps indicates that the people in Zion and in Samaria are not really two separate groups, though they are in different places, but are instead a ruling elite that shares personnel, probably intermarries (as did the royal houses, for a while at least), and shares similar responsibilities, thus making the expression *byt yśr'l* somewhat more realistic as a blanket term than we are wont to regard it. We imagine too that ambassadors and diplomats of the two nations are actually present in

each other's capitals, so that both groups are mixed, even though the proportions would be reversed in the different capitals.

2. The third Woe is aimed at essentially the same people as indicated in the great Woe of 5:18–20, those who hurtle along to the Day of Yahweh with eager expectations, unaware of the tragedy awaiting them or coming to meet them. We think the *yôm rā*ᶜ (day of calamity) in 6:3 is the same in all likelihood as the day of darkness without any light in 5:18 and 20.

3. The remaining Woes (4–7) all refer to the same group, indulging in various excesses as they celebrate, perhaps, the remarkable victories mentioned in 6:13, which they imagine will turn the tide in their direction and which foreshadow the triumphant Day of Yahweh they eagerly await.

II.B.2. THE OATH AND WOES (6:8–14)

This collection is somewhat less cohesive and more miscellaneous than the preceding one, but the main element continues to be the series of Woes, which winds up at the end of the chapter.

In 6:8–10 we have an oath by Yahweh, the second of three in the book of Amos, one in each major unit. Their importance lies in the depth of feeling and the degree of commitment by the deity. They are all totally negative. In the first case (4:2) the oath confirms the punishment of the proud women and their consorts in Samaria and condemns them to exile. In the third (8:7), the oath is made against the crushers of the poor (8:4–6, cf. 2:6–8) whose deeds will be remembered, not for good but for evil. In the present case, the oath is taken against proud Jacob, as also in 8:7; here as in 4:2 Yahweh swears by himself, though the specific words may be different— *běqodšô* in 4:2, *běnapšô* in 6:8—but the sense is the same. In accordance with the arrangement in BHS, we suggest the following:

> 6:8a   *nišbaᶜ ʾǎdōnāy yhwh běnapšô*
>   *nĕʾum-yhwh ʾĕlōhê ṣĕbāʾôt*
>   *mĕtāʾēb ʾānōkî ʾet-gĕʾôn yaᶜǎqōb*
>   *wĕʾarmĕnōtāyw śānēʾtî*
>   8b   *wĕhisgartî ᶜîr ûmĕlōʾāh*

> 6:8a   My Lord Yahweh has sworn by his life
>   —Oracle of Yahweh, God of hosts—
>   "I abhor the pride of Jacob,
>   its citadels I reject;
>   8b   so I will hand over the city in its entirety."

What we have in the latter part of 8a and 8b is apparently a tricolon with interlocking chiastic patterns. The first two cola have the verb forms at either end (*mt'b 'nky//śn'ty*) and the complementary or at least related nouns in the middle (*'t-g'wn y'qb//w'rmntyw*). As between cola 2 and 3, we have the verbs in the middle and the related nouns at the ends: *śn'ty// whsgrty* and *'rmntyw//'yr wml'h*. The parallelism of *mt'b* and *śn'* is confirmed by 5:10, where we have *śn'w//yt'bw*. This occurrence shows that there is a scribal error in 6:8 (unless it is some kind of by-form, which seems very dubious) where we should have *mĕtā'ēb* (with *'ayin*) for *mĕtā'ēb* (with *'aleph*), an otherwise unknown form. The root *t'b* means "to long for," which is not feasible here, and a supposed *t'b* II meaning "loathes" is created from this passage. The confusion in laryngeals would hardly occur before rabbinic times.

In interpreting the passage we suggest that the hating, like the loathing, is directed against proud Jacob, and that the citadels, like the city and its fullness (i.e., all of its inhabitants), will be turned over to the enemy. There is some slippage between the order and the sense, but all of the terms have a certain range beyond the immediate connection, and in any case the general sense is quite clear. The remainder of the unit deals apparently with the aftermath. A single house with ten men, all of whom die, symbolizes the death of the city. There is a curious connection with an earlier passage in Part II (5:3), where a city's army (the same city) is progressively decimated from one thousand to one hundred and then to ten. While the same people may not be involved, the same number is, and we can read it as saying that even the ten, the 1 percent, will also be swept away. The destruction is total and the death toll is 100 percent.

Verses 11–13 pick up the theme of the Woes again. There is an echo of the first formal Woe in the unit, 5:7, which was aimed at those who turn justice into wormwood; the same terms are used here, but the form is slightly different (i.e., 2d m. pl. perfect form of the verb *hpk* [*kî hăpaktem*] in 6:12 instead of the m. pl. participle [*hhpkym*] in 5:7). This Woe is followed by two more (v 13), which complete the roster for chaps. 5–6 with a total of eleven or twelve, the dominant block in this material and for the whole book.

Looking at the section a little more closely, we note that in v 11 Yahweh gives a command or charge, but the words of the charge do not appear until v 12, showing that vv 11–13 form a compact unit. The remainder of v 11 seems to be parenthetical, though the subject of the verb at the beginning of this part is not specified and is not clear:

> he will smash the largest house into pieces,
> and the smallest house into bits.

The ultimate subject is Yahweh, to be sure, but is the actual destruction to be carried out by an agent such as the destroying angel (cf. 2 Sam 24:16) or some other heavenly figure (cf. the Sword and the Serpent of 9:3–4)? In that case the command of v 11a might be connected with this bicolon; but the association remains awkward, and it is better to link the opening words of v 11 with direct speech by Yahweh. That appears in vv 12–13, which would be suitable as a continuation of v 11aA. Even more impressive, however, is the connection with v 14, where Yahweh says what he is going to do about all of the matters discussed in chaps. 5–6. In other words, the true continuation of v 11aA is v 14—"For soon I will raise up against you, O house of Israel . . . a nation that will overpower you. . . ."

According to this reckoning, 11aB–b contributes a parenthesis or digression explaining what Yahweh will do to the city mentioned in v 8, only the subject is in the third person (perhaps an agent). The destruction of the dwellings in the city is an expected, even automatic, outcome of its being delivered into the enemy's hands.

Then vv 12–13 provide the springboard for the conclusion in v 14. Essentially the point is that the Israelites, especially those indicted in the woes, have behaved in ridiculous, utterly ludicrous fashion; they have done things comparable to running horses on rocks (a potentially fatal blunder) or plowing the sea with oxen (even sillier). The behavior of the Israelites is at least equally foolish in turning justice into poison and the fruit of righteousness to wormwood. Turning justice into poison does no one any good and, more important, it offends Yahweh. They should have known better.

Verse 13 belongs to the same category. Victories are one thing, boasting is another. The latter is not only foolish but despicable, and it offends Yahweh even more. The Israelites above all peoples should know that only Yahweh can win battles and give victories, and to boast that by their own strength they had captured for themselves Lo-Dabar and Qarnaim is fatuous, foolhardy, and will prove ultimately fatal. In the end they will be oppressed from the entrance of Hamath to the Wadi Arabah. This statement is especially interesting because almost the identical words are used to describe the conquests of Jeroboam II in 2 Kgs 14:25. Historically speaking, the victories mentioned in 6:13 probably were the high points of a triumphant campaign that brought that large territory east of the Jordan under Israel's control. If the view adopted here is correct, then Amos' prophecies turned out to be wrong for the short run, or at least in the reign of Jeroboam. Only long after Amos was gone did things come about as he had foreseen. It would appear that the prophet who foresaw and predicted the victories and conquests of Jeroboam was the elusive figure of Jonah ben-Amittai (2 Kgs 14:25). As the editor of 2 Kings insists, Yahweh did not say he would wipe out Israel and its name, but on the contrary took pity on them and saved them through Jeroboam and by the hand of Jonah. Once more Yahweh relented or repented, and the course of history took an entirely different turn from that forecast by Amos. Only later would he be vindicated. Happily, this circumstance tends to support the authenticity of what he said rather than the reverse. It would even appear that the comment in 2 Kings 14 about Jeroboam's conquest of the same territory mentioned in Amos was intended as a rebuttal of Amos' prediction, as though the author knew that there were prophets who foretold disaster at that time.

In our opinion, chap. 6:13–14 serves not only as the conclusion of The Book of Woes (chaps. 5–6) but also as the summation of the entire work from the beginning of the Great Set Speech in chap. 1 to this point. When we analyze the historical connections between the victories recorded and condemned here and the political status of the Transjordanian states in chaps. 1–2, we suggest the following historical reconstruction. The oracles in the opening chapters presuppose, if they do not affirm, the independent status of those kingdoms, whereas the oracle in 6:13–14 affirms victories and assumes (if it does not require) the conquest of much of the same territory east of the Jordan, thus altering the picture presented in chaps. 1–2. We conclude, therefore, that 6:13–14 reflects a later development, after the victories of Jeroboam II, and that the oracles in chaps. 1–2 reflect the political situation before the ascendancy of that king. Thus, while we have urged and argued that the chronological order of the first six chapters of Amos proceeds mainly in reverse—in other words, The Book of Woes (chaps. 5–6) basically precedes The Book of Doom (chaps. 1–4, with 3–4 preceding 1–2)—the pattern is not observed with complete consistency and, in any case, 6:13–14 is a general summary marking the end of the whole process. Thus it is the last and most recent statement in the book of Amos to this point.

Part III. The Book of Visions (7:1–9:6)

Here we have a carefully structured account of the prophet's experience that lay behind and occurred before the messages in chaps. 1–6. We think there is a clear and inverted or chiastic correlation between the first two visions and the second group of oracles (chaps. 5–6) and between the second two visions and the first collection of oracles (chaps. 1–4). The culmination of the story is in the account of the confrontation that comes after everything in the first six chapters has been said and all four visions have been seen. The insertion of the story of the confrontation between the reports of the third and fourth visions shows that the association with that phase of Amos' experience is quite deliberate and that we must combine vision, message, and confrontation in our analysis and presentation of the material.

We are trying to make sense of the book as a whole by relating all of the messages to successive stages in Amos' career. The clearest guideposts are provided by the three sets of visions, which inaugurate and characterize three modes and moods in Amos' messages. The first pair could also have represented the experience of his being called to prophesy, for none of his activities need have taken place before them. In the time of conditional reprieve secured by his successful intercession as he receives the first pair of visions, Amos is able to deliver the messages of the first phase—the Woes and calls to amendment in chaps. 5–6.

At the same time a series of plagues is sent, and the prophet comments on them, explaining them as object lessons and talking points. In chap. 4 the perspective is clearer; the plagues are over and can be reviewed as a set. It is clear that the plagues are connected with the first pair of visions, and, as their scale and duration seem to have been mitigated by Amos' successful intercession, it is possible also that the plagues (or the first of them) represent the first events in Amos' public career (the locusts come first in the visions, but in the middle of the plagues).

In his visions Amos sees the real source and deeper meanings of the plagues. He, at least, makes the appropriate response in lamentations and prayers. But his vicarious repentance cannot cancel the judgment; it can only stay its execution, buying him time to proclaim his message, buying the people time to listen to it. While it is possible that the people were expected to interpret for themselves the plagues as calls to repentance (the commination rituals of the covenant should have been sufficient for that), it is more likely that the prophet's word gave them the needed commentary, explanation, and exhortation. Amos 3:3–8 points firmly to such a combination of calamity and commentary.

We think, accordingly, that chaps. 5–6 are a summary of messages given by Amos after the first two visions, while at least some of the plagues were still going on. It is a more subtle question whether, in the final write-up of the preaching that occurred in this earlier phase in Amos' career and its attachment to the Great Set Speech (chaps. 1–2), which came later in time, any touches were added from the perspective of this eventual outcome. This problem is discussed in detail in the general INTRODUCTION to The Book of Woes.

When it becomes clear that the people are not going to repent, no matter how many plagues are sent and no matter how much the prophet exhorts them, there is nothing left but judgment (4:12). The end of the reprieve is marked by the striking difference between the first pair of visions and the second pair.

The conjunction of the confrontation between Amos and Amaziah with the second pair of visions and with the associated judgment oracles in chaps. 1–4 is less easy to determine. The second pair of visions obviously forms a unit. Like the first pair they are presented in such similar terms as to give the impression that they are two facets of a single entity. From the placement of the report (7:10–17) in the middle of them it is clear that the association is close: but, by the same token, the connection and sequence are not evident.

Two developments can be seen as both cause and explanation of the drastic change in the situation represented by the differences between the first pair of visions, in which Amos has the effective say, and the second pair, in which he has no say at all. At the end of each of the latter two, Yahweh says, "I will never spare them again." Never again will he grant a reprieve as he has already done in connection with the first two visions. The first of these factors is the failure of the people to repent, as cataloged in 4:6–11; the second is the expulsion of Amos from Bethel, as reported in 7:10–17.

Either alone would be enough to explain the final exhaustion of divine patience. But if Amaziah's treatment of Amos is identified as the last straw —on top of the people's refusal to repent, which could lie behind Amaziah's remark that "the land cannot endure all his words" (7:10)—then we must suppose that the complete change in tone reflected in chaps. 1–4 when compared with chaps. 5–6, and representing the announcement to the people of what Yahweh meant by "I will never spare them again," came after Amaziah's conduct provided the final proof that the situation was without remedy. If so, it follows that Amos continued to be active, delivering such messages, even after the confrontation with Amaziah.

This reconstruction of the evidence is possible, but we do not think that it is the most likely one. Although we know nothing of the sequel, the impression conveyed by 7:10–17 is that it marks the end of Amos' career in public. That leaves no room for the development and delivery of the all-important messages of chaps. 1–4. Accordingly, we identify the climax of 4:12 as the end of the first phase (in the interval between the first and second pairs of visions and at the very end of that interval), and as another way of proclaiming the now inevitable judgment, as affirmed with equal finality in the second pair of visions. The oracles now presented in chaps. 1–4 were the result of this change, spelling out the message of doom.

It was, then, the preaching of the messages of chaps. 1–4 that caused Amaziah's reaction. Amaziah's behavior, in turn, made it even clearer that the new policy of granting no more opportunities for repentance was fully justified. Commentators have found it easy to imagine that Amos actually proclaimed the contents of chaps. 1–4, or something like them, within the precincts of Bethel. The threat against rulers and the prediction of exile for the people (7:11) is prominent in the Great Set Speech (chaps. 1–2). It is true that an explicit threat against Jeroboam, along with a prediction of exile for Israel as such, is not found in that speech. But it is certainly implied, and Amaziah's quotation of Amos' threat in 7:11 can hardly be his own invention. It would be entirely in keeping with chaps. 1–2 for Amos to say such words in an appropriate context; and it is quite possible that such words were actually present in one version of the oracle against Israel on some of the many occasions of its delivery up and down the country. The references to the several popular shrines located at widely separated places in the two kingdoms suggest that Amos could have turned up at all of them to speak his piece. The complaint, "the land cannot endure all his words" (7:10), implies as much.

Furthermore, preachers of repentance are easier to tolerate than preachers of doom, even though neither is heeded. The preacher of repentance still holds out hope, as Amos does in chaps. 5–6. It would be easier for Amaziah to brand chaps. 1–4 as sedition than chaps. 5–6.

We suggest, accordingly, that the second phase in Amos' career began with the second pair of visions; it was characterized by preaching of the kind now found in chaps. 1–4. It was climaxed by his proclaiming the message at the shrine of Bethel itself; and this act provoked Amaziah to take more drastic measures to silence the prophet. It is true that silencing the prophets is one of the reasons for the judgment listed in the Great Set Speech (2:12), and Amaziah's prohibition could be what was meant. But if Amos was able to deliver that message, he was not yet completely silenced. That charge is given in general rather than in personal terms, but it could represent a final revision of Amos' message in response to Amaziah's intervention and interdiction. Even so, we need not imagine that 7:10–17 records the first and only time that Amos encountered such a hindrance, or that Amaziah was the only person who ever tried to silence him.

What should be clear from this analysis is that the book of Amos contains a literary presentation of his message rather than a chronological account of his life. Yet reasonable, if not certain, conclusions can be drawn from the biographical information that dominates The Book of Visions. We can take its autobiographical form as a token of its complete authenticity, while the biographical (third-person) form of the account of the confrontation (7:10–17) is a mark of its secondary character, the work of a disciple. It presents its own kind of veracity as an eyewitness report, the authenticity of which has almost never been questioned by scholars. Its insertion at this point can be seen as the work of an editor, but this positioning does not necessarily mean that he is trying to place that event at the same moment as the second pair of visions, which embrace it, or that he is trying to identify it as the cause and explanation of those visions. We suggest that it is the other way around. The message of Amos' second phase, consisting of the second pair of visions and the associated judgment oracles of chaps. 1–4, when delivered in Bethel, triggered Amaziah's response and brought that phase to an end.

The cluster of material in 7:7–8:3 thus represents the whole of Amos' second phase, beginning with the dual vision—or at least the first of the pair—and ending with the altercation with Amaziah.

After the report of the fourth vision there is a transition to the fifth vision, and the intervening material would seem to belong to that phase, the third phase in Amos' career. From 8:4 on we are involved in a wrapping-up operation, with the fifth vision and its accompanying messages reinforcing and sharpening features of the earlier phases.

III.A. THE FIRST FOUR VISIONS (7:1–8:3)
III.A.1. THE FIRST PAIR OF VISIONS (7:1–6)

The first two visions are dealt with at length in the NOTES and COMMENTS. Here we wish to emphasize that they are visions of doom involving the larger entity, all of Israel. Amos, presumably at the very beginning of his mission as a prophet, is startled by a vision, which is an entirely new experience for him, and he reacts strongly, intercedes, and successfully induces Yahweh to reverse his decision. The theme of both accounts is that Yahweh has repented and will not execute the judgment inherent in the vision. That allows time for Amos to preach the word and for the people to repent. The result is the speeches in chaps. 5–6, with their emphasis on repentance and the possibility of saving the situation.

III.A.2. THE SECOND PAIR OF VISIONS (7:7–8:3)

The second pair of visions reverses the first pair. This time there is no intercession by Amos and no repentance by Yahweh. On the contrary, he says he will never do that again. The end has come. Here we can correlate the message in the visions with the oracles and preachments of chaps. 1–4. The somber implications of chaps. 5–6 (reflected in the Woes and the repeated warnings about death and exile) are fully brought out in chaps. 1–4. There are no calls to repentance, only irreversible judgment rooted in the total and repeated failure of Israel to turn back to Yahweh. A final judgment is pronounced.

If we are right in supposing that the bulk of what is contained in chaps. 1–6 had already been said by Amos, most of it publicly and some of it at Bethel, then confrontation and conflict were inevitable. Amos and Amaziah had been on a collision course for some time, and the explosion was quite predictable. The account is very much condensed and carefully and intricately structured, so it is not easy to reconstruct a coherent and reasonable account of what happened. We have tried to do so in the COMMENTS on the passage. In view of what Amos says about worship at the great shrines, including Bethel, and what will happen to the Temple there, and in view of his criticisms of the elite, including the priestly groups at the shrines, the atmosphere would be distinctly unpleasant and difficult from the outset. But when at a critical point in the proceedings Amos uttered damaging words about the house and family of the high priest himself and of the king as well, then for the first time, we may assume, the situation went beyond the usual sort of difference of opinion and expression and became a judicial matter. The priest accused the prophet of fomenting sedition, a capital offense; and we infer that Amos' career came to a halt at that moment. While no one can say exactly what happened to Amos, it is likely in our judgment that he was not allowed to continue and may well have been silenced permanently. There may have been a short period during which he was held prisoner pending an investigation by the king (who had been notified by the priest) and then a judgment. In view of what we have before us it is hard to imagine king and priest simply releasing Amos, allowing him to go on with his mission. The priest has a remarkably high score for veracity in what is recorded of his words in the passage (and they have a remarkable literary quality as well), and he says quite truly and factually that the land cannot hold all the prophet's words. Certainly the authorities could not permit any more.

So what is left in the book—the material in the second insertion (8:4–14), the account of the fifth vision (9:1–4), and the last hymn, which closes the section (9:5–6)—must have transpired or been provided by Amos during that interval before his own trial and judgment. In fact, a preliminary publication containing the first six chapters plus an account of the four visions may have been prepared by Amos before he set out on this most hazardous and perhaps ultimately fatal visit to Bethel.

III.B. THE FIFTH VISION (8:4–9:6)
III.B.1. SECOND INSERTION: WOES (8:4–14)

When we look at the second insertion leading to the fifth vision, we suggest that these oracles derive from the same period and in all likelihood are related to the fifth vision, just as the first six chapters are related to the first four visions. The fifth vision is in many ways the harshest of all, for the emphasis there is not only on the destruction of the Temple (at Bethel) by divine order and action (9:1) but on the ruthless and merciless pursuit of all survivors and escapees until they are brought to the bar of judgment and executed. If we are right in supposing that the fifth vision came to Amos while he was in custody at Bethel, then the association of the vision of a temple's violent destruction with *that* Temple becomes more likely. And the other elements in the vision (vv 1–4 of chap. 9) also no doubt have local connections. We should look in a similar way at the remaining oracles of chap. 8.

We have noted that 8:3 depicts a violent and tragic scene in the palace corresponding to the equally violent scene in the temple in 9:1–4; 8:3 may be a fragment of the larger depiction of a similar vision, or it may be complete as it stands. In any event it forms an envelope with the fifth vision around the oracle in 8:4–14, showing that they are all bound together in a graphic and dramatic portrayal of the End Time, when everything will crash in ruins.

The Woes and oath of 8:4–8 form a reprise with additional harsh data supplied about the crushers of the needy already attacked in 2:6–8 and again in 5:7 (and 10–12). Here Yahweh's anger is framed in an oath that "I will never forget any of their misdeeds" (8:7). A hint of the earthquake to be announced in the vision of 9:1–4 may be found in 8:8 (and cf. 9:5).

There follow in rapid succession oracles about the End Time, days of grievous mourning echoing 5:2 and 5:16–17, and a famine of the words, going back to 2:11 and to the role of the prophet in 3:8, 5:10–12, and 5:13. There is also an echo and contrast with the famine described in the plague series (4:6–11). The final piece (vv 13–14) brings us back to the battle scene of 2:14–16, which concludes the Great Set Speech against the nations. It also brings to a head the long series of woes that are concentrated in chaps. 5–6, but do not end there. The basic ineradicable problem for the nation is that its leaders and those with heavy responsibilities all over both countries swear by false gods; they are apostates and idolaters in irreconcilable conflict with their true God and under irreversible judgment.

III.B.2. The Fifth Vision (9:1–6)
III.B.2.a. Temple and Earthquake (9:1–4)

We now come to the fifth and final vision, which in our opinion must have come to Amos in those last trying days between the confrontation and the royal judgment, whatever it turned out to be. And the oracle about the vision, along with the other visions just discussed, constitute a final chapter or unit in the message to supplement or summarize them all in the light of the experience at Bethel and the vision of the fallen Temple.

As we have argued earlier, there is no essential difference in the message after the confrontation at Bethel and what was said before. What change there is comes out of that experience and is reinforced by Vision 5. The decisive words at Bethel had to do with the judgment of execution against the king and the high priest, another indication that they would do no less to Amos. (1) Even if the prophet himself was not an active conspirator in such a plot, as some prophets had been, he had pronounced a judgment of capital punishment on the king and priest that in their view would be an open invitation to any adventurer to engage in assassination and usurpation. (2) Assassination with usurpation was a frequently successful practice in Israel, while assassination without usurpation was the mode in Judah;

but the distinction would not make much difference to the target of such an attack. (3) So in Phase Three the added element is that the leadership will not even enjoy the privilege of exile, the certain threat against the nation, but will be hunted down and executed for the criminals that they are. The nation itself will fall, as already established; but some people will survive, either in exile or by being left behind. They will have been victims twice, first of the sinners who brought on the judgment of God by afflicting others, and second by the judgment itself. But for those who were guilty in the first place, beginning with king and priest—or perhaps priest and king—to survive under any circumstances will be too good for them, and, as Amos says in Yahweh's name, he will hunt them down in the remotest hiding places and even in exile, and capture them and bring them back for summary judgment and execution.

And with the final somber words of 9:4, the message of Amos reaches a certain conclusion:

> "For I shall set my eyes upon them
>   to do them harm and not good."

That is because they spurned the words of the prophet who said: "Hate Evil and love Good" (5:15).

III.B.2.b. HYMN (9:5–6)

Part III ends with the last of the three hymns, a potent and elegant reminder of just who this God of Israel is: the one who strikes the earth so that it melts and all of its inhabitants mourn; the one who has built his sanctuary with its upper stories in the heavens, while its lower structure he founded upon the earth; the one whose "name is Yahweh" (9:6).

Part IV. Epilogue (9:7–15)

The last part of the book of Amos is an Epilogue that pulls together the book's main themes and extends the vision of the future beyond anything found in the preceding material. It is a difficult and controversial section, but our purpose at this point is merely to describe. In its present form the section is the work of the editor; but then the whole book is. He is working with authentic material from Amos, certainly for vv 7–10, and perhaps for vv 11–15 as well. We will deal with Amos' ideas about the future elsewhere, and they need only be sketched in here. The unit breaks down into two major divisions, each of which can be further subdivided:

IV. Epilogue
    A. The end of the nation
        1. The wicked nation (7–8)
        2. The sieve (9–10)
    B. The restoration
        1. The booth of David (11–12)
        2. The calendar: superabundance (13–15)

IV.A. THE END OF THE NATION (9:7–10)

This section describes the way in which the judgment against Israel will be carried out. The sinful nation will be destroyed (the northern kingdom no doubt, but the southern realm will be destroyed too), as will the remainder of the eight nations listed in chaps. 1–2; and "All the sinners of my people shall die by the sword." That is the last of the Woes, and it summarizes all of them clearly and sharply. At the same time, there will be survivors, whatever the precise meaning of the simile of the sieve. Finally, from these survivors there will come a new people and a restored nation.

IV.B. THE RESTORATION (9:11–15)

This section ushers in Phase Four—renewal and restoration—also in two subsections. Verses 11–12 describe the restoration of the kingdom of David (under the obscure image or figure of the *sukkat dāwîd,* the exact meaning of which is uncertain and much debated). This involves the final elimination of the last of the eight nations, apparently the Edomites. Perhaps surprising is the participation of other nations, such as the Cushites (9:7), all of whom will become part of the commonwealth of Yahweh—not that they will be absorbed by the kingdom of David, which will presumably occupy the same territory as in the days of David and Solomon, but that the others will also worship and serve Yahweh and live in peace and harmony with one another.

The last oracle depicts the idyllic prosperity and security of the restored nation, and with this picture of permanent peace and plenty the book ends.

THE MULTIPHASIC STRUCTURE OF THE FUTURE IN AMOS' PROPHECIES

We have postulated a four-phase structure for the organization of the materials in the book of Amos, based essentially on the visions described in chaps. 7–9, but utilizing other clues to be found in the book. The time has come not only to set down this list in rational order and to indicate which parts of the book belong to which phases, but also to explain the order of arrangement of the phases. We also need to address the question of whether all of these phases and the associated materials can be attributed to the prophet himself or can only be dealt with together as part of the book. Because our primary task must be to deal with the book of Amos and all of its contents, we can safely leave the other question to one side as we pursue the task of description, analysis, and interpretation of the book as it has come down to us. In the end the major claim or test of our work will be whether we have accomplished that task—and the degree to which we have maintained some adequate standard of scholarship while doing so. Nevertheless, the other question, which concerns the extent of the prophet's own participation in his book, also needs to be confronted: how much consists of his words, how much is authentic information about him and from him, and how much has been added by followers and editors. The development of the book was most likely an involved and lengthy process culminating in a final version that ends the book's literary history and begins its textual history, although these separate stages may or often do overlap. In any event we would be remiss if we did not face the question and deal with it in terms of our assumptions and presuppositions as well as using the data available for making choices and decisions.

To put the cart before the horse, we can state the conclusion briefly: the literary product called the book of Amos is not merely the transcript of oracles uttered by the prophet and stories about his experience recalled directly by him or through an amanuensis. There is a significant editorial process as we move from the actual utterances of the prophet to a written literary record and adaptation. An editor is at work putting the book together, certainly using materials taken directly from the prophet. After all, it is the book of *Amos,* a person important enough to warrant the attention given to him and his words, because except for the book he would be totally unknown. No one would invent an otherwise unknown person because it would serve no describable or conceivable purpose.

So Amos himself and his words remain the central factor in the book, and we make our first assumption by arguing that the editor's purpose is to do precisely that—to make and maintain the centrality of Amos, man and prophet, words and deeds. In other words, there is a coherence and continuity between prophet and editor. It is conceivable that a prophet could be his own editor, as seems to be the case with Ezekiel (and possibly Zechariah, who can be postulated as editor of the book of Haggai and his own book, that is, chaps. 1–8; but concerning the remainder we can say only that it is very obscure). A more likely and common situation is reflected in the book of Jeremiah, concerning which we know who the first and most important editor was, Baruch the Scribe (Muilenburg 1970). The circumstances are entirely plausible and understandable, and while some of the details are unique and peculiar to Jeremiah's time and place, we can posit such a pattern for other prophets, unless there is compelling evidence to the contrary. Again it seems likely that the prophet and his editor were in close contact, and that the editorial work proceeded with the authorization and approval, as well as the critical appraisal and corrections, of the principal. To the extent that this is the way matters developed we can speak of the prophet as his own editor, one who was heavily involved in that process.

The importance of this aspect of the process of the literary embodiment of oracles should not be underestimated. It means that the transition from first oral presentation to ultimate or at least stable written form will have been done with the prophet's supervision and approval. The implication is that the materials can be well preserved, for that is the purpose of the exercise. It is important to note that secondary and tertiary uses—written records as opposed to initial presentation—serve different purposes from the original, and often (or at least sometimes) modifications are introduced when the transition occurs. It is not so much the supposed shift from oral to written forms, as there is no reason why one need be different from the other. Speeches presented orally can be written down verbatim and no doubt were, whereas speeches originally written down can and will be delivered orally. There may well be alterations as one moves from one medium to another, but the transfer itself does not require or even imply significant changes. Rather, it is the modification in purpose and function that dictates change in format, style, wording, and the like. The tendency in writing is to expand, as the wry comment about Baruch's second edition of Jeremiah's book makes clear:

> And Jeremiah took another scroll and he gave it to Baruch ben-Neriah the Scribe; and he [Baruch] wrote upon it at the dictation of Jeremiah all the words of the book [the writing] that Jehoiakim the king of Judah had burned in the fire; and again [even so] he added to them many words like those (Jer 36:32).

The point is that a good many of the oracles show signs of rewriting or adaptation, the product of editorial work designed to preserve material in context, or to link it with other materials presented at different times and places. Such editorial activity may be taken for granted, and scholars are constantly on the lookout for signs and clues showing that the preserved form of an oracle may not be the same as the form of the original presentation. Such analysis is both important and useful, and when successful can point us to the original utterance by the prophet. But it would be a mistake to relegate automatically the revised or updated form in which the oracles now appear to the hand of a later editor—and to deem it of less value than the reconstructed original. Two comments are in order.

1. The exercise is a hypothetical and speculative one. The recovery or reconstruction of so-called original versions of oracles or poems or narratives is an enterprise fraught with perils, obstacles, and difficulties; any results, however appealing, are still partly if not largely informed guesswork. In the end there is a significant difference between having something tangible in front of our eyes, and trying to draw inferences or argue cases on the basis of a reconstructed hypothetical original. What we reconstruct is finally of our own making; the text in its preserved form is what we have.

2. The revised form may be as much the work of the prophet as the original presentation. The editing or altering may well have been done with his approval and authorization if not with his direct participation. Poets often revise their work, and who is to say that one version is more authentic or authoritative than another? We must reckon with this possibility in the case of biblical books, and in the case of Amos (as well as others) we must give this option first consideration. Thus the intermixture of elements deriving ostensibly from different occasions may not be the work of clumsy later editors or contributors, but rather the revisions and rearrangements of the prophet himself, making the book serve purposes other than those of the originally presented oracles.

Amos is not alone in such arrangement of materials. The books of Jeremiah, Isaiah, and Ezekiel likewise combine biographical, autobiographical, historical, visionary, and oracular compositions. All four books have blocks of material containing prophecies against the nations, though none is as systematic, regular, and compact as Amos 1:3–2:16. Noteworthy is the combination of chronological and thematic sequences, with the latter often overriding the former. To judge from these other collections, we should not assume that the book of Amos will unfold along a time line. While the visions of Jeremiah 1 probably inaugurated his ministry, those of Ezekiel (chap. 1) could mark the close of his (Greenberg 1983:9, 39). Isaiah 6 could document Isaiah's "call," though it does not begin the book. Similarly Amos 7:1–6 (along with 7:15) probably marks the earliest known events in Amos' career as a prophet.

Even when exact dates are supplied in the major prophets, they do not come in sequence; and where they are lacking (almost completely in the case of Amos) the question of dating their first presentation remains open. That question is germane only if an oracle was used only once, because if oracles were used again and brought up to date in the light of later developments, then the date of them all is the date of the whole book's completion.

As explained earlier, the identification of phases in the book's message and the assignment or allocation of oracles and episodes to these phases are based on an analysis of the visions, which are organized in such a way as to indicate a logical progression from the first to the fifth. We should be less certain of chronological sequence, for historical experience rarely if ever follows a smooth rational course, and we should expect both overlapping and intermingling as the course of events unwinds—perhaps inexorably though not in a single straight line—toward its dénouement. While offering this important qualification, we also wish to attach it to the prophet's own experience of the Word of God and his perception of the same course of events. The question we will ask is whether the prophet himself moves sequentially from one phase to the next, either chronologically or logically, or whether from the beginning or at some important point in his career he does not see things from the standpoint of heaven, or, like God himself, surveys the whole range of phases from first to last and is cognizant of the whole sequence, including stages that have not moved into the realm of history and even those that are beyond such stages.

We pose a certain paradox here: inevitably the prophet is existentially involved in the current phase, and his message is directly and uncompromisingly addressed to people at that point in their history. Thus when it is a matter of warning, nothing must conflict with or qualify the ringing cry of danger and the absolute need to respond and repent. Words of comfort or reassurance, of promise and support, could only weaken the main message. But at the same time, must not the prophet have in view the possible results of the present phase, what will happen after the period of warning has run its course, and what should happen or must be said then? It would be very strange indeed if prophets spoke only out of and into a particular situation and were unable to consider consequential situations in which a different message based on a different aspect of the relations between God and his people would be needed and forthcoming. The burden borne by a prophet is foreknowledge of the future and the education of people about the most important decisions they can make regarding that future. Are prophets the only ones who are not allowed to harbor thoughts beyond the immediate scope of the current message entrusted to them? Or is there some rule that does not permit the prophet to range over all of the possibilities regarding the future of his people? This question is especially important with regard to a book that contains a variety of messages offered over an undetermined length of time, and which not only reflects the vicissitudes through which any nation is likely to pass but is also intended to serve as guide or lesson for the same people for a later time.

Now we proceed to a survey of the phases and a discussion of how the passages were assigned to appropriate phases; we offer as well a rationale for placing these phases in the context of the prophet's life and work. The phases we are talking about are outlined in what follows.

Visions 1 and 2 (locusts and fire: 7:1–6) represent Phase One, an early point in the pronouncement of judgment against Israel, Judah, and perhaps the other nations as well, a point at which it is still possible to avert disaster. The message of these visions is that judgment by Yahweh has already been rendered, and punishment in the form of natural catastrophe (i.e., an act of God) is about to begin. But the prophet's intercession has caused Yahweh to rescind the order. On the face of it the order is rescinded through the prophet's intercession, following the pattern of famous mediators and their interventions recorded in the Bible: Moses and Samuel, and the classic story of Abraham's intercession on behalf of Sodom and Gomorrah. The point to be made is that Amos' action only buys time; it does not permanently reverse the judgment. While the text does not say so explicitly the context invariably does, and in this case the direct linkage with Visions 3 and 4 demonstrates the temporary and provisional character of the first and second exchanges between Yahweh and the prophet.

While the first two visions deal explicitly with the impending judgment or punishment and the prophet's successful intervention, we wish to emphasize that the prophet's intercession keeps alive the possibility of repentance and a more abiding reversal of the decision. In the end, genuine repentance is reciprocal: human repentance will evoke its divine counterpart. Prophetic intercession is not a permanent substitute for the necessary interaction between the divine and human parties. The issue between them, of sin and judgment, punishment or forgiveness, cannot permanently be resolved by prophetic intercession but only by the parties themselves. It is direct because it involves confrontation between judge and those judged, while intercession involves a third party. The passages that reflect this phase are therefore the ones that speak of threatened judgment and punishment but also issue a call to repentance, with the implied promise that God will respond to such behavior—that genuine repentance will result in rescission of judgment and real reconciliation. Perhaps the passage that best reflects this phase is the formal statement in chap. 4 on the five plagues. All of these were warnings and signs of impending doom and destruction but were intended to evoke repentance. Hence the sad refrain that "you did not repent [return] to me" (e.g. 4:11). The oracle in its present form (and doubtless also the form in which it was first presented by the prophet) stands at the end of Phase One. The period of warning and exhortation to repentance is closing, for there has been no effective response on the part of the leaders or their people. Nothing is said in this sequence about the next phase, but it is implied in the ominous statement now attached at the end of the series: "prepare to confront your God" (4:12). Even so it shows clearly that there was a first phase and that it was expressive of the time in which Israel was being warned by signs and tokens of divine disfavor as well as by words of prophets bearing the divine message.

Another example of this phase can be found in chap. 5, where the exhortation to seek Yahweh and live is repeated. Here the door is still open to repentance and the restructuring of relations with Yahweh. We find along with these clauses a summary of phase-one messages in 5:14 in which the people are instructed in the basic requirement of the covenant faith: to seek the Good [One] and not the Evil [One]. That passage seems to epitomize the message when the threat of judgment hangs over Israel, in the prophet's view. Doom is in the air, but there is still time to stem the impending tide of ruin and reverse the impending judgment.

Right next to this passage is 5:15, containing the same exhortation in almost identical language, but it is addressed specifically to the "remnant of Joseph"—namely, those who are left after the projected catastrophe. According to our view this passage belongs to Phase Four, but it is modeled on and linked to the neighboring passage, which belongs to Phase One. It might be possible to argue that 5:14–15 is a unit with a single message to the same audience, as the only audience specified is that mentioned in 5:15 (the "remnant of Joseph"). If that argument prevails, then the whole passage belongs to Phase Four and is aimed at the surviving remnant, after the destruction has occurred. Nevertheless v 14 reads more like the passages in 5:4–6, which can only be construed as an early warning to an unrepentant Israel. In any case v 15 clearly applies to a future far beyond that contemplated in Phase One, and the message is addressed to projected survivors of the debacle to come. This verse poses in its clearest form the question we raised earlier. Can such a message only be addressed to the people or even thought of by the prophet after the other phases have come to pass historically, and thus be regarded as a message created by a later editor or writer and interpolated into the book to meet the needs of that future age? We argue otherwise. The point the prophet is making in this juxtaposition is that the message remains the same regardless, and that even in the great renewal of the age to come, exhortation and warning will still be necessary and important; only presumably the second time around people will heed the warning and repent, and thus the nation will be spared a repetition of the disastrous series of phases through which it now most certainly must pass.

If one were to pinpoint a historical moment for the book of Amos, a position in which the prophet stands and from which the rest of the book can be projected, it would be in Phase Two. Now in the perspective of the second pair of visions (ʾănāk, 7:7–9, and ripe fruit, 8:1–2) the die has been cast and the irrevocable decision for destruction reached. The period of amnesty is over, and the possibility of repentance and reconciliation has been lost, as the passage on the plagues (4:6–11) makes clear; the great bulk of the oracles stresses this point, especially the major utterance with which the book begins. Phase Three is a justification of Phase Two and arises out of the special question of what will happen to the leaders when disaster comes. The answer is that the nation's destruction and exile are insufficient punishment for the leaders, who will be pursued even into exile and put to death for their sins (Vision 5, 9:1–4). It seems clear that Phase Three is already in the prophet's thinking before Phase Two is concluded. None of the irreversible actions of Phase Two has actually taken place when the details of Phase Three are presented. In other words, the prophet combines these elements even though Phase Three can only occur when Phase Two has reached its culmination.

We come now to Phase Four, which deals with the survival of at least a remnant and restoration and renewal in the latter days. This material, which is concentrated in the latter part of chap. 9, can be reckoned as part of the prophet's message, in our opinion. He was capable of contemplating a future for the people whose destruction as a nation he had confidently predicted, along with the extermination of its leadership, even though that destruction had not even begun to happen and, if our view is correct, would not happen in his experience or lifetime. If he could clearly predict the disastrous end of the nation, which he apparently did, then it would not matter whether he saw it happen, because in a strange way that fact would be of little functional importance for him. The word of Yahweh was what counted: it was more real than the facts of history, and in any case it created them; and the only thing that could prevent the word from happening according to its content would be another word from the same God modifying, postponing, or superseding the previous one. It was the prophet's business to speak the word, and for Amos that would suffice. So even in the midst of Israelite prosperity he could assume that the divine word would come to pass and that, for him at least, the future was settled. As he had said repeatedly, Israel would cease as a nation, its cities would be destroyed, its people decimated with the survivors deported, and its leaders wiped out. What could be more thorough and final than that? Nothing, except that this story was about Yahweh and his people, and their story could not end in the manner described. While the evidence can only be drawn from literature that was written later than Amos in its present form, there can be little doubt that the basic theological premises and affirmations were part of a common tradition shared by prophet, priests, kings, and people alike. They might differ strenuously and violently on how it was to be interpreted and applied. But the basic story was an article of tradition and faith: Yahweh had brought his people out of bondage in Egypt and had established them in the land that he wrested for them from the Canaanites and gave to them to dwell on. In return they owed him service, worship, and obedience to his will. Fidelity in maintaining the terms of the covenant would ensure them continuing possession of the land, security, and prosperity. But failure to live by the commandments and to pursue justice and mercy in all their dealings would result in the opposite: end of nationhood, loss of the land, and punishment in exile.

This was the general picture, and all agreed in principle. In practice it was otherwise, and prophets could differ with kings and priests or with each other about whether Israel was obedient to the covenant or disobedient, and to what degree, and about what lay in store. There were those who were persuaded that the divine commitment especially to the house of David exempted Israel from the consequences of misbehavior or that almost by definition Israel could not violate the terms of its covenant.

It is our view that in spite of wide variations in the weight given to the different elements in the picture, and despite obvious differences in evaluation of a particular situation at a certain time, the great prophets were all agreed that the bond between God and Israel did not exempt Israel from possible judgment, and that in fact Israel would be held to a stricter accounting than other nations precisely because of its privileged position. Ultimately the result would be the dissolution of the relationship when it turned out that Israel was really like the other nations and unable to live up to the standards of the covenant. The holy God of Israel would not hesitate, finally, to pronounce judgment and execute it on his own people.

That judgment, however, did not necessarily mean the end of the story. The same prophets believed that beyond judgment, destruction, and exile there were also redemption and renewal, based entirely on the faithfulness of God and his commitment to himself and to the fathers. From the beginning it had been so. He was known to the world as the God of Israel, and would always be known that way. It is always possible that a prophet here or there did not believe in this fourth phase, and it is possible to isolate some of the minor prophets who spoke briefly and only to a single concern or to a limited number under special circumstances.

But the great message, with all its variety and differences in imagery and details, includes that essential last point, that God will not finally abandon his people, even if he is responsible for judging and destroying them, even if that action is necessary and there is no way to escape it. Covenant violations are punishable by death, and the nation as a whole cannot be treated differently. The prophets insist on this point against all other claims. Without repentance there is no possibility of forgiveness. But beyond execution there is the possibility of resurrection. It was the prophet Ezekiel who presented the case in its most radical terms: the criminal tried and convicted in the divine court must be executed, the nation must die. But the God who created the nation and committed himself to being the God of Israel throughout history will re-create the people as his own—not for their sake, but for his own. In that way the prophet Ezekiel resolved the paradox of election and judgment. In the Primary History it is expressed by the twin covenants of Abraham (divine commitment and promise) and Moses (human obligation and performance). Both function in history, with the former guaranteeing permanent divine commitment to his people and the latter insisting that Israel will always be held to the strictest standards of justice. An ultimate resolution is eschatological: in the new age the two covenants will become one because with a new heart and spirit the people will live up to the required standards (Jer 31:31–34; Ezek 11:19, 36:26), and by fulfilling the law and being righteous they will enable God to fulfill his promises of permanent possession of the land and prosperity and security forever.

Neither Ezekiel nor Jeremiah invented these ideas. Neither in our opinion did the great prophets of the eighth century; but they shared them and clarified them, acknowledging a basic paradox in the covenant relationships but insisting that both applied and were valid. God could not be indifferent to covenant repudiation by his people, but he also could not finally give them up. After execution there would be revival and restoration: this message was delivered by all of the great prophets, and we find no reason to suppose that it is a creation of exilic or postexilic scribes who carefully put it into the books of prophets who had never thought of the matter. Each prophet in his own words and thoughts articulated it, with differences in emphasis and coloration. But they shared a common vision and hope, and their message was carried on by their successors, refined and expanded but essentially the same. Amos was the first of this group, and his book has the same elements as the others. Phase Four was an integral part of the book to which he was the principal contributor, and in the compilation of which he may have had a role.

Jeremiah 25 is a prophetic composition that in several particulars resembles the book of Amos as a whole. It documents similar phases in the development of the prophet's career and serves a similar apologetic purpose.

Jeremiah's career was inaugurated in the thirteenth year of Josiah (Jer 25:3; cf. 1:2). It began with a pair of visions that threatened destruction. Similar autobiographical forms are used by Amos and Jeremiah to recount these experiences: the same question is asked, "What do you see?" (Jer 1:11, 13; Amos 7:7, 8:2). Like Amos, Jeremiah stood in the Lord's council (sôd; Jer 23:18), making intercession (15:11), at the same time calling the nation to repentance (25:5). In this activity both men identified themselves with "his servants, the prophets" (Amos 3:7; Jer 25:4). Jeremiah reports that this activity, corresponding to the first phase of Amos' ministry, lasted for twenty-three years in his case (25:3). At the end of that period Jeremiah was not allowed to make further intercession, just as no intercession occurs after Amos' first pair of visions. The people did not listen (Jer 25:3); they did not repent (Amos 4:6–11).

The time had come for total and unrevisable judgment. Jeremiah 25:8–14 matches Phase Two of Amos' career. The themes of Jer 25:30–38 are found in Amos 1:2—the roaring lion, the withered pastures, the mourning shepherds. The judgment is global (vv 29–33), and individual nations are named (vv 17–26). The list reflects the political realities of a later time than Amos', but six of Amos' original eight nations are cited (Israel and Aram are missing), along with more far-flung places—Egypt, several Arabian states, Babylon, Elam, Media.

The perspective and the theology are essentially the same as those of Amos. Jeremiah 25:15–31 reads like another vision, the final one in the book of Amos. The main difference between Jeremiah's summary of his career in chap. 25 and Amos' summary in his book is that Amos presents the climax of irreversible judgment first and then moves in retrograde fashion into the background and buildup of what went before (in time), while Jeremiah traces the development forward, logically and chronologically.

THE LIFE AND MISSION OF AMOS THE SHEPHERD AND PROPHET

On the basis of the information available from the book of Amos itself we can reconstruct the essential data of his life as follows (some items are less probable than others, but we think they are all plausible and make sense in the total picture):

1. Home and profession: He was a shepherd and orchard keeper in Tekoa, a village in the southern kingdom a few miles south of Jerusalem.

2. He was called to be a prophet by Yahweh during the reigns of Jeroboam of Israel and Uzziah of Judah (they overlapped during the decades from 790 to 750 B.C.E.). His call came through a vision or two, and there were others during his career.

3. The first two visions (7:1–6) are connected with a series of plagues (4:6–11) that afflicted Israel (by which we mean the composite of both kingdoms—when only one is meant we will specify). (Note that there are in fact eight plagues arranged in five sets: first set, famine [v 6]; second set, drought [vv 7–8]; third set, blight, mildew, locusts [v 9]; fourth set, plague, war [v 10]; fifth set, fire [v 11].) Two sets of plagues correspond to the first two visions: locust plague (first vision [7:1–3], corresponding to locusts [4:9] in the third set), and destruction by cosmic fire (second vision [7:4–6], corresponding to fifth set of the plagues, fire [4:11], compared with the destruction of Sodom and Gomorrah). We suppose that Amos was naturally concerned about plagues that clearly affected his livelihood and perhaps his survival. Everyone would understand the plagues as being inflicted by an angry deity (cf. the situation in the days of Elijah and Elisha), but Amos received specific enlightenment about the meaning of the plagues in his visions. These visions revealed a dimension of judgment not previously encountered: the end of the nation. The plagues might come and go, but the

visions were enough to convince Amos that the nation's future was in
jeopardy. It would not be a matter of replacing a dynasty or a priesthood,
so something more drastic was required: national repentance. Such repentance was not a question of formulas and sacrifices but of the heart and will
and action.

Amos interceded successfully, and Yahweh canceled the ultimate penalty. The plague had come or would come but in itself would not be fatal; it
would draw blood but not kill the victim, and enough time would be allowed for Amos to do something about it. Presumably he set out immediately on his mission to the house of Israel, preaching repentance. In all
likelihood he would not wait for a second vision to confirm the first. In this
case it is clear that he was convinced from the first and proceeded immediately. Perhaps on his first mission he preached essentially what we now
have in chap. 5 of the book. That would be most appropriate. Chapter 5 is
highly structured, and the essential ingredients of a preaching mission are
there: a call to repentance, woes and laments, the denunciation of injustice,
and the plea for justice with the assurance that repentance can secure salvation.

The second vision comes during the fifth set of plagues, and the clear
meaning is that the mission is failing—there has been no significant response, no sign of change. All is as before, and that is very bad. The vision
is also worse as we move from locusts, which, while distinctly dangerous
and terribly threatening are nevertheless familiar, and everyone in the Near
East in those days had lived through more than one such plague. The vision
of cosmic fire devouring the Great Deep must have seemed much worse
and immediately life-threatening to the whole portion of Yahweh (haḥēleq
[7:4]). Once again Amos intercedes successfully, and Yahweh cancels the
disaster; but this time, if our interpretation is correct, it was a very close
call—it was like Sodom and Gomorrah, symbol of total destruction by fire,
and in the end they were plucked like a brand from the burning. One would
think that Amos would have found a receptive audience, and with his
magnificent preaching style a response appropriate to the message. But
nothing of the kind occurred. It is reasonable to suppose that the second
time around his message was essentially what we find in chap. 6. Once
again the message is to all of Israel and specifically to Zion and Samaria,
and it consists predominantly of woes. We do not hear an explicit call to
repentance as we did in the first round; the stakes and tempo are being
escalated. The pressure is greater and the message is more intense. Having
survived the previous plague and with the apparent turnaround in military
fortunes (compare the victories in 6:13 with the defeats in the fourth set of
plagues) no doubt the people addressed were sure that the worst was over
and that Amos was 'way off base. So the second mission likewise ended in
failure. It may also be that Amos was already being warned to change his

tune or to stop prophesying altogether. As long as the plagues continued he may have had a better reception and perhaps made some points and some converts (there had to be a few, anyway).

4. The interval: we postulate that the mission (both missions) failed, as is confirmed by the account of the plagues. Neither plagues nor prophet had any effect on the people or the leaders, north or south. That claim is repeated five times in 4:6–11, so that section reports what happened after the plagues and before the second pair of visions. In addition, opposition to this gloomy prophet was also developing, and we can detect some personal experience behind the comments about the treatment of prophets and the necessity for the prophet to report what he is told (3:8), not what he might like to say or what people might like to hear.

5. Now we come to the second pair of visions. In them Yahweh announces to Amos that the period of grace is over and that he will no longer repent, relent, or show them any mercy. It is clear from the period of the plagues and the first two missions that the whole combined effort by Amos and Yahweh has been a failure. Neither prophet nor plagues has had any effect on the heart and mind of his people. Next is the period of judgment. Once again it is not clear whether the two visions come at the same time, so that the second reinforces the first, or whether they are separated in time and the prophet responds to each as it happens. By this time he does not require confirmation, and we think it is better to take them separately, for while the message is essentially the same the second of the pair (in both sets) is a little more threatening and ominous than the first.

Our impression is that after the third vision Amos delivered a new set of oracles, which are essentially to be found in chaps. 3 and 4. The shock effect of 3:1–2 on an audience must have been potent, and it contained the whole message in a nutshell. Because that one sentence would no doubt offend everyone, he must then defend himself by saying that those statements are not his ideas. They come directly and precisely from Yahweh (3:3–8). There follow the attacks on Samaria (3:9–12, 4:1–3) and Bethel (3:13–15, 4:4–5) in alternation, and the closing speech about the plagues that are now in the past; but by referring to them he makes clear that Yahweh has been trying to warn them, and he reminds them that he has been preaching on the same subject for some time. With the somewhat enigmatic but ominous 4:12 the mission ends: "prepare to confront your God, O Israel!" We are clearly in the sphere of the northern kingdom now.

Then follows the fourth vision with its quite explicit message, that the *end* has come for my people Israel. Once more Amos goes on the sawdust trail. He is no longer preaching repentance or even referring to the lost opportunities. Now we have the Great Set Speech of chaps. 1–2. We must point out that what we have in writing is a distilled and probably abbreviated form of the actual speech, which was probably given on a number of occasions with a number of variants. This version is the polished one for publication. So chaps. 1–2 correspond to the fourth vision. We can set up the correspondence as follows:

First pair of visions   :   chaps. 5–6
   1. Vision 1   :   chap. 5
   2. Vision 2   :   chap. 6
Second pair of visions   :   chaps. 1–4
   1. Vision 3   :   chaps. 3–4
   2. Vision 4   :   chaps. 1–2

The speech (chaps. 1–2) is the one given at Bethel on the occasion of his great confrontation with Amaziah. The whole affair begins with the speech, which is carefully organized and worked out, so that Amos can capture his audience before he throws down the gauntlet. There is something subtle and persuasive about the series of oracles against the nations, and if he got through the first six no one would stop him before he got through the seventh or part of the eighth. Maybe he was interrupted after 2:8 and never got to utter the terrible words about destruction by fire that should have followed. What does follow in 2:9–16 is more apologetic and defensive and perhaps was said under slightly different circumstances, though in the same setting.

6. The story of the confrontation must follow. While the big speech is threatening to Israel it is not sufficient to explain Amaziah's reaction, especially if the specifics of the punishment were left out or not stated explicitly. On the basis of that speech, Amaziah (who may have heard about Amos and had reports on some of his more inflammatory remarks, but had not heard him speak) now for the first time had grounds for action against Amos. He may well have interrupted Amos just as he was about to say, "And I will send fire" and told Amos to leave and go back to Judah.

From that point matters escalated, and Amos, after defending his role as prophet, finally revealed the secret messages he had for both Amaziah and the king. Once Amos had talked about the high priest and his family suffering death and degradation, he was probably trapped; and when he mentioned the king and his house dying by the sword, his doom was sealed. When Amaziah had heard enough to convince him that a charge of treason and sedition could be made to stick, he sent word to the king and arranged to detain Amos.

7. In our view Amos remained under arrest at Bethel until word came from the king saying what to do about him. The most reasonable explanation is that someone came from the king to interview Amos and to get testimony from others. Then he would make an appropriate decision either to dismiss the charges and let Amos go, or to bundle him off to Samaria for

trial and adjudication by the king himself or his deputy. During the early part of the sequence, we suppose that Amos would still be able to speak to disciples, some of whom may have accompanied him, or they might have been local adherents recruited during an earlier mission. In any event we should pick up the last group of prophecies along with the fifth vision in this setting—from 8:3 to 9:6.

8. What happened to Amos afterward is anybody's guess, but it is hard to believe that he was ever set free, especially by a tough and successful king such as Jeroboam. The only question is whether he was martyred or just kept under restraint. In any event, it would seem that his career as a prophet ended abruptly. The final visions or oracles come from the period at Bethel. Assuming that he was taken to Samaria, it is possible that he was also able to speak to someone there. We would like to think that 8:13–14 reflects the Samaria environment, but it is not necessary to make this assumption. There are also some other oracles to account for, the ones in the Epilogue. As for 9:7–10, they may well have been placed where they are for literary and structural reasons rather than because they were composed late. With respect to 9:11–15, it is hard to imagine circumstances under which Amos would have delivered them; it is even possible that, like Isaiah 2 = Micah 4, they come from a different period of his career entirely, when he may have hoped for repentance (cf. 5:14–15). But it is best not to speculate too much. Their placement at the very end is an editorial choice, and very likely Amos had nothing to do with that decision.

9. In our opinion we can connect the publication of the book with the earthquake, which was a devastating one and must have been seen as a partial vindication of the prophet's words, especially if the Temple at Bethel suffered any damage (always a possibility—but the Temple has not yet been located archaeologically, much less its stratification history). The book, however, had been finished two years earlier, if that is what the notice in 1:1 signifies. That could be the date of Amos' death, for it makes clear that there were no later oracles from that source. If our hypotheses are true, why was it not written up that way? It is difficult to say. Although they may contain biographical data, none of the prophetic books reports the death of the prophet whose name it bears.

So Amos' career extended from the first vision associated with the third set of plagues until two years before the earthquake, and can be dated during the reigns of Uzziah of Judah and Jeroboam of Israel, but not later.

We may add three brief notes.

1. If Amos prepared or dictated some material before he went to Bethel, it is possible that his followers also prepared something after he was arrested to aid in his defense, or that we are talking about essentially the same piece of writing, namely, chaps. 1–6 plus an account of the visions.

2. Of the eight oracles introduced by the formulas "in that day" (*bywm hhw'*) or "the days are coming" (*ymym b'ym*), six are in the last two chapters, beginning with 8:4, which starts the last major subunit, 8:4–9:6. There are three more in what is left of chap. 8, and then two others at the very end of the book, 9:11–12 and 9:13–15. This circumstance perhaps suggests an artificial arrangement grouping the eschatological oracles at the end (and leaving open the date of their composition). The question then concerns the remaining two oracles (one of each kind), respectively at 2:14–16 (*bywm hhw'*) and 4:2 (*ymym b'ym*). Are these oracles displaced from the original grouping with the other six or are they in their proper places, with the others deliberately arranged at the end? It is hard to choose. Our inclination is to think that the grouping at the end reflects both ideas: end things belong at the end, but the prophet himself may have uttered such oracles later in his career rather than earlier.

3. If Phase One is connected with the first pair of visions and points us to chaps. 5–6, and Phase Two involves the second pair of visions and points us to chaps. 1–4, then the transition to phase three is the confrontation (7:10–17) or the culmination of Phase Two (just as the plagues, 4:6–11, are the transition to Phase Two). Then Phase Three is the period after the confrontation and includes the material from 8:4 through 9:6; also, it is associated with the fifth vision. It is briefer and does not add a great deal, but it is distinctive and notably harsh. Finally, Phase Four is connected with the Epilogue and points to the future, and it is also in two sections: 9:7–10, the transition from Phases Two and Three, or the end of three; and 9:11–15, the full flowering of Phase Four, the restoration of the Davidic kingdom and the renewal of the land with peace and prosperity forever.

THE GOD OF ISRAEL IN THE BOOK OF AMOS

This essay will perforce be sketchy, but it may serve a purpose in providing a format and framework for dealing with the subject. Inevitably we will be influenced by the structure of the book, but our approach now will be topical so as to simplify, clarify, and organize the data in useful and comprehensible form. The arrangement too may be more congenial to a modern Western mind, but it is only for convenience. Our purpose is to present Amos' picture of the deity, not ours, and to keep it within the thought world of the ancient Near East and the Bible rather than to translate it into contemporary theological or philosophical language.

The God of Heaven and Earth

Yahweh, the God of Israel is universal God of heaven and earth.

Not only is this premise essential to any theology of the Hebrew Bible and certainly of the prophets, but in Amos it is explicit in the famous but suspect hymns, which are placed strategically in the text. Of the three, two (at 4:13 and 9:5–6) are ideally located at the close of important sections, while the remaining example seems to be out of place toward the beginning of a major unit (5:8–9).

Our first point is that even if the hymns, which are widely regarded as later additions to or insertions in the text, were removed entirely from consideration, we would have to draw the same conclusions about the power and authority, the majesty and might of the God of Amos or the Bible generally. There is no perceptible difference between the explicit and express statements of the unique universality of the deity in the hymns and the presuppositions, the premises, and the inferences to be derived from the rest of the book. The dominion over the world, nature, and history asserted in the hymns is taken for granted in the oracles and speeches that touch on or emphasize such matters. Everything is under divine control. He is the architect of the heavens and earth, the ruler of all things, and the one who wills as he pleases and executes what he wills. Whether by word or deed, he decides; and what he decides is what happens.

The basic position is not different from most sources in the Bible, though there may be differences in nuance or detail. However we may wish to modify, qualify, condition, or extenuate, Amos' theology is essential monotheism. There are other gods, to be sure, but that is just a convenient way of dealing with rampant polytheism both outside and inside the country. It would be going a little too far to say that Israelites had no perception of other deities as the nations conceived of or believed in them, because Israelites seemed to have little difficulty in absorbing or being absorbed in pagan religion, its cult or practice. Nevertheless, neither Amos nor his fellow prophets and their successors ever conceded that there was much more substance to another deity than the image that represented the god. They are rarely concerned with other gods or goddesses as such, rather with the undeniable and excruciating fact that many of their own people gave to these deities the worship and service that Yahweh claimed as his exclusive right.

In addition, there may be any number of other kinds of heavenly beings who belong to the divine court and make up his retinue. Amos hardly gets into this subject at all, but he implies that the prophet has access to the deity as a member of the heavenly court, and some of his visions and remarks reflect both the privilege and the experience. Other prophets are much more explicit or colorful in describing the heavenly scene, but for one reason or another, it is not a matter of great moment to Amos. What is most important to Amos is the truth of God's complete mastery of the forces of nature and the course of history. The world and the people in it are the primary focus of interest, but God's relation to that world has to be defined with great care. He exercises a monopoly of power and wisdom, of authority and will. At the same time, the world and in particular human beings have certain degrees of freedom and responsibility. The complexities of the theological or philosophical debates over the issues of divine sovereignty and human freedom, over predestination and foreknowledge are not dealt with in Amos. But the starting point with God is clearly his sovereignty in relation to the created world—and in relation to everything that is part of it. There are two categories only: God and everything else. Everything else is subordinate and dependent on the deity for its existence and whatever else it has or is.

A. S. Kapelrud (1961) finds the cosmic scope of Yahweh's activity in the book of Amos in his acquisition of aspects of the Canaanite El. This connection can be sustained only in a very general way, and the process lies remote from Amos' own immediate thinking; that is, such a connection derives from a much earlier stage in the evolution of Yahwistic theology, not in any thinking of Amos himself. First, Amos does not give Yahweh any of the names or epithets of El, the most distinctive of which would be "Father of gods and men" or "Creator of heavens and earth" (*qôneh šāmayim wā'āreṣ*); neither, for that matter, does he use other telltale Canaanisms, which would document such a syncretistic augmentation of Yahweh's supposed prior restriction to primal Israelite thought. Second, and in any case, El is benign or indifferent, as opposed to the passionate and violent destroyer, Yahweh, who uses all available "natural" means to send his disasters, as seen in Amos and in the book of Job. Finally, and with quite an opposite result, the fragments of ancient creation hymns, as used by Amos to set forth the high points in his theology, are distinctively Israelite; for example, his verbs are *br', yṣr, 'śh,* not *kn(n)* or *qnh* as found in Canaanite sources. The tradition that Yahweh was the Creator and Lord of heaven and earth (i.e., of everything) was not a new insight of Amos himself or a new development of his time; it was an ancient and essential ingredient of the faith of Moses, and certainly from that time on.

The God of the Nations and Israel: The God of History

In Amos' perspective, the ruler of the universe is also the Lord of history (human history, that is) and the sovereign of all nations. While the focus in Amos for the most part is somewhat narrower than in other and later prophets, the essential point is the same. Amos is primarily interested in the eight nations that make up the territory lying between the great powers Egypt and Assyria, but he is aware of peoples beyond that area, mentioning Egypt and Cush explicitly and Assyria by implication. The will and rule of Yahweh extend beyond the borders of the territories occupied by the peoples who worship him and even beyond the borders of the Davidic empire. Those nations may never have been under the suzerainty of Yahweh and may not now acknowledge it, but he is their Lord—just as he is and should be acknowledged Lord of Israel (and Judah).

The control of history and nations is expressed bluntly in the great oracle with which the book begins (chaps. 1–2). All eight nations are treated in similar, summary fashion under the impartial eye of the divine judge. Judgment and punishment are the themes of these chapters, and there is a pervasive emphasis on impartiality: all are guilty, charged in the same manner, and all are sentenced under the same judgment, though details vary a good deal. Along with and behind the judgment, other factors and elements are present. Yahweh is both creator and redeemer, not only of Israel, as the tradition emphasized, but also of the Aramaeans and Philistines, and doubtless of the others too. While the general statements about passing sentence and inflicting punishment are formulaic and depict Yahweh as rendering judgment and initiating the violent action ("I will send fire") against the nations, the details of destruction—namely, defeat in battle, execution, or exile—show that God uses various means, often human agents, to accomplish his purposes. His control of both nature and humanity is complete, so he can send plagues or armies as he pleases, one or the other or, as is often the case, both.

As already indicated, Yahweh is presented as judge of the nations, severe but just and impartial, exhibiting the characteristics enjoined on human judges in various documents of the Bible. In the instances of the nations, the crimes with which they are charged would be regarded as reprehensible behavior on anyone's part, anywhere, anytime. There seem to be underlying principles of justice and equity that are equally applicable to all. The details are somewhat cursory and insufficient to build up a case for a particular profile of violations, but the general principle seems to hold. It is of interest that the crimes charged to the other nations are international in character, against other nations usually on their borders, while the crimes charged against Judah and Israel are internal matters, involving their behavior to God and fellow citizens.

The general term used for all of the crimes in all of the nations is $pš'$, which is basically rebellion against authority, the revolt of a vassal against a suzerain, usually initiated by failure to pay the annual tribute (something like the interest payments on debts to international banks by third-world countries these days). It is a very strong term and should be interpreted as a deliberate and serious violation of the terms of a covenant. It is not usually regarded as an excusable breach, and the offended or aggrieved party is expected to take appropriate action, which is his right. Moab is reported to have rebelled ($pš^c$) against its suzerain, the king of Israel (after the death of Ahab; 2 Kgs 1:1). So the charge is made that each of these nations has committed $pš^c$ enough times and in enough ways to convince the sovereign that the breach is deliberate and requires summary retribution. The action is also the same throughout, punitive attack and destruction of the capital city by fire and either execution or exile for the recalcitrant and rebellious leadership. It is more difficult to reconstruct the case and circumstances of the nations in this situation than of Israel (and Judah), where the picture is much more detailed. But that it is essentially the same is guaranteed by the constant repetition of the expressions describing what the nations, including Israel, have done, and what Yahweh is going to do to them. For Israel the covenant violation involves abandonment of Yahweh for other gods and the adoption of different religious norms. Whether the apostasy is simple substitution of other gods (both male and female, as we know from 2:7–8; cf. 8:14) or a more complex syncretism involving the corruption of classic Yahwism, or whether it involves both approaches in a variety of different activities, is not entirely clear and for our purposes does not greatly matter, for whatever the specific form it represents a violation of the basic commandments and obligations. In addition, there is the overriding principle of justice. This comes through from beginning to end and is the central theme of the central chapter (5), which contains the first formulation of Amos' message. The issue of right behavior to one's neighbors is the ultimate test of true religion, if not its actual essence and substance. It is not a substitute for theology but its necessary adjunct. On both counts—its profession of faith and its practice—not only has Israel fallen short of minimum acceptable standards, but it is in a state of outright violation and rebellion.

What makes the situation all the more aggravated and pernicious is that Israel owes to Yahweh not only the obedience that the inferior owes to a superior, that a slave owes to its master, but also an immeasurable obligation of gratitude. Israel was the beneficiary, at a time of great need and anguish, of an act of divine grace and intervention to which it had no claim or right. In other words, Yahweh is ruler of Israel not only because he is ruler of the world, and not only because of his superior power to enforce his will, but because he is savior and redeemer, the gracious and compassionate one who took pity on these poor suffering slaves and delivered them from bondage in Egypt. Thus Israel, on top of everything else—or beneath and underlying everything—has an incalculable debt of gratitude that it can never pay off; but it can make a down payment by obeying the terms of the contract between them.

The same rationale applies to the nations who are under judgment. Yahweh can make the same claims on them for in every case he is also to be credited with creating, redeeming, or otherwise establishing each of them as a political entity. This claim is made explicitly of the Philistines and Aramaeans in 9:7, where the comparison is made directly with Yahweh's action in bringing them from distant places and his delivering Israel from bondage in Egypt, and it can be presumed with respect to the others as well. There are indications in the older traditions about Yahweh's role in establishing Edom, Moab, and Ammon (Gen 36:1, 19:30–38), which give us some information on this topic for seven of the eight nations. Only Tyre is left unaccounted for, but there is every reason to believe that Yahweh would have been credited with its foundation as a state. The major difference in all cases is that whereas Israel and Judah know their history and in particular that the God who saved them is the only true God, the other nations wander and flounder around in the darkness of idolatry. Furthermore, while they may know something of their history they would not be expected to know Yahweh's role in it. Perhaps one day they will learn the truth, but they are not to be blamed for failing to worship and serve Yahweh, whom they do not know as God. Hence they are not condemned for apostasy, because never having known him they have not been guilty of abandoning him. It is complicated, but an important principle is involved. As Paul of Tarsus might put it, "Is Yahweh God of the Jews only? No, he is God of the Gentiles also" (Rom 3:29). While Israel is special—after all, he is called "the God of Israel" and that is his title forever—so are all the other nations. It is not a matter of rejecting the idea of election; on the contrary, Amos affirms it and extends it. Every nation is elect; every nation has a special history created for it by the same God, Yahweh. It is an extraordinary feature of Amos' theology: election is universal.

It bears a heavy price, however. Election involves responsibility, and failure to discharge that properly brings on judgment and punishment. This rule applies impartially to all. The paradigm for Israel, then, is summed up in the breathtaking paradox of 3:2: "Only you have I known of all the families of the earth; *therefore* I will punish you for all your iniquities." In that sentence is summed up the meaning of the relationship of Yahweh with Israel: Israel was chosen by Yahweh and delivered, led, nurtured by him. He also required of Israel obedience to his laws, which were meant for their own well-being, not his. With them went a warning that behavior is the test of belief and commitment. The standards are set higher for those who know more and better, and highest of all for the one with the closest relationship —Israel. In spite of this intimate association, Israel had failed utterly. So destruction as judgment and punishment was in store for a recalcitrant, resistant nation.

In a situation of that kind, there is always the possibility of change: repentance on the part of the people, reciprocal repentance on the part of God. He is known as the one who repents over evil, that is, the damaging

judgment or punishment he has previously decreed. This theme of mutual
repentance is also stressed in Amos and is a major factor in the bulk of the
book. Yahweh can and does change his mind—the essential meaning of
repentance—and can and does reverse decisions, but not often and always
for cause. There are three main reasons. (1) The main cause is repentance
on the part of people, and the story of Nineveh in the book of Jonah is a
classic illustration, though Jeremiah documents a case in the time of Micah
and Hezekiah the king of Judah (Jer 26:19). (2) Another cause is in the
reassessment of a situation by the deity in view of unforeseen or developing
circumstances. In connection with the decision to send the Flood, Yahweh
repented that he had made mankind; something had gone wrong or contrary to expectations. The same is true in the case of Saul (1 Sam 15). God
repented that he had made Saul king because of Saul's behavior as king and
his failure, as Samuel puts it, to carry out the command of Yahweh. (3) The
third cause is prophetic intercession. There are very few instances of this,
but Moses (Exod 32:31–34) and Samuel (1 Sam 15:10–11) are regarded as
powerful if not always successful intercessors with God, while Amos makes
the same claims for himself in connection with the first pair of visions. For
an extended discussion of this topic, see the excursus "When God Repents."

In short, the relations between Yahweh and the nations are governed by
moral and ethical principles, and the closer the relationship the more strin-
gently the rule applies. But there is some flexibility in the arrangement: a
showing of good faith in an effort to change for the better and an appeal to
the deity's strong sense of compassion may produce a shifting away from
punishment in the direction of mercy. The lively interaction involving deity, people, and prophet is one of the highlights of the book. Only a moral
God can be truly merciful, and mercy can only be meaningful in a context
of justice and punishment. One without the presence of the other would
mean a God indifferent either to morality or to pain and anguish. The God
of the book of Amos and of the Bible balances both in an uneasy tension,
leaving uncertain the outcome. The book of Amos remains paradoxical.
What is the final word on the house of Israel? It is clear that time and
patience finally ran out in a historical sense and judgment must come, but is
there a future for this people and this nation beyond the date of its demise?
Is the last word something like 9:1–4 or 9:8–10, or is it like 9:11–15? Is
there life after death, resurrection for the lifeless where nations are concerned, as Ezekiel clearly supposed (Ezek 37:1–14)? As things now stand,
the last word in the book of Amos is for restoration and renewal, but it is a
reasonable question whether the last oracles are consistent with the tenor of
the rest of the book. Throughout we find a constant mood and tone of
judgment expressed by the prophet who does not neglect the matter of
repentance or the willingness of God to interrupt and abate his decisions

while awaiting some sign of repentance and regeneration. In the end we must allow for all kinds of possibilities and leave the resolution to those with greater wisdom and better judgment.

What is said here of Israel is also true of the other nations. Wherever information is available, it is clear that they are treated in the same manner, have experienced the same kind of history, have similar obligations, and are under the same judgment with the same possibility of being punished or rescued.

To understand a little more about the dynamics of the relations between the deity and humanity we should look at the relations between deity and prophet. The basic idea in Amos, which is developed in a similar fashion throughout the biblical literature and especially in the prophets, is that there is a special, personal, intimate relation between deity and prophet and that this relationship always serves a larger purpose. The prophet in his permanent primary role is Yahweh's messenger. It is his duty first and foremost to hear, understand, and transmit the word that Yahweh gives him to speak. The medium is essentially that of words and conversation, but it may also involve visions and often does. The communication is often directly in words, but visions and symbols can also communicate, and the prophet may thus translate a message from a visible to an audible form. In our age of audiovisual activity such interaction can easily be understood. In the case of Amos' visions there is always conversation. With respect to the first four visions there is dialogue between Yahweh and the prophet about the meaning of the vision or the deity's intentions, or implicitly of the prophet's role.

It is noteworthy that while there are clear connections between the content and the communication associated with the visions, the messages or oracles that the prophet actually gives or that are recorded are not identical in wording. It seems clear that not everything that was given to Amos to say was communicated in those five visions. There may well have been others, not recorded. Furthermore, it is always possible that Amos himself or his editors made adjustments and adaptations in the spoken and written form of the message. The prophet did not use a tape recorder, and he is not one himself. The speeches are at once his and Yahweh's and we must allow for the presence and participation of two personalities, not just one. It does not follow that the message is actually only the words and ideas of the prophet, who attributes them to the deity *pro forma* or because it is the appropriate convention. We should not treat such matters cynically. Whatever we may privately believe about prophets and prophecy, especially in the Bible, these were sincere men and women who believed that God was in touch with them and had spoken to them or otherwise communicated with them, and that it was their duty to report what they had seen or heard. Clearly they would report faithfully, and to the extent that they heard words spoken by Yahweh, they would try to reproduce them verbatim. Where they had a sense of the meeting or were interpreting a visual message, they would make every effort to be faithful to the meaning and import of what they had seen. It is clear too that reports range from verbatim transcripts to paraphrases and summaries in indirect discourse. The prophet's personal interest often shines through an oracle. The personality of the prophet is not suppressed, but he speaks the word of God. That is the mystery of prophetic religion.

In the book of Amos, the prophet's role looms large. That is not unexpected, and we gain some insights into the difficulties faced by the prophet and the way in which he fulfilled his mission. As we have seen, the main obligation is to report the word spoken by the deity, the word intended for a large audience. The prophet is the preferred or chosen means of that communication. On the basis of the recorded visions and other descriptive material, the picture we have is that of the prophet being present in the heavenly court and overhearing the deity speak or being addressed directly by the deity. Just how this picture is to be interpreted—in what sense the prophet was in the presence of God and what his own thinking about the matter was—is not at all clear. But as far as possible we should take these matters at face value. Certainly literary conventions are involved, and ultimately the imagery is derived from second- (or third-) millennium mythological motifs, which have lost operational force in Mosaic and post-Mosaic Yahwism. Nevertheless it is a powerful, colorful, and effective vehicle of communication and should not be attenuated or vaporized into a mere figure of speech.

Once the message has been received, the prophet must deliver it. Care is taken to make sure the prophet gets it straight, for there must be no confusion in his mind about what the message is or what it means. It must be conveyed in words that the mythical "ordinary person" can understand or, to switch the metaphor, so that he who runs can read and understand it. But as we know, Amos seizes the opportunity to debate the merits of the case in the first two visions. The message, even without being put into words at all, is nevertheless only too clear, and the thought of the termination of Israel the nation is more than the prophet can bear, much less repeat or deliver. So he takes advantage of his position to intercede. A prophet may assume this role because the situation makes such action possible, that is, he is in the presence of the divine king. That role, however, is not formally part of the status of prophet; it does not belong officially to the job description. Nevertheless the possibility and reality of dialogue open new areas for understanding the nature and personality of God. In the end Yahweh will have his way and the prophet must be his servant delivering his message, but there are moments in which there is genuine give and take, and if the prophets are to be believed (and we hardly have a choice) it is possible to sway God's mind and secure a change or modification of the message. Surely that must be the high point of any prophet's life, to have a say in the decision making and to help to shape the message he will deliver in due course.

What it finally comes down to is the nature of the God of the Bible, the person with whom the prophet must deal (and vice versa) and the person around whom everything turns. When all of the superlatives have been exhausted and when all of the authority or majesty have been accorded and the recognition given to the one incomparable deity who stands uniquely alone and against everything that is perishable, vulnerable, corruptible, and the rest, he nevertheless remains a person. That is the fundamental and ultimate category in the Bible, as without it nothing else matters. It may be a hopelessly inadequate metaphor for what God really is in himself and to himself, but it is the best that the Bible can do and the best we can do, because anything other than personality or personhood is not beyond it but beneath it. It is a question of the images: we are persons and we communicate in various ways, and if there is to be communication or connection between the divine and the human, then it has to take place on our terms. In a real sense God must empathize with humanity and human nature without relinquishing the realities of his own divine nature and being. And so he does, especially in the presence of the prophets. Once it is agreed that this God—creator and sustainer of heaven and earth, sole and unique—is the God of the Bible and Israel and Amos and the rest of us, then we may draw closer and ask him who he is, what he is like, and how things run in this world. There is more than enough in the book of Amos to show that he is the same God who revealed himself to Moses, among others, and said enough about himself to give us pause and make us think.

And Yahweh passed in front of him and he proclaimed: Yahweh, Yahweh, El the Compassionate and the Gracious, long-suffering, and very loyal and true; who maintains mercy for thousands of generations, who forgives iniquity and rebellion and sin; but he by no means acquits the guilty, but visits the iniquity of fathers upon sons and upon grandsons, upon those of the third and fourth generations. (Exod 34:6–7)

To which we may add from Joel and Jonah: "he is the one who repents over evil" (Joel 2:13 and Jonah 4:2; cf. Amos 7:3, 6).

AMOS' GEOPOLITICAL TERMINOLOGY

Evidence and Hypothesis

As was shown to be the case in Hosea (Andersen and Freedman 1980), the use of names for various geographic and political entities in Amos is both interesting and unusual. Principal concern centers on the word "Israel," which has been and can be used in a variety of ways to designate at least the following: the patriarch, the twelve-tribe group or nation as a whole, and the northern kingdom in its various historic borders. Subsequent to the time of Amos, and with the disappearance of the northern kingdom, the term "Israel" continued to be used either for the survivors, or for Judah itself as the only recognizable representative of the original people, or in an eschatological sense for the revived and reconstituted nation of the future. It is clear that in Amos both the second and third of the possibilities are realized, and the question is whether there is any clue or device by which the designations can be separated and fixed. In certain instances the context will be the determining factor, but in others the evidence is mixed or insufficient to make a decision. It is also true that in Amos there are several distinct phrases containing the word "Israel," as well as other political terminology. Whether "Israel," alone or in one or another of these several phrases, is used consistently, always with the same referent, remains to be determined. Israel occasionally stands alone but in other instances is qualified by the terms *běnê, bêt,* and *'ammî.* Does the use of these expressions make a difference and offer guidance to interpretation? An examination of the available evidence indicates that there is a code or system in the book and that the use of the qualifying words is meant to identify the entity labeled Israel in each case. The question is whether the use of these additional words—"sons of," "house of," "people of," and the like—secures distinctions among the several possible meanings of the word "Israel." In the course of the investigation we will also look at parallel and related terms, such as *ya'ăqōb, yôsēp, yiśḥāq,* and, as a reference point, *yěhûdâ,* though as we would expect the last refers regularly and exclusively in Amos to the southern kingdom of his day.

The proper noun Israel occurs thirty times, a considerable number for a short book like Amos, and we would regard it as an adequate sample for testing the following hypothesis. When the term is used by itself, it designates the northern kingdom only; the usage derives no doubt from contemporary practice, as that was the term used both in Israel and among its neighbors, and it is attested in an expression like *melek yiśrā'ēl,* used of

Jeroboam twice in the book (1:1 and 7:10). Thus wherever the term stands alone, it will refer to the northern kingdom. The usage is older than the disruption and split that followed the death of Solomon. Even before, the so-called united kingdom was rather a dual kingdom with a common monarch, designated either "Judah and Israel" (1 Kgs 4:20, 5:5 [E4:25]) or "Israel and Judah" (1 Sam 17:52, 18:16; 2 Sam 3:10, 24:1; 1 Kgs 1:35; etc.). This describes the political reality; the autonomy of Judah as David's kingdom prior to his acceptance as king of Israel (Saul's kingdom) is also attested. A related question is whether, at this early stage, additional terms such as "children of," "people of," or "house of" were used to distinguish the whole nation. Where, in Amos, other qualifying expressions are used in conjunction with "Israel," such as *byt, bny, btwlt,* or *ʿammî,* then the reference could be to historic Israel of the Exodus or the twelve-tribe league, or the united kingdom; it can also refer to an ideal entity of the future or even the two kingdoms together conceived of or interpreted as a whole, the combined descendants of Jacob//Israel.

Among the parallel or related terms we extend the hypothesis in the two directions. First, *yaʿăqōb* always stands for historic Israel, not for the northern kingdom as such, for that usage is never elsewhere attested. This claim holds whether *yaʿăqōb* stands alone or is qualified. The point is that the special use of "Israel" alone is dictated by the political reality, while as far as we are aware that kingdom was never called Jacob. This opinion is not the established one. It says in BDB (p. 785) that "Jacob" is used specifically of northern Israel, citing Amos 7:2, 5; Hos 12:13 (also 10:11 and probably 12:3); and other texts, or else it is used of Judah. The latter usage is considered to be postexilic. These allocations beg a number of questions. One is the possibility that such a name is fluid in reference, or that it changes with time. It is more likely that Amos would not only be consistent in his own usage, but that his usage would match what was current in his time. In particular, if there was recognized contemporary meaning for such terms, one would expect other eighth-century prophets to display similar vocabulary.

Second, *yôsēp* and *yiśḥāq* are substitutes for or parallels to "Israel" and stand for the northern kingdom only. This correspondence is to be expected with respect to Joseph, for the Joseph tribes constituted the heart and center of the northern group of tribes constituting Israel. The use of Isaac, which is rare enough in the Bible outside of Genesis (and in Amos with a peculiar spelling) is more difficult to explain, but the context implies strongly that the northern kingdom is intended (7:9, 16).

Let us examine the passages in order in the light of our hypothesis and see where the trail leads.

1. 1:1 *ʾăšer ḥāzâ ʿal-yiśrāʾēl,* "who had visions concerning Israel." According to the hypothesis the term specifies the northern king-

dom, and certainly that is the book's major topic and target. The immediately following references to the kings of Judah and Israel lend weight to the distinction. If the headline writer had intended a broader scope, he would have added "Judah" or described the target in other terms. Nevertheless, the visions in chaps. 7–8, as distinct from the message in its main contents, concern Israel overall, as we shall argue, so there may be some discrepancy at this point. Strictly speaking, in terms of the book as we have it, the reference should be to Israel as a whole, or Israel and Judah, as in the comparable case of Micah, where in 1:1 we read, *ʾăšer ḥāzâ ʿal-šōmĕrôn wîrûšālāyim*, "which he saw concerning Samaria and Jerusalem." But in the case of Isaiah, who also spoke of and to both nations, the heading (Isa 1:1) reads *ʾăšer ḥāzâ ʿal-yĕhûdâ wîrûšālāyim*, "which he saw concerning Judah and Jerusalem." While the book—or at least the parts we can attribute to First Isaiah—deals predominantly with Judah and Jerusalem, there are more than a few references to Israel and Samaria, and oracles addressed to the northern territories. The heading, however, can be taken as appropriate because it reflects the main concern and content of the book. We need not ask more of the heading of Amos. The book's main concern and content are certainly Israel, the northern kingdom; but that would not exclude consideration of other areas, including specifically Judah. The unequivocal terminology immediately following (items 2 and 3 below) introduces strain into the heading (1:1). On the one hand, the location of Amos' work in the reigns of two kings suggests that he is interested in both kingdoms (with Judah mentioned first); hence the impression that his visions concern all of Israel, here called simply Israel. On the other hand, such an interpretation gives "Israel" two distinct meanings in the same verse. The strain could be relieved somewhat if "Israel" does designate the northern kingdom as such in both of its occurrences in this verse. It identifies "Israel" as the prime focus of the visions and the main topic of the book, but the mention of Judah immediately thereafter shows that it is also part of the picture.

Allowance should be made for the fact that 1:1 is editorial and might not line up exactly with the book as a whole. But it would be going too far to infer that the editor mislabeled the contents. Neither should the reference to Judah in the title, immediately after the statement that the visions were about "Israel," be taken as only an indication of a date. It is even less appropriate that this analysis should lead to the removal of passages dealing with the southern kingdom from the body of the book on the grounds that because Amos dealt only with Israel, any references to Judah must come from a later editor or scribe.

2. 1:1 *bîmê ʿuzzîyâ melek-yĕhûdâ*, "in the days of Uzziah the king of Judah." In the case of Judah, there is no question about the reference, and no further comment is necessary.

3. 1:1 *ûbîmê yārobʿām ben-yôʾāš melek yiśrāʾēl*, "and in the days of

Jeroboam ben-Joash the king of Israel." There can be no question of the reference here: Israel is the northern kingdom *only* here, clearly distinguished from Judah. In fact, this phrase is the point of departure for the inquiry and the reason for or example of the usage we postulate in the book of Amos.

4. 2:4 *ʿal-šĕlōšâ pišʿê yĕhûdâ,* "For three violations by Judah." No question about the usage and no comment.

5. 2:5 *wĕšillaḥtî ʾēš bîhûdâ,* "And I will send Fire against Judah." No question.

6. 2:6 *ʿal-šĕlōšâ pišʿê yiśrāʾēl,* "For three violations by Israel." In view of the list as a whole and especially the preceding reference to Judah, there can be no question that the northern kingdom alone is in mind here. Even if the oracle on Judah were treated as secondary, the argument would hold, and the hypothesis would support the interpretation.

7. 2:11 *haʾap ʾên-zōʾt bĕnê yiśrāʾēl,* "Isn't that actually so, you Israelites?" Here, according to the hypothesis, the addition of the qualifier *bny* means that the prophet is referring to Israel as a whole rather than to the northern kingdom exclusively. The context itself (vv 11–12) could be interpreted broadly or narrowly, for presumably the charge could be leveled at the leadership in either or both nations, that is, of suppressing true prophets and nazirites, or, as we think, the specialized groups of naziritic prophets, those prophets who take naziritic vows, like Samuel, or those in nazirite communities who are called to be prophets. We associate groups such as the prophetic bands led by Samuel (the only attested naziritic prophet in the Bible), Elijah, and Elisha with the north, but that may be an unwarranted restriction. These prophets were not restricted to any one part of the nation. "The word of Samuel came to all Israel" (1 Sam 4:1). Note the equivocal attitude of Elisha to the three kings in 2 Kings 3, especially vv 13–14 (allowing of course, for its *Tendenz*). What tips the scale here in our judgment is the setting established in vv 9–10, in which the classic tradition of the Exodus and Conquest is cited by the prophet, a tradition belonging to all of Israel, of which both kingdoms were the heirs. The expression *bny yśrʾl* itself is characteristic of the narratives in the Primary History, so in the framework provided here we should see a reference to the larger Israel encompassing and embodying both kingdoms. Amos may in fact be addressing a northern audience, but with the dramatic shift at 2:9 he is talking about classic Israel and its heirs. The charges here include both kingdoms, just as the traditions cited do. And we must carry the thought through to the end of the pericope and chapter. The final dramatic and decisive battle, described in general but overwhelming terms, is not aimed precisely at Samaria, though it is included, but at Israel as a whole to ensure its demise. It may well be for this reason that the possible original ending, which would have used the standard formula previously attested seven times, has

been omitted in favor of this broader and vaguer one. In any case, the use of
the expression *bny yśr'l* seems distinctive and will bear the interpretation we
have suggested. It is consistent with the context. In this and in the following passages where *bny yśr'l* is used, attention switches from the kingdom as
a political entity to the people as such. Their identity is found not so much
in their contemporary citizenship as in their early history, shared equally
by the people of Judah. Amos is clearly playing on this fact by basing his
appeal on premonarchical traditions. The same tactic is seen when residents
of Samaria are addressed as *bny yśr'l*.

8. 3:1 *'ăšer dibber yhwh 'ălêkem běnê yiśrā'ēl,* "that Yahweh has spoken
about [or against] you, O Israelites." According to the hypothesis, the
reference should be to all of Israel, historic Israel or the combined nations
of the present day. There is an alternate reading, attested by the LXX,
namely, *byt yśr'l*. This reading is actually found in *Codex Petropolitanus,*
corrected to *bny* in the margin. But this piece of evidence would not affect
the position adopted, for that expression also designates historic Israel or
all of Israel. In this passage, the appositional clause that directly follows
confirms the interpretation:

'al kol-hammišpāḥâ 'ăšer he'ělêtî mē'ereṣ miṣrayim

> about [or against] the whole family that I brought up from the
> land of Egypt.

It is clear that the prophet is addressing the whole group who can rightly
call themselves "the Israelites"—not only the citizens of the northern kingdom but those of the south also. This fact may explain the choice of terms
in the first place, and this passage can be regarded as the point of departure
for the examination of the compound group involving Israel. Here the
group addressed is identified explicitly with the "whole clan" (see the note
on this term ad loc.) that Yahweh brought out of Egypt, in other words, all
who claim descent from the Exodus generation. It follows too that the
classic statements on the meaning of divine election and the certainty of
judgment apply equally to Israel and Judah in the present circumstances,
even though the prophet may be addressing a northern audience and even if
he has the northern kingdom uppermost in his mind.

9. 3:12 *kēn yinnāṣělû běnê yiśrā'ēl,* "in the same way shall the Israelites
be rescued." According to our hypothesis, the reference here should be to
Israel as a whole, along the lines of the analysis offered for 3:1. The difficulty, however, is that the rest of the statement makes clear that the
prophet is talking about the northern kingdom, specifically those residing
or ruling in Samaria. The larger context, vv 9–12, also specifies Samaria
and the northern kingdom as the subject of this discourse. So we might

regard this example as running counter to the hypothesis. In view of the clear statement of the prophet about the judgment to come on the northern kingdom and the people of Samaria, we might have expected the term here to be "Israel" rather than "Israelites." At the same time it is to be noted that the prophet is careful to qualify the broader term, *bny yśr'l*, by the phrase *hyšbym bšmrwn*, indicating that he is restricting the reference here to the northerners. The implication is that without the qualification the term *bny yśr'l* would refer to both kingdoms, which is not the intention of the speaker. So he uses the broader term and then reduces its scope by the qualification, a perfectly legitimate procedure, because northerners qualify as *bny yśr'l* just as the southerners do. We might wonder why the prophet used this roundabout method to arrive at the point—he might have used the word "Israel" by itself to achieve the goal, or he could have left out the expression *bny yśr'l* altogether and relied on the following phrase, *hyšbym bšmrwn,* to convey his meaning. As already mentioned under item 7, the terminology used identifies Samarians as the audience, but addresses them in their identity as members of the whole people. Regardless—and we are hardly in a position to rethink his thoughts or rewrite his script—the statement can be made to fit within the contours of the hypothesis. It is also appropriate to note that we do not have elsewhere the combination of the broader term with the restrictive qualification attached to it.

10. 3:13 *wĕhāʿîdû bĕbêt yaʿăqōb,* "Confirm what you have heard about [or against] Jacob's family." It is difficult to specify the precise identification of this group, "Jacob's family," but it seems to be a substitute for or equivalent to "the house of Israel." In that case we are looking at a term for the combined kingdoms, as in other places in which *byt* or *bny yśr'l* is used. It makes some difference whether we translate *b* before *byt* as "in" (neutral) or "against" (adversative), as the former rendering would fit better with the broader group and the latter would go better perhaps with the northern kingdom, which is under prophetic attack. The context may also supply helpful information here. In v 14, as we will observe in the next item, Israel is named and is clearly the northern kingdom. The question is whether the expression in v 13 is intended to be parallel to "Israel" in v 14 or is intended to be distinguished from it. Is the audience addressed in v 13 supposed to be the same as the nation under indictment in v 14? The answer, rooted in grammatical and syntactical considerations, would appear to be that it is not, for Israel is described in the third person in v 14, which would hardly be the case if the audience addressed in the second person were the same group. Of course, *byt yʿqb* is the broad term and can include the north, but the emphasis is on the non-Israelites in the audience. Comparison with the previous unit, vv 9–12, supports the view that outsiders are being addressed or summoned to observe and listen and spread the word about the deplorable situation in Israel and the drastic measures soon to be

instituted against it. We may also remark that the use of the rare expression
(in Amos anyway) *byt yʿqb* may document an effort to distinguish the
groups more sharply from the *yśrʾl* in v 14 and to avoid confusion that
might arise if the more usual *byt yśrʾl* were used.

Compare Exod 19:3, where *byt yʿqb* is the historic group in parallel with
bny yśrʾl; cf. 1 Kgs 18:31, *bny-yʿqb,* also 2 Kgs 17:34; Isa 2:5, 6; 8:17;
10:20//*yśrʾl;* 14:1; 29:22; 46:3; 48:1; 58:1; Jer 2:4; 5:20; Ezek 20:5; Amos
9:8; Obad 18; Mic 2:7; 3:9; 5:6[E7], *šʾrt* and 5:7[E8]; Mal 3:6, *bny yʿqb;* Pss
77:16[E15], *bny yʿqb;* 105:6, *bny yʿqb;* 114:1—*byt yʿqb*//*yśrʾl*—where the
usage is standard and different from what we have in Amos; 1 Chr 16:13,
bny yʿqb. Amos does not use "Jacob" in chaps. 1–2, where the distinct
political entities of his time are clearly in view. The use of "Jacob" to
designate political Israel (all of it, as we maintain) is suitable for prophetic
discourse of a more general and often symbolic character. As in the frequent use of "Jacob" in Second Isaiah, the shade of the patriarch himself is
still haunting the nation. Though now a royal shrine of the north, Bethel
retains its associations with Jacob from patriarchal traditions. No other
name could secure this effect.

11. 3:14 *kî bĕyôm poqdî pišʿê-yiśrāʾēl ʿālāyw,* "When I punish Israel for
its acts of rebellion." According to the hypothesis, this passage refers to
the northern kingdom only. It is to be connected through terminology and
content with 2:6, already discussed, where there can be no question of the
identity of Israel as the northern kingdom. The word *pšʿ* links this passage
with the oracles in chaps. 1–2. Furthermore, the immediately following
colon in 3:14 specifies Bethel as one of the sites to be attacked violently,
confirming the reference to the northern kingdom:

> *ûpāqadtî ʿal-mizbĕḥôt bêt-ʾēl*
> *wĕnigdĕʿû qarnôt hammizbēaḥ wĕnāpĕlû lāʾāreṣ*

> I will also punish [i.e., visit the transgressions of Israel upon]
> the altars of Bethel; the horns of the altar will be cut down, and
> will fall to the ground.

There can be little question, then, that Israel in this passage is the northern
kingdom and that the usage supports the hypothesis.

12. 4:5 *kî kēn ʾăhabtem bĕnê yiśrāʾēl,* "For that's what you love [to do],
O Israelites." Solely on the basis of this passage and the context, it would
be difficult to say which group is referred to, although the oracle itself, vv
4–5, is aimed at those pilgrims who practice their faith constantly and
enthusiastically as they go from shrine to shrine. In this context only Bethel
and Gilgal are mentioned. Bethel figures as the royal shrine of the north,

yet even so it might well have retained some of its ancient status as a national center. Gilgal, the first Cisjordan national shrine under Joshua and still in use as an assembly point in the time of Saul, doubtless retained its ancient prestige as much as, perhaps more than, Bethel, for it remained a pilgrimage center in spite of competition from the two great rivals, Bethel and Jerusalem, sponsored by the two competing dynasties of north and south. Elsewhere the list of shrines is increased to include Beer-sheba and still others (cf. 5:4–6 and 8:14, where Samaria and Dan are mentioned along with Beer-sheba). The implication of the latter passages is that making pilgrimages to the great shrines of both north and south involves the people of both kingdoms. It would be axiomatic that celebrations and observances at Beer-sheba would be attended by people of the south predominantly, though no doubt some northerners might be present too. The same should be said of southerners at the northern shrines. On the face of it Amos' presence at the Bethel shrine would be nothing remarkable. His prophesying there unbidden, and especially the contents of his prophecies, would make the visit unusual, though hardly unique in the annals of that place. Even if the story in 1 Kings 13 has been embellished, the motif of a southerner prophesying in the north need not be fanciful.

Our point here is that the population that is being told about the visits and worship at the shrines would presumably and plainly be one that included all of Israel, that is, Israelites and Judahites; and that is precisely what we believe the term *bny yśr'l* used here signifies in Amos. Logical support and confirmation of this interpretation will come from 5:4–6, where not only is the same population called by the equivalent term, *byt yśr'l*, but Beer-sheba is explicitly included in the list of objectionable sanctuaries. It is not necessary to prove that Israelites from all over frequented all of these shrines in order to sustain the point being made here. The reference of *bny yśr'l* is more nuanced. It does not have to mean all members of both kingdoms. A small group could be so addressed; then Amos is giving them an identity beyond their citizenship in one or other of the kingdoms.

13. 4:12 *lākēn kōh 'e'ĕśeh-llĕkā yiśrā'ēl,* "Therefore thus have I done to you, O Israel." According to our hypothesis, this term limits the application to the northern kingdom. The threat of punishment is repeatedly directed at Israel rather than Judah in the book, and this passage is no exception. Not that Judah is exempted, but clearly the immediate target of the prophet's remarks is the northern kingdom. Because v 12 comes at the conclusion of the set speech on the plagues we might expect the entire passage to have the same subject: namely, that the warnings and threats in the series on the plagues (vv 6–11) would be directed at the same people who are condemned in v 12. At the same time the passage immediately preceding the one on the plagues (4:4–5) has as its subject the larger group,

the *bny yśr'l*. An argument could be made that the subject of the discourse on the plagues is the larger group, both in view of the antecedent in 4:5 and because the geographic references include southern locations such as Egypt (v 10) and Sodom and Gomorrah. When it comes to the vagaries of climate and weather, no part of the land is immune. We may have to leave the question unanswered but affirm that the judgment in v 12 is nevertheless directed at the north, whatever the indications about the whole nation that may be found in vv 6–11.

14. 4:12 *hikkôn liqra't-'ĕlōheykā yiśrā'ēl,* "prepare [make ready] to confront your God, O Israel." In this passage, as in the immediately preceding one, the name used is the same—Israel—and whatever decision is made about the usage there should apply here equally. According to the hypothesis, here again we have the northern kingdom, and presumably that was to be expected in light of the same usage earlier in the verse. Items 13 and 14 go together. On the face of it they make sense if "Israel" means the whole nation, but the fact that they do does not prove that the choice of this name was intended in that sense. As our study will show when it is complete, most if not all of the occurrences of "Israel," unmodified, fit the hypothesis that the name means the north distinctively, while not necessarily leaving the south out altogether. (To do so the term "Samaria" could be used, and it is so used in this period.) But as with the heading (1:1), where a similar problem was encountered, we cannot be sure that the language and usage of Amos himself occur everywhere in the book. We do not intend to invoke editors and redactors lightheartedly to explain apparent inconsistencies in terminology and usage; but 1:1 is surely an exception. If items 13 and 14 also deviate slightly, in that here "Israel" could refer to the whole nation, not simply (or primarily) to the north as such, it could be because here Amos is not so free to use his own terms. While 4:12 remains obscure, it has features that remind us of a classic theophany (the following hymn fragment has that quality too) and could be a quotation from a traditional source, such as Exod 19 (see vv 11, 15).

15. 5:1 *'ăšer 'ānōkî nōśē' 'ălêkem qînâ bêt yiśrā'ēl,* "that I am going to utter about you, a dirge, O house of Israel." The usage here is to be compared with that in 3:1, where we have a similar introductory formula: *'ăšer dibber yhwh 'ălêkem bĕnê yiśrā'ēl,* "that Yahweh has spoken about [or against] you, O Israelites." Presumably the group addressed is the same, and as in 3:1 it can be identified certainly with all of Israel, or those who could claim descent from classical and historical Israel of the Exodus and Wanderings, so here in 5:1 there is no reason to alter the assessment. In Amos *byt* and *bny* before "Israel" are interchangeable and equivalent, so the group addressed in 5:1 must be the same as in 3:1. Needless to say, this conclusion is in accord with the hypothesis, which specifies that *byt yśr'l* describes the larger group. Or, to put the matter more cautiously (albeit

negatively), it cannot be shown that here "house of Israel" refers exclusively to the northern kingdom.

16. 5:2 *nāpĕlâ lō'-tôsîp qûm bĕtûlat yiśrā'ēl,* "The virgin Israel has fallen, she will never stand up again." This dirge is in the so-called prophetic perfect, describing the prophet's vision, which is in the past tense but refers to a future event. Because the phrase *btwlt yśr'l* is unique in Amos, we can only be guided in our interpretation by general rules and the context. Because qualifying constructs and appositional nouns affect the meaning of Israel and broaden its application from the northern kingdom to larger Israel defined in a variety of ways, we should imagine that the expression *btwlt* as the construct before Israel would do the same. In accordance with the hypothesis, we could say that "the virgin Israel" refers to all of Israel. There is nothing in the sense or the context to conflict with this interpretation, but it would be equally possible to apply it more strictly to the north. If the dirge transcribes a vision, then we could connect it with the other visions of chaps. 7–8; of them it can be said that they refer to the nation as a whole rather than to one part of it, which also seems to be the case here.

When we look at other instances of the expression *btwlt yśr'l* we find them, curiously, exclusively in Jeremiah (18:13; 31:4, 21), where obviously the term does not refer to the northern kingdom, long since vanished. But it also, at least in 31:4 and 21, seems to refer to a restored Israel of classic dimensions. (Does Jer 18:13 refer to Judah or Israel of old?) The only other occurrence (Deut 22:19) has to do with an actual *btwlt yśr'l,* not the nation. But because it is so unusual in Amos we need to ask if the occurrence of *btwlt* secures a nuance that none of the other qualifiers does. In particular, the contemporary use of *bĕtûlat-* (or *bat-*) for Jerusalem suggests possibly here "Samaria."

17. 5:3 *lĕbêt yiśrā'ēl,* "O house of Israel." It is difficult to interpret this phrase in relation to the rest of the verse. The *l* is probably vocative and thus connected with the opening formula, "For thus my Lord Yahweh has said." Or the *l* could be taken as the ordinary preposition in the same construction: "For thus my Lord Yahweh has said to the house of Israel." There are various ways in which the phrase can be linked to the text of the verse, but the description of cities at war and the decimation of armies is too general and common to make a judgment about the scope of *byt yśr'l.* There is no reason, however, to depart from the hypothetical pattern, so we assign the passage to all of Israel or the combined "house of Israel." Once more, however, it must be conceded that the language is so general that it makes sense whether applied to either kingdom or to both together. Without more identifying specifics, we cannot advance beyond this point. We have only the name to go on, but we allow cases like the present one, which are indeterminate when taken in isolation, to be defined by others such as

items 21, 22, 25, 32, and 44 in which there *are* specific indications, that
"house of Israel" means the entire people.

18. 5:4   *kî kōh 'āmar yhwh lĕbêt yiśrā'ēl,* "For thus Yahweh has said: O
house of Israel [or to the house of Israel]."   For our purposes the variant
renderings are equally satisfactory. Incidentally, we may note that the sequence here ties together the phrase *lbyt yśr'l* with the opening formula,
showing that the split arrangement in 5:3 is simply a variation of the order
in 5:4, and therefore the interpretation proposed earlier linking the opening
formula with the closing phrase is the correct one.

According to the hypothesis, the term *byt yśr'l* covers the double kingdom, and, as already indicated, the context not only offers no hindrance to
such an interpretation but supports it in rather impressive fashion. As previously noted in the comment on 4:5, the passage here deals with those who
worship at the major shrines of Israel and Judah; whereas the sanctuaries
mentioned in 4:5 include only Bethel and Gilgal (belonging to the north),
here Beer-sheba is added at a climactic point. The structure of v 5 is clearly
chiastic with five cola or components: the first and the fifth match up, both
speaking of Bethel; so also the second and fourth units, which speak of
Gilgal; in the center, the third unit, which is the passage on Beer-sheba,
stands by itself. The prophet is speaking to a transient population that
frequents the different sanctuaries, or he is addressing those who worship at
the different shrines. In either case—or if there is a combination of both—
people from the south and north alike would be included, as it is most
unlikely that only northerners traveled to shrines both north and south,
and southerners stayed home. No doubt southerners came north as northerners went south, and while a stable local majority made up the bulk of
worshipers at any particular shrine, pilgrims from every part of both countries would make up a sizable part of the throng at any of the major
sanctuaries. Amos' words are addressed primarily to those who go from
shrine to shrine, but that will include much of the double population over
time and certainly large groups of both kingdoms at any particular time.
There can be little doubt that in this context *byt yśr'l* refers to greater Israel.

The network of shrines and their cultic personnel, who were members of
the "Levitical" clans, represented a continuing factor in national life and
expressed the earlier unity and identity of the whole nation in terms of
religious festivals and institutions. This network antedated the monarchy
and cut across the formal divisions of the rival kingdoms as expressed in
the secular administration based on the palaces in Samaria and Jerusalem.
Even the attempts to integrate palace and temple—more evident in Jerusalem than in the north, where Samaria was the focal point of the royal sector
and Bethel of the cultic sector—did not override the ancient status of the
shrines, which remained national and, we suggest, places of pilgrimage for
people from both kingdoms. Jeroboam I set up centers in Dan and Bethel

precisely in an attempt to neutralize the attraction of Jerusalem and to divert northerners from visiting the shrine there, but there is no indication that he entirely succeeded in this effort. In Amos' time the older system is still in evidence in the Levitical towns, as listed in Joshua 21 and 1 Chronicles 6. Archaeological fieldwork has pointed to the prosperous times of Jeroboam II and Uzziah as the period in which nearly all of the traditional Levitical settlements were occupied; for some of them it was the only clearly attested occupation time. While generally confirming Amos' picture of a flourishing cult, they point also to what Boling and Wright (1982:495) call "a support system" distinct from the political superstructures.

19. 5:6 *pen-yiṣlaḥ kāʾēš bêt yôsēp,* "lest he rush [upon you] like a flame, O house of Joseph." The latter phrase, "Joseph's house," can be interpreted as vocative. The parallelism with *lbyt-ʾl* in the parallel colon ties the two names together, and the combination shows that the prophet has focused his attention on the northern kingdom. This conclusion seems certain in view of the use of the name "Joseph," for the two Joseph tribes, Ephraim and Manasseh, constituted the heartland, the bulk of the population, and the armed might of the northern kingdom. A little later, a somewhat truncated version of the northern kingdom will be called "Ephraim" (cf. Hosea and Isaiah and our remarks on the usage in Hosea [Andersen and Freedman 1980]). Our conclusion is that Joseph will refer only to the northern kingdom in this book, or wherever it is used of a nation, just as Judah will invariably refer to the southern kingdom when used in the same way. The qualifying nouns used as constructs in connection with Joseph do not affect the identity of the community named Joseph. Here *byt* is used; *śʾryt* in 5:15; *šēber* in 6:6 does not function in the same way, so *ywsp* is without qualification of this sort in that passage. The distinction we posit is restricted to Israel alone on the one hand and Israel with qualifiers on the other.

It is an interesting question whether the imperatives in v 6 (*dršw* and *wḥyw*) are addressed to the same audience as the same imperatives in v 4 (*dršwny wḥyw*). According to our analysis, and especially if *byt ywsp* in v 6 is vocative, the subjects are different and there is a shift from all of Israel to the house of Joseph (the northern kingdom). There is no problem, however, about the two being addressed in the same manner in such close quarters. "The house of Joseph" is an integral and essential part of "the house of Israel"—but there is an important shift in focus. The threat leveled here at Bethel, which will be consumed by fire, is more immediately relevant to the house of Joseph, because it is in their territory. Most of the specific threats are aimed at targets in the north, as we have observed.

20. 5:15 *ʾûlay yeḥĕnan yhwh ʾĕlōhê-ṣĕbāʾôt šĕʾērît yôsēp,* "Perhaps Yahweh the God of hosts will treat [you] kindly, O remnant of Joseph." Here again there can be little question that the reference is to the northerners, though "the remnant" clearly implies a restriction to the sur-

vivors of the coming disaster and destruction. Nevertheless, only northerners are addressed in this passage. There is an implication that v 14, which shares so many ideas and words with v 15, should then also apply to the north only, though the subject is not specified. The difference, if any, could be that v 14 is addressed to its audience before the catastrophe, while v 15, with essentially the same message, presupposes it. But if *š^eryt ywsp* is the delayed subject, acting as the object of direct address for the verbs in both verses, then the time frame is the same, and the middle verses of the book belong to the latest phase of the prophet's oracles and are addressed to the projected survivors of the north only.

21. 5:25 *hazzĕbāḥîm ûminḥa higgaštem-lî bammidbār ʾarbāʿîm šānâ bêt yiśrāʾēl,* "Did you bring me sacrifices and gifts for forty years in the desert, O house of Israel?" Here the picture is unequivocal. The people addressed are identified with classic Israel of the Exodus and Wanderings, those who spent forty years in the wilderness. There can be no doubt that "the house of Israel" here refers to all who claimed descent from and identity with the whole of Israel of the classic tradition. The term therefore would include current Judah as well as current Israel.

22. 6:1 *nĕqūbê rēʾšît haggôyīm ûbāʾû lāhem bêt yiśrāʾēl,* "the notables of the foremost of the nations, who have come for themselves to the house of Israel." This passage is a very difficult one from every aspect, but we believe that it forms a complement to the preceding bicolon, 6:1a. We also believe that the expression *byt yśrʾl* is parallel to *rʾšyt hgwym* (appropriated from Amalek, cf. Num 24:20, and applied to themselves by the self-confident and arrogant leaders of the double nation) and that it is to be combined with the construct *nqby* in the same fashion. Furthermore, we identify these nobles or leaders with the nominal forms in 6:1a—*hš^ʾnnym* ("those who luxuriate") in Zion, and *hbṭḥym* ("those who are secure" or "feel themselves to be secure") in Mount Samaria—and see a common compound subject throughout the couplet. In short it is the leadership in Zion and Samaria who are in charge of the house of Israel, the first of the nations who have returned home presumably in triumph and self-satisfied with their labors.

By hypothesis, *bêt yiśrāʾēl* refers to the double kingdom here, and in this case the context offers firm support. Whether our particular analysis of the grammar and syntax is correct, there can nevertheless be little doubt the *byt yśrʾl* of 6:1b is to be identified with both Zion and Samaria, the two kingdoms. This passage can be compared with 3:12, where the expression *bny yśrʾl* is associated with a participial construction, similar to those used here: *hyšbym bšmrwn* ("those dwelling in Samaria"). In that passage we argued that out of the larger group represented by *bny yśrʾl* (equivalent to the present *byt yśrʾl*) only "those dwelling in Samaria," that is, the people or leaders (it could be rendered "those ruling in Samaria") of the northern kingdom were intended. Here leaders in both capital cities are mentioned, so the full complement of "the house of Israel" is made up. If we assume the integrity of the passage and the interaction of the elements according to the syntax proposed, then the equivalence is clear, and this passage becomes a key one in identifying *byt yśr'l* with the double kingdom rather than with the north only.

23. 6:6 *wĕlō' neḥlû 'al-šēber yôsēp*, "They are not distressed at Joseph's crash." As in the other passages mentioning Joseph, the reference seems clearly to be to the northern kingdom. Traditionally the name Joseph stands for the two major tribes of the north (Ephraim and Manasseh), and the usage—whether historical, poetic, or prophetic—is consistent throughout the Bible. Historical passages using the particular or exact expression, *byt ywsp* (cf. 5:5), include the following: Josh 17:17; 18:5; Judg 1:22, 23, 35; 2 Sam 19:21[E20]; and 1 Kgs 11:28. Compare also Obadiah 18, where Jacob is parallel to Joseph; and Zech 10:6, where Judah and Joseph are parallel or complementary. Other passages have *bny ywsp*, and many have no qualifying element; but the meaning or identification seems to be the same throughout.

24. 6:8 *mĕtā'ēb 'ānōkî 'et-gĕ'ôn ya'ăqōb*, "I abhor the pride of Jacob." This is a difficult and enigmatic passage, with at least two problems. One, which seems to involve a scribal error, requires us to read *mt'b* for *mt'b* (cf. NOTE ad loc.). The emendation can be supported by comparing the sequence **mĕtā'ēb 'ānōkî . . . śānē'tî*, "I abhor . . . I hate" in 6:8 with *śānĕ'û . . . yĕtā'ēbû*, "they hate . . . and abhor" in 5:10. The other problem is more relevant to our inquiry because it concerns the meaning of the phrase *g'wn y'qb* ("the pride of Jacob"). Varying interpretations have been offered, but our concern here is with the scope of the term "Jacob." According to our hypothesis, the reference should be to greater Israel (the double kingdom) partly because it is very unlikely that the northern kingdom was ever denominated "Jacob." Further, we have argued that *byt y'qb* in 3:13 denominates the larger entity, which would predispose us to the same conclusion here. The context is hardly decisive, but that point in itself is a gain and an indication that the prophet has the larger political configuration in mind. In the immediate setting Yahweh affirms his abhorrence of "the pride of Jacob" (presumably, plausibly, or possibly the infamous leadership of both nations pilloried and assaulted in the main set of Woes, 6:1–7) and his hatred of "its citadels." He also asserts that he will deliver up the "city in its entirety." Such a statement certainly could and would be applicable to Samaria and Israel, as similar sentiments are voiced elsewhere in the book. But they could equally be leveled at Judah and Jerusalem, as other passages show, not least of which are ones already cited, 2:5 and 6:1.

A further consideration may be urged by examination of the adjoining passage, vv 9–10. This difficult and obscure unit can be compared and associated with the less enigmatic passage in 5:3, which describes the progressive decimation of the army of an otherwise unspecified city (it is a generic depiction). Here in 6:9–10 we seem to have the final demise of the few survivors of the previous slaughter, though admittedly the only visible link between the passages is in the repetition of the number ten; but the contexts are not dissimilar, and the mood is similarly somber. The point to be raised here is that the description in 5:3 is connected with the term *byt yśr'l* and in this passage (6:8) with the parallel term *y'qb;* thus they support and confirm the analysis that identifies the political entity as the double kingdom. Finally we may add that 6:11, which seems to carry on the same theme of the destruction of the city previously alluded to, this time focuses attention on the houses, great and small, and is also vague and general enough to apply to both kingdoms. Our conclusion is that there is no compelling reason to abandon the hypothesis and so we identify Jacob here with the double kingdom.

25. 6:14 *kî hinĕnî mēqîm 'ălêkem bêt yiśrā'ēl . . . gôy,* "For soon I will raise against you, O house of Israel . . . a nation." Here, according to our hypothesis, the reference should be to the double kingdom; and therein lies a problem. On the face of the matter, there is nothing disturbing in the idea that God would raise up a nation that in the course of time would oppress both Israel and Judah. In fact, it is hard to imagine a nation attacking one without dealing in some way with the other. And historically speaking, the Assyrians did just that, though in separate waves of attack. Beginning with Tiglath-pileser III, Israel was subjected to repeated attacks until it succumbed to the siege imposed on Samaria by Shalmaneser V and brought to a successful conclusion by him or by his successor Sargon II, who in any case claimed credit for the city's capture and the people's captivity (ca. 722). Judah, which had requested aid from Tiglath-pileser III in repelling attacks by Israel and Aram in 735–734 and had become a vassal of the eastern empire, ended up by rebelling in the reign of Hezekiah and being overrun by Sennacherib in 701. The country barely survived, but the experience of both kingdoms reflects not only the reality of eighth-century power politics but what a prophet might well have foreseen and predicted.

The difficulty lies in the context, v 14b, which states that this nation "will overpower you from the gateway of Hamath [Lebo-Hamath] as far as the Wadi Arabah." The description of the foreign onslaught restricts the territory to be attacked to the eastern areas, and in particular to those captured or dominated by Jeroboam II, according to 2 Kgs 14:25, where we read that "he restored the territory of Israel from the gateway of Hamath [Lebo-Hamath] as far as the Sea of the Arabah." The only difference is the use of *yām* in 2 Kings where in Amos we have *naḥal.* There may be a geographic distinction here and the two writers may have different territorial boundaries in mind, but the general picture is the same. It would appear, therefore, that Amos is saying that Yahweh will raise up a nation to come against Israel and in the initial instance overrun and seize from Israel the lands recently recaptured and restored by Jeroboam. That claim would mean in turn that the primary or perhaps exclusive reference here is to the northern kingdom, and that *byt yśr'l* is to be understood in the more restrictive sense of that kingdom. We would have to concede that this is not only a possible reading of the passage and interpretation of the phrase *byt yśr'l*, but even a reasonable or probable one.

Is the other option, which is in accord with our hypothesis, also possible? The answer will lie in the geography of the threat. No matter whether we speak of the Wadi or the Sea of the Arabah, it is difficult to imagine Jeroboam considering a campaign along the whole length of the east bank of the Jordan without having the approval and probably the assistance of Judah. We have suggested elsewhere that the two kings, Jeroboam and Uzziah, may have assisted each other while each pursued his own objectives, with Jeroboam operating in the east from Lebo-Hamath to the Arabah, and Uzziah in the west primarily expanding his domain into Philistine territory. But it is hard to imagine either operating so freely across national borders without an alliance or at least a cooperative understanding between them securing the internal border and allowing them to draw troops and equipment from that border in order to attack elsewhere. The prophet may have had such cooperation in mind when speaking of the oppressing nation to come. Clearly its first target would be Israel, but could the second one, Judah, also be in view? We suggest that the use of the expression *byt yśr'l* carries just that implication, and that the notion is not contradicted by what is in the text. We may also point out that the use of *byt yśr'l* in v 14 provides an echo of its use in 6:1, thus forming an envelope construction. We would expect the scope of the term to be the same in both cases. Furthermore, we recognize a similar pairing in 5:1 and 5:25, in which the same expression, *byt yśr'l*, likewise occurs and provides an echo or a closure. In both of those cases, as also in 6:1, the evidence strongly if not unequivocally supports the hypothetical interpretation, especially 5:25. Finally, it seems clear that 6:14 constitutes the conclusion of the major unit that begins with 5:1 and that the occurrence of *byt yśr'l* at the beginning and end of the whole unit entitles us to believe that the bulk of the material contained therein is directed at all of the surviving descendants of historic Israel.

Taking the unit as a whole, the word "Israel" occurs seven times, and in six of the seven occurrences the word is qualified by the construct *bêt* (*byt yśr'l:* 5:1, 3, 4, 25; 6:1, 14); the only exception is in 5:2 where we have *bĕtûlat*, which functions in the same way and within the special form of the dirge has the same significance. (Maybe this line is an instance of the single deviation from an established pattern, only it is the second out of seven, not the fifth as we have observed the phenomenon elsewhere in Amos.) According to the hypothesis, all of these expressions designate the larger entity. In this section (chaps. 5–6), therefore, when the prophet wishes to refer to the northern kingdom alone, he avoids possible confusion by using the identifying marker *yôsēp,* initially *byt ywsp* (5:6, the "house of Joseph"), then *šʾryt ywsp* (5:15 the "remnant of Joseph"), and finally *ywsp* alone (6:6, "Joseph's crash").

The clear implication of all of this evidence is that the section of the book bounded by 5:1 and 6:14 should be regarded as dealing primarily with the larger *byt yśrʾl,* and that while the northern kingdom—denominated by the term *yôsēp* or initially by the "house of Joseph," a classic term used in the historical accounts—plays an important role, the audience for the prophet is the whole "house of Israel."

26. 7:2 *sĕlaḥ-nāʾ mî yāqûm yaʿăqōb kî qāṭōn hûʾ,* "Please forgive! How can Jacob survive, as he is so small?" It is not easy to decide just who or what is signified by Jacob here. Clearly a political entity is intended, and the name "Jacob" signifies the descendants of the patriarch; but which ones and how many? The vision itself, which occasions the prophet's outcry, is geographically nonspecific and could apply equally to either territory or to both. If—as we maintain and shall attempt to demonstrate in detail at the proper place—the visions and the plagues are two sides of the same coin, the indications that 4:6–11 apply to all of Israel are an argument that the visions had the same coverage. Our hypothesis about the meaning of Jacob calls for a reference to the whole community, the large entity or double kingdom, and in our view this reference conforms to the nature of the visions as a whole and to the prophet's concern. We will develop the case further, but the main point is that the visions, the call to prophesy, and the message inevitably concern the fate of the whole enterprise, which for the prophet began as a national movement with the Exodus from Egypt. While the primary focus will be the northern kingdom, it was not the exclusive target, and Amos would have rejected the notion that he was called to prophesy only to or about the northern kingdom, just as he rejected emphatically the statement by Amaziah that he should restrict his prophetic activity to the south. He was a prophet of Yahweh, peculiarly the God of both nations, and he had visions encompassing the future of the double nation, with a message for the northern component initially or primarily, but not exclusively. At this point we hypothesize that Jacob refers to the descendants of the patriarch and in this instance to the double kingdom.

There is another aspect of Amos' intercession to be taken into account. If Jacob means only the northern kingdom, the threat of its extermination would not be as grave as a threat against the whole people. As we have already pointed out in the discussion of chap. 4, locusts are not likely to have respected territorial boundaries; and the next vision, a twin of the first, is clearly cosmic in its scope. If Judah were exempt, the case would not be so desperate, and Amos could have consoled himself with the thought that the nation would survive as the southern half. He might even have consented to this distinction as appropriate because the north was the worse of the two, at least in the opinion of some Judeans. Amos makes no such distinctions. Whenever he identifies Judah or Jerusalem explicitly, it is in the same predicament as (north) Israel and Samaria. If Judah were not to be included, it would have been easy enough to say so. The qualification in 9:8 does not contradict this view. Quite apart from the likelihood that it belongs to a different phase of Amos' ministry than the first pair of visions, in its context it promises that a remnant of all Israel will survive, not Judah alone. It is only in hindsight that we are aware of how differently things turned out for the two kingdoms. In Amos' perspective there is no hint that his vision included such eventualities.

27. 7:5 *ḥădal-nāʾ mî yāqûm yaʿăqōb kî qāṭōn hûʾ*, "Please desist! How can Jacob survive, as he is so small?" In this instance, the analysis, interpretation, and assignment or reference must be the same as for the previous instance of Jacob. It is the larger grouping, not just the northern kingdom.

28. 7:8 *wayyōʾmer ʾădōnāy hinĕnî śām ʾănāk bĕqereb ʿammî yiśrāʾēl lōʾ-ʾôsîp ʿôd ʿăbôr lô*, "My Lord said, 'Soon I will put grief (*ʾănāk*) in the midst of my people Israel. I shall never spare them again." This passage has certain difficulties, especially concerning the obscure word *ʾnk*, but our concern is with the identity of *ʿmy yśrʾl* ("my people Israel"). According to our hypothesis, the phrase could be interpreted as a reference to the historic and larger entity because the word *yśrʾl* is qualified by *ʿmy*, which functions in a way similar to the constructs *byt* and *bny*. Or Israel could be taken as the solo noun, with the appositional *ʿmy* as purely epexegetic; then Israel would be equivalent to Israel elsewhere in Amos, identifying the northern kingdom only. In this instance, the choice is a difficult one, but we are guided by the example of Jacob in the first two visions. We are inclined to identify the expression *ʿmy yśrʾl* with the other compounds and see here a reference to all of Israel as the target of Yahweh's wrath rather than a narrower designation of the northern kingdom only. The convenant connotations of "my people" also point to the larger entity. That the north is included in the judgment is obvious and does not need to be pointed out. That it is also the primary target is shown by the material that is sandwiched between the third and fourth visions.

29. 7:9 *wĕnāšammû bāmôt yiśḥāq*, "The high places [burial mounds] of Isaac will be devastated." The use of the name "Isaac" as a designation of the nation is very rare; in fact, the only explicit occurrences are in Amos (here and 7:16). All other uses refer to the patriarch either in stories about him or in formulaic association with Abraham or Jacob or both, so it would

not be obvious at first sight whether the reference would be to all of Israel, or classic Israel, or just the northern kingdom. One might expect the name to be used in the same way that Jacob is, namely, to refer to the descendants of the patriarch and hence to cover both nation states. That happens not to be the case in Amos, however, where we have adequate controls to determine the scope of the reference. In both instances *yśḥq* occurs in parallel with *yśr'l*, and in both cases the context shows that Israel (that is, the northern kingdom) is meant. Here in v 9 the "high places of Isaac" are in parallel construction with "Israel's sanctuaries," and it is clear that they will share the same fate. While theoretically the expressions could be complementary, it is most unlikely that the name "Isaac" would be used only of Judah and even less likely that it would be used of both kingdoms in parallel with a term designating only one kingdom, Israel. In this case, the noun "Israel" refers to the northern kingdom not only because of the hypothesis but because the immediately following clause, "and I shall attack Jeroboam's house," directs attention to an assault on the northern kingdom. In this instance (7:9), therefore, there can be no doubt that Isaac designates the northern kingdom only:

$$\text{wĕnāšammû bāmôt yiśḥāq}$$
$$\text{ûmiqdĕšê yiśrā'ēl yeḥĕrābû}$$

The high places [burial mounds] of Isaac will be devastated,
    and Israel's sanctuaries will be laid waste.

Note the perfect chiasm, with the verbs at the ends, and the construct chains in the center. Further, the terms *bmwt* and *mqdšy* form a combination locating the sanctuaries at the high places, while the names can also be combined (as is entirely appropriate) as *yiśrā'ēl* [*ben-*]*yiśḥāq*.

30. 7:9 *ûmiqdĕšê yiśrā'ēl yeḥĕrābû*, "and Israel's sanctuaries will be laid waste." *Ex hypothesi*, the term "Israel" here should refer to the northern kingdom only. That position is confirmed by the immediately following clause, in which a direct statement is made about an attack on the house of Jeroboam, the then-reigning king of Israel. In the passage the evidence is explicit and decisive. It also helps to establish that in Amos Isaac as a national designation also specifies the northern kingdom.

31. 7:10 *'el-yārob'ām melek-yiśrā'ēl*, "to Jeroboam, the king of Israel." This title is to be compared with the same one in 1:1, with the same comment. There is no question about the reference, and no doubt this title is the basis for the usage in the book of Amos. The natural meaning of the term "Israel" in the period of Amos (first half of the eighth century) would have been as a designation of the northern kingdom, and that is doubtless its most common use and the way in which most hearers and readers would have understood it.

32. 7:10 *qāšar ʿāleykā ʿāmôs bĕqereb bêt yiśrāʾēl,* "Amos has conspired against you inside the house of Israel."   The term used here, *byt yśrʾl,* may come as a surprise, in view of the circumstances and the context, but on the basis of careful analysis and reflection it may convey quite precisely and accurately what the prophet (or editor) had in mind. According to our hypothesis, the expression here should refer to the double kingdom, not to the north alone, which may seem peculiar in view of the setting and the message delivered by Amos and now reported to the king. We might have expected the reference to be to the northern kingdom only, where this particular drama is being played out. Certainly, if there is a conspiracy it must be directed at the north and can only come to fruition there. But where was the plot hatched, and where is the base of operations or head-quarters for this particular cabal? It is well known that plotters and seditionists often find refuge in neighboring countries and are often protected and abetted by their governments, if not funded and guided in their enterprise. There are enough examples in the Bible to suggest that Amaziah is deliberately including the south in the range of Amos' activities. But note that the reference to *byt yśrʾl* does not exclude the north, where obviously an important—perhaps the most important—part of this hypothetical conspiracy will be worked out. For in addition to these general considerations, Amaziah is fully aware that Amos is from the south, presumably a recent arrival in the north at the shrine in Bethel, and it is altogether likely that the priest would assume that the plotting and other conspiratorial activities were initiated in the south. Only now, with Amos' appearance on the scene at Bethel, has the center of plot and projected action shifted to the north. Not that it was a plot of the south against the north. Amos' messages would have been viewed with just as much alarm in Jerusalem as in Samaria or Bethel. This point is acknowledged in Amaziah's comment: "the land cannot endure all his words" (7:10). Hence the use of the combination *byt yśrʾl* would be singularly appropriate here, because of all of the information about the matter available to us, and it would be more important to Amaziah, the speaker of the words. In short, Amaziah seems persuaded that the plot or conspiracy against Jeroboam and his house is not limited to the northern kingdom but involves both south and southerners, the conspicuous example being Amos. This situation clearly would raise the level of risk, as it would involve the possibility of outside governmental support and an international crisis. With some amazement we ascribe the usage here to the double kingdom as an appropriate arena for this supposed conspiracy instead of the northern kingdom alone.

An alternate view is to take the expression *byt yśrʾl* literally ("the house of Israel") as a reference to the Temple at Bethel, where the damaging and, to Amaziah, self-incriminating words ("I shall attack the house of Jeroboam with my sword") were uttered by Amos. Because Amaziah describes the Temple as *byt mmlkh* ("temple of the kingdom") in parallel with *mqdš mlk* ("royal sanctuary"), the designation *byt yśr'l* ("temple of the nation Israel") would be entirely appropriate. In this context "Israel" would designate the northern kingdom, while "house" would refer to the Temple, where the plot fomented by Amos and his abettors was revealed—and nipped in the bud by the high priest.

33. 7:11 *wĕyiśrā'ēl gālōh yigleh mē'al 'admātô*, " 'and Israel shall surely go into exile from its land.' " According to hypothesis, "Israel" here refers to the northern kingdom only, and that supposition is confirmed by the preceding statement, which limits attention to that nation: " 'By the sword shall Jeroboam die.' " The association of Jeroboam with Israel, the northern kingdom, is too clear and obvious to require further comment.

34. 7:12 *ḥōzeh lēk bĕraḥ-lĕkā 'el-'ereṣ yĕhûdâ*, "O seer, go, run away to the land of Judah." The reference to the southern kingdom is obvious and requires no comment. The only point to be made is that, as the story in chap. 7:10–17 requires, the distinction between the two kingdoms must be made and maintained. Except for two instances (7:10, already discussed, and 7:15, see below) the terms used apply to one kingdom or the other, mostly to the north (ten in all, nine referring specifically to Israel, the other to Judah). That makes the two references to the combined or double kingdom of Israel all the more important for analysis and evaluation.

35. 7:15 *lēk hinnābē' 'el-'ammî yiśrā'ēl*, " 'Go prophesy to my people Israel.' " Here again we have an apparent anomaly, which, however, on closer inspection turns out to be revelatory—astonishing perhaps, but potentially and actually important for understanding the relationship of deity with prophet and the nature of the latter's call and commission. In view of the immediate circumstances and the context, one might expect Amos to say that Yahweh had instructed him to prophesy to the people of Israel, the northern kingdom; and certainly most scholars would interpret the expression *'ammî yiśrā'ēl* in that fashion. Because Amos came north to Bethel and is here justifying that action, that reading would seem to close the case, and we would have to accept the usage here as unusual or anomalous or concede finally that the terms, with and without qualifiers, are used indiscriminately to represent the different Israels that have been identified in the Bible. All of this is plausible, but we must explore the other possibility: that the choice of the term here, with its qualifier, signifies that Amos' commission included more than Israel, that he also had a message to deliver to Judah. There are several lines of argument and evidence to be considered before reaching a conclusion. The first point is that the expression *'my yśr'l* certainly does not exclude the northern kingdom, and even if it included Judah, that fact need have no effect on the prophet's initial decision to come to Bethel to proclaim the word. It is conceivable that he had previously delivered messages in Judah especially in connection with the first

two visions, because Visions 3 and 4 are wrapped around the visit to Bethel. But as we have no record of a ministry in or to Judah and a record only of his mission in Israel, we may concede that he might never actually have proclaimed the word in Judah. Even so, it does not mean that he was not called to do so, or did not plan to speak the word there also. There is every reason to believe that he understood his visions to encompass both nations, and hence that his message, with appropriate adjustments, would also be meant for the two kingdoms. Even if we exclude the explicit references to Judah in the book—and we are strongly inclined to retain them—it is difficult or impossible to imagine that the unfolding of the divine plan for Israel in the days to come did not also include Judah. If the ultimate crisis were about to confront the northern kingdom, could the southern one expect to be left alone?

In our view, just as the visions cover both kingdoms, so here does the commission to prophesy. The words Amos quotes are the actual ones he heard, not ones tailored to the present mission. He understood that within the broad commission he must make a particular and prior decision: to Samaria or to Jerusalem. Circumstances and doubtless another word from Yahweh made the fateful determination: first to Israel and later to Judah. There is an unconscious irony in the words of Amaziah to Amos in which he forbids the latter to prophesy in Bethel; he urges the seer rather to go to the land of Judah and "there prophesy." To do so would be quite all right with Amaziah for obvious reasons. Indeed, Amaziah's advice makes more sense if he is telling Amos to go back not to the farm but to his old stomping ground, and not to go and prophesy where he had never prophesied before. But Amos does not contradict Amaziah by his reply, at least with regard to Judah. What he says to Amaziah is that his mandate was not restricted to Judah only, nor was it restricted only to Israel. He was told to go and prophesy to "my people Israel," that is, all of Israel, both kingdoms. In due course, when he has finished his assignment in Israel he may well return to Judah, and "eat [his] food there, and there do [his] prophesying." Of all subsequent events we know little or nothing. Perhaps Amos never got back to his homeland. Even falsely accused seditionists did not fare well at the hands of frightened and angry kings, as the stories in the book of Jeremiah about Uriah and Jeremiah himself show. Or Amos may have been shut off from his prophetic calling afterward, before he was able to articulate and deliver his message to the south. We have no way of knowing. Certainly the major part of this message was aimed at the north, and a good deal of it was delivered there. But to insist that neither the visions nor his message had anything to do with the south, or that Judah was simply a blank in his thinking or speaking, is going too far. The frequent references to the Israel of the past, from which both Israel and Judah of Amos' day could legitimately claim descent, show that the prophet's thinking and

speaking come in line with those of other contemporary prophets who
spoke to and of the north and south as parts of traditional Israel, encompassing both peoples. Hosea, Micah, and Isaiah all addressed messages to
both north and south and considered the destinies of both nations as part of
the continuing story of Yahweh's relationship with his people. It is very
difficult to imagine that Amos had any other general understanding of the
situation. He was summoned, as were the others, to speak the word of
Yahweh to his people, Israel, wherever they were—certainly to the north,
but also to the south.

36. 7:16 *'attâ 'ōmēr lō' tinnābē' 'al-yiśrā'ēl,* "You say, 'Don't prophesy
against [or about, but presumably Amaziah would not object to favorable
prophecies about Israel] Israel.' "   Here the reference is clear and certain:
the term "Israel" refers to the northern kingdom only. That is true not only
because the usage conforms to the hypothesis, but because the priest
Amaziah, who is being quoted here, has a specific, exclusive interest in
preventing Amos from prophesying about or against the northern kingdom,
which is the point of the remarks in v 13. At the same time, Amaziah has
not only not forbidden, but has encouraged the prophet, however sarcasti-
cally, to do his prophesying elsewhere, specifically in Judah (v 12). So
without question the reference is specifically limited to the northern kingdom, and becomes a major support of our hypothesis.

There is, however, one aspect of Amaziah's words that indicates a distinction, in his mind at least, in Amos' status in north and south. He
acknowledges Amos to be a professional prophet. He suggests that he return to Judah and earn his living there (if that is what "Eat your food!"
means). But he must not do it in Bethel. Do Amaziah's words imply that
his prophecies "against Israel" would be welcomed and rewarded in Judah?
It seems incredible that Amaziah would treat such a dangerous person in
this way. This problem is only part of the much larger one of why Amaziah
told Amos to flee, at the very time that he has accused him to the king of a
capital crime. There is no indication that Amos had a positive attitude to
Judah, or even that he had nothing at all to say about the southern kingdom. The surviving tradition is that he sometimes denounced Judah explicitly along the same lines as the north (2:4, 5:5, 6:1). To delete these passages
in support of a theory that Amos spoke only about the north shows how
flimsy that theory is. If Amos was a partisan, an agent for the south, a spy
as well as a revolutionary, then there is even more reason for eliminating
him instantly. Amaziah's failure to do so is simply incredible. But, as we
have seen in our discussion of 5:5, in connection with item 18, and of 6:14
(item 25), there are indications that the two kingdoms were in league with
each other at this time. The freedom of movement between the two kingdoms (as indicated by the travels of Amos and the pilgrims) points to some

such arrangement and supplies more evidence that it was appropriate for Amos to treat the people of Israel as a whole.

37. 7:16 *wĕlōʾ taṭṭîp ʿal-bêt yiśḥāq,* " 'don't preach [anything] against Isaac's domain.' " The reference here is clearly to the northern kingdom, as the parallel clause, just discussed, shows. For the reasons indicated above, the term is restrictive, because the priest Amaziah is concerned only that Amos shall not prophesy in the north or against the north (vv 13 and 16). The usage of the name Isaac here agrees with that in 7:9, and the parallelism with Israel is the same.

38. 7:17 *wĕyiśrāʾēl gālōh yigleh mēʿal ʾadmātô,* " 'and Israel shall surely go into exile from its land.' " The passage is the same as v 11b, already discussed. The reference is to the northern kingdom only, as the context in both verses shows: in v 11, the association is with Jeroboam, and here it is with Amaziah. Nothing could be more restrictive or explicit. The use of the name "Israel," therefore, conforms with the hypothesis and our expectations. By this time our confidence in the hypothesis has increased perceptibly. It may be of interest to note that the northern kingdom alone is targeted for exile in the prophet's immediate horizon. No doubt a comparable fate was in store for Judah also, but the prophet does not discuss it in the preserved prophecies (cf. 5:27, however, for a possible expansion of the certainty of this sort of punishment to include both kingdoms and for references to their common tradition and history).

39. 8:2 *bāʾ haqqēṣ ʾel-ʿammî yiśrāʾēl,* "The end is coming for my people Israel." According to our hypothesis, the usage here, which corresponds exactly to that in 7:8, refers to the entire people and not to Israel alone. Whatever has been said in support of that view earlier also applies here. It is basically a question of the nature and scope of the visions, and of how the message is articulated. No more or less than the others, this vision is not specified for or restricted to Israel; it covers both kingdoms and perhaps others besides, as the great oracle in chaps. 1–2 suggests. But the northern kingdom surely is included, and the first and immediate application of the message is to that region, as the positioning of the story of Amos' visit to Bethel between Visions 3 and 4 shows. Without undermining in any way the specific application of the message to the destiny of the north, we nevertheless maintain that the divine message, like the vision preceding it, was inclusive, reaching beyond that kingdom. So the expression *ʿmy yśrʾl* belongs with the other compounds as designations of combined Israel, the two-nation complex.

40. 8:7 *nišbaʿ yhwh bigʾôn yaʿăqōb,* "Yahweh has sworn by the pride of Jacob." The reference here is general and somewhat vague, though the context (vv 4–6 especially) suggests a link with 2:6–8, in which the transgressions of the northern kingdom in particular are noted. That link would

perhaps imply a similar restriction to the northern kingdom here. The usage indicates otherwise, as our hypothesis implies. Jacob is a synonym for all of Israel, as we have argued in connection with other passages in which the word occurs. Our defense here would be that if indeed the reference to Jacob in this passage involves the crimes described in 8:4–6, that fact in itself does not require the reference be restricted to the northern kingdom. While the crimes of the south may have been different in kind and degree from those of the north, and we do not have an explicit catalog of them from Amos, it would be rash to argue that the malefactions described in 8:4–6 occurred only in Israel and not in Judah. The broader designation here may be intentional, but we must concede that the data are lacking. The situation is similar to what we found in 6:8, where the same expression, g'wn y'qb, occurs. In both cases, there is some slight indication in the context that the reference is to the north. But it is not conclusive, and we will stand by the hypothesis.

41. 9:7 *hălô' kibnê kūšiyyîm 'attem lî běnê yiśrā'ēl,* "Aren't you like Cushites to me, O Israelites?" According to our hypothesis, the reference here is to larger Israel. The context supports this view, for the immediately following clause describes the Exodus from Egypt, part of the tradition common to both Israel and Judah. In the concluding section, the framework is rather vague, but the general outlook as well as the words seem to favor the broader designation.

42. 9:7 *hălô' 'et-yiśrā'ēl he'ĕlêtî mē'ereṣ miṣrayim,* "Didn't I bring Israel up from the land of Egypt?" Here we seem to have the one flat contradiction of the hypothesis, for according to the latter the term "Israel" should refer to the northern kingdom only, while it is apparent that here it designates historical Israel of the Exodus from Egypt. The usage itself is not uncommon in the Bible, but in Amos it runs counter to the hypothesis. We acknowledge this point but look for help or at least an explanation in the usage itself, and suggest that Amos (or the editor) is simply quoting a standard expression, without altering it to suit the special requirements of his book (cf. item 14). To make the usage conform to the hypothetical pattern, the word *byt* or *bny* should have been inserted before *yśr'l*, on which compare the use in 3:1, where *bny yśr'l* is in apposition with the phrase used in the classic restatement of the Exodus theme:

[*'ălêkem běnê yiśrā'ēl*] *'al kol-hammišpāḥâ 'ăšer he'ĕlêtî mē'ereṣ miṣrayim*

[About you, O Israelites], about the whole family that I brought up from the land of Egypt.

In the case above, the prophet was able to use the traditional statement and at the same time identify the group properly in accordance with his scheme: *bny yśr'l* would be proper for the whole group that came out of Egypt, but he also did not have to introduce the compound phrase itself into the statement.

In 2:10, where the same statement is repeated, the 2d m. pl. pronoun is used instead of the word "Israel":

wĕ'ānōkî he'ĕlêtî 'etkem mē'ereṣ miṣrāyim

And as for me, I brought you up from the land of Egypt.

In this case there is no clear antecedent noun, though there is no doubt about the reference. It must be to historical Israel, regularly represented by *byt yśr'l* or *bny yśr'l*. In the context of the passage, which extends from 2:9 through 2:16, the nearest noun to which the pronoun can be attached is *bĕnê yiśrā'ēl* in 2:11. Once again we see how the prophet or editor handled the problem of not disturbing a classic statement and at the same time conforming to an important identification scheme in his book, which would otherwise be violated. Our suspicion is that by the time we near the end of the book the writer did not feel the same sense of obligation to conform to his own pattern and he may have let this one through without resorting to the various circumlocutions available to him. He probably should have used the pronoun in 9:7b instead of the word "Israel," because the antecedent *bny yśr'l* in 7a would have served admirably. But clearly he preferred to keep the name intact in 7b in association with Egypt, to correspond to the two other nations and homelands mentioned in the verse. (Other occurrences of this formulation with *'lh* in the *hip'il* and Israel as object [or a substitute] may be found in the following places: (1) the people identified as "Israel," directly or indirectly, in Exod 32:4, 8 [compare 1 Kgs 12:28, Neh 9:18]; 1 Sam 10:18; Hos 12:14[E13]; 1 Chr 17:5; (2) as *bny yśr'l*, in Josh 24:32; 2 Sam 7:6; Jer 16:14; 23:7; (3) as "fathers," in Josh 24:17; 1 Sam 12:6; Jer 11:7; and (4) with no noun, in Exod 17:3; 32:1, 7, 23; 33:1; Lev 11:45; Num 16:13; 20:5; 21:5; Deut 20:1; Judg 6:8, 13; 1 Sam 8:8; 2 Kgs 17:7, 36; Jer 2:6; Mic 6:4; Ps 81:11[E10].)

Elsewhere in the Bible we find the statement with *bny yśr'l* along with *yśr'l* alone, so there was nothing to prevent the prophet or editor from using the compound expression in 9:7 (for *bny yśr'l* cf. Jer 16:14, 23:7; Josh 24:32 and 2 Sam 7:6; for Israel alone cf. 1 Sam 10:18 and 1 Chr 17:5; in many other cases the appropriate pronoun was used). The usage in 9:7 remains anomalous, though the reference is entirely clear. Israel here refers to historic Israel of the Exodus.

This verse has to be interpreted and understood in the light of the oracles in chaps. 1–2. As we have shown elsewhere, the reference here to Israel, Philistines, and Aram is directly related to the oracles against those nations in chaps. 1–2 and provides the basic rationale for the judgment pronounced against them, namely, that they owe their existence to the gracious intervention of Yahweh in bringing them out of one place and settling them in another, their current homeland. Of the three, the story of Israel is the only one known to us in detail, but the opening words of 9:7, comparing the *bny yśr'l* to the *bny kšyym,* make it clear that the three deliverances and settlements are to be seen as equivalent actions on the part of Yahweh. What is especially intriguing about the structure of the elements in chaps. 1–2 (in particular 1:3–5 on Aram, 1:6–8 on the Philistines, and 2:6–16 on Israel) and 9:7 is that they are arranged chiastically (i.e., in reverse order). Israel, though last in chaps. 1–2, is first here; the Philistines are second both here and in the opening; while Aram is last here and first there. It is clear that not only are the two sections tightly bonded, but the arrangement is entirely deliberate. We note additionally that the whole section 9:7–15 is linked with other elements in the opening unit to form an envelope around the whole work (e.g., cf. Amos 1:2 and 9:13 with Joel 4:16–18[E3:16–18]). In view of this structure it is not surprising to find the same terms used for Israel in 9:7 that we find in the section on Israel in 2:6–16. In 2:6 we have *yśr'l* alone, a clear reference to the northern kingdom, comparable to the corresponding references to Aram and the Philistines. Then in 2:11, in association with the particular statement about the Exodus from Egypt (vv 10–11) we have the term *bny yśr'l.* In 9:7, however, the order is reversed, with *bny yśr'l* first in 9:7a, and *yśr'l* alone second in v 7b. It is clear that the artistic requirements of the great chiasm have dictated both the selection and the order of the terms in 9:7.

Furthermore, because of the association with chaps. 1–2, it was essential that both terms be used, Israel identifying the northern kingdom and *bny yśr'l* identifying the groups coming out of Egypt in chaps. 1–2; the second time around the terms are reversed but the sense is the same. Both groups are involved. (The point is that in the list in chaps. 1–2, Aram and the Philistines are associated with Israel, the northern kingdom, while the group in the Exodus is identified as *bny yśr'l;* the author had to use the same terms in his résumé in chap. 9 in reverse order, and the pattern was also reversed, bringing Israel into the Exodus and *bny yśr'l* into the current scene.) It may be, therefore, that the designations *bny yśr'l* and *yśr'l* alone have been reversed deliberately in this passage on account of the chiastic structure of the book, and in apparent contradiction of the basic pattern.

43. 9:8 *'epes kî lō' hašmêd 'ašmîd 'et-bêt ya'ăqōb,* "Nevertheless, I shall not utterly destroy the house of Jacob." According to our hypothesis, the reference here must be to the double kingdom, and there is nothing in the statement to contravene that position. The problem with the verse, how-

ever, is the apparent contradiction between 8a and 8b, because in the former it is stated by Yahweh that his eyes are on the sinful kingdom, and "I shall destroy it from the surface of the earth." If the sinful kingdom is the same as the house of Jacob in 8b, then there is a rather blatant contradiction, because in the former the sinful kingdom will be destroyed, and in the latter the house of Jacob will not be utterly destroyed. The usual scholarly view is that 8b is a corrective of 8a offered by a later editor, but it is hard to imagine such a procedure on the part of any editor, leaving a contradiction like that for the reader to cope with. In this case it is possible that our scheme may be of value. The nearest antecedent for the sinful kingdom is the unfortunate *yiśrā'ēl* in v 7, which shows that the sinful kingdom is Israel, the northern nation; that fact may help to explain the anomalous usage in 9:7 (already discussed). Because the identity of the sinful kingdom is now clear, the contradiction may be more apparent than real. Taking the sentence as a whole, we argue that the meaning is that Yahweh will destroy the sinful kingdom (Israel) but will not utterly destroy the house of Jacob (the larger unity comprising both kingdoms). Or to translate, we get the following:

> Indeed, the eyes of my Lord Yahweh are upon [against] the sinful kingdom;
> I shall destroy it from the surface of the earth.
> Nevertheless, I shall not utterly destroy the house of Jacob—
> Oracle of Yahweh!

Further discussion of this problem will be found in the NOTES.

44. 9:9 *wahănî'ôtî bĕkol-haggôyīm 'et-bêt yiśrā'ēl,* "I will shake the house of Israel among all the nations." As with the preceding designation, this one refers to the larger entity, the double kingdom. It is appropriate in the context, which is general and not geographically specific. At the conclusion of the book, the language is more and more universal and eschatological and properly, therefore, focuses attention on all of Israel, classical and to come. The incidental reference to *'ammî* ("my people"), v 10, brings to mind the expression *'my yśr'l* ("my people Israel"), which has already been associated with the same larger group. So the usage in the unit, vv 9–10, is consistent.

45. 9:14 *wĕšabtî 'et-šĕbût 'ammî yiśrā'ēl,* "Then I will restore the fortunes of Israel my people." According to our hypothesis, the term refers to Israel as a whole, and here we have an eschatological context for the future restored Israel, comparable to classic Israel, which came out of Egypt, or the united kingdom of David and Solomon. There is no reason to limit the reference to the northern kingdom in its historical existence. Here

it is present as part of a future restored commonwealth. The usage here conforms with and confirms our hypothesis.

Evaluation of the Hypothesis

The next step in this exercise is to evaluate the findings in terms of the degree to which each example supports or undermines the basic hypothesis, then to arrive at some conclusion as to its probability or validity. We will do so for all forty-five entries, making evaluations for each name before consolidating the results. We will then summarize all of the results in tabular form. To keep matters as simple as possible we have devised five categories in which to classify the results:

1. complete agreement or support of the hypothesis;
2. probable or likely support;
3. neutral: does not lean either way—no support, no hindrance;
4. improbable or unlikely; difficulties with the hypothesis;
5. contradiction of the hypothesis: most unlikely or impossible.

The basic hypothesis is that the term "Israel" when used alone refers to the northern kingdom only, just as Judah (which is always used alone in Amos) routinely refers to the southern kingdom. All other examples of Israel (with qualifiers) refer to an older or larger Israel, including the northern kingdom but not restricted to it. Of the other terms, Jacob refers to the larger entity, while Joseph and Isaac refer to the northern kingdom.

There is no need to repeat any of the preceding arguments when the identification is certain or virtually so. We will add a few summary comments only where the identification is problematic and the choice of a grade of certainty is debatable.

The occurrences of Israel and modifications in Amos, with confidence ratings:

	yśr'l	bny yśr'l	byt yśr'l	btwlt yśr'l	'my yśr'l
1 (1:1)	3				
3 (1:1)	1				
6 (2:6)	1				
7 (2:11)		2			
8 (3:1)		2	2		
9 (3:12)		2			
11 (3:14)	1				
12 (4:5)		3			
13 (4:12)	3				
14 (4:12)	3				

	yśr'l	bny yśr'l	byt yśr'l	btwlt yśr'l	'my yśr'l
15 (5:1)			3		
16 (5:2)				3	
17 (5:3)			2		
18 (5:4)			2		
21 (5:25)			2		
22 (6:1)			2		
25 (6:14)			3		
28 (7:8)					2
30 (7:9)	1				
31 (7:10)	1				
32 (7:10)			2		
33 (7:11)	1				
35 (7:15)					2
36 (7:16)	1				
38 (7:17)	1				
39 (8:2)					2
41 (9:7)		2			
42 (9:7)	4				
44 (9:9)			2		
45 (9:14)					2

Other names used in Amos with confidence ratings:

	yhwdh	y'qb	ywsp	yśḥq
2 (1:1)	1			
4 (2:4)	1			
5 (2:5)	1			
10 (3:13)		3		
19 (5:6)			1	
20 (5:15)			2	
23 (6:6)			2	
24 (6:8)		4		
26 (7:2)		2		
27 (7:5)		2		
29 (7:9)				1
34 (7:12)	1			
37 (7:16)				1
40 (8:7)		3		
43 (9:8)		2		

1. The evidence is generally in favor of the hypothesis, but the reference would also make sense if here Israel extends beyond the border of the

northern kingdom to include Judah, for the two kingdoms are immediately listed, and both are dealt with in the following oracles. Furthermore, if the book as a whole is in general about the entire people, it would be appropriate for the title to refer to greater Israel. Because the point cannot be decided either way, we give it a neutral rating.

7. The context strongly implies the descendants of the Israel of the Exodus but does not entirely rule out the possibility that only the northern kingdom is meant.

8. The association with the Exodus group is certain, but the exact identity of the current *bny yśr'l* is slightly uncertain, hence a 2 rating. The same judgment would hold if we were to adopt the variant reading *byt yśr'l*.

9. Even if the address was made to northerners, the expression itself almost certainly designates the larger group.

10. It is not clear whether the larger or smaller group is being addressed here.

12. The link with Bethel suggests that here northerners might be addressed exclusively, but Judeans could be included (or at least not excluded), and some could actually have been present.

13, 14. If these items depart from the prevailing pattern, it could be because the language is traditional.

15, 16, 17, 18, 21, 22. On the face of it, all of these references to *byt yśr'l* in chaps. 5–6 can be interpreted either way—either the northern kingdom, as commonly held, or the entire people (our hypothesis). The consistent usage in this part of the book suggests that they all be given the same rating. In our opinion, the reference to Beer-sheba in 5:5 tips item 18 in favor of the hypothesis, and the context of item 21 is even more unequivocal. Some doubt attaches to item 22 because of uncertainty over the syntax. If we could be sure of the integration of 6:1b with 6:1a, where both Zion and Samaria are mentioned, there would be no doubt that *byt yśr'l* in v 1b refers to the whole nation.

24. It is the most perplexing feature of the system that Jacob is evidently used for the whole nation while Isaac refers only to the north. This circumstance induces doubt in the present instance; hence we rate this instance as telling against the hypothesis.

25. In this case the context itself is in need of determination. The geographical frame is relatively wide, but we also need to know the political situation in order to decide whether the southern boundary simply reflects northern expansion at this time, or whether it takes us into the Judean sphere of influence. We cautiously give it a neutral rating.

26, 27. In addition to the intrinsic likelihood that the name "Jacob" here retains associations with old tradition and refers to all of his descendants, the universal perspective of the other visions favors a wide application. This interpretation must be offset, however, by the fact that "Isaac" seems to refer to the northern kingdom later in the chapter.

28, 35, 39, 45. The traditional associations of this term slightly favor a national rather than a regional reference.

42. This one seems to be in direct conflict with the hypothesis; but, as in other cases, it is possible that the prophet is singling out the smaller group for special attention (cf. 9:8).

44. This one is neutral, with a slight inclination toward the hypothesis.

SUMMARY OF RATINGS

		Israel	Others	Total
Certain	(1)	8	7	15
Probable	(2)	14	5	19
Neutral	(3)	7	2	9
Improbable	(4)	1	1	2
Impossible	(5)	0	0	0
		30	15	45

It is necessary to break down these ratings and examine the status of each entry and each column to test the hypothesis, but in general we can say there is more evidence in support of it than against it. According to our numbers, in thirty-four cases the evidence is in favor of the hypothesis, while the evidence seems to be against it in two cases; the remaining nine are neutral. Put another way, only two instances out of forty-five seem generally in conflict with the hypothesis; and, as we suggest in the NOTES, practically all can be explained or explained away in one way or another. We have found none that is in absolute contradiction to the hypothesis, though one (yśr'l in 9:7) comes close. If we vote the neutrals with those favorable we can say that the hypothesis accounts adequately for the phenomena, always remembering that the basic assumption is that if different terms are used, it is reasonable to suppose that they have different meanings. If we examine the individual expressions, we find varying degrees of certainty or probability, and some elements in the hypothesis and the argument seem stronger than others; in fact, some of the identifications seem to ride with the others and are specified chiefly in light of the others. It should be added that the individual evaluations were restricted in the first place to specific data available for each item, not on the basis of or in view of the system as a whole. The evaluations should therefore be regarded as minimal, and the case overall may well be stronger than the summation of the individual cases.

When we look at the names other than Israel and consider their occurrences separately, we find the following:

Judah: 4 certain occurrences
Isaac: 2 certain
Joseph: 1 certain, 2 probable
Jacob: 3 probable, 2 neutral, 1 improbable

There was never any doubt about Judah, and it was only included as a reference point. Certainty on this score also established certainty in a number of cases in which Israel is mentioned. The same is true of Isaac, because in the two cases it occurs it is parallel to and defined by equally certain examples of Israel. There is really no question about Joseph either, chiefly because the historical use of the name limits it to a certain group, and there is nothing in the material that runs counter to the normal interpretation. For these three names there is virtual certainty, and certainly no dispute about what each specifies or designates.

The case is somewhat different for Jacob. There are no truly compelling cases, and the most probable instance (9:8) is fraught with problems, chiefly because of the apparent contradiction between v 8a and v 8b, which throws the whole verse into doubt. In two instances (7:2, 5) there is some evidence in support of the hypothesis, while in two others (6:8 and 8:7) the context implies a contrary position. In the remaining case we find nothing better than a neutral or median position. Why stick with the hypothesis? Reversing it might help a little, but mostly we are in a state of uncertainty. Because the usage and distribution of Jacob are similar to those of Israel, it may be that we should examine more closely the forms and combinations used: *y'qb* alone in 7:2 and 7:5, where our interpretation of the use in those visions has been influenced by our overall view of the visions and the use of *'ammî yiśrā'ēl* in Visions 3 and 4. Presumably Jacob in these places has the same force as *'my yśr'l* in the others. While certainty is hard to reach with regard to the second set, the view we have taken is consistent with the evidence and the hypothesis that all of Israel is meant.

There are two instances of *byt y'qb,* in 3:13 and in 9:8. Here the identification according to the hypothesis seems stronger, and the correlation with the use of *byt yśr'l* would support the analysis.

Last, there are two instances of the phrase *g'wn y'qb* (6:8, 8:7). It is not clear whether the qualifier differentiates this pair from the others belonging to the same category (*y'qb*), but these instances pose the greatest difficulty in identification. In both cases the contexts seem to point to the northern kingdom rather than to the composite, but it is hard to reach certainty in the matter.

When we look at Israel and its combinations, we find the following picture.

1. Israel. The name occurs alone twelve times. Of these occurrences, the identification is certain in eight cases, neutral in three, and improbable in

one (9:7). The high probability of the view that Israel stands for the northern kingdom only is at the center of the whole hypothesis, and it seems to be strongly supported in most cases and not contravened in the others, with one possible but significant exception.

2. None of the other cases in which "Israel" is modified seems nearly as certain, though there are very few instances that run counter to the hypothesis.

First, the *bny yśr'l* group seems to offer general support for the hypothesis, for out of five instances in the MT (four in the LXX, which reads *byt* instead of *bny* at 3:1) four are rated probable, or leaning toward the hypothesis, and only one (4:5) poses a problem; even the last is rated neutral. Our conclusion is that *bny yśr'l* is used in a different way from *yśr'l* in the book of Amos.

Second, the case of *byt yśr'l* seems less strong, though the argument from analogy with *bny yśr'l* can be pressed, as the terms seem to be equivalent and interchangeable. In other words, if *bny yśr'l* is used differently from *yśr'l* then *byt yśr'l* should go with *bny yśr'l* rather than the other way, or its own way. Of the eight attested instances in the MT (nine in the LXX; see 3:1) we rate six (or seven) as probable and another two as neutral. One (6:14) is especially difficult, and on the face of it seems to run in the opposite direction. We have drawn attention to possible extenuating circumstances, but we rate the case as neutral, perhaps improbable. On balance the picture is not as bright as that for *bny yśr'l*, but it is certainly not dark either. We think the evidence favors the hypothetical distinction between *yśr'l* and *byt yśr'l*, but not one between *bny yśr'l* and *byt yśr'l*.

Third, the phrase *btwlt yśr'l* occurs only once (5:2) and can be folded into the much larger group of *byt yśr'l*, which dominates chap. 5. There is good reason to believe that whatever decision is reached about *byt yśr'l* will apply as well to *btwlt yśr'l*. It received a neutral rating, which is appropriate.

Finally, the remaining expression, *'my yśr'l*, occurs four times, but in none of the instances is there evidence that compels or even inclines toward a decision. Two of the instances are in the visions, and the same decision should be made about *'my yśr'l* in the third and fourth visions as about *y'qb* in the first and second. The other passages containing the expression can be interpreted either way, with the former (7:15) leaning away from the hypothesis slightly and the latter (9:14) leaning toward it. Perhaps a decision here cannot easily be reached, but we can point out that there is no significant obstacle to the hypothesis in any of the readings.

It is important to make a distinction between the people addressed and the people spoken about. Thus 6:1 is aimed at people in both Samaria and Zion, but could not have been addressed immediately to both at once. Indeed, the words might never have been spoken in either capital, or they could have been repeated in many places. It is not likely that Amos ever addressed an official national assembly of representatives of both kingdoms, a group that could be regarded as embracing the whole people. The nearest thing to that would have been the crowds at the major shrines during the great festivals, which drew pilgrims from all over, in spite of the rival and exclusive claims that might have been advanced for political purposes on behalf of Jerusalem and Bethel. Yet even if the composition of such assemblies were almost entirely local, it would still be appropriate to address any group of Israelites as Israelites, and not as citizens of either kingdom.

It is only by hindsight that we think that no reference to "Israel" (with or without qualifiers) includes Judah, because we know that while Israel was destroyed, Judah survived at least for a time. Amos did not know it. Whenever he mentions the two explicitly, they are on the same footing (2:4–8; 6:1). To conclude otherwise, we need to have a contrast that is explicitly made, an exclusion of Judah from the threat. No such point is made anywhere in Amos. On the contrary, whenever Judah (or Zion) is mentioned, it has the same status as Israel (or Samaria). Hence it is likely that references to the nation of Israel (as distinct from the state of that name) include Judah along with the north.

In conclusion, when we exclude the obvious and certain cases of such names as Judah, Joseph, Isaac, and Israel alone, the rest of the expressions, including the nouns compounded with Israel and the group associated with Jacob, seem less certain. That circumstance does not upset the theory but suggests further investigation, and the possibility of some changes and refinements to make the picture more focused.

The Distribution of the Names

Some observations are in order about the distribution of these names in the book of Amos:

For a variety of reasons we divide the book of Amos into the following major units:

		Words	
I. Chaps. 1–4			General and specific indictments
	A. Chaps. 1–2	426	
	B. Chaps. 3–4	422	
		848	
II. Chaps. 5–6		498	Woes
III. Chaps. 7–9:6		547	Visions
IV. Chap. 9:7–15		149	Concluding oracles
		2,042	

In the following tables we will show the distribution for Israel alone and in its various combinations, and of the other names in our group.

| | ISRAEL | | | | | OTHER | | | |
MT	0*	bny	byt (btwlt)	'my	Total	Jacob	Judah	Joseph	Isaac	Total
I.	6	4	0	0	10	1	3	0	0	4
II.	0	0	6 + 1	0	7	1	0	3	0	4
III.	5	0	1	3	9	3	1	0	2	6
IV.	1	1	1	1	4	1	0	0	0	1
	12	5	9	4	30	6	4	3	2	15

* "0," here and in subsequent tables, means "Israel" alone without a qualifier.

| | ISRAEL | | | | | OTHER | | | |
LXX	0	bny	byt (btwlt)	'my	Total	Jacob	Judah	Joseph	Isaac	Total
I.	6	3	1	0	10	1	3	0	0	4
II.	0	0	6 + 1	0	7	1	0	3	0	4
III.	5	0	1	3	9	3	1	0	2	6
IV.	1	1	1	1	4	1	0	0	0	1
	12	4	10	4	30	6	4	3	2	15

Looking first at the chart for Israel, we note that the name in general is distributed widely and rather evenly through the four sections, which themselves are quite uneven in length. The distribution of each variety, however, is highly restricted, so that each unit is dominated by one or at most two forms, while the others are sparse or missing. Thus we find that the use of Israel by itself (the northern kingdom) is restricted to Parts I (6) and III (5), while it does not occur at all in Part II (0). It occurs once in Part IV. Similarly, the form with bny (yśr'l) occurs only in Part I (four in the MT or three in the LXX) and, as with the others, once in Part IV. By contrast, the form byt (yśr'l) is predominant in Part II, occurring six times plus once for btwlt (yśr'l), which we regard essentially as a variant of byt in this chapter. Note that there are seven occurrences of the paired expression, the construct chain byt yśr'l, with one marked exception, btwlt yśr'l, with apparently the same meaning or scope: another example of the imperfect or incomplete pattern of seven that we have noted elsewhere, most strikingly in the case of the expression wĕšillaḥtî 'ēš, which occurs or should occur seven times in chaps. 1–2, as part of the oracles against the first seven nations listed. Only one of them is different, the fifth in 1:14, which reads wĕhiṣṣattî 'ēš, with the same meaning, as far as can be determined. Of course, *btwlt yśr'l* has a different meaning from *byt yśr'l,* and the imagery in 5:2 is quite different from that used elsewhere in the chapter; but the former expression describes or designates the same political entity, whether that be the northern kingdom by itself or the corporate nation. We have marked all of the occurrences in chaps. 5–6 with probabilities ranging from likely to neutral, with the majority as likely and with neutral for the exceptional cases. But the probability is that all should be interpreted in the same way, whether more or less likely when considered separately.

This form (*byt yśr'l*) occurs once in Parts III and IV, and either not at all (MT) or once (LXX) in Part I (at 3:1). We think that the distribution was probably symmetrical in the original form of the book and hence believe that the reading in the LXX (at 3:1) may be more original than that in the MT. We should note that the LXX version is supported by at least one important Hebrew manuscript, though the evidence is too slight to be decisive. Still, it is interesting that 3:1 is apparently the only place in which the shift between *bny* and *byt* is reflected in the surviving texts of Amos. It does occur in other books.

Finally, when it comes to the last compound phrase, *'ammî yiśrā'ēl,* we find this form only in Parts III (3) and IV (1), not at all in Parts I and II.

To summarize, the distribution of the name "Israel" in its several patterns is remarkably selective and symmetrical, showing the following features.

1. Parts I and III have corresponding reciprocal structures (following the LXX) with almost equal total numbers (10 for Part I and 9 for Part III). The dominant form is *yśr'l* alone (6 in Part I and 5 in Part III), and each has the form *byt yśr'l* once. Three occurrences of *bny yśr'l* in Part I are matched by 3 occurrences of *'my yśr'l* in Part III. The patterns may be shown as follows:

LXX	0	*bny*	*byt*	*'my*	Total
I.	6	3	1	0	10
III.	5	0	1	3	9

2. Part II is radically different. There are no occurrences of the forms that dominate Parts I and III: *yśr'l* alone is not used, but neither are the compound forms *bny yśr'l* and *'my yśr'l.* The form *byt yśr'l* is used exclusively (6 times), with one apparently deliberate variation, *btwlt yśr'l* (which is used nowhere else in Amos), making a total of 7.

3. Part IV (the concluding unit of the book) has the unique distinction of having a single example of each of the forms, *yśr'l* alone and *yśr'l* with *bny, byt,* and *'my.* Whether by choice or chance, the distribution in this last unit serves as summation for the whole book.

If we now look at the chart of the other names, we note a similar trend of selectivity and at least partial symmetry, so that each of the names is concentrated in a different unit and is either absent or nearly so from the others. Thus Judah is concentrated in Part I (3 times, in apposition with Israel [2]), and occurs only once more (Part III); Joseph occurs 3 times, all in Part II; Isaac occurs 2 times, both in Part III. Only Jacob occurs in all parts, but it is concentrated in Part III (3 times) and once each in the others. It is the only one that appears in Part IV.

Another interesting feature of the Jacob group is its distribution, which is precisely chiastic throughout the book.

JACOB

I.	byt yʿqb	(3:13)
II.	gʾwn yʿqb	(6:8)
III.	yʿqb	(7:2)
	yʿqb	(7:5)
	gʾwn yʿqb	(8:7)
IV.	byt yʿqb	(9:8)

In comparing the two tables, we note some other correspondences. There is a curious symmetrical correspondence between forms with byt in both lists. As observed, byt yśrʾl occurs in every part of the book (following the LXX), the only form with Israel to do so; correspondingly, in the second list there is also a single form with byt in each part. In Parts I, III, and IV the correlation is 1 to 1, but in Part II the matchup is 6 to 1, thus producing the seven occurrences of byt in this section (the missing byt yśrʾl was replaced by btwlt yśrʾl in 5:2). The correspondence may be seen as follows:

	Israel	Other
I.	byt yśrʾl (1)	byt yʿqb (1)
II.	byt yśrʾl (6)	byt ywsp (1)
III.	byt yśrʾl (1)	byt yśḥq (1)
IV.	byt yśrʾl (1)	byt yʿqb (1)

In conclusion, we suggest that the selection and arrangement of the names for Israel and its variants, including related terms, were deliberate and carefully and artistically disposed by the author/editor. We have noted a number of distinctions among the terms and other features in their distribution. Doubtless others will be located and identified in the course of further investigation.

Our study has attempted to establish the referents of Amos' geopolitical terminology in terms of contextual evidence within the book itself. It is possible that some of the usage is peculiar to the prophet himself, as is clearly the case with his unparalleled use of Isaac with a deviant spelling; or it could reflect contemporary but transient usage. Note, for instance, that he does not use Ephraim, a political term that became prominent shortly after his time, as usage in Isaiah and Hosea shows. At the same time, we might expect Amos' language to match general and traditional terminology.

The next most important point in our hypothesis is that "Israel" alone means the northern kingdom, but it refers to the whole people when modified. This distribution holds, for the most part, in the historical books. In Samuel and Kings, "Israel" usually means the northern kingdom, not only after the disruption but also under David and Solomon, when it describes the northern portion of their dual realm. The term *bny yśr'l* is not at all common. The majority of cases refers to the early nation, especially during the Exodus (1 Sam 10:18; 15:6; 2 Sam 7:6, 7; 1 Kgs 6:1; 8:9; 11:2; 14:24; 21:26; 2 Kgs 16:3; 21:2, 9) or the tribes (1 Sam 2:28) or the whole people contrasted with the Philistines (1 Sam 7:4, 6, 7, 7, 8; 17:53).

It quite probably refers to the entire nation in 1 Kgs 6:13; 8:63; 9:21; 19:10, 14; but there is a significant set of exceptions in which *bny yśr'l* refers to the northerners exclusively. This reference is certain in 1 Sam 11:8, where it contrasts with *'īš-yĕhûdâ;* but only in that instance does the usage of the books of Samuel differ from our hypothesis for Amos. It is different in Kings: there *bny yśr'l* refers to northerners (1 Kgs 12:24; 18:20; 20:15, 27, 27, 29; 2 Kgs 13:5). The usage in 2 Kgs 17 (vv 7, 8, 9, 22, 24) is Deuteronomistic, theological rather than political; and in this mode it can even refer to southerners (2 Kgs 18:4). We can accordingly maintain that *bny yśr'l* could be used for any or all Israelites. Even when used for northerners, it regards them as members of the larger entity, especially when reflective interpretations and editorial comments are being made.

The expression "all of Israel" would seem to be the clearest way of indicating that the whole people (twelve tribes or two nations) is intended. Even so, it is sometimes used for the northern kingdom as distinct from Judah, and later for the community as it existed after the Exile. "All of Israel" is used almost exclusively by the editors of historical books: sixty-five times in the Primary History (only once before Deuteronomy, so it is clearly Deuteronomic); forty-one times by the Chronicler. The Chronicler is dependent on the Deuteronomist for his usage, and there are only two occurrences outside these two historical corpora (Mal 3:22[E4:4]; Dan 9:11), both of them late and derivative, and linked to Moses.

Apart from Malachi, none of the prophets ever refers to the whole nation as "all of Israel," even though they often have the entire people in their sights. They prefer to use "house of Israel," especially Ezekiel, who accounts for more than half of the total occurrences of this expression (85 out of 148). The table that follows shows a clear complementary distribution.

The prophets account for 126 of the occurrences of "house of Israel"; and, apart from Zech 8:13 (where "house of Israel" is coordinated with "house of Judah"), the phrase is restricted to the four eighth-century prophets, Jeremiah, and Ezekiel (who does not use the name "Judah" very much). Deuteronomic usage ("all of Israel") has not intruded into the prophetic writings; neither has prophetic usage ("house of Israel") influenced the Chronicler. Our claim that Amos means "all of Israel" and not just the northern kingdom by "house of Israel" is fully supported by the larger picture of biblical usage:

	"All of Israel"	*"House of Israel"*
Genesis–Numbers	1	8
Deuteronomy	8	0
Joshua–Kings	56	10
Prophets	1	126
Chronicles–Ezra–Nehemiah	41	0
Other writings	1	4
Total	108	148

Israel rather than Judah is more commonly the apparent object of the prophet's charges, even when they are of a sufficiently general nature to be equally applicable to both parts of the divided nation. To put it another way, if the crimes and corruptions charged against Israel (Samaria) warrant the punishments attached, then there are no grounds for exempting Judah (Jerusalem). Judah is never exonerated. The argument that Amos, coming from the south, was more severe on the north and played down Judah's culpability out of patriotic sentiment or prejudice cannot withstand even casual scrutiny. His apparent silence about Judah in passages when he is speaking directly about Israel does not mean that he somehow implies that Judah was better, or even different. That argument can only be sustained by deleting the oracle against Judah (2:4–5) and the references to Judah or Jerusalem in a few other places. Such circular reasoning can only convince the converted and cannot be defended as serious scholarship. The surviving book of Amos shows that Judah is in the picture, and, when Judah is mentioned, it is on the same footing as Israel.

So the question is, why is Judah not mentioned more often in conjunction with Israel? The basic answer is that the northern kingdom is the primary target of Amos' message, but that Judah is also in the prophet's thoughts. In the many instances that reference is made to the "house of Israel" or "the Israelites," both nations are included and both are intended as the objects of criticism and condemnation.

It is a mistaken theory that Amos, in chaps. 1–2, is only interested in

Israel, the last of the eight nations, and that his long analysis of the crimes of every state in the region is just a rhetorical buildup, a feint to put Israel off guard before delivering the knockout punch, a trick to secure their moral consent to the verdicts on all of the neighbors before surprising them by adding their name to the list, on the analogy of Nathan's parable to David (2 Sam 12:1–15).

Amos is even-handed, but he does not give each of the eight nations equal time; neither does he give Judah and Israel equal time. Already in the Great Set Speech (chaps. 1–2) Israel is dealt with at more length than any of the others. That the house of Israel (both states) receives more attention than the other six nations is sufficiently explained by 3:2—greater privilege, greater punishment. But this circumstance does not mean that the others will not be punished at all. All will be punished alike.

Concentration on Samaria and Israel rather than on Jerusalem and Judah may reflect the political realities at the time. Address to "the Israelites" was not just a reminder of an ancient unity and common origin, now betokened by no more than memories, or at most by the shared religious belief that Yahweh was still the God of all the Israelites. It recognized a newly recovered, if transient, sense of national identity and unity. Since the disruption after Solomon's death, Israel and Judah oscillated between two relationships—hostility, often warring against each other (1 Kgs 14:30; 15:16; 2 Kgs 14:12; Isaiah 7), or alliance, sometimes joining forces against neighboring enemies (1 Kings 22; 2 Kings 3). The long and overlapping reigns of Jeroboam II and Uzziah (Azariah) represented a period of conciliation, if not close cooperation, in which each nation was free to renew the bid to recover old lost territory. Both were successful (2 Kgs 15:25; 2 Chr 26:5–15), each aided and abetted by a prophet (Jonah in one case, Zechariah in the other). The most likely political scenario is that each recognized the other's sphere; but joint activity is also a possibility, at least where they had common cause. The language of Amos 6 points to a period of such cooperation, their joint achievements ranging from Hamath (Israel's conquest) to Gath (Judah's conquest). While a treaty of nonaggression would have been enough to allow such moves, a closer alliance is equally possible. Most likely, it would have been under the leadership of Samaria. Samaria, not Jerusalem, attracted the main interest of the Assyrians in the region. Judah was the minor partner, the lesser entity, at least while Israel was strong and independent. It was, therefore, sufficient for Amos to talk about the kingdom of Israel (Samaria) much of the time, with Judah always in mind even if not always in view. As we have repeatedly seen and said, Amos' use of the distinct terminology "Israelites" and "house of Israel" recognizes the existence of one people in two nations.

We can infer further that the alliance between the two parts of divided Israel was at its strongest in the first phase of Amos' ministry (chaps. 5–6), when such terminology dominates his speech. By the time we move to the second phase (chaps. 1–4), it has become more appropriate to address Israel and Judah separately.

THE TEXT OF THE BOOK OF AMOS

We concede at the outset that our point of departure is the Masoretic Text of the book of Amos. We have studied other versions of Amos, including the Septuagint, the Peshitta, the Vulgate, and the Targum, as well as the materials from Qumran and other ancient caves, and we have cited and discussed alternate readings when these had some plausibility and interest. We have also tried to deal seriously and constructively with the numerous emendations and improvements in the Hebrew text proposed by colleagues and predecessors. Time, reflection, and reconsideration have eroded the appeal and value of many of the latter, while the few that have survived and warrant discussion and evaluation are dealt with in the course of the COMMENTS. For the most part, however, we find no serious alternative to the Masoretic Text, and with the few exceptions noted have clung firmly to the MT, difficult and problematic as it may be in numerous places.

We have not been overly sympathetic with efforts to remake the text in the interests of different theories about its evolution over the centuries, not because we believe that the text has come to us directly from the hands of Amos and his disciples or that it has been miraculously preserved from error (although its transmission is remarkable in many ways and for many reasons), but because we remain unconvinced by the results of numerous scholarly undertakings. We admire both the courage and the creative energy of those who have devoted much time and strenuous effort to the quest for the earlier stages in the composition and copying of the book of Amos and to the recovery and reconstruction of the pristine original; but we have concentrated our own efforts on the final product, chiefly because with minor variations that is what we have and that inevitably and invariably is where we must all begin. Where we end is another matter.

Every reader, ancient and modern alike, would prefer a clear text to an obscure one, and the temptation to "write your own" is understandable. Translation is interpretation, and it is no wonder that the LXX, Peshitta, Targum, and so on are more intelligible than the MT in many places. It is also suspicious that they present fewer unintelligible or difficult readings than the MT. It is precisely where such differences exist that we can see the fulfillment of the translator's desire to give his readers something that they can understand. He has a liberty not enjoyed by a person whose job it is simply to make a copy of the MT.

Yet even the latter may find himself under a similar constraint. He may find it intolerable to reproduce a text that does not make sense. He might even persuade himself that "Amos would never have said a thing like that" and that Amos said (or wrote) something else. It is, accordingly, quite possible that the "better" reading attested in one or more of the versions already existed in a Hebrew manuscript that came into the hands of those translating into Greek, or Aramaic, or Syriac. We even have textual evidence for it sometimes, though it is rare. 5Q Amos 1:3 refers to "pregnant women," just as the LXX does. The interpretive character of the LXX in 1:3 compared with the MT is transparent; it has explained a unique and obscure statement by using one that is familiar and clear. But it is doubtful if "threshing Gilead with iron sledges" means "ripping up pregnant women." And it is even more doubtful that any early—let alone the original—text of Amos 1:3 read in this way.

The study of the MT as it stands is a straightforward and intrinsically legitimate activity. If more justification is needed, then the MT is self-vindicating to the extent that it can be shown to make sense. Sometimes it is not possible to do so. There are instances in which the MT resists all attempts to understand it, or at least it presents a number of possibilities, none of which carries the day and all of which contain unsolved problems. What to do? We must emphasize that the student is not obliged to achieve intelligibility at all costs and by whatever means. Farfetched and even ridiculous vindications of the MT are self-destructive. The fault may be in the text, and it may be ineluctable. The assumption that the original text must have been immaculate and lucid is far from obvious. For all we know, the text that now baffles us might always have been that way. The fault could be with the author, who went too far in being enigmatic or who did not realize that an idea, clear to him, would not come across in the language he selected. Or the fault could lie in ourselves. We simply do not know what the word means. We have to guess. Already in antiquity readers had to do so. The most common procedure, then as now, was to help out the analysis of an obscure passage with the assistance of knowledge gained from somewhere else. The rare or unique was replaced by the familiar. We have illustrated this tendency by the movement of Amos 1:3 into the well-known atrocity of mutilating pregnant women.

Study Amos 5:25–27 with the LXX or with Acts 7:42–43, and we see it happening under our eyes. We know all about exile to Babylon; we do not understand exile "beyond Damascus." The LXX retained the latter; Stephen (or his source) supplies an obvious explanation by substituting Babylon for Damascus. But "beyond Babylon," while still in touch with the MT, is still unclear, and it received the further gloss *epi ta merē Babylōnos* (Bruce 1951:174). We do not know any gods called Sikkût or Kiyyûn, and the phrase "the star of your god(s)" is unmanageable by our usual understanding of Hebrew grammar. The MT vocalization itself is suspicious; the words seem to have been rhymed with *šiqqûṣ*. One must reckon with the possibility that a text of this kind was always accompanied not only by knowledge of how to *pronounce* the words, knowledge that existed and survived quite well in oral tradition, but in addition by concomitant knowledge of the *meaning* of the words. In the case of Amos 5:25–27 there was an understanding that the reference was to Saturn worship. The LXX's *kai anelabete* also shows an appreciation of the fact that Amos 5:26a is a continuation of the history of v 25, not part of the prophecy of v 27. The phrase "the star of your god(s)," for all its obscurity, shows that an astral deity or deities are intended, and the Greek preserves *ton astron tou theou* (but omits the possessive pronoun). The knowledge that the god is the planet Saturn has been recovered only in modern times. Behind the Hebrew words are *sakkut* and *kaiwanu,* Babylonian and Assyrian equivalents of Sumerian NINIB, Saturn. This knowledge was apparently still current in late pre-Christian times, but it came out in garbled form in the LXX. The first god was identified as Molok, not "your king," and his name, Sikkût, became "the tent." The latter indicates that the Hebrew *Vorlage* had defective spelling. The Alexandrian translator of Kiyyûn was already a practitioner of "contextualization" and found a cultural equivalent in Raiphan (or Rephan), for Repa, a name of Seb, the Egyptian deity representing Saturn. And this word in turn has undergone variations—Rempham, Romphan, and more.

Now, all of these byways and by-products of the MT are very interesting, but they take us farther and farther away from the MT. They belong to the history of interpretation. We are not prepared to paste them on top of the MT. We keep the MT in the first place of interest and with first claim to be Amos' text.

AUTHENTIC AMOS AND LATER ADDITIONS

Since the basic work of B. Duhm and J. Wellhausen, certain passages and phrases in the book of Amos have been marked off as not the work of the prophet himself; they were not included in the work until after his time, after the first publication, some being added quite late in its literary development. T. K. Cheyne, W. R. Harper, and S. R. Driver were mainly responsible for spreading these ideas to English readers, and George Adam Smith popularized them, making such observations respectable even for preachers.

Each scholar has his own list, for there is no surefire technique for distinguishing authentic Amos materials from the additions of later scribes; and each investigator arrives at his conclusions with various degrees of confidence, ranging from "perhaps" to dogmatic certainty (Fohrer 1968:436). By the same token, every thoughtful reader is likely to wonder about many parts of the book, especially when it is hard to see how they fit in with the rest of Amos' message or when they do not seem to belong in his times.

A full list of passages that have been questioned by someone or other at one time or another would be quite long. The following are the ones most commonly doubted: 1:2; 1:9–10; 1:11–12; 2:4–5; 2:10; 3:7; 3:14b; 4:13; 5:8–9; 5:13; 5:14–15; 5:26–27; 6:2; 8:6; 8:8; 8:11–12; 8:13; 9:5–6; and 9:8–15. Harper (1905:cxxxii) has an even longer list of secondary additions, and in his commentary he also deletes many other short phrases (cxxxiii), including all of the rubrics. For many writers in recent years the questions are settled, and it has been enough to refer to the great names of the past as warrant for repeating their conclusions. At most the reasons for doubting the authenticity of these passages are given in a summary and desultory manner (Mays 1969:13).

The most common grounds are historical, literary, or theological, or a combination of these. On historical grounds one or more of the oracles against the eight nations may be rejected because they are said to reflect the circumstances and concerns of a later time, the Exile or even afterward: Judah (2:4–5—the words "in Zion" are stricken from 6:1 for the same reason) and Edom (1:11–12) frequently, Tyre as well (1:9–10) quite often. The prophecy in 3:14b was rejected by Wellhausen (1893) as a *vaticinium ex eventu;* 5:26–27 likewise was written after the event, and 8:8 is rejected because it purports to predict the earthquake. Other passages "alleged to reflect a later stage of history" (Smith 1896:201) are 5:1, 2, 15; 6:2, 14.

Historical arguments are also brought against passages containing ideas deemed to be not yet current in Amos' time, especially the eschatological pieces at the end of the book—8:11–12; 8:13 (Smith); 9:8–15 (the references to the southern kingdom are an additional reason for rejecting these verses). In spite of its location and its quite advanced theological insight, scholars seem reluctant to take 9:7 away from Amos; they prefer rather to defend the authenticity of this verse as one of his major breakthroughs.

Some arguments—partly historical, partly literary, partly theological—depend on the results of research into other parts of the Bible. The Deuteronomistic scholars mainly responsible for composing D (the bulk of Deuteronomy) and for compiling the Deuteronomistic history of Israel (essentially Deuteronomy through Kings, but without possible subsequent Priestly additions, in the opinion of many scholars) are believed to have operated mainly in the seventh and sixth centuries B.C.E. Passages in Amos that seem to reflect their point of view, namely, 2:10 and 3:7, must have been added to the book of Amos after that. W. H. Schmidt (1965) published an influential study of this question.

Arguments, mainly literary, deny to Amos compositions that do not belong to any of the standard prophetic genres, in particular the three hymns or hymn fragments (4:13; 5:8–9; 9:5–6). To these passages are sometimes added 8:8 and 1:2, the latter with the supplementary argument that Amos did not work out of Zion. From another quarter, 5:13 "is the comment of one of the wise" (Mays 1969:13). In dealing with this kind of problem, it is important to distinguish between what Amos himself might have composed as original prophecy and traditional pieces that he might have quoted or adapted and worked into his messages.

The speech attributed to the merchants in 8:5 has caused trouble. The use of first-person plural and the repetition of "wheat" in v 6b is a link to the opening words of v 5, suggesting that it is all one speech. But Smith thinks that v 6 "may be a mere clerical repetition" of 2:6 (1896:183). Certainly 8:6 is an echo of 2:6, but not simply a repetition, for there are interesting differences in wording, so one is entitled to search for long-range connections between them; and the study of 2:6–8 and 8:5–6 side by side will help to solve the problems presented by each. As for 8:5b, difficulty has been felt from Wellhausen onward in retaining such words in the mouth (or mind) of the merchants themselves. W. Rudolph (1971a:262) tries to salvage the situation by suggesting that the last three words of v 6 had been dislocated. He relocates them to follow v 5 as another fraudulent practice contemplated by the merchants, along with those in v 5b. Some, however, regard vv 5b–6 as Amos' comment (NIV). In this, as in many similar problems, the arguments become very attenuated indeed. And when more emendations are required to fill in the cracks, the credibility of the result recedes even farther.

We recognize that no one can "prove" that these verses (or any other parts of the book for that matter) did or did not come from Amos himself, or from circles very close to him, which practically amounts to the same thing. We ourselves have great interest in these issues but do not believe that they can be solved either by scholarly ingenuity or by appeal to certain postulates about the nature and evolution of biblical literature. What concerns us most is the interpretation of the book of Amos as it now stands complete.

As long as one does not demand certainty in such things, as long as one does not affect to have attained certainty in such things, the question of the antiquity of any particular passage can always be raised; and, because the means to indubitable answers are not available, they will doubtless continue to be raised by biblical scholars. The enterprise seems to have exhausted itself in its conduct along the lines laid down in the nineteenth century.

The merits of each individual proposal will be examined in the NOTES on the passages concerned. If we finish with a reluctance to discard any part of the book as "certainly not Amos," it is partly because we have come to the conclusion, after working through the whole business many times and weighing all arguments, that there are no compelling reasons against accepting most if not all of the book as possibly, indeed probably (we can never say "certainly") Amos.

We have two main reasons for deviating from traditional criticism on these points. First is the cumulative demonstration of the *literary coherence* of all of the diverse ingredients in the whole assemblage, which is more than an assemblage; it is a highly structured unity. Second is the diverse and divergent (even apparently contradictory, sometimes) points of view we account for as reflecting successive phases in the prophet's career, which underwent quite substantial changes in both inner perception and declared messages.

Behind all of that, we have been compelled to question the hidden foundations of the old criticism at four points essential for its results. (1) We consider the "advanced" cosmic theology of the hymns to be, in fact, not late, but primal in the faith of early Israel and quite in tune with Amos' prophetic outlook as a whole (see the essay "The God of Israel in the Book of Amos"). (2) We consider that the roots of eschatological thinking are also ancient (see the COMMENTARY on "Yahweh's Day" at 5:18), so that there is no reason to assign eschatological passages to postexilic times just because they are eschatological. (3) We consider it to be far from demonstrated that (apparently) fulfilled prophecies could only have been composed after the events that *we* identify as their fulfillment. On the contrary, we shall argue that few, if any, of Amos' prophecies can be shown to have been successful in the sense that later apologists (and, as opposed to them, freethinkers) could take them as evidence of miraculous and accurate prediction of historical happenings. And we shall argue further that it is precisely because they were not fulfilled in this manner that they should be accepted as authentic (Jenni 1956). (4) We recognize the early prophets, and Amos in particular, as versatile verbal craftsmen, quite capable of using cultic and wisdom pieces as well as the more direct prophetic oracles in their speeches. So form-critical identification of ingredients as nonoracular is not sufficient grounds for excising them.

THE USE OF POETRY AND PROSE IN THE BOOK OF AMOS

In our commentary on Hosea (Andersen and Freedman 1980) we drew attention to a remarkable feature of its vocabulary. The so-called "prose particles" (the definite article, the relative pronoun, and *nota accusativi*) are not used uniformly throughout the book. They are found mostly in the first three chapters, and to a lesser degree or quite rarely in the rest of the book. The obvious distinction between the narrative of the first part and the prophecy of the second correlates with a greater use of poetic forms for oracular material. We can also say that Hosea's prophecies use a kind of Hebrew found elsewhere in archaic epic poems and in lyrical cult poetry.

The extent to which the "prose particles" are used is thus an independent diagnostic element or tool to be placed alongside form-critical considerations. F. I. Andersen and A. D. Forbes (1983) subsequently presented detailed counts of these particles for every chapter in the Bible, thus confirming the hypothesis and bringing to light in a systematic way the distribution of the phenomenon over the entire corpus. The results are quite clear-cut for whole chapters consisting entirely of pure narrative prose, and for chapters consisting entirely of poetry. But many chapters yield an intermediate score; and more detailed research is now needed to find out whether such a tally results from a mixture of prose and poetry, which averages out to a middle value over the whole chapter, or whether such chapters contain prose that uses the particles sparingly, or poetry that employs them more than usual.

In much prophecy it is found that by prosodic and rhetorical analyses, the form is neither prose nor poetry, but an intermediate mode. In a recent study D. L. Christensen (1985) has made so much of this kind of thing as to abolish the categories of prose and poetry altogether. This extreme position is unnecessary and unfortunate. In the limit cases there is certainly a difference between poetry and prose (Kugel 1981). There should be no doubt that the Joseph story is prose and that the dialogue in Job is poetry. Yet even in the Joseph story there are a few places in which the narrative or dialogue breaks out in parallelism; and even in the speeches in Job there are occasional lines that would pass for prose in a different context. Many of the problems that lead to inclusive theoretical arguments over Hebrew poetry arise from expecting too much regularity, or from concluding from the many irregularities that there were no rules at all.

When we come to prophecy it is not appropriate to manage extreme cases by identifying a verse or two of prose in an otherwise poetic oracle, or a patch of poetry in a prose discourse. It is regrettable that modern editions, such as BH³ or BHS, and most modern translations now feel obliged to classify each verse as one kind or the other. As a result there are some rather prosaic passages printed in poetic lines; and some poetic passages that have been presented as prose.

The degree to which the prose particles are used can provide an additional aid in making such decisions. Not that it can ever be unequivocal; it is only one of several diagnostics. As with *parallelismus membrorum,* this diagnostic reaches an insurmountable limitation when dealing with smaller and smaller units. A little bit of parallelism in prose is not enough to assert an embedded poem or poetic substratum. An abnormally high use of prose particles in one line of an oracle is not enough to prove that it is heterogeneous. Especially in prophetic discourse, such evidence is insufficient warrant for excising such a passage as a scribal addition that should be removed in order to recover the authentic poem in its original purity.

The need for such caution has been tacitly recognized from the beginning of modern studies of Hebrew poetry. In spite of the prominence given to parallelism as the *sine qua non* of Hebrew prosody, Bishop Lowth's third category ("synthetic parallelism") is not really parallelism at all, and many specimens of such long clauses, extending over two rhythmic lines, are virtually indistinguishable from prose. Such bicolons are very numerous, and there is rarely a basis for suspecting that they are not integral parts of the poems in which they occur.

The same is true of other departures from the norm (if it deserves that dignity) of a bicolon with parallelism. Three lines in parallel or a single line with no parallel also occur not infrequently, especially in prophetic discourse. The earlier critical practice of deleting such odd lines cannot be sustained. We are now more aware that such variations often serve important structural purposes in larger units such as stanzas and strophes.

The differing levels of use of prose particles in prose and poetry are a distinct indicator, independent of prosodic and structural arguments. This indicator has the advantage of objectivity, and it works very well with the limit cases. Its use in categorizing the compositional units of Amos is less clear-cut, however. Where necessary we shall draw attention to the extreme cases in the introductions to each section.

The figures and ratios for Amos show overall that Amos rates high for poetry and low for prose, but that is simply because prosaic and poetic elements are mixed in the book. There are some fairly straight prose passages, such as 2:9–13 and parts of the story in 7:10–17, but the dialogue tends to be poetic, as is frequently the case in the Bible. The most interesting aspect of this phenomenon is precisely where prose sentences are embedded in formulaic and otherwise poetic material. It would not only be difficult but probably foolhardy to try to sift out the prose, or to revise the material to meet the standards or refinements of true poetry; instead we should recognize that the prophets, in particular Amos, created a new style to serve as a vehicle for the divine message.

Because of the formulaic character of the oracles against Israel and the nations, it would be hard to argue that what we have is the edited written form of the oracle in contrast to its original oral presentation. In principle and partly in practice that may be true, but it would be very difficult to try to recover or reconstruct the original oracles on the basis of what we have. It could perhaps be done, but apart from its being an exercise in ingenuity, would scholars have any assurance that something was being recovered rather than created?

Strikingly, it is in the formulaic oracles, such as the plagues, the woes, and a few other catalogs (3:3–8; 9:1–4) that prose elements are quite prominent, while the standard poetic units lack the formulas and refrains. It may be that the formulas and fairly rigid framework were deliberately devised to allow considerable variation in content, length, and detail—and that this is a rhetorical oracular style deliberately devised by and for prophets like Amos. The framework and formulas provided a fixed but flexible structure, while the prophet indulged in free-form composition mixing prose and poetry categories, perhaps something like free verse or oratorical prose, styles known in other cultures and languages.

What emerges when the headings and other clear prose patches are set aside is a collection of oracles and other statements that are often poetic, occasionally formulaic, and generally free of prose particles except where these elements are embedded in the framework of a formal piece such as the Great Set Speech, or the one on the plagues, and perhaps one or two others. We may conclude that the book of Amos consists of three or four kinds of literary material with some mixture of elements:

1. Headings: 1:1; 3:1; 4:1; 5:1—standard prose
2. Prose units (with a possible admixture of dialogue): 2:9–13; 3:1–2; 7:1–8:3; 9:1–4; 9:7–8, 9, 11–12; 9:13–15
3. Formulaic structures with prose elements: 1:3–2:8, 14–16; 4:6–11
4. Other oracles and utterances—poetry or at least not prose

The division between prose and poetry does not mean that the poetry belongs to Amos and the prose to the editor. Certainly the various headings that are in prose could be assigned to the editor, and whatever poetry or nonprose compositions there are could almost by definition be assigned to the prophet. What of the remaining material? The formulaic pieces represent a genre in eighth century and later prophecy, and no one has suggested that these pieces in Amos are later fabrications: the question is largely about the prose elements found in them, and whether they are the work of the prophet or were added by one or more editors. It will be our contention that these set pieces are integral units and that the prose and the formulas alike belong to the pieces, that the individual items are not uniform in length or style, and hence that we have little or nothing in the way of criteria to sift out spurious or secondary materials and so isolate the primary ones. The same argument will apply to the wisdom piece in 3:3–8 and the catalog of places in 9:1–4, as well as to the plagues and the oracles against Israel and the nations.

There remain the prose units, which are concentrated at the front and back of the book but which also occur in chaps. 7:1–8:3, where we have the group of four visions (plus 9:1–4, Vision 5) and the story of Amos' encounter with Amaziah at Bethel. It would be difficult to deny these passages out of hand to Amos, though we may say that overall the narrative in chap. 7, including the visions, is about Amos rather than by him (the visions are autobiographical). Nevertheless the content, including visions and speeches, bears all the marks of authenticity, and the only difference is that the material is put in story form.

It would also be difficult to question the originality or authenticity of a statement like that in 3:1–2, even though the entire piece is prose. In our opinion the same would or could be true of 2:9–13. While it does not appear to be an original part of the oracle in chaps. 1–2, it is distinctive, clearly not Deuteronomic, and may very well stem from Amos along with other prose statements of an original and striking nature, such as 5:27. With respect to chap. 9, especially from v 7 to the end, there are difficulties and doubts, but they attach mainly to the content of the material and its supposedly different tone and theology rather than to the fact that they are written in prose. Provisionally we would accept everything up through 9:10 as by Amos and put a question mark on the material in the last paragraph, 9:11–15. Practically everything hinges on the term *sukkat dāwîd,* just what that is and what it means that it "has fallen." If it symbolizes the dynasty of David or the state of Judah, then it may well reflect the fall of the kingdom early in the sixth century B.C.E. But the expression is unique, and caution is indicated; pending clarification we may withhold judgment. Its being prose hardly affects the case one way or the other, and if it were the only consideration we would be reluctant to deny the material to Amos. In other words, we believe that in addition to the poetry and oracular utterances in formulaic style with their prose elements, there is other prose material that stems directly from Amos.

The book as we have it is the product of editorial labor including selection, modification, expansion, adaptation, and especially the incorporation of headings, closings, liturgical formulas, and the like. The narrative of chap. 7:10–17 and its context (7:1–8:3) are also the work of the editor, though the content of the visions and the dialogue reported seem to come from Amos himself. Drawing the line between what Amos said and did and may have written, and what the editor may have contributed has proved to be a difficult and ultimately unrewarding task. In the end we must deal with the book of Amos, not Amos and his editor, but what the two or more of them together produced.

To complete this general introduction it should be enough to point out that Amos was capable of composition all across the range, from pure prose to pure poetry. We do not need to include the narrative of 7:10–17 or the three creation hymns (which we do not think Amos himself composed, though we believe he deliberately incorporated them into his message).

Both the autobiographical sections of The Book of Visions, which come from Amos, and the narrative portions, admittedly brief, are in standard prose. In addition, some of the most notable oracles, which no serious scholars deny to Amos, are also in prose: for example 3:1–2, surely one of the most important statements in the book, which could hardly have come from anyone else—unless we recognize that the editor was as much a prophet as Amos, and then it would hardly matter. Or they can be in elegant poetry, like 5:24, the very center of his doctrine; 5:15a, a complex structure; and 5:2, a beautiful elegy.

A SELECT BIBLIOGRAPHY

COMMENTARIES ON THE BOOK OF AMOS

Anderson, B. W.
  1978   *The Eighth Century Prophets: Amos, Hosea, Isaiah, Micah.* Procla-
          mation Commentaries. Philadelphia: Fortress Press.

Bewer, J. A.
  1949   *The Book of the Twelve Prophets.* 2 vols. Harper's Annotated
          Bible. New York: Harper & Brothers.

Bič, M.
  1969   *Das Buch Amos.* Berlin: Evangelische Verlagsansalt.

Cheyne, T. K.
  1903–4 *Critica Biblica, or Critical Linguistic, Literary and Historical Notes
          on the Old Testament Writings. Isaiah and Jeremiah; Ezekiel and
          Minor Prophets; Samuel; Kings; Joshua and Judges.* London.

Cripps, R. S.
  1969   *A Critical and Exegetical Commentary on the Book of Amos.* Lon-
          don: SPCK.

Driver, S. R., and H. C. O. Lanchester
  1915   *The Books of Joel and Amos.* 2d ed. The Cambridge Bible for
          Schools and Colleges. Cambridge: The University Press.

Duhm, B.
  1911   "Anmerkungen zu den Zwölf Propheten." *ZAW* 31:1–43, 81–110,
          161–204.

Edghill, E. A., and G. A. Cooke
  1926   *The Book of Amos.* 2d ed. Westminster Commentaries. London:
          Methuen.

Guthe, H.
  1923   "Der Prophet Amos." Vol. 2, pp. 30–47 in *Die heilige Schrift des
          Alten Testaments.* ed. E. Kautzsch and A. Bertolet. 4th ed. Tü-
          bingen: J. C. B. Mohr.

Hammershaimb, E.
  1970   *The Book of Amos: A Commentary.* Trans. J. Sturdy. New York:
          Schocken Books.

Harper, W. R.
  1905   *A Critical and Exegetical Commentary on Amos and Hosea.* The
          International Critical Commentary. Edinburgh: T. & T. Clark.

Hoonacker, A. van
  1908   *Les Douze Petits Prophètes, traduits et commentés.* Études bib-
          liques. Paris: Gabalda.

Keil, C. F., and F. Delitzsch
    1986   *Biblical Commentary on the Old Testament.* Trans. fr. German ed. Repr. (15 vols. in 10). Grand Rapids: Eerdmans.

Kraft, C. F.
    1971   "The Book of Amos." Pp. 465–76 in *The Interpreter's One-Volume Commentary on the Bible.* Ed. C. M. Laymon. Nashville: Abingdon.

Laetsch, T. F. K.
    1956   *Bible Commentary: The Minor Prophets.* St. Louis: Concordia.

Löhr, M.
    1901   *Untersuchungen zum Buch Amos.* BZAW 4. Giessen: J. Rickes.

Marti, K.
    1904   *Das Dodekapropheton erklärt.* Kurzer Hand-Kommentar zum Alten Testament 13. Tübingen: J. C. B. Mohr.

Mays, J. L.
    1969   *Amos: A Commentary.* The Old Testament Library. Philadelphia: Westminster Press.

Nowack, W.
    1922   *Die kleinen Propheten übersetzt und erklärt.* 3d ed. Handkommentar zum Alten Testament 3–4. Göttingen: Vandenhoeck und Ruprecht.

Procksch, O.
    1910   *Die Kleinen Prophetischen Schriften vor dem Exil.* Erläterungen zum Alten Testament 3. Claw and Stuttgart.

Robinson, T. H., and F. Horst
    1938   *Die Zwölf Kleinen Propheten.* Ed. O. Eissfeldt. HAT 1.14. Tübingen: Mohr.

Rudolph, W.
    1971a   *Joel-Amos-Obadja-Jona.* Gütersloh: Gerd Mohn.

Schmidt, H.
    1917   *Der Prophet Amos.* Tübingen.

Smith, G. A.
    1896   *The Book of the Twelve Prophets Commonly Called the Minor. I. Amos, Hosea, and Micah.* The Expositor's Bible. New York: A. C. Armstrong.

Weiser, A.
    1929   *Die Profetie des Amos.* BZAW 53. Giessen: J. Ricker.

Wellhausen, J.
    1893   *Die Kleinen Propheten. Übersetzung, mit Notizen.* Skizzen und Vorarbeiten 5. Berlin: Alfred Töpelmann.

Wolff, H. W.
    1977   *Joel and Amos.* Hermeneia. Philadelphia: Fortress Press.

BOOKS, MONOGRAPHS, AND ARTICLES

Ackroyd, P. R.
1956–57 "Amos VII:14." *ExpT* 68:94.
1977 "A Judgement Narrative Between Kings and Chronicles? An Approach to Amos 7:9–17." Pp. 71–87 in *Canon and Authority.* Ed. G. W. Coats and B. O. Long. Philadelphia: Fortress Press.

Aharoni, Y.
1979 *The Land of the Bible: A Historical Geography.* Rev. and enlarged by A. F. Rainey. Philadelphia: Westminster Press.

Ahlström, G. W.
1981 "King Josiah and the *dwd* of Amos 6:10." *JSS* 26:7–9.

Albrektson, B.
1981 *"Difficilior lectio probabilior:* A Rule of Textual Criticism and Its Use in Old Testament Studies." *OTS* 21:5–18.

Albright, W. F.
1942 "A Votive Stele Erected by Ben-Hadad I of Damascus to the God Melcarth." *BASOR* 87:23–29.
1944 "The Oracles of Balaam." *JBL* 63:207–33.
1945 "The Chronology of the Divided Monarchy." *BASOR* 100:16–22.
1956 "Notes on Psalms 68 and 134." Pp. 1–12 in *Interpretationes ad Vetus Testamentum pertinentes Sigmundo Mowinckel septuagenario missae.* Oslo: Forlaget Land og Kirke.
1969 *Yahweh and the Gods of Canaan.* Garden City, N.Y.: Doubleday.

Alt, A.
1934 "Die syrische Staatenwelt vor dem Einbruch der Assyrier." *Zeitschrift der Deutschen Morgenländischen Gesellschaft* 88:233–58.
1959a "Archaeologische Fragen zur Baugeschichte von Jerusalem und Samaria in der israelitischen Königzeit." Vol. 3, pp. 303–25 in *Kleine Schriften zur Geschichte des Volkes Israel.* Ed. M. Noth. Munich: C. H. Beck.
1959b "Der Stadtsaat Samaria." Vol. 3, pp. 258–302 in *Kleine Schriften zur Geschichte des Volkes Israel.* Ed. M. Noth. Munich: C. H. Beck.
1959c "Judas Gave unter Josia." Vol. 2, pp. 276–88 in *Kleine Schriften zur Geschichte des Volkes Israel.* Ed. M. Noth. Munich: C. H. Beck.

Andersen, F. I.
1960 "Doublets and Contamination." *RTR* 19:48–57, 73–81.
1961–62 "The Diet of John the Baptist." *Abr-Nahrain* 3:60–74.
1966 "The Socio-juridical Background of the Naboth Incident." *JBL* 85:46–57.
1969 "Israelite Kinship Terminology and Social Structure." *Bible Translator* 20:29–39.

1971 "Passive and Ergative in Hebrew." Pp. 1–15 in *Near Eastern Studies in Honor of William Foxwell Albright.* Ed. Hans Goedicke. Baltimore: The Johns Hopkins University Press.

1976 *Job.* Tyndale Old Testament Commentaries. Downers Grove, Ill.: Inter-Varsity Press.

1977 "Slavery in the Ancient Near East." *Ancient Society* 7:144–90.

———, and A. D. Forbes

1983 " 'Prose Particle' Counts of the Hebrew Bible." Pp. 165–83 in *The Word of the Lord Shall Go Forth: Essays in Honor of David Noel Freedman in Celebration of His Sixtieth Birthday.* Ed. C. Meyers and M. O'Connor. Philadelphia: American Schools of Oriental Research.

1986 *Spelling in the Hebrew Bible.* Biblica et Orientalia 41. Rome: Biblical Institute Press.

———, and D. N. Freedman

1970 "Harmon in Amos 4:3." *BASOR* 198:41–42.

1980 *Hosea.* AB 24. Garden City, N.Y.: Doubleday.

Arieti, J. A.

1974 "The Vocabulary of Septuagint Amos." *JBL* 93:338–47.

Avigad, N.

1979 "Baruch the Scribe and Jerahmeel the King's Son." *BA* 42:114–18.

Bailey, J. G.

1981 "Amos: Preacher of Social Reform." *Bible Today* 19:306–13.

Barré, M. L.

1985 "Amos 1:11 Reconsidered." *CBQ* 47:420–27.

1986 "The Meaning of *ľ ʾšbnw* in Amos 1:3–2:6." *JBL* 105:611–31.

Barstad, H. M.

1975 "Die Basankühe in Amos IV, 1." *VT* 24:286–97.

1984 *The Religious Polemics of Amos: Studies in the Preaching of Amos II 7b–8, IV 1–13, V 1–17, VI 4–7, VIII 14.* Leiden: Brill.

Bartczek, G.

1980 *Prophetie und Vermittlung. Zur literarischen Analyse und theologischen Interpretation der Visionsberichte des Amos.* Europäische Hochschulschriften Reihe XXIII, Band 120. Frankfurt am Main: Peter Lang.

Bartlett, J. R.

1977 "The Brotherhood of Edom." [Amos 1:11]. *JSOT* 4:2–27.

Barton, J.

1980 *Amos' Oracles Against the Nations: A Study of Amos 1:3–2:5.* Cambridge: University Press.

Baumann, E.

1903 *Der Aufbau der Amosreden.* BZAW 7. Giessen: J. Ricker.

Beek, M. A.

1948 "The Religious Background of Amos II 6–8." *OTS* 5:132–41.

Bennett, B. M.

1972 "The Search for Israelite Gilgal." *PEQ* 104:111–22.

Bentzen, A.

1948   *Introduction to the Old Testament.* 2 vols. Copenhagen: G. E. C. Gads Forlag.

1950   "The Ritual Background of Amos 1:2–2:3." *OTS* 8:85–99.

Berg, W.

1974   *Die sogenannten Hymnenfragmente im Amosbuch.* Europäische Hochschulschriften Reihe XXIII, Band 45. Frankfurt am Main, Bern, and Cirencester: Peter Lang.

Bergren, R. V.

1974   *The Prophets and the Law.* Monographs of the Hebrew Union College 4. New York: Hebrew Union College.

Berridge, J. M.

1976   "Zur Intention der Botschaft des Amos. Exegetische Überlegungen zu Am. 5." *TZ* 32:321–40.

1979   "Jeremia und die Prophetie des Amos." *TZ* 35:321–41.

Bewer, J. A.

1901   "Lexical Notes." *AJSL* 17:168–70.

Bič, M.

1951   "Der Prophet Amos—ein Häpatoskopos." *VT* 1:293–96.

Bjorndalen, A. J.

1980   "Erwägungen zur Zukunft des Amazja und Israels Nach der Überlieferung Amos 7:10–17." Pp. 236–51 in *Werden und Wirken des Alten Testaments: Festschrift für C. Westermann.* Ed. R. Albertz. Göttingen: Neukirchener-Verlag.

1981   "Jahwe in den Zukunftsaussagen des Amos." Pp. 181–203 in *Die Botschaft und die Boten: Festschrift für H. W. Wolff.* Ed. J. Jeremias and P. Lothar. Göttingen: Neukirchener-Verlag.

Black, M.

1958   "The Zakir Stele." Pp. 242–50 in *Documents from Old Testament Times.* Ed. D. Winton Thomas. New York: Harper & Brothers.

Blaquart, J. L.

1977   "Parole de Dieu et prophètes d'Amos à Ézéchiel." *Point théologique* 24:15–30.

Boling, R. G., and G. E. Wright

1982   *Joshua.* AB 6. Garden City, N.Y.: Doubleday.

Botterweck, G. J.

1971   "Sie verkaufen den Unschuldigen um Geld. Zur sozialen Kritik des Propheten Amos." *Bibel und Leben* 12:215–31.

Bowman, R. A.

1944   "An Aramaic Religious Text in Demotic Script." *JNES* 3:219–31.

Bright, J.

1965   *Jeremiah.* AB 21. Garden City, N.Y.: Doubleday.

Brockelmann, C.

1956   *Hebräische Syntax.* Neukirchen: Verlag der Buchhandlung des Erziehungsvereins.

Bronznick, N.
1985   "More on *hlk ʾl.*" [Amos 2:7] *VT* 35:98–99.
Bruce, F. F.
1951   *The Acts of the Apostles.* London: Tyndale Press.
Brueggemann, W.
1965   "Amos 4,4–13 and Israel's Covenant Worship." *VT* 15:1–15.
1968   *Tradition for Crisis: A Study in Hosea.* Richmond, Va.: John Knox Press.
1969   "Amos' Intercessory Formula." *VT* 19:385–399.
Brunet, G.
1966   "La Vision de l'étain: Réinterprétation d'Amos VII 7–9." *VT* 16:387–395.
Buccellati, G.
1966   *The Amorites of the UR III Period.* Naples: Istituto Orientale de Napoli.
Budde, K.
1924   "Zu Text und Auslegung des Buches Amos." *JBL* 43:46–131.
1925   "Zu Text und Auslegung des Buches Amos." *JBL* 44:63–122.
1930   "Antwort auf Johannes Meinholds 'zur Sabbathfrage.'" *ZAW* 48:138–45. (See Meinhold 1930).
Carny, P.
1977   "Doxologies—A Scientific Myth." *Hebrew Studies* 18:149–59.
Childs, B. S.
1962   *Memory and Tradition in Israel.* Studies in Biblical Theology 37. London: SCM Press.
1974   *The Book of Exodus: A Critical, Theological Commentary.* Old Testament Library. Philadelphia: Westminster Press.
Christensen, D. L.
1974   "The Prosodic Structure of Amos 1–2." *HTR* 67:427–36.
1985   "The Story of Jonah: A Metrical Analysis." *JBL* 104:217–31.
Claassen, W. T.
1971   "The *Hiphʿil* Verbal Theme in Biblical Hebrew." Ph.D. diss., University of Stellenbosch.
Cohen, S.
1961   "Amos *was* a Navi." *HUCA* 32:175–78.
Collins, J. J.
1974   "History and Tradition in the Prophet Amos." *Irish Theological Quarterly* 41:120–33.
Cooke, G. A.
1936   *The Book of Ezekiel.* International Critical Commentary. 2 vols. New York: Scribner.
Coote, R. B.
1971   "Amos 1, 11 *RḤMYW.*" *JBL* 90:206–8.
1981   *Amos Among the Prophets: Composition and Theology.* Philadelphia: Fortress Press.

Coulot, C.
1977   "Propositions pour une structuration du livre d'Amos au niveau rédactionnel." *Revue des sciences religieuses* 51:169–86.

Cornfeld, G.
1976   *Archaeology of the Bible: Book by Book.* New York: Harper & Row.

Craghan, J. F.
1972   "The Prophet Amos in Recent Literature." *Biblical Theology Bulletin* 2:242–61.

Craigie, P. C.
1982   "Amos the *nōqēd* in the Light of Ugaritic." *Studies in Religion* 11:29–33.

Crenshaw, J. L.
1970   "A Liturgy of Wasted Opportunity (Am 4, 6–12; Isa 9, 7–10; 5, 25–29)." *Semitics* 1:27–37.
1972   *"Wĕdōrēk 'al-bāmŏtê 'āreṣ."* [Amos 4:3] *CBQ* 34:39–53.
1975   *Hymnic Affirmation of Divine Justice: The Doxologies of Amos and Related Texts in the Old Testament.* SBL Dissertation Series 24. Missoula, Mont.: Scholars Press.

Cross, F. M.
1947   "The Tabernacle: A Study from an Archaeological and Historical Approach." *BA* 10:45–68.
1953   "The Council of Yahweh in Second Isaiah." *JNES* 12:274–77.
1973   *Canaanite Myth and Hebrew Epic.* Cambridge, Mass.: Harvard University Press.
——, and G. E. Wright
1956   "The Boundary and Province Lists of the Kingdom of Judah." *JBL* 75:202–26.

Crüsemann, F.
1971   "Kritik an Amos im deuteronomistischen Geschichtswerk. Erwägungen zu 2 Könige 14, 27." Pp. 57–63 in *Probleme Biblischer Theologie: Festschrift für Gerhard von Rad.* Ed. H. W. Wolff. Munich: Kaiser.

Cutler, B., and J. MacDonald
1982   "On the Origin of the Ugaritic Text KTU 1.23." *UF* 14:33–50.

Dahmen, U.
1986   "Zur Text- und Literarkritik von Amos 6:6a." *Biblische Notizen* 31:7–10.

Dahood, M.
1966   *Psalms I: 1–50.* AB 16. Garden City, N.Y.: Doubleday.
1968   *Psalms II: 51–100.* AB 17. Garden City, N.Y.: Doubleday.
1970a   "Hebrew-Ugaritic Lexicography VII–IX." [Amos 1:11] *Bib* 51:391–404.
1970b   *Psalms III: 101–150.* AB 17A. Garden City, N.Y.: Doubleday.
1971   "Additional Notes on the *MRZḤ* Text." Pp. 51–54 in *The Claremont Ras Shamra Tablets.* Ed. L. R. Fisher. Analecta Orientalia 48. Rome: Pontifical Biblical Institute.

1978 "Amos 6, 8 *mĕtā'ēb.*" *Bib* 59:265–66.

1981 "Afterword: Ebla, Ugarit, and the Bible." Pp. 271–321 in *The Archives of Ebla: An Empire Inscribed in Clay,* G. Pettinato. Garden City, N.Y.: Doubleday.

Danell, G. A.

1951 "Var Amos verklingen en nabi?" *Svensk Exegetisk Årsbok* 16:7–20.

Davies, G. H.

1980–81 "Amos—The Prophet of Re-Union." *ExpT* 92:196–99.

Deist, F. E.

1978 *Towards the Text of the Old Testament.* Ed. W. K. Winckler. Pretoria: D. R. Church.

Diebner, B., and H. Schult

1975 "Edom in alttestament Texten der Makkabäerzeit." [Amos 9:11–12] *Dielhammer Blätter zum Alten Testament* 8:11–17.

Dietrich, M., and O. Loretz

1978 "Ugaritische *'bš, ībš,* Hebräische *šbs* (Amos 5:11), Sowie Ugaritische *īšy* und *šbš.*" *UF* 10:434.

Dion, P.-E.

1975 "Le Message moral du prophète Amos s'inspirat-il du 'droit de l'alliance'?" *Science et esprit* 27:5–34.

Dothan, T.

1982 *The Philistines and Their Material Culture.* New Haven: Yale University Press.

Driver, G. R.

1938a "Linguistic and Textual Problems: Minor Prophets II." *JTS* 19:260–73.

1938b "Linguistic and Textual Problems: Minor Prophets III." *JTS* 19:393–405.

1950 "Difficult Words in the Hebrew Prophets." Pp. 52–72 in *Studies in Old Testament Prophecy Presented to Professor Theodore H. Robinson.* Ed. H. H. Rowley. Edinburgh: T. & T. Clark.

1953 "Two Astronomical Passages in the Old Testament." *JTS* 4:208–12.

1955–56 "Amos 7:14." *ExpT* 67:91–92.

1973 "Affirmation by Exclamatory Negation." [Amos 7:14f.] *Journal of the Ancient Near Eastern Society of Columbia University* 5:107–14.

Driver, S. R.

1913 *Notes on the Hebrew Text and the Topography of the Books of Samuel.* 2d ed., revised and enlarged. Oxford: Clarendon Press.

Dussaud, R.

1941 *Les Origines cananéennes du sacrifice israélite.* 2d ed. Paris: Leroux.

Eichrodt, W.

1977 "Die Vollmacht des Amos. Zu einer Schwierigen Stelle im Amosbuch (3:3–8)." Pages 124–51 in *Beiträge zur Alttestamentlichen Theologie: Festschrift für W. Zimmerli.* Ed. H. Donner. Göttingen: Vandenhoeck and Ruprecht.

Eissfeldt, O.
1968   *Kleine Schriften.* Vol. 4. Ed. R. Sellheim and F. Maass. Tübingen: J. C. B. Mohr.
1970   "Gilgal or Shechem?" Pp. 90–101 in *Proclamation and Presence, the G. Henton Davies Volume.* Ed. L. Durham and R. Porter. London: SCM Press, 1984 repr.
1973   *"Marzeaḥ* und *Marzeḥa'* 'Kultmahlgenossenschaft' im spätjüdischen Schrifttum." Vol. 5, pp. 136–42 in *Kleine Schriften.* Ed. R. Sellheim and F. Maass. Tübingen: J. C. B. Mohr.

Even-Shoshan, A.
1985   *A New Concordance of the Old Testament.* Jerusalem: Kiryat Sefer.

Ewald, H.
1867   *Die Propheten des Bundes.* Band 1. "Jesaja mit den Übringen ältern Propheten." Göttingen.

Farr, G.
1958   "The Concept of Grace in the Book of Hosea." *ZAW* 70:98–107.

Fendler, M.
1973   "Zur Sozialkritik des Amos. Versuch einer wirtschafts- und sozialgeschichtlichen Interpretation alttestamentlicher Texte." *Evangelische Theologie* 33:32–53.

Fenton, T. L.
1977   "The Claremont *'MRZH'* Tablet, Its Text and Meaning." *UF* 9:71–76.

Fey, R.
1963   *Amos und Jesaja.* Wissenschaftliche Monographien zum Alten und Neuen Testament 12. Neukirchen Vluyn: Neukirchener-Verlag.

Finesinger, B.
1926   "Musical Instruments in the Old Testament." *HUCA* 3:21–76.

Fishbane, M.
1970   "The Treaty Background of Amos 1, 11 and Related Matters." *JBL* 89:313–18.
1972   "Additional Remarks on *rḥmyw* (Amos 1:11)." *JBL* 91:391–93.

Fisher, E. J.
1976   "Cultic Prostitution in the Ancient Near East? A Reassessment." *Biblical Theology Bulletin* 6:225–36.

Fisher, L. R., ed.
1972   *Ras Shamra Parallels I.* Analecta Orientalia 49. Rome: Pontifical Biblical Institute.
1975   *Ras Shamra Parallels II.* Analecta Orientalia 50. Rome: Pontifical Biblical Institute.

Fitzmyer, J. A.
1967   *The Aramaic Inscriptions of Sefîre.* Biblica et Orientalia 19. Rome: Pontifical Biblical Institute.

Flammer, F.
  1983   "Prophet und Tempel." [Amos 9:1–3] *Franziskanische Studien*
            65:35–42.
Fohrer, G.
  1968   *Introduction to the Old Testament.* Trans. D. E. Green. Nashville:
            Abingdon Press.
  1982   "Der Tag JHWHS." *EI* 16:43–50.
Foresti, F.
  1981   "Funzione   semantica   dei   brani   participali   di   Amos
            (4,13;5,8s;9,5s)." *Bib* 62:169–84.
Freedman, D. N.
  1963   "The Law and the Prophets." *VTS* 9:250–65. Leiden: Brill.
  1975   "Early Israelite History in the Light of Early Israelite Poetry."
            Pp. 3–35 in *Unity and Diversity: Essays in the History, Literature,
            and Religion of the Ancient Near East.* Ed. H. Goedicke and
            J. J. M. Roberts. Baltimore: The John Hopkins University Press.
            Repr. in Freedman 1980, pp. 131–66.
  1977a   "dor." Vol. 2, pp. 185–94 in *TWAT.*
  1977b   "Pottery, Poetry, and Prophecy: An Essay on Biblical Poetry."
            JBL 90:5–26. Repr. in Freedman 1980, pp. 1–22.
  1980   *Pottery, Poetry, and Prophecy: Studies in Early Hebrew Poetry.*
            Winona Lake, Ind.: Eisenbrauns.
  1981   "Temple Without Hands." Pp. 21–30 in *Temples and High Places
            in Biblical Times.* Ed. A. Biran. Jerusalem: Hebrew Union College
            Press.
  1983   "The Earliest Bible." Pp. 167–75 in *The Bible and Its Traditions.*
            [*MQR* 22.3] Ed. M. O'Connor and D. N. Freedman. Ann Arbor:
            University of Michigan Press.
  1985a   "But Did King David Invent Musical Instruments?" [Amos 6:5]
            Bible Review 1:48–51.
  1985b   "Who Asks (or Tells) God to Repent?" [Amos 7:1–6] *Bible Review*
            1:56–59.
  1987a   "Headings in the Books of the Eighth-Century Prophets." Pp.
            9–26 in *Seminary Studies Dedicated to Leona Glidden Running.*
            Andrews University Seminary Studies 25.1. Ed. K. A. Strand.
            Winona Lake, Ind.: Eisenbrauns.
  1987b   "The Structure of Isaiah 40:1–11." Pp. 167–93 in *Perspectives on
            Language and Text: Essays and Poems in Honor of Francis I.
            Andersen's Sixtieth Birthday, July 28, 1985.* Ed. E. W. Conrad and
            E. G. Newing. Winona Lake, Ind.: Eisenbrauns.
  1989   "Formation of the Canon of the Old Testament." in *Religion and
            Law.* Ed. E. B. Firmage. Winona Lake, Wisc.: Eisenbraun.
———, and A. Ritterspach
  1967   "The Use of *Aleph* as a Vowel Letter in the Genesis Apocryphon."
            RQ 6:293–300.

Friedman, R. E.
1979–80   "The *MZRḤ* Tablet from Ugarit." *Maarav* 2:187–206.

Fuhs, H. F.
1977   "Amos 1:1: Erwägungen zur Tradition und Redaktion des Amosbuches." Pp. 271–89 in *Bausteine biblischer Theologie: Festschrift für G. J. Botterweck.* Ed. H. J. Fabry. Cologne: Hanstein.

Garbini, G.
1977   "L'Inscrizione fenicia di Kilamuwa e il verbo *škr* in Semitico Nordoccidentale." *Bibbia e Oriente* 19:113–18.

Garrett, D. A.
1984   "The Structure of Amos as a Testimony to Its Integrity." *Journal of the Evangelical Theological Society* 27:275–76.

Gelb, I. J.
1979   "Definition and Discussion of Slavery and Serfdom." *UF* 11:283–97.

Gerleman, G.
1946   *Contributions to the Old Testament Terminology of the Chase.* Pp. 79–90 in *Humanistika Ventenskapssamtfundet;* Årsberättelse 1945–46. Lund.

Gese, H.
1962   "Kleine Beiträge zum Verständnis des Amosbuches." *VT* 12:417–38.

1979   "Das Problem von Amos 9:7." Pp. 33–38 in *Textgemäss: Aufsätze und Beiträge zur Hermeneutik des Alten Testaments: Festschrift für E. Würthwein.* Ed. A. H. J. Gunneweg and O. Kaiser. Göttingen: Vandenhoeck and Ruprecht.

1980–81   "Komposition bei Amos." *VTS* 32:74–95. Leiden: Brill.

Gevirtz, S.
1963   *Patterns in the Early Poetry of Israel.* Chicago: Oriental Institute.

1968   "A New Look at an Old Crux: Amos 5, 26." *JBL* 87:267–76.

1973   "On Canaanite Rhetoric: The Evidence of the Amarna Letters from Tyre." *Orientalia* 42:162–77.

Geyer, J. B.
1986   "Mythology and Culture in the Oracles Against the Nations." *VT* 36:129–45.

Gibson, J. C. L.
1971   *Textbook of Syrian Semitic Inscriptions.* Vol. 1, *Hebrew and Moabite Inscriptions.* Oxford: Clarendon Press.

Gilead, C.
1973   "Amos—from the Herdmen in Tekoa." *Beth Mikra* 54:375–81. (Hebrew with English summary)

Gitay, Y.
1980   "A Study of Amos' Art of Speech: A Rhetorical Analysis of Amos 3:1–15." *CBQ* 42:293–309.

Givati, M.
    1977   "The Shabbat of Prophet Amos." *Beth Mikra* 69:194–98. (Hebrew
                with English summary)
Glueck, N.
    1939   *Explorations in Eastern Palestine.* Vol. 3. Annual of the American
                Schools of Oriental Research 18–19. New Haven: American
                Schools of Oriental Research.
    1940   *The Other Side of Jordan.* New Haven: American Schools of Ori-
                ental Research.
    1951   *Explorations in Eastern Palestine.* Vol. 4, 2 pts. Annual of the
                American Schools of Oriental Research 25, 28. New Haven:
                American Schools of Oriental Research.
Gordis, R.
    1940   "The Composition and Structure of Amos." *HTR* 33:239–51.
    1943   "The Heptad as an Element of Biblical and Rabbinic Style." *JBL*
                62:17–26. Reprinted in Gordis 1971, pp. 95–103.
    1950   *"Na'alam* and Other Observations on the Ain Feshka Scrolls."
                JNES 9:44–47.
    1971   *Poets, Prophets, and Sages: Essays in Biblical Interpretation.*
                Bloomington: Indiana University Press.
    1976   "A Rhetorical Use of Interrogative Sentences in Biblical Hebrew,"
                pp. 152–57 in Gordis' *The Word and the Book.* New York: KTAV.
    1978   *The Book of Job: Commentary, New Translation and Special Stud-
                ies.* New York: KTAV.
    1979   "Edom, Israel and Amos—an Unrecognized Source for Edomite
                History." Pp. 109–32 in *Dropsie College 70th Anniversary Volume.*
                Ed. A. I. Katsh and L. Nemoy. Philadelphia: Dropsie College.
Gordon, C. H.
    1965   *Ugaritic Textbook.* Analecta Orientalia 38. Rome: Pontifical Bibli-
                cal Institute.
    1978   "New Directions." *Bulletin of the American Society of Papyrolo-
                gists* 15:59–66.
    1982   "Asymmetric Janus Parallelism." *EI* 16:80–81.
Gottwald, N. K.
    1979   *The Tribes of Yahweh: A Sociology of the Religion of Liberated
                Israel 1250–1050 B.C.E.* Maryknoll, N.Y.: Orbis Books.
Grabbe, L. L.
    1977   *Comparative Philology and the Text of Job: A Study in Methodol-
                ogy.* SBL Dissertation Series 34. Missoula, Mont.: Scholars Press.
Greenberg, M.
    1983   *Ezekiel 1–20.* AB 22. Garden City, N.Y.: Doubleday.
Greenfield, J. C.
    1960   "The Root 'GBL' in Mishnaic Hebrew and the Hymnic Literature
                from Qumran." *RQ* 6:155–62.
    1966   "Three Notes on the Sefire Inscription." *JSS* 11:98–105.

Gressmann, H.
1921   *Die älteste Geschichtsschreibung und Prophetie Israels (von Samuel bis Amos und Hosea)*. Ed. H. Gunkel. Die Schriften des Alten Testaments in Auswahl übersetzt und erklärt (3/1). Göttingen: Vandenhoeck und Ruprecht.

Gunkel, H., and J. Begrich
1933   *Einleitung in die Psalmen. Die Gattung der religiösen Lyrik Israels.* Handkommentar zum Alten Testament. Göttingen: Vandenhoeck und Ruprecht.

Gunneweg, A. H. J.
1960   "Erwägungen zu Amos 7, 14." *Zeitschrift für Theologie and Kirche* 57:1–16.

Hallo, W. W.
1977   "New Moons and Sabbaths: A Case Study in the Contrastive Approach." *HUCA* 48:1–18.

Halpern, B.
1979   "Landlord-Tenant Dispute at Ugarit?" *Maarav* 2:121–40.

Haran, M.
1967   "The Rise and Decline of the Empire of Jeroboam ben Joash." *VT* 17:266–97.

1968   "Observations on the Historical Background of Amos 1:2–2:6." *IEJ* 18:201–12.

1971   "The Graded Numerical Sequence and the Phenomenon of 'Automatism' in Biblical Poetry." *VTS* 19:238–67. Leiden: Brill.

Hare, D. R. A.
1985   "The Lives of the Prophets." Vol. 2, pp. 379–99 in *The Old Testament Pseudepigrapha.* Ed. J. Charlesworth. Garden City, N.Y.: Doubleday.

Harris, R.
1975   *Ancient Sippar: A Demographic Study of an Old-Babylonian City 1894–1595 B.C.* Istanbul: Nederlands Historisch-Archaeologisch Instituut te Istanbul.

Hellbing, L.
1979   *Alasia Problems.* Studies in Mediterranean Archaeology 57. Göteborg: P. Åström.

Hillers, D. R.
1964   "Amos 7:4 and Ancient Parallels." *CBQ* 26:221–25.

Hirscht, A.
1903   "Textkritische Untersuchungen über das Buch Amos." *Zeitschrift für wissenschaftliche Theologie* 44:11–73.

Höffken, P.
1982   "Eine Bemerkung zum 'Haus Hasaels' in Amos." *ZAW* 94:413–15.

Hoffman, H. W.
1970   "Zur Echtheitsfrage von Amos 9, 9f." *ZAW* 82:121–22.

Hoffmann, G.
  1883   "Versuche zu Amos." *ZAW* 3:87–126.
Hoffmann, Y.
  1977   "Did Amos Regard Himself as a *nābī'?*" *VT* 27:209–12.
  1982   "From Oracle to Prophecy: The Growth, Crystallization and Dis-
              integration of a Biblical Gattung." *Journal of Northwest Semitic
              Languages* 10:75–81.
Holladay, W. L.
  1970   "Once More, *'ănak* = Tin, Amos VII, 7–8," *VT* 20:492–94.
  1972   "Amos VI, 1bB: A Suggested Solution." *VT* 22:107–10.
  1986   *Jeremiah I.* Hermeneia. Philadelphia: Fortress Press.
Hoonacker, A. van
  1941   "Le sens de la protestation d'Amos vii, 14–15." *Ephemerides The-
              ologicae Lovanienses* 18:65–67.
Horst, F.
  1929   "Die Doxologien im Amosbuch." *ZAW* 47:45–54.
Houtman, C.
  1981   "Ezra and the Law." *OTS* 21:91–115.
Howard, G.
  1970   "Some Notes on the Septuagint of Amos." *VT* 20:108–12.
  1982   "Revision Toward the Hebrew in the Septuagint Text of Amos."
              EI 16:125–33.
Huesman, J.
  1956a   "Finite Uses of the Infinitive Absolute." *Bib* 37:271–95.
  1956b   "The Infinitive Absolute and the Waw + Perfect Problem." *Bib*
              37:410–34.
Huffmon, H. B.
  1983   "The Social Role of Amos' Message." Pp. 109–16 in *The Quest for
              the Kingdom of God: Studies in Honor of G. Mendenhall.* Ed. H. B.
              Huffmon et al. Winona Lake, Ind.: Eisenbrauns.
Hyatt, J. P.
  1947   *Prophetic Religion.* Nashville: Abingdon.
Isbell, C. D.
  1977   "A Note on Amos 1:1." *JNES* 36:213–14.
  1978   "Another Look at Amos 5:26." *JBL* 97:97–99.
Jacobs, P. F.
  1985   " 'Cows of Bashan'—A Note on the Interpretation of Amos 4:1."
              JBL 104:109–10.
Jacobsen, T.
  1946   "Mesopotamia." Pp. 137–216 in *Before Philosophy.* Ed. H. Frank-
              fort. Chicago: University of Chicago Press.
  1976   *The Treasures of Darkness.* New Haven: Yale University Press.
Janzen, W.
  1972   "Mourning Cry and Woe Oracles." [Amos 5:18–20, 6:1–7] BZAW
              125. Berlin: Walter de Gruyter.

Jenni, E.
1956   *Die politischen Voraussagen der Propheten*. Abhandlungen zur
        Theologie des Alten und Neuen Testaments 29. Zurich: Theo-
        logischer Verlag.
1968   *Das hebräische* piʿel. Zürich: EVZ-Verlag.
Kahlert, H.
1973   "Zur Frage nach der geistigen Heimat des Amos. Eine Prüfung
        der These von H. W. Wolff." *Dielhammer Blätter zum Alten Testa-
        ment* 4:1–12.
Källstad, T. E.
1980   "(Amos 4:11; Zech 3:2) 'A Brand Snatched out of Fire.' " *Archiv
        für Religionspsychologie* 14:237–45.
Kapelrud, A. S.
1961   *Central Ideas in Amos*. 2d ed. Oslo: H. Aschenhoug.
Kaufmann, Y.
1953   *The Biblical Account of the Conquest of Palestine*. Trans.
        M. Dagut. Jerusalem: Magnes Press.
1960   *The Religion of Israel*. Trans. M. Greenberg. Chicago: University
        of Chicago Press.
Kelly, J. G.
1976   "The Interpretation of Amos 4:13 in the Early Christian Commu-
        nity." Pp. 60–77 in *Essays in Honor of J. P. Brenan, by Members of
        the Faculty, St. Bernard's Seminary, Rochester, NY*. Ed. R. F.
        McNamara. Rochester, N.Y.
Kennicott, B.
1776   *Vetus Testamentum Hebraicum cum variis lectionibus*. Vol. 1. Ox-
        ford: Clarendon Press.
Klopfenstein, M. A.
1964   *Die Lüge nach dem Alten Testament*. Zurich: Gotthelf.
Knapp, A. B.
1985   "Alashiya, Caphtor/Keftiu, and Eastern Mediterranean Trade:
        Recent Studies in Cypriote Archaeology and History." *Journal of
        Field Archaeology* 12:231–50.
Knierim, R.
1965   *Die Hauptbegriffe für Sünde im Alten Testament*. Gütersloh:
        Gütersloher Verlagshaus (Gerd Mohn).
Koch, K.
1974   "Die Rolle der Hymnischen Abschnitte in der Komposition des
        Amos Buches." *ZAW* 86:504–34.
1976   *Amos. Untersucht mit den Methoden einer struckturalen Form-
        geschichte*. Alter Orient und Altes Testament 30. Kevelär: Butson
        & Berker.
Kraeling, E. G. H.
1918   *Aram and Israel, or the Arameans in Syria and Mesopotamia*. New
        York: Columbia University Press.

Kraft, R. A.
1979   "P.OXY. VI 846 (Amos 2:6–12) Reconsidered." *Bulletin of the American Society of Papyrologists* 16:201–4.
Krause, H. H.
1932   "Der Gerichtsprophet Amos, ein Vorläufer des Deuteronomisten." *ZAW* 50:221–39.
Krenkel, M.
1866   "Zur Kritik und Exegese der Kleinen Propheten." *Zeitschrift für wissenschaftliche Theologie* 9:266–81.
Kuenen, A.
1869   *De Godsdienst van Israel I.* Haarlem.
Kugel, J. F.
1981   *The Idea of Biblical Poetry.* New Haven: Yale University Press.
Kuhnigk, W.
1974   *Nordwest Semitische Studien zum Hoseabuch.* Biblica et Orientalia No. 27. Rome: Pontifical Biblical Institute.
Lambert, W. G.
1957–58 "Morals in Ancient Mespotamia." *Jaarbericht van het Voorziatisch-Egyptisch Genootschap Ex Oriente Lux* 15:184–96.
1960   *Babylonian Wisdom Literature.* Oxford: Clarendon Press.
Landsberger, B. L.
1965   "Tin and Lead: The Adventures of Two Vocables." *JNES* 24:285–96.
Lang, B.
1981   "Sklaven und Unfreie im Buch Amos (II 6, VIII 6)." *VT* 31:482–88.
Leeuwen, C. van
1974a   "Amos 1:2, Épigraphe du livre entier ou introduction aux oracles des chapitres 1–2." Pp. 93–101 in *Verkenningen in een stroomgebied* (*Festschrift* for M. A. Beek). Amsterdam: University of Amsterdam.
1974b   "The Prophecy of the *yôm YHWH* in Amos V 18–20." *OTS* 19:113–34.
Lichtenstein, M.
1968   "The Banquet Motif in Keret and in Proverbs 9." *Journal of the Ancient Near Eastern Society of Columbia University* 1:19–31.
Limburg, J.
1973   "Amos 7:4: A Judgement with Fire." *CBQ* 35:346–49.
1987   "Sevenfold Structures in the Book of Amos." *JBL* 106:217–22.
Lindblom, J.
1924   *Die literarische Gattung der prophetischen Literatur. Eine literargeschichtliche Untersuchung zum Alten Testament.* Uppsala: A. Lundequistska bokhandlen.
1955   "Wisdom in the Old Testament Prophets." *VTS* 3:192–204.

Liver, J.
1971   "The Israelite Tribes." Pp. 183–211 in *The World History of the Jewish People*. Ed. B. Mazar. New York: Jewish Historical Publication.

Lods, A.
1930   *Israel des origines au milieu du VIIIᵉ siècle*. Paris: Renaissance du livre.

Loretz, O.
1974   "Die Berufung des Propheten Amos (7, 14–15)." *UF* 6:487–88.
1976   "Vergleich und Kommentar in Amos 3, 12." *Biblische Zeitschrift* 20:122–25.

Luria, B. Z.
1973   "The Prophecies unto the Nations in the Book of Amos from the Point of View of History." *Beth Mikra* 54:287–301. (Hebrew)
1985   "Who Calls the Waters of the Sea and Spills Them on the Face of the Earth (Amos 5:8, 9:6)." *Beth Mikra* 101:259–62. (Hebrew)

Lust, J.
1981   "Remarks on the Redaction of Amos V 4–6, 14–15." *OTS* 21:129–54.

Maag, V.
1951   *Text, Wortschatz und Begriffswelt des Buches Amos*. Leiden: Brill.

MacCormack, J.
1955–56 "Amos VII, 14a." *ExpT* 67:318.

MacDonald, D. B.
1899   "The Old Testament Notes: Eccl. 3:11 and Amos 5:25." *JBL* 18:212–15.

McAlpine, T. H.
1975   "The Word Against the Nations." *Studies in Biblical Theology* 5:3–14.

McCarter, P. K.
1980   *1 Samuel*. AB 8. Garden City, N.Y.: Doubleday.
1984   *2 Samuel*. AB 9. Garden City, N.Y.: Doubleday.

McCaslin, D. E.
1980   *Stone Anchors in Antiquity: Coastal Settlements and Maritime Trade Routes in the Eastern Mediterranean*. Studies in Mediterranean Archaeology 61. Göteborg: P. Åström.

McKeating, H. M.
1971   *The Books of Amos, Hosea, and Micah*. Cambridge Bible Commentaries. Cambridge: The University Press.

Malamat, A.
1973   "Tribal Societies: Biblical Genealogies and African Lineage Systems." *Archives européennes de sociologie* 14:126–36.

Mandelkern, S.
1965   *Veteris Testamenti concordantiae*. Ed. M. Goshen-Gottstein and F. Margolis. 6th ed. Jerusalem: Schocken.

Markert, L.
1977   *Struktur und Bezeichnung des Scheltworts: Eine gattungskritische Studie anhand des Amosbuches.* BZAW 140. Berlin: de Gruyter.
Marmorstein, A.
1920   *The Doctrine of Merits in Old Rabbinical Literature.* London: Oxford University Press.
Mauchline, J.
1970   "Implicit Signs of a Persistent Belief in the Davidic Empire." *VT* 20:287–303.
Mays, J. L.
1959   "Words About the Words of Amos: Recent Studies in the Book of Amos." *Interpretation* 13:259–72.
Mazar, B.
1954   "Gath and Gittaim." *IEJ* 4:227–35.
Meek, T. J.
1940   "The Hebrew Accusative of Time and Place." *JAOS* 60:224–30.
1941a   "The Accusative of Time in Amos 1:1." *JAOS* 61:63–64.
1941b   "Again the Accusatives of Time in Amos 1:1." *JAOS* 61:190–91.
1958   "On Amos 2:7." *JAOS* 78:128.
Meinhold, J.
1930   "Zur Sabbathfrage." *ZAW* 48:121–38 (see Budde 1930).
Mendenhall, G. E.
1962   "Covenant." Pp. 714–23 in *IDB.*
1973   *The Tenth Generation.* Baltimore: The Johns Hopkins University Press.
Michaelis, D.
1772   *Deutsche Übersetzung des Alten Testaments.* Vol. 1. Göttingen.
Milgrom, J.
1964   "Did Isaiah Prophesy During the Reign of Uzziah?" *VT* 14:164–82.
Millard, A. R.
1978   "Epigraphic Notes, Aramaic and Hebrew." *PEQ* 110:23–26.
Miller, P. D.
1971   "The *MRZḤ* Text." Pp. 37–49 in *The Claremont Ras Shamra Tablets.* Ed. L. R. Fisher. Analecta Orientalia 48. Rome: Pontifical Biblical Institute.
1986   "The Absence of the Goddess in Israelite Religion." *Hebrew Annual Review* 10:239–48.
Mittman, S.
1971   "Gestalt und Gehalt einer prophetischen Selbstrechtfertigung (Amos 3, 3–8)." *Theologische Quartalschrift* (Tübingen) 151:134–45.
1976   "Amos 3, 12–15 und das Bett der Samarier." *ZDPV* 92:149–67.
Montgomery, J., and H. S. Gehman
1951   *The Book of Kings.* International Critical Commentary. New York: Scribners.

Morgenstern, J.

1931–32 "The Book of the Covenant, Part III—The *Ḥuqqim.*" *HUCA* 8–9:1–150.

1936 "Amos Studies I." *HUCA* 11:19–140 (also in Morgenstern 1941).

1937–38 "Amos Studies II." *HUCA* 12–13:1–53.

1940 "Amos Studies III." *HUCA* 15:59–304.

1941 *Amos Studies.* Vol. 2. The Sigmund Rheinstrom Memorial Publications. Cincinnati: Hebrew Union College Press.

1961 "Amos Studies IV." *HUCA* 32:295–350.

Mowinckel, S.

1914 *Zur Komposition des Buches Jeremiah.* Kritiania: Jacob Dybwad.

Muilenburg, J.

1956 "The Site of Ancient Gilgal." *BASOR* 140:11–27.

1970 "Baruch the Scribe." Pp. 215–38 in *Proclamation and Presence.* Ed. J. Durham and J. R. Porter. Richmond: John Knox Press.

Mulder, M. J.

1984 "Ein Vorschlag zur Übersetzung von Amos 3:6b." *VT* 34:106–8.

Mullen, E. T.

1980 *The Assembly of the Gods: The Divine Council in Canaanite and Early Hebrew Literature.* Chico, Calif.: Scholars Press.

Muraoka, T.

1970 "Is the LXX Amos VIII:12–IX:10 a Separate Unit?" *VT* 20:496–500.

Murtonen, A. E.

1952 "The Prophet Amos: A Hepatoscoper?" *VT* 2:170–71.

Na'aman, N.

1986 "Historical and Chronological Notes on the Kingdoms of Israel and Judah in the Eighth Century B.C." *VT* 36:71–92.

Nagah, R.

1981–82 "Are You Not Like the Ethiopians to Me (Amos 9:7)?" *Beth Mikra* 27:174–82. (Hebrew with English summary)

O'Connor, M.

1987 "The Pseudo-Sorites in Hebrew Verse," pp. 239–53 in *Perspectives on Language and Text. Essays and Poems in Honor of Francis I. Andersen's Sixtieth Birthday.* Ed. E. W. Conrad and E. G. Newing. Winona Lake, Ind.: Eisenbraun.

O'Rourke, M. B.

1971 "The Covenant Lawsuit of the Prophet Amos: III,I–IV,13." *VT* 21:338–62.

Orlinsky, H. M.

1983 "The Masorah on *'ănāwîm* in Amos 2:1." Pp. 25–35 in *Estudios Masoréticos.* Ed. T. E. Fernandes. Madrid: CSIS Institute.

Osten-Sacken, P. von der

1979 "Die Bücher der Tora als Hütte der Gemeinde—Amos 5:26 in der Damaskusschrift." *ZAW* 91:423–35.

Oullette, J.

1972   "The Shaking of the Thresholds in Amos 9:1." *HUCA* 43:23–27.

1973   "Le Mur d'étain dans Amos VII, 7–9." *Revue biblique* 80:321–31.

Overholt, T. W.

1979   "Commanding the Prophets: Amos and the Problem of Prophetic Authority." *CBQ* 41:517–32.

Paul, S. M.

1971   "Amos 1:3–2:3. A Concatenous Literary Pattern." *JBL* 90:397–403.

1978a   "Amos III, 15—Winter and Summer Mansions." *VT* 28:358–59.

1978b   "Fishing Imagery in Amos 4:2." *JBL* 97:183–90.

1981   "A Literary Reinvestigation of the Authenticity of the Oracles Against the Nations of Amos." Pp. 189–204 in *De la Tôrah au Messie, études d'exégèse et d'herméneutique bibliques offerts à H. Caselles pour 25 années d'enseignement à l'Institut Catholique de Paris.* Ed. M. Carrez et al. Paris: Desclée.

————, and W. G. Dever, eds.

1973   *Biblical Archaeology.* Library of Jewish Knowledge. Jerusalem: Keter Publishing House.

Pedersen, J.

1940   *Israel, Its Life and Culture.* London: Oxford University Press.

Pettinato, G.

1981   *The Archives of Ebla: An Empire Inscribed in Clay.* Garden City, N.Y.: Doubleday.

Pfeifer, G.

1976   "Denkformanalyse als exegetische Methode, erläutert an Amos 1,2–2,16." *ZAW* 88:56–71.

1981   "Amos und Deuterojesaja denkformanalytisch verglichen." *ZAW* 93:439–43.

1983   "Unausweichliche Konsequenzen: Denkformanalyse von Amos III 3–8." *VT* 33:341–47.

1984a   "Die Ausweisung eines lästigen Ausländers Amos 10:10–17." *ZAW* 96:112–18.

1984b   "Die Denkform des Propheten Amos (3:9–11)." *VT* 34:476–81.

Pitard, W. T.

1987   *Ancient Damascus: A Historical Study of the Syrian City from Earliest Times until its Fall to the Assyrians in 732 B.C.E.* Winona Lake, Ind.: Eisenbrauns.

Pope, M. H.

1977   *Song of Songs.* AB 7c. Garden City, N.Y.: Doubleday.

Porten, B.

1968   "The Marzeaḥ Association." Pp. 179–86 in *Archives from Elephantine.* Berkeley: University of California Press.

Porter, J. R.

1981   *"Běnê hanněbî'îm* (Amos 7:14 + 10x)." *JTS* 32:423–29.

Priest, J.
1965   "The Covenant of Brothers." *JBL* 84:400–6.
Pritchard, J. B.
1943   *Palestinian Figures in Relation to Certain Goddesses Known Through Literature.* American Oriental Series 24. New Haven: American Schools of Oriental Research.
Puech, E.
1977   "Milcom, le dieu ammonite, en Amos, 1:15." *VT* 27:117–25.
Rabinowitz, I.
1961   "The Crux at Amos III,12." *VT* 11:228–31.
Rahtjen, B. D.
1964   "A Critical Note on Amos 8:1–2." *JBL* 83:416–17.
Rainey, A. F.
1974   "Dust and Ashes." *Tel Aviv* 1:77–83.
Ramsey, G. W.
1970   "Amos 4:12—A New Perspective." *JBL* 89:187–91.
Rector, L. J.
1978   "Israel's Rejected Worship: An Exegesis of Amos 5." *Restoration Quarterly* 21:161–75.
Reider, J.
1948   *"dmšq* in Amos 3:12." *JBL* 67:245–48.
Rendtorff, R.
1973   "Zu Amos 2, 14–16." *ZAW* 85:226–27.
Reventlow, H.
1962   *Das Amt Des Propheten bei Amos.* Forschungen zur Religion und Literatur des Alten und Neuen Testaments 80. Göttingen: Vandenhoeck und Ruprecht.
Richardson, H. N.
1973   *"SKT* (Amos 9:11) 'Booth' or 'Succoth'?" *JBL* 92:375–81.
Riedel, W.
1902   "Bemerkungen zum Buche Amos." Vol. 1, pp. 19–36 in *Alttestamentliche Untersuchungen.* Leipzig.
Rivkin, E.
1969   "Prolegomenon." Pp. vii–lxx in *Judaism and Christianity.* Ed. W. O. E. Oesterly. Repr. New York: KTAV.
Robinson, T. H.
1923   *Prophecy and the Prophets in Ancient Israel.* London: Gerald Duckworth.
1947   *The Poetry of the Old Testament.* London: Duckworth.
Rosenbaum, S. N.
1977   "Northern Amos Revisited: Two Philological Suggestions." *Hebrew Studies* 18:132–48.
Roth, W. M. W.
1962   "The Numerical Sequence $x/x + 1$ in the Old Testament." *VT* 12:300–11.
1965   "Numerical Sayings in the Old Testament." *VTS* 13. Leiden: Brill.

Routtenberg, H. J.
1971   *Amos of Tekoa: A Study in Interpretation.* New York: Vantage Press.

Rowley, H. H.
1946   "The Unity of the Old Testament." *BJRL* 29:326–58.
1947   "Was Amos a Nabi?" Pp. 491–98 in *Festschrift für Otto Eissfeldt.* Ed. J. Fück. Halle: Max Niemeyer.
1950   "The Meaning of Sacrifice in the Old Testament." *BJRL* 33:74–110.

Rudolph, W.
1970   "Amos 4, 6–13." Pp. 27–38 in *Wort, Gebot, Glaube. Beiträge zur Theologie des Alten Testaments: Walther Eichrodt zum 80. Geburtstag.* Ed. H. J. Ströbe. Abhandlungen zur Theologie des Alten und Neuen Testaments 59. Zurich: Zwingli.
1971b   "Die angefochtenen Völkssprüche in Amos 1 und 2." Pp. 45–49 in *Schalom. Studien zu Glaube und Geschichte Israels: Alfred Jepsen zum 70. Geburtstag dargebracht von Freunden, Schülern und Kollegen.* Ed. K. H. Bernhardt. Stuttgart: Calwer.
1973   "Schwierige Amosstellen." Pp. 157–62 in *Wort und Geschichte. Festschrift für K. Elliger zum 70. Geburtstag.* Ed. H. Gese and H. P. Rüger. Alter Orient und Altes Testament 18. Göttingen: Neukirchener Verlag.

Sawyer, J. F. A.
1970   " 'Those Priests in Damascus': A Possible Example of Anti-Sectarian Polemic in the Septuagint Version of Amos 3:12." *Annual of the Swedish Theological Institute* 8:123–30.

Schmid, H.
1967   " 'Nicht Prophet bin ich noch bin ich Prophetsohn.' Zur Erklärung von Amos 7,14a." *Judaica* 23:68–74.

Schmidt, W. H.
1965   "Die Deuteronomistische Redaktion des Amosbuches. Zu den theologischen Unterschieden zwischen dem Prophetenwort und seinem Sammler." *ZAW* 77:168–93.

Schottroff, W.
1964   *"Gedenken" im Alten Orient und im Alten Testament: Die Wurzel zākar im semitischen Sprachkreise.* Wissenschaftliche Monographien zum Alten und Neuen Testament 15. Neukirchen-Vluyn: Neukirchener Verlag.
1979   "Der Prophet Amos. Versuch einer Würdigung seines Auftretens unter sozialgeschichtlichem Aspekt." Vol. 1, pp. 39–66 in *Der Gott der Kleinen Leute, sozialgeschichtliche Biblauslegungen.* Ed. W. Schottroff and W. Stegema. Munich: Kaiser.

Schoville, K. N.
1974   "A Note on the Oracles of Amos Against Gaza, Tyre, and Edom." *VTS* 26:55–63. Leiden: Brill.

Schult, H.
1971   "Amos 7, 15a und die Legitimation des Aussenseiters." Pp.
        462–78 in *Probleme biblischer Theologie: Festschrift für G. von
        Rad.* Ed. H. W. Wolff. Munich: Kaiser.
Schwantes, S. J.
1967   "Note on Amos 4,2b." *ZAW* 79:82–83.
Seilhamer, F. H.
1974   "The Role of Covenant in the Mission and Message of Amos." Pp.
        435–51 in *A Light unto my Path: Old Testament Studies in Honor
        of Jacob M. Myers.* Ed. H. N. Bream et al. Gettysburg Theological
        Studies 4. Philadelphia: Temple University Press.
Shea, W. H.
1977   "A Date for the Recently Discovered Eastern Canal of Egypt."
        BASOR 226:31–38.
Smalley, W. A.
1979   "Recursion Patterns and Sectioning of Amos." *Bible Translator*
        30:118–27.
Smelik, K. A. D.
1986   "The Meaning of Amos 5:18–20." *VT* 36:246–48.
Smend, R.
1963   "Das Nein des Amos." *Evangelische Theologie* 23:404–23.
Snyder, G.
1982   "The Law and Covenant in Amos." *Restoration Quarterly*
        25:158–66.
Soggin, J. A.
1970   "Das Erdbeben von Amos 1:1 und die Chronologie der Könige
        Ussia und Jotham von Juda." *ZAW* 82:117–21.
1971   "Amos 6:13–14 und 1:3 auf dem Hintergrund der Beziehungen
        zwischen Israel und Damaskus im 9. und 8. Jahrhundert." Pp.
        433–41 in *Near Eastern Studies in Honor of William Foxwell Al-
        bright.* Ed. H. Goedicke. Baltimore: The Johns Hopkins Univer-
        sity Press.
Speiser, E. A.
1940   "Of Shoes and Shekels." *BASOR* 77:15–20.
Sperber, A.
1966   *A Historical Grammar of Biblical Hebrew.* Leiden: Brill.
Stamm, J. J.
1980   *Der Name des Propheten Amos und sein sprachlicher Hintergrund.*
        BZAW 150. Berlin: de Gruyter.
Story, C. K. I.
1980   "Amos—Prophet of Praise." *VT* 30:67–80.
Strange, J.
1980   "Caphtor/Keftiu, a New Investigation." *Acta Theologica Danica*
        14:1–277.

Ströbe, H. J.
  1970   "Überlegungen zu den geistlichen Voraussetzungen der Prophetie
          des Amos." Pp. 209–25 in *Wort-Gebot-Glaube: Walther Eichrodt
          zum 80. Geburtstag*. Abhandlungen zur Theologie des Alten und
          Neuen Testaments 59. Ed. H. J. Ströbe. Zurich: Zwingli.

Strong, H. A., and J. Garstang
  1913   *The Syrian Goddess*. Translation of Lucian's *De dea Syria* with a
          Life of Lucian. London: Constable.

Stuart, D. K.
  1976   *Studies in Early Hebrew Meter*. Harvard Semitic Monographs 13.
          Cambridge, Mass.: Harvard Semitic Museum.

Super, A. S.
  1973   "Figures of Comparison in the Book of Amos." *Semitica* 3:67–80.

Szabó, A.
  1975   "Textual Problems in Amos and Hosea." *VT* 25:500–24.

Terrien, S. L.
  1962   "Amos and Wisdom." Pp. 106–14 in *Israel's Prophetic Heritage:
          Essays in Honor of J. Muilenburg*. Ed. B. W. Anderson and
          W. Harrelson. New York: Harper & Brothers.

Thiele, E. R.
  1965   *The Mysterious Numbers of the Hebrew Kings*. Rev. ed. Grand
          Rapids: Eerdmans.

Torczyner, H. (See also Tur-Sinai, H.)
  1936   "Presidential Address." *Journal of the Palestine Oriental Society*.
          16:1–8.
  1947   "A Hebrew Incantation Against Night Demons from Biblical
          Times." *JNES* 6:18–29.

Torrey, C. C.
  1946   *The Lives of the Prophets, Greek Text and Translation*. Journal of
          Biblical Literature Monograph Series 1. Philadelphia: Society of
          Biblical Literature.

Tromp, N.
  1984   "Amos 5:1–17: Towards a Stylistic and Rhetorical Analysis." *OTS*
          23:56–84.

Tucker, G. M.
  1973   "Prophetic Authenticity: A Form-Critical Essay on Amos
          7:10–17." *Interpretation* 27:423–34.

Tsirkin, Y. B.
  1976   *The Phoenician Culture in Spain*. Moscow: Nauka. (Russian)

Tur-Sinai (Torcznyer), H.
  1954   *halašon wehaseper: Essays by Harry Torczyner*. Vol. 1. Jerusalem:
          Bialek Institute.

Tzevat, M.
  1961   "Studies in the Book of Samuel." *HUCA* 32:191–216.
  1972   "The Basic Meaning of the Biblical Sabbath." *ZAW* 84:447–59.

Uffenheimer, B.
1976   "Amos and Hosea—Two Directions in Israel's Prophecy." *Dor le Dor* 5:101–10. (Hebrew)

Unger, M. F.
1957   *Israel and the Arameans of Damascus: A Study in Archaeological Illumination of Bible History.* Grand Rapids, Mich.: Zondervan.

Vaux, R. de
1934   "La Chronologie de Hazael et de Benhadad III, rois de Damas." *Revue biblique* 43:512–18.

Vesco, J.-L.
1980   "Amos de Teqoa, défenseur de l'homme." *Revue biblique* 87:481–543.

Vischer, W.
1975   "Amos, citoyen de Téqoa." *Études théologiques et religieuses* 50:133–59.

Vogels, W.
1972   "Invitation à revenir à l'alliance et universalisme en Amos IX, 7." *VT* 22:223–39.

Vogt, E.
1956–57 "Waw Explicative in Amos VII, 14." *ExpT* 68:301–2.

Vollmer, J.
1971   *Geschichtliche Rückblicke und Motive in der Prophetie des Amos, Hosea und Jesaja.* BZAW 119. Berlin: Walter de Gruyter.

Vriezen, T. C.
1970   "Erwägungen zu Amos 3,2." Pp. 255–58 in *Archäologie und Altes Testament. Festschrift für Kurt Galling.* Tübingen: J. C. B. Mohr.

Waard, J. de
1974   "A Greek Translation-Technical Treatment of Amos 1:15." Pp. 111–18 in *On Language, Culture, and Religion (Festschrift* for E. A. Nida). Ed. M. Black. The Hague: Mouton.
1977   "The Chiastic Structure of Amos V, 1–17." *VT* 27:170–77.
1978   "Translational Techniques Used by the Greek Translators of Amos." *Bib* 59:339–50.

Wagner, S.
1971   "Überlegungen zur Frage nach Beziehungen des Propheten Amos zum Südreich." *Theologische Literaturzeitung* 96:653–70.

Wal, A. van der
1983   "The Structure of Amos." *JSOT* 26:107–13.

Waldman, N. M.
1973   "On *hplyg, ʿbr,* and Akkadian Parallels," pp. 6–8 in Gratz College Annual 2. Philadelphia: Gratz College.

Watson, W. G. E.
1984   *Classical Hebrew Poetry: A Guide to Its Techniques. JSOT* Supplement Series 26. Sheffield: JSOT Press.

Watts, J. D. W.
 1958 *Vision and Prophecy in Amos: 1955 Faculty Lectures, Baptist Theological Seminary, Rüschlikon/Zürich, Switzerland.* Leiden: Brill.
 1972 "A Critical Analysis of Amos 4, 1ff." Vol. 2, pp. 489–500 in *Society of Biblical Literature Annual Meeting Proceedings* 108. Missoula, Mont.: Scholars Press.

Weil, G. E.
 1980 "Analyse automatique quantifiée en critique textuelle biblique: Limite des analyses statistiques." Colloque de l'ALLC, Tel-Aviv. *Bulletin of the Association for Literary and Linguistic Computing* 8.

Weimar, P.
 1981 "Der Schluss des Amos-Buches. Ein Beitrag zur Redaktionsgeschichte des Amos-Buches." *Biblische Notizen* 16:60–100.

Weinfeld, M.
 1972 "The Worship of Molech and the Queen of Heaven and Its Background." *UF* 4:133–54.

Weingreen, J.
 1939 *A Practical Grammar for Classical Hebrew.* Oxford: Clarendon Press.

Weiser, A.
 1928 "Zu Amos 4:6–13." *ZAW* 46:49–59.

Weisman, Z.
 1975 "Stylistic Parallels in Amos and Jeremiah: Their Implications for the Composition of Amos." *Shnaton* 1:129–49. (Hebrew with English summary)

Weiss, M.
 1967a " 'Because Three . . . and Because Four' (Amos I–II)." *Tarbiz* 36:307–18. (Hebrew with English summary)
 1967b "The Pattern of Numerical Sequence in Amos 1–2: A Re-Examination." *JBL* 86:416–23.
 1978 "These Days and the Days to Come According to Amos." *EI* 14:69–73. (Hebrew with English summary)

Westermann, C.
 1954 "Struktur und Geschichte der Klage im Alten Testament." *ZAW* 66:44–80.
 1967 *Basic Forms of Prophetic Speech.* London: ET.

Willi-Plein, I.
 1971 *Vorformen der Schriftexegese innerhalb des Alten Testaments. Untersuchungen zum literarischen Werden der auf Amos, Hosea und Micha zurückgehenden Bücher im hebräischen Zwölfprophetenbuch.* BZAW 123. Berlin: Walter de Gruyter.

Williams, A. J.
 1979 "A Further Suggestion About Amos IV, 1–3." *VT* 29:206–11.

Williams, J. G.
 1977 "Irony and Lament: Clues to Prophetic Consciousness." *Semeia* 8:51–74.

Winckler, H.
1895   *Geschichte Israels.* Leipzig: Pfeiffer.

Wolff, H. W.
1964   *Amos' geistige Heimat.* Wissenschaftliche Monographien zum Alten und Neuen Testament 19. Neukirchen-Vluyn: Neukirchener Verlag.

1970   "Das Ende des Heligtums in Bethel." Pp. 287–98 in *Archäologie und Altes Testament: Festschrift für Kurt Galling.* Ed. V. A. Kuschke and E. Kutsch. Tübingen: J. C. B. Mohr.

1973   *Amos the Prophet: The Man and His Background.* Trans. F. R. McCurley. Philadelphia: Fortress Press.

Wright, G. E.
1966   "Fresh Evidence for the Philistine Story." *BA* 29:70–86.

Wright, T. J.
1975   "Did Amos Inspect Livers?" *AusBR* 23:3–11.

1976   "Amos and the 'Sycomore Fig.' " *VT* 26:362–68.

Würthwein, E.
1947   "Amos 5:21–27." *TZ* 72:143–52.

Yadin, Y., et al.
1960   *Hazor II: An Account of the Second Season of Excavations, 1956.* Jerusalem: Magnes Press.

Zalcman, L.
1980   "Piercing Darkness at *bôqer.*" *VT* 30:352–55.

1981   "Astronomical Allusions in Amos." *JBL* 100:53–58.

Zevit, Z.
1975   "A Misunderstanding at Bethel, Amos VII 12–17." *VT* 25:783–90.

1979   "Expressing Denial in Biblical Hebrew and Mishnaic Hebrew, and in Amos." *VT* 29:505–8.

Zimmerli, W.
1980   "Das Gottesrecht bei den Propheten Amos, Hosea und Jesaja." Pp. 216–35 in *Werden und Wirken des Alten Testaments: Festschrift für C. Westermann.* Ed. R. Albertz. Göttingen: Neukirchener Verlag.

Ziu, Y.
1982   " 'Bōqēr ûbōlēs šěqamîm'—běTeqoaʕ?" *Beth Mikra* 92:49–51.

For further bibliographic reference see:
1983   *Amos: A Classified Bibliography.* Ed. A. van der Wal. Amsterdam: Free University Press.

1972–85   *Biblical Bibliography.* Ed. P-E. Langevin. Quebec: University of Laval Press.

1920–   *Elenchus bibliographicus Biblicus.* 1920–68 published as part of the journal *Biblica,* 1968– published as separate volumes. Rome: Pontifical Biblical Institute.

1951–   *Internationale Zeitschriftenschau für Bibelwissenschaft und Grenzgebiete.* Düsseldorf: Patmos-Verlag.

1978–   *Old Testament Abstracts.* Washington, D.C.: Catholic University of America.

AMOS:
TRANSLATION, NOTES,
AND COMMENTS

PART I

The Book of Doom
(1:1–4:13)

HEADING (1:1)

1¹The words of Amos—who was one of the sheep raisers from Tekoa—who had visions concerning Israel in the days of Uzziah the king of Judah, and in the days of Jeroboam ben-Joash the king of Israel, two years before the earthquake.

INTRODUCTION

The heading identifies the prophet and the date of his visions in relation to the reigns of kings of Judah and Israel. The information supplied is precise, but meager. On the one hand we are told Amos' hometown and his profession, and the visionary character of his prophetic experience. But on the other he is given no patronymic and is not even called a prophet. A precise date is given ("two years before the earthquake"), but the earthquake itself is not dated. His work is located in the days of two kings, but their reigns were among the longest on record and largely overlapped. The exact years are uncertain, but ca. 790–740 for Uzziah and ca. 790–750 for Jeroboam II are reasonable estimates. Where Amos is to be dated within these three or four decades is hard to say. There is no information about Amos outside this book, and there are no datable events reported in the book that might aid in narrowing the range.

Many scholars, assuming that the earthquake triggered Amos' career and dating the earthquake to about 760 B.C.E., assign his main activity to the later years of the contemporary kings. The language of 8:9 has been attached to a total eclipse of the sun that took place in 763 B.C.E. If 8:9 is seen as a comment on this event, not a prediction of it, then Amos' main work is dated to the 750s (Smith 1896:1.66). On the basis of the interpretation of various texts throughout the book against the historical background, we shall argue for an earlier date—possibly 780–770—recognizing freely that such arguments can only be oblique and circumstantial, and that certainty cannot be achieved.

NOTES

1:1. *The words of Amos.* The prophecy of Amos consists of oracles of Yahweh, not sayings of the prophet. Hence the title refers to the "matters" of Amos, that is, his "story," or rather materials connected with his name. (See Jer 1:1 and Andersen and Freedman 1980:150.) In other details the heading of Amos resembles Mic 1:1, but the latter's opening phrase, *dĕbar yhwh,* refers directly to an oracle of the Lord. This term is nearly always singular; and such a divine message, even though spoken by a human, is not referred to alternatively as that person's *words.* The difference is made quite clear in Jer 1:1–2, where "the word of Yahweh" that came to Jeremiah is distinguished from "the words of Jeremiah," which constitute the subject matter of the entire book.

It is only in much later retrospect and because of his unique role that the term "Torah of Moses" can be used interchangeably with "Torah of Yahweh." A similar identification of "the word of the Lord" is never made with the word of any prophet, but compare 1 Kgs 17:1, where Elijah refers to "my word" as having oracular force.

Mays (1969:3, 18) maintains that the title means that the book is a collection of "Amos sayings." It is, in fact, a series of Yahweh sayings that came to the prophet in prophetic visions. Some of these visions are reported in The Book of Visions (7:1–9:6), and the autobiographical form in which those visions are reported (7:1, 4, 7; 8:1; 9:1) shows that Amos himself told the story of those visions. In this sense the whole book can be titled "Stories about (or told by) Amos. . . ."

The expression itself, *dibrê N,* is used often enough at the beginning of Bible books or sections to show that it serves as a title. Thus we have it at Neh 1:1, Eccl 1:1, and Prov 30:1, among others. Note also Jer 51:64 and Job 31:40, where the same expression is used to mark the end of a literary entity. We also have the frequently repeated formula *yeter dibrê N,* referring to the activities of successive kings of Israel and Judah in Kings and Chronicles, also *sēper dibrê N* or *sēper dibrê hayyāmîm* (i.e., annals). The grammatical construction is itself ambiguous; the genitive may be taken as either the subject or the object of the construct "the words by *N*" or "the words about *N.*" The latter would be a broader expression and would signify the account or record of *N,* and might well include *N*'s words as part of the fuller account, as is certainly the case with the kings, whose record would contain both edicts and actions. Where the expression occurs at the beginning of a book the same seems likely, though in the case of the prophets the predominant element would be the utterances. Nevertheless, in the two prophetic books that begin in this fashion (Amos and Jeremiah) we have not only prophetic utterances but also biographical material about the prophets. Thus we conclude that *dibrê ʿāmôs* means "the Story of Amos," or "Amos' Record," or "Amos' Report." We must then interpret the following clauses in this fashion: "The record of Amos—who was one of the sheep raisers from Tekoa—who had visions concerning Israel," and so on.

It is equally appropriate to call a prophetic book "The Word of Yahweh" (Hos 1:1; Joel 1:1; Mic 1:1; Zeph 1:1; Mal 1:1; cf. Jonah 1:1; Hag 1:1; Zech 1:1), or "The Vision of *N*" (Isa 1:1; similarly Obad 1; Nah 1:1). The titles of Amos and Jeremiah are similar to each other and different from the rest, perhaps because of a somewhat greater interest in the person of the prophet himself, even though in the case of Amos the personal information available is minimal. But in other instances (Joel, Micah, Nahum, Habakkuk, Zechariah) there are no personal details at all. Nonetheless, the titles of both Amos and Jeremiah immediately restore the balance by adding "who had visions" (Amos 1:1) or "to whom the word of Yahweh came" (Jer 1:2).

Amos. It is only an accident that his name (*ʿāmôs*) sounds like the name of Isaiah's father (*ʾāmôṣ*) in languages other than Hebrew or cognates. The words have only one consonant in common. There is no connection between the two men. Nothing is known about Amos apart from what is provided in this book. Not even his patronymic is given, or his tribal affiliation. Coming "from Tekoa" presumes that he was a Judahite, and Amaziah in 7:12 apparently tells him to go back to his homeland.

The etymology of the name *ʿāmôs* does not contribute to our understanding of the man or of his message. It has been claimed, nevertheless, that the meanings of the root *ʿms,* "to carry" or "to load," are "highly significant and descriptive of the prophet's activity" (Laetsch 1956:137). It could be said of any prophet that he bore the Word and found it a burden. It can only be a fancy that such a connection was intended in the case of Amos. There is no indication that he was given this name to match his character. No use is made of the root within the book itself as part of its message.

The biblical name *ʿămāśāʾ ʿămāśay* cannot be equated with *ʿms* with any confidence; neither can *ʿămaśśay* (Neh 11:13). There remains only *ʿămasyâ* (2 Chr 17:16), which in Amos' day would have been **ʿămasyāhû.* A verbal root such as this one can generate quite a repertoire of personal names based on either perfect or imperfect, usually with a divine name. The divine name may be omitted to yield a shorter form. Two such sets are *yĕḥizqiyyāhû, yĕḥizqiyyâ, ḥizqiyyāhû, ḥizqiyyâ, ḥizqî, yĕḥezqēʾl; yĕberekyāhû, berekyāhû, berekyâ, bārakʾēl.* If the seal published by N. Avigad (1979) of Berekyahu ben-Neriyahu, the Scribe, actually belonged to Jeremiah's friend Baruch (*bārûk,* the only name by which he is called in the book of Jeremiah), then it would seem that a person's name could be used in longer or shortened forms. Names based on *ʿms* were widely used in the NW Semitic onomasticon (Stamm 1980), generally theophoric: *yaḥmus-AN* in Amorite, *ʿmsʾl* in Ammonite, *ʿmsmlk, ʾšmn ʿms, bʿlʿms, mlqrtʿms* in Phoenician; but *ʿms* alone is attested in both Phoenician and Ugaritic. All seem to come under the heading of thanksgiving names, celebrating the fact that someone has been carried (= supported, sustained) by the god. Either side of such an experience can be highlighted, as shown by the variants (*yĕberekyāhû*, God actively blesses, and *bārûk*, passive, the human is "blessed"). The problem in the case of *ʿāmôs* is whether it derives from a passive **ʿamus*, "Borne [by God]," or is an active noun, "Bearer." As the word stands, it could be a variant of the verbal component of the complete theophoric name, the infinitive absolute, and so quite generalized or deliberately ambiguous in voice.

The rarity of the name is matched by the rarity of the use of the verb to describe an act of God in the Bible. Ps 68:20b[E19b]—"day by day he carries the load for us"—is about the only case. If the idea had been exploited in the book of Amos, we might have expected the root in 2:13. But no hint of any such connection is given.

who was. The use of the past tense gives a historical perspective to this detail. It could be the past in relation to his career (he used to be a sheep raiser; he *became* a prophet), or the past as seen after his death. The precise nuance to be given to *hāyâ* depends on the meaning of the following preposition, *b-,* in the complete idiom. (See the next note.) Hence the choice: "who was among the shepherds" (RSV), or "one of the sheep-farmers" (NEB), or "who came from the sheep raisers." Amos' own testimony— "Yahweh took me from following the flock" (7:15)—suggests a clean break from his former vocation when he became a visionary.

one of. Further comparison of Amos 1:1 with Jer 1:1 raises the question of the meanings of the prepositions *min-* and *b-* and of the relations between them.

	PROFESSION	HOMETOWN
Jer 1:1	*min-hakkōhănîm*	*baʿănātôt*
Amos 1:1	*bannōqĕdîm*	*mittĕqôaʿ*

If the matching expressions are considered to be equivalent, then the semantic ranges of *min-* and *b-* overlap, and they are to some extent interchangeable. The possibility that *min-* can have a locative meaning "in," while *b-* can have a partitive meaning "from," has caused some anxiety among scholars (neither meaning was recognized by BDB), but routine translation of *min-* as "from" and *b-* as "in" leads to many awkward results.

The case for partitive *b-* is stronger than the case for locative *min-*. The constructions in Jer 1:1 and Amos 1:1 are not exactly the same (Jeremiah has *ʾăšer baʿănātôt,* so the prepositions need not be equated in each pair of expressions). Jeremiah was one of the priests *in* Anathoth; Amos was one of the sheep raisers *from* Tekoa. The choice of preposition could record a subtle nuance. Jeremiah was still regarded as belonging to the community of priests in Anathoth; Amos was no longer one of the *nōqĕdîm* in Tekoa. The Lord took him away from that (7:14–15). At least it gives the perspective from outside, just as Elimelek was *"from* Bethlehem" (Ruth 1:2) or "Goliath *from* Gath" was his name (1 Sam 17:4). The usual "the shepherds of Tekoa" (RSV) loses this detail. It is not only bland; it is careless, for that wording would be simply **nōqĕdê tĕqôaʿ.* The translation "among" (RSV) is a compromise between the locative and partitive meanings of *b-.* Compare the same translation of *b-* in Gen 17:23. The fine balance between these two possibilities can be estimated by study of the use of both prepositions throughout Amos. Without listing every example, it should be enough to point out that in the oracles against the nations *b-* has many meanings— temporal (*bîmê* [1:14, twice]; *bĕyôm* [1:14, twice]; *bĕqôl* [2:2]), circumstantial (scarcely distinguishable from temporal: *bitrûʿâ* [1:14; 2:2]; *bĕsaʿar* [1:14]; *bĕšāʾôn* [2:2]), and instrumental (*baḥărūṣôt habbarzel* [1:3]; *baḥereb* [1:11]; *bakkesep* [2:6], the latter sometimes distinguished as the *b-* of price). Its only spatial meaning is associated with movement, not rest—"into" or "against" (1:4, 7, 10, 12, 14, 15; 2:2, 5). *Min-,* by contrast, often has a spatial reference, and the translation "in" makes as good sense as "from" (1:5 [twice], 8 [twice]; 2:3), especially in 1:2 (see the note on *min-* in that verse).

sheep raisers. The similarity between Amos 1:1 and Jer 1:1–2 weakens Mays's argument that the reference to the *nōqĕdîm* is an addition to the original title (1969:18). There is no need to think of it as a gloss, especially as it contrasts with Amos' self-identification as *bôqēr,* "herdsman," in 7:14. The correctness of *nōqēd* as a designation for Amos was used by some scholars to throw doubt on 7:14, and to change *bôqēr* to *nôqēd,* an unnecessary harmonization.

As for Amos' profession, the word *nōqēd* is found again in the Bible only in 2 Kgs 3:4, where it is a title for Mesha, the king of Moab.

The word is evidently cognate with Arabic *naqadun,* a kind of small sheep, and *naqqādun,* "shepherd." The participle *nāqidu* is likewise used in Akk as *nomen professionis.* In spite of the coincidence, the adjective *nāqōd* (Gen 30:32, 35, 39; 31:8, 10, 12), which describes "speckled" sheep and goats, is probably not connected with *nqd* II (BDB) but with *niqqûd,* which describes some kind of biscuit (1 Kgs 14:3) or crumbs (Josh 9:5, 12) or ornamental jewelry (Cant 1:11)—*nqd* I (BDB).

It has been suggested (Gibson 1971:75) that *nqdy,* "my *nōqēd*s," be restored in the damaged Mesha inscription at the end of line 30. This change would match evidence from Ugarit that is abundant and clear. There the term *nqd* is found in various lists of functionaries (*UT* 62.55; 300.12; 308.12). In that society it seems to mean "high officials in charge of royal(?) herds" (*UT,* p. 447). (For full discussion and bibliography see Wright 1975 and Fisher 1976:63f.) Clearly, it can designate a wealthy pastoralist, which has made some people wonder whether Amos was a sheep owner and not merely a tender of flocks, as the language of Amos 7:14 suggests. Scholars who wish to cast Amos in the role of champion of the proletariat emphasize that the sycamore fig was the food of the poor, who scratched a subsistence wherever they might. But if Amos was in any way like the king of Moab, he would have been wealthy and influential. Amos 7:14–15 gives a different impression. Apart from possible seasonal employment as a (hired?) worker in the sycamore fig industry, itself a lowly task, he describes himself as "following the flock" (7:15), a phrase not applicable to the king of Moab, and with no hint of ownership of numerous flocks. If he was only one of several *nōqĕdîm* in a little country town like Tekoa, his social and economic status must have been fairly modest. Terms for social rank are notoriously unstable and tend to slide down the scale. Amos lived in a different country, in a different century, and in differing economic circumstances from Mesha, so similarity need only be slight. Suggested in part by the association of Ugaritic *nqdm* with *khnm,* "priests" (*UT* 62.55), and in part from a general theory that Israelite prophets were officers of the cult, Amos' status as *nōqēd* has been interpreted as that of either a supplier of sheep needed for sacrifice at the shrines or a diviner whose technique was the inspection of a sheep's liver (Bič 1951 and others). The arguments are tenuous and receive no support from the book of Amos itself. A. E. Murtonen (1952) presented arguments against the theory. There are no examples within the OT of any Israelite shrines having their own flocks and shepherds; and even if they did, it would not make the attendants cultic officers. In any case, the distance in time, space, and culture between Ugarit and Tekoa is even greater than that between Mesha and Amos. Amos' social and economic status cannot be reconstructed from this meager evidence. (See the discussion at 7:14.)

Tekoa. A village in the Judean hills about eight kilometers (five miles) southeast of Bethlehem. The country quickly passes into desert, but some valleys are fertile enough to yield grain and the usual fruits.

who had visions. Characteristic translations are "which he saw" (RSV), "which he received in visions" (NEB). These agree with the LXX, in which the relative pronouns *hoi* and *hous* make "words" the antecedent of both relative clauses. This interpretation derives support from Mic 1:1, which reads, "Yahweh's word, which came to Micah . . . , who had visions concerning Samaria."

In Mic 1:1 the antecedent of *ʾăšer* is "Yahweh's word," certainly in the first clause and plausibly in the second. Isa 2:1 demonstrates that the combination *ḥazâ dābār* is entirely in order. The point is, however, that in both Micah and Isaiah the word in question is that of Yahweh (explicitly in Micah and by implication in Isaiah), while the presumed antecedent in Amos 1:1 is "the words of Amos." For the unlikely picture of Amos seeing his own words there is no parallel whatever. It is instructive that in Jer 1:2 the "word of Yahweh" is introduced alongside the formula in 1:1 (the "words of Jeremiah"), showing that the two have independent meanings. In view of both Mic 1:1 and Jer 1:1–2, we might suppose that Amos 1:1 is elliptical and that the author or editor intended to say two different things, namely, "The story of Amos, who was one of the sheep raisers. . . . The word of Yahweh which came to him . . . , which he saw concerning Israel. . . ." But taking the text as it stands, we must interpret *ʾăšer* as the relative pronoun in both cases referring to Amos:

> who was one of the sheep raisers from Tekoa—
> who had visions concerning Israel.

A slight grammatical difficulty remains in this analysis. If both relative clauses have the same antecedent (Amos), we might have expected the second to be coordinated with the first. Otherwise we must resolve the problem by interpreting "the words of Amos" as "the word of Yahweh as reported by Amos." We have already rejected this interpretation of *dibrê ʿāmôs*. A better antecedent would be *ḥāzôn*, as in Isa 1:1; Ezek 12:27; or *haddābār* (Isa 2:1). The alternative is to take the verb *ḥāzâ* absolutely—"he had visions." The verb is often transitive, and characteristic objects are either things supernaturally perceived, or the cognate *ḥāzôn* (Ezek 13:16) or *maḥăzeh* (Num 24:4, 16). It only requires the omission of the implied, redundant cognate object to obtain the absolute usage (Isa 30:10; Job 27:12, 34:32; Prov 24:32).

visions. Amaziah called Amos *ḥōzeh,* "seer" or "visionary" (7:12), and Amos did not repudiate this designation, though he disowned the title "prophet." The "vision" is the experience in which the word of Yahweh is given. This book contains visions along with oracles, so the title is appropriate. Auditory and visionary components were integral to the prophet's close encounter with God. Hence it was possible to "see the word" (Isa 2:1) and to "write the vision" (Hab 2:2).

Behind this emphasis could be a belief that hearing a voice was not enough to legitimate a revelation—not that anyone could ever prove to another that he had received either experience. But for the prophet himself the autobiographical highlight was "I saw my Lord" (Isa 6:1; Amos 9:1) or "my Lord Yahweh showed me" (Amos 7:1, 4, 7; 8:1).

In the Atraḥasis epic of Mesopotamian mythology, because the god Enki did not show himself to Atraḥasis but only talked to the wall of the reed hut outside, the former could pretend that he had not revealed any divine secrets to the human being. Seeing the god himself was important, as the Balaam text from Deir ʿAllah shows:

| ʾš. ḥzh. ʾlhn (.) hʾ | He was a man who had visions of gods, |
| wyʾtw. ʾlwh ʾlhn. blylh. | and gods came to him in the night. |

Such night visions could be dreams. We have no information about the circumstances of Amos' visions.

The inclusion of the words "who had visions" in the heading of the book of Amos is appropriate because from beginning to end it attests to the visionary character of Amos' prophetic experience and message. This feature is conspicuous in The Book of Visions (7:1–9:6); but, as we hope to show, those visions are central and integral to the entire presentation, and similar pictorial, mythic, and cosmic imagery is encountered everywhere in the book. The visions also included auditions, to be sure. There was vigorous dialogue between Yahweh and his prophet in the "council" (*sôd* [3:7]), which was experienced as vision, along with debate, intercession, argument. And out of it came divine decrees and pronouncements, messages to be delivered and declared in the name of Yahweh by his spokesman the prophet. Almost everything in the book can be thus identified as divine speech, apart from the autobiographical and biographical material in chaps. 7–9. It is probable that all of the oracles came from the visions; hence we translate *ḥāzâ* as covering everything: he "had visions."

concerning Israel. Compare the similar use of *ʿal* in Isa 1:1 and Mic 1:1. The preposition can mean "about" or "against," but not that Israel was "the addressee of the sayings" (Mays 1969:18). This part of the title is problematical and was probably intended by the editor in a very general way. Amos' words are concerned mainly with Israel but include many other states. The title should not be allowed to define the book, so that prophecies about Judah are deleted and prophecies against other nations are seen as marginal, no more than a backdrop and buildup for an attack with Israel as the exclusive target. At the same time we have no explicit evidence of Amos in action in any other country; his messages were delivered in Israel and possibly Judah, as seems to be implied in the altercation with Amaziah. But that is not the meaning of *ʿal-yiśrāʾēl* in the title.

Israel. Our introductory essay on political terminology shows that the terms "Israelites," "house of Israel," and "my people Israel" cover the entire nation and therefore the two kingdoms of Amos' day. "Israel" alone usually means the northern kingdom as distinct from Judah, as it clearly does in its second occurrence in this verse. It would place a strain on usage to claim that the word has a different meaning in its first occurrence, namely, that Israel there designates the larger entity, including both Judah and the northern kingdom, Israel. We make this claim, nevertheless. The idea that Amos was a prophet mainly, or even exclusively, to the northern kingdom has had a profound influence on Amos studies. It has placed the book in a completely different focus from the binational and international perspective that it exhibits in so many places. It has led to suppression of the references to Jerusalem and Judah in the book as later additions, a circular argumentation that betrays the weakness of the hypothesis. It has led to the theory that the many nations mentioned, the inner zone represented by the nations of chaps. 1–2, and the outer zone represented by Egypt and Cush, are merely a framework for Amos' real concern: the northern kingdom.

There is, of course, a school of interpretation that plays up Amos' international perspective, especially approving of the question in 9:7. But more often than not this verse is seen as a reduction of Israel to the level of the heathen rather than recruitment of other nations into the community of Yahweh. All of these questions will be discussed more fully in the appropriate places. Here it is enough to remark that, even if the nomination of "Israel" as the subject matter of Amos' visions means major attention to the northern kingdom, Judah is not excluded. In the end the contents of the book must determine the meaning of the title, not vice versa. In the book as a whole, Amos—or we should say Yahweh—is evenhanded in his dealings with all of the nations within his purview. The set of eight opening oracles places all of the countries in the region on the same footing, as far as judgment is concerned. They are blamed, not just for crimes against Israel as Yahweh's special people (Gilead is mentioned twice [1:3, 13], and possibly Edom's crime against "his brother" [1:11]), but for wrong done to anyone (Moab against Edom [2:1]; and the captives in 1:6, 9 were not necessarily Israelites).

All eight oracles refer to the same "it," which will not be retracted or reversed. There was a single decree covering them all. This obtains whether or not "his voice" in v 2 is the antecedent of all of those pronouns. The Great Set Speech is a composition declaring judgment on the entire region as a unit. Whatever the various causes, the means of judgment are the same in every case except the last—fire from heaven. This unity suggests one cosmic holocaust, not just several invasions that would pick off these countries one by one. When several are mentioned together in a similar way (9:7–8) they are representative of all. Assyria (MT: Ashdod, but see discussion ad loc.) and Egypt are invited to come and inspect Samaria (3:9). Others (unidentified, presumably Israelites, but it could be anyone) are to tour the region to assess the situation (6:2). Egypt (4:10), Sodom and Gomorrah (4:11), and the Amorites (2:9–10) supply the models of judgment. Continual reference to the Exodus, not only of Israel (2:10, 3:1) but of other nations (9:7) reveals Yahweh as the master of geopolitics, and no bounds are set to his jurisdiction (9:2–4). The three hymns (4:13, 5:8–9, and 9:5–6) are vital to this presentation, for they ground the universal activity of Yahweh in his cosmic role as creator and manager of the entire universe.

It follows from the preceding that the opening reference to Israel is editorial, not definitive. The titles of other prophecies are similar. Isaiah deals with both Samaria and surrounding nations, even though the title of his book mentions only "Judah and Jerusalem" (Isa 1:1). Micah deals with "Samaria and Jerusalem" (Mic 1:1), closely bound, as shown by the circumstance that the preposition is not repeated.

the days of Uzziah. "The days" of someone usually means his lifetime (Job 1:5); of a king it means his reign. Approximate dates for Uzziah are 790–740; for Jeroboam 790–750. With such a large overlap, Amos' activity can be placed anywhere in the second quarter of the century. There are no clearly identifiable or datable events reported in the book, and few developments after 750 B.C.E. leave any mark on it. It was not until the reign of Tiglath-pileser III (745–728) that Assyrian imperialism began once more to press against the region. Amos does not know about this turn of events, though he hints at the possibility (cf. 4:2–3 and especially 5:26–27; also 6:14). Amos' oracles, while grounded in historical circumstances and reflecting geopolitical reality, do not project or reflect an actual course of military action and destruction but a vision of cosmic fire that ignites the whole region. Subsequent events bear a relation to prophetic prediction, but the correlation varies widely and the end results show a large gap between expectations and fulfillment.

The suspension of Assyrian aggression in the first half of the eighth century B.C.E., however, provided the opportunity for Israel (2 Kgs 14:23–25) and Judah (2 Chr 26:6–15) to recover some of the territory and the glory acquired through David's conquests. The resultant prosperity and complacency could supply the setting for Amos' comments on the leadership of both countries (6:1).

Uzziah. The short form of the name, ʿuzziyyâ, not ʿuzziyyāhû, corresponds to postexilic usage. Use of this form could indicate that the editorial note was written in association with a postexilic edition of the shorter prophetic writings; but it could also be due to an updating of the spelling in an older text. The spelling of Amaziah in chap. 7 is likewise short and late.

Jeroboam ben-Joash. The patronymic was used presumably to distinguish this Jeroboam (II) from the founder of the northern kingdom, Jeroboam ben-Nebat.

The dating formula is hardly enough to betray the hand of a Deuteronomic editor (Mays 1969:14, 18). Nevertheless, the fact that Uzziah's name precedes Jeroboam's implies that the heading was supplied by a Judahite editor. The same is true of Hosea, the only other prophetic book in which the title includes the names of kings of both nations. Here again the name of the Israelite king, Jeroboam, is at the end, following the names of the Judahite kings. As Hosea lived in the north and his prophecies were mainly about the northern kingdom, we would hardly have expected this arrangement of the kings. The conclusion must be that the editor of the book in its present form, as also in the case of Amos, was a Judahite. Hosea lists four successive Judahite kings, but only this one from the north. The discrepancy in the dates implies that Hosea's ministry in Israel was terminated during the reign of Jeroboam (because none of his successors is mentioned) but was carried on in the south, during the reigns of several kings of Judah. Amos' ministry did not extend beyond the reigns of the two kings mentioned. Because otherwise the similarities in the book titles of the four eighth-century prophets—Amos, Hosea, Isaiah, and Micah—point to the same final editor for them all, the specific differences among them show an awareness of the different dates of their activity. Amos was certainly the first, and could have preceded Hosea by as much as two decades (cf. Freedman 1987a).

two years. The RSV translation, "during two years," points to the question whether *šĕnātayim* means a point of time or a period of time *before* the earthquake. The grammar of this "accusative" (we must remember that the Hebrew language no longer had a functioning case system) was the subject of some notes by Meek (1940, 1941a, 1941b). He argued that "motion is always implied in the accusative" but settled for a point of time in this instance.

the earthquake. a. Palestine is intersected by the great rift valley of the Jordan River–Dead Sea–Arabah axis, and earthquakes are frequent (Num 16:31; 1 Sam 14:15; 1 Kgs 19:11; Matt 27:51f.; Acts 16:26). They were interpreted as signs of the impact of God on the world, usually in displeasure. They accompanied the theophanies of the past (Exod 19:18; Judg 5:4; Hab 3:6; Pss 18:7[Heb18:8], 29:6, 97:4, 114:4) and will be a feature of the End Time (Joel 2:10, 4:16[E3:16]; Isaiah 24, 29:6 [tempest and storm]; Mic 1:4; Nah 1:5; Rev 6:12, 8:5, 11:13, 16:18). Amos apparently foresaw and predicted an earthquake (cf. the vision in 9:1 and the description in 8:8 and 9:5), and *"the* earthquake" that serves to date his prophecies must be the one in question. Amos 1:1 thus records the fulfillment of the prediction "in the days of Uzziah." It must have been one of the worst on record, for it was remembered centuries afterward (Zech 14:5).

The definite article (*"the* earthquake") was sufficient to identify it when the book was published, which could only be done if the event were unique in recent memory. Later on it would have to be identified as the one "in the days of Uzziah, king of Judah" (Zech 14:5). In view of the frequency of earthquakes in that part of the world, some such additional identification would soon be needed, but the text of Amos was fixed before that need arose. And, once published, the book would suffice to identify the earthquake. The use of this dating device in the heading also serves to link that earthquake with Amos as the most notable and significant event of his times. The oracle that immediately follows (1:2) could be one of his predictions of that event. Micah made similar threats against Samaria (1:6) and Jerusalem (3:12) in language that would fit seismic devastation.

If we look for other references to such a calamity in the book of Amos we have the reported destruction of some of their cities, an event of which the mode and scale could be compared with the overthrow of Sodom and Gomorrah (4:11). Fire was involved, as is generally the case with earthquakes. But this disaster was only one of a series, not singled out from the rest as *the* one. And, if we are correct in our reconstruction of Amos' career, calamities described in 4:6–11 belong to the first main phase of the book. In the fifth vision (9:1), Yahweh commands someone to smite the capital of a pillar at a temple site, so that the thresholds shake (*yrʿšw*), most likely the one at Bethel (compare 3:14–15). An earthquake (*rʿš*) would bring about the result described. We have identified this vision as the last of the set. If its announcement was followed by an earthquake of unusual intensity, this event would have vindicated Amos and validated his message, at least in the opinion of his followers and disciples. If Amos' final messages of irrevocable doom, including the prediction of the Bethel shrine's demolition and the king's death by violence, led to his incarceration and possible martyrdom, then the prompt fulfillment of his word would have given irrefutable endorsement. We may therefore identify *"the earthquake"* not with the event reported in 4:11, the primary characteristic of which was an intense fire (which served as a warning and was not taken seriously), but with a later and more severe one, which had a very different effect. It therefore means "the earthquake predicted by Amos," which we know took place two years after he had his visions. If 9:1 is the last vision, and near the end of Amos' ministry, if not of his life, then the interval between his disappearance and his vindication was quite short.

This is the only instance in which a happening (the career of Amos) is dated with respect to an event that happened later (the earthquake). When an event is dated at its occurrence, it is attached to something prior ("after the flood") or coincident ("in the year that King Uzziah died"). This unique dating places Amos' prophecies in a clear perspective. It is remarkable for its precision. It also gives a note of finality to the book. Some inferences my be drawn from its unconventional character. (i) It is not intended to date the book in the usual way; that is done by the reference to the reigns of the two kings. The additional information at the end of v 1 is important in itself and in the way it is presented. (ii) The notice is final because the earthquake completed Amos' career, confirming his prediction and validating his message, possibly after his death. The disaster itself is not recorded anywhere in contemporary history. With the lapse of time its proportions diminished, though it was long remembered (Zech 14:5). But at the time, immediately afterward, it would loom large, and Amos' name would be linked to it as the predictor and interpreter of the event. The editor did not make that point; it was self-evident. It was enough to mention "the earthquake." (iii) The editor's work must have been done and the book published in its final form soon after the earthquake, during the reigns of the two kings. The book betrays no awareness of their deaths, or of any subsequent events. In fact, it predicts that Jeroboam would die by the sword (7:9)—he did not—and that Amaziah would go into captivity (7:17), which could only have happened, if it ever did, some decades later. The destruction of Bethel is implied (9:1), and we know from Hosea that the cult there was still active in his time. The fact that so many of Amos' prophecies had not been fulfilled was apparently of little concern to the editor. The earthquake was quite enough at the time, and for the time being, to warrant the publication of Amos' "words" as those of an authentic prophet. (iv) How could the editor have been so sure of Amos' seeing visions and giving oracles "two years before the earthquake"? The notice is so final that it must record the termination of Amos' career, not its inauguration—perhaps his death, but not his call. The editor is asserting a fact, so he is a contemporary. But the book is presented as though no more oracles or visions are to be expected either, now that the earthquake has come and gone. There can be only one explanation. Amos is dead. There are two possibilities. (a) He died two years before the earthquake, which is the easiest and most plausible explanation. He might have been put to death, for things moved rapidly at the end. If he was put to death—a not unlikely outcome for a person accused to the king of sedition (7:10) and something that happened to more than one prophet—it was not necessarily the immediate result of the showdown with Amaziah (7:10–17), though probably it was the eventual result (see the NOTES and COMMENT). If we are right (or largely right) in our interpretation of the book as a whole, that confrontation was the great turning point in Amos' career. The rejection of prophecy and the muzzling of the prophet was the beginning of the end. It marked the change from probation (an open situation in which the people might listen and Yahweh might repent—the plagues [4:6–12] and the first two visions [7:1–6]) to inevitable doom (the first eight oracles and the following visions). An interval must be allowed for the production of the oracles that declare this doom, and for the composition of the whole book. Even so, that interval need not have been a long one, and Amos' entire career could have been of quite brief duration, perhaps only a few years. (b) He stopped preaching two years before the earthquake (cf. 8:11) but lived until the earthquake and either died in it or at that time. It would be too ironic if the earthquake he predicted killed him.

In summary, we have established with some plausibility the following moments in the career of Amos ([   ] = stages of composition and/or editing):

    1. his call with visions;
    2. a period of probation, with the disasters of 4:6–11 and the preaching of chaps. 5–6 (of indeterminate length);
    3. more visions and the preaching of doom;
    [4.] composition of Amos' speech for Bethel;
    5. confrontation with Amaziah;
    6. final vision;
    [7.] composition of the book, or at least its main body (if Amos did it);
    8. Amos' death, possibly by martyrdom;
    [9.] editing of the book by a close follower (if Amos did not do it);
    10. the earthquake; and
    11. publication of the finished book.

This scheme makes the reference to "two years" even more enigmatic. If *ḥāzâ* is correctly interpreted as a general statement about his prophetic career (he "had visions"), and if we are correct in making the series of five visions in 7:1–9:6 the framework of that career, then two years is hardly long enough for all of the events that have to be fitted in, especially all of the plagues, one after the other. It would be straining the language too much to make it mean, "who had visions . . . for a period of two years [at an indeterminate interval] before the earthquake." It seems more natural to take the two-year period not as the interval of time during which Amos had visions but as pinpointing an event connected with the earthquake, which occurred two years before it.

The most eligible event to be connected with the earthquake in this way would be the termination of Amos' career, by whatever means. If the editor knew that Amos had been martyred two years before the earthquake, it is strange that he does not mention that fact. At the same time, it is very unlikely that Amos was still alive at the time of the earthquake, for the book presents his career as if it is finished. An immediate link with the earthquake would be a prediction of such an earthquake. Such a message can be identified with the fifth vision (9:1) and associated oracles (8:8, 9:5); and we have every reason to mark these drastic messages as Amos' last ones, and to connect them with the termination of his public activity, if not of his very life, in consequence of the clash with Amaziah.

Strain is created within Amos 1:1 by the fact that it has two dates—one conventional and general, followed by one unique and precise. This strain can be relieved if the last three words of v 1 are detached from the title of the book as a whole and joined to v 2, dating that verse as one of the prophecies of the earthquake given two years before it happened. Such a change would make 1:2 one of the last of Amos' oracles, rather than a secondary introduction to the oracles against the nations in 1:3–2:8. In any case, 1:2 is not a prediction of an earthquake as such.

There may be some value in this point, however, if the second date locates the Great Set Speech of 1:2–2:8 "two years before the earthquake." The result would not be much different from one already made: Amos' career ended two years before the earthquake. According to our analysis of the whole book, the speech in 1:2–2:8 is the public result of the second pair of visions, and Amos did not survive long after it was given. Joined to chaps. 3–6, it sums up Amos' career from the perspective given by the second pair of visions. It may well represent the substance of a speech given in Bethel, which provoked Amaziah's reaction. One wonders, if the showdown with Amaziah was as drastic and final as 7:10–17 suggests, whether Amos would have been able to do much afterward in the way of literary composition. Amos would have been naïve indeed if Amaziah's reaction had taken him by surprise. Expecting some such confrontation, and knowing what often happened to prophets who spoke the word of Yahweh, Amos could have prepared a comprehensive statement—a summary of his visions and oracles—as brief, *apologia,* and testament. It justified his behavior and his messages, and especially his defense of his role as prophet: "Yahweh has spoken, who could not prophesy?" Such a brief could have contained everything through the fourth vision (8:3) but excluding the confrontation. The book is well organized up to this point. The addition of 7:10–17 and 8:4–9:6, which are not so well organized, was the work of the editor (two years before the earthquake) and the book was published pretty much as we now have it. Things could have moved to their end quite quickly after the fifth vision supplied Amos with his very last messages.

We suggest that such an explanation of the phrase "two years before the earthquake" is both plausible and credible. More speculative is the question of the way this date and the earthquake relate to the production of the book of Amos itself. We suggest at several places in this study that the overall plan and thematic development in chaps. 1–6 identify that part of the book as a comprehensive statement in which Amos justifies his final oracles (chaps. 1–2) with reference to his earlier work (chaps. 3–6). It strikes an apologetic note, as shown by our study in comparison with Jeremiah 25. We suggest that such a statement could have been the substance of his preaching at Bethel in his last days. This proclamation stands alongside the narrative found in The Book of Visions (7:1–9:6). Both cover essentially the same ground; they complement each other. Because The Book of Visions undoubtedly comes from Amos himself (7:10–17) we can claim that the book's essential contents were already in existence before the close of Amos' life. Whether he himself wrote any of it down is another matter. The autobiographical character of The Book of Visions strongly suggests that Amos himself wrote it. Three connected events—the final vision and prophecy of the earthquake, the first edition of "the words of Amos," and the termination of his career—can all be identified as the climax "two years before the earthquake."

The first edition consisted of 1:2–9:6, which was largely if not entirely the work of Amos himself, perhaps in collaboration with a follower (as in the case of Jeremiah and Baruch). Some faithful follower (or followers) saved (or edited) the material, and the book was finally issued soon after the earthquake with little or no editorial expansion. The second edition added 1:1 and 9:7–15, the latter containing authentic Amos material (his very last words), probably produced during the two-year period and added after his death.

Earlier in this note we suggested that all four of the books of the eighth-century prophets were assembled and edited by a single person or group, as reflected in the similar headings and formulated probably not long after the critical events described in detail at the end of First Isaiah (chaps. 36–39). At the same time, the differences in the titles show that the works themselves were composed and compiled separately, and it is clear from the evidence presented and the explicit statements in the book itself that Amos was the first of them, produced shortly after the earthquake mentioned in 1:1 and alluded to in other places in the book. It is impressive and perhaps conclusive for this point, in our opinion, that the book of Amos betrays no awareness of the actual death of Jeroboam II or developments afterward. Similarly, the book of Hosea does not exhibit knowledge of the events leading to the fall of Samaria, including Assyrian invasions. Micah also, just like Amos, deals with Samaria and Jerusalem evenhandedly, predicting a similar fate for both. In the event, things turned out quite differently. The north went down, the south survived. The prophecies were not fulfilled; but they were not revised. They had already been certified as genuine and had acquired an authoritative status that would later be called "canonical." In the case of Amos, the evidence of the end of v 1 points to the early completion of the book in its basic form and content, even though we cannot exclude the possibility of editorial and scribal changes in subsequent transmission.

the earthquake. b. It is possible that Amos has influenced Isaiah. The shaking of the threshold at "the voice" (Isa 6:4) reminds us of Amos 9:1; the comparison with Sodom and Gomorrah (Isa 1:9; compare also "your cities are burned with fire" in Isa 1:7) reminds us of Amos 4:11. Compare the comment of the Deuteronomistic editor of Kings (2 Kgs 21:13, but now Samaria has become the city to cite as the example and warning). On Isaiah and the earthquake, see the illuminating article by J. Milgrom (1964:164–82).

the earthquake. c. Dating the earthquake itself is a distinct question.

Amos' career and the unforgettable earthquake are both dated to the reign of Uzziah (Zech 14:5), which by any reckoning was very long. In the excavations of Hazor (as well as Samaria) evidence was found of a major earthquake, dated to about 760 (Wolff 1977:124; Yadin 1960:24ff., 36f.) There is no contemporary confirmation of the occurrence of a conspicuously violent earthquake that might be identified with Amos 1:1, so as to date it.

General Introduction to The Book of Doom

The integrity of The Book of Doom (1:2–4:13), which properly begins in v 2 following the heading in 1:1, is shown by several thematic and structural particulars. Its end is marked by a brief hymn or apostrophe (4:13), and the next section, The Book of Woes (chaps. 5–6), begins with a note of lamentation that had not been struck before. Structurally the apostrophe (4:13) balances the brief initial oracle in 1:2. Within this inclusion the body of The Book of Doom is anchored by two solid blocks of material—the Great Set Speech (1:3–2:8) at the beginning, and the Plagues (4:6–12) at the end. These two blocks are characterized by the listing of similar items within a fixed frame. The intervening material is more varied in outward form and is marked by themes in contrary motion. The frequent use of the conventional rubrics for prophetic oracles (2:11, 16; 3:10, 11, 12, 13, 15; 4:3, 5, 6, 8, 9, 10, 11) shows that a considerable number of individual utterances have been assembled. The rubrics are positioned at the outset or at the end or sometimes inside each distinct message. The rubric might not be used at all, or twice in a single oracle, so there is no way of telling for certain how many of them might have been issued separately in their first, oral phase. The Great Set Speech and the Plagues show that a series of similar proclamations can be readily concatenated to yield unified compositions. Spoken messages have been turned into literature, apparently with very little if any editorial modification. The oracles between these two blocks (2:9–4:5) are more diverse in form and content and did not lend themselves to cohesive organization with the aid of sustained themes or repeated formulas. They retain their raw oral character and their existential immediacy. Apart from the wisdom piece in 3:3–8, the text is all oracular.

The audience is sometimes identified, indicating that different groups are being addressed. In 2:10–13 all of Israel is addressed as "you," a speech embedded in third-person material (2:6–9, 14–16). All of Israel is addressed again in 3:1–2, 11, and throughout chap. 4. In 3:9–10 and 12–15 the prophet (or the Lord) addresses an unidentified group (or groups). They are to call on the Assyrians (or Philistines) and Egyptians to observe the Israelites (3:9–10). They (or perhaps these foreign observers after their inspection) are to testify against the house of Jacob (3:13). The dramatic roles of these participants remain indeterminate. The moments and movements of a court trial (covenant lawsuit) can be glimpsed here and there, but the process cannot be reconstructed, as may be done to some extent in Isaiah 1 or Micah 6.

The themes of sin and punishment run through The Book of Doom—accusations of sin and threats of punishment. The accusations against the first six nations are specific; those against Judah and Israel are sometimes general (2:4, 3:2), but many particular crimes in the latter are also itemized (2:6–8; 3:9–10; 4:1, 4–5). This material is an essential complement of the plagues (4:6–12), in which it is said that they did not repent but does not indicate what they were supposed to repent of. This recital, in turn, is an essential complement of the judgment pronouncements that run through it all. It shows that penal provisions are of two kinds. Some, in the first stage of the process at least, are corrective rather than punitive; they are intended to lead to repentance. The calamities listed in 4:6–11 are what we would call "natural" disasters (not for Amos, of course; for him Yahweh does everything)—bad enough, to be sure, but still limited in scope and scale. Others are more tremendous, more obviously God-sent, and more complete. They represent the irreversible decision to destroy an unrepentant people. The essential point of 4:12 as the culmination of 4:6–11 is also made in 1:3–2:8, where it is the last of a series of violations that triggers the final judgment. In the first seven oracles against the nations a specific threat follows from a specific accusation. In addition to the constant threat to send fire, there are threats to kill rulers (1:5a, 8a, 15; 2:3), defeat armies (1:14, 2:2b), exile the population (1:5b), and exterminate the survivors (1:8b). The accusations against Israel that begin in 2:6–8 continue through chaps. 3 and 4. No threat is immediately given after 2:6–8; but several threats follow later—demolition of fortresses (3:11), shrines (3:14), and residences (3:15); defeat in battle (2:14–16), with few survivors (3:12); and exile (4:2–3).

If one pays more attention to the variety in form and mood, if one notes the discontinuities, abrupt endings, and sudden beginnings, one might conclude, along with many scholars, that what we have now is not much more than a loosely assembled congeries of short prophecies. Wolff finds "more than two dozen short individual oracles" in the entire book (1977:91). We recognize nearly fifty distinct literary units in our analysis (see TABLE OF CONTENTS). If one pays more attention to the literary organization of the complete book—unifying links and architectonic structural devices—one can take the original oral material only a certain distance toward coherence and unity on a purely formal level. These devices should not be exaggerated, but they cannot be ignored. It is not a freshly composed piece of literature. It is all still so close to the oral mode in form that one can imagine most of it being presented as extended speeches. The language of 3:9, 4:4, 5:4–5, 6:2, 8:14, and 9:7 gives a glimpse of itineraries that Amos himself pursued—at least in imagination, perhaps in actuality:

Ashdod (LXX: Assyria)
Egypt   } 3:9

Bethel
Gilgal   } 4:4

Bethel
Gilgal
Beer-sheba   } 5:4–5
Gilgal
Bethel

Samaria
Dan   } 8:14
Beer-sheba

Cush
Egypt
Caphtor   } 9:7
Kir

Calneh
Hamath   } 6:2
Gath

There is one circuit within Israel, embracing both kingdoms. There is another surrounding Israel. Both are present in the Great Set Speech against the eight nations, which sets the stage for the whole book. The repeated grouping of such widely separated places in clusters discloses a perspective that can embrace them all together in a common destiny under the governance of the one Creator God. But the presentation was not brought to a perfectly geometrical symmetry.

Whether Amos' frequent calls to people to do the rounds and go to all of these places were rhetorical or real, it sounds as if he himself had visited many of them, just as Elijah and Elisha did. It is easy to imagine him repeating his oracles wherever he went, and not just giving each as a one-time pronouncement, so that in the end he had quite an accumulation of items wrought into discourses. A street preacher is not a pulpit orator. Yet the collection (1:2–4:13) makes sense as a unified address. The beginning (1:2) and ending (4:13) are sharp and arresting. The control of such a speech is assisted by the firm and fixed form of the opening and closing blocks (1:3–2:8 and 4:6–12). The problematical use of the name "Israel" in 4:12 can be explained as a return to the starting point in 2:6, and goes with the fact that the eighth oracle against Israel does not end in the way the other seven do. The repetitions in the opening and closing blocks provide control within which the prophet has liberty to supply variable content. Between these two chunks of ballast he was free, on any occasion, to insert any number of messages—not so well ordered, held together more loosely than the others, but related nevertheless by recurrent themes and by their similar oracular character. The Book of Doom is an appropriate title for this great discourse: *Doom*—because it contains no promise of relief or remission of the punishment (as in The Book of Woes), no hope of recovery or reinstatement after punishment (as in the Epilogue); a *Book*, because it now exists as a piece of literature and could well be a transcript of one of Amos' characteristic presentations toward the end of his career, perhaps close to his actual proclamation at the shrine of Bethel.

Another way of looking at the structure of the Great Set Speech is the following: the eight units naturally fall into two groups of four parts, which in turn naturally divide into two pairs. First we wish to point out that while no two oracles are precisely the same, there are two basic types to which the oracles can be assigned: the first type, which we may call *A*, is somewhat longer, while the other, *B*, is somewhat shorter. All have the same opening formula, followed by a statement of the charge. The third element is the announcement of the threatened punishment, also in a repeated formula.

In the *A* type the accusation is presented in a single statement, prosaic in form, while in the *B* type the charge is given in the form of a poetic pair, a bicolon or couplet.

When it comes to the punishment, all repeat the basic formula concerning the sending of fire, but the *A* type expands to include consequences or effects on the nation, while the *B* type concludes with the formula.

Turning to the eight oracles, we find that the first group of four consists of two pairs: the first pair belong to type *A*, with the prosaic single charge and extended punishment; while the second pair have the poetic charge with parallel elements, and the abbreviated form of the punishment.

The second group, similarly, begins with a pair of oracles belonging to type *A*, with the single prose charge along with extended descriptions of the punishment. The second pair belong essentially to type *B*, with the charge given in poetic form while the punishment is restricted to the formula. This pattern holds true for the oracle against Judah, while the oracle against Israel represents a further elaboration and deviation from the basic pattern. Thus the charge against Israel is extended beyond that of any of the others, consisting of a quatrain, largely poetic, but including one prosaic statement as well. There is no punishment formula, however; and the oracle on Israel along with the whole Great Set Speech ends abruptly at 2:8. The following material (2:9–16) has been spliced onto the speech at that point to provide a different continuation and ending. A rationale of the divine decision and an apocalyptic vision of military destruction close the chapter. The deficiency in detail is more than made up in the following materials, especially 3:9–11, where similar terminology occurs (cf. 3:12–15, 2:14–16, etc.).

The following simple tables will exemplify the structural pattern:

	Type A	Type B
1. Aram (Damascus)	*	
2. Philistia (Gaza)	*	
3. Tyre		*
4. Edom		*
5. Ammon	*	
6. Moab	*	
7. Judah		*
8. Israel		*

	Type A		Type B	
	PROSE CHARGE	PUNISHMENT PLUS	POETIC CHARGE	NO PLUS
1. Aram	*	*		
2. Philistia	*	*		
3. Tyre			*	*
4. Edom			*	*
5. Ammon	*	*		
6. Moab	*	*		
7. Judah			*	*
8. Israel			*	*

As can be seen, the divisions and subdivisions match up quite nicely, each having distinctive characteristics while sharing others of the larger group.

There is a further element that should be mentioned with regard to the threat formula. Although it is essentially uniform throughout the first seven oracles, there is nevertheless a basic variant in form. In the first colon the opening words are wĕšillaḥtî ʾēš, with the single exception that in the fifth oracle the verb wĕhiṣṣattî is substituted for wĕšillaḥtî. There follows a phrase introduced by the preposition b-, which is then followed by a proper noun (or compound) directly or by a construct chain, or bound expression, the first word of which is ḥômat, "wall," while the second again is a proper noun. There is a corresponding alteration in the second colon, so that when

the preposition *b-* is followed directly by a proper noun in the first colon
there is a parallel proper noun in the second, following the constantly
repeated verbal clause *wĕ'ākĕlâ 'armĕnôt*. When, however, the common
noun *ḥômāt* occurs in the first colon, then a pronominal suffix *-hā* is subsumed for the proper noun at the end of the second colon. The information
can be tabulated as follows:

		First Colon	*Second Colon*
1.	Aram	*bbyt ḥz'l*	*'rmnwt bn-hdd*
2.	Philistia	*bḥwmt 'zh*	*'rmntyh*
3.	Tyre	*bḥwmt ṣr*	*'rmntyh*
4.	Edom	*btymn*	*'rmnwt bṣrh*
5.	Ammon	*bḥwmt rbh*	*'rmnwtyh*
6.	Moab	*bmw'b*	*'rmnwt hqrywt*
7.	Judah	*byhwdh*	*'rmnwt yrwšlm*
8.	Israel	*[bḥwmt šmrwn*	*'rmnwtyh]*

The second colon invariably begins with the verb *wĕ'ākēla* and then is
followed by the noun *'armĕnôt*. In some cases there is a third noun completing the construct chain, while in others the pronominal suffix of the 3d
f. s. is used. This arrangement also forms a pattern, as the following table
will show:

			Construct Chain	*Suffix*
1.	Aram	*'armĕnôt ben-hădād*	*	
2.	Philistia	*'armĕnōteyhā*		*
3.	Tyre	*'armĕnōteyhā*		*
4.	Edom	*'armĕnot boṣrâ*	*	
5.	Ammon	*'armĕnôteyhā*		*
6.	Moab	*'armĕnôt haqqĕriyyôt*	*	
7.	Judah	*'armĕnôt yĕrûšālāyim*	*	
8.	Israel	*['armĕnōteyhā*		*]*

While the formula for Israel does not occur in the text (after 2:8) we can
find an echo of it or equivalent for it in 3:11, where we read *wĕnābōzzû
'armĕnôtāyik*. While the verb is different, it fits into the pattern for *waw*-
conversive with the perfect as the following noun takes the suffix (here 2d f.

s.) just as we would expect from the pattern in the chart. The data in this table cut across the items in the previous chart, but nevertheless conform to the assumed requirements of symmetry. The balance is maintained in both the major segments and the subdivisions, though the actual distribution differs. Formulating the pattern, we can summarize it as *abba//baab,* while for the other features we had the following: *aabb//aabb.*

We can put it all in a single chart as follows:

	A		*B*		*A*		*B*	
	Aram	*Philistia*	*Tyre*	*Edom*	*Ammon*	*Moab*	*Judah*	*Israel*
	1	2	3	4	5	6	7	8
Opening	*	*	*	*	*	*	*	*
*Charge	S (pr)	S (pr)	L (po)	L (po)	S (pr)	S (pr)	L (po)	L (po)
Threat								
1C	——	ḥwmt	ḥwmt	——	ḥwmt	——	——	[ḥwmt]
2C	pr.n.	suff.	suff.	pr.n.	suff.	pr.n.	pr.n.	[suff.]
Addition	*	*			*	*		

* S = short; L = Long; pr = prose; po = poetry.

It will be noted that within a single general structure there are numerous variations, both subtle and significant, which support the view that the whole is a single artistic creation. While there are two basic variants, these in turn exhibit differences in detail, so that the correlations and divergences are both intricate and pervasive. The essential symmetry is preserved throughout, though with sufficient variety to avoid monotony. With very few exceptions, there are at least two examples of each slightly divergent type. Thus we may summarize:

1. Type A_1 Nos. 1, 6
   Type A_2 Nos. 2, 5*
2. Type B_1 Nos. 3, 8†
   Type B_2 Nos. 4, 7

* No. 5 is almost exactly the same in form as no. 2, except that the standard verb for the first clause of the threat, *wĕšillaḥtî,* which occurs six times, has been replaced in the oracle against Ammon by the synonymous *wĕhiṣṣattî.* Thus the second major division begins with this slight but notable difference.

† No. 8 differs notably from all others in two respects. First, the charge is considerably expanded beyond any of the others, though in principle it belongs to the group that has the long form of the charge. In other words, the pattern is appropriate but it has been stretched. Second, the final threat or punishment does not occur after v 8, where we would expect it. On the basis of all available data, we can reconstruct the form and wording, that is, the simplest of the formulas, as follows:

wĕšillaḥtî ʾēš bĕhômat šōmĕrôn
wĕʾākēlâ ʾarmĕnōteyhā

The omission of this closing formula in the written form of the Great Set Speech
was doubtless deliberate, though it may well have been uttered or at least intended or prepared by the prophet. Whether he was interrupted on the occasion
of its delivery, so that the fatally ominous words would not actually be pronounced by the man of God, we cannot say; but the omission in the written,
published form holds in suspense the clearly implied or intended outcome while
the prophet or his editor presents additional supporting data for the threats of
doom and condemnations to come.

I.A. ORACLES AGAINST THE NATIONS
(1:2–2:8)

INTRODUCTION

The basic division of The Book of Doom (1:2–4:13) comes at the end of
chap. 2, so that the two main parts consist of the Great Set Speech (1:2[or
3]–2:16) and then a collection of pieces relating to the main theme of the
section (chaps. 3–4).

The Great Set Speech is itself a composite, with the first clear break
coming after 2:8. Up to that point the speech is unified and follows an
established order, with fixed formulas and phrases. The sequence is interrupted by a historical recital in 2:9–12, and the speech is concluded with an
eschatological vision of a climactic battle (vv 13–16). A new address with
its own formula begins at 3:1 (with an echo at 4:1 and even 5:1), which
marks the second half of The Book of Doom. In maintaining the integrity
and unity of the long opening speech (1:2–2:16), in spite of the abrupt shift
at 2:9, we call attention to the following considerations.

1. It has been a common opinion among modern critics to doubt the
originality of one or more of the eight oracles in the cycle; but we consider
the list of nations to be complete as it stands. The nations completely ring
the compass around Israel; they are all contiguous; and they number seven.
Along with the eighth, Israel, in the center, Amos' list comprehends the
entire region from Egypt to the Euphrates, an expanse of territory of enormous importance in Israel's history and memory. It is a combination of the

ideal (one of the versions of the promised land) and the real (the fullest extent of David's empire, its sphere of influence if not of actual conquest).

The geopolitical facts are presented symbolically by means of a highly artificial literary structure. This artistry, along with a rich infusion of mythic imagery, makes it difficult to find the connections with political actuality. But there can be no doubt about the consistency and symmetry of the verbal craftsmanship.

2. In the organization of this speech three numerical patterns have been superimposed. One is the conventional parallelism $3//3 + 1$. Another is the significant number seven, produced by adding these two numbers: it is always important in biblical thought. On the use of the number seven here and elsewhere in Amos, as well as in biblical literature generally, see R. Gordis (1943) and M. Weiss (1967a, b). In addition we have the pattern of $7//7 + 1 = 8$, which also has symbolic meaning.

3. Each of the eight oracles against the nations begins with the same formula: "for three violations . . . and for four." The sequence $3//4$ is part of the traditional poetic conventions of Canaanite and Israelite litera-ture (Gevirtz 1963, 1973; Haran 1971; Roth 1962, 1965; Watson 1984:144–49; Weiss 1967a, b). There are several examples of this trope in Proverbs 30. It serves to introduce an inventory of things that resemble one another, and the aggregate or actual number of them is four. In some instances the fourth is a human who resembles three animals in some trait. The fourth one is different and gives a surprise twist to the discourse at the end. Amos does not use the figure in this way; he does not itemize the violations. Only one crime (or possibly two, but they form a single entity) is charged against each nation. Presumably the others in the group are passed over, and only the last and worst is actually specified.

4. The numerical pattern "three . . . four" also points to the symbolic total seven (Weiss 1967a, b). Although Amos makes only a single charge against each of the nations in this final reckoning, the sum is seven. Now that the full number has been reached, the judgment will fall. In each case the judgment takes the form of assault by fire from heaven; all of the nations will be devastated in the same way, possibly all together in one and the same act, precisely as the several cities of the plain were burned up (4:11) in a single action. By his presentation the prophet makes two points simultaneously: each nation will be judged individually, on the grounds of its particular crimes; and the whole region will be wiped out as a unit. They are bound together in a common destiny, the justice of which is indicated by their common guilt. Thus the numerical pattern is more than a stereo-type for a string of prophecies directed at each nation individually. It points as well to the total of seven nations, and their seven acts of rebellion against the suzerainty of the God of heaven and earth. With the enumeration of the

separate crimes of the group, the full measure is made up and divine judgment will be imposed on all.

5. There is a basis for this view of the region in earlier tradition. The number seven corresponds to the number of the traditional enemies of Israel who occupied the holy land and who were to be driven from it and dispossessed (cf. Deut 7:1; Josh 3:10, 24:11; Acts 13:19). The list is not always complete, but it is repeated often enough that we can be sure that the intended number was seven. The prophet has used the same pattern, but in a different setting. The precedent is quoted (2:9–10). The present occupants of the same region are, in fact, the ones brought in by Yahweh to replace those original seven inhabitants (we need not worry about the exact geographical extent in each case). These latter-day nations are now in their turn the object of a similar divine judgment; they too will be driven from their lands (1:5, 15) or exterminated (1:8; cf. 2:3). This time around, however, Israel is joined with them, and all will suffer the same fate (7:11 [17], 9:10).

6. The numerical pattern 3 // 3 + 1 = 4 (also making a total of 7) applies not only to the general structure of the oracle's first major section, but also to its internal organization. Thus the first three charges form a group with basic common features, which distinguish it from the second group of four (more precisely 3 + 1), which also have distinctive features in common. In the first three, cities are specified (Damascus, Gaza, Tyre) as the capitals, and symbols of their respective commonwealths or confederations; whereas in the latter group, the nations themselves are identified (Edom, Ammon, Moab, Judah). The former lie along the main routes of an invading army from the east and would be the first to bear the brunt of the attack. The latter all lie east of the Jordan River (except for Judah, which occupies a special place in the list, namely, the "1" of 3 + 1) and along a secondary line of march. We may point also to the fact that Edom, Ammon, and Moab are frequently associated in the biblical traditions.

We are not sure that this classification is what the prophet had in mind when he listed the eight countries in the order he did. No one, certainly no scholar who retains the text as it is, has yet succeeded in relating the inventory of states, in the given sequence, to any geopolitical or military reality. It is, in fact, one of the reasons why scholars feel obliged to remove some of the oracles from the set, especially when they wish to attach the oracles to known historical events. First in order as a point of reference for explaining the oracles is Assyrian imperialistic expansion. W. R. Harper (1905) relied heavily on this idea.

If Amos had in mind an actual invasion by Assyria, then Aram would be the first object of attack, and in fact Aram is first on Amos' list. This rather patent correspondence has encouraged scholars to plot a military campaign beginning with the assault on Aram and continuing until all nations in the area are overrun. While it is possible to make some sense out of the sequence given by Amos, at least in part, it only applies in a few cases: for example, an invading army would proceed from Aram to the coast, go south to conquer the Philistine pentapolis and then north to mop up the Phoenician cities. But in so doing the army would have to go through one of the major passes from the plain to the coast, which would require crossing Israelite territory. So while an Assyrian invasion might well proceed from Aram to Philistia and back up the coast to Tyre and the Phoenician cities, the omission of Israel from the list after Aram shows that the arrangement is not military but literary and theological.

It would be very difficult to explain the logic or logistics of a succeeding or separate campaign against the nations east of the Jordan in the order given in Amos 1–2: Edom, Ammon, and Moab. Assyria might attack them all, especially if they formed a defensive alliance; but the order of the states —Edom in the south, Ammon in the north, and Moab in the middle—does not make military sense. Excising Edom from the list, which is the solution of choice, would relieve that problem while creating a greater one, namely, the omission of a key member of the group of eight.

As we have seen, placing Judah or Israel at the end of the list reflects a literary and dramatic interest on the part of the speaker or author. Here again, however, military and political reality intrude on literary drama. While it might make sense to put the destruction of Judah and Jerusalem at the end or climax of this series of assaults, it would be impossible, or nearly so, to put the conquest of Israel after that of Judah. Not only strategy but history rules otherwise: Israel first and then Judah is the way it had to happen and did happen; but Amos has the order reversed. The only way that order would work is if the attack came from the south, from Egypt. But then we could not begin with the invasion of Aram, which would have to be at the other end of an Egyptian invasion. So we must look for another more viable possibility.

A better case can be made for a program in which invasion comes from both the south (Egypt) and the east (Assyria), their successive strikes being listed in alternation. Assyria conquers Aram (no. 1), Tyre (no. 3), Ammon (no. 5); Egypt conquers Philistia (no. 2), Edom (no. 4), Moab (no. 6). But if the region is to be divided between the two world powers, four in the north for Assyria, four in the south for Egypt, then once again the sequence of Judah and Israel does not fit the alternating pattern of the first six.

We conclude that the listing of the eight nations does not represent the order in which they would be destroyed by any massive conquest of the region. Indeed, its highly formulaic character makes it very unlikely that it would ever correspond to real historical events. The entire speech is planned along literary lines.

7. With respect to the individual pronouncements, we find a recogniz-

able balance in the arrangement. Thus the first two, against Damascus and Gaza, form a balancing pair; while the third, against Tyre, is noticeably shorter, though clearly related to the preceding. In complementary fashion, the second group consists of a balanced or parallel pair (Ammon and Moab) of substantial length, preceded by the briefer oracle on Edom. The arrangement is the reverse of the first group. The final indictment, against Judah, stands somewhat apart from the others and properly leads to the second major section of the general oracle, the statement on Israel itself.

8. Israel stands as the eighth in the series, separate from the other seven. This contrast makes dramatic and poetic sense. While Israel's fate will be the same, the circumstances differ. Here the prophet spells out in detail the crimes of Israel (according to our count four, confirming the original sense and use of the 3 // 4 pattern) that will bring the threatened punishment. At the same time, three of the four indictments are given in a paired formation with poetic parallelism, while the remaining one is a single charge with an ordinary prose structure, exemplifying the 3 // 4 pattern in a more literal fashion.

The prophet has taken traditional themes and patterns and reworked them to portray the new historical and theological situation in which he lived and to which he addressed himself. The tradition of the seven local enemies of Israel has been adapted to a different set of circumstances; at the same time the numerical device $N // N + 1$ has been used both with its original force and as a sum matching the number of irremediable acts of rebellion with the corresponding nations.

We cannot be certain that we have the original text of the oracle. It is probable that Amos and his followers repeated it on several occasions with appropriate changes in wording. The apparent confusion and conflation of the violations in 1:6 and 1:9 may reflect different forms of the same oracle, assigned to different nations in the process of transmission. It is possible too that Judah was lacking in the original listing, so as to leave a list of six nations with Israel (both north and south) providing the seventh and final name in the group of those to be judged by God. On the whole, it seems probable that the original structure has survived with its numerical patterns; it would be highly speculative to try to recover supposedly more original forms of the oracle, though this task is commonly attempted. The present text exhibits a structure entirely in accord with traditional patterns.

For ease of reference we list once more the catalog in 1:3–2:8:

1. Aram (Damascus)   (1:3–5)
2. Philistia (Gaza)   (1:6–8)
3. Tyre   (1:9–10)
4. Edom   (1:11–12)
5. Ammon   (1:13–15)

6. Moab	(2:1–3)
7. Judah	(2:4–5)
8. Israel	(2:6–8)

The Rhetorical Structure of the First (Eightfold) Oracle

As already noted, the oracle consists of a series of pronouncements on the nations surrounding Israel. It culminates in condemnation of Israel itself. Each of these components is introduced by the same oracle rubric, "Thus Yahweh said"; and the oracles themselves each begin with an identical expression, differing only in the name of the city or people:

> For three violations by ———,
> and for four,
> I will not reverse it.

This formula is used eight times (1:3, 6, 9, 11, 13; 2:1, 4, 6), and these occurrences form the outline or basic structure of the oracle as a whole. We may view the whole as eight distinct oracles, because each one has a new heading and a different target, and some have a closing colophon as well; or as eight sections or divisions of one integrated prophecy.

These stanzas, or strophes, are very uneven in length, however, and their contents vary considerably. Nevertheless they all share certain elements in common, in addition to the introductory formulas, and these elements provide a basic model or pattern for the pronouncements. These ingredients may be itemized as follows:

1. The opening oracle rubric.
2. The opening and fixed formula quoted above.
3. The charge. Following the sequence *ʿal . . . wĕʿal . . .* of the opening formula, the next clause always begins with *ʿal* for the third time, followed directly by an infinitive (the *wĕʿal* in 2:8 may be a further continuation of the series, and not the simple preposition). This clause specifies the particular act of rebellion with which the nation in question is charged. Except for the charges against Israel (no. 8), which are given *in extenso*, the statements are brief and belong to one of several patterns:

    a. A single clause, with the infinitive after *ʿal* serving as the only verbal form: Aram (no. 1), Moab (no. 6).

    b. The same as (a), but with an additional subordinate clause introduced by *l-* or *lĕmaʿan,* also followed by an infinitive: Philistia (no. 2), Ammon (no. 5).

    c. The same as (a), but with a balancing clause containing a finite verb: Tyre (no. 3).

d. The same as (c), but with an additional couplet containing two clauses, both with finite verbs: Edom (no. 4), Judah (no. 7).

e. The same as (d), but comprising a quatrain with several additional clauses: Israel (no. 8).

These constructions also vary in the referential pronoun used with the infinitive, the subject of which refers to the performer of the misdeed. These pronouns are all masculine, which is surprising, as the obvious antecedent is the name of the city or country, *běnê ʿammôn* being the exception. In most cases, the pronoun is plural, showing that the peoples are meant. It is singular for Edom and Moab. This detail, which could be important for interpretation, has been scrupulously retained in the RSV. But the LXX had already normalized all of these pronouns to plural (cf. NEB, "they" throughout). The NIV, taking liberties that show little respect for the text, confuses the picture by translating the first three as "she," the next three as "he," and the last two as "they."

4(A). Following the charge, there is a statement concerning the punishment to be inflicted. The opening words are always: *wěšillaḥtî ʾēš,* "and I will send Fire," with the single exception of Ammon (No. 5), which has *wěhiṣṣattî ʾēš,* "and I will kindle Fire." (The oracle against Israel is entirely different from this point on, and we will not consider it in this part of the analysis. The threatened punishment is omitted in the oracle on Israel [no. 8] after 2:8, but corresponding elements are found elsewhere in the book [especially 3:11].) The object of this attack is specified in different ways:

a. Only the name of the city or nation is given, Teman (no. 4), Moab (no. 6), Judah (no. 7).

b. The expression is amplified by the word *ḥômâ,* "wall": Gaza (no. 2), Tyre (no. 3), Rabbah (no. 5).

c. The phrase *běbêt ḥăzāʾēl,* "house of Hazael," is used in no. 1, to indicate either the nation (Damascus) or the actual palace of the king.

4(B). In every case the second colon of the punishment formula begins with the verb *wěʾākělâ,* "and She will consume," followed by the object, *ʾarměnōt,* "citadels." The latter is followed either by the possessive pronoun, referring back to the name of the people or the city involved, or by another proper noun parallel to the first:

a. Pronominal suffix, "its citadels": nos. 2, 3, 5.

b. Proper noun: Ben-hadad (no. 1); Bozrah (no. 4); Kerioth (no. 6); Jerusalem (no. 7).

5. In certain cases, the decree for destruction by Fire completes the pronouncement (nos. 3, 4, 7). In the others, additional details fill out the picture of national judgment. In each of the four more elaborate cases (nos. 1, 2, 5, 6), the standard formula common to all seven is followed by a double bicolon. In nos. 1 and 2 the same expressions occur: *wěhikrattî yôšēb* . . . , "and I will cut off the sovereign . . . ," followed by *wětômēk šēbeṭ* . . . , "and the scepter-wielder. . . ." In each case a geographical place-name follows: "from Biqʿat-

Awen" and "from Beth-Eden" (no. 1); "from Ashdod" and "from Ashkelon" (no. 2). In no. 6 the expressions have been modified considerably; in fact only the first word, wĕhikrattî, is the same. Number 5 is entirely different.

6. A closing colophon, "Yahweh has spoken": nos. 1, 2 (variation), 5, 6.

The findings may be summarized in tabular form:

		1	2	3	4	5	6	7	8
1.	Oracle rubric	X	X	X	X	X	X	X	X
2.	Opening formula	X	X	X	X	X	X	X	X
3a.	Charge ('al + inf.)	X	X	X	X	X	X	X	X
3b.	+ independent clause(s)	—	—	X	X	—	—	X	X
4.	Punishment formula	X	X	X	X	X*	X	X	—
5.	+ four-colon unit	X†	X†	—	—	X	X†	—	—
6.	Colophon	X	X	—	—	X	X	—	—

* This one reads hiṣṣattî for šillaḥtî, which occurs in all the others.
† Includes a formula, repeated in nos. 1 and 2, adapted in no. 6.

All of the pronouncements have the same three essential elements of a judgment oracle: opening formula, charge, and punishment formula (except for no. 8, which follows the pattern only through the charge). They all expand on this base with additional material, but in two different ways. They add details either to the charge or to the punishment, but not to both. Thus nos. 1, 2, 5, and 6 have a simple charge and complex consequences—a double couplet is added to the punishment formula. In nos. 3, 4, and 7, the charges are amplified by the addition of one or two clauses but the consequences are stated more simply. Number 8 is different from all of the others, but retains the essential form. The accusations follow the standard pattern, but are substantially expanded (2:6–8). The punishment formula is omitted at this point, but similar phrasing is found elsewhere.

With all of these combinations of major structural differences and minor stylistic variations, no two of the oracles are exactly the same in form. It would be a mistake to conclude that one pattern alone was authentic and original; that deviations from that pattern represent textual errors picked up in transmission; or that an oracle substantially different from the others can be seen, by that fact, to be not the work of Amos. The preceding table shows that nos. 3, 4, and 7 share a pattern that contrasts with the rest, and this fact has been used to support other arguments on historical grounds that the oracles against Tyre, Edom, and Judah are later additions. Such arguments can cut the other way. One oracle exactly like another could be dismissed as a deliberate and careful imitation! While it may be difficult to determine the reason for certain variations, there can be little basis for supposing that the prophet was not able or free to vary his formulas and structures as he proceeded. Within a fairly rigid framework, then, as defined by the repeated formulas, the prophet was nevertheless able to exercise considerable creativity.

Studies of oral literature, and especially of oral composition, have shown how the availability of stock phrases can facilitate spontaneous generation of artistic works. Here much of the framework common to all eight oracles is poetic, but much of the added material is hardly distinguishable from normal prose. We do not mean to deny that the language shows literary craftsmanship of a high order. It does. But there is not much achievement of regular prosody, and it is a mistake to look for that as a guide to the solution of textual or philological problems. The chief distinguishing mark of Hebrew poetry, parallelism, is not always present. The use of "prose particles" also shows that we do not have classical lyrical verse here (see below).

Thus the charges in nos. 1, 2, 3, 5, and 6 are prosaic both in form and sequence. Only nos. 4 and 7 have poetic features, and the second couplet of no. 7 may be questioned. In addition some of the charges in no. 8 may also be classified as prose. Thus 2:7 poses numerous problems: we may agree that v 7a was originally poetic in form, but v 7b reads like prose.

This admixture of seeming prose with poetry is found throughout the whole cycle. We may suspect that the prophet's procedure was deliberate and that he used language appropriate to his purpose without regard for niceties of style, relying on the fixed framework to provide the basic poetic and metrical structure for his oration. It is worth remembering that prophetic utterances were solo performances, not choral presentations for which a constant pattern may have been necessary.

With so many patterns and possibilities, there is little point in arguing about *the structure* of the whole speech, and no point in asking how consciously and deliberately the prophet composed this piece. We are not studying Amos' consciousness or intention, but his text. We have noted the total pattern of $7 + 1$; within the seven, $3 + 4$; and within the four, $3 + 1$. The table also shows an arrangement $2 + 2 + 2 + 2$. The first two threaten the punishment of the ruler; the second two elaborate on the crime, but not on the punishment; the next two fasten on the rulers again. Ammon and Moab are also a natural pair, as are the final two, Judah and Israel. Having said all that, we must emphasize again that no two of these oracles are exactly the same.

The observations we have made about the form and texture of this first great prophecy have important methodological implications. First, they permit the recognition that a prophecy may take the form of a sustained composition even when it uses a number of individual oracles. Second, prophetic oratory is a distinct mode that is only superficially described as a mixture of poetry and prose. It is not bits of poetry intermingled with bits of prose. The ingredients range along an unbroken spectrum from pure poetry to pure prose, and most of them are neither poetry nor prose. And they are all woven together so tightly that any attempt to separate the prose from the poetry would tear the fabric to shreds.

This distinctive and rugged style is characteristic of the entire book. It is quite different from that of Hosea, to name but the nearest of Amos' contemporaries. Hosea's clauses are much shorter, and enigmatic to the point of opacity. Amos is more generous in the use of prepositions and conjunctions, which makes his composition more lucid, also more proselike.

Additional evidence along these lines is to be found in the materials added to the oracle against Israel. Indeed, there is a noticeable change in style between 2:8 and 2:9, a significant shift in stance, and a striking departure from the established patterns of the oracles to that point. Thus vv 6–8 are clearly addressed to contemporary Israel, that is, the northern kingdom. The recital in vv 9–13, however, applies to classic Israel of the Exodus and Settlement (the common ancestor of contemporary Judah and Israel). This wider focus is shown by the content and by the use of the term "sons of Israel" (v 11). The language of vv 14–16 is even more expansive. It could apply quite suitably to all eight nations, rounding off the entire prophecy and including them all in a common fate. In 2:9–13 a basic structure is secured by the repetition of the first-person singular pronoun, *wĕʾānōkî* (vv 9, 10, 13) and the repeated use of first-person singular verbs: *wāʾašmîd* (v 9), *wāʾôlēk* (v 10), *wāʾāqîm* (v 11). Nevertheless, much of the material reads like prose; the use of *waw*-consecutive is sufficient proof. Although v 9b–c has characteristic poetic features, including parallelism and chiasmus, v 9a, "and I destroyed the Amorite before them," is prose. Verse 10 seems entirely prosaic, v 11a might pass muster as poetry, but v 11b would be exactly the same if composed as prose. Similarly, v 12b reads like prose, though if pressed we might concede a certain parallelism with v 12a. The chiasmus illustrated by the inversion of *prophets//nazirites* in v 11 to *nazirites//prophets* in v 12 could be the result of a conscious striving for poetic effect on the part of the author, but it needs to be remembered that such devices are not absent from biblical prose, especially prophetic rhetoric. Neither, in our opinion, is there anything notably poetic about the form of v 13, though the simile is a striking one. By contrast, vv 14–15 are clearly poetic in form and structure, and may be compared with 1:2 in both respects. Verse 16 has the form of prose, though it follows smoothly from the preceding material and fits into it quite well.

Parallelism and scansion are not the only hallmarks of Hebrew poetry. Prophetic discourse can be poetic in other ways, particularly in its preference for the vocabulary of poetry without the use of verse forms. Following observations of W. F. Albright on the scant use of the so-called prose particles *ha-,* *'et,* and *'ăšer* in archaic poetry, Freedman (1977b:6–10) developed frequency of their use as a general discriminant between poetry and prose. Application of this diagnostic to Hosea pointed up the striking difference between the narrative in chaps. 1–3 and the prophecy in chaps. 4–14 (Andersen and Freedman, 1980:60–66).

Andersen and Forbes (1983) have calculated this index for every chapter in the Bible. More sensitive analysis suggests that the article has less diagnostic power than the *nota accusativi* and the relative pronoun. In prophetic writing it gives a rough marker of prophetic comment (not necessarily editorial) as distinct from oracular utterance. The alternation of oracle and prose in Amos chaps. 1–3 in terms of the percentage of words that are the relative or *nota accusativi* is shown in the following table.

Section	Words	Particles	Percent	Genre
1:1	23	2	8.7	prose
1:2	13	0	0	poetry
1:3–2:8	291	5	1.7	oracle
2:9–13	63	7	11.1	prose
2:14–16	33	0	0	poetry
3:1–2	31	5	16.1	prose
3:3–8	72	0	0	poetry
3:9–15	104	1	1	oracle
Totals	630	20	3.2	

Discussion

In view of the observations that have been made about the opening prophecy in chaps. 1 and 2, we should not expect to find metrical precision either in individual lines or in the larger blocks of material. The individual oracles in the first long prophecy (1:3–2:8), as well as those in the rest of the book, vary both in length and in organization. No clear strophic patterns emerge anywhere. We must conclude that the author was under no constraint anywhere and in particular was under no constraint to adhere to formal regularities of a quantitative kind. This state of affairs in no way precludes the production of a clearly discoverable overall structure for the prophecy, one that has been worked out in great detail and with great care.

There are indications that the prophecy has been constructed on the basis of a numerical pattern, the key being the number seven (or $7 + 1 = 8$). We have already made some remarks about this phenomenon piecemeal, but it may be convenient to gather the evidence here.

First a note of caution and a disclaimer. There is a difference between a symbolic use of numbers and a mystical meaning of numbers. In later biblical studies a technique for extracting all kinds of meaning from texts on the basis of arithmetical calculations, gematria, enjoyed considerable vogue among cabalistic interpreters. The usual procedure was to give a numerical value to the letters in a word. "Numerics" (or numerology) is another pseudo-science that concentrates on counting the number of times that individual words occur in particular passages. Thus evidence of divine inspiration is discovered in the fact that the word "God" occurs twenty-eight times (4 × 7) in Genesis 1. These exercises discredit themselves when the enterprise is carried through relentlessly, mechanically, to absurdity. The best-known modern student of number symbolism in Scripture was E. W. Bullinger (a descendant of the famous reformer), an Anglican priest and a brilliant but erratic scholar—he produced seventy-seven books (one wonders, by the way, what he would have made of this number because, according to his system, seven meant *perfection*, eleven *disorder!*). His crowning work, *The Companion Bible*, published by Oxford University Press posthumously and anonymously, is replete with observations on numbers and numerical patterns, most of them contrived and arbitrary.

We do not wish our own study of number symbolism in Scripture to be confused with that kind of self-defeating extravagance. Nevertheless, in certain instances numbers do have symbolic meaning in Scripture; but it does not follow that any and every number always has a symbolic meaning (the same meaning!) whenever it is used.

It is thus legitimate to ask why Amos said "three . . . four," even though only one sin is itemized. At the very least the numbers show that the one mentioned is not the only one; but is it enough to interpret them as meaning no more than "crime after crime" (NEB), or "the people . . . have sinned again and again" (TEV)? The analogy of Proverb 30 suggests that *four* is climactic (3 + 1), not additive (four more). But in that chapter the literal value of four is shown by the list actually given. If Amos is like Proverb 30, the one crime mentioned is the fourth and the worst. But it is possible that the one given is the last and worst, whatever the aggregate. The charge against Israel actually conforms to the pattern in Proverbs 30—the real sum there (2:6–8 of Amos) is four, as in the examples from Proverbs.

It has been argued by Weiss (1967a, b) that the 3 // 4 pattern in the Amos oracles reflects an underlying concern with the sum, the number seven, signifying totality. In addition, Weiss points to the list of Israel's rebellious acts and finds there the number seven. We wish to point out in support of the general hypothesis, and to go considerably beyond Weiss's claims, that the number of nations attacked by Amos before he reaches Israel is seven, and that by adding the rebellious acts, one for each nation, we reach the total of seven, which completes the full measure and signals the coming of the judgment that falls on all of the nations as a group. These acts of rebellion would then match those of Israel and bring all to the point of judgment.

Another possibility is that each of the seven nations has committed seven crimes, the total being forty-nine.

In our opinion also, the list of seven nations (other than Israel) goes back to the ancient traditions of the conquest in which the inhabitants of the land of Canaan were identified as seven nations (cf. Deut 7:1ff.). The prophet has adapted the ancient pattern to a present purpose. If it is objected that Judah should not be included in such a list, the answer must be that of geopolitical necessity. In dealing with Israel and its neighbors, Amos could hardly omit Judah, which was there on the scene and, while not as immediately exposed to threatened attack as some of the others, could not finally escape a day of reckoning like the rest.

Furthermore, we are persuaded that the 3 // 4 pattern not only signifies the breakup of the desired total, seven, but serves as a structural guide in its own right. Thus there is a legitimate division in the list of the seven nations after no. 3 (as argued above). The group of three is followed by a group of four (or more precisely 3 + 1). In support of the latter point we may also call attention to the interesting pattern at the end of the prophecy. The catastrophic military disaster that is forecast for Israel (2:14–16) applies symbolically to all of the other nations as well. The fate of one is the fate of all. To emphasize the totality of the destruction, the poet lists seven categories of military personnel (Weiss 1967b:420). Again we can easily divide the seven into two groups, 3 and 3 + 1.

I.A.1. YAHWEH ROARS FROM ZION// JERUSALEM (1:2)

1:2a   And he said:
　　　　　Yahweh—from Zion has roared,
　　　　　　　and from Jerusalem has given forth his voice;
　　2b　　and the pastures of the shepherds are in mourning,
　　　　　　　and the peak of Carmel is withered.

INTRODUCTION

Verse 2 is considered by some to be a self-standing oracle, a suitable commencement for the whole book. For others it is the preface and preamble to the following set of oracles. As such it would mark the extension of the first prophecy through 3:8, which is identifiable as a complement of 1:2, forming an inclusion or envelope. Both of the verbs in 1:2a occur again, in 3:4 and 8, embracing the long discourse or collection of oracles in 1:3–3:7. Both 1:2 and 3:8 declare that Yahweh has spoken with the roar of a lion. In this larger structure the "imperfect" verbs of v 2a must be preterit, and, by the same token, the following "perfect" verbs are stative, in agreement with archaic syntax (so LXX). This arrangement is the inverse of classical prose, which has imperfect verbs in clause-initial position and statives in circumstantial (nominal, in the meaning of classical Arabic grammarians, that is, with a noun as the first member) clauses.

Traditional interpretation regards v 2 as more hymnic than oracular, a general heading for the book as a whole, in fact part of the title and therefore not from Amos himself at all. The reference to Jerusalem contributes to this doubt. Translation of the imperfect literally as future (KJV) has given way to a modern preference for a bland present (NEB, NIV, NJPS). In that case the roar of the lion that will devastate Carmel is not the same as the roar that has uttered the word (3:8, where the verbs must be past tense). Pertinent here is the use of a virtually identical line in Joel 4:16aA (E3:16aA). The continuation there shows that in that context at least the event is eschatological and certainly cosmic. But in view of all that is to follow in the book of Amos it would be appropriate to begin with a statement that the Lord has already spoken and that disasters have already been experienced.

The third colon in Joel 4:16aB (E3:16aB), however, is different from Amos 1:2b: "and heaven and earth will quake." The use of the same root ($r\check{s}$) as in Amos 1:1 is suggestive, and Joel 4:18 (E3:18) is like Amos 9:13b (the lines have four words in common). The conservative opinion that Joel is earlier than Amos made it possible to interpret the latter as dependent on the former. There are other options: Joel could be using Amos. Or both could be drawing on commonly circulating oracles. The circumstance that it is the first line of a bicolon that is shared while the second line is different points to the third explanation. To the extent that each prophet uses the material independently, there is less need to interpret the same line in the same way in each place.

Even so, the verbs in Joel 4:16aA (E3:16aA) can be taken as preterit, especially if v 15 is part of the unit. The verbs in v 15 are perfect, and the perfect verb in v 16aB need not be consecutive (future) if the system is archaic. The darkening of heavenly luminaries and the shaking of heaven and earth are all part of the same event, caused by the divine lion's roar. There is no need to deny that Joel's words are a prediction in order to sustain the *grammatical* result that the verbs are past tense in function. The prophet has seen these things. They happened in a vision. He recounts the vision in a historical mode, but he is repeating a forecast of the future. We may speak of the prophetic preterit along with the prophetic perfect.

So comparison of Amos 1:2 with Joel 4:16 (E3:16) does not settle the question of the verb tense. Jer 25:30 is another variant:

> *yhwh mimmārôm yiš'āg*
> *ûmimmě'ôn qodšô yittēn qôlô*
> *šā'ōg yiš'ag 'al-nāwēhû*
>   *hêdād kědōrěkîm ya'ăneh*
>   *'el kol-yōsěbê hā'āreṣ*

> Yahweh from the Height has roared,
>   and from his holy dwelling has given his
>   voice;
> he has roared loudly from his habitation,
> a shout like the treaders (of grapes) he sang out
>   to all the inhabitants of the earth.

The rendering of *'al-nāwēhû* as "from his habitation," in contrast with the RSV, "against his fold" (cf. Bright 1965, pp. 159–61, and Holladay 1986), is based on the following considerations.

1. The first is parallelism. *Nwh* is regularly used for the abode of the deity. A striking example is to be found in Jer 31:23, where we find the double pair:

> *něwēh ṣedeq*   abode of righteousness!
> *har haqqōdeš*   the mount of the holiness!

The reference is first of all to the heavenly residence and probably also to the temple mount in Jerusalem. The association of *mmrwm* and *mm'n qdšw* in Jer 25:30 shows that the heavenly abode is intended along with its earthly counterpart. In that context *nwhw* should signify the divine residence rather than a human one. The pastoral setting goes back to the earliest poetry of Israel, where the divine residence is called *něwēh qodšekā,* "your holy habitation" (Exod 15:13). The primary reference here is to the desert sanctuary, Mount Sinai, but also to the heavenly counterpart. The long-range parallel expression, using terms already familiar to us in Jeremiah, is to be found in Exod 15:17—*har naḥălātĕkā*, "the mountain of your possession"—which likewise refers to the actual mountain with which Yahweh was associated from earliest times, along with the heavenly correlative from which Yahweh descends to the top of the mountain. The language of Jeremiah is derived from the older source and its traditional if not archaic terms. (For *ʿal*, "from," see provisionally Dahood 1970b: 396, 475; 1966:322; 1968:386; and esp. 1966:26, where supporting evidence is presented for this usage in the Psalter and elsewhere.)

The verbs display the same ambiguity in the matter of tense. The heavenly location and global scope require a cosmic scale for the action (as in Amos 1:2), the principal difference being that in Joel and Amos the setting is the earthly Temple, so the proceedings are primarily cultic and representative rather than mythic and heavenly. Like Amos, Jeremiah mingles several images. The lion's roar marks the commencement of universal judgment.

The passages common to Joel and Amos present another feature. In Joel 4 (E3) the roar of the lion, which devastates the cosmos (vv 15–16), is followed by renewal. In the future paradise "the mountains shall drip sweet wine" (v 18). Amos has the same idea, in similar words, and likewise in the closing scenes of his book. The two ideas, which are in the same place in Joel, are separated as widely as possible in Amos. Amos 9:13–15, if it is at all like Joel 4:15–18 (E3:15–18), makes Amos 1:2 a prediction of the general devastation that will be followed by universal reconstruction. And the lion's roar is the boast of the predator after he has made the kill. If, however, Amos 1:2 is connected with Amos 3:8, which is clearly in the past tense ("the Lord has spoken"), the lion's roar is the announcement of coming judgment (1:3–2:8). We suggest that the ambiguity in the verb forms of v 2 (preterit or future) leaves it open for a double connection shown by the literary structure. Verse 2 thus serves as an opening statement for the entire book but also as the preface to the oracles against the eight nations. With its animal imagery it is a kind of *mashal*, a riddle with more than one possible solution.

2. A second consideration in our rendition of *ʿal-nāwēhû* as "from his habitation . . ." is:

> *yahwēh miṣṣiyyôn yišʾāg*
> *ûmîrûšālēm yittēn qôlô*
> *wĕʾābĕlû nĕʾôt hārōʿîm*
> *wĕyābēš rōʾš hakkarmel*

Yahweh—from Zion has roared,
  and from Jerusalem has given forth his voice;

and the pastures of the shepherds are in mourning,
and the peak of Carmel is withered.

The quatrain consists of two couplets in sequence. The action described in v 2a precedes and is causally linked with the effects in 2b. The poetic structure is apparent; typical and classical devices are employed. The word "Yahweh" serves as the subject of both cola and is specially placed for emphasis. The normal position of the subject is after the verb, in particular when the imperfect form is used. In the first colon the subject (Yahweh) is followed by the prepositional phrase (*miṣṣiyyôn*) and the verb (*yišʾāg*). The construction in the second is parallel, with minor stylistic variations. The colon begins with a prepositional phrase (*mîrûšālēm*) corresponding to *miṣṣiyyôn* in the first colon. There follows the verb and predicate object (*yittēn qôlô*), which together provide a parallel for the verb of the first colon. The longer expression, used in the second colon, makes up for the omission of a term to match the subject (Yahweh) in the first colon, thus achieving metrical balance. The poetic structure can be schematized as follows: *ABC//B'C'* (two words), where *C'* consists of a ballast variant (rhythmic compensation) or extended parallel. In this pattern the subject (*A*) serves both cola.

Continuing the analysis, we find that the cola of the second couplet are exactly parallel in structure: verb followed by subject, which consists of a construct chain. The verbs in v 2b are perfect in form, in contrast with the verbs in v 2a, which are imperfect (the time reference remains the same throughout); and they are positioned at the beginning of the cola, in contrast with the verbs of v 2a. This structure appears to be the result of conscious artistic composition. The poet has taken a traditional couplet (v 2a, cf. Joel 4:16 [E3:16]) and combined it with fresh material to form a polished quatrain.

The metrical structure may be described in terms of accents or stresses as 3 : 3 :: 3 : 3. Using a somewhat more precise syllable-counting system we have 7 : 9* :: 9 : 7 (*vocalize *mîrûšālēm* following the kethib), which may reflect more accurately the symmetrical pattern of the double couplet.

Whether Amos himself composed this four-line poem is another question. As it stands it could belong either to the title as a kind of superscription, or to the prophecy that follows as a general heading for all of the oracles that follow. The point is a fine one, and it leaves unaffected the observation already made, that 1:2 is picked up and balanced by 3:8.

NOTES

1:2a. *And he said.* Here we have the familiar *waw*-consecutive of narrative. The subject is not identified. It could be Yahweh, so that the rest of the verse is his direct speech (it is not uncommon for divine utterances to be in the third person, as in this case: Yahweh = he). The fact that "Yahweh does not speak in the first person" (Mays 1969:21) does not in itself prove that he is not the speaker. It is altogether appropriate that Yahweh should introduce his own oracles with such rubrics as "Thus Yahweh said" (1:3, 6, 9, 11, 13; 2:1, 4, 6) or "Yahweh said" (1:5, 15; 2:3). The speaker refers to himself in the third person in order to use his name and identify himself before switching to the first person. The same can happen in the body of an oracle (as in 2:4, "his statutes") that is spoken by Yahweh himself. It would be easier to maintain that v 2 is an oracle if Yahweh had been mentioned in the title. So the subject is probably Amos. This conclusion would not have been possible without the help of some background already supplied for the listener or reader. In the present form of the book, the antecedent is the name "Amos" in the title. This antecedent is essential for the intelligibility of v 2, which means that vv 1–2 belong together and that the heading and first oracle were introduced by the same person, the editor.

Zion//Jerusalem. a. Zion was Yahweh's headquarters, the Jerusalem Temple his earthly residence. From this palace he issued his decrees. Verse 2 should not be removed on the grounds that Amos was a prophet to the north and therefore Jerusalem was not part of the picture. On the contrary, as we shall try to demonstrate in detail, the whole nation is in Amos' view most of the time. Judah has an oracle (2:4–5); Zion balances Samaria in 6:1; the future of the nation is connected with David (9:11). To state the point negatively, it is hard to believe that Amos had no views on Judah, or that he never expressed them. True, he concentrates mainly on the northern kingdom; but even then Judah is not excluded. There is not a hint in the book that Amos thought that Judah was different from Israel, that the south might be spared, on whatever grounds. Other eighth-century prophets such as Hosea and Micah shared the same outlook, though the case of Isaiah is separate and special. Ultimately the miraculous escape of Jerusalem in 701 B.C.E. was attributed to Hezekiah's repentance (Jer 26:19).

The identification of Zion//Jerusalem as the source of the prophecies that follow suggests further that this place is also where Amos received them. There is no record of such an event, admittedly. Amos himself tells us that the Lord took him away from following the flock, as if he received his call while actually engaged in this task (7:15). But Jerusalem is an eligible location for his visions, his interactions with Yahweh, and his commissioning as a prophet, especially when we take note of the use of cultic pieces at several high points in the prophecy. It was as a worshiper at the temple, not as one of its officers, that he had this contact with the major outlet for messages from Yahweh—Zion//Jerusalem. His experience could have been similar to that of Isaiah (Isaiah 6). There is every reason to believe that he joined in the festivals that brought country folk to the central shrines, including Jerusalem, from time to time (4:4; 5:5).

Zion//Jerusalem. b. This is the usual poetic sequence. Psalm 147:12 is an exception. When the sequence Jerusalem//Zion is met, it usually follows the conventional sequence in chiasmus (Isa 52:1–2), perhaps after several lines of poetry (Lam 2:10, 13; Isa 37:22, 32). The exact opposite occurs in Zech 1:14 and 17. Such patterns make it appropriate to point out that Jerusalem (2:5) and Zion (6:1) follow in chiastic sequence in Amos.

from Zion. A number of grammatical questions are raised by the word sequence in the first clause. The clause-final position of the verb could be an indication that it is preterit (see the following note). The placement of both subject and locative before the verb suggests that *yhwh miṣṣiyyôn* (the whole phrase) is the subject; that is, *miṣṣiyyôn* is not an adverb modifying *yiš'āg,* rather it is an attribute modifying *yhwh.* In the religion of Israel's neighbors it is common to have a god identified by his/her shrine or main city of residence. Thus we find *bʿl ṣdn, bʿl lbnn,* and *bʿlt gbl,* to name a few. Such phrases can be explained as titles, *bʿl* or *bʿlt* being common nouns in the construct "the lord of *X,*" "the lady of *X.*" The point is a fine one. In their absolute use *Baʿl,* "Lord," and *Baʿlat,* "Lady," are essentially personal names, so the phrases violate the general rule that a proper noun cannot be in the construct state. It is much harder to find an analogous construction with Yahweh in Hebrew, perhaps because of a constraint on particularizing or localizing him in this way. Now we have evidence from Quntillet ʿAjrud of precisely this construction in the phrases *yhwh šmrn,* "Yahweh of Samaria," and *yhwh tmn,* "Yahweh of Teman." The title *yhwh ṣĕbāʾōt,* "Yahweh of hosts," is an apparent exception, though originally in this expression *yhwh* may have retained its verbal force. Besides *bʿl ṣpn* (*KAI* 50:2–3; 69:1), the blessing *ybrkk bʿl mn ṣpn* compared with *tbrk bʿlt gbl* (*KAI* 10:8) suggested to R. A. Bowman (1944) that *bʿl mn ṣpn* identifies the God in terms of his chief shrine, "Baal of the North." Dahood (1970b:229) drew attention to *yĕbārekĕkā yhwh miṣṣiyyôn* (Pss 128:5, 134:3); cf. *bārûk yhwh miṣṣiyyôn//šōkēn yĕrûšālāyim* (Ps 135:21). The last phrase is certainly a title, compare *yōšēb ṣiyyon* (Ps 9:12[E11]); the parallelism of Zion //Jerusalem is the same as in Amos 1:2. The parallelism of Ps 135:21 suggests that *yhwh mṣywn* is a title, as is *bʿl mn ṣpn.* Humans are often identified in exactly this way, as with the Edomite kings (Gen 36:31–39;

1 Chr 1:43–51). This comparison has a bearing on the meaning of *mn* in Amos 1:5a (twice).

Yhwh mṣywn as a title resembles *zh syny*, "the one of Sinai," equivalent to *yhwh missînay* (Deut 33:2). *Yhwh mṣywn* can be identified as a title in Ps 110:2. Zion is where Yahweh *is*, not where he comes from. *Mn* is locative. Compare *ʾĕlōhîm bĕṣiyyôn* (Pss 65:2[El], 84:8[E7]), *yhwh bṣywn* (Ps 99:2; Lam 2:6).

That *mṣywn* or *bṣywn* is a modifier of the subject, not an adverb modifying the verb, is suggested by the fact that the phrase is never broken in the sequence Subject + Verb + Location. The verb is either first (Pss 110:2, 128:5, 134:3, 135:21) or last (Joel 4:16 [E3:16]; Amos 1:2; Ps 99:2) in the clause, never in the middle. Note the pattern in Ps 135:21, *yhwh mṣywn// škn yrwšlm*.

When the sequence is Verb + Location + Subject, the locative phrase is clearly adverbial: 2 Sam 22:14 and Ps 18:14(E13):

> *[way] yarʿēm [ba-]min-šāmayim yhwh*
> *wĕʿelyôn yittēn qôlô.*

> Yahweh thundered from the heavens,
> and the Most High gave forth his voice.

Compare 1 Sam 2:10, where we have a similar expression, *ʿālāw baš-šāmayim yarʿēm:* "the Exalted One thundered from the heavens" (*ʿlw* being the divine appellative known from Ugaritic and suspected in several places in the Bible). Here the prepositional phrase is more evidently adverbial.

has roared. The closest affinities of Amos 1:2 are with cult poems, particularly with those celebrating a theophany. The parallelism of *yittēn qôlô* with *yarʿēm* in 2 Sam 22:14 = Ps 18:14 (E13) points to the thunderstorm. But the imagery in Amos 1:2 is confused. While the peal of thunder may be compared to the roar of a lion, the connection with Amos 3:4 and 8 shows that the utterance here is oracular. Even so, the voice is destructive: not the destruction of tempest, but, it would seem, of drought. So the role of Yahweh as storm-god, whose "voice" wreaks widespread havoc (Psalm 29), has been somewhat demythologized. Furthermore, the change of location from the sky (2 Sam 22:14) to Zion (Amos 1:2) makes it easier to equate his "voice" with prophetic revelation (Isa 2:3b). At the same time the proximity of the reference to "the earthquake" (1:1) leaves open the possibility that it is the noise caused by the roar of the (divine) Lion.

The word *yišʾag* is commonly translated as future (KJV, RV), or as a neutral and somewhat bland present tense (NEB, NIV, NJPS). We suggest that the tense is preterit, for the several reasons given above. Therefore it reports and explains, but does not predict, a disaster. The affinities with cultic poetry and the syntax both point that way.

Amos 3:8 reports that "the lion has roared," and that verse forms an inclusion with Amos 1:2. Both verses together show that the roar of the lion is the declaration of an angry word, the giving of the message that the prophet delivers. It is not just a threat, a prediction, that the lion will roar later on.

has given forth. In parallel with "roar," "give voice" could mean "growl" (Jer 2:15). The idea of oracular utterance is not excluded. It has connections with thunder as the voice of God (Exodus 19; Job 37:1–5), to be interpreted by a prophet as an oracle (1 Sam 7:10; John 12:29).

voice. The word *qôl* is often translated "voice," but does not refer so much to the facility for speech as to the "sound" made. The term *qôl* is sometimes used for "articulate speech" (BDB 877) or for an utterance as such. In Ezra 1:1 *qôl* is a proclaimed decree.

Amos 3:8 indicates that the Lord's utterance, which the prophet has heard in the divine council, is like a lion's roar; and this metaphor further indicates that the declaration in this case is an angry threat. In other contexts, this vocabulary has associations with the role of Yahweh as weather-god. The peal of thunder is like a lion's roar:

Job 37:2	*šimʿû šāmôaʿ běrōgez qōlô*	Hearken to the thunder of his voice,
	wěhegeh mippîw yēṣēʾ	and (to) the rumble (that) came from his mouth
4	*ʾaḥărāyw yišʾag-qôl*	After it [the lightning] he roared (with) (his) voice
	yarʿēm běqôl gěʾônô	he thundered with his majestic voice
5	*yarʿēm ʾēl běqôlô . . .*	El thundered with his voice

Recognition of the double-duty preposition in v 4 improves the analysis and translation.

2b. *mourning//withered.* Decisions made about the verbs in the first bicolon will flow on to those in the second bicolon. In strictly formal terms the constructions are ambiguous: either *waw*-consecutive and therefore future; or simple coordination with perfect (stative) verbs. The syntax favors the first, which would be almost enough if the medium were classical prose. Furthermore, in that medium, the ambiguity is easily avoided by postponing the verb, putting the subject first (a nominal, stative clause in the classical sense). But all of the verse's affinities are with archaic cult poetry, and the arguments for past tense are so strong in the first bicolon that the second should fall into line.

the pastures of the shepherds are in mourning. The first colon of v 2b offers a bold poetic image: the literal rendering as in the KJV, the RV, and the RSV is eased somewhat by the translation of *'ăbĕlû,* as "languish" (NJPS). Logically the subject should be the shepherds, not the pastures, but prophets and poets can anthropomorphize Nature as rejoicing, or as mourning. The latter activity of mourning (*'bl*) is often projected onto the objects of grief (Isa 3:26, 33:9; Hos 4:3; and frequently in Jeremiah).

It is possible to consider people rather than "pastures" the subject of *'ăbĕlû* and the "pastures" as an indirect object, though no prepositions are used. The less laconic speech of Jer 9:9 (E9:10) shows that "mountains" and "pastures" are the object or possibly the location of mourning.

> Over [or: upon] (*'al*) the mountains I will raise weeping and wailing, and over (*'al*) the pastures of the steppe a dirge.

In the end, however, the parallel passage with its construct chain (*rʾš hkrml*) as subject supports the traditional understanding of the first colon as having the same construction and syntax.

The second incongruity within v 2b is that the two verbs are not parallel —*mourn* and *withered.* The powerful influence of the doctrine of synonymous parallelism in Hebrew poetry is seen in many translations and commentaries on this verse. In some, the frequent use of the roots *'bl* and (*y)bš* in similar contexts has suggested secondary meanings or textual adjustments to bring them closer together here. The verb *'ăbĕlû,* "they mourned," can be changed to *nābĕlû,* "withered" ("dry up" [NIV], "scorched" [NEB]), or simply given that alternative meaning (*'bl* II in KB, not in BDB). Or, *yābēš* can be brought into line by reading *yēbōš,* "it is ashamed," continuing the figurative language. We do not think such changes are needed. The doctrine of synonymous parallelism in a bicolon should not be overstressed. The shift in focus from colon to colon permits both aspects of the disaster to be included in a single picture. Everything has dried up; people mourn everywhere. There is merism between the two colons. Not just the meadows and the peak are ruined by drought, but everything in between as well.

The incongruity between v 2a and v 2b lies in the fact that a lion does not cause a drought by roaring. The withering of pasture is usually the effect of the hot desert wind. In Ezek 19:7 the desolation of the land by the lion's roar is the result of devastation in war. The use of the word "shepherds" suggests in addition that they are mourning the ravaging of the flock by the lion (3:12), who roars when he has taken prey (3:4; Ezek 22:25; Pss 22:14[E13], 104:21).

Other chains of cause and effect are recognized. The lion's roar of Yahweh's voice ("from heaven," i.e., thunder [Psalms 29, 68:34{E33},

77:18; Jer 25:30]) causes earthquakes (2 Sam 22:14; Pss 18:14[E13], 46:6[Heb 46:7]). This result appears in Amos too (8:8; 9:5, 9), to be followed by mourning (8:8).

The incongruities among the images in Amos 1:2 thus foster a cascade of associated ideas, and there is no point in asking which of them were in the prophet's conscious intention.

pastures of the shepherds. The disasters of 4:6–11 (compare 7:1) could be the background of 1:2. The reference to shepherds' grazing grounds takes us close to Amos' personal interests.

Carmel. Realism and myth are combined in the picture. The peak of Mount Carmel has dried up. As a comment on actual events, this preface probably refers to the devastations described in 4:6–11. The refusal of the people to repent under these chastisements is the reason why the Lord will not retract his decree of judgment (1:3a, 6a, 9a, 11a, 13a; 2:1a, 4a, 6a). There can be mourning without penitence. Mourning for the devastation of nature was a part of pagan cults ("weeping for Tammuz") and would do more harm than good, as far as prophets were concerned. For them "returning" to Yahweh (4:6, 8, 9, 10, 11) consisted of doing justice, not singing songs, whether of grief or joy (5:23–24; cf. Is 1:10–17).

There was more than one Carmel in Israel, but in prophecy (as in Amos 9:3) this place is usually the luxuriant mythic mountain garden where everything grows to perfection. Its inclusion here suggests the cosmic scope of the devastation. Compare the great abyss of Amos 7:4. It is unimaginative to identify Carmel with the well-known headland prominent in the west of central Palestine. It is only five hundred feet high, and a disaster restricted to its peak would not be as serious as what is needed to open a prophecy like this. It is not simply a symbol of the northern kingdom in general (Mays 1969:21).

Verse 2 achieves a balance and synthesis between the realistic and the mythic. The references to Zion and Jerusalem are historical, but Carmel takes us into fantasy. It is true that there was more than one real Carmel, but the four compass points in Is 33:9—Lebanon, Sharon, Bashan, Carmel (cf. Is 35:2)—take us to the boundary between the geographical and the cosmic. The disaster described or predicted in Amos 1:2 was not restricted to one small mountain peak. Like the Lebanon of Isa 40:16 and Hos 14:5–6, this Carmel represents a region at least as wide as the territory occupied by the eight nations in the prophecy that follows. The mourning of the shepherds for damaged pastures (v 2bA) is real enough, but the literal form of the statement, "the pastures mourn," is fanciful. A god who roars like a lion takes us into myth, but the giving out of a statement in Jerusalem is a concrete event of revelation in history at a known place and time. The statements are poised between the actual and the imaginary and can be pushed in either direction—figurative descriptions of a natural disaster, or the use of familiar terms for an indescribable eschatological event.

This literary technique is worth emphasizing at the beginning of our study, because it is characteristic of Amos' craftsmanship throughout the entire book. It is grounded in his visionary experiences, but it is always in contact with the phenomenal world. The prophet as visionary is not interested in a transcendental world, inaccessible to the rest of us. Thus he betrays no curiosity about what the Lord looks like. (See the note on 7:7.) He is a messenger to tell us what the Lord has decided to do (3:7).

I.A.2. THE EIGHT NATIONS (1:3–2:8)
I.A.2.a. SIX NEIGHBORS (1:3–2:3)
I.A.2.a.i. ARAM (1:3–5)

1:3a   Thus Yahweh said:
　　　　　For three violations by Damascus,
　　　　　　　and for four,
　　　　　　　I will not reverse it:
3b　　　Because they threshed Gilead with iron sledges.
4a　　　So I will send Fire against the house of Hazael,
4b　　　　　and She will consume the citadels of Ben-Hadad.
5a　　　And I will break the bar of Damascus,
　　　　　　　and I will cut off the sovereign from Biqʿat-Awen,
　　　　　　　and the scepter wielder from Beth-Eden—
5b　　　and the Aramaean people will go into exile to Qir.
　　　　　　　　　Yahweh has spoken!

NOTES

1:3a. *Thus Yahweh said.* This phrase is the customary formal opening of an oracle. It is part of the messenger formula; the courier who delivers a letter repeats what the originator *said,* with a written copy of the speech as an aid to his memory or as confirmation that he has said it. The connections between prophecy and epistle are ancient. The telltale *wĕʿattâ* that typically introduces the main content of a letter is used in Amos only at

7:16. In literary presentation of collected oracles, the initial formula serves to identify the onset of each distinct speech. It is used for each of the eight components of the opening oracle (1:3, 6, 9, 11, 13; 2:1, 4, 6). It is characteristic of Amos (3:11, 12; 5:3, 4, 16; 7:17) but rare in the other minor prophets (Obad 1; Mic 2:3, 3:5; Nah 1:12).

The significance of this formula (kōh 'āmar Yhwh) was first thoroughly investigated by J. Lindblom (1924: Appendix). It is exclusively prophetic in location, but note the use of the same formula when X is human. A. Bentzen (1948 I:187) concluded that the language was ritualistic, as suited to priestly Torah as to prophetic oracle. But there does not seem to be any evidence for use that is not strictly prophetic.

for . . . and for. The preposition is usually interpreted as "on account of," "because of," the whole phrase giving the reason why the Lord "will not reverse it." Because we do not know what "it" refers to, the logic of the preposition remains elusive. The series continues in the next line, where 'al is followed by an infinitive that identifies one crime. In its meaning "on top of," 'al can describe the accumulation of one thing upon another, especially when the preposition is repeated (Greenfield 1966)—"for crime upon crime." It is not clear whether it means four crimes on top of three—in other words, seven in all—or for the addition of the fourth, the one named in the next line. It is persistence in sins, not just committing them that is condemned. A tally has been kept. Presumably warnings have been given, impending and threatened judgments suspended or canceled, to give a reprieve, a moratorium during which the situation might be rectified. In the case of Israel it is clear from the visions and plagues (4:6–11) that many opportunities for repentance had been given. Final judgment did not come without adequate warning.

There is no indication that the progress of culpability was monitored in all of the surrounding nations with the same intensity and detail as in Israel. But, because all eight nations are on exactly the same footing in the opening prophecy (1:3–2:8), we may suppose that this final word was not Amos' first word to any of them. Complacency is one of the evils he attacks (4:1; 6:1, 6). The postponement of the day of reckoning was interpreted as divine indifference or even approbation, so that they could say to themselves, "Calamity shall not even come close, much less confront us" (9:10) and even have high hopes for the Day of the Lord (5:18).

three . . . four. As already pointed out, Amos' use of this formula does not follow the conventions found in wisdom literature (e.g., Proverbs 30). He mentions only one "rebellion," but more than one is implied. The Bible continually asserts that God is very reluctant to punish sinners; he gives them plenty of time to repent. But there is also a limit to the divine patience, and there is the notion of a quota (Gen 15:16) of accumulated sins that, when reached, triggers the change from forbearance to anger. The rabbis took the numbers seriously, arguing that a sin could be forgiven three times, but the fourth one was unpardonable (Mishna *Yoma* 86b; cf. *Sanh.* 7a).

God is notably exasperated when his self-restraint is misinterpreted as indifference or acquiescence, when a stay in punishment, granted so that they may have every possible opportunity to repent, is used as an opportunity to commit more sins (Rom 2:1–11). The detailed analysis of Amos 4:6–11 shows this process at work. It is clear that God's first priority is to forgive sin, and he welcomes every excuse for putting off the day of doom. A similar process lies behind the numerals *three . . . four* in all of the oracles. In the early stages of the process sin after sin is met with call after call to repent. In each case a disaster could be sent as a warning and a sample, identified as such by a prophet and used as a talking point in a sermon on repentance. Amos 4:6–11 shows this treatment at work in Israel, though the successive sins are not itemized and the prophet's accompanying efforts are not reported. But both ingredients are clearly implied, for they are present in other biblical cases.

We have no way of telling how far such a ministry of Yahweh's prophets extended to Israel's neighbors, so that the final crackdown is seen to be just and, indeed, long overdue. They had been warned often enough, and they are without excuse.

violations. Heb *piš'ê*, "acts of rebellion." The term is used of treaty violations in which the vassal rebels against his suzerain, cf. 2 Kgs 1:1; 3:5, 7; 8:20, 22; cf. 1 Kgs 12:19. It is essentially a covenant term, and in the framework of Israel's relations with God signifies the violation of the major terms of the covenant, that is, rebellion against God. In the present context it is often referred to as the violation of general standards of international morality—universal laws of God—expressed in inhumane treatment of one nation by another. That offenses against Yahweh's law are involved is clear from the fact that punishment is to be meted out by Yahweh himself. (On *pš'* as rebellion see Knierim 1965:113–43.)

It need not be denied that Amos' moral teaching fits into a scheme of universal humane ethics. But he does not present his oracles in such terms. They are specific and concrete. Although we cannot equate any of the charges with documented atrocities of the period, the crimes are those of nation against nation (not person against person). Most of them have to do with conduct in war—atrocities during attacks (1:3, 11, 13) and cruelty afterward (1:6, 9; maybe 2:1). The setting is international; the issues are political. Tyre is accused of violating a parity treaty (1:9); and although the other party is not identified, Israel is the best candidate, remembering the long-standing alliance between the two countries (1 Kgs 9:10–14, 16:31). So one must ask more precisely whether these "acts of rebellion" were just offenses against conscience in days long before any declarations of human rights as such, or more specifically willful violations of formal agreements, which made them directly answerable to Yahweh himself.

In the case of Judah (2:4) the nature of the "acts of rebellion" is made clear, though no specific acts are cited. They rejected the law and commandments of Yahweh and followed "lies" instead. The indictment of Israel is the inverse—specific charges, but not identified as breaches of covenant stipulations.

In all cases the offenses are double—crimes against humanity and rebellion against Yahweh. The difference in emphasis between the six non-Israelite nations, whose crimes are international, and the two Israelite kingdoms, whose crimes are domestic, should not be exaggerated. All are equally classified as "acts of rebellion"; all receive similar punishment (Yahweh will send Fire on seven of the eight; some are threatened with exile).

The condemnation of the six neighboring states is often seen as no more than a buildup to the real point, the condemnation of Israel. The argument is that the indignation of Israelites against these surrounding people over acts of aggression and cruelty, many of them against Israel itself, robs them of any excuse when the prophet finally points his finger at them. This view is certainly one of the effects of the total presentation. But the issues raised in the oracles against Judah and Israel were not new. They were all too familiar.

Yahweh claims jurisdiction over all the region. All eight nations are responsible to him. It is precisely because he will judge the world with equity and the peoples with truth (Ps 96:13) that all of the oracles have to be taken with equal seriousness.

Another way of facing this issue is to ask whether the Israelite prophets, when they addressed oracles to neighboring countries, did so purely for home consumption: "His utterances concerning foreign nations, Syria, Moab, etc., like the similar utterances of Isaiah, Jeremiah and Ezekiel, were intended for the ear of Israel" (Harper 1905:5); or whether they delivered their messages outside the bounds of Israel. The prophets, from Elisha (2 Kings 9) to Jeremiah (27:3—which lists four of the six nations charged by Amos) delivered oracles to, not just about, other nations. Jonah was not as exceptional as he is sometimes made out to be.

Israel is central and special. That is not denied. Amos emphasizes it (3:2); but that fact does not leave the others out. In historical perspective the entire region was settled under Yahweh's supervision (Deut 2:5, 9, 19; Judg 11:15–27; Amos 9:7—five of the six). There are good historical memories here; Israel knew that the Phoenicians had been in their land much longer than the others. As history developed all of these nations had a connection with Yahweh through their contacts with Israel.

So the nature of these "acts of rebellion," as rebellion against formal and known obligations to Yahweh, can be clarified in historical and political terms. These eight nations comprise the entire region of Syria and Palestine. The places mentioned in the oracle about Damascus suggest that the prophet has the entire Aramaean territory in mind. The whole corresponds to David's sphere of influence, to one of the definitions of the Promised Land. In its full extent, the region was also considered to be Yahweh's particular domain. The association of Yahweh with David his "messiah" in governing the region is clear in Psalm 2 and other passages. In concluding various kinds of treaties with subjugated or allied peoples, sanctions would be imposed and oaths sworn in the name of Yahweh (Amos 9:12). It is hardly likely that David, the stronger party, would have reciprocated with oaths in the names of Hadad, Chemosh, and the rest. However the Moabites, Aramaeans, and the others may have viewed their position, from Israel's point of view they had entered into obligations to Yahweh. However unreal it might seem to be invoking a long-dead political establishment, it is clear that this model ("as in the days of old" [9:11]) retained its vitality as an idea and an ideal. Israelites dreamed about the future along precisely these lines. For Amos the undiminished claims of Yahweh on the loyalty of these peoples were a present reality, and any repudiations of those claims were "acts of rebellion."

I will not reverse it. a. The statement is used eight times. There can be no doubt about the correctness of the text, but its interpretation presents three problems: (i) the meaning of *lōʾ;* (ii) the meaning of the verb; and (iii) the meaning, especially the referent, of the pronoun suffix.

i. On the assumption that *hēšîb* means "pay back" (1 Sam 6:8, 17), a negative meaning for *lōʾ* is impossible in a threat of punishment. Its force can be canceled if it is actually a rhetorical question: "Shall I not make requital?" It requires the slightest change to obtain *hălōʾ;* in fact, the letter could have been lost by haplography after the *he* at the end of the preceding word. Or the statement could be construed as a question, even without *h*- (cf. Gordis 1976:152–57).

A similar result could be reached by reading *lʾ* as asseverative, "I will certainly punish them" (TEV). If *l-* is preferred, the extra *ʾ* can be explained as dittography. This explanation was favored by W. F. Albright (1969:216 n. 23, 240), who read, "I will verily requite him."

Leaving the full discussion of the pronoun object "him" until later, we observe no more at this stage than that it does not agree with "Damascus" as the implied object, which would be feminine, or with the plural "they" that follows. Furthermore, when *hēšîb* has the required meaning, the person requited is governed by *l-* (Hos 12:3[E2]; Prov 24:12, 29:2; 2 Chr 6:23). The meaning "requite" for *hēšîb* entails too many difficulties and should be abandoned.

ii. On the basis of an almost identical expression in the oracles of Balaam it is better to find in *lōʾ ʾăšîbennû* an expression of strong conviction and assurance that a decision has been made, and will not be reversed. The example is in Num 23:19b–20:

19b	*hahû² ²āmar*	Has he [God] said?
	wĕlō² yaʿăśeh	and will he not do it?
	wĕdibber	And has he spoken,
	wĕlō² yĕqîmennâ	and will he not make it stand?
20	*hinnēh bārēk lāqāḥtî*	Behold to bless I took [him]
	ûbērēk	and he will bless,
	wĕlō² ²ăšîbennâ	and I shall not reverse it.

This ancient oracle presents numerous problems, not the least of which is the puzzling object *-ennâ* on two of the verbs, a feature resembling Amos 1:3.

Albright (1944:212 n. 23) proposed to solve this problem by identifying the ending *-ennâ* as simply energic, thus eliminating the object altogether. It is not so easy to dispose of the suffix *-ennû* in Amos 1:3 in this way; and the two details must be explained in similar fashion. In the case of Num 23:20 the feminine could be explained as a vague neutral reference ("it"), or by supposing some feminine noun, such as "blessing" as the implied object of the preceding verbs, *²amar . . . dibber . . . bērēk,* and serving as antecedent for the pronoun. In Amos 1:3 we must then find a corresponding masculine noun. At least Num 23:20b establishes that *lō² ²ăšîbennâ* means "I won't take it back," that is, "what I have said." Compare Esth 8:8, where *²ên lĕhāšîb* refers to an irreversible decree.

iii. But even if this argument settles the meaning of *²ăšîb,* the referent of its pronoun object remains to be identified. Most translations resort to paraphrase: "I will not turn away the *punishment* thereof" (KJV, RV); "the punishment" (RSV); "my word" (NAB); "my decree" (JB). The NJPS translates "it" and footnotes "the decree of punishment." The NEB paraphrases "I will grant them no reprieve." The NIV has "my wrath."

It is hard to believe that Amos was being deliberately vague, saying that Yahweh "will not reverse *it,* " but not telling them what "it" is. It is possible that the pronoun is cataphoric, referring to the punishment that follows immediately after the charge in the following oracle. Somewhere in the prophecy we should be able to find the referent for the pronoun. To aid the search we ask whether the pronoun object has the same referent for all of its eight occurrences, or whether there is a distinct reference for each of the eight nations severally. If the latter, then it cannot be an anticipation of the specific judgment pronounced on each, for in the case of Israel no such pronouncement follows. We suggest rather that the repetition of the identical words eight times shows that it is one and the same decision, covering all of them equally and all together, that will not be reversed. We need a referent that blankets the whole set of oracles in the coherent prophecy of 1:3–2:8.

The repetition also includes the formula "for three violations . . . and for four" in each case. In this association it could mean, "this time I will not change my mind as I have done on previous occasions." Such a resolution corresponds to the repeated "I shall not spare them again" of the second pair of visions (7:8, 8:2).

The nearest candidate for antecedent of "it" is "his voice" in verse 2 (suggested to us first by Edgar Conrad at the University of Queensland; found already in Matthew Henry and many others since). This referent makes sense if the utterance described in v 2 is an oracle of judgment on all of these nations. It also makes literary sense if v 2 is a preface to the comprehensive prophecy in 1:3–2:8. Verse 2b hints at a cosmic fire that will dry up even the mythic realm of Carmel, and Amos 7:4 is explicit that the fire will destroy the great subterranean ocean. The same language is used of the cosmic fire that will engulf all of the countries in the region (1:4, 7, 10, 12, 14; 2:2, 5). Everything thus fits together, and the links between these oracles against the nations and the visions reported in chaps. 7 and 8 show that the events develop from an initial threat that was temporarily averted by Amos' successful intercession (7:1–6). Amos bought time during which the disasters could have become occasions for repentance (4:6–11). There is a continuing play on the root *šwb*, the *hip'îl* being used eight times in chaps. 1–2, while the *qal* occurs five times in chaps. 4:6–11. In every case the word is governed by a negative particle, with overtones of despair and irretrievable consequences. The opportunity was missed. Rebellion persisted in (three, four, perhaps a total of seven times [1:3, 6, 9, 11, 13; 2:1, 4, 6]) finally exhausted the divine patience. The double comment on the third and fourth visions—"I shall never spare them again" (7:8; 8:2) corresponds to the eightfold "I will not reverse it," all referring to the decree of judgment (the "statement" in v 2) not to be revoked or even postponed any longer.

It follows that the oracles presented first do not come from the opening phases of Amos' ministry. Rather they represent the climax and close after every means of averting the catastrophe, by canceling the decision or staying its execution, has been tried and exhausted, to no avail.

The possibility of divine repentance and the reversibility of divine decisions and decrees are a constant of biblical religion, and Amos himself exploits this element in the account of the visions of chaps. 7–8. Intercession by the prophet is one of the ways in which divine judgment can be put off, modified, or even abandoned, and such is the case with the first two visions. In the third and fourth, however, the period of vacillation or flexibility is terminated, and the decision becomes hardened and no longer subject to revision or reversal. The oracles in chaps. 1–2 reflect the time of hardening; the decision to conquer and destroy has been fixed and is not subject to reversal: "I will not reverse it." In terms of the fourth vision, the end has come for all of the nations listed, including and especially the last of them, Israel.

At the time the oracle was given, it must have seemed more foolish than ominous, especially if we are right in supposing that it came fairly early in the reign of Jeroboam, at a time that the future must have looked bright, and indeed proved to be so for Israel. No doubt king, priest, and people would have been much happier with the words of a rival prophet, a northerner with more acceptable credentials, Jonah ben-Amittai of Gath-hepher. According to 2 Kgs 14:25, his words of promise and success were fulfilled, and Jeroboam enjoyed victory and prosperity during his long reign.

It is possible that the oracles of Amos and Jonah were structurally similar, and both dealt with the fate of the nations surrounding Israel. In both cases a divine judgment was proclaimed against those nations and perhaps for similar reasons—violation of a covenant commitment to the Lord of Israel, or perhaps an atrocity committed against the people of God. From that point the oracles would move in different directions: for Jonah the beneficiary of divine intervention would be Israel because it was the chosen nation of God, the recipient of the divine promises of old. The agent of victory or salvation would naturally be the anointed king, Jeroboam. For Amos, on the contrary, precisely because Israel was the elect of God, it must suffer the necessary consequences of its defection and apostasy. It is revealed as the ultimate target of denunciation, the last of the nations to be destroyed in the judgment to come. Immediate success and acclaim lay with Jeroboam and Jonah, but in the end Amos' analysis proved more durable and true. Whatever temporary success was achieved in the days of Jeroboam proved to be ephemeral, and the long night of disaster and destruction that Amos predicted descended on Israel and its neighbors— though perhaps not precisely in the way and order stated. For Israel the end came just as he said (cf. 8:2).

I will not reverse it. b. Although we are satisfied that the conclusions reached in the preceding note are the best possible, other possibilities have been tried, and we will mention them briefly (for a detailed survey of proposed solutions of the meaning of *lō' 'ăšîbennû* and a new interpretation see Barré 1986). The LXX reads *ouk apostraphēsomai* ("I will not turn away") in each instance, but varies the object, *auton* (1:3, 13; 2:1, 4, 6), *autēn* (1:9), *autous* (1:6, 11). The departures from *auton* are unaccountable. Although the latter agrees with the MT, the plural shows a tendency to agree with the subject of the following infinitive. The feminine could agree with "fire"—"I will send her—and not bring her back."

It is most unlikely that Yahweh is saying that he will not turn back the Assyrian invader from the area. We do not accept the idea that the disasters threatened here are simply prophetic language for military aggression

(Harper 1905:11, 20). And we date the prophecy before that development was on the horizon.

The word *hēšîb* sometimes means "bring back" (from exile). Exile is threatened in 1:5, 15; 7:11, 17. The expression *lōʾ ʾăšîbennû* could be the finishing touch—"I won't bring him back." This sentence would represent the most severe grade of punishment. The first grade is cautionary trouble (4:6–11); the second is to wipe out some, but leave a remnant (7:1–6; also 3:12, 4:11, 5:3); and the third in severity is to send them into exile (4:3, 5:5, 6:7, 7:17). But then it would be possible to restore a remnant, bring back exiles (9:14). Never to bring them back would be just as bad. Although these ideas are found in Amos, they do not apply equally to all of the nations that are under judgment. And this theory does not explain the object pronoun "him" (or "it").

3b. *threshed.* The vivid description of cruelty and violence in warfare is based on agricultural practice. There are at least five different words *ḥārûṣ* in Hebrew. The one used here means "threshing sledge." The word *môrag* is a synonym (2 Sam 24:22; 1 Chr 21:23), and the two terms are combined in Isa 41:15, *môrag ḥārûṣ.* The description of Leviathan as a *ḥārûṣ* whose scales on his underbelly are sharp postsherds (Job 41:22[E30]) gives the picture. The glimpse of agricultural life in Isa 28:23–29 connects the *ḥārûṣ* with the verb *dwš,* as here. The design of this piece of equipment has been described by modern travelers. It was either a sledge dragged across ears of grain or a low-slung wagon with wheels, the underside mounted with teeth of flint or iron. Commentators usually take this part of Amos' indictment literally. The Aramaeans used such machines to commit atrocities against the inhabitants of Gilead. Harper (1905:18) states: "Only prisoners of war were thus tortured; the custom was not uncommon of placing them on the ground like grain, and driving the machine over them." As far as we have been able to discover, there is no explicit attestation in any ancient war reportage that such an act was performed. Quite apart from the practicalities of such an elaborate form of torture and the availability and known use of more efficient techniques, the execution or mutilation of prisoners would go against one of the main purposes of such conquests—to recruit slaves for the national workforce or for trade (1:6, 9).

The words of 2 Sam 12:31 are often cited as evidence of similar atrocities committed by David. The passage is notoriously difficult, and the parallel in 1 Chr 20:3 does not ease the difficulties much (it replaces *wayyāśem* with *wayyāśar* and *magzĕrōt habbarzel* with *mĕgērōt,* repeating the first word on the list, and omits the detail about assigning the captives to the brickworks). The use by David of *ḥārîṣê habbarzel* matches *ḥărûṣôt habbarzel* of Amos 1:3. The *ḥārîṣ* is an unidentified "sharpened" tool. In 2 Sam 12:31 it comes in series with *mĕgērâ* and *magzĕrōt habbarzel,* "saws, iron threshing boards, and iron axes" (NJPS). The instrumental use of *b-* is the same in both passages.

The translation "under" (RV) has been accommodated to 1 Chr 20:3. But the several adjustments in that version already attest to a shift in interpretation similar to that in the LXX of Amos 1:3. The fact that the variant *wayyāśar* is reflected in the LXX[L] *kai deprisen* does not make it a "patently superior reading" (McCarter 1984:311). It does not even establish the meaning "and he saved [them]" for *wayyāśar*. This unique meaning for the root *śr (r)* rests entirely on the evidence of the Greek translators: BDB is unhappy with it; KB does not recognize it. There is some evidence for a root *nsr (samek!)* in Aramaic and Arabic, and Heb *maśśôr*, "saw" (Isa 10:15), could be derived from it. It is more likely that *wayyāśar* in 1 Chr 20:3 has the meaning it has in Judg 9:22, namely, that David became prince of the Ammonites. Apparently what has happened is that the legendary embellishments of old stories with lurid details about bizarre atrocities have determined the renditions in the version. Thus "he made them pass through the brick-kiln" (2 Sam 12:31 KJV) requires the *qere*, and Amos 2:1 has been used to corroborate the idea that this was simply an act of cruelty. As for a torture that forces a person into a brick mold . . . ! Josephus (*Antiquities* 7.161) made no use of the details of 2 Sam 12:31, saying briefly "and the men he tortured and put to death." David's treatment of the Moabites (2 Sam 8:2) could be in mind. Once this "meaning" gains currency, the obscure old texts are assumed to have that meaning, and the necessary meanings are forced on the Hebrew vocabulary—*śr* means "saw"; *b-,* means "under." It is even possible that the text itself is then moved in this direction: 1 Chr 20:3 by abbreviation and simplification; but even 2 Sam 12:31 by variants, such as *bmlkn > bmlbn*, which involves a very minor scribal change. The difference between "he made [them] pass" and "he made them work" is also minimal, and the latter emendation has proved convincing (details in McCarter 1984:311). So deeply entrenched is the tradition that 2 Sam 12:31 describes atrocities that C. F. Keil and F. Delitzsch (1857–58:5.396) declare, "the cruelties inflicted upon the prisoners are not to be softened down . . . by an arbitrary perversion of the words into a mere sentence to hard labor, such as sawing wood, burning bricks, etc." Yet there seems to be little room for doubt that the latter is the meaning of 2 Sam 12:31. But neither interpretation of 2 Sam 12:31, torturing or enslaving of prisoners, is applicable to Amos 1:3b.

The ancient trend to interpret an obscure passage such as 2 Sam 12:31 or Amos 1:3b in the light of other sources is already evident in pre-Christian Hebrew recensions of Amos. In 5QAm4 we find *hrw* [*t.*] (DJD, 3:173), clearly a contamination from 1:13 (on the textual process of contamination in both transmission and translation of texts see Andersen 1960). The LXX has the same gloss—*tas en gastri echousas*. This wording is probably due to connection with 2 Kgs 8:12 (Hazael!). But it is completely different from the idea that Amos is condemning atrocities committed on prisoners of war. And it shows that ancient commentators were guessing just as desperately as their modern counterparts.

Amos says that Damascus "threshed Gilead." In Isa 41:15 Israel is described as a threshing sledge, new, "with many spikes" (NJPS), which will *thresh* mountains to powder and make hills like chaff. It is a metaphor for the savage conquest of a territory. The war machine is like a gigantic threshing board, which slashes and pulverizes the whole land. The harvesting imagery can be elaborated in several ways. The devastation of Israel by Aram in the time of Jehoahaz is described in precisely this manner— *wayĕśīmēm keʿāpār lādūš*, "and he made them like the dust of threshing," (2 Kgs 13:7; cf. Isa 41:2; Jer 13:24; Ps 83:14[E13]). The comparison is also found in Assyrian war dispatches.

4a. *send.* Compare Hos 8:14. He will dispatch an agent (cf. Amos 9:1–4, in which the deity commands "the snake" and "the sword" to carry out his punitive decision against survivors of the destruction of the city and sanctuary). As in 4:10, where Yahweh sends "pestilence," "Fire" is a mythic being (a messenger) not much different from the fire gods (Nushku, Erra, Ishtum) of neighboring religions. The idiom is restricted to acts of the deity. When humans start a conflagration they burn *bāʾēš.*

Traditional interpretation has identified the messenger of fire to be sent by Yahweh not with the cosmic destroyer of mythological texts (Gen 19:24; Num 16:35; Deut 32:22; etc.) but with the destruction of cities in warfare, and specifically as a threat of the Assyrian invasions. In view of that understanding, "I will not bring him back" means "I will not call off the Assyrians." All of this theory is quite beside the mark, because Amos is never specific or explicit about the human agent of the disasters to come. Although Assyria is not explicitly mentioned in the MT of Amos, there is a probable reading at 3:9 on the basis of the LXX; and there are other indications that Assyria (like Egypt) is in the picture somewhere or at least behind the scenes. The formula "I will send Fire" may well be mythic language and description of purely historical events. Prophecy always remains attached to historical actualities, even when its language breaks the bounds of historical possibility. In the present oracles the burning of cities, the defeat of armies (2:14–16), the killing of rulers, and the exile of populations (1:5b, 15) are the punishments sent by God. While the prophet is not much interested in the details of military engagement, these are typical actions and outcomes of war.

4b. *consume.* This is the usual verb for fire (7:4); *ʾēš ʾōkēlâ* is one of the terrifying omens—"thunder, earthquake, loud noise, tornado, tempest, flame of devouring fire" (Isa 29:6). We translate the subject "She" because there is more than personification here. Fire is a living agent, like the angel with the sword in 2 Sam 24:15–17 or the angel of pestilence in 2 Kgs 19:35; consider also the serpent and the sword as agents of the deity in Amos 9:3–4.

Once again we see how the oracle is made up of cosmic, mythic components, but conveys a truth that will be realized in historical events. Prophecy is closely related to event, and in biblical thinking influences and produces the events described in its content; but prophecy and fulfillment are not mechanically linked, and prophecy is not simply an account of what is to happen, as a record of the occurrence composed after the fact would be. So we can say that the terms and elements in Amos' oracles are not themselves oriented to contemporary history only, but rather belong to the realm of the heavenly council and divine decision making. Once the message is transmitted to the prophet and uttered by him, it will have dynamic influence in the historical realm and will produce effects that are in line with the prophetic content and are produced by the divine words. The outcome will be historical and will be related consequentially to the prophecy; but they will scarcely be identical because they function in different realms.

house//citadels. The target of the divine fire is identified in each of the oracles, and it is usually the capital city and its defense works, and within it the complex of fortified buildings that constitutes the king's administrative headquarters. Amos never uses the term "palace" (*hêkāl*) in this connection; in its one occurrence (8:3) that word refers to the temple. The political establishment, not the religious hierarchy, is in his sights; the crimes charged are those of the military, the merchants, the magistrates, not those of priests. At least that is true of the six outside nations. Judah and Israel are a different matter. It is an irony that the point on which the chosen people congratulated themselves and assured themselves of exclusive divine protection (9:10), "we are not idolaters like the heathen," is not considered in 1:3–2:3, where nothing is said about the gods and temples of these nations. The gods of these nations are nothing anyway; but when such gods are introduced into Israel they acquire real status as "lies" (5:26, 8:14). The other nations are not condemned for idolatry. This feature of their life is not even mentioned. It was Y. Kaufmann (1960, especially chaps. 1 and 2) who pointed out the extraordinary interest of this simple, but generally overlooked, fact.

The following is a list of the targets of the divine fire.

    1:4   *byt-H//'rmnwt-H*
    1:7   *ḥwmt-C//'rmntyh*
    1:10   *ḥwmt-C//'rmnwtyh*
    1:12   *C//'rmnwt-C*
    1:14   *ḥwmt-C//'rmnwtyh*

2:2   *L//ᵓrmnwt-C*

2:5   *L//ᵓrmnwt-C*

H = Human; *L* = Land; *C* = City.

In every case the target of the divine fire includes the *ᵓarmĕnōt,* usually of a city that is either named (Bozrah [1:12], Kerioth [2:2; or "the cities," i.e., of Moab], Jerusalem [2:5]) or referred to by means of the suffix "her," linking to a name of a city in the preceding colon (Gaza [1:7], Tyre [1:10], Rabbah [1:14]).

When the name of the city appears in the second colon, the first colon has the name of a land (Moab [2:2], Judah [2:5]) or another city (Teman [1:12]). When the second colon says "her *ᵓarmĕnōt,*" the first colon has the wall of the respective city (1:7, 10, 14). The two main patterns thus occur three times each. The targets in the first country (Aram) and the eighth country (Israel) are not identified in either of those two ways. For Aram the targets are connected with the king, and "house" instead of "wall" is used in the first colon.

If the pattern of 2:2, 5 is being followed, "the house of Hazael" could be a name for the country, which is probably the meaning of "house" in v 5, as also in the phrases "house of Jacob" (3:13), "house of Joseph" (5:6), and "house of Isaac" (7:16).

In this case the land or state of Damascus is being identified as "the house of Hazael," just as Israel was known as *bīt ḥumri* in Assyrian records. It does not necessarily imply that Hazael was still alive; see the following note.

A city could also be known as "the house of *X*" (*X* often the titular god of the city, or the name of his or her temple serving as a sufficient designation for the entire town). When the city is named in the first colon it is either the same as the city name at the beginning (Gaza, Tyre) or a city, presumably the capital, of the country named at the beginning (Edom, Ammon). The development thus passes through three sequences, which come in pairs:

Nos. 2, 3   City, City, her *ᵓarmĕnōt*

Nos. 4, 5   Country, City, (her) *ᵓarmĕnōt*

Nos. 6, 7   Country, Country, *ᵓarmĕnōt* of capital

The oracle against Damascus in Amos does not follow any of these patterns, leaving the denotation of "house of Hazael" indeterminate, whether country or city. The similar oracle in Jer 49:27 has "wall of Damascus" instead of "house of Hazael" in the first colon, which comes nearer to the pattern in Amos 1:7, 10, and 14. It is more likely that Jer 49:27 is derivative, being modeled on Amos 1:14a (note use of *hiṣṣattî ʾēš*) and 4b (exact duplicate), rather than a survival of Amos' original reading. Amos 1:4 should not be changed to agree with Jer 49:27. Rather, Jer 49:27 has leveled the text to get rid of the difficulties in the phrase "house of Hazael." In any case Amos does threaten "the bar of Damascus" (v 5aA).

We also know that "house" as residence could be an object of destruction (3:15), while in 7:9 "house" means "dynasty" or royal family. If these are the models it is the residence or even the person of the king who is in view. But unlike 7:9, which can be heard as a threat against the king's life (7:11), 1:4 does not concern Hazael personally. Verse 4b, however, though directed against the *ʾarmĕnôt*, names Ben-Hadad. In any case, the ruler is dealt with in v 5.

citadels. If the pattern is purely verbal, the first four occurrences constitute a chiasmus.

1. *ʾrmnwt*	5. *ʾrmnwtyh*
2. *ʾrmntyh*	6. *ʾrmnwt*
3. *ʾrmntyh*	7. *ʾrmnwt*
4. *ʾrmnwt*	[8. *ʾrmnwtyh*]

To achieve a similar but inside-out pattern with the rest, the missing eighth term would have been "her citadels." But the uniqueness of the total pattern in the first oracle makes us hesitate to say that the eighth one originally completed the symmetry. Whatever may have been true of the original, presumably oral presentation, the omission of the final punishment in the surviving text and the abrupt shift to another theme can only be regarded as deliberate on the part of the compiler and editor.

Because a standard form of the oracle against Damascus was available (as shown by the example preserved in Jer 49:23–27), the failure of the first oracle to follow the pattern of the following six oracles could, then, reflect differences in the perceptions on the part of the prophet in the targets themselves. The rhythmic alternation of the two basic patterns, as shown in the chiastic arrangement above, with very minor variations, shows that the combinations serve to describe the essential features of all of the cities. As observed earlier, the oracles are grouped essentially in pairs, and the alternation of the patterns in these pairs is intended to include pertinent information about both members. Thus each pair has a single reference to the wall, while the citadels are mentioned in both. It may be deduced that the Fire will attack the wall and devour the citadels in both instances. Similarly, in the oracles with extended descriptions of the punishment to be meted out, nos. 1, 2, 5, and 6, the first in each pair is sentenced to exile, while the second is threatened with extinction. Thus Aram (v 5) and Ammon (v 15) will go into exile, while the remnant of the Philistines (v 8) will perish, as will Moab (2:2–3) with the slaughter of its leaders. Our impression is that not only is the pairing deliberate but the combinations are intended to extend to both nations in each case. The twin consequences of defeat by the enemy are death and captivity—precisely the fate in store for Israel.

What then of the corresponding targets in Israel, which are not specified in the manner found in the oracles against the other seven nations? Something like them is found in 5:6 (the target is Bethel, cf. 3:14, 7:9b, and 5:9). Amos says that the ʾarmĕnōt of Samaria hoard, plunder, and loot (3:10) and will be demolished (3:11). He threatens to demolish their houses (3:15, 6:11; cf. 5:11aB). The failure to round off the eighth oracle (against Israel) with a stereotyped expression like the one used, albeit with variations, with all of the others does not necessarily mean that the speech was interrupted, or that an original ending in that form has been lost from the text, although both are possibilities. The relentless repetition of the formula of accusation (eight times) implies that the repetition of the punishment, the formula for which is repeated with certain variations in a prescribed pattern, was equally persistent. That the expected final formula can be reconstructed with considerable confidence indicates that it was intended, or may even have been spoken on the occasion that the speech was actually given, presumably on the momentous occasion at the sanctuary at Bethel. Of this event we have no certain knowledge. In its present form—without the ending, but with a very different continuation—we must acknowledge the handiwork of an editor, compiling the dibrê ʿāmôs, the book of Amos, with an altered purpose or different objectives. That the essential ingredients of the missing closure are found elsewhere in the book serves to show not only that the prophet was capable of pronouncing this doom on the people of Israel, but that the strategy of the editor was to build the case against Israel beyond the limits imposed by the format of the opening address.

Because we believe that the Great Set Speech represents a late stage in Amos' message and ministry, it was incumbent on the compiler to postpone the conclusion until he could incorporate earlier observations and arguments, which are to be found in later parts of the book.

The ʾarmĕnōt could be the battlements on the defensive walls of the city, so well known from Assyrian reliefs. It was part of siege warfare to set them on fire by igniting the timbers that were part of the construction. This reading would follow the assumption that we take the reference to fire literally; if it is a divine fire sent from heaven it will burn anything and everything. Alternatively, the movement from wall to citadel could describe the conflagration of the city from outer defenses to acropolis. The architecture implied by 1 Kgs 16:18 suggests that the destruction at Tirzah happened this way (cf. 2 Kgs 15:25). We do not need to spend time on the romantic fancy that the ʾarmĕnōt are the luxury apartments of a well-

stocked harem. T. F. K. Laetsch (1956:12f.) thinks that they are the ostentatious dwellings of the rich, "rivaling in size and beauty and grandeur of
construction the palaces of kings." Although it occurs only once (v 4), the
connection of the citadels with the king is clear.

Hazael. a. The names used in the oracles exhibit these patterns in the
"Fire" bicolon throughout the speech:

1. Damascus	Hazael	Ben-Hadad
2. Gaza	Gaza	
3. Tyre	Tyre	
4. Edom	Teman	Bozrah
5. Ammon	Rabbah	
6. Moab	Moab	Kerioth
7. Judah	Judah	Jerusalem
[8. Israel	Samaria	]

The patterns, as far as they go, are chiastic. In each case the middle pair
(nos. 2 and 3, 6 and 7) have the same name at the beginning and as the first
object of fire. When it is the name of the city, it is the only object of the fire
(nos. 2 and 3); when it is the name of a country (nos. 6 and 7), the object of
the fire is the country followed by the capital city. The flanking items in the
first set (nos. 1 and 4) have two names as objects of fire. They do not really
match, because the first pair are humans, the last pair cities.

The second set is incomplete. We speculate that a completed oracle
against Israel would resemble the one against Ammon, with the capital city
the object of the fire.

Hazael. b. Only in the case of Damascus are the names of kings mentioned. The most likely dates for this monarch are from 843 B.C.E. (Unger
1957:75) to early in the eighth century, ca. 796 B.C.E.; but there is no
definite evidence indicating when his reign ended. The date of his accession
is fixed before 841 B.C.E. by two facts. First, Shalmaneser III, in the eigh-
teenth year of his reign (841 B.C.E.), reports his sixteenth expedition across
the Euphrates, with an attack on *Haza'ilu* of Damascus (Albright 1942:28
n. 16), supplying in addition knowledge that Hazael was a usurper ("son of
nobody" [*ANET* 280]), which confirms the biblical account (2 Kgs 8:7–15).
Second, Hazael warred against Israel during the reign of Jehoram (2 Kgs
8:28–29), who was wounded defending Ramoth-Gilead (2 Kgs 9:14–15)
and died in 842 B.C.E.

Hazael continued aggression against Israel throughout his reign, with
unrestrained atrocities (2 Kgs 8:12). To judge from 2 Kgs 10:32–33 he must
have seized from Jehu all of Israel's territory in Transjordan and subsequently "oppressed Israel throughout the reign of Jehoahaz" (2 Kgs 13:22).
Unless some of the territory captured from Jehu had been recovered in the

meantime, these further invasions could have involved incursions west of the Jordan, such as occurred under an earlier Ben-Hadad (2 Kings 6). Even Moabites were able to make similar attacks (2 Kgs 13:20). We do not know what the historian means by his ameliorating comment in 2 Kgs 13:23 (cf. 2 Kgs 14:13–23). It could mean no more than that Hazael did not conquer Israel completely. Y. Aharoni (1979:341–42) thinks that Israel's territory was "reduced to the confines of Mount Ephraim." Hazael's conquests may have extended to other countries besides Israel. The wording in Adad-nirari's inscription concerning his sixteenth campaign (LAR 1.379) not only gives prominence to Hazael, but mentions in addition only Israel, Damascus, and Edom and in a manner that suggests that Aram controlled the rest of Transjordan (Gilead, Ammon, Moab) and probably exercised hegemony over a region comparable in extent to David's empire. The expression *běyad* (2 Kgs 13:3) implies dominion, which continued into the reign of Ben-hadad.

It is likely that Hazael extended his power as far as Philistia (2 Kgs 12:17 [Heb 12:18]; see Mazar 1954). It is possible that Amos 6:2 reflects the boundaries of Hazael's empire. We know that Israel's army was reduced to ten chariots (2 Kgs 13:7) and that Hazael attacked Jerusalem, stripping it of its treasures (2 Kgs 12:17–18[Heb12:18–19]).

Ben-Hadad. His name, not his patronymic. The LXX has *huiou Ader,* reading *dalet* as *resh*. The parallel construction Hazael//Ben-Hadad might have been used as a poetic convention, even though it inverts the usual rule that such pairs represent the full name of a person (given name + patronymic, or other title), split up and spread over the bicolon (2 Sam 20:1). The patronymic can, however, precede the given name (1 Sam 10:11). This Ben-Hadad was the son of Hazael, and the choice of the name was doubtless intended to secure a pretense of legitimacy by setting up a pattern of papponymy (the practice of naming a male child after the grandfather in a dynastic sequence, thus producing an alternating pattern of names). M. F. Unger (1957:83) says that "he assumed the dynastic name at the death of his sire." We are not aware of the existence of any evidence to support this assertion. If the name was reserved for royal personages (the rich onomasticon of a city like Sippar suggests the opposite; naming people after the chief god was very popular, just as with Yahwistic names in Israel under the monarchy), then his father may well have given this name to his heir designate.

Whether there had been one or two Ben-Hadads ruling Damascus before Hazael we do not know, and it does not matter at this point. Hazael had murdered the previous Ben-Hadad. Whether Hazael had also claimed to be the son (adopted) as well as the successor of the Ben-Hadad he had murdered, we do not know. If he had done so, the parallelism of v 4 could be more conventional. The contemptuous reference in the annals of Shalmaneser III's sixteenth campaign could be a knowing rejection of such a pretense. "The house of Hazael" could then be the dynasty founded by the usurper, and the Ben-Hadad of v 4 was his son and successor.

This Ben-Hadad ruled about 796–770 B.C.E. Precision in dating either his accession or his demise is unattainable in the present state of knowledge (Unger 1957: chap. VIII). As already mentioned, Hazael could have died as early as 801 B.C.E., but for our purposes the termination of Ben-Hadad's reign is of more interest. As he was probably still on the throne when Amos' oracle was given, we might be able to narrow the date of its possible delivery to a brief range, for it must also coincide with the reigns of Uzziah and Jeroboam (1:1). The third decade of the eighth century B.C.E. is indicated.

Ben-Hadad's reign represented a transition between the domination of the region, including Israel, by Aram during Hazael's time (2 Kgs 8:7–15, 28–29; 10:32–33) and the conquest of Damascus by Jeroboam II (2 Kgs 14:28). But whether the change took place during or only after the reign of Ben-Hadad becomes an important question in the dating of Amos' career.

Jehoash, Jehoahaz's son, had three successful campaigns against Ben-Hadad, Hazael's son, recapturing all of the towns that "he" had taken in battle from Jehoahaz. The relative clause is ambiguous, but Hazael, not Ben-Hadad, seems to be intended, because Ben-Hadad did not begin his reign until after Jehoahaz's death, as far as we can establish the chronology of the period. One gets the impression from 2 Kgs 13:25 that Jehoahaz's reign might have overlapped Hazael's and Ben-Hadad's; but 2 Kgs 13:22 implies that Jehoahaz died during Hazael's reign.

The identity of the Aphek mentioned in 2 Kgs 13:17 is not known with certainty; it could be a site east of the Sea of Galilee, and a victory in that region would have represented a significant recovery of Transjordanian territory. But 2 Kgs 13:18–19 shows that Jehoash's success was limited (or even ephemeral, if it was only made possible by Assyrian attacks on Damascus in the closing years of Hazael's reign). At the same time his other reported successes should not be underestimated. His war with Amaziah (2 Kgs 13:12), rashly instigated by the latter, resulted in the worst defeat ever suffered by Judah at Israel's hands (2 Kgs 14:8–14).

One might ask whether the victories celebrated in Amos 6:13 belong to that time, or whether they were episodes in Jeroboam II's later and more substantial reconquests (2 Kgs 14:25). The similarity of the language of 2 Kgs 14:25 to Amos 6:14 suggests that Amos is predicting a reversal of Jeroboam's achievement, and this issue has considerable bearing on dating Amos' ministry, or at least on dating that oracle. The coincidence in terminology could have arisen from its conventional meaning, as generally recognized by scholars, not from historical correspondence. It is a traditional way of describing the extreme limits of Israel's territorial claims. That is,

Amos' comment does not necessarily mean that Jeroboam had already accomplished what is recorded in 2 Kgs 14:25 when Amos uttered 6:14. There is always the possibility that Amos 6:14 is a later addition to the book of Amos, derived from 2 Kgs 14:25, and reflecting "knowledge after the event"; but we have serious reasons, given in other places, for rejecting this explanation.

In any case we do not have an exact date for Jeroboam's restoration of the old boundaries of Israel from Lebo-Hamath to the Arabah Sea. It could not have occurred early in his reign. Unger (1957:90) has no tangible grounds for supposing that Jeroboam simply kept up the momentum generated by his predecessor. Even if Amos 8:14 shows that Dan had now been recovered (it is possible that it had been in Aramaean hands since the time of Ben-Hadad I), there is no evidence that any of the Transjordan territories had likewise been retrieved. If the locations of Lo-Dabar and Qarnaim (Amos 6:13) have been correctly identified by modern research, their recovery by Israel did not necessarily represent a full dislodgment of Aram from previous conquests. Lo-Dabar is only a few kilometers east of the Jordan. Qarnaim is on the southern approaches to Bashan. It is impossible to connect Amos 6:13 with 2 Kgs 14:25. If they had reached Lebo-Hamath and the Arabah Sea, they would surely have been boasting about the achievement, not about small incidental successes like Lo-Dabar and Qarnaim. There could be sarcasm in Amos' words about this exaggerated boasting over victories that did not really amount to much.

We suggest that a better case can be made for linking Amos 6:13 with 2 Kgs 13:25. Apart from the reference in Amos 6:14, which can be explained as conventional, and Amos 6:13, which is not grand enough, we have no proof in Amos that Jeroboam or Uzziah had yet regained the former territories of imperial Israel when he gave his prophecies. The prosperity implied by his criticism of the opulence and luxurious living of the ruling classes is generally advanced as evidence that great successes had been achieved; but the other side of that argument is that Amos exposes poverty and exploitation in a way that suggests that the wealth of the upper classes had been derived from social injustice on the domestic front, not from plunder in foreign wars.

The references to Hazael and Ben-Hadad take us back to the beginning of the eighth century. Additionally, 2 Kgs 14:28 states that Jeroboam actually recovered Damascus and Hamath. The textual difficulties of this passage are notorious, at least as far as the words "to Judah in Israel" are concerned. A reference to Yaudi is now widely accepted (NEB, NIV) as a likely solution to this part of the problem. It could equally well be evidence of Judah and Israel acting together in that enterprise. But there is no need to declare the rest of the claim "absurd" (Montgomery and Gehman 1951:444). Whether Jeroboam's action was conquest and annexation, or simply reduction to some kind of vassaldom (or even, less than that, the achievement of hegemony over a regional entente), the term *hēšîb* represents it as a recovery (its political legitimation). We have to go back to David's reign for anything like it (2 Samuel 8), and doubtless that is what the historian had in mind by the terminology he used. This explanation could also apply to the problematical reference to Judah.

As already indicated, the biblical sources contain no clues as to when in Jeroboam's long reign he finally achieved this apogee of power. As a political reality it could not have lasted long. The situation had changed back by the time the Assyrians renewed their attacks in the region under Tiglath-pileser III. Jeroboam II could only have achieved his successes when the Aramaean states were weakened and when the Assyrians were too busy elsewhere to retaliate against a rival power that had moved into a sphere in which they had such a vital interest. Neither of these conditions was met in the early years of Jeroboam's reign as king. We must look rather to a later period, which also coincides, suggestively, with a blank page in the history of Damascus. At that time (after 770), we do not even know who reigned there, if anyone, between Ben-Hadad II (or III), who died about 770, and Rezin, with whom documentation resumes. The latter is known from the Bible, and his name appears as a tributary to Tiglath-pileser III in 743. The arrival of the last-named monarch on the scene changed the situation forever, and the Assyrian conquests in the region covered by Amos' oracles (chaps. 1–2) proceeded relentlessly over the next few decades.

The book of Amos contains little evidence of such a development; Assyria is not directly mentioned in the MT (though see 3:9, where we read "Asshur" rather then "Ashdod"). But Assyrian absence from the region was not alone sufficient to account for Jeroboam's restoration, certainly not on the scale that includes the recovery of Hamath and Damascus, which modern historians have found so hard to believe. Adad-nirari III, in the fifth year of his reign, had subdued Damascus and extracted tribute from its ruler (called Mariʾ, "Lord"). That Hazael was the king in question is supported, if not altogether confirmed—others might have borne such a title— by an inscription on a piece of ivory found at Arslan Tash, evidently part of Assyria's spoils. It reads *lmrʾn ḥzʾl*, "(belonging) to our lord Hazael" (de Vaux 1934:512–18). Another Assyrian attack on Damascus is recorded for the year 773, but none after that until the rise of Tiglath-pileser III thirty years later (Thiele 1965:99).

To understand why Damascus did not recover all her old power and prestige during the period of Assyrian indifference (or rather distraction with other matters), we must note the evidence in Aramaic inscriptions of the period, that is, in the first quarter of the eighth century. According to the Zakkur stele, a coalition of a large number (the exact number cannot be established because of damage to the inscription) of kings of city-states in northern Syria was led by "Bir-Hadad son of Hazael, king of Aram" in war against Zakkur, king of Hamath. (New evidence [Millard 1978] shows that his name was Zakkur, not Zakir.) The impressive title "king of Aram" was not new; 1 Kgs 15:18 documents its use by (or at least for) an earlier Ben-Hadad. It is significant, nevertheless. Damascus was still able to claim seniority, if not suzerainty, over the Aramaean people. Equally impressive is the formidable array of allies, though there is more than a hint that not all of the members of the alliance actually fielded troops, which, along with the defeat itself, points to a limitation in Damascus' real power. In spite of the powerful combination of forces (which Zakkur might have exaggerated in order to enhance his own achievement), the attack on Zakkur's capital city Hazrek was not successful, and Ben-Hadad himself was not heard of again. It would be reading too much into this silence to infer that Ben-Hadad died in the fighting (Kraeling 1918:115). If that had happened, we might have expected Zakkur to have reported it. Ben-Hadad's fate is only one of many questions arising from the Zakkur stele that remain unanswered. For our purposes the most vital of these questions is the date of the stele, or rather of the situation it reports concerning Aram.

The reason for naming the king in the opening oracle in Amos 1 is to provide a synchronism for the date of the oracle. As observed, we have Jeroboam, Uzziah, and Ben-Hadad, which points to early in the second quarter of the eighth century, 780–770, perhaps 775. Unfortunately, the Zakkur stele supplies no exact synchronisms, and paleography is not precise enough to supply more than a range early in the eighth century. J. A. Fitzmyer says "from 780" (1967:26); M. Black says that about 755 "is generally accepted" (1958:242), but this is a minority view, if not a misprint. The motives for the war can only be guessed. Black is too dogmatic that Zakkur was an Assyrian puppet as the only explanation that fits the facts (244).

We can, however, attribute the weakness of Damascus in the second quarter of the eighth century to the compounding of Hazael's defeat by Assyria with Ben-Hadad's defeat by Zakkur. These events gave Jeroboam II his opportunity. The claim that he recovered Hamath as well as Damascus "for Judah in Israel" (2 Kgs 14:28) must also be assessed in the light of Ben-Hadad's failure to defeat Hamath at an earlier, unknown date. That failure might have come near the end of Ben-Hadad's reign and not long after the beginning of Jeroboam's reign. Time must be allowed between the battle against Hazrek and the erection of the stele, for Zakkur also reports numerous other activities after the victory, including the building of the city of 'pš, where the stele itself was erected. In other words, Hamath was still independent and strong as late as 770 B.C.E., and possibly for some time after that.

Amos betrays no awareness of Damascus' decline. On the contrary, he has in memory Aram's devastating conquest of Gilead (1:3) with 6:13 as evidence of only partial and possibly exaggerated countermeasures. He thinks of Aram's rebellions against Yahweh in terms of Hazael as well as Ben-Hadad, and the several places mentioned in 1:3–5, as well as the reference to "the people of Aram" as a whole, suggest a political state of affairs very similar to what is attested in Zakkur's stele before the debacle of Hazrek. It is the situation in the second decade of the overlapping reigns of Jeroboam and Uzziah, say 780–770 B.C.E. The decline of Damascus after Ben-Hadad's reign rendered the contents of Amos 1:3–5 obsolete.

We can now draw out the consequences of a remark made earlier, namely, that Amos gave his prophecies before Jeroboam and Uzziah had achieved their major successes. If Amos' predictions of gloom and doom, all made, as we have concluded, before 770, were followed by the very opposite—conquests and glory the like of which had not been seen since the days of David, then Amos would have been thoroughly discredited. We could see Amos as opposing and contradicting Jonah's program. But could it not be that Jonah opposed and discredited Amos' prophecies? See a full discussion at 6:14. In such circumstances only extraordinary faith in Amos' prophecies on the part of some faithful followers—in the face of all of the facts of history—could account for the preservation of his messages. The heading (1:1) does, nevertheless, suggest that the earthquake, if nothing else, identified as the fulfilment of the fifth vision and its associated oracles by at least some disciples, vindicated him in their eyes sufficiently to secure the preservation and publication of his "words."

5. The tetracolon in this verse exhibits the well-known envelope construction. The second and third lines constitute one bicolon; the first and fourth lines constitute another bicolon in which Damascus//Aram. Verse 8 has four similar lines, but there the two bicola come in sequence. That circumstance is no warrant for rearranging v 5 into a similar pattern by moving the first line next to the last line, as done by Morgenstern (1961:300, 314). The conjunction of the cosmic-visionary (v 4) and the historical-realistic (v 5) sides of Amos' prophetic perception, which we have already analyzed in the NOTES on v 2, is beautifully illustrated in these two related actions of God (sending fire, breaking the bar). The latter is easier to identify with military action, a prophecy (or *vaticinium ex eventu*) of Tiglath-pileser's capture of Damascus in 732 B.C.E. (It could have been Jeroboam II [2 Kgs 14:28].) The sequence is logical: capture of the city (v 5aA), execution of rulers (v 5aB//5bA), deportation of inhabitants (v 5bB).

5a. *break.* Why is the *qal* used to describe the action of God, when this "conjugation" is held to refer to a simple action? The usual doctrine is that when a root such as *šbr* has both *qal* and *pi'el,* and both *binyanim* are monotransitive, the *pi'el* describes a more intensive activity (*GKC* 52–53).

The word *šbr*, in fact, is the parade example of this supposed distinction (Weingreen 1939:105). Illustrations can often be found to support the theory. The object of the *qal* is often a stick (Isa 14:5) or bone (Exod 12:46) or weapon (Hos 1:5; Jer 49:35), which might be simply "snapped" in two. The object of the *pi⁽el* is often stone (Exod 32:19; 34:1) or metal (Jer 52:17), objects that have to be "smashed" to fragments.

E. Jenni (1956:182–83) worked out the difference between *qal* and *pi⁽el* in terms of a "resultative" *pi⁽el*. Against this theory, however, in the case of *šbr* at least, it can be pointed out that both *binyanim* can be used with the same object (e.g., *pi⁽el* with "bars" in Lam 2:9), with no hint that the result was different in the two cases. Data of this kind convinced A. Sperber (1966:6, 13) that there was no difference at all between the *binyanim*: "the so-called verbal stems were interchangeably used in order to indicate one and the same meaning without implying the slightest differentiation."

A study of every occurrence of the root *šbr* suggests that neither of these explanations is entirely satisfactory—neither Sperber's that there is no distinction nor Jenni's that *pi⁽el* is resultative. It should be remembered that in most cases (apart from the participles) the only difference between the *qal* and the *pi⁽el* is in the Masoretic pointing, not in the original orthography of the manuscripts. Looking at all possible variables, a number of other distinctions seem possible. Combining the factors of effort and result, there could be four degrees of intensity.

1. Minimum effort and effect—one thing broken into two pieces with one easy blow (such as a stick)
2. Medium effort—one thing into many pieces with one blow (such as a pot)
3. More effort—many things to be broken with at least one blow each (bones)
4. Most effort—many blows needed, and much force, solid object smashed to smithereens (a stone idol)

If the *binyanim* distinguish the effort needed by the doer, the distinction will depend on not only his strength but also the strength of the object. Classifying by subjects yields the following:

Subject	Qal	Pi⁽el
God	39	15
Man	8	20
Other	6	1
Total	53	36

Classifying by objects yields the following:

Object	Qal	Pi'el
Singular	39	1
Plural	14	35
Total	53	36

The major difference lies in the fact that the *pi'el* is preferred when the object is plural. Even the one instance of a singular object (Ps 46:10[E9]) can be construed as collective. This fact suggests that *pi'el* pluralizes the action of the *qal* (many blows are needed, not necessarily more energetic). It is true, as Jenni points out, that *qal* is used more characteristically for small objects (stick, bone, etc.), *pi'el* for objects of stone or metal, suggesting that a greater effort or more blows are needed to break the latter. The distribution of subjects between *qal* and *pi'el* is less clear-cut. The higher use of *pi'el* for human action is due partly to the frequency with which humans smash idols or similar cult objects—many of them and perhaps many blows needed for each. But more impressive is the fact that *qal* most frequently describes a divine action, even when done to as mighty an object as a great world power. Perhaps the distinction being made here is that it is easy for God to destroy an object with one light blow, while humans must make a greater effort. In any case the distinction does not lie in the result, the final state of the object, but in the number and possibly also in the strength of the blows given.

bar. The LXX reads *mochlous* (pl.). The full expression is "bar and [double] doors"—*bĕrîaḥ ûdĕlātayim* (Ezek 38:11; Job 38:10) or the inverse (Deut 3:5; 1 Sam 23:7; Jer 49:31; 2 Chr 8:5). Sometimes "bars" (Neh 3:3; 2 Chr 14:6[E7]). In Nah 3:13 it appears to be a wooden pole; but bronze (1 Kgs 4:13) and iron are also specified. The bar was a feature of an *'armôn* (Prov 18:19). The word can be used by synecdoche for the complete gate-system (Judg 16:3; 1 Kgs 4:13; Jer 51:30; Lam 2:9).

cut off. As with the *nip'al* in its technical use in the P and H sources of the Pentateuch, the verb is ambiguous. It could describe removal by execution or by excommunication (in this case exile, which is clearly in mind at other places [1:5, 15]). Its meaning in the Torah, especially as it might require humans to carry it out, engendered much debate and disputation and gave rise to a treatise (*kĕrîtôt*) in the Mishna. Here there is no question that it is God who will cut them off (not excluding the use of human agencies). Violent or premature death would be viewed as evidence that God had inflicted the death penalty (Morgenstern 1931–32:31ff. and Tsevat 1961:197ff.). It would also signify extermination of the line, not just of the individual.

The LXX's *exolethreusō,* "I will utterly destroy," is interpretive and, as usual, more sensational than the original. In the next line it supplies *katakopsō,* which matches nothing in the Hebrew. But it omits *tômēk.* The same thing happens in v 8, where, however, the verb *exartēsetai,* "it will be shattered," is used. The LXX evidently could not manage *tômēk* and interpreted *šēbeṭ* as *phylē,* "tribe," not "staff." None of these variations points to a competitive alternate Hebrew "original.

sovereign. Three interpretations are available for *yôšēb* (1:5, 8):

    1. With the meaning "resident" it can signify "inhabitant" (KJV, RV) or, as collective, "dwellers" (*katoikountas* [LXX]) (RSV, NJPS); similarly in v 8.

    2. With the meaning "sitter" (i.e., upon the throne) in the capital city, it is a title of a human ruler.

    3. Or it can designate a divine ruler whose chief residence is a shrine in a city.

Each one of these usages can be paralleled in the Bible and other ancient documents. In what sense does Amos use the term?

In favor of the second interpretation is the fact that Ben-Hadad is called *melek 'ărām hayyôšēb bĕdarmeśeq* (2 Chr 16:2). The verb is used without qualification in parallel with *mlk* in *KTV* KRT 1.16:IV:37–38, 52–54 (= *UT* 127:37–38, 52–54):

> *rid la mulki 'amluka*
> *ladurkatika 'aṯiba 'anā*

> Descend from [your] kingship, [so that] I may be king
> from your rule [so that] I may sit.

The title *yšb* (= *yāṯib*) in the Tell Fekherye bilingual shows that it was in current use for Aramaean kings or gods. It can be followed directly by the name of the city, or it can use the preposition *b-* (Num 21:34, 33:40; Deut 1:4, 3:2, 4:46; Judg 4:2). In all cases it could be an abbreviation of *yôšēb* (*'al-*)*kissē'* (*b-*) city name (1 Kgs 1:48, 3:6, 8:25; Jer 22:30, 33:17; 2 Chr 6:16).

This terminology identifies the capital city, not just the residence, of a monarch. The title *yôšēb* is characteristic of kings in northern Transjordan in early traditions. It can also be used of Israelite judges (Judg 10:1).

The word *yôšēb* is also a title for Yahweh (Isa 40:22) notably as *yôšēb hakkĕrūbîm* (1 Sam 4:4; 2 Sam 6:2; 2 Kgs 19:15; Isa 37:16; Ps 80:2[El], 99:1; 1 Chr 13:6) or "upon [his] throne" (Isa 6:1) or "in heaven" (Ps 2:4). Just as an Aramaean god could be called *yāsib Sikan,* so Yahweh was *yôšēb ṣiyyôn* (Ps 9:12).

The article can be used in these titles: *hayyôšēb 'al-kis'ô* (Exod 11:5,

12:29) or *hayyôšēb ʾel-kissēʾ dāwīd* (Jer 29:16, a variant characteristic of that book); or *hayyôšēb bĕdammeśeq* (1 Kgs 15:18; 2 Chr 16:2—title of Ben-Hadad). The references to Amorite kings make the meaning clear: Sihon is *melek hāʾĕmōrî hayyôšēb bĕḥešbôn* (Josh 12:2), *melek hāʾĕmōrî ʾăšer mālak bĕḥešbôn* (Josh 13:10); the same is true of Og (Josh 12:4, 13:12).

The following terms are used in the oracles:

yôšēb//tômēk šēbet	1:5, 8	Aram, Philistia (death)
malkām//śārāyw	1:15	Ammon (exile)
šōpēṭ//kol-śāreyhā	2:3	Moab (death)

As in the ensuing oracles against Israel, the focus of the judgment is on the rulers, and various titles are used for them; not on the inhabitants at large, or even the residents of the cities (not that they are excluded).

In Amos 1:5 and 8 *yôšēb* is used without any further definition or modification. While it cannot be absolutely proved that he does not mean "inhabitant(s)," there are several reasons, with cumulative force, for translating it "sovereign."

1. Even if *tômēk šēbeṭ* is not another title for the same person as ruler in another town in a dual kingdom, but the title for a vassal or deputy in Biqʿat-Awen (Ashkelon in the Philistine oracle, 1:8), the parallelism nevertheless suggests a similarity in meaning, if not an identity of reference.

2. The use of clearer designations ("king," "judge") in later oracles suggests that *yôšēb* is part of a series of equivalent titles. It is possible that the choice of terms represents actual differences in usage from kingdom to kingdom.

3. There is more than enough evidence listed above that *yôšēb,* when defined or modified in some way, refers to a sovereign and is even a formal title.

4. More specifically, the term is used for and by Aramaean kings (*ysb* [Tell Fekh.]; *yšb* [Sefire 3.17]; 1 Kgs 15:18; 2 Chr 16:2).

5. The interpretation lines up with the mention of Ben-Hadad by name.

This result does not, however, rule out the possibility that the main god of Damascus is meant, for gods enjoyed analogous titles. Amos concentrates on human rulers and has no identifiable polemic against the gods of other nations. He denounces the worship of foreign gods in Israel, but that is quite another matter. We conclude that *yôšēb* in 1:5 and 8 refers to the human sovereign.

The variety of titles used shows that Amos is not just recycling a stereotyped construction for each nation in turn. Just as the crime of which each is accused is specific and reflects some historical actuality, so we suggest that the terminology used reflects political reality. The eight nations are independent. Damascus exercises some authority over other Aramaean cities. The Philistines are a league of cities, but Tyre is not linked with any other Phoenician city. With respect to Ammon and Moab, however, the terms "king" and "judge" are probably complementary and meant to refer to both rulers, along with the "princes" mentioned in both oracles (cf. Is 33:22, where both words occur in parallel construction).

The pattern and terminology used to refer to the rulers of Ammon and Moab show that the parallel terms need not be synonyms. Furthermore, the term "prince" sometimes refers to the viceroy of a city, especially the military commander of an occupying garrison (Judg 9:30; 1 Kgs 22:26; 2 Kgs 23:8). When several cities are under consideration it is the chief official in each (the king in the capital) who is specially in view. The oracle against the Aramaeans is more complex than the others in this respect. Verse 5 refers to two or more Aramaean rulers. It is possible that they are additional titles of Ben-Hadad himself, as common sovereign of three states. But because they will be cut off "from" their respective cities (see the following note), it is more likely that three individuals are in view. The information does not permit us to go farther and to work out whether the rulers in (or of) Biqʿat-Awen and Beth-Eden were Ben-Hadad's deputies, or vassal princes under his suzerainty, or autonomous allies under his hegemony. We are, however, clearly in a situation in which the Aramaean empire or entente was still reasonably intact and quite extensive.

from. The preposition *min-* is used with the four place-names: Biqʿat-Awen, Beth-Eden, Ashdod, and Ashkelon (1:5 and 8). Its common meaning makes sense. A question remains, however. If we have correctly identified *yôšēb* as "sovereign" in these verses, they are the only places we know of in which this word is used absolutely with that meaning. Everywhere else it is modified, and its meaning "sovereign" made clear by information about where the ruler "sits"—*on* a throne or *in* a city (cf. the discussion of *yhwh mṣywn* at 1:2). Doubtless the persons mentioned by Amos were sovereigns *in* the places named and would be cut off *from* those cities.

Biqʿat-Awen. Two places besides Damascus are mentioned in the oracle against Aram. Neither can be identified with certainty. The valley of Awen is probably the Biqʿah Valley in present-day Lebanon, and "the house of Eden" is almost certainly the Aramaean state of Bît-Adini, located between the Upper Euphrates and the River Baliḫ. It was conquered by Shalmaneser III as early as 855 B.C.E., and Assyrian penetration into the region is now attested by the Tell Fekherye bilingual inscription in the ninth century.

The successes of Hazael in the last decades of the ninth century changed the picture, while the Bible emphasizes his devastating attacks on Israel (2 Kings 13).

As with the similar case of Philistia, where several cities are mentioned after the oracle begins with Gaza, we cannot tell whether Amos is speaking about a political entity, a coalition, or simply an ethnic group. The use of the term "people of Aram" in v 5 suggests the last; but otherwise his interest in rulers rather than people suggests a major concern with states. This observation still does not define the political connections among Damascus, Biqʿat-Awen, and Beth-Eden. The title "king of Aram" (Alt 1934) given to Ben-Hadad in the Zakkur stele suggests hegemony, if not suzerainty, over an extraordinarily large area. Indeed, the circumstances of the war against Zakkur suggest that he might have been the only Aramaean king who had not joined the alliance, and that the purpose of the war was to force him to do so or to replace him by a king who would.

The extension of Damascus' influence to the Biqʿah in the west is not all that remarkable, but doubtless served the same strategic purpose that the Syrian military presence in the same locality does at the present time. The extension of Damascus' influence to Bît-Adini is surprising. Although it is not mentioned as one of Ben-Hadad's allies in the Zakkur stele, other Aramaean states as far north, but west of the Euphrates, are mentioned. Just as Amos 6:14 gives the northern and southern limits of Israel, so Amos 1:5 gives the southern and northern limits of Aram.

The evidence of the Zakkur stele shows that at this time one king could rule two cities. It is therefore possible that one and the same person, namely Ben-Hadad, is identified as the sovereign in Biqʿat-Awen and the scepter wielder in Beth-Eden. But the same Zakkur stele also indicates that the contingents from the many cities that joined Ben-Hadad for the campaign were led by their own kings. It would seem, then, that Amos expects all of the cities and rulers of the Aramaeans to be wiped out. A similar situation probably obtained in Philistia.

The LXX translates Biqʿat-Awen as "the plain of On." It is correct to read ʾāwen as ʾôn in Ezek 30:17; the LXX has *Hēliou poleōs*. The Egyptian city of the sun-god is correctly called Beth-Shemesh in Jer 43:13. It has been inferred that Amos 1:5 refers to Baʿalbeq, which, as the Syrian Heliopolis, was called On after the Egyptian Heliopolis. The cult of the great *dea Syria* (Atargatis), the goddess of Hierapolis, was described by Lucian. (See Strong and Garstang 1913 for translation and commentary; also Pritchard 1943.)

5b. *scepter wielder.* This title is used only in Amos 1:5 and 1:8.

Beth-Eden. See the preceding note on Biqʿat-Awen. The LXX reads *ex andrōn Charran.* It might have had a manuscript that read *bny* for *byt,* for the exchange occurs elsewhere (the opposite way in 3:1). Harran is geographically correct; it is a substitute term, not a transcriptional error.

Aramaean people. The use of this term embraces the cities already mentioned as a group. The whole nation is the target. It does not necessarily imply that Damascus enjoyed hegemony over the whole region at that time, though that is possible. Compare "Aram-Damascus" in 2 Sam 8:3–8 and 1 Chr 18:3–8.

Qir. The Lord had brought them from Qir in the first place (9:7). The fulfillment of this prophecy is recorded in 2 Kgs 16:9, but that is well after Amos' time (732) and the king was Rezin, who was put to death. The passage in Kings does not correspond exactly to Amos 1:5. The latter specified that "the people of Aram" will go into exile, and the limits of Aramaean territory, Biqʿat-Awen to Beth-Eden, suggest total depopulation; 2 Kgs 16:9 mentions only that "she" (Damascus) was deported to Qir.

Its location is not known. In Isa 22:6 Qir is parallel to Elam. Numerous suggestions have been made. The LXX did not know *qîr* as a place name. It has *epiklētos* as if from *qārî'*. In other contexts the word means simply "city." The parallelism of Amos 9:7 requires a region. Harper (1905:20) lists a number of attempts to replace *qîr* by a more suitable word. Replacing it by some other word achieves nothing, because the biblical evidence is consistent.

As the later discussion of Amos 6:14 shows, the connections between Amos and the book of Kings are not clear. If the historian mentions the circumstances of deportation to Qir (2 Kgs 16:9) because he knows Amos' prophecy, why did he not follow through and make the point with the usual commentary "according to the word Yahweh which he spoke by the hand of Amos the prophet"? For all we know the Israelite historian's "knowledge" of what the Assyrians did could have been derived from Amos' prophecy—not based at all on knowledge of what the Assyrians actually did. Further doubt on the originality of the word *qîrâ* in 2 Kgs 16:9 is cast by the fact that it is missing from the LXX. The detail is not confirmed by the Assyrian annals.

The occurrence of *qîr* in Amos 9:7 implies a knowledge of Aramaean origins that is not found elsewhere, and the basis of which we can only guess. It matches knowledge of Philistine origins that can be found in other places. Amos 1:5 implies a cancellation and reversal of this ancient action of God. It is quite unlikely that Amos 1:5 was added later on the basis of 2 Kgs 16:9; and the authenticity of Amos 1:3–5 does not seem to have been doubted by any modern scholar.

I.A.2.a.ii. PHILISTIA (1:6–8)

1:6a   Thus Yahweh said:
>> For three violations by Gaza,
>>   and for four,

I will not reverse it:

6b   Because they took into captivity an entire captivity,
            to hand [them] over to Edom.
7a   And I will send Fire against the wall of Gaza,
7b   and She will consume its citadels.
8a And I will cut off the sovereign from Ashdod,
    and the scepter wielder from Ashkelon;
8b and I will bring back my hand against Ekron,
    and the Philistines will perish, even to the remnant.
                        My Lord Yahweh has spoken!

NOTES

6a. *Gaza.* Jeremiah's prophecy against the Philistines (chap. 47) likewise concentrates on Gaza, and mentions Ashkelon as well. While we may suppose that Ashdod in its heyday was the leading city of the Pentapolis, Gaza must have become the head of the coalition in later times. Assyrian inscriptions mention Ashdod, Ashkelon, and Gaza in the eighth century.

6b. *an entire captivity.* Compare v 9. The expression *gālût šĕlēmâ* is unusual. In other combinations *šĕlēmâ* signifies "full, sound measure," as with weights. A similar use of the adjective is met in the expression *'eben šĕlēmâ,* "whole stone(s)" (Deut 27:6; Josh 8:31), originally, in the tradition of Exod 20:25, undressed stones, but later given the contrary meaning of building blocks made exactly to specifications.

Here the cognate object *gālût* anticipates the end point of the process. The seizure of captives from Judah in the reigns of Amaziah (2 Kgs 14:14) and Ahaz (2 Chr 28:8–15) illustrates the practice. The Chronicler uses the more familiar *šebî* (2 Chr 28:17—Edom) and *šibyâ gĕdôlâ* (v 5—Aram). We take the phrase to mean a captivity of the whole population, in contrast to the more usual partial, selective captivity reflected in biblical accounts. Compare 2 Kgs 24:14–16, 25:11–12; and Jer 52:28–30 for the number of captives. Such a total captivity must have been regarded as peculiarly cruel and repulsive (cf. Jer 13:19).

The nationality of these captives is not identified, or the size of the group. They no doubt were Israelites, but this fact does not contribute to Amos' point. He refers to the incident as if it were something notorious and recent, which listeners would recognize without further explanation. In terms of opportunity, they might have carried off the whole population of a nearby Judahite village, as the Amalekites did to Ziklag (1 Sam 30:1–2). The use of such prisoners as domestic slaves is illustrated by the Israelite girl in Naaman's household (2 Kgs 5:1–3—the language of v 3 suggests that these raiders might have been no more than kidnappers); but to capture a "complete captivity" must be a national enterprise. On the scale and economic significance of slavery in the ancient world and its motivation of military excursions, see the literature reviewed by Andersen (1977) and I. J. Gelb (1979). Edomites attacked Judah in the time of Ahaz (2 Chr 28:17) and took slaves. Philistines made raids at the same time. On the use of slaves in Edomite mining operations, see N. Glueck 1940:60.

The LXX reads *šlmh* as "Solomon." Targum is literal, *gālû šelmā*'.

Edom. Perhaps the point is that a concerted enterprise is involved, with Aram and Ammon attacking from the north and south (on the east), while Philistia and Phoenicia attack from the west (both Israel and Judah apparently). The statements are representative and exemplary and reflect a major attack from both sides. Otherwise there is a logistical problem regarding how Philistines could hand captives over to Edom without using the most obvious lines of access across Judean territory. The problem is even more acute if the Tyrians were middlemen. The suggestion has been made that Aram is a more feasible destination (Haran 1968:203–7).

We know from 2 Kgs 5:2 that Israel was a source of slaves for Aram at this time, but the notice gives no idea of the scale. The Aramaeans raided directly. There is no other evidence of a large-scale trade involving three cooperating nations. And with Philistines as the originating supplier, Judah rather than Israel is the most likely source. Confusion of Edom with Aram (and vice-versa) is usually considered easy because of the similarity of the Hebrew letters *daleth* and *resh* in square characters. But there is another consideration. Edom is always spelled *plene* in the Bible, a practice that requires that any confusion of Edom and Aram occur before this style of spelling came into vogue.

The LXX reading is *Idoumaian.*

7. See NOTES on v 4.

8. This four-line unit resembles v 5; but here the bicolon with city// people is continuous. Both use *waw*-consecutive verbs in the same way: all first person, so that the action of God is immediate with no concern for means, agents, or instruments.

8a. See NOTES on the matching lines in v 5.

8b. *Ekron.* Three cities are mentioned in the oracle against Aram, Damascus twice for a total of four. Here four Philistine cities are listed, each once, producing a rough equivalence between the sets. A fifth, Gath, is mentioned in Amos 6:2.

bring back. The LXX *epaxō* is less precise. For the Hebrew idiom see Isa 1:25; Jer 6:9; Zech 13:7; Ps 81:14. It means "strike with repeated blows" (Harper 1905:26).

perish. The plural verb agrees with the *nomen rectum* "Philistines" rather than with the *nomen regens.* It emphasizes that they will perish to the last person. The singular verb is used in a similar construction at Jer 40:15, *wbdh šryt yhwdh,* but masculine plural pronouns occur in concord with *šĕērît* (2 Kgs 21:14; Jer 23:3); it is the subject of a masculine plural verb in Jer 42:15. Both features are found in Jer 44:28. These examples show that the agreement is with the meaning of the whole phrase; *šĕērît* is not formally an adverb. Our somewhat paraphrasing translation is not based on formal grammatical analysis. As with the use of *gālût* in v 6, *šĕērît* anticipates the end result; it does not describe their condition at the onset.

Amos mentions also "the remnant of Joseph" (5:15) and "the remnant of Edom" (9:12). The term usually refers to the survivors of a catastrophe that greatly reduces the population, usually war. Even a small remnant (Isa 1:9 —there the word is "survivor") gives some hope of posterity. When the "remnant" is liquidated the group is exterminated (Jer 11:23). The severity of the law could be mitigated by exempting some members of a family, to ensure "a name and a remnant" (2 Sam 14:7). No exceptions would be made in extreme cases (e.g. Achan, Josh 7:24). The sentence against Philistia is, accordingly, very drastic (cf. Jer 15:9). It is poetic justice. Complete extermination is fitting punishment for exiling a whole population.

Four cities are listed: Gaza, Ashdod, Ashkelon, and Ekron. We need not suppose that Gath is exempted; the "remnant" of Philistines (end of the list) would cover all others, not just the survivors of the four cities. Compare the positioning of *šĕērît* of Ashdod in the list in Jer 25:20 and *šĕērît* of the island of Caphtor in Jer 47:4 (the phrase containing *šĕērît* in the next verse is less clear—"Anaqim"?).

I.A.2.a.iii. TYRE (1:9–10)

1:9a   Thus Yahweh said:
        For three violations by Tyre,
           and for four,
           I will not reverse it:
  9b   Because they handed over an entire captivity to Edom,
        and did not remember the covenant of brothers.
  10a   And I will send Fire against the wall of Tyre,
  10b   and She will consume its citadels.

NOTES

1:9–10. The oracle against Tyre is briefer than the others. No other cities are mentioned. In the two preceding oracles additional cities are mentioned in the elaboration of the judgment, which is lacking in this case. Perhaps it is because the city of Tyre was the whole nation. The accusation is similar to that against Gaza, and the identical phrase *gālût šĕlēmâ* suggests that they have cooperated in the same venture. The wording is not identical, however. The Philistines "took captive" "to hand over"; the Phoenicians "handed over," suggesting that they were the middlemen in this transaction, as in so many other trading ventures.

9b. *entire captivity*. See the note on v 6. On slaves as a commodity in the Phoenician trade catalog, see Ezek 27:13. Export to Mediterranean countries with the aid of their vast fleet is understandable. (See Tsirkin 1976: chap. 2.)

remember. The root *zkr* means not only to recall or recollect, but also to observe, regard, and deal with something as real and substantial (Schottroff 1964:245–51; Childs 1962:12). It thus involves activity as well as memory: to remember the Sabbath is to keep or observe it. So here to remember the covenant is to adhere to its terms.

brothers. A pact between brothers is presumably a parity treaty in which mutual obligations are equally binding on both parties to the covenant. Compare the pact between Laban and Jacob (Gen 31:43–54).

The "brothers" of Tyre in this treaty are not identified. Behind the allusion may lie the treaty between Hiram of Tyre and Solomon (1 Kgs 5:26[E12]; the word "brother" in 1 Kgs 9:13). The relationship goes back to David (2 Sam 5:11) and continued into the ninth-century alliance with Samaria (1 Kgs 16:31). This circumstance suggests that the victims of the covenant breach were Israelites, perhaps including Judahites. If so, then the Philistines were probably involved in the same enterprise.

COMMENT

The list of nations in Amos 1–2 can be considered to embrace all of the accountable states that occupied the buffer zone between the great empires of the second millennium B.C.E.—Egyptian, Hittite, Mesopotamian—a zone that all three desired, claimed, and occupied from time to time. Israel occupied the heart of that region, ringed around by all the others, desiring, claiming them all and sometimes subduing, annexing, occupying one or more. Israelite hegemony over the region was never more than partial, fragile, transient; but it enjoyed enough definition and glory in David's time to provide a model, a pretext, a hope, and a drive, usually unrealistic in political-military terms, but irrepressible and irresistible when projected into eschatological prophecy and apocalyptic expectation.

There is no indication that Amos had in mind, in picking off all of Israel's neighbors one by one (or all together), a renewed expansion of Israel, now in one direction, now in another. Even if Judah and Israel had not been included in the list at its end, it is clear from the taking of the Aramaeans into captivity to Qir (1:5) that for them at least the aggressor would come from the east.

The list of neighbors might be regarded as a catalog of traditional enemies, such as might be found in ritual cursing texts (Bentzen 1950); but the inclusion of Tyre on the list has been considered a problem, for there is no record of armed clashes between Israelites and Phoenicians. At least in the time of David and Solomon, the whole emphasis is on the parity treaties and trade agreements between the two friendly countries. Always a political pragmatist, David had concluded a variety of peace treaties with the several states he defeated, ranging through annexation with settlement, installation of garrisons, acceptance of fealty, tribute, and mutual assistance pacts. Doubtless these expedients were viewed differently from Jerusalem, where one and all were seen as both Yahweh's subjects and David's (Psalm 2). Certainly in the memory and perspective of later times the old technical distinctions between vassal, client, and ally were forgotten or ignored, and even Tyre could be placed on the same footing as all the others.

After the Assyrian conquests Aram and northern Israel were permanently absorbed, and the circle became smaller. In Jeremiah's day it consisted of Edom, Moab, Ammon, Tyre, and Sidon (Jer 27:3).

Psalm 83 documents an occasion on which most of the nations on Amos' list made a concerted alliance against Israel based on full diplomatic consultation and negotiated treaties (vv 3–8)—a formidable combination. The coalition consisted of the following:

	Psalm 83	*Amos*
		[No. 1—Aram]
1.	Edom	No. 4
2.	Ishmael	
3.	Moab	No. 6
4.	*Hagrîm*	
5.	Gebal (Byblos)	
6.	Ammon	No. 5

7. Amalek
8. Peleshet   No. 2
9. Tyre   No. 3
10. Assyria
11. Sons of Lot

Only Aram is missing, replaced by Assyria in that quarter. The order of the others is quite different from that of Amos. If we assume that "the sons of Lot" are equivalent to Moab and Ammon (uniquely without *bĕnê*), then the aggregate is ten, rather than the traditional number, seven (cf. however, Gen 15:19–21, where there are ten). It is hard to tell whether the presence of Gebal and Peleshet places this incident before Amos' time, or whether the absence of Aram and the presence of Assyria place it after Amos' time. The occurrence of Gebal, however, is an indication that we have an old tradition, going back perhaps to the time that Gebal was claimed by Israel (Josh 13:5). The main value of the inventory in Psalm 83, besides its partial overlap with Amos' list, is its indication that Phoenicians, at some time or other, were allied against Israel with all of Israel's neighbors in almost a complete circle. Amos 1:6–10 also shows a consortium triangulated around Israel, organized for slave trade, the victims presumably Israelites, though the text does not identify them.

I.A.2.a.i.v. EDOM (1:11–12)

1:11a   Thus Yahweh said:
              For three violations by Edom,
                   and for four,
                   I will not reverse it:
11b   Because he pursued his brother with the sword,
                   and he destroyed his allies;
              and his anger tore perpetually,
                   and his rage persisted always.
12a   And I will send Fire against Teman,
12b   and She will consume the citadels of Bozrah.

NOTES

1:11–12. The elaborated charge in four lines uses ellipsis between parallels to achieve a compact effect:

11bA	ʿal-rodpô	baḥereb	ʾāḥîw
11bA	wĕšiḥēt		raḥămāyw
11bB	wayyiṭrōp	lāʿad	ʾappô
11bB	wĕʿebrātô	šĕmārâ	neṣaḥ

The parallelism points to poetry, as does the sparse use of prepositions, and the fact that there is not a single prose particle. The syntax presents several problems, doubtless due to the poetic character of the composition. "His brother" and "his compassion" are complementary parallels (see the ensuing explanation), which leaves "with the [i.e., his] sword" to do double duty. Or *rdp ḥrb* may be parallel to *šḥt,* because the latter does not occur with *ḥrb.*

When the parallel members are linked synthetically, *rdp//šḥt* means "pursue and destroy." Compare the sequence "pursue, overtake, destroy" (*šmd*) in Deut 28:45 (cf. Exod 15:9, where *rdp* and *ḥrb* also occur in the same context). Both verbs have the same object. The word *šḥt,* with the meaning "damage, spoil, ruin, destroy" can govern a range of objects, usually things—crops, buildings, cities—often with total obliteration and extermination, as in the Flood, Sodom and Gomorrah, the demolition of Jerusalem, and the like. The Edomites must have totally liquidated some Israelites on an occasion that is no longer on record. Destruction on that scale is permitted to God, not to humans, a consideration that applies to the verb *nṭr* as well, if it is adopted in v 11b.

With respect to the verb *šḥt,* there does not seem to be any distinction between *piʿel* and *hipʿil,* unless the latter is elative. In a moral sense both can mean "pervert" or "corrupt." There is no other place in which the object is as abstract as "compassion," and a special meaning ("stifled" [BDB, NIV, NEB] or "repressed" [NJPS]) has to be assigned to *šḥt* to accommodate the unique idiom. *Ad hoc* meanings such as "cast off" (RV) do not solve the problem.

It is true that *raḥămîm* are the tender feelings naturally felt for close kin, a combination of affection and concern that is more than "pity" (KJV) or "compassion." The latter are evoked by perception of need or distress in the object, whereas *raḥămîm,* in God and man, are spontaneous surges of love for someone, no matter what state he is in. Genesis 43:30, where

Joseph's "heart yearned for his brethren," is the classic instance. To judge from the traditions, these feelings never developed between the twins Jacob and Esau, and the agelong vendetta between their descendants is recognized and prophesied in Gen 27:40, where the sword is already in Esau's hand. In Amos, "Jacob" refers to the whole nation, both Judah and Israel. To judge from all of the other oracles, Amos seems to have in mind the eruption of this ancient and endless feud in an episode of exceptional savagery. *Raḥămîm* is natural affection for closest kin, of father for children (Ps 103:13), even more of a mother for "the children of her womb" (*reḥem;* Isa 49:15; cf. Lam 4:10), and between children of the same womb (uterine siblings were felt to be much closer than half-siblings with the same father; cf. Gen 43:30), and most of all for twins. The parallelism of "brother" with *rḥm* secures this association; and just as the parallel verbs constitute a combination with just one object, so the concomitant phrase *'āḥîw//raḥămāyw* should be integrated to mean "his brother of his affections," that is, the brother to whom he was bound by the strongest of natural kinship ties, as Israel was taught (Deut 23:7). Or, taking *rḥm* more literally, it could mean "the brother of his [mother's] womb" (the tradition in Gen 25:22, 26). For the latter usage, note that Job calls his mother's womb simply "my belly" (Job 3:10).

The charge is that Edom pursued his uterine brother and destroyed him with the sword. It sounds like an act of *ḥērem*. We do not know which of the many wars between Israel and/or Judah and Edom Amos has in mind. Something recent would suit best; but nothing eligible is recorded in the history of the eighth century. On the contrary, Amaziah, Uzziah's predecessor, defeated Edom (2 Kgs 14:1–20; 2 Chronicles 25) but did not, apparently, annex it completely, because it remained for Uzziah to restore Elath to Judah (2 Kgs 14:22). These brief notices, however, give the impression that Judah had the upper hand with Edom during the first half of the eighth century. There was never any love lost between those two, and perhaps some incident in recent conflicts went beyond the bounds of the usual cruelties, if that were possible.

Because we know more about the hostilities that flared up again in the sixth century, and because the prophets of that period (Obadiah; Jeremiah 49; Psalm 137) were vehement in denouncing Edom's treachery and inhumanity toward Judah, many scholars have inferred that this oracle too should be attached to those later developments.

11. The LXX seems to be floundering in places. It translates *wšḥt rḥmyw* as *kai elymēnato mētran epi gēs,* "and destroyed the mother upon the earth," apparently rendering *rḥmyw* as *mētēr.* Other recensions have the more appropriate *splagchna* at that place. It interprets *lā'ad* as *eis martyrion,* "for a witness," which confirms MT but misses its meaning. Aquila

correctly translates *eis tous aiōnas*. We cannot explain how *'appô* becomes *phrikēn autou*.

11b. *pursued.* This wording sounds more like hot pursuit after battle (Gen 14:15) than going to war. The adverbs "perpetually"//"always" suggest that the contemporary incident is an outburst of the age-old feuding between the brothers that Amos is condemning. The following "destroy" gives the aim of this relentless pursuit, to eliminate Israel "completely," and this, rather than "always," is a possible meaning of (*la-*)*nesaḥ*.

The worst defeat is the kind from which no survivors emerge. The mopping-up operations are thorough. Such a disaster can be a symbol of divine anger (Jer 29:18; [cf. Deut 28:22] Amos 9:4; Hos 8:3). It is rage that drives the human or divine swordsman to track down relentlessly and destroy unmercifully all survivors (Lam 3:43, 66), showing that the words for anger in v 11bB are to be linked with the verbs in v 11bA.

his brother. This expression must mean all of Israel, that is, the populations of both kingdoms or, in particular cases, either kingdom.

destroyed. As already intimated in the introductory notes on this verse as a whole, it is better to take *šḥt*, in parallel with *rdp*, in its literal meaning, with the human victims (Israel) rather than an abstraction ("compassion") as its object. There is no other supporting example of this latter usage. The word *šḥt* can mean "murder" a person (2 Sam 1:14) or "destroy" a nation (Hos 11:9). Compare Gen 6:17, 9:15; 2 Sam 14:11; Ezek 5:16, 20:17.

his allies. In recent years, a new interpretation of the clause *wšḥt rḥmyw* has been proposed. The second word has been analyzed as a concrete noun, defining a person or a group in a covenant relationship with another person or group. The meaning is "ally, associate, companion." While there may not be any decisive biblical examples as yet, the term with this meaning is found in Genesis Apocryphon 21:21, where we must translate: "my allies, companions." Just as the root *'hb*, "to love," has been shown to have fundamental and extensive use in the framework of covenants and treaties in the ancient world, we may accept it that the root *rḥm*, with a very similar meaning, does too. Thus the root meaning (*rḥm* = womb) leads easily into *raḥămîm* (= love, tenderness, compassion), and now for those who are partners in covenant relationships. If we take the two terms *'ḥyw* and *rḥmyw* together, they would identify the Edomites as the brothers and allies of Israel and/or Judah. The relationship would be rooted in traditions about their common parentage and expressed historically in their ongoing relationship as allies. The latter is exemplified by the joint expedition of Israel, Judah, and Edom against Moab, recorded in 2 Kgs 3.

Such an analysis is attractive and merits serious consideration. We would agree that the term *rḥmyw* is not an abstract term, but refers to a person or a group; that the basic meaning is derived from the root *rḥm*, meaning "womb"; and that it describes an intimate friend or close associate. We would say that it reflects both kinship and covenant associations. Edom and Israel (including Judah) have the closest kinship ties, and their political history also reflects a long term and intimate association, not always friendly, but always close. Amos may well have combined these ideas in his selection of the term *rḥmyw* to go with *'ḥyw* to express both the unique kinship relationship (the closest of all possible relationships) and the covenant tie. (Cf. Barré 1985; Fishbane 1970, 1972; Coote 1971:206; Paul 1971:402–3.)

Joseph and Benjamin had the same mother (Gen 43:29), hence deeper affection. In the case of Jacob and Esau, the characterization is unique: they were not just brothers, even full brothers, but twins, whose struggles began already when they were in Rebekah's womb (Gen 25:22–23).

11bB. The bicolon has all the elements for complete synonymous parallelism with chiasmus:

wayyiṭrōp	(A)	*lā'ad*	(B)	*'appô*	(C)
wĕ'ebrātô	(C₁)	*šĕmārâ*	(A₁)	*neṣaḥ*	(B₁)

The preposition *l-* does double duty: *neṣaḥ* nearly always occurs with it, and the LXX already reads *eis nikos*. For these reasons, older commentators from Wellhausen onward wanted to "restore" the preposition; see BHS. The words *'ad* and *neṣaḥ* are synonyms, as are *'ap* and *'ebrâ* (Gen 49:7). The other pair (*ṭrp* and *šmr*), however, have less evident semantic links. They raise two quite distinct problems. The first is the suitability of these two words to be in parallel; the second is the suitability of their collocation with the other words in the bicolon. Genesis 30:2 shows that *'ap* is m. s., in spite of the rule that names of paired anatomical organs (*'appayim*) are feminine. The agreement of masculine verb and noun in the first colon, and of feminine verb and noun in the second colon, suggests that the grammar of each clause is the same, *'appô*//*'ebrātô* being the subjects (Mays 1969:35).

The verb *ṭrp* means "to rip," and "anger" is not a very suitable subject for it. The figure is that of a savage animal that tears at its prey: *ṭōrēp napšô bĕ'appô*, "tearing out each one's throat in his anger" (Job 18:4). It is not Job who is tearing himself to shreds (Gordis 1978:188) in his anger. That reading does not fit, and the NEB discarded it. Bildad accuses Job of treating his friends like animals, snaring them with words and then savaging them. The imagery is quite concrete, and *napšô* is not reflexive but distributive. Job has accused God of treating him in exactly the same way (16:9):

'appô ṭārap . . .	In his anger he tore me . . .
ḥāraq 'ālay bĕšinnāyw	He slashed me with his teeth.

Psalms 35:16, 37:12, 112:10; and Lam 2:16 show that "teeth" goes with *ḥāraq* and should not be transferred to *ṭārap* in Job 16:9.

Here, as in Amos 1:11b, *'appô* is apparently the subject of *trp*. But the idiom of Job 18:4 shows that *'appô* is instrumental, and in Job 16:9 the necessary preposition is available for retroactive double duty in the next line. Whether, in this parallelism, and with the animal imagery, *'ap* means "snout" rather than "anger" (Andersen 1976:181) is a minor detail. What Job 16:9 shows is that an item lacking in one line may be supplied in the following one, and this principle applies to *'ālay*. Applied to Amos 1:11bB, these observations permit both *'appô* and *'ebrātô* to be parsed as instrumental, despite the lack of the appropriate preposition. Therefore, "Edom" can continue from the preceding lines as the subject of *wayyiṭrōp*. To compare a savage human with a rapacious beast is an old tradition (Gen 49:27; Deut 33:20, where "arm" is likewise instrumental), the wolf or lion providing the image.

If *'ebrātô* is not parsed as the subject of *šěmārâ,* then the semantic incongruity is relieved: "his wrath" is not a suitable subject for "watched." But the feminine gender remains unexplained, and the meaning "watched" is not a parallel, at least not a synonymous one, for "ripped."

There are several ways of solving this cluster of problems. One strategy retains the existing text, but gives the words new meanings more suited to the context. Another is to replace one or two words with others that fit better. Attention focuses mainly on the verbs.

The morphological problems presented by the MT *šěmārâ* are the easiest to handle. First, the vocalization, which—if the verb is third f. s.—is neither the contextual (*šāměrâ*) nor the pausal (*šāmārâ*) form, might be accounted for as retraction of accent to avoid two stressed syllables in sequence. But if "his fury" is not the subject, no alternate feminine subject is available, and it would achieve desirable continuity and coherence if "Edom" were the subject of all of the verbs. A solution with some appeal supposes that "his fury" is the preposed object, and *-āh* the resumptive object: "and his fury, he kept it for ever"; cf. the RV (Harper 1905:34). On this view *mappiq* was somehow lost from the final *hē.* In addition, grammatical congruence between the two cola is forfeited. But "fury" as object of the verb is not much better than "fury" as subject.

A possible, but remote, alternative is that the form is masculine, that the primal ending of *šamara,* "he watched," was preserved.

Continual efforts have been made to retain the established meaning of *šmr,* "watch, guard protectively." It has usually been considered farfetched to suppose that Edom's wrath was perpetually on guard in a hostile way. "Lies in wait" was Ewald's (1867) explanation, which retains the imagery of the predator. But *šmr* is usually transitive, and if its common meaning is retained an object must be found for it. The victim is "his brother," carrying on from the previous lines. The word occurs first in the Bible in Cain's cynical question, "Am I my brother's keeper (*šōmēr*)?" In this good sense the Lord is *šōmēr yiśrā'ēl* (Ps 121:4). The usual meanings of *šmr*, "guard," "protect," "keep safe" (people in custody [Josh 10:18; 1 Kgs 20:39], property), or "observe" (rules, religious duties), do not fit here, though they can be stretched to include surveillance with hostile intentions (Jer 20:10; Pss 56:7, 71:10).

Otherwise, a different meaning altogether must be sought. J. A. Bewer (1901) adduced Akk *šamāru*, "to rage." This verb is most commonly used of divine or demonic ire. But it is too long a shot to suppose that such a common Hebrew word has an exotic meaning in this one occurrence. It has, however, been accepted by the NEB, the NIV, and the NJPS. Another possibility is *šmr* III, "sharp, hard," as in *šāmîr*, "adamant" (cf. Ezek 3:9; Zech 7:12).

Preserving *šmr* with its usual meaning and bringing the preceding verb into line with it yields an ancient solution (Albrektson 1981:12). Replace the verb "he tore" with **wayyiṭṭōr*, "he kept," for which *'appô* is a somewhat more suitable adjunct, if not object, and *šmr* is a closer parallel. This adjustment has already been achieved in Syriac and Vulgate ("hug his enmity" [Knox]). The defense of the emendation can become quite tortuous. It is difficult to keep up with the reasoning, which uses the parallelism between v 11bA and v 11bB to emend the first colon into agreement with the second, then to declare the second colon redundant because it merely repeats the first, and finally to discard it as a gloss (Harper 1905:33, 34). The tradition represented by Syriac and Vulgate is preferred by many modern critics. Rudolph (1971a:127) does not think that it commends itself; he asks who would have altered so smooth a text (as does Wolff 1977:130–31). The answer is that *'appô* attracted a verb (*ṭrp*) with which it occurs in other places (Job 16:9, 18:4). But this argument cuts both ways; for *nṭr* occurs nowhere else with *'ap*, a difficulty that needs to be surmounted by defenders of the emendation.

The emendation *wyṭr*—or variant, if we wish to give the evidence of Syriac that status—can be viewed in two quite distinct ways. It could be no more than a translator's interpretive decision, relieving the strain in the idiom "his anger tore" with help from the following parallel, which confirms, incidentally, the usual meaning for *šmr*. Quite different is the conclusion that the Syriac translator had **wayyiṭṭōr* in his Hebrew *Vorlage* and simply translated it. In that case **wayyiṭṭōr* could be either the original Heb reading, replaced in ancestors of the MT by *wyṭrp* because this verb goes with *'ap* (Job 16:9, 18:4); or a solution already made by a Hebrew scribe to the problems still presented by the MT. The point is finely balanced, and the changes are minimal either way, simply adding or deleting *p*.

Dahood (1968:201) had it both ways, reading *wayyiṭṭōr* and retaining the

MT version by identifying the *p* as the conjunction "and." We think this proposal is farfetched (cf. Barré 1985).

The fact that *ntr* is never used with any word for wrath, while *trp* and *'p* do occur together, can be invoked both for and against the proposed emendation. The similarity of Amos 1:11 (MT) to Job 16:9 and 18:4 makes it an impeccable Hebrew idiom, so why should we change it into an idiom (*ntr 'p*) found nowhere else? But the problem we still face with *ntr 'p* could account for the MT as an ancient emendation in the direction of Job.

The root *ntr* with the meaning "keep" has its best attestation in Aramaic, and its distribution in Heb is restricted. Its clearest occurrences are in Canticles (1:6 [twice]; 8:11, 12), where it means "guard" in a general way; but the object is something valued, and there are overtones of jealousy. The *nōṭĕrîm* of Cant 8:11 have been identified as "tenants" (NIV), and elaborate attempts have been made to relate the term to ancient agroeconomics. "Custodian" might be better, if *maṭṭārâ,* "ward," as used in Jeremiah, is derivative; but the use of this word with the meaning "target" (1 Sam 20:20; Job 16:12; Lam 3:12) complicates the evidence from that quarter. In view of the dialectical character of the language of Canticles, it is not safe to use the meaning of *ntr* in that book as definitive of its occurrences in other parts of the Bible. There are only five. In one case it occurs in parallel with *šmr,* lending support to the emendation as a restoration, but perhaps providing the model for the variant as an ancient emendation:

> *hăyinṭōr lĕ'ōlām*
> *'im-yišmōr lāneṣaḥ*
>
> Will he keep [?] for ever?
> Will he watch for ever? (Jer 3:5)
>
> Will he be angry for ever,
> Will he be indignant to the end? (RSV—adopting *šmr* II)
>
> "Will he be angry for ever?
> Will he rage eternally?" (NEB)

The similarity to Amos 1:11 is impressive; but the verbs have no objects. "His anger" is supplied by analogy. The subject is apparently God.

Besides the arguments that *ntr* means "guard" in Aramaic and in Canticles, and that it occurs in parallel with *šmr* in Jer 3:5, a third point is its similarity on both of these counts to *nṣr.* The parallel *šmr//nṣr* occurs in Deut 33:9; Ps 105:45; Prov 4:6; and reversed in Ps 119:34, 145–46. This watchfulness is beneficial, praiseworthy. God "watches" people protectively (Prov 22:12, 24:12). He guards (*nṣr*) a vineyard, clearly cognate with *ntr* in Cant 1:6. In Job 7:20 God is *nōṣēr hā'ādām*, with humans under apparently hostile surveillance. Job is bitter in this context and is not sure of God's intentions. A usage with ironic overtones is not the best way to establish the normal meaning of a word. Even if *ntr* in Canticles is cognate with Heb *nṣr* (Pope 1977:34), it does not follow that there is only one Heb root *ntr* with the same meaning, "guard," wherever it occurs in the Bible (as in BDB). Neither does it follow that two words that are found in parallel with the same word (*ntr//šmr* in Jer 3:5 and Amos 1:11 [emended] and *nṣr//šmr* documented above) must themselves have the same or close meanings. The reasoning becomes attenuated. Aramaic *ntr*, "guard," cognate with Heb *nṣr*, occurs as a delimited dialectal feature of Canticles, not necessarily an Aramaism; but its Aramaic character accounts for its use in the Syriac version. There are too many uncertain steps to take *ntr* from these places back into an eighth-century Hebrew prophecy.

If *wytr* is to be restored at Amos 1:11, its affinities should be sought in the occurrences of *ntr* in the mainstream of Hebrew usage, not in a sidestream such as Canticles. Nah 1:2 reaffirms some of the most elemental names and titles of God built around a threefold recital that "Yahweh is the Avenger."

> *'ēl qannô' wĕnōqēm yhwh*
> > *nōqēm yhwh ûba'al ḥēmâ*
> *nōqēm yhwh lĕṣārāyw*
> > *wĕnôṭēr hû' lĕ'ōyĕbāyw*

> Yahweh is El the Passionate and the Avenger.
> Yahweh is the Avenger and the Lord of Wrath.
> Yahweh is the Avenger to his foes,
> > and he is the *nôṭēr* to his enemies.

The word *nôṭēr* clearly defines an attitude and a response to enemies. In God's case it is based on justice (he is *nōqēm*) and expressed in anger (*ḥēmâ*).

Because *ntr* is a particular response and not a constant attribute, it represents occasional and transient divine behavior. Other passages emphasize the fact that it does not last for ever, such as Ps 103:9:

> *lō' lāneṣaḥ yārîb*
> *wĕlō' lĕ'ōlām yiṭṭôr*

> He will not dispute for ever,
> and he will not *ntr* for ever.

This statement follows, just as Nah 1:2 precedes, quotations from Exod 34:6, and goes on to emphasize that

> He does not treat us as our sins deserve,
> nor repay us according to our iniquities.

Jeremiah 3:12 gives a similar explanation of the fact that God's anger is relatively light and brief when compared with his unfaltering and unfailing *ḥesed:*

> *kî-hāsîd ʾănî . . .*
> *lōʾ ʾeṭṭôr lĕʿôlām*

> For I practice *ḥesed* (loving-kindness)
> I will not be *nṭr* forever.

The questions in Jeremiah 3:5 are thus rhetorical. The close similarity of Isa 57:16 to Ps 103:9 adds another piece to the picture:

> *kî lōʾ lĕʿôlām ʾārîb*
> *wĕlōʾ lāneṣaḥ ʾeqṣôp*

> For I will not dispute forever,
> and I will not be angry eternally.

In God, then, *nṭr* describes a just and angry response, appropriate but restrained and measured. It defines an attitude to the wicked. In none of these occurrences does *nṭr* have an object. It might mean "to be (justly) angry" but it does not demonstrably mean "to maintain (anger)."

In Lev 19:17–18, such an attitude and behavior are forbidden to humans. It is the exclusive prerogative of deity:

17 *lōʾ-tiśnāʾ—ʾet ʾāḥîkā bilbābekā . . .*
18 *lōʾ-tiqqōm wĕlōʾ-tiṭṭōr ʾet bĕnê-ʿammekā*
    wĕʾāhabtā lĕrēʿăkā kāmôkā

17 You shall not hate your brother in your heart . . .
18 You shall not take vengeance or bear any grudge against the sons of
    your own people,
    but you shall love your neighbor as yourself.

The prohibition is framed by the antithetical

> You shall not *hate* your brother in your heart, . . .
>
> but you shall *love* your neighbor as yourself.

In other words, you must not seek revenge, you must not *nṭr.*

In none of these passages does *nṭr* mean "keep." The traditional "bear a grudge" implies an inner object. *Nṭr* itself implies anger rather than resentment, and a different root from *nṭr,* "guard," is indicated (*nṭr* II KB 613) perhaps cognate with Akk *nadāru,* "hate" (NJPS note on Jer 3:5). Amos 1:11 (emended) would then be the only place in which the connotation "anger" was made explicit.

If *wyṭr* is read at Amos 1:11, then Edom is accused of violating precisely the law of Lev 19:18. In becoming *nōṭēr* to his *brother* (the word occurs in Lev 19:17 and Amos 1:11) he is usurping prerogatives reserved exclusively by God. More than that, he is keeping up this attitude and behavior, taking vengeance into his own hands instead of leaving it to the Lord, forever, whereas with God anger is mild and momentary in contrast to his deeper and everlasting kindness.

We are left then with these options:

> ripped//watched (*šmr* I)
> ripped//was angry (*šmr* II)
> watched (*nṭr* I)//watched (*šmr* I)
> avenged (*nṭr* II)//watched (*šmr* I)
> avenged (*nṭr* II)//was angry (*šmr* II)

No matter which verbs are preferred, and with which meanings, the parallel references to anger are adverbial and qualify as neither subjects—"his anger kept watch" (Mays 1969:35)—nor objects—"he maintained his fury" (NASB). He ripped, or watched, or took revenge "(in) his anger."

Verse 11b presents two figures, each of which can be documented elsewhere (ripping and watching). There is no need to mix them or to make one conform to the other.

To judge from the other oracles in which the first reason (*ʿal* + inf.) is followed by one or more explanatory clauses, it would better if all of the clauses in v 11B described actions of Edom, that is, if Edom were the subject of all of the verbs. Taking them as a set of four eases the pressure to find close parallelism within each pair of colons. To "rip" in v 11bB is similar to "ruin" in v 11bA, leaving *rdp* to be brought into line with *šmr* (chiasmus). This pairing makes it easier to account for the apparent anomaly of following the infinitive in v 11bAa with a perfect verb. Of course one could repoint *šḥt* as an infinitive, governed remotely by *ʿal.* To have the simple preterit perfect followed by a *waw*-consecutive is impeccable Hebrew: *wĕšiḥēt . . . wayyiṭrōp;* whereas to have the latter followed by another (apparent) perfect, *šmrh,* is disturbing, though acceptable in view of the chiasmus that is achieved. The total picture is then one of watching and chasing in order to rip and destroy.

In this context, *šmr* (chiastic parallel to *rdp*) could have the military connotation of guarding prisoners. The composite picture then contains or implies all aspects and stages of war: attack, defeat, pursuit (*rdp*); capture, guarding (*šmr*); mutilating (*ṭrp*); exterminating (*šḥt*); cf. Barré 1985.

Reading all four colons together also permits the *b-* in the first one to do duty in the last two as well, confirming that "his anger" and "his wrath" are instruments, not subjects or objects, as we have already pointed out. The objects of the first two verbs are also the understood objects of the last two, so that v 11bBa means "and he ripped [him] continually [in] his anger" (Aquila and Symmachus *en orgē autou;* cf. Job 18:4).

12. *Teman//Bozrah.* Teman could be a district or a clan, with the eponym being Esau's grandson (Gen 36:11; 1 Chr 1:36). Here it is clearly a town; and, to judge from the other oracles, a leading city if not the capital of Edom. Elsewhere it is a prime target for prophetic judgment speeches (Jer 49:20; Ezek 25:13; Obad 9). N. Glueck (1940:24–26) identified it with Tawilân.

12b. *citadels.* The LXX has *themelia teicheōn autēs.* It is hard to see how "walls" can be a translation of *bṣrh. Themelia* ("foundations") translates *ʾarmĕnôt* in 1:4, 7, 10, 14; 2:2, 5.

Ta teichē translates *ḥwmt* in 1:7, 10, and 14 as if it were plural, an orthographic possibility. *Themelion* is a satisfactory translation of *môsād,* but it is not clear that *ʾarmon* is a synonym. Logically, if the fire were set by besiegers, it would burn the walls right up to their battlements or crenelations. Or, in another picture, found in other Greek recensions, the *ʾarmĕnôt* are considered to be the fortresses, or citadel, perhaps a central stronghold on an acropolis. The conflagration then spreads from the outermost to the innermost defenses, effectively burning the entire city. The LXX text presents another picture again. The fire burns the walls down to their foundations, as if struck by lightning from above.

The words in parallel in 1:7, 10, and 14 are inverted in 1:12 in the LXX.

COMMENT

Only the first colon of the accusation is reasonably clear and can be understood as a reference to defeat in battle and its aftermath. Pursuing the defeated foe after battle was standard operating procedure (Exod 15:9). Presumably the reference is to some recent battle between Edom and Israel.

Because Israel is identified as Edom's "brother," the point would have most power if the victim was both kingdoms, that is, all of Israel. Why highlight mopping-up operations rather than, say, a treacherous attack or cruel battlefield tactics? Interpreters have been influenced by the known behavior of Edomites against Judeans after their defeat by Babylon in the sixth century, as denounced so bitterly by Obadiah (cf. Jeremiah 49; Psalm 137). It was not the pursuit of the remnants of a defeated and scattered enemy so much as the denial of sanctuary, indeed the harassment, imprisonment, and murder of survivors and fugitives (Obad 14) that brought prophetic indignation against Edom to fresh vehemence after the Babylonian sack of Jerusalem.

Amos' language seems to condemn a general policy or practice. Pursuit with the sword could characterize a policy of violent animosity and hostility. It might also refer to the pursuit of anyone who might be a victim or a refugee or a bystander by an armed person or persons. When Job accuses God of savaging him (Job 16:9) he says *wayyiśṭĕmēnî*, and the same verb describes Esau's settled feelings about Jacob, hatred that relishes the thought of doing harm (Gen 27:41). This connotation is the remote background of Amos' words about Esau "watching" Jacob or "seeking revenge" for the injuries and insults suffered at the latter's hands. In Genesis itself the historian is remarkably evenhanded in his treatment of the twin brothers. His only adverse comments on Esau are that he "despised his birthright" (Gen 25:34) and entertained murderous thoughts about Jacob (Gen 27:41–42). His actions did not correspond, and the reader's sympathies tend to be with him rather than with Jacob. Later, however, the picture of endless enmity and warfare between Edom and Israel (including Judah, or especially Judah) becomes common and constant. Edom more than any other of Israel's neighbors becomes a symbol of hostility and meanness. It is also worth mentioning, and the point is ironic, that the endless struggle between these two most closely related nations, even as the Bible records it, alternates between subjugation of Edom by Judah and successful recovery of independence by Edom, the swing both ways predicted in Gen 25:23 and 27:40. In Amos 1:11 the emphasis is on Edomite aggression and brutality; yet it is difficult to pinpoint a specific instance, especially if we accept the authenticity of the oracle, and look for an occasion in recent memory, say in the early years of the eighth century. If this oracle is a postexilic insertion (Mays 1969:36) it was clumsily done, for the oracle represents *Amos* as saying that Edom had already done these things, and had done them perpetually. The language of Amos 1:11 is so unclear that it is impossible to insist that it can only be referring to events in the sixth century B.C.E. The discovery of a circumstance prior to Amos' time, and preferably still large in memory at that time, is made more difficult when Amos is located in the second half (765–750 [Harper 1905]) rather than in the first half of the reign of Jeroboam II. A brief notice in 2 Kgs 14:7 attributes to Amaziah a smashing victory over Edom. The Judean atrocities, as elaborated in 2 Chr 25:12, make Amos' words seem like the pot calling the kettle black. In 2 Kgs 14:22 it is reported that Uzziah built Elath, which suggests continuation or renewal of Amaziah's restoration of Judaean control over Edom. Admittedly the *hû'* at the beginning of 2 Kgs 14:22 is ambiguous; it could refer to Amaziah, and some Greek manuscripts actually make this identification (Montgomery and Gehman 1951:442–43). But the ascription is obscured by the date "after the king slept with his fathers." Achievements of Amaziah and Uzziah are likely to be confused, in view of the extended coregency needed to solve the chronological problems in the sources and amounting to nearly half of Uzziah's long reign. If the words at the end of 2 Kgs 14:22 were intended to distinguish an act of Uzziah as full king, it could have been as late as 765. Elath, and presumably Edom, remained in Judean control until Rezin "restored" them to Aram (2 Kgs 16:6), which probably happened before Rezin became a tributary to Tiglath-pileser III in 738.

There is not enough evidence from which to establish the case. But we can say that Amos does not speak about Edom as if it were currently a vassal of Judah. Our failure to link Amos' charge against Edom with any known historical event should be viewed in the context of the entire book. To put the matter bluntly, the only historical data in Amos that can be identified, equated with, and confirmed by information in other sources are the Exodus and forty-year desert period (2:10; 3:1; 5:25; 9:7). Even the accompanying migrations of Aramaeans and Philistines are uncorroborated, for the exact locations of Caphtor and Qir are uncertain. The individual crimes charged against the six foreign nations are similarly elusive. Not one of them can be pinpointed. The first six oracles are a combination of stereotyped indictment and identical judgment, followed by only one specific charge, or at most two. We need to ask, accordingly, whether the approach is mistaken that tries to deal with each of the nations on an individual basis, tries to interpret each oracle as an independent item.

When we view chaps. 1–2 as a Great Set Speech, not just a collection of similar oracles, we can use one to fill out the others. Even commentators who discard two or three of these items as later additions still concede that the original core constituted a single composition the rhetorical effect of which depended on the whole thing being delivered at once. This circumstance does not rule out the possibility that each oracle separately was intended for the nation named. Whether Amos himself actually made the rounds, roving as far afield as Elijah and Elisha, preaching over the whole region, we do not know. The heading of the book says that his visions concerned Israel (1:1), and Amos himself says that he was called to prophesy to Israel (7:15). Yet 3:9 requires proclamation to be made in Assyria (or

Ashdod) and even in Egypt. Is Amos only "pretending" (Mays 1969:63)? Amos 1–2 is not the only part of the book that boxes the compass. The circuit from Calneh to Hamath to Gaza likewise encompasses essentially the same large region.

All are accused alike of rebellions against Yahweh; all are condemned alike to Fire from heaven, which Amos 7:4 describes as a cosmic conflagration that threatens to consume the whole world. Each nation is charged with four (maybe seven) transgressions, but only one crime is listed for each. Does the numerical pattern imply that each was guilty of all? Although each crime seems to be specific and individual, there are connections among them all.

1. Damascus threshed *Gilead* with an iron sledge.
2. Gaza captured an *entire captivity* to deliver to *Edom*.
3. Tyre delivered an **entire captivity** to **Edom**, violating the covenant of *brothers*.
4. Edom pursued his **brother** with his sword.
5. Ammon ripped open pregnant women in **Gilead.**
6. Moab burned the bones of the king of **Edom** to lime.

It all adds up to an indictment of war's savagery, ferocity, and inhumanity, of "total" war with atrocities even against the most innocent (no. 5), unrestricted fighting (no. 1), no mercy for survivors (no. 4), taking whole communities captive (no. 2), slave trading (no. 3), desecration (no. 6). The terminology is either conventional (nos. 1 and 5) or obscure (nos. 2, 3, 4, and 6), but each presents a facet of war, and in any war all of them could happen. Each nation might thus be implicated in more than one violation. Connections among all of the single items are shown by repetitions of certain words—Gilead, Edom, brother—which encourages us to believe that a single comprehensive bill of particulars was intended. Transjordan was the main scene; but even the coastal nations, Phoenicia and Philistia, were involved. It is a fair summary of the whole region's history since the collapse of David's empire. All of his former vassals have been in rebellion "against the Lord and against his anointed" (Ps 2:2b).

The most specific of the charges is the one against Moab, even though we have no idea what it means. We are not suggesting that all of the others had a hand in it. All we are saying is that all of them had been doing the kind of thing that each is charged with, and there are indications of collusion and cooperation. It cannot be shown that Israel provides the common factor, as the victim of crimes by all her neighbors. Israel, in fact, is never mentioned at all, unless indirectly as Gilead (nos. 1 and 5) or as "brother" of Tyre (no. 3) and of Edom (no. 4). Number 6 shows that any crime done by any one against any other one was equally likely to arouse the divine displeasure. All were guilty and all might have been victims too.

In contrast to the first six particular charges, the seventh, against Judah, is quite general and comprehensive. The term *peša*ʿ, repeated in all eight oracles, implies more than violations of treaties among themselves, though doubtless that was involved in every case. The Lord's interest in the matter arises from the fact that such actions are viewed as rebellions against Yahweh himself, whether the treaties were sworn in his name or not.

We return to the case of Edom, which is mentioned in three of the other oracles. In 1:11 Edom is portrayed as aggressor, in 2:1 the victim. In 1:6 and 9 Edom is the final station in a complex trade in captives (slaves?). In view of the operation's extent and intricacy, the implication is that Edom shares the guilt of the crimes of Philistines and Phoenicians, that it is an accessory to them. Evidently Edom had the need for and the means to acquire large numbers of slaves, perhaps in connection with a military buildup. Somewhat later Edom invaded Judah to get slaves (2 Chr 28:17). In that civilization slaves had two functions: domestic, which is well-documented, and public. We know practically nothing about the scope and scale of state slavery in this period. So we can only surmise that Edom used gangs of slaves in industries such as mining, or in great public construction works, especially defense projects.

Apparently Edom was on the move and making its presence felt among the neighboring countries in those days. Several nations were struggling for control of the entire Transjordan area. The key territory of Gilead, always claimed by Israel and repeatedly won and lost, could fall into the hands now of Aram (1:3), now of Ammon (1:13), or could be a victim of a joint attack. Aram, Moab, and Judah especially contended for mastery of Edom, in order to control the outlets to the Red Sea such as Elath and trade beyond. That situation itself contains the possibility that slaves were shipped to Edom for trade with points farther east.

It all adds up to endless hostility and hatred among those countries in every imaginable combination, now allies, now enemies. What we have in all the piled-up charges are glimpses of continuing belligerence across every frontier. Doubtless treaties and trade agreements were also made in every possible combination; for example, we find Israel, Judah, and Edom united against Moab (2 Kgs 3:9). It would seem that the main purpose of a treaty was to provide an opportunity for treachery, for the next time around we might find Israel and Aram against Judah. Everyone had plenty of grievances to recite against the others, from the long history of dispute and conflict among them all. The reference to the bones of the king of Edom in the charge against Moab remains obscure, but it may also reflect continuing hostile relations between those countries, not unexpected considering the long history of dispute and conflict between them, similar to the case of

Israel and Judah. Edom was related by culture, tradition, and ancestry to the Moabites, and conflicts over the ill-defined boundaries between them and over control of trade routes, especially for access to the lucrative frankincense trade, would be expected.

Edom is mentioned in the Great Set Speech more often than any other country. Just when it achieved the prominence and importance recorded and reflected in these passages is problematic, but the conclusions already reached in the case of Aram (assuming that the presentation of all of the oracles in one coherent speech shows that they all reflect the conditions in the whole region at the same time) point to a period between Amaziah's success against Edom and the later successes of his son and successor Azariah (Uzziah). Instead of assuming that Uzziah's restoration of Elath to Judah (2 Kgs 14:22) was a continuation and completion of his father's successes against Edom (2 Kgs 14:7), so that Edom remained under Judah's domination during that interval, we must allow for a complete loss of Amaziah's gains as the circumstance and cause of Azariah's countermove after his father's death, when he became full king (possibly as late as 767 [Thiele 1965:80]). Two important points should be made in this connection. The first is the disinclination of court chroniclers to record defeats and disasters. So it is no surprise that Edom's recovery of independence is not recorded. This kind of censorship did not prevail as completely in Israel as in other countries, for there they had prophets to tell the bad side of the story and to point out the moral; and prophets had the final say in how the history would be recounted and interpreted. Even so there were many failures and setbacks that were never recorded but which we must infer as the explanation of a situation that later comes to light. The most conspicuous case is the almost complete silence of the records over the dismemberment of David's empire. Indeed the account of Solomon's reign in 1 Kgs 4:21–25 and other notices, which suggest that Solomon maintained the status quo, are belied by the indications in 1 Kgs 11:14–40 not only that his international alliances had fallen apart (Pharaoh gives harbor to his enemies), and that the provinces had successfully revolted (Zobah, Damascus), but that cracks were already showing in the united kingdom itself.

The reports of Amaziah's reign are mixed, and one is not sure what to do with the additional details found in 2 Chronicles 25. It is one thing to moralize on facts and another thing to fabricate them. The capture of Sela was clearly the high point, his one recorded positive achievement; and afterward he went downhill. In any case a devastating defeat at the hands of Israel followed his success over Edom. The wall of Jerusalem was partly demolished, and a huge amount of plunder was taken. The Bible does not spell out the consequences; but it is hard to imagine Amaziah retaining his hold on Edom after such a crippling defeat.

Second, it was Jehoash (the father of Jeroboam II) who dealt this blow and who, according to the Chronicler (2 Chr 25:23), actually captured Amaziah at Beth-Shemesh. How long he remained a prisoner we do not know. It is possible that Uzziah was not only coregent, but sole regent for a period in place of his father. According to 2 Kgs 14:17–21, Amaziah perished in a conspiracy, and afterward Uzziah recovered Elath.

The important result of these details, at this point in our argument, is that because Jehoash died around 782, Amaziah's defeat and the ensuing loss of Edom (as we surmise but with a high degree of plausibility) must have occurred before the end of the second decade of the eighth century. Thiele (1965:76–89) fits the long reigns of Amaziah (twenty-nine years) and Uzziah (fifty-two years) into the first half of the eighth century by recognizing an extended coregency of twenty-four years. He argues for a similar coregency with an overlap of twelve years to compress the connecting reigns of the successive kings of Israel, Jehoash (sixteen years) and Jeroboam (forty-one years).

Thiele then goes on to suggest that this coincidence in coregencies was occasioned by the same circumstance, namely, the major battle between Jehoash and Amaziah (1965:84). The only difference in policy was that in the north, Jeroboam was made coregent out of prudence, before his father went to battle; while in the south Uzziah was made coregent out of necessity, after his father had been defeated and made a prisoner of war. This explanation is admittedly more speculative than the general hypothesis of coregencies, which has gained widespread acceptance. What is of interest to us, in the wake of the data and arguments given above, is that we can provisionally fix the date of the capture of Jerusalem by Jehoash to ca. 792. Thus Amaziah's invasion of Edom must have occurred a few years before. The change in Edom's status from vassalage to independent foe of Judah probably followed soon after. In any case, the next swing of fortune against Edom (Uzziah's recovery of Elath) did not occur until Uzziah became king in his own right (2 Kgs 14:22), possibly as late as 767.

In summary, the events of 2 Kgs 14:7–14 (2 Chronicles 25) *could* have taken place as early as 792 and must have occurred by 782, when Jehoash died. The events of 2 Kgs 14:22 probably did not occur until after 767, when Amaziah died. Edom could have regained independence from Judah as early as the 790s, but certainly between 780 and 770 the situation was favorable for Edom to make a comeback. We have already shown in the comments on 1:3–5 that this is the very period for which Amos' oracle against Aram matches the political situation in that region.

It is possible, of course, that in the Great Set Speech of chaps. 1–2 Amos is not listing the latest crimes of all of those countries but is assembling memories from the past that could not be erased, a catalog of representative events that could not be forgotten, whenever they occurred. Except for Moab's crime against Edom, the "violations" were actions that might have happened repeatedly. How many times was Gilead invaded? The catalog could stretch back over the entire period from the breakup of David's empire, but the impression is that these nations have now filled up the quota of tolerated and pardonable crimes. The one listed is the last of four or seven, and it is the one that finally exhausts Yahweh's patience, so that he says of each of them, "this time I will not reverse the decision to punish them." The first priority for interpretation is to find a period in which all of the things in the Great Set Speech could be true simultaneously, when the events described were of current or recent vintage. So far we have found the decade of 780–770 to be the time that suits the circumstances best, in which the actions can be placed most reasonably, and in which we have the fewest contradictions and implausibilities.

I.A.2.a.v. AMMON (1:13–15)

1:13a   Thus Yahweh said:
        For three violations by the Ammonites,
            and for four,
            I will not reverse it:
13b   Because they ripped open the pregnant women of Gilead,
            in order to enlarge their territory.
14a   And I will kindle Fire upon the wall of Rabbah,
            and She will consume its citadels;
14b   with shouting on the day of battle,
            with a tempest on the day of windstorm.
15a   And their king will go into exile,
15b   he and his princes together.

                                    Yahweh has spoken!

NOTES

1:13b. *ripped open*. The LXX attributes the same crime to Aram in v 3.
territory. The word gĕbûl is usually translated "border," but the sense is that a wide boundary means vast territory. See 6:2.
    14a. *kindle. hiṣṣattî*. This word is conventionally derived from yṣt (BDB 428a; Mandelkern 1965:501 also proposes ṣwt), but the only evidence for

this root seems to be Kethib *whwṣtyh* (Qere *wĕhaṣṣîtûhā*) in 2 Sam 14:30. All attested forms except *'ăṣîtennâ* (Isa 27:4) can be derived from **nṣt*. Here it corresponds to *šillaḥtî* as used in all the other oracles. The words are metrically identical, and no significant difference in meaning can be detected. The two verbs seem to be interchangeable, and both are used outside of Amos in other occurrences of the same construction (Jer 17:27, 21:14, 49:27, 50:32; Lam 4:11; Ezek 21:3[E20:47]); all have *'kl* as following parallel, and some are very similar to Amos' refrain (so also Jer 43:12). These fires consume gates, walls, buildings, cities, battlements, and defense works of all kinds. Any human agency is quite lost sight of in the overwhelming realization that it is God who sends the fire; and sometimes a note is added that it is unquenchable, like God himself (Heb 12:29).

In view of the use of identical vocabulary in the repeated parts of the eight oracles, this exceptional departure from the fixed formula is startling, to say the least. The LXX attests the variation. It uses *kai exapostelō* (= *wĕšillaḥtî*) in 1:4, 7, 10, 12; 2:2, 5, but *kai anapsō* ("and I shall inflame") in 1:14. The only difference in meaning between the two verbs is that *šlḥ* can have a variety of objects, while *yṣt* means specifically "kindle." Because of this difference, the object "fire" has to be specified with *šlḥ*, with the thing ignited governed by a preposition such as *b-*, as here. In contrast, derivatives of *yṣt* usually have the thing ignited as object, with *bā'ēš* as instrument. Here, however, and in many occurrences, including those cited above, *yṣt* has followed the syntax of *šlḥ*, which makes the meanings indistinguishable. The variation is purely artistic. It follows a pattern that we might almost regard as a law of composition when a stock formula is used many times; there is likely to be one deviation.

We cannot be certain that the prophet delivered the speech exactly this way, if that is what happened, or how his editor composed it. It could have been no more than a variation in the choice between the two words with identical meaning in the oral phase. The word was used in war stories about times earlier than Amos, and is epic-poetic in tone (Josh 8:8, 19; Judg 9:49). But the idiom with the same syntax as *šlḥ* comes to the fore in the sixth century (cf. Jer 17:27, 21:14, 43:12, 49:27, 50:32; also Jer 32:29, 51:30; Ezek 21:3; and Lam 4:11); so the one occurrence in Amos could be an intrusion from this later usage. The tendency, however, is generally the other way, to normalize such a dominant pattern by eliminating deviations. Its preservation here confirms that the variant is original. Thus the LXX has lost the two occurrences of singular pronouns in the opening charge. It has made them all plural. We shall not attempt here a march-past of all of the scholars who have pronounced for and against the authenticity of this detail. Wolff thinks that *hṣty* replaced *šlḥty* to bring it into line with Jer 49:2 (1977:131, 161). But Rudolph points out that other parts of Amos' speech have not been adjusted to parallel places in Jeremiah (1971a:127). The text should be retained, not only because there is no compelling argument against it and because its antiquity is confirmed by the LXX, but because it lines up with other places in Amos in which a form or formula appears many times, but with a single deviation.

14b. In some oracles in the Great Set Speech the judgment consists simply of Fire against the capital city. In others extended consequences are added. Verse 14b adds color to the account of the destruction of Rabbah. It supplies circumstances and indicates that the destruction will come about by "war." None of the preceding oracles is quite that explicit. They allow a cosmic (mythic) meaning, especially the repeated first-person verbs in the first two oracles. It could all be done by fire from heaven. By the time we reach 2:14–16, however, the historical (realistic) side is apparent. Amos 1:14b falls between these extremes. There are no verbs. There are two circumstances, war and storm. The storm could be divine; the war could be anyone.

The two lines of v 14b do not have synonyms in close parallelism, but they could be descriptive of the same event. Note the alliteration of the fourfold *b-* in *bitrû'â běyôm . . . //běsa'ar běyôm.* Compare *bitrû'â//běqôl šôpār* in 2:2bB. The language could hardly be more economical; its sparseness leaves room for the imagination to fill in the details, an exercise that would not be triggered if the prophet had painted a fuller canvas. The emphasis is on noise and confusion, and the statements could be taken literally or as similes. The first, *těrû'â,* is the war cry, with voice or trumpet, especially the alarm at the onset of combat. It is an important indication that, in spite of the mythic imagery that dominates the repeated formula "I will send Fire," the agent could be a human assailant, the occasion "war" (*milḥāmâ*). The second colon takes us back to the supernatural. It evokes memories of great occasions in the past, celebrated in legend and song, in which military victory was achieved (Exodus 14–15) or assisted (Joshua 10; Judges 4–5; 1 Sam 7:10, 14:15) by meteorological or seismic acts of God. The same two words occur in Nah 1:3.

tempest. The same parallelism occurs in Ps 83:16(E15):

kēn tirděpēm běsa'ărekā	So pursue them with your tempest
ûběsûpātěkā těbahălēm	and with your hurricane terrify them!

This verse follows a reference to the wind in v 14(E13), a dramatic simile of God's contribution to the war, a flame that ignites the mountain forests (*yā'ar . . . hārîm* is a discontinuous construct phrase split across the bicolon) in verse 15(E14). As in many old stories (e.g., 1 Kings 19), wind (*rûaḥ* [Amos 4:13]), earthquake (*ra'aš* [Amos 1:1]), and fire (*'ēš* [Amos 7:4 and chaps. 1–2]) are God's most available agents. Compare the combination in Isa 29:6. The metaphysics involved has more in common with the earlier stages of Near Eastern theology, when no distinction was made between the divine being and the element that was his manifestation (Jacobsen 1946; 1976). The categories of natural and supernatural are not distinguished in this kind of thinking. It is, therefore, inappropriate to ask whether Amos 1:14bB describes a "miracle" or not. The radical difference between Israel and the rest is that in Israel the mighty winds and fireflashing clouds of tempest storms (the most terrifying combination of phenomena) are no more than creatures, attendants, messengers, transportation for Yahweh (Ps 104:3–4). They commonly accompany military action, as in Psalm 83.

The expression *kassûpâ* can be a simile for the tempestuous attack of the chariots of the heavenly army (Isa 66:15–16 [fire is prominent too]; it is possible that the army described in Isa 5:26–30 is likewise celestial, as the reference to clouds in v 30 suggests; Jer 4:13 is a similar vision).

15a. *king.* See the note on "ruler" at 1:5. The terminology is unmistakable in the oracles against Ammon and Moab. The differences might correctly reflect the local practice in the several countries. In Ammon and Moab the association of "king" or "judge" with "princes" points to a more highly unified state and centralized administration.

15b. *princes.* Either top bureaucrats in the capital or governors of regional towns are intended. While some may have been princes by blood, the main interest is in their function. Jeremiah 49:3 predicts similar judgment for Ammon, Jer 48:7 for Moab:

Amos 1:15a *wĕhālak malkām baggôlâ*
            And their king will go into exile

Jer 49:3   *kî malkām baggôlâ yēlēk*
            for their king shall go into exile

Jer 48:7   *wĕyāṣā' kmyš baggôlâ*
            and Chemosh [kethib *kmyš,* as apparently at Ebla; Dahood, 1981:291–92] shall go forth into exile

Amos 1:15b *hû' wĕśārāyw yaḥdāw*
            he and his princes together

Jer 49:3   *kōhănāyw wĕśārāyw yaḥdāw*
            his priests and his princes together

   48:7   *kōhănāyw wĕśārāyw yaḥdāw*
            his priests and his princes together

If this line is a set piece, it is more likely that Amos has omitted "his priests" than that Jeremiah has added it, for it is in line with Amos' emphasis. He never condemns the other heathen nations because of their heathen religion. In his other oracles kings, not gods, are named as candidates for judgment of various kinds. The reference to priests goes along with Chemosh in Jer 48:7, which suggests that *mlkm* in Jer 49:3 could be "Milkom," god of Ammon, as in the LXX, which presents Melchhol, Melchom, Molchom. But it is more appropriate to accuse "their king" rather than their god of dispossessing Gad (Jer 49:1). The LXX version of Amos 1:15 conforms to these other passages in reading "priests," but it does not name their god: "And her kings [sic!] will go into captivity, their priests and their rulers together." The Greek translation is based on a Hebrew text that varied from MT (four of the six words being different), though the wording in Hebrew or Greek may have been influenced by the corresponding passages in Jeremiah, such as the reference to "the priests." But why the plural "kings"? Also the LXX version of Amos 1:15 is not just an imitation of them, for they have *apoikia,* while it has *aichmalōsia.*

Comment on Chapter 1

The first five oracles, which occupy chap. 1, are distinct from the remainder in that they have links among themselves lacking among or with the following three. It is true that Edom figures again in the oracle against Moab; but there it is victim, whereas in chap. 1 Edom is either culprit (1:11–12) or accomplice (1:6, 9). The connections among the second, third, and fourth oracles suggest that all three countries named—Philistia, Phoenicia, and Edom—were somehow involved in related if not joint activities. They represent the extreme points of a triangle around Israel. Both Philistia and Phoenicia are accused of handing over "an entire group of captives" to Edom. The identity of these prisoners, destined to be slaves, is not disclosed. That Edom's crime is the other side of the same coin is suggested by the repetition of the word "brother." Note the staircase connections:

> 1:6   exile a *gālût*
>   to hand over to Edom
>   to hand over a *gālût* to Edom
>   forget a covenant of brothers
>   pursue   brother//allies

If "brother" has the same referent in both occurrences, as the structure suggests, then identification with Israel is obvious. The term "covenant of brothers" could refer to a political treaty between Tyre and Israel, violated when they handed over captives to Edom. It could also indicate that handing over Israelites to Edom violated the terms of their association, rooted in their common heritage and expressed in an appropriate pact. According to biblical traditions they were the closest of brothers.

In any case, there seemed to be a network among Philistines, Phoenicians, and Edomites, although how the slaves were shipped from one country to the other may be difficult to explain.

The repetition of vocabulary between no. 2 and no. 3 and between no. 3 and no. 4 is matched by repetition of "Gilead" between no. 1 and no. 5, making a frame around the others. We do not know whether the two invasions of Gilead were separate and independent enterprises of Aram and Ammon, or the concerted action of an alliance that would divide the territory between them. Both aggressors had traditional claims on Gilead (Judges 11; 1 Samuel 11—Ammon; and Aram throughout the ninth century), and were more likely to contest each other's than to join forces. But the possibility of cooperation, as in 2 Samuel 10, cannot be ruled out, for every conceivable combination of friend and foe seemed to come about at one time or another.

Though never identified as such, Israel could have been the common victim of the covenant violations listed against the five neighbor countries of chap. 1. Hence the belief, often stated by scholars, that Amos is really addressing Israel, not Aram, Tyre, and the rest, stirring up indignation against these other nations not just for crimes against humanity, but for crimes against the Israelites themselves. If such was the pattern and his intention, then the next oracle, against Moab, breaks the pattern and expresses indignation on behalf of a victim (Edom) that so far has been the most prominent evildoer.

If the five nations covered in chap. 1 have been partners in the crimes listed there, they are also marked down for a common fate. The obvious indication is the use of the identical formula to describe it. In the cases of Tyre and Edom this formula is all that is said; but we should not imagine that it is all that will happen. The supplemental tetracolons that follow this threat in 1:5, 8, and 14b–15 enlarge on defeat in war (14b—the language suggests pitched battle in the open field), the killing of rulers (vv 5, 8), or their exile (v 15), the exile of all of the people (v 5bB), and the extermination of the remnant (v 8bB). We do not wish to assemble a composite picture mechanically and say that all these things will happen to all of them. The fate of king and people could be either extermination in the homeland or deportation. But Amos 7:17 and 9:4 show that even prisoners and refugees could be subsequently executed to complete the destruction of a nation. The individual details are representative. The total effect is comprehensive.

I.A.2.a.vi. MOAB (2:1–3)

2:1a Thus Yahweh said:
>For three violations by Moab,
>>and for four,
>>I will not reverse it:

1b   Because he burned the bones of the king of Edom to lime.

2a   And I will send Fire against Moab,
>>and She will consume the citadels of Kerioth.

2b   And Moab will die in tumult,
>>with battle shout,
>>with trumpet blast.

3a   And I will cut down the judge from its midst,

3b   and all her princes I will slay with him.
>>Yahweh has spoken!

NOTES

2 1–3. The ingredients now familiar from the five oracles in chap. 1 appear once more with variations in this oracle against Moab. Such variants are more likely to be original than the result of textual divergence from a stereotype fixed for all of them. The versions show that the tendencies in textual transmission go the other way, toward leveling and uniformity. Here v 2b resembles 1:14b but differs in many details; v 3 is like 1:15 but also diverges. It is possible to bring these two oracles closer together. Thus by omitting 1:14bB as a gloss and by moving 2:2bA to follow 2:1b, a similar sequence of lines is obtained (Harper 1905:38). When there is no textual or versional support for the outcome, there seems to be little point in such an exercise.

1b. *king of Edom.* The identification of the victim makes it clear that not all of the "violations" condemned in the prophecy were against Israel. The main problem concerns the nature of the criminal act involved and its relevance in the context. As in 1:3b, the charge in 2:1b is a single infinitival

construction. Harper, following G. Hoffmann (1883) and guided by considerations of parallelism and scansion, arrives at

ʿl śrpw ʿṣmwt mlk ʾdwm
lšdd hmt bśʾwn mwʾb

because they burned the bones of the King of Edom,
in order to desecrate the dead because of violence done to (or suffered
　　by) Moab.

The result is hardly a poetic bicolon, and v 2bB is left as an unmatched line.

In spite of the obscurity of the expression, the LXX for once translates
literally, the only interpretive shift being *eis konian*, "to ashes," which, as
in Vulgate (*cenerem*), is only an internal object. Targum explains that he
used the lime to plaster his house. This aside does not supply us with a
variant reading in the Heb original, but it confirms the meaning of *śîd* as
"lime," not just "(white) ashes," which blocks the need to read *śēd* (cf. Ps
106:37; Deut 32:17, where the plural is written *šdym*) or *šdd* (Harper
1905:43).

According to 1 Sam 31:11–13, burning a king's body prior to burying
was a pious act. The "violation" perpetrated by Moab has been interpreted
either as an act of desecration on an already dead person or as a sacrifice.
Acts of posthumous sacrilege are not uncommon. Human sacrifice is attributed to the Moabite king in 2 Kgs 3:27. Albright (1969:240) accepted Tur-
Sinai's (1954:40) emendation of Amos 2:1 to *mōlek ʾādām laśśēd*, "a human
sacrifice to a demon." But more is involved than "simply changing the
pointing," for two *matres lectionis* have to be disposed of. And the verb
remains a problem. For sacrifice we would expect *zbḥ*, for holocaust *hʿlh*.
And why the focus on "bones," which were not as such burned in sacrifice,
but removed and buried? When "bones" are mentioned alone it is often a
reference to a dead body, especially in the context of burial. A similar
combination of terms in Isa 33:12, *miśrēpôt śîd*, "burnings of lime," supports the MT of Amos 2:1b, and the victims there are human. It suggests a
fire of unusual intensity. The expression remains obscure, but the simplest
interpretation for the text as it stands is a violation of the sanctity of a
tomb. This sacrilege was feared in antiquity, and graves were protected by
curses (*KAI*, nos. 13, 14). By removing and burning bones a person would
have to believe that he was doing more harm to the dead than could be
done to him by the protective curse. Such a risky act must have been
motivated by intense vindictiveness. Jeremiah 8:1–2 describes such an act
of exposure (no burning is mentioned, however). As no king is named, it is
possible that *mlk* is collective—the royal tombs were desecrated.

2. The divine origin and cosmic nature of this fire is more evident at this

point. It lies within the power of a human invader to set a city on fire, but it takes a God to burn up a whole country, which is what will happen to Moab (2:2) and Judah (2:5).

2a. *Moab.* The LXX confirms that the country, not a city, is the target of the fire in this case. The need to make this oracle like the others in this detail is felt less strongly when the following oracle against Judah is retained as authentic, for it has a similar pattern. There is no need to supply "the cities of" (BH³) or the like.

Kerioth. The patterns in other oracles suggest that this is the name of a city. The LXX lacked this knowledge and translated *tōn poleōn autēs* (cf. the NEB; Targum: "the city").

The authenticity of the name is confirmed by Jer 48:24, and the *Mesha* inscription (line 13) shows that it was an important center for the cult of Chemosh. There are hints in that passage that Israelite inhabitants of Ataroth were slain as some kind of offering (*ryt,* meaning unknown) to Chemosh, and that the *ʾrʾl dwdh* (meaning unknown) was taken to *kmš bqryt* (compare the discussion of *b-* in 1:1) for a similar purpose. This background provides a tenuous link with v 1b and supports slightly the idea that the "violation" mentioned likewise involved human sacrifice.

The location of Kerioth is not known. Because they are never mentioned together, it has been identified as another name for ʿAr, the capital. Both are dialectal variants of words meaning "city."

2b. *die.* There are problems of gender in this oracle. The pronoun "he" (subject of "burned") in v 1b refers to Moab, and the verb here is likewise masculine. So "Moab" could mean the king, not the country. The longer phrase "land [f.] of Moab" occurs ten times, but "field [m.] of Moab" also occurs ten times, and this phrase could account for the masculine pronouns referring to the country. But the most suitable subject for *die* is human; yet the death of the ruler is only threatened in v 3. Otherwise the singular *mēt* refers collectively to the death of the entire Moabite army in battle (cf. 2:14–16). The NIV translation "will go down" is evasive. The feminine suffixes in v 3 then refer to the city, even though *qěriyyôt* is formally plural.

tumult. The word *šāʾôn* refers to the tumult of battle (Isa 17:12—*hāmôn//*), followed by *qôl* in Jer 51:55, as here. Compare Hos 10:14; Jer 25:31; Pss 40:3(E2), 74:23. The following expressions are clearly military, including the verb "slay." The LXX rendition of *šāʾôn* as *adynamia,* "weakness," is inferior.

battle shout. "war-cries" (NEB), "fanfare" (Wolff 1977:132).

3a. *judge. šôpēt,* "chief executive"; the old Israelite term for a charismatic community leader with mainly military duties. Why this term is used here, rather than "king" or *yôšēb,* as used in 1:5 and 8, is unclear. The term was still used in the eighth century as a divine (royal) title (Isa 33:22).

COMMENT

All of the oracles climax with a threat of destruction by fire. The oracles against Tyre, Edom, and Judah end at that point. Those against Damascus, Gaza, Ammon, and Moab add more details, coincident with or consequent to the siege, capture, and gutting of the city by fire. Each supplement is different, touching on one or another aspect of warfare and its aftermath. The threat of fire alone, with its cosmic perspective and mythic language, could be contained in a divine action, like the destruction of Sodom and Gomorrah; so the oracles against Tyre, Edom, and Judah could be interpreted as if no human agency were involved. The supplementary remarks in the other four cases, however, make it clear that mundane forces are at work, either as concomitants of divine actions or as the "natural" forces that are seen in prophetic vision as executing the divine will. The oracles against Ammon and Moab both mention war and its tumult. The oracles against Damascus, the Philistines, and Moab include the death of the cities' rulers. The oracles against Damascus and Ammon predict exile for king, princes, and people. The oracle against the Philistines says that even the remnant will perish. In summary:

1. Fire against the city (all cases)
2. War and tumult (1:14; 2:2)
3. Death of rulers (1:5, 8; 2:3)
4. Exile (1:5, 15)
5. Remnant perishes (1:8)

The specific threats are expected to be carried out not only against the cities named in those oracles, but against others as well. Nor does it mean that the cities left unmentioned in the text will be spared such consequences. Rather, we are to suppose that these things, all very much a part of war, are likely to happen to all of the cities on the list and others besides, in short, to the nations as a whole.

Before proceeding with the oracles against Judah and Israel we will review the crimes specified in the charges against the foreign nations and propose historical circumstances under which these charges may have been shaped. We have already described the probable circumstances under which the attack against Gilead may have taken place. It looks as though Aram and Ammon coordinated plans for a two-pronged assault or pincer movement from north to south to overrun Gilead. It would not have been the first time for Aram, which had fought many bloody battles with Israel over that disputed territory.

In the latter part of the ninth century Hazael, the usurper of Damascus, overran large parts of the whole region, including Transjordan. But we are told that after further humiliating defeats in the reign of Jehoahaz there was a reversal in the time of his son Jehoash, who achieved some successes against Ben-Hadad the son of Hazael. Presumably they included the recovery of Gilead from the Aramaeans. Now at the time that Amos spoke, and presumably in reference to an assault by the separate forces of Aram and Ammon, Gilead was invaded and overrun once more. Later, as we know, Jeroboam II was to retrieve all of that territory once again from the Aramaeans and Ammonites, and in the process overwhelm those countries east of the Jordan. It is possible that Amos is looking back to the earlier conflicts of Hazael; but the clear implication of the oracle is that circumstances described are current and obtain at the time of Amos' utterances.

Because the early eighth century B.C.E. is largely blank as far as extrabiblical sources are concerned, we can only speculate about the situation. We suggest that the invasion by Aram and Ammon, otherwise unattested, actually took place during the transition from Jehoash, who held the Aramaeans at bay during his reign, to the accession or in the early years of Jeroboam, before he consolidated his forces and, encouraged by the oracles of Jonah, set about restoring the kingdom of Israel to its ancient borders, or retrieving the territories, especially those is Transjordan, that had been lost in the past.

When we look at the oracles against Gaza and Tyre we must develop a different scenario. A dual action against an unspecified victim is described (but we may assume that the target is Israel, as also in the cases of Aram and Ammon, though conceivably Judah could also be involved as victim). The two nations seem to be involved in a joint scheme to traffic in captives taken in raids across the border of Israel (cf. 2 Kgs 5, the story of Naaman the Syrian, which begins with the account of an Aramaean raid and the capture of an Israelite girl, who then serves as a domestic slave in Naaman's household). The charges are similar, but a sharp distinction is made between the Philistines, who are accused of actually capturing these people, and the Tyrians, who are accused of delivering the captives to Edom. The actions are part of a single plan, because it is said that the Philistines captured the victims in order to turn them over to Edom. In other words, these are not separate transactions but a two-part plan of which the first component is carried out by the Philistines (the raids) and the second by the Tyrians (delivery to Edom). It all seems bizarre and unusual and very difficult to explain or rationalize, but for precisely that reason we should be wary of facile emendations (Edom to Aram). See the NOTES on 1:6.

Of course it would be much easier for the Tyrians to deliver captives to Aram than to Edom, especially because Phoenician territories were contiguous with those of Aram along the coast, and it would make sense for the Phoenicians to act as middlemen between the Philistines and the Aramaeans. But after all Edom is by far the more difficult reading. Perhaps for that reason we should consider the possibility that it was in fact the end term in this complicated traffic in human beings, and we must ask certain questions and make certain points before proceeding with our scenario.

1. What was the nature and purpose of this traffic in human bodies?

2. In most of the cases examined, the crime charged is not typical or ordinary but unusual and dramatic. The general action is all too typical—namely, acts of war—but the specific crime is described in lurid terms. In each case there is something horrifying or spectacular to set it apart, which thereby justifies the charge and leads to the appropriate judgment and punishment prescribed by the prophet.

So we are looking for something both special and heinous, something out of the ordinary and at the same time obviously criminal. In the case of the Philistines, the rather commonplace practice of raiding across the border to capture a few slaves for the domestic market (cf. 2 Kgs 5:2) is heightened and transformed by the expression *gālût šĕlēmâ,* something quite out of the ordinary. The repetition of this unique expression suggests that it is this detail, not just slave trading as such, that represents the acme of Philistine and Phoenician wickedness. The emphasis here seems to be on the extent of the raid, namely, that the capture includes the whole population of the village or other settlement. Whether it includes women and children or just male adults is not clear, but in any case it is regarded as different and worse in kind because it is so drastic in degree. In order to determine the reason for the mass deportation we must look at the objective, namely, delivery to Edom. Why does Edom need so many slaves? And why do the Tyrians have to be brought into the picture? If the destination were Aram instead of Edom, the Tyrians could serve as the conduit or relay station; it is also possible that the captives could be sent by ship along the coast. The case would make some sense if we had a reason for the Aramaean demand and need for slaves. As we know from the story of Naaman, the Aramaeans could pick up slaves from Israel directly without going about it in such a time-consuming and roundabout method. Perhaps they preferred to buy their slaves (although by the time they had paid both Philistines and Phoenicians the price could have been much inflated), but we must still account for the increased demand. The only way to account for such presumed large numbers is by supposing that these slaves were intended for public state use and not just as domestic servants. Would Aram have need or use for such—perhaps in building projects, more likely for work on public enterprises and in particular in mines? The next question is whether the

Aramaeans had mines like those in Sinai, which were worked by slaves. We have to think especially about iron mines and the incessant warfare over those well-known mines in Transjordan, which must have come under Aramaean control from time to time. Certainly Israel's persistent interest in the Transjordanian territories was occasioned in large part by these mines. We do not know very much about the traffic in state slaves and in mine working, especially in that area, but certainly this explanation is possible for a text that has suffered in transmission, especially the supposed change from Aram to Edom.

Note that in BHS the first mention of Edom in 1:6 is left uncorrected, indicating that the traffic from Philistia to Edom could have been conducted overland. The correction is made in 1:9 where the Tyrians are involved, it being deemed unlikely, if not impossible, for the Tyrians to be involved in a deal with the Edomites; but that may be just the point. The Tyrians managed to be in contact with all nations and traded in everything with everybody (see Ezekiel 27 for a marvelous description of that mercantile empire in the heart of the seas). In our opinion the weakness of the position is that it is overwhelmingly likely that Philistines and Tyrians are engaged in a joint enterprise with divided responsibilities, and that there can be only one destination for delivery of the slaves. Therefore we conclude that we must read the same name in 1:6 and 1:9, either Edom or Aram but not both.

Now let us consider the more difficult reading, "Edom." What if the objective were to deliver large groups of slaves, adults and children, male and female, to Edom?

It has been proposed that Edom itself was a center of the slave trade, receiving them from neighboring countries and transferring them to other nations in Arabia and elsewhere along the spice route. At the same time, no doubt some slaves were kept for both public and domestic purposes. Presumably able-bodied males would be put to work in the copper mines at Punon (Feinan), though there may be some question of how extensively they were worked in the Iron II period and by whom.

Assuming that it was a joint venture on the part of Philistines and Phoenicians, how would they carry out the plan? The first option would be to transport the captives by land from Philistine territory (Gaza) through the southern Negev and part of Sinai to Edom. The settlement at Quntillet ʿAjrud may well have served as a way station for such caravans. Inscriptions there attest to the presence of Phoenicians and perhaps Philistines, as well as Israelites and Judahites, about 800 B.C.E. If, however, the captives were themselves Israelites and/or Judahites, then it is not likely that the consortium of Philistines and Phoenicians would or could use such a route.

The alternative would be to transport the captives by ship, and this suggestion may explain more reasonably the role of the Tyrians, masters of the sea. It may seem unlikely, but it is not impossible to imagine that the captives were taken down the Mediterranean coast and then transported through the Egyptian canal to the Red Sea and thence around the Sinai peninsula to the ports on the Gulf of Akaba, then presumably under Edomite control. The existence of this canal has been demonstrated from the time of the 25th Dynasty in Egypt, and earlier versions can be traced as far back as the 20th Dynasty (Shea), so there is good reason to believe it was in existence and operational in the days of Amos. Even less likely is the notion that the Phoenicians might have transported the captives completely around the continent of Africa, though we know that the intrepid made such trips, as suggested in the Bible (1 Kgs 10:22) and confirmed by the Periplus.

I.A.2.b. JUDAH AND ISRAEL SEPARATELY (2:4–8)
I.A.2.b.vii. JUDAH (2:4–5)

2:4a   Thus Yahweh said:
   For three violations by Judah,
    and for four,
   I will not reverse it:
4b   Because they rejected the instruction of Yahweh,
    and his statutes they failed to observe;
   and their falsehoods led them astray,
    after which their fathers went.
5a   And I will send Fire against Judah,
5b   and She will consume the citadels of Jerusalem.

NOTES

2:4–5. The oracle against Judah resembles all of the others in general outline. It is similar to those against Tyre and Edom in detailed structure: Edom more than Tyre, in the use of a four-line unit for the charge. It is like the oracle against Moab in the pairing of country and the capital city in the threat clause: Judah and Jerusalem (v 5) is paralleled by Moab and Kerioth

(2:2a). It contrasts with them all, however, in having a more general accusation and in relating their violation directly to Yahweh. These details, and the labeling of the language of v 4b as "Deuteronomistic," have convinced many scholars that this oracle is not an Amos original, but one added much later by an editor with a "Deuteronomic" point of view (Schmidt 1965). The elimination of this oracle from the original set in turn facilitates the removal of the ones against Edom and Tyre, which resemble it in structure. There are also historical and theological reasons for these decisions (Mays 1969:42).

In terms of plan and style, Amos 2:4–5 is not much different from 1:3–2:3. But that similarity does not prove anything. It could be no more than a good imitation. Not even that, for most of it is simply repetition of the common formula. Only v 4b is distinctive; and there are two questions: (1) Is it so different from genuine Amos that we cannot leave it with the rest of his words? (2) Does it resemble Deuteronomistic writings, so that its source can be discovered or at least suspected? These questions will be taken up after we have presented the NOTES on v 4b. But before we do so it is important to stress, as we did in the general introduction to the Great Set Speech, that *no two of the oracles are exactly alike.* In the notes on 1:5 we resisted the tendency to reorganize the lines so that the structure would be the same as 1:8. We similarly rejected the proposals to rewrite 1:14b and 2:2b extensively in order to make them more alike. This critical approach and activity have pushed too far the valid observation that all of the oracles have the same general design, claiming that the authentic originals resembled one another more closely in detailed structure than they do now. The four "genuine" ones (Aram, Philistia, Ammon, Moab) are touched up to make them even more uniform. The other three (Tyre, Edom, Judah) are too different from those four to be brought into line; so they are discarded. The technique is heavy-handed, and the hypothesis is a weak one when every oracle in the series has to be touched up or else crossed out to make the theory work. Without pretending to know that Amos was the author of all of them (or any of them, for that matter), at least we can point out that variation within a common framework, rather than mechanical repetition, is the method of literary composition throughout the entire book. Therefore the variations that run through all of the oracles of the Great Set Speech cannot be used as evidence that Amos did not compose what we have now, or something very close to it.

4b. The charge against Judah resembles the one against Edom in having four lines. They use the verb forms similarly:

	Edom (1:11b)	Judah (2:4b)
Infinitive	ʿal-rodpô	ʿal-moʾŏsām
Perfect	wĕšiḥet	loʾ šāmārû

Waw-consecutive	*wayyiṭrōp*	*wayyatʿûm*
Perfect	*wĕ- . . . sămārâ*	*ʾăšer-hālĕkû*

Both indictments have a similar perspective. Edom's behavior goes back to Esau's. Judah's goes back to its fathers'. The problems of interpretation presented by 1:11b were solved above (at least provisionally) by recognizing the sequence between the second and third cola. The one *waw*-consecutive construction in 2:4b occurs in the same structural position and invites a similar analysis.

rejected. The verb *māʾas* is characteristic of prophetic thought. It is *not* distinctively or exclusively a Deuteronomic word. Neither is it used in later Priestly works (never in Ezra, Nehemiah, or Chronicles). Its use in the Pentateuch is restricted to H (Lev 26:43–44); Num 11:20 (J—"you rejected Yahweh"), 14:31 (J—"you rejected the land"). The verb is common in Job, and it is used quite often in the Psalms. Its frequent use in the classical prophets (Amos, Hosea, Isaiah, Jeremiah, Ezekiel) shows a range from outright rejection of the Lord himself to rejection of his word. In response, the Lord "rejects" the person who rejects him. The prominence of the root *mʾs* in the story of Samuel betrays the ancient source of this prophetic motif.

It began with the request for a king, tantamount to the rejection of Yahweh (1 Sam 8:7 [twice], 10:19). Then Yahweh "rejected" Saul (15:23 [twice], 26 [twice]; 16:1, cf. 16:7) because he rejected "the word of the Lord," specifically he disobeyed an order delivered by the prophet. There is no suggestion that this terminology is Deuteronomic. The characteristic repetition of the verb—"He rejected me, so I rejected him"—is found in Hosea 4:6, and the same balancing statements are distributed in Amos between 2:4 and 5:21. The verb enters the narrative (as distinct from the dialogue) of the Primary History only in the last stages of redaction. It can hardly be maintained that the majority of the occurrences in the prophets, even in Jeremiah and Ezekiel, are due to subsequent influence from 2 Kgs 17:15, 20; and 23:27, or even that its use in Jeremiah, Ezekiel, and Kings comes from the same editorial circles. The long comment in 2 Kgs 17:7–23 works the repeated *mʾs* into a homily: "They rejected his statutes . . ." (v 15); so he rejected all of the seed of Israel (v 20). The language is highly conventional and shows more signs of being based on long current prophetic discourse than the other way around. The verb is linked with more familiar Deuteronomic terms in 2 Kgs 23:27, where it is Jerusalem that is rejected.

instruction. Hosea agrees with Amos that Israel rejected (spurned) the knowledge of God, his *tôrâ,* his statutes. No information is supplied to help us to identify this *tôrâ* and so discover the specifics of the accusation.

Many studies have attempted to trace the history of the usage of the word *tôrâ* in the religion of Israel, and specifically in the prophets (Bergren 1974). It is generally assumed that it passed through successive stages, corresponding to quite different kinds of religion. The earliest mode of divine instruction was prophetic *torah*, oracular and occasional, the same as "the word of the Lord" (cf. the parallelism of Isa 2:3). Rejecting such *torah* would then be the same as spurning or silencing the prophets. The historian represents the succession of prophets as the purveyors of such *torah*, commandments, statutes (2 Kgs 17:13).

A different kind of *torah* was issued by priests. It had to do with the right conduct of the liturgy and the correct performance of ritual acts. This technical *torah* was part of the traditional lore of priests, and a decision in each case did not require prophetic afflatus (we leave aside the related question of whether a shrine would have a special cult prophet to assist in answering questions put on such subjects).

In either case it has been generally assumed that the use of the term *tôrâ* in these ways, its charismatic origin and impermanent status, shows that in preexilic times there was no standing body of established *torah*, statutes, ordinances, of fixed and constitutional character; no corpus resembling the *torah* of Moses, publicly acknowledged and providing the prophets with a talking point when it came to rebuking the people. That compilation is seen as the end of the process, a development not complete until well after the Exile.

A third kind of *torah* was defined by Harper (1905:45) as "direction as to the general duty of an Israelite." The Deuteronomic historian assesses the conduct of kings in terms of obedience to the *torah* of Yahweh (2 Kgs 10:31), usually without specific illustration, but in contexts that often imply that the maintenance of the calf cult at Dan and Bethel was the major breach.

Finally, it is supposed, the *torah* of Yahweh "by the hand of Moses" or "the *torah* of Moses" in short, as now found in the Pentateuch, was made available by compiling such material along with all kinds of other traditions. Resort to this corpus for guidance, rather than to prophet or priest, represented a major shift in Israel's religion.

This development was complete by the time of Ezra and was probably completed by Ezra himself (Freedman 1983). For a reductionist assessment of Ezra's place in history (or rather of our knowledge of his contribution to Jewish religion), see Rivkin 1969:vii–lxx. For a full review of opinions ranging from willingness to find a substantial historical basis, to the traditions about Ezra, to an almost completely negative evaluation of the story that has come down, see Houtman 1981.

In the one case Ezra is seen as a reformer. He reactivated, (re-)published the *torah* of Moses (= the Pentateuch?) and elevated it to special canonical status by separating the first five "books" of the established written traditions of Israel, the Primary History, from the following portions, which are now known as Former Prophets. These writings already existed, perhaps long before Ezra's time, possibly from the sixth century (Freedman 1963, 1983, 1988) or even before the Exile.

The farther back we try to trace the origins of the Pentateuch, the more conjectural our suggestions become. The references to *torah* in pre-exilic sources, such as Amos 2:4, which we are now studying, are not clear enough or specific enough to permit us to say that Amos and others who use the term had the *torah* of Moses in their minds, let alone in their hands. The infrequency of such references and the low profile of Moses in the few that there are suggest that any such body of received *torah* and statutes, whether written or still only or mainly oral, did not yet enjoy the kind of canonical status as sacred scripture that it eventually acquired by the time of Ezra. The truth probably lies between the one extreme, which identifies the *torah* of Yahweh mentioned by Amos here with the Pentateuch we now have (and uses that reference as evidence that the Pentateuch existed and was recognized as canonical in his day), and the other extreme, which denies all connection between the *torah* of Amos 2:4 and the *torah* of Ezra's day.

The argument becomes circular when passages that seem to reflect knowledge of the Pentateuch, and specifically of Deuteronomic ideas, are explained as later additions to the book. We have already discussed this question, which is distinct and separate (cf. p. 296), and we discuss it further below. Arguing in another direction, the references to patriarchal and Mosaic traditions found in Amos and in the other eighth-century prophets are frequently different in both vocabulary and fact from what we now have in the Pentateuch. The prophets rebuked the people, and especially the rulers, for not keeping *torah,* which they are supposed to know. This *torah* is "the knowledge [of God]" (Hos 4:1, 6) of which the content, when spelled out, resembles sections of the Pentateuch, such as the Decalogue (Hos 4:2), but cannot be tracked down as literal quotations from the texts we now have (cf. Mendenhall's view that originally *torah* was the text of the covenant [1962:719]). Certainly the prophets never say, to lend more weight and authority to their words, that they are quoting from official and established scriptures.

Steering a middle course, we can say that material that eventually found its way into the Pentateuch, or at least material closely resembling it, already existed in the time of the monarchy, some of it coming down from the age of Moses himself. This traditional moral code provides a prevailing backdrop to prophetic judgment speeches. The language of Hos 4:6, Jer 6:19, and Isa 5:24 is similar to that of Amos 2:4, but each has a different parallel to *torah.* In Jer 6:19 "my words" is followed by "my *torah,*" "and they rejected it." In Hos 4:6 *torah* is paralleled by "knowledge":

> *kî-ʾattâ haddaʿat māʾastā* . . .
> Because you have rejected the knowledge, . . .

> *wattiškaḥ tôrat ʾĕlōheykā*
> and forgotten the *torah* of your God.

This charge is spoken against a priest, Amaziah perhaps, or more likely a successor, if our early date for Amos is correct. In Isa 5:24 is the parallel "word of the Holy one of Israel":

> *kî māʾăsû ʾēt tôrat yhwh ṣĕbāʾôt*
> For they have rejected the *torah* of the Lord of Hosts,
> *wĕʾēt ʾimrat qĕdôš-yiśrāʾēl niʾēṣû*
> and the word of the Holy One of Israel they have despised.

The parallel terms used here (*daʿat* and *ʾimrâ*) do not permit a more precise identification of *torah* or of the actions that could be so described. There are three main possibilities:

1. Rejecting *torah* means breaking the stipulations of the covenant. The immediate context of Hos 4:6 points to this idea (4:1–2, with "knowledge" as the link). The same is true of Isaiah 5, in which the woes are similar to those in Amos. There can be no doubt that "rejecting *torah*" means doing the kinds of things that are deplored in Isa 5:8–23. Amos 5:7, 15, 24 and 6:12b show that it is the same as denying righteousness and justice, defined in terms of social evils. The term *tôrâ* can well bear this meaning in all of its prophetic occurrences. It is not to be identified with the present Pentateuch, and so declared anachronistic; but it is not to be isolated from the codes in the Pentateuch either.

2. When Amos 2:4b is read in the light of 2 Kgs 17:15, 20; and 23:27, the rejection of *torah* is identified not as the desire for a human king, as in Samuel, or as social injustice, as in Hosea and Isaiah, but as idolatry. So "their lies" are identified as idols.

3. In some prophetic passages the object of the verb *māʾas* is "the word of the Lord" (Jer 8:9; Isa 30:12), so that this can be identified as the *torah* in those contexts (Isa 2:3) and the crime is the rejection of the prophetic message itself. In the context of Amos 2:4 it means the contrary acceptance of false prophecies—"their lies." All of these components are present in Isa 30:9–12. They are "lying (*kehāšîm*) children," a rebellious people. These epithets do not imply that the people tell lies; they prefer to be told lies rather than to hear the truth. There are two matching statements:

> They don't want to hear the *torah* of Yahweh (30:9b).
> You have rejected this *word* (30:12a).

Between them is the famous passage that shows how this rejection works. They tell the seers to stop seeing, the visionaries to stop having visions about what is right. Rather, in 30:10b:

> Speak to us falsehoods,
> prophesy delusions. (NJPS)

Nothing could be clearer. Rejecting the prophets and rejecting the *torah* of Yahweh are one and the same thing. More than that, the prophets are abused in 30:11, verbally and physically:

> Get out of the way,
> get off the path.

The same language is used by Amos in 2:7 to describe the treatment of the poor. To silence the prophets (2:12; 7:12–13) is to reject Yahweh himself.

These interpretations need not be mutually exclusive, especially when the language is so general. Ezekiel often has "my judgments" and "my statutes" as objects of *māʾas* (5:6; 20:13, 16, 24); and one does not have to choose between a body of traditional regulations (priestly *torah*) or occasional oracular utterances (prophetic *torah*), for the prophets spoke as custodians and restorers of the requirements of the covenant (2 Kgs 17:23). Amos' indictment is accordingly quite broad.

statutes. These are the particulars of *torah.* The parallelism of *tôrâ// ḥuqqîm* is not Deuteronomistic. It is mainly found in the latest installments of the Old Testament, when such terms tended to pile up, as in Psalms 19 and 119. Nehemiah 10:29–30 lists *tôrâ, miṣwōt, mišpāṭîm.* In 1 Chr 22:12 *tôrat yhwh* is followed by *haḥuqqîm* and *hammišpāṭîm,* "which Yahweh commanded Moses concerning Israel"; it is followed by singulars in Ezra 7:10; 7:11 shows that these new rules are all in a book. It would be a mistake to read this usage into Amos 2:4, just because of the parallelism *tôrâ//ḥuqqîm.* As already mentioned, these later texts never use the verb *māʾas.*

observe. The idiom "keep (*šmr*) statutes" is standard and cannot be used to diagnose a source or tradition that supplied these words to Amos, whether to the man originally or to the book subsequently. The sequence *tôrâ//ḥuqqîm* and the placement of a negative word ("reject") in parallel with a negated positive word ("did not keep"), with chiasmus of the verbs, is good poetic composition. Nonetheless, it is not quite classical, because Amos uses *ʾet,* whereas Hosea, in an otherwise similar statement (4:6), does not.

falsehoods. Once again Amos is clearly outside the range of Deuteronomistic influences.

The root *kzb* occurs four times in the Primary History, twice as the verb, twice as the noun. None of these instances can be connected even remotely with any Deuteronomistic source.

Verb: 1. Num 23:19:
          lō' 'îš 'ēl wîkazzēb
          El is not a human that he should lie.
          2. 2 Kgs 4:16:
          wattō'mer . . . 'al tĕkazzēb bĕšiphāteka
          And she said . . . do not lie to your maidservant.

The passage in Numbers is from the Oracles of Balaam, an old poem incorporated into an early source. The passage in Kings is part of the Elijah-Elisha cycle.

Noun: Judges 16:10, 13:
          wattĕdabbēr 'ēlay kĕzābîm
          And you have told me lies.

This passage (which occurs twice) is from the story of Samson and Delilah.

There is no hint of Deuteronomic usage in any of the passages cited; hence we can say that the root, whether verbal or nominal, is not part of Deuteronomic vocabulary or usage.

No matter how we analyze v 4b, it is important to recognize that it is an integral tetracolon, not just two bicolons in sequence. The behavior described in v 4bB is the consequence of the rejection of prophetic instruction by Yahweh in v 4bA.

"Their lies" (or "delusions"; NJPS) are commonly interpreted as "idols" or "false gods" (NIV, NEB, TEV, and many commentators). Several arguments support this conclusion. First, there is the assumption that "their lies" is the antecedent of v 4bB, along with the fact that "walking behind" someone means following a leader; and this expression can be used for devotion to a god, the opposite of "following Yahweh."

This argument is supported further by expressions used elsewhere. In the Deuteronomic strand of the Primary History, apostasy is "going after *hăbālîm*," that is, vain gods; Deut 32:21; 1 Kgs 16:13, 26; and Jer 8:19 show that these are idols. Jeremiah 2:5 uses the expression "walk after the *hebel*"; Ps 31:7(E6) expresses detestation of idolaters, "who keep" (*šmr*) *hablê-šāw'*. It requires only the equation of *hăbālîm* with *kĕzābîm* in Amos 2:4 to complete the circle: lies = vanities = idols.

Amos 2:4b is close to 2 Kgs 17:15:

wayyim'ăsû 'et-ḥuqqāyw . . .   They despised his statutes . . .
wayyēlĕkû 'aḥărê hahebel   and went after worthless idols.

Yet even there the identification of *hebel* as "worthless idols" (NIV, NEB; but NJPS has "delusion") is not compelling. It could cover any kind of deflection from the true way. It is the opposite of keeping the statutes of Yahweh; it means following any other code. It would include idolatry, but it could be any violation of the covenant, which 2 Kgs 17:15 also mentions.

The use of a common word like "walk" is not enough evidence of Deuteronomic influence, especially when the texts differ in the use of specific terms. As observed earlier, *kzb* does not occur in any Deuteronomic or Deuteronomistic passage in the Bible. Furthermore, the meaning "idols" for *kĕzābîm* is hypothetical for Amos 2:4b and unattested and unproved anywhere else. Once the door is opened to equating "lies" with idols, this meaning can be found in other passages (Dahood 1966:23–24, 245–46 on Ps 4:3[E2]; 40:5[E4]). But such an identification cannot be recycled as evidence that the equation is correct.

The interpretation nevertheless is ancient. The LXX has *ta mataia autōn, ha epiēsan.* The term *mataia* itself does not specify idols, as it is quite general. The added clause shows how the translator understood the term. It translates eleven different Hebrew words. *Mataia* also translates *hăbālîm,* which can mean "lies" as well as "futile things."

In spite of this apparent consensus of ancient and modern interpreters, we reject the identification of "their lies" with "false gods" for several reasons:

1. Adequate sense can be made out of the salient meaning.

2. There is no other certain instance of *kāzāb* meaning "idol."

3. The identification assumes what it has to prove.

4. False words and false gods can both be called *hăbālîm,* but it does not follow from this usage that *kĕzābîm* has the same two denotations.

5. The passage reflects immediately Amos' reiterated condemnation of Israel (including Judah) for rejecting the authentic word of prophecy and following false oracles; so this meaning for "lies" is quite suited to the context.

6. The prevailing interpretation identifies the subject and object of *wayyat'ûm,* "and *they* led *them* astray" as being "their lies" and "Judah," respectively; but there are good reasons for doubting this reading. The subject of *hit'â* is usually human, namely, false teachers or prophets (see the following note). Here we have synecdoche: "lies" for lying prophets and other leaders. There is no indication that "lies" can be the subject of such a verb, let alone "idols."

7. The interpretation concedes too much actuality and capacity to idols. Is it conceivable that Amos would say that idols can do anything?

8. All of the eighth-century prophets had to cope with competition from false prophets. The latter are the ones who delude and mislead the people. The people do two things: they reject the true words, they follow the false words.

Hebrew has three main roots for falsehood: *kzb, khš,* and *šqr.* The Bible contrasts God, who speaks the truth, with men, who tell lies. See, for example, Num 23:19:

> *lō' 'îš 'ēl wîkazzēb*
> *ûben-'ādām wĕyitneḥām*

> El is not a man that he would lie,
> nor a son of Adam, that he would change his mind (Num 23:19).

The point is that he will keep his word.

God insists that he did not give an untrue oracle to David: *'ăšaqqēr// 'ăkazzēb* (Ps 89:34[E33], 36[E35]).

The root *kzb* (verb or noun) has the simple meaning of untruthful speech (Judg 16:10, 13; Job 24:25). The *pi'el* is factitive (Klopfenstein 1964:176ff.), and like many such verbs of speaking (Jenni 1968:216) it does not need an explicit object. The word field is well represented in Prov 14:5:

> *'ēd 'ĕmûnîm lō' yĕkazzēb*
> *wĕyāpîaḥ kĕzābîm 'ēd šeqer*

> A truthful witness does not lie,
> but a false witness breathes lies.

Note the perfect double chiasmus (subjects at the extremes and verbs in the middle), which sets off the passage.

More specifically, a false promise can be called a lie; that is, a liar is a person who does not keep a vow (Ps 78:36). This meaning is mainly found in connection with oracular promises made by God. The Shunammite said to Elisha, "Don't lie to your handmaiden" (2 Kgs 4:16), in other words, do not give me empty hopes by making a false prediction/promise. The prophet's response is not recorded; but the incident shows that the woman suspected that a prophet might give such a pleasing but groundless message. For then as now there would be charlatans preying on the hopes of the superstitious. When she repeats the question she says "Don't give me false assurance" (*tašleh;* 2 Kgs 4:28).

In most instances *kzb* refers to false prophecy. A vision from Yahweh "will not lie" (Hab 2:3), it will certainly come to pass. A prophecy that comes out of the human mind ("heart") will deceive, and the person who makes up such an oracle is *ʾîš šeqer,* or *ʾîš . . . rûaḥ* (Mic 2:11).

Isaiah denounced the alliance with Egypt as a compact with hell, because it was based on alleged prophetic "vision." The word *ḥōzeh* in Isa 28:15 and *ḥāzût* in Isa 28:18 should retain this meaning and not be changed to "covenant." A policy based on false prophecy is called *kāzāb//šeqer.*

The problem of the false prophets was long-standing in Israel. It cannot be traced continuously from the opponents of Micaiah ben Imlah (1 Kings 22), but it would seem from the preoccupation of all eighth-century prophets with it that the outspoken messengers of Yahweh sometimes encountered violent opposition from rivals who were evidently part of the political and religious establishment. Likewise Jeremiah and Ezekiel denounced rivals whom they considered to be impostors. They continue to use some of the language of their predecessors, but some new factors enter. In the eighth century false prophecy was linked with drunkenness (Isa 28; Hos 4:11 and chap. 7; Mic 2:11; Amos 2:8). At the end of the era, false prophecy is linked with divination. Ezekiel (13:6–9) says the prophets utter

ḥāzû šāwʾ	false vision
wĕqesem kāzāb	and lying divination

when they say "Oracle of Yahweh," but Yahweh did not send them. This charge is repeated in v 7 with similar language: "surely it is *false visions* you have seen, and *lying divination* you have spoken"; or

$$mahăzēh\ šāwʾ\ .\ .\ .\quad ûmiqsam\ kāzāb$$
$$\text{(v 7; cf. 21:34[E21:29])}$$

By means of chiasmus in v 8 the verbs and nouns are interchanged:

They spoke	(*šāwʾ*)	false things,
they saw	(*kāzāb*)	lying visions.

And the prophets are called

hahōzîm šāwʾ	Those who see "vanity" in visions
haqqōsĕmîm kāzāb	and who discover "a lie" by divination. (v 9)

In Amos 2:4 the identification of "their lies" as false prophecies also secures continuity with the preceding lines. These spurious oracles are put in place of the genuine but rejected statutes of Yahweh.

astray. Our literal translation is not entirely satisfactory. Were it not for the availability of "their lies" as a possible subject of the verb, one would prefer continuity with the preceding verbs. The people accused of rejecting the *torah* of Yahweh are the ones who lead astray by means of lies, which replace the true statutes.

In Jer 23:30–32 the same kind of thing is described, as perpetrated by "the prophets." They steal Yahweh's words from one another, that is, they plagiarize the recognized modes of utterance and sound like real prophets talking. But Yahweh did not send them (v 32b), they made up the messages out of their own heart. They are "dreams of falsehood (*šeqer*), oracle of Yahweh. So they report them, and they lead my people astray with their lies" (*wayyat'û 'et- 'ammî běšiqrêhem*).

This passage enables us to identify the subject (false prophets), the object (the people), and the instrument ("their lies"). Each prophet has a select preferred vocabulary. Jeremiah is partial to *šeqer;* Ezekiel uses *kāzāb;* Isaiah has both. Hosea and Amos prefer *kāzāb;* Micah leans toward *šeqer.* But they are all talking about the same phenomenon: false prophecy. The kindred passage in Ezekiel 13 studied in the preceding note culminates in the charge in v 10 "they have led my people astray" (*hit'û 'et-'ammî,* the key verb of Amos 2:4); "they say 'peace' when there isn't any peace." They are like Isaiah's rivals who prophesied "smooth things" (Isa 30:10; in Ezek 12:24 *miqsam hālāq,* "soothing divination" [NJPS], in parallel with *hāzôn šāw'*). They are like Amos' rivals who promised a bright "day of the Lord"; like Micah's "liar and deceiver" (2:11); like Hananiah who prophesied a speedy end to the Exile (Jeremiah 28). These prophets led the people astray *with* their lies. They lied to the people, who listened to lies (Ezek 13:19). There is no instance (unless it be Amos 2:4) in which the word "lie" or "lies" is the subject of a verb. Hence Amos 2:4 should be analyzed on the basis of and lined up with Jer 23:32 and Ezek 13:10.

This approach also agrees with the general use of *hit'â.* The priest led the people astray by means of the spirit of fornication (Hos 4:12—see Andersen and Freedman 1980:366–68). The (false) prophets lead the people astray *mat'îm* (Mic 3:5); compare Isa 3:12. See also Jer 23:13: "Among the prophets of Samaria I saw a disgusting thing, they prophesied by Baal and they led astray (*wayyat'û*) my people Israel."

The image of the shepherd and his flock is present in the verb *t'y.* The *qal* describes the aimless wandering of a lost animal (Exod 23:4; Ps 119:176; Isa 53:6); of a human who is unintelligent (Isa 35:8) or drunk (Isa 28:7), or simply lost (Gen 21:14, 37:15). The duty of the shepherd is to keep the sheep on the right path (Ps 23:3); a shepherd who actually leads the flock astray by false directions is doubly at fault. The only occurrence of the verb that could be Deuteronomistic is found in 2 Kgs 21:9; Manasseh led the people astray (cf. 2 Chr 33:9).

fathers. What is the antecedent of this relative clause? The nearest eligible noun is "lies," and the passage is usually interpreted this way, especially when the lies are identified as idols. With the resumptive "after them" the antecedent must be plural, and "his statutes" is possible. The idiom "walk behind" is used for following a person (Gen 24:61), including Yahweh (1 Kgs 14:8). By the same token, apostasy is walking behind the rival god, such as Baal (Deut 4:3; 1 Kgs 18:18), and this circumstance makes the usual interpretation plausible. The idiom "walk *in* statutes" is also met (1 Kgs 6:12; 8:61; Ezek 5:7; 11:20; 18:9, 17; 20:13, 19, 21; 36:27); Amos' usage does not quite match. The question is thus whether Amos is accusing them of deserting the statutes that their fathers followed, or of imitating their fathers by following lies. Two quite opposite points of view on this matter are found in the Hebrew Bible. Sometimes the faithfulness of the fathers contrasts with the errors of their descendants. Sometimes they are all accused of straying from Yahweh from the beginning. Amos does not say enough about the ancestors to enable us to say how he viewed it. Amos 5:25 is too obscure to settle the point; 2:10–12 gives the impression that they have always been that way. If we reject the identification of "lies" with idols, then this word is less appropriate as an antecedent. If the false prophets led them astray with their lies, then those prophets were the ones they followed. The antecedent is the implicit subject of the verb *wayyat'ûm.* Those whom their fathers followed also led them astray by their lies.

5. The oracle against Judah is less focused in its target. Those against Aram, Philistia, Ammon, and Moab specify the leaders, at least by titles, including individual rulers. The vaguer language of 2:4 leaves open the question of whether all of the Judahite people are accused or whether their leaders are considered responsible. Verse 5 too leaves this question open. Fire is sent against Judah, but Jerusalem is the main target.

I.A.2.b.viii. ISRAEL (2:6–8)

2:6a   Thus Yahweh said:
         For three violations by Israel,
             and for four,
             I will not reverse it:
    6b   Because they sell for money the righteous,
                 and the poor for the sake of a pair of sandals—
    7a   those who trample upon the dust of the earth the head of the
             destitute,
                 and they push the humble out of the way—

7b   and a man and his father go to the Girl,
                so as to desecrate my holy name.
8a   And because they spread out garments pledged for debt be-
            side every altar,
8b   and drink the wine of those who have been fined,
                in the house of their God.

INTRODUCTION

2:6–8. The oracle against Israel begins in the same way as all the others, but it does not follow the common pattern for very long. The charge is elaborated and seems to go on without an end. The switch to the use of a participle at the beginning of v 7 is unmatched by any similar construction in the preceding seven oracles. It marks the inauguration of a series of "woes" couched in participial constructions, which continue almost to the end of the book. They occur in all major sections, spanning and integrating the whole. *Haššōʾăpîm* in 2:7 and 8:4 forms a conspicuous inclusion. There are, in fact, many connections between vv 6–12 and the rest of the book, so that the oracle against Israel serves not only as one of eight in the Great Set Speech but also as an announcement of themes that will be repeated and elaborated later.

Just as 2:9–13 elaborates the background and justification for Yahweh's punitive act against Judah and Israel (the last two in the set), so the same sort of explanation is given at the end of the book (9:7) for those two and the first two in the Great Set Speech (Aram and Philistia, 1:3–8). In the same way there is an elaboration of the indictment in 2:6–8 and in 8:4–14, especially 8:4–8, 13–14. The latter verses also have connections with 2:14–16. If, then, 2:6–16 and 8:4–14 throw light on each other, we may discover in 8:14 the name of the divine "Girl" in 2:7. In other words, we have the same situation and the same people in 2:6–8 and 8:4–8, 13–14. If the *nšbʾym* of 8:14 are the same as the *šʾpym* of 2:7 and 8:4, then clearly the temple is linked with the business activities. We may detect a three-way alliance of priests, merchants, and magistrates, with most of the personnel drawn from a few large and influential families.

The oracle against Israel does not go on to pronounce judgment ("and I will send Fire . . ."), as do all of the others. Not that such threats are absent from the ensuing text. All of the ingredients—destruction of cities, defeat in battle, death of leaders, exile of people—turn up in one form or another, sooner or later. But the formulation is different. It is noteworthy that no one seriously questions that the oracle against Israel was composed by Amos because it is different from the others.

The fact that the oracle against Israel suddenly (at v 7) goes off in a direction different from all of the others makes it difficult to say where it ends. There is a significant break at v 9 clearly marked by "As for me." Even so, vv 9–12 are a continuation of charges. There is a marked change in the target. The historical recital of vv 9–11 applies equally to all Israelites, and we have shown that "sons of Israel" (v 11b) means the people of both kingdoms.

In modern translations and commentaries, there is considerable variety in the division of Amos 2:6–16 into paragraphs. Mays (1969:42) treats it as a single unit. Most find a break after v 8. The NIV has five paragraphs. Verse 13 is sometimes joined to vv 9–12 as its culmination; but more often it is seen as the preamble to the judgment in vv 14–16. The connection is not smooth in either direction. A new beginning is more evident at 3:1, but there is also continuity (cf. the NOTES to that verse).

The material (vv 9–16) that grows out of the oracle against Israel (vv 6–8) can be viewed as an expansion of the picture in two steps, so as to round off the Great Set Speech of chaps. 1–2.

The first step is taken in vv 9–12(13), which link Judah and Israel. That all of Israel is in mind is shown not only by the term "Israelites" (v 11) but by the more certain fact that the recital of vv 9–11 cannot leave Judah out. In addition, if we are correct in our interpretation of v 4, v 12 is its complement. The silencing of true prophets and the fostering of lies are two sides of the same violation, and the whole nation is guilty.

The second stage is reached in vv 14–16. This passage picks up threats of punishment through military defeat which was hinted at in 1:14 and 2:2, but which would be suited to all eight nations equally.

The prime sin of Israel is the abuse and oppression of the poor. It is in the domestic scene, not on the international stage, that Israel's crimes are exposed. Amos returns to this matter again in 5:12 and 8:4–6. All three passages have vocabulary in common, and each helps to clarify the others. The poor are abused by the powerful in several ways.

First there was exploitation that denied them compassion; then there was corruption that denied them justice. Amos' language is somewhat general; it lacks the specifics of Micah (2:1–2) and Isaiah (5:8), who highlight the seizure of family lands. As the case of Naboth shows (1 Kings 21; see Andersen 1966) there were ways of legalizing such robbery. Impoverishment was doubtless the most common route to total loss of property—first land, then the clothing from one's back, and finally one's own body. All three acts were forbidden in Yahweh's *torah,* and redress through the law courts was available to citizens. Indeed magistrates, and especially kings, were expected to take the initiative to see that those who lacked both means and advocates—orphans and widows were the extreme cases—would have champions in the seat of justice.

To succeed in their crimes, the oppressors needed both the power and audacity to break the basic laws; also the money and influence to bribe judges and subvert the process of justice. The poor were forced off their land, enslaved, and denied access to the courts.

The commercial and the juridical sides of such developments were not necessarily distinct moments or separate events, involving first merchants in the markets and then magistrates in the court. The making and repaying of loans, foreclosure and redemption of property, were public transactions in which the community had an interest. They were conducted under supervision and certified by witnesses: an assembly of citizens (Genesis 23, 34) or an *ad hoc* committee of elders (Ruth 4), presided over by "nobles" (1 Kgs 21:8, 11). The traditional location for transacting all such business was the open air near the city gateway. Everyone had a right to be there, and all citizens had a right to speak. Everything was given publicity, and even without written titles and affidavits, the community as a whole would be able to keep track of the property of its members. Promises were confirmed and protected by oaths, which is where God came into it. Things were done "in front of God," which might require the presence of principals and witnesses at the shrine. See the COMMENT on "the house of their god(s)" in v 8 and the swearing described in 8:14.

Both stages are reported in 2:6–7; 5:12; and 8:4, 6. The pattern is chiastic, with the law court in the center:

> 2:6b   *ʿal-mikrām bakkesep ṣaddîq*
> Because they sell for money the righteous,
> > *weʾebyôn baʿăbûr naʿălăyim*
> > and the poor for the sake of a pair of sandals—
>
> 7a   *haššōʾăpîm ʿal-ʿăpar-ʾereṣ*
> those who trample upon the dust of the earth
> > *bĕrōʾš dallîm*
> > the head of the destitute,
> > *wĕderek ʿănāwîm yaṭṭû*
> > and they push the humble out of the way—

> 5:12b   *ṣōrĕrê ṣaddîq*
> you who harass the upright,
> *lōqĕḥê kōper*
> and hold them for ransom,
> *weʾebyônîm baššaʿar hiṭṭû*
> who thrust the poor from the gate.

> 8:4a   . . . *haššōʾăpîm ʾebyôn*
> . . . you who trample upon the poor,
> 4b   *wĕlašbît ʿăniwwê-ʾāreṣ*

and put an end to the wretched of the land;
6a   *liqnôt bakkesep dallîm*
who buy the needy for money,
  wĕʾebyôn baʿăbûr naʿălāyim
and the poor for a pair of sandals

NOTES

6. Each of the preceding oracles mentions "three . . . four acts of rebellion," but only one or two are cited in each instance. In the case of Israel we have a list that could be analyzed as three or four:

1. selling the righteous poor into slavery (v 6b);
2. abusing the humble indigent (v 7a);
3. going to the Girl (v 7b);
4. misbehaving in the shrine (v 8).

There are even more, if the indictment continues through vv 9–12. We have concluded, however, that the latter section is aimed at both kingdoms.

6b. Selling the poor for a pair of sandals is one of best known of Amos' expressions; but when it is looked at closely, it is hard to work out what exactly is meant. The correlative "buy" occurs with the same objects in 8:6.

righteous . . . poor. The terms *saddîq* and *ʾebyôn* are not really synonymous expressions (cf. Beek 1948:140–41) though standing in parallel relationship; rather they are complementary. The prophet's meaning is brought out in combining the terms "righteous poor" instead of the "poor" in general. In the same way, the words *dallîm* and *ʿănawîm* in v 7 are to be taken together to signify the "humble destitute." The terms "wicked" and "rich" are similarly paired (and combined) in Isa 53:9 and other passages. Neither poverty nor wealth is in itself good or bad, but there is an inevitable tendency in the Bible to associate wealth with the wicked and poverty with the pious in spite of opposite traditions from earliest times, which saw wealth as a sign of divine favor (blessing) and destitution as a mark of divine disapproval (curse). This ambivalence to wealth as a mark of either wickedness or virtue, and poverty as a sign of punishment or righteousness, is present throughout the biblical materials, but attention is focused primarily on the anomalous situations in which the wicked were wealthy and the righteous were poor.

money . . . sandals. Chiasmus. The principle of complementarity in poetic parallelism points to a discontinuous construct phrase, "the price . . . of a pair of sandals."

The statement has a formal similarity to lines 7–8 of the Kilamuwa inscription (*KAI* 24; cf. Garbini 1977):

| ʾlmt ytn bs | A girl he sold | for a sheep |
| wgbr   bswt | and a man | for a garment. |

A proverb is suspected, but it is so pithy as to remain opaque. Rosenthal thought it meant that Kilamuwa got a bargain in his deal with Assyria (*ANET* 654). It resembles Amos 2:6b in that humans are sold for an article of attire, which is assumed to represent a very low price.

In the larger context of the indictment, the action has been identified not as commercial payment but as bribery (Speiser 1940). In Kilamuwa 7–8 the *b-* of price is repeated; in Amos 2:6 *b-* is paralleled by *baʿăbûr,* perhaps a synonym in that position, but perhaps with the nuance "for a consideration." Pursuing the idea of a bribe, Gordis tracked down the word *naʿălām,* "bribe" (1950). The orthographic adjustment is minimal, but in the context of *mkr* the focus is commercial, for this verb is often used for the sale of human beings as slaves (Gen 37:27, 28, 36; 45:4, 5; Exod 21:16; Deut 21:14; 24:7).

Gordis' suggestion that some derivative of the root *ʿlm,* "conceal," in other words, to cover up some fraud in business or some perversion of justice, receives support from the language of 1 Sam 12:3–5. In this *apologia pro vita sua,* Samuel challenges the people to produce any evidence of corruption during his career as a magistrate.

First we note the parallelism of *ʿšq* and *rṣṣ* as in Amos 4:1. Samuel also specifies ways in which such wrongs might be done—taking someone's ox or ass (i.e., unlawfully depriving anyone of property). It does not necessarily mean that Samuel personally acquired the animals; it could mean that he gave the wrong verdict in a dispute over the ownership of such beasts. In addition he protests that he had never received a bribe (*kōper*), "to look the other way" (NJPS)—MT *weʾaʿlîm ʿênay bô,* "that I should cover my eyes with it." The LXX version is quite different, *kai hypodēma apokrithēte kat' emou* "even a sandal, bear witness against me." In Sir 46:19 there is a paraphrase, which corroborates the tradition that Samuel had not taken anyone's property, "not so much as a pair of sandals."

The retroversion *wnʿl(ym) ʿnw by* differs considerably from the MT. The reference to sandals may be "arcane" to us (McCarter 1980:209–10); but if the language of Amos 2:6, 8:6; Sir 46:19; and 1 Sam 12:3 in the LXX reflects either a proverb or else an actual custom, is it likely that a Jewish scribe would have found it "arcane" and changed it into the even more obscure MT reading? The Hebrew of Sir 46:19, *kwpr wnʿlm mm[y lqḥ]ty wkl ʾdm lʾ ʿnh bw,* "a bribe and a pair of sandals from who[m did I receive] and every man did not answer him," is another paraphrase. Both the LXX and Ben Sira are somewhat midrashic, and the reference to "sandals" could have entered the oral tradition of interpretation that went along with the written Hebrew text by linking it with the well-known and intriguing references in Amos. In view of the singular of 1 Sam 12:3 in the LXX (contrast Sir 46:19), one must also ask if the idiom is closer to Gen 14:23, where a sandal thong represents an item that a scrupulously honest person would not accept, in spite of its petty value. With arguments going in either direction so finely balanced, it would be rash to declare either the MT or a retroverted LXX reading of 1 Sam 12:3 original. We do not have to make that decision in order to use 1 Sam 12:3. Whether the Hebrew text of 1 Sam 12:3 was originally closer to Amos 2:6 and 8:6 than it now is, or the texts were brought into association by ancient interpreters or scribes, the LXX reading, whatever its textual status, does attest a situation in which a judge might be accused of improperly receiving a pair of sandals as a bribe. Again, this point stands whether we interpret *kpr wnʿl(ym)* as hendiadys, a bribe consisting of a (pair of) sandal(s), or whether we accept the paraphrase in the Greek version of Sir 46:19 ("not so much as"). We do not know if the sandal (or a pair) was a proverbial bribe or merely a symbol of a paltry sum. The real issue is whether there is anything in common between commercial transactions in which sandals changed hands and the use of sandals as bribes. The use of the verbs *mkr* and *qnh* in Amos 2:6 and 8:6 points to sale and purchase. The word *kpr* in 1 Sam 12:3 points to bribery. The two could be combined if the bribe is given to the judge to certify an illegal or unjust commercial transaction. S. R. Driver (1913:88–89) had difficulty with the LXX reading because he could not see that a sandal would have any force as a bribe. The difficulty can be overcome if the point is that an avaricious judge would accept even a bribe of small value. Speiser (1940:18) found the idea of buying and selling a person for a pair of sandals "economically improbable." The significance of sandals lies not in their commercial value (or lack thereof) but in their symbolic legal value as formalizing transactions. He found evidence for this practice at Nuzi. If we assume that similar customs prevailed in Israel, why should Samuel and Amos consider the exchange of sandals, whether in the market or in the law court or at the validation and certification of a sale before a magistrate, to be reprehensible, indeed the extreme example of the low value set on a poor person and of the low price at which a judge could be "bought?"

The ceremonial and symbolic use of sandals in legalizing contracts, commercial or quasi-commercial such as a marriage agreement, as discussed by Speiser, was proper and respectable. The crime that Samuel denies and that Amos charges—receiving a petty bribe—was serious because it was trivial. The symbolic value of the sandal in both connections could derive from the basic fact that sandals have enormous significance as a sign of identity and status. Likewise the cloak; the two often go together, as in Speiser's examples. Both are mentioned in Amos 2:6–8. Removal of both (Isa 20:1–3) represents ultimate destitution, the lot of slaves and prisoners of war. The value of the sandal is thus ambivalent, lending pathos to the symbol. The person who lost it was impoverished; the person who took it was not enriched. This view of the matter is not to deny that collusion of magistrates was also involved, and that bribes also changed hands.

In considering the meaning and significance of the charge against the people of Israel in v 6b, the following points can be made.

1. If the text is taken literally, they are accused of selling the "righteous poor" for a paltry sum: the value of a pair of sandals.

2. If the criminal activity in view is the sale of people into slavery, then the price or value of the persons sold would not seem to be relevant or consequential. Would it diminish the crime if the value of the persons were set higher? Or does it make the crime worse if a lower figure is used? Such an evaluation seems improbable (see Speiser 1940). We may conclude that this distinction was not the point of the statement.

3. Alternatively, the pair of sandals is interpreted as a bribe paid to the judge for a favorable verdict. While it is possible to explain the reference to the meagerness of the bribe as showing how venal judges could be, the usual purpose in mentioning trivial objects such as sandals, or even the latchet on a sandal, is to attest to the incorruptibility of judges, as in the case of the patriarch Abraham. To argue the case in reverse, that is, to claim that the judges will sell to even the lowest possible bidder, is unusual but not implausible.

4. The remaining possibility is to see a reference to and description of debt slavery: the pair of sandals is the value of the debt for which the "righteous poor" are being sold as slaves. Even for such a trivial debt, harsh leaders and rapacious creditors are forcing "the righteous poor" into debt slavery. In such a case, perhaps the amount involved does make a difference along with culpability. Someone who is heavily in debt and blameworthy might legitimately be sold into slavery. Amos does not find fault with the principle—he says nothing about it. But he criticizes severely those who for a paltry debt owed by a person, who has suffered reverses but is without fault or complicity, will seize the man (and his family) and sell them into slavery to satisfy such a trivial amount.

While the other explanations are possible, especially the notion of bribery, this one also deserves consideration.

7. There are numerous difficulties in the text. On the syntax see Meek (1958:128). We derive *haššōʾăpîm* from *šʾp* II, "to crush, trample," as in several other passages in the OT, cf. Amos 8:4; Pss 56:2(El), 3(E2); 57:4(E3). The verb *šʾp* I, "pant" (KJV, RV) has been taken as a colorful description of avarice, "They begrudged him the very dust, which is sign and token of his poverty and misery, he had placed on his head" (Laetsch

1956:13). The verb *š'p* I describes the quickening of breathing under various stimuli: a woman in labor (Isa 42:14); a wild ass, thirsty (Jer 14:6) or sexually aroused (Jer 2:24); an athlete (Eccl 1:5) longing for various things (Job 5:5, 7:2, 36:20). Beek (1948:135) lists Ezek 36:3; Amos 2:7, 8:4; Pss 56:2–3(El–2), 57:4(E3) here as well ("the eagerness of the enemy for his opponent"), but these passages are generally translated "trample" (RSV). Such meanings make it hard to distinguish between *š'p* I and *š'p* II. The problem is complicated by the existence of *šwp,* "bruise (by trampling)," as in Gen 3:15.

Since Wellhausen it has been common to argue that the participle *šāpîm* acquired *alef* as *mater lectionis* (Deist 1978:44) and was subsequently identified incorrectly with the root *š'p.* By the nature of the argument, it is impossible to say with any confidence that this sequence of changes actually occurred in any particular case. Only the attestation of *špym* in a Hebrew text could make the variant reading viable; retrojection from the LXX *patounta* is not enough, for this could be an interpretation of the MT.

It is true that the use of *alef* as a *mater lectionis* for spelling long *ā* intrudes slightly into the orthography of the MT as a late Aramaic influence, especially at the end of words. Even in Aramaic its use for a word-medial long *ā,* when *alef* is not etymological, is restricted (Freedman and Ritterspach 1967). Nevertheless, some examples do occur in the MT: for example, *wq'm* (for *wěqām,* Hos 10:14). The usage was wrongly identified by the LXX translator of the minor prophets in a number of cases where the *alef* is part of the root: for example, *t'šm* (Hos 14:1)—*aphanisthēsetai,* "to be utterly destroyed," as if from *šmm.* It is less likely that the LXX *Vorlage* read *tšm* (*tiššōm* or *tēšam*), that this form is original, and that the MT results from a scribe who pronounced the word *tāšōm* and fixed that pronunciation with the aid of *alef.* There are several places in the LXX where a *prima alef* root has been read as if the *alef* had been dropped in its Hebrew *Vorlage* (*y'spw* [Hos 4:3], *y'šm* [Hos 13:1, root *šym*], *yšmw* [Hos 5:15, 10:2; cf. 14:1; Joel 1:18, root *šmm*], *yqr'hw* [Hos 11:7, root *yqr*]); but it is also possible that the LXX *Vorlage* was the same as the MT's and that the translator read the *alef* as a *mater lectionis.* For examples of omission of etymological *alef* in the MT see Andersen and Forbes 1986. Amos 2:6 is not quite the same, because *šp* and *š'p* II seem to be variants of the same root.

Accepting that *š'p* does not mean "pant after" the dust of the earth (RV) but rather "trample," "the head of the poor" is a more suitable object, "they grind the heads of the poor into the earth" (NEB). But, no matter what meaning is given to *š'p,* the rest of the clause is cumbersome and its length quite disproportionate by comparison to the next line (v 7aB).

It is difficult to construe both prepositional phrases with the single verb. The problem is resolved in NIV by making the first a simile,

> They trample on the heads of the poor
> as upon the dust of the ground.

A simpler expedient is to regard the reading as a conflation of alternatives, "panting after the dust of the earth" or "trampling on the head of the poor." It is usual to delete the first phrase. But the LXX attests it, and has an additional verb:

> Those trampling upon the dust of the earth,
> And they strike [with the fist] the heads of the poor.

Because the LXX can take the liberty of paraphrase, the second verb is doubtless the translator's remedy for the difficulties in the MT that we still face. He has done the same thing in Mal 3:5. There a list of miscreants has been expanded by breaking up the phrase "hireling, widow and orphan"— [*kai epi tous aposterountas misthon*] *misthōtou* [*kai tous katadynasteontas*] *chēran* [*kai tous kondylizontas*] *orphanous* "and against them that keep back the *hirelings* wages, and them that oppress the *widow*, and afflict *orphans.*" In neither place does *kondylizō* match anything in the MT, so it would be unwarranted to use the LXX to recover a Hebrew variant by retroversion. Even so, the LXX interpretation does help by indicating that each phrase can be taken as an object. The term *ʿăpar-ʾereṣ* seems to match the *ʿanwê-ʾereṣ* of other texts (Isa 11:4; Ps 76:10[E9]).

In contrast to the wordiness of 2:7a, 8:4 is as brief as can be: "they trample the poor." Note the parallels:

2:7a	*ʿal-ʿăpar-ʾereṣ*	//	*běrōʾš dallîm*
	upon the dust of the earth	//	the head of the destitute
8:4	*ʾebyôn*	//	*ʿăniwwê-ʾareṣ*
	the poor	//	wretched of the earth

This connection suggests an equivalence of *ʿpr* with *ʿnw,* expressions for the lowly, those in the dust. Dust is of course the essential material of the human body (Gen 2:7, 3:19, etc.), and remembering this fact is a feature of divine compassion (Ps 103:15[E14]). It can be used figuratively of human beings ("the dust of Jacob" [Num 23:10]) and as a mark of humility or lowliness (Gen 18:27). (See Rainey 1974.)

In summary, the problems of v 7a can be solved in any of four ways: first, by deleting the first phrase (JB); next, by taking it as simile (NIV); third, by taking it as an object, with a second object in apposition. Finally, the simplest solution is to accept the complete clause, recognizing the first prepositional phrase as locative, the second as the object. This reading does more justice to the prepositions. The preposition *b-* is sometimes deleted, but

Wolff (1977:133) defends its accusative function ("against") with verbs of assault. There is a clash, however, between the singular "head" and the plural "poor." In view of 8:4, the proper object of *hš'pym* is *dlym* (//*'bywn*); *br'ṣ* is then another adverbial phrase (*r'ṣ* has this meaning without a preposition in Gen 3:15).

The accumulation of phrases brings out the deliberately malicious treatment of these unfortunates, who are not only denied justice, but treated with physical abuse and bodily harm. They smash them on the head, they shove them off the street and trample them in the dust.

7a. *push.* Verse 7aB is to be interpreted in the light of 5:12; Job 24:4; Isa 10:2 and 29:21:

2:7	*wdrk 'nwym yṭw*	and they push the humble out of the way
5:12	*w'bywnym bš'r hṭw*	who thrust the poor from the gate
Job 24:4	*yṭw 'bywnym mdrk* (//*'ăniyyê-'areṣ*)	they thrust the poor out of the road (//the wretched of the earth)
Isa 10:2	*lhṭwt mdyn dlym*	to turn aside the needy from justice
Isa 29:21	*wyṭw bthw ṣdyq*	and they thrust aside into the wasteland the righteous

While the action could be no more than pushing someone out of the way (cf. Num 22:23), the expression usually occurs in longer lists of accusations. Compare Job 24:1–4 with Mal 3:5, both of which involve defrauding people and depriving them of legal redress. The nouns that are the object of *hṭh* in these passages confirm our analysis of v 6b and identify the *righteous* poor, that is, those who are destitute through injustice. If the adverbs are equally interchangeable, the series *mdyn, bš'r, mdrk* shows that these poor people, who have a legitimate case (= *bĕrîbô* in Exod 23:6), are driven out of the place of judgment—"the gate." So in Amos 2:7 and Job 24:4 the *drk* is *drk hš'r*, where Absalom stood (2 Sam 15:2) as judge. We conclude that *'nwym* is the object and *drk* is adverbial, but without the usual preposition "from." Compare *wĕligzōl mišpaṭ 'ăniyyê-'ammî* (Isa 10:2), which is interpreted (RSV—"and to rob the poor of my people of their right") as if *mišpāṭ* were an adverb; but in Exod 23:6 *mišpāṭ* is the object of this verb.

It is not clear whether *hṭh* describes the wrongful physical ejection of a litigant from the courts or is a figure for the deflection of justice through partiality (Deut 16:19, Prov 17:23—the term *'rh* here suggests that *drk* in Job 24:4 and Amos 2:7 could be short for "the way of justice") or bribery (Prov 18:5; 1 Sam 8:3); compare the parallel "twist" in Isa 29:21.

To sum up, the object of the verb can be either a person, or the *mišpāṭ* of a person (Deut 24:17; 27:19), or simply *mišpāṭ* (Deut 16:19). *Rîb, dābār, dîn,* and *mišpaṭ* can also be present adverbially, with or without the preposition *b-* or *min.* Locatives *(b)šʿr, (m)drk* are also found. Warnings against this kind of corruption are made so frequently that the terms can be used laconically with all of their associations still present.

The procedures for perverting the course of justice are described in Isa 29:21:

maḥăṭîʾê ʾādām bĕdābār	who pronounce guilty the person with a word,
wĕlammôkiaḥ baššaʿar yĕqōšûn	and for the one who reproves in the gate they lay a snare,
wayyaṭṭû battōhû ṣaddîq	and they thrust aside into the wasteland the righteous.

This passage is to be compared with Amos 5:10 and 12, where we find closely related terms and behavior:

10a	*sānĕʾû baššaʿar môkîaḥ*
	They hate in the gate the reprover
b	*wĕdōbēr tāmîm yĕtāʿēbû*
	and the one who speaks truth they abhor.
12bA	*ṣōrĕrê ṣaddîq*
	those who harass the upright
	loqĕḥê kōper
	those who hold them for ransom,
	wĕʾebyônîm baššaʿar hiṭṭû
	and they the poor from the gate thrust.

The repetition of verbs and nouns shows that Isaiah has in mind much the same situation as Amos. As we argue in the passage Amos 5:10–12, the one who reproves in the gate must be the prophet himself or the prophets as a class. The parallel in Amos 5:10 is "the one who speaks truth," an apt designation of the prophet. Similarly we must interpret *ʾādām bĕdābār,* "the man with the [his] word" as another designation of the reprover in the gate, or the prophet. "The word" in this case is the word of Yahweh.

Both Amos and Isaiah use the verb *nṭh* in the *hipʿil* to describe the maltreatment of others. Amos in 5:12 and 2:7 speaks of thrusting the poor/afflicted out of the gate/road, while Isaiah (29:21) criticizes the same leaders for abusing the righteous. There is no significant difference, however, for both prophets link the righteous with the poor, and they are complementary and overlapping terms (cf. Amos 2:6–7 and 5:12). Hence *bthw* is to be understood as the counterpart or opposite of *bš'r*, that is to say, they thrust them away from the city gate into the terrifying wasteland outside the bounds of city or civilization.

7b. *a man and his father*. This simple phrase remains obscure. Already the LXX reflects an interpretation that has become conventional. It translates *'îš* as *huios*, an obvious correlate of "father" ("Father and son" [NIV, NEB]), and adds "to the *same* girl." Even though the verb is "walk," not "go," the connotations of the latter for sexual intercourse are assumed. If the sin lies in the identity of "the girl," then the question is whether she is a (cult) prostitute or *"the* goddess." Any such activity could be branded as profanation, so v 7bB does not resolve the issue.

The reference to the culprits as "a man and his father" is the opposite of the expected "father and son" and suggests that *'îš* is used here with its distributive meaning "each." Not just two men, but everybody is doing it. If incest was in mind, it would have been easy to say that a man had intercourse with his father's wife (cf. Lev 20:11). The verb "walk" suggests religious pilgrimage, resort to a shrine.

If *'îš* is distributive, we would expect "everybody" to be *'îš werē'ēhû* or *'îš we'āḥîw*. Hence *'îš we'ābîw* is distributive in time (cf. *hēmmâ we'ābōtêhem*— Deut 13:7, 28:36). They have been doing it for generations.

the Girl. The article points to a specific and well-known personage. Verse 8 connects the unjust acquisition of garments and wine with an altar and a shrine—"their god," so not a Yahweh temple. Verse 8:14 introduces a female deity called *'ašmat šōmĕrôn*. The geographical references given there suggest a popular and widespread cult, all the way from Dan to Beer-sheba. The noun *na'ărâ* has a range of associations but is characteristically used of a nubile woman—eligible (Genesis 24, 34), betrothed (Deuteronomy 22), widowed (Ruth), a concubine (Esther, Judges 19, 1 Kings 1), a slave (2 Kgs 5:2–4); cf. Barstad 1984. In the series *ṣaddîq, 'ebyôn, dallîm, 'ănāwîm, ḥăbûlîm, 'ănûšîm, na'ărâ* (makes seven) could be a slave girl, sexually exploited. The fact that this noun alone has the article could suggest that one well-known "girl" needing no further identification is in mind.

There is no biblical occurrence in which "the girl" is a prostitute. Identification as a cult prostitute because of the background in v 8 is possible. (Compare Herodotus's description of Babylon, *History* 1.199, and the *Code of Hammurapi,* lines 178–182. See also Cutler and MacDonald 1982:35.) There are several connections between 2:6–8 and chap. 8: 2:6b and 8:6a; 2:7a and 8:4; 2:7b–8 and 8:14. The expression "in that day" (2:16; 8:13) also links 2:14–16 with 8:13–14 as aspects of the same destructive judgment on the same people for the same sins. For a start, 2:6–8 is focused on the northern kingdom; 8:14 shows that the same thing is happening all over the country. Possibly oaths could be sworn by these gods in any location, but the greatest solemnity and force would be secured if the act were performed in front of a statue in a shrine. "The house of their god" (v 8b) points to such a building, and "every altar" suggests a multitude of such installations.

so as to. The use of the preposition *lĕmaʿan,* "so as to," implies witting and willful intention. Weaker translations have "and thereby" (NJPS), "and so" (NIV).

desecrate. Verbs based on *ḥll* refer to pollution through violation of various moral laws and ritual taboos. They often describe defilement of sacred precincts by bringing in some forbidden object or person, or by violating any covenant rule. Not only objects—the land, the shrine, the altar—can be "profaned" by such actions, but also God's name and even God himself (Ezek 22:16, 26). Because such profanation can result from so many different things, the outcome does not help us to find out what the man and his father are doing with "the Girl."

holy. The LXX reading is "the name of their God," contamination from v 8.

Actions described as profaning God's holy name include reneging on an oath sworn in his name (Lev 19:12; Jer 34:16), sacrificing children to *mōlek* (Lev 18:21, 20:3) or idolatry (Ezek 20:39, 36:20–23). (See Weinfeld 1972.)

In Leviticus 21 the term covers actions forbidden to priests (including the code of sexual taboos), and Lev 22:2 forbids the use of "the holy things of the people of Israel, which they dedicate to me." This definition suggests that the *yyn ʿnwšym* could be legitimate temple dues, misappropriated or misused by the priests, like the behavior of Eli's sons (1 Samuel 2), who were "blaspheming God" (1 Sam 3:13).

8a. *And because.* We take *ʿal* as a conjunction (cf. *ʿal ʾăšer,* Deut 29:24[E25]) rather than a preposition, in parallel with *ʿal mikrām* in v 6; see also Gen 31:20; Ps 119:136.

spread. There is a play on the word *yaṭṭû,* already used in v 7; but it is hard to see how it can have the same meaning in each occurrence. The different object requires the meaning "spread" in v 8, but the *qal* is commonly used for hanging a curtain or pitching a tent. The connection is found in the fact that the garments used in v 8 are the property of the poor who were deprived of justice in v 7a.

garments. As often happens, the poor of Israel (v 7) have fallen from destitution into debt, from which there is no feasible recovery. In the end, a person's last remaining asset would be his *beged* or *śimlâ,* a cloak by day and a blanket at night. It was forbidden to take a widow's *beged* as a pledge (Deut 24:17).

According to Exod 22:25–26(E26–27), when a person raises a loan on his clothing, the garment was taken into pawn only as a formality. It was to be given back to the owner at nightfall so that he would have something to sleep in. Compare the plights of the poor citizen of Nippur and of the reaper of the Meṣad Hashavyahu inscription; cf. Job 22:6; Prov 20:16, 27:13.

pledged. The parallelism within v 8 invites comparison of *bgdym ḥblym* with *yyn ʿnwšym.* The NIV translation (cf. the NEB) brings the two participles into line:

> garments taken in pledge//wine taken as fine

The root *ḥbl* generally means "bind," but in this context "distrain." While the pretext for seizure was doubtless security for a loan or foreclosure on an unpayable debt, the use of *gzl, pšṭ* or *lqḥ* as a parallel (Deut 24:17; Isa 10:2; Job 24:9; Prov 20:16, 27:13) brands the action as robbery with violence. See Job 22:6, where "the garments of the naked" matches *bgdy(m) ḥblym* of Amos 2:7:

kî-taḥbōl ʾaḥeykā ḥinnām	For you have exacted pledges of your brothers for nothing,
ûbigdê ʿărûmmîm tapšîṭ	and stripped the naked of their clothing.

A vital piece of legislation forbids reducing widow and orphan to destitution (Exod 22:21–26[E22–27]). Much of its language is used in Job 24:1–12. The use of the same vocabulary by Amos illustrates his point that they have rejected the *tōrâ* (v 4). The threatened punishment, "your wives will be widows and your children orphans" (Exod 22:23[E24]), is the basis for Amos 7:17.

The discord in number makes it impossible to take *ʿnwšym* as an attributive modifier of *yyn.* It is simpler to take both participles as references to the victims, who have been both pledged and fined. If the phrases are also congruous in syntax, *bgdym* and *yyn* are both constructs, the former with enclitic *mem.* If the persons are pledged, they could be family members handed over into debt slavery, who are then deprived of their clothing.

One wonders, however, if people who have fallen to that level of destitution would have cloaks of sufficient quality to be used by the luxury-loving exploiters condemned by Amos (6:4–6). It is hard to take the details literally, even though commentators have found the effects colorful. The language is probably elliptical. In the shrines they are using fabrics and wine, both symbols of indulgence, acquired by fraudulent loans and unjust fines. If the sources of the mulct had been real criminals, there would have been nothing wrong with lodging the fines in the shrine. The fact that temples had been enriched shows that the priests were the beneficiaries of collusion with merchants and magistrates in the social injustices condemned by Amos.

every altar. a. It was happening all over, at the shrines listed in 4:4, 5:5, and 8:14. Some modern scholars have concluded that Amos did not locate these injustices in the shrines. The phrases "beside every altar, and in the house of their god(s)," originally a single expression, were added to the text by way of commentary. Their arguments are partly based on the observation that the two clauses in v 8 are far too long to be lines of poetry. Verse 7bB is likewise considered to be an addition in the same vein (Wolff 1977:133–34). Such criticism begs several questions. To judge from the book as a whole, Amos did not compose his oracles in accordance with the rules of lyrical or epic or cult poetry. And we cannot say that his targets were the secular institutions and leaders, omitting the temples and their priests.

every altar. b. The LXX refers to only one altar, but its paraphrase bears little resemblance to the MT: "and joining their garments together with cords, they make curtains protecting the altar."

8b. *fined.* The root *ʿnš* can mean "to punish" in a legitimate sense (Deut 22:19). In 2 Kgs 23:33 (2 Chr 36:3) it refers to an indemnity placed on the land by Pharaoh. Other occurrences (Exod 21:22; Prov 17:26, 21:11, 22:3, 27:12) are not specific enough to permit exact denotation. Deuteronomy 22:19 (the fine of a rapist) suggests payment of damages in money. Amos 2:8 then means payment in kind. Amos does not indicate whether the act was sinful because such wine should not be drunk in the shrine or whether the fine was unjust (Prov 17:26).

their God. In view of the links with 8:14, the plural "gods" could be read in both places, the gods being *ʾšmh* and *drk.* If "the house of their God" is one of the Yahweh temples (Dan, Bethel, or one of the other shrines mentioned by Amos), why does he distance himself in this way by saying "their"? The series "so as to profane my holy name," "beside every altar," and "in the house of their God" marks a change of focus from law court (vv 6–7) to shrine. This shift suggested to Beek (1948:137) that a set of secondary religious offenses followed the judicial offenses.

COMMENT

In spite of the several concrete details, the exact nature of Israel's "act(s) of rebellion" remains undetermined. Although the whole nation is at risk, the fault clearly lies with only a section of the people. Their loci can be discerned:

1. the markets where people are sold (v 6b);
2. the assemblies where loans are certified (v 8a);

3. the courts where fines are paid (v 8b);
4. the shrines with their altars (v 8).

The locations of the acts described in v 7 are less clear. Verse 7a probably
goes with v 6b, and would also fit in with v 8a if those reduced to destitution (v 6b) fail to obtain redress in the courts (v 7a) so that their garments
are retained (v 8a). The fact that such a garment finishes up beside an altar
identifies the priests as the culprits, or at least as accessories. They are not
named, but the reference to the shrine in v 8b and threats against the shrine
and altars (note the plural!) of Bethel elsewhere (3:14, 4:4, 7:9, 9:1) show
that the cultus is one of the prime targets. Amos 5:10–13 shows that the
magistrates must have been part of the conspiracy; injustices such as those
itemized in 2:6–8, blatant violations of well-established rules (*tôrâ* [2:4b]),
could only occur if the judges had been corrupted.

It is possible to analyze 2:4 into three crimes of Judah, and 2:6–8 into
four crimes of Israel, seven in all; but from another view these crimes are
only aspects and specimens of general and total corruption. The climactic
lines (2:4bB, 7bB, and 8bB) point to apostasy, not in fringe groups and
underground paganism, but in official prophets and priests.

Each of the preceding seven oracles ends with a threat to send fire. There
is no similar ending to the eighth oracle against Israel. That oracle takes a
different turn with vv 9–12. From the form-critical point of view it introduces a new genre, historical recital, with covenant associations. While
it is still rhythmic and some quite good bicolons can be found in it, it is
much more like prose than the highly formulaic material in 1:3–2:8.

It makes more use of "prose particles" than any section we have met so
far. Yet vv 9–12 stand out from the rest in this respect partly because the
piece itself is longer than any unit in 1:3–2:8. The eight oracles are not
lacking in "prose particles." They are found in some quite important lines,
for example:

> 1:3b, which has no parallelism, no discernible meter, along with
> one *'t* (true prose particle) and two examples of *h-;*
> 1:6b, which has no parallelism and no meter;
> 1:9b, the same problem, though there is a balancing clause,
> which, however, is not parallel to it;
> 1:13b, no parallelism and no meter; it also has *'t* (one example)
> and one *h-,* and is simply not poetic;
> 2:1b, again no parallelism and no meter;
> 2:4b, there is some parallelism and possible meter, but examples
> of *'t* (one) and *'šr* (one) point strongly in the direction of
> prose;

> 2:7b, once again there is no parallelism and no meter; there is an example of 't and one of *h-*.

In the clauses just given, we have all of the examples of 't and 'šr in the whole passage. It will be noted that in every case the passage cited constitutes the whole or part of the indictment or charges against the culprit nation. To excise these passages on the grounds that they are prosaic, which admittedly they are, would leave the unit incomplete. Neither would it improve matters merely to delete the prose particles. It would be necessary to substitute something quite different. Such a procedure seems to us to be unjustifiable. We must recognize that at least in the book of Amos and no doubt elsewhere oracular utterance has this character: it seems that the incorporation of prose lines in poetic structures is part of the prophet's technique. Perhaps the insertion of the plain prose sentence in the midst of a poetic oracle had a shock effect. We repeat that in every case the statement constitutes the whole or an integral part of the indictment, and that in five of the seven cases there would be no indictment without it. In the other cases excision would be almost as harmful. Nevertheless the next section, vv 9–13, is quite different in character, being a complete unit in itself and more like prose, though there are many features that we commonly associate with poetry, such as parallelism, chiasm, unusual figures of speech, and the like.

If each of the eight oracles was delivered separately before being worked up into the Great Set Speech now in the book, it is possible that the one against Israel was originally like the others, ending with the threat to send fire. But we should point out that the repeated formulas have their effect only when all of the oracles are joined together. The different direction taken by the Israel oracle at the end achieves precisely the literary effect of not closing off the set of eight, but making it an integral and continuous part of the larger book.

I.B. ORACLES AGAINST THE WHOLE OF ISRAEL (2:9–3:8)

I.B.1. HISTORICAL RECITAL AND THREAT (2:9–16)

I.B.1.a. YAHWEH'S GRACIOUS ACTS (2:9–11)

2:9a   As for me, I destroyed the Amorite before them,
        whose height was like the height of cedars,
        and he was as powerful as oak trees;
 9b   and I destroyed his fruit from above,
        and his roots from beneath.
10a   And as for me, I brought you up from the land of Egypt,
10b   and I led you in the wilderness for forty years,
        so that you could take possession of the land of the
        Amorite.
11a   And I raised up some of your sons to be prophets,
        and some of your choice young men to be nazirites.
11b   Isn't that actually so, you Israelites?
                The solemn declaration of Yahweh!

I.B.1.b. THE PRESENT SITUATION (2:12)

12a   And you made the nazirites drink wine,
12b   and against the prophets you gave commands,
        saying, "You shall not prophesy!"

INTRODUCTION

The prophecy develops and unfolds in various new ways; and Israel remains the main target for the rest of the book. The historical perspective of vv 9–12 makes it clear that the whole nation is in the prophet's mind. Even when the northern kingdom is being addressed, Judah is not left out.

Whereas the complaints against the six surrounding nations are restricted to one conspicuous crime each and the indictment of Judah proceeds in rather general terms, the charge against Israel grows into a long list, which continues through chap. 8. Social injustice and religious apostasy head the list (vv 6–8). Ungrateful forgetfulness of Yahweh's goodness in the past culminates in rejection and refusal, and finally to suppression of prophecy (v 12). Judah's case is essentially the same, though stated more briefly. The sins of the entire nation are twofold: first, in rejecting the *torah* (v 4), which leads to the evils of vv 6–8; second, in silencing the prophets who called them to repent. For the first sin there could be forgiveness. But when the offer of forgiveness is refused, nothing more can be done. Yahweh has reached his limit (v 13). In vv 14–16 there is a sudden shift to the eschatological denouement, the final military defeat "in that day."

Verses 9–12 offer additional charges against Israel, but within a framework of traditional covenantal statements about the relations between Yahweh and his people and a brief account of the divine intervention and gracious acts in their behalf. The Exodus, the Settlement, and the divine provision of prophets and nazirites are all listed, though the order of the first two is reversed, no doubt deliberately and for special effect. The emphasis in vv 9–12 is on the Israelite mistreatment of prophets and nazirites sent to them by God, which symbolizes the nation's resistance to the will and word of God, its failure to respond to those mighty acts of grace and condescension by which God created and sustained the whole people. The unit leads to an extraordinary picture of God suffering under the burden of his people, like a cart that labors and creaks under a full load of sheaves (v 13).

The historical recital in vv 9–11 is reminiscent of the traditional prologue to covenantal formulations. It serves several purposes. As in the original Sinai covenant, the story of Yahweh's dealings with Israel up to that point provides grounds for his claims on their love and loyalty. It also vindicates God, for it proves his steadfastness in the agreement, especially when the account is brought up to date with the reminder that through nazirites and prophets he continued to deal faithfully with them. Their continued occupation of the good land is a further token of divine favor.

The central creed of the Bethel cult was originally, "This is your God, O Israel [cf. 4:12], who brought you out of the land of Egypt" (1 Kgs 12:28), and a ritual recitation like that in Amos 2:9–11 doubtless continued at national assemblies and festivals at that shrine up to his day (cf. 3:1–2).

But there was more than history and reminiscence in such recital. It could serve to renew the covenant, provided the people reaffirmed their adherence, with reformation if necessary (Joshua 24). Otherwise the review could serve as preamble to an indictment, a covenant *rîb*, followed by release of the curses (4:6–11) threatened against violations (*pěšā'îm*, as in the eight preceding oracles) of the covenant.

The continuation of the charge against Israel (including Judah) consists of two parts:

1. Yahweh's gracious acts (2:9–11);
2. the present situation—Israel's response and the threatened calamity (2:12–16).

The first part consists of two subdivisions, each introduced by *wě'ānōkî* and followed by a *hip'îl* form of the verb in the perfect tense (vv 9a and 10a). These verbal forms are then balanced by a *hip'îl* form of the same or related verb in the imperfect tense with *waw*-consecutive (9b and 10b). There are minor differences in structure between 9 and 10 (9aB has a relative clause, while 10bB is an infinitive construction), but the pattern is essentially the same. The second subdivision (vv 10–11) is expanded, however, by a second clause introduced by the *hip'îl* form of the verb in the imperfect tense with *waw*-consecutive (v 11a), and a concluding question that sums up the unit. The break is marked by the phrase, "The solemn declaration of Yahweh." Thus we have the following structure: (1) v 9, the destruction of the Amorites; and (2) vv 10–11, the deliverance from Egypt and guidance through the wilderness (v 10); the raising up of prophets and nazirites (v 11).

The second part falls naturally into two subdivisions: (1) vv 12–13; (2) vv 14–16. The first is clearly transitional, picking up the theme of v 11 but specifying Israel's response to Yahweh's action. The pattern in v 13, beginning *hinnēh 'ānōkî* and followed by a *hip'îl* participle, is similar to that of vv 9 and 10 and suggests a possible continuity with the preceding section. Nevertheless, because of the shift in subject in v 12, and in the time and tense of v 13, it is better to separate these verses and regard them as a bridge to the conclusion in vv 14–16. It is because of Israel's negative response to the nazirites and prophets sent by him that Yahweh has reached the end of his patience and endurance (v 13). The final defeat of Israel (along with or immediately after that of the other nations) will follow. Thus the first subdivision consists of two couplets of approximately equal length: v 12, the response of Israel; v 13, the present reaction and mood of the deity. The second subdivision consists of an account of the fate of the various military personnel in the final disaster. It may be analyzed as follows: (1) v 14, a tricolon listing three classes of soldiers; (2) vv 15–16, a complementary list of four classes of military personnel, which may be further divided: (a) v 15, a tricolon specifying three branches of the military; and (b) v 16, a bicolon identifying the seventh and final category (a special one), with a concluding notice.

NOTES

2:9–10. The autobiographical form (cf. Josh 24:2–13) lends pathos to the recital, and the concluding question (v 11b) gives it passion. Unlike Hosea, who makes considerable use of patriarchal traditions, Amos begins with the Exodus. He does not even highlight the Sinai events, or the role of Moses (except as the latter may be in mind as the first in the long line of prophets).

The emphasis is entirely on the extermination of the Amorites and the installation of Israel in the land (vv 9, 10bB—six lines). The briefest possible account of the escape from Egypt and the desert journey (v 10a–10bA—two lines) has been inserted into this conquest account, just before the last line (v 10bB), highlighting its function as an inclusion with v 9aA.

These two lines describing the Exodus and wilderness phase have attracted suspicion for four reasons: (1) they present the events out of chronological order; (2) they are prosaic and longer than the more poetic lines that describe the eviction of the Amorites; (3) the grammatical number changes; and (4) their language is Deuteronomistic. None of these observations is strong enough to warrant the deletion of these two lines as a later scribal addition; or, less drastically, to accept them as the words of Amos but to move them in front of verse 9 to secure the correct chronological sequence.

1. If v 10a has been dislodged from its original position before v 9 as the first moment of the story, the explanation could be that both verses begin with $wĕ'ānōkî$. But the present sequence is not only satisfactory; it achieves a special effect. It is not uncommon for a narrator to work backward from the present when reviewing the past. This sequence is found not only in the Bible but also generally in the ancient Near East, in visual, as well as verbal, art. In the present case, the spotlight is on the purpose and goal of the Exodus and journey, and on the present condition of the people. The backward sequence of the verbs $'ašmîd$ and $he'ĕlêtî$ in 2:9–10 prepares for the chiastic sequence $he'ĕlêtî$ . . . $wĕhišmadtî$ (and $hašmêd$ $'ašmîd$) in 9:7–8, with the telling point that just as the Amorites were destroyed for

defiling the Lord's land (Gen 15:16), so Israel will be destroyed for the same reason.

2. The argument that v 10a–bA is an intrusion of prose into poetry has little weight as a test of authenticity. This kind of thing happens throughout the entire book, as we have already seen in the oracles against the nations. The use of the *nota accusativi* (twice) and *waw*-consecutive identifies the *language* as that of normal prose, but poetry is first a matter of *form*. Whether construed as two lines (5 : 5) or as four lines (3 : 2 :: 3 : 2), the rhythms are good, even though the parallelism is not the usual synonyms in bicolons.

3. The change in grammatical number is inconsequential. It happens frequently (e.g., 4:1–3), and often the literary integrity of the whole piece is so patent that critics are more prone to normalize the pronouns than to excise the deviant. We do not think that either of these expedients is a convincing solution except in the trivial sense of removing the evidence that is seen as a problem. It happens so often that it is better to accept such changes of pronominal person within discourse as acceptable in Hebrew composition.

4. As for Deuteronomic language, the statistical odds are too long to permit a statement of ten words to be diagnosed as the distinctive and exclusive utterance of one author or school, unless it can be identified as an exact quotation of quite original or at least highly idiosyncratic and original combinations of words. Such a result can be made more plausible if at the same time it can be shown that the expressions (vocabulary, syntax, style) are quite different from those usually employed by the author in whose work the suspected statement is now found.

It can hardly be claimed that v 10a–bB could not have been said by Amos. As we have already pointed out, the same operational verbs are used again in 9:7–8, and, although these verses are sometimes assigned to Amos' disciples (Wolff 1977:348), other vocabulary, such as "house of Jacob," is hardly Deuteronomic. Even the claim that the traditional language of v 10a–bB is Deuteronomic is exaggerated. Here we will mention only one detail. The verb *hʿlh*, "bring up," describes the Exodus only once in Deuteronomy (20:1); it prefers *hwṣyʾ*, "bring out" (twenty times). See also the NOTES on v 10.

Yet even if it could be shown that v 10 contains Deuteronomic language and is dependent on Deuteronomic traditions, this fact would not prove that it was added later to the book by a Deuteronomistic editor. There are sufficient indications that the eighth-century prophets knew and used Deuteronomic traditions as if they could count on their recognition by their audiences. Whether any of these traditional materials was already written before the seventh century is quite a different matter, and not germane. It would be gratuitous to declare that Deuteronomic traditions did not exist in any form before the seventh century, and therefore that Amos could not have known and used them in the eighth century. It is also possible, given a late date for Deuteronomy, that Amos and other prophets were the originators of some of the prophetic content (Krause 1932:221–39).

9a. *as for me.* The repeated pronouns and the first-person verbs underscore the vital fact that it was entirely the Lord's own personal achievement. All secondary causes and agencies are kept out of view.

destroyed. This verb, used twice here, describes violent and complete destruction. The point is driven home by the repetition in v 9b. While used in Deuteronomy (2:21), it seems to be pre-Deuteronomic (Josh 24:8). It is associated with the Amorite tradition (Deut 31:4).

the Amorite. This term is used in so many ways that it is impossible to tell which tradition Amos has in mind. As an ethnic group (an eastern branch of West Semitic peoples), the Amorites have a history extending over the entire ancient Near East, ranging from Lower Mesopotamia from the Ur III period onward (Buccellati 1966), with strong development in Upper Mesopotamia (Mari) in the Middle Bronze Age, and a kingdom in Syria in the Late Bronze Age (Ugaritic and Amarna texts). Biblical notices are mixed. Amorites are affiliated with Canaanites (Gen 10:15–16) and are sometimes listed as one of the (seven) traditional pre-Israelite occupants of the Promised Land (Gen 15:19–20; Exod 3:8); and sometimes the word is used as a generic term for all of the previous inhabitants of the land of Israel (Gen 15:16). More specifically two Amorite kingdoms, Heshbon and Bashan, are located in northern Transjordan (Josh 2:10, 9:10, 24:8; Judg 10:8, 11:19–23), and here the traditions emphasize their replacement by Israelites as an act of God, in line with Amos' thought. Another tradition locates Amorites in the hilly territory centered on Hebron (Josh 10:5) and to the south of the region allotted to Judah (Deut 1:19, 27, 44). They are not explicitly connected with the territory occupied by the kingdom of Israel in Amos' day, another indication that he has the whole nation in mind in vv 9–12.

height . . . powerful. The parallelism in this bicolon is well developed, but it is not quite symmetrical. The noun "height" is followed by an adjective *ḥāsōn,* which requires the free pronoun as subject. The MT is asymmetrical in another way, too. The preposition *k-* permits an article to be supplied to "oaks," but "cedars" lacks the article, as befits a poetic image. The grammatical point is worth making, for the Masoretes were doubtless correct in taking the nouns as definite; but they did not venture to add the obvious *hā-* to *'ărāzîm.* The contrast is all the more impressive when we note that this poetic phrase, *kgbh 'rzym,* follows immediately *'et, hā-,* and *'ăšer,* as if the language were prose.

The simile is somewhat of a cliché, and these are fabulous trees, usually located in a mythic Lebanon. The description calls to mind "a people great and tall" (ʿam-gādôl wārām), the Anaqim (Deut 9:2), also rather mythic giants, located in the region of Hebron (Josh 15:14). Deuteronomy 3:11 indicates a tradition that the Transjordan Amorites were tall. The tradition that reached Amos has blended the Anaqim and Amorites and lost the geographical restriction.

9b. *fruit . . . roots.* The sense is "I totally destroyed them." Compare the English idiom "root and branch"; hence "from the top of the tree with its fruits to the bottom with its roots."

from above. Paralleled by "from beneath." These adverbs do not indicate the direction of an action but the location of the object. This usage is illustrated by the expression in Deut 4:39; Josh 2:11; and 1 Kgs 8:23:

baššāmayim mimmaʿal	in the sky above,
wĕʿal-hāʾāreṣ mittaḥat,	and on the earth below.

Compare with Job 18:16:

mittaḥat šorāšāyw yībāšû	his roots dry up beneath,
ûmimmaʿal yimmal qĕṣîrô	and his branches wither above.

The image itself is a commonplace, a wisdom motif for judgment on the ungodly (Psalm 1; Jer 17:5–8; Isa 40:24). The theme runs through Job (8:16–18, 14:7–9, 15:30–33, 18:16).

10a. *you.* Mays (1969:23) sees in this departure from the third person a clue that Israel is the actual audience of this and, in fact, of all of the oracles. But because God does address Israel in either the third person or the second person (compare 5:1–3), it is possible that in the opening cycle each nation is addressed (indirectly) in turn. The switch to the second person in 2:10 may be due to the use by Amos at this point of traditional material already familiar in the second person, which he incorporates into his oracle without altering that feature.

brought you up. There is an important link among 2:10, 3:1, and 9:7. All state the same premise for Yahweh's judgment against Israel—the classic recital of Israel's election and God's supervening grace. They match the threefold recital of cosmic hymns, combining belief in Yahweh as Creator and Redeemer. The verb *hʿlh* is used in a wide range of sources to describe the Exodus. It is preferred to *hwṣyʾ* in old credal statements (Gen 50:24; Exod 17:3; 32:1, 7, 23; 33:1; Lev 11:45; Num 16:13; Deut 20:1; Josh 24:17; Judg 6:8,13; 1 Sam 10:18; 12:6; 2 Kgs 17:7, 36; Jer 2:6; 16:14; 23:7; Hos 12:14[E13]; Mic 6:4; Amos 3:1; Ps 81:11[E10]; Neh 9:18; 1 Chr 17:5).

led. Deuteronomy 29:4(E5) is the same, except for word order (cf. Deut 8:2, 15). The argument is stretched when such widely used language is declared to be Deuteronomic wherever it is met (Hos 2:16[E14]; Jer 2:6, 17; Ps 136:16); cf. Kuhnigk (1974) on Hosea and Brueggemann (1968).

11–12. Verses 11–12 lead to a specific charge, central to the prophecy. Amos accuses them of subverting two related institutions, supplied by God for their benefit: nazirites and prophets. The unit shows the usual combination of poetic and prosaic language and features. Verse 11a is an unexceptional bicolon, and its parallelism is used again in v 12, in chiasmus. But v 12 is quite unbalanced, and the article and *nota accusativi* identify prose. The long final line does not scan with the rest; yet it ends the unit in a powerful way by saving the most shocking sin of all until last.

These four lines (vv 11a and 12) are interrupted by a question, addressed to the "Israelites," the whole nation (v 11b). It also marks a division between the full recital of what God has done (vv 9–11a) and what Israel did (v 12).

11a. *nazirites.* Nazirites, like prophets, formed a special class of those dedicated to the service of Yahweh. Appropriate vows were taken for life, or more commonly for a limited period of time. The stipulations included abstinence from alcoholic beverages, from cutting the hair, and from contact with corpses. Samson was a nazirite (Judg 13:5, 7; 16:17); apparently Samuel was a nazirite as well as a prophet; cf. 1 Sam 1:11 and the added material in 4QSam[a], which states the matter explicitly (McCarter 1980:53–54). Compare the rules in Num 6:1–21.

The mention of nazirites is completely non-Deuteronomic. The only occurrences of *nzyrm* in Deuteronomic literature, Deuteronomy 33 and Judges 15–16, are independent of the Deuteronomic editor. The only extended discussion of nazirites is in P, but there is no literary link between Amos and Numbers.

The mention of nazirites is unusual, as they are never referred to in any of the other prophetic literature, and the only extensive treatment is in Numbers 6 (P). Aside from Samson and probably Samuel, no historical nazirites are known. The association here of the two groups suggests that the statement originally referred to them as examples of failure on the part of Israel to deal with those whom God had chosen and sent to serve his people. These terms have been utilized here in connection with Amos' own mission as a prophet. There is no suggestion that he was even a temporary nazirite, but it is possible that he combined both callings in one verse to emphasize his own total dedication and the common source of a double commission.

The collocation of nazirites with prophets gives to the latter a distinctive connotation in Amos' mind. The old-time prophets are the true prophets of Yahweh, and Amos does not wish to be labeled *nābîʾ* as the term is now used (7:14). The verb *ʾāqîm* contrasts the charismatics of the olden days with the institutionalized and perhaps hereditary (*ben-nābî* [7:14]) professionals of Amos' time. Samuel is clearly the model, but the succession of Elijah and Elisha is also in mind, and these formidable instruments of the divine will would still be in living memory if we are correct in dating Amos to the first quarter of the eighth century. There was also a military side to the old nazirites, as the case of Samson shows. The early prophets likewise played a vital role as the directors of military operations—Deborah (Judges 4); Samuel (1 Samuel 7, 12); and Elisha (2 Kings 3–6). Samuel could even be listed as a judge (1 Sam 12:11—but the texts fluctuate between Samuel and Samson [McCarter 1980:211]). It was the prophets who determined victory or defeat. More ominously, prophets from Samuel onward would make and break kings. The role of Elisha in terminating the dynasty of Omri (1 Kgs 19:17) was not long before, and it was a political necessity for a king to have an entourage of prophets who would endorse his policies (1 Kings 22; 2 Kgs 3:13). Amos brings prophets and nazirites very close, almost to identification. At least he suggests that the prophets of recent times resemble the nazirites of earlier days, with Samuel overlapping and uniting the two successions. Elijah complained that the true prophets of his time, presumably of his type, had been slain by the sword (1 Kgs 19:10, 14).

choice. The parallelism indicates that it was the choicest of Israel's young men who were raised up to be nazirites, and the cadet prophets were also *baḥûrîm.* The related *bāḥîr* is always used of someone "chosen" by God. *Bāḥûr* is sometimes coordinated with *zāqēn,* so there is a component of "youth." More often (thirteen times) it is coordinated with *bĕtûlâ,* indicating that the choice young men were virgins. The rules for the *nāzîr* in Numbers 6 do not prescribe celibacy; but sexual abstinence was part of a warrior's dedication (1 Sam 21:5–6; 2 Sam 11:11). There were also lifelong nazirite vows, especially with persons chosen or dedicated even before birth (Samson, Samuel, Jeremiah). The stories of Samson and Samuel show that celibacy was not an essential component of this state. Taking a wife could be part of a prophet's calling (Hosea); but marriage could also be forbidden (Jeremiah).

There is no one pattern or norm, but elements of the nazirite vow were clearly optional for prophets. Amos indicates a connection between the two movements, possibly the survival into the ninth century of an identification of the two roles exemplified in Samuel. Elijah and Elisha resemble Samuel in presiding over communities of ecstatic prophets, located in such ancient cult centers as Gilgal and Bethel (2 Kgs 2:1–3). These "sons of prophets" could be married (2 Kgs 4:1). In spite of Elijah's lament (1 Kgs 19:10, 14), these groups were still flourishing at the end of the ninth century. There is no trace of them in the eighth century. The classical prophets are not seen to be operating out of groups like those associated with Samuel and Elijah/Elisha. Indeed, Amos insists that he is not a *ben-nābî.* Amos' anger expressed in v 12 points to a persecution more recent than that under Ahab and Jezebel. Jehoash revered Elisha (2 Kgs 13:14), but the animus of the prophets against his son Jeroboam II and Amaziah's attitude to Amos point to a radical change of policy toward the old-style prophets. Amos clearly knew what to expect when he went to deliver his messages at Bethel, and perhaps at other shrines. He identifies himself with the genuine prophets (3:7) and speaks about their harassment as something recent and current, something central to his indictment of the authorities of his day. Amos regards the corruption of the nazirite communities and the silencing of the prophets as a particularly wicked repudiation of the God of Israel and proof that the judgment will fall with great force on the nation and especially its leaders. There is a desperate as well as a defensive note in 3:3–8, and Amos' *apologia* in 7:14–15 shows that he saw his own call as prophet as an emergency measure on the part of God in view of the suppression of what he considered to be the voice of true prophecy.

12a. *wine.* Several eighth-century prophets connect the abuse of wine with false prophets (Isaiah 28; Mic 2:11; Hos 4:18). Priests were forbidden to use liquor when performing their duties (Lev 10:9). Amos' indictment specifies the abuse of the nazirites in forcing them to drink wine with an implication concerning the prophets, if they took similar vows. There is also an implication, in juxtaposition to v 8, that these persons lacked the dedication of the old nazirites.

12b. *You shall not prophesy!* In our introductory essays we have emphasized the important connections between this charge and the language in 3:8 and 7:10–17. In hindsight, rejection of Yahweh's messenger-prophets was seen as the prime cause of the destruction of Judah by the Babylonians (2 Chr 36:16).

I.B.1.c. A TRANSITIONAL STATEMENT (2:13)

2:13a   Indeed, I am creaking underneath you,
13b   just as the cart that is full of sheaves creaks.

NOTES

2:13. The Psalmist said he was distraught, with inner tumult (*'āhîmâ*) because of "the pressure of the wicked" (*'āqat rāšā'*) (Ps 55:4[E3]). The simple parallelism of *'ôyēb* and *rāšā'* does not warrant the replacement of the *hapax legomenon* *'āqat* by a synonym for *qôl*, "voice," *ṣa'ăqat*, even though the change is minimal. For *ṣa'ăqâ* is the outcry against wrong. The Psalmist experiences anguish, he is agitated with horror; he is suffering from internal pressures as well as external hatred.

If the picture in Amos 2:13 is a cart loaded with sheaves, then the pressure that makes Yahweh groan is the external burden of the people. The spatial reference of the preposition *taḥtêkem* suggests such a picture. But the *hip'il* requires an active meaning for the verb; hence the popularity of the emendation to *mēpîq//tāpûq*, "totter." The use of the article with *'glh* suggests that the image is proverbial. Strictly, *'āmîr* is a swath of newly cut grass; and it requires no change in consonants to read "the heifer who has glutted herself with grass." Some fresh fodder generates gastric gas, which can be very painful, even fatal, if not relieved. The pressure is internal.

13b. *creaks.* The verb *'yq* or *'wq* occurs only here. The meaning is unknown, and this context is the only clue. The simplest approach is to regard both verb and participle as intransitive internal *hip'il*, "groan heavily." Some meaning like "creak, groan, totter, tremble" can be hazarded simply because that is what an overloaded cart might do.

The sense of the simile then would be that Yahweh groans under the burden of Israel, just as a cart groans under the burden of the sheaves that fill it. As v 12 indicates, the breaking point has been reached. The figure should not be pressed unduly, because Yahweh's reaction will naturally be different from that of the cart. But the general idea of Yahweh suffering under the burden of an ungrateful and rebellious people is not unique to Amos. The Pentateuchal stories of the wilderness wanderings emphasize this aspect of the relationship, and the point itself is made by Hosea and Isaiah among Amos' contemporaries (cf. Hos 11:8–9; Isa 1:13–14). Moses, as servant of Yahweh, also complained about bearing the burden of the people (Num 11:14–17; Deut 1:9–12). The image itself may be unusual, but then Yahweh is portrayed in the prophetic literature under a variety of extraordinary, bizarre, and exotic figures.

The preposition *taḥat*, "underneath," confirms the correctness of this picture. The indignity of the language as applied to God is no reason to ignore the preposition completely and to give the verb a different meaning:

"I will crush you as a cart crushes" (NIV); "I will slow your movements" (NJPS).

the cart. The use of the article suggests a gnomic image, as we might expect in a simile of this kind. Because such wisdom sayings often involved animals, it is possible that an *'glh* is a heifer "full" of fresh fodder, which can easily cause painful, even fatal bloating. Compare Elihu's similar comparison (Job 32:18–20), vulgar to our taste, but very effective.

I.B.1.d. THE THREATENED CALAMITY (2:14–16)

2:14a Then flight will fail the swift,
            and the mighty will not prevail through his strength,
    14b   and the warrior will not save his life;
    15a The archer will not survive,
            and the swift of foot will not save himself,
    15b   and the charioteer will not save his life.
    16a Even the most stout-hearted among the warriors
            will run away naked in that day—
                            The solemn declaration of Yahweh!

INTRODUCTION

Once again there is a major shift as the final passage (vv 14–16) begins abruptly with the description of a crushing military defeat and the demolition of an entire army. While no names or designations are given, this unit seems to supply the conclusion to the judgment against Israel; but it could apply to all of the nations listed in the catalog of oracles. The last words of the passage, *bayyôm hahû',* suggest an eschatological component: this is the last battle of all, at least for Israel.

What seems to be missing is not only the divine threat and imminent action but also the early stages of the attack. What follows is the end of the battle, which will then lead to the destruction of the capital city and country, the exile of the people, and the end of the nation. These events correspond to Phase Three of the overall development; so at this point the prophecy anticipates that eventual result. Before the battle, however, we

expect something about Yahweh's response and the preparations and actions leading up to the battle. These elements are to be found distributed
throughout the book, and the reader is invited to pursue this central issue
by reference to those passages, which specify the threats made and actions
taken and those prepared for the days, months, and years ahead. The implication is that the different parts of the book are integrated around the first
major oracle, and that the supposed gaps in the latter are to be made up by
reference to other statements and comments positioned in the remaining
units.

The first of these statements is the next oracle, chap. 3:1–2, where the
theme of the Exodus finds an echo (cf 2:10) and the basic response to
Israel's persistent resistance, rebellion, and refusal to heed the words of its
suzerain:

1. 3:2: "Only you have I known of all the families [tribes or clans]
of the earth; therefore I will punish you for all your iniquities [I will
visit upon you all your iniquities]."

2. 3:11: "The foe indeed surrounds your land, and will pull down
your fortresses in your midst, and your strongholds will be sacked."

3. Cf. 3:12 and 3:14–15 for details of the destruction and damage.
Exile is mentioned in 4:3.

4. The dirge over the fallen virgin Israel in 5:2—"The virgin Israel
has fallen, she will never stand up again; she has been left lying on her
land, and no one raises her up."

5. Cf. also 5:3 and 5:4–5—decimation of the army, destruction of
the cities, and exile are all depicted.

6. 5:16–17—lamentation.

7. 5:27—exile beyond Damascus.

8. 6:7—exile for all of those addressed in the Woes (6:1–6).

9. 6:8—deliver up the city to destruction.

10. 6:11—destruction of houses.

11. 6:14—raising up a nation against you that will oppress you.

12. 7:9–17—especially 9 and 17 (cf v 11).

13. 8:3—slaughter and wailing (in reverse order).

14. 8:7—oath by Yahweh that he will make an appropriate response.

15. 8:9–10—"in that day"—the term is a link with 2:16—specifying
the actions, mourning after disaster. Also 8:13, where the same theme
is elaborated.

16. 8:14—they will fall and never rise again (cf. 5:2).

17. 9:1–4—"I shall set my eyes upon them" for evil, also no survivors or escapers (cf. 2:16).

18. 9:8—eyes against wicked kingdom, destruction from the face of the earth, but not total destruction.

19. 9:9–10—further detail, even more final.

The eventualities that we have identified as Phase Three, irrevocable and total destruction, are thus anticipated throughout the entire prophecy. In certain contexts such warnings could be conditional. When given during Phase One, when the possibility of repentance is recognized and hoped for, such threats are part of the call to amendment. As the situation deteriorates, however, the predictions are more unqualified and more specific. In particular, attention is focused on the elite leadership of Israel, especially the army, as already here in 2:14–16; and on individuals (Jeroboam and Amaziah, by name!). And military defeat and exile are followed by complete and systematic execution of "all the sinners of my people" who are tracked down (9:2–4) and killed by the sword (9:10). These notes are struck in every chapter, but it is only in chap. 9 that they rise to a crescendo. And only afterward are promises of restoration (9:11–12) and renewal (9:13–15) given in a new unequivocal mode.

In trying to locate 2:14–16 in this total scheme, we confront once more a feature of the book's composition that we can either appreciate or deplore. The motif of military catastrophe appears throughout, mostly as very brief glimpses. The present passage is, in fact, the most coherent and systematic.

To put these events in logical order, we may begin with the general divine pronouncements, proceed to the more detailed references, and then advance to the various stages of the crisis and its ultimate issue:

1. Previous warnings in the form of plagues, also woes:

     3:1–2   "I will punish you for all your iniquities."

     8:7   Oath by Yahweh—"I will never forget any of their misdeeds."

     9:4   "For I shall set my eyes upon them to do them harm and not good."

2. Preliminary

     6:14   "I will raise . . . a nation that will overpower you." The identity of the nation is never specified, but the mechanism of catastrophe is clearly military-political. Natural disasters serve as warnings, as do internal upheavals: class conflict, socioeconomic dislocation, and the like, along with religious defections and apostasy. The climactic struggle leading to dissolution of the state is warfare. God will bring a nation to conquer, dismember, and destroy the political entity and disperse its population.

3. Defeat and Destruction

     a. Siege and defeat (central action)

6:8   "I will hand over the city" (cf. 6:11)

3:11–15 Military action

b. Fall of city and nation (central action)

5:2   Virgin Israel (cf. 5:3–5)

8:14   "They shall fall and never rise again" ("fall" is the link). If the
         casualties of 5:3 are cumulative (two campaigns), only one per-
         cent survive. Yet even that fraction will later perish in the city of
         refuge (6:9).

c. Lamentation and mourning (aftermath)

5:16–17 In city and country

8:3   In the palace (contrast 6:5)

8:9–10   General

d. Exile of survivors, end of dynasty

4:3   Upper-class women (?) taken from city

5:27   Exile—beyond Damascus

6:7   (Cf. 6:1–6 = all of those addressed) worst first

7:9, 17 (Cf. 7:11)—dynasty destroyed and exile of population

e. No survivors even in exile

9:1–4   (Cf. 2:14–16)—they will not just die there; they will be killed.

There is little or no interest in secondary causes or agencies. Yahweh will do it, as is shown by the "I" clauses of judgment speeches.

Any of these threats would fill the gap after 2:8 due to the lack of anything corresponding to the "punishment formula" in the first seven oracles. What is lacking in the oracles against Judah and Israel is more than made up in the chapters that follow.

The threats run the whole gamut of responses and judgments following on the charges and the condemnation of the guilty. Any one of them would fit after 2:8, but it is likely that the standard expression "and I will send Fire and She will consume" was intended to be understood here, to be followed by vv 14–16 as they stand. Why was the standard refrain omitted? Perhaps it was deliberate, perhaps accidental: the form might have been, "And I will send Fire against Samaria, and She will devour its citadels"; or perhaps Samaria and Bethel were mentioned: "I will send Fire against the wall of Samaria and She will consume the citadels of Bethel." In any event, the basic prophecy was fulfilled: in the course of the 730s and 720s, Israel was demolished as a nation. This circumstance makes it all the more re-markable that no such passage is now present in the Israel oracle. This lack shows that later scribes did not supply "prophecies after the event" as readily as is often alleged.

The series consists of eight charges and seven threats of punishment. The oracle on Israel turns in a different direction from the others. There is a prose interpolation consisting of 2:9–13. If the conclusion in vv 14–16 is intended to match the punishment clause of the other seven oracles, it differs from them all in its concentration on military defeat. It is also quite general (no names) and so could apply to all of the preceding. It also uses the eschatological formula "on that day" (2:16). Nothing is gained by speculating on what the Israel oracle might have been in an earlier (oral) phase. We would defend the surviving text and argue that we must deal with what has come down to us, whether original or not. We recognize the hand of an editor here and agree that the purpose and function of the book of Amos that he compiled are not the same as the oracles pronounced on specific occasions and under distinct circumstances by the prophet. Those were spoken for immediate effect, while the written form was meant to be read and pondered many times over. The prophet's message was to warn Israel of impending divine judgment. The book was compiled at least in part to vindicate the prophet: to record what he said, but also to make the case that he was a true prophet and that Israel added to its sins the unpardonable error of refusing to receive a prophet who spoke under divine compulsion.

As it was the editor's intention to preserve for posterity the words of Amos, it would not serve that purpose to distort and destroy them. We assume therefore that the substance of the book and the oracles in particular are accurate. Nevertheless the arrangement, the selection—including condensation and expansion, perhaps adaptation and structuring—are part of an editor's work and should be identified and recognized whenever it is possible to do so.

The concluding section (vv 14–16) returns to a numerical pattern. There are seven lines, or rather clauses (the last is long enough for two lines of poetry). The language is palpably that of poetry, in contrast to vv 9–13. Three opportunities to use *'t* were not used. The nouns are definite, but the article is used only when the noun is *nomen rectum* (exactly the syntax of Isaiah 40), and in *bayyôm hahû*.

The opening and closing bicolons contain the same roots in chiasmus—inclusion. The series *kōḥô, napšô, napšô, libbô* constitutes another chiasmus. The two outer clauses enclose five statements, each with *lō*. The first pair have an object after the verb, the second pair have a two-noun subject before the verb; the fifth one combines both of these features, so it is the longest line in the poem (eleven syllables). The verb "save" is used three times, repeating the certainty that none will escape.

Against those who would excise portions for various reasons, we point out that the list of seven classes of military personnel is comprehensive. We have a characteristic recapitulation corresponding to the seven nations and their seven acts of rebellion, paralleled by Israel with its seven transgressions. The list of seven military types is presented as two groups—3 and 3 + 1.

1. *qāl*, the swift	In this group, each
2. *ḥāzāq*, the strong	type is characterized
3. *gibbôr*, the warrior	by a single word.
4. *tōpēś haqqešet*, the bowman	Here each type is
5. *qal běraglāyw*, the swift of foot	characterized by a
6. *rōkēb hassûs*, the horseman	pair of words.
7. *'ammîṣ libbô baggibbôrîm*	Three words.

The last category describes the most courageous of all of the crack troops, the king's elite bodyguard, and receives two lines. Even they will run away naked.

The verbs describe the various outcomes for the warriors. Some will not "stand," in other words, hold their ground or survive; some will not save their lives; it is implied that even those who flee will not escape.

To summarize: those involved in the decisive military action are divided into seven classes. These classes are further organized into two groups, of three and four elements, as follows. The first group consists of generic types: (1) the swift; (2) the strong; (3) the warriors. In the second group, the identification is in accordance with the military role or function: (4) the archers who fight from fixed positions; (5) the infantry ("swift of foot"); (6) the chariotry (or cavalry). The last unit (7) belongs to the second group but stands somewhat apart, as befits the elite corps ("the mighty in will," that is, the most courageous), presumably the personal bodyguard of the king or commander. When they finally break ranks, abandon their weapons, and flee, the battle is over.

NOTES

2:14 *save his life.* The idiom "run away (*nws*) and save (*mlṭ*) your life (*npš*)" is standard (1 Sam 19:10–12; 2 Sam 19:6[E5]; 1 Kgs 1:12; Jer 48:6, 51:6). Sometimes *brḥ = nws*. The *nipʿal* of *mlṭ* is used as a middle in Genesis 19 and Job 1. There is no object with the verb *yěmallēṭ* in v 15aB, and it is recommended that the *nipʿal* be substituted here, partly on the basis of the LXX *diasōthē*. At the same time, we can retain the *piʿel* here, with the implied object (*npš*) provided by the other two occurrences of the combination *ymlṭ npšw* (vv 14b, 15b). Otherwise the *piʿel* usually has *npš* as object (2 Kgs 23:18 is a rare instance in which the object is not a living person).

15b. *charioteer.* Originally the driver of horses, but by Amos' day cavalry had been introduced to Palestine, so this unit could describe "riders" of horses.

16b. *naked.* Compare Isa 20:1–6.

Summary of Chapters 1 and 2: The Great Set Speech

Now that we have completed our study of the first large unit of the book in chaps. 1–2—the Great Set Speech—we can make some observations about its overall structure and possible editorial history.

1:1. Heading. This extended title was provided by the editor of the work to give essential information about Amos and in particular the date of his oracles and his book. It is prose, naturally, with a complex sentence structure, including two parallel subordinate clauses introduced by *ʾăšer.*

1:2. Introduction to the book of Amos. While the couplet of two bicola leads into the great oracle against the nations including Israel or against Israel among the nations, it also serves as an introduction to the whole work. It serves a dual purpose, being at once an introductory part of the prophecy that follows and a suitable exordium for the work as a whole. It doubtless was placed here by the editor, who now and then displays a Judahite bias, certainly because the book was preserved in the Judahite canon and must have been put together and edited in a Judahite environment. The editor's tendency is evident in the order of the kings in 1:1 with the Judahite king(s) first and the Israelite king second, in both Hosea and Amos, even though the major content of both books centers on the north. Whether Amos was responsible for this expression is not clear, and many would argue that he was not, for there is specific mention of Zion//Jerusalem; it is contended that Amos never referred to the southern kingdom or its capital, and wherever these terms appear they are interpolated by editors or others. There is no way to defeat such an argument, for its proof is incorporated into its assumption, namely, that Amos did not speak against or for the southern kingdom and hence any reference to it must be spurious. All we can say is we do not agree with the logic and are not sure of the substance. As we have shown in the introductory essay on Amos' political terminology, many of Amos' references to "Israel" are to the nation as a whole (both kingdoms). If the more explicit references to Judah and Jerusalem attract suspicion, each passage must be dealt with on its own merits and not on the basis of some *a priori* certainty or general position. We believe, for example, that the passage containing the word "Zion" in 6:1 is authentic, whereas we share well-nigh universal doubts about the last unit in the book, 9:11–15, where the "booth of David" is mentioned. About the oracle against Judah in 2:4–5 we have some misgivings but cannot automatically rule the passage out as inauthentic.

With respect to 1:2, there is another question. Verse 2a may not be original with Amos because we find the same wording in Joel 4:16(E3:16). It may have been part of the prophetic corpus, without clear authorship or attribution, and hence claimed by or for more than one. The figure is not unique—that of Yahweh as a roaring lion—but it characterizes much of the material in the book of Amos, or serves as a fitting introduction. It also has more direct links with certain units in Amos, especially 3:3–8, where the association between lion roaring and Yahweh speaking is made explicit.

It also needs to be mentioned that v 2b is distinctive as v 2a is not, but that together they form an unusual couplet. The mourning of the pastures and the drying up of Carmel seem to be separate, not related, items, or related only through widely varying characteristics of the deity as lion. As Amos 3:4 points out, the lion's roar is associated with the capture of prey, and the typical prey of a lion is precisely what makes shepherds and pastures mourn at its capture. At the same time, the roaring of the divine lion is associated with the hot winds from the desert, which dry up everything and scorch even the sylvan headland of Carmel—here symbolic of the worst kind of drought. There are verbal associations with remote units of Amos, namely 9:3 and 5 (cf. 8:8), which are sometimes suspected of being editorial additions. Perhaps we can recognize the work of an editor here, creating an envelope around the entire composition.

1:3–2:16. This composite passage may be called "The Oracle Against Israel and the Neighboring Nations." It is often designated as "oracles against foreign nations" but, as the content and organization make clear, the eventual emphasis of the emerging theme is the judgment of God on his own people, Israel. While the other nations are important and receive due attention, they constitute a framework or backdrop for the main part of the message, which is directed against Israel.

In our judgment the piece as it now stands is a composite, the work presumably of the editor, who could have been Amos himself. At least it is possible that the organization, which makes such excellent sense of the whole, more than any portion would in isolation, derives from Amos, with very little more for an editor-scribe to do in order to produce the present book. While there may be slight editorial touches (and occasional textual errors) in the piece as a whole, we find only one major adjustment in the text, namely, the inclusion of a prose piece in chap. 2:9–13 between the main part of the oracle (1:3–2:8) and the conclusion (2:14–16). While the concluding unit differs in some respects from the standard formulas and set phrases of the major unit, these differences are insufficient to treat the closing part as also an editorial intrusion or supplement. Put briefly, the argument is as follows: The major group of oracles ends abruptly at 2:8; the analogy of the other oracles in the group and the requirements of sense and completeness require a statement about the judgment against Israel, how it will be executed, and what the results will be. Comparison with other statements in chaps. 1–2 and with statements about the fate of Israel in ensuing times elsewhere in the book provides an outline of what such a statement should be and what it should contain. We would expect a statement comparable to the constantly repeated threat of the other oracles:

> *wĕšillaḥtî ʾēš bĕḥômat šōmĕrôn*
> *wĕʾākĕlâ ʾarmĕnōteyhā*

> and I will send Fire against the wall of Samaria,
> and She will consume its citadels.

That passage would have ended the oracle if not the whole address. This oracle would have conformed to the pattern for nos. 2 (Philistia), 3 (Tyre), 7 (Judah), and more particularly to no. 3. In other respects it conforms to nos. 3, 4, and 7, with longer charges and briefer judgments. Combining features, we come out with a reconstruction or restoration of the expected formula for Samaria. Because it is the last in the series, however, the oracle may have varied from the norm in its original (and subsequent) presentations.

Needless to say, no such formula is found in 2:9–13, which introduces other themes and in fact expands on the charges made against Israel and its ruling classes in 2:6–8. Neither are these points made in the concluding verses, though they reflect a disastrous ending for the nation: what we have is a fairly elaborate description of the components of an army that share in a totally destructive defeat. Nothing is said of invasion, siege, or exile, but defeat is total; the end has come for the nation, and other features of the final defeat can be imagined or supposed. No doubt the insertion of the prose unit (vv 9–13) between the utterance of this complaint and the picture of the aftermath of the decisive battle with its eschatological overtones has affected the form and character of the final component (vv 14–16). The latter can be connected with the immediately preceding material, though a gap remains (because v 13 closes the earlier unit by expressing Yahweh's unhappiness with his people, who have become an intolerable burden).

It would be difficult to decide whether the final part has been added along with the prose insertion, was part of the original oracle, or is a separate piece appended to the entire oracle because of this apparent lack of a conclusion. Because it fits as well with the main oracle as with the inserted piece, we will opt for the first solution while allowing that the three pieces do not now fit together smoothly. Something has fallen out or been dropped, something has been inserted, and there are some troubling discontinuities among the surviving parts. The basic theme and thrust of the oracle are not seriously compromised by these rearrangements and adjustments toward the end, but it is necessary to point them out and to deal with the materials separately as well as together.

The section from 1:3–2:8 is one of the major set pieces of the book of Amos, and we assume that it is substantially the product of Amos' own thinking and preaching. While the authenticity of a number of parts has been questioned, and a number of individual phrases and words have been challenged as to their originality, their meaning, and the sense they make syntactically and grammatically, we believe that arguments in defense of the unity and authenticity of this part of the work are at least as good as those against them, and conclude therefore that the oracle as a whole is the work of Amos, and that except for the threat and description of the doom of Samaria, which might have come after 2:8, in line with the preceding seven oracles, the piece is essentially complete and unchanged.

A word about the format and style may be in order. The format is fairly rigid, consisting of an infrastructure of formulaic statements. These constitute a framework within which the essential content of the numerous oracles is bound. There are variations in the formulas themselves and different ways in which the content is handled—so that no two oracles are exactly the same even in format, but all are recognizably part of a continuum. The individual oracles vary in length as well, but there are two basic types: (1) Type *A*, which is longer, averaging about forty words, and of which there are four examples; (2) Type *B*, which is shorter, averaging about thirty words, and of which there are three examples. While many scholars have seized on this difference to strike the three shorter oracles as spurious or secondary, it seems to us that, in principle at least, the variation is not suspicious in itself, and that other and more persuasive evidence is required to make the case against authenticity. The formulas and contents give the whole a structured appearance, and we may denominate them as prophetic or oracular utterances: the prophet speaks in the name of God and with his words, that is to say, it is for the most part first-person address by God himself. As far as texture and rhythm are concerned there is a good deal that would qualify as poetry, and some elements that decidedly are not. We have pointed to the statement of charges made in each instance, and almost without exception they qualify in whole or in part as straight prose, having none of the features normally associated with poetry. Because they are essential to the composition as a whole and to each oracle in particular, it is impossible to drop them as secondary insertions. At the same time, it is difficult to deal with them as constituent elements in material that otherwise qualifies as poetic and even as poetry, even though the framework of each oracle reduces the original or nonformulaic content to just a line or two. The prose particle count for the whole piece likewise is low, clearly within the range for poetry rather than for prose, though the prose sentences in which these particles are concentrated stand out all the more by contrast with the surrounding material. What is one to make of such a phenomenon? Unless we are prepared to rewrite the entire oracle, or to assume and argue that in each of five or six cases the charge against the nation has been revised by a prose-writing editor, we must conclude that the prophet himself mixed these elements in a way and in a proportion that are strikingly unlike the pattern in most of the Bible, in which prose and poetry are quite different and readily separable. Prose elements, including our diagnostic particles, may have crept in through the inadvertence of scribes, who might be inclined subconsciously to add prose particles because the majority of their biblical and nonbiblical training and practice would tend to stress standard prose writing. It is remarkable that so little of such change has happened in the course of transmission. When we find this sort of mixture in Amos we must regard it as a genuine and distinctive style and try to understand and interpret rather than tamper with it.

Except for the unit (2:9–13) already discussed, we accept the rest as belonging to the speech, though we may share some doubts and difficulties about other parts of it, including 2:14–16 (also discussed) and the oracle on Judah (2:4–5). In the end we think that the arguments against the originality of the latter oracle are outweighed by the arguments for it, and we wish to retain the piece as part of the composition. The main arguments are negative:

1. It is hard to imagine a set of oracles against all of the nations in the quadrant between Egypt and Assyria (or Syria-Palestine) that would omit one as important as Judah. It is foolish to say that Amos included it in the oracle against Israel when that is obviously not the case. While Israel and Judah shared common traditions, had a common origin, and had a common history for a limited period, Amos uses the word "Israel" in different ways, and it is almost always quite clear when it is used for the whole people (usually in reference to the past, or possibly in connection with the future, but hardly as a present reality or even a potential one) and when for the northern kingdom alone. Certainly in this oracle the northern kingdom is in his mind, as it is in much of the book.

2. The prose elements in the oracle on Judah are limited to the charges (note 't and 'šr), but that is true in at least five other cases, so it is not unusual, much less unique. In other words, it is no more prosaic than the others, and in some respects rather poetic. The contents pose problems, but it should be emphasized that there is no visible influence from or dependence on the Deuteronomic tradition, and the distinctive terms (e.g., kzbyhm) and ideas are either not Deuteronomic at all, or are pre-Deuteronomic and therefore part of the common tradition. As to the remaining

oracles, there is even less reason to question them, especially the so-called short statements on Tyre and Edom, simply because they differ from the so-called major four: Aram and Philistia, Ammon and Moab. There are in fact two basic models for these oracles, and to argue that one set is spurious because it is not the same as the other set is no more convincing than to argue the other way around.

What remains compelling as far as we are concerned is the argument from the number of oracles and the role that numbers play in the whole structure of the speech. While the number is not specified independently of the group itself, there is no need to defend the number seven as structurally important in the composition of biblical units. There are too many examples to have to labor the point. The fact that there are seven oracles for seven nations in a repeated format should be enough to persuade the unbiased that a deliberate literary action has been taken. Clearly, the arrangement is purposeful, and it does not serve a useful purpose to try to dismantle this patently intentional structure in the interest of recovering a supposedly more original presentation. It may be argued that the present literary structure is the work of the editor and that, while we may stop briefly to admire his handiwork, we have a more important calling to locate the real message of the real prophet beneath and behind this verbiage. Conceivably this point is valid, but instead of attempting to carve out the "pure original" from the supposedly corrupted transmitted text we are content to stop when we find an undoubted work of literature. We think that it means that we have reached the prophet, but if by chance it means that we have only reached the editor, so be it. It could mean that the editor is the literary genius who took the prophet's words and put them in writing, as Baruch is reported to have done for Jeremiah. We would not wish to neglect or impugn the words of Baruch in the search for the true Jeremiah. Who after all is likely to know better what Jeremiah thought and said and meant than his faithful companion and scribe? Surely not we. In other words, we take it as axiomatic that when a work meets rational and honorable standards of literary quality, our task is to understand and interpret, expound and explain, but hardly to dismember and disperse the parts. So once we have reached the number seven for the oracles against the nations we have a secure platform on which to build the rest of the inquiry. It may be questioned whether the structure should be construed as 7 + 1 (Israel) or 6 + 1 (omitting Judah), and it is possible to argue on both sides of this point. The question of Judah is different from the others. It does not threaten the main conclusion that all of 1:3–2:8 should be kept. If we leave Judah out we have 6 + 1. If we keep it in we have 7 + 1. Both are good schemes. Israel is last in either case. But if we delete 2:4–5 as the one interpolation, we must then take 2:6ff. as referring to both kingdoms as "Israel." At least 2:9ff. is *common* tradition. But 2:6–8 is like material about Samaria in other parts of the book. The pattern is basically an eight-part structure, presented in pairs: 1–2, 3–4, 5–6, 7–8. There are other pairings as well, but the numbers always add up to or presuppose a total of eight. The question boils down to whether Judah and Israel are to be combined and both represented in the oracle on Israel (2:6–8); but that scenario is highly unlikely, not least because the Israel oracle is incomplete and leads to the extended treatment in the balance of the book. Hence we can take the passages in sequence: 4–5 (Judah), 6–8 (Samaria), 9–13 (all of Israel), 14–16 (everybody—these verses identify *no* audience). But once it is clear that the real target of the denunciation is Israel, and when the traditional background of Israel's occupation of the land by dispossessing the seven nations then in residence there is recalled (cf. Deut 7:1), it becomes clear that the right arrangement is 7 + 1, as here in Amos.

There remain numerous questions about readings and meanings, words and phrases, and some of them still defy solution. But analysis and evaluation may be found in the NOTES. Here we are concerned with the larger perspective and picture. Because of the formulaic structure, Amos presents a unified picture of impending doom and disaster for the whole area and all of its nations: eight times charges are leveled (7 + 1) and seven times threats are made—in fact the same threat with minor variations against seven nations, with similar implications for the eighth. The statement itself has a certain cosmic flavor; the ultimate source is Yahweh, who himself will kindle the fire that sets the whole area ablaze. There is a subtlety in the formula that restricts the action to deity, a strong indication that there is a single unified plan by which a universal conflagration will engulf this all too combustible territory. It is equally clear, however, that there is to be a human agent, that God will raise up a nation to accomplish his fell purpose, particularly if vv 14–16 are seen as the terrestrial counterpart to the cosmic action and if they enwrap all eight oracles. Yet it may be that the final battle scene involves only Israel and represents the end of the campaign that has obliterated the seven other nations.

The mechanism or instrument is not identified by name in the book of Amos, and it may be best to leave the human agent unidentified. But some things can be said. There is one such instrument, not more. Not only does a law of parsimony apply here, but the outworking of the divine plan probably requires a unitary instrument. Thanks to our knowledge of subsequent history and the insights provided by roughly contemporary and later prophets, we can identify this invader and conqueror as Assyria. Perhaps Amos did not wish or need to do so—Assyria had fought great battles in that area in the past, and its illustrious all-conquering kings had washed their swords in the waters of the Great Western Sea; it would not take a great prophet to suppose that the Assyrians would attempt to do so in the future. Doubtless some day they would succeed, or perhaps it would be some other equally fearsome people from the north (or the east by way of the north). But it would take a great prophet to see that such an invasion was not merely the move of an expansionist superpower, but the act of an omnipotent God who meant to deal with his world and his people according to principles and protocols laid down in the dim past. Amos saw that the long-postponed day of reckoning was about to break—and break over their heads. We are not dealing here with another round of internecine battles to shift boundaries and alter relations, but rather with a decisive action that would end the world of petty principalities in that part of the Near East and bring all under the sway of that great and terrible nation to the east.

All of the specific and positive indications point in that direction, not only the various references elsewhere in the book, but specifically those in the oracles in chaps. 1–2. There are two main emphases in the specific threats attached to the general and repeated statement about sending fire against the walls and burning the citadels of the capital cities of each of the nations: slaughter and exile. These emphases are found in the two pairs of such pronouncements: (1) on Aram and Philistia in the first two oracles; Aram will go into exile and the Philistines will perish where they are (1:3–8); (2) similarly, the Ammonites or at least their king and his princes will go into exile, while Moab's ruler and its princes will perish by the sword (1:13–2:3). Thus are bound together the twin themes of slaughter in battle and concomitant exile, reflecting the standard operating procedure of the Assyrians from at least the ninth century. While the taking of prisoners and hostages is a common procedure among nations and in itself not an identifying feature, the wholesale transfer of populations from their current homeland to distant places was characteristically Assyrian (though it could be imitated and used by others, such as the Babylonians). Two things can be said about it: (1) It served a political purpose evolved by the Assyrians— to intimidate (as shown also by their calculated brutality and cruelty), and to break decisively local ties in order to compel peoples to adopt a higher loyalty to the empire. The latter policy seems largely to have succeeded in reverse: it only embittered and enraged such peoples, but it may have succeeded in effectively breaking local resistance. (2) In order to carry out these enormous population shifts it was necessary to have both the means and the territory, which could hardly be true of the smaller nations who were the targets of the accusations and charges. Israel at the height of its power in the days of David and Solomon was not large enough or strong enough to carry out such plans, assuming that they contemplated them. It is hard to imagine any people other than the Assyrians at this time able to mount such an offensive or to carry out so vast a rearrangement of the political map. When Amos spoke, Assyria was a vague and distant threat. But the memory of the past, as when Shalmaneser III forced his way to the west and held the combined forces of Aram and Israel and all their allies at bay at Qarqar, would make people aware of and sensitive to this possible danger.

Within a few decades of the time of Amos, Tiglath-pileser III was to bring Assyrian armies back through this area and commence a campaign that would finally in the days of his successors fulfill the prophecies, in most respects, against the small nations. Because Amos prophesied at a time that the threat from the east was not proximate or imminent, it would not have been necessary to spell out all of the details. Time would fill them in. It was also unnecessary to give a timetable of events. Suffice it to make an authentic prediction, one that concerned nations and their destinies and one that conveyed theological meaning. It was not a matter of clever political analysis, though prophets no doubt were aware of what was going on in the international scene and what had happened before. And it was not a matter of mechanical divination—discovering the details written down in the tablets of destiny. Prophecy shares some features both with political analysis and insight and with divinatory power and practice, but it has its own ethos and effectiveness. The prophet speaks for God, for his plan, his decision, and the historical impact and effects those moves will have. It is enough for the prophets to know the mind of God and his purpose; the rest will follow.

In speaking of prophecy and prediction we want to emphasize its reality. It was not a bluff or an exercise in literary adjustment. Prophets made predictions, and they could be tested against events. It was a centrally important part of their ministry, their commission. There were always conditional elements, so prophecies were rarely if ever absolute. Not only could the intercession of prophets themselves make a difference, so could the repentance of people. And finally there were the mind and will of the biblical God, who could and did alter his own decisions on the basis of new data—those mentioned above—and his own private reasons, whatever they might be. Micah's credentials as a prophet were not negated by the fact that his flat prediction about the wreck and ruin of Jerusalem failed to come about, at least during his lifetime and for a century or more thereafter. It does not mean either that his status was held in abeyance until his prophecy could be tested or fulfilled or found wanting in history. That the prediction was fulfilled in 587/586 would hardly have mattered, for what was important was that he was a real prophet who spoke the word that he had received from God. The test of a prophet was just that: was he chosen and commissioned by God? Ultimately there were no objective tests by which such claims could be confirmed or denied. So it was with Amos; he was called and commissioned, he delivered the word he was given. It included dire predictions about the future, but his role and status as prophet depended finally not on whether his words came out—they would have their effect, but the ultimate outcome lay in the hidden future, where the interaction between God's will and man's response produces historical events—but on whether he had responded to the summons and on how he carried out his commission.

Now we wish to return to the oracles of Amos. As previously mentioned, the general threat of invasion and conquest is particularized in relation to four of the nations, and, in those elaborations, death in war and captivity are emphasized. For Aram its destiny is to go into exile in Qir. We do not know exactly where that is but it is a place and it is in the east, and we are told later on (2 Kgs 16:9) that Tiglath-pileser III captured Damascus and carried the population captive to Qir (about 734/733). This event is striking fulfillment of a prediction, though nothing else is made of the point either in Amos or in Kings. It may be argued that the item in Amos is an editorial expansion specifying just where the exile would take place, and that it was not in the original prophecy. It is more likely that it was, and that the reason for its being mentioned was not the later information but rather the interesting fact, if it is a fact, that the Arameans (or some of them) came from Qir in the first place (cf. Amos 9:7).

With regard to the reference in 2 Kings, it looks as though it is independent of the passage in Amos, although scholars may argue that the two are related in different ways: that 2 Kings is based on Amos but that neither is correct or accurate because there is no extrabiblical information about Qir at all. It may also be argued that the passage in Amos has been doctored to fit the later information derived from Kings to indicate that Amos predicted the event accurately. Our concern is not with the historical fulfillment of prophecy, even though that is an important matter. We believe that the data should be taken at face value because that is the simplest way to interpret them and because it is a reasonable view. For the institution of prophecy to have survived for centuries in Israel and Judah predictions must have come true, with some frequency if not always. And often predictions could be made with a high probability of being fulfilled on the basis of common sense and good judgment. But we do not wish to rationalize them away into informed guesses. Other factors were at work, and these, including the all-important interaction of God and prophets, were generally recognized in those countries. We conclude that the prophecy was authentic, and it implies that Amos had in mind that great military power in the east as the agent of the divine judgment. He was sure, in any case, that Aram would be taken captive and exiled to the east, back to the place from which that people had come centuries before. Israel would also go into exile in the east, an exile to be engineered by the same great power. Exactly where they would end up is not spelled out, but it would be in the region beyond Damascus, another indication that the nation that would accomplish this result had its power base in the east.

The connection of Qir with Aram, as not only the destination of the soon-to-be exiled inhabitants of Damascus but as their place of origin, offers an explanation of a fundamental issue underlying the oracle. What is the basis or rationale for Yahweh's judgment on the nations? With respect to Israel the basis is clearly spelled out in the great tradition that goes back to the Exodus if not to the Fathers and is expressed succinctly in the Decalogue, "I am Yahweh your God who brought you up from the land of Egypt" (Exod 20:2). God not only redeemed the Israelites from slavery in Egypt but created them a nation. On the basis not primarily of his power (or his role as creator) but of his saving activity, Yahweh has a claim on his people. The covenant between them, based on his gracious act of deliverance, imposes obligations on Israel, and Israel is honor-bound to obey them. Failure to obey is a fundamental violation of the agreement and additionally an act of gross ingratitude; it incurs guilt and brings with it the threat of punishment. The basis of claim and threat is the original and initiating act of grace in the Exodus—a point made repeatedly in the book of Amos (albeit in prose—cf. 2:9–10, 3:1–2, and 9:7).

Now how does the same demand and threat work with the other nations? Two ideas have been put forward, both meriting serious consideration. The first is the general authority exercised by God as lord of creation. He created and hence controls everything, including all of the nations, whether they recognize him or not. There are several passages in Amos in which the power and authority of God over his creation are emphasized (4:13, 5:8, and 9:5–6), and certainly this idea lies behind much of the thinking about God and the created world in the Bible. Ultimately it is the basis for the doctrine of redemptive grace just mentioned, and the fundamental reason for divine demand and threat is his supreme authority over the whole of the creation. But even in view of the passages cited above (and many scholars deny that they come from Amos) no connection is made between Yahweh as Creator and the charges and threats to the nations. We may rest the case with the observation that the authority of God originates with his work of creation; but that is not the operative reason for Amos in the oracles against the nations.

A second view is more subtle but also more speculative. It is held that at one time or another, but especially in the days of David and Solomon, all of the nations listed in Amos 1–2 belonged to their empire and were therefore subject to the authority of Israel's king and Israel's God, namely, that they were bound by oath to the worship and service of Yahweh. This claim may be true in part, though we may question whether in fact all of these nations and peoples were incorporated into Israel or made subject in some formal way to Israel's God. We do not know the truth of the matter with Tyre or other Phoenician cities, though presumably in any parity treaties made between Israel and Tyre the authority of the gods of both nations would be acknowledged by both parties. But this situation hardly accords with Amos' announcement of Yahweh's authority over all of these peoples and the way in which it is exercised. There may be some merit in the general idea of Yahweh's suzerainty over the nations conquered and integrated into the Davidic empire, but that too is not the basis for the inherent authority Amos claims for Yahweh. The notion of Yahweh's authority over other nations being extended by conquest may receive some slight support in the usual reading of Amos 9:12, which seems to speak of "all the nations over whom my name was pronounced"; but we read the clause differently, and in any case it is hard to say just what such an expression means.

The real reason for Yahweh's authority over the other nations is suggested in Amos 9:7, where notice is taken of God's action in bringing Israel from Egypt, the Philistines from Caphtor, and the Aramaeans from Qir. Just as Yahweh's claim to and demand on Israel is based on his act of unmerited kindness and grace in bringing them out of Egypt, so he has acted in comparable fashion by bringing the Philistines to Palestine from Caphtor (perhaps Crete or another Aegean location) and the Aramaeans from Qir. The implication of the passage is quite clear; the relationship is essentially the same: one of grace. Because he has acted on behalf of Philistines and Aramaeans he has the right to impose demands and to insist on compliance with rules and requirements, just as in the case of Israel. The difference, and it is not a small one, is that these nations obviously are unaware of that all-important truth. They have their own gods and explain their history in a different fashion, no doubt; but Amos insists that the truth is as he has stated it. Whether the nations are aware of the action of divine grace in bringing them out of one place to another and establishing and providentially guiding their history, they are not less responsible because of their ignorance. Or because such ignorance is probably a mitigating circumstance, they are not as responsible as Israel because Israel knows the truth of its history, who its benefactor and suzerain is, while the others do not. But each is answerable, and basically for the same reason. We may assume that Amos would make the same claim and the same argument about the rest of the nations on the list: that Yahweh brought them to their present territory and has overseen their historical experience. They are answerable for their behavior to him primarily because he is their benevolent sovereign. This doctrine is unusual, especially because it emphasizes divine grace in the lives of other peoples—not that it reduces Israel to the level of common humanity but that it raises others to the level of Israel's special status. Till now Israel's unique status has persisted and been protected by the fact that the other nations are unaware of Yahweh's providential involvement in their history; but the underlying facts make the truth the same for all. All have received the grace of God and all are answerable to him, each in accord with the measure of grace received and acknowledged. Isaiah's doctrine concerning Assyria as the agent of divine judgment is doubtless similar to that held by Amos, but neither speaks of acts of grace in Assyria's early history, though it is possible that Amos and even Isaiah would uphold the same view. In any case, Assyria along with the others is answerable to the Lord of the whole earth.

It only remains to tie up a few loose ends. The picture presented in chaps. 1 and 2 is that of a final total conquest of the buffer zone between Egypt and the east—western Syria including all the nations between Hamath to the northeast and the Philistine cities to the southwest, Edom in the southeast, and the Phoenician cities along the coast to the northwest. The use of the same formulas for all of the nations points to a unified program of invasion and conquest to be achieved by a single chosen agent, and all within the brief span of a single campaign. The picture is conceived in theological terms and in a cosmic geography rather than in realistic geopolitical terms. While the action contemplated is military and the effects only too plain to those who lived in the area in the first part of the first millennium B.C.E., the order of events and the sequence of nations do not follow military or diplomatic logic but rather fit the perspective of one viewing the scene from heaven and the position of the Almighty. On the one hand the outcome is certain and inevitable and historical, that is, the destruction of all of these small nations will be accomplished; on the other, the timetable does not fit historical requirements, and the supposed events do not suit some actual military campaign by real armies.

Thus the list of nations is complete for the territory described, and it is difficult to imagine an earlier truncated list as serving the prophet's purpose or conveying the divine message. All of the nations in this area will be overrun and overwhelmed. The arrangement expresses inclusiveness and totality rather than an invader's actual line of march. Thus the divine action moves from the northeastern corner of this region—Damascus—to the southwestern limit—Gaza. From here up the coast to the northwestern boundary (Tyre, as representative of Phoenicia) and thence to the southeastern extreme (Edom), then up the eastern side to the northeast again (Ammon, bordering on Damascus), and finishing on that side with Moab. Once more across the Jordan to the west and Judah, bordering the first nation mentioned on that side (Philistia), and finally northward to Israel to complete the list on the west, moving in the opposite direction from that on the eastern side. It is hardly the way an actual conqueror would move or the way the historic invaders moved; but this is a divine conquest, and the arrangement reflects the point of view of no fixed geographic position but rather of an extraterrestrial observer. It would be possible to parcel out the targets between invaders from two places, northeast (Assyria) and southwest (Egypt), and posit alternate strikes until the land was divided between the rival conquerors; but this is hardly the picture presented by or deducible from the text and only leads to unnecessary complications, such as the prospect of a final great conflict between the superpowers (surely not contemplated by Amos). The uniformity, regularity, and repetition of the actions strongly suggest that there is a single underlying plan, and a single agent is contemplated. In effect the conditions inaugurated with the Iron Age, when the area of Canaan was invaded and occupied by migrating peoples from sea and land and from all directions, will finally be reversed, and the whole territory will fall again into the hands of a single conquering empire (as for example in the Middle Bronze and Late Bronze periods, when Egypt ruled or claimed to rule the Asiatic province as far as the Euphrates).

The plan is schematic but it follows a logical order, boxing the compass and then proceeding in spiral fashion to the inner core and final bastion, Israel itself. All eight nations that fill the space are accounted for—the order is dramatic and eschatological rather than military and political. The corner outpost regions are rolled up first and then the inner regions, ending up in the mountains of Judah and Samaria, the most remote and difficult of access but the original and ultimate target of the divine decision and action.

The scheme proposed in Amos 1–2 does not fit any particular historical scene or sequence of events, and it would be difficult to construct an order of events that would translate vision and prophecy into reality without drastic alterations and adaptations. We can suggest, however, a general time and situation in which an oracle of this nature could have been uttered. While the relations among the peoples of the area were constantly in flux and yesterday's foes were today's friends only to be enemies again tomorrow, the basic requirement would be that each of the eight nations be autonomous with its own government and free (or more or less free) to make decisions and act on them not only within its borders but beyond them. During the era in which Amos prophesied, when Jeroboam reigned in the north and Uzziah in the south, there must have been such a period, perhaps earlier in their reigns than later, as both were active beyond their borders and often successful in interfering in their neighbors' affairs and dominating them. In fact, we are told that Jeroboam conquered the whole eastern territory from Lebo-Hamath to the Arabah, which would in effect remove three of the nations from our list. It has been suggested that this development is reflected in Amos' condemnation of the four nations east of the Jordan and that the possibility of conquest from within the group should not be overlooked—in other words, at least a partial restoration of the Davidic empire (perhaps in conjunction with conquests to the west by Judah, actually achieved by Uzziah through an invasion of the Philistine territories).

While such events took place during the period in question, they hardly meet the needs and concerns of the passages under consideration. Amos does not speak of these preliminary and provisional exchanges of territory and sovereignty but rather of a final resolution, an end to the individual histories of these nations when they will be invaded and destroyed for the last time. So whatever vicissitudes they undergo, defeats suffered and victories won, territories surrendered or added, all such changes have little meaning in the light of a permanent settlement to be achieved at a time in the future. The certainty of the outcome is determined, but the time itself, while imminent, is hardly fixed. It would seem that the oracles must come from a time either before the expansionary conquests of Jeroboam and Uzziah, or after the collapse of their respective empires. The latter, however, would bring us into the period of Assyrian revival and its own expansion westward (beginning with the accession of Tiglath-pileser III in 745)— and turn Amos' predictions into recollections, a view we reject. It may well be, therefore, that Amos' oracles are to be dated earlier than the common view (760 or later), perhaps as early as 780 or in the early years of the two kings (whose reigns overlapped from perhaps 790 to 750), before their aggressive expansionist activities had commenced or proceeded very far.

THE INTEGRITY OF THE GREAT SET SPEECH

From time to time one scholar or another has suspected one or more of the eight oracles of being later compositions inserted "during the exilic or post-exilic periods" (Mays 1969:25). The most widely held opinion seems to be that only five oracles derive from Amos (or his circle), the ones covering Tyre, Edom, and Judah having been added in the light of later historical developments.

Doubts about the authenticity of certain oracles arise from two expectations, one literary, the other historical. If all of the oracles had been composed by Amos, they would all follow exactly the same pattern. The oracles against Tyre, Edom, and Judah are different from the others; therefore Amos did not compose them. This argument cuts both ways. First, if a later reviser of the book was not simply augmenting the collection with new oracles of his own, but inserting and presenting them all as the work of Amos, why not follow the original models more carefully? But, as a matter of fact, the four or five oracles deemed to be the authentic work of Amos are by no means identical in design among themselves. The close analysis given above shows that each is distinct and unique in one way or another; we have a set of eight variations on a theme. Furthermore, the variations themselves make a pattern, which is exhibited in its full beauty and symmetry only when all eight oracles are left as they are and where they are. We cannot find a geographical or a historical pattern in the complete set, but there is certainly a literary pattern. Each of the separate oracles must have been composed with individual peculiarities so that an overall pattern would be achieved when all of them were put together. This highly integrated final result does not mean that each oracle might not have had prior use as a self-standing prophetic message. What we now have is a total statement for which each of the oracles has been specially written or rewritten—whether by Amos himself or his immediate editor, who knows? But if the whole thing was not really finished until two or three hundred years after Amos' time, then this later author did not simply slip two or three more into an earlier set of five or six; he must have rewritten the whole thing in order to attain the uncanny balance of variety within unity that we now have. There is an "all or nothing" quality about verbal craftsmanship of this kind.

Second, the historical approach assumes that oracles must match real events. In its most skeptical form this argument assumes that all predictive prophecy must have been written after the events it purports to forecast. Therefore the set of oracles against these eight nations could not have existed until after all of them had been destroyed. The destruction of these eight nations took place in two broad phases. The Assyrian conquests in the second half of the eighth century removed all but Tyre, Edom, and Judah. Oracles against these three could not have been present in an early version of the book of Amos, such as might already have existed by the beginning of the seventh century; for in that case the survival of Tyre, Edom, and Judah would show that Amos' prophecies were false.

This whole approach is under the spell of an attitude to prophecy, as prediction of historical events, that is postbiblical in origin and essentially modern in its more rationalistic forms. In the case of Amos' younger contemporary Micah we know that an unfulfilled prophecy against Jerusalem was retained in his book, with no thought that its nonfulfillment weakened Micah's case. On the contrary, that very fact was seen as vindicating him, as long as it is realized that repentance can avert or at least postpone a threatened disaster.

A difficulty with this approach is that we are dependent on our very limited knowledge of the history of those countries to find matches between Amos' statements and actual events. To be candid, there is comparatively little certain historical actuality in any of Amos' statements in these oracles, whether in the crimes (for example, we have no documentation of Tyre selling a whole set of captives to Edom), or of the punishments (we have no documentation of the burning of Bozrah). The whole speech could be regarded as nothing but fantasy, and no item in the speeches should be crossed out just because it lacks external corroboration, or even because it is found to be contrary to known historical fact.

CONCLUDING COMMENT ON THE GREAT SET SPEECH (1:2–2:16)

The oracles in chaps. 1–2 show signs that they emerged from visionary experiences like those reported in chaps. 7–9. Out of the visions comes the certainty of the destruction of the kingdom and its cities, and of the end of the royal dynasty, and the temple and its priesthood, along with the exile of the people. Amos' message reflects the visions and is itself the description of an eschatological vision of ruin—of the entire area between Egypt and Assyria, or at least to the Euphrates. The picture given in chaps. 1–2 is therefore realistic in the sense that actual kingdoms and their crimes are recounted; but the plan of action and particular occasions and instances of their destruction are colored by the heavenly perspective of the prophet. Yahweh himself will encompass their destruction in an order that defies military or geopolitical logic but which makes eminent dramatic and theological sense, if we understand that Yahweh sends his fire from heaven to consume the rebellious kingdoms (as in the Elijah stories). The idiom *šlḥ ʾš* is used exclusively of God, whereas when human beings are involved in such fire storms, a different Hebrew expression is used (*šlḥ bʾš*).

The picture, then, in Amos 1–2 is one of the wholesale liquidation of the small kingdoms in the Syro-Phoenician-Palestinian region; and while, in fact, that objective will be achieved historically and militarily by the Assyrians and finally the Babylonians in the ensuing centuries, the picture presented by Amos does not fit those specifications and is not intended to do so. There is a correlation between the heavenly vision and the earthly counterpart, and Amos is speaking from and into real human historical conditions. But the language is that of the heavenly council and of vision and audition involving the celestial and terrestrial, and in his prescription for doom and destruction Amos here focuses attention on the divine warrior who sends fire and destroys cities, walls and ramparts, citadels and palaces, and wreaks destruction on the population. While the charges are painfully particular and the consequences are specified for the several peoples, the framework is both eschatological and cosmic: the results are not only irreversible but will make permanent changes in the landscape of this western region. An end to the nations is foreseen and described, and survivors, if any, will be scattered to other areas of the world. It is noteworthy that after this all-embracing vision of the region, little if any attention is paid to the nations mentioned. Although they continue to exist and function in the scene of Amos' activity and ministry, it is as though their fate were sealed, their destiny already fulfilled. Amos has seen them destroyed in his vision, and by his message the future reality enters the world and will complete its work.

The open-endedness of the eighth oracle, the one against the northern kingdom of Israel, shows that the fate of that state is Amos' main topic. At the same time the shift in focus in 2:9–13 has brought the whole nation of two kingdoms into his sights. This shift sets the perspective for the rest of the book, in which all of Israel, mainly the northern kingdom but never excluding Judah, is under attack.

The rest of the book, in particular chaps. 3 and 4, expands the charges and condemnation of Israel and spells out the details of attack and devastation. The ultimate target of the divine wrath is Israel itself, and the great weight of the argument is thrust upon Israel, which was the immediate and direct objective of Amos' trip to Bethel (7:13). There is no evidence that Amos visited the other nations and their capitals to deliver his messages, but there is no doubt that he went to Israel and Bethel to do so. Within the general framework of chap. 2:6–16 with its charges, its argument, and its forecast of apocalyptic defeat, the details and particulars of all of these aspects are provided in subsequent chaps., beginning with 3 and 4. The oracle in chaps. 1–2 is to be seen as a final word, as the single most complete message of the prophet on the basis of his experience in the divine assembly. There the decision has been reached; destruction is ordained for all eight nations, and it remains only to carry out the divine decree. The picture provided is that of direct divine intervention: fire as the personal or, in any case, the direct agent of the deity. All will be devastated and in such order and manner as to leave Israel alone and helpless at the last. The compass is boxed, cutting off aid or escape on all sides, and then Israel itself is overcome in a final battle. Needless to say, the order in the list does not conform to any known historical sequence of events, and actual conquest by the Assyrians followed a standard and rational pattern based on strategic and geopolitical considerations. Some of the nations disappeared earlier than others, while others survived long past the period envisioned in the prophecy (such as Tyre). Perhaps the most glaring inconsistency concerns Judah, which did not precede Israel in the path of destruction but followed it by more than a century, and even then was overcome not by the Assyrians, who themselves disappeared from the map toward the end of the seventh century B.C.E., but by the Babylonians.

Even if we regarded Sennacherib's invasion and near conquest of Judah in 701 as a partial realization of Amos' prediction, nevertheless the order of events would still not conform to the sequence in Amos 1–2, for Israel was conquered and dismembered long before the attack on Judah commenced. It is thought by many scholars that Judah is a secondary insertion in the list, and it would be difficult to disprove such an assertion, though there is no hard evidence that the book of Amos or any precursor ever existed without it. It has been argued many times that insertions of oracles against Tyre, Edom, and Judah were made after the Fall of Jerusalem in the sixth century, to make it appear that the prophet's words were in fact fulfilled. The insertion would nevertheless run counter to the chronological implications of the oracles in chaps. 1–2.

It cannot be proved that the prophet believed that the nations would fall in the order in which they are listed; but if any kind of chronological scheme were in his mind, that seems the most natural way to interpret the arrangement. Still, there can be little doubt that he had in mind a single general campaign, directed from heaven, which would engulf the entire region. And it is reading real history back into a visionary oracle to attempt to match the oracles with what actually happened over the succeeding centuries. In our opinion it is not likely that anyone knowing the true history of what happened, especially to Israel and Judah but also to the other nations, would have inserted Judah before Israel in the list, or several of the other nations (such as Tyre and Edom), because each had a distinctive and continuing history, which hardly conforms to the picture Amos presents of a general conflagration and destruction. It is equally unlikely that anyone would have inserted this oracle on Judah after the destruction of Israel and while Judah was still in being. At that stage, pointed distinctions would be made between the two kingdoms in the light of their very different fates. The oracle would have had to be reshaped entirely to accommodate such an unexpected development. In a somewhat better position to judge the matter, a later contemporary of Amos, Micah, flatly predicted the end of Jerusalem and Judah—a prophecy well remembered more than a hundred years later in the days of Jeremiah. Micah was honored for such forthrightness, and his failure to predict accurately was not regarded as an instance of false prophecy, because it was in effect conditional. The survival of the kingdom was attributed to adequate repentance on the part of king and people (as in the case of Nineveh in the story of Jonah), so the prophecy was considered to have worked an alternative effect. But it retained its force as a warning, and thus it could be renewed in the days of Jeremiah. It is perfectly possible that Amos' prophecy about Judah was interpreted in the same manner, but is it likely that anyone would invent such a prophecy and attribute it to Amos when in fact it had not been fulfilled and might not be in the future? It is axiomatic that prophecies after the event are historically accurate because that is the purpose of the author in creating them. It is hard to imagine anyone attributing a false prophecy to an earlier prophet with the object of enhancing and strengthening his reputation. So in the case of the Judah oracle, its position before the one against Israel and its history of unfulfillment make it difficult to believe that it was inserted by someone else at a later or much later date. Rather, it logically and obviously belongs to the general picture of destruction and conquest, presented as a single overwhelming campaign conducted by God from heaven. The picture is conformable in many ways with the official view of the Israelite conquest of the land of Canaan—a single overwhelming invasion (with stages and strategy and particular objectives) which brought the whole land under Israelite control. It is recognized that this picture is not historically accurate and that pockets of resistance remained, along with unconquered areas; but the intention was to depict the conquest as divinely inspired, divinely executed. If pressed about the mechanism by which battles are fought and won, Amos and the other prophets would point to natural and historic forces available for these purposes, but would emphasize the divine figure and force behind and controlling them all. While human participation is rarely if ever excluded, it may be severely limited, as in the case of the Israelites who were mere spectators when the sea overwhelmed the Egyptian host (compare this situation with the role of Israel in the defeat of the Canaanite forces at the Wadi Kishon—which was undoubtedly more substantial but still minuscule compared with Yahweh's hand in the proceedings, which was dominant and decisive). In the current picture in Amos, essentially the same idea is present. The divine role is dominant, and the catastrophe is all but total. The reflection of human activity is to be found in the statement that this or that nation or group will go into exile and that there may be a survival or a remnant after the military actions, including invasion, investment and reduction of the capital city, and conquest of the nation.

In similar fashion, while Judah is to be finished off along with the other nations, nevertheless among the oracles directed at the northern kingdom, its capital city, Samaria, and other sites such as Bethel, there is also the mention of Jerusalem or more specifically Zion and the reference to Beersheba, which was part of the southern kingdom. These mentions can all be explained on the grounds that they continue to exist in the world of the prophet, even though they have been wiped out in the heavenly vision— even indeed as Israel also has disappeared. There is no rule that requires the prophet to obliterate them from the text as well as from the world, though it is clear that his prime concern is with Israel, with the northern kingdom, and only in tangential ways with the others, including Judah. But in the inaugural speech all are on the same footing, awaiting divine destruction while engaging in their personal and petty violence against one another.

Before proceeding to a more detailed examination of Part IB, we will suggest another way of looking at the book of Amos. If, as we have suggested, the visions offer a clue to the classification of the materials in the book, perhaps then an assignment of parts can be made in relation to the sequence of visions in the following manner. As is well known, visions (or dreams) often come in pairs, so that the first is backed up or reinforced by the second. This is surely the case with the first two pairs of visions in the book of Amos in chaps. 7–8. The point stands whether each pair came in close succession, even in a single night (or day), or whether they were separated by a time interval. The interactions of deity and prophet in each pair are the same, showing that while the visions are different, their messages and meanings are the same. With respect to the first pair, the prophet who receives revelations in the presence of God (and we believe essentially in the presence of the heavenly court or with the latter as the framework in which to understand what is going on or what is going to happen) is shocked and intervenes, pleading for mercy for "little Jacob." The response in both cases is compassionate: the judgment is withheld, the decision is put off, the punishment is postponed. The possibility of divine forbearance is always there—and in this case as in others (notably 1 Kings 22, Isaiah 6) Yahweh responds to the intervention of the prophet as a member of the heavenly congregation where plans are made, proposals are debated, and decisions rendered. With these visions and decisions we should therefore connect the oracles and utterance that speak of the need for repentance and the acts of warning that have already occurred and demand a response.

1. In chap. 5 there are two such sections, vv 4–6, "seek me and live"; and vv 14–15, "Seek Good and not Evil, so that you may live."

2. Presumably a part of the call to repentance would be a specification of charges or a description of those things which are contrary to the will of God and which are the basis of the threatened judgment. There are many such passages, but they are more often connected with threats of doom and judgment than with calls to repentance. Nevertheless they would be presupposed by either possible outcome, and certainly the call to repentance is linked to the specification of charges in the form of woes. A list of some representative passages is given below.

3. The plagues, five in number, that have been sent against Israel also constitute a warning of worse to come in the event of nonrepentance and failure to turn around (4:6–11). The refrain here after each plague, "yet you did not return to me," indicates that time is running out for Israel and that soon the other five plagues will be loosed on the people, with catastrophic results. The number five is doubtless deliberate and incomplete in the same sense that the full scale of plagues in Egypt is either seven or ten. In any case, the full number has not yet been reached, but if the significance of the refrain is clear, these warnings have not been heeded. Any future warnings are not likely to be either, and in the end the plagues to come will not serve as warnings but will be the instruments and markers of doom. The last of the five plagues—the overthrow of cities—is compared with the fate of Sodom and Gomorrah, a standard lesson in morality and divine judgment. In the present instance the "overthrow" did not wipe out the whole population, but the implication is clear. Israel is in the same danger and will suffer

the same fate. The conclusion of the matter is that a fateful and fatal confrontation is at hand. The repeated statement—that in spite of these terrible afflictions, which are universally regarded as acts of God, Israel has not turned back (šûb) to God—will lead to the next phase in which the same verbal root occurs also as a repeated refrain, "I will not reverse it (ʾăšîbennû)," meaning that the judgment has been made, the issue has been decided and is now irreversible.

At that point we come to the second phase, represented by the second pair of visions in which again, while the details of the visions vary, the message is the same: the end has come and God will not forgive or overlook the sins of the nation. Now the situation has advanced beyond the point of no return. According to the statement, a final decision has been reached, and in principle at least, neither intercession nor repentance is possible. This state of affairs is reflected in Visions 3 and 4 (chaps. 7:7–9 and 8:1–3), which have as their refrain the same words: "I shall not spare them again." Embedded in this complex is the story of the confrontation between Amos and Amaziah, showing that the confrontation belongs to the second phase, when the possibility of repentance and rescue has passed and when a final determination has been made for the whole area and for Israel in particular. The oracles of chaps. 1–2 reflect this phase of the book and speak repeatedly of the irreversibility of the decision and the certainty of punishment. These are not the only passages, as the book is full of similar judgments and irreversible threats; but they are typical. The threats that extend to the whole area, though concentrating on Israel, include two principal themes: invasion and the destruction of population centers on the one hand, and the exile of the survivors on the other. In themselves these threatened events do not require or assert annihilation but rather characterize the end of national existence. The force of the second central phase of the message and book of Amos is twofold: (1) the chance for repentance and survival, escape from the verdict of guilty and the sentence of death has passed; that door of opportunity has closed; and (2) on the contrary, attention has shifted from the verdict and decree, which were temporarily suspended in view of the prophet's intercession and the desire of the high judge to give the defendant every opportunity to escape the penalty by turning his heart and mending his ways. Attention has now shifted to the means of judgment and the execution of the sentence. At the end of the series of plagues (4:6–11), the transition from warning and threat to pronouncement of doom, the beginning of final judgment, is signaled by the portentous words in 4:12,

> Therefore thus have I done to you, O Israel! . . .
> prepare to confront your God, O Israel!

The bulk and heart of the book belong to this second phase of the prophet's mission and undoubtedly give the whole book its tone and color. The book as a whole was prepared after this second phase was over, and some or several messages from the first phase that were incorporated into the final report are presented in the light of their disappointing consequences. Warnings, which at first could be taken as conditional and which were doubtless intended to be received in that light, enabled the people to experience a disaster either as a discipline and an exemplary lesson, or as a taste of more to come, a corrective. If they had repented, it would have been gratefully seen as a timely and kindly curb on their slide into the pit. Unheeded it becomes the first installment of a series of punishments that are penalties for unrepented sins, and they take their place as such within the book as a whole. Chapters 1 and 2 are an uncompromising message of doom and destruction set within the classic framework of covenant formulation with its threats and promises, with its obligations, sanctions, and consequences. There is nothing surprising in this design, though the particular presentation in Amos is distinctive and, instead of following an established pattern, sets one for the other eighth-century prophets and those who followed in subsequent periods. And the solemn tone and punitive air of the prophecy should be attributed to its proper source, the God of heaven and Israel, rather than the prophet who has been charged with vindictiveness and callousness about the fate of Israel (and Judah), not to speak of other nations. It is precisely the role of the prophet to speak the heart and mind of God rather than his own, to deliver a message not his own and one with which he may disagree viscerally and emotionally, as we know explicitly in the case of Jeremiah (and of Moses, according to the stories about him in the Pentateuch). As to Amos' real feelings in the matter, his report of the visions is as close as we are likely to get, and his response to the first two visions clearly reflects the spontaneous reaction of one who is deeply concerned about the destiny and well-being of his countrymen, particularly those in the sister kingdom of Israel.

While the second phase, following or closely associated with the second pair of visions, is reflected in the bulk of the book and most of the oracles express the certainty of final judgment on the nation and describe the effects on the country and its people, there is a third phase, which pinpoints a special group within the larger population and a consequence that goes beyond what is in store for the nation generally. This later picture is to be associated with the fifth and last vision (9:1–4). While the form is slightly different from the others and there is a spatial separation (8:4–14 contains a series of oracular utterances, which echo the sections beginning with *šimʿû* in chaps. 3–5, and a continuation of the series of woes begun in chap. 5), it nevertheless belongs to the series and serves as a kind of climax. The purpose of the vision is to center attention on the destruction of the sanctuary (at Bethel, we assume). Yahweh himself gives the order, apparently to an angelic attendant but not to the prophet, who is an observer. The picture is similar to what is presented in Ezek 10:1–22 and 11:22–25, but especially 10:1–8, which describes the coals of fire to be used in the destruction of Jerusalem.

The theme of divine Fire, that is, a source of fire directly associated with the deity, is to be found in a number of passages in the OT: thus there is fire on the altar of the Temple in Isaiah's vision; the burning coal is taken by the Seraph to cleanse and cauterize the lips of the prophet (6:6–7). Here the fire is associated with the altar, but it is in the heavenly temple (as well as in the earthly counterpart). Similarly, when Yahweh descends upon Mount Sinai in the Exodus theophany he brings fire with him (Exod 19:16–20, esp. 18). It is this fire that is recalled by Moses in Deut 5:22–27 and that frightened the people, for it is a consuming fire, an expression used of Yahweh himself elsewhere in the Bible. The importance of the divine fire at Sinai/Horeb is emphasized at great length and in great detail through chap. 4 of Deuteronomy. Related to it is the pillar of fire associated with Yahweh during the period of the Exodus and Wanderings (Exod 13:21–22 J[E], cf. Neh 9:12, 19). Yahweh as a devouring fire is mentioned in the theophany in Exod 24:17 and Deut 4:24 and 9:3. More pertinent to Yahweh's role as warrior and firefighter from heaven are the stories of Elijah at Mount Carmel in 1 Kings 18 (vv 24, 38), at Mount Horeb in 1 Kings 19 (v 12), and in the confrontation with armed troops: 2 Kgs 1:9–16 (especially 10–14). See also Job 1:16, and compare the destructive fire from Yahweh in Num 11:1–3 (J), 26:10 (P), Lev 10:2 (P). It is used figuratively or mythically of Yahweh's anger: Ps 89:47 [E 46]; Nah 1:6; Lam 2:4; Ezek 21:36[E31], 22:31, 36:5, 38:19. See also the fire at the bush in Exodus, as symbolizing the presence of the deity. The close association of Yahweh with fire is amply attested, along with the use of divine fire in violent and punitive actions connected with warfare. There can be little doubt that in Amos 1–2 the fire that Yahweh sends produces this violent and destructive conflagration. Siege operations often involve fires, and warfare is inevitably associated with fiery destruction. But we need to distinguish between the military action of nations and those of God as divine warrior, for the latter are presented in mythopoeic language. It seems clear that Amos is relying on an extended and ancient tradition to make the point: the general destruction envisaged in Amos 1–2 is directed from heaven by the God of fire, who personally sends this violent destructive agent to encompass the ruin of all nations in the area. We have shown that the idiomatic usage is restricted to divine action, and the action described accords with the usage attested in the many passages cited.

One other essential element in divine warfare is the weapon of slaughter that precedes the general conflagration, as in Ezekiel 9. Usually this weapon is the sword, symbolic of all such activity and often associated with Yahweh. In Amos the direct connection is made in the oracle against the house of Jeroboam in 7:9 and then repeated for emphasis in 9:1 and 4. In the latter, the "Sword" is the personified agent of the deity, corresponding to the "Fire" that he will send against the nations: the combination will produce utter devastation. Yahweh has another agent of destruction, a "serpent" mentioned in Amos 9:3; just who is this "serpent" is not clear, though it is natural to associate this mythic monster with Leviathan and Yam(mu) or the seraphim, who are generally thought to be dragons, monsters shaped like snakes but with added features, such as wings and breathing fire (cf. Deut 8:15 and Num 21:6; a flying serpent or dragon in Isa 14:29 and 30:6; and of course Isaiah 6, where the seraphim are mentioned and described). In view of all of these data it seems clear that Amos is thinking in mythic and cosmic terms as well as in historic ones when talking about the destruction of the nation, its cities and its people.

It is to be noted that in connection with the total destruction of the temple at Bethel there is also involved the annihilation of the people associated with it. In an elaborate and extended image the prophet says that God will personally, and through his agents, pursue and relentlessly overtake all of them, regardless of the distance they flee and the inaccessibility of their hideouts. No one will escape. In fact, the description goes to an extreme in emphasizing that not a single person will escape the vengeance or retributive justice of God. But we believe that the material belonging to this third phase is intended to cover not the whole population but particular groups and individuals. In the light of the altercation between Amos and Amaziah in chap. 7 it is little wonder that Bethel is singled out for utter and total destruction, or that the prophet insists that no one connected with this corrupt and iniquitous sanctuary will survive. While in chap. 7 the word for Amaziah is that he will die in an unclean land as an exile, here it is emphasized that exile will not be the last punishment or indignity heaped upon the temple personnel but rather that Yahweh will send the Sword (another agent of divine punishment) to slay them. The division between leaders (in this case the religious hierarchy, but the monarchy is also included) and people made here is strengthened in the following verses, where it is specified that "All the sinners of my people shall die by the sword" (9:10), which we take to be a clarification of the statement in 9:8 concerning "the sinful kingdom," a reference to the governing hierarchy and civil and ecclesiastical establishment. It may be that those passages are in conflict, but it seems wiser to recognize that in Phase Three a distinction is made between the more culpable and the less culpable, and between victims and oppressors. This problem continued to trouble prophets and theologians, because on any ground they were determined to protect the justice of God against the charge of indiscriminate punishment or vengeance. This issue is raised in the debate between Abraham and God over the fate of Sodom and Gomorrah, and, as we know, the subject of Sodom and Gomorrah was an important one in the prophetic oracles, especially as that ancient tradition concerning the destruction of sinful cities by an angry and judgmental God was applied to the contemporary examples of Samaria and Jerusalem. It would be contrary to the basic principles of divine justice (*mišpāṭ*) and righteousness (*ṣĕdāqâ*) to inflict the same terrible consequences on guilty and innocent alike; and it would be especially repugnant to condemn to further suffering those who were themselves the victims of the oppressors whose wicked deeds were responsible for the imposition of divine judgment. The problem was never fully resolved, because destructions and devastations as well as plagues and earthquakes hardly distinguish between individuals on moral grounds, and in great calamities good and bad seem to suffer equally, or sometimes in inverse proportion to their merit. This inversion of what seems just and right is a frequent complaint of the Psalmist and the prophets, and it is incorporated as a basic thesis in the book of Job. How the problem could be solved in any realistic historical sense is hardly ever discussed, and no practical measures for doing so are offered. Ezekiel spends the most time and effort on the subject and is only able to say that God is not guilty of lumping good and bad together. But Ezekiel's hypothetical cases hardly satisfy: he only says that the truly righteous will be spared and the truly guilty will be punished and denies that the categories can ever be mixed.

In the third phase, then, Amos concentrates attention on the leadership of the nation and focuses interest ultimately on the royal house and the priestly hierarchy as targets of extermination. Yahweh will destroy those ultimately responsible for the coming disaster root and branch, and they will indeed be annihilated. Even in the opening oracles against the nations, rulers are specifically mentioned as special, almost the only, targets of the divine anger. In addition to the passage cited, the fifth vision and associated commentary, there are a number of others that reflect the basic distinction between groups and individuals in the population. Thus the Woes, including both the set piece in 6:1–7 and the scattered examples in chaps. 5–8 (with an echo in chap. 9 and perhaps some anticipation in chaps. 3 and 4) identify elements in the population who are guilty of covenant breaches and violations of the rule of God, both in matters of faith and in practice between person and person. The Woes in effect divide the population between the violators and the violated, between those who have power and position and those who are victims of the gross failure of those in authority, thus preserving the sanctity of the covenant community or providing remedies for the breaches that may and will occur. It is important to recognize that these distinctions are at the very root of God's justice, are embedded in the earliest legislation, and are part of the essential message of the material in chap. 9. Already in the basic charges against Israel, which will serve to implement and support the judgment of condemnation and the sentence of national punishment, the distinction between oppressors and oppressed is made (2:6ff.). It is true that the whole nation is condemned and the punishment is nothing less than execution, wholesale destruction and slaughter, and exile of people. The innocent will clearly suffer with the guilty, but that can hardly be because the prophet is ignorant or unaware of what he is saying, or because he or the God he represents does not care. The same general options or possibilities are presented by Abraham and Ezekiel and may be presupposed in all such instances. It is unthinkable that good and bad, innocent and guilty should share the same fate once the decision is made to destroy the whole community. The first proposal is to spare the city for the sake of the righteous in it, thus in effect allowing the guilty to escape the consequences of their evil. Yahweh tends to lean toward this solution, temporary and unsatisfactory as it is; but what precipitates the crisis is the unwillingness to continue with the compassion or condonation indefinitely or the failure to find sufficient righteous to warrant sparing the city. The other extreme is to destroy the city and all in it on account of the guilty ones there. This solution too is ruled out as being unjust, unfair, unkind, and basically contrary to the principles of biblical religion and the spirit of Yahweh himself, whose two primary attributes (once his divinity as creator, Lord and executive authority are established)—those of justice and mercy—are deeply involved in resolving the human predicament and dilemma. The resolution of the problem is found in destroying the city on account of the overwhelming wickedness in it, and at the same time sparing the righteous or protecting them from the worst consequences of the judgment. Such acts are never carried through lightly or for marginal reasons. This by implication is the solution in the case of Sodom and Gomorrah: Lot and his family are delivered while the rest perish in the destruction of the city. So for Ezekiel the solution will be much the same: Jerusalem and its sinful population will be destroyed, but the three great heroes of faith and righteousness (Noah, Job, and Daniel) will be spared—although their righteousness will not suffice to save anyone else, not even their families. (In the original traditions, Noah and Lot *did* bring their families to safety.) We must suppose a similar view on the part of Amos. The judgment against iniquity and sin has been pronounced, and the cities and nations will be destroyed. Furthermore, the leadership will be rooted out, and the leading figures, the king and priest, will be cut off. But there will be survivors and they will be spared—presumably they will go into exile and continue an identifiable existence elsewhere. There may be a remnant in the land as well, although here the prospect is bleak, if indeed there is one at all.

The fourth and final phase is represented by the last sections of the book, which have little echo or counterpart in the rest of the prophecy and are generally regarded as secondary. These passages seem to presuppose the destruction of the kingdom, but in particular the end of the dynasty of David (assuming that this is the essential meaning of the enigmatic and curious expression *sukkat dāwîd*—"David's booth" or "tent"). And a restoration is promised: "I will restore the fortunes of Israel my people" or "return their captivity." Again we find an echo in the root *šûb,* which plays such an important role in the rest of the book by linking the several phases by changes in the verb's form and force:

Phases One and Two (1). Yet you have not "returned" to me (in repentance)—in phase one or the transition to phase two, signaling the end of the chances for repentance and reconciliation.

Phases Two and Three (2). I will not "reverse" it, affirming repeatedly, as in the earlier case, that the judgment has been made, the condemnation pronounced, and the sentence of death passed—it only awaits execution, and it is irreversible. God will not repent or relent.

Phases Three and Four (3). The "restoration" of Israel, my people (9:14). It may be that the passage or passages at the end of the book are secondary and added by a later editor. It is hard to explore the prophet's mind, much more difficult to inquire into that of the heavenly council or of God. In his sovereign freedom, God through his prophets may declare an end, even a final end at any time. But the logic of the situation forces the prophets and the biblical writers to a different resolution. Unless we opt for some theory of total human depravity or universal sinfulness in which no distinctions are allowed, or submit to the fatalistic view that the workings of God must not and cannot be questioned and can only be accepted, then it is clear that the issue of justice and righteousness, of concern and compassion, forbids a final indiscriminate destruction. The nation may and will end, and its leaders will be pursued relentlessly and punished in accordance with their deserts. But what of the pitiable residue, the exiled remnant, including those who have suffered twice? Surely their lot is not just to be ignored or lumped in with those who deserved destruction in the general judgment. It is this double suffering by those who first suffered at the hands of the oppressors of their people, and then in the judgment of the nation that Second Isaiah may refer to in chap. 40. Elementary justice and a simple sense of fairness would require an end to accumulated inequities and a balancing and settlement of all accounts; in short, the replacement of the current world by a new one. But is there nothing here in this world and in this life? Someone obviously thought so and pointed to a future restoration. Perhaps it was not Amos; but it supplied an essential element in the requirements of biblical religion, covenant theology, and the workings of divine justice. Those who were victimized in the first place by the oppressive leadership, and in the second place by the indiscriminate judgment of God, could not and should not suffer a third miscarriage of justice and indignity by being swept into the dustbin of history along with the others. They had suffered double, perhaps not even for sins but for being part of a miscreant people; and at some time in the future their plight would have to be recognized and their claims validated. They should have been protected to begin with and spared in the second instance—and in the third place restored and their city and nation renewed, even as it is said in 9:14–15, the message at the end of the book of Amos.

General Introduction to Chapters 3 and 4

The second part of the first major section seems to consist of chaps. 3–4, but there is continuity into The Book of Woes, as indicated by the use of the standard heading, repeated with very slight variations at the beginning of chaps. 3, 4, and 5. In chap. 6 there is a shift to another formal category, "the Woes," which, however, has been anticipated in chap. 5 (beginning at v 7, but note also v 18) and will carry beyond the main section (6:1–7) to the end of chap. 6, also finding an echo in chap. 8. The lesson to be learned from the scattering of Woes in the book is that none of the divisions is sealed off from the others, but, on the contrary, there are interlocking elements linking each with the others. In these circumstances it is natural to see important connections between chaps. 1–2 and chap. 3, especially because in many ways chap. 3 picks up themes and thoughts from the earlier chapters and expands and elaborates on them. More specifically, chap. 3 is an exposition and explanation of elements in the last section of chap. 2, the one dealing with Israel. Chapter 3 can be divided as follows:

1. 3:1–2 Summation of the threat—prophetic condemnation of the people whom Yahweh delivered (cf. 2:10–11, also v 9);
2. 3:3–8 The role of the prophet—empirical-logical consequences (cf. 2:11–12);
3. 3:9–11 The condemnation of Samaria and all of its works (cf. 2:6–8);
4. 3:12 Interlude—separate utterance on the fate of the Israelites. (It seems to reflect the situation mentioned in 2 Kgs 14:25–28, especially v 28, which is difficult but implies that Jeroboam captured Damascus.)
5. 3:13–15 The fate of Bethel—the ecclesiastical counterpart of Samaria.

It will be noticed that the chapter divides into two virtually equal parts: vv 1–8 = 103 words; vv 9–15 = 104 words. The first half sums up the prophetic condemnation of Israel and explains the true role of the prophet as a member of the divine council and appointed messenger of the deity. The second part spells out in some detail the consequences of divine judgment (explicitly expressed in vv 1–2) for the nation. Here we may find the missing threat in the oracle on Israel in 2:6–13; 2:14–16 describes the outcome of the final battle, while 3:9–15 depicts the destruction and devastation of the two major and symbolic cities of Israel: Samaria (vv 9–11; 12) and Bethel (vv 13–15). It is likely that v 15 combines the references to Samaria and Bethel and is a summation of the national disaster. The point about Samaria and Bethel is that one is the national capital and the other is the national shrine. This division does not exclude religious components from Samaria or political ones from Bethel, for the two establishments were interwoven, as chap. 7 makes clear and as we understand from the whole story of kingship and priesthood in Israel and Judah and the rest of the Near East. While formal distinctions are made and there is a division in duties and differences in prerogatives and privileges, the two groups interacted, with power and influence flowing from one to the other and back. To destroy a nation effectively one must wreck both establishments. Normally they are combined in one center, as for example Jerusalem, where palace and temple were parts of the same enclave and belonged together in the administration of the common life; but in the north the prestige and authority of an ancient shrine and cult center such as Bethel ensured its religious primacy even though the political capital was elsewhere, and in spite of obvious efforts on the part of successive dynasties to build up the importance of Samaria as a religious center including the presence of temples and other shrines. It is notable, however, that the cult of Samaria seems to have been more syncretistic than that at the traditional Yahweh shrines (such as Bethel and Dan), and we know of temples there dedicated to Baal and probably Asherah (cf. 1 Kgs 16:32–33; Amos 8:14; and Hosea passim).

We may observe that chap. 4 is to be subsumed with chap. 3 as part of the comment on the latter part of chap. 2. The first part of chap. 4 echoes themes in chap. 3: Samaria and Bethel are targeted again. The central content of the chapter concerns the series of five plagues that constitute a sort of final warning to Israel. The unit closes with an elaborate apostrophe to Yahweh (4:13), also consisting of five elements.

OUTLINE OF CHAPTER 3: "HEAR THIS WORD"

1. Oracle (3:1–2)   The first two verses summarize the case against Israel, emphasizing at the same time its unique relation to the deity and its extreme culpability.

2. Riddles (3:3–8)   This passage constitutes a discourse on causality and connectedness in the life of nature and human beings. The heart of the message has to do with the indissoluble link between the word of God and the mission of the prophet. The connection between the speaking of Yahweh and the prophesying of his servant is essential and fundamental—they are two parts or sides of the same reality. The word of God and the word of the prophet must not and cannot diverge if the word is God's and the prophet is his true servant. They are one and the same, and in that fact are bound up the issues of the prophet's role and obligation, and the even more agonizing one concerning authenticity and authority. There can be no higher authority than God himself, and his word bears the stamp of that authority. The prophet's burden is enormous and weighty, but the authority attached to his words is correspondingly great, though only if his words are indeed the words of God. So the prophet, if true, is everything through his words—the spokesman and delegate of the deity—or nothing, just another person speaking his mind and heart, truly or falsely, if his words do not come from that same deity but from some other source. This passage, but especially vv 7–8, offers an important clue to understanding the prophet's role and the significance of his message. The complex of ideas about the prophet's status and role in relation to Yahweh is put in somewhat elliptical form, but the following elements can be isolated and identified. Going from the simple to the more difficult, it is clear that the conclusion of the matter is: "Yahweh has spoken; who could not prophesy?" Or, paraphrased: when Yahweh has spoken, the chosen instrument, the prophet, must respond. In fact, the content and purpose of prophecy are quite clear, to report the words of Yahweh as he or she has heard them. The hearing takes place in the *sôd* or privy council of the royal deity. Such scenes are described in detail by Isaiah, Micaiah, and Ezekiel, but the visions of other prophets seem to be related and may take place under similar circumstances. Two items may be mentioned here: the *sôd* is originally the place or setting in which divine decisions are rendered and allocutions or decrees issued. The word is then used to describe the decision or decree itself; but it is essentially the same thing, the decree or the setting in which it is made. The meaning of v 7 can be brought out by the following paraphrase: unless he has revealed his secret decision to his servants the

prophets, and his counsel or decree is revealed in the meeting of the privy council to which the prophet has been summoned, there can be no message from God. As a member of the council, the prophet not only has the privilege of an auditor but also the right or obligation of speaking. The decision is not reached, sealed, and promulgated until the matter has been broached and discussed. Once it is decided, then, the prophet is under obligation in accordance with his calling and commission to carry the message to his audience—to the people or whatever group or individual within it to whom he is sent. The second point is that, while in the visions and instructions to the prophet no explicit statement is made about the setting and we do not have a description of the heavenly court such as we are given in various other places in the Bible, the material in Amos is not only compatible with such a setting, but makes better sense and can be drawn together into a unified package if we understand such a scene and setting as background for his message. It is to be observed here that before Yahweh carries out his decrees, he reaches the decision in the presence of his aides and counselors, including the prophet(s) summoned for that purpose. The prophet, therefore, learns of the decision-making process before the decree is executed. Once the decision is reached, then the prophet's task is to communicate it to his people, to bring the message. This act is itself part of the process of actualization whereby the decision or decree made in the heavenly council becomes a force and a fact in the lives of the people to whom the message is directed. The delivery of the words is itself a stage in their fulfillment and initiates their realization in history. How they come out or what the ongoing effects and results may be are directly affected by the prophet's pronouncement and the response of those to whom he is sent. It is precisely this experience and this commission to deliver the word that are at the heart of Amos' sudden involvement in the prophetic role, and of his insistence on carrying out his commission. Having been present at the *sôd* of God and having had the decision made there revealed to him, he is then not only prepared for his mission but obligated to carry it out forthwith. In summary—Yahweh has spoken; one cannot avoid or escape the obligation to prophesy.

3. Proclamation (3:9–15) This unit naturally divides into two sections, with a transitional element between:

    a. 3:9–11 "Come to Samaria and see"
    b. 3:12 The end of Samaria
    c. 3:13–15 The demise of Bethel

It is quite possible that the final verse covers both cities and sums up the destruction to be visited on them. The unit that comes between the two oracles on Samaria and Bethel is difficult to interpret chiefly because of the elliptical character of the final phrase. It is also not entirely clear how to interpret and apply the figure of speech. Certainly there is an analogy here between the shepherd rescuing pitiful remnants of the animal or the flock from the mouth of the lion and the rescue of the children of Israel. By using the passive or reflexive form of the verb (the rendering is probably passive) the author avoids the question of identifying those in the roles of lion and shepherd. In the case of Israel, we are not told from whom Israel is to be rescued or by whom. In view of 1:2 and 3:8 an identification of the lion with Yahweh would be altogether in order, and there are other places in the Bible in which Yahweh is so depicted (cf. Hos 5:14, 11:10, 13:7–8). The question, then, is who is the rescuer; and here again we have explicit statements that no one can rescue from Yahweh's grasp (Deuteronomy 32, Hosea). It is possible that the rescuer is Yahweh, but then we must ask who the seizer and the lion figure is. And because the purpose of rescuing a bit or two of the animal is for identification and to provide proof to the owner that the shepherd was not negligent, and that the animal from the flock was actually eaten and not merely a stray (or indeed taken by the shepherd for his own purposes), the whole figure seems to break down. The real point of comparison, and perhaps the only one intended or open for consideration, is the dreadful fate of the people of Israel—of whom only a few bits and pieces will survive, sufficient for purposes of identification and no more. Thus the statement, "in the same way shall the Israelites be rescued [or: rescue themselves]—those who dwell in Samaria—only the corner of a bed" is understandable as a comparison with the rescue of the remnants of the sheep or goat from the lion's mouth. All that will be left of "those who dwell in Samaria" will be a piece of a bed—not merely in terms of what they will be rescued with, in other words, that is all they have left; but rather, that is all that will be left of them. After the devastation the city will be destroyed, and its surviving population will be taken captive. All that will be left of the city as well as in it will be these pitiful fragments. Verse 12 should then be seen as a comment on or expansion of the closing words of v 11. The verse (12) then describes the consequences of the violent action initiated in v 11, and the comparison is between the lion (v 12) and the enemy (v 11), both yielding equally disastrous results. By the time the rescuer arrives or is able to act, all that remains are a few fragments suitable for identification purposes, just sufficient to identify the victim. The implication is that there will be no rescuer or that he will not be able to save them. The use of the word *nṣl* here surely is heavily loaded with irony, if not sarcasm. Such rescuing will be of no benefit to the rescued, because the enemy in this case (the lion) is ordained and commissioned by God himself. Here again we must recognize that the "enemy," while described in human terms and performing human acts—setting a siege and then attacking the city, tearing down walls and despoiling towers—is also a cosmic and eschatological figure like the other heavenly agents of Yahweh (cf. the Fire in chaps. 1–2, and the snake and sword in chap. 9). We must ask whether even the *gôy* of chap. 8 is not a symbolic and eschatological figure as well as a historical and geographic one.

We arrive now at the beginning of the oracle in 3:9ff., and the question of the 2d m. pl. verbs (all four of them imperatives), to whom they are addressed and by whom. It seems clear that this passage constitutes a divine utterance, and whether the words are proclaimed by God or through the prophet as his authorized agent is neither clear nor very important once we understand that they are part of the heavenly proceedings. It is likely that they are instructions given by God directly to some of those attending the heavenly council designated to carry out the divine decision and in obedience to his will. The first pair of verbs are parallel, *hašmîʿû . . . weʾimrû,* "make heard . . . and say." The people who are to utter the proclamation, which can only be from God, are his messengers. They are to cause the announcement to be heard upon the citadels or ramparts of Assyria (MT: Ashdod) and in the land of Egypt. The content of the message follows, but it would appear that the announcement is aimed at peoples beyond the sphere of imminent or accomplished destruction. The oracles in the book of Amos are not in any sort of chronological arrangement, and it has proved difficult to the point of impossibility to extract any sort of chronological sequence (we have tried to settle here and there for a logical or reasonable order, but not at all with the intention or expectation of arranging or rearranging the materials). Nonetheless, the mention of Egypt, about which there is no textual doubt, shows that the particular instruction in 3:9a is aimed at a country beyond the range of chaps. 1–2, one that is not included in the list of the condemned or as an agent of divine judgment, one not otherwise involved in the area of activity so far defined. This consideration makes the reference to Ashdod in the parallel position somewhat puzzling and disturbing. The people of this place and Egypt are summoned to be witnesses to the case against Samaria and should therefore not be included among those to be judged. We would expect therefore that a nation that balances Egypt politically and geographically would be named, and the more than logical candidate, as we know from the repeated pairings in Hosea, is Assyria, not Ashdod. Assyria is actually the reading in the LXX here; and while the LXX is not without its problems in this verse as elsewhere in the book, that reading is to be preferred to the anomalous Ashdod, which is never used in parallel with Egypt elsewhere in the Bible. When it occurs in conjunction with other cities or nations it is always mentioned with other Philistine cities, as in Amos 1:8 and elsewhere. The peculiar pattern whereby *ʾrṣ* is used with one of the countries and not the other is to be found in Hosea in all positions—so this arrangement is attested: *bʾšwr . . . bʾrṣ mṣrym;* cf. Hos 7:12, *kʾšr* (for *kʾšwr?*), and 7:16, *bʾrṣ mṣrym* (long-range enclosure); 11:5, *'rṣ mṣrym//'šwr;* 11:11 *mmṣrym//m'rṣ 'šwr.*

In our judgment the heavenly messengers are ordered to proclaim the coming trial of Israel and to summon representative outside peoples who are not currently involved with the high court to come and see, to attend the proceedings and to observe as witnesses. The second set of plural imperatives in v 9b is addressed to the inhabitants of the citadels and fortresses of Assyria and Egypt: "Assemble on the mountains of Samaria, and observe the great tumults in its midst, the acts of oppression within it." In other words, the heavenly messengers (cf. Isa 40:1; Mullen 1980:209–26) are instructed to proclaim a message to the inhabitants of outlying countries, summoning them and their representatives to Israel to observe what is happening within its borders and in particular within the confines of the capital city. The summary statement (3:9–10) about upheavals and oppressions reflects the comment about Israel's acts of injustice specified in 2:6–8 and repeated with modifications and elaborations elsewhere in the book: for example, 4:1–5; 5:7, 10–12; the Woes in 6:1–6, 8:4–6. Verse 10 is a slightly different sort of summary: the basic problem is lack of knowledge, a frequent emphasis in both prophetic and wisdom literature, that essential knowledge which is ethical and moral in nature and which comes from direct experience of God and experiential knowledge of his character and ways. This lack of knowledge is not excusable ignorance but willful disregard of the knowledge of God that is immediately available and accessible to Israel more than to any other people because of its long-term and intimate association with this deity. So it is all the more punishable because of deliberate and willful resistance to the God to whom they owe everything, but above all obedience. The condemnation of those who store up violence and destruction is perhaps the earliest of the Woes in which particular groups and individuals are identified as especially guilty and therefore targets of unrelenting pursuit and punishment. Here no doubt it is the fruits of lawless destructive acts of robbery and raiding that are intended; at the same time, "the rewards" (v 10b) may be meant ironically and retributively. Because they have stored away the fruits of their violent and lawless acts, so they will be punished in the same manner; they are unconsciously and unintentionally storing up the same kind of lawless destruction against themselves that they practiced against others. Whether that is the actual meaning or implication of the language cannot be demonstrated, but it is consistent with the theme of retributive justice in Amos and the Bible generally. The specific threat enunciated in v 11 is not unlike the standard threat repeated against all of the other nations in chaps. 1 and 2 but not stated in connection with Israel. Here and elsewhere similar statements are made about the attack on and destruction of Israel and its cities, beginning with Samaria and continuing with Bethel (we are not speaking chronologically but in terms of their appearance in the book and the logic of the situation). The "enemy" there can be compared with the "Fire" in chaps. 1–2 as the otherwise unspecified agent of God who is commissioned to carry out the order of destruction and empowered to do so. He will bring down Samaria's fortresses and despoil her citadels. The picture is similar but not identical; nevertheless, the result will be the same, the destruction of the city and the end of the nation.

The transitional verse, 3:12, has an independent heading but can reasonably be attached to the preceding oracle because it elaborates the theme of destruction and emphasizes the completeness of the ruin. "Rescue" here is certainly ironic, for the only value to the shepherd of what he rescues from the lion is proof that the sheep or goat was completely destroyed; so it will be with Israel. In the second following oracle we have the same plural verbs, and they match directly and intricately with the first pair of verbs in v 9 rather than the second, though there may be some linkage among all three sets: note that in v 9 we have a *hipʿil* 2d m. pl. form followed by a *qal* form, *hašmîʿû . . . wěʾimrû*, whereas in v 13 we have the reverse order, *šimʿû . . . wěhāʿîdû*, while in v 9b we have a *nipʿal* form followed by the *qal: hēʾāsěpû . . . ûrěʾû*. The question is whether the imperative verbs are spoken to the angelic messengers assumed to be addressed in the first two verbs of v 9 or to the nations summoned in the second pair of verbs in the same verse. The choice is not an easy one, but while structurally the two imperatives from v 13 balance better with the first pair of v 9, their content seems to suggest that the second set of subjects is intended. It is also possible that a different set of messengers is addressed here and instructed to carry tidings of the heavenly council's decision directly to the house of Jacob (which is parallel with the "Israelites" of v 12 and more remotely balances the "sons [or house: LXX] of Israel" in v 1). In v 13 the verb *šmʿw* is a typical and standard parallel for *rʾw* in 9b. This pairing might imply that the nations (Assyria and Egypt) are not only to witness—by seeing what is going on and hearing the charges, accusations, and threats—but also to testify to what they have seen and heard and pronounce the judgment of God on his own people. This reading is possible but rather unusual, as the nations, in the eighth-century prophets, are rarely called on to do more than attend and witness the proceedings. A more active role, such as is here suggested, seems to be reserved for heavenly messengers and prophets who fill the same functions because they are considered agents of the divine court, as we have seen.

Therefore we conclude that the persons addressed in v 13 in the imperative plural are the same angelic group addressed in v 9a, whose mission includes a direct visit to the house of Jacob with the instruction to testify against the guilty nation what was decided by the privy council in heaven, a decision that they were in a position to hear. We do not want to force all of the data into a rigidly logical pattern because the whole picture belongs in the realm of vision, but within the framework of heavenly proceedings there should be a reasonable sequence of words and actions. In the charge itself in v 14 we have echoes of the great oracle of chaps. 1–2 (*pišˤê yiśrāˀēl*), while the promise of punishment is conveyed in the same wording as the summary statement of 3:1–2. The point is that the general destruction of chaps. 1–2 is presupposed here, while a particular assault within the larger universal attack is specified. This assault is aimed at Bethel, where the great sanctuary of Israel was located and which figures more and more prominently as the story develops and the book progresses. The horns of the altar symbolize the whole temple precinct and have special associations with the holiness of the place. The hacking off of the horns signifies the end of the useful existence of the altar(s) and the end of the Temple altogether. Further details are offered in different parts of the book, with respect to both the guilt and culpability of the Temple personnel and worshipers there (4:4–5) and the consequences for all involved, both people and buildings (cf. 5:5–6, 7:9–17, and 9:1–4). With the assault on Samaria (vv 9–11, 12) and Bethel (v 14), the charges and threats against Israel have become more specific, and details not included in the picture given in chap. 2 have been supplied. In v 15 we have a direct attack on the winter and summer houses and the elaborately ornate dwellings, which must be the palaces of the king and perhaps other members of the ruling aristocracy. The primary reference would seem to be to Samaria, but it is likely that there were royal dwellings elsewhere, almost certainly at Bethel. As Amaziah notes, the Temple at Bethel was a royal chapel; it was supported by the king, and as in the case of Jerusalem it is likely that a royal palace was nearby. The focus of attention on Samaria and Bethel in this chapter makes it clear that the nation's leaders are of particular interest to the prophet both because they symbolize the whole nation and its people and because they are specifically responsible for the current crisis. They are not the only guilty ones, but they bear the heaviest responsibility, will be pronounced the most guilty, and will endure the worst and most drastic punishment.

I.B.2. ORACLE AND RIDDLES (3:1-8)
I.B.2.a. THE WHOLE "FAMILY" (3:1-2)

3[1a]Hear this word that Yahweh has spoken about you, O Israelites, [1b]about the whole family that I brought up from the land of Egypt: [2a]"Only you have I known of all the families of the earth; [2b]therefore I will punish you for all your iniquities."

NOTES

3 1-8. In our introductory outline we highlighted the shift in focus that occurs between 2:6-8 (clearly the northern kingdom) and 2:9 (clearly the whole nation) and the change of address to foreign nations in 3:9. The change at 3:9 also brings Samaria back into focus as the center of attention of surrounding nations. In this framework 2:9-3:8 can be viewed as a unit with internal continuity, in spite of the break between 2:16 and 3:1.

Chapter 3 begins with an address to the "Israelites" (the term in 2:11), with 3:1 picking up the theme of Exodus from 2:10 (chiasmus). Clearly 3:3-8 is a unit, with the lion image a firm link between vv 4 and 8. But, by the same token, 3:8 forms an inclusion with 1:2 (the same verb, *š'g*). Amos 3:3-8, with its theme of prophecy, is an *apologia* for the compulsive behavior of prophets, in the light of the treatment received in 2:12.

Viewed in another perspective, there is a clear break at the end of chap. 2 with the oracle formula; and a fresh series of exhortations marked by the verb "Hear!" begins with 3:1. This kind of thing happens throughout the book. Even when there is a clean formal break, as at 3:1, there is thematic continuity, as we pointed out above. Indeed, the whole of chaps. 3–4 is essentially an expansion of the latter part of chap. 2, elaborating the end of Israel. And just as 2:9-11 contains a quick review of Israel's history back to the distant past, so chap. 4 contains a more detailed review of Israel's history in the recent past, especially the series of plagues still in living memory (4:6-11).

Amos 3:1-2 would make a good introduction to the combined oracles against Judah and Israel in chap. 2 (3:1b matches 2:10a). It serves as a colophon and supplies the missing sentence "I will punish you." The nature of the punishment is not specified here, but can be found in 2:14–16 and in other places in the book. The identification of Israel as just one of the clans of the region also places it once more in the total setting and perspective of the Great Set Speech in chaps. 1–2.

By the salient test of the number of "prose particles," Amos 3:1–2 has a very high count. The unit is too short to attach much statistical significance to the percentage; but its indubitably prose character is no warrant for branding it as secondary, Deuteronomistic, or otherwise editorial. There is no reason to believe that Amos was incapable of speaking or writing prose, but the main point is not the authenticity of this passage as his *ipsissima verba*. It contrasts completely with the units that precede (2:14–16) and follow (3:3–8) it. It succeeds in launching a whole new phase of the book (exhortations and woes, which continue through chap. 8), at the same time tying the rest of the book securely into chaps. 1–2 by formal, thematic, and verbal links, which we have pointed out on numerous occasions. Its function is clearly redactional; but it is not simply an adhesive between two otherwise independent blocks of material. It also contributes very important content not found elsewhere in the book. Its language is not conventional. It is rightly regarded as one of the most important and original statements in Scripture, and because it is so interesting and provocative, critics are reluctant to ascribe it to anyone but Amos. The interaction of two personalities, the prophet and his scribe or editor, may better explain the resultant text; but we must be careful not to suppose that the two of them differed significantly in any way, or that the editor lived long after Amos and that he invariably corrected and distorted the prophet's views and statements.

1a. *Hear.* There are three collections of oracles that begin in this characteristic way, at 3:1, 4:1, and 5:1. These collections (3:1–15, 4:1–13, and 5:1–17) are of approximately the same length, while a new series (of Woes) begins at 5:18 and extends through chap. 6.

Yahweh. Yahweh himself is the speaker, as the continuation in the first person (v 1b) shows. The identification of himself in the third person is conventional, especially in formal, royal usage. It shows that Yahweh can be identified as the direct speaker of other third-person passages, even when there is no switch to the first person.

Israelites. Literally, "sons of Israel," *oikos* in the LXX; presupposes *byt,* which is the reading of the Hebrew manuscript Codex Petropolitanus.

about. The LXX has *kai,* as if from *w'l,* for MT *'l.*

family. In ancient Israelite tribal lists and genealogies the kinship groups range in size from nation (*gôy, 'am, l'ôm, 'ummâ*) through tribe (*šēbeṭ, maṭṭeh*) to family (*bêt 'āb*) or simply household (*bayit*). The latter is literally "father-house" or "house," that is, an extended family under the authority of a patriarch (paterfamilias). This terminology could also be applied to larger units—the nation is *bêt yaʿaqōb,* a tribe likewise can be *bêt yôsēp,* etc.

The *mišpāḥâ* is the largest subtribal unit, between tribe and family, and could be called a clan or phratry. There is a certain amount of movement up the hierarchical structure. The tribes can be called "peoples," as in Isaac's blessings of Jacob (Gen 28:3). A large clan can acquire the status of a tribe, legitimated by fictitious adoptions (Genesis 48) and revision of genealogies. The use of these terms in Joshua 7, especially in vv 14–18, reveals three levels in the hierarchical structure (Andersen 1969). The nuclear family was not a functional unit in the sociopolitical structure (military, judicial, fiscal) of Israel; it did, however, define a zone of close kinship within the "family" excluding otherwise endogamous marriages, and mapping moral solidarity. Thus Achan's children, but no other kin, were executed with him (Josh 7:24).

Many problems arise in our use of such terminology as tribe or phratry, drawn from the classical world. The Latin and Greek terms acquire predominantly political significance in the developed constitutions of Mediterranean city-states. At the other extreme, the kinship structures of "tribal" societies are not entirely suitable either as a model for Israelite society during the biblical period. Transitions can be traced from Semitic nomadism to urbanization. In the former, blood relationship is paramount; in the latter, political affiliation (cf. Malamat 1973; Liver 1971). Eventually a person's place in society is defined by the town in which he resides. In the transition from patriarchal to political social structures, the ancient tribe becomes first a territorial unit, as in the allocations of "fiefs" (this term is not entirely suitable either, for the setup was not really feudal) in the book of Joshua. At this stage, in theory at least, the region is defined by the group occupying it. With the rise of centralized administration under the monarchy, this determination is inverted; the group is identified by the region it occupies. The continual use of kinship terms to describe the resultant political entities and their affiliations does not mean that the genealogies are pure fictions and projections. The genealogies doubtless served to legitimate political decisions, as outsiders were brought in by various means of aggregation, such as political alliances with provisions for intermarriage (Genesis 34).

The Israelite ethnic stock, with roots of great antiquity in the patriarchal age, was the nucleus for such growth, fostered during the formative Mosaic era by the active proselytism of the new monotheistic faith (Mendenhall 1973:177–83). The multiracial constitution of Israel during this transitional period should not be exaggerated, however, to the point that the nation is no more than a melt of previously unrelated peoples (Mendenhall

1973:180–81). This thesis has been carried to an extreme by Gottwald (1979:237–343).

This discussion of Israelite kinship terminology underscores the unique and puzzling use that Amos makes of the term *mišpāḥâ*. It normally describes a subtribal unit; and, just as a tribe can be given the rank of a nation when it is big enough and can be considered autonomous, so a *mišpāḥâ* can be given the rank of a tribe, as a major unit in a nation. But a *mišpāḥâ* is never viewed as an autonomous political unit. Amos 3:1 is the only place in which Israel is called a *mišpāḥâ*.

This unique and atypical use of antiquated terminology requires explanation. In old sources Israel itself is never called a *mišpāḥâ*. Israel consisted of about seventy *mišpāḥôt* (Andersen 1969). In Micah 2:3, Judah is a *mišpāḥâ* (cf. Jer 8:3, 33:24). There can be no doubt that Amos has the whole nation in mind; "the Israelites . . . that I brought up from the land of Egypt." It would seem a slight to refer to them as merely a subtribal unit. If v 1 were all we had, knowing that Israel was made up of scores of *mišpāḥôt*, we might take *kol-hammišpāḥâ* as collective, "all of the clan(s) [of Israel]," that is to say, every clan; compare *kol-mamlākâ* (2 Chr 9:19). But v 2 puts that point out of doubt. Israel is only one of the *mišpāḥôt* of the world. The phrase echoes Gen 12:3 and 28:14 (both J); compare "all the nations of the earth" (Gen 18:18, 26:4, 28:14).

This usage is downgrading. It also places Israel beside all of the other nations ("families") as members of a larger unit, a single tribe. It corresponds to the pictures in chaps. 1–2, where the two "houses" of Israel (= one *mišpāḥâ*) are listed with six other "peoples" of the region to constitute one regional entity, all equally under the jurisdiction of the one God.

2a. *have I known*. It is clear from chaps. 1–2 that Yahweh knows "all the families of the earth" equally well, also that he punishes them all for their iniquities. The verb "know" as used here must indicate special intimacy. For this meaning of the root *yd*ᶜ see Dahood's comments on Ps 1:6 (1966:5). Equally pertinent is the use of *yd*ᶜ in marital relations (BDB 394a), where the English equivalent would be "to make love to" (cf. Gen 4:1, 17, 25, etc.). The representation of Yahweh as husband and lover of Israel is frequent in the prophetic literature (especially Hosea, Jeremiah, Ezekiel), so a similar reference in Amos is entirely appropriate. The figure is simply a vivid and dramatic expression of the covenant relationship of Yahweh and Israel, which constitutes the fundamental premise and point of departure for the prophets. It is the real meaning of that relationship that Amos expounds with characteristic vigor and irony in this verse. Contrary to the common opinion, the intimacy of the covenant relationship of Yahweh and Israel was no guarantee of the latter's continued prosperity and security. Built into the covenant was a burden of responsibility commensurate with the gifts bestowed: "To whom much is given, of him much is required."

Without the covenant background and the stipulations and sanctions imposed at Sinai, the prophet's argument would be meaningless. The close relations between Yahweh and his people were nevertheless conditioned morally, and the divine grace was balanced by or consisted partly in divine demands. The consequences of disobedience would be disastrous.

In Exod 33:12, "I knew you" has as a parallel "you found favor in my eyes." The use of *bḥr* is Deuteronomic. Amos 9:7 shows that Israel was not the exclusive object of Yahweh's historical activities, nor the sole recipient of his favors. Amos does not define Israel's special status in terms of such traditional fundamentals as the call of Abraham or the Sinai covenant. He reports the migration and settlement in a new land (2:9–10), but in this matter Israel is no different from other nations whom Yahweh has moved around the stage of the world (9:7). While the earlier prophets focused attention on their own people, they did not leave everyone else out completely; at least Elijah and Elisha roamed beyond the borders and brought the word of the Lord to Phoenicians and Aramaeans. Even so such excursions were rare, and may be considered exceptional. Yahweh is "God of Israel," also God of the whole earth, but never specifically the God of any other nations as such. Israel is his homeland; Jerusalem his headquarters (1:2). While Yahweh knows all of the nations and moreover asserts his claims on them all, Israel is the only nation that knows Yahweh. Although v 2 states the case in absolute terms, these should be taken as relative rather than exclusive: I have given you more attention than any other people; therefore I expect more from you than from them. I will punish you more than them. Amos 3:2 is thus related to chaps. 1–2, but moves to a new point. In the Great Set Speech Judah and Israel are placed on exactly the same footing as the six nations that surround them. All are judged evenhandedly. The question recurs in 6:2b; but Israel continually supposed that they enjoyed most-favored-nation status in the area of justice. "Calamity shall not even come close, much less confront us" (9:10). But they will be punished *all the more,* that is, more than the others.

2b. *iniquities.* This is the only occurrence of *ʿāwōn* in Amos. It goes with *pqd* and is matched by *pišʿê-yiśrāʾêl* in v 14a. Both are the implied object in v 14b. The use of *pqd* twice in v 14 is a firm link to v 2, unifying the whole chapter.

Amos 3:1–2 emphasizes one of the central themes of the whole book. It goes right back to what is behind the threatened punishment of Israel. The special status of Israel and the favored treatment received are the leitmotif of the whole of the Hebrew Bible, and especially of the Primary History. Because Yahweh chose Jacob and saved Israel from bondage in Egypt, he has a right to demand devoted obedience and will judge Israel all the more strictly for its shortcomings. The statement is argumentative and provocative. "Therefore" (v 2b) goes against the usual interpretation, or the infer-

ence easily made by people who believe that they have been specially chosen by God: he will be indulgent toward our faults. The prophets did not
take this view. They agreed that the covenant relationship, once entered
into, was indissoluble. But the relationship with a sinful people was sustained by punishments, not by indifference. The punishments became a
token and proof of divine concern and commitment, and when they were
received and endured in that spirit they became disciplines, a corrective,
occasions for restoring the relationship to harmony by repentance and return to respect and obedience (4:6–11).

I.B.2.b. SOME RIDDLES (3:3–8)

3:3a	Do two go together,
3b	unless they have arranged to meet?
4a	Does a lion roar in the forest,
	if it has no prey?
4b	Does a young lion thunder from its lair,
	unless it has seized [a victim]?
5a	Does a bird alight upon a ground trap,
	if there is no lure for it?
5b	Does a trap spring up from the ground,
	except to make a capture?
6a	If a trumpet is sounded in a city,
	will not the people be disturbed?
6b	If a disaster befalls a city,
	is it not Yahweh's doing?
7a	For my Lord Yahweh does nothing,
7b	unless he has disclosed his plan to his servants, the prophets.
8a	The lion has roared;
	who is not frightened?
8b	My Lord Yahweh has spoken;
	who could not prophesy?

INTRODUCTION

Amos 3:3–8 is a wisdom piece that provides further background for the
Great Set Speech of chaps. 1–2. It ties together the roaring lion of 1:2 and
the prophets of 2:11–12 with Amos' own role as prophet. It gives his *apologia:* a true prophet has no choice, regardless of consequences for himself or
anyone else.

The verses in Amos 3:3–8 constitute an independent unit, but serving as
a comment on the asseveration in 3:2 and perhaps included in the text here
for that reason. Amos 3:2 is already a riddle, puzzling and paradoxical.
How do these two statements fit together? "I know you . . . *therefore,* I
will punish you." The standard argument would have been just the reverse.
"I know you . . . therefore I will bless you and save you." The remaining
verses read like a string of riddles, and the recourse to the wisdom genre is
another reason for regarding them as a digression. But they fit too snugly
into the context to be regarded as an intrusion. In vv 3–8 we have a series of
paired statements or consequences, which have a superficial resemblance to
the protasis-apodosis sequence in v 2. Furthermore, the ominous tone of the
figures in vv 3–8 echoes the note of doom sounded in v 2.

AMOS 3:3–8

		Syllables		
3:3	*hăyēlĕkû šnayim yaḥdāw*	$4 + 1 + 2 = 7$ $\Big\}$ 13	$\Big\}$ 13
	biltî 'im-nôʿādû	$2 + 1 + 3 = 6$		
3:4	*hăyišʾag 'aryēh bayyaʿar*	$3 + 2 + 2 = 7$ $\Big\}$ 11		
	wĕṭerep 'ên lô	$2 + 1 + 1 = 4$		28
	hăyittēn kĕpîr qôlô mimmĕʿōnātô	$3 + 2 + 2 + 5 = 12$ $\Big\}$ 17		
	biltî 'im-lākād	$2 + 1 + 2 = 5$		
3:5	*hătippōl ṣippôr ʿal-paḥ hāʾareṣ*	$3 + 2 + 1 + 1 + 2 = 9$ $\Big\}$ 14		
	ûmôqēš 'ên lāh	$3 + 1 + 1 = 5$		29
	hăyaʿăleh-paḥ min-hāʾădāmâ	$3 + 1 + 1 + 4 = 9$ $\Big\}$ 15		
	wĕlākôd lōʾ yilkôd	$3 + 1 + 2 = 6$		

Syllables

3:6	*ʾim yittāqaʿ šôpār bĕʿîr*	$1 + 3 + 2 + 2 = 8$
	wĕʿām lōʾ yeḥĕrādû	$2 + 1 + 3 = 6$

$\left.\begin{array}{}\\ \end{array}\right\}14$

	ʾim-tihyeh rāʿâ bĕʿîr	$1 + 2 + 2 + 2 = 7$
	wyhwh lōʾ ʿāśâ	$3 + 1 + 2 = 6$

$\left.\begin{array}{}\\ \end{array}\right\}13$ $\left.\begin{array}{}\\ \end{array}\right\}27$

3:7	*kî lōʾ yaʿăśeh*	$1 + 1 + 2 = 4$
	ʾădōnāy yhwh dābār	$3 + 2 + 2 = 7$

$\left.\begin{array}{}\\ \end{array}\right\}11$

	kî ʾim-gālâ sôdô	$1 + 1 + 2 + 2 = 6$
	ʾel-ʿăbādāyw hannĕbîʾîm	$1 + 3 + 4 = 8$

$\left.\begin{array}{}\\ \end{array}\right\}14$ $\left.\begin{array}{}\\ \end{array}\right\}25$

3:8	*ʾaryeh šāʾāg*	$2 + 2 = 4$
	mî lōʾ yîrāʾ	$1 + 1 + 2 = 4$

$\left.\begin{array}{}\\ \end{array}\right\}8$

	ʾădōnāy yhwh dibber	$3 + 2 + 2 = 7$
	mî lōʾ yinnābēʾ	$1 + 1 + 3 = 5$

$\left.\begin{array}{}\\ \end{array}\right\}12$ $\left.\begin{array}{}\\ \end{array}\right\}20$

There is a neat, even elegant group of items in vv 3–6. It is complete in itself and is a piece of wisdom/prophetic literature. The basic proposition is that two things do not go together unless they belong together, as is shown by the three pairs of examples that follow. They are all intermeshed and interlocking, and the piece ends with a satisfying conclusion mentioning Yahweh for the first time (v 6bB). The balance is very good, and while the number of lines varies, the total number of syllables or words works out nicely. We also note the use of particles in a highly sophisticated way. They reach out across natural boundaries to show how interlocking the whole thing is:

		Words	Syllables
3:3a	*hă*	3	7
b	*biltî ʾim*	3	6

$\left.\begin{array}{}\\ \end{array}\right\}6$ $\left.\begin{array}{}\\ \end{array}\right\}13$

		Words	Syllables
3:4aA	*hă*	3	7
B	*ʾên*	3	4

$\left.\begin{array}{}\\ \end{array}\right\}6$ $\left.\begin{array}{}\\ \end{array}\right\}11$

bA	*hă*	4 ⎫		12 ⎫	
		⎬ 7		⎬ 17	
B	*biltî 'im*	3 ⎭		5 ⎭	
3:5aA	*hă*	5 ⎫		9 ⎫	
		⎬ 8		⎬ 14	
B	*'ên*	3 ⎭		5 ⎭	
bA	*hă*	4 ⎫		9 ⎫	
		⎬ 7		⎬ 15	
B	*lō'*	3 ⎭		6 ⎭	
3:6aA	*'im*	4 ⎫		8 ⎫	
		⎬ 7		⎬ 15	
B	*lō'*	3 ⎭		6 ⎭	
bA	*'im*	4 ⎫		7 ⎫	
		⎬ 7		⎬ 13	
B	*lō'*	3 ⎭		6 ⎭	
Totals		48		97	

The seven double questions divide one way into five with *hă*- and two with *'im;* and another way into four with *biltî 'im* and *'ên* and three with *lō'* in the second member. The use of *'im* in the first and third balances the use of *'im* in the last two. The alternation of *'im* and *lō'* within the last two pairs matches the alternation of *hă*- . . . *biltî 'im* and *hă*- . . . *'en* in the first four double questions as a set. The fifth one shares *hă*- with the first four and *lō'* with the last two. This last detail is worth dwelling on. The fifth item in a series is often a variant; this one combines features of both groups and makes a transition. The structure is not symmetrical in the geometrical sense, but it creates a strong impression of a set of interlocking questions, asked, however, in several ways so that it is not at all obvious what the implied similarities are or what is to be taken as cause and what as effect.

The author has not only rung the changes on the available interrogative and negative particles; he has also used a wide range of grammatical constructions, even in lines that seem to have the same movement. The closest in syntax are 5bB, 6aB, 6bB, yet even here the verbs are different in each.

In all of them the second colon has three words, the first three or more, with seven as the average total. The lengths of the individual colons, by syllable count, show a wide range (four to twelve syllables); but the effect of combining them into bicolons evens out to an average of fourteen syllables (plus or minus three).

The grammatical patterns in vv 3–8 could provide a clue to the causal relationship of the paired statements:

3       $\Big\{$ a   interrogative + imperfect verb + subject + adverb
No. 1

         b   negative + conjunction + perfect verb

4       $\Big\{$ a   interrogative + imperfect verb + subject + adverb
No. 2

         b   "and" + subject + existential + adverb

No. 3 $\Big\{$ a   interrogative + imperfect verb + subject + object + adverb

         b   negative + conjunction + perfect verb

5       $\Big\{$ a   interrogative + imperfect verb + subject + adverb
No. 4

         b   "and" + subject + existential + adverb

No. 5 $\Big\{$ a   interrogative + imperfect verb + subject + adverb

         b   "and" + infinitive + negative + imperfect verb

6       $\Big\{$ a   *'im* + imperfect verb + subject + adverb
No. 6

         b   "and" + subject + negative + imperfect verb

No. 7 $\Big\{$ a   *'im* + imperfect verb + subject + adverb

         b   "and" + subject + negative + perfect verb

7   a   conjunction + negative + imperfect verb + subject + object

           b   conjunction + perfect verb + object + indirect object

8       $\Big\{$ a   subject + perfect verb
No. 8

         b   question

No. 9 $\Big\{$ a   subject + perfect verb

         b   question

The theme of the series in vv 3–8 is expressed at the beginning (v 3): "Do two go together, unless they have arranged to meet?" In the standard interpretations, the sentence is taken to refer to two people who agree to meet and proceed together. Unless prior arrangements are made they are likely to miss connections. In some commentaries the picture is suggested of travelers in the wilderness who are able to join forces only through previous agreement on a meeting place. Though somewhat cryptic, the question is rhetorical and self-answering, and apparently trivial. But no prophet could be frivolous; obviously some deeper, perhaps sinister meaning lurks within the enigma.

Verse 3 can better be understood as an introduction to the series of examples, rather than as the first of them; as a statement of the underlying principle rather than as an illustration of it. Thus the "two" mentioned in v 3 are not necessarily people or anything else material, but anything at all, in this case propositions or statements. The principle is that two such items belong together if they are in essential harmony with each other. The statements that follow, drawn from common experience, admirably illustrate the principle.

According to this analysis, then, the introduction (v 3) is followed by a series of seven statements, three pairs plus one (vv 4–7), each of which links two related phenomena and thus validates the principle of association adumbrated in the introduction. In each case there are two things that naturally go together. In one perspective the seven riddles consist of five (beginning with hă-) plus two (beginning with 'im). In another there are four dealing with natural history plus three dealing with humans; or six dealing with various analogies followed by one dealing with God; or one (v 3), which states the basic principle that things come in pairs, followed by six examples of such paired events; or one (v 3) followed by three pairs of riddles. If the last is the basic design, then the connection between Riddles 2 and 3 (lion) is clear; between Riddles 4 and 5 (bird), likewise; but the connection between Riddles 6 and 7 (people and Yahweh) is more enigmatic.

The first clause in each paired statement has the interrogative hă- (first five) or 'im (last two) followed immediately by an imperfect verb. All of these clauses could be taken as timeless generalities, but the use of different verb forms in the accompanying clauses points in different directions for the time sequence or chain of causality for these pairs of related events.

The second member uses three kinds of negation: biltî, 'ên, lō', with or without "and." The "and" clauses all have the same syntax: "and" + X + negative + predicate. Two have the syntax "and" + subject + 'en + l + pronoun. Three have the syntax "and" + X + lō' + verb, where X is either the subject or the infinitive absolute. The verb is twice prefixed, once suffixed. The question is, then, whether these are merely artistic variations, or whether they secure real distinctions.

The seven riddles are linked as in a chain. The second and third describe two aspects of the hunting practices of lions, their behavior in forest and den. Kĕpîr is a conventional parallel to 'aryēh; ṭerep (v 4a) is the implied object of lākād (v 4b). Riddles 4 and 5 are likewise a pair linked by the common word paḥ. Riddles 2 and 3 are also linked to Riddles 4 and 5 by their common theme of catching (the verb lkd is used in both pairs) and by their similar poetic and grammatical patterns. Riddles 6 and 7 are linked to each other by the common word "city"; the first of the two resembles Riddles 2 and 3 in discussing a loud noise (the trumpet blast resembles a lion's roar). The entire series is pervaded by an atmosphere of terror. Bad things are happening. Only at the end is it indicated that the Lord is behind it all.

The distinctions among the Hebrew verb tenses are largely lost by translations that translate them all as bland present tense. The first parts of the double statements (labeled "a" above) all have an imperfect verb. The second parts ("b") vary: three have a perfect verb; two an imperfect; two the negative existential *'ên*.

When a perfect verb is used in the protasis the riddle makes sense if the perfect verb describes the anterior cause, the imperfect the subsequent effect. The two made an appointment; then they walked together. (Or they did not make an appointment, so they did not walk together.) The young lion did not make a capture, so he did not cry out from his den. Likewise for the existentials. The snare does not have a spring (or trigger), so it will not catch anything. The lion does not have prey; so he will not roar in the forest.

    1. Two persons made (perfect) an appointment, and so walk (imperfect) together: b ⟶ a.

    2. The lion has prey (present), and so roars (imperfect): b ⟶ a.

    3. The lion has caught (perfect) and so growls (imperfect): b ⟶ a.

    4. There is a lure (present), so the bird alights (imperfect): b ⟶ a.

    5. The snare goes up (imperfect) and so catches (imperfect) something: a ⟶ b.

    6. The trumpet blows (imperfect) and the people are agitated (imperfect): a ⟶ b.

    7. Yahweh did something (perfect), so a disaster happens (imperfect): b ⟶ a.

The first four riddles thus have a similar logic. When the second verb is imperfect, however, the causal connection or temporal sequence is less clear. The trap springs up from the ground and then it catches something; or perhaps the two events are simultaneous. Likewise in v 6a we cannot decide whether the trumpet is blown in the city because the people are alarmed, or vice versa, though it is more likely the latter than the former.

The seventh question (v 6b) involves God. It is clearly climactic. It also has a perfect verb in the protasis, but this time the events are identical even though the verbs have different forms.

The question of interpretation (how the riddles work) goes off into the still unsolved problem of the meaning of the Hebrew verb forms, whether tense, aspect, or mood, or some combination of these. The use of negative and interrogative particles and of conditional conjunctions introduces three additional, different kinds of indefiniteness or uncertainty into the situation. Riddles of this kind are real brain twisters.

The seventh riddle also serves as the connection with vv 7–8, which must be viewed as the solution to the conundrum. These verses contain three more pairs of statements, each pair involving negation. This unit consists of one long statement (v 7) followed by two very pithy ones (v 8). The last two (v 8) ask questions. Here it is clearer that the perfect verbs describe the prior action; the imperfects describe the consequences. The three prior actions are connected; indeed they can be viewed as three aspects of the same event: the lion has roared; in other words, God has spoken; in other words, he has revealed his decision to the prophets.

The three consequences are likewise connected, but not identical: (1) The hearer must take fright—the prophet himself in the first place, when he hears the word immediately in the divine council (as they invariably report on their own reaction); the people in the second place, when they hear the word from the prophet (or at least they should fear). (2) The prophet must prophesy. (3) God will do what he said (the statement [the only one of the ten that is not a question] actually asserts that the Lord will not do anything unless he has previously revealed his plan to his servants the prophets).

The three concluding statements (vv 7–8) have verbal and thematic connections with the seven preceding riddles. The pattern is introverted.

> Riddle 2 $\check{s}^{\circ}g$ ——⟶ v 8aA
> Riddle 6 yr° ——⟶ v 8aB
> Riddle 7 $\acute{s}h$ ——⟶ v 7

Other elements in vv 7–8 correspond to themes in vv 3–6 as if it were all a cluster of parables. The lion's roar is clearly the voice of God, the trumpet blast the voice of the prophet. The discrepancy is that Amos prophesied (v 8b) but the people did not fear (v 8a).

To sum up the linkages among the paired statements of vv 3–8:

> Riddle 1 has the same syntax as Riddle 3 and the same theme as v 7;
> Riddle 2 has the same syntax as Riddle 4 and the same theme as Riddle 3 and v 8a;
> Riddle 3 has the same syntax as Riddle 1 and the same theme as Riddle 2 and v 8a;

Riddle 4 has the same syntax as Riddle 2 and the same theme as Riddle 5;

Riddle 5 has the same syntax as Riddle 6 and the same theme as Riddle 6;

Riddle 6 has the same syntax as Riddle 5 and the same theme as Riddle 7;

Riddle 7 has syntax like v 8a and the same theme as Riddle 6 and v 8b [Yahweh]; and

V 8a has the same syntax as v 8b, different from all of the others, with statement (perfect verb) first, then question (*mî*) and the same theme as Riddles 2 and 3.

The statements are not repetitious; indeed, each is different. And the grammatical, logical, and thematic structures of the whole are not isomorphous.

Verse 7 reads like prose rather than poetry, having no distinctively poetic features. Under the circumstances it is not surprising that certain scholars regard the passage (v 7) as a prose addition to an otherwise tightly constructed series of couplets, which is then completed by the clearly poetic couplet in v 8. Because the connection between v 6 and v 8 is not immediately apparent, it is argued that v 7 was composed to provide the needed transition. That may be so, but v 7 is not merely explanatory or even editorial. It seems to be another example of a necessary if prosaic component in an otherwise poetic composition. We have already encountered this phenomenon in the Great Set Speech.

Furthermore, it is possible to discover a compelling numerical pattern in the poem without the prose comment in v 7. Counting v 3 as the first in the series of pairs, we would have a total of seven such affirmations through v 6. Then v 8 with its couplet of pairings summarizes and concludes the series. Because a deliberate and repeated pattern of sevens has been demonstrated for chaps. 1 and 2 of Amos, and the same pattern occurs elsewhere in the book of the prophet, it is not unlikely that such a pattern is to be found here as well. Nonetheless, it is risky at best to discover such a pattern through a process of excision, and thus by forcible means to arrive at a previously anticipated goal.

Against the case suggested above, and in defense of the integrity and authenticity of the poem as it stands, the following considerations may be urged. While v 7 clearly is prosaic both in substance and form, it cannot be ruled out either as an authentic utterance of the prophet or as an integral part of the poem (3:3–8). The reason is that, disconcerting as they may be, such prosaic sentences and expressions occur repeatedly in the midst of otherwise unexceptionable poems by the prophet. And in several decisive instances it is virtually impossible to exclude the material in question from the original composition because it bears an essential part of the content, and its omission would disfigure the unit irreparably. Thus in the series of condemnations in chaps. 1:3–2:3, the specific charge against the nation mentioned is often stated in a form indistinguishable from prose, and in a structure that is not obviously compatible with the poetic meter of the surrounding material. For example, we have in 1:3 *ʿal-dûšām baḥărûṣôt habbarzel ʾet-haggilʿād,* "Because they threshed Gilead with iron sledges." This clause does not conform in style to the clearly poetic couplets in vv 3a, 4, and 5. Nevertheless, without it we have only the framework of a stanza consisting of a series of stock phrases made specific by the insertion of particular names and places. In short, the key phrase or something like it must have been part of Amos' original utterance. It is possible to suppose that an original poetic expression was lost and replaced by the present prosaic one, or deliberately altered to suit some circumstance; but it is hardly probable that such a procedure will have been adopted repeatedly throughout the series just where the specific charge is involved. It is more likely that the poet himself is responsible for the flat charge, prose form and all, as part of an otherwise metrical format, as a deliberate and perhaps shocking device to focus attention on the part of the hearer. But whatever the reason, we are compelled to reckon with the phenomenon.

In 1:6 we have a similar prosaic charge, "Because they took into captivity an entire captivity, to hand (them) over to Edom"; while in 1:9 we have a variation of it, which might be construed as more poetic because it consists of a couplet: "Because they handed over an entire captivity to Edom, / and did not remember the covenant of brothers." It can be argued that the charge in 1:11 is poetic and consistent with the context, but the charge in 1:13 is just as clearly prosaic and not metrically conformable with its context: "Because they ripped open the pregnant women of Gilead, in order to enlarge their territory." The charge in 2:1 is similarly prosaic in form, though its precise meaning remains in doubt. Other examples of such prosaizing in the middle of poetic units occur in Amos, but perhaps the preceding will suffice to indicate the existence of the phenomenon, and warn us against too facile a treatment of such elements elsewhere in poetic contexts. As it can be argued too that 3:7 contains the crucial content of the whole passage, we should be doubly careful about rejecting it. Perhaps the fact that the prophet shifts here from metaphoric language to the substance of his argument—that is, from parallel circumstances in nature and in human experience—is sufficient to explain the break in the previously established pattern. It is to be remarked that certain basic ingredients remain, which show that the composer was following the line of thought of the earlier affirmations. There are two elements juxtaposed that belong together. The action of Yahweh, alluded to in v 6, is predicated on his revelation of his intention to the prophets. The catchword method by which v 7 is linked to both v 6 (cf. *lōʾ ʿāśâ//lōʾ yaʿăśeh*) and v 8 (cf. *ʾădōnāy yhwh// ʾădōnāy yhwh; dābār//dibber; hannĕbîʾîm//yinnābēʾ*) is used throughout the poem: for example, *lākād* (4), *wĕlākôd . . . yilkôd* (5); *paḥ* (5a), *paḥ* (5b); *bĕʿîr* (6a), *bĕʿîr* (6b); *ʾaryēh* (4), *ʾaryēh* (8). Of course, any attentive reader of the poem could have composed a connecting link between vv 6 and 8 making use of the devices already present in the poem, which would leave matters as undecided as before.

The question of a numerical pattern is in a similarly ambiguous state. There are in all ten statements of varying length, but each makes a connection between two presumably related items or ideas. Eight of them occur in double pairings or couplets (such a couplet occurs in each of vv 4, 5, 6, and 8). Single affirmations occur in vv 3 and 7. Because the numbers seven and ten occur elsewhere in combination (i.e., $7 + 3 = 10$, as in Psalm 29 where, for the body of the poem, vv 3–9, we have the expression *qōl yhwh* seven times plus *yhwh* alone three times, making a total for *yhwh* of ten and for *qōl* seven; or the ideal family pattern in Job of ten children, seven sons plus three daughters [cf. also Baal in Canaanite mythology]), there is initially some reason to suppose that the poem is complete as it stands. If we assume further that the larger number, ten is to be broken into smaller components, namely seven and three, then the most obvious division (A) would come after v 6, with the first unit consisting of the single element of v 3 plus the three pairs of vv 4–6, and the second unit of the single element in v 7 plus the concluding pair in v 8. In such an analysis, v 7 serves as the connecting link between the examples and the conclusion. Another possibility (B) hinges on the meaning of the cryptic statement in v 3. If, as we believe, it is actually an introduction to the series, then it should be separated from the examples in vv 4–6, which should be tied to v 7, constituting the major unit of seven elements. The minor unit would consist of the introduction (v 3) and the concluding pair (v 8). The difference between these analyses is not great, and both require an overall structure of which v 7 is an integral part. It is perhaps unnecessary to pursue the matter further at this point.

	A				B		
I	v 3	(1)			Intro. v 3	(1)	
	v 4	(2)	7			v 4	(2)
	v 5	(2)		= 10 = 3	+ 7	v 5	(2)
	v 6	(2)	+			v 6	(2)
			3			v 7	(1)
II	v 7	(1)					
	v 8	(2)			concl. v 8	(2)	

NOTES

3:3. The obscurity of the Hebrew verb is reflected in the variety of preferred translations, ancient and modern.

The LXX version, "unless they know (or recognize) each other," suggests a variant *nwd'w* (influenced by *yd'ty* in v 2). The Aquila reading *syntaksōntai* supports the MT and interprets it as "make an arrangement" or "come to an agreement." The Theodotion reading *synelthōsin*, "unless they meet," is perhaps a little banal. The Hebrew root has the idea of meeting by appointment, as in Job 2:11 (which also uses *yaḥdāw*), a meeting followed by a journey, hence a reciprocal rather than a passive meaning. It is useless to speculate on the identity of the pair. It could be Yahweh and Israel, or it could be any couple (*wayyēlĕkû šnêhem yaḥdāw* [Gen 22:6, 8]).

Two people might meet by accident; but if they travel together, it was probably planned. Nothing could be simpler. The basis, the relation between the two, could be anything, as could the aim of the trip. Those details have nothing to do with the point. There is no warrant for making the riddle into an elaborate allegory. In the series that follows, the "two things" that go together are more specific, and the relations between them are quite varied. One thing accompanies another or perhaps triggers it. The first one is not the generalized case, for the ensuing pairs are not linked by prior arrangement. As in *Sesame Street*, things go together, the roaring of a lion and the taking of prey; the bird comes down because someone set a lure; the trap is sprung because the bird triggers it. The shofar is blown because there is alarm in a city; or perhaps there is alarm because the trumpet is blown. The statements are banal. The twist is in the last one. The two statements about the lion are parallel; the two statements about the bird are similar. Wisdom statements about animals and birds are often thinly veiled figures of human conduct. Yahweh has already been presented as a lion (1:2) who savages human prey (Hos 5:14), and gods often catch humans like birds in a net (Enlil; Hos 7:12). In verse 6a disaster (*rā'*) strikes a city, but the second half contains the surprise ending—only because Yahweh does it.

The last of the seven questions then becomes the starting point for further analysis. Not only is it true that evil befalls a city because Yahweh does it, he does not do it without telling a prophet. The links in the chain are firm. The Lord makes a decision; he tells a prophet; the prophet announces it (he must); it comes to pass (it must). The only missing connection is that the people do not heed the warning.

3b. *unless.* This is the only place in which the construction *biltî ʾim* is followed by a verb (cf. Gen 47:18; Judg 7:14). But *lĕbiltî,* the standard negation of an infinitive, is sometimes followed by a finite verb (Jer 23:14, 27:18; Exod 20:20; 2 Sam 14:14).

4. The parallelism among the following three pairs of riddles decreases as we go along. It is closest in v 4. This progression may be seen from the following matches:

hăyišʾag	//	*hăyittēn . . . qôlô;*
ʾaryēh	//	*kĕpîr;*
bayyaʿar	//	*mimmĕʿōnātô;*
ʾên	//	*biltî ʾim;*
ṭerep . . . lô	//	*lākād.*

The parallels are synonyms in each case, except for the last pair, which are complementary. The tendency to balance prepositions, especially those with similar or overlapping meanings, suggests that v 4aA could read "from the forest." In 1:2 the identical verbs have *min-* in each case.

4a. *forest.* The LXX says *ek tou drymou autou.* In the underlying Hebrew, *w* has been transferred from the following "and" under the influence of the suffix on the following *mmʿntw.*

prey. Does the lion roar when he spots the prey, to paralyze it with terror (matching vv 6a and 8a)? Or does he roar in triumph after the catch? Psalm 104:20–21 suggests that the roar is the lion's prayer to God for his meal (*bqš*). In Isa 5:29 and Ezek 22:25, the lion roars and seizes; in Ps 22:14(E13) he tears and roars. In other words, he may roar before, during, and after the kill, or at any other time; but the association was part of folklore.

4b. *seized.* The implied object is *ṭrp* in the preceding line. The LXX supplies *ti,* as in v 5. Note also the addition of *tis* to both lines in v 8.

5. The second pair of statements deals with birds and traps, thus adding a human dimension (the trapper) to the animal world of the first pair. Each statement, as before, links two phenomena: (1) the bird alights because of the lure set for it; (2) the trap is sprung by the pressure of the intended victim. Unlike v 4, however, the statements in v 5 are not duplicate or parallel statements of the same phenomena, but express a sequence of actions, namely, they tell a short, sad tale of the unwary bird, which is attracted by a lure on the ground attached to a hidden trap. The bird alights to investigate the lure, and in so doing triggers the mechanism of the trap; thus we have the inevitable combinations of bird and lure, trap and capture, here all interlocked to produce the anticipated disaster.

The linkage of 5a and 5b is confirmed by a series of literary and poetic devices, some of which have already been used in previous verses. Thus the poet balances *ʾên* in 5a with *lōʾ* in 5b; the sequence *ʿal paḥ hāʾāreṣ* (5a) is echoed with different meaning in *paḥ min hāʾădāmâ* (5b); note too the deliberate contrast between *npl* (5a) and *ʿlh* (5b); the bird comes down // the trap springs up. The theme of the bird carries through the verse, for it is the implied object of the final clause, "except to make a capture."

The verse presents three philological difficulties. One is the meaning of the phrase *paḥ hāʾāreṣ* (*hapax legomenon*). Because of the parallel *ʾrṣ*// *ʾdmh* and because v 5b says that the snare springs up from the ground, v 5a is usually paraphrased to mean "a snare [on] the earth" (RSV).

Second, *ʿal-paḥ* is found nowhere else; *ʾel-paḥ* is found in Proverbs. The idiom *npl ʿal* is used, and means "attack." This idiom accounts for the preposition in Amos 3:5. This difficulty seems to explain why the LXX has nothing corresponding to *ph*.

The third is the referent of the feminine pronoun "her" ("it") in v 5aB— "there is no *môqēš* for her [it]." Neither of the available referents (*ṣippôr* or *paḥ*) is feminine; but because some words can have either gender, *ṣippôr* can be taken as feminine in this one occurrence (BDB 861b), as the verb shows also. The solution depends in part on the identification of *môqēš,* whether it is part of a trap or whether it is something a bird might take (bait?).

In trying to solve the double riddle of v 5, insufficient attention has been paid to the verbs *tippōl*//*yaʿăleh,* clearly correlated. The bird comes down (Prov 7:23), the trap goes up. The usual translation, "fall," is unfortunate. The act of falling can be enforced, accidental or voluntary. A bird might be brought down by a net (Hos 5:1), but it plummets down onto a snare because it sees the bait; or rather it does not alight on the trap unless there is a lure for it.

In descriptions of such enterprises, references to equipment often involve metonymy; any one part can identify the whole mechanism (Gerleman 1946). *Paḥ* is often parallel to *môqēš,* as here (cf. Isa 8:14; Hos 9:8; Ps 69:23 [E22]), or used with the verb *yqš* (Pss 91:3; 124:7; 141:9), or sometimes with *rešet* (Hos 5:1). It can be a net with cords (Ps 140:6[E5]) to be thrown over the victim, or a concealed noose, or a pit for the animal to drop into (Hos 9:8). *Paḥ* seems to be the generic term.

Môqēš can be any enticement. Most of the occurrences of *môqēš* are figurative, and it is no wonder that it turns up in many enigmatic proverbs. A common snare is to trick someone into saying something that he cannot get out of afterward (Prov 20:25, 22:25, 29:5–6 [cf. 12:13]). The smooth talk (*ḥlq* [as in Qumran]) of the *ʾîš rāʿ* or *geber mahălîq* (con man) sets traps of cursing, deceit, oppression, mischief, iniquity by his mouth//tongue (Ps 10:7–10). It is useless to set the trap in the sight of the intended victim (Prov 1:17). Seductive speech is the lure (Prov 7:21–23). Proverbs 29:25 is obscure, *ḥerdat ʾādām* cannot be the subject of *yittēn,* as in RSV; but it suggests that the scoundrel plays on someone's fear to intimidate him. He makes the trap look like a safe refuge. Another tradition designates idols a *môqēš* (Exod 23:33; Deut 7:16; Judg 2:3; 8:27; Ps 106:36). In such proverbs the behavior of the bird or animal is a picture of human conduct. Amos 3:5 thus connects with 2:4b; the people of Ephraim have become like a silly bird (Hos 7:11), led aside by the lure of false prophecy (in contrast to the genuine word [vv 7–8]) and ensnared.

The LXX lost the picture: "Does a bird fall to the ground without a bird-catcher?"

6. The role of the trumpet in v 6 may be determined from the context and parallel usage in similar passages of the Hebrew Bible. It seems certain from the repetition of *bĕ'îr* that v 6a and v 6b are sequentially related (as are 5a and 5b) and that the military disaster indicated in v 6b is anticipated by the sound of the trumpet in v 6a. A similar pairing of *šôpār* and *rā'â* is to be found in Jer 6:1, "In Tekoa blow the trumpet . . . for disaster from the north has been observed."

A primary function of the trumpet in such a situation is to warn the people of an approaching enemy. Thus the sentry in Ezek 33:3 who "sees the sword coming against the land, will blow the trumpet in order to warn the people." The trumpet is also used to summon the army to action, to defend or attack as the case may be (Josh 6:5, 20; 1 Sam 13:3; 2 Sam 2:28, 15:10, 18:16, 20:1, etc.). Both elements may be present in the Amos passage. The effect of the trumpet blast is to rouse the people to a state of high tension. Whether the tension consists more of fear than excitement is not clear, but doubtless some mixture of these components is intended (cf. Isa 18:3). The same combination of the blast of the *šôpār* and the ensuing agitation among the people occurs in the description of the assembly at Mount Sinai (Exod 19:16–19). As in the other pairings in this section, the two actions are inevitably and inescapably related: the sound of the trumpet and the trembling of the people. In this case, the second element follows the first, as also seems to be the case in v 5b. In v 6b, however, the order in time is reversed, with the decision reflected in the second element preceding the event described in the first, as is also the case in v 5a and throughout v 4.

6a. *trumpet.* The figure is transparent. The prophet is like the *šôpār* (Hos 9:7–8).

city. Because he speaks about the people as *'am* ("armed forces") rather than *yôšēb*, it is a city under siege. It links to the Great Set Speech, for capture of the (capital) city is the end of the nation (1 Sam 5:9).

disturbed. In Hos 11:10–11 it is the lion's roar that produces "trembling" like a bird—a blend of three of Amos' riddles.

6b. The sense is that if or when disaster occurs in a city, it must have been caused by Yahweh. Because only a single action or event is under consideration here, the question of pairing is dealt with in a different manner from the other examples in the series. Here the concern is with cause and effect, that is, with disaster in the city, which is the result of Yahweh's decision and action. Or, put in other words, behind the observable occurrence is the will and previous decision of God. The action of Yahweh is identical with the disaster in the city (9:4).

doing. The object understood is the subject (*ra'â*) of the previous clause. The perfect verb points to something specific and concrete, "disaster," not just "bad."

7. With v 7 there is a significant alteration in the previous pattern of couplets in the series. In vv 4–6, there are three pairs of statements, each linking two related elements. Thus v 4 is essentially iterative, with v 4b repeating v 4a in different words; whereas vv 5 and 6, as we have argued, are sequential, with v 5b completing the action initiated in v 5a and v 6b complementing v 6a. But in each verse, there is a single subject, and the theme is carried through both bicola consistently. In v 7, however, the pattern is broken, for we have a declarative sentence instead of a question or supposition. In addition we have a single run-on sentence consisting of two associated elements, rather than the couplets of such pairings as in the previous verses.

7a. *does.* The verb *'āśâ* is general and can have a variety of objects. Because the word *dābār* can mean "decree," it is possible that the idiom here means that the Lord will not execute a decree without first telling a prophet and having him announce it. The verb *dibber* in v 8 then means that "Yahweh has issued a decree." The idea could, however, be more vague. In 1 Sam 20:2 Jonathan says:

> *hinnēh lō' ya'áśeh 'ābî dābār gādôl 'ô dābār qāṭōn*
> *wĕlō' yigleh 'et-'oznî.*

> Look! my father doesn't do anything, great or small,
> without confiding in me. (NIV)

The analogy casts the prophet in the most intimate and trusted role as the ruler's right-hand man and closest confidant. We should not, therefore, assume that the meeting and discussion always take place in a plenary session of the Lord's celestial court. Elijah was able to identify Yahweh as "the one before whom I *stand*" (an important technical term) and to claim such an exclusive executive role that "there will be neither dew nor rain . . . except at *my* word" (1 Kgs 17:1). The host of heaven was present when Micaiah and Isaiah saw the Lord (1 Kings 22; Isaiah 6), but the meetings with Moses, Samuel, and Amos seem to have been private. Yet even Amos contains hints of other agents present, though he does not name or describe them. He hears God issuing commands to "Fire," or commanding "the Sword"; and the title "Yahweh, God of hosts" (4:13, 5:27) shows awareness of the existence of celestial beings.

In neither Jonathan's nor Amos' case can *dābār* mean "anything." Obviously God does most things without first telling a prophet. And even Jonathan's qualification "great or small," meant to be all-inclusive, cannot be taken literally. In the context the *dābār* is a specific course of action in response to an unusual situation, one requiring forethought and planning—not a situation for a routine, predictable response, but a departure from the norm that needs to be identified and explained as an act of God.

7b. *plan.* *Sôd* is usually the conclave in which plans are made, an intimate circle (Jer 6:11, 15:17; Job 19:19), including God's consultative committee (Ps 89:8[E7]; Jer 23:18, 22; Job 15:8). By metonymy it could be the plan itself, otherwise secret (Prov 11:13, 20:19, 25:9). Both meanings are suitable in Amos 3:7; cf. the LXX *paideian,* as if from *ysr* (the usual word is *mûsār*).

servants. The phrase "servants [slaves] of Yahweh" can be used in a general way to refer to any and all of his worshipers (2 Kgs 10:23; Pss 113:1, 134:1, 135:1). The phrase "my [his] servants the prophets" is Deuteronomistic (2 Kgs 9:7, 17:13), but it occurs widely (Jer 7:25 = 44:4, 26:5, 29:19, 35:15; Ezek 38:17; Zech 1:6). All occurrences can hardly be assigned to a Deuteronomistic editor, but except for the present instance, they are late.

prophets. There is no indication that more than one prophet at a time was ever admitted to the divine council. Several individuals (Moses, Micaiah, Amos, Isaiah, Jeremiah) can be glimpsed in this setting. The plural word used here probably indicates this line and succession of individuals (2:11), not the presence of a group of prophets in the assembly at any one time. Elisha and his servant together saw the heavenly host (2 Kgs 6:17), but this is not the same as joining the assembly. The plural verbs at the beginning of Isaiah 40 were interpreted by the Targum as a call to "prophets" to comfort the people. The setting of that chapter is the divine assembly (Cross 1953). But the plurals can be interpreted otherwise (Freedman 1987b). In view of the fact that the prophets are present one at a time, the experience reported here reflects Amos' own encounter with Yahweh. The statement that God "took" Enoch (Gen 5:24) is usually understood to mean that he was taken into heaven, and later legend embellished this event into fantasies that Enoch was admitted to the divine society and initiated into heavenly secrets that he was able to impart to mankind. Amos' statement that "Yahweh took me from following the flock" (7:15) could document a similar experience, issuing in the inescapable task of announcing the divine decree (*dābār* [v 7a]). We must interpret Amos' visions in chaps. 7–9 as products of such a rapture, as part of the prophet's experience as a member of the divine assembly. His *apologia* (7:14) is rightly located in the midst of the visions, and Amaziah correctly calls him "visionary." In short Amos became a prophet with a message from God as a result of his vision of God in the divine assembly of which he, the shepherd and farmer, was an invited member. These visions, which are presented in stylized form, nevertheless reflect the circumstances of the divine court, because there is opportunity for discussion. There is time for intervention before the final decision is rendered and the plan ordered into execution. The remarkable thing is that the Lord shows a readiness to listen to other suggestions; he virtually invites the prophet to make intercession. So easily is he influenced, in fact, that he has to prohibit Jeremiah from making intercession and perhaps delaying or altering a divine decision to act in judgment.

8. Verse 8 serves as both summary and conclusion. The opening words pick up the image of the lion in v 4 (*yiš'ag 'aryēh//'aryēh šā'āg*), and in effect the whole series of images in vv 4–6. At the same time it leads directly to the final statement on Yahweh, for the figure of the roaring lion is regularly used of Yahweh. The figure drawn from nature in v 4 has been subtly adapted in v 8 to the divine imagery normally used by the poets of Israel. Comparison with 1:2 clarifies the point; and it is immaterial whether 1:2 was part of the original proclamation of Amos or not, for the figure of speech was part of the stock in trade of the prophets and poets of Israel. In v 8, therefore, the roaring lion is not only the beast of the forest in 3:4, but Yahweh himself, whose thunderous shout inspires terror in the hardiest but also compels the prophet to perform his inescapable duty of transmitting the exact words intended by God. With these words, the prophet's argument closes. It is tempting to see in this exposition a defense of the prophet's right and obligation to speak the word of Yahweh when he hears it. It is a cleverly reasoned response to those who may and indeed have ordered the prophets to be silent (2:12; cf. 7:10ff., especially v 13, where Amos himself is commanded not to prophesy at Bethel). Just as certain matters are permanently linked in the process of nature and history, so the word of God compels the utterance of the prophet, and no mere mortal or combination of human forces can sever the link between the one and the other or effectively suppress the prophetic utterance once Yahweh has pronounced his word.

8a. *The lion has roared.* According to Harper (1905:73–74) this phrase is Amos' way of saying that he has heard the tramp of the Assyrian army, and the following question shows that "he does not understand why others should be deaf to it" (74). We do not know how much stimulus to prophetic vision and audition might have come to him through brooding on the politics of his own day, and his prevision of rising Assyrian militarism. Except possibly for 6:14, the book contains no hint that he foresaw in any detail the scenario of Assyrian conquest that took place in the generation after him.

8b. *prophesy.* The emendation of *yinnābē'* to *yḥrd* to improve the parallelism with v 8aB and to link it to v 6aB (Wellhausen 1893) is misguided.

Parallel statements do not have to be synonymous; neither do the events have to be reported in their natural sequence. The prophet is fearful in the presence of God; this dread compels him to prophesy. The people *should* panic when they hear the warning of impending disaster.

I.C. MESSAGES FOR ISRAEL//SAMARIA (3:9–4:3)
I.C.1. THE INTERNATIONAL SETTING (3:9–12)

3:9a   Proclaim upon the ramparts of Assyria [MT: Ashdod],
         and upon the ramparts of the land of Egypt.
 9b   Say:
       "Assemble on the mountains of Samaria,
         and observe the great tumults in its midst,
         the acts of oppression within it.
 10a   They have no interest in doing right—
                        Oracle of Yahweh—
 10b   those who store away the rewards of lawless behavior in
                        their strongholds."
 11a   Therefore thus my Lord Yahweh has said:
       "The foe indeed surrounds your land,
 11b   and will pull down your fortresses in your midst,
         and your strongholds will be sacked."
 12a   Thus Yahweh has said:
       "Just as a shepherd rescues from the mouth of a lion
         two legs or a piece of an ear,
 12b   in the same way shall the Israelites be rescued—
         those who dwell in Samaria—
         only the corner of a bed—
         only the *dmšq* of a couch—"

I.C.2. ISRAEL (NORTH)—BETHEL (3:13–15)

3:13a   Confirm what you have heard about Jacob's family—
13b   Oracle of my Lord Yahweh, God of the hosts—
14a   When I punish Israel for its acts of rebellion,
14b   I will also punish the altars of Bethel;
            the horns of the altar will be cut down,
            and will fall to the ground.
15a   I will smash the winter palace
            as well as the summer palace;
15b   the ivory palaces will be destroyed,
            and the magnates' palaces will be swept away—
                        Oracle of Yahweh!

INTRODUCTION

Amos 3:9–15 is a fairly coherent unit. The only indication of a group to apply it to is "Jacob's family" in 3:13. This "family" may be equivalent to "the Israelites . . . who dwell in Samaria" (3:12). The two expressions are close enough to be equated, which makes better sense than seeing "Jacob's family" as another entity, for the obvious focus in 3:9–15 is the northern kingdom. The references to Samaria (vv 9, 12) and Bethel (v 14) make that conclusion certain. We have shown that "Israel" is Amos' usual term for the northern kingdom as such, and the failure to use it in the main oracle (3:9–13) here could be puzzling. We have shown that piš'ê yiśrā'ēl in 3:14 and "Israel" (twice) in 4:12 constitute echoes of 2:6, embracing and unifying this part of The Book of Doom (2:6–4:13) as the expanded and extended eighth oracle against Israel. But, as we have also seen, a variety of materials has been gathered into this discourse, some of it applicable to Judah and Israel alike. The focus shifts back and forth between the northern kingdom and the whole nation, sometimes imperceptibly.

Because of the break between 4:3 and 4:4, one might regard 3:9–4:3 as a set of related oracles. Each of the three units threatens disaster; each contains aspects of military action. Verse 11 describes the plundering of pelf and wealth that were accumulated as loot in the first place. Verse 12 implies much the same. What is left is hardly worth saving. Verse 14 describes the destruction of the shrine at Bethel; v 15 the demolition of luxury residences; 4:2–3 describes the removal of prisoners after the capture of the city. These four vignettes apply to Israel, and specifically to Samaria and Bethel—threats like those found in the Great Set Speech. Here, as there, it is possible to explain such actions as the result of military defeat and conquest. But it is also the action of Yahweh. In fact, in 3:14–15 the action is direct: "I will. . . ." An earthquake would do it. The four vignettes are arranged chiastically, so that both sides of such disasters—the supernatural cause, the natural means (our distinctions, not Amos') are recognized.

3:11	An enemy will overrun	Human agent
3:14	I will destroy	Divine agent
3:15	I will tear down	Divine agent
4:2–3	You will be [passive]	No agent

The mythic mode achieved by the use of direct divine speech in 3:14–15 is an important link with the fifth vision (9:1–4), which includes not only the demolition of the temple but also military defeat, exile, and extermination of survivors. There, however, the sword is not simply the weapon of a human invader, but the angel known elsewhere as "The Sword of Yahweh." The words of 4:1–3 also introduce an eschatological note (*hinnēh yāmîm bāʾîm*), which we meet again in 8:11 and 9:13. This little series ties together the three definitive stages of the End Time, in Amos' view. First the cessation of prophecy (8:11–12); second, the destruction of the nation (4:1–3); finally, the restoration of the fortunes of "my people Israel" (9:13–15). The study of these three passages together with the aid of their common eschatological rubric enables each to complement the others. It is easy to dispose of 9:13–15 as a later addition; but 8:11–12 is an integral part of the threefold oracle in 8:9–14, all of which is authentic Amos. Harper (1905:cxxxii–cxxxiii) discards 9:9–15, of course; but only 8:11a (a "Messianic addition") out of 8:9–14. He also salvages 4:2a as original. If this pin holds firm, then the kindred passages in chaps. 8 and 9 are also secured by it. But, by the same token, if these more eschatological oracles reflect the program inaugurated by the fifth and final vision (and we have now found several links between 3:9–4:3 and chap. 9), not only must chap. 9 be retained as authentic Amos tradition, because The Book of Doom depends on chap. 9, but also the whole book must finally have been composed in the perspective secured by the completed set of visions.

On the first reading, and even after many readings, 3:9–15 seem like a loose assemblage of unrelated oracles, or even fragments of oracles. There are some obscure passages, and whether we take each bit separately or even try to make sense of the whole unit, the difficulties are severe.

There are enough indications, structural and thematic, to encourage the search for some unifying principle, at least in the thinking of a redactor, if not in the mind of the prophet himself.

The quotation formulas are used five times in four different forms, suggesting a catena of oracles. The elaborate proposals in BH³ for trimming the one in v 13, deleting the one in v 15, and moving the one in v 10 into v 9, as well as dismembering v 12 and relocating the parts before v 9 and after v 13, draw attention to the problems but do not solve them.

All of the utterances are oracles; but who speaks them for the Lord? And to (or about) whom? Only v 11 contains a 2d f. s. pronoun "you," clearly addressed to Samaria. If we are correct in recognizing the participles in vv 10 and 12 as continuing the series of Woes that began in 2:7 and ends in chap. 8, then there is a speech about (or to) the residents of Samaria. The first and second oracles are linked by ʾarmĕnôt, which comes at the end of each. Scholars are usually inclined to see it as no more than a catchword used by an editor to put together two otherwise unrelated oracles by another editor (domino pattern). If this word were the only link, it would be hard to prove any more. But the first oracle has links with each of the following ones.

Besides the verbal link between the first and second oracles, the phrase hayyōšĕbîm bĕšōmĕrôn in the third oracle links back to "Samaria" and "those who store away" in vv 9–10. The fourfold use of the word "palace" in v 15 balances the twofold use of ʾarmĕnôt in vv 9–10, with the concluding bāttîm rabbîm as an inclusion with mĕhûmōt rabbôt in v 9. The process continues into the next chapter, with "Mount Samaria" (4:1) as a link to "mountains of Samaria" (3:9). The connections are not smooth enough to indicate a single original composition out of whole cloth; but they are not so disjointed as to indicate only disjecta membra.

The scenario is complicated by the involvement of observers and assessors who are summoned from Assyria and Egypt (v 9). The LXX reads en Assyriois (Assyria) here rather than the MT "Ashdod." While the MT is the more difficult reading, it may be too difficult. The Philistines are under the same judgment, while the Assyrians and Egyptians are not. It is not Amos who is instructed to collect these witnesses, for the verbs "proclaim" and "say" in v 9 are plural. There are two other places in which similar calls are issued: people are told to go to Bethel and Gilgal (4:4), to go to Calneh, Hamath, and Gath (6:2). In neither instance are we to take the proposal literally. They are exercises for the imagination. The challenge here is addressed to Israel, specifically to the residents of Samaria: "What do you think the Assyrians (or Philistines) and Egyptians would say if they saw what is happening in Samaria?"

There is balance between the double command issued to the unidentified messengers (*hašmí'û wě'imrû*) and the double command issued to the Assyrians (or Philistines) and Egyptians (*hē'âsĕpû . . . ûrě'û*). The double command in v 13 continues the instructions to the foreign observers. They are to assemble and observe, hear and testify.

The RSV and other translations display vv 9–15 as verse, except for v 12. The decision is arbitrary; it is the same rhetoric throughout. It abounds in parallelism, and v 12 has its share. But it is hopeless to try to scan it into "lines" with regular beats. Such lines vary in length from one or two beats (a few syllables) to statements of considerable length, which to all intents are indistinguishable from prose. One can appreciate the unwillingness of modern scholars to force v 12 into the patterns of classical lyrical verse. Theory prefers as many lines as possible to have three beats, and it can accept a few with two or four beats (or it can find an extra beat in the former, and reduce the beats in the latter, by counting or ignoring a secondary stress or even by adding a needed word, deleting an excess word).

Such heavy-handed criticism is essentially self-defeating, and it becomes unnecessary once the text is accepted as it is and perceived to be "prophecy" in a mode that is midway, in language and rhythms, between poetry and prose. For example: in v 9bB there is a four-beat line from which BH[3] wants to delete *rabbôt,* thus reducing the length and improving the parallelism. Likewise in v 9aB the editor did not know whether to delete *'armĕnôt* or *'ereṣ.* If it were not for modern theory and certain assumptions about the structure of Hebrew poetry, a long line such as v 10b and a short line such as v 14bA would not necessarily come under suspicion.

One observes a number of units in which a long line with no parallel is followed by two shorter ones with parallelism (v 9b, 11, 12a, 12b); or by another long line with parallelism inside it (v 10b).

Verse 12 is the centerpiece. It represents the last scene in the process of destruction threatened and described in vv 11 and 14–15. From the quantitative point of view also, the whole composition is balanced. The first two oracles (vv 9–11) not only match the last two (vv 13–15) with thematic content and verbal links; the two parts are about the same length (about twelve lines, about one hundred syllables).

NOTES

9. The LXX version reads *apaggeilate chōrais en Assyriois kai epi tas chōras tēs Aegyptou,* "proclaim it to the regions among the Assyrians (in Assyria), and to the regions of Egypt." While it is difficult to retroject Hebrew variants from such a loose translation, the LXX clearly read *b'šwr* for *b'šdwd*

and renders *'rmnwt* as *chōrai.* We have adopted *b'šwr* "in Asshur" as a better reading than "Ashdod" (see note below). In the Great Set Speech, the LXX translates the numerous occurrences of *'rmnwt* as *themelia,* but in Amos 3:10, 11 and 6:8 (as well as twice in this passage) *'armnwt* is represented by *chōrai.* This has led many to believe that the LXX presupposed *'dmwt* (Harper 1905:75) or *'rṣwt* (Wolff 1977:189) instead of *'rmnwt* in the rest of the book.

upon. The sense is ambiguous; it could mean "concerning" or "against," as in 1:1, or "over" (Wolff 1977).

ramparts. The nouns are definite, and in prose this phrase would be *hā'armĕnōt 'ăšĕr b-.* While a preposition in a construct phrase is not impossible, it is best to recognize here that the usual prose particles are simply not used. The *'armĕnōt* are targets for demolition in the Great Set Speech, while those of Israel are mentioned in 3:10, 11; and 6:8. See the note on 1:4.

Assyria. We read *b'šwr* along with the LXX as a more suitable parallel to *b'rṣ mṣrym* than the MT *b'šdwd.* Ashdod is one of the four Philistine cities mentioned in 1:6–8. Gath is mentioned alone in 6:2 (cf. Zeph 2:4). It is hard to see why the Philistines should be singled out for this task, or why they should be linked with Egypt. There are other reasons why "Assyria" is a better reading. Assyria is not otherwise mentioned in Amos, but in other eighth-century prophets it is commonly paired with Egypt. Because all eight nations of chaps. 1–2 have been placed in the same jeopardy, it is not sensible to threaten a nation with destruction and then invite it to be a witness or observer. If "Egypt" is correct, and it must be, then Ashdod is wrong, and something else is needed. The only reasonable possibility is Assyria.

9b. *mountains.* The plural is unusual; the expected singular is used in 6:1 and is found in the LXX, an obvious leveling. The subsequent pronouns focus on the city, but v 11 shows that the whole land is affected.

tumults . . . oppression. Compare these passive forms with *ḥăbūlîm* and *'ănûšîm* in 2:8. The term *'šwqym* could refer to various classes of the oppressed. It looks like a combination—the tumults arose from the oppression of the poor—an interesting idea of social upheaval resulting from oppression.

10. This verse changes the focus to a more direct address to the leaders who have accumulated treasure through lawless acts and failure to administer justice (*nĕkōḥâ*), as described in 2:4–8.

10a. *right. Nĕkōḥâ* has the general meaning of honesty or rectitude. It has associations with correct speech, the opposite of mockery or deception. In the context of Amos chaps. 2–3, with the negative particle, it is the opposite of heeding the word of prophecy and *torah* (2:4). Compare Isaiah 30:10:

> *ʾăšer ʾāmĕrû lārōʾîm lōʾ tirʾû*
>   *wĕlaḥōzîm lōʾ teḥĕzû lānû nĕkōḥôt*
>   *dabbĕrû lānû ḥălāqôt*
>   *ḥăzû   mahătallôt*

Who say to the seers, "See not";
    and to the prophets, "Prophesy not to us what is right;
      speak to us smooth things,
      prophesy illusions. . . ."

This context shows that *nĕkōḥâ* is the opposite of plausible deceptive speech. It is the plain talk of an honest prophet, which people do not wish to hear.

10b. *rewards of lawless behavior.* The literal version is hendiadys, "the spoil of violent action." As the object of *ʾṣr,* these treasures could be actual war plunder. But it might be Amos' way of describing wealth and luxury items accumulated by the exploitation and unjust spoliation of the poor within Israel. The word *šōd* has various associations, coordinated with or parallel to such words as *šēber* (Isa 59:7, 60:18; Jer 48:3) as well as *ḥāmās* (Jer 6:7; 20:8; Hab 1:3; Ezek 45:9) and *kāzāb* (Hos 12:2[El]). As in Amos 5:9, *šōd* also describes the ruination of a country through war and could imply that the wealth in the treasury was booty. The main connections are with internal injustice. The word *ḥāmās* is linked with both covenant violation and physical violence. In Deut 19:15–18 *ʿēd ḥāmas = ʿēd šeqer,* "false witness."

strongholds. The meaning of *ʾarmōn* was discussed at 1:4. Verse 10 has switched from "it" (Samaria) to "they," the residents or more particularly the rulers, the ones with the treasures of rapine in their strongholds. Although Amos does not name the kings of Israel or Judah in his prophecies of chaps. 3–6 (he may have done it in other oracles not reported), Amaziah has cause to brand his activities as seditious against the king and the whole country (7:10–11), especially because 2:4–8 shows that the wealth had been acquired through neglect of the king's prime duties. Amos' sustained hostility against the *ʾarmĕnōt* is due to their use as storage for plunder, not their legitimate use for military defense.

11. To plunder the plunderer is poetic justice. The identity of the agent is not mentioned here; and there is no indication of the nation (cf. 6:14) or "adversary" that Amos has in mind.

This verse presents several philological problems. Verse 11b is clearly intended to be a poetic bicolon, and the tendency of modern students is to bring the two cola into closer synonymy. Thus the RSV translates *ʿōz* as "defenses." But the singular probably denotes the outer wall (cf. *ḥômâ* in 1:3–2:5) with many *ʾarmĕnôt* inside. The verbs have likewise been brought into line by making both passive, a change rendered easy and plausible by the *defective* spelling of *hwrd*.

The most serious problem is v 11aB, which is unintelligible or at least ungrammatical—literally, "an adversary and around the land." It requires more drastic emendation to read *yĕsôbēb*. The LXX attests the preposition, but it levels to "your land" and reads *ṣr* as "Tyre," which is often *defective*. This interpretation is a case of misreading the text but confirming it. "Tyre" would be out of place because it too is targeted for total destruction. We share the desire of the LXX translator to know who the agent of divine retribution will be. His identification creates an unfulfilled prophecy; Tyre never plundered Israel.

your. The form is feminine and refers to Samaria.

12. The oracular formula "Thus Yahweh has said" shows that a prophecy can take the form of an extended simile such as is found in a proverb. Here the image of the predatory lion is used once again. The picture is not very reassuring. If there is a glimmer of hope, it is a very faint one: only enough will survive to prove who the victim was.

It was a rule among shepherds that the remains of an animal that had been taken by a predator could be produced to exonerate the shepherd in charge (Gen 31:39). The flock in this case is "the children of Israel." Elsewhere the lion is Yahweh, as in Hos 5:14–15; but if there is to be a remnant, Yahweh would be like the shepherd who rescues it. The simile cannot be forced into a detailed allegory. The focus is not on the responsibility of the shepherd but on the devastation of the flock.

12a. *legs.* The word is always dual; the numeral pleonastic, one pair of legs, nor four legs. But only a bit of an ear. The image is ambivalent. If Israel is like one sheep, the loss is total, the scraps no more than evidence of that. If the organs represent individual Israelites, the term "rescue" contains a slight hint that a few persons might survive. But the picture has to do with identifying the victim, a total loss, not with saving anyone.

12b. *Samaria.* Compare 4:1.

corner. The rest of the verse is very difficult. The LXX did not recognize the references to furniture, translating *miṭṭâ* as *phylē* ("tribe") and *ʿareś* as *hiereis* ("priests"). It also saw Samaria//Damascus. The difficulties compound to the point that the LXX can hardly be used to recover a better Hebrew original.

Little progress has been made in solving the textual problems of v 12bB since Harper (1905:80–82) reviewed the numerous proposals available in his time. Nothing worthwhile has been recovered from *katenanti* (for *bpᵓt*), which Theodotion retained, even though he corrected *phylē* to *klima*.

The remainder of the verse is equally beyond recovery. If the Hebrew text is correct, it is unintelligible to us. The crux is *wbdmšq*, and we have to explain why the Masoretes did *not* read Damascus, even though this reading was apparently obvious to ancient and modern readers. The MT, however, is probably correct here, *bdmšq//bpʾt*, and they both refer to parts of the bed//couch.

The LXX *hiereis* was perceived by Jerome to be an inner-Greek corruption arising from simple transliteration of *ʿareš*. This explanation is still the best one, though it lost favor after Hirscht (1903) pointed out that *ʿrš* is correctly translated in 6:4. But the LXX also missed *mṭh* = "bed," and was clearly off the track. The Greek revisers increasingly recognized that the passage was about furniture. But how do the scraps of furniture fit into the picture? In particular, what is the function of the preposition *b-*? The KJV translation, "who dwell in Samaria *in* the corner of a bed," is literal, but meaningless.

Because an elaborate simile links v 12a and v 12b, one expects close correspondence, not only in the things compared but also in the grammar. But v 12b does not have anything to match the lion or the shepherd. It changes the active *yaṣṣîl* to the passive or reflexive *yinnāṣĕlû*. The scraps of furniture somehow resemble the bits of the animal, suggesting that all that will be salvaged will be a few miserable and useless pieces. Or rather, the few survivors will be like such scraps (*bet essentiae*). The NEB changes *b-* to "like," which makes "the Israelites who dwell in Samaria" the subject. This reading leaves *wbdmšq* as the last and hardest piece to fit into the puzzle. The preposition *b-* supplies two options, because it is used in two preceding phrases and *bdmšq* could be parallel to either of them. (1) Read *dmšq*, as many versions did, and identify "the Israelites who dwell in Samaria . . . and in Damascus." This reading is strange but not altogether impossible, because in times of peace Israelites and Aramaeans probably had trading colonies in each other's capitals (1 Kgs 20:34). (2) In the second option, *bpʾt mṭh//bdmšq ʿrš*, and *dmšq* is identified a part of a couch (perhaps the covering or quilting) or a kind of couch, even a Damascus couch, an imported luxury item. It is not likely, however, that such a modifier would precede its noun. There have been endless attempts to find a more acceptable word, preferably one parallel to *pēʾâ*. G. R. Driver's proposal to read *bmqrš*, "on the frame of a bed" retains most of the consonants (albeit rearranges them) and uses the more salient meaning of *yšb* (1950:69). But the word *mqrš* is a mere invention. The NEB's "a chip from the leg of a bed" is ingenious; it fits the rest of the picture, and it requires minimal alteration of the text. It derives from a suggestion of Rabinowitz (1961), *ûbad-miššôq ʿareš*. Wolff (1977:196) rejects this proposal because *šôq* is never used for a foot of a bed (it means "thigh," especially of an animal), but the term could be metaphorical and appropriate in the context. *Bd* is a pun on *bdl*. The comparison between a bed and a sheep is worked out in chiasm:

two shanks
earlobe
corner of a bed
"thigh" of a couch

J. Reider explained *dmšq* as a compositum of *d(ᶜ)m šōq,* "prop-leg," securing parallelism and congruity (1948).

Wolff (1977:196) prefers H. Gese's suggestion, *bĕᵓāmešet,* compared with
Akk *amartu/amaštu,* "the <headboard> of the couch" (1962). This reading retains the picture of idling and luxuriating presented again in 4:1 and
6:4–6, lolling on divans of ivory in houses of ivory. A connection between
3:12 and 6:4 is certainly to be sought; but as 3:15 threatens the demolition
of such houses, v 12 likewise anticipates the smashing of the furniture.

The images are mixed, perhaps incongruous. The relations between
bones, beds, and people could be two pictures of the remnant of Israelites.
The number of Israelites who survive the disaster will be like the few bits of
a mutilated sheep left by the lion; or like a few scraps of furniture salvaged
from a looted city. All that is left are two pairs of leg bones and a piece of
an ear; or the legs of a couch and another small piece.

13a. *Confirm.* Israel has refused to listen to the native prophets, so the
Lord will send them foreign ones. The sequence resembles Isa 1:2, where
heaven and earth are the witnesses against Israel.

Jacob. Here we find the first occurrence of this term, which occurs again
in an introverted pattern:

House of Jacob	(3:13)
Pride of Jacob	(6:8)
Jacob	(7:2)
Jacob	(7:5)
Pride of Jacob	(8:7)
House of Jacob	(9:8)

Compare Mic 2:7, 3:9; Obadiah 17, 18.

14–15. This oracle consists of seven lines, three in the first person, four in
the third person. The first-person statements are made by God and predict
(or threaten) acts of judgment. There is a time reference (v 14a) followed by
two clauses with consecutive future verbs, *ûpāqadtî* (v 14bA), . . . *wĕhik-
kêtî* (v 15a). These lines are long (twelve, ten, and eleven syllables). Each
threat is followed by two lines that spell out the consequences; all four
clauses use consecutive future verbs. These lines are shorter (nine, six,
eight, and seven syllables), so each bicolon has fifteen syllables. This structure is spoiled when v 14bA is deleted as a later addition (Wolff 1977:199).

The use of singular and plural nouns secures a chiasmus:

> 14b   altars//horns of the altar
> 15a   palace//palace
> 15b   palaces//palaces

14a. *acts of rebellion.* The phrase *piš'ê-yiśrā'ēl* constitutes an inclusion with 2:6, so that this threat of destruction supplies the otherwise missing conclusion to the eighth oracle in the Great Set Speech.

14b. *punish.* (Literally, "visit.") The verb *ûpaqādtî* matches *wěšillaḥtî* and *wěhiṣṣattî.* A discrepancy has been found between the plural of v 14bA and the singular of v 14bB. Amos sees the multitude of altars as sinful, including the possibility of many at one shrine. The singular "altar" in v 14bB, then, either refers to the great and main altar of Bethel as a special target, or it is distributive (each). The singulars ("palace") in v 15a are similarly related to the plurals ("palaces") in v 15b.

horns. Special sanctity is attached to this part of the structure (Exod 27:1–2). The horns could be quite prominent in some designs (Ezek 43:15). The horns received the blood of solemn offerings (Lev 4:30, 16:18). They provided sanctuary (1 Kgs 1:50, 2:28). Their destruction means the loss of the last refuge; the destroyer will be undeterred by the holiest taboos.

15a. *winter . . . summer.* The climate of Palestine is not as uniform as some people think. Winter can be severe, summer intolerable. The height of luxury would be to have a separate residence for each season. Ahab's two palaces, one in Samaria and one in the plain of Jezreel (1 Kgs 21:1) may have served such a purpose. The king of Sam'al, Bar-Rakib, characterized the simplicity of his ancestors' lifestyle by saying that they used the same house all year round, not having a special winter residence (*byt štw'*) and summer residence (*byt kyṣ'*) (Zenjirli i:18–19).

as well as. The usual translation of *'al* as "(together) with" is not entirely satisfactory. J. C. Greenfield, in a study of *pgr . . . 'l pgr* in the Sefire inscription, has demonstrated the widespread use of the idiom to describe total destruction, the nouns being generic (1966).

15b. *magnates' palaces.* The attributive phrase *bāttîm rabbîm* does not match the construct *bāttê haššēn. Rabbîm* could mean "great," that the houses were large as well as ornate. The term "other" (LXX) is not needed. Recognition of enclitic *mem* would lead to another construct, "palaces of the great ones."

The oracles in 3:9–15 grow out of the preceding material and develop it further. The image of the lion from 1:2 and 3:4 is worked out, making it clear that the lion is Yahweh, the prey Israel. If they will not listen to a true prophet from their own kin (2:11), God will raise up against them accusers from outside (Deut 32:21; Rom 10:19). The picture in 1:2–2:3 is thus turned inside out. There Israel was looking around on all the crimes and atrocities committed by its neighbors; here other neighbors are looking in on the oppressions within Israel. All stand equally condemned.

Introduction to Chapter 4

Chapter 4 continues the clarification and elaboration of charges and threats made against Israel in chap. 3:9–15, a development that grows out of the initial oracles of 2:4–8. Chapter 4, which we associate with Chap. 3 in the structure of part 2 of The Book of Doom (chaps. 1–4), can be analyzed and outlined as follows:

A. vv 1–5: Charges and threats against one or two groups of people (2d m. pl. and 2d f. pl.).
    1. vv 1–3   The cows of Bashan
    2. vv 4–5   Sinful worship at Bethel
B. vv 6–11: The plagues
    1. v 6   Famine: *nātattî lākem*
    2. vv 7–8   Drought: *mānaʿtî mikkem*
    3. v 9   Blight: *hikkêtî ʾetkem*
    4. v 10   Pestilence: *šillaḥtî bākem*
    5. v 11   Earthquake: *hāpaktî bākem*
C. vv 12–13: Conclusion
    1. v 12   Final threat
    2. v 13   Apostrophe

The plagues constitute the centerpiece. The structure of this unit is similar to what we found in the opening oracle against the nations, with a formula providing the framework in each case. The openings are similar with a perfect verb in the first person, sometimes reinforced by the independent pronoun, *ʾny* and *ʾnky* in the first two cases, and followed by a preposition with the 2d m. pl. suffix (*ʾt* in v 9, the sign of the definite direct object, which is a preposition in the strict sense, though not generally reckoned with the standard forms). In two instances (second and fourth) an additional pair of first-person verbs occur. In the first instance (v 7) the verbs are from the same root and conjugation (first-person perfect and imperfect forms, *wĕhimṭîr//ʾamṭîr*), and they match up in an elegant chiasm. In the second case, the same perfect-imperfect arrangement is found, but the verbs are different (v 10: *hāragtî//wāʾaʿăleh*). Note the reverse usage of the conjunction. In the first example the *waw* occurs with the perfect and not with the imperfect with its special aspectual force, but the selection is influenced if not occasioned by the chiasm in the structure; in the second case we have the more normal pattern of perfect followed by the imperfect with the *waw*-conversive. While questions have been raised about the originality and authenticity of the expanded second plague, the similarity in part to the structure of the fourth plague shows that we must reserve judgment about what is or is not part of the prophet's oracle. With the addition of the two perfect 1st s. verbs we have a total of $5 + 2 = 7$, which may be of some significance. If we also reckon with the two first-person imperfect forms in vv 7 and 10 (*'mṭyr* and *'lh*) and add in the verb in 12a (*'śh*) we have three of them for a total of ten first-person verbs in the unit. That in turn suggests that v 12 should be linked with the plagues thematically, though grammatically and syntactically it stands by itself. Here we have 2d m. s. forms in contrast with the 2d pl. used throughout the plague sequence. Nevertheless we can mark v 12 as transitional, serving as closing comment on the plague series and leading to the final hymnic element with which the subunit and the whole unit close.

The curious repetition in vv 12a and 12bA can be explained in terms of direction: v 12a expresses the consequence of Israel's failure to repent, while v 12bA leads to the final ominous warning to Israel of a confrontation between God and people that is imminent now that previous signs and actions have proved unavailing. The closing words, "prepare to confront your God, O Israel!" have an unusual structure, with the subject of the imperative verb placed at the end, thus forming an envelope around the middle elements (a prepositional phrase with an infinitive taking a direct object) with the verb, which comes at the beginning.

Verse 12 is a comment and a warning: v 12a, comment on the plagues and Israel's failure to respond; v 12b, on the basis of Israel's resistance to warnings, and a decision reached by Yahweh, a final ominous warning is now given—"prepare to confront your God, O Israel"—as the first section of the book comes to a close with v 13, a hymnic apostrophe. In this unit Yahweh is apostrophized in a sequence of five participles (cf. the other hymnic units of similar nature in 5:8–9 and 9:5–6; in both of the latter there are only three participial forms, but they are balanced by two finite verb forms, making a total of five verbs with Yahweh as subject). In our view this hymn of praise to Yahweh rounds out the first large section of the book and leads into the middle section of the book, represented by chap. 5.

We have suggested that chap. 4 in effect continues the account of Israel's sins and crimes developed in chap. 3. The target of the attack is the same as in chap. 3, though there is some difficulty in untangling the apparent confusion in the opening unit (vv 1–5). Destruction and exile are prominently on the agenda. Of special interest to the prophet are the religious devotion and activity of those condemned for high crimes against God and fellow human beings. Speaking with great sarcasm, he invites and encourages, even commands them to come to Bethel and Gilgal, shrines with historic ties to Israel's early days. They were the sites of special revelation and other religious activity going back to patriarchal times and to the early days of the invasion and settlement of Canaan. Bethel is central to the patriarchal tradition, especially in relation to Jacob, while Gilgal figures prominently in the early phases of the conquest and settlement on the west side of the Jordan. There is still considerable controversy about the precise location of the town with its sanctuary, but it must be in the general vicinity of Jericho, where the conquest of western Canaan was launched; no doubt one of the several sites proposed by scholars will turn out to be correct.

The opening unit, then, combines the explicit threat of exile as a consequence of violent military action against Samaria with these heavily ironic orders to the population to multiply their sinful rebellions against God (once again the root $p\check{s}^c$ is used prominently, thereby identifying the action threatened with that proclaimed in chaps. 1–2 in an almost hypnotic eightfold repetition). As also in 3:14, so here in 4:4–5 the root is used to identify those engaged in the most sacred acts as rebels and seditionists—that is, treaty-covenant breakers against God. Not only will their display of piety fail to help them, it is precisely their practice of religion and the faith that lies behind it and guides it that are the root cause of the problem. The heavy irony here reflects that already noted in 3:12, where the salvaging of a few miserable bones from the mouth of the lion is characterized as "rescue." So here the summons to worship at the major shrines is associated with the worst sort of rebellion against God, worship as an act of sedition against the divine suzerain. Acts of worship associated with the shrines are considered acts of rebellion; religion for Israel is resistance to God. So cause and effect are combined but, as is often the case with the prophets, in reverse order.

The whole unit requires careful analysis especially because of the curious and apparently illogical combination of 2d m. pl. and 2d f. pl. forms in vv 1–5, without clearly marked lines of demarcation or distinction. It must first be noted that the opening verb of 4:1 is an imperative 2d m. pl.—*šim'û*, exactly the same as in 3:1, 5:1, and elsewhere, including 3:13, 8:4, and so on. The initial clause is abbreviated, in contrast to 3:1 and 5:1, but the elements present in the others, including *'ălêkem* and *bny* or *byt yśr'l* (cf. 3:1 and 5:1) are to be found scattered through the pericope in 4:1–5. The word *'ălêkem* in 4:2 follows a different eschatological formula: "behold, days are coming upon you" rather than "this word which Yahweh has spoken about you" or "which I am about to utter about you." But the basic idea is the same, for in 4:2 an oath is involved that promises to fulfill the words spoken in actions taken against Israel (note also the connection between "hear this" and an oath of perpetual hostility in 8:4 and 8:7, which is parallel to this material in other ways too). Finally, the *bny yśrʾl* are identified as the m. pl. subject of the imperative at the beginning of 4:1 and with the m. pronominal suffixes in 4:2 and in 4:5 at the end of the verse. They are also the subject of the verbs in vv 4–5, but this issue is not in question. What binds the two subunits together, then, is the 2d m. pl. forms that occur at the beginning of v 1 and sporadically in v 2, then in vv 4–5 to the exclusion of all others. There are, in fact, seven imperative verbs in vv 4–5a; all are 2d m. pl. forms, with the single exception of *wqṭr* in v 5—there is no need to emend this form *qaṭṭēr,* which is interpreted as imperative 2d m. s., to the plural to make it conform to the others. It should be read rather as the *piʿel* infinitive absolute, used here as an imperative (cf. *zākôr* and *šāmôr* in the different versions of the Decalogue, which have imperative force but are in fact examples of the infinitive absolute). The verbs occur in pairs except for the infinitive absolute, which is the deliberate deviation from a standard pattern. This pattern of varying from a repeated series is so well established as to be a recognizable and expected element in almost any series. We have already observed this variation from a norm several times in Amos (e.g., chaps. 1–2 and chap. 6), so it should come as no surprise here:

> v 4 *bōʾû . . . ûpišʿû*
> *harbû . . . wĕhābîʾû*
> v5a *. . . wĕqaṭṭēr . . .*
> *wĕqirʾû . . . hašmîʿû*

The first two pairs are in normal order. The first pair matches verbs in the *qal* stem, while the second matches *hipʿil* forms. Then comes the distinctive separate term *wĕqaṭṭēr,* while the final pair matches one *qal* form with one *hipʿil* form, in chiastic order. The first verb has the conjunction *waw,* while the second does not. Note that it is the fifth item in the list that differs from the others. The same variation turns up in the other two lists of seven items, which we have identified in the book of Amos. (1) The threats against the cities in chaps. 1 and 2: six of the seven instances have the form *wšlḥty ʾš,* but one (the fifth) has the form *whṣty ʾš,* with essentially the same meaning. (2) The targets of the "woe" pronounced in 6:1–6: of the seven groups identified, six have the definite article preceding the noun or participle, but one (the fifth) lacks the article (*wʾklym*). Verse 4:5b has an eighth verb with a 2d m. pl. pronominal subject, but this form diverges even farther from the norm because it does not have imperative meaning or force.

The principal question we face in the opening section concerns the so-called "cows of Bashan." Who are these people? The "cows" of course are females, but is the group they represent in the figure of speech necessarily female also? It is clear that the cows stand for people who are in Mount Samaria, and like others located there are guilty of serious crimes, especially against the poor and powerless (cf. 2:6–8 and 8:4–7, among other passages). The participial forms are used elsewhere in the book in connection with the woes, and we may have an anticipation of that series (which begins formally in 5:7 and ends formally in 6:13, but which has echoes and leaves imprints elsewhere in the book, beginning as early as 2:7 and in this passage). It would be natural to suppose that female animals represent female persons, and a majority of scholars and commentators has interpreted the usage in that way. That view is reinforced by the use of 3d f. pl. participles in 4:1a–b:

> Those who oppress the destitute
> Those who crush the poor
> Those who say to their lords. . . .

As this reference is obviously not to animals but to human beings, it is conceivable, but not likely, that the feminine forms result from the influence of the original figure's gender, but it is more reasonable to suppose that the real subjects of the verbs are women who wield power and can do the things attributed to them. If we question the power of women in their right both to hold property and to exercise influence in the court or in life, then we must reconsider the situation. But is it clear that it is the women of Samaria and in particular the wives of the leaders and nobles who are charged with greedy oppression and partying at the expense of the poor? The charges are essentially the same as those made against other groups and classes in Israel, and it is certainly possible to see the great, sleek women of the city engaging in the same oppressive practices. That women could be so involved is attested in a number of places and especially in Proverbs 31, where the model housewife runs the family and the family business almost entirely on her own.

The simple sense of the passage could point in this direction, but scholars have demurred in the past and continue to do so. They argue that the feminine gender is only in the figure of speech and that it is part of the prophet's charge against these people to characterize them as female cattle, an insult in any case and a worse one if directed against men. This interpretation is not intended to annul a charge of male chauvinism against the prophet because, whether by attacking the women directly or by characterizing men as members of the weaker sex, the prophet or editor may well display an antifeminine bias. It is said that the civic leaders, whether in military or civilian life, behave like women or rather cows, but that they are men who hold the levers of power and do the things that elsewhere are charged against men. Furthermore, the mixture of feminine and masculine forms in 4:1–3 simply shows that men are meant throughout; the occurrence of feminine forms arises from the use of the imagery of "cows" and an attempt to carry the figure through the oracle. In short, here as else-where, with participles and woes, a distinctive group (categorized or char-acterized as cows of Bashan) in Israel is singled out for condemnation and punishment. Just who that group is remains a question.

After reflecting and reconsidering, it still seems best to take the state-ments at face value and see here the lordly women of Samaria, whose husbands dominate the government, as the oppressors and crushers of the poor. These women soon shall suffer the same consequences as they have meted out to the helpless and defenseless. They are, nonetheless, part of the larger group, the people of Israel, and will share in the common fate. In the meantime, all Israel is headed toward its appointed doom, being hastened on its way by a distorted view of religion and by enthusiastically practicing and pursuing a faith and a life-style that are hateful to God. This situation is spelled out more explicitly and in detail in 5:21–27 and in 2:6–8, where both the crushing of the poor and abhorrent practices, cultic and otherwise, are mentioned. The first unit of the chapter ends with v 5.

In connection with the large centerpiece on the plagues (vv 6–11 and 12) it is necessary only to point to its formal structure and in particular the number. The plagues themselves are typical experiences in the Holy Land and would be remarkable only in their concentration in a single period of time and in their severity. The order does not necessarily have to be chro-nological, and the connections, while reasonable, are not necessarily se-quential. Plagues tend to multiply, and one disaster often leads to another. The first four often accompany one another, because famine frequently follows drought, and the weakening effect on flora and fauna is not difficult to predict. Blight of different kinds, affecting trees and vines and their products, only adds to the general misery, while people in a comparably weakened state are easy prey to epidemic disease. Such plagues in turn undermine the strength and morale of the army and make it an easy target for military action, so the calamity of defeat is added to all of the other woes. It was not until the twentieth century that armies began to lose more manpower to military action than to disease, so the association of war-making with epidemic disease is quite natural. What is portrayed here is a list or series of calamities that are compatible with one another and rein-force one another's effects. They are also causally related, reaching a kind of climax in the familiar theme of defeat in battle and perhaps exile (if that meaning can be extracted from 4:10).

The fifth plague stands apart from the others, though once it occurs it can contribute its share to the realization of the others. It is an overturning, an earthquake perhaps, though it has its cosmic and eschatological dimen-sions as it is associated with the legendary cities of Sodom and Gomorrah, which were destroyed in similar fashion. The word "earthquake" is not used, but the plague emphasizes "burning" like the terrible fire that destroyed Sodom and Gomorrah. The earthquake was a major disaster, perhaps the one mentioned in Amos 1:1 and in Zechariah, although the terms used there are different from the one here; but whether described as an overturning or a vigorous shaking, no doubt the same sort of experience is intended. Apparently there was a narrow escape for the people of Israel, for they are described as being like a brand rescued from the burning. One figure is mixed with another, but the implication is that the earthquake laid the country low and narrowly missed being an irreversible disaster. Despite all of these calamities, all of which could be taken and would be taken as signs of divine displeasure and as warnings of worse to come, there has been no discernible change. The nation goes on its merry way to that unavoidable and inescapable meeting with its destiny, also described in a variety of figures and images, which will only compound and consolidate all of the power of the plagues suffered and result in the rapid demise of the nation. What had been samples of warnings and threats now will become realities. Israel has had ample time to repent, and that time and opportunity have passed. The decisive meeting with God is at hand. We have now reached the end of Phase One in our recapitulation. The preliminary warnings have been uttered and gone unheeded; the same message in a series of natural disasters has likewise failed to produce changes in the people or in their leaders (i.e., "Yet you did not return to me"). So now that period of possibility has ended, and the next phase is about to begin. We need to remind ourselves that we are speaking of the detailed comments of chaps. 3–4 on chaps. 1–2, and that it is in the recapitulation that we have reached this point, a circumstance that will be presented and argued again in chap. 5. But the reader will understand that the perspective of the prophet (and editor) is that of a later vantage point, when all of the remedies have been exhausted and the decree of final judgment against the nations has been issued (chaps. 1–2). The prophet has already seen in vision and heard in words the end of all of those nations in the battleground between great powers to the northeast and the southwest, and has spelled all of it out in the great speech contained in the opening chapters of the book.

I.C.3. MOUNT SAMARIA (4:1–3)

4:1a   Hear this word, you cows of Bashan who are in Mount Samaria,
            oppressing the poor,
            crushing the needy,

1b   saying to their lords, "Bring, that we may drink!"

2a My Lord Yahweh has sworn by his holiness:
         "Indeed, behold, days are coming upon you,

2b   when they will take you away with grappling hooks,
            and your rear guard with fishhooks.

3a Through the breaches you will go out,
         each one through the gap in front of her,

3b and you will be cast away beyond Harmon—"

Oracle of Yahweh!

INTRODUCTION

"Hear this word" marks the beginning of major sections at 3:1, 4:1, and 5:1. The exhortation is addressed to Israel in 3:1 and 5:1; in 4:1, specifically to "the cows of Bashan who are in Mount Samaria." This audience can be identified only from what is said here; but the mixture of masculine and feminine gender forms in the passage creates great confusion, not to speak of the grammatical discord in violation of one of the simplest rules of Hebrew, the agreement of a verb with its subject.

1a Hear (2d m. pl.) this word
      You cows (f. pl.) of Bashan who are in Mount Samaria
         Oppressing (f. pl.) poor
         Crushing (f. pl.) needy

1b   Saying (f. pl.) to their (m. pl.) lord(s)
         "Bring (m. s.) that we may drink!"

2a My Lord Yahweh has sworn by his own holiness:
      Indeed, behold days are coming upon you (m. pl.)

2b   When they will take you (m. pl.) away with grappling hooks,
      And your (f. pl.) rear guard with fishhooks.

3a And you (f. pl.) will go out the breaches,
      Each (f. s.) straight ahead of her (f. s.)

3b And you (f. pl.) will [be] cast beyond Harmon.

Summary:

      šimʿû
        pārôt
        ʿōšĕqôt
        rōṣĕṣôt
        ʾōmĕrōt

                                    -hem
                                    hābîʾâ
                                    -kem
                                    -kem
                        -ken
                        tēṣeʾnâ
                        ʾiššâ negdāh
                        hišlaktenâ
            bōʾû

The display brings out the remarkable fact that there are four masculine words inside two blocks of four feminine words each. One of the masculine words ("bring") is, of course, addressed to the "lord"; it is what these females say. Otherwise the speech is coherent only if the referent is the same "cows" throughout, and we would expect all of the pronouns to be feminine, as are the nouns and participles. The discord occurs between immediately connected words, "hear" (m. pl.) . . . "cows" (f. pl.); "saying" (f. pl.) . . . "their" (m. pl.); and within vv 2–3. Except for the opening verb, the deviants are all pronoun suffixes. The impossible grammar is glaring, and the remedy obvious and simple, to change them all to the feminine, as recommended by BH[3] and many commentators. Harper suggested that *šimʿû* is masculine because it comes first (1905:88); and Wolff cites Joel 2:22 and other examples (1977:55, 203).

Some commentators have suggested that the entire speech is directed at males who are addressed insultingly as females. Switching to masculine forms would show that the audience is male, the feminine forms being figurative; if the audience were female, the occasional masculine pronouns would indicate that the women are being addressed as if they are behaving like men. Because Greek pronouns do not always distinguish gender, the inconsistencies in the MT do not come through in the LXX. The participles are all feminine, along with the noun, "cows." In the Targum, by contrast, everything has become masculine.

The majority of commentators has taken the oracle as an attack on the women of the upper classes, "fat and ferocious" (Harper 1905:86), the accomplices and beneficiaries of their husbands' oppressions. That they have acquired such power is seen as a usurpation of a man's position, and there is also a criticism of the men who have permitted it, for they allow their wives to dominate them (v 1bB). With this interpretation, the passage continues to be a favorite of antifeminist preachers. As the following notes will show, this result can be sustained only by changing the text at several places and by giving some of its words strained meanings.

The parallelism of masculine and feminine within v 2b suggests complementarity. Both males and females will be removed on hooks. It needs to be

remembered also that whereas the Hebrew feminine gender refers specifically and exclusively to females, the masculine gender serves also as common gender, when the group referred to consists of both males and females.
The masculine is thus ambiguous; the feminine is not. It is only by switching to the feminine gender that the speech shows that women are included.
But the same mode of address could be no more than a parody (the bulls
are called cows). To make it clear that the group includes both sexes, the
author could have said "bulls and cows" or, in v 3a, *ʾîš negdô wĕʾiššâ
negdāh*. The lack of such constructions leaves the matter indeterminate.

NOTES

4 1a. *cows.* The use of animal names—buffalo, ram, stag, stallion, bull
(*šôr*)—for strong brave men, especially warriors, was popular among North
Semitic peoples. The usage is often met in the Bible, including *pārîm* (Ps
22:13[E12]; Jer 50:27). To call men who fancied themselves such heroes
"cows" would then be a parody and an insult. Such a taunt or curse is
found in other texts, where soldiers behave like women. The military background of v 2 supports this result.

Bashan. An area celebrated for its pastures, so the animals are fat and
sleek (Deut 32:14; Ezek 39:18; Ps 22:13[E12]).

mount. The word is plural in 3:9; singular in 6:1. While the term can
refer to the actual mountain on which the city was built, it can also include
the entire mountainous region of which the city was the capital, especially
when the plural is used. Concentration on one conspicuous example does
not mean the exclusion of similar cases in other parts of the nation. Similarly, highlighting the women (or effeminate men) in Samaria does not
leave out the similar culprits in other towns.

1b. *their.* The switch from second person to third is due to the fact that a
participle with the article is virtually a relative clause.

lord(s). The usual term for "husband" is *ʾîš* or *baʿal.* The general Semitic
mutu with this meaning was not retained in Hebrew. The Levite living in
Ephraim who had a concubine from Bethlehem is called *ʾădōneyhā* in Judg
19:26–27, so the term, even the majestic plural, can be used for that kind of
"husband." If the lord(s) here are the husbands of the "cows," then the
usage is sarcastic, for this exalted title is used of persons who are ordered
about like slaves. The picture has appealed to commentators, especially if
they think it is demeaning for a husband to wait on his wife; and scenes of
lazy self-indulgence have been recreated by linking 4:1 with 3:15 and 6:4–7
(note the similarity between 4:2 and 6:7). But this result is far from certain.
To translate "their husbands," the pronoun must be emended to feminine.

There is a discrepancy also between *ʾădōnê-* (*kyriois* in the LXX) and the singular *hābîʾâ* (plural in the LXX). It is possible, of course, that the imperative is distributive (it is what each woman says to her husband). But the singular verb could equally well show that *ʾădōnê-* refers to only one "lord." The majestic plural is generally used for Yahweh as "Lord," just as *ʾĕlōhîm* is God. It is a moot point whether both words retain this meaning even when used of rival gods, referring as a majestic plural to the chief rival (usually Baal) and not to the multitude of other gods.

If, again, the pronoun *-hem* with this noun is left alone, and accepted as evidence if not proof that the words are addressed to males and that the feminine nouns, participles, pronouns, and verbs are all part of a metaphor, then *ʾădōnê-* cannot mean "husbands" and almost certainly refers to a deity, the same as "their god" (2:8b), in whose house those who are oppressing the poor are drinking wine.

2a. *sworn.* God's most conspicuous oaths are those sworn to Abraham (especially the promise to give the land) and to David. There are six places in which prophets report an oath to back up an oracle—twice by "My Lord Yahweh," twice by "Yahweh of Hosts," twice simply "Yahweh." Three of them are in Amos (4:2, 6:8, and 8:7). The others are Isa 14:24, 62:8; and Jer 51:14. In each of the oaths in Amos the Lord swears by something different, "his holiness," "his life" (cf. Jer 51:14), "the pride of Jacob." In Isa 62:8 it is "by his right hand and by his mighty arm" (cf. Deut 32:40). Others swear "by the life of Yahweh" and/or "by the life of my soul" (cf. Amos 8:14). Because an oath is likely to become a stereotype, the variations in Amos are noteworthy. In each instance the oath carries a judgment speech of great solemnity and finality.

days are coming. This prophetic expression occurs twenty-one times—fifteen times in Jeremiah; three times in Amos; plus 1 Sam 2:31; 2 Kgs 20:17; and Isa 39:6. Amos applies it to future judgment (4:2, 8:11) and to future restoration (9:13).

2b. *take you away.* No agent is identified. The nearest eligible antecedent is *ṣar* in 3:11, an unidentified "enemy." Some translations make the verb passive (NJPS, NEB). The form itself is ambiguous; 2 Kgs 20:17 also has *hinnēh yāmîm bāʾîm* and continues, "and everything that is in your house . . . will be carried [*wĕniśśāʾ, nipʿal*] to Babylon." But the ancient versions all translated as active and plural, in other words, reading the form as *piʿel.*

grappling hooks. Several proposals have been made about the meaning of *ṣinnôt.* Controls are sought from six directions: (1) identification with other Hebrew words that have the root *ṣnn;* (2) connection with suitable words in other Semitic languages; (3) parallelism; (4) the context; (5) versions; and (6) emendation.

1. In Hebrew a *ṣinnâ* is the largest kind of shield, such as is used by Goliath (1 Sam 17:7, 41). The phrase *māgēn wĕṣinnâ* (hendiadys?) is used

several times. While shields (including the huge ones used to protect engineers conducting a siege) would be used in an assault on Samaria, to bring about the "breaches" described in v 3, the use of such weapons to carry people away would imply the removal of corpses, an unlikely action of a victorious enemy. The LXX and Targum identified *ṣinnôt* as "shields" (cf. NEB), but the plural *hopla* is mainly used in a more general way for any kind of weapon or battle harness, or even for ships' tackling or cables. The rest of the LXX betrays a loose and very interpretive treatment, "They will take you *en hoplois,* and those with you fiery destroyers shall throw into seething cauldrons." It is impossible to recover any viable Hebrew variants from this wording.

Another Hebrew word is *ṣinnîm* (Job 5:5; Prov 22:5), or *ṣĕnînîm* (Num 33:55; Jos 23:13), meaning "thorns," which is always used figuratively. Its parallel *sîrîm* also means "thorns," or rather "thornbush," used as fuel (Eccl 7:6), or "to make a fence" (Hos 2:8[E6]). They grow in the wasteland (Isa 34:13), where the outcast scratches for a subsistence (Job 5:5). In Amos 4:2 both words (if they are the same) present unique feminine forms of the plural. The association with *dûgâ* (another *hapax legomenon*) suggests that both words are being used figuratively to denote fishhooks. The words *hôah* and *hah* have a similar range of usage and refer to the ring or hook that might be placed in the nose of a beast to lead it around.

Ibn Ezra, interpreting Job 5:5, identified *ṣinnîm* as a basket woven out of thornbush. The NEB has given *sîrôt dûgâ* the meaning "fish-baskets," with "baskets" as a possible meaning of *ṣinnîm* to match. The metaphor has thus changed from leading cows away by the nose (cf. Isa 37:29) to hauling in captives like fish (cf. Hab 1:14–17).

2. The use of cognates in languages other than Hebrew is more tenuous and more like emendation. Wolff is partial to the idea of "ropes," which is better if the people are being described as cows rather than fish (*ad loc*). But this suggestion, deriving from S. J. Schwantes (1967), presupposes the equation of Akk *ṣerretu* and *ṣinnitu* (*CAD* 16, p. 201).

3. Synonymous parallelism cannot be assumed as a firm basis for solving the problems: *ṣinnôt* and *sîrôt,* with the same preposition, seem to be parallel, but *'etkem*//*'ahărîtken* present serious problems, made worse by the clash in gender in the pronouns.

4. The context does not yield the needed controls. The active verbs in v 3 suggest free if not voluntary actions. Verses 1 and 2 present mixed metaphors (cows and fish), and vv 2 and 3 seem to have different pictures.

5. As partly discussed above, the versions are in a state of chaos. It is hard to see how Targum gets "daughters" (unless "progeny") out of *'hryt.*

6. Some ingenious emendations have been proposed to alleviate the incompatibility of *'tkm* and *'hrytkn* (Duhm 1911:6; Marti 1904; Nowack 1922; and Procksch 1910, who understand the victims to be animals,

change 'ṭ to 'p; cf. Isa 37:29). The pronoun suffixes can be leveled either way. Developing the picture further, because 'aḥărît is not attested as a counterpart of 'p, "nose," meaning backside or rear end of an animal, a further change is proposed to 'ăḥōrê-, as in Exod 26:12, 33:23; 1 Kgs 7:25; Ezek 8:16. But the more changes needed, the less plausible the result.

rear guard. Another rendering might be "remnant." "Remnant" is a marginal meaning for 'aḥărît, and šĕ'ērît, the usual term, is used by Amos in 1:8, 5:15, and 9:12. In military contexts, as here and 9:1, it could refer to the tail end of an army. "Rear guard" suggests some kind of order, while the picture in 4:2–3 and 9:1 is one of panic and disarray. "Stragglers" includes both ideas, as in Ezek 23:25. The word has both a temporal and a spatial reference, like its counterpart rē'šît (beginning/ending; past/future; first/last; origin/destiny) Job 8:7. It can mean "posterity" (Ps 37:37–38) or "death" (Num 23:10). To cut off the 'aḥărît (Prov 23:18; 24:14, 20) is to deny a person any future (or "hope"—tiqwâ [Jer 29:11]). Contrast Job 42:12.

3a. *breaches.* The verb prṣ describes a breakthrough, a break-in, or an outbreak. The characteristic object is a wall (Neh 1:3, 2:13, 3:35[E4:3], 4:1[E4:7]), breached by a besieging army or broken down by animals escaping from inside (Mic 2:13). Both ideas seem to be combined here, for the usual picture of heroic warriors as strong bulls is inverted. In assaulting a besieged city each man went up "straight before him" ('îš negdô [Josh 6:20]). So it was an irony and an insult to say that these effeminates would "go out (through) the breaches"—'iššâ negdāh—like animals escaping from a pen.

The word "breaches" can be adverbial without a preposition. Even so, commentators have proposed reading something else. The LXX wording *gymnai,* "naked," suggests 'ărummôt (Marti 1904), which could hardly be a misreading of wprṣym. Fewer changes are needed to obtain wmṣrym, "Egypt" being a match for "Harmon." But Egypt and Harmon do not match up at all. Harmon is a minor city, Egypt a great nation. This emendation may be easier, but it is also meaningless.

go out. The LXX has *exenechthēseste. Ekpherein* normally translates the hip'îl of yṣ'; this is the only place in which it corresponds to the qal. There is, however, no warrant for reading the Heb as hop'al. The entire rendering of the LXX version is very loose; it also interprets the following verb as passive.

each. The noun 'iššâ is used as an indefinite distributive pronoun in this idiom, which keeps up the figure of the defenders of Samaria as females, or else is addressed to the women of the city.

3b. *cast.* The unusual ending, -tenâ (for normal -ten), does not need to be explained away now that we know from Qumran texts that the longer alternate ending was not uncommon on pronouns and pronoun suffixes.

There is thus no need to delete the *h* as a dittograph (*GKC* 44k). It secures rhyme, but it was not created for that reason; other specimens are known, such as 2 Sam 1:26, *niplĕʾatâ* (but Freedman [1980:271] read this word as *nplʾ ʾth*, the *alef* written only once when the words are written consecutively). Why did the Masoretes point the verb as *hipʿil* when there is no available object and the passive sense seems obvious? It needs to be remembered that this verb occurs only as *hipʿil* and *hopʿal*, and that the same problem is presented by *hišlîk* in 8:3. There is no need to emend to *hopʿal*, however. The absolute or intransitive *hipʿil* can be an internal elative (Dahood 1970b:389–90). This category has not been accommodated to the theory that the *hipʿil* is essentially causative, or even denominative. Available explanations are strained or evasive (Claassen 1971:108–13). The apparent interchangeability of *qal* and *hipʿil* does not mean that there are no distinctions in meaning (Sperber 1966). Just as *hēbîʾ* can mean "go right in" or "go right through" (Ezek 12:5, 6, 7b, 12—the orthography precludes reading *qal*, and four occurrences together are not accidental). G. A. Cooke found the apparent omission of the object with the *hipʿil* forms unacceptably "harsh," and followed the versions and emended to *qal* (1936:134). M. Greenberg considered that an object was understood in each case (1983:207–8). The form *hāšîb* can mean "come right back" (Ps 80:4[E3]), so *hišlîk* can mean "go right away."

Harmon. While the location is not known, plausible identification has been made (Andersen and Freedman 1970). It must be in the region beyond Damascus in Aram (cf. 5:27, where exile to the same region is also mentioned).

I.D. MESSAGES FOR ALL ISRAEL
(4:4–13)

INTRODUCTION

The oracle in 4:4–5 strikes a distinctive note. It is the clearest condemnation of the official cult as sinful. The concluding messenger formula in its fuller form "Oracle of my Lord Yahweh" completes the catena of prophetic materials that began with 3:1. The phrase *bny yśrʾl* echoes *bny yśrʾl* in 3:1, and together they form an inclusion. The root *pšʿ* in 4:4 also occurs in 2:6–8 and again in 3:14, forming a sequence. The oracle against Israel began with criticism of activities "beside every altar," presumably in the shrines of Bethel and Gilgal. These places also serve as one end of a forward linkage with 5:4–5, and the inclusion of Beer-sheba in that itinerary supports the view that all of Israel is in mind, even though the main focus is on the political and religious centers of the north.

In the full national setting of 5:4–6 Amos refers to both the "house of Joseph" and the "house of Israel." Our study of Amos' political terminology has shown that these terms are not equivalent and interchangeable. References to Samaria, Bethel, Joseph, and "Israel" (unmodified, which means the northern kingdom as such) throughout The Book of Doom alongside references to the "house of Israel" or "Israelites" focus on specific cases within the more general description. Remarks about the northern kingdom are thus representative, not exclusive.

The crowning threat of immediate encounter with the God of Israel in 4:12 has been placed between the plagues (4:6–11) and the final apostrophe of The Book of Doom (4:13). Some connection between 4:12 and 4:13 can be found, for *hikkôn* means "Get ready (for a theophany)" (Exod 19:11), which is what 4:13 describes. The words "thus" and "this" in 4:12 apparently refer to what Yahweh intends to do next, when Israel meets its God; and we would expect them to be followed by explicit and specific threats. No referents are available, not in the immediate context, anyway. So the ending of The Book of Doom is somewhat disjointed. In 4:12 Israel is referred to by that simple title, and addressed as "you" (in 5), in contrast to the plural used elsewhere throughout chaps. 3–4, except for one f. s. instance in 3:11. Too much should not be attached to this alternation, perhaps; but, for what it is worth, all of the plural pronouns could refer to the whole of Israel, otherwise identified as "Israelites" or "the house of Israel," while "Israel" ("you" [in 5]) in 4:12 is the northern kingdom. Amos comes back to this nation at the end of The Book of Doom to finish off the eighth oracle (2:6–8), which was not developed like the other seven but went off into historical recital (2:9–12), wisdom (3:3–8), and various judgment speeches, which apply to Judah just as much as to "Israel." The oracles about the plagues (4:6–11) contain no clues that permit us to say to whom they were addressed. The plural pronouns permit us to suggest that they applied to more than the northern kingdom. After all, Judah needed to repent just as much as Israel. The plagues give the impression of widespread regional disasters, even though they could be selective (4:7).

I.D.1. CONDEMNATION OF THE CULT
(4:4–5)

4:4a   Come to Bethel
　　　　　and rebel at Gilgal
　　　　　—rebel repeatedly!
　4b   Bring your sacrifices for the morning,
　　　　　your tithes for the third day;
　5a   Burn sacrifices without leaven,
　　　　Thank offerings—and announce
　　　　Freewill offerings—proclaim.
　5b　　　For that's what you love, O Israelites—
　　　　　　　　　Oracle of my Lord Yahweh!

NOTES

4:4–5. The translation and arrangement of the parts represent our best judgment about the form and sense of this brief oracle, and the intention of the poet. In the normal or standard analysis, the passage is divided into four lines or bicola, the first three of which exhibit a fairly regular 3 : 3 pattern (matching cola with three stresses each), while the fourth has a 2 : 2 meter, followed by the closing formula (with three stresses).

Such an arrangement is quite reasonable and might well reflect some stage in the history or transmission of the passage. Nevertheless, we believe that a better arrangement is possible, which will bring out more effectively the subtle nuances and overtones in the material, and that the principal clues to the proper division are to be found in the extraordinary series of verbs and the use (or omission) of the conjunction with them. Thus there are three principal verbs in each of the first and third lines (4a and 5a), while only one (which serves for the full bicolon) in the second line (4b). Concerning the latter, there is no question that we have a standard bicolon of 3 : 3 (9 + 9 syllables). With regard to the others it seems to us preferable to analyze the lines as tricola, 2 + 2 + 2, rather than as bicola, 3 : 3. The structure of the passage would then take on a different appearance, with somewhat different shadings of meaning and force:

		Accents	Syllables
4:4a	*bōʾû bêt-ʾēl*	2	4
	ûpišʿû haggilgāl	2	6
	harbû lipšōaʿ	2	4
		6	14

The first two clauses are clearly parallel and augmentative. We understand both verbs to apply to both places, as is clearly the poet's intent: "Come to and rebel at Bethel and Gilgal." The arrangement is in accordance with poetic canons, to emphasize the parallel or, better, the complementary character of the pairings. The use of the conjunction with *pšʿw* shows that the verbs are to be taken together and with both proper nouns. The omission of prepositions with indirect objects is also common practice in poetry. In this case the omission serves the purpose of allowing both verbs to govern both objects: come to and rebel at.

The third clause, separated by the *absence* of the conjunction with *hrbw,* is a general statement covering both of the previous assertions: namely, rebel repeatedly (= multiple rebellion) at Bethel and Gilgal. The suggestion that the instruction is somehow increased or escalated as the prophet speaks of Bethel and Gilgal, while a frequent feature of poetic parallelism, is not present here. The prophet is not suggesting that they sin more at Gilgal than Bethel, but rather that they should rebel continuously or with increasing frequency at both shrines. In other words, just as the first verb (*bʿw*) operates with Gilgal and Bethel alike, so the remaining verbs function with both places too. Hence the paraphrase: "Come to and rebel at (both) Bethel (and) Gilgal, that is, rebel repeatedly (=continue to rebel, or rebel more and more frequently)."

No change in the structure or treatment of v 4b, the second line, is needed. But it may be noted that the single verb (*whbyʾw*) does double service with both sets of objects. Gapping is a prime feature of poetry, as everyone acknowledges; but what is insufficiently recognized is that it works in both directions in Hebrew, backward as well as forward.

In v 5a once again we have three principal verbs; there are indications that the line should be divided into three cola of two words each:

	Accents	Syllables
wĕqaṭṭēr mēhāmēṣ	2	6
tôdâ wĕqirʾû	2	5
nĕdābôt hašmíʿû	2	6

In the first colon we note the use of the infinitive absolute *qaṭṭēr* as a substitute for the normal m. pl. imperative, which is used in the other six instances. Not only is the substitution perfectly acceptable (in the face of the proposed emendation made by many scholars, cf. BHS), but it seems to be a deliberate deviation from an established pattern. Curiously, the same kind of deviation is to be found in the sequence of repeated instances of *wĕšillaḥtî* in chaps. 1–2, which is varied once, and only once, in the text. In the series of seven instances the fifth is *wĕhiṣṣattî;* and here *wqṭr* is the fifth of the seven verbs used in vv 4–5.

With respect to *mēḥāmēṣ,* it is difficult to decide whether the *min* is privative or partitive, whether it means that the sacrifice is to be made "without leaven" or "with some of the leaven." There are arguments for and against both interpretations, but it would appear that Amos is advocating procedures and practices not merely contrary to established rules, but in excess of and going beyond them. We have opted for the former meaning, "without leaven," on the grounds that normally leaven would be used; but the opposite may be the case, as Wolff holds (1977).

In the second colon, the presence of the conjunction between *tôdâ* and *qirʾû* may be an example of the emphatic *waw,* used to enhance the force of the imperative verb. Also possible, and perhaps more likely in this instance, is the recognition that *wqrʾw* and *ndbwt* form a natural pair: "and announce freewill offerings," while *twdh* and *hšmyʿw* form a frame or envelope around them: "thank offering(s) proclaim." Because the verbs are essentially synonymous and the nouns are complementary, the meaning would not be altered, while the intricacy of the arrangement testifies to the poet's skill and ingenuity.

Superficially, at least, the tricola in vv 4a and 5a are very much alike, while the deeper structures are quite different. Nevertheless, for each verb there is an object, direct or indirect, or adverbial in force. There is a repeated pattern of 2 : 2 forms in these lines as also in 5bA, while 4b has the standard 3 : 3 meter along with 5bB, with which the piece closes.

The overall structure for this oracle would be as follows:

	Accents	Syllables
4a	2 + 2 + 2 = 6	4 + 6 + 4 = 14
b	3 + 3 = 6	9 + 9 = 18
5a	2 + 2 + 2 = 6	6 + 5 + 6 = 17
b	2 + 2 = 4	5 + 5 = 10
	3 = 3	7 = 7
	25	66

Dimeter	8 cola × 2 = 16 stresses	41 syllables
Trimeter	3 cola × 3 = 9 stresses	25 syllables
	11 25	66

The effect is somewhat disjointed no matter how it is construed. Its terseness is enhanced by the limited use of grammatical particles, characteristic of poetry. The two place-names in v 4a have no prepositions. The objects in v 4b do not receive the *nota accusativi* to which they are entitled. The parallel nouns in v 5a should have pronoun suffixes "your." The verb "love" in v 5bA needs an object. Thus each of the seven lines has something missing. The only article is an integral part of the name Gilgal; the nouns in v 5 do not have it. The connections between related words *across* poetic lines enable us to link *zbḥ* and *tôdâ*. The phrase *zibḥê tôdâ* occurs in Ps 107:22 and 2 Chr 33:16; *zebaḥ tôdat šĕlāmāyw* in Lev 7:13, 15; *wĕhābîʾû zĕbāḥîm wĕtôdôt* in 2 Chr 29:31. Similar connections between "tithes" and "vows" show that these are not routine tithes, but special offerings promised on the eve of some hazardous enterprise or in a crisis (Jonah 1:16). Jephthah's vow (Judg 11:31) is an example. Abraham paid tithes to Melchizedek in thanksgiving for victory (Genesis 14). So it all hangs together, and it ties in with 6:13, for such vows would be fulfilled with rejoicing and thanksgiving.

4a. *Bethel.* This cult center is mentioned by Amos more often (seven times—3:14; 4:4; 5:5, 6; 7:10, 13) than any other place in Israel—Samaria (3:9, 12; 4:1; 6:1; 8:14), Gilgal (4:4; 5:5), or Dan (8:14). In Judah Beersheba is the only place mentioned (5:5, 8:14) besides Zion.

Gilgal. It is associated again with Bethel in 5:5.

The failure of Joshua 15 to supply details of the eleventh district of Judah is due to the fact that it originally belonged to Benjamin (18:21–24). The mapping of boundaries there agrees with the system in Joshua 15. It contrasts with the system used to describe the boundaries of the northern tribes. Note, for example, the distinctive use of *pēʾâ* for "boundary" (15:5; 18:12, 14 (twice), 20. Joshua 15:5 is explicit that the eastern boundary of Judah was the Salt Sea as far as the mouth of the Jordan River; and Josh 18:20 sets the Jordan as the eastern boundary of Benjamin. The distinction between Judah and Benjamin is thus clear. Furthermore, the northern border of Judah, as described in Josh 15:5–11, matches the southern border of Benjamin in 18:15–20. If the Chronicler may be trusted, for a kernel of fact if not in all details, Abijah secured (or recovered?) part of Benjaminite territory for Judah (2 Chr 13:19).

Each account boxes the compass counterclockwise (ENWS), so the list of names in Josh 15:5–11 is matched by the list in Josh 18:15–20, but in reverse. The detailed listings of towns that follow in each case (15:21–22; 18:21–28) are arranged in districts. Benjamin consists of two cantons, one east, one west of the watershed. Two towns in the latter appear as the only towns assigned to the tenth district of Judah, in spite of the fact that these towns would be north of the northern boundary of Judah (15:5–11 = the southern boundary of Benjamin [18:21–28]). Thus it is tempting to identify the eastern half of Benjamin (mainly in the Jordan valley) with the missing hypothetical eleventh district of Judah; or rather, we should say, of the eleventh administrative district of the southern kingdom when it consisted of Judah and Benjamin.

Comparison of the list of towns belonging to Judah (Joshua 15) with those assigned to Benjamin (Joshua 18) suggests that "the eastern half of the territory of Benjamin (that is, the section that extended across the Jericho plain to Jordan) became Judahite District XI" (Boling and Wright 1982:430). The old Benjaminite territory actually included Jerusalem; Josh 18:16 is explicit that its southern border ran south of Jerusalem (compare the northern boundary of Judah in Josh 15:7–8). Jerusalem was considered a Benjaminite city (1 Chr 8:28). Much of the western half of the old Benjaminite tribal allotment gôrāl must have passed into Judahite control with the establishment of Jerusalem as David's capital, though the national frontier between the divided kingdoms was not very far to the north of Jerusalem. Alt and Noth maintained that Gilgal was originally a distinctively Benjaminite cult center. Kaufmann (1953:67–69) has disputed this claim.

Modern research has not been able to relate the particulars of these boundaries and of the political affiliation of the towns to the changes in the ever-disputed claims of north and south to the territory that lay between them. In general terms this was the land of Benjamin, with its northern border just south of Bethel and its southern border just south of Jerusalem. There were even times that Bethel was within this domain (Josh 18:22), reflecting in all likelihood a temporary annexation of the territory by Judah under Abijah (2 Chr 13:19) or Josiah (2 Kgs 23:15–19).

Y. Aharoni considers the administrative organization of the tribal region of Benjamin, as reported in Joshua 18, to go back to Solomon (1979:315). F. M. Cross and G. E. Wright (1956) point to 2 Chr 13:19 as evidence that Abijah seized old Benjaminite lands as far north as Bethel (which strictly belonged to Joseph [Josh 16:2]). A. Alt dates this tradition to Josiah, who expanded Judean influence to the north (1959c). We do not know what happened to Gilgal, or indeed to the Jordan valley portion of Benjamin during that time. The actions took place up and down the central ridge (Hos 5:8; Isa 10:28–32).

We can say at least that Gilgal did not seem to retain the strategic importance it had at first, when Joshua used it as his base and Saul as his mustering point. Once the tribes were established in the central hills, their military stance changed to defense. Interest in Gilgal in the eighth century had become purely religious.

Although Joshua mentions dozens of cities and assigns them to their respective tribes, Gilgal is not one of them. The Gilgal of Josh 15:7 (= Geliloth of 18:17) is too close to the Ascent of Adummim to qualify. It must have been southwest of Jericho. There is no indication that Gilgal ever became a settlement, that is, a center of permanent population, worthy of listing in the usual administrative documents. It was a camp, an assembly point for muster of the tribes, a headquarters for the military campaigns, a haunt of prophets, a cult location, and a center for pilgrimage. It is possible that it remained an open-air installation, belonging to all tribes and to none, and that it retained this status down through the eighth century, when the attention given to it by the prophets shows that it was enjoying a revival as a purely religious center for all Israelites.

The tribal affiliation of Gilgal is not clear. For one thing, we are not sure of its precise location. Its general location is in the Jericho plain, nearer to the Jordan River than that city. But study of the most eligible site (Tell en-Nitleh) yielded no confirmatory evidence (Muilenburg 1956:20). More likely candidates are sites a little to the north of Khirbet el Mefjir (Muilenburg 1955:22–27) or a little to the west (Bennett 1972). This region abuts on Benjaminite territory to the northwest and on Judahite territory to the southwest. The mapping of tribal boundaries in this region is uncertain. It was a disputed area and doubtless was annexed at different times by north or south, with the changing fortunes of political power.

The status of Benjamin itself was in question as the two kingdoms wrangled over this tribal territory, especially the areas adjacent to Jerusalem. Originally Benjamin was the southernmost of the northern group of tribes (hence the name, which means "Sons of the Right Hand" = South).

The division between north and south (Israel and Judah) did not originate in the time of Rehoboam (Judah) and Jeroboam (Israel) but goes back to premonarchic times. It is reflected in stories concerning the accession of David as king first of Judah (capital at Hebron) and then of all-Israel (capital at Jerusalem), cf. 2 Sam 19:44(43) in which Israel, the northern group, is described as having ten shares in David, leaving the southern group with two. The same division is also found in the tribal listing in the Song of Deborah, showing that the two groupings preceded the formation of the monarchy. It is clear that throughout these periods Benjamin was reckoned as a northern tribe, while the one tribe associated with and in fact absorbed by Judah in the south was Simeon. Hence, when 1 Kings 11 speaks of "one tribe" being assigned to Judah, that one must be Simeon. The LXX version, which may be more original, confirms that the southern kingdom will consist of two tribes. The effect of Rehoboam's strenuous military and political efforts was to annex at least parts of Benjamin into the southern kingdom, those guarding the approaches to the city of Jerusalem, thus adding at least part of a third tribe to his territory. In spite of the continuing association of Benjamin with Judah through the centuries, Benjamin continued to be claimed as part of the northern kingdom. With the fall of the latter, the kings of Judah resumed efforts to incorporate the territory of Benjamin into Judah and on various occasions were successful in doing so. As Simeon had long been part of Judah, it is possible that the biblical writer or editor, one of the Deuteronomists, misinterpreted or misrepresented the situation to mean that Yahweh had also assigned Benjamin to the kingdom of Judah. Such a development would have changed the ratio or proportion of north and south from 10:2 to 9:3, but the latter figures are never mentioned.

We cannot determine whether Gilgal belonged to Israel or to Judah in Amos' time. Most likely, it was still a common shrine, as it had been before the division, still being claimed by both after the division. This status would be affirmed more by use than by any formal assignment in a territorial-political sense, and befits its listing with Bethel and Beer-sheba in Amos 5:5. At the least we cannot insist that Amos restricted his denunciations to the northern kingdom.

rebel repeatedly [over and over again]. Literally, the phrase is "multiply transgressions."

5a. *Burn.* The related nouns refer to various kinds of smoke, with interest in the odor as well. The burning of incense and other substances, including flesh and cereal foods, was generally practiced in the religions of the ancient Near East. It is often mentioned in criticism of pagan cults on "high places" (2 Kgs 23:5; Isa 65:7) or roofs of houses (Jer 19:13, 32:29).

leaven. The preposition (*min*) with *ḥāmēṣ* could be interpreted as privative ("without") or partitive ("with some"), and there is evidence to support either usage. Some ceremonies specified the use of leavened bread, and in some the use of leaven was forbidden. Leviticus 2:11 prohibits the burning (*lōʾ taqṭîrû*) of such offerings. Amos' sarcastic imitation of the priestly call to worship labels the burning of something leavened as a sin (*pešaʿ*), but not because it violates the rule of Lev 2:11. "The sacrifice of thanksgiving" of Lev 7:11–13 (*zebaḥ hattôdâ* or *zebaḥ tôdat šĕlāmāyw*), which has the same vocabulary as Amos 4:4–5, was accompanied by both unleavened and leavened (*ḥāmēṣ*) cakes. So it was not the use of leaven as such that constituted the wrongdoing. There is no indication that it was paganizing, or that the bans in Leviticus represent a later purist reaction against the practice.

COMMENT

This oracle reads like a mock call to worship, a sarcastic invitation to sin even more by going to the shrines. The root $p\check{s}^c$ secures firm links with the Great Set Speech of chaps. 1–2 and with 3:14. Some commentators have read this and similar critiques throughout the prophets as an indictment of the cultus as such, but that judgment is too categorical. The attitude of the prophets to the political and religious institutions and officials of Israel was ambivalent. They could commend or condemn as occasion required. This passage is not a general rejection of all the festivals; it is a specific pronouncement against a particular festivity, a national celebration.

What is described here is a pilgrimage to the great shrines that involved all of Israel and lasted three days. Its purpose was thanksgiving and fulfillment of vows. In 6:13 we have a glimpse of rejoicing over a recent military victory. That, or something similar, could have been the occasion of the assemblies that Amos (rather, Yahweh) considers to be violation on top of violation. It is the use of religion to legitimate militarism, to equate victory with divine blessing, to use such tokens of divine approval as evidence to contradict the argument that oppression of the poor has made them forfeit the favor of heaven. In this way the priesthood is corrupted, the sacrifices defiled, the sanctuaries profaned, so that all become the chief target for judgment and destruction (3:14; 5:6, 21–23; 7:9, 17; 9:1).

Our association of these scattered verses as glimpses of a single event, a great and special national celebration in thanksgiving for the victories over Lo-Dabar and Qarnaim, touches on an important methodological question. The usual theory about prophetic oracles is that they were brief occasional addresses aimed at a specific moment. Not only was the message terse, pithy, and enigmatic; it took for granted the knowledge of the immediate situation shared by the prophet and his audience. Even when the oracles were collected and written down, this background information about the concrete circumstances in which the prophecy had its function is not supplied. The listeners saw the meaning of the oracle with the aid of this knowledge (they could hardly miss the connection). But because we lack this knowledge, the prophecies often remain obscure to us. Only once in Amos (7:10–17) are we told the story of the oracle. As each oracle is brief, any inference about the situation that we attempt to make from its meager and obscure content remains meager and obscure. And if each short oracle is a single message for a particular situation, they cannot be joined together to make a composite picture. Or else they are seen in quite general terms. Thus Amos 4:4–5 is taken to be a general critique of the cultus as such, or of the formalism of "Northern religion" (Harper 1905:93), rather than an attack on one quite specific event. We suggest that an event can be identified, and its objectionable nature properly understood. We need to recognize that the whole book of Amos documents a time of crisis in Israel, epitomized in the confrontation with Amaziah and catalogued in the visions. The numerous links among all parts of the book and the many links between the oracles and the visions point to similar links between the visions and oracles and the events and circumstances in Israel and on the world stage. Even if the individual oracles, correctly identified by the appropriate techniques of form-criticism, were originally given from time to time on specific occasions throughout the phases that we have reconstructed, they have been presented in the light of the final outcome, which was the refusal to listen (4:6–11) and eventual silencing of the prophet (2:12, 7:12–13). From this perspective we can see connections among the situations that we can only glimpse behind the surviving oracles. The synthesis in the final literary presentation corresponds to the coherence in the career of Amos. A fundamental difference between Amos and his opponents was the interpretation of good and bad times. Amos saw disasters as calls to repentance (4:6–11); they did not. They saw successes as occasions for rejoicing; Amos did not. They should have grieved over the smashing of Joseph (6:6). "The pride-of-Jacob" in his military buildup (6:8), for them clear proof that the Lord is with them (5:14), so that "Calamity shall not even come close" (9:10), was abhorrent to the Lord (6:8), the fortresses a special target for destruction.

Amos 4:4–5 is part of this scene. In view of commercial prosperity and military successes, it is clear that the Israelites are enjoying the favor of heaven, and they acknowledge it enthusiastically (and doubtless quite sincerely) by their crowded attendance at the shrines and their generous donations. In such a situation a call to penitence, mourning, and self-affliction is completely unnecessary. More than that, it is unpatriotic, irreligious, seditious. No wonder that Amos was reported to the authorities, run out of town, or possibly incarcerated and executed.

I.D.2. PLAGUES (4:6–11)

4 ^{6a}Indeed it was I who decreed cleanness of teeth in all your cities, and shortage of bread in all your districts; ^{6b}yet you did not return to me—Oracle of Yahweh!

⁷ᵃAnd I also withheld the rain from you, although there were still three months before harvest; and I would make it rain upon one city, and upon another city I would not make it rain: ⁷ᵇone section would receive rain, while the section upon which it did not rain would dry up. ⁸ᵃAnd two or three cities would take refuge in one city, to drink its water; but there would not be enough to satisfy them; ⁸ᵇ yet you did not return to me—Oracle of Yahweh!

⁹ᵃI smote you with blight and with mildew repeatedly, your gardens, and your vineyards, and your fig trees, and your olive trees the locust devoured; ⁹ᵇyet you did not return to me—Oracle of Yahweh!

¹⁰ᵃI sent against you Pestilence in the way of Egypt; I killed with the sword your choice young men [soldiers], along with your horsemen; ¹⁰ᵇand I made the stench of your camps rise up, even into your nostrils; yet you did not return to me—Oracle of Yahweh!

¹¹ᵃI overturned a number of you, as God overturned Sodom and Gomorrah, and you were like a brand plucked from what was burned; ¹¹ᵇyet you did not return to me—Oracle of Yahweh!

INTRODUCTION

As with the Great Set Speech (1:3–2:8) the presentation of the plagues cycles through five case studies using a fixed frame. The language is formulaic and repetitive.

No times or places are mentioned, so we do not know if it is just a selection of instances that could have happened anywhere, anytime. Wolff has an excellent chart showing the relations between the plagues of Amos 4:6–11 and the disasters threatened in the promises of rewards and threats of punishments in the blessing/cursing texts of Leviticus 26 and Deuteronomy 28 (1977:213). Solomon's prayer in 1 Kings 8 (2 Chronicles 6) refers to similar events as occasions for penitence and prayer. All of these lists have certain items in common. Actually *deber* is the only word found in all four passages, but there are several items that are found in three of them, and all are clearly drawn from a common tradition; even so, literary connections or interdependence among them cannot be demonstrated.

The only element common to all five constituents is the final statement "yet you did not return to me—oracle of Yahweh." Each is preceded by a statement by Yahweh of what he has done, in two (I, III, V), three (IV), or seven (II) clauses. These clauses can hardly be called poetic lines, though there is literary artistry here and there.

Each of the autobiographical recitals by God begins with a perfect verb, as if initiating a narrative. The first two begin with "and also I," each with a different form of the pronoun; the other three begin immediately with a perfect verb. The first constituent has only one event, one perfect verb, "I decreed (gave)," while the others offer pairs or larger groups of plagues.

Only v 11 develops the story using classical syntax: perfect plus *waw*-consecutive with imperfect: a story with two events, which could not be briefer. Verse 10 likewise uses a *waw*-consecutive verb for the sequential event; but it is preceded by two perfect verbs. The clauses are paratactic, which gives the impression that there were two distinct actions, plague and sword, both contributing to the stench in the camp, so possibly two aspects of a disaster that overtook an army in the field. These verb forms show that everything discussed has taken place in the past.

In the other two constituents the initial perfect verbs are not followed by the *waw*-consecutive plus imperfect of classical narrative. The one additional verb in v 9a is imperfect (*yōʾkal*). There is a problem with *harbôt*, which could go with either the preceding or the following words. In any case, v 9aB consists of object–verb–subject, with imperfect *yōʾkal* in parallel with *hikkêtî* and evidently in the same tense (past). Any distinction intended probably points to the sustained or continual inroads of locusts on the various crops.

Verses 7–8 are more complex than the others. Here two of the continuing verbs are *waw* plus perfect, normally future; but following a simple perfect the verbs could be coordinated and past tense. But why not use the normal *wayyiqtōl* construction? Of the other clauses, three have an imperfect negated with *lōʾ*. Verse 7b seems to be parenthetical (no "and"), and it uses a simple imperfect. The whole account refers to past events, and every verb is in the past tense. If a distinction is intended by using so many imperfect forms along with perfects, it is hard to see what the nuance could be. It is hardly iterative. The section without rain simply "dried up" (v 7bB), simple past or preterit. Wolff thinks that such inconsistent use of verb forms "can hardly be expected of Amos" (1977:214).

In each of the five constituents the opening perfect verb is followed immediately by "you" with a variety of prepositions:

v 6a	*wĕgam-ʾănî*	*nātattî lākem*	and I gave to you
v 7a	*wĕgam ʾānōkî*	*mānaʿtî mikkem*	and I withheld from you
v 9a		*hikkêtî ʾetkem*	I smote you
v 10a		*šillaḥtî bākem*	I send against you
v 11a		*hāpaktî bākem*	I overthrew (some of) you

Afterward, each piece goes its own way. The brief opening and closing formulas are the only constants. The paragraph structure of each one is different. Compare the similar compositional technique in the Great Set Speech (1:3–2:8). The authenticity of the piece can hardly be doubted; moreover, it is not just a collection of small oracles originally autonomous and unrelated. (We do not deny that each could have been given originally at the time of the plague it discusses; this timetable could even help to explain in part the peculiar use of the verb forms in vv 7–9.) The final presentation depends for its effect on the accumulation of examples. Yet they are not all cast in the same mold.

The composition cannot be called poetry as such, even though most modern editions lay it out as if it were. The vocabulary is that of prose. The three "prose particles" (*ha-, ʾet, ʾăšer*) are all used in accordance with the rules of standard grammar; and some verbs—not all (see above)—are used as in standard prose narrative. More telling still is the almost complete lack of parallelism, and the use of some long and quite prosaic clauses, notably vv 6aA, 7aA (ten words!) 7bB, 8bA, and 11aA. The longer constituents have a little parallelism (6a, 7aB, and 10a), but even then the patterns are not classical, and the wide range of lengths forbids any kind of scansion. Rigid observance of poetic rules was not Amos' interest. His genius shines in rhetoric of a different kind; and clearly 4:6–11 betrays no attempt to write poetry, except in vv 7–8, where there are six lines that achieve rhythms characteristic of high-flown prophetic oratory. Numerals are used to good effect; there is repetition of the root *mṭr* and of the key nouns *ʿîr* and *ḥelqâ*. There is chiasmus in v 7aB. But v 8a has a line of nine words followed by one of two words. Amos 4:6–11 is not poetry. The point requires emphasis. It corrects the view, often stated, that prophetic oracles, especially those from the earliest and "classical" prophets, were regulated by forms of speech that were necessarily poetic. It is true that the pioneers of form criticism, and especially the great masters Gunkel and Gressmann, studied "form" as "formula" with primary interest in content rather than in poetic form. The formulas were identified by key words, and the distinctive technical vocabulary of each form was the prime target for study and the best diagnostic for investigation. Special attention was paid to opening and closing formulas. At the same time it was generally maintained that authentic classical prophetic oracles were poetic in form, even though the brevity of these messages did not permit "elaborate versification" (Robinson 1947:53). Robinson goes on to maintain that

> It is also fairly clear that, within the limits of an individual poem, the dominant "metre" *remains unchanged* [our italics]. It is sometimes difficult, for various reasons, to be certain of the original "metre" of a short poem, but where this can be definitely ascer-

tained, and we find ourselves passing from one rhythm into another, we may be practically certain that we have reached the end of one oracle and have started a fresh one. (Ibid.)

By such criteria and expectations, it was difficult to find very many original prophecies that had survived unaltered into the prophetic books. C. Westermann (1967:105–6) maintained that a prophetic message "must be short" and that only from Ezekiel on does the prophetic speech become long.

So, according to form criticism, prophetic oracles in their originating oral creation and delivery were simple, brief, and poetic. The longer complex forms so frequently encountered are due to the elaboration of an original prophetic message by redactors (commentators). The occurrence of miscellaneous and heterogeneous components is due to "dissolution of the form" (Westermann 1967:205–9). The prosaic character of many of Jeremiah's prophecies is due to rewriting by a Deuteronomic scribe (Mowinckel 1914).

By all such tests the speeches we have recognized in the book of Amos cannot be his: they are long, they are mixed in form, and they are irregular in poetic rhythms, some almost devoid of parallelism. It is ironic that the one place in 4:6–11 that moves in the direction of poetry, vv 7b–8, was rejected by Harper (1905:98) as a "very tautological" interpolation.

While many commentators are reluctant to deny such an excellent and powerful piece of prophecy to Amos, by numerous tests it fails to demonstrate the required properties. Wolff finds that many details of vocabulary and style are not found in any of Amos' other (undisputed) oracles and concludes that "a five-part homily has been attached to the old reproach of Amos in 4:4–5" (1977:214). He dates it to the time of Isaiah (224) on the occasion of the supposed destruction of the sanctuary at Bethel (220).

It is hard to know where to begin in an exercise of this kind. The numerous attempts that have been made to sift out Amos' personal, distinctive, and original compositions have not arrived at anything like unanimity. With such small specimens very little confidence can be attached to statistical arguments. In such a small book there are likely to be many words and expressions that the author would use only once. The problem is compounded by the practice of using older traditional material in making up the message. Amos 4:6–11 uses language that is drawn from the schedule of curses that are threatened against covenant violators; and to that extent the contents are not completely fresh.

The five constituents are not neat and regular, and there does not seem to be any way of assigning such defects in craftsmanship (as they might seem to our taste) to the rugged speech of Amos himself, to hasty redaction, or to subsequent interference by one or more scribes. Except for the words *harbôt* (v 9aA) and *tamṭîr* (v 7bB), as well as some problematical "ands," the text is philologically clear and clean.

NOTES

4:6. In chapter 4:6–11 Amos enumerates seven plagues: (1) famine (v 6); (2) drought (vv 7–8); (3) blight (v 9); (4) locusts (v 9); (5) pestilence (v 10); (6) sword (v 10); and (7) "overthrow"—earthquake? fire? (v 11). There is no canonical schedule of plagues, curses, destructions. Ezek 14:21 lists "my four evil judgments"—*ḥereb* (sword), *rāʿāb* (famine), *ḥayyā rāʿâ* (evil beasts), *deber* (pestilence). Amos' first, famine, corresponds to the second of Ezekiel's. In 1 Kgs 8:37 there is another list: *rāʿāb* (no. 1), *deber* (no. 5), *šiddāpôn* (no. 3), *yērāqôn* (no. 3), *ʾarbeh* (no. 4), *ḥāsîl-kol-negaʿ, kol-maḥălâ.*

In addition, 1 Kings 8 mentions drought (v 35; no. 2) and defeat in war (v 33; no. 6). Matches can be found for six of Amos' seven plagues; only his seventh is lacking from conventional inventories. The vocabulary overlaps only partially. He describes famine as "shortage of bread" or "cleanness of teeth."

7. Drought would logically precede and cause famine. Amos uses *gešem* where Deut 28:24 and 1 Kgs 8:35 use *māṭār,* but Amos uses verbs with the latter root four times.

The details are quite specific, and the consequences are vividly described.

7a. *one city.* There is no analysis of the rationale behind this selectivity, as if one city were more wicked than another. Amos consistently speaks of cities rather than countries as targets of divine judgment (chaps. 1–2; 3:6, 9; 4:1; 6:1). It is cities that field armies (5:3). In his terminology *ʾereṣ* is usually the whole world and *ʿîr* is a city-state, what we could call a country or a nation. Amos is describing drought that affected now one country, now another. The migrations described in v 8a are not just from one town to the next, but to neighboring countries, as in Gen 12:10; 26:1; 47; Ruth; or 2 Kgs 8:1–6. The setting is more like the international stage of chaps. 1–2 than a purely local problem restricted to the northern kingdom of Israel. The term *ḥelqâ* refers to an allotted portion of arable land ("farm") to focus on crop failure. But in this context it could refer to national territory (Jacob is Yahweh's *ḥēleq* [Deut 32:9]; cf. Amos 7:4).

7b. *receive rain.* There is a problem with the verbs in v 7. We have already pointed out the difficulty in fixing the tense/aspect of the imperfect forms. Each of the oracles is framed by a pair of perfect verbs with simple past-tense meaning, "I smote you . . . yet you did not return to me" (v 9). In continuity with this envelope the four imperfect verbs in vv 7–8 would

likewise be past (preterit), and even the coordinated perfects that commence in ʿv 7aB and 8aA are past, not *waw*-consecutive, as is shown in our
translation. BH³ removes the stress by deleting "and" from *whmṭrty* but,
strangely, does not do the same with *wnʿw*. But if the six lines inserted into
the frame of vv 7–8 are not in continuity of tense with the frame, and if the
"and + perfect" constructions are consecutive, as in the Masoretic pointing, then there is a choice between future (which is hardly acceptable,
though the LXX translated it that way, as if vv 7aB–8a were a prophecy)
and iterative past (as in Gen 2:4b–6). The latter would mean that the
circumstances in vv 7aB–8a were repeated again and again—"I would
cause it to rain . . . and they would wander. . . ." (cf. Wolff's 1977 translation). Yet this reading does not fit in with the precise (punctiliar) statement of v 7aA that the rains failed three months before the harvest. We
conclude that the imperfects in vv 7–8 encode the preterit tense, and that
the *waw*s commencing vv 7aB and 8aA are not consecutive. There are
difficulties either way, and many scholars explain the inconsistency by identifying vv 7aB–8a as an "explanatory gloss" (Cripps 1969:172), and Löhr
despairs of the whole passage and deletes vv 7–8 altogether (1901). For a
full discussion see Weiser 1928.

   Of unusual interest is the use of *nipʿal* rather than *hopʿal* in v 7bA as the
passive of the *hipʿil*s in v 7aB. The form is unique. Strictly speaking it is not
a well-formed passive transformation (Andersen 1971) because *himṭîr* is not
transitive. It is a causal denominative with an inner object—"he caused
[rain] to rain." The extrinsic "object" ("city," "plot,") is marked by *ʿal*, as
in the three other clauses that have the verb. "Upon" has to be supplied to
v 7bA in translation. Why use the passive at all? The problem is compounded by the fact that the following verb, synonymous with *timmāṭēr*, is
once more *hipʿil*. Even if the *nipʿal* is "ruled out" as impossible (Wolff 1977,
following many previous scholars), we still have the problem of *tamṭîr*. The
plene spelling, if we take it seriously, forbids reading another *nipʿal*. The
LXX's *breksō* has simply leveled the verb to the two preceding ones. It can
be used to emend the MT to *ʾamṭîr* only if we dismiss the MT's *tamṭîr* as a
crude and inexplicable error. *Tamṭîr* has been identified as an impersonal
feminine, resembling *tašlēg,* "it snows" (Ps 68:14; Wolff 1977:209). (The
difficulty with this proposal is that *ḥelqâ* is clearly the subject of *tamṭîr*.)
Regrettably, Claassen does not discuss this verb in his monograph on the
hipʿil (1971).

   dry up. Compare 1:2.

   8a. *take refuge.* Literal renderings of *wĕnāʿû* would be "wandered" or
"staggered." The LXX has *synathroistēsontai,* "they will gather together,"
as if from *wĕnôʿădû;* perhaps an instance of contamination from 3:3,
nôʿădû?

   9a. *blight.* The words *šiddāpôn* and *yērāqôn* are always used together

(Deut 28:22; 1 Kgs 8:37 [= 2 Chr 6:28]; Hag 2:17) to form a stock phrase that cannot prove dependence of Amos on any other passage containing it except in the general sense that the curses of the covenant are the common background.

repeatedly. The attachment of *harbôt* to the following nouns achieves better poetic balance, but it breaks up the phrase of four nouns, which as a unit makes an appropriate object for "devoured." The BHS assists the division by deleting "and" from "your fig trees." The LXX already moved this way, but it lacks "and" with the second noun. Its verb, *eplēthynate,* partly confirms the MT (**hirbêtem*) and puts the antithesis in v 9b. The other versions likewise support the MT. A more drastic solution is to replace *harbôt* by a verb in chiastic parallelism with *hikkêtî.* The most popular proposal is Wellhausen's *heḥĕrabtî* (1893), which has been widely adopted—"I laid waste" (NEB). Less drastic is the retention of *harbôt* and its recognition as equivalent to *harbēh,* the infinitive absolute, which is often used as an adverb meaning "repeatedly." The MT punctuation should also be retained, so that *harbôt* modifies *hikkêtî* chiastically (cf. NIV). Alternatively, *harbôt* could be attached to *yōʾkal* (NJPS); cf. Prov 25:27, eating greedily and to excess.

The blight and mildew ruin the cereal crops (*šĕdēpâ* is often applied to standing grain), while locusts devour all of the fruits.

10a. *I sent.* All of the disasters cataloged in vv 6–11 are presented as direct actions of God, whether withholding rain or sending pests. Here the concepts are mythic, as in the Great Set Speech, and the same verb is used, indicating that *Deber,* like Fire, is an agent in Yahweh's entourage (Hab 3:5) to be commanded (cf. 9:4). The use of *deber* to name this pestilence has restricted occurrence in the OT. It is found in J material in Exodus and Numbers, and once in Deuteronomy 28. It may occur in Hosea 14, but otherwise it is not found in eighth-century prophets (Isaiah and Micah). Jeremiah uses it; although Ezekiel often lists the destroyers, he mentions *deber* only once.

With this uneven distribution, it is impossible to locate the vocabulary in any recognizable tradition. Neither can doubt be cast on its authenticity for that reason. The book contains many little touches that appear only once, and the fact that something does not occur anywhere else in Amos is not an argument against it. There is no reason (except the desire to tidy things up a bit) to suppose that originally each of the five oracles in 4:6–11 contained only one plague, so that either v 10aA or v 10aB should be deleted from this one. Pestilence and sword often go together, both inflicting casualties on armies in the field (Exod 5:3; Lev 26:25). The word "captivity" points to a defeat.

way. The word *derek* can also mean "manner" (RSV; cf. Isa 10:24–26; Ezek 20:30). There could be an echo of Deut 28:60, which threatens covenant rebels with the diseases of Egypt. A pestilence was not one of the plagues of Egypt in Exodus, but popular wisdom held that it was endemic in that land. At the same time, "the way of Egypt" may simply refer to the highway leading there (Jer 2:18), and Amos could be talking about something that happened to an army traveling that way.

sword. Here the victims—choice young men and horses (perhaps infantry and cavalry)—and the mention of your "camps" point to a terrible military defeat, with so many casualties that the dead could not be buried. No historical identification is possible, even though a particular event is probably in Amos' mind. Hazael had reduced the horses in Israel's military stables to a mere handful (2 Kgs 13:7), and Amos could be reminding them of that event. We have suggested, however, that everything reported in 4:6–11 was of recent occurrence, experienced by Amos' listeners and commented on by the prophet as an object lesson in repentance that they refused to learn.

10b. *stench.* The verb is often used metaphorically for an odious reputation (Gen 34:30; Exod 5:21; 1 Sam 13:4, 27:12; 2 Sam 10:6, 16:21). It applies literally to putrefying carcasses: frogs (Exod 8:10[E14]); fish (Exod 7:18, 21; Isa 50:2); flies (Eccl 10:1), soldiers (Isa 34:3; Joel 2:20). The picture is a complicated but realistic description of a defeated army camp: killing of men; the presence of plague, with the resulting stench of death. "The way of Egypt" is geographical, and it is hard to place an Israelite army in such a setting—where and when?—in some serious defeat. There are possible examples involving Israelites in campaigns in the south, mainly in Transjordan, but they may have been involved with Judahites in war with the Philistines; going down to Ashdod, Ashkelon, or Gaza would put them on the road to Egypt.

The inference is that there was an abortive and disastrous campaign early in the reign of Jeroboam II or perhaps a predecessor that Amos understood as a divine judgment and warning, but which did not produce the desired effect. There was no repentance. On the contrary, Jeroboam adopted more successful tactics and later ran up a string of victories; the background here seems to be earlier than the main oracles. This reverse occurred earlier, but its meaning was missed, as was the case with the other plagues.

11a. *overturned.* The destruction of the cities of the plain as reported in Genesis 19 is the parade example and traditional object lesson of God's anger against wicked cities. The root *hpk* is used in this connection in Gen 19:21, 25, 29 (both noun and verb); Deut 29:22[E23]; Jer 20:16, 49:18, 50:40; and Lam 4:6, as well as Amos 4:11. It served both as a warning and as a measure of later acts of similar severity.

Along with Isa 13:19 and Jer 50:40, Amos preserved the phrase *kĕmahpēkat ʾĕlōhîm,* which might once have existed in Deut 29:22[E23] as well, for the Codex Severus had it. In keeping with the model, the object of similar treatment is often a city: Jerusalem (2 Kgs 21:13); Nineveh (Jonah 3:4); or Babylon (Isa 13:19; Jer 50:40). It is also used of nations: Edom (Jer 49:18) or Israel (Deut 29:22[E23]). Selected groups can receive the same treatment. The conventional "overthrow" connected with the traditions of Sodom and Gomorrah is often associated with seismic forces; but the cause named in Genesis 19 was "fire from Heaven," as in Amos 1–2. The meaning of *hpk* is quite general. It can describe the changing of anything into anything. For instance, in Leviticus 13 it refers to various clinical signs of dermatitis. It always describes an extreme or complete change. The result in the case of Sodom and Gomorrah is described in Deut 29:22[E23]: "the whole land brimstone and salt, a burnt-out waste, unsown, and growing nothing, where no grass can sprout" (cf. Zeph 2:9). Compare the description of Edom in Isaiah 34.

a number of you. The partitive use of *b-* is unusual, but it seems to be the only plausible explanation here. See the note on "in" in 1:1. As with the second plague, the disaster was partial and selective.

Sodom and Gomorrah. In the context of Amos 4:6–11 the comparison with these cities is more apt in the light of the tradition of Jer 23:14, where the false prophets of Samaria and Jerusalem make those cities like Sodom and Gomorrah because they "walk in lies" (cf. Amos 2:4), so there is no repentance.

brand. The image is a cliché, but it fits in with the picture of destruction by fire.

The fifth plague is unlike the other four, in that it does not correspond to any of the conventional curses of the covenant, as Wolff's chart (1977:213) shows. It is the last on the list, the most drastic, for the obliteration of Sodom and Gomorrah represented the most extreme case of divine judgment. It is climactic, and possibly the most recent. It is not clear what happened, but it seems to have been a great disaster in one or another of the major cities (perhaps an earthquake) resulting in a devastating fire (usually an accompaniment to and consequence of a quake, and causing more loss of life and damage to property than the tremor itself). From the almost total conflagration only a bit of charred wood was rescued (cf. 3:12).

plucked. This wording suggests rescue, not just survival.

COMMENT

To interpret these oracles (or this literary unit), we need to discover the connections among the plagues and their accompanying messages; the connections of the messages with cursing texts and commination rituals; the connections of the disasters with real events, whether long past history or something recent and still in everyone's memory as an actual experience; and the connections of these events and messages with the career and proclamations of Amos.

We suggest that actuality and immediacy have the first claim on interpretation. We suggest that the harm inflicted by these disasters corresponds to the destructive acts seen in the visions of chaps. 7–9 (we do not have to find one-to-one equations in order to prove this point). The interpretation of the catastrophes as corrective disciplines and summonses to repentance, implied by the complaint that they did not repent, matches accusations of Amos, found mainly in the schedule of woes and in the exhortations to amendment that are either implicit in such reprimands or explicit in chaps. 5–6. The persistence in transgression, culminating in some final and blatant sin with no sign of felt guilt or contrition balances the accumulation of sins (three, indeed four) noted in chaps. 1–2; and the consistent refusal to repent (*šwb;* the refrains of 4:6–11) matches Yahweh's decision not to change his decree of judgment (*hšyb;* the refrain of 1:3–2:8). The disasters of 4:6–11 are thus central and pivotal to the development of Amos' career and to the presentation of his message as a whole in its written form.

In this perspective, the plagues are as cosmic as the visions and as global as the oracles of the Great Set Speech. There is no reason to regard them as merely local. Drought, locusts, and the others do not observe political boundaries. The catastrophes were not uniformly spread; there was famine "in all your cities," but the drought did not occur everywhere (4:7b), and only "some of you" were overthrown (4:11).

The "you" of the unit is not identified. Framed in 4:4–5 and 4:12, the piece applies immediately to Israel, and more precisely to the northern kingdom, if "Israel" has the meaning in 4:12 that it has in the rest of the book (except for 1:1a)—note also "Samaria" in 4:1. Yet even if Israel is the target, and the messages were actually delivered within the territory of the northern kingdom and nowhere else (Bethel suggests itself as one place, Samaria another, as 4:1–3 were certainly addressed to people in the capital, and 4:4–5 were addressed to people going to Bethel and Gilgal from other places), the message applied equally well to Judah. Returning to Yahweh was expected of the covenant people, hardly of the other six nations of the Great Set Speech; yet even they are held accountable on the same basis as the more favored people.

Following immediately on 4:4–5, 4:6–11 pushes farther the point that religiosity is not the same as repentance. At the same time the juxtaposition of these two passages highlights another problem. In the first two visions Amos is horrified at the threat to "little" Jacob. Amos 4:6–11 gives the impression that the region had suffered from many severe catastrophes. If these calamities are connected with the visions, their severity was not mitigated by the people's repentance, but solely by the prophet's intercession.

There are other indications in the book that terrible disasters have already been experienced (5:2; "Joseph's crash" [6:6]) as well as predicted (3:13–15; 5:3, 16–17; 6:9–10), even before the more drastic predictions in the closing phase (8:9–10; 9:2–4). Yet there are just as many indications of prosperity (3:15; 4:1; 5:21–24), success in war (6:13), well-being (6:4–6), and complacency (6:1).

The two pictures are very different. Did they coexist, assuming that all of the information should be retained? There is no documentation of a series of setbacks such as listed in Amos 4:6–11 for the reigns of Uzziah and Jeroboam; but then such ills were endemic to the region. It would have been an irony, and a bitter one for Amos, if the mitigation secured by the prophet's intercession were construed not as "the goodness of God leading them to repentance" (Rom 2:4) but as a sign that no repentance was required. On the contrary, there were many tokens of divine favor they could point to, including military success, along with their enormous enthusiasm for religion and their pious comments on their prosperity (5:18, 9:10b).

Scholars find the high points in the overlapping reigns of Uzziah and Jeroboam as the best time for Amos' references to national prosperity and pride; somewhere in the decade 760–750 B.C.E. has appealed to many. An even later date appeals to those who feel that Amos' prophecies, especially his prediction of exile beyond Damascus (5:27), could only have been made if the Assyrian conqueror Tiglath-pileser III were already on the move (about 745). Cripps (1969:172) proposes a date of 741 for Amos and uses Isaiah 5:25 to date the earthquake to about 740, so that the disasters come after the successes. We do not altogether rule out the possibility of equating the convulsion of 4:11 with the earthquake of 1:1, but even then we would locate the entire career of Amos much earlier, and place the review of the plagues in 4:6–11 at the transition point between the first phase of his ministry, when there was still a chance to repent, and the second phase, when that chance had been missed. The events reviewed in 4:6–11 could have taken place over a period of any length of time prior to that; but it need not have been long. In any case, we do not believe that the picture was ever clear-cut or one-sided; there were always good circumstances to set against the gloom and doom of the prophet, and such evidence clearly made it difficult for Amos to drive his point home. He does not deny such facts, but he sees their prosperity as unjust and self-indulgent, their pride and complacency unfounded and unjustified. The annals of the century indicate that none of the kings took any notice of the prophets until Hezekiah, who entreated the Lord, who repented so that Jerusalem's fate was different from Samaria's (Jer 26:16–19).

Among our reasons for placing 4:6–11 at the midpoint of Amos' career is not only its perspective—it comes after messages like those in chaps. 5–6, in which the situation is still open; but before those in chaps. 1–3, when it is too late—but also the correspondence between the visions of chaps. 7–9 and the plagues. The number of plagues is indeterminate (there could be as many as seven in the five oracles), and they match the visions at only one or two points; but at least both series begin with locusts.

I.	4:6	(1) Famine	
II.	4:7–8	(2) Drought	= Cosmic fire that destroys the underground water supplies (7:4)
III.	4:9	(3) Blight	= Connected with 8:1(?)
		(4) Locusts	= Locusts (7:1)
IV.	4:10	(5) Pestilence	= The aftermath of war (6:9–10)
		(6) Sword	= The disaster of 5:3 (7:17)
V.	4:11	(7) Earthquake(?) or Fire(?)	= The destruction of 9:1(?)

The threat of destruction in the first two visions and the stay secured by Amos' intercession requires the preaching of repentance. The repeated reproach, "yet you did not return to me," in 4:6–11 indicates that this call was given, also that it was not heeded.

We are not to suppose that the people were left to work out for themselves that the famine, drought, locusts, and so on were divine visitations and that the correct response was penitence and amendment. Amos stated that there was no evil done in a city (the targets in vv 7–8, 11) unless Yahweh did it; and that Yahweh never did anything like that without first telling a prophet, who was bound to declare it (3:6–8) as warning before, analysis during, and reproach afterward. Each of the plagues would have been accompanied by suitable preaching, and the refusal to listen to such preaching (2:12, 7:12–13) was a major factor in the eventual irrevocable judgment of Visions 3 and 4 and of chaps. 1–2. Amos 4:6–11 is the heart of Amos' *apologia*.

The length of the series must have weakened his point as time went by. Each of the five oracles in 4:6–11 concludes with *nĕʾūm-yhwh*, as if each were a complete word presented as a final message at the time.

Amos was exonerated because he had faithfully but futilely delivered the message as plague succeeded plague. The people were culpable because they had not only willfully and repeatedly ignored the prophet's call to repentance, they had also silenced him. Amos 2:11, then, is not just a review of past treatment of Amos' predecessors. It was his experience too, and not just from Amaziah (7:10–17). Amos knew that they were not repentant by the way in which they responded to his proclamations.

I.D.3. THREAT TO ISRAEL (4:12)

4:12a   Therefore thus have I done to you, O Israel!
12b   Because I have done this to you:
                    prepare to confront your God, O Israel!

INTRODUCTION

4:12. The plagues (vv 6–11) end with a final threat (v 12) reinforced by
an apostrophe (v 13). These three disparate pieces are only loosely connected and may well have had an independent use before they were brought
together in this way by Amos or by his editor. They strike a final note,
which rounds off the long indictment of all of Israel that began at 3:1, itself
an outgrowth of the oracles against Judah and Israel in chap. 2. Verses
12–13 are thus a fitting conclusion to The Book of Doom (chaps. 1–4) as a
whole.

Even so, the arrangement does seem to be somewhat makeshift. As political terminology used throughout the book, the term "Israel" (unmodified
in any way) refers regularly to the northern kingdom, which was singled
out as an exclusive target in 2:6–8. But 2:9–4:5 expanded the scope of the
discussion to include both kingdoms, or rather to address all of the house
(or people) of Israel in deep historical perspective. Even when attention
switches briefly to Bethel (3:14, 4:4) or Samaria (3:9, 4:1), the larger reference to the whole nation is not lost. Amos' political entities are city-states,
not territories. The threat against "Israel" (simply) in v 12 can then be seen
as another return to the northern kingdom as part of the wider picture
presented in chaps. 3–4. But, in view of the cosmic perspective of the hymn
that immediately follows, it would be more appropriate if the transition
from vv 6–11 to v 13 retained the broad reference found in the rest of
2:9–4:11. Verse 12 could be the one place in which "Israel" (alone) is used
to refer to the whole nation. It might well be that this verse concludes the
condemnation of the northern kingdom, which is under immediate threat
in Amos' view. He has already dealt with the other seven nations, but the
judgment against Israel was postponed for an elaborate expansion, now
being completed. Here at last the oracle beginning in 2:6–8 is brought to a

conclusion. The traditional elements in v 12 seem to derive from memories of the Sinai theophany (Exodus 19). As the people prepared then for the display of the divine splendor, so once more they must prepare to meet their God, as he is identified by v 13.

While it is legitimate to ask at each stage just who is being addressed by the prophet, it is too much to expect that the answer will always be clear to us. The individual groups itemized in the Woes may be quite small, but whether they are the businessmen in the marketplace (2:6, 8:6), the garrison of Samaria (4:1), the revelers in the palace (6:4–7), or the pilgrims at the shrines (4:4–5), they represent the whole nation, and talking to or about them does not leave anybody else out—similarly for the two nations of Israel and all eight nations of the region. There are no exemptions. It would be overly precise to maintain that cities and countries are included only when they are explicitly named. We should not infer from the absence of Gath from the list of Philistine cities in 1:6–8 that it was somehow immune; or from the sole mention of Gath in 6:2 that all of the other Philistine cities are left out.

The verse itself is irregular in construction, and the repetition of one entire line has attracted the attention and suspicion of critics:

12a	lākēn kōh ʾeʿĕśeh-llĕkā yiśrāʾēl
12bA	ʿēqeb kî-zōʾt ʾeʿĕśeh-llāk
12bB	hikkôn liqraʾt-ʾĕlōheykā yiśrāʾēl

It is only by using very flexible rules that regular rhythms can be found in these three lines. The last line clearly requires four beats, and such long lines are not uncommon in Amos. The small words in the other two lines can be counted or not, depending on theory, to yield from two to four beats, but the rules have to be applied differently to the first two to make them match. It looks as though 12bA is the culprit, as the first and third lines match very nicely with a count of 4/3 // 4 and 9/10 // 10/11. The imbalance is mainly caused by the presence of "Israel" in the first line; but it evidently serves to link the first line with the third, and should not be deleted just to improve the meter. In any case, the "Israel" here must be the northern kingdom, which is the proper culmination of chaps. 1–4, and in particular completes the eighth oracle, which began in 2:6–8.

NOTES

4:12a. *Therefore thus.* The interpretation of this passage depends on finding connections between v 12 and other passages. The pronouns *kōh* and *zōʾt* clearly refer to some act of God. The problem is how to interpret the tense of the imperfect verb (*ʾśh*): whether it is something that God "is doing" (present), "has done" (past), or "will do" (future). We have translated as follows:

> 12a   *lākēn kōh ʾeʿĕśeh-llĕkā yiśrāʾēl*
>   Therefore thus have I done to you, O Israel!

We take the verb to be preterit and the reference to be to the series of plagues described in vv 6–11, all of which have already taken place. The next lines read as follows:

> 12b   *ʿēqeb kî-zōʾt ʾeʿĕśeh-llāk*
>   *hikkôn liqraʾt-ʾĕlōheykā yiśrāʾēl*
>
>   Because [or inasmuch as] I have this done to you:
>   [and because you have not returned to me]
>   prepare to confront your God, O Israel!

The passage makes sense, though there is a slight ellipsis to be supplied by the closing formula for the series of plagues. After each plague or group it is said: "Yet you did not return to me" (vv 6, 8, 9, 10, 11). It is not only or primarily because of what Yahweh has done, but rather because of what Israel has not done—repented and returned to Yahweh—that the flash point of judgment has been reached. In this setting, then, it seems clear that the pronoun *zʾt* refers to previous actions already taken. This would seem to be the normal usage of *zʾt*, namely, that it resumes an antecedent unless there are clear indications of different usage. In this instance the context as well as the use of *zʾt* supports the view that the verbs (*ʾśh* in both cases) are preterit rather than future.

The six other occurrences of *zʾt* in Amos fall into the same pattern.

1. Amos 2:11b:

> *haʾap ʾēn-zōʾt bĕnê yiśrāʾēl*
> Isn't that actually so [true], you Israelites?

The reference is to a series of actions in the past by Yahweh culminating in or including the assertion in 11a:

> And I raised up some of your sons to be prophets,
>   and some of your choice young men to be nazirites.

2. Amos 4:12 is discussed above. It refers to the past deeds of Yahweh

(the plagues enumerated in 4:6–11) and is the concluding remark about the plagues.

3 and 4. Amos 7:3, 6:

> niḥām yhwh ʿal-zōʾt
> Yahweh repented of this.

The reference is apparently to the preceding vision in each case and to that vision's portrayal of divinely authorized destructive actions against Jacob// my people Israel. In both cases the following statement confirms the interpretation:

> lōʾ tihyeh (v 3)
> It shall not happen

> gam-hîʾ lōʾ tihyeh (v 6)
> This also shall not happen

5. Amos 8:4:

> šimʿû zōʾt
> Hear this!

Here the reference is forward, and we believe it covers the statement beginning in v 7. The remainder of vv 4–6 is really the address to the targets of the Woe and a lengthy description of who they are and what they do. But what they are supposed to listen to is the statement in v 7,

> Yahweh has sworn by the pride of Jacob:
> "I will never forget any of their misdeeds."

6. This statement is followed by 8:8:

> haʿal zōʾt lōʾ-tirgaz hāʾāreṣ
> For this reason, should not the earth tremble?

To what does "this" refer? One might suppose that the catalog of sins and crimes in 8:4–6 was intended, and then we should shift our interpretation of zʾt in 8:4 so that they come out at the same place. But it is more likely that the sins and misdeeds, the crimes summed up in v 7 are the more remote cause, and that the more proximate cause is the divine oath. After all, in the biblical view the violent actions and demonstrations of nature in the world are the result of the decisive word of Yahweh. It is Yahweh's oath that produces the action described in v 8. So the two instances of *z't* in the passage refer to the same item, namely, the oath of Yahweh that is quoted in v 7. The occurrence in v 4 refers forward to the oath in v 7, while *z't* in v 8 refers backward to the same oath. The double use of *z't* also supports our view that the material in vv 4–8 comprises a single unit.

7. Amos 9:12:

> *nĕʾūm-yhwh ʿōśeh zōʾt*
> Oracle of Yahweh, who will do this.

In this phrase we have the normal usage. The reference is grammatically backward, covering all of the things that Yahweh says he will do along with those which he has already done. The first statement in 7a is contemporary, while 7b refers to the past in a temporal sense. The rest of vv 8–12 refers to future action, but the expression at the end treats them all the same: Yahweh is the doer par excellence, and the guarantee implicit in the brief clause is that he will do what he says, as he has done in the past and as he does now.

There are seven occurrences of the pronoun *z't* in the book of Amos. It is never used as an adjective but always as the independent pronoun, so it stands alone. It has a specific theological sense: it always refers to something or, more specifically, to the thing that Yahweh has done, is doing, or will do, or has said, or has revealed in a vision. The *z't* in every case is a result of divine decision. The connection with the verb *ʿśh* and the subject *yhwh* is basic to the entire usage in Amos.

From a grammatical point of view all of the occurrences function in the same way. With one exception they regularly refer back to a preceding statement or clause that provides the content of the word: (1) Yahweh's actions in raising up prophets and nazirites; (2) Yahweh's action in bringing the plagues; (3 and 4) Yahweh's action in producing the visions; (6) Yahweh's oath concerning the *śpym;* (7) Yahweh's actions and promised actions in the section from 9:7 through 9:12. The one exception is no. 5 (8:4), where *z't* has a forward reference to the oath previously taken but not mentioned or quoted until 8:7. This is also the only case in which the word *z't* is used twice in connection with the same action or utterance by Yahweh. So out of the seven one is exceptional in at least two ways, and it turns out to be the fifth instance.

I.D.4. COSMIC HYMN (4:13)

4:13a   For behold!
       The Shaper of the mountains,
       and the Creator of the wind,
       and the One who declared his secret thought to Adam;
       the Maker of dawn out of darkness,
       and the One who treads upon the mountains of earth—
13b   Yahweh, God of hosts, is his name!

INTRODUCTION

There are three hymns (or hymn fragments) in Amos (4:13; 5:8–9; 9:5–6). Their presence in the book raises numerous critical questions. The literature on the subject is vast. J. D. W. Watts (1958: chap. III) admirably reviews the debate up to that time. F. Foresti (1981) brings the discussion up to date, with special interest in the movement of old cosmogonic traditions into an apocalyptic setting.

It is generally acknowledged that these pieces are not original compositions of Amos. They belong to a distinctive genre. They recite the achievements of God as a series of mighty acts. The participles are in effect titles, almost names. As such there could be any number of them and in any kind of arrangement. They celebrate notable deeds and doubtless derive from actual stories, but in their present form they no longer tell any story. Two fragments of a flood narrative do survive in 5:8b and 9:6b, where the use of the *waw*-consecutive construction requires that the preceding participle be construed as past tense also:

> [the One] who summoned the waters of the sea,
> and poured them out on the surface of the earth.

The same is true of the participle in 9:5a. In 5:8a and 9:6a, moreover, there are perfect verbs (*heḥšîk* and *yāsad*) that secure the past tense; but they are parallel, not sequential to the preceding participles. An imperfect *yābô'* occupies a similar position in 5:9, however. The verbal roots of the participles come from a stock of creation terms that are found elsewhere in various traditional pieces (hymns, mythic fragments) dealing mainly with divine activities of cosmic scope: *bōrē᾽, ῾ōśeh, yôṣēr, bôneh*. Other participles document struggle and combat: *dōrēk, hōpēk, mablîg, nōgēa῾;* a third set recounts the speech of God, commanding (*qôrē᾽*) or revealing (*maggîd*). The activities are thus diverse, almost miscellaneous. As such they could be no more than an arbitrary selection of such statements from one or more hymns of that genre, or even imitations of such ingredients made up by Amos (or the editor) to achieve some special and intended effect, which we have yet to ascertain, in the prophecies in the book.

A related question is whether all of these quotations come from a single source ("an old hymn" [Watts 1958:51]), which one might even attempt to recover and reconstruct from these three fragments. It has not been possible to reconstitute an original hymn by simply regarding these three pieces as "strophes." They present neither thematic unity nor regularity in composition, and a poem recovered by simply excerpting them from Amos and stringing them together would have to be accepted as falling short of classical prosodic standards. The objects of Yahweh's celebrated acts are mountains, wind, man(?), morning, the ridges of the earth, the Pleiades and Orion (perhaps other constellations), darkness, the waters of the sea, heaven, and earth. In addition there is 5:9, which is suspiciously separated from the other statements in that it seems to be dealing with history rather than with primal creation events. There does not seem to be any order or system in either the selection or the arrangement.

Attempts to find regular verse forms without recourse to drastic emendation have not been successful. Whether by syllables or by beats, the lines vary widely in length. And that other hallmark of classical poetry, parallelism, is present only to a minimal extent. There is a bicolon in 5:8aB with chiasmus of the verbs, and another in 5:9 (same pattern, with repetition of *šōd* and *῾al* as well). The bicolon in 9:6a shows complete introversion—A : B : C :: C' : B' : A'. The parallelism in 9:5b is climactic. In sum: there are four bicolons in about twenty lines. The language is mixed. Sometimes pure poetic diction is used—the nouns, even when definite, do not have the article. But in 5:8b and 9:6b the article is used along with the *waw*-consecutive, as in standard prose. The first seven participles do not have the article, the last five do. *Nota accusativi* is not used at all. The syntax shows some affinities with epic hymnic verse. The clearest example is 9:6aA, which has the adverb ("in heaven") coming before the object, an abnormal sequence often used in similar clauses in Deutero-Isaiah. The use of the preposition in 5:8aB permits the recognition of a similar pattern, with *lbqr* as the second object. Furthermore, the parallelism and introversion here lead to the recognition that the preposition does double duty: he "darkens the day *into* night." But 4:13aB has been read as if the syntax were normal, leading to the error of "He makes morning darkness" (RSV), instead of recognizing the similarity to 5:8aB.

The listing of achievements as a string of participles used as titles is tantamount to reciting the numerous names of God. The climax is the declaration of *the* Name—Yahweh! It is done four times, each time differently. The simplest, *yhwh šĕmô,* comes in its usual place at the end of the third unit; but it falls in the middle of the second. The first one ends with the more elaborate "Yahweh, God of hosts, is his name." A similar name leads the third, "My Lord Yahweh of hosts." This last one is unique, but it agrees with Amos' own frequent use of *'ădōnay yhwh.*

Some themes overlap, providing continuity from one fragment to the next. The middle one shares the motif of light and darkness with the first, and 5:8b is repeated verbatim in 9:6b.

It must be admitted that, from the formal point of view, the craftsmanship is not impressive; yet at the same time the effect of these pieces in their context is powerful. And, no matter who did it (Amos himself or an editor), we have to ask why they were placed in these positions.

H. Guthe identified these hymns as doxologies placed at the end of the main collections of prophecies in the book (1923:37). This theory works for the first one and possibly the third, but hardly for the second. We think it is probably significant that there is one hymn fragment in each of the three "books" into which we have divided the prophecy. The Book of Doom (chaps. 1–4) ends with an apostrophe (4:13). The third apostrophe comes at (or near) the end of The Book of Visions (chaps. 7–9). But it is hard to see any reason for placing the second one where it is, near the beginning of The Book of Woes (chaps. 5–6).

It should be noted in conclusion that four of the ten *qal* active participles have /ō/ spelled *plene,* well above the average for the OT as a whole, and in this practice the hand of a postexilic scribe can be detected; but whether he was just a scrivener or a glossator is hard to tell. All of the minor prophets including Amos seem to have had their spelling updated more toward later practice than other books in the canon.

NOTES

4:13. This apostrophe has five participles, perhaps a deliberate pattern to match the five plagues in 4:6–11. There are four *qal* participles in two pairs, with a *hip'il* in the middle. These three sets present three distinct aspects of Yahweh's activity in Amos' theology. The first two may be referring to original creation. The last two refer to ongoing activity, the regular diurnal changes and special visitations of the world. All four can be found in old myths. The middle one is different. God reveals his musings or meditations to man. Yahweh is not only the originator and sustainer of the universe; he reveals his mind to mankind.

13a. *Shaper of the mountains.* The verb *yṣr* describes the potter's craft. It is used in Genesis 2 to describe the modeling of Adam's body. The verb is a favorite with Deutero-Isaiah, who, like Amos, uses it in parallel with *brʾ* (43:1, 7; 45:7, 18). Genesis 1–2 does not go into the creation of mountains. For that we have to go to Ps 90:2 (where they are born) or Isa 40:12 (where they are weighed out) or Prov 8:25 (where they are shaped [*ṭbʿ*]).

Creator of the wind. In Genesis 1 "the spirit of God" is already soaring over the face of the waters of chaos when the action begins. In Genesis 2 the spirit that gives life to Adam is God's own breath imparted to him. Only in this place does the Bible speak of the creation of "the spirit." The LXX translated *pneuma,* but in the context a cosmic and "natural" element is more likely to have been intended.

thought. While the pronoun of "his thought" is formally ambiguous, there does not seem to be any support for the view that Amos is saying that God can tell a man what he (the man) is thinking. That is obvious in any case (Jer 11:20; Ps 94:11). Rather, God declares what he (God) is thinking. The remarkable use of the word *śēaḥ* rather than, say, *dābār,* which would be quite familiar, resembles *sôd* in 3:7. It is his secret thought, his inner musing, that he reveals. But, by the same token, Amos cannot mean that God discloses his private meditations to "man" in general. The implication of 3:7 is that disclosure of God's "plan" is an exclusive privilege of a few chosen confidants, perhaps only one at any particular time. It would complicate 4:13 to make it mean that God reports his thought to mankind through prophets. In the context of traditions from ancient creation myths, we may ask if *ʾādām* here means Adam the individual, a memory of the primal communing that took place in the garden, according to Gen 3:8.

darkness. The vocabulary is closer to myth here. But *šaḥru,* "Dawn(-god)" is demythologized. H. Torczyner recognized in *ʿēpâ* the singular of *ʿptʾ,* which occurs in the incantation text from Arslan-Tash, where it is a female demon who flies around in the dark (1947:20). Sheol is the land of *ʿēpātāʾ.*

mountains. "heights" or "ridges." Another glimpse of myth. Applied to a human, the image implies triumph (Hab 3:19; Ps 18:34[E33]). In God's case it contains an echo of trampling the primordial dragon, whose humps are the ridges, or even the waves of the sea (Job 9:8). The mythic details had probably been washed out long ago, and the phenomenology of the cliché was currently found in the storm, the thunder being the sound of God's chariot wheels rumbling across the world. The trampling is then done by the horses (Hab 3:8). Otherwise we must think of a warrior-god who strides across the mountains and dominates the world (Hab 3:12; Isa

14:14). This connection is important. Amos' sketch of the theophany could be intended not just as a reminder of God's exploits of old but as a warning that such theophanies have occurred from time to time, and will occur again. It is in such capacities that they must prepare to meet their God.

13b. *Yahweh, God of hosts.* The simplest ending for such a hymn is *Yahweh šĕmô* (Exod 15:3; Jer 33:2; Amos 5:8, 9:6). There are indications that the repetition of the name (Yahweh Yahweh, as in Exod 34:6) could be developed into a simple affirmation in two short lines, as in

> *yhwh ʾîš milhāmâ*
> *yhwh šĕmô*   (Exod 15:3)

> *yhwh ʾĕlōhênû*
> *yhwh ʾehād*   (Deut 6:4)

> *w-yhwh ʾĕlōhê hassĕbāʾôt*
> *yhwh zikrô*   (Hos 12:6[E5])

The virtual identity of *zikrô* and *šĕmô* in such recitals is shown by the parallelism of Exod 3:15:

> *zeh šĕmî lĕʿōlām*
> *wĕzeh zikrî lĕdōr dōr*

There it is a question of "the God of the Fathers," Abraham, Isaac, and Jacob; but the name Yahweh alone is so described in Ps 135:13, and other names, such as *gādôl* (Pss 76:2[E1]; 99:2, 3); *kābôd* (Pss 29:2; 66:2; 96:8; 1 Chr 16:29—do not read "construct"!); *qādôš* (Isa 57:15); *nôrāʾ* (Ps 47:3[E2]); sometimes in combinations with *gādôl* (Dan 5:21) or *qādôš* (Ps 111:9). The prophets favor *yhwh sĕbāʾôt šĕmô* as the closer (Isa 47:4, 48:2, 51:15, 54:5; Jer 10:16, 31:35, 32:18, 46:18, 48:15, 50:34, 51:19, 51:57), which makes more conspicuous Amos' unique *yhwh ʾĕlōhê sĕbāʾôt šĕmô* (4:13), which is used again in the oracle formula in 5:27.

PART II

The Book of Woes
(5:1–6:14)

Amos 5–6 is marked off as a distinct "book" of prophecy by the definitive conclusion of The Book of Doom at the end of chap. 4, and by the clear opening of The Book of Visions at the beginning of chap. 7. The Woes that begin at 6:1 divide this section into two distinct parts. Chapters 5 and 6 each end cleanly, with similar judgment oracles carried by rubrics with the same name for God (5:27; 6:14).

The note struck in the central section of the book is one of woe rather than of doom, warning rather than judgment. There is commiseration and concern. In the intercessions that take place in the first two visions, Amos stands with Jacob against Yahweh. In the condemnations that go with the second two visions, Amos stands with Yahweh against Israel.

"Woes" are prominent in chaps. 5–6, especially in 5:7, 18–20; 6:1–7, 13(–14). Linked with similar statements in other parts of the book, they constitute an extensive inventory of the persons and activities that are the targets of Amos' indignation or, rather, of Yahweh's wrath.

Because the "Woe" is one of the oldest and most persistent of the prophetic forms or genres, we can safely attribute the whole collection to Amos.

The Book of Woes is not isolated from the rest of the prophecy. The threefold šim'û (3:1, 4:1, 5:1) serves as a link with earlier material, and šim'û in 8:4 is a later link. Although the audience seems to be the same throughout, our study of political terminology showed a concentration of the terms "house [or virgin] of Israel" and "Joseph" in these chapters.

"Woe" is the chief note struck in chaps. 5–6. It serves as a rebuke, a denunciation, a warning. It is not the same as condemnation, rejection, judgment; they come at a later stage, after the admonitions have failed. The Woes express grief, commiseration, and can even take the form of a mourning song or dirge (qinah). They are accompanied by earnest calls to changed conduct, so the prophet still has hope that repentance might avert the final catastrophe. No such feelings or hopes are expressed in The Book of Doom (chaps. 1–4).

Formal expressions of woe are not confined to The Book of Woes. The word *hôy* itself occurs only twice (5:18, 6:1). This exclamation is followed typically by a participle, usually with a prefixed *he* as a sign of the definite article or the vocative particle. This pattern leads us to ask whether other participles similarly used throughout the book are part of an extended series of "Woes," even when the word *hôy* is not used with them. The book contains nineteen such participles in all, and when they are taken all together they give a comprehensive picture of the wrongdoers in Israel against whom Amos directs his reproaches, along with a list of the evil deeds of which they are guilty.

1.	2:7	*hš'pym*	those who trample upon the dust of the earth the head of the destitute
2.	3:10	*h'wṣrym*	those who store away the rewards of lawless behavior
3.	4:1	*h'šqwt*	oppressing the poor
4.	4:1	*hrṣṣwt*	crushing the needy
5.	4:1	*h'mrt*	saying to their lords, "Bring . . ."
6.	5:7	*hhpkym*	those who turn justice into wormwood
7.	5:18	*hwy hmt'wym*	Woe to you who long for Yahweh's Day
8.	6:1	*hwy hš'nnym*	Woe to you who luxuriate in Zion
9.	6:1	*hbṭhym*	you who feel secure in Mount Samaria
10.	6:3	*hmndym*	you who rush along toward the day of calamity
11.	6:4	*hškbym*	those who lie on beds of ivory
12.	6:4	*w'klym*	those who devour lambs from the flock
13.	6:5	*hprṭym*	those who improvise on the lyre
14.	6:6	*hštym*	those who drink from basins of wine
15.	6:13	*hśmhym*	you who are delighted over Lo-Dabar
16.	6:13	*h'mrym*	you who say, "Have we not captured Qarnaim for ourselves by our might?"
17.	8:4	*hš'pym*	you who trample upon the poor
18.	8:14	*hnšb'ym*	those who swear by the Guilt of Samaria
19.	9:10	*h'mrym*	those who say: "Calamity shall not even come close"

The nineteen participial statements that we have identified as "Woes" and the twelve participles (or titles) that occur in the three hymns display several similar compositional details. Each statement may be simple or absolute, apparently complete; or it may be developed, explicated, or expounded in various ways by means of additional clauses, either in poetic parallelism or in grammatical sequence. The patterns used to link one or more additional clauses to the lead participial construction are particularly interesting: there may be no conjunction, or there may be coordination with "and" or use of *waw*-consecutive.

1. A single participle
   A. Woe: 3:10b, 5:18, 9:10
2. Two or more such statements in immediate sequence, without conjunctions
   A. Woe: 4:1 (thrice), 6:13 (twice)
3. Two or more such participles in sequence, coordinated by "and"
   A. Woe: 6:1 (twice), 6:4a (twice)
   B. Hymn: 4:13a (thrice), 4:13b (twice)
4. Participle//a colon with no verbal element
   A. Woe: 6:4b
5. Participle//clause with imperfect verb at the end
   A. Woe: 2:7, 6:6
   B. Hymn: 5:9
6. Participle//clause with perfect verb
   A. Woe: 6:5; at the end: 5:7
   B. Hymn: 5:8aB, 9:6
7. Participle//clause with *waw*-consecutive and imperfect verb
   A. Hymn: 5:8b = 9:6b; 9:5a
8. Participle//clause with *waw*-consecutive and perfect verb
   A. Woe: 8:14
   B. Hymn: 9:5 (three following clauses)
9. Participle//infinitive construction
   A. Woe: 8:4

The fact that there are nine different patterns bespeaks the author's versatility and flexibility, and renders nugatory any appeal to regularity as a mark of original components. It is surely remarkable that four of the five constructions used in the Hymns are used in the Woes as well. This connection shows, at the very least, that the compositional technique of the two series is so similar that we have no grounds for doubting the common authorship of both sets. As far as the Hymns are concerned, because they attract the most suspicion, their similarity to the Woes in this matter (and the difficulty of finding sources or models for them in the cult poetry to which they have the closest genre affinity) points to Amos as their presumptive author or at least adapter. They were deliberately composed, and both series were composed to go together. They are not only parallel in form; they are interwoven in presentation. The Hymns are spread throughout the book, like the Woes. At the central point one of the Hymns is actually inserted into one of the Woes. As with the insertion of the confrontation with Amaziah into a pair of visions in chap. 7, this placement combines the two closely.

The Woes and the Hymns resemble each other formally; they stand in stark opposition conceptually. They are placed in juxtaposition to secure a contrast. The celebrated activities of God stand out against those of the humans; the one series for awesome approbation, the other for revulsion and condemnation. A sharp contrast is thus drawn between the majesty of the divine activity and the misery of human behavior. This counterpoise is another good reason for retaining the three Hymns as an integral part of the treatment.

Besides these formal similarities, the two series are connected by various verbal and thematic links, the most conspicuous of which is the root *hpk.* The verb describes one of the most celebrated of Yahweh's deeds, the obliteration of the Cities of the Plain, and describes the quintessence of human depravity, turning justice to wormwood. We see that this statement supplies the twin pillars that support the entire structure of The Book of Woes (5:7, 6:12). Similar links extend the web to other parts of the book. Thus the root *hpk* already occurs twice in 4:11, pointing to a disaster already sent. Another disaster is predicted in 8:9–10, using similar language. This oracle picks up the language of the Hymns, especially the notion of turning light into darkness (8:9; cf. 4:13aB, 5:8) and joy to grief (8:10; cf. 5:1–2). This notion completely reverses the human state of mind, which expects the Day of the Lord to be light, not darkness (5:18) and which rejoices (6:13). The verbs of 5:8 (*hpk//hḥšyk*) are used again in 8:9–10 chiastically.

We might add a comment on a curious detail. The one pattern in the Hymns that is not used in the Woes—no. 7 above—is the one that comes closest to the syntax of classic narrative in standard Hebrew prose. It is the more surprising that this pattern is found where we would expect more archaic language, and is not used where we would expect to find an account of human doings in the usual grammar of storytelling.

The Woes are concentrated in chap. 6, where half of the participles are found. The block of seven in 6:1–6 is at the center of it all, and smaller sets are grouped around it in some kind of symmetry. It is not clear whether the one participle in the Epilogue (9:10) is part of the series or a summary of the whole. Neither is it clear whether the three feminine participles (4:1) belong with the others. The use of the same participle twice, at the beginning and near the end, encourages us to believe that there are long-range connections among them all. It is apparent that the present arrangement is symmetrically structured and that one and all apply to the same group or at least to very closely related and interconnected groups.

Viewed in this way, the eleven participles in The Book of Woes proper (chaps. 5–6) consist of the central block of seven (6:1–6) flanked by two pairs (5:7, 18 and 6:13). At a greater distance this book is tied into The Book of Doom by two participles in 2:7 and 3:10 and to The Book of Visions by two participles at 8:4 and 14. Although 8:4 and 8:14 are separated by other material they belong together, and because 2:7 and 8:4 are almost identical the latter must be seen as a long-range link between the chapters. Amos 2:7 and 3:10 are also separated, but we have shown that chap. 3 is a deliberate elaboration of 2:6–8, so there are grounds for linking the first two participles. These links show that the whole prophecy has the same target from beginning to end.

One final observation: all of the participles except one (*ʾklym* in 6:4) have the article. Its omission in this case could be due to coordination; the article with *škbym* modifies both of the participles in that verse. But we consider this instance to be another example of a pattern or even a rule found in Amos, that when the same form is used many times, one of them will have a variation (see NOTES on 1:14).

If all of the participles in chaps. 5–6 go together, all go equally well with the opening word of chap. 5—"Hear!"—and the opening word of chap. 6—"Woe!"—even when neither of these key words is used immediately with the participle. There is no reason to claim that the people who desired the Day of Yahweh (5:18) were different from those in 5:7, 10–12; or 6:1–7, 13. They came from different walks of life—merchants, magistrates, soldiers—but their general outlook was the same, and they amounted to one consolidated class, which doubtless embraced all branches of public leadership, including clergy.

Besides the Woe participles, which produce a measure of coherence in The Book of Woes, there is another element that reflects and confirms the remarkable balance or symmetry of a planned structure. Amos 5:14–15 happens to be the physical center of the book: that is, it divides the whole into two equal halves by word count—1:1–5:13, 1,009 words; 5:16–9:15, 1,006 words. If we count *byt-ʾl* as a single word (as it is written in some manuscripts), instead of two, then the totals for the two halves are exactly the same: 1,004 // 1,004 (1,009 − 5 = 1,004 // 1,006 − 2 = 1,004). Whether this kind of symmetry was planned or accidental, there can be no doubt that the theme of 5:14–15, "justice," is central to the message of the book. It is a classic exhortation on the vital topic of good and evil, tightly bound to the demand for *mišpāṭ*.

This pivot of the whole book has an elegant chiasmus:

5:14a	*diršû-ṭôb wĕʾal-rāʿ*	Seek Good and not Evil,
	lĕmaʿan tiḥyû	so that you may live!
15a	*śinʾû-rāʿ wĕʾehĕbû ṭôb*	Hate Evil and love Good,
	wĕhaṣṣîgû baššaʿar mišpāṭ	and establish justice in the gate.

Note also that 5:14a harks back to the theme of 5:4–6:

diršûnî wiḥyû

diršû ʾet-yhwh wiḥyû

Similarly 5:15a is linked with a trio of verses (5:7, 24; 6:12b), the structure of which will be discussed shortly. Thus 5:14–15 is a nexus for several themes in The Book of Woes.

Another symmetrical pattern in The Book of Woes highlights a key theme and confirms our isolation of this unit. We have identified 5:7 as the first of the Woes; it forms an inclusion with 6:13. The accusation in 5:7 is matched by the language of 6:12b. In 6:11 there is an echo of 5:6, and 6:14 is related to 6:2. The accumulation of small pieces at the end of The Book of Woes, not immediately connected among themselves, can then be understood as a series of echoes or inclusions:

5:1–2 ⟶	5:16–17
5:3 ⟶	6:9–10
5:4–5 ⟶	6:11
5:6 ⟶	5:14
5:7 ⟶	6:12b
5:7 ⟶	6:13
6:2 ⟶	6:14

With much vocabulary in common, the major prongs are 5:7 and 6:12b. They are not at the very beginning or end of The Book of Woes, but far enough apart to span the whole effectively. It is not unusual for an echoing element to be found toward the end of a major unit instead of precisely at the end. Thus, chap. 6 ends with an accusation (v 12b) matching the Woe of 5:7, a Woe (6:13) matching the accusation of 6:8; a judgment (6:14) matching the Woe and accusation of 6:1–2. It is usual for the key word to be at the very beginning, even though its counterpart comes a little before the end. For example, in Psalm 23 the echoing word is "Yahweh," the first word in the poem, which is not used again until the last verse. It is not the last word, however, but the third from the end. For other similar examples see Psalms 3, 94; and Lamentations 5.

While 5:7 is not the beginning of The Book of Woes, it is the first of the series of Woes, with 6:12b as its echo just before the end.

5:7	*hahōpĕkîm lĕlaʿănâ miš-*	[Woe to] those who turn justice into worm-
	pāṭ	wood,
	ûṣĕdāqâ lāʾāreṣ hinnîḥû	and equity in the earth they bury.

6:12b   *kî-hăpaktem lĕrōʾš mišpāṭ*   But you have turned justice into poison,
        ûpĕrî ṣĕdāqâ lĕlaʿănâ   and the fruit of righteousness into worm-
                                         wood.

Note the repetition of *hpk* and the chiastic placement of *laʿănâ* when the four lines are read as a unit.

Comparison of the two couplets yields insights into the basic meaning or purpose of both. The second (6:12b) evinces a more classic parallelism, along with a characteristic chiasm:

$$lr\'š\ mšpṭ$$
$$\ldots\ ṣdqh\ ll\'nh$$

The single verb at the beginning governs both objects; the corresponding extra term in the second colon makes the comparison more precise. It is, after all, not justice and righteousness that are turned into wormwood and gall, but the fruit of those virtues, the acts or effects stemming from those required and virtuous dispositions. Hence *pry*, "fruit," should be understood as the real term of comparison not only in 6:12 but also in 5:7. In the latter (5:7), four of the elements are the same or nearly so—*hhpkym, llʿnh, mšpṭ,* and *wṣdqh*—while the last two words diverge considerably. Whether some items have dropped out, namely, the two missing terms, *pry* and *lrʾš,* and the replacement words actually belonged to a third colon, which added a complementary or completing idea (planting these noxious weeds in the ground or something similar) is hard to say; but we must suppose that *llʿnh* in 5:7 stands for *lrʾš* as well, while *pry* is to be understood as qualifying *mšpṭ* and *ṣdqh* throughout.

The central thought is the same: these perverters of the judicial process turn the fruits of justice and righteousness into poisonous flora, which they plant in the earth with all ceremonial propriety (cf. Baal's order to Anat that she put love in the earth, *UT ʿnt*:III, 11–14).

The key words *mišpāṭ* and *ṣĕdāqâ* are paired once more in 5:24, perhaps the most famous of Amos' words:

        wĕyiggal kammayim mišpāṭ   But let justice roll on like the ocean,
        ûṣĕdāqâ kĕnahal ʾêtān   and equity like a perennial stream.

Note also that the positive thrust of the central statement (5:24) combats the negative connotation of the two flanking ones (5:7, 6:12b).

These three bicolons are clearly part of an extended composition. Perhaps it is not just coincidence that the block of material they encompass has an almost perfect internal symmetry:

5:7	6 words
5:8–23	200 words
5:24	6 words
5:25–6:14	200 words (not counting 6:12b)
6:12b	7 words

The usual techniques of form criticism identify a great variety of genres in The Book of Woes. The paragraphing of most modern translations reflects a similar impression. A dozen or a score of individual compositions are recognized, and some of them are taken to be prose. The material is reckoned to be so heterogeneous by these criteria that much of it is considered to be secondary editorial comment or scribal addition. We recognize that three categories of contributors, including prophet, editors, and scribes, have produced the final result, but we contend that efforts to sort out those contributions are not always successful or convincing. We do not think that the usual tests of original and authentic prophetic utterances (regular rhythm, parallelism, elevated language) are invariably or necessarily valid. The varied results achieved by many scholars do not inspire confidence in the presuppositions or the method. As a matter of fact, there is little indication that Amos composed his pieces according to the norms of classical lyric verse. His literary technique is quite different from that of his great contemporaries—Hosea, Isaiah, and Micah. Poetic form alone is not decisive. Neither can genre classification get us very far, unless we already know before we begin that the prophet used only certain genres and not others. To deny 5:14–15 to Amos because it is "a construction of purely sapiential character" (Wolff 1977:250) seems quite inconclusive, indeed irrelevant to us. We think that unit is central and integral, not only to the structure of The Book of Woes, but also to its message. Amos often slips into a wisdom mode, and he weaves wisdom talk into his oracles at many points and quite effectively.

When form and genre are indecisive, the content alone may be judged unsuitable for Amos. Amos 5:6 is an example. We have already pointed out some of its verbal, thematic, and structural connections with the rest of The Book of Woes. Furthermore, we are willing to recognize in the switch from direct divine speech (5:4, second person, "seek me") to indirect speech (5:6a, third person, "seek Yahweh"), the addition of a prophetic exhortation to a core oracle. But when it is argued that the encouraging note struck in 5:6 must be later "interpretation," not from Amos, because of "its alteration of the uncompromising sentence of judgment into a forewarning" (Wolff 1977:240), we are not inclined to accept the argument. Our entire treatment emerges from taking such warnings and exhortations seriously as an essential part of Amos' message in its first phase. Even when the note of irreversible doom is finally struck (in The Book of Doom and in other parts of the prophecy) it presupposes that they had prior and ample opportunity to escape the judgment. It is only after repeated violations ("three . . . four") that an irreversible decree is issued (the refrain of the Great Set Speech). Not only sins persisted in, but repeated refusals to repent (4:6–11) lead to the final confrontation (4:12). It is precisely in The Book of Woes that we find those exhortations to repentance which, when rejected time and again, eventually (but only after every effort had been made, every chance given) exhausted the divine patience. Of course, 4:6–11 can be deleted as a later homily. But what is now to be crossed out as scribal addition is not a few marginal notes, but at least one-quarter of The Book of Woes, including verses that give integrity and structure to the whole.

As a distinct unit in The Book of Woes, chap. 5 has its own inner organization and structure. The occurrence of "house of Israel" in the opening and closing units (vv 1, 25) constitutes an inclusion that is forfeited when vv 25–27 are regarded as a later addition. This identification is important, especially in association with the tradition of the forty years' wandering; for it shows that the "you" addressed throughout the chapter is the entire nation. The specificity of the woes might seem to suggest that a more restricted group is in mind, but defined in the context of references to the whole "house of Israel." The charges enumerated in the woes are appropriately directed to the leadership responsible for the manner and practice of the cult and for the perversion and subversion of justice in official proceedings. This is the group primarily responsible and the only group in a position to initiate and achieve national reformation, the group on whom the fate of the whole nation—either way—depends.

The contents of chap. 5 may be outlined as follows:

A. Exhortations for Israel and Judah, separately and together (5:1–27)
    1. Exhortation to the house of Israel (5:1–6)
        a. The fallen virgin (5:1–2)
        b. Decimation (5:3)
        c. The sanctuaries (5:4–6)
            i. "Seek me and live" (5:4–5)
            ii. Threat against Bethel (5:6)
    2. First Woe (5:7–13), including the Second Hymn (5:8–9)
        a. First Woe (5:7)
        b. Second Hymn (5:8–9)
        a (continued). First woe (5:10–12)
        c. The wise man (5:13)
    3. Exhortation and lamentation (5:14–17)
        a. Repentance (5:14–15)
        b. Lamentation (5:16–17)

4. Warning and Woe (5:18–27)
    a. The Day of Yahweh (5:18–20)
    b. Justice (5:21–24)
    c. Threat of exile (5:25–27)

The chapter divides into two equal parts (by word count) between v 13 and v 14. Several of the elements in the two halves are comparable, though located differently in each half. The pairings are shown in this two-column display:

vv 1–13		Words		vv 14–27
1–2	Dirge	22	28	14–15 Seek
3	Decimation	16		
4–6	Seek	41	31	16–17 Dirge
7	Woe	6	39	18–20 Woe
8–9	Apostrophe	26		
10–12	Woe (they hate)	41	41	21–24 I hate
13	The wise man	9	21	25–27 Threat of exile
	Totals	161	160	

There are links of various kinds—verbal, thematic, formal—among four of the units in each half. Three of the others have more long-range links with material outside chap. 5. The theme of decimation (v 3) is resumed in 6:9. The apostrophe (vv 8–9) is one of three hymn fragments. The reference to the wilderness (v 25) echoes 2:10, and the threat of exile (v 27) is made repeatedly throughout the book. The only piece without a mate is v 13, the center of the chapter; but even this passage could have a connection with 6:10 through the motif of silence.

Even though there is not much formal similarity between vv 10–12 and vv 21–24, the confrontation between divine and human "haters" is dramatic. The juxtaposition of the words is another example of the Bible's preoccupation with exact retribution (i.e., poetic justice—Ps 18:26–27).

There is another important consequence of viewing all of these materials in relation to one another instead of treating each oracle as an isolated, autonomous, and self-interpreting statement. Much harm has been done in Amos studies by taking small oracles as categorical and absolute declarations. A woe such as 5:7 can be reduced to simple moralism, without reference to the larger framework of religion. An oracle like that in 5:4–6 can be seen as driving a wedge between seeking Yahweh and frequenting the shrine. But 5:14–15 brings these threads together; and 5:10 fits another piece into the puzzle, because it goes to the heart of ethics in terms of attitude and intention, not just behavior. It is their total life-style—the

1. General view of Samaria referred to by Amos, "Assemble on the mountains of Samaria" (3:9). Amos refers to the mountains as God's creation in 4:13, and to the security of the mountain of Samaria in 6:1. *(Israel Department of Antiquities and Museums)*

2. Israelite masonry from Samaria. Amos 3:15, "I will smash the winter palace as well as the summer palace...and the magnates' palaces will be swept away." Compare 6:11, "he will smash the largest house into pieces, and the smallest house into bits." *(Israel Department of Antiquities and Museums)*

3. Israelite masonry from Samaria. Amos refers to houses made of hewn stone, instead of field stones, in 5:11, "the houses of hewn stone that you have built—you shall not dwell in them." *(Israel Department of Antiquities and Museums)*

4. This photograph illustrates Amos' reference to a straight wall of hewn stone (7:7): "Yahweh showed me: Indeed he was standing beside a plastered wall, with a lump of tin in his hand." *(Israel Department of Antiquities and Museums)*

5. "Mesad Hashavyahu" Letter, Hebrew Ostracon, Mesad Hashavyahu, near Yavne-Yam, late seventh century B.C.E. The letter describes the subject of garments taken in pledge and not returned to their owner at the prescribed time (cf. 2:8). *(Israel Department of Antiquities and Museums)*

6. Bronze copy of seal of "Shema, servant of Jeroboam," Jasper, Megiddo, eighth century B.C.E., depicting a lion:

> The lion has roared;
>   who is not frightened?
> The Lord Yahweh has spoken;
>   who could not prophesy? (3:8)

(Compare 3:4, 1:2, 5:19.)   *(Israel Department of Antiquities and Museums)*

7. "Woman in the window" ivory from Samaria, ninth–eighth centuries B.C.E. This ivory depicts Amos' reference to the fact that "the ivory palaces will be destroyed" (3:15). It also illustrates Amos' view of rich women (4:1). *(Israel Department of Antiquities and Museums)*

8. Altars from the high place (Holy of Holies) in the fortress of Arad, ninth century B.C.E., Israelite period. ''I will also punish the altars of Bethel; the horns of the altar will be cut down, and will fall to the ground'' (3:14). *(Israel Department of Antiquities and Museums)*

combination of ruthlessness with religiosity, their values, attitudes, and actions in court and cult—that makes the religion they profess and practice in their rites abhorrent and abominable to God. It is not simply the cult as such or in itself that is objectionable, even though the prophet fastens on the cult as the ultimate expression of rebellion and sinfulness. Rather, it is the smugness and self-satisfaction of those who presume to violate the covenant and at the same time act as though nothing were amiss. They revel in sacrilege and injustice yet believe that they are welcome in the Lord's house, at the altar of sacrifice and the communal table. It is the gap between unrighteous doing and living and the profession and practice of official and formal piety which disturbs the prophet or, more properly, the God who sent him.

There could be something personal behind this view. They not only hated and thwarted the reprover in the gate (5:10), they hated and ejected the reprover in the shrine (7:10–17).

In summary, chap. 5 is a compendium of major themes and elements from the whole book of Amos. It is built in concentric circles around the center of the chapter, which is also the middle of the book, namely 5:14–15. Here the major exhortation of the whole book of Amos is given, 5:14–15 buttressed by vv 4–6 and by vv 23–24, which balance each other as well. The great exhortation arises out of the first pair of visions and represents the initial phase of the commission and ministry of the prophet. There is a great danger for Israel, but there is still time; there is great urgency because the time is very short and the need for change very great. Nothing less than a complete about-face is needed. All of the key theological terms are present or implied, and taken together these words constitute the first and primary message of the prophet.

There is more, however. At the beginning of the chapter there is mourning for the fallen virgin Israel and at the end the unmodified threat of exile. These passages, reinforced by others in the chapter, reflect a later and more disheartening stage in the story: Israel is doomed, and already in vision or imagination, and in accord with the classic formulation of the dirge or qinah, the prophet sees Israel as a fallen (= prostrate, dead, and deserted) virgin, a scene already played out and past. Only mourning is in order now; the decision is irreversible, and in vision and word already carried out. Here we clearly have Phase-Two material forming an envelope around the central exhortation of Phase One. The dirge is echoed by the lamentation in vv 16–17, while the ominous threat of exile at the end of the chapter is anticipated in the exhortation of vv 4–6.

II.A. EXHORTATIONS FOR ISRAEL AND JUDAH, SEPARATELY AND TOGETHER (5:1–27)

II.A.1. EXHORTATION TO THE HOUSE OF ISRAEL (5:1–6)

II.A.1.a. THE FALLEN VIRGIN: INTRODUCTION AND QINAH (5:1–2)

5 ¹Hear this message that I am going to utter about you, a dirge, O house of Israel:

2a   "The virgin Israel has fallen,
            she will never stand up again;
2b   she has been left lying on her land,
            and no one raises her up."

INTRODUCTION

5 1–2. Verse 1 is the introduction, v 2 the qinah. The unit is unusual in several ways. The call to listen to "this message" leads us to expect an oracle of conventional type—an accusation or a judgment speech or a reproach in the form of a Woe, as in 4:1, which begins in the same way.

The "message" is then identified as a qinah (Heb *qînâ*), a song of grief, the text of which immediately follows. The introduction is in prose; the three "prose particles" are used (note that there is no *'et* in the otherwise similar introduction in 4:1). The last three words dangle rather awkwardly. Comparison with 3:1 shows that "house of Israel" is vocative. It also shows the equivalence of *dibber yhwh* and *'ānōkî nōśē'*, which suggests that Yahweh is the singer of the qinah.

The song itself is brief, a fragment perhaps, one stanza at the most. It is not long enough to disclose any regular verse design, but what there is conforms reasonably well with the standard qinah, as seen, for example, in the book of Lamentations. The prevailing pattern in Lamentations 1–3 is 3 : 2 in stresses and 8 : 5 (or 7 : 6) in syllables; but there is considerable variation in individual lines.

The construction is rather close to the several units of Lamentations. We should read as follows:

2a	*nāpĕlâ lōʾ-tôsîp qûm*	$3 + 1 + 2 + 1 = 7$	(3 stresses)	⎫ 13 (5)
	bĕtûlat yiśrāʾēl	$3 + 3 = 6$	(2 stresses)	⎭
2b	*niṭṭĕšâ ʿal-ʾadmātāh*	$3 + 1 + 3 = 7$	(2 stresses)	⎫ 11 (4)
	ʾēn mĕqîmāh	$1 + 3 = 4$	(2 stresses)	⎭

The only significant deviation is in 2bA, where we only have two stresses instead of the expected three. But the syllable count is the same as for 2aA. If we restored the original long form of the 3d f. s. suffix in 2b, the two bicola would be the same in total length. Compare Lam 1:2bA, *ʾēn-lāh mĕnaḥēm* (which is similar to *ʾen mĕqîmāh*), used in both first and second cola (with chiasm) in 1:2b, 9bB, 17aB, and 21aB; cf. 7cB. See also Lam 1:14cB for *qwm* and 15cB for *btwlt*.

There is parallelism between the two negative statements: *lōʾ-tôsîp qûm//ʾēn mĕqîmāh*. The root *qwm* is repeated, climactically. Not only is she unable to get up again; there is no one to help her to get up. The same intensification is found in the parallel verbs *nāpĕlā//niṭṭĕšâ*—"fallen"// "abandoned." The most striking feature of all is the insertion of *lōʾ-tôsîp qûm* into the clause *nāpĕlâ . . . bĕtûlat yiśrāʾēl,* which otherwise would be a perfectly acceptable parallel to *niṭṭĕšâ ʿal-ʾadmātāh.* We see no reason to rearrange the text into something more conventional.

NOTES

1. Both verses have unusual word order. In v 1 the relative clause comes before two items in apposition: "this message . . . a dirge," "that I am going to utter about you . . . O house of Israel."

utter. The noun *maśśāʾ,* "burden" or "message," would be a suitable implied object of *nśʾ.* The use of the participle instead of, say, the rubric *kōh ʾāmar yhwh* indicates that the "word" is not a decree that has been determined, but something that will be uttered, perhaps in some indeterminate future.

dirge. The qinah is a song of mourning for the dead. A prophetic oracle in the form of a *qînâ* could express the sincere grief of the prophet (or of Yahweh) at the demise of the nation, which is felt as a personal bereavement. It is made all the more touching by describing the victim as a "virgin." But this qinah oracle is spoken "against" or "concerning" Israel. It therefore serves to predict the death of the nation and anticipates the mourning to follow. As such it is tantamount to a death sentence. But the form chosen softens the tone of the judgment speech and does not allow the customary note of vindictiveness; rather it describes the hurt and loss suffered by God himself at the breakdown of his relationship with his people. Indeed the term "virgin" suggests that Israel is viewed as a bride or fiancée. The allegory is not developed; the point is that the extreme of grief was considered to be that of a young man who loses his intended before the marriage. The pathos is that the relations possible in the covenant between Yahweh and Israel were never fully realized.

Ezekiel has four prophecies in the form of dirges (19:1, 27:2, 28:12, 32:2). These, however, are not expressions of grieving love but of bitter hatred. The dirge is sung in mockery, to taunt a fallen foe.

2a. *fallen.* The two perfect verbs suggest that the disaster has already taken place. But nowhere else in Amos is there record of a calamity so complete and final as to be death with no prospect of revival. Even the plagues of 4:6–11 leave the nation intact and unrepentant, though badly damaged. The verb "fallen" evokes pictures of defeat in battle, for this term often describes war dead. As such, v 2 could be an extreme statement of a major military defeat as described in v 3.

2b. *she has been left.* Implicitly, it is by God, as the use of the verb elsewhere shows. There was a covenant promise that Yahweh would never abandon his people (Ps 94:14); yet he abandoned Shiloh (Ps 78:60). The ambivalence of the covenant engagement, at once unqualified and conditional, left Israel in a state of existential uncertainty, except for those who affirmed only the absolute commitment in a smug and careless way (9:10b).

her land. Elsewhere Amos predicts exile of the people "from its land" (7:11, 17). Here we have the corresponding picture of the abandoned land. The virgin Israel is prostrate on her land, just as in Lam 1:1. Sometimes a city is called a virgin, for example, Jerusalem (2 Kgs 19:21). The following reference to a city (v 3) supports this idea. On the supposition that these oracles are directed solely against the northern kingdom, the "virgin" has been identified as Samaria. But the reference to "her land" is to the whole land. The qinah mourns not just the destruction of one city but of Israel (the "virgin").

raises . . . up. Because God was renowned for his ability to raise up the fallen, the statement that Israel has no one to do so for her represents an even worse dereliction than refusal to help on the battlefield. Here God rules out all prospect of ever restoring the nation to life. In the context of The Book of Doom it would be another statement of final and irreversible punishment, the end of the nation. In the context of The Book of Woes, however, we must ask if this anticipation serves as a warning of a very likely outcome, not as an announcement of its inevitability. Verse 27 also predicts "exile beyond Damascus," a fate not inconsistent with that in v 2, but appropriate as a threat that might still be averted if the exhortations contained within this inclusion (vv 2 and 27) are heeded in time. These fates are the same pair as in the Great Set Speech: death in battle and exile of the survivors. Because vv 4–6 hold out the possibility of life, the threat of death in vv 2–3 is not final.

COMMENT

The formula at the beginning is almost identical with that found at 3:1 except that the message is identified as a dirge. Just as 3:1–2 constitute the essential message after the elaborate introduction, so here the essence of the message is embodied in a single verse (5:2). Amos 3:2 was ominous and menacing, explaining in threatening terms the real relationship of Yahweh and his people: the unique intimacy between them would result in a harsher judgment, perhaps the opposite of general expectation. So here in 5:2 the matter is summed up briefly. In vision or stereotyped expression the prophet laments the death of Israel, a virgin fallen on her land, never to rise again because there is no one to raise her up. This image is no flight of fancy—visions participate in reality, and words turn pictures into facts. The dirge is not fantasy; it is poetry that creates events. The mourning may be premature, but it sets in motion the course of events that justifies it. What the prophet sees and says is going to happen. The words are the means by which the series is begun, by which it is defined and will be concluded. There is a supplement or complement to this qinah in vv 16–17, where the picture is generalized in terms of the country and its people. Both partake of the same reality and its articulation in the words of a divine message.

II.A.1.b. DECIMATION (5:3)

5:3a   For thus my Lord Yahweh has said:
         "The city that marches forth a thousand strong
         shall have only a hundred left;

3b   and the one that marches forth a hundred strong
         shall have only ten left—
          O house of Israel!"

NOTES

5:3. With its brief form and cryptic comment, this oracle can pass the usual tests of authenticity. Approximating the rhythm of a qinah, it could be taken as the second stanza of the dirge in v 2. "House of Israel" then makes an inclusion with v 1, and the conjunction *kî* makes the logical link. This passage confirms that the virgin Israel lies prostrate as the consequence of an overwhelming military defeat. There is, however, a major difference between the two verses. The verbs in v 2 are perfect; those in v 3 are imperfect, in parallel with participles; v 3 reads more like a prediction.

In analyzing the structure of v 3 we have a choice between two long lines, 5 beats // 4 beats; or four short lines with interleaved parallelism. We must also ask if the report concerns two cities of different sizes, each of which suffers 90 percent casualties; or only one city, which, after two successive campaigns, suffers 99 percent casualties. The latter is more drastic, and seems to be indicated by the fact that the word "city" is used only once.

3a. *my Lord.* Wolff (1977:227 n. f) says that "the messenger formula in the book of Amos regularly uses only *yhwh.*" It is true that *kōh 'āmar yhwh* is preferred in the Great Set Speech (1:3, 6, 9, 11, 13; 2:1, 4, 6), and again in 3:12. Without *kōh, 'āmar yhwh* is a colophon in 1:5, 15; 2:3; and 5:17. The stock formula is preceded by *lākēn* in 7:17. Amos is fond of the title *'ădōnāy yhwh,* which occurs twenty times in the prophecy, and this fuller title sometimes occurs in the messenger formula (3:11; 5:3—preceded by a conjunction) or colophon (1:8; 7:6). Amos is also remarkable in using *nĕ'ūm 'ădōnāy yhwh* (3:13; 4:5; 8:3, 9, 11) as well as the stock *nĕ'ūm yhwh* (2:11, 16; 3:10, 15; 4:3, 6, 8, 9, 10, 11; 9:7, 8, 12, 13). He also has both *lākēn kōh-'āmar yhwh ṣĕbā'ōt 'ădōnāy* (5:16) and *nĕ'ūm yhwh 'ĕlōhê ṣĕbā'ōt* (6:8, 14), and even *'āmar yhwh 'ĕlōhê ṣĕbā'ōt šĕmô* (5:27). The book ends with *'āmar yhwh 'ĕlōheykā* (9:15). Presented with such variety, it seems a little mechanical to declare only one of these formulas authentic and to use the others for detecting the hand of a later scribe.

marches forth. The verb *yṣ'* describes a military expedition (cf. Gen 4:16; Deut 20:1; 1 Sam 8:20; etc.).

3b. *house of Israel.* It is easy enough to delete this phrase as a dittograph from the following verse (NIV). The force of the preposition is not clear. Either it is a delayed modifier of "the city," or it completes the messenger formula in v 3aA, just as the same phrase does in v 4. Then again it could echo the vocative "O house of Israel" in v 1, making an inclusion or envelope. Compare *lĕbêt-'ēl* at the end of v 6.

COMMENT

The image in v 3 may be associated with the preceding. It describes the results of defeat in war and the corresponding decimation of the army. This decimation is compounded so that we are actually talking about a tenth of a tenth or 1 percent of the original population group rather than the usual 10 percent. In fact, decimation can be interpreted or applied in two different ways: it may refer to the loss of 10 percent, meaning that 90 percent survive, which is severe enough in terms of military casualties and losses; or it may mean loss of 90 percent and survival of 10 percent, which for all practical purposes means the end of the army and of the nation. For the prophet even this disaster was not enough (as also in the case of Isaiah, cf. 6:1–13, especially v 13). He compounded the decimation so that finally from the original thousand only ten survived—first one hundred were left after the first military engagement, and then of the hundred only ten, after the second engagement. Apparently there is a postscript or addendum to this woeful account, though the linkage is purely numerical. In chap. 6:9–10, we hear again of ten—ten men in a house who are left—from what we do not know, and even the verb is not the same. But it may be the same ten, or 1 percent, who survived the catastrophic defeats of chap. 5:3. If so, they will be gathered into a single house and then die. In the end there are no survivors at all if we have interpreted the passage correctly, or at most one person out of ten, a third round of decimation leaving only one-tenth of 1 percent, or literally one in or out of a thousand. The possible association of v 3 and its military catastrophe with the mourning of v 2 (and cf. vv 16–17) is obvious enough and need not be pressed. Similar imagery is to be found in Lamentations.

II.A.1.c. THE SANCTUARIES (5:4–6)
II.A.1.c.i. "SEEK ME AND LIVE" (5:4–5)

5:4a   For thus Yahweh has said:
   "O house of Israel,
  4b Seek me and live!

5a   But don't seek [me] at Bethel,
           and to Gilgal do not come,
           and to Beer-sheba do not cross over;
5b   because Gilgal will certainly go into exile,
           and Bethel will become nothing.

II.A.1.c.ii. THREAT AGAINST BETHEL (5:6)

5:6a   Seek Yahweh and live,
6b   lest he rush [upon you] like a flame,
               O house of Joseph,
               and it consume [you] with none to quench [it],
               O house of God!

NOTES

After the opening formula (v 4a), the oracle consists of an exhortation in seven lines, enveloped by the repeated verb *diršû*, followed by a subordinate clause (*pen-*) that states the consequences of refusal to heed the exhortation. The arrangement of the three place-names in the inner five lines achieves a perfect introversion:

		Syllables
4a	*kî kōh ᵓāmar yhwh lĕbêt yiśrāᵓēl*	5
4b	*diršûnî wiḥyû*	5
5aA	*wĕᵓal-tidrĕšû bêt-ᵓēl*	7
5aB	*wĕhaggilgāl lōᵓ tābōᵓû*	8
5aC	*ûbĕᵓēr šebaᶜ lōᵓ taᶜăbōrû*	8
5bA	*kî haggilgāl gālōh yigleh*	8
5bB	*ûbêt-ᵓēl yihyeh lĕᵓāwen*	7
6aA	*diršû ᵓet-yhwh wiḥyû*	7
6bA	*pen-yiṣlaḥ kāᵓēš bêt yôsēp*	8
6bB	*wĕᵓākĕlâ wĕᵓên-mĕkabbeh*	9
	lĕbêt-ᵓēl	4

The chiastic arrangement, in which Bethel is listed first and last (*Bethel—Gilgal—Beer-sheba—Gilgal—Bethel*), makes it clear that Bethel is the prime target, as elsewhere in the prophecy (3:14; 4:4; 7:10, 13); but it is not the only one. The mention of Beer-sheba is important because it shows that the region of Judah is included. It is straining things to argue that it is only included because northerners went there on pilgrimage (Keil and Delitsch 1986:10, I:279).

5:4a. *house of Israel.* In view of the occurrence of the same phrase in vv 1 and 3, it could be vocative here as well. The matching phrase at the end of v 6 can likewise be taken as vocative, so that vv 1–3 and vv 4–6 have similar inclusions. If this point can be sustained, with the structural equivalence of *bêt-yiśrāʾēl* and *bêt-ʾēl* in these units, then the reference of the latter should be controlled by the former, not vice versa. That is, instead of arguing from the prominence of Bethel that the message is restricted to the northern kingdom and that therefore this is what "house of Israel" means, the reference of "house of Israel" to the whole nation (two kingdoms), which we have proposed on other grounds, shows that Bethel, as the most prominent of the national shrines, was visited by the people of both nations. Similar logic applies to "house of Joseph" in v 6. There is no question that the spotlight is on the heartland of the northern kingdom and its major shrine. But silence alone (the failure to name Judah or Jerusalem explicitly in this connection) is not sufficient to exclude any part of the nation from the general message. Beer-sheba clearly belongs to Judah, but the fact that it is not openly threatened with destruction and exile, like the other two, does not necessarily mean that it is exempt from danger. Pilgrimage to it is forbidden just as definitely as to the other two.

4b. *seek.* "Seeking" is a major theme of the chapter—vv 4, 6, 14.

5b. *Gilgal.* By using the infinitive absolute, the consonants *g-l* occur four times. On the topography, see the NOTES on 4:4.

nothing. In a similar oracle, Hosea (4:15) warns against frequenting the shrines of Gilgal or Bethel:

| weʾal-tābōʾû haggilgāl | Don't go to Gilgal, |
| weʾal-taʿălû bêt ʾāwen | Don't go up to Beth Awen. |

Hosea calls Bethel "house of *ʾāwen*" several times (5:8, 10:5; cf. 10:8)—"iniquity" or "nothing," with either meaning suggesting "idol(s)" (Andersen and Freedman 1980:372). Because Amos plays on the sound of Gilgal, some play on "Bethel" is likely, *ʾāwen* contrasting with *ʾēl*. It is no longer the house of the true God; it will become the house of "Nothing."

6b. *lest.* The use of the conjunction shows that there is still the possibility of averting the threatened disaster, but we have moved beyond the stage represented in the second vision (7:4–6), where the prophet's intercession

was sufficient to reverse the divine decision. Now, however, full-scale repentance on the part of the people is required.

rush. The verb is used characteristically of the onset of the Spirit (Judg
14:6, 19). The subject here is God; in similar passages (Jer 4:4, 21:12) we
find his wrath:

pen-tēṣē' kā'ēš ḥămātî	Lest my wrath go forth like fire,
ûbā'ărâ wĕ'ên mĕkabbeh	and burn with none to quench it.

In spite of Wolff's endorsement of the MT, his translation adopts the interpretive version of the LXX, which makes the verb *analampsē,* "catch fire,"
with "house of Joseph" as subject.

flame. There is an incongruity between v 6bA and v 6bB. In v 6bA "fire"
is a simile for the onrush of Yahweh himself, unless *k-* marks the grammatical complement (*"as* fire," not *"like* fire"). In v 6bB the feminine verb
shows that Fire is now the agent, as in the Great Set Speech. The Great Set
Speech, in fact, announces as inevitable what is here threatened. In both
places the image is strongly mythopoeic.

house of Joseph. Because the prepositions *'el* or *'al* are the usual idiom
with *ṣlḥ,* the unique use of *l-* here could indicate that "house of Joseph" is
vocative, in line with other names in vv 1–6.

quench. Compare the similar participial construction at the end of v 2.
The purport of each is the same. Yahweh is the only one who can perform
such rescue acts, and if he does not intervene (after all, he caused the
calamity in the first place!) no one can help them. Compare Lamentations
1, with different verbs but the same picture. The LXX avoids the clash of
gender.

Bethel. The LXX version levels to "house of Israel" and implies that *byt'l*
here stands for *byt yśr'l.*

COMMENT

In 5:4–6 once again an oracle is addressed to the house of Israel (also
mentioned in vv 1, 3, and 25). Here, as already noted several times, we have
an example of Phase-One oratory. It is an exhortation to seek Yahweh (a
standard expression for seeking an oracle or message) and thereby live—
have life and not die, which will otherwise be their fate. The exhortation
continues in vv 5–6 and spells out the negative side of what seeking Yahweh
in order to live means. The positive side is stated in v 14. Verse 5 picks up a
matter that was mentioned earlier in 4:4–5. The reference in v 5, "Don't
seek . . . Bethel," is elliptical. The meaning as shown by v 4 (cf v 6) is

certainly, "Don't seek me at Bethel," just as at the other shrines. In the earlier passage Israel is instructed, commanded to go to the shrines at Bethel and Gilgal (the latter is mentioned for the first time there, for only Bethel was mentioned earlier [3:14]) and there rebel repeatedly by performing acts of worship. In the current passage the matter treated ironically before is now handled in a forcefully direct manner but with the same meaning: Seek me, but do not seek me at Bethel or Gilgal. Now a third sanctuary city is added, Beer-sheba. The sequence seems deliberate. Other cities with shrines will be added later, including Samaria and Dan. Here the count adds up to three, as though the prophet were closing off different options. All of these shrines and their cults are equally corrupt, and all are under the ban of God through his prophet. Going to one rather than another or from one to another will be of no avail: do not seek me at any of these shrines; they are places of corruption, and their festivals are occasions of sin. The injunction is absolute and uncomplicated: "Seek me and live" (v 4) and "Seek Yahweh and live" (v 6), which form an envelope around the denunciations of the various shrines. We know that Amos is talking about the weightier matters of the law, and in particular justice and righteousness, which are at the core of the covenant whether the word itself is used, or should be. The imperative is balanced by a warning. Failure to do so would result in disaster, but the injunction must have been maddening to the pious of Israel, who were constant in their devotion, frequent in their attendance, fully participant in their services, and generous in their pledges and contributions. What more could they do? And what did it really mean "Seek me! . . . but don't seek [me at] Bethel," or the other shrines? How else to do as instructed, or to find what was needed? As with the paradox in 3:2, where election guaranteed punishment rather than redemption, so here too there seemed to be a contradiction in intentions, an insistence and rejection in the same breath. Where else and how else did anyone seek Yahweh in the past or present, or how would they in the future if not at the great shrines hallowed by traditions going back to the patriarchs and the generation of the conquest? But going there was forbidden in the same words that made the demand. The explanation comes a little later in the instruction in vv 14–15, where we are brought face to face with reality. The sharp and specific contrast between the behavior of those condemned in vv 10–12 and that which is approved and commanded to those in vv 14–15 makes clear what is in the mind of God and his prophet. Whereas "they" shove the poor away from the gate (v 12), "you" are to establish true justice in the gate (v 15). Seeking God is seeking "Good and not Evil." It is the same as hating evil and loving good. While the prophet presents the alternatives as mutually exclusive, that seems to be for rhetorical effect. The point is that if there is injustice in the gate and oppression and mistreatment of the poor and helpless, then the worship of the perpetrators at whatever shrine, however elaborate and fully in accordance with tradition and ancient precept, is false and worthless. It is only an occasion for greater sin. If the goal of religious faith and practice is the person and presence of God, then he is to be found in association with the "good" and away from the "evil." Let these earnest seekers forget about the shrines they frequent and search rather for goodness, abandoning evil. To do so is the secret of the divine presence and the divine approval. Then he will be found of them wherever they worship and on whatever terms. There will be no problem once the essential distinction between good and bad has been recognized and made. The key is in finding not the right place to go, but the right thing to do and the right way to do it. The true search for God, like the search for the true God, begins in the heart (i.e., the mind and the will); and in the practice of justice and righteousness, in attachment to the good and detachment from the bad, the presence and person of God become more real. It is the people who, following this prescription, will transform the sanctuaries, beginning with Bethel; and only then will it be possible to find Yahweh at those places in which his name is hallowed. As of now, however, their search is doomed before it begins. He cannot be found at the sanctuaries in which sin and oppression are condoned not condemned, in which those who deceive and mistreat their fellows celebrate their faith and profess their success. For them and for the sanctuaries they support there will be total destruction and disaster. The formula involving fire, which consumes the sanctuary city, is similar to the one used repeatedly in chaps. 1–2 of all of the other nations. Once again, but in the central section, we are provided with a variant of the missing formula of punishment for Israel, directed at the principal northern shrine at Bethel (if the reading in the MT of v 6 is correct).

II.A.2. FIRST WOE (5:7–13), INCLUDING THE SECOND HYMN (5:8–9)
II.A.2.a. FIRST WOE (5:7, 10–12)

5:7a   [Woe to] those who turn justice into wormwood,
7b   and equity in the earth they bury.

NOTES

5:7. This is the first of the Woes in The Book of Woes. The Introduction (p. 462) shows that they are spread throughout the book of Amos, though concentrated in The Book of Woes (chaps. 5–6), sometimes in clusters, the largest group being seven in 6:1–6. This one is stranded between the denunciation of worship in vv 4–6 and the apostrophe in vv 8–9. One could hardly imagine more disparate units; it is easy to see why so many scholars think that here we have no more than miscellaneous scraps of oracles, unconnected in any way with the neighboring material. Even so, v 7 does have several connections, or at least possible connections. First, it could be a vocative, to complete vv 1–6, identifying the people who are there exhorted to seek the Lord, and threatened with grief: "you who turn justice into wormwood." NJPS even adds "[Seek the LORD]" to v 7 to round off the unit. Second, we have already pointed out that the parallelism of *mišpāṭ* and *ṣĕdāqâ* links 5:7, 5:24, and 6:12, with 5:15 as a stepping stone. It should also be pointed out that the verbal, thematic, and structural connections unify these three well-formed bicolons, in spite of differences in genre. Thus, 5:7 is the only one in the form of a "Woe." We note, however, that when a Woe that begins with a participle is expanded, the description of wrongdoings is continued by means of a finite verb: *haššōʾăpîm . . . yaṭṭû* in 2:7; and *hahōpĕkîm . . . hinnîḥû* in 5:7. The verbs in vv 10–12 could be a continuation of this pattern, giving more details about how they turn justice into wormwood, so that vv 7 + 10–12 constitute the complete Woe.

This possibility then leads to the question of why the Hymn fragment (vv 8–9) has been sandwiched into the Woe. The genres are completely different, as are the topics. Yet those differences are the very means for bringing out the great contrast between the acts of humans and the actions of God. The same verb (*hpk*) is used, and "the earth" is the common location of their deeds. Verses 7 and 10 constitute a parody of vv 8–9, to show how completely opposite to God humans have become (Maureen Jeffrey—private communication). Commentators usually explain the juxtaposition of the two participles as no more than the association of "catchwords," a trivial reason for sliding the Hymn inside the Woe where it does not fit at all.

7a. [*Woe.*] This verse is so obviously a Woe that some scholars wish to restore *hôy* at the beginning. We accept the identification, but see no need for the emendation. In fact only two of the nineteen participles in Amos have *hôy*, but all are members of an extended series of Woes. Otherwise it can be seen as an extension of the exhortation addressed to the house of

Joseph in v 6. In either case, the use of the third person in the next line does not tell against this connection; such a change is acceptable in a dependent clause.

7b. *bury*. The images in the two lines of this bicolon do not seem to be congruent. They are both at once vague and suggestive, so that the imagination can create strong pictures without having to equate "casting righteousness to the earth" with any specific act. Indeed it could describe any kind of wrongdoing. There is one similar passage (Isa 28:2bB, *hinnîah lā'āreṣ bĕyād*), which is roughly contemporary and is included in a Woe against Samaria. Unfortunately it too is obscure; but it seems to describe an action of God in bringing the beauty of Samaria down into the dust.

In spite of these difficulties, there does not seem to be any textual reason for doubting the authenticity and accuracy of v 7. It fits firmly into the overall structure of The Book of Woes by its connections with 5:14–15, 24; and 6:12b. This function relieves the need to find integral connections between 5:7 and its immediate context, though they are not lacking. Failure to make sense of v 7 as it stands explains the freedom with which the LXX interprets it, not as a Woe against the unjust, but as a celebration of the justice of God. The LXX text has thus blended v 7 with vv 8–9:

> *kyrios ho poiōn eis hypsos krima*
> *kai dikaiosynēn eis gēn ethēke*

> The Lord is the one who makes judgment on high,
> and justice on earth he established.

As a textual variant, a few connections with the MT can be found. *Eis hypsos* suggests that *ll'nh* was read as *mlm'lh* (the LXX managed *l'nh* in 6:12b). But "doing" usually renders *'śh* or *p'l*, and it is hard to think of a *Vorlage* that can be connected with *hhpkym*. *Kyrios* could reflect an original text that began with *hwy*. The second line preserves the original Hebrew much better, including the word order, but the verb has been harmonized to singular.

COMMENT

As observed earlier, we have here one of the Woes, anticipating the fuller statement (with *hôy*) in v 18 and the central statement of seven Woes in chap. 6:1–6. It seems clear that *hôy* is to be understood with this participle (*hhpkym*) as with all of the other instances on the strength of the two actual occurrences in 5:18 and 6:1. In our opinion, the former governs all of the pairs beginning in 2:7 (eight in all), while the latter governs the group in 6:1–6 plus the last one in 9:10 (also eight). In any case, 5:7 forms a boundary with 6:12b, for the two verses are built around the traditional—and, in Amos, vital—pair: justice and righteousness. They also point to the middle unit in 5:24, where we have a positive expression about the same terms—the well-known exhortation, "let justice roll on like the ocean, and equity like a perennial stream." In 5:7, as in 6:12b, the statement has a negative tone and attacks those who turn (the fruit of) justice and righteousness into wormwood and thrust them down or place them on (literally, "to") the earth. Once again we have a chiastic construction in 5:7, with the verbal forms at the extremes and the repeated pair, *mišpāṭ ûṣĕdāqâ,* in the center. The same words in the same order (though not consecutively in the third instance) occur in the other two key places, 5:24 and 6:12b. In 6:12 we have the standard pair, *rš̄//lʿnh,* in the normal order (cf. Deut 29:17; Jer 9:14; Lam 3:19 and 3:15, where a different word is used with *lʿnh*). In Amos 5:7 only *lʿnh* is used, and it is in the initial position contrary to the placement in 6:12b, thus forming an envelope construction or echoing pattern for the unit described earlier, which extends from 5:7 through 6:14. While the echoing passage (6:12b) does not come at the very end of the unit, it is sufficiently close to mark the closing. Apparently the editor also wished to end the unit with a pair of woes to match the woes in the earlier part, thus framing the central set of seven woes: 5:7 and 18 and 6:13–14 form an envelope around the woes in 6:1–6. The curious thing is that 5:7, which contains the fundamental pair of moral and ethical requirements that constitute the center and edges of this unit, is itself in the form of a Woe. But 6:12b, which matches it in using the same pair, is not; instead, an additional pair of Woes is appended to balance structurally the ones in chap. 5.

The precise meaning of the second clause of 5:7 is not clear, but presumably it corresponds to or complements the first clause, which is reasonably clear (and is paralleled and confirmed by 6:12b). Just how this works is a problem, but there may be a play on the basic meaning of *hpk,* "to turn over" or "overturn." Perhaps the evildoers who exchange justice and righteousness for wormwood are also guilty of overturning those principles. Another possibility (though more remote) is that justice and righteousness represent attributes or attendants of the divine king, which are cast down to the earth or even the underworld by the actions of the corrupt leaders. Such a shift would be unusual but not impossible. It may be that we have missed an important element in the picture or that an allusion has escaped us. The best parallel to the usage here seems to be in Isa 28:2, where we read:

> *hinnîaḥ lāʾāreṣ bĕyād*
> He brought [them] down to the earth by force.

The context shows that an act of judgment and violence is involved, which would correspond to the setting of Amos 5:7 even though the subjects and objects are different. The phrase *byd* in Isaiah provides the added element of power and could well be understood in the Amos passage. It may be, then, that the real object of the verb in Amos is not the abstractions, justice and righteousness, but those who have been denied their rights and their claim to justice and who are the victims of those who practice the opposite: injustice and unrighteousness. These victims are first described by the terms *ṣdyq* and *'bywn* in 2:6, and they recur elsewhere in the book (cf. 5:12; 8:4, 6). It may even be that we should interpret the abstract f. s. *ṣĕdāqâ* as standing for a concrete m. pl., namely, "the righteous who are brought down to the earth forcibly" by these evildoers to whom the Woe is directed —the effect, then, rather than the equivalent of their action in turning justice into wormwood. This interpretation is rather drastic, but then the complementary bicolon in 6:12b has a much more traditional set of pairs and utilizes a single verb for both objects. Here we have something quite different, and the difference requires a more dramatic interpretation. Either way, the whole picture would be consonant with other pronouncements of the prophet on the subject of justice and its perverters, and the innocent victims of these malpractitioners.

II.A.2.b. SECOND HYMN (5:8–9)

5:8a   The One who fashioned the Pleiades and Orion,
          who transforms pitch darkness into daylight,
          who darkens the day into night;
  8b   the One who summoned the waters of the sea,
          and poured them out on the surface of the earth—
          Yahweh is his name!
  9a   The One who makes destruction burst upon the stronghold,
  9b   and destruction upon the fortress when he comes.

INTRODUCTION

The relations among the three hymn fragments and their place in the overall structure of the book have already been discussed in connection with 4:13. There the apostrophe serves as a fitting conclusion to The Book of Doom. The position of the third one (9:5–6) is less clear-cut. It comes toward the end of The Book of Visions; but the resumption of the theme of 9:2–4 in 9:9–10, and the inclusion of the very problematical 9:7–8—to say nothing of the Epilogue in 9:11–15—give the impression that each of these pieces represents the addition of a new ending to the whole book. It is even more difficult to account for the position of 5:8–9 in The Book of Woes. It is near the beginning. It seems to break right into one of the Woes, for vv 7 and 10–11 would make an acceptable unit if the Hymn were removed. As already pointed out, the root *hpk* is used in 4:11, 5:7, and 5:8, and a contrast could be intended between the activities of God and those of humans. The latter are entirely detrimental. God's transformation can be destructive (4:11), but it can also be the miracle of creation, converting total darkness into the light of morning (5:8).

This apostrophe contains seven lines, five before the Name, two after it. The first line stands by itself but is structurally linked with the following pair to form a tricolon. Verses 8aB//C and 9 have a similar chiastic structure, owing to the clause-terminal position of the verb that follows the participle; but the verbs are different—perfect in v 8aC; imperfect in v 9b.

The second Hymn resembles the others in having as a climax the affirmation of the divine Name. Here the name Yahweh is used in its simplest form, as in 9:6b. In 4:13 it is elaborated, and in 9:5 it also precedes. Each Hymn fragment uses the Name differently, and 5:8–9 has this line at the end of v 8, that is, in the middle of the piece. Alternatively, this detail could show that v 8 is the Hymn fragment and v 9 is something else. These details do not support the theory that Amos (or more likely some scribe after him) was simply quoting a few lines from a well-known Hymn. No source is known for these quotations. Some of the vocabulary is unparalleled, and some remains obscure to us. So the questions remain: What are these pieces doing in the book of Amos? Are they annotations that someone thought appropriate at these points (but we cannot see how)? Are they pieces of Hymns known to Amos and his audience, selected to bring into his messages not only their immediate content but a penumbra of rich connotations and associations? Are the verbal links between the Hymns and the rest of the book (admittedly few) accidental and coincidental, or were they sufficient in the mind of the prophet (or editor or scribe) to make a connection that he considered significant? Or, more telling, were these pieces written in imitation of such familiar Hymns as used in the cult, but set up deliberately so as to dovetail into the book—into the immediate context; into one another; into the complete book as integral components of its total structure?

If the matter is as studied and contrived as our last remark suggests, then we have something quite unconventional and original, so that guidance and illumination cannot be obtained by studying other examples elsewhere of the same thing.

The second Hymn makes four distinct affirmations: (1) creation of constellations; (2) turning darkness into light and vice versa; (3) pouring water over the earth; (4) doing something to a fortress.

The designation of the three "doxologies" as "creation" Hymns or fragments is due to the fact that creation titles (or glimpses of characteristic creation myths) are found in all of them, leading the way in the first two, embedded in the third, with the roots $y\d{s}r$ (4:13); brʾ (4:13); ʿ$\check{s}h$ (5:8); bnh (9:6); and ysd (9:6). But that is only part of the story. Only five of the twelve participles used in the Hymns can be tagged with certainty as creation activities. Each Hymn is distinctive in this detail. The third uses the image of constructing a building (9:6); the first uses the image of shaping or molding (the potter's craft) along with the more abstract and theological "create" (brʾ). The second one uses the most neutral and colorless of all of the creation verbs (ʿ$\check{s}h$). An act or event referred to in the first and second Hymns deals with light and darkness. The theme occurs twice in Genesis 1 —the creation of light as such on the first day (darkness already exists when the story begins) and the creation of luminaries on the fourth day.

In the interpretation of Genesis 1 it is rarely appreciated that day and night are identified as light and darkness; the creation of light means the creation of "day." They are the domains of, respectively, sun and moon, who appear and "rule" in their realms. Genesis 1 does not recognize the sun as the source of light and the cause of day. And, as anyone may observe, the light of day exists before the sun rises (whatever the actual or ultimate source), and light persists after the sun has disappeared. Although the sun itself may be called both $h\bar{a}$ʾ$\hat{o}r$ and $m\bar{a}$ʾ$\hat{o}r$, $\check{s}eme\check{s}$ and ʾ$\hat{o}r$ are distinct creations (Eccl 12:2). In any case, Amos does not talk about sun and moon. Verse 8aA speaks of the creation of two constellations (further references to constellations have been discovered, or rather fabricated, in v 9). Otherwise Amos speaks of "dawn" (i.e., the predawn twilight), "morning," "day," and "night," with the nouns ʿ$\hat{e}p\hat{a}$ and $\d{s}alm\bar{a}wet$ for "darkness" and the verb $h\d{h}\check{s}yk$. What do these references mean? At the very least we can say that they disclose no obvious connection with the best-known creation story that explains the origins of light and of luminaries.

Although v 8a mentions the making of two constellations, the main emphasis is on the making of darkness. Verse 8aC is clear on this point, even if none of the others is, for the verb is unequivocal—"he makes it dark," that is to say, he turns day into night. Verses 4:13aC and 8aB are similar in having words for darkness, "dawn," and "morning." To give $\check{s}ahar$ and $b\bar{o}qer$ their strict meanings, we have "daybreak" and "sunrise." It seems best to take both of them as the opposite of 5:8aC—the transition from night to day: "Who turns blackness into daybreak" (NJPS), not "Who makes the morning darkness" (RSV). The latter interpretation seems to be harmonistic with 5:18 and 8:9; but the preposition *l-* settles the issue in 5:8aB, and similar syntax can be identified in 4:13aC, even though no preposition is used there. The same preposition does double duty in 5:8aC. The picture is balanced (darkness into light and light into darkness) and suggests the management of regular diurnal changes (Ps 104:19–23) rather than an account of the primal creation of day and night. This view is entirely in line with the biblical understanding of God as Creator, the one who keeps things going, who makes everything happen that happens. Origins are included (mountains, wind); but it is surely remarkable—so surprising as to be unaccountable, if these are supposed to be "creation" songs —that the essential recital of faith in God as the sole cosmic creator, "Maker of heaven and earth," is not used at all. The focus is quite definitely on ongoing and current "creative" acts.

Such acts can also be recounted in a more threatening mood. Are they exceptional events that interfere with the regular and orderly operation of nature, undeniably due to special interference and intervention by God? Are they more examples of the disasters sent by God, like the many plagues and calamities discussed in every part of the book? In the case of darkness, are we dealing with an eclipse (cf. 8:9, using the *hip'îl* of *ḥšk* once more)? We do not think that the references to morning and night go that far. But there can be no doubt about 9:5a. It is positively eschatological. It describes the dissolution of the earth at the touch of God, the opposite of its solidification out of the primal water, as in various creation stories. The reference to the waters of the sea, which is used twice (5:8b, 9:6b), achieves the same effect. It is too dramatic to be merely the story of the creation of rain or even of water. The sea exists. Pouring the water over the earth is a deluge, the *mabbûl,* more like a huge tidal wave than even the most devastating cloudburst. The mythological character (and probably also the source) of this snippet is betrayed by its language and general scope (at least no limit is set for it), and it conjures up memories of the great Flood, a primeval but still historical act of God even more universal than the overthrow of Sodom and Gomorrah. These are examples of cosmic deeds that God has achieved in the past; and it is well to remember them, in case one is tempted to say, "Calamity shall not even come close, much less confront us" (9:10). In that context, and to serve the same purpose, it is entirely appropriate to bring the list down to something more recent and contemporary—the devastation of strongholds (v 9). This patently historical detail is made all the more impressive because the traditional recital is rounded off in the usual way with *yhwh šĕmô,* and then the additional point is made. It could happen again!

The activities of God brought together by the twelve participles in the three Hymns thus cover a wide range of activities, from the beginning to the present. They celebrate his limitless, terrifying power, his control of all the elements and forces in his creation, and his continued supervision and deployment of these agencies and forces. The most ominous threat of all is that every act of creation can be canceled, the work reversed and undone.

He shapes mountains (4:13)	He treads on the earth (4:13)
	He touches the earth and it melts (9:5)
He turns darkness to light (4:13; 5:8)	Light to darkness (5:8, 18–19; 8:9)
He moves the water from the earth, so that dry land appears (Gen 1:9–10)	He brings the water back over the earth (5:8; 9:6)

NOTES

5:8. *the Pleiades and Orion.* It is a very wooden and quite doctrinaire criticism that refuses to accept a single line as a valid component of a poem of this kind, arguing that it "is apparently either secondary or we must suppose that an originally parallel colon has been lost" (Wolff 1977:229). Job 9:5–10 has many affinities with the three Hymns in Amos. It mentions mountains and earth, sunrise and eclipses. It uses the verb *hpk.* It has *wĕdôrēk ʿal-bomŏtê-yām* (9:8b—*ʾāreṣ* in Amos 4:13). Most important for Amos 5:8 is *ʿośeh-ʿāš kĕsîl wĕkîmâ* in Job 9:9; cf. Job 38:31–32. *ʿš* is probably *ʿyš* (contraction) and may have been lost in Amos by haplography; cf. Job 9:9. The composition of Job 9:5–10 has just as much variety as the three Hymns in Amos, including several different ways of following the lead participle—including perfect verb, imperfect verb, or another participle. The meter is nearly perfect: 36 accents (6 × 6 [3 + 3]) and 94 syllables (minimum count) against an expected total of 96. The fact that this passage is metrically quite regular suggests that the text is intact. The single line in Amos 5:8aA can therefore be accepted. What is more likely, however, is that we have a tricolon in v 8a, as the use of the conjunction "and" at the beginning of the second and third cola of 8a shows. The bicolon in v 8b does not begin with "and." Compare Isa 40:22–26, especially v 26, where there are similar structures and associations of stars (note the verb *qrʾ*) with creation activity.

transforms. See the note on *hpk* at 4:11. It describes a complete change. The change can go either way—darkness to light, light to darkness—and God controls both. The language describes "natural" phenomena, and especially the orderly succession of daybreak and nightfall; but it is highly symbolic, as shown in the parallel or comparable passage from Isa 45:7:

yôṣēr ʾôr	Shaper of light
ûbôrēʾ ḥōšek	and Creator of darkness
ʿōśeh šālôm	Maker of Wholeness
ûbôrēʾ rāʿ	and Creator of Harm

Deeds of this scope mark the ultimate power of a supreme God. Yahweh was not the only deity of the ancient world, however, whose achievements were hymned in such terms. The Mesopotamian goddess Inanna is described as follows:

> She darkens the bright daylight
> and turns the midday light into darkness.
> (*in-nin šà-gur₄-ra*, lines 49, 177)

pitch darkness. The popular interpretation of *ṣalmāwet* as "shadow of death" is a secondary development due to an (historically) incorrect division of the word into *ṣl-* (*ṣēl* means "shadow") and *-māwet* ("death"). Such compound words are quite foreign to Hebrew morphology; but words of that shape derived from a single root (in this case *ṣelem;* Grabbe 1977:27–29) are also unusual. While the insistence of most modern scholars on the essential meaning, "deep darkness" or the like, is fundamentally correct, we should not exclude possible associations with "death," for that is the realm of ultimate darkness.

8b. *the sea.* What Amos is describing is surely a catastrophe of cosmic proportions, not just the creation or production of rain. A whole ocean is tipped over the entire world. There are two possible interpretations of the disaster, depending on whether the background is a creation story or a flood story. If it is a creation story, then the point is that what was done in the beginning will be undone at the end. The threat and vision are eschatological. The process is the reversal of the action of the third day, when the sea was divided from the land (cf. Job 38:8–11; Prov 8:29); or of the second day, when the celestial waters were contained above the firmament. This heavenly *tĕhôm*, counterpart of the abyss (*tĕhôm rabbâ*), could be the "ocean" poured down on the earth in Noah's deluge, if the Flood Story were in the poet's mind.

In spite of the undertaking of Gen 8:21, Amos seems to be warning that another similar inundation is definitely possible. We have already pointed out the many similarities in form, vocabulary, and ideas between the Hymns and the Woes, and between the Hymns and the plagues of 4:6–11. This is a convenient place to point as well to links between the hymns and the visions. Both are cosmic in scope and conception. In addition, the activities of God are similar in both. Note the use of *yôṣēr* as the lead participle in both series (4:13; 7:1). In 7:4 God "calls" (*qōrēʾ*) the fire, just as he "calls" the water in 5:8.

9. The apparent completion of the Hymn in v 8 in the usual way with *yhwh šĕmô* and the altogether different character of v 9 arouse suspicion that the latter is not part of the apostrophe, at least not originally. It seems to be a clumsy addition. If accepted, it means (among other things) that we can no longer call it a creation Hymn. We need to ask, however, why the person who brought v 9 into it—whether it be Amos, his editor, or a later scribe—should have been so inept. It was surely as obvious to him as it is to us that a Hymn of that kind ends with *yhwh šĕmô*. So, if he were going to improve the composition by adding two more lines, it would have been a simple matter to put them before rather than after this conventional conclusion. We see little merit in the proposal to fix the flaw at this late date by moving *yhwh šĕmô* to its "proper" place; even less in the more drastic solution of striking v 9 out altogether. Verse 9 presents two problems: its position apparently after the Hymn proper and its inappropriate content. Is it part of the Hymn at all? Perhaps it is another Woe, the only one with a singular participle. But that very fact brings it into line with the other participles in the hymns.

The contrast between v 9 and the rest of the Hymn series could be reduced if it were a celebration of creation rather than a description of an act of historical destruction. The verse is notoriously obscure and an obvious target for emendation. The LXX is quite different from the MT; either it had a different *Vorlage* or else it too is floundering and guessing. V. Maag describes it as a "hymnic splinter" (1951:25); Wolff calls it "stylistically tortured" (1977:230 n.w.). A drastic rewrite by G. R. Driver (1953) brings it into line with v 8a; hence NEB: "who makes Taurus rise after Capella and Taurus set hard on the rising of the Vintager." Such emendations, which change almost every word or at least invent hitherto unheard-of meanings for the words there, are ingenious but unconvincing. Driver overcomes the difficulty of *mablîg* by emending to *mĕgabbēl* (the same consonants rearranged; 1938a:262). He then proposes "knead" as the meaning of *gbl,* as in the Peshitta of Psalm 94:20. J. C. Greenfield has refuted this proposal (1960).

9a. *makes destruction burst.* The verb *blg* in the *hipʿil* appears several times in the Hebrew Bible, but the meaning is often obscure. Our choice of an English equivalent for *mablîg* recognizes that the only hint supplied by the MT is that the action must be suited to the other items in the clause: "he . . . devastation against strong." The nouns in v 9a can be retained, because one is repeated in v 9b and the other is paralleled by *mibṣār,* "fortress." Verse 9 describes the destruction of a strong fortress. In its other occurrences *hblyg* means "to be cheerful" (Job 9:27, 10:20; Ps 39:14); cf. the noun *mablîgît*, "cheerfulness," in Jer 8:18. With a little help from the Arabic cognate, the meaning has been extended to "flash" (RSV, NIV). The LXX wording *ho diarōn*, "distributes," suggests *hammabdîl*, "he who divides," to which Wolff gives the meaning of "appoint." But an action, not just a decree, is required.

destruction. It is not an argument against the word *šōd* that its repetition "violates the law of variation within *parallelismus membrorum*" (Wolff 1977:230 n.w.). We have seen repeatedly that Amos' poetry is bound by no such rules, and there is no warrant for rewriting it to fit our rules. The usual adjustment of *šd* to *šbr* has textual support from the LXX, which does not repeat the corresponding words. It has *syntrimmon//talaipōrian.* The former is used only a few times (about five) in the LXX, so retroversion is insecure. When *syntribē* and *syntrimma*, which are more common, are included in the picture, it can be seen that they mainly translate *šeber* and other nouns from the same root. But we also find *syntribē* = *šōd* in Isa 13:6 and *syntrimma* = *šōd* in Isa 22:4, 59:7, and 60:18. The last two cases are interesting because *šōd wāšeber* is translated *syntrimma kai talaipōria.* Now *talaipōria* is the favored equivalent of *šōd* and cognates; but the phrase *syntrimma kai talaipōria* is the idiom preferred for "devastation and destruction." This set phrase, familiar from the catena of quotations in Rom 3:10–18, has found its way into the LXX at Psalm 13(= Heb Ps 14):3, and from there back into a Hebrew manuscript (Kennicott 1776:649). The point is that these correlates are used, even when the Hebrew *Vorlage* has the same word twice, as in *šeber ʿal-šeber* (*talaipōria* [*kai*] *syntrimmon*) in Jer 4:20. It would be unwarranted to emend *šeber* to *šōd* in Jer 4:20 because the LXX has two different words; likewise, there is no warrant to emend *šōd* to *šeber* in Amos 5:9 because the LXX has two different words.

fortress. Mibṣār is characteristically associated with a city and may well signify a fortified city, even when *ʿîr* is not used. Amos is very much concerned with the cities of the region, especially their destruction, a topic in each of the first six chapters. So the theme in v 9 is quite in keeping with Amos' thought.

9b. *comes.* Emendation of *yābôʾ* to *yābîʾ* improves both the parallelism and the grammar. The translation "brings" is widely favored and finds support from the LXX *epagōn*. But it has not carried the day. It is patently harmonistic, and the rule *lectio difficilior potior* has a certain edge. Thus NJPS makes the second line a result clause, "So that ruin comes upon fortresses." This reading is possible; *šōd* can be the subject of *bwʾ—miššōd kî yābôʾ* (Job 5:21). In Isa 13:6 it is "the day of Yahweh" that comes "like *šōd.*" Compare Joel 1:15. But it is better to keep the parallelism closer than that, with *šōd* as the object of *mablîg* in both lines and *ʿal-ʿāz//ʿal-mibṣār* having the same function in both. This pattern can be maintained if *yābôʾ* is part of a subordinate clause, as in Job 5:21 (but without the conjunction). If it means "[when] he [i.e., Yahweh] comes," it is different from other verbs in the Hymns, but it is not unlike the threat in 4:12.

COMMENT

Amos 5:8 is the second of the three apostrophes to the God of creation and history. The structure is similar to that of 4:13 and 9:5–6, but each is slightly different from the others. Here we have the standard quota of five verbs (three are participles, two of them being balanced by finite verb forms, the second and third participles each having a corresponding verb). There are verbal and literary links, but each is an independent construction. While the central emphasis in Amos is on the redemptive activity of God as deliverer of Israel from bondage and establisher of the nation, other aspects of this deity are not neglected, including especially his role as creator of the universe and lord of nature. These attributes are presented in the three passages cited and are often excluded as secondary additions. Similar sentiments and elements are found elsewhere in the book of Amos, however, and throughout the text the presuppositions and implications point in the same direction. For the redemptive deity to accomplish his ends he must have unchallenged and unchallengeable power and authority. A God who charges, judges, and threatens nations with destruction clearly must be in control of the visible order of things. The comment and elaboration of the fifth vision (9:1–4) have a series of cosmic features, which again reflect the sway and governance of a universal deity. His power and perception penetrate everywhere, and no one can escape either his watchful eye or his long arm—extending to the upper reaches of heaven or the nether depths of Sheol—and the whole terrain of earth between.

Amos 5:9 seems to be appended to the apostrophe just described and shares some of its features, including the pairing of a participle and a finite verb (*hammablîg//yābô'*). The bicolon itself is extremely difficult to analyze and interpret, and may in the end be a loose fragment. But the subject of the verbs seems to be Yahweh, and the content apparently links the God of the created world with the particulars of violent destruction incident to warfare, especially siege operations. This utterance could be related to any of the threats made against Israel and the other nations, especially the capital cities.

II.A.2.a (CONTINUED). FIRST WOE
(5:10–12)

5:10a They hate the reprover in the gate,
10b   and abhor the one who speaks truth.
11a   Therefore, because you trample upon the needy,
             and extract levies of grain from them,
                 the houses of hewn stone that you built—
                 you shall not dwell in them;
11b   the prized vineyards that you planted—
                 you shall not drink their wine.
12a   I am aware that your rebellions are many
             and your sinful acts are numerous—
12b those who harass the upright,
         those who hold them for ransom,
         and the poor from the gate they thrust.

INTRODUCTION

Verses 10 and 12b form an envelope around the body of the passage, vv 11–12a. The clearest indication of this arrangement is that the outer lines have 3d m. pl. verbal forms while the interior lines have 2d m. pl. verbal and pronominal forms. The same group(s) are targeted, however, for their mistreatment of the righteous poor (12b; cf. 2:6 and elsewhere) and for their unethical and oppressive behavior. The clear-cut and impressive chiasm at the beginning of v 10 and end of v 12b confirms the analysis and sharply delineates the unit:

10a *śānĕʾû baššaʿar*   they hate . . . in the gate
12b *baššaʿar hiṭṭû*   from the gate . . . they thrust

The subject is the same in both cases, and it is supplied by the successive participles in 12bA:

| ṣōrĕrê ṣaddîq | those who harass the upright |
| lōqĕḥê kōper | those who hold [them] for ransom |

In turn, vv 10 and 12b are constructed chiastically, thus completing a complex interlocking structure that surrounds the center of this unit. In v 10 we have the following pattern:

		Syllables
10a	śānĕʾû baššaʿar môkîaḥ	$3 + 2 + 2 = 7$
10b	wĕdōbēr tāmîm yĕtāʿēbû	$3 + 2 + 4 = 9$
12bA	ṣōrĕrê ṣaddîq lōqĕḥê kōper	$3 + 2 + 3 + 2 = 10$
12bB	wĕʾebyônîm baššaʿar hiṭṭû	$4 + 2 + 2 = 8$

| 10a | They hate the reprover in the gate, |
| 10b | and abhor the one who speaks truth. |

12bA	those who harass the upright,
	those who hold them for ransom,
12bB	and the poor from the gate they thrust.

In v 10 the two verbs (note the classical poetic sequence of perfect and imperfect, each without *waw* and clearly sharing the same tense and aspectual features) are at the ends, while the objects (direct and in participial form: *môkîaḥ wĕdōbēr tāmîm*) are in the center. The objects in turn may balance the two active participles in v 12bA, *ṣōrĕrê//lōqĕḥê,* which for their part provide a counterweight for the verb ending 12bB. These groups, variously identified and described, are tracked through the book of Amos as the particular and proximate cause of the crisis in Israel's affairs. They link the charges specified from the beginning against Israel (2:6–8, etc.) with the groups singled out in the "Woes" as the special objects of divine wrath, and they are among those who will be pursued to the end of the universe and finally annihilated by a just and retributive God.

Turning now to the interior section, we note that it too is composed in layers and suggest that vv 11aA and 12a form an envelope around the kernel or hard core of the passage: the double threat in v 11aB–b. Logically 11b is the continuation of 11a (after *lākēn*), but it forms a pattern of its own; structurally the balance of 12a, which is an internal summary, with 11a is striking:

		Syllables
11aA	lākēn yaʿan bôšaskem ʿal-dāl	$2 + 1 + 3 + 1 + 1 = 8$
	ûmaśʾat-bar tiqḥû mimmennû	$3 + 1 + 2 + 3 = 9$

Syllables

12a   *kî yādaʿtî rabbîm pišʿêkem* $1 + 3 + 2 + 3 = 9$

       waʿăṣūmîm ḥaṭṭōʾtêkem $4 + 4 = 8$

Therefore, because you trample upon the needy,
and extract levies of grain from them,

I am aware that your rebellions are many
and your sinful acts are numerous.

The heart of the whole piece is the threat in 11aB–b, which echoes similar threats in the Deuteronomic speeches of Moses and reverses the marvelous blessings of the initial occupation of the land, namely, that they would dwell in houses that they had not built and eat the crops that they had not planted or cultivated). Here the threat is absolute (note that there is practically complete and perfect parallelism across both bicola, but no chiasm):

Syllables

11aB   *battê gāzît běnîtem* $2 + 2 + 3 = 7$

        wělōʾ tēš ěbû bām $2 + 3 + 1 = 6$

11b   *karmê ḥemed něṭaʿtem* $2 + 1 + 3 = 6$

        wělōʾ tištû ʾet-yênām $2 + 2 + 3 = 7$

11aB   the houses of hewn stone that you built—
         you shall not dwell in them;

11b   the prized vineyards that you planted—
         you shall not drink their wine.

If conditional, this threat belongs to Phase One of Amos' ministry, when repentance could still avert the calamity; if unconditional, it belongs to Phase Two of the prophet's message when judgment, final and irrevocable, is pronounced. It is only a matter of time and a question of details, but the decision has been rendered, and execution has been ordered.

Verses 10–12 are clearly a continuation of v 7, which could be rendered in either the second or the third person. Verse 7b is clearly in the third person, but v 7a could be either. The absence of the word "woe" leaves the matter open. Third-person descriptive speech is more distant; second-person address is more direct. After the implied "Woe" in v 7a, making it the second person, a following dependent clause in the third person is grammatically acceptable. A similar mixture is seen in vv 10–12. We have already noted that the participles of the Hymns balance and contrast with the participles of the Woes. The insertion of vv 8–9 into vv 7–12 brings the two descriptions (God and man) into the closest possible connection. There is no need to transpose v 7 to follow v 9 (NEB, JB).

NOTES

5:10a. *They hate.* Each distinct Woe begins with a participle, which may be elaborated in the following clauses using other verb forms. The verbs in v 10 are without a specified subject. Because there are no grammatical links with vv 8–9, we must look elsewhere and find their subject in v 7. The two participial phrases in v 12b are a recapitulation. We do not mean that the miscreants identified in v 7 are exactly the same as those in v 12b; the situation is quite complex, and several groups are in collusion. Their conspiratorial contributions to communal crime can be distinguished, but not separated.

Three parties are traditionally found "in the gate," the operational phrase in vv 10a and 12bB; cf. Isa 29:19–21, where there is a similar analysis of the situation in which the downtrodden (*ʿănāwîm*) and the poor (*ʾebyônê ʾādām*) confront the ruthless (*ʿārîṣ*) and the scoffer (*lēṣ*) and all of those who are on the lookout for an opportunity to do evil (*šōqědê ʾāwen*):

> Isa 29:21 *mahăṭîʾê ʾādām bědābār*
> *wělammôkîaḥ baššaʿar yěqōšûn*
> *wayyaṭṭû battōhû ṣaddîq*

> They declare a man with a just cause to be a criminal,
> And the reprover in the gate they entrap,
> And they thrust into the wasteland the upright.

Five of these words are used in Amos 5:7 and 10–12 and may be given the same reference in both passages.

The victim is a man (*ʾādām*) with a (just) suit (*dābār*). Generally he is one of the poor (*ʾebyônîm* [v 12]—in Isa 29:11 *ʾebyônê ʾādām//ʿănāwîm*, as in Amos 2:6–7; or *dallîm*). In view of Amos 8:4, *ʾādām* in Isa 29:21 could mean "the poor of the land." It is assumed that the plaintiff is in the right—*ṣaddîq* (Isa 29:21; Amos 5:12) or *tāmîm* (Amos 5:10; cf. Gen 6:9). As plaintiff he is the "speaker" (*dōbēr* [Amos 5:10] or "accuser" *môkîaḥ* [Amos 5:10; Isa 29:21]). It is possible, however, that the *môkîaḥ* is a reprover ("arbiter" [NJPS]), a third party or advocate who takes up the case of the poor against the rich, and thus is hated. There is no need for exploiters to hate their miserable victims; but the prophet, as champion of the oppressed, delivers exposures and accusations and, as we know in the case of Amos, becomes a main object of detestation.

The magistrates are not identified by any nouns or titles, only verbs and participles. They take bribes (*lōqĕḥê kōper* [v 12b] = *šōqĕdê ʾāwen* in Isa 29:20[?]). They turn justice into wormwood (v 7). They are enemies of the righteous (*ṣōrĕrê ṣaddîq* [v 12b]); they abhor the faultless person (*tāmîm yĕtāʿĕbû* [v 10]); they hate the accuser (v 10). If Isa 29:20 may be added into the mix, they are tyrannical and cynical.

In court (the gate) they push aside the petitioner (dismiss the case with force)—*wayyaṭṭû . . . ṣaddîq* (Isa 29:21) = *wĕʾebyônîm . . . hiṭṭû* (Amos 5:12). Or they ensnare the accuser—*yĕqōšûn* (Isa 29:21)—or condemn the innocent—*mahăṭîʾê ʾādām* (Isa 29:21), contravening Deut 25:1; cf. Prov 17:15, *maṣdîq rāšāʿ ûmaršîaʿ ṣaddîq*, the only use of the *hipʿil* with this meaning (it is often elative [Claassen 1971:109–11]). Justice is miscarried for a bribe (*kōper*). The expression in Isa 29:21, *wayyaṭṭû battōhû ṣaddîq*, "and they thrust into the wasteland the upright," is to be compared with similar passages in Amos 2:7, *wederek ʿănāwîm yaṭṭû*, "and they push the humble out of the way," and Job 24:4.

Some of these descriptions might apply equally well to the oppressors and exploiters as to the judges; and in any case it is not likely that the courts were conducted by professional judges quite independent of the powerful and rich. What is going on in the gate involves both justice and business, commercial as well as criminal proceedings. The transactions of buying and selling were supervised and certified by a quorum of citizens of seniority and standing; and as men of property and prestige they would one day be the magistrate and the next day the merchant.

The repentance or change of heart urged on those who "hate the reprover" is to "Hate Evil and love Good, and establish justice 'in the gate' " (v 15a, clearly linked to the woe of vv 7, 10–12).

10b. *abhor.* Note the repetition, with orthographic variant, in 6:8.

11a. *trample.* The usual root for treading on something—often of a warrior standing or striding on a prostrate victim—is *bws*. The *poʿlel* form *bōsēs* is used in Isa 63:18 and Jer 12:10. It is hard to believe that *bšs*, as it appears here, is a real Hebrew root. The root *bwš* generates a stative *qal* meaning "be ashamed," or rather "to feel shame." A *poʿlel* could be factitive; but *bōšēš* in its two occurrences in the OT means to delay one's return from an unsuccessful mission because one is ashamed to face people (Exod 32:1; Judg 5:28).

The LXX *katekondylizete*, along with *ekondylizon* in 2:7, seems to be a desperate and adventurous attempt to achieve some kind of meaning for unintelligible Hebrew. In neither case can a viable Hebrew original variant be retrojected. There has been no lack of ingenuity in proposing a substitute for *bwšskm*. The most popular is *bôskem* (Harper 1905:118), but many other suggestions, close to or distant from the MT, have been floated. The proposal of Tur-Sinai (= Torczyner 1936:6–7; Wolff 1977:230) to connect the word to the Akk *šabāšu*, "to levy taxes," has the double merit of retaining two of the Hebrew consonants (albeit with metathesis) and securing parallelism with the next line; hence NJPS, NEB. Neither argument is firm. Verse 11aB is too unclear to provide a starting point for reconstructing v 11aA as similar, even assuming that parallelism is present in discourse of this kind. It is a very long shot to import into Hebrew a technical word from Akkadian, especially when that word itself has to be rearranged, by both metathesis and dissimilation. In any case, the nature of such taxation would still be unknown. The term suggests a government levy. Wolff, however, drawing on the double meaning of *šibšu* as tribute or rent, interprets the injustice here as extortionate rent. If we remain with Hebrew, sound text-critical method requires not only a plausible emendation (the easier part), but an explanation of the actual reading—how it arose and why it survived. The points already made in 2:6–8 show Amos' concern for the poor as victims of injustice, but also as objects of physical abuse and personal insult. The humane laws of the Torah aimed not only to preserve human rights but to affirm human dignity. The two best candidates for emendation involve leveling of the sibilants one way or the other, *bs(s)*, "trample," or *bš(š)*, "shame." Both ideas suit. It would be easy to confuse either with the other because of homographs *š/ś* and homophones *ś/s*. The reading we have could be an unreal "mixed" spelling that incorporates these alternatives into a single composite.

needy. (Hebrew *dal.*) The singular is generic and gnomic, especially without the article. It also occurs in moral exhortations in legal passages (Lev 19:15). Amos elsewhere uses the plural (2:9, 4:1, 8:6). In Hebrew, *dal//ʿāšîr* (needy//wealthy) are both relative concepts. In the present setting we would like to know the exact economic status of a *dal:* whether he is able to supply "grain" (v 11aB), albeit under duress and in hardship, to say nothing about paying rent—albeit excessive (if that is what v 11aA means).

grain. The crime of which these people are accused in v 11aB cannot be identified. The verb "take, receive" is neutral, but its salient meaning is to obtain legitimately, as by purchase. It does not mean or even imply fraud or theft. The problem is compounded by the uncertainty of the noun *maśʾat.* Its basic meaning is "gift," perhaps "ration" (Gen 43:34; 2 Sam 11:8; Jer 40:5). In each of these examples the gift comes from a superior and is seen as bounty. This sense does not fit Amos 5:11 except by elaborate and roundabout explanations. The meager food these destitutes receive as alms is taken away by the rich; or it is tax, or rent, or interest on a loan. The best clue is supplied by the immediate context, if, as so often in the Bible, the punishment fits the crime. Because the victims are identified as "poor," not workers deprived of a daily allowance, we must consider what obligations an Israelite, especially one with a fine house and good vineyards, had toward the poor. The answer is that they were to be generous, and there was a means for dispensing largesse that was more than a handout. The institution of gleaning preserved the honor of the destitute. It recognized them as sharers in the produce of the good land that the Lord had given to them all. And it enabled them to enjoy the dignity of work. A really kind person like Boaz could go out of his way to supply more than was his obligation, by a subterfuge. To go back and collect the residue of grain, normally left for the poor, would be an infringement of the basic rule of compassion, a sin even though not a crime in the legal sense. The parallelism would seem to be: "you impose a burden on the poor, and you take from him even the measure of grain to which he is entitled."

The rest of v 11 picks up the theme of Deut 6:10–11, 28:30, 38–40; and Josh 24:13. In the promised land they received houses they did not build, enjoyed fruit from trees they did not plant. When this blessing is forfeited through covenant disobedience, the reverse will happen. Then it will be reversed once more in the future (9:15).

hewn stone. This detail contains a criticism of the opulence and ostentation of the oppressors (3:15; 4:1; 6:1, 4–6). Hewn stones (*'abnê gāzît*) were not to be used for an altar. David (1 Chr 22:2) and Solomon used them (1 Kgs 5:31; 6:36; 7:9, 11, 12), but the plural here suggests more than the kings' residences; compare Isa 9:9. The explicit relative pronouns in the prose of Deuteronomy make it mandatory to read the perfect verbs in v 11 as part of relative clauses; the relative pronoun is simply not used by Amos in this passage. Most translators have missed this detail.

11b. *prized.* The attribute *ḥemed* means "desired, prized" as applied to possessions such as fields (Isa 32:12), vineyards (Isa 27:2), houses (Deut 8:11–12), or young men (Ezek 23:6, 12, 23).

12. Verse 12a is a well-formed, albeit rather conventional, bicolon. With the Deuteronomic overtones of v 11, the adjectives remind one of the destiny of Israel to be a great and powerful people (Gen 18:18; Exod 1:9; Deut 26:5). They turned out to be great and powerful in sins.

that. The conjunction *kî* cannot be the usual subordinating particle, for there is no suitable principal clause in the vicinity. Elsewhere *kî* with a predicate adjective such as *rabbîm* is either elative, "how many," or else assertative, "indeed." Here it is discontinuous with the word it modifies.

12b. *hold them for ransom.* An alternative would be "take a bribe." Bribery involves two equally punishable crimes, giving and receiving. The double reference to "the gate" unifies the two verses (5:10 and 12), but both commercial and judicial processes are probably involved. They could be two sides of a single transaction, in which the authorities certify a dishonest deal. In that case the witnesses might simply be citizens who happen to be available. But some of the terms, such as *môkîaḥ* ("accuser"), suggest

something more formal in the way of charges. In that case we have a
judicial proceeding: the receivers of bribes are the magistrates, the givers of
bribes are the wealthy exploiters who are under indictment. In either situation "the poor" are the victims, and they are doubly helpless. They suffer
economic oppression in the first place; they are denied fair process, which is
their due, in the second. That the magistrates rather than the merchants are
the prime target at this point is likely from the fact that they, more than
any group in the community, were responsible for justice. Injustice in the
marketplace can be curbed if the wronged can count on justice in the
courts; but what recourse is there if the judges are corrupted by bribes?
Furthermore, when criminals control the verdicts, they can do as they
please. It is possible, then, that those who attack the righteous are the
criminals, the receivers of bribes are the magistrates, and together they
drive the poor from the gate.

The poor are not completely friendless, however. They have a champion,
a reprover-speaker. *Môkîaḥ* and *dōbēr* are clearly parallel, while *ṣaddîq* and
'ebyônîm form a distinctive pairing, as in 2:6, in spite of the difference in
number. The connection of *tāmîm* is less clear. Is it an adverb ("uprightly,"
RV); or part of a construct chain, with adjectival force ("forthright
speaker"); or the noun object of "speaks" ("the truth" [NIV])? A *tāmîm* is
an innocent person, and the word is practically synonymous with *ṣaddîq*
(Gen 6:9). If the *dōbēr tāmîm* is the spokesman for the innocent, then the
expression complements *môkîāḥ*. Grammatically the first clause of v 10 is
to be rendered "they hated the one who reproves [them]," the pronoun
being omitted when its referent is the subject of the preceding verb. The
double role of the prophet is now clearer. He speaks in defense of the
innocent, righteous poor; he denounces those who wrong them, both the
exploiters who have impoverished them and the judges who deny them
their rights.

II.A.2.c. THE WISE MAN (5:13)

5 ^{13a}Therefore the wise man remains silent at such a time, ^{13b}for it
    is an evil time.

NOTES

5:13. Where does this verse fit in? Does it belong at all? It recommends,
or at least predicts, silence as the policy for such an evil time. This attitude
is quite the opposite of Amos' (3:8, 7:15); so the wise man is not a prophet,
unless the time has come for revelation to be discontinued (8:11–12). In
that case the *maśkîl* would be God, an unparalleled appellation. Or it could
be the prophet; but he would only be silent if no oracle was given to him.
The problem focuses on the logical connection of the conjunction *lākēn*.
The preceding woe already has one at the beginning of v 11. A judgment
oracle sometimes contains an accusation or verdict of guilt and a sentence
or prediction of punishment; the latter often occurs with *lākēn* and the
messenger formula (Jer 23:15). An additional statement of charges can
follow, introduced by *kî*, "because" (Jer 23:15b). So in Amos 5, the Woe of
v 7 is followed by charges (v 10) and judgment (v 11), which includes a
further accusation (v 11a). All of these elements are followed by an additional and more general *reason* for the sentence using *kî*, which should be
rendered "indeed" (v 12a), followed in turn by more specific accusations
(v 12b), which match and round off points already made in vv 7, 10, and
11a.

The construction is thus quite elaborate and could include a second
"therefore" clause. "Such a time" would then be either the time of the
social wrongs, when the prudent man learns to hold his tongue because the
rebuker and speaker of truth is hated (v 10)—in that case, the "evil" is
what the oppressors do—or the time in which the threats of v 11 are carried
out—in that case, the "evil" is what Yahweh does (Mic 2:3).

The verse or bicolon contains effective repetition of *ʿēt* and *hîʾ*, but it is
too short and unbalanced in length to reflect any poetic design.

13a. *wise.* The root *śkl* has many connotations. It describes the ability to
cope in prudent and practical ways through trained perception and culti-

vated intelligence. Such a person could be silent because he realizes the futility of speech. Or the silence could mean that no such person exists in the community. Wisdom has perished. If we had some grounds for identifying the *maśkîl* with a prophet (Amos himself, whose riddles and gnomic discourse show that he could couch his message in the words of a wandering wise man), then the silence could reflect the phase in which all that the messenger can report is that there is no oracle from the Lord. Heaven is silent. And the matching silence of the spokesman (Isa 53:7–9; Mark 14:61) is then a condemnation and a judgment of those who refused the word when it was current.

remains silent. There is a slender possibility that *yiddōm* here means "wails," because of the parallelism *dōmmû//hêlîlû* in Isa 23:1–2 (*dmm* II in BDB 199a). There may be no need to evoke another root. Torpid silence and frenzied keening are both expressions of extreme grief—the person is struck dumb with stupefaction and horror, Lam 2:10, 3:28; Job 2:13. The Book of Woes recognizes both wailing (5:1, 16–17) and silence (6:9–10) as fitting responses to the situation. If anything, silence expresses the most intense grief (Mic 1:10). Such an interpretation seems better than identifying the silence as mere discretion, to keep out of trouble.

13b. *time.* We have here the only occurrence of *ʿēt* in Amos; cf. Mic 2:3; Jer 51:6.

COMMENT

The central point of the whole book (5:14–15) is flanked by verses beginning with "therefore" (vv 13, 16). Just as vv 14–15 are symmetrical, so we might suspect that the placement of vv 13 and 16 is part of the same symmetry, and that the conjunction "therefore" does not necessarily provide a logical link to the immediately preceding text, as it does in normal prose. "Therefore" typically introduces a judgment after an accusation. Verses 14–15 are not an accusation, but an exhortation to repentance. And vv 16–17 are not exactly a judgment speech; rather, they predict mourning after an act of judgment, here the demolition of houses and the devastation of farmlands, which would be a fitting penalty for the sins exposed in 5:11. The prudent man remains silent in the evil time. In biblical wisdom the *maśkîl* usually does the right thing; and, although his behavior here is not commended, it is not censured either. Verse 10 shows that those who speak up on behalf of the victims of injustice are wasting their effort, because the courts are corrupt (v 12b). Even so, the good man—and certainly a prophet—is still obliged to speak out. We must ask accordingly whether the silence of the wise man in v 13 represents a voluntary act that has a certain prudence about it, or that shows he has given up public protest as futile, or that he chooses it in the interest of self-preservation. As such this silence could be another sign of the collapse of community values, but in that case the word "wise" would be sarcastic and bitter.

Verses 10–13 are a unit, or rather vv 7–13, with vv 8–9 as a contrastive intrusion. The accusation has four parts—vv 7, 10, 11a, 12b—and the consequences are stated in vv 11aB–b and 16–17. Verse 13 is part of the total situation. Amos' persistent complaint is that the leaders have refused to listen to the word of God delivered by prophets. Indeed, they have silenced the prophets (2:12, 7:12–13), and that action is the final provocation. No possibility of repentance remains. Similarly in the law courts, those who speak the truth are hated, indeed ejected. We conclude that the silence of the *maśkîl* in v 13 is not voluntary, but enforced. The wise teachers of ethics were resource persons whose mastery of customary procedures enabled them to give moral guidance "in the gate." When they are silenced along with the prophets, the times are indeed evil.

Verse 13 is a sapiential statement closely connected with neither what precedes nor what follows but suitable at any turning point in the book and especially as marking the midpoint both of the chapter and of the book as a whole. (The midpoint of the chapter comes between vv 13 and 14, while for the book as a whole vv 14 and 15 are directly in the center. The difference is slight and need not detain us.) Verse 13 seems also to be in prose and constitutes perhaps an editorial comment on the predicament of the reprover and speaker of truth, who is the object of hostility and abuse in v 10. It is nevertheless a curious comment, for it constitutes good practical advice for unpopular speakers or those who, like the men mentioned in v 10, have a distinctly unpopular message and are attacked for speaking the truth. The advice is that wise men should or do keep silence at such a time, when tyranny and oppression are rampant and the price of nonconformity and outspokenness can be disastrously high. But this advice would seem to be the exact opposite of Amos' intentions and practice. He deliberately sought a public platform and announced his devastating message under conditions that were guaranteed to compromise him personally in the worst way. If the advice or the general comment in v 13 were meant seriously, then it could hardly have been taken seriously by the prophet whose name is on this book. Perhaps it was intended as an ironic comment on what actually took place, proving at once the truth of conventional wisdom and its total inapplicability in the present situation. Alternatively, it may be a rueful comment by the prophet or his followers in the light of the outcome, or at the time of the confrontation with authorities at Bethel, which took place when the prophet delivered his message.

It may be a comment on a slightly different class of person, the wise man, and contain prudential if not conventional advice. At such a time as is described in the preceding unit (vv 10–12), there is no occasion for further words, wise counsel, or prudent advice. If our view is correct, then by Phase Two all reasonable hopes for change and the realistic possibilities of avoiding disaster have been exhausted. The end truly is at hand, and the time of the wise man has passed; even the time of the prophet is running out. It only remains to pronounce or set down the final words of judgment and the matter is out of everyone's hands, except those of God, who decides and disposes the affairs of all.

II.A.3. EXHORTATION AND LAMENTATION (5:14–17)
II.A.3.a. REPENTANCE (5:14–15)

5:14a Seek Good and not Evil,
           so that you may live!
  14b And let it happen so—
           let Yahweh, the God of hosts, be with you as you have
                                                               claimed!
  15a Hate Evil and love Good,
           and establish justice in the gate.
  15b Perhaps Yahweh the God of hosts will treat [you] kindly,
           O remnant of Joseph.

INTRODUCTION

In terms of position, this unit is the midpoint of the chapter and the middle of the book. It also contains the heart of the message. Here at the center of the book is a basic statement about the religion of Israel and a pithy digest of the prophet's proclamation. On the face of it, the passage belongs to Phase One. It is an exhortation to repentance and amendment of life, which also holds out the possibility of reciprocal behavior on the part of God—to be gracious and merciful and to restore the penitent.

These verses pick up the theme of 5:4–6, on which comments have already been made. The key words are *diršûnî wiḥyû* (v 4), "Seek me and live"—which are also echoed in v 6, forming an envelope around a series of chiastic cola:

In 5:4–6 the enveloping idea is to seek Yahweh in order to live, but presumably not to seek him at the official and traditional shrines, which the prophet characterizes as centers of sin and stimulants to commit crimes and covenant violations (cf. 4:4).

The catchword *diršû* is picked up in 5:14 with the object *ṭôb,* but with essentially the same comment, *lĕmaʿan tiḥyû,* "so that you may live." It is arguable that *ṭôb* stands here not for the abstraction or generalization "goodness," though that is suitable in the context, but for God himself who is the embodiment or essence of goodness: the Good One. Dahood has shown that this epithet or title is used a number of times in the Psalms and elsewhere in the Bible for Yahweh (1968:296). The duplication of the verb here in Amos supports the view that the object is the same in both passages. In the same way, *rāʿ* ("evil") may be personified (see discussion in Andersen and Freedman 1980:476–77); we may find this counterdeity in the Canaanite pantheon. Presumably Baal would already qualify; and in fuller form and at a much later date (cf. Matt 10:25; 12:24, 27; Mark 3:22; Luke 11:15, 18–19), we find the chief of devils called Beelzebul (correct for *bʿl zbl* in Ugaritic) or Beelzebub, which is the form found in the OT, perhaps a derogatory play on words, namely, *zĕbûb,* "flies," for *zĕbûl,* "prince" or "noble one." The modified repetition of this theme in 5:15 could be analyzed in the same manner: "Hate evil and love good," in other words, "hate the Evil One and love the Good One"—in both cases titles of deities, false and true, characterized by these fundamental attributes. Perhaps we can leave the question unsettled by including both meanings in the translation:

> Seek the Good [good]
> and do not [seek] the Evil [evil]
> so that you may live.

Because *ʾal* is normally used with the verb in the imperfect, we suppose that there is an ellipsis here, with the verb (*tidrĕšû*) being understood, its force carrying over from the imperative. The construction would be equivalent to a negative imperative, which is what is needed.

The parallel passage in v 15a reads as follows:

> Hate the Evil [One]
> and love the Good [One]
> and establish in the gate justice.

The additional lines in 14aB and 15aB, *lmʿn tḥyw,* "so that you may live" (v 14a), and *whṣygw bšʿr mšpṭ,* "and establish justice in the gate" (v 15a), fit satisfactorily into the context, but they are not themselves parallel to the preceding clauses or to each other. Together they form a vivid and expressive combination, however. The logical order would be:

> and establish justice in the gate (v 15a)
> so that you may live (v 14a).

In both cases the consequence may be not only survival but revival and renewal—"that you may live"—and the realization of the proud but now pathetic boast that "Yahweh is with us."

> And let it happen so—
> let Yahweh, the God of hosts, be with you as you have claimed! (v 14)

The corresponding passage in v 15 brings out the same point, only more poignantly and less self-righteously:

> Perhaps Yahweh the God of Hosts will treat [you] kindly,
> O remnant of Joseph.

The verb expresses another of the fundamental attributes of Yahweh, revealed in the creedal proclamation originating in the ancient formula found in Exod 34:6–7 (ʾēl raḥûm wĕḥannûn, "a God merciful and gracious") and elsewhere in the Bible. These formulas emphasize the mercy and kindness of the covenant deity, and their use everywhere brings out the ultimate hope and confidence of Israel that even in the worst situations and most threatening crises the grace and compassion of God will prevail, even over his rectitude and retributive justice.

Here the operative word is "perhaps," and while we attribute the passage to Phase One of the prophet's commission, its force and pathos may cover the entire message and mission. Even *in extremis* there is some residue of hope, not necessarily before the catastrophe but during and even after. In other words, the key message may be placed in this strategic and pivotal spot for a reason beyond its own content and applicability to a sinful and recalcitrant Israel: to encourage and exhort to repentance and change of ways not only while there is still time, as in 5:4–6, but even when time runs out and all is seemingly lost, because what appears to be true may not be. Perhaps, only perhaps—there remains a small window, a slim hope, but better than none at all. Supporting a shift in interpretation of this passage is the subtle change from bêt yôsēp ("O house of Joseph") in v 6, which is an unusual but understandable reference to the northern kingdom (at least its main parts: Ephraim and Manasseh), to šĕʾērît yôsēp ("O remnant of Joseph") in v 15. While it is not necessary to suppose that this passage reflects the partial destruction and devastation of the land following the invasion by Tiglath-pileser III in 732 B.C.E. or the total destruction of the state of Israel in 722 after the capture of Samaria, there seems little doubt that the prophet has in mind such a stage in Israel's fortunes and fate. The terms seem to be used proleptically, anticipating the fall of the city and the nation, or at least its dismemberment. The fall of the northern kingdom happened in several phases, beginning with the civil wars and rival kings of the 740s and 730s, continuing with the Assyrian raids on border territories, and ending with the conquest and annexation of what was left of the kingdom by Shalmaneser V and Sargon II in the 720s. This interpretation would place the passage not solely in Phase One of the prophet's commission but across several phases, presupposing Phase Two (of irrevocable judgment) and Phase Three (the actual destruction of the kingdom and the ruthless search-and-kill operation against the most criminal and guilty elements, beginning at the top with king and priest) and even Phase Four, with its confident expression of hope in a renewal and restoration. The statement here is much more cautious and provisional, and the tone is hesitant: the operative word is "perhaps," and perhaps that is the proper word after all, for Israel in the time of Amos, for all the rest of the nations of that time (as we have seen, whatever is appropriate for Israel must apply *pari passu* to the others in the same situation and relationship with God, which they all can claim), and for nations and their people of any other time and place. Perhaps the God of hosts will be gracious to the remnant—perhaps!

NOTES

15b. *perhaps.* Compare "who knows?" with the hope of life if Yahweh is gracious (2 Sam 12:22). The prophet does not give an ironclad guarantee either way. It is never absolutely predictable that God will punish the sinner or pardon the penitent.

remnant. The word *šĕʾērît* occurs three times in Amos, once in each of the three books into which we have divided the whole:

    1:8   šʾryt plštym
    5:15 šʾryt ywsp
    9:12 šʾryt ʾdwm

The use of the word in the Epilogue (9:12) gives to them all a continuing reference to the End Time (Phase Four). Compare "Joseph's crash" in 6:6. In discussing the fallen "virgin Israel" in 5:2 we could not determine whether the event had occurred or was still in the future. The same is true here. We suggest that Amos is interpreting the troubles already experienced (4:6–11), interpreting them as warnings and early stages of judgments, which could become more and more severe or which could be mitigated by repentance. The same vocabulary in the opening lines of vv 14 and 15 divides the two verses into a twofold message. Verse 15 is more specific than v 14. It spells out precisely how they are to love and seek good: by establishing justice in the gate, that is, by reversing and correcting all of the ills and evils that are cataloged in the inventory of woes.

At the same time, there is a specific mention of the "remnant of Joseph." The location of this moment, whether in the several phases through which we have traced the career of Amos or in the unfolding of the judgments in historical events, depends on how far the nation must be diminished before it can be called a "remnant." The points reached in 4:11 and 5:3 suggest that the nation had found itself in sufficiently serious trouble to give the prophet his chief talking point. We do not see how these statements can reflect the last stages of the Assyrian dismemberment of the northern kingdom, for then the setting would be at least a decade after the reigns of Jeroboam and Uzziah. We take the information in 1:1 with complete seriousness, and we do not accept a "solution" that identifies passages like those in 5:14–15 as additions made long after the time of Amos with the benefit of hindsight. In 6:6 Amos rebukes people for not grieving over "Joseph's crash," an expression that seems to echo "the remnant of Joseph" in 5:15. Amos 5:4–5 and 14 belong together, and in vv 4–5 the nation is intact, and indeed flourishing. Yet even when it is possible to speak of Israel as fallen and of Joseph as a ruin and a remnant, the situation is not that of 730 or 720, because they have not yet gone into exile (5:5, 6:7); that event is still a threat, a more ultimate threat.

The specific denotation of "the remnant of Joseph" thus changes with changing historical circumstances, but the principle ("it may be that Yahweh will be gracious to the remnant") remains in force, no matter what the remnant is at any particular time. In the setting of The Book of Woes (5:15), the remnant is the nation injured and diminished under the disciplinary plagues of 4:6–11. In the setting of The Book of Doom (1:8), the remnant are the survivors (if any) of the punitive judgments of the Great Set Speech. In the Epilogue (9:12), a remnant would be anything left even after the final mopping-up operations of Phase Three.

COMMENT

Throughout this study we have done our best to find dates for the oracles in order to interpret them as far as possible in a specific historical context. We are unable to establish absolute dates, because we cannot attach a single verse in the book of Amos to any identifiable event or situation attested and dated in other sources. There are only oblique connections and partial or provisional identifications. An accumulation of indirect and circumstantial links points to the early decades of the eighth century as the most probable period for Amos' activity, say 780–770. The numerous references to plagues and troubles, setbacks and disasters must reflect a period of trials and tribulations that the other histories do not report, because these bad times were forgotten in the spectacular recovery that took place later in the reigns of those two long-lived monarchs, Jeroboam II and Uzziah; and the Primary History tells us nothing more. In Amos' view these disturbances were all acts of God and indications that the end was near, very near indeed (4:12). Not only should there be mourning (5:1–2), there would soon be occasion for an outpouring of sorrow and grief (5:16–17). But not inevitably: it is still possible that Yahweh will be gracious to the remnant of Joseph (v 15b). How? After 740 such grace would be to restrain the Assyrians, so that Israel would not be attacked. After 730 such grace would be to defeat Assyria, so that the diminished Israel would survive and even recover. After 720 such grace would require greater exertion, the preservation of exiles and their repatriation. There is no indication that Amos was thinking in these terms. He was not in any of those situations.

Events in the intervening period, especially about 760–750, pointed exactly the other way. It was not "an evil time" (v 13); it was a time of military success and economic prosperity. Signs of these conditions are already reported in the book of Amos (6:13; 6:4–6). Amos' day of doom did not come immediately. In this matter he was mistaken, or at least premature.

The preservation of his messages, in spite of their apparent nonfulfillment, gives them a different status in relation to concrete historical situations. It is clear from the fact and manner of their preservation that their apparent nonfulfillment was not considered as invalidating them. We have seen that the whole book was written at a time and with a perspective corresponding to the end and apparent failure of Amos' mission. In what we have called Phase Two inevitable judgment is announced (The Book of Doom, chaps. 1–4). Yet representative prophecies from Phase One (The Book of Woes) are preserved and included along with these later messages, which have superseded and replaced the earlier ones. So why preserve them at all, if they no longer applied? Just for the record? At least that. The full background supplied by the materials from Phase One (the first two visions and The Book of Woes) serves as a defense of Amos and as a justification for his final messages. Ample opportunity has been given to the people for amendment; they are doubly inexcusable and rightly condemned, for their violations in the first place and in the second place for their impenitence.

Yet this background is not just given for the record. It remains an integral and vital, indeed central part of the message. As long as there is a remnant of Joseph (a tenth, a hundredth, a thousandth [5:3, 6:9]), perhaps Yahweh will be gracious.

Some of the oracles from Phase One preserved in The Book of Woes are not strictly applicable to Israel in later phases of Amos' program of judgment. The "house of Joseph" in 5:6 is still able to resort to the shrines, even as far as Beer-sheba. It was possible to talk about "Joseph's crash" at the very time that some of the people were living in luxury and while exile is still a threat (6:4–7), and while they are not grieved over that ruin (6:6). The reason could be either that they are not concerned about the destruction threatened by the prophet or that they are not distressed by a measure of ruin already sustained. We think that the latter is true, because The Book of Woes contains a call to mourning (5:1–2). It also contains anticipations of further mourning (5:16–17). It records decimation (5:3); it anticipates further decimation (6:9–10). The remnant will get smaller and smaller. The "remnant of Joseph" in 5:15 is addressed when it is still possible to secure grace by establishing justice in the gate. Such an exhortation would have its best impact when national life and community institutions were reasonably intact, and when there was still hope of their preservation. But such an exhortation never loses its relevance. In later interpretation such a message would view "grace" as recovery from national destruction and return from exile. The conditions for grace remain the same, repentance by doing justice (Dan 4:24[E27]). The "remnant of Joseph" would be identified differently: Ephraim, after Assyria had carried off most of the northern kingdom; then the survivors after the total destruction of Samaria, whether remaining in the homeland or scattered in exile. In spite of the drastic language used for Phase Three—no survivors, not even in exile (9:1–4)—there is still a chance, even after the worst has happened; but only a chance, not a certainty. Restoration would come after repentance, not before and not independent of it. Perhaps Amos 9:11–15 reflects a further stage in this process, in which return, rebuilding, and restoration are promised without such conditions; but perhaps the conditions are assumed to have been fulfilled.

II.A.3.b. LAMENTATION (5:16–17)

5:16a   Therefore, thus has said Yahweh the God of hosts, my Lord:
            "In all the squares let there be lamentation,
                and in all the streets
            Let them say, 'Alas! Alas!'—
16b   and let them summon the field hands
                            to mourning and lamentation—
                                to those trained in wailing.

17a   And in all the vineyards let there be lamentation,
17b   when I pass through, in the midst of you."
                                        Yahweh has spoken.

INTRODUCTION

This unit continues the series of *lākēn* oracles from vv 11 and 13. The *kî* clause in v 17b continues from v 12. The theme of mourning continues from vv 1–2, but the focus is different. There the prophet takes up the lamentation as if the nation were already prostrate. Here the mourning is predicted as a result of Yahweh passing through in the midst of the people.

Verses 16 and 17 are framed by the familiar formulas of prophetic utterance:

16a   *kōh 'āmar yhwh*
17b   *'āmar yhwh*

Note the repeated usage of the same or similar patterns in the Great Set Speech of chaps. 1–2 (e.g., 1:3, 5; 6, 8; 13, 15; 2:1, 3). The structure of the poem is intricate and interlocking, but most of the features are familiar to us and characteristic of Hebrew lyric poetry. The basic pattern is established by the repetition of phrases and particles, and constitutes a three-part structure in which the opening and closing are parallel in form while building up to the climactic first-person assertion by the deity. The central section has a slightly different structure and consists of a pair of emblematic and allusive references to the public announcement of a summons to mourning.

The key to the poem's structure is provided by the repeated prepositional phrases (*bkl . . . wbkl . . . wbkl*) and by the corresponding expression, also repeated three times (*mispēd . . . 'ēbel ûmispēd . . . mispēd*). Thus the opening and closing sections are introduced and defined by the parallel and complementary cola, as follows:

v 16   *běkol-rěḥōbôt mispēd*
v 17   *ûběkol-kěrāmîm mispēd*

At the same time, the middle unit is bounded by the same sort of expression but split up between the opening words and a place near the end of the unit:

ûběkol-ḥûṣôt . . . 'el-'ēbel ûmispēd

Just as there is an added phrase at the end of the second section, so there is an additional and concluding clause at the end of the third section and the piece as a whole. Within the middle part we can identify a pattern of concentric circles or spiral construction, in which layers are built up around a core statement. With all of these factors in mind we may now attempt an analysis of the structure of this call to public mourning:

		Syllables		*Accents*
16a	**bĕkol-***rĕḥōbôt* **mispēd**	$2 + 3 + 2 = 7$		3
	ûbĕkol-*ḥûṣôt*	$3 + 2 = 5$		2
	yō^ʾmĕrû hô-hô	$3 + 1 + 1 = 5$		2
16b	*wĕqārĕ^ʾû ʾikkār*	$4 + 2 = 6$		2
	ʾel-ʾēbel ûmispēd	$1 + 1 + 3 = 5$		2
	ʾel-yôdĕ^ʿê nehî	$1 + 3 + 2 = 6$		2
17a	**ûbĕkol-***kĕrāmîm* **mispēd**	$3 + 3 + 2 = 8$		3
17b	*kî-ʾe^ʿĕbōr bĕqirbĕkā*	$1 + 2 + 3/4 = 6/7$		2

The opening colon of the poem (v 16a) forms an envelope with the first colon of v 17. The wording is almost identical, the exception being the second term: *rĕḥōbôt* is balanced by *kĕrāmîm*. They are hardly synonyms but complement each other well, the former referring to the city while the latter reflects the countryside. Together they cover both areas. Along with the remote correspondence, there is a more immediate one in the traditional pair *rḥbwt//ḥwṣwt* (v 16aB): only the order is reversed. In any case, the second unit expands on the theme of plural mourning by identifying the participants or procedures in more detail. Once again the references are complementary rather than synonymous, and distinctive terms are used for the different classes represented at the public gathering. The "plowman" of v 16b represents the rural constituency including the vintners (and others), as we know from the parallel passages in Joel 1:5–14. More broadly, they participate in the rites or ceremonies of mourning as lay people, without special status or qualifications. The other group or class mentioned consists of professional mourners, representing the leadership in such public demonstrations. By the judicious use of distinctive yet representative terms, the poet is able to identify specific constituents and participants in the rites of mourning. At the same time he conveys the depth and extent of the tragedy by the repeated use of the word "all"—the total involvement of the entire community in both the tragic devastation of the land and the decimation of the populace on the one hand, and the pervasive lamentation or mourning to follow, on the other hand.

The envelope construction is maintained through the middle section. Thus the first two cola with their clauses are joined by the second pair in such a way that the first verbal clause is grammatically linked with the second prepositional phrase, while the second verbal clause merges directly into the first prepositional phrase. The effect may be diagrammed in the following manner:

> yō᾿měrû hô-hô
> wĕqārĕ᾿û ᾿ikkār // ᾿el-᾿ēbel ûmispēd
>   ᾿el-yôdĕʿê nehî

We would render the poet's syntactical intention as follows:

> Let them say, "Alas! Alas!" . . .
>   to those trained in wailing
> and summon the field hands
>   to mourning and lamentation.

The rearrangement in the rendering is intended only to facilitate the interpretation and understanding of the poem. The text in its present arrangement reflects the subtlety and sophistication of the prophet-poet and has been preserved correctly.

It remains only to mention that the verbs in the body of the text have anonymous or unidentified subjects, presumably those responsible for the enterprise. In the similar passage in Joel 1, they are the priests of the sanctuary, responsible for public worship or the rites pertinent to the outpouring of grief and sorrow. For the poet what is presumably important is not the status or even identity of the speakers but their message, authoritative and effective. Mourning appropriate to the tragedy in the making is in order.

The final words of the oracle do not fit easily into the structure or are, rather, a comment on the summons to or preparation for the great public mourning. While the words pertaining to mourning are part of the divine oracle, they reflect the prophet's mood or voice. The closing clause is the very word of Yahweh himself, spoken in the first person.

> kî-᾿eʿĕbōr bĕqirbĕkā
> "when I pass through, in the midst of you."

Clearly the tone is ominous, and the sense is that of impending disaster and destruction. The language itself is reminiscent of the threat expressed in Exod 12:12, where God announces that he will pass through the land of Egypt and strike down all the firstborn:

> wĕʿābartî bĕ᾿ereṣ-miṣrayim ballaylâ hazzeh wĕhikkêtî kol-bĕkôr
> bĕ᾿ereṣ miṣrayim mē᾿ādām wĕʿad bĕhēmâ

> And I will pass through the land of Egypt on this night and I will strike down all the firstborn males in the land of Egypt including humans and domestic animals. . . .

In view of the many references to the Exodus tradition we need not doubt that the words in Amos 5:17 are ominous and threaten the same violence against the land of Israel and its inhabitants. In view of the account of the series of plagues in Amos 4:6–11, the correspondence between the treatment to be accorded Israel for its defiance of God and that which was meted out to Egypt at the time of the Exodus seems both plausible and probable. The march through the land of Israel will have the same or equivalent disastrous consequences and result in universal mourning in the land, just as the earlier destructive attack did. Compare Exod 12:29–30, especially: "and there was a great outcry in Egypt, for there was not a house where there was not one dead."

NOTES

16a. *Yahweh . . . my Lord.* The title is cumbersome and unusual. The messenger formula begins and ends the piece, so that the repetition of *Yahweh* in 16a and 17b forms an inclusion. This structure could partly explain the inversion of the normal "my Lord Yahweh." But the latter is not only reversed (cf. Hab 3:19), it encloses "God of hosts." Amos uses this title mainly in The Book of Woes (5:14, 15, 16, 27; 6:8; cf. 4:13), twice with the definite article (6:14; cf. 3:13) rather than *yhwh ṣbʾwt,* preferred by others (once in 9:5, with the article). The LXX omits *ʾdny,* throwing doubt on the MT. The peculiarity of the expression in v 16 should be viewed in relation to the equally unique rubric in v 27b:

> *ʾāmar yhwh ʾĕlōhê ṣĕbāʾôt (šmw)*
> said he, whose name is Yahweh, God of hosts.

This line balances v 16a, and both serve as a frame to embrace and unify vv 16–27 as a larger ensemble of oracles and related pieces.

all. Its use three times emphasizes that there will be mourning everywhere.

squares . . . streets. The normal sequence is here reversed:

> Wisdom shouts in the streets (*ḥwṣ*)
> In the squares (*rḥbwt*) she gives out her voice.
> (Prov 1:20; cf. Prov 5:16, 7:12, 22:13)

Proverbs has a pattern of balancing singular and plural forms. Prophets use plurals (Nah 2:5[E4]; Jer 5:1; Isa 15:3), but Jer 9:20 is like Proverbs:

> Death has climbed into our windows,
>   he has entered into our citadels,
> to cut off the suckling from the *street,*
>   the choice youths from the *squares.*

lamentation. Of the three nouns with this meaning, one (*nehî*) occurs again in Jer 9:19–20, where the affinities with Amos 5:16–17 have been noticed. There *nehî//qînâ.*

16b. *field hands.* In Joel 1:11 we have plowmen//vinedressers. Here the parallel *ʾkr/krmym* is elliptical. The plowman stands for both groups, and the vineyards stand for both locations, in other words, there is merismus. The professionals summon farmers from their fields and vinedressers from their vineyards.

trained in wailing. Apparently they are members of a professional guild with special skills. In addition to knowing and singing the traditional dirges, they may also have esoteric skills to assist in the crisis, warding off the dangers of death and demons. Compare the priests who minister in the temple in Joel, who also arrange matters for the vinedressers and plowmen who will mourn and be abashed. Here too there are two groups—those who direct and lead in mourning and those who join them.

17b. *when I pass.* In Exod 12:12, Yahweh passes through the land of Egypt to kill the firstborn.

midst. The usage is unique. Otherwise *ʿbr bqrb* is used of Israel passing through the lands of the peoples (Deut 29:15[E16]; Josh 24:17[E]) or of the people passing through the camp (Josh 1:11, 3:2). None of these passings is either destructive or beneficial. Applied to God the expression is not altogether clear. Either it contrasts with the common idea that the presence of God "in the midst" is beneficial (Deuteronomy); or he is in the midst now to do harm (Hos 11:9), and they are in mourning as a result. Compare *ʿbr* in Amos 7:8 and 8:2.

you. The masculine singular pronoun suggests the northern kingdom rather than the larger entity of two kingdoms, but the point should not be pressed. The same detail was not decisive in 4:12. Because 5:16–17 has some kind of connection with 5:2, in which there is mourning for "virgin Israel," singular or plural words may equally refer to the whole nation.

COMMENT

Because of its prominence in a cult setting, the communal lament as a distinct literary genre has received most attention from form critics in connection with Psalms studies. The pioneering research of H. Gunkel (Gunkel and Begrich 1933) remains basic for such work, augmented and adjusted by C. Westermann's subsequent study (1954). Wolff drew attention to an associated genre, the "Call to Communal Lamentation" (1977:21). While such calls must have been issued from earliest times, the formal evolution of the compositional conventions, in his judgment, was not completed until quite late in OT times, on the basis of Joel 1:5–14, with which he connects Isa 23:1–14. In Amos 5:16–17 this mode of address has already been adapted to a distinctly prophetic use: to predict and warn of an impending disaster that will require such a call to lamentation. It is thus proleptic and protreptic. The prophet himself could also engage in such lamentation by way of dramatic anticipation, which may be what Amos is doing in 5:1–2. Micah likewise describes himself as wailing like the ostriches (Mic 1:8), and his long, partly incoherent, almost hysterical dirge (Mic 1:10–16) could be his response to wholesale devastation, either as perceived in prophetic vision or as it actually transpired.

It is important to recognize the intensity with which the prophets internalized and personally endured the wounds of divine punitive judgment, suffering on behalf of the people. Their identification and concern lend spiritual authenticity to their warning messages and correct the false image attributed to them as harsh and vindictive announcers of doom.

Isaiah 13:6–22 is an important specimen of the call to lamentation because it identifies the time for mourning with "the Day of Yahweh." Moreover, it describes that day as a day of universal judgment and of cosmic convulsions, including the conversion of light into darkness (Isa 13:10). Such motifs are typical of later apocalypses, but their roots are in the ancient theophanies. The conjunction of mourning with the Day of Yahweh in Amos 5:16–20 is thus an important transitional development.

II.A.4. WARNING AND WOE (5:18–27)

II.A.4.a. THE DAY OF YAHWEH (5:18–20)

5:18a Woe to you who long for Yahweh's Day!
18b   What does it mean to you?
        Yahweh's Day will be darkness rather than light.
19a   It will be as though a man were to escape from the lion,
            only to have the bear meet him;
19b   or, having reached his house,
            to rest his hand on the wall,
            and have the snake bite him.
20a Is not Yahweh's Day darkness rather than light,
20b   pitch darkness without a glimmer of light?

INTRODUCTION

This unit is the first of the formal "Woes," explicit in using *hôy* (cf. 6:1). We have argued that most of the other participle constructions also come under this rubric. This Woe is unlike the others in that it denounces an outlook or point of view mainly religious, even theological, in character, whereas the others are mainly concerned with acts of social injustice or self-indulgence. This Woe is a rejection of a false estimate of "the Day of Yahweh." It plays on the themes of light and darkness. Verses 18 and 20 are an envelope around the gnomic wisdom piece in v 19. The language is prose, but the composition achieves several striking effects.

18a *hôy hammit'awwîm 'et-yôm yhwh*
18bA *lāmmâ-zzeh lākem*
18bB *yôm yhwh hû'-ḥōšek wĕlō'-'ôr*

20a *hălō'-ḥōšek yôm yhwh wĕlō'-'ôr*
20b *wĕ'āpēl wĕlō'-nōgah lô*

There does not seem to be any basis for describing the rhythm as qinah (Cripps 1969:194), whether for the whole unit or for the wisdom piece in v 19. The latter bears only a superficial resemblance to the qinah in that the balancing second lines are shorter than the lead lines, but the entire section (vv 18–20) is prosaic. More important than consideration of scansion is the fact that v 19 is simple narrative. At the same time the use of the verb forms is peculiar. The imperfect in the first clause is followed by four clauses beginning with *waw*-consecutive and a perfect verb. In standard Hebrew this verb would be future, a prediction. The use of the definite article throughout is gnomic, but it could point as well to "the lion," "the bear," "the snake," who are the stock characters of such moralistic tales. Amos may have adopted or adapted familiar folklore, or he may have created a little story out of traditional materials derived from the common store of the ancient Near East.

NOTES

18a. *Woe.* The "Woe" category is exclusive to the prophets. It may be added that the term itself, *hwy,* is exclusive to the prophets in the Bible, except for one occurrence in Kings (1 Kgs 13:30). It occurs in all of the major prophets and half of the minor ones, including three of the four belonging to the eighth century; only Hosea does not use it. The most frequent user is First Isaiah (eighteen times, while in Second Isaiah it occurs only three times); the most concentrated use is found in Habakkuk (five times in the second chapter alone; it does not occur in the first or third chapter). The grand total is about forty-eight.

The formal and functional aspects of "Woe-Cries" have been repeatedly, extensively, and thoroughly studied by form critics. The whole matter has been reviewed and summarized by Wolff (1977:242–45), especially as it has a bearing on Amos' usage. Wolff's work has been helpful in drawing attention to affinities between Woe pieces and wisdom materials. The association is close and central in Amos and tends to validate the wisdom material in other parts of the book as authentic. The point should not be pushed to the point of making Amos merely a "wise man." Insofar as wisdom modes and motifs are the possession of the community, they were available both for general use and for highly special and original adaptations and applications by a prophet. In case after case, Amos adopts wisdom speech, not to change his role but to develop a special kind of oracular discourse, as in 3:3–8 or 5:18–20.

long. The associations of the word are with craving for personal gain, like the people in the wilderness (Num 11:10–34) who lusted for meat (quails;

Ps 106:14). Amos seems to be using the word in the same way. Their inordinate desire for the Day of Yahweh will result in its coming. They will get what they asked for, but it will not be what they wanted.

Yahweh's Day. The phrase is used three times, and three times it is stated that it is not light, but darkness. We are not told much about what the people were expecting who desired the Day of Yahweh, or why Amos contradicted them in these terms. To judge from the analogy of v 19, they were expecting it to provide refuge and safety from some threatening danger, as well as success and victory. It would only bring greater danger, indeed final disaster.

This passage is one of the earliest occurrences, if not the first, of a term that becomes a leitmotif in prophetic discourse and is central to a theology of the Bible. It is possible that Amos 5:18–20 is the earliest attested use of the phrase "the Day of Yahweh" as a technical term. It has not yet acquired a fixed meaning, for Amos and the people he addresses have opposite interpretations of its meaning and import. As Amos is reacting to their strongly held opinion, it would seem that the idea had already taken hold before the prophet was obliged to contradict it. Because he says that it is darkness, not light, should it be understood that they believed that the Day of the Lord would be light, and said it that way? Or did Amos produce this terminology as his way of telling them that the Day of Yahweh would be the exact opposite of what they thought? Whether "light" was their word in the first place or was introduced into the debate by Amos, we cannot advance beyond "light" and "darkness" to give precise and specific content to their expectations. The terms are abstract and almost metaphysical, as is Amos' use of "good" and "evil." The only clue is provided by the fact that *'āpēl* and *nōgah* are theophanic terms (Hab 3:4, 11), applied in due time to apocalyptic events. Amos' interpretation of the "Day" then marks an important moment in the reinterpretation of *Urzeit* terminology for *Endzeit* phenomena. All we can say is that the Day of Yahweh is the day of his manifestation or epiphany; but just what he will do when he comes is not explained. Everywhere Amos criticizes his opponents' hope that God will be "with them" (5:14) and their belief that "Calamity shall not even come close, much less confront us" (9:10). The eager expectation and longing for the Day of Yahweh clearly involve more than a mere avoidance of trouble. The people addressed obviously had quite well-developed and definite ideas about what the Day would bring. At least they expected safety. But more than that, it is suggested that the hope for the Day of Yahweh goes back to old traditions and arises from continued belief that Yahweh would come as the warrior-god, fighting on Israel's behalf, overcoming Israel's enemies, bringing in security (6:1) and prosperity (6:4). The old theophanic-apocalyptic tradition of God rising like the sun on the world (2 Sam 23:4) could be expressed in the opposite terms of darkness (2 Sam 22:8–16). Which would it be?

19. The narrative seems simple and straightforward, but there are some subtle features. It could be a pseudo-sorites, for each danger in turn would seem to be inescapable (O'Connor 1987). The predicament of the people who desire the Day of Yahweh is like that of a man (the word does not have the definite article) who tries to escape from the lion, only to be overtaken by the bear (these words have the definite article). Perhaps v 19b is a continuation of the same story, but "goes" is neutral; it could be another simile. He goes into "the" (= his) house and puts his hand against the wall. The significance of this action is not clear. Perhaps it is just a casual, thoughtless act. In any case, when he thinks he is safe, even in the shelter of his own home, nemesis can overtake him.

The continuity in the string of verbs, along with the fact that the subject is used only once, supports the view that there is here a single story with five successive moments. This question cannot be settled in purely grammatical terms, and Wolff (1977:256 n. 15) dismisses too abruptly Brockelmann's suggestion that there are two little stories here (1956:41k). The question is whether the encounter with the bear is fatal, or whether we are to understand that the fleeing man escaped from that animal as well as from the lion, and made it safely to the shelter of his house. In 4:6–11 the people are described as continually surviving a series of disasters, only to be confronted in the end with God himself (4:12). The same could be happening here. But there are three good reasons for reading v 19 as a pair of similar illustrations. First is the practice of making a solemn point twice. Second, inescapable doom overtakes people wherever they are, outside or inside (Deut 32:25). Third, the illustrations match the simple distinction made between two theories of the Day of Yahweh if each experience is a simple reversal of expectation. The first man thinks he escaped from the lion, but a bear took him. The second man thinks he is safe inside, but a snake kills him. So the person who thinks that the Day of the Lord is light will discover that it is darkness.

19a. *lion.* With such a familiar image, it is unlikely that this lion has anything to do with the lions in 3:4–8, which represent Yahweh.

19b. *snake.* The use of the same verb in 9:3 brings the two passages together. In the light of 9:3, 5:19 may contain the idea that even an accident like being bitten by a snake in one's own home is under the sovereign direction of Yahweh and achieves his judgment.

II.A.4.b. JUSTICE (5:21–24)

5:21a I detest, I loathe your festivals,
 21b   I have no satisfaction in your solemn gatherings.
 22a Whatever you sacrifice to me
           —your burnt offerings and gifts—
           I cannot accept
 22b   —your peace offerings and fat cattle—
           I cannot approve.
 23a Take your loud songs away from me!
 23b   I won't listen to your instrumental music.
 24a But let justice roll on like the ocean,
 24b   and equity like a perennial stream.

INTRODUCTION

The remainder of the chapter (vv 21–27) is the direct speech of Yahweh, ending with a colophon that is a meld of the messenger formula and the end line of the creation hymns (v 27b). The passage may be divided into two major sections: (1) vv 21–24 and (2) vv 25–27; these sections in turn may be subdivided as follows: (1a) vv 21–22; (1b) vv 23–24; (2a) v 25; and (2b) vv 26–27. The divisions, however, are permeable, and it is clear that various elements serve as links (vv 22a and 25 are associated in vocabulary and syntax) or transitions (v 25 resumes the 2d m. pl. forms after a shift to 2d m. s. pronominal elements in v 23, thus establishing a connection with vv 21–22 on the one hand and vv 26–27 on the other).

Section 1a. 5:21–22

The first portion (vv 21–24) is an angry denunciation (vv 21–22) followed by an earnest plea for repentance in both its negative aspect ("stop what you are doing," v 23a) and its constructive side ("achieve justice," v 24).

1a. Verses 21–22 constitute a poetic unit with a symmetrical structure in terms of stresses and syllables.

Verse 21 consists of a bicolon 3 : 3 (accents) and 9 : 10 (syllables) with parallelism in nouns and suffixes (*ḥgykm//bᶜṣrtykm*). The verbal pattern is overbalanced with two perfect forms in the first colon matched by a nega- tive imperfect in the parallel colon (all first-person singular, the most direct form of divine utterance).

Verse 22 closes with an exactly matching bicolon: 3 : 3 and 10 : 9 (the syllable numbers being in a chiastic arrangement). Preceding and occupy- ing the space between the bicola is a conditional clause, *ky ʾm-tᶜlw-ly,* which can be construed with the following cola but does not conform well to the normal interpretation and understanding of the prophetic denunciation. This clause, while embedded in v 22, nevertheless has apparent links with v 25 (on which see below) and anticipates the comparison and contrast between current sacrificial practices and those carried on in the wilderness wanderings.

The cola of v 22aB and 22b match up in excellent parallelism with paired nouns (*ᶜlwt wmnḥtykm,* a conjunctive expression balanced by *šlm mryʾykm,* a construct chain, but in both cases only one of the nouns is suffixed) followed by the negative particle (*lʾ*) preceding a first-person imperfect form of the verb. These verbal forms are in turn matched in the preceding and following verses, showing linkage across sectional lines:

v 21	*wlʾ ʾryḥ*	
v 22	*lʾ ʾrṣh*	*lʾ ʾbyṭ*
v 23		*lʾ ʾšmᶜ*

Note has already been taken of the paired verbs at the beginning of v 21.

Section 1b. 5:23–24

This unit has a similar structure; there are two sets of bicola with slightly varying stress and syllable counts:

v 23: 4 + 3 and 9/10 : 9/10
v 24: 3 + 3 and 7/8 : 8

In both verses there is extensive chiasm: of both verbs and nouns in v 23, and of nouns and prepositional phrases in v 24 (one verb does double duty for both cola).

The whole unit may be displayed as a poetic composition, in nine lines of fairly uniform length and without a single prose particle.

		Syllables	*Accents*
21a	*śānēʾtî māʾastî ḥaggêkem*	3 + 3 + 3 = 9	3
b	*wĕlōʾ ʾārîaḥ bĕᶜaṣṣĕrōtêkem*	2 + 2 + 6 = 10	3

22a	kî ʾim-taʿălû-lî	$1 + 1 + 2 + 1 = 5$	2
	ʿōlôt ûminḥōtêkem lōʾ ʾerṣeh	$2 + 5 + 1 + 2 = 10$	3
b	wĕšelem merîʾêkem lōʾ ʾabbîṭ	$2 + 4 + 1 + 2 = 9$	3
23a	hāsēr mēʿālay hămôn šîrêkā	$2 + 3 + 2 + 2/3 = 9/10$	4
b	wĕzimrat nĕbālêkā lōʾ ʾešmāʿ	$3 + 3/4 + 1 + 2 = 9/10$	3
24a	wĕyiggal kammayim mišpāṭ	$3 + 2/3 + 2 = 7/8$	3
b	ûṣĕdāqâ kĕnaḥal ʾêtān	$4 + 2 + 2 = 8$	3

The point of the oracle is made by means of six first-person singular verbs. The first two are perfect forms (v 21a), followed by four negated imperfects of increasing severity—I won't be mollified, . . . I won't be pleased, . . . I won't even look, . . . I won't (even) listen. Three of the verbs cover the primary senses of smell, sight, and sound, but none of these sensuous components of the cult will give pleasure (the fourth verb). The display of the objects of these perceptions cuts across the usual poetic designs:

> Whatever you sacrifice to me
> —your burnt offerings and gifts—
> I cannot accept
> —your peace offerings and fat cattle—
> I cannot approve [look at them].

All of these parts of v 22 go together; the two more specific sacrifices (grain and flesh) spell out the "burnt offerings." The verb "smell" in v 21 anticipates them.

Verse 23 likewise means "Take your loud songs away from me! [mēʿālay matches lî in v 22] I won't listen to your instrumental music." Ezekiel 26:13 is a parallel, with hămôn šîrāyik//qôl kinnôrayik. And the ban on music in v 23 applies also to the assemblies of v 21 and the sacrifices of v 22.

NOTES

21a. *detest* or (*hate*). The verb śnʾ generally has a direct object, usually a person. Its standard use in legal texts indicates formal renunciation or severance of a relationship, as in divorce. There are not many examples with Yahweh as subject; Hos 9:15:

⌐─ *kol-rā'ātām baggilgāl*	All their evil was in Gilgal
⌐─ *kî-šām śĕnē'tîm*	for there I hated them.
⌐ *'al rōa' ma'ălêlêhem*	On account of the evil of their doings
└─ *mibbêtî 'ăgārĕšēm*	from my house I drove them.
└─ *lō' 'ōsēp 'ahăbātām*	I will never love them again
└─ *kol-śōrĕhem sōrĕrîm*	All their princes are rebels.

The symmetrical structure shows that the first and last lines go together. Likewise the second and next to last go together with "hate"//"love." The middle statement gives the reason for the antipathy. Other examples are:

> Jer 12:8—"I hated her."
> Ps 5:6 (E5)—"you hate all workers of iniquity."
> Ps 11:6 (E5)—"his soul hates the lover of violence and the wicked one."
> Mal 1:3—"I hated Esau."

Elsewhere Yahweh hates "robbery" (Isa 61:8), "this abominable thing" (=] serving other gods, Jer 44:4; cf. Deut 12:31); a *maṣṣēbâ* (Deut 16:22); "your new moons" (Isa 1:14). Here as in Amos 5:21 we can read an elliptical formulation: "I hate you because of your feasts . . . ," and because religious services are no substitutes for justice.

Even when the formal object is not a person—it is a thing or an abstract quality—the real object is the person and the other item is adverbial. So Amos 6:8 means, "I abhor and hate Jacob for his pride in his strongholds."

loathe. (An alternative would be "reject.") *M's* is the opposite of *bḥr*. It has a connotation of hatred, just has *bḥr* has connotations of love. In Hos 4:6 God rejected the priest because he had rejected "the knowledge [of God]" and "because you forgot the *torah* of your God," an interesting verbal link with the oracle on Judah in Amos 2:4. As is the case with the correlative *bḥr, m's* can have a person or thing as the object, with the implication that the person is rejected because of a specific fault. A preposition may be used with the noun object of *m's*, or it may be omitted. Where it is used, the preposition is normally *'et* or *b-*, as is also true of *bḥr*. That the three idioms are equivalent is shown by their occurrence in the same discourse:

w't-mšpṭy m'sw	but they rejected my ordinances (Ezek 20:13)
y'n bmšpṭy m'sw	because they rejected my ordinances (Ezek 20:16; cf. 5:6)
whqwty m'sw	but they rejected my statutes (Ezek 20:24)

When God rejects persons or things it is always with *b-*. Compare Jer 2:37,

kî-māʾas yhwh bĕmibṭaḥayik
For Yahweh has rejected [you] because of the things in which you trust.

In Amos 5:21 the object has no preposition. The apparent exception to the normal usage is due to the influence of the other verb: I hate (and) reject (you) (because of) your feasts.

21b. *have no satisfaction.* (Alternatively, "smell.") The next verb does have a preposition (*b-*), but it is not the usual idiom. Whether the subject is God or man, the object may be marked with *ʾet* (Gen 8:21, 27:27), with *b-* (Exod 30:38; Lev 26:31), or with no preposition (1 Sam 26:19).

In v 21b we have *b-* after the verb but not with the expected idiom. The usage implies that one smells an odor, of clothes as in the case of Isaac (Gen 27:27); but with Yahweh it is always the sweet-smelling odor of sacrifices. So here it must be the soothing odor that comes from the sacrifices offered in the solemn assemblies. This soothing odor occurs numerous times in P and Ezekiel. The context involves various sacrifices, and 1 Sam 26:19 shows the usage in narrative—to smell the *minḥâ* that we find in vv 22 and 25.

In Gen 8:20–21 Noah offers sacrifices (*wayyaʿal ʿōlōt*) on the altar, and Yahweh then smells the soothing odor of these sacrifices. Note Amos 5:22, in which the first sacrifices mentioned are *ʿōlôt* with the same verb. This connection may help to explain the curious placement of v 22aA, which is tied more directly to v 25a (see COMMENT). Verse 21b is therefore elliptical and should be understood as meaning, I will not smell the sweet odor of the sacrifices you offer in your solemn assemblies. The same may be implied in 21a, the rejection being aimed not only at the feasts but at the sacrifices offered during the feasts and the people who make the sacrifices.

22a. *accept.* As with the two opening verbs, *rṣh* can have as its object either a person or his deed or offering (Mal 1:10, 13; Ps 51:18[E17]). It also governs the object with either *ʾet* or *b-*.

22b. *peace offerings.* The word *šelem* is a *hapax legomenon.* Otherwise the plural is used. Compare the unique *kebed* in Isa 1:4.

23. The new exhortation given here raises the question of whether v 23 should be associated with 6:5 rather than with vv 21–22, repudiating both the musical culture of the palace and the religious culture of the temple. The immediate connection has the first claim, especially as Yahweh commands the music to be taken "away from me." This detail preserves and affirms the belief that Yahweh's presence is localized in the shrine (it is his "palace"), and the worshipers come there to perform for his entertainment

and pleasure. A connection with 6:5 can still be found, however, in that David was responsible for the music of the temple and the palace alike.

23a. *your . . . songs.* The singular pronoun contrasts with the plurals of vv 21–22. There is no need to normalize to plural as recommended by BHS. This kind of alternation happens frequently in prophetic exhortations. If an individual is intended, it could be Amaziah the priest or more likely Jeroboam II the king, who had a prominent role in both palace and temple.

24. In purely quantitative terms v 24 is the middle of the unit (5:7–6:14) defined by the words "justice" and "righteousness." It is simplest to give these key words the same connotation throughout. The faults of 5:7 and 6:12 are to be corrected by responding properly to 5:24.

This exhortation is less direct than v 15aB. The term *ʾêtān* is poetic and cosmic, and a *naḥal ʾêtān,* like the *ʾêtānîm* of Mic 6:2, is mythic, the more so because a *naḥal* as such is usually only a seasonal stream (but cf. Deut 21:4). Amos' point then is that righteousness should be constant, not intermittent. It has been suggested that the reference to "water" is rather pedestrian, especially because the verb *gll* describes the powerful roll of waves or billows, not just the ordinary flow of water. An emendation changing "water" to "sea" has been proposed, without altering the consonantal text by reading *kĕmô-yām,* with the familiar heavier form of the preposition. It may be more fitting to recognize in "the waters" an allusion to the mythic *mayim rabbîm,* "the vasty deep" or "great ocean" (cf. Mays 1959). In Ps 36:7 we have

ṣidqātkā kĕharerê-ʾēl	Your righteousness [is] like the mountains of God
mišpāṭ(e)kā tĕhôm-rabbâ	Your judgment(s) [like] the great abyss.

Nevertheless, there is no need for such a procedure if we recognize that *mym* and *nḥl ʾtn* form a combination in which the torrential waters of an ever-flowing wadi are specified.

COMMENT

This unit needs to be studied along with 4:4–5, 5:5, 8:14, and threats against the Bethel shrine (3:14, 7:9, and 9:1). It explains why they are not to seek Yahweh at Bethel, Gilgal, or Beer-sheba, namely, that their sacrifices are intolerable. Such preaching would inevitably stir up a reaction from the priests (7:10–17), who would identify their interests with those of the whole nation (7:10b). Amaziah's attempt to gag Amos (7:16) would in turn generate an even more radical denunciation of the cult and all of its workings.

The vehemence of Amos' retort and the intensity of Yahweh's loathing of the whole business have to be understood in the context of the crisis in Israel at that particular time, and most of all in terms of Amos' own career. The book of Amos is an intensely personal document, a testament and an *apologia.* Its pronouncements should not be absolutized into standing indictments of the cult as such, no matter how conducted, no matter what the accompanying state of the nation. The Bible generally has a very negative estimate of religions, because most of them are false and even the true one is continually liable to corruption. The shrines and ceremonies, sacrifices and songs here denounced and renounced were, after all, instituted by Yahweh and expected by him. It is precisely for this reason that it was so easy for the people to deceive themselves into believing that their conscientious and doubtless sincere obedience to this part of Yahweh's Torah assured his presence (v 14) and their safety (9:10b). It also explains why it was so difficult, unexpected, and unacceptable for the prophet to carry his point. It was because they were so religious that they did not repent. It could even be that, in the face of the plagues of 4:6–11, they intensified their shrine attendance and increased their offerings as activity likely to secure God's favor (v 15b) and avert further disasters. These were precisely the measures adopted so effectively in counteracting the successive plagues in the Atraḥasis epic. But the substance of true repentance is defined otherwise by Amos. It is when they establish justice in the gate that the Lord will be gracious (v 15); when righteousness rolls down Yahweh will listen, look, smell, and accept their worship (v 24).

Cripps's commentary contains a useful survey of biblical affirmations that good deeds are as good as or better than sacrifice, or even render it unnecessary (1969:342–48).

II.A.4.c. THREAT OF EXILE (5:25–27)

5 ²⁵Did you bring me sacrifices and gifts for forty years in the desert, O house of Israel? ²⁶ᵃBut you shall carry Sakkuth your king, and Kaiwan your star-god, ²⁶ᵇyour images, which you made for yourselves, ²⁷ᵃwhen I drive you into exile beyond Damascus, ²⁷ᵇsaid he, whose name is Yahweh, God of hosts.

INTRODUCTION

This strange conclusion to the chapter contains a question (v 25) and a threat of exile (v 27) with the enclosed detail about carrying the images of various gods. The questions about the content of these three verses severally, their possible links with one another, and their connections with the rest of the book are among the most puzzling and problematical in Amos studies.

It is easy enough to declare v 25 a gloss (Würthwein 1947: col. 150), but what would be the point of it? Each of the three verses is a very long single clause with no indications of poetic structure or pattern. The language is that of prose. Verse 25 is the longest individual clause in Amos, consisting of interrogative + object + perfect verb + indirect object + location + time + vocative. Verse 26 has a verb with a very long object (three noun phrases), made even longer by a relative clause. Verse 27 contains a single threat and the concluding messenger formula with an elaborate title for God.

The unit has important connections with the rest of the book. The bringing of sacrifices has already been criticized in v 22, but only the word *minḥâ* is common to both, and even then the singular of v 25 contrasts with the plural of v 22. Nevertheless, formal indications that 22a and 25 are to be linked can be found in the use of the nouns without suffixes (in contrast to v 22b) and in the repetition of *lî* with chiasmus:

> 22aA   *ky ᵓm tᶜlw-ly*
> 25a   *hzbḥym wmnḥh hgštm-ly*

The phrase "forty years" in the wilderness was mentioned in 2:10, and "house of Israel" is characteristic of the middle section of the book.

The threat of exile is often made in the book, and the more precise specification in v 27 matches the detail of Qir as the destination of the Aramaeans (1:5).

The middle portion (v 26), with its reference to the idolatrous worship of unfamiliar deities, does not seem to have a direct relation with the rest of the book.

NOTES

25. The syntax presents several unusual features:

(1) The curious vocalization of the initial *h* with *paṭaḥ* and *dagesh,* which makes it look like the definite article, results from the juxtaposition of two vocal schwas, the *dagesh* being used to conserve the short vowel with *he.*

(2) The position of the vocative at the end is peculiar. Compare 3:1a, 4:12.

(3) The word for "bring" is uncommon. In 2 Chr 29:31 the command "draw near and bring sacrifices" could be equivalent to *haggîšû.* Otherwise the verb "draw near" describes any approach prior to speaking, kissing, sex (Exod 19:15), war (Judg 20:23; Jer 46:3) or litigation (Exod 24:14; Isa 41:1, 50:8), or the approach to a holy place for worship (Num 8:19).

(4) The object is positioned oddly. It is intended to apply the question to the object, not the verb or any other individual clause-level item. The only alternative would be to question the total clause as a single package, but in this case the verb should be first. Anything placed in a preverbal position is inevitably brought into focus as the questioned item. What is presupposed by the question is that the Israelites did bring something into the desert. The question is, was it sacrificial gifts? Or something instead? Or something in addition?

This word order rules out the inference that the expected answer is "nothing." Far-reaching conclusions have been drawn from this inference, as if Amos imagined that Israel had no cult whatever in the desert and idealized this situation. Scholars who accept Amos' statement as reflecting historical fact find a memory of the acquisition of ritual sacrifice from the Canaanites *after* the conquest (Dussaud 1941; Hyatt 1947; Pedersen 1940:317). But there are other possibilities. Indeed, the idea that the Israelites had no cult at all in the desert seems *a priori* incredible. The only question is, what kind of cult did they have? This issue goes back to the question of what cult the Israelites might have practiced while in Egypt, to say nothing of the patriarchal age before that. Apart from the matter of a professional (and hereditary) priesthood and the use of permanent shrines, the sacrifice of animals and vegetables by a residential community in Egypt is highly probable. But in that context it is also likely that the style was more Canaanite than Egyptian. Hence the Canaanite background, if not origin, of the Israelite sacrificial system may be acknowledged, without conceding that it was acquired only by a kind of syncretism after the Conquest. (On the tradition of a shrine in the desert period see Cross 1947 on the Tabernacle.)

A. Lods sees the Israelite sacrificial system as a heritage from common pre-Mosaic Semitic practice (1930). D. B. MacDonald, in the light of the expression used, inferred that the question meant, "Was it only flesh-sacrifices and meal-offerings that ye brought me in the wilderness?" (1899). The expected answer was, "We brought more than this; we brought true worship of heart and righteousness." This teaching seems to be the message of Jer 7:21–23, but it is no different from Samuel's assertion that "to obey is better than sacrifice" (1 Sam 15:22). Without necessarily accepting the pious inference, H. H. Rowley has argued that Amos 5:25 cannot be used to infer that Amos thought there was no cult in the desert, as if he did not know, or did not believe, the abundant testimony of tradition on this point now found in the Pentateuch (1946). He considers Jer 7:22 to be an example of the idiom, where negation serves for comparison "not this but that" means "that is more important than this."

(5) The meaning of the phrase *zĕbāḥîm ûminḥâ* requires further remark. It can be interpreted in two ways: first, as hendiadys—"gift sacrifices." In this case it is sacrifices as such, and precisely animal sacrifices, that are in view. Second, it has been read to mean that two kinds of oblation are distinguished by strict use of technical terms—"flesh-sacrifices and meal-offerings" (MacDonald 1899:214).

Because there is no doubt that Israel sacrificed animals in the desert, the question is, did they also bring produce, as now, or was this feature an addition, learned from the Canaanites, that contaminated the true offerings (Cain's sacrifice not acceptable, while Abel's is)? It is doubtful that Amos is making such a point, for nowhere else does he denounce produce but endorse animals as valid sacrifice.

house of Israel. Because the "house of Israel" was in the desert for forty years, Amos is still using the term to embrace the whole nation, that is, both kingdoms. If v 25 continues without a break into vv 26–27, as the plural pronouns suggest, then exile is threatened against the whole nation without distinguishing the north from the south.

26. Does v 26 go with v 25 or with v 27? If with the former, then it could come under the morpheme *ha-*, and the same answer is expected for both. A major difficulty in connecting v 26 with the desert period is to explain a tradition that they were already then carrying around these gods. The issue is not whether such a tradition could have any basis in fact, but how it could have arisen at all. Neither this passage nor 2:9–11 permits us to determine whether Amos believed that Israel was better in the desert period than it is now, or whether it had always been sinful. The reference to the "fathers" in 2:4 suggests that apostasy had been practiced for a long time, but not necessarily from the beginning.

There are several reasons for linking v 26 to v 27. It predicts something that will happen when they go into exile. They will carry their gods with them. This reading is supported by the natural meaning of the *waw*-consecutive used with the initial verb. Because the gods in question are most probably Assyro-Babylonian astral deities, they are probably a feature of contemporary worship in Israel, already infected by influences from that quarter. The association with Mesopotamia probably reflects common unofficial cultural interchange, and we can speculate that Israel was on friendly terms with Assyria in a time of open warfare between Israel and Aram (cf. 2 Kgs 14:28ff.). When they go into exile they will take with them the gods whom they worshiped in Israel, and they will worship them in their new homeland.

The text of v 26 presents a number of structural and grammatical problems that make it difficult to identify the gods and to determine their functions and relationships. All are characterized as "your gods, which you made for yourselves." The verb *ʿāśâ* and the fact that they are carried show that Amos is describing idols.

There are two or three names (*sikkût, kiyyûn,* and *kôkab*) and two or three titles (*malkĕkem, ṣalmêkem,* and *ʾĕlōhêkem*). Analysis is complicated by the fact that whereas the first two are governed by *ʾet* and joined by "and," "star" has neither particle and seems to stand in apposition with the preceding. Yet it is singular, and the Masoretes made it construct with the following noun—"the star of your gods" or, unless we take the plural *ʾĕlōhê-* as generic and virtually singular, "your astral deity" (NJPS). Another complication is the fact that the first title is singular, "your king," made even worse by the fact that the preceding word *sikkût* could be feminine. "Your king" might not be the title of a god at all, but a reference to a king in Israel who was responsible for making the idol.

26a. *Sakkuth.* The Masoretic vocalization is probably artificial, as is *kiyyûn,* to resemble *gillûl,* "idol," or *šiqqûṣ,* "abomination." The LXX *tēn skēnēn* presupposes *sukkat* (defective), "booth," and this reading is still favored by some modern translations (NEB, NIV). The parallel *kywn* is then brought into line with the meaning "pedestal." The identification of *kywn* with Akk *kayyamānu,* "Saturn," seems certain, especially as it is supported by the word "star" (Meinhold 1930:134–38 and Budde 1930:138–44).

If Israelites ever worshiped this planet, it was most likely a practice lately borrowed from Assyria. That Israel anciently worshiped Saturn was conjectured by A. Kuenen (1869:260). Because Exod 35:3 forbade the lighting of a fire on the Sabbath, it was suggested that Kenite smiths avoided work on Saturn's day as unlucky. Moses learned the custom from his father-in-law.

Each of the gods is an astral deity—images that you made for yourselves

—but "your king" is involved; perhaps the god Saturn (= El) is regarded as ultimate king of the nation. Perhaps the king is Jeroboam, the king of Israel, who is involved in the cult of these images. These gods are said to have been made by the Israelites, and perhaps it was in conjunction with the ratification of a treaty of friendship with Assyria, a logical step for Jeroboam, who had scores to settle with the Aramaeans and who could threaten their rear by a treaty with a weak but potentially threatening Assyria. Such an alliance would suit Israel and Jeroboam before the emergence of Tiglath-pileser and the renewal of Assyrian power. Before that time Assyria posed no serious threat, and an alliance would make sense. By contrast, Ahaz's seeking help from Tiglath-pileser III was seen as an act of folly by Isaiah, resulting from a crisis and the fear of Aram and Israel. While forging an alliance with Assyria relieved the pressure on Judah and resulted in short-term deliverance and gain, inviting Assyria into the picture only hastened the disaster that overwhelmed Judah in the days of Hezekiah. While Jeroboam's proscribed act was equally condemned, there was more sense in such an alliance in his day. At least for the short run Jeroboam was eminently successful.

Both gods, if that is the right interpretation of the names, are astral deities and represent the same heavenly body—Saturn. This god was Kronos = Saturn in Greco-Roman mythology, the father of the reigning king of the gods: Zeus-Jupiter. In Canaanite religion these gods are, respectively, El and Baal. Both deities play a significant role in Israelite religion, especially in the north during this period (ninth–eighth centuries). The cult of El, which goes back to patriarchal times, was merged with that of Yahweh, who at the time was the dominant figure in Israelite religion. Hosea (perhaps a little later) was to argue that the cult of Baal and one or more of his consorts—Asherah, Anat, Astarte—was all too rampant in the north and was widely promoted by the authorities. Nevertheless, it is possible that the inclusion of these deities in the pantheon of Israel was regarded by the king and priests as a small accommodation in the interest of beneficial relations with a foreign power. Such an arrangement was not viewed as a compromise of their religion, for the gods in question could be regarded as equivalent to El, or as attributes or local manifestations of the same chief God. With other images being used, the bull calves for El (= Yahweh) and the female goddess ensconced in Samaria, the addition of these two would not change the essential picture particularly, though the whole development was bound to shock and affront true prophets.

For Amos, as for Hosea, idolatry was one of the leading indications, perhaps the most important, of the basic religious problem in the country, the apostasy from Mosaic religion and the corrupt mingling of the worst features of pagan religion with vestiges of Yahwism. It may be objected that Amos is talking here about an imported cult while Hosea is dealing with a local one, and that different gods are involved. How can that be? The first part of the answer is that neither prophet is exhaustive in his charges and accusations. The second is that they carried on their polemics at somewhat different times. Third, they operated out of different sets of circumstances and experiences: Hosea was an insider, the only northern prophet of this period whose oracles are recorded (we have a little information about Jonah's message in 2 Kings 14), while Amos was from the southland.

The remaining question is what to make of v 26 in relation to v 25 on the one hand and v 27 on the other. The simplest solution is to regard it as a link between the verses, capable of being read with either and intended to be a bridge between them. Grammatically it is possible to connect the verse with v 25 and see it as a continuation of the question concerning the period of the Exodus, with the expected negative answer:

> Did you bring me sacrifices and gifts for forty years in the desert,
> O house of Israel?

or:

> During the forty years in the desert did you bring me sacrifices
> and gifts? Or did you raise up (and carry) . . . your images,
> which you made for yourselves?

The expected answer to both questions would be the same: No! Such a reading is possible and has a certain superficial plausibility. It has captured a certain group of scholars, including Wolff, and is enshrined in some modern translations (e.g., RSV). But the connection is difficult, especially the sequence *higgaštem* . . . *ûněśāʾtem,* in which the second verb is also taken as a true perfect in the past tense. The natural sequence after a perfect in the past tense is the imperfect with *waw*-consecutive. It is much more in keeping with standard Hebrew grammar to read *wnśʾtm* as the perfect with *waw*-consecutive, which would be consistent with *whglyty* read the same way, "and you shall carry . . . your images . . . and I will drive you into exile." While the logical order of the clauses would seem to be "and I will exile you—and you will carry your images," reading them in reverse order is not impossible or implausible and is clearly a feature of the existing text of this prophet and others. A phenomenon that is preserved as often as this one in the surviving text of the Hebrew Bible should be considered and evaluated before being removed, and in the present case there are good reasons for this so-called reversal, not the least of which is the balance between vv 25 and 27. Compare for example the sequence 2:9–10, where the chronological order is reversed. But it is mechanical and pedantic to rearrange the text just because the order puts the later event (Conquest) before the earlier event (Exodus). Literary considerations often take precedence over purely historical ones, and those priorities seem to be observed here.

It is argued by Wolff (1977:265–66) that the reference to these Assyro-Babylonian deities here cannot come from Amos or the period of the Amos prophecies. He suggests that they reflect the circumstances in the country after the conquest by Assyria, the deportation of many Israelites and the importation of foreign peoples and religions. While there is a certain plausibility to his proposal and we do not want to rule out the possibility that a disciple of Amos edited the oracles after the fall of Samaria in the light of that experience, the evidence points in a different direction. Thus, the details do not agree, and the events and interpretations are incompatible.

The account in 2 Kgs 17:28–30 deals with foreigners who brought their own gods with them. Amos is talking about Israelites who have adopted foreign gods and made images of them for themselves. Furthermore, Amos is talking about the Israelites taking these foreign gods into exile with them to a region around and perhaps beyond Damascus. In 2 Kings the discussion concerns the period after the exile of the people of Samaria, when foreigners brought their gods to Samaria. In all but one of the cases there is no resemblance among the gods involved. In other words, there is no specific connection between the accounts, only the vague notion that Mesopotamian gods are under discussion. Had the presumed editor knowingly made the connection, it would have been much more explicit and to the point, so that the reader could confirm for himself that the prophet's predictions had been fulfilled. There is little reason to doubt that the obscure statement about the foreign gods worshiped by Israelites in the eighth century B.C.E. was anything other than a statement of fact by the prophet or his editor. While it might have been true of those remaining in the country after the fall of Samaria, it is just as likely to have been the case with those who were contemporary with the prophet and who in so many other ways offered evidence of the apostasy and idolatry that the prophet eagerly condemned.

Against the arguments offered by Wolff, that there is much secondary Deuteronomic material here and that the various components must be read in consecutive order, we would say the following: the Deuteronomic argument is debatable. Concerning the crucial item, Wolff (1977:265–66) argues that the Deuteronomist picked up a theme from Hosea, which was then incorporated into Amos. Even if the direction is correct, and it is always possible that common elements in books such as Hosea and Amos are derived from an earlier source, there is no need to posit an intermediate Deuteronomic editor. The evidence for Deuteronomic influence and interference in the book of Amos is debatable at best and can only be argued on the basis of known and provable usage and vocabulary, not on the basis of a

general tone or impression. After all, the Deuteronomist was himself a
copier influenced by earlier materials, as Wolff recognizes. Specific usage in
Amos is rarely identical with that of the Deuteronomist and often in direct
conflict with prevailing practice in the Deuteronomic work. Where there is
a correspondence, the same usage generally turns up in pre-Deuteronomic
sources, so the case cannot be made. While we are prepared to accept the
notion of a final exilic editing of Amos among several other Minor
Prophets, we think that the great bulk of the book had already reached
fixed form long before this final editing and that there is very little in the
book that can be attributed to any Deuteronomic editors. Each claim and
case must be examined carefully, and casual judgments about Deuteronomistic style and vocabulary are to be resisted.

27. The prediction of exile is both definite and vague. It is located with
reference to Damascus, but "beyond Damascus" could be almost anywhere
in northern Syria or Mesopotamia. The adverb *hālĕʾâ* refers to both space
("beyond") and time ("afterward"). The commonest idiom (occurring
eleven times) is *min-X wĕhālĕʾâ*—"from a time and after that," "from a
place and beyond it." In the less common *mēhālĕʾâ l-X* (Gen 35:21; Jer
22:19; Amos 5:27), the place marked by *l-* is the beginning of the space. The
goal of the exile could thus lie just on the other side of Damascus. Exile to
Mesopotamia is not necessarily indicated, though it may be implied.

27b. *whose name.* A link with the hymn in 5:8–9, which does not end in
the usual way.

Concluding Comment on 5:16–27

Reviewing this unit as a whole, it looks as though some separate and
perhaps disparate materials from different times and locations have been
worked into a cohesive continuum. The opening and closing statements
form an inclusion:

> 16a *lkn kh-ʾmr yhwh ʾlhy ṣbʾwt (ʾdny)*
> 27b   *ʾmr yhwh ʾlhy ṣbʾwt (šmw)*

Clearly these lines are the work of the editor, but we rely heavily on this
person to guide us through the intricacies of the text and to show us how he
grouped the oracles, thereby creating literary units. To strip away such
editorial clues and niceties in a fruitless search for the so-called original

prophecies is to deprive us of the best clues to the structure of the book and to leave an incoherent collection of unmanageable fragments.

In the present arrangement the opening oracle (vv 16–17) speaks of the impending visitation of Yahweh in judgment (*ky ' 'br bqrbk*) and the consequent prayers and lamentations offered by the people through their leaders (those skilled in mourning, i.e., the professional lamenters, summoned by the priests).

Drawn from the leadership are those who avidly seek the Day of Yahweh in the next section (vv 18–20). Even if the connection with *ywd'y nhy* is secondary the editor probably intended us to understand that the subject of v 18 is defined by the most immediate antecedent. The nature and content of the prayers are defined as seeking the confrontation with Yahweh rather than avoiding it. The self-satisfaction and overweening confidence about the future on the part of leaders and the led alike provoke the prophet's bitter comment and explanation. Contrary to this extraordinary display of assurance about the great and terrible Day of Yahweh, it will in fact be darkness and not light, defeat and not victory, disaster and not salvation or redemption for Israel. The gnomic image of the householder fleeing for his life and finding fatal confrontation instead of safety at home is proleptic of an Israel that is not even aware of its true peril but glides from crisis to crisis, falsely imagining that these are minor predicaments from which a major deliverance will take place shortly. Nothing could be further from the truth; each narrow escape will lead to a further strait until at last there will be no way out at all.

The last section (vv 21–27) includes several components that have been woven together in an intricate pattern. The first unit (vv 21–22) deals with Yahweh's fierce rejection of the cult and liturgy of Israel as then practiced. Beginning with the double verb sequence, *śn'ty m'sty,* expressing the strongest hostility (the absence of the conjunction only emphasizes the power of the statement; cf. Deut 32:15aB and Exod 15:9, where three verbs follow one another in direct sequence), the theme of rejection is picked up by a series of negative assertions—*l' 'ryḥ . . . l' 'rṣh . . . l' 'byṭ*—all in relation to aspects of the sacrificial system. It is important to note that the three verbs are each connected with all of the specific actions and procedures and not narrowly to the particular activity mentioned in its colon. Thus smelling the sweet odor is not restricted to the solemn assemblies but rather is to be linked with the sacrifices mentioned in v 22, while being pleased and looking with favor refer to the sacrifices offered in the solemn gatherings. In other words, we have a typical case of poetic distribution in which the elements are arranged in accordance with metrical and aesthetic considerations but are to be combined to fill out a single composite picture. We might render the whole unit (vv 21–22) as follows:

I hate I despise your solemn gatherings and festivals in which you perform cultic acts and offer all kinds of sacrifices including burnt offerings, sacrifices (gifts), and the *šelem* sacrifices of fatlings. Concerning the latter I won't take any pleasure at all either smelling their sweet odor or looking with favor upon them.

The series of negative responses is echoed in the following unit, vv 23–24, by the verbal expression *l'-'šm'*, which belongs to the sequence *l'-ryḥ–l' 'byt*, I won't smell–I won't look–I won't listen, though the particular reference may be to a different kind of group activity (royal revelry, perhaps).

Superficially at least, v 22aA seems to fit into this sequence because it deals with one of the major essential sacrifices; but both the structure and the grammatical features point beyond the immediate context to a link with v 25a and a role in a different part of the current complex. It need not be emphasized that vv 21–22 constitute a central element in the prophet's message and a special feature of the outcry of the four eighth-century prophets. The denunciation of the elaborate cult of the temples, whether north or south, is one of the common themes of these prophets, and no one has ever doubted that both the thesis and the particular formulations are part of their original authentic message. If anything, the prophets have too often been portrayed as modern free-thinking rationalist monotheists who rejected the cult entirely on the grounds that it was a vestige of primitive conceptions of deity and worship. There is no doubt that they believed that obedience was better than sacrifice and that doing justice and righteousness was more important than practicing the liturgy. Still, it is difficult to imagine, especially in that setting, that they wished to do away with public worship at the temple or the great festivals, with their multiform sacrifices and other ritual acts. A judicious balance needs to be struck, one in which the prophet's role as conservator of ancient tradition is blended with that of radical critic of current behavior and intention. The prophet stood as a vigorous denouncer of the dichotomy between worship at the temples and practice in all other areas of life. In view of the current crisis and impending disaster the prophets (perhaps first of all Amos) drew attention to the most pressing problem, that of false worship. Sharp contrasts were drawn between the elaborate ritual of the temples, sponsored by king and priest, and the neglected requirements of justice and righteousness, love and mercy. Had there been a better mixture of all of the ingredients, the prophets might not have been so emphatic or even critical on the point of the cult. But the gap between ritual practice and ethical behavior—or, in their terms, failure to obey the whole will of God—vitiated the services that they did perform and only made more glaring the discrepancies and deficiencies in the areas of omission. If there is some exaggeration or hyperbole in the prophetic speeches, they were successful practitioners in a rhetorical tradition of long standing, one that can be traced and followed through the whole of biblical literature.

The prophetic emphasis on the importance of obedience to Yahweh and behavior in conformity with the ethical and moral demands of the covenant is to be measured in the context of formal religion. They did not advocate the abolition of the cult but rather regarded the impending destruction of the nation and its temple as God's final judgment and his punishment for persistent apostasy. The end of the cult was proclaimed as a judgment visited by a justly angry God on his people, not as a goal devoutly to be wished and sought.

The second unit (vv 23–24) is at the heart of this section and constitutes one of the best known and highly regarded of all prophetic utterances in the Bible. Verse 24 especially strikes the keynote of OT prophecy and summarizes in positive form the true goal of Israelite society, and God's intention for his people. The simile is apparently original with Amos, though it is echoed in Deutero-Isaiah (48:18—"If only you had given heed to my commandments, then your well-being would have been like the River, and your vindication like the rolling waves of the Sea"). The comparison is striking and apt—the simile forms a combination in which justice and righteousness are likened to the torrential flow of a perennial wadi—emphasizing permanence and power as well as reliability. It is in contrast to all of those treacherous riverbeds that are filled only in the rainy season and then dry up soon after the downpour, remaining that way for the long months of summer when their water is most needed. What is specially interesting about the simile is the depiction of *mšpṭ wṣdqh* as the subject of the verb *wygl* rather than as object, which would be normal. Both nouns originate in action or decision; *mišpāṭ* is a judgment in a case, a judicial decision leading to action, while *ṣĕdāqâ* seems to operate in the realm of executive decision and action, a righteous deed, that in battle would spell victory. They retain the element of event while being used more and more in the mode of principle by which attitude and behavior are measured. They are also regarded as essential elements in the universal scheme of divine government and appear as attributes and in mythopoetic terms as attendants in the divine court about the throne of the king himself. The words *mišpāṭ* and *ṣĕdāqâ* are not personified here but rather are described in terms of the mighty stream. Behind this figure there may be mythic allusions, as is more clearly the case in the related passage, Isa 48:18, and in many other places in which *yam* and *nahar* are personified with full mythic regalia and flow at full strength continuously (cf. Pss 74:13–15, 77:17–20[E 16–19]). Nevertheless, some reflection of the autonomous status of these divine attributes is to be found in the passage here, held up as the goal of Israelite society and in particular of its civil and religious establishment.

There is a curious shift in v 23 from 2d m. pl. pronominal forms to

2d m. s. This shift is also reflected in the singular imperative form of the verb *hsr* at the beginning of the verse. The shift is awkward especially as the 2d m. pl. forms are resumed in vv 25–27. Such changes from plural to singular and the reverse occur with sufficient frequency to caution us against facile or wholesale emendation, even though the significance of the shift is not readily apparent. Why in the midst of a series dealing with the nation or its leaders as "you (plural)" is there a verse with the singular pronoun (the threefold occurrence of the singular shows that it is not an accidental slip)? Whether the change goes back to the prophet or is the result of juxtaposing passages originally separate can hardly be determined. It would be valuable if adequate criteria and evaluative procedures could be devised to make such a determination, which would not simply confirm a prejudgment about the composite nature of such material. It is possible that the singular forms here are a collective representing the same group defined by the plural pronouns that are dominant in the surrounding materials, as seems to be the case with the singular pronominal form in v 17 (*ky-ʾbr bqrbk,* "when I pass through the midst of you [singular]," meaning Israel). At the same time we must consider the possibility that a particular individual was on the prophet's mind when the lines were uttered and that the use of the singular pronoun was a deliberate effort to preserve the identification of the person addressed. The two logical candidates in the book of Amos are the priest Amaziah of the temple at Bethel and the king, Jeroboam II. In the context of ritual and worship, of feasts and sacrifices, a reference to the high priest would seem most appropriate, and it is possible that the priest is intended here (compare, for example, the condemnation of a particular priest, possibly the same Amaziah or his successor in Hosea 4). Nevertheless, and in spite of the link with the surrounding materials established by the words *lʾ ʾšmʿ* in v 23 (continuing the sequence in vv 21–22), the content of these verses is quite different and suggests a different setting, a different activity, and finally a different person. The musical jamboree described in v 23 might be connected with temple services but the terms are not necessarily or conspicuously religious or cultic. It would be easier to suppose that revelries at the palace are intended, royal banquets being the target of prophetic denunciation throughout Scripture, and especially in eighth-century prophecy. In particular, the presence and activity of songsters are mentioned (e.g., Amos 6:5, 8:3) in connection with royalty and palace celebrations. It should be noted that among the captives taken by Sennacherib from Hezekiah after the siege of Jerusalem were male and female musicians and singers. Reliefs and other illustrations throughout the Near East well represent the sort of activity described in v 23.

The use of the imperative (*hsr*) in v 23 indicates direct address. Both form and content correspond to characteristic condemnations spoken by prophets to kings and other officials. Here the injunction to put away such revelry, along with the powerful emphasis on justice and righteousness, points to the reigning monarch (or his surrogate) as the specific target of the prophet's rage. It is in keeping with the tenor and context of the speeches in the book of Amos that the criticism is extremely sharp and the threat both immediate and strong. Nevertheless, there is also—at least in the initial phases—with the threat of punishment an exhortation to repent so as to avoid these disastrous consequences. This opinion is confirmed by the series of visions in chaps. 7–8, which reflect a development in seriousness and intensity, from threat with the chance of averting judgment to the certainty of a final destruction. The possibility of averting the threatened judgment through a change of heart and of practice is present in the oracles, though finally overbalanced by the certainty of the destructive outcome because there is no sign of radical change and no hope of genuine repentance. Here vv 23–24 represent the transition between the statement of the case against the nation, and the threat of condign punishment that will culminate in exile from the land (v 27). Between indictment and the pronouncement of judgment is the warning to put away the noise of parties and festivities that symbolize the frivolous lack of concern for the weightier matters of government, and let justice and righteousness roll on like a mighty, ever-flowing torrent. Let the noise of the latter drown out the noise of the former, and in this way the judgment of God may be averted. The second-person imperative and third-person jussive (with the implied command to the same person to stop merrymaking and attend to those things which achieve the establishment of justice and righteousness in the land) combine to give the key word of warning and the only hopeful possibility in the situation.

The next verse (25) picks up the theme of the opening unit (vv 21–22) and specifically hooks onto v 22aA, as we have shown in the detailed notes on these verses. It concludes the discussion of contemporary sacrifice and ritual by contrasting them with the presumed practice of the time of the wilderness. There can be little if any doubt that the initial *h* in v 25 is the interrogative particle and that the question is asked in such a way as to require or expect a negative reply. In other words, by the standard of the wilderness experience, current practice in the realm of cult and sacrifice is so deficient as to be worthless. Unless there is a dramatic change across the board and in the direction of the standard of the wilderness then there is no hope for the nation, and the ultimate consequence of loss of nationhood and deportation from the land will be inevitable.

Verse 25 matches 22aA beautifully in content and structure with the alternation of perfect and imperfect verbs, along with chiasm of verbs and objects, as well as the repetition of the prepositional phrase *ly*. The total correlation can hardly be accidental, and we are therefore justified in connecting these clauses. Verse 22aA functions in both the context of vv 21–22, with its condemnation of contemporary worship, and that of v 25, with the question about sacrifice in the wilderness.

The final unit consists of vv 26–27. As we have seen, v 26 can be read with v 25 as a continuation of the question, though it is quite awkward to read *wnś'tm* as a parallel to *hgśtm*, especially after a *waw* that would normally be taken as *waw*-conversive producing a future tense or incomplete action. It is possible to understand v 26 as a question about idolatry in the wilderness period, though the wording again requires a negative answer. The purport of the verse would be that in the present age the Israelites have been carrying images of foreign (Assyro-Babylonian) gods, which they themselves have made, which was obviously not the case in the halcyon days of the wilderness. The force of this statement would be almost the opposite of v 25, because the leaders conducting worship at the temples would claim ancient authority for doing so and Amos' question would be a startling and remarkable challenge to received tradition. But the assertion that they did not carry their Assyrian deities around in the wilderness half a millennium before could hardly be challenged. A more general statement about apostasy and idolatry might fit better, but the precision of this one suggests a different orientation and interpretation.

It seems much more appropriate to link v 26 with v 27 and see the content of v 26 as relating to the exile announced in v 27. In that case it is easier and better to understand *wnś'tm* as future after the *waw*-conversive, in the same way that *whglyty* in v 27 is interpreted. Logically and chronologically, v 26 would follow v 27 and we may have to reckon with another reversal in order, the purpose being to close the unit with the climactic statement about the Exile. But in both Hebrew and English it is perfectly permissible to put a logically prior clause after another clause, rather than in correct chronological sequence. In view of the standard paratactic treatment of clauses in Hebrew, subordination of different kinds and means is the option of the interpreter; so it is perfectly reasonable to read:

> And you shall carry . . . your images, which you made for yourselves, when I drive you into exile beyond Damascus.

The order of the clauses does not determine the precise chronological relations between them, and the sense does not depend on the order as long as the relationship is recognized. It would be equally accurate to render the passage as follows:

> So I will drive you into exile beyond Damascus, and you shall carry . . . your images, which you made for yourselves.

If this is the correct interpretation of the relation of the two verses then we may observe that the prophet is speaking about the adoption of Assyrian gods in Israel in the period of Jeroboam II if not earlier, but not necessarily after the conquests of Tiglath-pileser III and his successors. As already noted, the story in 2 Kings 17 describes an entirely different situation in which foreign groups are brought to Samaria by the Assyrians; these people naturally bring their own gods with them. It is possible that the remnants of the local population adopted these gods in the period after the settlement of the foreigners, but the statement in Amos 5:26 has nothing to do with that circumstance. Here it is the Israelites who have adopted Assyrian gods and made images of them for worship, who will take those gods with them into exile—ironically, back to the place of their (the gods') origin.

II.B. WOES AND WARNINGS (6:1–14)
II.B.1. WOES (6:1–7)
II.B.1.a. THE SEVEN WOES (6:1–6)

6:1a   Woe to you who luxuriate in Zion,
     and [woe] to you who feel secure in Mount Samaria;
 1b   the notables of the foremost of the nations,
     who have come for themselves to the house of Israel!
 2a   Cross over to Calneh, and see;
       proceed from there to Greater Hamath,
 2b   and go down to Gath of the Philistines:
        Are you better than these kingdoms?
        Or is their territory greater than yours?
 3a   [Woe] to you who rush along toward the day of calamity,
 3b   who draw ever nearer to the reign of lawlessness!
 4a   [Woe] to those who lie on beds of ivory,
     who sprawl upon their couches;
 4b   and [woe] to those who devour lambs from the flock,
     and calves from the stall.
 5a   [Woe] to those who improvise on the lyre
 5b   —like David—
     who compose for their pleasure on musical instruments!
 6a   [Woe] to those who drink from basins of wine,

who anoint themselves with the best oils!
6b   They are not distressed at Joseph's crash.

II.B.1.b. THE EXILES (6:7)

6:7a   Now indeed they shall go at the head of those who go into exile,
7b   they shall depart,
            these sprawling "mourners."

INTRODUCTION

This section consists mainly of a highly rhetorical sevenfold Woe along with two additions, an expansion of the first pair of Woes (v 2) and a summarizing conclusion (v 7). It is plausible to suppose that the oracle, when originally composed and proclaimed by the prophet, comprised the seven Woes, and that the other elements were added in the course of editing and publishing. All that is available to us is the final edited version, and we will present it and comment on the current MT, while indicating how the original oracle may have looked and sounded.

The boundaries of the sevenfold Woe are easily noted. The opening *hôy* is distinctive of this sort of prophecy, and it controls all seven of the individual Woes. Its usage implies as well that the seven classes or groups are closely related and overlap to a considerable degree. In fact we shall try to show that the series embodies and expresses the classical dramatic elements of time, place, and action—so that the Woe, while being addressed to different and overlapping groups, concerns a certain set of circumstances and applies to a particular event. The end of the series is marked by a tricolon (v 6), which provides a climax or conclusion to a series of bicola. The same pattern may also be observed in other poems, such as Psalm 94, which is a nonalphabetic acrostic poem: the poem is composed in standard bicola of sixteen syllables (8 : 8 with 3 : 3 stresses), but the closing line (Ps 94:23) is a tricolon. The passage in Amos has the same structure and the same meter. The last colon of Amos 6:6, "They are not distressed at Joseph's crash," is grammatically linked to the subject of v 6 (*hštym*, "those who drink"), but at the same time includes all of the subjects of the series of Woes; because the subjects themselves are all related, the assumptions are self-confirming.

The structural features, namely, the form of closure and its reciprocal position in relation to the initial *hôy,* establish and demonstrate the literary artistry of the composer and help to determine the meaning or force of the piece.

The last verse of the unit (v 7) is a fitting summary and shows affinities with the oracle proper. It may have been added at the time of composition, perhaps more likely when it was first written down as part of the book of Amos. The case of the expansion of the first double Woe in v 2 may be slightly different. While the passage has literary qualities (note the sequence of four imperative verbs), the latter half is clearly prosaic, while the first part is indeterminate. It seems likely that it too was added at the time of the Amos scroll's preparation and its publication later in the eighth century. Whether it comes from the prophet and belongs to the period before the Assyrian invasion or reflects some of their conquests is hard to say, chiefly because the analysis of the comparison clauses in v 2b is problematic. Whether the cities named in v 2a had already been attacked and destroyed or were only inviting targets depends partly on the reading of the text and partly on how we understand the message. Had the cities already been overrun, we might have expected a more explicit statement to that effect, as for example in Amos 6:13, where he speaks about two other cities.

Now we may look at the piece as a whole, along with the parts that make it up.

		Syllables	*Stresses*
6:1a	**hôy haš** *šaʾănannîm bĕṣiyyôn*	1 + 4 + 3 = 8	3
	*wĕ**habb**ōṭĕḥîm bĕhar šōmĕrôn*	5 + 2 + 3 = 10	3
1b	*nĕqūbê rēʾšît haggôyīm*	3 + 2 + 3 = 8	3
	ûbāʾû lāhem bêt yiśrāʾēl	3 + 2 + 1 + 3 = 9	4
2a	*ʿibrû kalnēh ûrĕʾû*	2 + 2 + 3 = 7	3
	ûlĕkû miššām ḥămat rabbâ	3 + 2 + 2 + 2 = 9	4
2b	*ûrĕdû gat-pĕlištîm*	3 + 1 + 3 = 7	3
	hăṭôbîm min-hammamlākôt hāʾelleh	3 + 1 + 4 + 3 = 11	3
	ʾim-rab gĕbûlām miggĕbūlĕkem	1 + 1 + 3 + 5 = 10	3
3a	**ham**ĕnaddîm *lĕyôm rāʿ*	4 + 2 + 1 = 7	3
3b	*wattaggîšûn šebeṭ ḥāmās*	4 + 1 + 2 = 7	3
4a	**haš** *šōkĕbîm ʿal-miṭṭôt šēn*	4 + 1 + 2 + 1 = 8	3
	ûsĕrūḥîm ʿal-ʿarśôtām	4 + 1 + 3 = 8	2
4b	*wĕʾōkĕlîm kārîm miṣṣōʾn*	4 + 2 + 2 = 8	3
	waʿăgālîm mittôk marbēq	4 + 2 + 2 = 8	3
5a	*hap pōrĕṭîm ʿal-pî hannābel*	4 + 1 + 1 + 2 = 8	3
	kĕdāwîd	3	1
5b	*ḥāšĕbû lāhem kĕlê-šîr*	3 + 2 + 2 + 1 = 8	3
6a	*haš šōtîm bĕmizrĕqê yayin*	3 + 4 + 1 = 8	3

	wĕrēʾšît šĕmānîm yimšāḥû	3 + 3 + 3 = 9	3
6b	wĕlōʾ neḥlû ʿal-šēber yôsēp	2 + 2 + 1 + 1 + 2 = 8	3
7a	lākēn ʿattâ	2 + 2 = 4	2
	yiglû bĕrōʾš gōlîm	2 + 2 + 2 = 6	3
7b	wĕsār mirzaḥ sĕrûḥîm	2 + 2 + 3 = 7	3

SUMMARY

Standard Hebrew meter calls for a 16-syllable line with 6 stresses. The normal line is a bicolon with 8 syllables and 3 stresses (or accents) in each colon. There are numerous variations in most poems; here we come quite close to target figures:

	Syllables	Stresses
1a	8 + 10 = 18	3 + 3
b	8 + 9 = 17	3 + 4
3a–b	7 + 7 = 14	3 + 3
4a	8 + 8 = 16	3 + 2
b	8 + 8 = 16	3 + 3
5a–b	8 + (3) + 8 = 16 (+3)	3 + (1) + 3
6a–b	8 + 9 + 8 = 25	3 + 3 + 3
Totals	55 + 59 + 8 = 122 (+3)	21 + 21 + 3 = 45 (+1)
Norm	56 + 56 + 8 = 120	21 + 21 + 3 = 45

As we have already observed, the series of Woes begins with the word *hôy* and closes with an added colon at the end of v 6. The internal structure of the Woe is built around the seven groups to whom the Woe is addressed. The normal pattern consists of a balanced bicolon (3 : 3 and 8 : 8) in which the opening word is a participle or equivalent noun, with the definite article and a variety of predicate terms; the second colon is normally introduced by the conjunction *waw* and offers a selection of different verbal forms to balance the first colon. There are a number of exceptions, and in the end no two lines or bicola are exactly the same. Thus the first pair of prophetic targets are combined so that the two groups are identified in the first bicolon, while descriptive material about them is added in the second bicolon. The external structure is maintained by using the conjunction at the beginning of each second colon. The effect is to displace the second group, which is placed in the second colon of the first line instead of being in the first colon of the second line. We have

1a   (hwy) hš'nnym . . . whbṭhym . . .
1b   nqby . . . wb'w . . .

where we would have expected something like

(hwy)hš'nnym (w)nqby . . .
[ ]hbṭhym wb'w . . .

There is no reason to question the preserved arrangement: it is clearly deliberate. The purpose is to combine or amalgamate the first two groups, and this objective is reinforced by the second bicolon, in which joint characteristics and activities are mentioned. The "notables of the foremost of the nations" include both the dignitaries who reside in Zion (=Jerusalem) and those who dwell in Mount Samaria. They are the "notables" who have come to the house of Israel.

Another exception is to be found in v 4, in which the two bicola are treated as a single couplet and the three clauses after the opening participle with the definite article (hškbym) are all connected by the conjunction *waw*. Thus we have

hškbym . . . wsrḥym
w'klym . . . w'glym

We would have expected h'klym instead at the beginning of the second bicolon, especially because 'klym fits the pattern of participles that normally (six times) begin the lines. The result is that of the seven participles or nouns identifying the different groups, six have the definite article, while only one ('klym) does not. We can list them to show the variants:

1. hš'nnym
2. whbṭhym
3. hmndym
4. hškbym
5. **w'klym**
6. hprṭ ym
7. hštym

It is uncanny that once more it is precisely the fifth item in seven that varies from the established pattern, as elsewhere in Amos. When we compare the first pair of Woes with the last two we note some verbal similarities or echoes. Thus in v 1b and vv 5b and 6b we find the following:

1b	rʾšyt *hgwym*	5b	ḥšbw **lhm**
1b	wbʾw **lhm**	6b	wrʾšyt *šmnym*

The repeated words are *rʾšyt* and *lhm,* and they are in reverse order in vv 5 and 6, providing a form of chiasmus, echoing or envelope construction. The purpose is deliberate and tends to bind the ends of the poem together, thus emphasizing along with *hôy* and the final colon of the poem (6b) the unity of the Woe. It is the same people who are mentioned in the opening and in the closing of this piece.

In the second colon of each line, a variety of verb forms is used, and in one case the verb is omitted. We can set up the double column as follows (allowing for the displacement in v 1, where the two bicola have been combined):

Woe	Verse	Column A	Column B
1	1a	hšʾnnym	whbṭḥym
2	1b	nqby	wbʾw
3	3	hmndym	wtgyšwn
4	4a	hškbym	wsrḥym
5	4b	wʾklym	
6	5	hprṭ ym	ḥšbw
7	6a	hšym	. . . ymšḥw

Of the six forms in Column B (including *nqby* in v 1b rather than *whbṭḥym*) there are three different verb forms with two examples of each: (1) qal perfect 3d pl.; (2) imperfect 2d m. pl. and 3d m. pl.; and (3) qal passive participle, m. pl., one construct, one absolute. In each pair one of the forms has the conjunction *waw,* the other does not. Normally the verbal form comes at the beginning of the colon, but there is one exception: *ymšḥw* comes at the end of the colon, while its companion *wtgyšwn* comes at the beginning:

1b. *nĕqūbê*//4a. *ûsĕrūḥîm*
1b. *ûbāʾû*//5b. *ḥāšĕbû*
3b. *wattaggîšûn*//6a. . . . *yimšāḥû*

The omission of a verbal form in v 4b is still another variation or exception to the normal pattern. The result of this process of subtle variation is that no two bicola are exactly the same but the prevailing pattern is quite distinct or regular.

On the basis of these structural components, there is a presumption that the whole piece is a unity or that the various elements belong to a single picture. We believe that the contents also point in that direction.

We have already noted that the last four Woes seem to be directed at the same group of people, and that they describe and condemn behavior associated with parties and festivals. The eating and drinking all fit into a common pattern. The condemnation is not limited to excessive and intemperate indulgence, but there seems to be a cultic or religious component as elsewhere in the book of Amos. We have echoes and reflections in this passage of others in the book, such as 4:4–5 and 5:21–23, in which the elements of worship and sacrifice are identified alongside the self-indulgences criticized here. Perhaps the feature that tips the scale and decides the question here in favor of religious observance and celebration is to be found in the third Woe. A group is specified as moving rapidly or uncertainly or behaving in a reprehensible fashion that will hasten the coming of the "evil day" in which violence or lawlessness will hold sway. The expression $yôm\ rā^c$ is unique in the Bible, though similar terms occur. More common and clearly related is the opposite expression $yôm\ ṭôb$, which is used for festival occasions or appropriate religious or cultic observances. We would interpret the $yôm\ rā^c$ as the actuality in the view of the prophet, while the celebrants obviously see it in its ordinary sense as the $yôm\ ṭôb$, a festive occasion, whether one of Israel's great feasts or some other solemn but exuberant celebration like the $marzēaḥ$.

We can then determine that a cultic purpose or framework informs and surrounds the occasion or its sacral and convivial meals. For the prophet, the celebration itself is a desecration of a sacral event and location, a form of blasphemy against the God of Israel.

Now we can consider the opening pair of Woes in the light of these observations. The rearrangement of the Woes whereby the two groups are identified in the first bicolon indicates that they are closely associated, even though their geographical locations are at a considerable distance, Zion (= Jerusalem) and Mount Samaria. The next colon (v 1b) should be regarded as describing both preceding groups, not just one, "the notables of the first (foremost) of the nations." While on the face of it this may seem to be an unusual if not peculiar way to describe those luxuriating securely in Zion or Samaria, the usage is plausible, even reasonable, and the association of the groups in some joint undertaking is implied if not presupposed.

When we come to the remaining clause there are several possibilities, owing to the freely flying pronouns: rendered literally we have "and they will come to them, the house of Israel." The meaning is not clear however we interpret the syntax of $byt\ yśr^2l$, subject, object, or indirect object. It is similarly not clear whether the pronouns (both 3d m. pl. presumably) refer to the same antecedent or to different ones. It would be possible to interpret the clause as stating that they (the luxuriants in Zion) come to them (the secure ones in Mount Samaria), or vice versa. We could then account for $byt\ yśr^2l$ as a parallel to and synonym for $r^2śyt\ gwym$ in the first colon. These speculations are grammatically and syntactically feasible, but they do not take us very far or provide a helpful guide to the scene or the action. If we follow the structure and flow of the sentence as we find it, then we should see as the subject of the verb *wbʾw* the antecedent plural noun, *nqby rʾšyt hgwym,* who are in turn identified with both groups in v 1a. They are joined in a common purpose and a common experience. The question remains where they have come together, and the answer must be supplied by the remaining expression, *byt yśrʾl.* The construction is the same as in Amos 4:4, where we read *bōʾû bêt-ʾēl,* "Come to Bethel," or in 5:5, where we read *wĕhaggilgāl lōʾ tābōʾû,* "and to Gilgal do not come." In both cases the verb is a *qal* form of *bōʾ* and there is no preposition with the locative object. In both cases, too, the object is a place with a name. The same should logically be the case here, and we suggest that along with its other frequent meanings, *bêt yiśrāʾēl,* "the house of Israel," can and does signify a place. We suggest that in this instance, as perhaps elsewhere, *byt yśrʾl* is a surrogate or alternate name for *bêt-ʾēl* and that it refers to the major central shrine of the northern kingdom. Thus in 5:6 the threat of consuming fire is leveled against the "house of Joseph" (*bêt yôsēp*), which is in parallel with *lĕbêt-ʾēl!* Curiously, the LXX at this point has *tō oikō Israēl,* which would be suitable in the context as a complement for *byt ywsp.* The latter too may refer to the temple at Bethel, for it was located in the heartland of the territory of Joseph (in this case Ephraim, though close to the border with Benjamin).

Another passage to be considered is Amos 7:13. In it the high priest Amaziah tells Amos that Bethel "is a royal sanctuary (*miqdaš-melek*) and a house of the kingdom (*bêt mamlākâ*)—that is, a national temple. The second phrase, referring to the temple at Bethel, would be equivalent in meaning and significance to *bêt yiśrāʾēl.*

Similarly at Hos 10:15 the MT has *byt-ʾl* while the LXX again reads "house of Israel." We are not proposing that *byt yśrʾl* is an error for *byt-ʾl* in Amos 6:1, but rather that the former expression stands for the major sanctuary of the northern kingdom located at Bethel. The apparent interchange of these terms in Amos 5:6 and Hos 10:15 as between the Hebrew and the Greek suggests that in their range of meaning they overlapped and that either could be used to designate the Yahweh shrine at Bethel. It is our conclusion, therefore, that the two groups mentioned in 6:1a joined forces at the *bêt yiśrāʾēl* in Bethel and that it was there that the fateful festivals took place, which are so cuttingly described and passionately denounced by the prophet in the succeeding verses. We would render, therefore: "And they have come on their own recognizance (for their own benefit) to the house of Israel." We have interpreted *lhm* in this verse as an ethical dative or dative of advantage, referring back to the subject of the verb (a form of the reflexive); it can be compared with the same kind of construction in Amos 6:5: *ḥāšĕbû lāhem,* "they compose for themselves."

The conclusion of the matter is that the series of seven Woes in Amos 6:1–6 is directed against a group of national leaders from the capital cities of both countries, who have gathered at the great shrine at Bethel in order to celebrate a festive occasion. The use of the rare term *mrzḥ* in v 7 (which summarizes the same event) may signify a wake or funeral observance and accompanying revelry, perhaps that of a royal or priestly figure. The whole diatribe is aimed at a particular assembly in a particular place (Bethel) and on a particular occasion—a matter of considerable moment in that it brought together leading citizens from both Zion and Samaria.

Verse 2, which has been added to the Woes, though how soon and by whom can hardly be decided, has its own interest. The subjects, presumably the same notables of both southern and northern kingdoms, are urged by four imperative verbs to cross over (or pass through), observe, go, and go down to the several cities of Calneh, Greater Hamath, and Gath of the Philistines for comparison with the cities mentioned in 6:1a, Zion and Samaria. While the syntax is obscure and the meaning somewhat uncertain, the general idea is that those cities are vulnerable to attack, with their destruction either imminent or already past. It is clear that in the prophet's view, no immunity or exemption has been conferred on either the northern or southern kingdom, and hence they can expect no better outcome or destiny. The fate of those others will be the fate of these cities. And the designated leaders should ponder the lesson of this journey to the neighboring territories.

In any case, we can argue for the integrity of an original Woe oracle consisting of vv 3–6, perhaps minus the word *kdwyd* in v 5. The intrusive material in v 2 is an oracle addressed to the house of Israel, as are many others in the book of Amos. Nonetheless, the Woes are characteristically aimed at particular groups within that society.

If we look at the reconstructed version of the Woe oracle (6:1–6, v 7 being a summary or conclusion), we can make the following observations.

There are exactly seven Woes, each consisting of a bicolon (roughly 3 : 3 in stresses with about eight syllables per colon, ranging from seven to ten). The first unit begins with the word *hôy* (whence the designation "Woe" for this class of oracle), which also serves for all of them. The word following *hôy* and the first word of each succeeding unit is a substantive, almost always with the definite article. In six of the cases it is a participle, and in five of the six it is the *qal* active participle. In the remaining case it is pointed as a *piʿel,* but the verb is difficult and the meaning of the clause is obscure. So the standard pattern begins with *hôy,* present or implied, followed by the noun (participle) with the definite article.

There are two exceptions. The first noun is not a participle but a curious formation based on the root *šʾn* with duplication of the third stem consonant of the word. The noun is derived from the so-called *peʿalal* conjugation of the presumed root, the only one that occurs in the Bible. We may infer that the verb really has a quadriliteral root *šʾnn* and that the noun is based on this root, with a curious doubling of the final *nun*. Because the verb is well attested and the noun occurs elsewhere in contemporary literature (Isaiah 32), the meaning is not seriously in doubt, and its sense conforms to that of the other nouns (participles) in the series. There is no reason to delete or emend simply because it is not an ordinary participle. Compare *GKC* 84b–k and, for example, *rʿnn-*, which has a similar structure; the ground form is *qatlal*. It is classed under intensive stems, which suits the basic meaning and context. These people are thoroughly comfortable with themselves and completely at ease in their situation (reflected in what Isaiah or Jeremiah and Ezekiel have to say about the people of Jerusalem). We note two parallels. First, the immediate connection is with the second Woe, directed at those who feel secure in (*bṭḥ,* "trust in") Mount Samaria. Whether the verb is stative or active, the sense is that they feel secure behind the mighty walls of the capital city and have confidence in its defenders. Second, the more remote but necessary connection of the opening bicolon is with the final clause of v 6 (6b). The words *wělōʾ nehlû,* literally, "they are not distressed at," in other words, they show no concern, worry, sympathy, or empathy about the "crash of Joseph," must refer to the northern kingdom and in particular the tribes of Ephraim and Manasseh.

The linkage of v 1a with v 6b is essential to the structure of the Woe oracles but poses an immediate problem: why connect the people of Jerusalem (= Zion) with the breach of Joseph (the imminent breakdown of the northern entity)? The connection is made through the second colon. It makes sense to link the final clause of the Woe oracle with the second group, those who live in Mount Samaria, the capital of the house of Joseph, and then by extension to the people in (Mount) Zion. No doubt the final clause is put where it is as a summation. Thus it applies effectively to all of the groups mentioned in the list, including the first pair.

At the same time, it must be acknowledged that there is substantial doubt among scholars that the opening Woe is original and authentic as it stands. The reference to Zion in 6:1 is considered suspect by many scholars, who also include the other references to Jerusalem and Judah in the same category. The description of the noble citizens of Zion here is directly parallel to that of the inhabitants of Samaria and reflects a common pattern among eighth-century prophets. According to the evidence of the texts as preserved, all four of the eighth-century prophets shared a common view about both nations: they were both guilty in the sight of God, and both would be punished. Clearly Amos and Hosea concentrated their attention, concerns, and utterances on the northern partner, whose fate was more imminent. Isaiah and Micah were more concerned about the southern kingdom and referred to the experience of the north by way of example and warning for Judah. It may be argued that neither Amos nor Hosea had anything to say about the southern partner, and all such passages may be excluded as secondary. But that claim leaves us with a blank, not with evidence for what they actually thought or may have said on the subject. It is easier and more logical on the whole to imagine that they were in general agreement with their fellow prophets of the south than to imagine that they had contrary views or none at all or that they never expressed them. As all were in agreement about the merited fate of the north, it is hard to imagine that they could have differed radically about the south. Certainly there could be differences in emphasis and insight. We can detect such divergences between the oracles of Isaiah and those of Micah, especially about the ultimate fate of Jerusalem and Judah. Isaiah thought that in the end Jerusalem would survive after undergoing terrible punishment and that a new order would be built out of a tiny remnant. Micah apparently thought otherwise, that Jerusalem would be totally demolished and that salvation and restoration, if they came, would come in the form of a new order, a new establishment. But these points may be argued, defended, and explicated elsewhere.

On the assumption that the text is relatively intact, the opening Woe should be linked closely with the immediately following one. The two together define the population or populations with which the prophet is concerned, namely, a specific group who occupy positions of leisure and pleasure, if not of power, in the capital cities of the two kingdoms. Because of the unusual sequence or close ties connecting 1aA and 1aB, we must similarly link 1b with both constituents of 1a. Thus it is not only the self-secure citizens of Mount Samaria but also those in (Mount) Zion who are associated in this denunciation. Note that *hr* serves double duty here, for the expression *hr-ṣ ywn* occurs frequently in Isaiah and Psalms and can be understood here without doing violence to the text. Curiously, *hr-šmrwn* is less common than *hr-ṣ ywn* but sufficiently frequent to show that the usage is parallel to that of *hr-ṣ ywn* (cf. Amos 3:9, *hry,* and 4:1, *hr*).

We should read the two clause-initial nouns as complementary: the combination of terms adds the element of security to that of ease (cf. Judg 18:27, where we have *sqṭ* and *btḥ* together). It is the term *š'nn* that provides the element of arrogance and self-indulgence, a necessary ingredient for this genre of Woe. Compare Isa 32:9–11, where there is a similar tone.

The third colon likewise should be understood as applying to both groups. Because the expression by itself only mentions the leading citizens of "the foremost of the nations," it should be interpreted as ironic and sarcastic. That the leaders are meant is straightforward enough, though the term itself is relatively rare. The phrase *r'šyt hgwym* requires further analysis. It would seem to refer to a single nation, the first or leading one. Should we understand this reference as applying to the ideal or traditional nation of God of which Israel and Judah are parts? Or can we interpret the expression as distributive and speak of the two leading nations? According to our analysis, the reference is to the leaders of both nations, Israel and Judah, and we must therefore understand *rʾšyt hgwym* as also referring to both nations rather than to one of them. The "first" should be understood as ironic. If they are first in anything it is only in self-esteem. The real view is expressed by Deuteronomy: Israel was the least of the nations, not the greatest by any means (Deut 7:6–8). The designation "first" can only be a matter of self-esteem. Here the leaders of both nations are instructed to travel to various points outside of their borders to compare themselves with their neighbors. The list of nations includes those bordering on both the northern and southern kingdoms and supports the view adopted above.

We have pointed out that the first pair of targets form the audience for the series of Woes. The opening pair thus constitutes a broad classification that literally and factually contains the internal content, that is, all of the people to be mentioned belong to the same constituency. The third Woe is aimed at the same group and identifies them in a slightly different way. These very confident people, at ease about the situation in the capital cities, are nevertheless rushing headlong (*hmndym*) toward the "evil day" (or "the day of the evil one"—cf. Andersen and Freedman 1980:476–77). The parallel or complementary colon is generally rendered, "And you bring near the seat [= rule?] of violence." We suggest first of all that the *waw*-conversive is inappropriate in this context. The simple *waw* with the imperfect would be correct. Note, for example, that the corresponding Woe in structural terms is 6:6, in which the parallel to the participle is the imperfect *yimšāḥû,* which has no conjunction at all. Second, we believe that *šbt ḥms* in v 3b forms an elaborate combination with *lywm rʿ* and that the single preposition serves double duty or governs the whole phrase. Then we would read the verb as the internal *hipʿil* rather than as the causative: "and you draw very near." Note also that the *yod* indicative of the *hipʿil* does not occur in the Aleppo Codex, though the vocalization is the same as in the BHS Leningrad Codex. It is possible, therefore, that the form was originally *qal*. We read the two pairs of words together as follows: "You rush along and have drawn ever nearer to the day of the lawless reign of calamity." This rendering would seem to capture the sense of the passage:

> [Woe] to you who rush along toward the day of calamity,
> who draw ever nearer to the reign of lawlessness!

The first two Woes—or rather their targets—clearly belong together, as shown by the identification of the two groups with the respective capital cities of south and north. The noun *šʾnnym* and the participle *bṭḥym* also complement each other, and the use of the conjunction with the second member (*whbṭhym*) supports the linkage.

We have suggested that the third Woe stands apart from the others, having no clear parallel (in a group of seven that pattern would be expected). In addition, its internal parallel is unique in being 2d m. pl., while all of the others are either 3d m. pl. forms or are left unspecified. We would expect the Woes to be addressed directly to their targets and hence can assume that the first pair are to be interpreted as second-person forms (they are not specified, and either second or third person can be used with them). Nonetheless, v 1b employs a third-person verb with the subjects, thus pointing toward an indirect address. In v 2, however, all four verbs are 2d m. pl. imperatives.

The third group is clearly second-person, the only one so specified (*tgyšwn*). Beginning with the fourth the third person is specified, and the same is true of the sixth and seventh as well. The fifth is ambiguous, but because it pairs up with the others in the second grouping (especially no. 7) we can also read it as third person. The final colon on the piece is also in the third person (*nḥlw*), consistent with the immediately preceding material. The final clause is attached to the seventh woe but is probably to be associated with all of them and is a summary of the essential problem with the groups seen together. Thus we would have a structure with three units in the second person (vv 1–3) and four in the third person (vv 4–6), if we were to assign v 4b, which is unspecified, to the second-person forms. As the definite article can also be interpreted as a vocative particle, the second person may be better represented than just by a single verb (*wtgyšwn*). Nevertheless, the ambiguity in the use of the initial *he* illustrates the uncertainty, which is perhaps deliberate. If we assume or suggest that the *he* before the series of nouns and participles (mostly participles) is the vocative particle rather than the definite article (the form appears to be the same), then we note a fairly frequent shift from second to third person and back, beginning with the first Woe.

The whole structure reveals a myriad of planned details, which together form an artistic mosaic. The basic scheme is easily recognizable as a seven-part Woe series. In spite of one radical intrusion (v 2) the scheme has been preserved relatively intact. The remaining Woes are each in the form of a standard bicolon except for the concluding one, which is a tricolon. The variations between pairs and among the group are slight but significant, with the result that no two bicola are identical. As previously pointed out, the first two Woes are tied together in complementary fashion defining the limits of the audience, the targets of the accusation. The third Woe applies directly to this double group and gives a general picture of what awaits them. The combination here is complex and requires careful analysis; still, we can posit a connection with the Woe in 5:18–20, which is the only other place in Amos where *hôy* is used explicitly. *Hôy,* though, is implied in all cases in which the form of these accusations is followed, perhaps eighteen or nineteen in all (cf. 5:7 and other references already given). In effect, these are the people eagerly awaiting and seeking the Day of the Lord, a day that will turn out to be the opposite of what they expect. So here the key word is "day," and while the language is slightly different, the result is the same. The four following Woes describe various aspects or details of the lives of the people already identified in v 1, the leadership of both nations, as self-indulgent, self-assured merrymakers careless of the future.

The banquet depicted in nos. 4–7 is a parody of the celebration that they anticipate when the Day of the Lord arrives. The symbolism of the great feast, the celebration of victory, peace, and prosperity, is deeply embedded in the hopes of Israel and ultimately becomes the emblem or token of the messianic age. Just as he reverses conventional wisdom about the election of Israel (3:2) and the Day of Yahweh (5:18–20), so here he caricatures the great banquet or celebration of victory as a drunken orgy that will precede the destruction and devastation so vividly described elsewhere in the book. The theme of dissolute behavior on the part of the elite of both nations, specifically in the capitals, is to be found in all four eighth-century prophets and especially in the condemnation of the Samarian nobility by Hosea and Isaiah.

This banquet is the one that foreshadows or celebrates the great day toward which they hasten. The people are eating, drinking, making merry, reclining on splendid furniture inlaid with ivory, and sleeping off their gluttonous drunkenness. The scene described in the four last Woes seems to be unified. Certainly "eating" and "drinking" go together—you would hardly have one group eating and another drinking, or the same group eating on one occasion and drinking on another—so nos. 5 and 7 belong together, and each carries with it its partner into the whole tableau. The sequential order seems to be inverted, with the actions described in reverse for emphasis and dramatic effect. Thus the anointing with oil is properly the preliminary or preparation for the banquet to come (cf. Ps 23:5); and it is possible that *ymšḥw* should be read as a *nipʿal* or perhaps as a *qal* passive formation: **yimmāšĕḥû,* "they anoint themselves," or *yumšāḥû* ("they are anointed"). The phrase *rʾšyt šmnym* is not to be taken as the direct object of the verb but as a dative of means or instrument. We can appropriate the preposition *b-* from the first colon, though it would have different meanings or uses in the two cola "from flagons of wine" and "with the best of the oil." The double use of *b* in v 6 would correspond to the double use of *l* in v 3 and of *ʿl* in v 5. While none of these proposals has been accepted generally, they are all persuasive or at least plausible.

The set of seven participle constructions itemizing the persons who are marked down for "Woe" (vv 1–6) is interrupted by a command in v 2 to visit and inspect several neighboring countries in order to make comparisons:

> 2a Cross over to Calneh, and see;
> proceed from there to Greater Hamath,
> 2b and go down to Gath of the Philistines:
> Are you better than these kingdoms?
> Or is their territory greater than yours?

The oracle is unitary with respect to time, place, and circumstances. It is to be compared especially with Isa 10:5–11, in which some of the same cities are mentioned; but the time and circumstances are markedly different. In Isaiah the period is after the fall of Samaria (722), cf. v 11; whereas in Amos both Samaria and Zion are independent and apparently flourishing. Again in Isaiah it looks as though the series of comparisons is between cities that have all been destroyed, but some more recently than others. Presumably the second in each pair is the more recent casualty, while the former represents a well-known conquest of a more distant past. In Amos, by contrast, there is no clear indication that any of the cities mentioned has been destroyed, rather that they are to be compared with "these kingdoms" (Samaria and Jerusalem) as to wealth and size. The implication is that the same fate will overtake all of them, namely, conquest at the hands of a foreigner. Whether that foreign agent was thought by the prophet to be Assyria or some other empire is not clear, but the line of march implied by the order in which the towns are listed points to the northeast as the place of origin and the Assyrians as the likely instrument of divine retribution, as indeed the passage in Isaiah makes explicit.

Under the circumstances it seems best to interpret v 2b as a continuation of v 2a, focusing on the force of the imperative *wrʾw*—hence "and see whether . . . ," which is the normal usage of the interrogative *he* after this verb. The question is, then, noncommittal in the sense that the nations mentioned may be better and greater or not, and in fact the three listed may belong to both categories; but in any case they and all others along the line of march, including finally Israel and Judah, will fall to the invader. It is not necessary to suppose that the other nations have already fallen, though in fact they did in the course of Assyrian expansion and invasion under Tiglath-pileser III and his successors. With the example of earlier expansionary Assyrian monarchs (e.g., Ashur-nasir-pal, Shalmaneser III, and Adad-nirari III) before them, kings and priests as well as prophets and ordinary citizens could easily imagine a renewal of those marches to the west. It is hardly necessary to regard a prophecy such as this one as a product of the events rather than as a prediction of them. The address to both Jerusalem (Zion) and Samaria precludes a date after 722, and in view of developments in both countries after the death of Jeroboam II and the rise of Tiglath-pileser III, a date after 750/745 is highly unlikely. We may therefore treat the whole unit as belonging to the same period as the bulk of the oracles in Amos and as an authentic expression of the prophet's message.

While the direct address to Zion is unusual (cf. 1:2 and 2:4–6) it is hardly out of keeping with the prophet's stance on the fundamental issues of true religion. In the light of the oracles of Isaiah and Micah we know that conditions in the south were not very different from those in the north, and the comparison of the two kingdoms is a standard image in both of those prophets and in Hosea as well. While the book of Amos concentrates attention on the north, it is hard to imagine that the prophet Amos would not have had an opinion, and a negative one at that, about his own country. The reason for the paucity of data on the subject of Judah must be found in the purpose and process of selection related to the book itself; this oracle as a whole fits the general prescription. But because of the formal structure of the oracle, with its series of vocative nouns and participles, the reference to Zion could not be avoided or eliminated, especially because it led the list.

We conclude, therefore, that this short passage in Amos belongs to a group and a pattern of prophetic threats describing the line of march of an enemy that as the agent of Yahweh will mete out just retribution to the nations filling the area between the great empires of east and west, north and south. Isaiah 10:5–11 represents a later stage in the same series, after much or most of the damage had been done, and only Judah was left of all of the nations that formerly were free; it too would shortly undergo invasion and siege. In Amos' day none of these events had yet taken place, but a discerning prophet could foresee the probable path of action and predict the likely course of events, selecting representative and geographically important cities to symbolize the grand scheme of conquest.

With reference to Calneh, or Calno (cf. Isaiah 10:9, presumably the same city), and Gath of the Philistines, the choice of these places depends on their location at strategic points on the line of march and the grand Assyrian scheme of conquest. In fact, Calneh was captured by Tiglath-pileser about 738, while Hamath fell a short time later; Gath had already been overrun by Uzziah of Judah during his reign.

NOTES

6:1a. *Woe.* The initial *hôy* governs the whole unit through v 7, and indeed all of the following participles until the end of the book; they similarly identify the objects of the prophet's denunciation and describe their misdeeds.

luxuriate. The word *š'nn* is a pseudo-participle, perhaps from a quadriliteral root. The word is known to Isaiah, who also uses it with *bṭḥ* as a parallel (Isa 32:9, 11—the order is reversed in 32:18 and has different correlates in 33:20).

The LXX has *tois exouthenousin,* "those who despise Zion," as if both lines are addressed to Samaria. The parallelism of Zion//Mount Samaria is obvious, and it suggests that the faults of one are the faults of both. The association with Zion does not exclude those who are luxuriating in Samaria. Amos' central target is Samaria and its self-indulgent aristocracy (4:1), but the people of Zion are involved as well. The other woes do not name cities and can be taken as applying to both groups.

Zion. The only other occurrence of this word is at 1:2. The arrangement is standard; the first bicolon has the normal sequence, with the conjunction at the beginning of the second colon, while the second bicolon follows the same pattern:

      1a   *hôy . . . whbṭhym*
      1b   *nqby . . . wb'w*

Mount Samaria. The use of *hr* with Samaria but not with Zion here, though the phrase *hr ṣywn* is very common, suggests the possibility (as noted previously) of the double-duty usage of *hr.* At the same time the omission in one case is reminiscent of the similar selectivity in the use of *'ereṣ* with Egypt and Assyria in the book of Hosea (11:5, *'rṣ mṣrym . . . 'šwr;* 11:11, *mṣrym . . . 'rṣ 'šwr*).

1b. foremost. Babylon is *rē'šît mamlaktô* in Gen 10:12; Amalek is *rē'šît gôyīm* in Num 24:20. The epithet could register priority in time or prestige. The LXX has *archas ethnōn,* plural. If v 1a–1bA is a tricolon, then "notables of the first of the nations" would apply to the complacent residents of both Jerusalem and Samaria.

for themselves. If "house of Israel" is the subject of *ûbā'û,* and the latter is future, the nearest available antecedent for *lāhem* is *haggôyim* in v 1bA. The LXX translated *lāhem* by *autoi,* as though it were an ethical dative reinforcing the subject. We have rendered it "who have come for themselves" or "on their own account." We analyze *byt yśr'l* as locative rather than nominative, and interpret the colon to mean "they have come to the house of Israel."

2a. Calneh. The LXX has *pantes,* as if it read *kl.* Compare the similar problem in Gen 10:10, where, however, the LXX reads *Chalannē.*

2b. Gath. This city alone of the Philistine pentapolis was not named in 1:6–8. Its mention here makes up the tally. No inferences about its political status at the time can safely be made from this circumstance. The question is whether the three cities named in v 2 were chosen at random as representative of many more such places, or whether they had some special lessons to teach. But because the questions that follow speak of kingdoms and territories, it seems best to take Gath as representing the entire Philistine domain. (On the location of Gath at Tell esh-Shariʿa see Wright 1966 and Boling and Wright 1982:315.)

3. The third Woe condemns those who try to avoid (or distance themselves from) the evil day, while at the same time bringing near "the seat of violence." The participle in the first colon and the nominal phrase in the second colon are both obscure. The notion that the preposition *l-* here is the Aramaic *nota accusativi* (Harper 1905:146) seems farfetched.

The participle *hmndym* could be the *piʿel* of *ndh,* the only other biblical occurrence of which is in Isa 66:5, where it means "expel from the community" or else "to taunt." The action seems to be physical, and it is strained to say that Amos 6:3 means they "refuse to think of it," though JPS has adopted this rendering (hesitatingly). The best clue is supplied by the parallel verb *ngš,* but we can use it only if we can decide whether the parallelism is synonymous or antithetical. "The day of calamity" and "the reign of lawlessness" are similar and complementary, though by no means synonymous. In chap. 5 Amos warned that the Day of Yahweh would be an evil time (5:13), but those addressed thought everything would be fine (5:14b, 9:10b). Another possible root is *ndd* or *nwd.* They are running toward the evil day and yet at the same time bringing nearer (or approaching) the seat of violence. Identifying the evil day as the Day of Yahweh, the picture is the same as 5:19. Like the man fleeing from the lion only to have the bear overtake him, so here they are fleeing from the evil day but will thereby only draw near to the reign of lawlessness. The LXX has simply *erchomenoi,* "coming."

We would then interpret *mĕnaddîm* as the *piʿel* participle of a root *ndh,* which has the same basic meaning as *nwd* and *ndd,* and the force would be emphatic or factitive but hardly causative or transitive.

3b. *draw ever nearer.* The problems presented by this verb were examined in the Introduction in connection with the overall structural analysis. The *waw-* is problematic, and no translations opt for past tense. The revision of the Masoretic pointing to *wĕ-* is minimal. The *binyān* is another problem, for "reign of lawlessness" is not a suitable object for a transitive (causative) *hipʿil.* The second person is an additional complication, but it is supported by the Vulgate; the LXX participle can be dismissed as its usual leveling. There are second-person pronouns in v 2 in any case, and emendation to *wayyaggîšûn* (Wolff 1977:272) is too drastic and too easy. The orthography of the Aleppo Codex is suggestive: *wtgšwn,* written *defective* (without the *yod*). It has Masoretic pointing with *hireq,* of course, but it permits consideration of *qal,* "you approach the reign of violence" as a tribunal—the verb often describes entry into litigation; cf. the LXX term, *eggizontes.* Even the *hipᶜil* permits such a result, for it can be construed as intransitive (elative).

If *yôm rāᶜ* and *šbt ḥms* are essentially complementary, then we should expect the two verbs to be related in similar fashion. Just as the second colon charges the culprits with bringing near or approaching very closely to the "reign of violence," so the same group is accused of rushing headlong toward "the day of calamity."

reign of lawlessness. (Alternatively, "reign of violence.") Is it the violence they are doing themselves, or the violence that awaits them? JPS says, you "convene a session of lawlessness," and *ḥāmās* usually describes human violence; but the verb can be used for God's act of judgment (Lam 2:6).

The LXX reads *šbt* as "sabbath," perhaps under the influence of 8:5.

4–6. The next four Woes (vv 4–6) present scenes of revelry and self-indulgence that add up to a single picture. The ancient Near Eastern literary conventions for describing banquets are discussed by M. Lichtenstein (1968). It is not clear whether the beds are for sleeping in after the party or for reclining on during it. And the components are not presented in a natural or logical sequence. The anointing with oil (v 6aB) probably describes the preparation for the party. The opening scene of people "sprawled" on their beds suggests dissipation and disorder. There are some other contemporary accounts, which may be placed alongside this one: Isa 22:12–14, 28:7–8; and Hos 7:3–7. In the first, the feasting and revelry are a defiant reflection of the call to mourning (Isa 22:12), the same contrast as in Amos 6. The motives, however, are quite opposite. In Amos 6 they are giving thanks (*tôdâ* in 4:5) for good times (6:13) and looking forward to even better ones (5:14, 9:10b). In Isaiah 22:13, which is later, they are resigned to inevitable death. This passage is, in fact, the origin of the famous slogan: "Eat, drink, and be merry; for tomorrow we die!"

4a. *beds . . . couches.* The same parallel occurs in 3:12. The parallelism requires that "ivory" modify "couches" as well as "beds" and that "their" modify "beds" as well as "couches."

ivory. The ivory is inlaid, as exemplified by Phoenician craftsmanship; cf. the famous ivory inlays from Samaria.

4b. *devour.* The LXX confirms that this participle lacks the article. This bicolon is unlike the others used in these woes, where the participle is followed by a verb. Here the participle covers both lines, a classical poetic construction. The parallels *krym mṣʾn//wᶜglym mtwk mrbq* show rhythmic compensation in the second colon (or ballast variant) to make up for the missing verb. The details of the menu supplied by v 4b indicate the unconscionable extravagance of the feast; cf. Isa 22:13. The sumptuous provision of beef and lamb, and young and tender animals as well, points to eating on a scale far beyond the means of the ordinary worker or farmer. Besides that, the banquet in 6:4–6 could hardly be a purely secular celebration. Meat was rarely eaten in ordinary life, and for most people it was available only on the most important cultic and sacramental occasions. The excessive behavior described here was its own condemnation.

5. This verse is unusual in its structure. There is apparently a superfluous word in the middle of the bicolon (*kdwyd*). It is not clear whether it qualifies the preceding colon or the following one. Although the punctuation of the MT places it in the second colon, thus associating "David" with the latter clause, it may be regarded as modifying both (the so-called double-duty modifier described by Dahood 1970b:439–44). Without it the two cola match precisely (3 : 3 stresses and 8 : 8 syllables), and it has been targeted by most scholars for deletion as secondary. They may be correct, but it is a curious gloss (admittedly the spelling is relatively late, corresponding to the practice in Chronicles rather than that in Samuel-Kings) and may have been included by the prophet or the first editor of these oracles. It may also be noted that we would normally expect a *waw* (conjunction) at the beginning of the second colon, but if *kdwyd* is suspended between the cola then the *waw* would be excessive and its omission required. The preposition *l* would apply to both compound nouns, *py-hnbl* in the first colon and *kly-šyr* in the second. The meaning of the first colon is unclear chiefly because the root *prṭ* is very rare, and the sense of the participle here is obscure. Whether the action involved is singing or dancing, whether it is carefully orchestrated or carelessly improvised are matters of speculation. Certainly, activity typically associated with instrumental music is involved, and traditionally it has been regarded as either singing or perhaps humming. The phrase *py-hnbl* can be rendered "the music of the lyre" or the "sound of the stringed instrument." Note the usage with *kĕlî:* in Ps 71:22, *kĕlî-nebel* is parallel to *kinnôr;* in 1 Chr 16:5, the plural form *kĕlê nĕbālîm* is parallel to *kinnōrôt*. We may assume either that the same instruments are meant in both cola or that *kly-šyr* is the more general term, encompassing a wider variety. The second colon can be rendered "they devise [compose] for themselves on musical instruments," in other words, they improvise songs to the accompaniment of musical instruments (or compose music with the instruments). It is most unlikely that musical instruments were frequently or even rarely invented at such gatherings, though anything is possible. Amos is referring to typical, not unique, behavior; finally, David is chiefly noted in the Bible as a gifted musician and composer, but Ps 151:2 (LXX and Qumran) also credits him with inventing or at least making a lyre. In Genesis 4 the origins of music and musical instruments are traced back to antediluvian times, and their invention is credited to the offspring of Cain.

The creation of songs, lyrics and melodies, is attributed to the vocalists and instrumentalists at these parties. Whether members of the musical guilds were involved as entertainers or whether these participants were amateurs demonstrating skills and training received in formative years is not clear. No doubt the musicians of temple and court belonged to the elite of Israelite society along with members of other professions and guilds, such as scribes, wise men, artisans, and the like. So they, along with their lords sacred and secular and the other managers and manipulators of society, are targets of prophetic attack and denunciation.

5b. *David*. Compare 2 Chr 5:11–13, 7:6.

instruments. (See Finesinger 1926.) The Chronicler continually mentions the patronage of David in connection with temple music and provides many descriptions. Here the antecedent could be either "instruments" or "song(s)." The expression *bkly dwyd* (2 Chr 29:26) suggests the former; *bkly šyr dwyd* (Neh 12:36) suggests the latter. Amos has split up one of the standard expressions. His inversion also achieves chiasmus with *šr* and *nbl* (both plural) in 5:23. The concentration of references to David as the organizer of temple music in the work of the Chronicler throws some doubt on the solitary occurrence of the same idea in Amos. At least it strengthens our suspicion that the phrase *kdwyd*, if nothing more, may be an intrusive gloss from that source.

In the LXX v 5b reads, "Like those who estimate that they are standing and not like those who flee." It seems to have no connection at all with the MT, and we can hardly speculate where it may have come from or how it got into the text.

6. The basic question seems to be the mode of drinking. The phrase *bĕmizrĕqê yayin* is unique and strange, though the separate words are well known. The word *mzrq* describes a wide open bowl used in a variety of rituals. Thus it was used to contain the blood of sacrificial animals; the blood was then splashed against an altar (Exod 24:6–8; 2 Kgs 16:13–15). In Numbers 7 the *mizrāq* contained an offering of flour mixed with oil. Whenever the material is mentioned, it is gold. We do not know whether such a vessel was ever used to contain wine.

Aside from this passage in Amos, no one ever drinks out of a *mizrāq*. For drinking purposes they normally used a *kôs*, "cup." The mention of the *mizrāq* in this setting suggests unusual and objectionable behavior, not just gluttonous and boorish but blasphemous. Perhaps the best parallel would be the behavior of the participants in Belshazzar's feast, in particular their drinking wine from the gold and silver vessels taken from the temple in Jerusalem (Daniel 5:2–4, 22–23).

The LXX has *diylismenon*, "filtered wine."

best. Compare *bĕrōʾš kol-bōśem*, "the best of spices" (Ezek 27:22—the preposition is the *bet essentiae*).

distressed. (Alternatively, "sick.") The *nipʿal* is probably a middle voice, identifying the subject and emphathizing with the sick person. Even the *qal* can be used in this way, as in 1 Sam 22:8; Saul complains that they did not feel sorry (sick) for him. Even if the MT *ḥōleh* is a mistake and the LXX "pity" (*ḥml*) is better in that passage, the idiom passed muster with the scribes. Compared with Jer 5:3, which uses *qal*, it is possible that *lʾ nḥlw* means that they shared the injury but did not recognize it:

> You smote them and they were not sick;
> you destroyed them—they refused to accept instruction;
>> they made their face harder than a rock
>> they refused to repent.

Jeremiah's explanation ties in with Amos' theme. It enables us to equate the *šēber yôsēp* with the injuries sustained under the plagues of 4:6–11 (blows inflicted by God), which were not accepted as disciplinary chastisements and which were not felt as an illness needing a cure, a fault requiring repentance (cf. Hos 5:13).

Elsewhere *ḥlh* seems to have a literal meaning, being sick from disease or injury. Here it refers to those who are not distressed or miserable about the breaches made in Joseph, presumably the disasters that have already occurred internally: natural calamities and the breakdown of justice in the society. Isaiah 1:5ff. must be similar: the body politic is smitten, wounded, but people act as though nothing had happened.

crash. The word *šēber* means "breach" or "fracture," an injury due to a heavy blow. In Isa 30:26 we have "the hurt of his people"//"the injury of his blow" in chiasmus. In prophetic writing it has the meaning "crushed" and is applied to the ruin of the nation in war. In warfare, "smashing" refers particularly to the braining of captives, either with a blow from a mace or by dashing them against a rock. The phrase "Joseph's crash" thus has many horrible associations. The rabbis, however, found another side to the word, playing on the sound of *šeber*, "hope," *Genesis Rabbah* 91:1. The prophets, too, did not regard the scattering of the broken pieces of the nation as the end. There could be gathering and mending. Compare the use of *šēber* in Isa 30:26 as the breach of his people. "When Yahweh will bind up the breach of his people and the smiting of his wound he will heal." Compare Jer 8:21, "concerning the breach of my people I am broken up"; also Jer 8:11, "They heal the breach of my people lightly, saying 'Peace, peace,' when there is no peace."

Here there are threats about the future, implying that the breach is internal and not necessarily visible. The point is that if Israel or Judah were suffering serious reverses in the field or tumults at home people would know it and do something about it, even if wrong in the view of the prophets. But they could be truly oblivious about something that was not

readily discernible, or so it would seem. In the Jeremiah passage it is difficult to tell whether the prophet is speaking about actual disasters that have
caused the breach in his people, or whether the illness and wounds among
them have weakened the fiber of resistance and will make them vulnerable
to the onslaughts yet to come.

Joseph. On the use of this term see the essay on geopolitical terminology
in Amos in the INTRODUCTION and the NOTES on 5:6 and 5:15. As a
designation of the northern kingdom, it suggests a diminution to a group
consisting only or mainly of the Joseph tribes, Ephraim and Manasseh.
Hosea does not use this terminology. Rather, he speaks of Ephraim. Amos
does not use the latter, an indication that the two prophets are dealing with
different political situations.

7a. *Now indeed. Lākēn ʿattâ* is very emphatic. It is dubious in Judg 11:8,
where the LXX reflects *lōʾ kēn;* cf. Gen 4:15.

This verse picks up the themes of the preceding Woes and rounds off the
whole set. The unique *gōlîm* as a *qal* active participle lines up with the
seven participles in the Woes. *Sĕrûḥîm* is repeated from v 4aB and its
positioning at the end of the colon makes a chiasmus, for *srḥym* comes first
in v 4aB. The revelers sprawled out is the last scene of the drama, which
was anticipated from the beginning of the report in v 4a.

head. There is an ironic play here on the root *rʾš,* for the word *rēʾšît* has
already appeared twice. They (i.e., the subjects throughout the Woes) are
"the *foremost* of the nations" (v 1b); they "anoint themselves with *best*
oils"; they will become the *first* of the deportees. We must also reckon with
the dual meaning of the preposition in *brʾš*—locative or *essentiae.* Thus Mic
2:13, "Yahweh is their head" or "Yahweh is at their head"; and Mic 4:1 (=
Isa 2:2), "Zion is the chief of the mountains" or "Zion is at the top of the
mountains." The same ambiguity occurs in 1 Kgs 21:9, 12.

exile. For sound play on the consonants *g-l* see 5:5b (based on Gilgal).
The chiastic placement of the words *hsr//ygl* (5:23–24) and *yglw//sr* (6:7)
brings out another point. If they do not want to be "exiled and set aside"
(*gōlâ wĕsûrâ,* Isa 49:21), they should set aside (*hsr*) their revelry and let
justice flow down (*ygl*). The LXX has *dynastōn,* as if it read *gĕdōlîm.*

7b. *depart.* *S-r* is another motif. The classic definition of a perfect man is
that he fears God and eschews evil (*sār mērāʿ,* Job 1:2). Here the alliteration of *sr . . . srwḥym* in v 7b balances *yiglû . . . gōlîm* in v 7a.

mourners. The traditional rendering, "revelry," for *mirzaḥ* in v 7 should
be qualified in view of the light now cast on the *marzēaḥ* institution by
recently discovered texts and associated research. On the institution at Elephantine, see Porten 1968. The funerary association probably owned a
community house where they had great feasts for the dead. The Claremont
Ras Shamra Tablet no. RS 1957.702 shows the existence of the institution
in Canaanite society at an earlier stage, and postbiblical sources document

its long continuance. (For discussion of the *MRZḤ* tablet see Miller 1971; Dahood 1971; Fenton 1977; Halpern 1979–80; and Friedman 1979–80.) The word occurs once more in the Hebrew Bible, Jer 16:5, where the *marzēaḥ* house is a place of mourning: not "a house where there is mourning," but a special place set up and maintained for such purposes. Note the chiasm,

> *ʾal-tābô bêt marzēaḥ* (16:5)
> *ûbêt-mišteh lōʾ-tābôʾ* (16:8)

The second might be not a distinct prohibition but an aspect of the first. The famous *marzēaḥ* text from Ugarit suggests that the institution was a kind of funeral cooperative to provide facilities for the burial rites and the care of the dead. Verses 4–7 then show us what was going on in one of these places in Amos' time. It was not a regular wake, because mourners did not anoint themselves with oil in the usual way (2 Sam 14:2). Jeremiah was forbidden to enter a *marzēaḥ* house because he was not allowed to mourn. Amos objects to their celebration because they should have been grieving for the ruin of Joseph (v 6b). Their behavior would have been all the more frivolous and reprehensible if they were carrying on in a *marzēaḥ* instead of using that institution for its intended purpose.

These festivities could be a way of mocking death while at the same time making provision for it (Isa 22:12–14). Jeremiah reflects the appropriate attitude to the *byt mrzḥ* of his day: no mourning, no revelry for the dead.

Verse 7b in the LXX reads, "And the neighing of horses will be taken away from Ephraim." The verb is the only point of contact with the MT. "Neighing" shows that the significance of *marzēaḥ* was not understood, but it supports the belief that the root means "to shout" rather than "to join" (Eissfeldt 1968:286–90). "Horses" (*swsym*) is a misreading of *srwḥym*. The word "Ephraim" has no claim to originality, for Amos never uses it.

Amos does not identify the occasion or location of the festivities described in vv 4–6. Many of the circumstances would suit a cultic festival: the use of *mizrāq* cult vessels; the use of music after the manner of David; the eating of the flesh of animals commonly sacrificed. Even the beds could be part of the setup if this furniture was provided for the comfort of those enjoying a communion meal in the shrine; cf. 2:8. These factors are not enough to identify the ceremony as formally religious. In view of Amos' evident distaste for the forms and practices of official religion, it is doubtful that he would overlook a chance to add or emphasize charges against the priesthood and its ceremonies. Even so, the religious overtones of the description may be taken seriously. There are three possibilities.

1. The touches in the description that suggest that there is something

cultic about the festivities are due to the prophet. It is part of his criticism; they devote themselves to merrymaking, as if it were their religion.

2. Accepting the statements that they were actually using the *mizrāqîm* normally reserved for sacral acts, and the musical instruments and songs as composed by David, we may conclude that the secular feasts of the ruling classes had some of the trappings and characteristics of religious festivals, including participants from both spheres of activity. The clue is the expression *yôm rāʿ*, which is a parody or adaptation of the normal phrase, *yôm ṭôb,* used in the Near East for a festive occasion. These people are engaged in such a festival; only what they treat as a *yôm ṭôb* will turn into a *yôm rāʿ* for them and for their nations.

3. We accept the reference to *marzēaḥ* as an indication that the banquet was taking place in a mourning house, or at least was intended as a wake for the dead—"for the *šēber* of Joseph," which could be any of the plagues cataloged in 4:6–11 or 5:3. But their behavior under the circumstances was the exact opposite of what was fitting. It shows how they did *not* repent. In the end the line of separation between secular and sacred was not sharply marked, and any festivity involving the elite was likely to have important implications for the life of the nation. That was the point of the prophetic message. It was precisely because all of these people were in positions of responsibility and authority, on whose plans and deeds the well-being of the whole people depended, that their behavior under all conditions was subject to detailed scrutiny. Wrong behavior had multiple consequences, so it made their callous self-indulgence all the more reprehensible. Amos and the other prophets were not merely against ostentatious displays of wealth, or excessive luxury and self-indulgence as such, but against the people who engaged in such diversions, because they had other and weightier responsibilities that they were rendered incapable of discharging properly. On the contrary, they carried this pattern of behavior and the psychology behind it into their official duties and thereby made a mockery of the justice and equity that were the foundation and cornerstone of Israelite society and the only good reason for calling themselves the elect of Yahweh, the chosen people.

The first pair of Woes and the last pair exhibit a notable balance in wording and sense. All seven combine to form a picture of the corruption and contamination of a great festive cultic celebration. In the last colon of v 6, we have a general statement about the abject failure of the aristocracy to be deeply concerned, to be sick, figuratively or literally, over the widening breakdown of Joseph. This charge sums up the case against all of the individuals and groups identified in the list: those who are at ease in Zion, those secure in Mount Samaria, those who flee from or go headlong toward the evil day, those who lie on beds of ivory, those who eat lambs from the flock, those who strum on stringed instruments and drink wine from basins.

All are guilty of the same neglect of duty and concern regarding the wounds of Joseph, bleeding internally, but soon to be revealed as fatally injured and beyond cure or care. They should be sick at heart, sick indeed over the impending and growing tragedy; and they are not.

The consequence is all too plain: for their sins, their self-indulgence, neglect of duty, oppression of the poor, abandonment of Yahweh, they will go into exile at the head of the exiles. The last colon is almost beyond recovery, but apparently it echoes deliberately the final word on the revelers—hung over, sprawled out on their beds—they will lead the parade.

II.B.2. THE OATH AND WOES (6:8–14)
II.B.2.a. THE OATH (6:8–10)

6:8a My Lord Yahweh has sworn by his life
      —Oracle of Yahweh, God of hosts—
      "I abhor the pride of Jacob,
      its citadels I reject;
  8b   so I will hand over the city in its entirety."
  9 So it will be,
      that, if ten men are left in a single house, they shall die.
  10a Then the nearest relative and his *msrp*
      will arrive to remove the corpse from the house.
      One will say to the other in the remote corners of the house,
      "Is anyone still with you?"
      He will reply,
      "No one."
  10b Then the former will say,
      "Silence! For we must not invoke Yahweh's name."

INTRODUCTION

The second half of chap. 6 (vv 8–14) is the concluding portion of The Book of Woes. It begins with an oath (v 8) and ends with a judgment speech (v 14). The latter completes the series in vv 8b and 11, and threats or predictions of a similar kind are found throughout the entire book. These pronouncements are built around an additional Woe (v 13), which we are inclined to identify as the key to the whole piece. It includes another pair of riddles (v 12a; cf. 3:3–6), followed by an accusation (v 12b) that echoes 5:7. It also contains a very strange passage (vv 9–10), perhaps the most obscure in the entire book, which seems to reach back to 5:3. The address to the "house of Israel" in v 14 and the geographical boundaries recognized there indicate that this unit, like the whole of The Book of Woes, is addressed to all of Israel.

The bounds of the unit are marked by the use of the same rubric, "Oracle of Yahweh, God of [the] hosts," in vv 8 and 14. They are identical except for the definite article, which is unique in the latter. Similar formulas are used to open and close the unit in 5:16–27. The *nĕ'ūm* formula is not used at the very beginning of an oracle, like the messenger formula ("Thus Yahweh has said"). The one in v 8 is in a satisfactory position near the beginning of the unit. The LXX lacks the phrase entirely in v 14, which throws doubt on the authenticity of the colophon. Also problematic is its awkward position in the middle of a clause; it divides *mqym 'lykm* from its object, *gwy.*

It is not certain that vv 9–10 should be linked with v 8, though some logical connection can be found. The gruesome scene in vv 9–10 could be the consequence of delivering up the city "in its entirety" to total destruction.

The structure of v 8 is chiastic and circular and quite regular, if we exclude the oracle formula from formal consideration. There is a four-colon unit, 8a, comprising an introduction followed by a tricolon:

	Syllables	Stresses
8 *nišbba'* [*'ădōnāy*] *yhwh bĕnapšô*	10	4
mĕtā'ēb 'ānōkî 'et-gĕ'ôn ya'ăqōb	11	4
wĕ'armĕnōtāw śānē'tî	8	2
wĕhisgartî 'îr ûmĕlō'āh	9	3

In order for the first line to fit in with the others as first-person speech, it is necessary to recognize "Yahweh" as the speaker's reference to himself. "Yahweh = I" is not uncommon usage; but *'ădōnāy,* "my Lord," does not fit so well, especially if it is taken literally. The title "my Lord Yahweh" is a favorite of Amos and could easily become a variant where only "Yahweh" is needed. The LXX has only *Kyrios* here, so we are inclined to remove *'ădōnāy* in this instance. There is some poetic parallelism in the oath, but it is not well developed. The second line (with prosaic *'et*) is rather long, but the syntax (participle + pronoun) is not normal; the sequence secures chiasm in the middle bicolon, and the verb *śānēʾtî* at the end of the line closes that small unit.

The oath itself is found in the last line. The perfect form of the verb with *waw*-consecutive follows correctly from the opening affirmation. It can also be tied to the preceding bicolon, which gives the reason for the threatened judgment.

Verse 11 can be recognized as a continuation of the threat of v 8bB. Verses 9–10, with a more prosaic and narrative style, are then a vignette of the vicissitudes of a city in wartime.

NOTES

8. The LXX version differs extensively from the MT. It lacks the *nĕʾūm* formula, along with *ʾădōnāy*. It begins with *hoti* (nothing in the MT) and has *dioti* in the second line. It tones down "by his soul" to "by himself." It has *chōras* for "citadels," as in chaps. 1–2. It also adds "all" twice. None of these variants merits retrojection.

8a. *sworn.* In 8:7 the Lord swears "by the pride of Jacob."

abhor. Mtʾb should be read with medial *ayin* rather than *alef.* The root *tʾb* means "long for," whereas the meaning "loathe," which is the suitable parallel for *śnʾ*, requires *tʿb*, as in 5:10. These parallels occur in both sequences: *śnʾw//ytʿbw* (Amos 5:10; cf. Pss 5:6–7, 119:163). In Mic 3:9 *tʿb* comes first in parallel with the root *ʿqš*, "to twist."

pride. This noun is commonly used with the name of a city ("Jerusalem," Jer 13:9) or a country ("Moab," Isa 16:6 and others). In Hos 5:5 and 7:10, "the pride of Israel" seems to be God in his majestic aspect. In Ps 47:5 God loves "the pride of Jacob," and in Nah 2:3 he restores it. There are clearly two sides to this idea. In the present context it is Jacob's misplaced confidence in the fortifications of the city. The linkage between *gʾwn* and *ʾrmnwt* could be hendiadys, "the majestic citadels of Jacob." The use of *ʾet* to mark this object is notable because the next three nouns do not have it. The parallelism also shows that it is the fortresses, more than anything else, that are the evidence of Jacob's pride and the object of Yahweh's detestation, as they will also be the prime target of his destructive judgment.

8b. *hand over.* In 1:6, 9 this verb describes the crime of handing over a captivity to the slave trade. We infer, therefore, that the "entirety" of the city is its population, and that its fate will be similar. In Deut 32:30, however, Yahweh "hands over" the people so that they suffer defeat like that in Amos 5:3. The human agent is insignificant (cf. Ps 78:50; Lam 2:7).

city. The indefinite *ʿîr* is poetic usage if a specific city is in mind. The chief object of an attack would usually be the capital city, and, as both are named in v 1, the phrase could be distributive—each city and its inhabitants.

9. Here the picture is that men are dying in a house; but how it comes about and why it is described in this way are far from clear. Ten is a large number of men to reside "in one house," if it means a dwelling in a city, especially if they are described as survivors. The logical structure of vv 9–10 is also indeterminate. Is *wāmētû* still part of the protasis (if ten men are left in a single house and they die [there], then his kinsman will lift him up, etc.)? Or is it the beginning of the apodosis, as usually translated: If ten men are left . . . then they shall die . . . ? In either case, there is a problem in the shift to singular pronouns in v 10. The LXX has relieved the strain by continuing with plurals—*hoi oikeioi autōn,* "their relatives." It also solves the problem of how all ten could die (v 9) and there still be someone to bury them (v 10) by adding, *kai hypoleiphthēsontai hoi kataloipoi* ("and the remaining ones will remain"). Nevertheless, that line still contradicts the preceding. Harper has a long catalog of available rewrites of vv 9–10 (1905:152). Compare the extensive emendations suggested by T. H. Robinson (1923). *Hypoleipein* is used in Amos 5:3, 9 (twice each). The equivalent would be *š'r.* The reference to the kinsman (*dôd,* "uncle" or perhaps "cousin") suggests a family situation.

The houses in v 11 are clearly buildings, but it is not certain that the "one house" is a family residence. The picture of ten refugees in a single house could be explained if they have crowded into a city, perhaps after the defeat of 5:3. Note the reference to "house of Israel" there. It could be the same "ten." The cause of death in such a siege could be pestilence (4:10), which could account for the extraordinary behavior in the presence of the dead described in v 10.

10. The conversation between the kinsman who comes to make a burning for the corpse (literally, "bones," in the sense of a dead body) and someone else in the house may suggest that there is just one survivor, cowering in the innermost recesses of the house.

10a. *nearest relative and his* msrp. It is unclear whether there is one person or two people involved here. If the *dwd* and the *msrp* are the same person, the "and" is epexegetic, but the construction is awkward. We would expect, "lift up his bones to bring them out of the house." The meaning of *msrpw* (literally "the one who burns him") is also uncertain. Although the verb *nš'* is singular, we have taken it to include another individual accompanying the "nearest relative."

corpse. Commonly *'ṣmym* are the bones of a living person, *'ṣmwt* those of a corpse.

10b. *Silence!* It is not clear who is speaking, the kinsman or the lone survivor. Neither is it clear whether the following words, literally, "for not to memorialize [the dead] in the name of Yahweh," are spoken by the person who says *hās!* or whether it is an explanation supplied by the editor. In either case, it would seem that normal burial rites are not being observed (contrary to the anticipations of 5:16–17). As with the death of Jehoiakim, there will be no wailing (Jer 22:18). Jeremiah and Ezekiel were both forbidden to mourn in extreme situations.

invoke. The use of *hizkîr* with the object *šēm* is discussed in Schottroff 1964:245–51. The word *šēm* can be used alone (Exod 23:13; Ps 45:18; Isa 26:13), with *b-* (Josh 23:7; Ps 20:8), or with *'et* (Exod 20:24). If there is a distinction it could be that without a preposition it means mentioning the name as such; with *b-* it is saying or doing something "in the name of Yahweh." But Josh 23:7 and Exod 23:13 are hardly distinguishable. In some contexts the idiom can mean to call someone by a name, or to swear by a name (both in Isa 48:1).

COMMENT

In Amos 6:9 it is the context rather than the terms that suggests memorializing the dead; *zkr* with the name of God does not have to be related to funerary rites. Here it seems that the occasion does not warrant or allow the use of the name of God. But who says so? If two men come to get the bones, then one must say it to the other. In sequence it would be the one on the outside rather than the one inside, or in the recesses looking for bodies or bones. If we take the whole thing in order we may come out with the following analysis.

The initial description seems to be a consequence of the siege we posit in v 8—the effect of the judgment pronounced in v 7 but described in more detail in 6:13–14. Among the harmful and damaging effects or accompaniments of a siege are famine and epidemic disease, and these disasters may combine here to produce the tragedy in the house, ten men who die. There is no indication here of invasion and killing, only of dying. The vivid description of the effects of a siege in 2 Kgs 6:24–7:20 brings out the point quite effectively.

The figures may be symbolic, but in any case we probably should read the last verb in v 9 as an apodosis: "It will be that if ten men [people] are left in a house" (it may be that the others if any have already gone to fight or have died during the course of the siege). So the ten die and none are left in the house, only bodies and bones(?). Then come two men, the *dôd* and the *msrp* of whom or what; the 3d m.s. suffix could be for anyone or anything. Perhaps they are related to the head of the house or to the household (*bayit*). The *dôd*, uncle or cousin (Jer 32:7), may be the nearest of kin here or the next in line of inheritance. Who the other person is we do not know, but it may be someone responsible for funeral arrangements. They seem to have come to the house (is it a palace or a temple?) to bring out the bones (not a single body but the bones of all of those in the house). Once they have gathered what bones they could, one is sent into the inmost recesses to look for either more bones or more people. There is an ellipsis here, but it is possible that they do not find any bones (most unlikely) or that, having found some, they are looking for more. The one in the street calls to the other in the farthest corner to ask whether he has found anything. The Hebrew here may imply that the person has been in the back of the house and is one of those who were there before (we do not read of someone going back there). If he is a survivor, then the statement in v 9 seems to be misleading, because on the face of it, it indicates that there are no survivors. Keeping the number of people to a minimum, we suppose that the two men engage in a dialogue. If the order is the same in the dialogue as in the listing, then the *dwd* says to the *msrp* who is in the back end of the house, "Is there any [one or thing] [there] with you? Have you [found] anything in the recesses of this house?" The man in the back answers "No! Nothing!"—no one or nothing. Then the first one (or the second) says, "Silence! For we must not invoke Yahweh's name." Perhaps more directly related to the funerary aspects of the scene, it is forbidden to conduct funeral services for these people, that is, to invoke the blessing in Yahweh's name on the dead in the house.

The last item in turn may reflect the view that the siege and its consequences were the just recompense of the rebellion against Yahweh. Hence there should be no mourning and no invocation of the name of Yahweh; cf. Jeremiah (chap. 16), who is forbidden to go to the house of mourning, or Ezekiel (chap. 24), who is forbidden to mourn for his wife.

It may be that in vv 9 and 10 the final *w'mr* is the apodosis and all the rest is protasis. When everything happens, then one will say, *hās*, "that's it!"

II.B.2.b. LAST WOES (6:11–13)

6:11a   For behold, Yahweh is commanding;
            he will smash the largest house into pieces,
  11b   and the smallest house into bits.
  12a   "Do horses run upon the rocks?
            Or does one plow the sea with oxen?

12b   But you have turned justice into poison,
                  and the fruit of righteousness into wormwood.
13a   [Woe to] you who are delighted over Lo-Dabar;
13b   [woe to] you who say,
                  'Have we not captured Qarnaim for ourselves by our
           might?' "

NOTES

6:11–12. In v 11 we have the conclusion of this drama, with the successful end of the siege and the demolition of the great house and the little
house. There is clearly a merismus covering all of the houses from great to
small, but it can be a specific reference to the royal palace and other great
houses on the one hand and ordinary houses on the other.

This demolition is the result of a command from Yahweh, probably given
to a heavenly agent, as is expressly the case in 9:1, where the command is
wy'mr hk hkptr, "He said: 'Strike the capital(s)!' " Here the command is
indirect, and the form *wĕhikkâ* could be rendered as passive. In Masoretic
punctuation 11aB–b is a bicolon, with incomplete synonymous parallelism:

>   *wĕhikkâ habbayit haggādôl rĕsîsîm*
>   *wĕhabbayit haqqāṭōn bĕqī'îm*

While the passage has features often associated with poetry, it also exhibits
prosaic elements, such as the extensive use of the definite article and more
particularly the noun with the adjective in the attributive position. Phrases
of the latter kind are rare in biblical poetry. The constraints of poetry
would certainly limit their frequency, for they tend to make a line too long.
With the average line containing three beats, and the typical clause consisting of three items—Verb + Subject + Object, Verb + Object + Adverb,
or the like—complex noun phrases consisting of two nouns can be used,
especially when a clause has only two items or when the parallelism is
incomplete. In fact, a construct phrase often serves for rhythmic compensation in incomplete synonymous parallelism. So why not attributive phrases?
Part of the answer may rest in the fact that an attributive adjective can be
used as a parallel in a neighboring line; that is, an attributive phrase is
broken up and spread over the two colons. See the NOTES on *ṣaddîq* in
2:6b. Even so, the rarity of normal contiguous attributes suggests a convention against this construction as unpoetic.

11a. *commanding*. Such a use of a participle with *hinnēh* indicates the intention to act in the immediate future. The verb has no explicit object. To judge from other instances, there are three possibilities.

1. No object is implied or required. Amos 9:9 has a similar construction:

> Indeed I will command:
> I will shake. . . .

Here "commanding" is the same as deciding, rendering a verdict. Yahweh himself carries out the decree (Pss 33:9, 148:5). Compare 2 Sam 17:14— "Yahweh had decided to subvert. . . ." The decision is internal; it reflects a decision that is prior to the following action, but which both defines and ensures the outcome. It does not deny the possible use of agents and instruments; they are simply unimportant.

2. In fact, because the idea of God giving a command to himself is somewhat outlandish, a suitable agent, such as a member of the divine retinue, is implied. The language is mythic or at least metaphorical. Indeed, in Amos 9:3–4 it may be taken more literally, the snake and the sword, albeit mythic, representing real destructive forces.

3. A third and somewhat more abstract idea is that the word of command, once issued, becomes a force or agency that produces the effects contained in the words: for example, the mode of creation in Genesis 1; cf. Isa 55:10–11 and 34:16.

smash. See the discussion at 9:1.

largest . . . smallest. The articles qualify the words as superlatives: the largest house and the smallest house. By merismus it means all houses, from biggest to littlest.

pieces . . . bits. Both words are rare. The first is an absolute *hapax legomenon* in the Hebrew Bible, that is, there is no other occurrence of any word with the same root. There is a homonym *rss* occurring as a verb ("moisten," Ezek 46:14) and as a noun (*rěsîsê lāylâ*, "dewdrops" // *ṭal*, Cant 5:2). Although the connotation of droplets of liquid might be a bit farfetched, perhaps there is only one word, *rsysym*. The parallel noun, *běqîʿîm*, occurs once again in Isa 22:9, referring to the city of David. The verb *bqʿ* is common and describes breaking, cleaving, or splitting. The object is commonly wood or rocks, but there are many others, including the war atrocity of ripping open pregnant women. Both complements go with both objects—all of the houses will be reduced to splinters and rubble as a result of the demolition ordained and carried out by Yahweh.

12. This verse begins with two riddles. These riddles are so enigmatic that they remain unsolved until the present day. It is not apparent what the point is or how it relates to the surrounding text. Verse 11 sounds a note of

final judgment, which could grow out of the oath in v 8 and which could represent a further and final stage in the death of a city after the scenes of vv 9–10. Does v 12a continue this theme, the point being the *futility* of building up defenses against Yahweh? Or does v 12a go with 12b, examples of seemingly foolish things that no sane person would do—run horses on rocks or plow the sea with oxen?

It is no wonder that puzzles of this kind can be read in more than one way. If that were the author's intention, it would be a mistake on our part to touch them up so as to give them a single simple and transparent meaning. Are the two statements meant to be congruent, so that one may be used to help interpret the other? The riddles in Amos 3:3–6 lined up in pairs to some extent, but no two of them were exactly the same in formation or import. That this is a twin riddle is suggested by the standard parallelism of *hă-* and *'im-* in successive interrogations (not used in 3:3–6). This sequence is reversed in the possible linkage between 5:22aA and 5:25a. The parallelism of "horses"//"oxen" supports this expectation; but that is as far as it goes. Which of the components of the two riddles is the main focus of the enigma, and therefore the node in which their commonality is to be found? Plowing is not the same as running. Horses running (the verb is plural) is not like someone plowing (the verb is singular) *with* oxen. The word "rock" has no parallel in v 12aB in the MT. Assuming that this word operates equally in both lines, we could read:

> Can horses gallop on a rock?
> Can one plow [it] with oxen?

Both are ludicrous suggestions—as foolish as thinking to build fortifications that Yahweh cannot smash; or as turning justice to wormwood. Perhaps these riddles are in the same class as "pigs might fly."

Such a reading of the text as it stands gives a literal interpretation to the preposition *b-* in each of its occurrences. The result is asymmetrical. In the first riddle, horses run *on* a rock; in the second, someone plows *with* oxen. By making the prepositions do double duty, the first would mean, "Can [people] race against horses?" (compare Jer 12:5). But if that is the point, it would not make any difference where the race was held. And it is different from the idea that horses cannot run safely on a rock.

The two riddles can be made even more similar by finding something in v 12aB to match *sela'*. On the face of it the question, "Does he plow with oxen?" is inane; for obviously one does. It is usual to supply "there" (i.e., on the rock) to bring v 12aB into line with v 12aA and to facilitate the answer "No!" A solution, as simple as it is ingenious, was proposed by D. Michaelis (1772), and his emendation enjoys almost universal acceptance. He read *bbqr ym*, "Can you plow the sea with an ox?" Harper lists four objections to the proposal, none of them very weighty (1905:158). The reading of *bbqrym* as two words involves an absolutely minimal adjustment, and it gets around the difficulty that the plural of *bqr* is itself very dubious. The only other occurrence of *běqārîm*, in 2 Chr 4:3, is needed to describe the bulls that support the "sea" in Solomon's Temple; and *bqrynw* in Neh 10:37 is the result of the *plene* spelling of /ē/ in the singular, coordinated with the equally unique *ṣ'nynw*, which is likewise a pseudo-plural form due solely to *plene* spelling. *Bāqār* itself is collective, especially when used in concord with plural forms. The individualizing singular is *ben-bāqār* (Gen 18:7). The omission of the article with *yām* is of no consequence. *Yām* occurs in parallel with *selaʿ* in Isa 42:10–11. Isaiah 32:2 collocates "streams of water" with "a great rock." Note also that the emendation reveals chiasmus between these two parallels.

The intricacies of the LXX text are discussed by Rudolph (1971a:226). They have nothing to offer for the improvement of the MT.

In ancient proverbs and fables about birds and beasts, their wise behavior is usually contrasted with the foolish behavior of humans. This contrast will work better for v 12aA if the horses are running free, not being ridden or drawing a chariot. Horses know better than to run on rocks. But in v 12aB the ox (or oxen) is being used for plowing. Both could be combined in stories about simpletons who tried to have a horse race on the rocks, and the animals refused, or who tried to plow (the sea or the rock) with an ox, and the animal refused. In any case the suggestions are ridiculous, and the corresponding human behavior equally absurd.

12a. *run.* Hebrew *rûṣ;* it is commonly used of a human messenger, also of an animal. For the idiom *rwṣ b-*, cf. Joel 2:9.

12b. The structural connections between 5:7 and 6:12b and the connections of both with 5:24 have been discussed in other places. The placement of *rōʾš* and *laʿănâ* in v 12b achieves a partial chiasmus similar to that in v 12a (reconstructed). Compared with 5:7, v 12b has the same pair of words in chiasmus, but *mišpāṭ//ṣědāqâ* retain their usual sequence in all three related verses. Verse 12b develops the horticultural image a little further by adding "fruit" as the ballast variant. It also comes closer to Jeremiah's remark about eating wormwood and gall (Jer 9:14, 23:15).

When a pair of words in poetic parallelism is repeated in chiasmus, it is harder to speak about a conventional sequence. Is the unusual sequence used first to prepare for the chiasmus, or does the normal sequence come first so that the less common sequel in chiasmus alerts the reader/listener to look for a connection that may be long-range (5:7 to 6:12 in this case)? The suspense is even greater when the lead word (*laʿănâ* in 5:7) does not have its familiar parallel at all (*rōʾš*, as in Jer 9:14, 23:15; Lam 3:19). We have to wait until 6:12b for the parallel. The sequence of 6:12b is used in Deut 29:17.

But. It is likely that v 12b connects logically with v 12a as a comment on vv 8–11. It is foolish and dangerous to run horses up a cliff; but these people have achieved something even more foolish and damaging, by turning justice into wormwood.

fruit. The image of the "fruit of righteousness" (Prov 11:30), meant to be wholesome and nourishing but turned into poison, implies that the product will be eaten. While in the first place it is bitter for their victims, in the end they will be forced to eat the fruit of their own doings; hence the Woe. Compare the fruit of wisdom (Prov 8:18–19) and contrast the fruit of lies (Hos 10:13).

wormwood. In Deut 29:17, the "poisonous and bitter fruit" grows from the root of idolatry.

13. Verse 13 constitutes a double Woe composed of a single tricolon, similar in some ways to the double Woe at the beginning of the main group (6:1), and should be read as follows:

6:13	Syllables	Stresses
haśśĕmēḥîm lĕlōʾ dābār	4 + 2 + 2 = 8	3
hāʾōmĕrîm hălōʾ bĕḥozqēnû	4 + 2 + 4 = 10	3
lāqaḥnû lānû qarnāyim	3 + 2 + 2 = 7	3
Totals	25	9

[Woe to] you who are delighted over Lo-Dabar;
[woe to] you who say,
    "Have we not captured Qarnaim for ourselves by our might?"

What is clear is that the two participles are complementary and that the two cities are parallel and also combinatory. In addition, there is a single statement that emphasizes and overemphasizes the first-person pronoun (three times in three successive words: "by *our* might, *we* have seized for *ourselves*"). This last represents precisely the *hubris,* conceit, and self-satisfaction against which the great speeches of Deuteronomy constitute a severe warning. When people are preoccupied with their own achievements, their own accomplishments, then they forget the God who made the whole thing possible; cf. Deut 8:11–20, especially v 17: "And you say in your heart, 'my strength and the power of my hand have made for me all this wealth.' "

In 6:13 we should render as follows (in this paraphrase we only rearrange the elements to bring out the sense, not to recover a supposed original):

Those who rejoice about Lo-Dabar [and] Qarnaim, who say "Have we not by our own strength captured [them] for ourselves?"

The point is that they are rejoicing about the capture of both cities, boasting about the fact that they did so by their own strength and strategy. Clearly they are not rejoicing over one city by saying that they captured the other; neither are there two groups, each talking about a separate city. There is one group who rejoice by saying (they speak exultantly) that they have captured the two cities mentioned all by themselves. The verb *śmḥ* is used with the preposition *l* to express joy or exultation with respect to persons or things, and clearly we have here the exultation resulting in victory over and capture of cities. Technically *l'-dbr* is the object of *hśmḥym,* while *qrnym* is the direct object of *lqḥnw;* but it is clear that both cities must be the objects of both verbs to make sense out of the passage. Thus it becomes clear that, contrary to the arrangement of the verse in BH³ or BHS, there is nothing missing in v 13, or displaced, least of all v 6b, which belongs precisely where it is. What we have instead is an intricate, unbalanced, but artistic structure with a more subtle symmetry than we normally see. Each part opens and closes with the participle and the name of the city:

13a   *hśmḥym ll' dbr*
13b   *h'mrym . . . qrnym*

Then with telling effect the redundant first-person references are packed together in one part (the second for delayed effect), instead of being distributed between the two cola:

hlw' bḥzqnw lqḥnw lnw

This is one of the more unusual tricola in the book of Amos, or anywhere else, but it makes excellent sense as it is.

13a. *are delighted.* Several different prepositions are used with *śmḥ. Min-* (Prov 5:18) and *b-* (Deut 12:7) mean "because," and so can *'al* (1 Chr 29:9). In *byhwh* the preposition expresses appreciation; but *l-* can express hostility or malicious glee over the defeat of an enemy (Obad 12; Isa 14:8).

Lo-Dabar. The deliberate puns make it difficult to assign the words to either of the two possible meanings (see the Hebrew text below, in the COMMENT on this verse). Translations choose between them and may place the alternative in a footnote. Literally "not a thing" implies that Lo-Dabar is a nonentity anyway, and its capture no big deal. The name Qarnaim likewise plays on the meaning "horns," a symbol of strength. A similar pun could be intended in Ps 83:11, where the assonance in *dōmen la'ǎdāmâ* suggests that Adamah is a place.

Lo-Dabar is spelled in a variety of ways: *lw dbr* (2 Sam 9:4–5), *l' dbr* (2 Sam 17:27), or *ldbr* (Josh 13:26). The last citation could be another reference to the same city, which would place it in a cluster of Transjordanian towns in the territory of Gad. Jonathan's son Mephibosheth took refuge there. The reference in 2 Sam 17:27 shows that it was a power center of some significance; one of the barons of Gilead from Lo-Dabar provisioned David in Mahanayim.

13b. *Qarnaim.* The place intended is Ashtarot Qarnayim, the city of the goddess with the two horns.

COMMENT ON VERSE 13

While vv 13 and 14 are formally and syntactically distinct, they nevertheless are juxtaposed and have literary links. The prophet utters his woe against those who are happy about *lō' dābār*—a city in Transjordan (Gilead) presumably taken by Israelite forces, as indicated in the parallel passage. "You who say" in v 13b are the same people who rejoice, "Have we not captured Qarnaim for ourselves by our might?" Qarnaim (and there may be a play on the name, literally, "two horns," which is also a symbol of strength) is another city in Transjordan, apparently also captured recently by Israelite forces. By interweaving the two woes, we find the Israelites celebrating the conquest or recapture of Transjordanian cities that had been in dispute for centuries and that had been lost to Aram and others in the preceding century (cf. Hazael who oppressed Israel, 2 Kgs 13:4 and 23). According to 2 Kgs 14:23–29, Jeroboam II restored the territory of Israel from Lebo-Hamath as far as the Sea of the Arabah, and he did so in fulfillment of the words of the prophet Jonah. The self-satisfied rejoicing of the people in Amos 6:13–14 is easily understood in the light of the 2 Kings passage, especially because the territory described is the same. There is a slight difference in the wording: Amos speaks of *naḥal hā'ǎrābâ,* while Kings has the more general term *yām;* but it seems clear that the same territory is meant, the whole of the eastern region from Hamath down to the region of the Dead Sea. The conquest of these territories would evoke enthusiastic memories of the great days of David and Solomon. In light of Jonah's prophecy, the victories could be construed as a fulfillment of the divine plan and an expression of divine approval of the nation and its leaders. Amos' assessment is much less generous: there is no fulfillment of divine purposes, only selfish and self-satisfied pride are involved, and the disastrous consequences cannot be postponed for very long. We are inclined, then, to tie the territorial reference at the end of 6:14 to the woes of 6:13. The two cities named belong to the territory recaptured by Jeroboam and succinctly defined by its northern and southern boundaries (6:14). The Israelites are rejoicing over the restoration of their borders as a result of the military exploits of Jeroboam II, but that happiness will be shortlived. Yahweh, according to the prophet, is raising up a nation that will oppress Israel. As the consequence of all of their sins, in particular their arrogance, their self-righteousness, and their claim of independent and autonomous power, the kingdom will be destroyed.

The terms used evoke the Egyptian experience, primarily the oppression and enslavement, which serve as a model, symbol, and standard of all of their subsequent suffering. They also reflect the oppression imposed by many national groups during the period of the Judges from which Yahweh would deliver them from time to time. And it echoes specifically the most recent of these oppressions, inflicted by Hazael, king of Aram, in the later part of the ninth century. The new oppression will be imposed on the house of Israel in the near future. The obvious continuation, describing the limits of the expanded territory of Israel, can be justified on the grounds that the oppression will cover the entire territory; and such an interpretation can be defended. The emphasis, however, is on the people rather than on their territory. It is the people who have rejoiced about the recent expansion of their territory, and it is they who will be oppressed. The reference to the territory is more in keeping with the rejoicing over captured territories, and therefore it belongs with the opening Woe and the context of v 13. At the same time, it can be read in the immediate context as referring to the area of oppression or punishment, of which the cities just mentioned are a part. The closing phrase fits with its counterpart at the beginning of the unit (v 13a), forming an envelope, and at the same time it connects plausibly with the immediately preceding clause. So the territory in which they rejoice now will be the same in which they will suffer oppression later.

The last two verses of chap. 6 bring the whole unit, 5:7–6:14, to a close. We must consider whether 5:4–6 also belongs with this material, because it uses terms that recur in the larger unit. *Byt yśrʾl* in 5:4 recurs in 5:25 and in 6:1, and the chain is completed in 6:14; *yôsēp* also occurs in 5:6 and again in 5:15 and 6:6. The key factors are the two woes at the beginning and the judgment at the end. The Woes sum up the charges that here are depicted as excessive self-reliance, forgetfulness of Yahweh, unreflective pleasure in success, and by implication all of those faults and shortcomings indicated in other Woes. Similarly, the judgment, which is aimed directly at the house of Israel, sums up all of the threats and ominous hints about oppression. This usage is no doubt designed deliberately to evoke memories of the great original oppression in Egypt and all oppressions since, which are detailed in the books from Judges to Kings. The most recent, which may equally foreshadow the next, last, and culminative one, was that of Hazael, king of Aram, who inflicted notable damage on the body politic and economic of Israel. There is a certain irony in the linkage between the boasting over the extended territory of Israel acquired through the recent conquests (viz. "restoration" of a military nature) of Jeroboam II and the suffering that will be inflicted on the whole population through its enlarged borders.

II.B.2.c. THE FINAL THREAT (6:14)

6:14a For soon I will raise against you,
　　　　O house of Israel
　　　　　　　—Oracle of Yahweh, God of the hosts—
　　　　a nation

14b　　　　　　　　that will overpower you from the gateway of Hamath as
　　　　　　　　　　　　　　　far as the Wadi Arabah.

INTRODUCTION

This verse, with which the whole section closes, provides an adequate response to the boasters of v 13: the victories will prove evanescent and ephemeral, and soon they will suffer the fate of those over whom they are now exulting. The victors will be vanquished. So also with the people in 9:10, who similarly boast that no harm will come to them.

It is a useful rule for dating a prophetic oracle that it must have been written after the situation out of which it speaks but before events that it patently predicts. The rule is better in theory than in practice. All too often the historical allusions are too vague to permit us to say "This independently known and datable event has already occurred; he is speaking about and obviously after that occurrence, presumably soon after." Thus 6:13 was given after the capture of Lo-Dabar and Qarnaim, because the audience is addressed as though they were in the midst of celebrating the victory. Unfortunately, we have no information about these events, so the references are of little use for dating. The prophecy in v 14, by contrast, presupposes the occupation of much more territory than those victories would have secured. So why were they not celebrating that larger acquisition? At the same time, v 14 clearly forecasts that an unidentified *gôy* will "oppress" them from the entrance of Hamath to the Wadi Arabah. So that disaster has not happened yet.

Another difficulty in applying the rule is that the "prophecy" before the fulfillment of which the prediction had to be given, if it was a genuine prediction, is either so vaguely stated that we cannot be sure what to identify as its fulfillment, or else it is so clear, specific, and unequivocal that we rightly suspect it of being a *vaticinium ex eventu.* In the latter case, we must say that the prophecy (or this addition to the prophecy) must have been written after the event it so accurately predicts. Then either the whole prophecy is seen to be inauthentic or at least the editorial addition is, and that detail cannot be used for dating.

Very few if any biblical prophecies are so obviously written with the benefit of hindsight that we can categorize them as predictions after the event. We have been persuaded that there are none such in Amos, at least. Modern readers naturally associate 6:14 with the Assyrian conquests, and doubtless it is valid to see those developments as a fulfillment of Amos' prophecy. But it is very difficult to match his words with any specific details of Assyrian aggression. The language does not describe invasion as such, but "oppression" as if by an occupying power. The geographical limits set for that activity fit generally with the historical experience of the northern kingdom but not in detail. They show no awareness of the quite different fates of the northern and southern kingdoms under Assyrian occupation. In fact, it is so hard to make a match that we cannot be sure that Amos even had Assyria in mind as the *gôy.*

The argument should not be overplayed, so that every successful prediction is dismissed as a concoction after it has happened. Such skepticism is quite uncalled for. As if no prophet could ever be right in his forecast! Even if they were only guessing, they would get it right sometimes. Some prophets would be right more often than not and more often than others. They would be remembered and recorded, while the others would be rejected or forgotten. A perfect success rate was by no means required or expected, for it could always be argued that something changed the plan: the prophet interceded, the people repented, Yahweh relented. Even so, the prophets expected their predictions, which were always warnings and forecasts, to be taken seriously; and sometimes they were. But the prophet had to be prepared for a genuine prophecy to be discredited by apparent nonfulfillment, as the story of Jonah shows (cf. also Mic 3:12 and the citation and comment in Jer 26:17–19).

There is another side to this question. An unfulfilled prophecy in a book like Amos is validated as original and authentic by that very fact. For instance, we do not believe that Amos' prophecy against Amaziah and his family (7:17), which is very precise, was ever fulfilled as stated. There is no supporting evidence, and it does not fit what we know about the subsequent history of Bethel and its shrine. The latter continued to flourish in the time of Hosea, and it survived intact when Israel was conquered and Samaria captured. At that time (722 B.C.E.), the priests at Bethel were carried off, but one of them was later brought back to officiate at the temple there (2 Kgs 17:6 and 27–28). As these events took place at least forty or fifty years after the prophecy, they could hardly have concerned Amaziah or his wife and children. We have no doubt, however, that Amos said those words to Amaziah; and there is no indication that their nonfulfillment was an embarrassment to later readers.

The question of this prophecy in relation to the history of the time has already been discussed in the NOTES on Hazael and Ben-Hadad at 1:4. The relation of 6:14 to 2 Kgs 14:25 is the nub. There are several interconnected problems here. The passage in which we find the information that Jeroboam II "restored the boundary" (gĕbûl, perhaps territory—see the NOTES on 6:2) of Israel from Lebo-Hamath as far as the Sea of the Arabah, according to the word of Yahweh, God of Israel, which he spoke by the hand of his servant Jonah ben-Amittai the prophet who was from Gath-hepher, is more editorial than annalistic. The prophet Jonah is carefully identified, but the story relating the circumstances and actual wording of his prophecy is lost to knowledge. The telltale idiom dibber bĕyad, used with a named prophet or prophets in general, usually called as well "his servant" (or servants), is characteristic of the Deuteronomistic historian or school mainly responsible for compiling the Primary History. Twelve of its eighteen occurrences are found in Kings (plus two in the Pentateuch, one in Samuel, one in Isaiah, one in Jeremiah). Prophets whose work is described in this way are Moses (Exod 9:35; Num 27:23; 1 Kgs 8:53), Joshua (1 Kgs 16:34), Samuel (1 Sam 28:17); Ahijah (1 Kgs 12:15, 14:18, 15:29); Elijah (1 Kgs 17:16; 2 Kgs 9:36, 10:10); Isaiah (Isa 20:2); and Jeremiah (Jer 37:2). Jonah is the last one named by the historian. Afterward he looks back on the whole succession (2 Kgs 17:23, 21:10, 24:2). His intention is not to vindicate the prophet by showing that his word came true; rather to legitimate or justify the outcome by means of the word of the Lord, which requires no validating action. The notice in 2 Kgs 14:25 is the most elaborate and strikes almost a polemical note, denying that Yahweh ever said that he would wipe out the name of Israel from under the heavens (2 Kgs 14:27). Yet just such divine decisions to "cut off him that is shut up and him that is left at large in Israel," with reference to the dynasties of the first Jeroboam and Ahab, had been made by earlier prophets and were preserved by this historian (1 Kgs 14:10, 21:21; 2 Kgs 9:8). Deuteronomy 32:36 says that when the nation had been reduced to this condition, the Lord repented and restored their fortunes. It is emphasized in 2 Kgs 14:26 that the Lord saw how bitter was their affliction and how helpless their plight, so he saved them by the hand of Jeroboam.

This position is the exact opposite of Amos'. The historian does not explain how Israel got into the perilous state described in 2 Kgs 14:26. It sounds quite desperate, as though the calamities enumerated in Amos 4:6–11 had actually occurred, especially the fourth, total military defeat. These plagues were intended to bring Israel to repentance, and they failed completely to achieve the result. The Lord had already repented (Amos 7:3, 6) in mitigating the severity of these plagues and limiting their duration. Finally he declared he would never repent again (7:8, 8:2; and the opening words of the eight oracles in chaps. 1–2 make the same affirmation). So the situation in which Amos says that the Lord would *never* repent is precisely the one in which somebody could quote Deut 32:36 as an assurance that the Lord had repented and raised up a savior, in this case Jeroboam II. Because his successful military action consisted in restoring the frontiers of Israel from Lebo-Hamath to the Sea of the Arabah, this recapture of lost territories would be an impressive sign of divine favor, in contrast with the miserable conditions described in 2 Kgs 14:26. If Amos' prophecy of 6:14 had been fulfilled, it would have created just such a situation. The developments described in 2 Kgs 14:25–27 would then represent a *later turn of events,* that is to say, later than the fulfillment of 6:14.

Amos also predicted that Yahweh would raise up a *gôy* that would oppress the house of Israel over the full range of its traditional territory, in wording almost identical with that used in 2 Kgs 14:25. There are several issues raised by Amos 6:14. We have presented arguments in several places in this book that most if not all of Amos' oracles belong to the decade 780–770 B.C.E., and that the situation implied by the language of chaps. 1–2 matches the politics of the region during that same period. There is no indication in those oracles that Israel has any power or even presence in Transjordan. On the contrary, all of the states in the region—Aram, Ammon, Moab, Edom—are active militarily.

The limited success of Jehoash against Ben-Hadad, and the transitory success of Amaziah against Edom (see NOTES on 1:11) imply loss of Israelite territory in Transjordan, with both Ammon and Aram involved in an invasion of Gilead (1:3, 13). Amos speaks of a *gôy,* as if there were only one; but he also says that *"they* will oppress you" over the entire region. It is doubtful that any one nation could operate with full freedom over the territory named in the first half of the eighth century B.C.E., unless it be Aram. Everybody claimed the region as his own, and Aramaean interests extended as far as Elath (2 Kgs 16:6). The latter action was clearly a countermove to Uzziah's capture of Elath, because the expulsion of Judeans is expressly mentioned; but it happened much too late to provide the setting for Amos 6:14 and 2 Kgs 14:25. In fact it does not fit at all, for Israel, far from being "oppressed" by this campaign, was a partner in it. Indeed, as we have argued at some length in the essay on Amos' geopolitical terminology (in the INTRODUCTION), 6:14 makes sense only if the "house of Israel" there refers to all Israelites, members of both of the kingdoms of the day.

We can, then, identify the fulfillment of Amos 6:14 with a successful counterattack against Israel and Judah by the Aramaeans, assisted by other states, including Edom (*qere* of 2 Kgs 16:6, strongly supported by the *plene* spelling of *ô*, even in *kethib*), hence the plural verb *lḥṣw*. *Gôy* is usually in concord with singular pronouns, adjectives, and verbs. Followed by the plural verb as here, it is either collective or distributive. This grammatical argument cannot be pressed, however, for Amos occasionally uses collective nouns with plural verbs—*wglw ʿm-ʾrm* (1:5), *wʾbdw šʾryt plštym* (1:8).

It has always been taken as obvious that the *gôy* of 6:14 is Assyria (Harper 1905:157 ["of course"]; Edghill and Cooke 1926:68 ["of course"]; Keil and Delitzsch 1986:10:1.304; Mays 1969:123 ["clear candidate"]); Rudolph 1971a:228 ["no one can deny"]). The identification, however, is far from self-evident. To say the least, the word *gôy* is very vague. It could be anyone. The prophecy does not predict total invasion (Rudolph 1971a:228) but oppression or harassment. As a prediction of what the Assyrians eventually did, it is wide of the mark, and, by the same token, it is a failure as a *vaticinium ex eventu*. Until 732 B.C.E. the region in question had not been "oppressed" by Assyria. The language of Amos 6:14 shows that Israel and Judah were to be oppressed *together*. In the late 730s, Judah under Ahaz (along with Ashkelon, Moab, Ammon, and Edom) was a voluntary tributary of Assyria in order to secure help against Pekah and Rezin. This situation bears no resemblance at all to the language of Amos 6:14.

Another observation worth making is that the territory bracketed by Lebo-Hamath and the Wadi Arabah, while it might remind us of Genesis 14, never coincided with an Assyrian campaign or even with Assyrian interests. With the aim of eventually invading and conquering Egypt, as well as for good strategical reasons, the Assyrians preferred to strike down the western corridor. Philistia was of more significance to them than southern Transjordan. Wolff (1977:289) takes seriously the doubts expressed by E. Meyer about Assyria as the *gôy* and refrains from any identification (cf. ibid. 266). But he rules out the Aramaeans on the grounds that they "had just been defeated" (ibid. 289). Presumably he has Amos 6:13 in mind. Whether the scale of those victories implies the reduction of Aram to impotence is another matter (see the NOTES on v 13).

The reports of Jehoash's three victories over the Aramaeans (details not given), his recovery of cities (names not given), and the involvement of Elisha (2 Kgs 13:14–25) are not part of the formal annals of Jehoash (2 Kgs 13:10–13), which report only his war with Amaziah. They are an independent tradition appended to the annals. Whatever the scale of Jehoash's successes against Aram (and it is admitted that they were limited), the fact that Jeroboam II had to restore the frontier of Israel (2 Kgs 14:25) all over again shows that losses had been sustained. The claim often made that 2 Kgs 13:24–25 and 14:25–28 record "military successes through which Jeroboam II rounded out the victories of his father Joash" (Wolff 1977:89) is not at all evident and depends on dates, especially dates for Amos, that are not necessarily convincing.

The language used in Amos 6:14, *hinneh* + participle, points to an incipient future, if not to events already in train. Language like this would be appropriate for Assyria after the rise of Tiglath-pileser III, but less appropriate in the two or three decades before his accession.

Without making excessive claims regarding a problem that may be insoluble, we call attention to the essays in the INTRODUCTION on the contents of the book of Amos, and on the phases in the prophet's life, which show that chaps. 5–6 come earlier in time than chaps. 1–2, so that the situation in chaps. 1–2, with its recent memories of terrible events in Transjordan involving atrocities committed by all of the countries in that region, could be the sequel and result of the oppression predicted in 6:14, thus identifying this verse as one of the earliest of Amos' oracles. The position argued in 2 Kgs 14:25–27 reflects an even later development, later than anything to be found in the book of Amos. We can go farther and state that the point of view expressed in 2 Kgs 14:25–27 is so strongly opposed to Amos' assessment of Jeroboam II (regardless of the secondary question of whether Amos 6:14 is an adverse reaction to the passage in Kings, or vice versa), that the idea that the book of Amos received its final redaction at the hand of Deuteronomistic editors (Wolff 1977:112–13) seems self-contradictory. As far as dating is concerned, the final edition of Kings is not earlier than the sixth century B.C.E., even though material in it—including, doubtless, the detail about Jonah found in 2 Kgs 14:25–27—goes back to earlier sources or traditions. The theological comment bears the marks of late redaction. The same cannot be said about Amos 6:14, which is not editorial.

The thesis that Amos 6:14 represents polemic against 2 Kgs 14:25 (Amos versus Jonah) was worked out by Eissfeldt (1968:140). We suggest the opposite: 2 Kgs 14:25–27 hails the achievements of Jeroboam II as canceling and condemning the words of Amos as found in Amos 6:14 and, indeed, the position taken by Amos throughout his book.

The stage is now set for a new section of the book, the unit on the visions that extends from 7:1 to 9:6 (at least) and perhaps beyond. It may be noted that the proper close for the present unit would be *n'm yhwh 'lhy ṣb'wt* in v 14a, which seems to be out of place where it is, between *byt yśr'l* and *gwy*. It would fit better at the end of the verse. We should also bear in mind that such refrains and formulas do not always come where they are expected and that, in some cases at least, the displacement may be deliberate.

COMMENT

At various places in this study, and more particularly in the essay on the life of Amos, we have tried to link the five visions, each marking a stage or moment in the development of Yahweh's changing attitudes, with Amos' messages and with the people's response. Chapters 5–6 go with the first pair of visions, and, as far as we can make finer distinctions and correlations, chap. 6 with its greater intensity of condemnation and diminished exhortation to repentance marks the end of the period of remission and probation.

At the same time, we recognized that the messages in their preserved form are not necessarily the same as they were when first delivered. We postulate that the visions enabled Amos to report to the people that each catastrophe as it came was a fresh installment from God of escalating wrath, of actions that were either destructive judgments or corrective disciplines, depending on how they took them. If they had repented, they would have affirmed the plagues as timely warning and samples of worse to come. Whatever Amos might have said when the plagues were going on has not been preserved. We can suppose that when the second plague followed the first, the message would include a reminder that they had missed the first opportunity, as in the words of 4:6. These messages would have expanded cumulatively, plague by plague, until the series was complete and all could be presented in retrospect (4:6–11).

The present arrangement of chaps. 1–6 represents a similar accumulation on an even larger scale. The earlier messages of chaps. 3–4 (associated with the third vision) were attached to the latest oracles (chaps. 1–2, associated with the fourth vision). They were followed by the even earlier messages of chaps. 5–6, associated with the first pair of visions. The extensive review of Amos' past career and summary of his messages during the earlier phases of his work served to justify the severity and finality of the oracles in chaps. 1–2, which are first in the book but the last in time of chaps. 1–6. The present arrangement has a logical function, amounting to Amos' *apologia pro vita sua.*

Viewed in this perspective, the whole of chaps. 1–6 could be the great final speech given by Amos at Bethel and evoking Amaziah's drastic response. At least it could be a literary presentation toward the end of his career of the materials of Amos' most developed and comprehensive messages. If that is so, it would not be surprising if chaps. 5–6 show marks of revision in the light of the outcome, the end of the matter as found in chaps. 1–2. For the most part chaps. 5–6 contain condemnation (in Woes) and calls to repentance. But at one or two places judgment is declared in absolute terms, more in keeping with chaps. 1–2. The conclusion of chap. 6 (vv 11–14) certainly sounds that way. That oracle could equally well belong to what we have called Phase Two. The command to smash the houses (6:11) could be another aspect of the earthquake that will also demolish the temple (9:1; cf. 3:13–15). Deploying an unidentified nation (6:14) could be the last and worst of a series of military disasters, of which they already had received a foretaste in the plague of Phase One (4:10). This outcome, threatened in 5:3, plays a prominent role in the oracles against the nations in chaps. 1–2, which culminate in 2:14–16; and it comes to final fruition in 9:10. The wording of 6:14 thus could be influenced by the final perspective of the whole book.

Concluding Comment on The Book of Woes

We have already observed that various oracles reflect various stages or phases in the message of the prophet or of his book. The literary presentation is logically organized but may be less compelling with regard to the original sequence or chronology. Nevertheless, we have distinguished four phases in the prophet's message, determined largely by reference to the data in the book itself and specifically the biographical and autobiographical information in chap. 7 and elsewhere. These phases may be summarized as follows.

Phase One. There is an initial period of warning, while there is still a chance to repent and be spared. The phase is defined by the first two visions and such utterances as may convey the central idea. These exhortations, along with 5:21–25 (at least), belong to Phase One of the prophetic denunciations of sinful actions documented here and elsewhere, which have attracted divine attention and concern and which will bring on a verdict of guilty and ultimately an irreversible judgment. In view of the first two visions, however, there may still be time and opportunity for a change, for a remission or relenting, and some hope of staving off disaster and reestablishing a right relation between God and his people. The commitment to practice *mišpāṭ* and *ṣĕdāqâ* is the key to the situation: the failure to meet these standards is the cause of the present crisis and its imminent, ominous threats. A reversal of spirit and a new dedication to these fundamental principles of divine order and human behavior could radically alter the present situation and the future prospects. There is relatively little material that can be assigned to this phase, but it must have been essential to the prophet and for his career.

Phase Two. The main phase is reflected by the second pair of visions and especially the biographical sketch sandwiched between them. The insertion shows exactly how this final, irreversible decision to destroy the kingdom (particularly the north, but Judah is not entirely overlooked) and to take the people captive was forced on Yahweh. The principal oracular utterance reflecting this phase is the Great Set Speech of chaps. 1–2. The decision has been made. The whole area, but Judah and Israel in particular, is doomed.

It is essential to an understanding of the phases, the prophet's circumstances, and the historical and chronological associations that we date this great oracle. The main point seems to be that all eight nations are autonomous entities, each free to make decisions and hence responsible to the supreme divine Lord for its actions, past and present. Because both Jeroboam and Uzziah are credited with conquests that would bring one or more of these territories under the sway of either of these nations, we must consider whether the opening oracle must therefore be dated before the conquests of either Jeroboam or Uzziah. We cannot date any of them precisely, but they are more likely to have been started early in their reigns rather than late, which would put us back in the decades of the 780s and 770s (roughly from 780 to 770 or from 785 to 765). In other words, Amos' view of the northern kingdom (and probably the south) had been fixed long before anything had happened: neither the expansion by conquest nor certainly the later tragic loss of nationhood and territory is evident in his words. There is good reason to believe that Amos' solemn warnings and conditional predictions of disaster were almost immediately invalidated by a course of events that seemed to prove the opposite, namely, success on every side. This development discredited the prophet long before circumstances altered, vindicating Amaziah and others like him—doubtless the majority—who considered Amos not only seditious but blasphemous. Already before anything happened, Amos was convinced that an unalterable judgment had been pronounced and that in only a short time disaster would strike. But the subsequent military victories favored prophets such as Jonah, whose *"shalom* prophecies" were fully realized. We can assume much the same in Judah, with the words of Zechariah, counselor to the king (Uzziah), being fully vindicated by the extraordinary successes of the king in military and diplomatic forays. The opening oracle (chaps. 1–2) requires a different political situation, one that obtained before the conquering armies of Jeroboam and Uzziah set forth against their neighbors. That time must be early in the reigns of both monarchs, but belongs to Phase Two of the prophet's ministry.

The passage now under consideration—The Book of Woes (chaps. 5–6) —in the opinion of many scholars reflects the later situation, in which the expansion is complete and the work of both kings largely accomplished. We may have to make rather fine distinctions in order to pinpoint the moment that the prophecies were uttered and the prevailing conditions.

If we take the woes together from 5:7 through 6:13, we note that the main theme is the misreading of the signs and the messages of God by those in both capitals, who are celebrating victories and congratulating themselves on the fulfillment of the promises of the covenant. The mention of Lo-Dabar and Qarnaim suggests that the process of conquest, at least in the north, has only begun, for these places are in Transjordan, probably in territory traditionally occupied by Israel (= Lo-Dabar) or on the border of such land (apparently Qarnaim, an Aramaean city). Nothing is said here (in 6:13) of Judahite campaigns or successes, and it seems plausible to date the activities of Uzziah as beginning somewhat later than those of Jeroboam. So the Woes, while undated in relation to the opening oracle (chaps. 1–2), seem to come shortly after the initial victories of Jeroboam II. We combine the Woes and see the celebration in 6:1–6 as reflecting the victories in 6:13, and the "rejoicing" in 6:13 as corresponding to the more elaborate description in 6:1–6, especially vv 3–6. It is possible, however, that the earlier unit reflects a later stage in which the conquests are further advanced; but about such an inference there are numerous points or questions to be discussed.

We note that the concluding verse (6:14) describes the retribution to be inflicted by Yahweh as covering the whole territory from Lebo-Hamath to the Wadi Arabah. This statement must come after the main conquests of Jeroboam (2 Kings 14:25), a later stage than that indicated by the celebrations reflected in the woes as such. It is possible to recognize a midpoint in the sequence because nothing is said specifically about the capture of Damascus and Hamath (itself) in Amos, while they are mentioned in 2 Kings. Because the conquered territory is limited on the north to Lebo-Hamath in both Amos 6 and 2 Kgs 14:25, it is reasonable to suppose that Damascus had not yet been taken over by Israel. Because nothing has been said about Judahite conquests, although we must assume some activity to justify the luxuriating in Zion, we may suppose that Uzziah's moves, especially in the southwest, have also just begun (cf. 2 Chronicles 26). A difficulty confronts us in 6:2, which seems to be extraneous to the list of woes though inserted deliberately as a challenge to those who are taking their ease in Zion and in Samaria. They are told to travel to or beyond the borders of their own countries and observe three city-states, with the idea of comparing them with their own states, Israel and Judah. As the text stands the intention is not to elevate one group over the other or to denigrate one as inferior to the other but to indicate that they are not better or worse than the others: "Are you better than these kingdoms? Or is their territory greater than yours?" (Amos 6:2) Whatever minor variations there may be, basically they are all regarded as being on an even footing; and the point of the comparison is that all are vulnerable and will ultimately share the same destiny—defeat, capture, and loss of independence by being incorporated into somebody's empire. The main question is whether the three city-states—Calneh, Great Hamath, and Gath of the Philistines—are still standing at the time of the oracles, or whether they have been captured or destroyed. If the latter, then it would appear that the words come from the time of the Assyrian incursions of 738–734, when Tiglath-pileser III overran just the territories that are mentioned here. But it is to be observed also that Jeroboam is credited with the capture of Hamath (not just Lebo-Hamath, already discussed) and that Uzziah is credited with "breaking down the wall of Gath"—so we have the further problem of deciding which of these conquests or captures the prophet or his editor has in mind. Of Calneh we know only about the capture by Tiglath-pileser III, but it is at least possible that Jeroboam conducted a campaign in that area too along with his invasions of Hamath and Damascus. Wolff maintains that only the conquests of Tiglath-pileser III can be considered, presumably disregarding the evidence of Kings and Chronicles, especially the latter. But then he dismisses the references to Zion and Judah as secondary.

We may now summarize the position. The main point is to grasp 6:2 as an integral part of 6:1–6 or, more particularly, of 6:1–3. We cannot talk here of the possible difference between the original oral presentation by the prophet and the subsequent edited form of the same oracle. Nevertheless, it is reasonable to suppose that some time elapsed between the one and the other, and that the second written form is not only what we have, but reflects changes that were made by the prophet himself or his editor. So the original form of the oracle, in view of its structure, may have omitted v 2, which varies significantly from the material included in the others. As we have tried to show, 6:1 matches well with 6:3–6, though there is a significant variation in the pattern because the first two woes are lumped together, with the corresponding second colons filling out the Woe initiated in the first colon of each Woe. In v 1 we have the initial colon of the first Woe followed by that of the second Woe, and only then is the second colon of each added as a pair. If the others are symbolized by a pattern a/b (e.g., 3ab, 4aA and B, 4bA and B, etc.), the first verse can be described as follows: 1aA/1aB followed by 1bA and 1bB, in which 1aA is matched with 1bA and 1aB with 1bB. Together they form a combination in which Judah and Israel are bound together as the $r\check{s}yt$ $hgwym$ (the first of the nations). Although v 2 may have been added when the oracle was set down, it was intended as a direct comment on v 1 and must be read and interpreted in the light of its current (and original) context.

In 6:1–7 we have the main group of Woes, already described and analyzed structurally. It is part of a larger grouping dispersed through the book, in particular through chaps. 5–6. We have another specific Woe addressed to one group in 5:18–20 (where we seem to have another intrusion, a comparison with local experience and the risks and uncertainties of village life—see the COMMENT). While the genre can be extended back to 5:7 (and perhaps elsewhere), which lacks the word itself (*hôy*) but otherwise has the genre's necessary characteristics, it is not necessary to supply the word, as suggested in BH³ and BHS, but rather to understand it, as it is used only twice in the entire book. A further observation may be made: the single use in 6:1–7 may strengthen the view that the prophet has in mind essentially a single group of people (or in this case the two groups specified in v 1 and directly governed by the initial *hôy*) and that all the other clauses beginning with participles refer to the same people rather than to separate and distinct groups. It seems obvious that the people described as eating and drinking, as reclining and improvising on musical instruments, are all participants in the same noisy banquet celebrating the recent victories, though individually they may not have engaged in all of the activities described.

The same can be said for the people addressed in the Woes generally. The prophet has targeted the same group with minor variations and eight major overlaps, specifying different aspects of the group as a whole or identifying smaller units within the group for special condemnation. In an envelope construction the initial Woe (5:7) is repeated in slightly different language, not precisely in the same form but as a continuation and summation of the basic charge against the group, the perversion of justice (6:12). This combination defines the major arena for the Woes, although the echo of 5:8 is in 6:12, and the final pair of Woes occurs in 6:13. The slight reversal at the end was occasioned probably by the linking of the last Woes (6:13) with the conclusion of the whole unit in 6:14. Thus there was a practical problem in tying up the various threads that come together at the end of both smaller and larger units.

The argument would then be that the target is the same throughout, and that the dual identification in 5:7 and 6:12 focuses attention (through repetition) on the leadership, on the one hand the military-political complex and no doubt on the other hand the ecclesiastical authorities, all bound together by the monarchy and more mundane ties of kinship, wealth, and common interest. These people are extremely eager and anxious for the Day of Yahweh to come, being confident that recent days of victory and revelry are a foretaste of greater blessings and celebrations ahead. They are, however, actually rushing headlong toward a day of a different sort—not the *yôm ṭôb* of Yahweh's salvation but the *yôm rāʿ* of his ultimate judgment. The day that is darkness and not light (5:18, 20) is also the day of disaster and tragedy. Finally, we can link the rejoicing and boasting of the leaders in 6:13 (who rejoice in and boast about the victories at Lo-Dabar and Qarnaim) with the opulent celebrations described in 6:1–7, especially 6:4–6.

Taking everything together, we have a picture of self-satisfaction and complacency along with excessive celebration. Hosea and Isaiah describe the drunken orgies of the leadership, especially in the northern kingdom, which are also the subject of Amos' condemnation (if not the same people and the same events, they belong to the same persistent and ongoing tradition).

In placing the Woes in their proper historical and social context, we wish to make two points.

1. The prophet's attitude and approach are the same as what is expressed vividly in the Great Set Speech (chaps. 1–2). This major statement condemns all of the nations, using identical language for the threatened and now irreversible judgment against them. If the language concerning Israel differs, it is only to emphasize even more strongly that not only will Israel not escape this international judgment, but it will be dealt with even more severely because of its special relationship with deity. The same view is expressed in 9:7, in which the essential equality before God and the equivalence in the treatment meted out to the several nations are affirmed. The same idea is articulated in 6:2, where a direct comparison is made with several kingdoms and the implied, actually required, answer to the implied question—are you better and bigger or smaller or worse, or is there any consequential difference between Israel and other nations of similar size and location?—is "No."

2. The other factor is the historical setting and the place in the sequential pattern of Amos' oracles that the Woes hold. In other words, where in the chronological framework of Amos' oracles do they belong? Our proposal is that, whereas the great utterance at the beginning of the book belongs in Phase Two of Amos' message, it comes before the great battles and victories of Jeroboam and certainly before he took over territories belonging to some of the nations listed in chaps. 1–2. In chaps. 5–6 the setting for the Woes involves the rejoicing and celebration after initial victories on the part of Israel (and Judah?) but before the completion of the campaigns of restoration on the part of Jeroboam and Uzziah. These initial victories at Lo-Dabar and Qarnaim were achieved in areas long claimed by Israel or bordering on Israelite territory, and hence must reflect an early phase of the campaign. There are no explicit references to Judahite victories, but some must be presumed, to account for the euphoria of the leadership in Jerusalem. Because the first recorded victory of Uzziah was at Gath (2 Chr 26:6), which is precisely the city mentioned in 6:2, and because Gath was still standing when that verse was uttered (or written), therefore the period reflected in the Woes is near the beginning of the campaigns. The passage at the end of chap. 6 (v 14) reflects a somewhat later stage, when Jeroboam's major campaigns were completed but apparently before his additional conquest of Damascus and Hamath. Lebo-Hamath is a different city, apparently on the border of the kingdom, which serves as the gateway

to Greater Hamath. Its mention in Amos 6:14 signifies that while the traditional borders of Israel on the east had been restored, the additional victories over and conquests of Damascus and Hamath had not yet taken place, or perhaps that they were ephemeral raids and only temporary acquisitions.

Now we are ready to consider the statements in 6:1–2. In v 1 it is to be noted that the prepositional phrases are not the objects of the respective participial forms, or at least their verbal force, but rather qualify the nominal elements. To bring out this point we may render as follows:

> Woe to you who luxuriate in Zion
> and to you who feel secure in Mount Samaria

The descriptive nouns or participles are complementary and should be combined to describe the mood of relaxed self- (or over-) confidence that pervades both cities, or at least their leadership, because of these recent victories.

The next bicolon may be rendered as follows:

> The notables of the foremost of the nations!
> who have come for themselves to the house of Israel.

The reference is to the leadership of the two nations, here treated as a single entity because of their association in the past during the great events of Exodus from Egypt and settlement in Canaan. We would like to find an implication in the verb $wb^{\circ}w$ and the associated pronominal phrase (*lāhem*), which serves as an ethical dative or dative of advantage, that these leaders are going to Bethel to celebrate the victories achieved against their foes. The clause remains difficult and obscure, but the structure of these Woes indicates that the subject of the verbal forms is the same throughout, which seems to be the case here (cf. the INTRODUCTION for II.B.).

It is precisely these leaders who are then told to "cross over to Calneh," to "go to Great(er) Hamath," and to "go down to Gath of the Philistines" and observe (as in chap. 3). Just what it is they are to look at is not made clear immediately, but whatever content there may be must be found in the sentence itself. In general the purpose is for those told to go to learn something during the projected travels. If they go and look they will find out something. What? The answer is not so easily derived, though we believe it is in the following words. The basic lesson, as we have already stated, is that Israel is not essentially different from these other nations and therefore can expect to share a similar destiny. But why these three nations, and what makes them important at this time? The usual answer, as for example in Wolff's standard commentary, is that the visitors will learn an important lesson by visiting these places because, one and all, the cities have been captured, their armies defeated, and their walls breached. Just as Jeremiah instructs the people of Judah and Jerusalem to go to Shiloh to see the ruins of the house of God in order to learn something about the vulnerability of their own temple, so it is argued that the lesson for Israelites and Judahites to learn is that their own capital cities can, may, and will suffer the same fate as these kingdoms, which have been overrun and their cities destroyed. The line of argument is impressive, and the fact that the cities mentioned were all captured along with dozens of others by Tiglath-pileser III (738–734) makes the case all the more so. It is also perfectly possible that Amos was still alive at that date and personally supervised the organization of the material to emphasize this point. It is equally possible that it is the insertion in the work by an editor concerned about the situation in the 730s rather than in the 750s or earlier.

What can be made of this argument? It is both plausible and persuasive, but is it really the point of v 2, and does v 2 imply or presume that the cities up for comparison have been destroyed or captured, or only that the fate in store for them will also be that of Jerusalem and Samaria? Thus we are convinced that v 2 makes the point that the cities, all five of them, are in the same situation and may well experience the same destiny, but that what may happen has not yet come to pass, and therefore Amos' statement precedes the capture or destruction of any of them.

There are other possibilities. There is the apparently undeniable fact that Tiglath-pileser III captured all three cities in the space of a few years (738–734), and it fits with the general idea that Amos or a successor (more likely the latter) is urging the listeners to go to those cities to see what happens, can happen, or better still has happened to states that are neither better nor worse, larger nor smaller than Israel (or Judah). The ruined cities would provide vivid and convincing evidence that the leaders of Judah and Israel should be less smug and complacent about their own condition and should be alert to the parallel cases of disaster. What has happened to the three mentioned can and will happen to the two being addressed. The basic problem with this position is that the text neither states nor implies that the cities in question have been destroyed. That notion is added to the text by hindsight and a certain specious logic. The only explanation we have for the directive to go and see these places is the set of rhetorical questions that follows and offers a comparison of Zion and Samaria with the three. As the comparison in its present form implies strongly that there is no significant difference between the group of three and the group of two, it alone indicates that they share a common status.

If one group were captured or destroyed and the other not, the glaring difference would spoil the comparison unless one were to spell out that the comparison was a progressive one: you used to be alike, now some malign destiny has overcome the three, so if the analogy holds, the two will suffer the same fate as the three. But not only is this scenario not spelled out, the normal mode of comparison used signifies that the three and the two share a common status. The question is clearly, "Are you better than these kingdoms?" referring to Jerusalem and Samaria on the one hand and to the group of three on the other. The required answer is "No!" But the reverse, namely, that they are better than you, is not required or even implied. The corresponding question would be, "Are they better than you?" to which the answer would also be "No!" This point is confirmed by the following question, "Is their border greater than your border (or territory)?" to which the required answer, again, is "No!"

In spite of the common proposal to emend the text of the second question to read along the same lines as the first, we agree with Wolff in resisting the idea. The emendation is based on the view that the prophet is affirming the contrary of the question: that the "No" to the question of goodness and bigness implies the opposite, namely, that the other nations are both better and bigger. But that inference is highly questionable. The point of the second question is to provide a balance to the first and to show exactly where the prophet's thought lies—in the middle. The two questions in fact form a kind of merismus, because taken together they imply two others and thus cover the full range of assessments. All of the questions require a negative response, and the end result is an equivalence: Judah and Israel have the same standing as the other three. Without expecting precision in such a matter, the status and condition of the cities are roughly the same, and hence comparisons are legitimate. If the purpose of the statement is to assert equivalence, then the natural inference is that the cities are truly equivalent; and to claim that some are destroyed while others are flourishing is to offer an apparent contradiction to that assertion. The real point the prophet is making is that all of the cities are vulnerable and subject to judgment and destruction, even though they currently enjoy prosperity or feel secure. A message of this kind is rather subtle and might be lost on the inhabitants of Israel and Judah, as doubtless it was. But fifty years later a message that concerned cities in ruins would hardly be needed for the inhabitants of Samaria and Judah, which had suffered severe depredation by that time from a variety of invaders and hardly needed to be reminded that their position was precarious. They understood it full well, and the question was how to shore up the defenses and how to survive in the midst of such great peril.

The question may be asked why Amos picked these three cities out of many, if in fact they were thriving along with many others; and is it not curious that these three were in fact captured or destroyed by Tiglath-pileser III? One might as well ask why these three were chosen as examples of captured cities when in fact there were so many others to choose from in the days of Tiglath-pileser's conquests. Thus in the course of events the status of the three cities (and of all five in fact) would not vary greatly, and differences in destiny would only be a matter of time and sequence, or of some special circumstance (such as Jerusalem's miraculous escape from destruction in 701 B.C.E.). Hence present conditions would hardly distinguish the three from many others at either period, that of Amos or that of Tiglath-pileser III.

There is another curious point: two of the three cities apparently were captured or destroyed by the armies of Israel (Hamath) and Judah (Gath of the Philistines). Long before Tiglath-pileser was on the scene, these cities could have been used as examples of divine punishment by the prophet, had that been his objective. But what of Calneh, about which we know very little apart from its capture by Tiglath-pileser III and its destruction at a still later date by Sargon II? In view of these complications, the best conclusions are either that all three were standing and thriving or that all three were captured and destroyed. If we assume that the words are those of Amos and belong in the immediate context, then the former solution will carry weight; whereas if we regard 6:2 as a later interpolation, then the latter will have greater merit. But the plain meaning of the passage supports the former interpretation.

Then why would Amos have chosen these three cities? Ultimately for the same reason that Tiglath-pileser III did: they occupied important strategic positions in the area of all of those nations. From Amos' point of view they were particularly vulnerable or could be expected to fall before the attacks came against Israel and Judah, so they could and would serve as object lessons. Perhaps their earlier history was characterized by violent onslaughts, bitter sieges, and destructive conquests. Their location, both generally and in relation to Israel, made Hamath and Gath logical candidates; while Calneh remains a puzzle, though its proximity to Hamath (along with other Aramaean cities) may have suggested its name. An invader from the northeast would sweep across the Fertile Crescent, attacking and capturing those cities on his way down to Egypt—the actual route of the Assyrian armies not only in the eighth century but also earlier, in the ninth century. So there was ample precedent for similar choice by marauding and invading kings and prescient prophets. And it is not surprising that Israel and Judah should reach out to attack and destroy the cities just beyond their borders. Little love was lost between neighboring states in the Near East, and when opportunity presented itself it was seized. As we have seen, both Jeroboam and Uzziah were encouraged and abetted by nationalistic men of God. They took full advantage of favorable circumstances to advance their causes, subdue and annex territories that bordered on their own and could be claimed for Israel or Judah on the basis of some text or tradition. For Judah the Philistine territories were always both an attraction and a threat, and there were good reasons to attempt to recover them or at least to neutralize the enemy in them, especially as attacks against the land of Judah could be expected from that quarter. The complex history of relations between Philistia and Judah could offer justification for attacks and invasion from either against the other at any time. But it was probably more of a surprise to Amos than he would have wished, to see his implied prediction about Gath fulfilled at least in part by the very people who were the target of his condemnation: the leaders of Judah. No doubt the same should be said of Hamath and Israel. While it was certain that Hamath was under judgment, it doubtless did not figure in his thinking that Israel would be the instrument of that capture, especially because such a turn of events would only strengthen the self-assurance and complacency of the winners. Any idea of comparing victorious Israel with defeated Hamath would be lost on the winners, as also the suggested comparison of Judah with Gath. This development alone makes it unlikely that Amos was talking about defeated city-states when he urged the leaders of Judah and Israel to visit those cities.

No doubt these startling events were a problem and an obstacle for the prophet. If we are right in our reconstruction, the main speech in chaps. 1–2 and the Woe series in chaps. 5–6 were presented to an unsuspecting nation not only when things generally were quiet and peaceful but on the eve of coordinated ambitious military campaigns on the part of the two rulers early in their reigns, and when an era of success, prosperity, and security such as had not been seen since the storied days of David and Solomon would ensue. The oracles in chaps. 1–2 only make sense before the conquests of Jeroboam and Uzziah, and the same can be said for the Woe oracles in chaps. 5–6.

After these violent denunciations, what followed was almost the exact opposite of what could have been expected by Amos and by those who heeded his words. The successes of Jeroboam especially and Uzziah as well might fulfill in part the actual words of the prophet concerning some of the other nations, but he could hardly have intended or expected any such outcome.

Considering all of the circumstances of his call and his questionable status as a prophet, as well as the experiences already undergone or yet in store, Amos must have been in a very difficult position during these years, when everything seemed to go the other way. Just where the episode with Amaziah fits into the picture is not clear, but it would seem that in the career of Amos and at least during Phases One through Three of the messages contained in the book, little if anything occurred to validate the prophet's ominous message. We gain an insight into the prophet's character to note that he endured the attacks and persecution of the ruling elite. His oracles, which were the source and at the root of his troubles, were per-

ceived as classical misstatements of the case. Far from being the words of
Yahweh they were seen and heard as merely the peevish remarks of an
alienated countryman, who could not bear to join in the general celebrations not only of the achievement of victory and peace but also in anticipation of even better times to come. It is fairly easy to read the book of Amos
in the light of the cataclysmic events of the late eighth century and to
observe how correct he was. But the oracles must be considered in their
own time and context and in the light of the circumstances of the man who
launched the divine thunderbolts when the land was at peace and enjoying
unusual prosperity—when, as almost a direct response and consequence of
his words, victories increased, borders were expanded, and the words of
rival prophets were being amply fulfilled.

We now turn to the Woes as a group to see whether some structural
patterns and symmetries can be derived from the material in its present
arrangement. If we view the groups of Woes as a whole in chaps. 5–6 (there
may be a few others scattered through the book), we can make the following observations.

The two groups of Woes form two concentric and interlocking rings, as
follows: first, 5:7 and 6:12. Here the repetition of theme and actual words
makes it certain that together they form a single Woe, the structure of
which is very much like that of the next Woe, which is found in 5:18–20. In
both cases the essential content is repeated at beginning and end, while in
the middle there is an appropriate wisdom saying that can be tied to the
central thought but derives from popular wisdom motifs. This is what they
look like:

		Syllables	
5:7	*hahōpĕkîm lĕlaʿănâ mišpāṭ*	$4 + 3 + 2 = 9$	$\Big\}$ 18
	ûṣĕdāqâ lāʾāreṣ hinnîḥû	$4 + 2 + 3 = 9$	
6:12	*hayĕrūṣûn basselaʿ sûsîm*	$4 + 2 + 2 = 8$	$\Big\}$ 15
	ʾim-yaḥărôš babbāqār yām	$1 + 2 + 3 + 1 = 7$	
	kî-hăpaktem lĕrōʾš mišpāṭ	$1 + 3 + 2 + 2 = 8$	$\Big\}$ 17
	ûpĕrî ṣĕdāqâ lĕlaʿănâ	$3 + 3 + 3 = 9$	

If we regard these clauses as a unit, then the wisdom saying sandwiched
between the two parts of the Woe can be regarded as an interpretive comment. It would be anyway, in view of its direct association with 6:12b. No
one does the absurd things recorded in 12a; but the leadership has done

something even more egregious, namely, to transform justice and righteous-ness into wormwood and gall.

Because 5:7 and 6:12b are so similar, it may be worthwhile to examine again not only the similarities, which are obvious, but the differences.

From 6:12b it is clear that the verbal root *hpk* governs both objects, which are complementary, synonymous, and interlocking in any case. The action applied to the pair *mšpṭ* and *ṣdqh* (or strictly to their fruit) is trans-formation: they are changed from fruit into poisonous products. The same must be the case in 5:7, where the meaning can be expressed in the follow-ing resorting:

> *hahōpĕkîm lĕlaʿănâ*
> *mišpāṭ ûṣĕdāqâ*

This wording expresses in slightly different and abbreviated form almost exactly what is affirmed in 6:12b, which is a slightly fuller version with a parallel term for *lʿnh,* namely, *rʾš.* The pair is attested elsewhere. The other addition, *pry,* provides an essential but easily understood clue to the nature of the image in the poet's mind.

We are left with *lāʾareṣ hinnîḥû,* a clause that does not fit well with the preceding and in any case does not make much sense when applied to the apparent object, *ṣdqh.* What is clearly in mind for the latter is transforma-tion, not being thrust down to the earth, even if we emphasize that it is the fruit of this tree that is being mistreated. Transformation from one sub-stance to another is what is happening or has happened to "justice and righteousness"; but what is the picture or intent behind the picture de-scribed in the words, "they have placed [or thrust] to the earth [or possibly: underworld]?"

We may point out in passing that the use of the perfect verb in both 5:7 and 6:12b qualifies the participle in the Woe as also past tense, describing actions that have taken place, not as a present tense. In the remaining Woes the presence of perfect verbs in association with the participles shows that a past tense is involved and that the prophet is talking about actual events of the past, however recent, and not about customary or even (though it is possible) continuing behavior. Compare the following:

> 6:5   *hprṭym . . . ḥāšĕbû*
> 6:6   *hštym . . . yimšāḥû . . . neḥlû*

The appearance of perfect *nḥlw* shows that *ymšḥw* is not the ordinary future (imperfect) but a preterit. That inference is reinforced by the appear-ance of imperfect with *waw*-consecutive in 6:3, *hmndym . . . wattaggîšûn.* While the usage is possible and fits our analysis of the tense of the action, we suspect that the imperfect here, as in v 6, is preterit, apart from the occurrence of the *waw*, which probably did not affect verbs in poetic or quasipoetic patterns.

We can also point to 6:1, where the fourth clause has the verb *ûbā'û*, and suggest that the conjunction here also is not the *waw*-consecutive. Therefore, the verb must be read as a standard perfect in the past tense: those who are luxuriating at ease in Zion and Samaria have recently returned ("come home," as in an unrelated passage 5:19) from triumphs in the borderlands (cf. 6:13).

Now we return to *lā'āreṣ hinnîḥû*. Just what is it that these perverters of justice are accused of having done? Their behavior is described elsewhere in the book of Amos, and it involves physical oppression of the poor and helpless, which we believe is also what is described here. They thrust (them) down into the ground, as in 2:7, where their treatment is vividly described and would correspond to the action depicted here (cf. also 8:4). The nearest connection with 3d m. pl. verbs of disagreeable action against the poor and weak is in 5:10–12, where there is an explicit description of such activity against the *dāl* (v 11) and the *'ebyônîm* (v 12).

Other examples doubtless can be recovered, but it is clear that the implied object of the verb in 5:7 has to be the targets of those in authority, who cavalierly and contemptuously mistreat the righteous poor, a constant theme in the book of Amos (cf. the NOTES for II.A.2.a. for further discussion).

The only exact parallel passage to this clause is in Isa 28:2, where Yahweh is described in terms of a violent storm: with great power he thrusts down to the earth the objects of his anger. It is obviously important that the passage in Isa 28:1–4 is a Woe with the same sort of envelope construction and that the object of the verb is a group of people, as we also suppose in Amos 5:7. The two Woes complement each other; Yahweh will punish the "drunkards of Ephraim" (Isa 28:1) in the same fashion and by the same means that the "perverters of justice" (Amos 5:7) crush their victims. It is a basic and pervasive principle of justice in the ancient world that punishment should not only fit the crime but inflict on the guilty party the same treatment as he meted out to his victims.

The conclusion is that the clause *l'rṣ hnyhw* qualifies the participle *hhpkym* and constitutes an integral part of the Woe (most of the Woe formulas combine the participle with a finite verb or another participle). Nevertheless, it does not have as its object "justice and righteousness" or the fruits thereof, but rather the people who seek and need such decisions and actions, and who are denied them. Not only are they being given wormwood and gall in place of the good fruit, but these perverters of justice are heaping physical abuse on their victims, as the prophet explicitly stated elsewhere. The verb here is seen to have the same subject as the verbs in

5:10–12, namely, those who are guilty of the greatest injustices. We may compare the following verbs: simple perfect and imperfect in vv 10–12: (10) *śnʾw . . . ytʿbw;* and (12) *hṭw.*

The next interlocking ring under consideration is in 5:18–20, which is formally introduced by the word *hôy.*

The Woe in 5:7/6:12 mixes 3d pl. forms with 2d pl. forms (6:12), which is also a feature of the main series in 6:1–7. The Woe here is apparently restricted to the 2d pl. (v 18), though that restriction may not be determinative for v 20, which does not specify the person and could be construed as third person. In that case it would reverse the order in 5:7/6:12.

Here again we have a sandwich construction in which the Woe and its description of the *yôm yhwh* (avidly sought by the subjects of the Woe) are interrupted by the piece of painful wisdom expounded in v 19. While the connection between the messages of the Woe and the wisdom saying is not immediately apparent, the main point of contact may be that complacency is a mistake and that the unexpected happens often enough to serve as a warning to those who have confident expectations about the future. Just as the man in the parable runs into one misfortune after another, even in the supposed safety of his own home, so those who seek the Day of Yahweh will not find the "light" they expect so confidently, but a dreadful "darkness" for which they are totally unprepared.

The people targeted by the prophet in this telling Woe—and by inference in all of the other peripheral Woes we are now considering—are the same ones pilloried by the prophet in 6:1–7, though that unit also stands by itself (hence the separate beginning with *hôy*). In short, the individual Woes are addressed to the same general group, though they identify and specify particular elements in it.

Whence the optimism and confidence of these people eagerly awaiting the victorious Day of Yahweh? It may well have been occasioned by the recent conquests celebrated by the same group in 6:13. Just as 5:7 is joined to 6:12, so we may perceive a link between 5:18–20 and 6:13. We need only add 6:14 to bring the whole unit, chaps. 5–6, to a crashing climax. It will be observed that 6:14 forms an envelope with 5:1, with numerous points of contact. There are other links as well, between 5:1 and 5:27 and between 6:1 and 6:14, but one set of connections does not preclude another, and all pivotal points in the book can be tied to several others, though they will vary in input and importance.

Verse 13 contains two Woes, though clearly the same people are intended in both. The structure of the pair of Woes of 6:13 is unusual, for there is no matching colon for the first Woe. The second one also is more of a run-on sentence than a bicolon, but it can be divided plausibly toward the middle. There is, however, a partial analogy in 6:1, where the first two Woes are conjoined. The difference is that the first two cola of 6:1, expressing parallel and interlocking Woes against the leaders in the two capital cities, have two more cola to match up with, thereby constituting together an acceptable couplet or tetracolon. Here we have an unbalanced pair with the second line just about twice as long as the first. Nevertheless they match, because the people rejoicing in the first line are also the speakers of the second line, and what is said of the capture of Qarnaim in the second line clearly applies to the first. If one asks what the "rejoicing of Lo-Dabar" is all about, the answer is that it has been captured just as Qarnaim was. All of these remarks are obvious enough, and the next question is whether the imbalance between the two lines is deliberate or accidental or, if the latter (or even the former), whether something has fallen out; and if so, what it is and where it is. What this speculation leads to is a look at the difficult clause in 6:6b, which makes the last of the Woes in that group a tricolon. The last clause, *wĕlōʾ neḥlû ʿal-šēber yôsēp*, has been regarded with suspicion by generations of scholars. It has become almost axiomatic to regard it as secondary and to detach it from v 6 and attach it here in v 13. The result eliminates at one stroke an anomalous (so it is said) tricolon in 6:6 and an equally or more anomalous monocolon in v 13a. Our response is that such a transfer is too tempting to be true or acceptable, but it points to an association between the peripheral Woes and the central group that deserves both recognition and emphasis. The plain truth is that the final colon of v 6 belongs everywhere and nowhere. It can be read meaningfully with all of the Woes, but it is not integral to any of them. It is a negative to begin with, describing what these people are not doing and have not been doing. Because we believe that all of the Woes are aimed at essentially the same group of people, this particular remark, which occurs at the end of the group in 6:1–6, applies to the whole list, that is, to the group in all of its attitudes and activities. So clearly we would not move it from its location: it expresses the prophet's evaluation of what is basically wrong with these people. What they are doing is bad enough, especially the mindless celebration of those minor or meager victories; but what they are failing to do is at least equally important: to grieve over Joseph's crash (6:6b).

We may digress for a moment to discuss the problems of the statement itself. Does the crash of Joseph signify that something terrible and tragic has already occurred, or only that the breach is there, but it is internal and only a few cracks have appeared on the surface? If the latter, then we could contemplate the paradox of the situation in which the prophet is accusing these same people of causing these inner cracks and of being responsible for the breakdown, but at the same time of being oblivious to the damage they themselves have done. But it is argued (by Wolff among others) that the breach is all too real, that "Joseph" (= Ephraim/Manasseh) has been shattered, and hence that we are talking about a much later period, when the Assyrians were making mincemeat of the smaller nations, including

Israel. The implication is, then, that not only are these words added by an interpolator (or editor) but they are addressed to a group in a situation different from the one faced by Amos. Thus these later people, already ravaged by the Assyrians, are eating and drinking and celebrating ancient or nonexistent victories as though they were happening and at least pretending to be unconcerned about the fatal injuries and illnesses from which Joseph is palpably suffering. Somehow interpretation links the material in its later form with the astute observations made by Hosea and Isaiah about the leaders of their day, who also celebrate and carouse and seem to be oblivious of the judgment descending on them. There may be some truth in the comparison, and it is not at all unlikely that Amos' words influenced the responses of later prophets and could in fact have been applied to the situation in the latter part of the century. But it seems to us that Amos is addressing a different situation, and that the colon on the crash of Joseph should be interpreted in the light of surrounding materials. Therefore, the breach of Joseph refers to the inner wounds being inflicted on the body politic by the leadership through its transmutation of justice and righteousness, its oppression of the poor and helpless, its disregard of its responsibilities toward God and humanity, and its mindless rejoicing over meaningless victories.

The conclusion seems to be as follows: If the passage (6:6b) is original or at least part of the edited version of the book in the eighth century, then it serves at least two clear purposes.

1. It ties together all of the woes of 6:1–6 by attaching this accusatory remark to the end of the list. Along with what each segment of the group in its various roles and practices is criticized for doing, there is now added this most grievous omission, failing to be deeply concerned and distraught over the disastrous fate of Joseph.

2. It also serves as a link to the peripheral group of Woes, both in a general way—because the subject and the subject matter are broadly the same—but more specifically as the apparently missing colon in v 13. This specific connection is more apparent than real, for the statement does not fit more appropriately in the middle of the double Woe in v 13 than it does elsewhere (and perhaps less so). The fact remains that the colon is an apparent plus in v 6, producing a tricolon that, while entirely plausible, is unique in that series. Additionally, the tricolon itself is somewhat suspect because the third colon is only remotely tied to the preceding pair, which form an excellent bicolon by themselves. It can hardly be denied that the couplet in v 13 is somewhat lopsided as it stands, and the increment from v 6b would balance things out somewhat more than they are at present. Adding the observation to include the peripheral Woes could be appropriate, though we have no intention of shifting clauses and/or phrases from place to place in the text. Not that we are committed to the idea of a

sacrosanct text with everything permanently in place from the beginning; but before making shifts, we need to know a lot more about how books were formed and what principles governed and what methods were used to arrange groups of oracles and other pieces. Only then, itself an unlikely outcome, might we be able to offer an opinion as to why an element that seems to belong in one place is actually found in another. Sometimes a reason or explanation can be offered and sometimes not; but the phenomenon is too widely spread to be called a recurring error or inadvertence. We contend that the practice is neither haphazard nor arbitrary, but we have not devised a general theory or overriding principle to explain the occurrences. In any case, the colon can serve to link the two groups of Woes, and it may be for that reason that it is located where it is.

However one interprets the varying lengths of the individual Woes, it is clear that the structures are similar in size and in their organization. It is not farfetched to see here a master plan in which the Woes form a framework with an introductory pair of Woes and a closing pair, while in the center is the main list of seven Woes. Embedded in the framework are a variety of materials with independently ordered units, which nevertheless are explicated to some extent by the Woes and contribute to their clarification. Thus the unit 5:10–12 elaborates on the sins of those targeted by the Woes and identifies the victims. In turn 5:7 provides the subject and information about those criticized in the later passage.

Other linkages have been noted, not only between the Woes and the intervening passages but among the latter, usually stretching across the two chapters: for example, 5:3, with its description of the repeated decimations of a city that began with a thousand troops and ends with ten, and 6:9–10, in which the ten men are described as ending in complete annihilation.

The interlocking aspects of chaps. 5–6 are so numerous, with the features spread across both chapters, that we can outline the structure of the book as a whole in the following manner:

Part I. Chaps. 1–4, with a clear division between chaps. 2 and 3. There are thus two units of approximately equal length:
A. Chaps. 1–2: the Great Set Speech
B. Chaps. 3–4: miscellaneous collection characterized by the opening formula, "Hear this Word . . ." or the like

Part II. Chaps. 5–6: the Woes and related items

Part III. Chaps. 7–9: the visions and their complements, including the sketch of the confrontation between priest and prophet at Bethel

While the divisions are hardly of equal length, they may prove to have a calculable relationship, indicating the order and the size of the units. Part I would appear to be longest, with the major address holding pride of place (chaps. 1–2). Spinoffs of that unit fill up the remainder of Part I, chaps. 3–4. In chaps. 5–6 we reach the midpoint and climax of the book, in the middle of chap. 5 (vv 14–15, itself a balanced two-part unit). But these verses may reflect different times and are aimed at different audiences. They lie at the very center of the whole book and by chiastic repetition emphasize the main theme: love Good and hate Evil.

But the former (v 14) belongs to Phase One and is addressed to the house of Israel, while there is yet time for reconciliation and survival. The latter (v 15) belongs to the Last Phase (four), which lies beyond the horizon of the book and any historical experience. It enunciates essentially the same doctrine, the one for humanity whether in Israel or outside, but it is addressed to the remnant of Joseph, those who will ultimately survive all threatened disasters. Their only hope is the same as it was when Amos began: to love Good and hate Evil. The message has come full circle: originally it was intended to offer existing historical Israel a final chance before the coming of judgment and destruction. At the end the same offer is made—or will be—to the future survivors of the catastrophes brought on by the refusal of the first group to heed the request. That offer will be the last chance for the survivors as well.

PART III

The Book of Visions
(7:1–9:6)

Introduction

VISIONS 1–4

This section of the book of Amos is dominated by a series of five visions, the first four of which are given in chap. 7 and the first part of chap. 8. They are presented in sequential pairs, except that between nos. 3 and 4 there is an insertion, the account of Amos' historic visit to the temple at Bethel and the fateful confrontation with Amaziah, the high priest there (7:10–17). The reason for the insertion and its being sandwiched between Visions 3 and 4 will be given elsewhere. Here we wish to deal with the form and structure of the visions themselves.

Vision 5 stands apart from the others and follows a collection of oracles (8:4–14) found after the end of the fourth vision. The visions may therefore be listed as follows:

First Pair $\left\{\begin{array}{l} \text{(1) 7:1–3 \quad Locusts} \\ \text{(2) 7:4–6 \quad Cosmic fire} \end{array}\right.$

Second Pair $\left\{\begin{array}{l} \text{(3) 7:7–8 \quad The } \textit{'ănāk} \text{ (lump of tin?)} \\ \text{(4) 8:1–2 \quad Ripe fruit} \end{array}\right.$

         8:3   Summation: provisional (the destruction)
    (5) 9:1–4   Destruction of altar and Temple
              Annihilation of survivors
      9:5–6   Apostrophe: conclusion of the unit and of the body of
                            The Book of Visions

The visions have a formal structure, which is similar in its features to the series of oracles on foreign nations (chaps. 1–2) and the series on the plagues (4:6–11). In some ways this group is more like the latter than the former, for there are five units in each and each concludes a major unit, at which point there is a hymnic description of the deity we call an apostrophe: 4:13 and 9:5–6.

The first four visions follow the same pattern with only minor variations, whereas the fifth not only stands apart but varies widely in form, length, and content from the others. The first four visions divide into two pairs, with each member of a pair resembling the other very closely. The concluding lines of each pair are practically the same, with the final words of Yahweh in each member of the pair being identical. It is clear therefore that the message is the same for the members of a pair, and the second vision of each is intended to reinforce or confirm the first. This procedure is regular in the Bible: visions and dreams often come in pairs, so that the second confirms that the first is not a happenstance and makes sure that there is no misinterpretation. Customarily also signs and wonders come in pairs (or greater numbers) to confirm that such things happen not by chance but rather by divine plan and purpose.

Now we may have a closer look at the structure of the visions, beginning with the openings of each:

1. 7:1	kōh hirʾanî	ʾădōnāy yhwh	wĕhinnēh
2. 7:4	kōh hirʾanî	ʾădōnāy yhwh	wĕhinnēh
3. 7:7	kōh hirʾanî		wĕhinnēh
4. 8:1	kōh hirʾanî	ʾadōnāy yhwh	wĕhinnēh
5. 9:1	rāʾîtî		

It will be noticed that with one exception, the first four visions begin with exactly the same words, while the fifth conveys essentially the same idea but differently. Explicit reference to the initiating act of the deity, represented by *kh hrʾny ʾdny yhwh,* is faithfully repeated in three of the first four.

The only difference among the first four is the omission of *ʾdny yhwh* in 7:7, the third vision. Naturally scholars have assumed that the text is defective here and have supplied the missing words; but there is no manuscript or versional evidence for the emendation, and we prefer to be cautious and await the results of further inquiry. In any event the sense is not affected, and we may go along with the idea, already demonstrated for the great oracle against the nations, that minor variations are characteristic of repeating patterns in Hebrew prophecy. Even minor deviations seem to have a purpose and reflect a certain style, so it is unwise to erase the distinctions in the interest of a presumed but unproved and unprovable uniformity.

We may note in passing that the formula *ʾdny yhwh* is used frequently in the book, and systematically in the visions, but not with absolute uniformity. Thus it occurs twice in the first vision, but four times in the second. In the third the full form does not occur at all, though the formula is split between the two clauses in v 8. It reappears, however, in the fourth vision, and then is used as well in the summation. We should be wary then of expecting or requiring uniformity in a collection of similar units, even when a standard pattern is perceived and clearly is being used as a model by the prophet.

After the opening formula, the vision proper is introduced by the exclamatory term, "And behold!" (*whnh*), which is often left untranslated in modern versions. It is intended to attract attention, to interrupt the line of dialogue, and to alert the reader or hearer to something important that is about to be communicated. After the word *whnh* comes the vision itself. In the first pair of visions, the description is that of a natural or supernatural phenomenon and is somewhat detailed. No further explanation is offered, but the prophet is fully aware of the vision's meaning and interrupts with words of his own. In the second pair, the vision consists of a supposedly ordinary object, or at least one with which the prophet is familiar. He is asked to identify it, so as to provide a point of departure for the next statement by Yahweh, and through repetition to emphasize the central element in the message. By a rhetorical twist, which is apparently in the form of a play on words in the first instance (though there is a so far unsolved mystery about what the common object in the third vision actually is), certainly in the second (the fourth vision) the hidden ominous significance of these harmless domestic objects is brought out in a final statement by the Lord, which terminates the discussion. We shall look more closely at the details of each pair, while recognizing that the pairs are also related to each other, and that the four together contain and constitute not only the initial and central messages of the book, but also a rare insight into the prophet's personality, character, and inner experience.

Turning to the first pair of visions (7:1–6), we find that the first vision is about the beginning of a locust plague, one of the more common of dreadful experiences in the ancient Near East. These devastating blights, which came frequently if not always on schedule, were uniformly regarded as divine punishments and universally dreaded. References to the appalling effects of locust plagues are scattered through the Bible; it is well known that the prophet Joel uses that image to provide a harrowing description of the Day of Yahweh. Amos himself lists the locust among the various natural calamities that serve as warnings in his set piece on plagues in chap. 4, which follows a pattern similar to the one used for the visions. In spite of the familiarity of the scene, the text has a number of unusual terms, and the picture presented is itself out of the ordinary. The threat is too obvious to miss, however, so the prophet responds without being invited to describe what he has seen or to have the vision interpreted for him.

If the first vision describes a common tragedy of life in the Near East, nevertheless portentous of a final judgment because of the path of total destruction achieved by the locusts, the second vision portrays a supernatural source and mechanism of destruction. In this case divine fire—that is, fire summoned and dispatched by Yahweh—is the cause of total ruination. The fire in question turns up frequently elsewhere in the Bible, as for example in the story of the fire-bombing of Sodom and Gomorrah or the numerous descriptions of theophanies in biblical poetry (e.g., 2 Sam 22:8–16 =

Ps 18:8–16, esp. vv 9, 13, 15). Reference should be made to the theophany on Mount Sinai and the negative theophany to Elijah at the cave in Horeb (where "fire" is rejected as a typical manifestation of the power or presence of the deity, 1 Kgs 19:12) and positively for the contest at Mount Carmel (= 1 Kgs 18:21–38, esp. v 24, where the point about divine fire is stipulated, and vv 37–38, where the fire comes down from heaven). The fire factor is emphasized further in the familiar story in 2 Kings 1, in which Elijah's powers and prowess in calling down fire from heaven are celebrated (2 Kgs 1:1–14, esp. vv 10, 12, and 14). Amos himself refers to destructive fire to be sent by Yahweh against the nations in chaps. 1–2 and against the house of Joseph in 5:6. We may connect the message with the vision, which depicts a violent and pervasive destruction of both sea and land by the supernal fire. The text is difficult in places, but the overall meaning is clear. In this instance as in the other, a devastating threat against the nation is vividly portrayed, so that total disaster is imminent and the prophet is impelled not only to respond but to intercede.

In both cases the opening exclamation is followed by a *qal* active participle, masculine singular, each of which confirms the other: *yôṣēr* in 7:1 and *qōrē'* in 7:4. The subject is not mentioned in the first vision but is specified in the second: *'dny yhwh* (placed at the end of the clause). We should understand the subject in the second vision to serve also for the first; that Yahweh is the subject of the participle can be inferred from the context, but this is only another in a long list of examples of retrospective nouns that govern pronominal antecedents. Lacking a subject, the LXX misinterpreted the word (no doubt written *yṣr* without the *waw* marking the active participle, a late spelling characteristic of the MT in the Minor Prophets but apparently not of the *Vorlage* of the Greek version) and turned it into the noun *yēṣer* (Greek *epigonē*).

At the end of the description of the danger and the damage already done, the prophet intrudes. His intervention is introduced by the verb *'mr* in the first-person *qal* imperfect with *waw*-consecutive: *wā'ōmar,* "and I said."

The prophet then addresses God with the same phrase used at the beginning of each vision—*'dny yhwh*—which emphasizes the formal status of the deity and the occasion. The phrase is used seven times in the course of the four visions and then again in the summation at the end of the fourth vision (8:3). But it does not occur as such in Vision 3, though both terms occur separately in that vision.

Visions 3 and 4 are structured differently from 1 and 2 in the following way: in the first two visions, Yahweh shows the prophet a scene that horrifies him so that he cries out to Yahweh to forgive or to cease and desist; and on both occasions Yahweh changes his mind and reassures the prophet that the disaster will not occur. Put another way, in the first two visions there is a single interchange between the prophet and Yahweh, initiated by the prophet and concluded by the deity. In the second pair of visions the dialogue is extended slightly: the conversation is both initiated and concluded by the deity. It is also controlled by him, so that the prophet is asked to answer a simple question but otherwise has no voice in the proceedings. If there is a spontaneous outburst on the part of the prophet in the first two visions, there is none in the second pair. In fact, the prophet is clearly and emphatically excluded from the deliberations and is entirely restricted to the role of seer and listener, and later to that of bearer of the message. In view of the dramatic impact of the prophet's intercession in the first two visions, in which the effect is immediate and drastic—Yahweh repents and reverses the preliminary decisions—it looks as though the second pair of visions is structured so as to prevent even the possibility of another reversal. In other words, Amos is so carefully and tightly restricted that he has no opportunity to voice an opinion or to intervene in the matters of substance. All he is asked to do is identify the obviously familiar objects that are presented to him. Presumably the intention is to avoid any mistake or misunderstanding, but doubtless it is also done for rhetorical purposes to convey the simple but subtle import of these two visions. The first two were great visions, which overwhelmed the prophet; but his instinctive response resulted in the derailment of the divine plan of judgment. The next two visions were more effective in the sense that at first sight they seem innocent and harmless, items of familiar appearance and use to the prophet, but containing or concealing a more devastating message. Not only did they forecast judgment and destruction, but they carried with them the tone or accent of finality. We have no way of knowing the prophet's reaction, because none is recorded. But he was only allowed to answer the question, "What do you see, Amos?" And then, before he could interpose or offer some plea for his people, the final historical judgment was pronounced, and in such a way as to allow no further rejoinder. The prophet was effectively silenced or, as suggested earlier, reduced to being a spectator, controlled and dismissed to perform his real mission as messenger and no longer to be seen as interlocutor and intercessor. The interview was ended abruptly.

By asking a simple question about a familiar object, Yahweh draws Amos into saying the operative word before he can realize its true or intended meaning. It is then assumed that simply by saying the word, he has affirmed the meaning the Lord intended, a meaning that Amos himself would not have accepted, had he realized the consequences. But once he has said the word it is too late to back out, too late to cancel the sinister second meaning.

Thus in the first two visions the prophet and Yahweh each speak once, the prophet immediately after seeing the terrible vision, and then Yahweh responding to his words. In the second set, the vision has no obvious meaning in itself—just an ordinary, everyday object that one can hold in the hand or carry—so the dialogue begins with Yahweh asking Amos to identify the object. In itself neither object conveys a message, so Amos, not knowing the significance of the vision, of which the object is at most a symbol, cannot interpose, though he may have considered doing so or may have had some suspicion about the process. Abruptly he is told what the object signifies, and in such a way that a rejoinder or further plea is ruled out entirely. There is no doubt a play on words in the second case (Vision 4) and probably in the first case (Vision 3), though we are handicapped by not knowing what an *ᵃnāk* actually is, or what the other meaning might be if a play on words were involved, which to us at least seems likely. The closing statement by Yahweh, the same in both cases, clearly reflects the decision reversals in the first two visions, because any such possibility is now entirely excluded. If the situation was fluid in the first two visions, as the effective intercession by Amos on behalf of his people showed, then in the last two it has frozen solid. Not only has the final decision been made but discussion of the subject is closed. It may be that further conversation is prohibited precisely because Yahweh fears that the prophet will prove persuasive again and he will feel he must reverse the decision, which he does not wish to do. This may seem a curious interpretation of an emphatic irreversible statement, but the situation is very much like that described in Jeremiah (15:1; cf. 14:11–12). There the prophet is told emphatically not to intercede for his people because it is too late. The judgment will proceed regardless, and incidentally the prophet would be wasting his breath because Yahweh will not listen. Even if those great intercessors of the past, Moses or Samuel, were to add their voices to the chorus of pleas, it would not matter: nothing can help; the decision is made; the die is cast. But if that were truly the case, then Yahweh would not have to insist that the prophet keep silent in the presence of the deity, and instead deliver the latter's message to the people without dissenting comment. The divine insistence on silence is rather an admission that God might still be influenced by his messenger, who is devoted to the well-being of his people, sinful and deserving of ultimate punishment though they be.

So in the second pair of visions we have three speeches each, the opening and closing addresses by Yahweh sandwiched around a brief observation by the prophet. The sequence is introduced by the following formulas:

	1. *wayyōʾmer yhwh ʾēlay*	And Yahweh said to me
Vision 3	2. *wāʾōmar*	And I said
(7:8)	3. *wayyōʾmer ʾădōnāy*	And my Lord said
	1. *wayyōʾmer*	And he said
Vision 4	2. *wāʾōmar*	And I said
(8:2)	3. *wayyōʾmer yhwh ʾēlay*	And Yahweh said to me

It will be seen that with one exception the elements are the same (verbs and nouns). Note that the order is reversed, so that we have an envelope construction with the same formula introducing Yahweh's words in Vision 3 and closing Vision 4. A more abbreviated form is used in the middle elements: *wy'mr* is repeated, with *'dny* in the latter part of the third vision, or without any expressed subject in the early part of the fourth vision. It will also be noted that the alternation of *'dny* and *yhwh* begins in 7:7 and continues through 7:8 in the order: *'dny* (7:7), *yhwh* (7:8), and *'dny* (7:8). Then in 8:1 we have a resumption of the full form at the beginning of the vision story, just as in 7:1 and 7:4 (but omitted in 7:7). Resuming the dialogue, we have *yhwh* in 8:2, giving us the two split pairs spread over the two visions. Finally, in 8:3 we have *'dny yhwh,* the full form, to close out the four-vision sequence in chaps. 7–8. For the second pair of visions and the closing summary (8:3), we have two full formulas (*'dny yhwh* in 8:1 and 8:3) and two split ones containing the same elements in the appropriate order: *'dny* (7:7) and *yhwh* (7:8); *'dny* (7:8) and *yhwh* (8:2).

Finally, we can identify the form *'dny* alone in 9:1 at the beginning of the fifth vision, corresponding to *'dny* in 7:7 and thus confirming both as correct, while the full formula *'dny yhwh* (*hṣb'wt*) occurs at the end of the last vision, closing The Book of Visions and in fact balancing the second half of the book against the first half. It also forms the bridge to the final apostrophe that ends The Book of Visions and concludes the main body of the book of Amos. The formula, which is so distinctive of the vision sequence, belongs with the fifth vision and closes it, not with the apostrophe, even though the Masoretes attached it to v 5 (as comparison with the apostrophe that closes off chap. 4 [v 13] shows).

For the visions as a whole we have the following data: including the five visions between 7:1 and 9:5 there are nine instances of the combined expression *'dny yhwh,* and there are three instances of each separately in contexts in which the longer expression would be appropriate. Altogether, then, there are twelve pairs, nine actually together and three separated, but overall in alternating order: *yhwh* (7:3); *'dny* (7:7); *yhwh* (7:8); *'dny* (7:8); *yhwh* (8:2); and *'dny* (9:1).

Looking at the distribution of *'dny yhwh* in the entire book, we observe the following points. There are twenty-two occurrences of the formula, three of which are expanded to include (*'lhy*) (*h*)-*ṣb'wt*. These three are strategically distributed, with one of them in The Book of Doom (3:13), another at the close of The Book of Visions (9:5), while the third is located very close to the center of the book (5:16). The last mentioned is distinguished by being the only one in the entire list in which the formula is reversed:

3:13 *'dny yhwh 'lhy ṣb'wt*
5:16 *yhwh 'lhy ṣb'wt 'dny*
9:5   *'dny yhwh hṣb'wt*

The common elements include *'dny, yhwh,* and *ṣb'wt; 'lhy* is omitted in the third instance but is present in the other two. The formula with the inverted sequence occurs as the middle term at the center of the book, forming a chiastic chain in both directions with the outer parallel members.

A chart of the formula's distribution follows:

Chapters	*'dny yhwh*	*'dny* (alone)
Part I: 1–4		
A. 1–2	1	
B. 3–4	6	
Part II: 5–6	3	
Part III: 7:1–9:6	11	3
Epilogue: 9:7–15	1	
	22 +	3

The title is thus highly characteristic of the more explicitly autobiographical portions of the book, while not lacking in the rest.

Now we will deal with the formal structure of the visions, listing the essential features in tabular form so as to be able to compare similarities and differences. In the following we will treat the first four visions in synoptic fashion and the fifth by itself, because in most respects it differs significantly from the others.

   I. Opening formula
       A. First pair
          1. 7:1 *kōh hir'anî 'dny yhwh*
          2. 7:4 *kōh hir'anî 'dny yhwh*
       B. Second pair
          3. 7:7 *kōh hir'anî* —— ——
          4. 8:1 *kōh hir'anî 'dny yhwh*

As noted, the only difference among the four is the omission of the compound subject in Vision 3, the first of the second pair. As there is no question about the subject or the meaning, this case could be regarded as a stylistic variant (rather than a scribal omission or error, which seems unlikely). The restoration in the fourth vision may be the result of the editorial decision to insert the story of Amos' confrontation at Bethel between Visions 3 and 4. Thus it was deemed appropriate to mention the subject again explicitly. Had Vision 4 followed Vision 3 directly, the subject might have been left out there as it was in Vision 3.

II. The vision itself (particle followed by participle)
    A. First pair
        1. 7:1–2   *wěhinnēh yôṣēr . . . hāʾāreṣ*
        2. 7:4   *wěhinnēh qōrēʾ . . . haḥēleq*
    B. Second pair
        3. 7:7   *wěhinnēh ʾdny niṣṣāb . . . ʾănāk*
        4. 8:1   *wěhinnēh kělûb qāyiṣ*

In all four cases the account of the vision begins with the exclamation *wěhinnēh*. In the first pair the particle is followed by a *qal* active m. s. participle, the subject not specified but clearly understood to be Yahweh himself (or at least the power and authority behind the action, which may be carried out by some other agent). In the third vision there is also a participle, in the *nipʿal*, however, and here the subject (*ʾdny*) is specified, perhaps because it was omitted in the opening formula. Such a double variation compensates for an omission in one phrase by a corresponding addition in the neighboring one. In the fourth vision there is neither verb nor subject: the whole vision is given abruptly in three words. The contents of the first two visions are given at greater length. With Visions 3 and 4, there is considerable reduction because the vision consists not of an action but of an object (unlike the first two). The reduced length of the vision's description is compensated for somewhat in the second pair by the extended dialogue. Thus we have the following quantitative data, counting orthographic words:

Number	Opening	Vision	Dialogue	Epilogue	Total
1.	4	18	19		41
2.	4	13	22		39
	8	31	41		80
3.	2	8	22		32
4.	4	3	21	14	42
	6	11	43	= 60 + 14 =	74

Closer scrutiny shows that the dialogue and associated materials are about the same for all of the visions and that the main difference is in the description of the visions, in which the reduction from first to last is dramatic but regular: $18 \longrightarrow 13 \longrightarrow 8 \longrightarrow 3$. The discrepancy in overall length between the first pair and the second ($80 \longrightarrow 60$) is compensated for somewhat by the closing statement (8:3), which belongs strictly with the second pair, though it closes off the first four visions with an appalling description of the devastation now on its way. In this respect it fills out the very terse or laconic description of Visions 3 and 4, especially the latter, which as noted is summarily described in three words (partly repeated by the prophet). Verse 3 elaborates that vision along with Vision 3, which is also described laconically; and the total, then (8 + 3 + 14 = 25), is a little closer to what we have for Visions 1 and 2 (18 + 13 = 31). Except for that noticeable and significant discrepancy, no doubt also deliberate, the figures come out about the same:

Vision	Opening		Dialogue		Total	
1	4	+	19	=	23	⎫ 49
2	4	+	22	=	26	⎭
3	2	+	22	=	24	⎫ 49
4	4	+	21	=	25	⎭

There is some variation in detail, but overall the pattern is quite symmetrical and well balanced.

A closer analysis of the dialogue follows. In Visions 1 and 2 there is a single exchange, whereas in Visions 3 and 4 there are three statements: two by Yahweh and one by the prophet. We can set them up as follows:

VISIONS 1 and 2

Prophet	Opening:	1.	*wā'ōmar 'dny yhwh*
		2.	*wā'ōmar 'dny yhwh*
	Body:	1.	*sĕlaḥ-nā' mî yāqûm ya'ăqōb*
			kî qāṭōn hû'
		2.	*ḥădal-nā' mî yāqûm ya'ăqōb*
			kî qāṭōn hû'
Yahweh	Transition:	1.	*niḥam yhwh 'al-zō't*
		2.	*niḥam yhwh 'al-zō't*
	Reply:	1.	*lō' tihyeh*
		2.	*gam-hî' lō' tihyeh*
	Close:	1.	*'amar yhwh*
		2.	*'āmar 'dny yhwh*

The main parts of the two visions are practically identical, thus stressing the point that they are intended to convey the same message. However different the visions themselves may be in their content and color, they are meant to say the same thing about the future. And the second confirms and reinforces the first. Then the only changes between the first and the second are the substitutions of the less specific *hdl* for the more theological *slh* in the prophet's intervention. The first time he uses the more polite and proper "forgive," while the second time around it is the colloquial and somewhat peremptory "cease," or in colloquial English, "lay off!" or "stop it!" In either case, the divine response is the same. He changes his decision, accedes to the prayer of the prophet, and assures him, "It shall not happen." Again there is one small change: the second time Yahweh adds the words *gm-hy*, "This also [the judgment or threatened action in the second vision] shall not happen," or "that shall not occur." There may be a note of finality in the message here, as if to say that it is also the last time. But that implication may be imparted into the case on the basis of our knowledge of what is in store for this prophet, namely, the second pair of visions, in which the conclusion is directly opposite to what we have here.

When we look at the second pair of visions, and in particular the central part or dialogue between Yahweh and the prophet, we find that the structure is quite different from that of the first pair. It conveys a different message, not only in a different framework but with a shift in the center of gravity. Thus in the first pair the initiative lies with the prophet, who is quick to intervene as soon as he grasps the vision's import. Yahweh, while initiating the contact with the prophet through the vision, is the respondent and must deal with the prophet's importunate demands: "Forgive!" and "Cease!" Yahweh has no chance to pursue the purpose of the vision to its logical verbal conclusion, namely, the message that the prophet is supposed to hear, understand, and then deliver to his audience. On the contrary, Yahweh backs off, literally obeying the prophet's imperatives; and without ever even stating the message, he turns off the judgment: "It shall not happen." The effect is sensational.

The second set of visions is handled in an entirely different fashion, as though to avert the possibility of diversion, suspension, or reversals of judgment. That idea carries over into the Great Set Speech of chaps. 1–2, in which, eight times over, Yahweh insists that "I will not reverse it," an echo not only of the refusal to consider leniency or amnesty in the final comment on the second pair of visions, but beyond that of the first pair, where in fact he was persuaded to cancel the decision to destroy and give Jacob//Israel another chance. In the second pair the dialogue is set up in a way that does not permit the prophet either initiative or freedom to interpolate his own feelings and thoughts. It is as though Yahweh, now finally determined on a course of action, wished to prevent the prophet from intervening in any way, and to compel the prophet to carry out his appointed mission. He is to bear a message and not assume the role of helping to shape the message or in fact—as happened with the first pair—to veto it and derail Yahweh's purpose. Thus there is not only an air of stringency in the second pair of exchanges between Yahweh and the prophet, but a certain terseness and perhaps asperity in Yahweh's words to him. The only purpose of the dialogue the second time around is to make sure that the prophet understands the vision and the message that goes with it. Not only is he not asked for an opinion about the merits of the matter, he is cleverly prevented from voicing any reaction at all. The opportunity for an intervention is simply closed off.

There is no reason to suppose that Amos' basic attitudes and feelings changed in the slightest. We judge that he would have been willing and eager to intercede for all of Israel whenever the opportunity presented itself. The same would be true even after the message of doom and destruction was understood to be irreversible, the decision final and unchangeable. The interview ended with the deity's closing words, in direct opposition to the words at the end of the first pair of visions. "It shall not happen" is reversed totally by "I shall not spare them again." What we have is a second reversal. The words in the first pair, "Yahweh repented [= changed his mind—his decision] about this," apply to the second pair, only the change has taken place in the interval between the two sets of visions. In other words, from the beginning of the first set to the end of the second there is a double set of reversals, whereby the original plan is reaffirmed and put back on course. The original visions, with all their terror and threatened woe, are effectually reinstated, and the terse and laconic reaffirmation made in the course of the second pair brings back the cosmic power and scope of the first pair.

Because the two sets of visions are tightly bound together by all of these connections, it is understandable that they should be grouped in a single unit, whatever the historical circumstances and the distinctions of time and place that may have characterized the prophet's experience of the divine. When it came time to put them in literary form it was both advisable and necessary to link them in sequence and thus demonstrate the interconnections and the dynamics of the relationship of deity and prophet. Needless to say, after the fiery confrontation between prophet and deity, the prophet—once subdued and committed to his mission—was not likely to be diverted, distracted, or prevented from carrying out his task. He was not likely to be cowed or intimidated by a mere high priest or a king, or any combination of human powers on earth.

The placement of the confrontation with the official representative of the same deity (with whom Amos had been dealing in the starkest and most intimate terms) in the midst of the vision sequence (and in particular between the members of the second pair) was doubtless deliberate. Among other things, it marks the absolute contrast—even contradiction—between the priest and the God he is supposed to represent. The visions, with their hard divine judgment, likewise make a mockery of the time-serving and equivocal words of the priest who is bargaining for a little breathing room, for a superficial and spurious tranquility, while the prophet is trying his best to convey the overwhelming terror and tragedy of the real situation. They are in two different worlds, but the point of contact between them has explosive consequences. We can read with the advantage not only of hindsight (namely, that Amos proved to be right) but more importantly with the help of the editor who thoughtfully juxtaposed the two confrontations so that we cannot miss or escape the point. There is a world of difference between the true and false representatives of the same God.

If we look at the second pair of visions, we can set up the parallel dialogues in the following manner:

OPENING:
7:8 *wayyō'mer yhwh 'ēlay*
8:2 *wayyō'mer*

RESPONSE:
7:8 *wā'ōmar*
8:2 *wā'ōmar*

CLOSING RESPONSE:
7:8 *wayyō'mer 'dny*
8:2 *wayyō'mer yhwh 'ēlay*

The sequence of introductory or framing words is almost the same throughout, and the content (the same common verb repeated in slightly different form six times) hardly makes for exciting reading. Once again, we note slight changes in the use and distribution of the divine names, and a mirror-image or envelope construction. The three-word formula used at the beginning of the dialogue in the first vision of this set is also used at the end of the second, producing an echo and envelope construction; the two inner formulas (7:8 and 8:2) are correspondingly shorter, though slightly different because of the concern about divine names (discussed earlier).

When it comes to the actual dialogue we have it in three parts, one more than we found in the first pair of visions:

DIALOGUE: *WORDS*

Yahweh	7:8	*mâ-ʾattâ rōʾeh ʿāmôs*	4
	8:2	*mâ-ʾattâ rōʾeh ʿamôs*	4
Amos	7:8	*ʾănāk*	1
	8:2	*kĕlûb qāyiṣ*	2
Yahweh	7:8	*hinĕnî śām ʾănāk*	
		bĕqereb ʿammî yiśrāʾēl	6
	8:2	*bāʾ haqqēṣʾel-ʿammî yiśrāʾēl*	5

CLOSE:

| Yahweh | 7:8 | *lōʾ-ʾōsîp ʿôd ʿăbôr lô* | 5 |
| | 8:2 | *lōʾ-ʾôsîp ʿôd ʿăbôr lô* | 5 |

In the dialogues recorded above, Yahweh is positively loquacious, in contrast to Amos, who is practically silent. Yahweh has four words in the first speech and eleven (or ten) in the second in each vision account, making a total of fifteen in the first and fourteen in the second. Amos manages to utter one word in the first and two in the second,

	Vision 3	Vision 4	Total
Yahweh	15	14	29
Amos	1	2	3
	16	16	32

If we compare these figures with those calculated for the first two visions, we note an impressive shift. In the first two, Amos is comparatively talkative while Yahweh hardly speaks at all:

	Vision 1	Vision 2	Total
Amos	10	10	20
Yahweh	2	4	6
	12	14	26

	Vision 3	Vision 4	Total
Yahweh	15	14	29
Amos	1	2	3
	16	16	32

	1st Pair	2nd Pair	Total
Yahweh	6	29	35
Amos	20	3	23
	26	32	58

The tables have been turned dramatically. Overall, Yahweh dominates the scene, as is only fitting. The word count and the shape of the dialogue reflect the undoubted fact that Yahweh has the last word (though not necessarily the first, at least in conversation with the prophet) and that ultimately the prophet's visionary experience is initiated, directed, and controlled by the deity.

In view of the close connection and interlocking relations between the two sets of visions, the concluding remarks in Amos 8:3 wrap up the entire sequence and are as much a commentary on the first pair of visions as on the second pair, because in effect the first two have been reinstated by the second two, and the original decision to proceed with destruction, by plague and fire, has been reaffirmed. It will be noticed that the second pair of dialogues emphasizes the certainty of judgment and destruction, but not the means or method, while the first pair describes the means and initial effects. Amos 8:3 carries the story farther to include the devastation in the palace and the wholesale slaughter of the inhabitants of city and country.

Thus the whole unit from 7:1 through 8:3 is a carefully constructed composite, linking the two sets of visions and dialogues in dramatic fashion and showing how the deity and prophet interacted until a final resolution was achieved of their respective roles and of the content of the message that the prophet was to deliver and in fact did deliver. Yet inside this sequence of visions is the confrontation with Amaziah, a balancing picture of the other dialogue. Here Amos, fresh from the second pair of visions and dialogues with the deity and his mind firmly fixed on the course set by Yahweh, confronts the priest at Bethel, the leading cult figure of Israel, the man who directs the worship of Yahweh and symbolizes the religion of Israel for the whole population. The contrast between the real God of Israel and this official representative could not be greater, and the juxtaposition of the two confrontations enhances the drama of the situation. Viewed from Amos' angle, the direct experience of the series of exchanges with Yahweh has set him on his course of action as a prophet and has shaped his message and responses. At the same time, it has prepared him for any eventuality in his meetings with Amaziah and the king (Jeroboam II), if that meeting should come about. After facing Yahweh in vision and voice, in dialogue and decision, the prophet is fully equipped to perform his earthly mission. In many respects the confrontation with Amaziah is anticlimactic, for Amaziah is mostly concerned with superficialities, with decorum and protocol. Proceedings at the temple of Yahweh should be conducted decently and in order, and Amos should not rudely disturb the peace or make terrible threats against the order of the sacral or secular establishment. The contrast between reality and triviality could not be greater, and perhaps with the second, human encounter, Amos too became convinced that Israel was doomed and that nothing could be done about it, except to announce the divine decision.

We will now summarize the findings about 7:1–8:3, in particular the visions, and then deal with two elements in the picture in a somewhat more extensive way: first, the use of the terms "Jacob//my people Israel" in the pairs of visions; and second, the meaning and import of the verb *nḥm* when used of the deity, as it is in the first two visions (see "Excursus: When God Repents," below).

We believe that the visions and the account in which they are embedded bring us as close to the person of Amos and his self-understanding as a prophet of Yahweh as we are likely to get. A close reading of the text (along with other passages but especially the story of the confrontation with Amaziah) will tell us things we are not likely to find elsewhere about the inner workings of the prophet's mind and of his relations with the deity. This account illuminates the prophet's struggle with his role, his message, and his relations with God and will also shed considerable light on other passages and places in the book of Amos.

It is the second set of visions that provides the framework for defining the actual and essential role of the prophet. His task as prophet is to bear Yahweh's message and to deliver it to the appropriate audience. He is above all a messenger, one who is given the privilege of seeing the vision, of hearing the word directly, and who has the responsibility of bringing the message to his people. In the second set of visions, Amos is shown something apparently quite ordinary and is asked to identify the object (so that there is no mistake). Immediately thereafter he is given a message based on the name or description of the object, which through a play on words turns into an oracle of menace and doom. The prophet is then dismissed with the expectation that he will give the message, and an example of such activity is provided in the story of his visit to the sanctuary at Bethel.

The account of the second set of visions is sufficient to describe and explain the prophet's role and the source of the words he proclaims under the formula: "Thus has said the Lord" (*kōh 'āmar yhwh*). Nonetheless, we must also consider the first set of visions, to which there is obvious reference in the closing words of Yahweh in the third and fourth visions, "I shall not spare [forgive] them again." That forgiveness was precisely what happened in the case of the first two visions, and the later reference shows that the earlier experience is still palpable and important in the second round of visions. What happened was that the first set of visions was not played out according to the plan, but in a different and unexpected fashion. Each of these first two episodes began with a vision that was cosmic and life-threatening in character. Before the standard dialogue could commence—with Yahweh asking the basic leading question and then, when the obvious response was given, pronouncing the formal judgment and sending the prophet to carry out his task—the prophet interrupted and injected a different note entirely, intended to halt the proceedings and change the outcome. He was successful not only in making himself heard by the deity but in reversing the decision implicit in the vision of doom and destruction. Yahweh, apparently taken off guard, acceded to the importunate request, and canceled his decision and judgment. The locust plague was halted before it was fairly under way, and the celestial fire was contained before it reached the holy territory. This reversal is called repentance and refers to a deliberate change of mind and direction on the part of the verb's subject, whether the subject be human or divine. Thus the prophet disrupted the original proceedings and clearly brought about a new situation, the cancellation of the original plan by its author. The intercession was effective. Strictly speaking, that was not or should not have been the prophet's role. As the account of the second set of visions shows, he was simply supposed to hear a message and deliver it, not to question the implied message of the vision and then seek to reverse it and succeed in doing so. But the role assumed by Amos in this instance is one that other prophets are known to have assigned themselves. Amos' behavior is not entirely surprising or unusual, except that it seems to come at the very beginning of his ministry, before he had served in any external way as a prophet. His intervention appears to have been quite spontaneous, not a formal action, and while the language is polite enough the first time around, the second intervention seems colloquial to the point of brusqueness. Clearly the prophet was quite agitated by what he had seen and believed to be the certain destruction of his people Israel, and he was determined to stave it off and do something to stop the judgment before it became operational. And he succeeded. Yahweh accepted the intervention and acceded to the intercession: "It shall not happen." The decision was reversed and the judgment suspended.

Then the reversal itself was reversed, for the second set of visions, which must follow the first, reports a renewed decision to impose judgment and bring destruction on the state. Apparently this about-face occurred in the interval between the two sets of visions. There must have been some significant time lapse to permit the deity to reevaluate the situation and to permit the prophet to bring a message of dire warning to the people threatened in the first two visions. Seemingly both parties recognized that the agreement to cancel the punishment was only conditional and thus temporary. Intercession is no substitute for repentance, and the latter is the only sure mechanism to reverse hostile judgments on a permanent basis (unless repentance produces permanent changes in attitude and behavior; then its effects will be transitory as well). So what the prophet's intercession did was to buy time, to spare the people until the situation could be reviewed and another decision reached. The second set of visions reflects this process and shows that after due consideration the deity has decided to reinstate the original visions and judgments. The intercession and its effect have lapsed; Yahweh has reconsidered the reconsideration, and the second time around has rendered an irreversible, permanent judgment. Whatever efforts the prophet may have made in the interim to transmute the intercession with its temporary restraining order into genuine and long-lasting repentance seem clearly to have failed (although we believe we can document some of these efforts, in those passages in which the people are exhorted to repent while there is still time). We want to emphasize that the sequence of visions is no charade; the principals were not going through motions. The visions were real, as were the dialogues. The intercession by the prophet was heartfelt and spontaneous, and the response reflected a deep thought and a difficult decision by Yahweh. The plan was reversed and suspended. Then came reconsideration and reinstatement. The period of suspension ended with renewed determination to carry out the original decision. The prophet succeeded the first two times, but the second pair of times he was not allowed to say anything other than what he was asked, to identify the objects shown him. His role was redefined; he was not allowed to go beyond that of messenger. If there was an implied rebuke, it is not stated. But now there is no time for a response, and the prophet must go his way with the message entrusted to him. Nevertheless, the comment made by Yahweh at the end of Visions 3 and 4 ("I shall not spare [forgive] them again") shows that the previous visions were still in mind, but that Yahweh had firmly and finally decided that matter. The nature of that irreversible decision and its finality are further emphasized in the main oracle in chaps. 1–2. The same point is stressed eight successive times in reference to each of the eight nations specified as the target of judgment and attack: "I will not reverse it" (*lōʾ-ʾăšîbennû*).

In the end the prophet bowed to Yahweh's will and delivered the classic uncompromising message of doom and destruction for which Amos is so well known. The outcome for Israel at least, forty or fifty years later, is equally well known, and the fall of Samaria and the destruction of the northern kingdom not only vindicated the prophet but had a profound effect on the surviving kingdom, Judah, and all of the prophets who followed. Amos' prediction and expectation about Judah were much longer in coming true, as were the prophecies of Hosea in all likelihood and Micah certainly. In the strict sense, and within the usual time frame of the prophets, they did not come true at all. But the effect of the message may have been greater in the south than in the north, and in the end that is where it was preserved. And precisely because it was more readily heard and taken to heart, the prophecy remained unfulfilled (at least for a long time).

In the course of this analysis of the visions, much has been learned about prophet and deity that belies the image of a stern and unyielding preacher of bad tidings and an unrelenting divine judge. The prophet's initial intervention, not once but twice, reveals his basic nature and his commitment to his people. He sought not judgment or retribution, but mercy. He did not justify his client, but presumed upon the leniency of the court. His defense was helplessness—"Jacob is weak and pitiful"—appearances to the contrary notwithstanding. There is no reason to suppose that this attitude on the part of the prophet ever changed. The case of Jeremiah is very similar and better documented (cf. 15:19–21, 20:7–9, and esp. 15:10–12 and 17:14–18). Amos' sympathies were with his people, north and south; and although his ultimate message was harsh and uncompromising, his intention was for their good. In spite of the total inflexibility of the final position, there must always have been the chance of a last-minute divine reversal. Amos, after all, had already achieved such a reversal twice, and in spite of repeated assurances to the contrary, or because of them, the prophet could sense the possibility, however remote, that things might be otherwise. And beyond the immediate fate of the kingdom there was the question of survivors and exiles and what might be done for and with them, and not less the question of the southern kingdom, clearly under the same judgment but perhaps with some leeway and more time to repent and be saved.

What we see in the prophet as he struggles with his vocation as a messenger of God we also see in the God who chose him and sent him forth. Within the setting of this encounter we see a divine as well as a human struggle. God is not working with a puppet or robot. The messenger wishes to participate in the message making, not only in the delivery. He has an argument and makes a case to which God finds himself responding positively. Against the intention and the call and commission of the prophet Yahweh rescinds the order, not once but twice. He accepts intercession for reconsideration. Until a final verdict can be reached, he suspends the process. Surely this hesitation was not expected—and yet, was it surprising? Prophets have a history of talking back. Moses was the great arguer, protester, and insister, as before him was Abraham. The greater the prophet, the greater the insistence and the interference. The story of Jonah (which may reflect pre-exilic conditions regardless of the date of final composition) exhibits the same idea in reverse. In that situation the prophet is so sure that Yahweh will forgive on evidence of good faith and repentance that he tries to escape his responsibility and then is extremely angry when his message of doom results in repentance and restoration. The conviction that Yahweh is permanently and predominantly the God of grace and mercy, compassionate and long-suffering, is so deeply embedded in the tradition of Israel that it is always present in the background of Israel's experience and frequently surfaces in the literature. Whether it is the people picked to be prophets or the nature of the God they serve, the issue of morality and its consequences in judgment and mercy are the constant in Israel's history and in biblical literature. Small wonder it emerges so directly and forcefully in Amos.

This God turns out to be as susceptible to the importunities of the prophet as the prophet is to the great tradition of a gracious and merciful God in which no doubt he was raised. The initial impact of each on the other is electrifying and startling: the prophet is heeded; judgment is rescinded; Jacob is spared; and the way is open to repentance, reconciliation, renewal, restoration. But that bright picture fades quickly from view.

Reconsideration and the passage of time reopen the lines of communication, and Amos' career as a prophet of doom, which almost ended (happily) before it began, is set on track again. The rescission is itself rescinded; the evidence is all too plain and overwhelming. The respite is over because nothing has changed. Five plagues have intervened while the prophet has been energetically plying his trade, preaching the good word of repentance while it is yet light, but all to no avail. The period of grace has ended, and now the final decision is rendered. The interaction between deity and prophet must be recognized as real and open-ended. Each can persuade the other until a decision is finally reached. It is true that power and authority rest with God alone; it is not the free cooperation of equal individuals, but within degrees of constraint the prophet is free to voice his views and make his opinions known. We are not to suppose, therefore, that the decision had been reached prior to the engagement with the prophet or that the discussion was *pro forma* and meaningless because in the end the decision was the same as at the beginning. It was a difficult struggle for both, and not less for God, to arrive at a final determination. But after the data available are weighed and the heart and mind of the divine subject are explored, the verdict is then firm and final, and now at last the prophet must do his part.

As we learn from elsewhere in the book, there remain qualifying factors, and the initial impression we have of both prophet and deity as concerned and desirous that no one, kingdom or person, should perish, but that all should live (cf. Ezekiel 18), is confirmed. Judgment, terrible and drastic, is on its way, certainly not because God wills it, though he does, but because the people deserve it and their persistently wicked behavior demands it. But as there must be punishment and execution, there will nevertheless be survival (in exile if nowhere else) and ultimately the chance and certainty of restoration and renewal. The end is not the end; as noted elsewhere there is a double future, one immediate and short term that is totally disastrous, the other long range, which is much more hopeful.

In this trial by fire neither would emerge unscathed.

JACOB//MY PEOPLE ISRAEL IN THE VISIONS

The word "Jacob" is used in each of the first two visions by the prophet (7:2, 5) to designate the people of God, who are threatened by the judgment implicit in the vision. In the second pair of visions, it is God who speaks of the judgment against "my people Israel" (7:8 and 8:2). Clearly the terms are parallel across the visions, and they almost certainly refer to the same entity. But what is the entity envisioned? It would appear that there are only two possibilities: either the northern kingdom, Israel, or the combined entity, Jacob-Israel, which would include both north and south. Elsewhere we have studied the frequency, distribution, and use of these names in the book of Amos, and we need not repeat that information here. The conclusions, however, may be stated in general: the terms "Jacob" and "Israel" are used for the larger entity both in Amos and in the rest of the Bible, with a single very important exception. From very early times (as far back as the song of Deborah) the name Israel alone was applied to the ten northern tribes, which later (under Saul) became the northern kingdom of Israel. Specifically, in Amos, with a possible exception or two, when the name Israel is used alone it refers to the northern kingdom only, but when used in combination with any other expression, such as *byt*, *bny*, or, as in this case, *ʿmy* (*ʿammî* = "my people"), the reference is to the larger entity, historic Israel, or the future Israel. So unless there are strong indications to the contrary, our present supposition is that, as elsewhere in Amos and throughout the Hebrew Bible, the usage here of the parallel terms *yʿqb*// *ʿmy yśrʾl* points to the larger entity, the double kingdom or classical Israel. In other words, the visions encompass and concern both kingdoms, the whole territory of the people of God, including Israel *and* Judah (cf. Num 23:7 [*yʿqb*//*yśrʾl*], 23:10, 24:5; Deut 32:9, 33:4, 33:28; 2 Sam 23:1; 1 Kgs 18:31 [*bny yʿqb*//*yśrʾl*]; Hos 10:11 [*ʾprym*//*yhwdh*//*yʿqb*]; cf. Micah 2:12, 3:1, 3:9; Jacob is not used in the book of Kings for the northern kingdom, which is always Israel; in Isaiah, Jacob and Israel are equivalent). Except for one case in Micah (1:5), the usage seems to be the same everywhere: Jacob refers to the patriarch or to the people descended from him, especially when construed with *bny* or *byt*. There seems to be no distinction in usage without or with qualifiers. It is very often in parallel with Israel, but never in Amos, where Israel alone refers to the northern kingdom only; and apparently Jacob cannot be or is not used in that way. The name "Jacob" occurs six times in Amos, including these two; in no case does it occur in parallel with Israel alone (here with *ʿmy yśrʾl*, which we take as a variant of *byt* or *bny yśrʾl*), and in no case does it seem to be identified clearly with the northern kingdom alone. (1) In 3:13, the context might imply that the northern kingdom is meant, but it is not required by the sense. (2) In 6:8 we have a similar situation in which Jacob is addressed, but it is not clear that the audience is restricted to the north. (3) The context of 8:7 is much like that of 6:8, and because it too is a heading in which Jacob is addressed, it is difficult to define or delimit the audience. If Amos were concerned only with the north or spoke only about the north, then clearly Jacob must refer to the north. But that is not an argument, only a circular assertion. (4) The text at 9:8 is difficult because of an apparent contradiction, to wit, "I shall destroy it [= the sinful kingdom just mentioned] from the surface of the earth. Nevertheless, I shall not utterly destroy the house of Jacob." If "the sinful kingdom" and the "house of Jacob" are the same, then there is a contradiction that can only be resolved by assigning the conflicting state-ments to different hands at different times or on different occasions. But if, in fact, "the sinful kingdom" is the northern territory (cf. the antecedent "Israel" in v 7), then the implication for "the house of Jacob" is that it refers to something else. It could refer to Judah alone, though we have no evidence for that identification. But much more likely and consistent with the previous statement, it refers to the larger entity, comprising both north and south. The destruction of "the sinful kingdom" will wipe out a large part of the combined entity but not the whole of it, for the remaining part will survive. Only if *byt y'qb* refers to an entity other than the northern kingdom alone can we accept the statement in the Hebrew text as it stands. If the analysis is correct, then we can say that the term "Jacob" in Amos is never used unequivocally for the northern kingdom, and in the one context in which the issue can be drawn and a distinction made, it cannot refer to the northern kingdom alone, but must refer to a larger entity, including Judah.

When we turn to the two instances in chap. 7, we find no evidence to indicate the extent or the exact identity of the reference. Neither vision restricts the territory under consideration to one kingdom or the other, though the holy land, *ḥēleq* (7:4), is certainly in view. One cannot say that the land must be Israel or that it must be Judah. In the nature of the case, we might expect visions to be broad and nonrestrictive, and in fact the language does not pinpoint or otherwise identify the territory involved. This fact suggests that the whole land is the object of concern and thus that Jacob refers to the larger entity, the combined kingdoms, so that the threat-ened judgment is against the whole country, not just one part of it. Such a view would support the impression derived from the oracles in chaps. 1–2 and the Woes in chap. 6, that Amos' message of judgment was aimed impartially at both north and south, the combined entity, namely, Jacob.

The same line of reasoning would apply to the name "Israel" in the second pair of visions, and the balancing of Jacob in the first set with Israel in the second implies that the same political entity is intended. Furthermore, because the name Israel alone has been preempted in this book as a designation of the northern kingdom, the qualifier *ʿammî* is attached to it to show that the designation is not restricted to the single kingdom in the north. The expression *ʿmy yśrʾl* is then equivalent to *bny yśrʾl* and *byt yśrʾl*, insofar as the terms refer to a larger Israel not limited to the northern kingdom. Other factors may be involved in the selection, but they cannot be determined on the basis of present methods and available data. These variations in the qualified usage of Israel with other nouns may be compared with the use of "Joseph" in chaps. 5–6 and "Isaac" in chap. 7. Both apparently designate the northern kingdom only, but it is not clear why one form is used in one section of the book and the other term in a different section.

It could be argued that these distinctions in the use of the name "Israel" are too finely drawn and that the second set of visions refers specifically to the northern kingdom, especially because it is the one directly under threat in the book of Amos. Even more supportive of this position is the fact that the episode at the temple in Bethel is sandwiched in between Visions 3 and 4, thereby demonstrating that those visions and messages have to do with the northern kingdom just as the narrative in 7:10–17 does. We can agree substantially with this argument and would have employed it ourselves except in terms of the restriction to the north or the exclusivity of the visions and message (which is repeated). The point is that the northern kingdom is always and emphatically included in all uses of the name "Israel." The only distinction we are suggesting is that when the term is used alone it refers to the north only, but certainly when the expanded expressions are used (*bny, byt, ʿmy*) we are not to suppose that the north is excluded, only that more than the north is intended. When it came to carrying out his mandate, Amos may well have felt that the most urgent need for his message was in the north, and that his primary obligation was to go there. That emphasis in itself does not mean that he spoke only in the north or that he never delivered any oracles in the south, only that the bulk of the material in the book of Amos may have been delivered in the north, and that his primary mission may have been in that kingdom.

The expression *ʿmy yśrʾl* is used four times in the book of Amos: twice in the visions we are studying and twice elsewhere. One of these instances is in the account of the confrontation at Bethel; that is, it is enclosed between the two occurrences in the visions. We would have every reason to expect that the same terms would have the same meanings in the same context. At first sight the presence of the expanded expression *ʿmy yśrʾl* in a story about Amos' presence in the north, which deals with a supposed threat to the king's life and begins and ends with a prediction of the captivity of the northern people, would strongly imply that other expressions involving

Israel would have the same restricted scope, but not necessarily. In the section 7:9–17, the word "Israel" occurs seven times; five of them are Israel by itself, and in every case the meaning is certain: the northern kingdom alone is intended.

7:9   (1) *wĕnāšammû bāmôt yiśḥāq*
             ûmiqdĕšê yiśrā'ēl yeḥĕrābû
             wĕqamtî 'al-bêt yārob'ām beḥāreb

             The high places of Isaac will be devastated,
             and Israel's sanctuaries will be laid waste;
             and I shall attack Jeroboam's house with my sword.

The context shows clearly that the north is intended, for the military action involved will be against the northern dynasty.

7:10   (2) *'el-yārob'ām melek-yiśrā'ēl*

             to Jeroboam, the king of Israel.

This one is absolutely certain.

7:11   (3) *baḥereb yāmût yarob'ām*
             wĕyiśrā'ēl gālōh yigleh mē'al 'admātô

             By the sword shall Jeroboam die,
             and Israel shall surely go into exile from its land.

Here again the context shows clearly that the northern kingdom is intended. The death of Jeroboam and the fall of his dynasty will signal the end of the kingdom and the captivity of its population.

7:16   (4) *'attâ 'ōmēr lō' tinnābē' 'al-yiśrā'ēl*
             wĕlō' taṭṭîp 'al-bêt yiśḥāq

             You say, "Don't prophesy against Israel,
             don't preach against Isaac's domain!"

Amos is quoting Amaziah as forbidding him to prophesy against or concerning Israel (with Isaac used as a synonym for Israel here, as also in v 9). The implication surely is that Amaziah is speaking of the realm in which he exercises some authority, which would be the northern kingdom. The actual statement attributed to him in vv 12–13 is even more precise and restricted about where Amos may or may not utter prophecies: "Run away to the land of Judah . . . and there do your prophesying. But at Bethel never prophesy again." In view of this statement, "Israel//Isaac" in v 16 can only refer to the northern kingdom and to it alone.

7:17 (5) *wĕyiśrā'ēl gālōh yigleh mēʿal 'admātô*

> and Israel shall surely go into exile from its land.

This one is an exact repetition of the statement in v 11, already discussed. It must have the same reference and same restriction: the northern kingdom only.

If the five occurrences of the name "Israel" alone all refer certainly to the northern kingdom and to it alone, what about the other two occurrences of the name in conjunction with qualifiers, (6) *byt yśr'l* (7:10) and (7) *ʿmy yśr'l* (7:15)? While the initial assumption about the use of the term in this story (with or without qualifiers) would be that it applied to the north only, more careful study may show otherwise or at least allow for other possibilities or plausibilities. Let us look at the cases.

7:10 (6) *qāšar ʿāleykā ʿāmos bĕqereb bêt yiśrā'ēl*

> Amos has conspired against you inside the house of
> Israel.

Amos is accused of conspiring against the king "inside the house of Israel." If the expression here has its normal application to the larger geographical and political entity (i.e., both kingdoms) then the charge should be interpreted to the effect that Amos' conspiracy against Jeroboam was hatched in Amos' homeland (Judah) and is being aided and abetted by both Judahite and Israelite factions.

An alternative proposal is that the phrase here should be understood literally as a designation of the temple at Bethel (i.e., the house of [the God of] Israel), a synonym of the terms used by Amaziah in v 13: *miqdaš-melek//bêt mamlākâ*. We believe that *byt yśr'l* has the same meaning in Amos 6:1 (see the discussion there and at 7:10, 13). Such an identification would signify that Amos was accused of plotting against the king and the kingdom, in the temple itself, which is where Amos uttered the fateful self-convicting words about the end of Jeroboam's reign and dynasty. The "land" in the following sentence would refer to the country or nation that Jeroboam rules.

7:15   (7) *lēk hinnābē' 'el-ʿammî yiśrā'ēl*

Go prophesy to my people Israel.

In many ways one's view of the book of Amos and of his prophetic mission and career hinges on the interpretation of this verse and of its possible links with the visions and other passages in the book. According to our view, *ʿmy yśr'l* must have the same meaning that it does elsewhere in the book of Amos and especially in this complex of material that includes the second pair of visions and the story of the incident at Bethel. We have already discussed the usage in the two visions. What does the expression mean here? In the immediate context of the visit to Bethel, one might well or easily conclude that the northern kingdom is in view, and certainly it cannot be denied. The way the story is placed, it would appear that in response to Yahweh's commission, Amos went to Bethel to deliver his message. We will only repeat that *ʿmy yśr'l*, like *bny* and *byt yśr'l*, clearly and always includes the northern kingdom. That claim cannot be in dispute, so that in every case in which those words are used, the north is included and Amos could interpret the charge in the way he did without deciding the question of the exact meaning of the expression. The only way to achieve the latter is to make a decision about the southern kingdom. Was the divine commission to Amos limited to the north? Did Yahweh, whether in vision or audition, say to Amos that he should go only to the north and not to the south? We find no evidence for this restriction and believe that Amos was called as a prophet to the larger entity in common with all of the prophets of whom we know enough to be able to form an opinion. The different prophets whose missions are specified may in practice have restricted their ministries to certain locations, but they did not hesitate to speak to and about other places as well. The other three eighth-century prophets were not limited to one kingdom or the other but spoke fully to and about both, even though the proportions may vary widely from one prophetic book to another and the prophets themselves may have stayed in their own countries. If we think of prophets such as Elijah and Elisha, they did not restrict themselves or their activities to the territory of the northern kingdom, though we call them northern prophets. They did not hesitate to exercise their prophetic mission outside the borders or to give counsel and warning to kings other than the kings of Israel. So unless there is compelling evidence to the contrary, we have every right to assume that Amos was called to be a prophet to all of Israel and that he responded to the call by going to Bethel. But that course of action does not mean that he was restricted to the northern kingdom. As the oracles in chaps. 1–2 show, his prophetic mission included many nations outside of Israel, among them specifically Judah. So we credit Amos here with very accurate use of the appropriate terminology.

We may also observe that, as in the unit involving chaps. 5–6, there are seven occurrences of the name "Israel" in the story in 7:9–17. Here, unlike the situation in chaps. 5–6, the predominant expression is "Israel" alone, which occurs five times; the other two instances have qualifiers, but the arrangement is symmetrical and would seem to be deliberate.

1.	7:9	*yiśrā'ēl*
2.	7:10	*yiśrā'ēl*
3.	7:10	*bêt yiśrā'ēl*
4.	7:11	*yiśrā'ēl*
5.	7:15	*'ammî yiśrā'ēl*
6.	7:16	*yiśrā'ēl*
7.	7:17	*yiśrā'ēl*

The conclusion of the matter is that the pair "Jacob"//"my people Israel" in the four visions refers to the larger entity and not exclusively to the northern kingdom. As far as we are aware, whenever the combination is used (or the terms are in some proximity to each other), the reference always goes beyond the local entity Israel and is never restricted to it. We do not discuss the usage after the fall of the northern kingdom, for it would not be relevant to the issue under consideration here. There was an Israel that embodied the promise and experience of the past as well as the hopes and expectations of the future along with the present reality, whatever its borders and limits may have been. It was the twelve-tribe or ten-tribe league, the united monarchy of Saul or David and Solomon, the divided kingdoms from the tenth to the eighth centuries, the exilic community, the postexilic restoration, or any combination of them.

As a footnote to this exercise, we may point out that the combination is found in Isa 1:3, only there it is divided and in reverse order (*yśr'l*//*'my*). The verse itself and Isa 1:2 do not offer clear evidence to indicate which political entity is intended, but the passage beginning with v 4 seems clearly to refer to Judah and Jerusalem. So if the expression in v 3 has a purely local reference, it would have to be to the southern kingdom, just as the usage in Amos 7:15—if it has a restricted scope there—would have to refer to the northern kingdom only. It is hardly likely that roughly contemporary prophets would use the same expression with mutually exclusive meanings. It is more reasonable to suppose that the expression *'my yśr'l*, in whatever sequence, refers to the same larger entity, combined Israel, while the prophet himself may be addressing only one part of it. In other words, both Israel and Judah are legitimate heirs to and parts of "my people Israel." The usage in First Isaiah generally seems to run parallel to that of

Amos, but it would require a detailed study of the actual occurrences to demonstrate the presumption.

There remains one other use of the expression ʿmy yśrʾl in the book of Amos: It occurs in 9:14, where we read wĕšabtî ʾet-šĕbût ʿammî yiśrāʾel, "I will restore the fortunes of Israel my people." We know from the occurrence of the same idiom in Job (42:10, wayhwh šāb šĕbût [Kethib šbyt] ʾiyyôb) that it is not restricted to the idea of return from captivity, but has a more general application to the reversal of misfortunes, which is the sense in which to understand it in Amos 9. The context is eschatological, and it is altogether likely that all of Israel is intended. Just as references to early Israel involve the whole people, so future and final references normally include both kingdoms, for a restoration of the halcyon days of David and Solomon or of Moses and Joshua is contemplated. So here we do not hesitate to interpret "my people Israel" as referring to the larger commonwealth. What follows is a description of the rebuilding of ruined cities and the replanting of abandoned vineyards. Emphasis is placed on a firm and permanent planting in their own land, from which they will not be taken again. In spite of the remarks above about the meaning of the expression šwb šbwt, this passage reads like a return and restoration after destruction and exile. Whatever the specific circumstances, and they may well be exilic, the expression ʿmy yśrʾl would encompass the larger ideal kingdom. No return and renewal were thought by any prophet to be restricted in nature. In those passages in which the restoration is described, it invariably involves a return to the old order and the renewal of all of Israel. So here we are to understand ʿmy yśrʾl in both the historic sense (past) and the eschatological sense (future) as meaning all of Israel.

Many other passages referring to the restoration either specify all of Israel, or both kingdoms by name, or a unified kingdom as in the days of David and Solomon. There seems little doubt that in Amos 9:14 the larger commonwealth is in view. The usage with respect to ʿmy yśrʾl always refers to the larger entity and not to the northern kingdom alone, although in the same way the latter is always included, never excluded.

EXCURSUS: WHEN GOD REPENTS

The verb nḥm occurs twice in the book of Amos, in exactly the same form, in the transition sentences from Amos' interposition to the divine response in each of the first two visions (7:3, 6). The lines read as follows:

niḥam yhwh ʿal-zōʾt
Yahweh repented [= changed his mind] over this.

On the basis of parallel usage elsewhere in the Bible with *nḥm ʿal* (or occasionally *ʾel-*) we can identify the pronoun *z't* with the noun *rʿh*, "evil, calamity, disaster," either threatened or actual. The verb form is ambiguous and could be either the *nipʿal* or the *piʿel* 3d m. s. perfect, but there is no question here that it is the former. On the basis of both common usage and the context here, the meaning is quite certain. Yahweh changed his mind about what he had planned to do, as shown by the visions, though not put into words, and, because of the prophet's intercession, repealed or reversed the decision: "It shall not happen" (*lōʾ tihyeh*). Again the reference is to the *rāʿâ* that was threatened in the vision. The second time around the reversal is reaffirmed with the recognition that the decision had already been canceled once: "This [calamity] also shall not happen," *gam-hîʾ lōʾ tihyeh*.

Thus the two visions and dialogues are to be seen as separate events, and if we are to follow the sequence closely, it means that the second sequence begins at the same point that the first one did. Even after the initial decision is reversed, it would seem that the particular mode of judgment, the locust plague, has been canceled but that a more permanent decision has been delayed. The second vision carries with it the same portent of utter doom, in fact worse in its cosmic aspects and implications for destruction than the first. Once again the prophet intervenes, and once again Yahweh cancels the decision. This cancellation can and should be interpreted literally and narrowly in the sense that the particular decision to destroy by fire (as, e.g., the destruction of Sodom and Gomorrah and that of all of the nations in chaps. 1–2) has been reversed. The decision is neither permanent nor general; it does not mean that all further negative judgments are ruled out, or that other means or methods of destruction may not be used, only that this particular decision has been negated.

It also seems clear, however, that the particular set of circumstances that gave rise to the decisions embodied in or illuminated by the visions will not be the direct basis for or occasion of another decision for destruction. Yahweh has accepted the prophet's intervention and will not now act against his people, pending a later determination on the basis of new evidence of intention and behavior. A period of grace has been granted to allow the people to solidify the position by genuine repentance and for the prophet to try to reach the people with due warning concerning their peril. At most, intercession buys time, and the decision made as a result of it must be regarded as temporary in the sense that the future course of the relations between God and people will depend on further developments and in particular on a show of genuine repentance. There is an interlocking reaction that involves repentance on both sides, one stimulating and requiring a radical change of mind and will in the other if the relationship is to survive and if the threat of drastic punishment is to be averted, not merely arrested.

Thus the first two visions and the dialogues associated with them assure a respite for "Jacob," so that the imminent threat of national obliteration has been canceled, and there is time to establish a more permanent reconciliation and stabilize the relationship. To do so requires a corresponding change on the part of the people, for the future of the relationship depends on a satisfactory reciprocal attachment of each to the other, of love on both sides, but of grace and goodwill on the part of the divine sovereign, and obedience in true service and worship on the part of the human vassal.

In the interim, Yahweh, having made his decision to cancel the immediate threat and withhold judgment for a space, both prophet and people have an opportunity to remedy the situation. The prophet must warn urgently on the basis of the visions (and their cancellation) and the conditions that brought on those decisions to begin with (as richly documented throughout the book). The people must then follow by responding in genuine repentance for their past and current rebellions and violations of the terms of the agreement between them. That sort of response would lead to an extension of the truce and to the establishment of a more permanent peace between the parties. Failure to act in this period of grace and on the kindly reversal of the deity would, however, ensure a reinstatement of the judgment and a renewed decision to punish the people for intransigent disobedience, intensified by the added guilt of rejecting the pardon and refusing to negotiate a permanent settlement.

As we know from the account of the second pair of visions, the extension failed, the period of grace produced no convincing evidence of genuine repentance, and the judgment was reaffirmed. The important difference is that the second time around, the prophet was not permitted to intercede or, recognizing that further extensions would not be granted and that the case was futile, did not even try. A second set of reversals had taken place, and the decision now, expressed in identical terms in the second set of visions, was both explicit and irreversible. Yahweh had changed his mind again, twice more, to come back to the original set of decisions. While the four visions have been gathered in the space of a little more than a chapter (7:1–8:3), with only the account of the visit to the temple at Bethel and the altercation with Amaziah intervening, we must suppose a sufficient time between the pairs of visionary experiences for the period of grace and suspended judgment. In fact, we suppose that the prophet must have engaged in a desperate effort to prod or provoke the people from bottom to top, but especially at the top, to restructure their lives and the conduct of the nation in political and ecclesiastical as well as social and economic matters, not to speak of personal affairs, so as to prolong the deferment of judgment and initiate or inaugurate an era of authentic peace, šālôm. The utter failure of the supposed campaign is underscored by the absence of any reference to or suggestion of changes on the part of Israel (or Judah for that matter) in the book of Amos. The exhortations, or at least some of them, are preserved along with the warnings. But of responses we have nothing except the occasional explicit (7:10–17), more often implied, rejection of the prophet and his message, the very word of God that they most needed to hear (chaps. 2–3).

The point now is to understand that in spite of the hopeless failure of the salvation mission, we must not question the reality of the reversals recorded in Amos 7–8, and we must seek to comprehend what Amos and the other biblical prophets and writers meant when they talked or wrote about the repentance of God. In spite of the apparent futility of the gesture and the effect of a double set or pair of reversals bringing us back to the original decision and starting point for the action of judgment against the people, a real transaction took place, which revealed the mind of Yahweh in action, and there was reciprocal influence and response between prophet and deity.

While the pair of events in which this action and response took place is isolated in Amos' story and vocabulary, and although we can infer that a second set of similar but opposite reversals took place offstage between the two sets of visions, the phenomenon itself of divine reversal is well documented elsewhere in the Bible and constitutes an important, perhaps essential feature of biblical theology, that is, the biblical interpretation of the divine status and involvement in human affairs.

It is to this combination of circumstances and features, attitudes and activities that we now turn. But first the following presentation may help to clear the air of possible misunderstanding. What follows is not an attempt to discuss theological matters *per se,* or to invade an area of investigation for which we are not qualified, and in any case for which the Anchor Bible series is not designed. Our concern here is strictly with the understanding of the way biblical writers and books deal with the figure of God; the way they interpret his being and presence, his thinking and acting in connection with the world that he created; and, most of all, the way his interactions with human beings are to be grasped. In order to understand properly the biblical positions on fundamental theological issues, it is necessary to enter into the world of the Bible and accept its presuppositions and affirmations, participate in the dramatic portrayal of the deity as person in relation to other persons, whether divine or human, in the action that takes place between heaven and earth. This action is both dramatic and dialogic, involving both conversation and action; it is framed by history or at least chronology; and it requires the presence of Yahweh as actor on the stage and participant in the course of historical events. As a living, acting person, he is subject to defining characteristics if not limitations that are not normally associated with attributes of deity, and he will demonstrate a full range of passions and compassions, convictions and attitudes, and a corresponding group of words and actions that are characteristic also of human beings. The vocabulary, with occasional modifications and exceptions, is much the same, as inevitably it must be.

While recognizing the vast metaphysical gap that separates human beings from God or the ideas of God, human beings, regrettably, are bound by circumstances beyond their control, and all ideas and their embodiment in words remain stubbornly human, locked within our own limitations. So even the effort to speak or write about God, the truly other, is doomed to failure even as we take the problem and its consequences into account and admit the truth while we are enunciating our views. At best we may talk about correspondence and correlation, about similarity and simile. While admitting that we cannot break into the divine realm we can affirm that for the biblical writers God managed to break into their world; they caught a glimpse of him within the limitations of the world we all inhabit, they heard him speak (in their language, of course), and they saw his actions.

The form of presentation is narrational (the Bible is essentially though not exclusively narrative, e.g., the Primary History—the great narrative of the Bible—is about half of its content, and if we add the Chronicler's history and the narrative materials in the latter prophets and their writings, perhaps two-thirds or more of the total), and the rules and conventions of narrative writing apply to all of the participants, including God. Special effort is made and precautions taken to affirm and constantly remind that this person is unique and shares certain characteristics with no one and nothing else, but he remains a person in the story nonetheless. We judge that the Bible is successful in conveying both facts of theological experience adequately, that he is God and that he is a person. The whole presentation is finally a metaphor for reality; no external evidence can be brought to bear to confirm or support the biblical picture. For our purposes it is enough to say that we will make the assumption and attempt to describe the deity of the Bible as the Bible does by implication and inference, and therefore take the biblical picture and portrayal at face value, leaving more difficult philosophical and theological questions concerning the truth claims of belief in transcendence and immanence, especially in their supposed simultaneity, to other times and places and persons for discussion.

Ours may seem like a rather primitive approach to a book that has been examined, studied, and restudied by millennia of theological thinkers and endlessly modernized and updated for the benefit of sophisticated and unsophisticated readers. We think the ultimate sophistication is to go back into the biblical world and live and work inside its literature for a more significant experience of the realities the biblical writers dealt with, and for a better understanding of both the story they wrote and the God who is its central figure and hero.

We remind the reader that this remains an effort to describe, analyze, and re-present. Decisions about belief and commitment are properly theological and personal and lie outside the scope of our assignment and of the series. We try to deal positively and sympathetically with the literature assigned to us, but exactly what we believe in theological terms, while doubtless important in the shaping of our approach, method, and results, is not germane to this discussion, and neither is what the reader believes about such matters, important as it is in influencing perceptions and inferences about the original text and the commentary. We are simply interested in *what* the text says, in *how* the editor told the story of Amos and his God.

It may be suggested or even urged that the biblical picture of the deity, with the possible exception of some books like Job and Second Isaiah and isolated theologically lofty passages elsewhere, is very little different from the portrayal of deities in the polytheistic religions of Israel's neighbors, and that by adhering to the biblical stance and style we overemphasize such similarities and do not give sufficient weight to the much more significant and important differences between the one and the other. It would be much more appropriate, they say, to present the biblical deity in the light of the best and later views, those that lean toward and may have been influenced by philosophical views emanating from Greece for example, and that a particular paradigm must be adopted, one more in keeping with later Jewish and Christian theological interpretation and exposition, than to revert to a best-forgotten and properly abandoned past.

We would prefer, however, to steer a course between what we perceive to be extremes, and which is consistent with the biblical writers' actual thinking and depicting. On the one hand they were insistent on the vast difference between their religion and that of any and all neighbors. They stressed two points, though many others are derivative from them: (1) Yahweh was the sole God worthy of the name or title, for he alone had actual power and authority. All of the other gods together were literally nothing or nobody, and they were consistently and constantly identified with images of wood and stone and anything else. Whether this is polemical argument rather than accurate reasoning about pagan religion, it clearly is a sufficient expression of the standard view on the subject in the Bible. (2) Yahweh was alone, without consort or children, without companions. This point goes with the other but refutes the notion that there is any conventional mythology in the central stream of biblical tradition. There is a large host of beings in heaven, but they are all creatures, having no independent existence or power base, and in that respect they are no better off than or different from humans.

The fact that in spite of these global differences Yahweh is treated as a person and shares attributes that in other cultures are attributed to their gods is hardly surprising. In the Bible, because comparison with other gods is ruled out, the same correspondences can be noted in heavenly and earthly beings, including especially human ones. Precisely because humans are made in the image of God (and so too the angels, at least those who visit the earth) it is possible for there to be communication and mutual understanding as well as empathy, sympathy, and antipathy. The deity's personality is central to the biblical picture and does not change from the earliest to the latest sources. He may be viewed from different angles and seen under different aspects; different traits or characteristics may be emphasized in different passages; but that he is a person with the many-faceted features of personality is affirmed from first to last. So in many ways the Bible remains true to its "primitive" past and is less compatible with philosophical notions of an abstract being, or ultimate reality or ground of being. Just as there is an important and unbridgeable distance between Yahweh and the gods of Canaan, or those of Mesopotamia or Egypt or Greece or Rome, so there is at least an equal or greater distance from an Aristotelian unmoved mover, or even a Platonic Idea (or Ideal). The biblical God is always and uncompromisingly personal: he is above all a person, neither more nor less.

At the same time care is taken by the authors not to present God as merely Superman or like the gods of other religions. In the case of our root *nhm,* an important qualification if not contradiction is introduced by the statement, made at least twice, that Yahweh does not repent because he is not a man, implying that repentance belongs to the human rather than the divine sphere and personality repertoire (see Num 23:19; 1 Sam 15:29). What is meant, we believe, is that Yahweh does not change his mind (= repent) the way human beings do, who often do so frivolously, capriciously, or arbitrarily, whereas Yahweh does so only for cause, as human beings should. While the case is not explained in general terms, it is clear that Yahweh's repentance is limited to situations of a certain number and kind and occurs only under certain conditions. Thus his repentance is limited entirely to his dealings with the created world and almost if not exclusively with human beings. It only takes place in response to a situation, event, or circumstance and is never initiated arbitrarily or capriciously. In other words, divine repentance is always a response to human behavior or action, and it is never undertaken or attributed to God independently of a specific human condition.

Overall, repentance on God's part occurs under the following conditions:

1. It can be a reaction to certain events or developments in the human scene.

2. Specifically, it can occur in response to an intervention or intercession on the part of a prophetic figure (e.g., Moses, Samuel, Amos, etc.), although it is significant that in the story of Abraham's intercession for Sodom and Gomorrah, the term *nhm* does not occur, perhaps because there is no real change of mind on the part of the

deity in the account. It seems clear that God never intended to sweep the innocent away with the guilty but would find a way to save the innocent (Lot) while punishing the guilty.

3. It can be a response to a showing of genuine repentance in word and deed on the part of people.

Divine repentance can move in either of two directions: from judgment to clemency or the other way around. It can also move in both directions sequentially, as in the instances in Amos, from judgment to forgiveness (first two visions) and then back to judgment in the interim between the two sets of visions (as expressed or reflected in the second pair). In view of the multiplicity of options and actualities, it will be of value to look at several examples scattered through the Bible; while the study is not exhaustive, it should prove to be representative. Throughout and in every case, it should be understood that the divine repentance is real; that the meaning and value of the story depend on the transaction between God and prophet, or God and people; and that if it is not real on the part of God (i.e., that he does not and cannot change his mind), then the story is a charade without significance. Admittedly we are using a metaphor, involving stories and persons that include God and humans; but within the metaphor—and we believe that nobody can get closer to the reality behind the metaphor—we must be faithful to the data. Once it is understood that Yahweh enters into the drama as fully and wholeheartedly as the other participants, then we can proceed with the analysis.

1. *Genesis 6:6–7.* The first example to claim our attention is at the beginning of the Flood Story in Gen 6:6–7 (J). We read:

> ⁶And Yahweh repented (= regretted, *wayyinnāḥem*) that he had made mankind on the earth, and he afflicted himself to his heart. ⁷And Yahweh said, "I will wipe out mankind, whom I have created, from the face of the earth—including man and beast, creeping things (reptiles) and birds of the skies, because I have repented (= *niḥamtî*) that I made them.

In this case the divine decision (the change of mind about the human race and other living creatures) results from the observation of human corruption and wickedness: "and Yahweh saw how great was the wickedness of mankind in the world, and that the whole structure of the thoughts of his mind was exclusively wicked at all times" (6:5). The reversal of the decisions made in the original creation comes about because of the activities of human beings, who behave wickedly and imagine more wicked things all the time. Hence the decision is reached to wipe out humanity and the rest of terrestrial life. The context is entirely clear that the fault—the evil and sinfulness—is entirely humanity's responsibility, and the punishment is aimed at mankind, and that the animal kingdom will share their fate, but only because of the close association of animals and humans. It may be observed that when the king of Nineveh and his people respond to Jonah's preaching, the domestic animals also put on sackcloth and join in the rituals and acts of repentance (Jonah 3:7–8).

The decision based on the change of will, and the pain and agony of the act of reversal of previous decisions and acts, are expressed sharply by the use of a remarkable *hitpaᶜel* form from the root *ṣb,* which means literally that he inflicted pain on himself (= he tortured himself or he agonized); the added phrase, "to his heart [= mind]," only strengthens the force of the affliction. Coming to a new decision was no light matter; it involved an agonizing reappraisal (as the expression goes) and was reached with great personal pain.

While the passage is commonly attributed to the J source, which is considered somewhat primitive theologically, no one can challenge the mastery of this writer as a storyteller or narrator. And while he presents the deity in highly personal terms and conveys a person who feels deeply, thinks sharply, and acts dramatically, there is nothing primitive about the stories either in content or style. Once we accept the requirements of this medium (narrative about persons), we can acknowledge the storyteller's remarkable achievement.

The decision is carried out in the course of the subsequent narrative. At the end, Yahweh makes another decision with regard to the survivors, in effect reversing or modifying the earlier one, although, strictly speaking, the latter is no longer in force once its objective has been achieved. In 8:21 (J) we read,

> And Yahweh said to his heart:
> "I will not ever again curse the earth for the sake of mankind,
>   even though the heart of man is wicked from his youth;
> and I will never again destroy all living things as I have done."

The new decision represents a shift from the preceding one in that the commitment is made to sustain life on earth not only irrespective of human behavior but in full recognition of humans' evil tendencies and proclivities:

6:5   *wĕkol-yēṣer maḥšĕbōt libbô raq raᶜ kol-hayyôm*
And the entire shape of the thoughts of his heart [reason] is exclusively evil all the time.

8:21   *kî yēṣer lēb hāʾādām raᶜ minnĕᶜūrāyw*
Even though the shape of the heart of the human is evil from his youth.

The first statement provides support for the decision to wipe out humanity, while the second modifies the commitment never to do so again. We can speak therefore of a new decision based essentially on the same data, in which God promises not to do what was done before; thus, although the term is not used in connection with the second statement, we can speak of a second repentance or change of mind (= heart). This situation is similar to that of Amos 7–8, where the first two reversals of a decision are signaled by the use of the word "repent" (*nḥm*), but the next set of reversals is subsumed or presupposed in the next decisional statement.

2. *Exodus 32:10–14* (J). In this famous episode, Moses intercedes with God, who has decided to destroy his people in the wilderness because they have made and are worshiping a golden calf. The intercession is effective and Yahweh changes his mind, reversing the earlier decision as follows:

> ¹⁰And now let me alone that my anger may burn against them, and that I may destroy them; then I will make you into a great nation.
> ¹¹And Moses placated the face of his God Yahweh. And he said, "Why, O Yahweh, should your anger be kindled against your people, whom you brought out of the land of Egypt with great strength and a mighty forearm?
> ¹²Why should Egypt say as follows, 'For evil he brought them out to kill them in the mountains and to destroy them from the face of the earth. Turn from your hot rage and repent about the evil to your people. . . .' "
> ¹³ . . .
> ¹⁴And Yahweh repented concerning the evil that he had said he would do to his people.

In this case the divine repentance occurs in response to the intercession of Moses, a prophetic figure. In the preceding material Yahweh told Moses that the people had made a molten calf and were worshiping it and crediting it with the deliverance from bondage in Egypt. Yahweh also told Moses that he, Yahweh, intended to destroy his people because of this unacceptable behavior and instead make Moses and his descendants into a great people. In v 10 the writer makes it appear that Yahweh is asking Moses to release or allow him to go ahead with this plan. Whatever the possible meaning of the terms, Moses seizes the opportunity to intercede and does so effectively. Here, as indicated, Yahweh has made a decision to destroy based on the same sort of data used to reach a similar judgment to wipe out humanity in Genesis 6 (all of these passages are J). In that situation the decision to destroy was denoted as the act of repentance, Yahweh's change of mind. Clearly a similar change of mind about his act of grace, in bringing

Israel out of Egypt, has taken place, and he will now punish the people who abandoned him for an idol. That decision, however, is not the one connected with divine repentance, though clearly it could have been. In this case it is the next reversal that is called repentance. Moses urges God to turn back from his fierce anger and to repent about the evil that he has decided to do to his people. Yahweh in turn accedes to the interceder and reverses the decision. The situation is now back where it was before Yahweh determined to destroy the nation. But the reprieve is only temporary, because the people are still in open rebellion and obviously Yahweh will not tolerate apostasy and idolatry. Something dramatic needs to be done, and Moses prepares for drastic action. Unless there is a radical change on the part of the people, the grace period will elapse and the judgment will be reinstituted. As we have suggested, intercession can only produce a temporary reversal; the basic situation must be rectified.

Moses does two things: first, he puts an end to the apostasy by destroying the image and by taking full charge of the situation; and second, he recruits the Levites to restore his authority through a blood bath in which the ringleaders and most visible followers of the new idolatrous religion are wiped out.

Only then is Moses prepared to renew the dialogue with Yahweh. He informs the people that in order to stabilize the situation after such a traumatic experience he must attempt to atone for their great sin. Moses asks Yahweh to forgive the people and adds pressure with a threat: "If you won't, then wipe me out of your tablet which you have written" (Exod 32:32). Yahweh is receptive but will not budge on the ultimate question of justice. The people will be spared, but the guilty parties (presumably the remaining leaders and those in responsible positions) will be punished.

We see in Exodus 32 a complex interaction between deity and people, with the prophet acting as mediator. The episode is precipitated by a deliberate and scandalous act of apostasy. The first reversal on the part of Yahweh is the decision to destroy his people. There is a curious element in the presentation, in which Yahweh asks Moses to do something (leave him alone) so that he, Yahweh, can go ahead with the decision, almost as though he were asking for Moses' approval or as though Moses were holding him back, and unless he released him he could not go ahead with it. Perhaps it implies that Yahweh wants the opposite of what he says and is really inviting Moses to take a part in the crisis. There is also the curious promise to Moses that if God destroys Israel he will nevertheless create a new nation out of Moses, thereby stressing the distinction between his faithful servant (Moses, cf. Num 12:7) and faithless and apostate Israel. This announcement implies, but without an explicit assertion, that the decision is not as solid and firm as it might appear. In any case Moses is able to intercede effectively, and Yahweh in response reverses the judgment. Moses asks him to repent (which is explained in the words "turn from your fierce wrath"), and he does (*hnḥm,* v 12, and *wynḥm,* v 14).

As we have noted, the account does not end there. Yahweh has been persuaded to reverse his decision and to hold off from settling accounts with his people. But the reprieve is only temporary. Moses must act quickly and decisively if he is to salvage anything from the situation. If nothing is done the judgment will be reinstated, and then Moses will be unable to intercede. The situation here casts some light on the circumstances in Amos 7–8. After the first two visions and dialogues there is a reprieve, time for action on the part of the leaders and people of Israel. But the period of grace is limited, and failure to produce tangible and visible results will bring about a second reversal. In this case the principal leader, Moses, is able and willing to do something. What he does is drastic but also effective. In the days of Amos no one could be found to bring about the change, so according to Visions 3 and 4 nothing happened, the judgment was reinstituted, and in the end disaster came. The prophet was powerless to intercede a third or fourth time in the same set of circumstances. At the end of the episode in the wilderness we are reminded that repentance and forgiveness on God's part do not entirely eliminate the requirement of justice. The parting word on the subject is,

> Whoever has sinned against me, I will wipe him out of my tablet.
> (Exod 32:33)

Moses' vicarious offer is politely but firmly rejected. In the end everyone must answer for himself (or herself) and be judged.

Note that Moses uses the imperative *hnḥm* in Exod 32:12 along with *šûb.* Apparently only Moses in the Bible expresses this idea quite so forcefully, commanding God to repent. Thus we have an echo of the statement in the story in Ps 90:13, where we read:

šûbâ yhwh ʿad-mātāy	Return Yahweh—How long?
wĕhinnāḥēm ʿal-ʿăbādeykā	and repent concerning your servants!

We note that Psalm 90 is attributed to Moses, thereby connecting it with the story in Exodus 32 and confirming the view that in the Bible only Moses uses such forceful language with God. While these are the only places in which *hnḥm* is used in the imperative (and furthermore addressed to God), the parallel root *šûb* is used more frequently and addressed to both God and humans. To instruct God to repent (using this verb with its connotations and overtones) is a privilege claimed by Moses and restricted to him.

Amos will also use the imperative but of a different verb, focusing attention on the resultant action ("forgive") rather than on the prior decision ("turn and repent").

3. *1 Samuel 15:11, 29, 35.* These verses tell the story of Saul's rejection by Yahweh, as transmitted through Samuel. It is the third story about divine repentance in which the root *nḥm* is used. The interactions between deity and prophet, and prophet and king, and the significance especially of the radical disjuncture between vv 11 and 35, which form an envelope around the rejection story itself, and v 29, which offers a drastically different insight into the nature of God, all require careful attention, but we will limit our study to the specific occurrences of *nḥm* and refer to the rest of the narrative as needed.

> ¹⁰And the word of Yahweh came to Samuel as follows:
> ¹¹I have repented [regretted = changed my mind] about making Saul king because he has turned from following me and my commands he has not established [= carried out].

At the end of the story we read the following (v 35), "And Yahweh repented (*niḥām*) that he had made Saul king over Israel."

In this story the repentance of God, that is, the reversal of his decision to make Saul king, comes about because of Saul's failure to carry out the divine command concerning the Amalekites, in not slaughtering the captured cattle and in keeping alive the king, Agag, who had been taken prisoner. Thus the divine repentance is spontaneous, as in the first story in Genesis. The sinful or rebellious behavior of a man or of mankind initiates a sequence in which Yahweh reconsiders a previous decision and then makes a new decision, reversing the former one. In the light of new evidence, and because Saul has failed in his responsibility as the anointed king of Israel, he is now rejected. The new decision is communicated to Samuel, who as prophet and messenger of Yahweh must deliver the message to Saul.

The details are spelled out in the remarkable colloquy recorded in vv 12–26, in which Samuel makes the charge that Saul has disobeyed the specific command of Yahweh, while Saul tries to defend his action and himself. Finally Samuel pronounces the dire words, "Because you rejected the word of Yahweh he has rejected you from being king" (v 23).

Saul then concedes that he is at fault and begs for forgiveness, which is the appropriate procedure under the circumstances (vv 24–25). But Samuel refuses to accept the confession and plea, and merely repeats the condemnation:

> SAUL: "I have sinned; indeed I have transgressed the command of Yahweh and your words, because I feared the people and listened to

what they said. But now forgive my sin and return with me so that I may supplicate Yahweh." (vv 24–25)

SAMUEL: "I will not return with you, because you rejected the word of Yahweh and Yahweh has rejected you from being king over Israel." (v 26)

The situation here is significantly different from the case with Moses and the golden calf. In the latter Moses interceded with God and secured a reprieve of the sentence and a grace period during which remedial action could be taken. In the current episode Samuel is not in a position to intercede, though it is possible that he attempted to do so the night before, when Yahweh informed him of the decision to reject Saul. That at least is a reasonable interpretation of the statement that Samuel was upset and cried out to Yahweh all night long (1 Sam 15:11). The next day, however, it was too late. For Samuel the issue is now settled, and his role is to carry out his mandate and deliver the judgment of God. We might suppose that if Saul's confession and repentance were genuine Yahweh might relent; but that opportunity is not offered either. Nevertheless, the prophet is in an awkward situation. While Saul was chosen to be king and anointed by Samuel, at Yahweh's instigation and with his approval, the prophet still has been troubled by the latter's behavior and finds reason to support Yahweh's latest decision.

On the face of it Samuel is simply representing the deity and reporting the latter's decision, but in an important sense it is also the prophet's decision. As we know from other stories, Samuel was regarded as an effective intercessor with the deity (cf. 1 Sam 7:5–9), and he had a reputation in this respect that linked him with Moses and persisted through the centuries (cf. Jer 15:1). His attempt at intercession in behalf of Saul had failed, and the latter's repentance came too late. The case is much like the one reported by Jeremiah about his own efforts on behalf of Judah. Yahweh forbade him to intercede because the matter had been decided and would not be changed. There is no evidence to suggest that Saul's repentance was hypocritical or false, though his attempts at self-defense are dismissed peremptorily by the prophet. Samuel does not question the sincerity or genuineness of Saul's repentance; he only says it is meaningless because it is too late. Yahweh has made a firm decision, an irreversible one; and while Saul may live out his days as king, he has been permanently rejected.

There is an important insight here into the nature and process of divine repentance. The contrast between an act of repentance that is a change of mind by God one day and the refusal even to consider a change the next day, in the same episode but with a dramatic shift in the position of the affected party, illustrates the conviction that divine repentance is neither automatic nor predictable (or compellable). God cannot be forced to change his mind once made up, and he cannot be prevented from changing it if he chooses. In this case one reversal is occasioned by Saul's failure to carry out orders, but a second reversal is refused even though Saul has confessed and repented on his own.

The outcome here is very different from what we saw in the other cases. Moreover, there is an added complication. When Saul appeals for a third time, v 27, Samuel rebuffs him yet again, thus making the decision in the human and literary sphere final and irrevocable. Just as Saul has inadvertently torn the corner of Samuel's robe, so Yahweh has deliberately torn the kingship of Israel away from Saul. Then Samuel adds the following in v 29: "And indeed the Eternal One of Israel does not lie and does not repent, for he is not a man that he should repent [= change his mind]."

Several things must be said about this statement. It is offered as an explanation or justification of Samuel's rejection of Saul's repentance and as an affirmation that Yahweh has made an irreversible decision in Saul's case. The general argument is that Yahweh is not a human being and hence neither lies nor repents. Human beings may be expected to do one or the other—especially to change their minds—or to do both, but not God. In view of the fact that, in the same story as well as elsewhere, not only is God said to change his mind but it is essential to the understanding of his relation to his world and especially to his people that he should be able to change his position so as to respond properly to changing circumstances, it is very difficult to comprehend such an unqualified statement, which seems to be in direct conflict with the other view. It is particularly paradoxical in this context because the story is one of divine repentance, in which it is stated explicitly not once but twice (vv 11, 35) that Yahweh has repented about having made Saul king.

Except for the fact that the statement in v 29 has a general and timeless or permanent quality, we could explain the apparent contradiction in the following way: Yahweh clearly changed his mind about Saul and repented that he had made Saul king. That event is essential to the story, and we cannot dispense with the divine decision in this matter or deny that it reversed a previous decision, namely, to choose Saul as king. Further, when Saul pleads for forgiveness and expresses his own change of heart and mind, the prophet rejects this act of repentance, or states rather that Yahweh has rejected it, perhaps as an instance of too little and too late. Certainly there can be no quarrel with a divine decision not to change, any more than one can quarrel with a decision to change. Of all persons, Yahweh himself must be free to make his own decisions, so that the element of repentance, the willingness to reconsider, carries with it the ability and right to reverse a previous decision, also to confirm it and not reverse it. The fact that a refusal in the face of an act of repentance on the human side runs counter to the usual and repeated statements about God's willingness to forgive penitent sinners and eagerness to accept and restore them to favor is an important comment on the general position. Saul too is a special case, not least because of his status and the high standard of expectation and responsibility that a king must fulfill. But we must go beyond this point and deal with the general scope and implication of the statement that "the Eternal One of Israel does not lie and does not repent, because he is not a man to repent" (1 Sam 15:29). The statement here is very similar to one in Num 23:19, where it is said, "El is not a man (*ʾîš*) that he should dissemble (*wîkazzēb*) or a human being (*ben-ʾādām*) that he should repent (*wĕyitneḥām*)." The accompanying line (v 19b) shows that what is meant by the statement concerns God's reliability and consistency, "Shall he say something and not do it / or speak and not establish it?" The conclusion would be in both places that God is different from man in that he is faithful and just; he does what he says he will do. He does not say one thing and do another, neither does he change his mind for frivolous reasons or no reason. He is not capricious or arbitrary but is truthful, consistent, and reliable. In that sense he does not repent: he does not change his mind and then change it again without cause.

We have added the last phrase in order to emphasize that in the Bible Yahweh does change his mind and does repent. But human beings repent or change their minds for bad reasons as well as good ones, for real reasons and for fake reasons or no reason. To be more explicit, humans may repent hypocritically and falsely, and they may pretend or deceive. The association of *nḥm* with *šqr* in Samuel and with *kzb* in Numbers carried a pejorative and suspicious tone, as if to say that *nḥm* may be a questionable activity on the part of humans. Whether in words or prayers, repentance may be, as it often is, a sham. Divine repentance, on the contrary, has nothing in common with this sort of activity. When Yahweh repents, it is always for cause and is never deceptive or false. The reality is that there is an important difference between divine repentance and the human variety; at the same time, there is a significant similarity, for otherwise the same word would not be used.

So we are left with the apparent paradox: Yahweh has repented in the case of Saul as he has and will in other cases recorded in the Bible, but at the same time he is God and not human and is therefore not given to repenting or prevarication (= lying, dissembling, misrepresenting). In the end, it may be truer to affirm both statements and risk contradiction instead of asserting one and explaining away the other, in order to achieve a false or superficial consistency. In the story at any rate, the meaning is clear: Yahweh has repented that he made Saul king and has rejected his continuation as king (although in fact Saul will continue to be king for a long time yet). When Saul apologizes, confesses, and renews his obedience, Yahweh through Samuel nevertheless rejects these actions and confirms the decision

that he had made previously. The story concludes with the statement that
Yahweh repented (changed his mind) that he had made Saul king.

In comparing this story with the episode of the golden calf, aside from
significant differences in the details and circumstances, we observe the radically different roles played by Moses and Samuel. In both instances there is
divine repentance and a decision to reject the people or a man formerly
chosen and blessed. While *nhm* is used in different places in each story, the
pattern is similar at a certain point in the crisis. Once Yahweh has made a
new decision, whether to destroy Israel or to reject Saul, he reveals this
information to his prophet, Moses or Samuel. Moses responds by interceding on behalf of his people. That intercession is accepted. The decision is
suspended, thus allowing Moses time to salvage and ultimately to rectify
the situation. While the final outcome is not clear-cut, in any case the
people are saved. And we can say that without Moses' intervention the
rescue operation could not have taken place.

With respect to the other situation, Samuel does not intervene successfully, though he apparently tried very strenuously to do so. Yahweh rejected the intervention. There is no further divine reversal, and the judgment against Saul is allowed to stand. Had Moses acquiesced in the divine
decision against Israel, then Israel would have suffered the consequences,
for the intention and decision on both sides of the conversation must be
taken seriously, at face value. They meant what they said, also what they
did not say. Had Samuel interceded successfully on behalf of Saul as Moses
had done for his people, the outcome would have been very different, although Saul would still have had to repent. We cannot say certainly, for
God is free to change or stand by a decision; but the possibility remains.
Both parties are free to make and change decisions or to influence the
outcome. In the end the prophet must do as he is told, but until a final
determination is made he may speak as he pleases. In this respect the two
stories complement each other and show the dynamics of the relationship
of deity and prophet, how they affect and influence each other and how
decisions are shaped by this mutual interaction. The specific act of repentance in each case is quite different, though we can identify similar stages in
the development of each episode. In the Exodus story the divine repentance
comes only after Moses' intervention and as a direct result of his imperative
pleading: "Turn back from your fierce anger and repent. . . ." (Exod
32:12).

In the Samuel story, the divine repentance is prior to the notification of
the prophet. Intercession is not successful on this occasion, and the verdict
that resulted from the prior change of mind stands. In both cases, curiously
enough, the action or inaction of the prophet confirms the decision reached
by the act of repentance. In Moses' case, the prophet induces the act; in
Samuel's case, the prophet confirms the act already taken.

If there is any concern about the relation between the private transaction involving prophet and deity and the actual course of external history, at least insofar as we can recover it from the Bible, there is an important correlation. Moses was able to salvage the movement and the faith of Israel in spite of the gravest crisis of the whole experience. The story of the golden calf struck at the heart of the new faith and the new community, and drastic and determined action was necessary. Moses' intervention at the earthly level was as successful as it was at the heavenly level; and although the cost was high, the damage was contained and Israel survived.

In Saul's case, the break between him and Samuel was clearly damaging to the former. Although he was able to hang onto his throne until he lost his life in battle with the Philistines, Saul clearly was on the losing side in the struggle to maintain his kingdom and his dynasty. Samuel acted consistently with his vision. After intervening unsuccessfully, he acquiesced in the divine repentance over Saul and transmitted the message by word and deed. His break with Saul was a message of rejection that translated the divine repudiation into historical terms. The biblical writers were able to trace the decline and fall of the dynasty from that point. In the same way, the story of Samuel's secret anointing of David also reflects at ground level the heavenly decision to transfer the royal mandate from Saul to someone else.

In summary, we can see that the two stories about Moses and Samuel and the roles of the prophets in them complement each other, though different actions and stages are emphasized. We may outline them as follows.

1. Background: in light of a divine prohibition (Exodus) or command (Samuel), there is a violation on the part of the people (they made and worship an idol) or the leader (Saul fails to carry out the rules of Holy War).

2. Yahweh repents or changes his decision about the lawbreaker(s). Thus he decides to destroy the people he has brought out of Egypt into the wilderness, and he decides to reject Saul, the person he had previously chosen to be king.

3. Yahweh informs the prophet of his decision. Moses intercedes on behalf of the people, reproves the deity, and urges him to repent (change his mind or reverse the decision). Samuel apparently attempts the same thing, interceding to secure a reversal of the divine decision, and cries all night in an effort to reinstate Saul as Yahweh's anointed.

4. Moses is successful in his intervention, while Samuel fails in his intercession. Yahweh repents with respect to the people, thereby providing Moses with an opportunity to rectify the situation and to secure the people's repentance, which in turn will satisfy God's requirements. Samuel, however, is unsuccessful, and Yahweh's decision stands. The deity will not be dissuaded: Saul is rejected and will not be reinstated.

5. Moses brings the words of the divine repentance to the people and they in turn repent, while the final issue is yet to be decided. In the case of Samuel, he brings Saul word of the latter's rejection. Saul repents, confesses his fault, and seeks forgiveness and restoration to divine favor, but to no avail. Samuel assures him that the decision, having been made and confirmed by a divine utterance, is irrevocable.

Taken together, the stories portray the different ways in which a crisis of obedience in the relations between God and his people may be mediated by a prophet. The lesson to be learned is that Yahweh's judgments are his own, as is his repentance. The prophet may intercede, as in fact Moses and Samuel do, but Yahweh is free to respond positively (in the case of Moses and the people) or negatively (in the case of Samuel and Saul). The same is true of the response to human repentance. Yahweh may respond favorably (in the story of Moses and the golden calf) or unfavorably (in the case of Saul and Samuel). The outcome remains in doubt until Yahweh seals the decision by his action.

4. *2 Samuel 24:16 = 1 Chronicles 21:15*. The passage in question is substantially the same in both texts and reads as follows: "Then the angel stretched forth his hand at Jerusalem to destroy it, and Yahweh repented concerning the evil and he said to the angel who had been attacking the people: 'It is enough now. Lower your arm.' "

Yahweh's repentance here is not the result of prophetic intercession or of any act of repentance on the part of the people. It is spontaneous in that he sees the effect of the judgment he himself pronounced on Israel, because of King David's sin, and suspends further punishment. The specific punishment itself was the result of a choice on David's part. He was told to choose among three disastrous consequences: seven years of drought and famine, or three months of military defeats at the hands of his enemies, or three days of pestilence and plague. He chose the last, with the interesting remark that it was better to fall into the hands of Yahweh, because his mercy is great, than to fall into the hands of humans (v 14). This comment only explains the rejection of the second option, but the other choice, between the first and the third, is not explained. It is not much of a choice, but one would suppose that the lightning strategist and decisive man of action would choose a disaster that was over quickly so that one could recover and rebuild, instead of the protracted, debilitating experience of a seven-year drought, which in the long run might cause even greater suffering and death. So he chose the plague. On the first day, seventy thousand are said to have fallen (v 15). Then presumably on the next day (or possibly at the end of the first, for the plague continued until the *minḥā,* the late afternoon sacrifice, which leaves only a short time until the beginning of the new day at sundown), when the angel stretched out his arm against Jerusalem to devastate it by a new attack of the same plague, Yahweh repented (changed his mind, reversed the decision) and stayed the plague. As far as we are aware it was not resumed.

This case is just the opposite of the decision in Genesis 6, where, as a result of human sin, Yahweh painfully reverses the decision to create humanity and decides to destroy them. Here it is the prospect of disastrous destruction in the holy city, Jerusalem, that disturbs him, and he reverses the decision, thus sparing the city and the rest of the country from the ravages of the plague. No doubt the effect of the previous day's slaughter is also to be reckoned with.

The story itself is rather complicated, and there is a special problem arising from a divergence between the account in 2 Samuel and the one in 1 Chronicles. In the former it is Yahweh who incites David to take the notorious census of the nation, because he (Yahweh) is very angry at Israel and clearly wishes to inflict great harm on the nation (2 Sam 24:1). In the Chronicles version, however, nothing is said of these circumstances; rather, the idea of conducting a census originates with Satan, who then incites David to go ahead with it. In both accounts the sequel is the same. David proceeds with the census in spite of Joab's misgivings and reluctance, and finally it is completed. Then David acknowledges that he has committed a great sin, but his confession does not result in remission or cancellation of the judgment, only in the offer of a choice among the three devastating punishments mentioned earlier.

Our concern is primarily with the act of repentance on the part of God and not with the beginning of the story, but because the question of the originator of the census idea is presented in dramatic form we must consider it briefly. In the Samuel account it is made clear that Yahweh was looking for an occasion to punish his people, which was the intention behind the census proposal. Once the census was carried out, then the punishment was justified, presumably because conducting a census was contrary to the proper worship and service of the deity. We must consider too the reason for the elaborate procedure in order to justify punishment and vent the divine anger. The implication would seem to be that there was insufficient cause for punishing Israel and that the anger arose for some other reason and was itself not justified or merited by the behavior of king or people. This investigation leads to a much more tangled and complex collection of problems, and it is perhaps better to let it drop. The shift from Yahweh to Satan in Chronicles no doubt reflects a similar judgment on the part of the Chronicler. Because Satan's hostility to humanity generally and to Israel in particular was axiomatic in earlier days and explicit in later ones (in Israelite thought), there was no problem in attributing this malicious move to the archprosecutor of mere mortals. By contrast, the attribution of this act to Yahweh himself could only cause troubling thoughts about motives and intentions, along with an intense curiosity and concern about the unexplained hostility against his own people. In the end, however, the Chronicler's solution does not really solve the basic problem, though it does shift attention from the deity to a subordinate. If indeed Satan is an officer of the divine court, the first officer in many respects, that is, the chief prosecuting attorney, then it is clear that the agent cannot be entirely independent of the court (and its ruler) that he serves, and whether he acts on his own or is under orders, the one he reports to (and in the Hebrew Bible there is no question about that point: he invariably reports to God, is answerable to him, and is under divine authority) has ultimate authority over him and is answerable for what he does. The Chronicler only shifted the focus of the problem, not the problem itself. And the problem of external evil, not manmade and presumably not god-made either, remains as a substantive concern for all monotheistic religions.

The reason that this matter of the beginning of the story affects our understanding of the divine repentance is that the unresolved anger that underlies the whole account is itself resolved by the repentance in v 16. The repentance reflects a reversal of the decision to punish, which itself arose out of the hot wrath mentioned in v 1. The proximate cause of the repentance was the appalling prospect of the punishment imposed by Yahweh and elected by David. Certainly that threat was the triggering factor, but underneath there must also have been a resolution of the initiating anger. The decision to punish was reversed by divine repentance, and thus the cloud in the relationship was removed. As we are not told anything about the original cause, we equally know nothing of the reason for its removal. While the initial phase of the punishment was directly caused by the census, it could also have stimulated a reconsideration of the whole situation and thus have led the way to a complete reversal, not only of further punishment but of the anger directed at Israel in the first place. Then it may be easier to understand the later phases of the story: the purchase of the threshing floor from Araunah, the offering of sacrifices, and the consecration of the place as the future site of the temple. These actions constitute the necessary prelude to the climactic act of the joint reigns of David and Solomon, namely, the erection of the temple in Jerusalem; but before the latter could be undertaken, the divine anger and the peril of the people had to be resolved. Thus the underlying issue was only brought to the surface by the census matter, and this problem was the one that had to be settled, and was, through the repentance of Yahweh.

While that decision could only be regarded as a suspension of the agreed-upon punishment, David interceded with Yahweh in order to make it permanent and thus permit the initiation of the great temple project. In a proposal similar to that of Moses in Exodus 32, David exculpates the people who are the innocent victims all around: they are the target of both the divine anger and the census that was David's idea, so David urges that

Yahweh exonerate the people and vent whatever remains of his anger or demand for satisfaction on David and his house. There is no direct response from God, but the subsequent activity in preparing the sacred place and offering sacrifices shows that David's offer was not taken up, but a general amnesty declared instead. At the very end, the efforts at reconciliation proved successful, as the last words of the chapter demonstrate: "And Yahweh was appeased [heeded the supplications] for the land, and the plague was restrained from upon Israel" (2 Sam 24:25).

In this situation, Yahweh's spontaneous repentance not only averts the further depredations of the plague but also overcomes the unexplained hostility and anger of the deity and opens the way for the renewed reconciliation of God and people and the establishment of the temple at Jerusalem.

5. *Jeremiah 26:3, 13, 19*. There are a number of passages in the book of Jeremiah in which the term is used: 15:6, 18:8, 18:10, 20:16, 42:10, and 26:3, 13, and 19. We will deal with most of them briefly and more extensively with the last.

a. Jeremiah 15:6: "You abandoned me, oracle of Yahweh, you kept going backwards. So I stretched out my hand against you and I destroyed you, (because) I was weary of relenting [repenting, *hinnāḥēm*]."

The reference is to Jerusalem and must date from the period of the final capture and destruction of that city. The statement is revealing about Yahweh's final decision, apparently at the end of a long series of reversals and changes of mind. There would, however, be another change—at least one—later on.

b. Jeremiah 18:7–10, the philosophy of divine repentance:

> [7]Any time that I speak concerning a nation or concerning a kingdom to pluck up and tear down and destroy,
> [8]and that nation turns from its wickedness . . . then I will repent [*wěnihamtî*] concerning the evil that I planned to do to it.
> [9]And any time I speak concerning a nation or a kingdom to build and to plant;
> [10]and it does what is evil in my sight by not listening to my voice, then I will repent [*wěnihamtî*] concerning the good that I said that I would do to make things good for it.

This statement embodies the general theory of divine repentance in the Hebrew Bible and expresses it as succinctly and directly as we can imagine it being done. Further elaboration in specific details would only cover additional possibilities, but this basic statement deals with the essentials. Divine repentance moves in either direction—from good to bad or vice versa—and on a convincing showing by the human party. The governing principle is applied impartially to any and all nations.

c. Jeremiah 20:16, no repentance: "And let that man be like the cities that Yahweh overturned [*hāpak*] because he did not repent [*wĕlōʾ niḥam*]."

This passage is an interesting comparison and an unusual comment. The reference is to the man who reported the prophet's birth to his father as a happy event. It is a strange curse, but our interest is in the comment about Yahweh's destruction of the cities of the plain (there is no question about what the prophet has in mind because the verb here, *hpk,* is used specifically of the catastrophe that engulfed Sodom and Gomorrah and the other cities of the plain). The added words are, "he did not repent [= change his mind]." This statement not only affirms the unswerving decision to destroy, but may be an allusion to the discussion with Abraham about the fate of the cities, with the comment that in the end Yahweh did not change his mind. Strictly speaking, the discussion in Genesis 18 does not involve the theme of repentance (and certainly not the root *nḥm*). In the first place, Yahweh says that he has come down to evaluate the evidence for and against the cities, so a decision has not been reached. But Abraham—who obviously knows the conditions in the cities or has a good idea about what the decision will be if made strictly on the merits of the case—begins to bargain with Yahweh in order to save the cities and their inhabitants. While Yahweh ultimately agrees with Abraham's final figure, the whole discussion happens before the investigation is completed and before a judgment is made. The subsequent event, the destruction of the cities, tells us what the decision was, which also included the provision to remove Lot and his family, perhaps partly because Lot was a resident alien and not directly involved in the crimes of the local people, but also because of Abraham's righteousness. What Abraham had urged was that the cities be saved with all of their wicked people in them for the sake of the righteous; but Yahweh's agreement to this stipulation was nullified by the failure to find even the minimum number, ten. The solution achieved by Yahweh was to avoid the legitimate charge that it would be unjust to sweep away the righteous with the guilty. Presumably Yahweh had no intention of doing so because it would violate the underlying principle on the basis of which the judgment against the cities was being made. But this solution, to rescue the righteous, would only be applicable after Abraham's remedy proved inoperative. In any case, the reference in Jer 20:16 is to the decision to destroy the cities. Once that decision was made, God did not repent or relent. But why say it, especially because there is not the slightest evidence of any change on the part of the people of the cities? We suspect that the statement may reflect the divine response to some further intercession on Abraham's part. It is clear that Abraham hoped to save the cities, not just his nephew Lot and his family. Having failed in the ingenious attempt to save the cities by an argument about the presence of enough righteous people in it, he may have tried some other argument or more likely appealed to the grace and mercy of the sovereign. This course of action certainly would have been in character for the patriarch, who, like Moses and Samuel, was famous for his intercessory powers (cf. Gen 20:7, 17). But the hypothetical plea was rejected; Yahweh did not repent, and that is what Jeremiah is referring to in this passing comment.

d. Jeremiah 26:3, 13, 19, repentance in the temple court.

If the passage in chap. 18 gives us a working definition of divine repentance in the world and life of nations, the story in chap. 26 is a prime illustration of the doctrine in action, how it worked on that extraordinary day when Jeremiah showed up at the temple with a message from Yahweh (to which an obvious parallel with Amos' experience at Bethel can be drawn). The significant passages are to be found in vv 3, 13, and 19, which can be read as follows:

> [3]Perhaps they will listen and they will turn each one from his wicked way, and then I will repent concerning the evil that I was planning to do to them on account of the wickedness of their doings.

The reference is to the message that Jeremiah is to deliver to the people at the temple (cf. also chap. 7) and the possible response of the people to that message. Yahweh is prepared to repent after finding satisfactory evidence of a genuine turning on the part of the people from their wicked ways.

> [13]And now make good your ways and your works, and listen to the voice of Yahweh your God, and [then] Yahweh will repent concerning the evil that he declared [he would do] concerning you.

This passage is part of Jeremiah's oracle to the people and embodies the private expression of the same message in v 3:

> [19]Did Hezekiah the king of Judah and all Judah even think of putting him [Micah] to death? Did he not fear Yahweh and appease the countenance of Yahweh; then Yahweh repented concerning the evil that he spoke about them. But we are about to do a great evil against ourselves.

This verse is the climax of the episode, in which the citation of Micah's well-known words about the destruction of Jerusalem becomes the rallying point for the defenders of the beleaguered prophet Jeremiah, and he is saved from the wrath of the priests and prophets. The point being made is that when Micah made the prophecy, the king and people responded, not by efforts to put him to death, but by acts of repentance, and that these acts in turn evoked a comparable repentance (using the word *nḥm*) on the part of Yahweh, who changed his mind and reversed the decision announced by the prophet Micah. The passage from Micah (3:12) is quoted verbatim, a significant point because it was remembered long after it had been uttered and its current applicability had been exhausted. It constitutes one of the major unfulfilled prophecies of the eighth century, a fact that did nothing to discredit the prophet. On the contrary, his prophecy created a more important result through the dynamics of repentance both human and divine, even if in the process the prophecy itself remained unfulfilled. An explanation is offered here for the fact that in spite of the overwhelming Assyrian invasion, the city of Jerusalem was spared, while the sister city, Samaria, had been destroyed. Different explanations are offered in the Bible, and Sennacherib, the Assyrian king, offers one through his emissary that has the advantage of being contemporary and the disadvantage of being self-serving. Proximity in time does not guarantee a similar proximity to the truth, although where the biblical and Assyrian accounts agree we can reasonably conclude that the special interests on both sides have been neutralized and that we have the facts. Both Sennacherib and the Bible refer to a huge indemnity paid by Hezekiah, while the books of Isaiah and Kings add a possible second campaign along with a highly militant angel who does not merely disperse but slaughters the whole Assyrian army. In any case the city was spared, the dynasty continued, and in Jeremiah's day the nation's survival was seen as a vindication of the doctrine of mutual and interactive repentance.

e. Jeremiah 42:10, the promise:

If you will surely remain in this land, then I will build you up and I will not wreck [you], and I will plant you, and I will not pluck you up; because I have repented concerning the evil that I did to you.

The scene is set after the destruction of the city and during the turmoil following the assassination of Gedaliah, the governor appointed by Nebuchadnezzar as a replacement for Zedekiah, the last and now removed king, to look after the remaining population and to represent the Babylonian authority. A group led by Johanan ben-Kareah decides to abandon the land and seek refuge in Egypt, partly at least because they fear Babylonian reprisals for the murder of Gedaliah and a number of Babylonian officials by Ishmael, a royal prince who has fled in the other direction. Before acting on this decision they ask Jeremiah for advice, that is, to intercede for them with Yahweh and to find out what Yahweh wishes them to do. The verse quoted is part of the answer. The story is told at length in chaps. 42–43, but the gist of it is that Jeremiah assures them that Yahweh has already repented of the harm done to Judah and Jerusalem. He has changed his mind and wishes them to stay in the land. He forbids them to go to Egypt, which they would like to do, but promises to build them up and plant them if they stay where they are. Furthermore, he tells them that he will influence Nebuchadnezzar on their behalf so that the Babylonian emperor will treat them kindly and allow them to remain in the land. He promises them that if they stay, they will prosper and flourish.

Johanan and the others reject the message from Jeremiah and claim that he was unduly influenced by Baruch, who had his own nefarious reasons for wanting them to stay and be punished by Nebuchadnezzar. So they go off to Egypt, despising the word of the prophet, and, adding insult to injury, drag him and Baruch along with them. With the close of this narrative in the book of Jeremiah (in chap. 44), the group vanishes from the pages of history, swallowed up in the land of the Nile.

Regrettably, they did not take advantage of the opportunity to test the repentance of Yahweh, pronounced by Jeremiah along with the divine promise of respite and renewal in the land. We are left with an unrealized commitment in the form of an act of repentance, a change of mind about a historic event of the gravest proportions—the destruction of the city of Jerusalem, the temple in the city, the disappearance of the nation, and the captivity of its leading citizens. Already in the few months since that catastrophe, Yahweh, according to Jeremiah, was ready and willing to begin again with the remnant left behind.

6. *Joel 2:12–14.* This passage is an important instance of double repentance:

> [12] And also now, it is the oracle of Yahweh, Return to me with all your heart, and with fasting and with weeping and with lamentation.
> [13] And tear open your hearts, and not [only] your garments, and return to Yahweh your God for he is the embodiment of grace and compassion, long-suffering [= very patient] and one who repents concerning evil.
> [14] Who knows if he will turn around and repent, and leave behind him a blessing

The prophet urges the people to return, return to Yahweh their God. Then comes the classic description of Yahweh as the epitome of grace and compassion. He is the personification of these attributes, and the terms used are unequivocally applied to him. The passage is a paraphrase of Yahweh's description of himself in his revelation to Moses at the mountain in Sinai (Exod 34:6–7). Not included there is the phrase *wĕniḥām ʿal-hārāʿâ,* "and a repenter over the evil" (the form is a *nip'al* ptc m. s.). On this occasion Yahweh's known tendency to the compassionate virtues, celebrated repeatedly in similar passages, is expanded to include repentance.

While the number of actual instances is small, the indication has been given that if the evidence warrants, Yahweh is prepared to repent, that is, to change his mind about the evil—the evil that he has done or plans to do. The vital condition is repentance on the part of the people who seek Yahweh's repentance, only the word *nḥm* is not used of the people here, but the more basic and general *šwb* ("turn, return, turn around"). The same term is used of Yahweh in the concluding statement, "Who knows whether he will *turn* and repent . . . ?"

No one can be sure, and Yahweh alone always retains his sovereign freedom to decide and to do as he pleases. Nevertheless, the introductory "Who knows?" is not a neutral expression and certainly does not have a negative expectation. It is a polite way of expressing a positive hope for an affirmative response without being overbearing. And the prophet's expectation has already been expressed in his characterization of Yahweh as "one who [normally or characteristically] repents over evil" (*nḥm 'l-hr'h*), "one whose nature it is to repent over evil." It would be out of character for Yahweh not to respond positively to repentance on the part of the people. Repentance, in short, is mutual and interactive. One stimulates the other and produces reconciliation and the exchange of blessings.

7. *Jonah 3:9–10, 4:1–2.* Here we find another example of double repentance:

> 3 ⁹"'Who knows whether God will turn and repent, and turn from his hot anger so that we will not perish?"
> ¹⁰And God saw their works, that they had turned from their wicked way, and God repented concerning the evil that he had said he would do to them and he did not do [it].
>
> 4 ¹And the matter was a great evil to Jonah, and he was very upset.
> ²So he prayed to Yahweh and he said, "Alas Yahweh was not this my word while I was still on my own soil? Therefore I went directly to escape to Tarshish, because I know that you are God, gracious and compassionate, long suffering and very kind [full of lovingkindness] and one who repents of evil."

The passage here is verbally related to the one in Joel. The difference is that the theory of double repentance is fleshed out in a story in Jonah, while in Joel it is in the form of a prophetic utterance or oracle. In this account the truth of Jeremiah's general statement about Yahweh's willingness to repent (Jer 18:8–10) is confirmed in an international setting, and the characterization of Yahweh as "the one who repents over evil" is attested by an actual experience (within the story form used).

The passage in Jonah uses many of the same words as the one in Joel but in a slightly different order. And the story in Jonah is much more detailed. The repentance of king, people, and cattle is spelled out in full and provides the basis for God's repentance.

The question "Who knows whether the God will turn and repent?" is the transition to the affirmation that when he saw that the people really had turned around from their wicked ways to a new way, he was convinced and reversed the decision he had made about destroying the city. The sentence affirming his repentance ends with the all-important words concerning the evil he had planned to do: "he did not do [it]."

The words of the credo are still to come, those which emphasize Yahweh's grace and compassion. These words, ironically, are put in the mouth of Jonah, who is exceedingly upset and bitter about the whole affair. It is bad enough that Yahweh repents in response to repentance on the part of the Ninevites, but worse that he, Jonah, was dragged in as the effective mediator of possible reconciliation with people who did not deserve such benign treatment. Nevertheless, it is Jonah who recognizes and affirms the inescapable conclusion. A God who describes himself and is described as "the one who repents over the evil" clearly *will* repent over evil he has done or has planned, as in this instance, when given a chance to do so. Jonah knew this fact from the beginning, which is why, as he explains in prayer to Yahweh, he fled to Tarshish. He knew that a God known as "one who repents [= the repenter]" would do exactly that in an actual situation, and he wanted no part of it. This story confirms the impression of the similar statements in Joel. The latter prophet also knows that a God who calls himself "the repenter over the evil" will do so in fact when people test him with a genuine repentance. The people of Jerusalem and Judah can expect as good a response from their God as the Ninevites received from the same God.

8. *Zechariah 8:14–15.* Here there is first no repentance and then repentance.

> [14]For thus has said Yahweh of Hosts, "As I planned to do evil to you when your fathers provoked me," said Yahweh of hosts, "and I did not repent (*wĕlō' niḥāmtî*).
> [15]Indeed I have turned. I have planned in these days to do good to Jerusalem and the house of Judah. Do not be afraid!"

The interest of this passage lies in the juxtaposition of the flat assertion "I did not repent" with the affirmation that he has now reversed that decision, and as he planned evil in the past so now he plans to do good to Jerusalem and the house of Judah. This is a case in which God did not repent, but it was followed in due course by an act of divine conversion (*šwb*): not precisely repentance (*nḥm*), but the effect is the same. In all likelihood the prophet avoids using the same term twice in succession for purely stylistic reasons. It may also be that the shift in direction is not quite the same as repentance because the judgment against Jerusalem was actually carried out and the punishment inflicted. It still requires a new decision to do good to those who have been on the receiving end of bad. Such a decision is called a turning, and the same expression is used in conjunction with *nḥm* elsewhere to describe Yahweh's change of attitude to those who survived the destruction of the city.

In the end the city was destroyed because, as said here, Yahweh did not repent; he did not rescind the order to wreck the place. The reason, however, was that there was no initiating action on the part of the people, a showing in good faith of repentance on their part. Throughout all of this material, the repentance of God is conditioned by the behavior of people who are the potential beneficiaries or victims of divine repentance.

9. A few passages remain to be considered. Their content does not affect the findings already discussed in any significant manner, but there may be value in completing the list.

a. Judges 2:18: And if Yahweh established for them judges, Yahweh would be with the judges and deliver them from the hand of their enemies all the days of the [= that] judge, because Yahweh repented on account of their outcry because of their oppressors and mistreaters.

The statement here is part of a description of the general pattern developed by the Deuteronomic historian for the sequence of Judges. This pattern is a familiar one and includes a series of stages, as follows: (A) In response to the outcry of the people, Yahweh raises up a judge who is successful in delivering the people from their oppressor. (B) The period of prosperity lasts through the lifetime and administration of the judge, and then the people rebel against Yahweh, turn to other gods, and violate their fundamental covenant commitment. (C) As punishment for their sins Yahweh brings them under the power of an oppressor. (D) Then when they have suffered for a time and cried out to Yahweh, he responds by raising up another judge to save them. Thus the cycle repeats.

As far as the book of Judges is concerned, the only time the repentance of God is mentioned as being a stage in the process is in the description in Judg 2:16–23, at v 18. The repentance of Yahweh comes about in response to the people's outcry on account of the oppression under which they suffer. He reverses the decision under which they are being punished and, in accordance with the new decision, raises up a deliverer. This repentance is a result of the people's outcry, but because the appeal is directed at

Yahweh, it is also a sign of repentance on their part. It means that they are turning away from the gods they turned to at an earlier phase of the cycle and back to Yahweh, whom they had abandoned. Thus we can classify this example of divine repentance with those that occur as a response to repentance on the part of the people. This is a model case and stands for an unspecified number of actual instances. It is of interest, however, that the verb *nḥm* is not used in any of the specific instances in the book of Judges, though a number of occasions would have been suitable for its use if they did not actually call for it. It is only in the general statement that the word is used, which may signify that it is only in retrospect, and in recovering and restructuring the history of those times according to the pattern prepared in this chapter of Judges, that the historian (or editor) identified and defined the divine action at that point in the cycle as repentance.

b. Ezekiel 24:14, Yahweh unrelenting: "I, Yahweh, have spoken. It shall come to pass, and I will do it. I will not refrain [= hold back?], and I will not have pity, and I will not repent. According to your ways and according to your deeds they have judged you [*versions:* I will judge you], is the oracle of my Lord Yahweh."

The reference here is to Jerusalem, the bloody city (represented by the 2d f. s. pronoun), and the specific statement is that Yahweh will not repent, he will not change his mind about the sentence of judgment. It is not surprising that the single instance of *nḥm* in the *nipʿal* with God as subject in Ezekiel is a negative statement. In view of the historical context and the prophet's known opinions on the subject of Jerusalem and Judah, the king of that country, and its leadership, there is no possibility of a change of mind or heart on the part of God. The decision has been made and the judgment rendered. Divine repentance is out of the question; Jerusalem must be destroyed.

In contrast with Jeremiah, for whom divine repentance is not only a possible but even a necessary element in the dynamics of the divine-human encounter and the turbulent course of Israel's history, Ezekiel rules it out entirely. Yahweh does not repent; everything happens in accordance with his determinate will and in accordance with a plan arranged from the beginning. The judgment cannot be averted because it has been decided. But the same is true of the promised return, restoration, and renewal. They are equally determined because they also have been decided by divine decree. What he wills happens, not for the sake of the people or because of their desire or outcry, but for his own name's sake. Human repentance, while a necessary feature of the nation's restoration, does not function in the process to evoke a corresponding divine action. On the contrary, it is the end product of the divine initiative. Only afterward, when the restoration has occurred, they are back in their own land, and the new age has been inaugurated, will Israel repent and thoroughly repudiate its former evil ways (cf. Ezek 36:22–32). But even here the term *nḥm* is not used.

c. Psalm 106:45, covenantal repentance: "And he remembered for them his covenant, and he repented according to the multitude of his mercies."

The divine repentance here is connected with a cycle of vicissitudes similar to what we observed in Judg 2:18 (here the broader statement includes vv 34–46, in which the history of Israel is portrayed as a series of deliverances punctuated by apostasies and punishments). The point in the cycle at which it functions is in response to the people's outcry on account of their suffering under their oppressors (see vv 40–44). The portrayal of Israel may also include the monarchic period, for there is an apparent reference to captors and captivity in v 46, though it may be insufficiently specific to pinpoint a particular captivity. Nevertheless, the psalm may reflect the experiences of the eighth and seventh centuries, if not of the sixth. The concluding verses also express the idea of a dispersion among the nations, which implies the exilic period.

We have here not only a link with the cyclical repentance of Judges 2 but a clear reference to the initiation of divine repentance in Israel's history and experience, when Moses interceded with God at Mount Sinai during the crisis of the golden calf. While the word is not used, clearly that incident provided the model and established the precedent for divine repentance in dealing with Israel (cf. vv 19–23). From an examination of this material, we propose that the portrayal of divine repentance as a constant in Israelite history and an essential attribute of the deity, whose nature it is to "repent over evil," actually derives from a single decisive incident near the beginning of the story, when Moses interceded with Yahweh to save his people from the divine anger, and uniquely commanded (i.e., the pleading imperative) the deity to repent: *hinnāḥēm . . . wayyinnāḥem* ("'Repent . . . and he repented,'" Exod 32:12, 14).

d. Psalm 110:4, God does not repent: "Yahweh has sworn, and he will not repent [= change his mind]."

This usage belongs in all likelihood with two passages already discussed: 1 Sam 15:29, where it is said that Yahweh does not lie and does not repent, because he is not a man to repent; and Num 23:19, where we have a different form of the verb (*hitpaʿel*) and a synonym for *šqr*, namely *kzb*, but the sense is the same. God does not prevaricate and he does not repent. In both cases the emphasis is on the reliability of divine utterances and the assurance that not only does God not speak untruth but he does not equivocate or vacillate, in other words, change his mind. Because the context in Ps 110:4 specifies an oath, it is clear that the same assurance is being sought and claimed. It is taken for granted that Yahweh will not lie under oath, but neither will he change his mind, that is, depart in any way from what he has sworn.

10. There is also a small group of occurrences of the root *nḥm* with God as subject in which the *hitpaʿel* is used rather than the *nipʿal*.

    a. Numbers 23:19, no repentance.

This passage, which is very similar to the statement in 1 Sam 15:29, has been discussed in connection with the latter. It is a general statement about the constancy and consistency of the deity, whose word is reliable, and who neither lies nor equivocates (= changes his mind). Generally speaking, a statement like this one comes from and is directed to circumstances quite different from those in which the repentance of God is affirmed. The dramatic juxtaposition of essentially opposed or even contradictory asseverations in 1 Samuel 15:11, 29, and 35, in which the negative statement is sandwiched between repeated affirmations, may be purely coincidental and reconcilable in view of the narrative. Nevertheless, this juxtaposition serves to show that the concept was (and is) not an easy one to accommodate and use, and under any circumstances had to be qualified in such ways as to make it clear that while there were obvious points of contact and correspondence with the human varieties of repentance, there were marked differences, for certain kinds of human repentance would be excluded entirely and the rest were not exactly the same.

    The two passages may be compared as follows:

Num 23:19

lōʾ ʾîš ʾēl wîkazzēb	Not a man is El that he should lie,
ûben-ʾādām wĕyitneḥām	Or a human that he should repent.
hahûʾ ʾāmar	Has he, has he said [it],
wĕlōʾ yaʿăśeh	and will he not do [it]?
wĕdibber	Or spoken [it],
wĕlōʾ yĕqîmennâ	and will he not establish it?

1 Sam 15:29

wĕgam nēṣaḥ yiśrāʾēl	and also as for the Eternal One of Israel—
lōʾ yĕšaqqēr wĕlōʾ yinnāḥēm	He does not lie, and he does not repent;
kî lōʾ ʾādām hûʾ lĕhinnāḥēm	For not a man is he to repent.

    The verbal links are few, but they are enough; and the ideas are the same. Numbers 23:19 is more ample, but *šqr* (1 Samuel) is stronger than "lie." It means to be a traitor, and the content of Num 23:19 shows that *kāzāb* does not specify "untruth," that is, a statement contrary to fact. It means not to do something you said you would do. Now how can you change your mind without committing *šqr*//*kzb*? Or, when does changing your mind become *kzb* or *šqr*? Answer, when you swear an oath, which is what *dbr* means in

Num 23:19. All three terms come together in Psalm 89:33–37, a passage in which Yahweh swears by his holiness to support the dynasty of David. Compare *wĕlōʾ-ʾăšaqqēr* (v 34) // *ʾim-lĕdāwīd ʾăkazzēb* (v 36).

An oath (preferably two) makes all the difference. So we must locate the double oath in Amos 6:8//8:7 (clearly a matching pair) in the multifaceted scheme. It is structurally interesting that these oaths are placed where they are, and especially that the last one comes between Visions 4 and 5.

b. Deuteronomy 32:36, there is repentance: "For Yahweh has vindicated his people, and concerning his servants he has repented."

The RSV reads "For the Lord will vindicate his people and have compassion on his servants." While the verbs are imperfect and customarily rendered as future, there is good evidence to show that in this poem they do not follow standard prose Hebrew practice but conform rather to the usage of early Hebrew poetry, in which the imperfect is normally or regularly a past tense. The sense of the passage is that Yahweh has acted in defense and on behalf of his servant people, that he has rendered judgment in their favor and executed it. In keeping with this affirmation is the motivation clause; he has acted so because he has changed his mind about them. In the preceding section of the poem, vv 15–35, there is very harsh condemnation of Israel (vv 15–25) followed by a transitional section concerning the enemy, and the suggestion that Yahweh has reversed his field. This suggestion is made explicit in v 36, which affirms the new decision to vindicate his people against their enemies, rooted in his (God's) repentance, his change of mind about his servants (cf. the very similar expression in Ps 90:13). The reversal was occasioned not by any intercession by a prophet or by any sign of repentance from the people, but rather by concern on Yahweh's part about the effect of his actions on the enemies or adversaries of Israel and a possible misperception of what has really happened (v 27). The presentation here has echoes in the story of the golden calf and Moses' argument about why Yahweh should repent, namely, that the Egyptians will misconstrue the event and misrepresent Yahweh as the butcher of his own people without legitimate cause. Because this poem, like Psalm 90, is attributed to Moses and the resemblances between the two poems and the story in Exodus 32 (J's version) are noteworthy, we may have here some indication of the reason for the two poems being attributed to Moses. In any case, Yahweh's repentance in Deuteronomy 32 is connected with some episode or experience in the wilderness wanderings, not after the settlement in the land (i.e., the conquest of the western territories). The central theme of the poem is the people's apostasy and idolatry, of which the classic instance in Israel's history is the making and worshiping of the golden calf. So the repentance of Yahweh in Deuteronomy 32 may be a stylized poetic version of the repentance in the story in Exodus 32.

c. Psalm 135:14, parallel to Deut 32:36.

The passage is identical with Deut 32:36, as is the setting. The poem deals specifically with the early history of Israel, including the plagues in Egypt and the Exodus from that country, the wanderings in the wilderness, the victories over Sihon and Og, and the settlement in Canaan. That historical survey is followed by the statement in v 14 and doubtless has the same meaning and force that it does in Deuteronomy 32. The passage reflects the crisis in the wilderness described in detail in Deuteronomy 32, when Yahweh, faced with rampant apostasy, nevertheless reversed the decision to destroy his people and gave them victory over their enemies instead. Behind the whole account is the single great act of divine repentance at the beginning of Israel's existence as the people of Yahweh. It was achieved by Moses through a unique intervention in the divine process; he interceded with God, instructed the deity to repent, and thus a history of the people of God was made possible. We can still hear echoes of that constitutive event in the poems attributed to Moses, Psalm 90 and Deuteronomy 32, and even in this psalm, though the direct connections with Moses have been removed.

Summary

In this study we have examined all instances of the verb *nḥm* in the *nip'al* and *hitpa'el* conjugations with God as subject. Of them, the ones expressing the central meaning of repentance, change of heart and mind, have been listed and discussed. A few in which a different meaning is indicated (e.g., Isa 1:24, 57:6) have been set aside. What are the highlights of the research?

The principal finding is that the repentance of God is an important aspect of his character and his behavior; it is mentioned frequently enough to warrant careful study. We should add that the phenomenon is more extensive than the use of the term *nḥm* itself. Thus the episode of the golden calf, which constitutes a principal example of divine repentance (Exod 32), is also described at length in the book of Deuteronomy (chap. 9), but while the second account is essentially the same and the respective roles of Moses and Yahweh are depicted in the same way, the word itself is not used in the Deuteronomic passage, perhaps because the writer preferred not to describe the mind and will of the deity in this fashion. We recognize a similar situation in a comparison of the books of Jeremiah and Ezekiel. The two prophets share essentially the same opinion and viewpoint about the situation in Judah and Jerusalem in the fateful days before the fall of the city. Both believe that the nation and the city are under divine judgment and will suffer dreadful consequences. Both believe too that afterward there will be a return and restoration initiated and carried out by the same deity. Jeremiah speaks eloquently of the possibility of Yahweh repenting before the fall of the city if the people for their part will repent. He affirms also the reality of divine repentance after the fall, involving a promise to rebuild and replant the survivors in their own land. Ezekiel for his part has nothing to say about any of these possibilities. He does not accept the idea that Yahweh repents (the only time he uses the verb in this sense with Yahweh as subject, he also prefixes the negative particle). Yahweh simply does not and will not change his mind. As to the future, it too has been determined, but it reflects a previous decision made by the deity and not a change of mind precipitated by anything that happens in the interim after the fall of the city.

Returning to the use of *nḥm* to express divine repentance, we note that God may repent by reversing a decision to do either harm or good, and that the change of mind may be a spontaneous action resulting from observing and reacting to a variety of situations in the world. Thus, as a result of observing the corruption in the world after the creation of humanity he repents that he made man and makes the decision to destroy humanity. Or when he sees the angel about to devastate Jerusalem as part of the punishment imposed on Israel because David took a census of the people, Yahweh changes his mind and cancels that part of the punishment.

The other reasons for divine repentance are either an act of repentance on the part of people under judgment or the intercession of a prophet. The former may be illustrated by the example of Nineveh and Jerusalem at different times and under different circumstances. Thus in the book of Jonah we read that under divine threat communicated by the reluctant prophet, the king and people of the city of Nineveh repented, and as a result God repented and spared the city. A similar case is made with regard to the city of Jerusalem. In the book of Jeremiah it is reported that in the days of Micah the prophet, the latter proclaimed the judgment of Yahweh against the city. In response, the king and people changed their ways and, as in the case of Nineveh, made a concerted effort to appease the deity. As a result Yahweh repented and the city was spared.

The principal example of divine repentance resulting from prophetic intercession is the case of Moses and the episode of the golden calf. In Exodus 32, the verb is used twice: Moses commands (the pleading imperative *hinnāḥēm*) and Yahweh complies (*wayyinnāḥem*). While Yahweh is described as "the repenter over the evil" in the prophetic version (Joel and Jonah) of the classic list of divine attributes first found in Exod 34:6–7, and there are general statements in a number of places about his tendency and willingness to repent, this is the only major public instance in the Hebrew Bible of a prophetic intercession successfully resulting in divine repentance, at least before the time of Amos. It should be noted that while Samuel is also considered an effective intercessor, ranked with Moses in the book of Jeremiah, the results he achieves are never described by the crucial term *nḥm*. In the one instance in which the term is used (three times), the divine repentance is not the result of Samuel's intervention, and Samuel's role in the account is to report to the repentant Saul that Yahweh has rejected the king and his repentance because "the Eternal One of Israel does not repent, for he is not a man." In fact, in this episode we find a classic example of intercessory failure, in which Samuel tries all night to persuade Yahweh to reverse a decision (itself an act of repentance) but does not succeed. It is in stark contrast to Moses' successful intervention on behalf of Israel in the episode of the golden calf. Jeremiah, who uses the word more than anyone else in the Bible and reports at least two acts of repentance on Yahweh's part, nevertheless confesses that he himself was forbidden by Yahweh to intercede for his people. His case reflects a third possibility.

The single major example of early successful prophetic intercession remains that of Moses, and it alone constitutes a model or precedent for Amos' intervention recorded in Amos 7:3, 6. Doubtless it was this dramatic and all-important action of Moses, and the repentance of God in response to Moses' intervention, that provided the basis for the prophetic designation of the deity as not only gracious and compassionate, long-suffering and merciful, and the rest of the qualities derived from the great self-revelation of Exod 34:6–7, but also as the one who repents concerning the evil (that he plans or has done). This interaction between prophet and deity was seen by Israel as decisive for its history and ranked with the other two great events of the Exodus: the deliverance from bondage in Egypt, highlighted by the Song of the Sea celebrating the destruction of Pharaoh's forces; and the establishment of the covenant community at the foot of Mount Sinai, including the giving of the Ten Words, the building of the Tabernacle, the making of its furnishings and equipment, and the institution of the sacral system reflecting and protecting the divine presence in the camp. The third element was the intervention by Moses to save the community from certain destruction by an angry deity who was offended by mass apostasy objectified in idolatry. The episode embodies central themes in the whole story of Yahweh and Israel and reveals the elements that determine that nation's fate. From this early stage there is a God determined to make a people for himself from the slave group hauled out of Egypt, a new society bound to its suzerain by solemn promises and commitments on both sides; and there is a people equally determined to wreck the agreement by committing the cardinal sin, to worship and serve another god (cf. the oldest form of the commandment in Exod 34:14, "You shall not worship another god," lō' tištaḥăweh lĕʾēl ʾaḥēr). Here at the beginning is also the ultimate confrontation. Because the people had repented first in the wrong sense—that is to say, they had reversed their decision to be the people of Yahweh, worshiping and serving him only—he also repented by changing his decision about them. His judgment against them was the inexorable consequence of their decision about him. Only the intervention of Moses prevented the immediate end of the glorious experiment in peoplehood begun forty days before. It is clear that without it, there would have been no Israel at all. And the divine repentance is the direct consequence of the Mosaic intercession. There is no other cause because the people are entirely oblivious to the situation, though presumably they are aware of having made a damaging breach in the commandments that hold the covenant between them together and make it valid.

As observed, Moses' action bought time only, time to remedy the situation, because a holy God cannot dwell in the midst of an idolatrous people, and unless the idolatry and the apostasy are eliminated the great experiment will end at its birth. The outcome through drastic and bloody measures is well known. Moses achieved a more permanent rescission of the judgment. The temporary suspension of judgment was confirmed, and with some reservations Yahweh agreed to keep his people and lead them to the holy land. Other crises that developed were met in similar fashion, but it is interesting that the term *nhm* is used only of the first and most important crisis in the history of the people.

In another sense, the problem exposed by that initial crisis was never resolved permanently. The revelation that there was a deeply rooted incompatibility between Yahweh and his own people, expressed by the people's irrepressible drive to worship other gods, cast a long shadow over the relationship and ensured an ultimate rupture. In truth, the prophet's intervention reversed the decision and suspended the judgment. But in spite of the best efforts of the prophet and his faithful followers the judgment was only suspended and would later be reinstated. Moses bought time for his people, a lot of it; but the judgment remained suspended, and six hundred years later it would be executed. It is the central conviction of the prophets and the biblical writers that Israel (including both kingdoms) remained incurably idolatrous throughout the history of the first commonwealth, and that ultimately this idolatry was the cause of divine rejection and the fall of the kingdoms; Israel and Samaria first, then Judah and Jerusalem. Already in this first episode after the ratification of the covenant, the basic and pervasive problem was uncovered and, in spite of Moses and all the prophets, could never be permanently corrected. The role of the prophets as agents of the divine word and as representatives of God's people is also seen in its full dimensions in this story and serves as a paradigm for the rest of Israel's history.

Moses and the repentance of God constitute an essential chapter in the story, which exerted a profound influence in its formulation and elaboration. It became a model for prophecy and history writing in Israel and helped to define the role of prophet as mediator between God and his people. While the prophet was first and foremost the proclaimer of God's word, he could aspire to the other office of intercessor, a role created by

Moses and enacted under the greatest pressure at the most critical moment in Israel's early history. Later prophets could aspire to such a complex and critical role, but few could attain it. Samuel apparently came closest (1 Sam 12:23), but all we know about it is by reputation and hearsay, because no actual instance of intervention on behalf of the people resulting in divine repentance is recorded. Although Samuel is credited with successful intercession, the one case of divine repentance in the story of Samuel shows the prophet as failing in this role.

Of all other candidates, strangely enough, the only successful example is Amos himself, and by his own admission. His was a limited success, a brief respite in the story of judgment. He intervened effectively, just as Moses had, though Amos did not use the verb itself in the imperative (*hinnāḥēm*) as Moses had. He found suitable substitutes and maintained the imperative form. Yahweh truly repented, but Amos was in no position to influence the people and their leadership or to effect desired results. No doubt he put forth his best effort. The contrast with Jonah is ironic, for Jonah was a very reluctant prophet who wanted to fail, and his message succeeded in winning a double repentance: first by king and people and then by God. Amos was eager to succeed, like Moses, to save his people, and he persuaded Yahweh to repent—the hard part, perhaps—but failed with king and people. They did not do so (4:6–11), and the suspended judgment, suspended now and again no doubt since the days of Moses, was reinstated.

The relation between Amos and Jonah is more complex and is not limited to the books under their names. Jonah was a historical prophet, a contemporary of Amos and apparently attached to the court of Jeroboam II, the king against whom Amos directed Yahweh's terrible words of judgment. The king preferred to listen to encouraging words from his own prophet and, according to 2 Kings 14, they were largely fulfilled. Yahweh did indeed grant a respite to this king and his people at about the time that Amos was bringing a word of final judgment. It might well appear that the major obstacle in the way of a genuine repentance and renewal of the covenant in Israel was precisely this other prophet who had the ear of the king and could and probably did frustrate (along with the high priest Amaziah) every effort on the part of Amos to get leaders and people to listen to the real message of Yahweh. Yet it is this prophet, Jonah, who is the permanent hero (or should we say antihero) of a story in which a repentant king and people unite with a repentant deity to save a great city (Nineveh). But that is only a story, and things often work out in stories much better than they do in real life. It is too bad that the same prophet could not have turned his efforts in real life to the rescue and salvation of the city and state in which he lived. While Jeroboam, his priest, and his prophet were superficially successful in those years of victory and prosperity, no doubt that very success at home and abroad ensured that life would continue in the same way, that Amos and his dire warnings would go on being ignored or dismissed, and that the doom of city or country would be guaranteed precisely because Jonah was considered and considered himself a true prophet.

Looking again at Amos and his work as prophet, we see that he did not hesitate to assume the mantle of the first and greatest of the prophets, Moses himself, perhaps along with Samuel. In fact, he was an intercessor before he became a prophet and tried to shape and modify the message he was to deliver. Surprisingly, he was successful, and as a result of his intervention Yahweh repented. The only earlier instance of specific divine repentance as a result of prophetic intervention is precisely the intercession of Moses in the story of the golden calf, as we have discussed. Because the story is assigned to the old narrative source in the Pentateuch we may conclude that Amos was aware of it, as he was of the basic traditions of the Exodus and Conquest. The connection, therefore, is not accidental or coincidental. As a prophet, Amos conceived his role to be that of intercessor as well as messenger. He aspired to save his people from destruction and took on the onerous and dangerous burden of prophecy to achieve that goal. Before accepting a mission, he tried to shape the message he was supposed to deliver, and succeeded in changing it from judgment to warning. When he failed to persuade the leaders of the people of both the reality and the urgency of the threat to their survival, not just their prosperity, he carried out the mission originally intended for him; but while he held out no hope for the nation, he knew that God had repented of the evil at least provisionally, as he had long ago, and in principle might do so again. Amos would have approved of the book of Jonah, though he may have had little use for the man himself. The refrain in Amos 7 (vv 3, 6), when the report of the first two visions is made, "and Yahweh repented of this," stands out in the biblical record. Not since the days of Moses and the beginning of the state had God repented specifically at the request of a prophet, and he did so twice; he would not do so again, at least not in the lifetime of Amos.

In view of the brevity of the accounts in Amos 7 and the inconsequential results of the prophetic intercession in the first two visions even for the prophet's mission, much less for Israel's history, it may seem an exaggerated effort to probe the meaning of the terms expressing divine repentance. It may also seem excessive to draw such dramatic and far-reaching conclusions about its significance for the biblical story and the understanding of the nature of the God of Israel. But one should not be misled by appearances even if they are real. The biblical experience is peculiar in that respect: the most important transactions between heaven and earth are often private and personal and defy the usual procedures of analysis and evaluation. Verification in the usual terms is almost impossible to achieve, and we are left with a bundle of claims and assertions, many of which challenge belief and defy rules of evidence and logical debate. The same is true of public events that often leave no trace in external records or archaeological excavations. Such questions, valid in themselves, must nevertheless be set aside once we enter the world of the Bible and attempt to read with understanding and appreciation. Thus, with respect to God's repentance in the story of Jonah we are entitled to ask questions about the historicity and reliability of the account because it purports to record an episode in the history of one of the greatest and best known cities of the ancient world. We are also entitled to a full measure of skepticism about the story as a whole and about many of its details, not just the credibility of the digestive capacities of the great fish. Nevertheless, the story has a meaning and import for understanding biblical religion and the particular matter of divine repentance quite apart from the questions just asked, as we have tried to show.

If our primary concern here is with the nature and character of the biblical God, then there are fewer and fewer external criteria by which to judge the extant data. Does God repent? Did he? Just to grapple with the meaning of the terms may be as much as we can handle or more, and it will be quite safe to leave decisions about veracity and validity to personal and public tribunals beyond the confines of this book. We will content ourselves with internal examinations and comparisons of the data and stay within the biblical world, where the interaction of God and his people is a matter of continuing concern. Channels are open, and special people called prophets have access to them.

It is in this light that we can speak of the decisive importance of Moses' interaction with Yahweh at Sinai in the episode of the golden calf. From the biblical perspective it was a public event. There were specific visible and verifiable consequences, including the destruction of the calf, the decimation of the community, and finally its survival as the people of Yahweh and not of some other god. That there are no external data to support or contradict the story in its essential content is one of the accidents of data preservation, a very haphazard affair, and of archaeological dispute among scholars over where Mount Sinai was and which peak among many it may have been. We would not even know where to look for, much less expect, any remains of the Israelite settlement at Sinai (in passing we can say that the search for such data at Qadesh Barnea, where the chances of finding something should be much better, has also proved frustrating); so we cannot expect to find anything about this story anywhere except in the Bible. We can make a relatively plausible case for the public events and perhaps agree that there was a great crisis in the wilderness about the essentials of the new faith, and that Moses and his coterie (the Levites) emerged victorious in that struggle, symbolized by the golden calf. In its present form there is little question that the episode in the desert has been affected by the tradition of the bull images used in the worship of the northern kingdom at

Bethel and Dan, but we need not conclude that the story in Exodus 32 is mere invention. About the private meetings between Moses and God, whether up on the mountain or down in the tent, even less can be said in terms of verification or external testimony. What actually went on in these head-to-head (mouth-to-mouth, face-to-face are the biblical metaphors) sessions? Only those who have been in them can say, but supporting testimony is hard to come by because in most cases there is no third party, and even when others are in attendance they are not privy to the details of the conversation. In the end we can only study the record and attempt to understand and appreciate it; assessing it objectively may be impossible and is, in any case, the responsibility of the reader. For biblical history the encounters between prophets and their God were of the utmost importance because it was believed firmly that both parties were affected by the interaction. The critical point in the story of the golden calf was the exchange between Moses and God (*hnḥm . . . wynḥm,* "Repent . . . and he repented"); the rest followed as a natural consequence. To trace the story from the original experience until it reached the form in which we have it is both difficult and speculative, and the trail is very murky. But it became the official accepted version, and that is what we have to work with.

The situation in many ways is even worse in the case of Amos. Here the transaction was entirely private, and the repentance of Yahweh reported in the book of Amos was canceled shortly thereafter, so that it has become merely a group of words, a brief refrain or footnote to the laconic account of the initiating visions. In a literal sense we have only the word of Amos to vouch for the experience or for any of the other experiences by which the word of Yahweh was transmitted. We do not have to validate Amos' experience or assess the reality of his vision or his viewpoint. It is enough—and this point is very important—to describe it and to show what its role was in the prophet's message and in the context of the book that bears his name. The visions were central to his understanding of his calling as a prophet and his mission to his people, Israel. That much is clear. And it is equally clear that, like Moses and perhaps Samuel before him, he aspired to and in his own judgment fulfilled the role of intercessor, a role that other prophets aspired to and in their own judgment did not succeed in fulfilling. That success puts Amos in a very select unit of a very select group. Of true prophets there are a very limited number, and of them only the barest handful could qualify as effective intercessors: Moses, Samuel, Amos; we might add Jeremiah; but for him the time of intercession passed, and he was not allowed even to try.

This insight into Amos' career and character also has large implications for understanding his message and in the end his book. It is striking that Amos the intercessor stands in sharp contrast to his fellow eighth-century prophets, with whom he otherwise has so much in common. None of the others deals in divine repentance at all. The word is not used at all in this sense with God as subject by any of them. Where it does occur in a story about a contemporary prophet, Jonah, the prophet is adamantly opposed to the idea altogether.

As in the case of Moses and Samuel, so with Amos, behind the facade of fierce and uncompromising loyalty to Yahweh—which demanded the most drastic measures to achieve conformity to his will—there was a passionate concern for the survival and well-being of the people to whom they were sent, but whose interest they chose to represent before the deity with daring and at great risk to themselves. They and they alone succeeded in reshaping the message they were to deliver, in reversing the divine decision, and in redirecting the divine activity, but only for the benefit and salvation of their people.

VISION 5

We turn now to Vision 5, Amos 9:1–4. As already noted, it is not only separated physically from the unit containing the other four visions (7:1–8:3), which also includes the story of the confrontation with Amaziah at Bethel, but it differs notably in form and content. For example, the opening formula, *kh hr'ny,* which is repeated precisely the first four times, is varied here by *r'yty,* "I saw." The sense is the same, but the change is important. The remaining words of the opening of the fifth vision remind us of the wording of Vision 3, which varies from the others in the main group:

7:7	(3)	*kōh hir'anî wĕhinnēh*	*'ădōnāy*	*niṣṣāb 'al-*
9:1	(5)	*rā'îtî*	*'et-'ădōnāy*	*niṣṣāb 'al-*

This echo shows that the fifth vision is connected with the earlier ones, but not as closely. It is instructive that it stands alone and is not paired with a parallel or reinforcing vision, as is true of the others. At first glance, because it deals with the destruction of a temple, it would seem to fit the context of the altercation at the temple in Bethel, in which case the story of that episode ought to have been brought into closer contact with this vision. But the fact that the location of the temple and the identity of the people to be destroyed are not specified indicates that Amos may not have had the Bethel temple and its personnel directly in mind, though certainly they cannot be excluded. The vision is of Yahweh standing at the altar and commanding the violent destruction of the sanctuary, while committing himself to the slaughter of the personnel gathered there. The vagueness with respect to identity or location is in keeping with the tone of the other visions, which, as we have seen, can apply to a scope beyond that of the northern kingdom, even if it was the target nearest at hand. Thus, while the application to the temple at Bethel is more or less obvious, an application to Jerusalem would not be out of the question. In fact, the vision may symbolize the destruction not of a single temple of Yahweh but of any or all of them. We should not assume that the vision must be specific in terms of place and time but may imagine rather that it was a vision of the desecration and destruction of the earthly sanctuary of Yahweh. The one at Bethel would come to mind naturally, but the ones at Gilgal, Beer-sheba, Samaria, and even Jerusalem would not be excluded; their turn would come.

The impending destruction begins as Yahweh commands his cohort to strike the capitals of the temple. The first group of verbs includes two that are m. s. imperative and are addressed to this aide, who must be present with Yahweh at the scene. That person could conceivably be the prophet, but because prophets as a rule are not physically active, are not wreckers or executioners, we should see in this unnamed person one of the leaders of the heavenly host (perhaps the commander; cf. Josh 5:13–15), here with Yahweh to carry out the violent orders. There is no need therefore to emend the text, but we should recognize that the *b* serves both *rʾš* and *ʾḥrytm*, which are balancing terms in any case. It seems equally clear that the suffix on *ʾḥryt* ("their") serves *rʾš* as well, although with one 3d m. pl. suffix on the verb and another on the pronoun *kl*, it is hard to escape the obvious reference even if *rʾš* stands by itself. So we understand the statement to mean that the destruction will begin with the temple, possibly in a divinely ordered earthquake, and with it there will be a slaughter of the temple personnel. Because of the switch from second-person m. s. imperative to first person indicative in v 1aB, it is clear that Yahweh and his angel will collaborate, the angel cutting them off at (their) head, while Yahweh himself will slay with his sword (at) their rear. That point is clearly enunciated in the concluding bicolon of the verse.

9:1a   *rāʾîtî ʾet-ʾādōnāy niṣṣāb ʿal-hammizbēaḥ*
        wayyōʾmer hak hakkaptôr
            wĕyirʿăšû hassippîm
            ûbĕṣaʿam bĕrōʾš kullām
            wĕʾaḥărîtām baḥereb ʾehĕrōg

9:1a   I saw my Lord standing beside the altar.
        He said: "Strike the capitals
            so that the thresholds shake!
            and smite them on the head [or cut them off at (their) head]
                    —all of them;

and their remainder [or (at) their rear] I shall slay
with the sword;

1b *lōʾ-yānûs lāhem nās*
    wĕlōʾ-yimmālēṭ lāhem pālîṭ

1b no fugitive among them shall make good his flight,
    no survivor among them shall escape."

The second part of the report consists of a series of conditional clauses, all referring to the ultimate fate of any who may escape from the debacle at the temple. This is a case of "pseudo-sorites," in which there is a series predicated on possibilities contrary to expectation (O'Connor 1987). Thus: (1) no one will escape, (2) but even if some do, they will not finally escape either, (3) because if they go to the remote parts of the world or beyond it, they will be tracked down and destroyed. We have interpreted this final vision as representing a special judgment against the leadership (whether in Samaria or Jerusalem), who will be held strictly and without exception to account and will be made to pay a final forfeit. We have described this time of judgment as Phase Three, the details of which can be traced back to the confrontation with Amaziah and the specific judgments pronounced against him and his family and against the royal house. In the present series the consequences are spelled out in universal terms for temple personnel, just as in 8:3 the palace dwellers were dealt with. We take the repeated reference to "them" in v 1—*bṣ'm, klm, w'ḥrytm, lhm* (bis)—to be to the people associated with the temple (chiefly the priests, but also civil and military leaders and not excluding the royal house); the reference to "them" in v 4b concludes the series (*'lyhm*).

9:2a *ʾim yaḥtĕrû biš'ôl*
            miššām *yādî tiqqāḥ***ēm**
  2b *wĕʾim-yaʿălû haššāmayim*
            miššām *ʾôrîd***ēm**
  3a *wĕʾim yēḥ ābĕʾû bĕrōʾš hakkarmel*
            miššām *ʾăḥappēś ûlĕqaḥ***tîm**
  3b *wĕʾim yissātĕrû minneged ʿênay*
            beqarqaʿ hayyām
    miššām *ʾăṣawweh ʾet-hannāḥāš*
            *ûnĕšāk***ām**
  4a *wĕʾim-yēlĕkû baššĕbî*
            *lipnê ʾōyĕbê***hem**
    miššām *ʾăṣawweh ʾet-haḥereb*
            *wahărāgāt***am**

4b   *wĕśamtî ʿênî ʿălêhem*
lĕrāʿâ wĕlōʾ lĕṭôbâ

Verse 4b forms an envelope with v 1b around the conditional series included in vv 2–4a. The emphasis is on "them," as already suggested, which links this unit to v 1a, the initial description (which has a triple use of the 3d m. pl. suffix, matching the triple use in vv 1b and 4b), and to the conditional series in which the 3d m. pl. suffix is stressed a total of six times: once at the end of each threat: *tqḥm* (2a), *ʾwrydm* (2b), *wlqḥtym* (3a), *wnškm* (3b), *whrgtm* (4a), making five, and once internally, *ybyhm* (4a). The grand total is twelve occurrences of the 3d m. pl. pronominal suffix, which is an impressive number, especially when compressed into four verses. The fact that the group is not otherwise specifically identified reflects the impression of the vision's broad applicability. As suggested earlier, while Amos may have thought, and we naturally think, of the temple at Bethel so recently under discussion, the description is devoid of explicit reference, and hence the vision was more basic and general, and the threat would more likely be aimed at all of the temples in which the idolatries and apostasies Amos complained of were being practiced.

The distribution and arrangement of the suffix forms are symmetrical in the opening and closing of the unit (vv 1 and 4): *-ām* three times in v 1a and *-hem* three times in vv 1b and 4b. In the body of the vision report, the other six occurrences are similarly and symmetrically arranged, with some variations. In the first three conditional clauses, we have the pattern *-ēm* (2a), *-ēm* (2b), *-îm* (3a), while in the last two the sequence is *-am* (3b), *-hem* (4a), and *-am* (4a). In each group there is an equivalent or matching pair (*-ēm* as the suffix of the imperfect form of the verb in the first group and *ām* as the suffix of the perfect form of the verb in the second group); each group also contains a single divergent form, *-îm* (3a) in the first and *-hem* (4a) in the second.

In this series of conditions, there are five instances of the pair *ʾim* (or *wĕʾim*) + *miššām* introducing the two clauses, "if . . . from there. . . ." The second term requires some explanation. In the first three instances it suits the context and can be given its normal translation "from there, thence," for retrieving from a place is involved. In the last two the connection is not so clear, and the precise meaning of the expression may elude us because what follows does not fit well with the rendering "from there." Nevertheless, the pattern is clearly established and at work in these members of the series, so it is best to keep the term *mšm* and to translate and interpret *ad sensum*. It may well be that we have an ellipsis in the latter statements and that the last preceding verb, *wlqḥtym*, or one of the others used earlier is also operative in the context. So the sense would be that just as he will search them out at the top of Carmel and take them from there, so also if they hide themselves at the bottom of the sea he will do the same, and having seized them will then command the great serpent to bite them. The same logic would apply to the last condition. One or another of the verbs of seizing and bringing down would be applicable in the last two situations, and, equally important, the punishments described in the last two would be appropriate for the first three as well.

Reviewing the data in the list of five conditions, we find the general scheme that the "if" clauses describe various attempts at escape: thus the first four deal with mundane or mythic possibilities, while the fifth appears to be a rather odd means of escape, that is, being taken away captive. Yahweh's response may be divided into two parts: (1) retrieval or recapture of those fleeing, again clearly applicable to the first four instances, less clear in the case of the last, which may be an exaggerated case to express in absolute terms the determination of Yahweh that none of the miscreants associated with the temple shall escape the judgment passed against them. If they flee they will be pursued implacably until captured, not only to the ends of the earth and sky and sea and mountains, but even if they are led away captive. Captivity in itself will be insufficient punishment; it will be viewed as a form of escape, and Yahweh will not allow even that to happen. (2) After capture there will be punishment, which will be inflicted by the serpent and the sword. While each may be particularly appropriate to the specific context in which it occurs, it would also be usable in the others. We conclude therefore that there will be two consequences of the attempt to escape in every case: capture (or recapture), and corporal (actually capital) punishment, because the serpent's bite will be just as fatal as the sword. Just as the escapes include the mundane and the mythical, so the punishments are symbolized by the ordinary and exotic weapons available to the deity. His sword has already been mentioned (v 1), and the serpent is clearly no ordinary snake.

The structure of the unit also deserves attention. The pairs of statements (*'im . . . miššām*) become progressively longer and more detailed, and the links between them become more intricate. Thus the first pair is clearly balanced and provides a framework for the others. Hell and Heaven (*še'ōl* and *haššāmayim*) represent the usual cosmic limits of the biblical universe; no one can go farther, and even these limits are inaccessible to human beings. The prophet says that even if they were to escape and go as far as is conceivable, to the ultimate limits, they would not escape the power of the deity. Psalm 139 affirms the same in almost identical language (vv 7–9), though that context and the poet's purposes are different.

Thus the first pair expresses the general position in universal terms and affirms that Yahweh will not permit any to escape no matter how far they flee, namely, to Hell or Heaven. The next two give specific examples of remote regions, with probable mythic associations, while the last gives a special situation, which can only be ironic. Captivity and exile are treated as a possible form of escape. But even that escape will not be permitted, and those people will be plucked from captivity to face an implacable judgment. All five initial statements begin with the particle 'im ("if"), and each of them describes an attempted escape to some possible refuge—even the last, though it is a special case. The second clause in each case begins with *miššām*, which is to be rendered, "from there." Because the first clause always begins with '*m* and the second always begins with *mšm*, we would expect the particles to retain the same meaning. The use of such formulaic devices is very common in Amos, and we can point to a similar grouping of five components with opening or closing formulas in chap. 4:6–11 (the plagues). There is no problem with '*m*, but one develops with *mšm* after the first two occurrences, where the meaning is quite satisfactory. In the third case we read, "If they hide themselves on the top of Carmel, *from there* I will seek them out at once, and seize them." The particle *mšm* does not go well with the first verb but can be used with the second, so it is simply a matter of connecting the adverbial expression with the second verb and cutting it loose from the first. In ordinary prose we would render, "If . . . Carmel, I will seek them out at once, and seize them from there." In the next case the first clause is closely parallel to the first clause of the third example, so we should render it similarly: "If they conceal themselves from my eyes on the bottom of the Sea, from there I will command the Serpent and he shall bite them." The initial particle seems to refer not to where they have hidden but to where Yahweh is, but that reading would be inconsistent both with the prevailing usage and with good sense. The same problem recurs with the fifth item in the series, where the same words turn up. Once again the potential escapees will go somewhere, into captivity before their enemies. Then we read: "From there I will command the Sword and it will slay them." The construction is the same, the problem is the same, and any solution should fit all cases.

We propose that while in every instance the "if" clause involves movement on the part of "them"—that is, they go somewhere, and therefore the expression *mšm*, which follows, naturally refers to the place to which they have gone—the *mšm* clauses that follow next do not share the same consistency. Some (the first three) speak of recapturing the fugitives, while the last two speak of punishing them. While we tend to bring them together as though they all involved the same kind of action, they do not necessarily do so. As noted above, we see instead two phases or stages in the action of Yahweh: capture and judgment. We believe that both actions are required in all five cases, but in the interests of brevity and poetic conciseness only the first phase is mentioned in the first three cases and only the second phase is indicated for the last two. The interpretation of the first three cases is somewhat easier to manage. After the escapees have been apprehended in the first three cases, they will be judged and executed in the fashion mentioned in the last two cases, by snake and by sword. Perhaps one would be more appropriate in one case and the other in another, but we think the terms are exemplary rather than specific or exhaustive. It is also possible that no particular punishment is specified in the first cases because the consequence could be imagined and taken for granted. But in view of what follows it is best to regard both sets of apodoses as reciprocal and operational across the board. So for the first three the punishments are to be added, while for the remaining two the "search and seize" procedure enunciated in the third case is to be understood as preceding the punishments. It is the presence of *mšm* in both instances that symbolizes the first phase of divine response, namely, the recapture of the miscreants, and that requires us to supply the necessary verbs at least in our minds before proceeding to the punishment. Admittedly, this reading involves a modification of the usual picture of punishment in the last two cases, in which Yahweh is supposed to send out these agents of doom to track down the fugitives and kill them on the spot, which departs from the earlier cases, in which seizure is emphasized. And that is the important point: recapture is necessary and obligatory in all cases (especially because the first pair, as we have seen, includes all of the possibilities). The first pair provides us with the clear requirement of capture, while the last pair makes it equally clear that the final word is execution, administered by divine agents. The middle entry serves as the transition and shows that the parallel cases of hiding on top of a mountain or at the bottom of the sea are to be handled in a sequential manner. First there is search and seizure for both groups, and then summary punishment at the command of the supreme judge when they are brought before him. So after *mšm* in the fourth and fifth cases we would understand that the words on "search and seizure" in the third case would apply, or the ones in the other cases to the extent that they would be applicable. But it is not necessary to spell everything out. The general meaning seems clear enough. In every case the fugitives from divine justice will be apprehended, and when they are brought before the divine tribunal they will be judged and the sentence executed by the agents appointed for the purpose. It may well be that the serpent is particularly appropriate for those hiding in the sea and that the sword is peculiarly appropriate for those carried off into captivity; but the principle is applicable to the other cases, just as seizure or recapture is appropriate as a preliminary step before sentence is carried out. We think too that the word "I will command" fits better in the context of judicial procedure than if they were being sent out to administer the punishment where the fugitives were found. In the latter case we would expect a verb such as *šlḥ* in place of *ṣwh*.

INSERTED ORACLES (8:4–14)

In principle at least the material in Amos 8:4–14, sandwiched between the fourth and fifth visions, should have some relation to the visions, and there should be a rationale for the arrangement of the various elements, perhaps along the lines of the way in which the story of the confrontation between Amos and Amaziah has been inserted between the third and fourth visions. In view of the heterogeneous character of the group of small units in 8:4–14, in contrast to the single story in 7:10–17—which itself is a carefully constructed literary achievement—we should not expect much from such an inquiry, but there should be some reason for the arrangement we have, apart from accident or the haphazard efforts of bumbling editors.

After v 3 (III.B.1.a) the material in question breaks down into two major parts: (1) vv 4–8 and (2) vv 9–14; while these parts in turn can be subdivided as follows: (1.b) vv 4–6 and (1.c) vv 7–8; (1.d) vv 9–10; (1.e) vv 11–12; and (1.f) vv 13–14. The first large unit is somewhat more cohesive than the second and deals with charges against merchants for a variety of malpractices all stemming from a cardinal vice, the eagerness to maximize profits at the expense of the customers and in defiance of the law. The passage is similar in some respects to the initial charges brought against Israel in 2:6–8 and to 5:10–12. There are also divergent elements, so this passage should not be regarded simply as a secondary assemblage of the earlier pieces, but rather as an alternative or reinforced indictment of the same or other groups. In fact, the identity of the group is not clear, though one might expect it to be the same as the one charged in 2:6–8, for the accusations are essentially the same and the wording is very similar:

> 2:6 *ʿal-mikrām bakkesep ṣaddîq*
> *wĕʾebyôn baʿăbûr naʿălāyim*
>
> Because they sell for money the righteous,
> and the poor for the sake of a pair of sandals—
>
> 8:6 *liqnôt bakkesep dallîm*
> *wĕʾebyôn baʿăbûr naʿălāyim*
>
> who buy the needy for money,
> and the poor for a pair of sandals.

Except for the obvious difference between selling (2:6) and buying (8:6) and the use of a closer parallel to *'bywn* in 8:6 (*dlym*, though note the plural) in place of the combinatory *ṣdyq* (2:6), the passages are very close in spirit and the rest of the wording is the same. The prophet clearly is talking about the same kind of behavior in both places, and no doubt about the same kind of people. But are they the same people in the same place?

2:7 *haššōʾăpîm ʿal-ʿăpar-ʾereṣ běrōʾš dallîm
      wĕderek ʿănāwîm yaṭṭû*

those who trample upon the dust of the earth the head of the
     destitute,
and they push the humble out of the way—

8:4 *šimʿû-zōʾt haššōʾăpîm ʾebyôn
      wĕlašbît ʿăniyyê[qere; ʿnwy kethib]-ʾăreṣ*

Hear this, you who trample upon the poor,
     and put an end to the wretched of the land.

There is also a long-range chiasm that must be seen to be appreciated, but it indicates that the prophet or editor wished to draw the noose tightly around his prey and bind all of the people of the woes, in their various occupations and pursuits, into a single parcel:

2:6 **ʿal-mikrām bakkesep ṣaddîq**
     wĕ **ʾebyôn** *baʿăbûr naʿălāyim*
2:7   **haššōʾăpîm** . . . **běrōʾš dallîm**
          wĕderek **ʿănāwîm** *yaṭṭû*

8:4   *šimʿû-zōʾt* **haššōʾăpîm ʾebyôn**
          wĕlašbît **ʿăniyyê-ʾăreṣ** . . .
8:6 *liqnôt* **bakkesep dallîm**
     wĕ **ebyôn** *baʿăbûr naʿălāyim*

These passages are obviously connected, but to regard one as a corruption of the other, or both as derived from a common original goes beyond the evidence and either the requirements or the implications of the case. Each passage can well be considered on its own merits, and the interpretation of each can be helpful in understanding the other. The interchange between *ʾl-mkrm* in 2:6 and *lqnwt* in 8:6 shows that we are dealing with a deliberate pattern on the part of the editor or author, rather than inadvertent and approximate duplication. The essential difference between the passages is that in 2:6 the words quoted constitute that particular charge in full, while in 8:4–6 the lines quoted serve as a framework for a more detailed and elaborate description and analysis of the crimes these people are committing. We have a classic description of what is known as short-weighting, apparently as much a problem in antiquity as in more recent times, "to make the ephah small, and to make the shekel great," and to "rig the scales deceitfully" in order to achieve those goals.

The major question raised by the comment, v 7, is the identity of the people described by the phrase *g'wn y'qb,* "the pride of Jacob," about which there is both confusion and controversy. Because an oath by Yahweh is involved, it is a matter of the greatest importance and urgency, and the comment is ominous: "Yahweh has sworn . . . 'I will never forget any of their misdeeds.'" We can recognize a sharpening and focusing of the charges and an escalation of the rhetoric. Yahweh is recorded as making oaths on three occasions in the book of Amos: 4:2, where he swears by his holiness that dire judgment will come on the "cows of Bashan" for their oppression of the same *dlym//'bywnym* mentioned in our passage; 6:8, where he swears by his soul that he abhors the same "pride of Jacob" we have here, and promises to deliver up the city; and the present passage (8:7). At the least we can say that the three passages complement each other, that we can identify "the pride of Jacob" as the target on two occasions (6:8, 8:7), and that no doubt the people in 4:2 also belong to the same group.

Exactly who or what "the pride of Jacob" was is not altogether clear, and parallel passages do not settle the question (cf. Nah 2:3 and Ps 47:5). It could be translated "Proud Jacob" or "Exalted Jacob" or the like and simply epitomize the political group, or it could be a reference to a capital city, perhaps Jerusalem in particular, as the elevated center of the nation. In our study of the name "Israel" and its cognates in the book of Amos, we were able to determine that Jacob stands for the larger entity, equivalent to Israel when the latter is used in its classical sense or in any future sense, whether Jacob alone (as in the visions, 7:2, 5) or in the chain *bêt y'qb* ("the house of Jacob"; 3:13 and 9:8). We are disposed, therefore, to interpret the phrase *g'wn y'qb* in the same way and have not found in either passage in which it occurs any compelling evidence to think otherwise, though the data do not necessarily support any specific interpretation of the title. That on both occasions the "pride of Jacob" is the target of a minatory divine oath may be significant in itself, and it might not be amiss to see here again a special animus against the leaders of the country. In 6:8 it would be the civil and military authorities; in 8:7 it would be the merchants as a whole, not excluding the royal establishment, which doubtless was the chief group of the country. It is also possible that 8:7 is not directly connected with

vv 4–6 and is a general indictment of the same group as in 6:8, where both
the divine oath and the pride of Jacob are also mentioned.

If we suppose, however, that v 7 is a comment on vv 4–6 and that the
same people are involved, then we would say that the charges in vv 4–6 are
not limited to the merchants of the northern kingdom but include the
larger Jacob/Israel. Perhaps we can speak of an expansion and escalation of
charges reflecting the growing intensity in the rhetoric and the increasing
sense of doom hanging over the nation in the transition between Visions
3–4 and Vision 5.

Turning to the unit vv 4–6, we find an intricate interlocking structure,
which deserves a closer look. Two subthemes are intertwined to produce
this curious effect: (1) the eagerness of the merchants to open their shops as
quickly as possible after the new moon and the sabbath and (2) the cheating
and other immoral and illegal activities associated with business. The following arrangement will illustrate the interlocking structure. The passage
divides neatly into two parts:

A. Description and dialogue

		Words	Syllables
1.	4a	4	9
2.	5a	9	22
3.	6b	3	6
Totals		16	
			37

B. List of charges

		Words	Syllables
1.	4b	3	7
2.	5b	7	19
3.	6a	6	13
Totals		16	39

The opening words (v 4a) provide the basis for both continuations, because
the same group—defined here as the oppressors of the poor—is the subject
throughout. The direct continuation of the address is in 5a, where these
oppressors are quoted as being eager to pursue their business (5a, 6b). In
the parallel unit (4b, 5b, 6a) there is a list of charges introduced by infinitives, with the preposition lĕ specifying what is wrong with the way they
conduct the business they are eager to promote, and why they do so. The
two interlocking units complement each other and fill out the picture, but
in order to understand the procedure it is necessary to pull it apart and
show how the parts fit together before putting them back in their places. It
may be asked why the prophet or editor bothered to make things complicated when they could have been handled more simply, but our task is not

to improve on the work of the writer or editor but to describe, analyze, and explain as far as possible.

		Syllables	
4a	*šimʿû-zōʾt haššōʾăpîm ʾebyôn*	$2 + 1 + 4 + 2 = 9$	A
b	*wĕlašbît ʿaniyyê-ʾāreṣ*	$3 + 3 + 1 = 7$	B
5a	*lēʾmōr mātay yaʿăbōr hahōdeš*	$2 + 2 + 2 + 2 = 8$	
	wĕnašbîrâ šeber	$4 + 1 = 5$	22 A
	wĕhaššabbāt	$4 = 4$	
	wĕniptĕḥâ-bār	$4 + 1 = 5$	
b	*lĕhaqṭîn ʾêpâ*	$3 + 2 = 5$	
	ûlĕhagdîl šeqel	$4 + 1 = 5$	19 B
	ûlĕʿawwēt moʾzĕnê mirmâ	$4 + 3 + 2 = 9$	
6a	*liqnôt bakkesep dallîm*	$2 + 2 + 2 = 6$	13 B
	wĕʾebyôn baʿăbûr naʿălāyim	$3 + 2 + 2 = 7$	
b	*ûmappal bar našbîr*	$3 + 1 + 2 = 6$	A

Both series proceed from the initial statement and tie into the principal clause by an infinitive with the preposition *lĕ*. The main series continues the direct address by quoting the merchant group, who speak for themselves in the first person: 5a, introduced by *lʾmr*—their speech includes 5a and 6b, forming an envelope around the catalog of charges, which begins in 4b, also an infinitive introduced by *lĕ* and continuing then through 5b and 6a. The list of five infinitives in this group constitutes a charge sheet, giving specifics of the merchants' illegal and immoral behavior. The list is similar in shape to the lists in Hosea 4 and Jeremiah 7, in which the covenant violations are spelled out; but in the latter the infinitive absolute is used without qualification, while here we have the infinitive construct forms with the preposition *lĕ*. We can translate and indicate the dependence of these phrases on the main clause, as follows: "Hear this, you who trample on the poor: (a) and put an end to the wretched of the land; (b) who reduce the quantity (*ephah*); (c) while raising the price (*shekel*); (d) and cheat with crooked scales; (e) and buy the needy for money." This series also reflects a balanced envelope construction.

The inner group, v 5b, has three infinitives, but the first two together constitute a single misfeasance, that is, reducing the *ephah* automatically increases the *shekel* and vice versa; together they match the third in the group, the manipulation of the scales in order to cheat, which is associated with the previous statement and may provide the means of achieving the former trick, that is, making the *ephah* small and the *shekel* large. The outer group (4b, 6a) consists of two infinitive clauses, but the second extends its force to the final colon, which has no verb. This unit resembles 2:6 and echoes the sentiments expressed there, although there are differences as noted, including an inversion in the order. Here the emphasis is on the victims of exploitation and mistreatment. Three terms are used in parallel order: ʿnyy (kethib ʿnwy) ʾrṣ//dlym//ʾbywn (bis), the last term forming an inclusion with ʾbywn in the opening line (v 4a).

Turning to the other side of this communication (vv 5a, 6b), we find a number of interesting structural features. It interlocks with the other so that the opening of the quotation with lʾmr (5a) corresponds to the opening of the parallel group with lšbyt (4b). There it forms an envelope around the main body of the first group considered, with the principal statement (5a) preceding; but there is a small piece at the end (6b) that must be linked grammatically with 5a (the verbal forms correspond), so 6b cannot be fitted onto 5b–6a. This unit consists of a single statement by the merchants branded hšʾpym at the very beginning of the section. They are quoted in the first person, and it could well be a faithful transcript of what they would say. It is quite realistic and expresses a typical eagerness to get on with business, impatiently awaiting the end of the new moon or the sabbath to open the bins and sell the goods. It is only at the very end of this unit that there may be a suggestion of excessive greed and possible infraction of the law. They apparently scrape up every last bit of the leavings of the grain, that is, the grain that has fallen in the furrows or by the way, which should be left for the poor. The expression may mean no more than that they sell every grain in their bins—in other words, they are eager to sell the lot. In the meantime, however, we learn from the encased material that the eagerness to serve their customers is only exceeded by their corrupting greed and their avidity to fleece the latter. While they are presenting themselves as affable and accommodating shopkeepers, the voice in the background is explaining what they are really up to, and that is the voice of the prosecuting attorney reading a list of their crimes from a court docket. The dramatic juxtaposition of self-assertion by the merchants and merciless exposure by the prophet justifies the curious interweaving of the parts. Once we have analyzed the elements and traced each sequence through we can put them back together again.

The opening statement (5a) presents us with a classic example of forward gapping or the extended double-duty service of the verb:

8:5a mātay yaʿăbōr haḥōdeš
wĕnašbîrâ šeber
wĕhaššabbāt
wĕniptĕḥâ-bār

When will the new moon pass,
so that we may sell our grain;

> and the sabbath,
> so that we may open our stores of grain?

The single initial verb covers both clauses, which are exactly parallel in form and structure, and combinatory or complementary in context and meaning. Taken literally and in order, we can render as follows, "When will the new moon [holiday] end so that we can trade [our] *šeber* (grain)? And when will the sabbath end [pass] so that we can open up [our sacks] of *bār* (grain)?" Two different actions are mentioned, which describe the process of offering and selling grain of different kinds or characteristics. Two different holidays are mentioned, one that observes the beginning of the month and one that is weekly. But we are not to understand that the second action takes place only in connection with the weekly sabbath. The same double action (the two features mentioned are representative of the whole process of selling agricultural products) is involved once the holiday is ended, whichever it is. We can summarize by paraphrasing the merchants as follows, "When will the holiday end [= any interruption in our business activity] so that we may do business in the grain market and dispose of our stocks to customers?"

We note too that the two first-person verbs (imperfect 1st pl.) have the so-called cohortative *he* endings (usually translated "let us . . ."), but here they are to be interpreted as the old subjunctive forms (in -*a*) expressing an oblique mood, equivalent to ". . . so that we may."

At the end of this section, v 6b, we have the conclusion of the first-person plural address, "and that we may sell the husks of the grain." This line is in a chiastic arrangement with the preceding statements in 5a, where the verbs are first and the objects last. Two of the three words are the same as or nearly identical with words in both parts of 5a, showing that it is a resumption and a conclusion (which often is the function of chiasm):

5a **wĕnašbîrâ** *šeber* . . .
   wĕniptĕḥâ-**bār**

6b   . . . **bar** *na*š**bîr**

The next unit (vv 7–8) would seem to be associated with the diatribe against the *šᵓpym* ("tramplers of the poor") of 4a, for the 3d m. pl. suffix on the last word of v 7 (*mᶜśyhm*) requires an antecedent, and this is the nearest suitable one. The immediate reference is to the "pride of Jacob," but that identification requires further specification because a particular set of misdeeds is in mind. As a very specific and utterly reprehensible set of crimes has just been described, it seems reasonable to suppose that the wrongdoings of v 7 refer to them and that the 3d m. pl. pronoun at the end refers back not only to the "pride of Jacob," which as we have proposed includes everybody in both kingdoms or perhaps primarily the leadership, but especially to grasping, greedy, and oppressive merchants who are front and center.

> 7a   *nišbaʿ yhwh bigʾôn yaʿăqōb*
> b   *ʾim-ʾeškaḥ lāneṣaḥ kol-maʿăśêhêm*
> 8a   *haʿal zōʾt lōʾ-tirgaz hāʾāreṣ*
>   *wěʾābal kol-yôšēb bāh*

> Yahweh has sworn by the pride of Jacob:
> "I will never forget any of their misdeeds."
> For this reason, should not the earth tremble,
> and everyone who dwells in it mourn?

At the same time, the judgment and threatened punishment have a universal tone that seems to extend beyond the borders of both kingdoms to envelop the whole world, as the added comment in v 8 shows. The pronoun *zōʾt* can cover a great deal of ground, and no immediate specific antecedent for it emerges. It is a summary of the preceding *kl-mʿśyhm,* which itself may encompass a great deal more than the sins of the merchants that may have been the point of departure for the prophet. They are typical and representative of all of those denounced in the Woes, and while vv 4–6 do not, strictly speaking, constitute a Woe form, the participial construction demonstrates that there are close affinities between the "Hear this" pattern and the "Woe" pattern (cf. in particular 4:1–3, where we have a similar combination of "Hear this" and participial constructions).

In v 8 it is not easy to decide the extent of the land, and it is possible that an ambiguous term was used deliberately. It could be restricted to a particular country, in this case the one or ones covered by the term "Jacob" (presumably both kingdoms, though either could be meant in particular cases) or the whole earth, with all of its inhabitants. Whether countrywide or worldwide—and we probably opt for the former—within that space the mourning is total. For total wrongdoing (*kl-mʿśyhm*) there must be mourning by everyone (*kl-ywšb bh*).

The remaining line has a near duplicate in 9:5, so the two of them must be studied together:

> 8:8b   *wěʿālětâ kāʾōr kullāh*
>   *wěnigrěšâ wěnišqâ kîʾôr miṣrāyim*

> Shall it not all rise like the Nile,
> and be tossed about,
>   then sink like the Nile of Egypt?

9:5b   *wĕ'ālĕtâ kay'ōr kullāh*
       wĕšāqĕ'â kî'ōr miṣrāyim

It all rises like the Nile,
       and subsides like the Nile of Egypt.

With respect to the first line there is only one slight difference, in the
second word, spelled *k'r* in 8:8 and *ky'r* in 9:5; clearly the reference is to the
Nile, so we must adopt the reading in 9:5 and supply the missing *yod* to the
word in 8:8. The latter reading (in 8:8) seems to be an error, though in view
of the vocalization of the word in the second colon of 8:8b and 9:5b the *yod*
serves as a vowel letter and might have been omitted at some point in the
transmission. In any case, there is no question about the reading or what is
meant: it all shall rise like the Nile. The subject presumably is "the land"
(*h'rṣ*) of v 8a, and the picture is a very accurate description of one of the
more frightening effects of a major earthquake: the land rises and falls like a
body of water.

When it comes to the second line, the differences in the two texts are
concentrated on the verbs. There are two verbs in 8:8 and only one in 9:5,
but all three are different. In view of the exact symmetry of 9:5b and the
suitability of the verb *šq'* as a complement for *'lh* in the first colon, it is clear
that 9:5 has a correct and unassailable text. For 8:8, we would imagine that
the two verbs are alternates and the present text has a conflate reading of
two possibilities. The second of them, *nšqh,* looks suspiciously like a defective *nip'al* form of *šq'h* in 9:5, and it turns out that the *qere* reflects the
augmented reading *wĕnišqĕ'â,* with presumably the same meaning as the *qal*
in 9:5. That solution would suit the sense, and we may regard it essentially
as an acceptable alternate or parallel to the verb in 9:5. With respect to the
first reading in 8:8, *wngršh,* that word apparently is omitted in the LXX but
may be a viable parallel to the verb *šq',* whether *qal* or *nip'al,* because *grš* is
used in the *nip'al* with a body of water in Isa 57:20. That passage reads,
"The wicked are like the sea when it is driven, for it is unable to remain
still; and its waters stir up (*wayyigrĕšû*) mire and dirt." The verb in Isa
57:20 reflects the constant restless motion of the sea and does not seem
quite so apt for the annual rise and fall of the Nile; but we should not rule it
out as another possible reading in the second colon in Amos 8:8. To sum
up: there is no problem with 9:5b—the reading is intact and original. For
8:8b we have two possibilities for the second verb: *wĕnigrĕsâ* or *wĕnišqĕ'â.*
While the meanings are different and the second clearly fits well as a complement (not as a synonym) to the verb *'lh* in the first colon, the first—
because it is unusual and perhaps unexpected—may have at least equal
claim to recognition. We would write this text as follows:

		Syllables	Stresses
8:8b	wĕʿālĕtâ ka[y]ʾōr kullāh	4 + 2 + 2 = 8	3
	wĕnigrĕšâ	4	
	wĕnisq[eʿ]â } kîʾôr miṣrāyim	4 } 2 + 2 = 8	3
9:5b	wĕʿālĕtâ kayʾōr kullāh	4 + 2 + 2 = 8	3
	wĕšāqĕʿâ kîʾōr mišrāyim	4 + 2 + 2 = 8	3

We have here one of the very few places in the book of Amos where there is adequate textual information available to make a serious attempt at a reconstruction of the text. Thanks to the control passage in 9:5b it is possible to make two or three highly probable decisions about the original and subsequent forms of the passage in 8:8b. It is quite likely that there are other passages in Amos in which similar developments have taken place, but without suitable controls it is generally inadvisable to make substantive changes.

The remaining oracles in this unit (vv 9–14) all come under the category of eschatological forecasts or, to be more neutral about them, future projections introduced essentially by the words

1. "And it shall happen on that day" (wĕhāyâ bayyôm hahûʾ) or the shorter "On that day" (bayyôm hahûʾ); or

2. "Behold! The time is coming" or "Behold coming days" (the form is ambiguous and depends on whether we consider the adjective to be in the attributive or predicate state), hinnēh yāmîm bāʾîm.

Altogether these expressions are used in Amos in the following places:

1. [whyh] bywm hhwʾ: 2:16, 8:3, 8:9, 8:13, and 9:11, of which only 8:9 has the long form; and

2. hnh ymym bʾym: 4:2, 8:11, and 9:13.

In the prophets generally, the former expression is much more common than the latter, and whether there is any difference between the two expressions in meaning is difficult to determine. It should be added that a third expression, perhaps the most specifically eschatological of them all— bĕʾaḥărît hayyāmîm, "at the end of the days"—does not occur in Amos.

We will treat the two expressions in Amos as broadly equivalent and regard the selection as a matter of stylistic variation. Here we wish to note that the first six occurrences all introduce forecasts or predictions of hard times and disasters, while only the last two forecast a happier future. There is also a certain order, although in view of the small number of examples, the pattern may be accidental. In sequence, the eight units fall into natural and symmetrical groupings, as follows:

1. *bywm hhw'* (2:16) ⎫
2. *hnh ymym b'ym* (4:2) ⎬ Part I

3. *bywm hhw'* (8:3) ⎤
4. *whyh bywm hhw'* (8:9) ⎫ │
5. *hnh ymym b'ym* (8:11) ⎬ Part III
6. *bywm hhw'* (8:13) ⎦

7. *bywm hhw'* (9:11) ⎫
8. *hnh ymym b'ym* (9:13) ⎬ Epilogue

The three pairs (nos. 1–2, 4–5, and 7–8) combine the two types of utterance in the same way and are identical, except that the middle unit is slightly expanded by the addition of *whyh* at the beginning of no. 4. The three-part pattern forms a pyramid with an anchoring structure at each end (Part I and Epilogue), while the center unit is more elaborate. The effect is further enhanced by nos. 3 and 6, which serve as buffers between the basic elements but also are associated in an envelope construction around the core elements, nos. 4–5. The whole structure is impressively symmetrical and presumably reflects deliberate placement and organization of the components.

A rapid survey of the events forecast under these two headings shows that disaster is the most prominent feature, but there is a broad spectrum of ways in which that day is or the coming days are depicted. Thus we find the following.

A. *First Set.*

1. In 2:16 the expression comes not at the beginning of the oracle but at the end, a stylistic curiosity but hardly to be rejected on that account. The scene is the great climactic battle in which the army of the kingdom (presumably the last of the eight kingdoms condemned in the Great Set Speech of chaps. 1–2, and perhaps symbolic of all of them) is destroyed and the end of the nation comes.

2. In 4:2 Yahweh swears an oath against the "cows of Bashan" that terrible days are coming and that they will be taken captive to a distant land. It could be part of the aftermath of the preceding debacle (in 2:16).

B. *Second Set.*

3. In 8:3 we have another scene of destruction and disaster, involving slaughter in the royal palace, again a fitting aftermath of the decisive engagement in 2:16, perhaps a matching accompaniment of the forecast in 4:2.

4. In 8:9 we have a description of consummate grief and despair for

the whole people, which seems to reflect much the same circumstances presented in the earlier examples.

5. In 8:11 there is a significantly different treatment of that future date. Here we have no bloody battles with an aftermath of weeping and wailing or people being dragged into exile, but a rather spiritualized forecast of plagues to come, famine and thirst, not literal deprivation but rather the absence of the word of Yahweh. We might think such a passage was out of place in a book like this, with all its gore and violence, but Amos has been urging from the beginning that it is precisely in the rejection of prophets bearing the divine word that the true disaster lies and incidentally the guarantee of the truth of the other, bloodier forecasts. In the coming days, when there is no word of Yahweh because there are no prophets to bear witness to it, then the real disaster will have occurred, which will lead directly to all the others. In our judgment this picture of the futile search for the word of Yahweh belongs at an early stage of the final period, leading to an ending in the disasters vividly described in the earlier pieces.

6. In 8:13 we revert to the same general pattern as the earlier ones, not like no. 5. We catch a glimpse of the younger generation suffering the consequences of the terrible tragedy forecast in 2:16—the beautiful virgins faint away from thirst, while the chosen warriors fall, not to rise again. This description is sandwiched around a Woe, one of the last in the book of Amos, aimed at those who are guilty of the worst sin of all—apostasy—revealing the root and ultimate cause of everything that has gone wrong, and why the forecasts to this point fill in a picture of unrelieved disaster and tragedy.

C. *The concluding unit.* With these oracles the tone and mood change entirely. They point to a future beyond anything depicted or contemplated in the first six instances of our terms. Most scholars regard these items as additions by an exilic or postexilic editor who wanted the book to serve a different purpose from the one intended by the prophet or his disciples, at least in his authentic speeches. We have suggested elsewhere reasons why these oracles at the end of the book may be regarded as authentic and as consistent with what we know of the prophet's message, his own character as man of God, and his insight into the nature and durability of the relationship between Yahweh and his people. It is difficult to believe that the ultimate goal of his messages was simply to provide an obituary for a people, his people and Yahweh's people. As the only documented successful intercessory prophet other than the revered Moses himself, Amos certainly shared the hopes along with the fears and concerns of his great predecessor. While uncompromisingly forecasting the tragedy that ensued as a result of persistent disregard of covenant, Amos could not himself give up his own people or wash his hands with respect to their ultimate destiny. So whatever the actual status of those final oracles, we believe they reflect an aspect of Amos' own convictions and of the message he delivered. Negatively, we do not believe they are a product of the exilic or postexilic periods, for they bear little relation in terms of vocabulary, construction, or other details to known materials from that time. The points of difference are too well marked to be passed over lightly. The controversial phrase *'et-sukkat dāwîd hannōpelet*, which is taken to be proof of a late postexilic date for that oracle, is itself unique and has no parallel elsewhere. It can hardly be regarded as indicative of any particular date, certainly not until we know what it means and to what it refers.

7. In 9:11, as already indicated, we have a radically different forecast of the future, a future that is not a substitute for any of the preceding descriptions. It lies beyond them in a more distant time, when the nation and its fortunes would be restored. Further discussion will be postponed until we take up the concluding section of the book, but here it can be said that the passage does reflect the earlier sets, previously discussed, dealing with the destruction of the kingdom(s). Here the wreckage will be rebuilt and the fallen ruins restored, along with the prediction of victory over traditional and hated foes.

8. In 9:13 we have the book's final forecast. As with the previous one, here the tone and mood are completely positive and the forecast radiant with hope and promise of great things. The key words are in 9:14 (*wšbty 't-šbwt* . . .), which reads: "Then I will restore the fortunes of Israel my people." Compare Job 42:10 where the same expression (*šb 'et-šbwt* [qere]) is used to describe the complete reversal of his circumstances from utter misery to complete happiness. The words here reverse Amos' predictions of the downfall of the kingdom(s), which he expected to be fulfilled. But beyond the ruin and the ransacking was return, restoration, and renewal of all things, and that is what the last prediction in the book of Amos presents.

We will now look at the second set of three oracles in 8:9–14 in some detail, starting with 8:9–10.

		Syllables
8:9	*wĕhāyâ bayyôm hahû*	$3 + 2 + 2 = 7$
	nĕʾūm ʾădōnāy yhwh	$2 + 3 + 2 = 7$
	wĕhēbēʾtî haššemeš baṣṣohŏrāyim	$4 + 2 + 3 = 9$
	wĕhaḥăšaktî lāʾāreṣ bĕyôm ʾôr	$4 + 2 + 2 + 1 = 9$

Here we have a heavy but balanced bicolon. While the text can be read in a straightforward manner as follows,

> And it shall happen on that day
>   —Oracle of my Lord Yahweh—

> that I shall make the sun set at noon
> and I shall make the earth dark in broad daylight,

it is likely that other or additional meanings and information can be gleaned from the arrangement of words, meanings intended by the author but somewhat obscured by the laconic style and the sequence of the different parts of speech. What is involved here is the precipitate setting of the sun at midday, an event described in the usual language for the movement of the sun across the sky and its daily descent into the nether world or lower sea. So we see the phrase *l²rṣ* as the sun's ultimate destination, namely, the underworld, a complement to *hšmš*, obviously not a parallel. The parallel terms are at the beginning and end of each line. The verbs match up, with *hb²ty* taking *hšmš* as its direct object, while *hḥškty* is probably absolute without a clear object, to produce darkness as a consequence of removing the sun at midday from the sky. The final phrases likewise are complementary if not precisely synonymous. They refer to the brilliant light of noonday in order to dramatize the sudden change from the brightest daylight to the deepest darkness.

		Syllables		*Stresses*	
8:10a	*wĕhāpaktî ḥaggêkem lĕ²ēbel*	$4 + 3 + 2 = 9$	$\Big\}$ 17	3	$\Big\}$ 6
	wĕkol-šîrêkem lĕqînâ	$2 + 3 + 3 = 8$		3	
	wĕha⁽ălêtî ⁽al-kol-motnayim				
	śāq	$4 + 1 + 1 + 2 + 1 = 9$	$\Big\}$ 15	4	$\Big\}$ 7
	we⁽al-kol-rō²š qorḥâ	$2 + 1 + 1 + 2 = 6$		3	
10b	*wĕsamtîhā kĕ²ēbel yāḥîd*	$3/4 + 2 + 2 = 7/8$	$\Big\}$ 14/15	3	$\Big\}$ 6
	wĕ²aḥărîtāh kĕyôm mār	$4 + 2 + 1 = 7$		3	

> 8:10a I will turn your festivals into mourning,
> and all your songs into a dirge.
> I will put sackcloth on every pair of thighs,
> and baldness on every head.
> 10b I will make it like the mourning for an only son,
> and its climax like the bitter day.

In all there are five verbs in this set (vv 9–10), all perfect 1st s. with the *waw*-conversive to express future time. While alliteration is not difficult to achieve in Hebrew it is of interest that four of the verbs begin with *he,* with one deviation at the end (three of the verbs are in the *hip⁽îl,* while one has a natural *he* as the first root consonant). In the first bicolon, there are balancing verbs, but in the remaining bicola there is only one verb, which controls parallel or complementary objects.

In the first of these bicola (10aA) in which the verb does double duty, the objects form a combination "all the songs at your feasts." It would be a question whether the pronoun *kl* applies to the feasts as well as the songs, but either option can be adopted because we can expect a compensatory backward gapping to complement forward gapping in poetic units. The final phrases, *l'bl* and *lqynh,* are parallel or complementary terms. So we would translate, "And I will transform all your songs at [all] your feasts into dirges of lamentation [mourning]."

It may be after all that *'bl/qynh* are a combination too, because *qynh* describes a vocal lament while *'bl* may have a broader meaning and refer to the rite of mourning generally. Then the two sets of objects, direct and indirect, would be combinatory in nature and function.

For 10aB, the single verb operates on both prepositional phrases, which are complementary, not synonymous. In this case, representative actions denote the marks of the mourning and lamentation just mentioned. So we read,

> And I will bring up
> upon all loins sackcloth
> and upon every head baldness.

With respect to v 10b we have some intricate details to untangle and clarify. In this case also there is a single verb that runs the whole sentence. The remainder, while ostensibly a pair of parallel phrases, is actually a continuous expression in which the parts fit together in a complex manner. The first question is the identification of the 3d f. s. suffix on the verb and on the noun *'hryt* in the second colon. The nearest suitable f. s. antecedent would be *qynh,* "lamentation," in 10a, which is not a great distance in prophetic or poetic discourse. That word is a likely candidate, although an alternative is possible, to regard the suffix object as indefinite, referring to the general situation, the circumstance of mourning. Either would suit the circumstances, but as a rule it is better to go with something definite than with something indefinite and vague. In either case we take the noun *'hryth* as the object of *śmty* implied or assumed in the suffix *-h* on the verb. Thus we would render literally, "And I will set her [= it]," namely, "the end of it"; or, paraphrasing, "And I will make the end of it [of the period of mourning lamentation]. . . ."

The remaining two-word phrases introduced by *k* are hardly parallel but, when threaded together, form an interesting combination: "like the bitter day of mourning for [the death of] an only son." The terms are interlocking and help to define and explain each other. Just set in parallel arrangement the results (in English) would be rather wooden:

> And I will make it like the mourning for an only son,
> and the end of it like a bitter day.

We prefer the interaction of the several parts to produce the following interpretation, "And I will make the end of it like the bitter day of mourning for an only son."

	8:11–12		Syllables
8:11a	*hinnēh yāmîm bāʾîm*		
	nĕʾūm ʾădōnāy yhwh		
	wĕhišlaḥtî rāʿāb bāʾāreṣ	$4 + 2 + 2 = 8$ ⎫ 13	
11b	*lōʾ-rāʿāb lalleḥem*	$1 + 2 + 2 = 5$ ⎭	28
	wĕlōʾ-ṣāmāʾ lammayim	$2 + 2 + 2 = 6$ ⎫ 15	
	kî ʾim-lišmōaʿ ʾēt dibrê yhwh	$1 + 1 + 2 + 1 + 2 + 2 = 9$ ⎭	
12a	*wĕnāʿû miyyām ʿad-yām*	$3 + 2 + 1 + 1 = 7$ ⎫ 15	
	ûmiṣṣāpôn wĕʿad-mizrāḥ	$4 + 2 + 2 = 8$ ⎭	
12b	*yĕšôṭĕṭû*	4	32
	lĕbaqqēš ʾet-dĕbar-yhwh	$3 + 1 + 2 + 2 = 8$ ⎫ 13	
	wĕlōʾ yimṣāʾû	$2 + 3 = 5$ ⎭	

8:11a	Behold! The time is coming
	—Oracle of my Lord Yahweh—
	when I will send famine throughout the earth:
11b	not a hunger for food,
	nor a thirst for water,
	but a famine of hearing Yahweh's words.

12a	They shall wander from sea to sea,
	and from north to east,
12b	they will run back and forth,
	seeking the word of Yahweh—
	but they shall not find it.

We have already commented on the unusual features of this oracle, especially in terms of the theme and the language. In contrast to and perhaps as a comment on the plagues in chap. 4, we have here explicitly a different kind of plague—a famine, not of food and water, but of the mind, of a hearing of the words of Yahweh. The prophet switches from the physical trials and tribulations vividly portrayed throughout the book and picks up a theme that is close to his heart, the availability of the word of Yahweh. He has dealt with the problem of prophetic calling and responsibility and the reaction of the people to the proclamation of the word. He charged them early with forbidding and preventing prophets from delivering that

word and has portrayed himself as a prime example in the confrontation
with Amaziah. The crisis is close at hand. The famine to come will inaugurate the whole series of disasters to follow, because without the word of
Yahweh to guide them the land and its people will be destroyed, like a ship
wrecked at sea without a pilot or "a star to steer her by."

There are interesting structural features and one significant problem in
an otherwise clear and relatively uncomplicated text. The first couplet has
an envelope construction, with the inner pair of cola matching exactly. The
parallelism in 11b (1 and 2) is complementary or exemplary, not synonymous, while the opening and closing sections form the main sentence (11a
and 11b [3]).

> 11b (1 and 2): "NOT a hunger for food
>   and NOT a thirst for water"
> 11a and b (3): "And I will send out hunger in the earth
>   . . . but of hearing the words of Yahweh."

In v 12 we have a problem about the proper placement of the key verb
yšwṭṭw, which can be connected either with the preceding or with the following words, or with both. The Masoretes attached it to what follows
(putting the *athnāḥ* under the preceding word *mzrḥ*), which seems the most
natural way to read the unit. At the same time, such an arrangement spoils
a beautiful chiasm in 12a and severs the link between synonymous verbs,
wnʿw//yšwṭṭw, and complementary forms (perfect balancing imperfect).
But placing the verb with the preceding seems to break the natural link
with the following infinitive, and in effect spoils a chiasm with the closing
verb (*yšwṭṭw//ymṣʾw*). The final problem is that in either place the verb
yšwṭṭw seems to overburden the line, making it disproportionately long in
relation to the other lines in the text.

In an effort to salvage everything and sacrifice nothing, we might opt for
the two-way double-duty use of the verb *yšwṭṭw* in this passage, appealing
to examples assembled by C. H. Gordon (Janus function, 1978, 1982) and
Dahood (1970b:435) as follows:

8:12	Syllables	Stresses
wĕnāʾû miyyām ʾad-yām	$3 + 2 + 1 + 1 = 7$ ⎫ 15	3 ⎫ 6
ûmiṣṣāpôn wĕʾad-mizrāḥ	$4 + 2 + 2 = 8$ ⎭	3 ⎭
yĕšôṭĕṭû	$4 = 4$ 4	1 ⎫
lĕbaqqēš ʾet-dĕbar-yhwh	$3 + 1 + 2 + 2 = 8$ ⎫ 13	⎬ 6
wĕlōʾ yimṣāʾû	$2 + 3 = 5$ ⎭	2 ⎭

In this two-way position *yšwṭṭw* can form a chiasmus with both verbs,
wnʿw and *ymṣʾw,* as the closing word of the first bicolon and as the opening

word of the second; the other verbs are also in a chiastic pattern, as the first and last words in the whole unit. The lines seem to be in better proportion, while the key word *yšwṭṭw* is at the center of the whole verse (out of fourteen words it is the eighth).

Adopting this view, however, may not serve the real purpose of the analysis, especially with regard to the structure of the couplet. In the end, we think the Masoretes had it right, and dividing the verse at *mizrāḥ* suits the prosody best.

The first bicolon would have a balanced structure, with six stresses and fifteen syllables divided 3 : 3 and 7 : 8, very close to the standard line of Hebrew poetry. The verb in the first colon would function with both prepositional phrases, a very common construction, while the phrase in the second colon serves as a ballast variant, supplying additional stress and syllables to balance the line.

The second bicolon is divided unevenly, with the pause not in the center but about two-thirds through the line. Thus we have four accents and twelve syllables in the first colon and two accents and five syllables in the second, for a total of six accents and seventeen syllables. The bicolon is fairly close to the norm; although the division into cola is unusual, it is not unattested. The totals for the couplet are unexceptional, twelve accents and thirty-two syllables, precisely equal to the count for standard Hebrew meter. It may also be noted that *wěnā°û* at the beginning and *yimṣā°û* at the end form a balanced chiasmus, alternating perfect and imperfect forms, as well as an echoing and envelope construction. Apart from the marked deviation in the position of the caesura in the second bicolon, the couplet is entirely normal and natural.

The question of the extent of the land or earth can be settled by reference to the geographic terms in v 12. Simply put, they constitute the boundaries of the Holy Land: "from sea to sea" probably means from the western sea (Mediterranean) to the southern sea (the arm of the Red Sea at the Gulf of Aqaba). Then with respect to the northern and eastern boundaries, the mountains and the desert are generally mentioned (cf. Notes at 8:12). The order would then be west, south, north, east, which is plausible but does not occur elsewhere in the Bible. The alternative, beginning with the south (the Red Sea), then the west (Mediterranean), then the north (Mount Hermon or Mount Casius), and then east (the Transjordanian plateau bordering on the great Arabian desert), is also unattested.

As already indicated, we place this oracle, with its picture of future deprivation, toward the beginning in the sequence of the last things, when the prophetic word will disappear. Only then will people miss it and remember perhaps when the word was still with them and they ignored it and persecuted the prophets who brought it. Amos doubtless saw himself as among the last of the prophets still able to bring the word of Yahweh to the people. The company of prophets was sadly depleted, and those who were active were in the employ of the governmental and religious leaders; so a man like Amos, not a prophet at all in the professional sense, had to be recruited by God directly. And when people persisted in ignoring the prophet, then the timetable of doom was fixed. Without prophets the word(s) of Yahweh could not be delivered, and without the word of Yahweh to guide or warn, threaten or encourage, the nation would be lost and ultimately destroyed. So this set piece, while unusual, is not out of keeping with the other parts of Amos, and it belongs in the series of last things or of the "days are coming."

	8:13–14	Syllables
8:13	bayyôm hahû'	$2 + 2 = 4$
	tit'allapnâ habbĕtûlōt hayyāpōt	$4 + 4 + 3 = 11$ } 23
	wĕhabbahûrîm baṣṣāmā'	$5 + 3 = 8$
14a	hannišbā'îm bĕ'ašmat šōmĕrôn	$4 + 3 + 3 = 10$
	wĕ'āmĕrû hê 'ĕlōheykā dān	$4 + 1 + 3/4 + 1 = 9/10$ } 25/26
	wĕhê derek bĕ'ēr-šāba'	$2 + 1 + 2 + 1 = 6$
14b	wĕnāpĕlû wĕlō'-yāqûmû 'ôd	$4 + 2 + 3 + 1 = 10$

8:13   On that day
        the loveliest virgins will faint,
        and the choicest youths from thirst.
14a   [Woe to] those who swear by the Guilt of Samaria,
        who say:
        "By the life of your god!"
        and: [from] Dan
        "By the life of your pantheon!"
        [to] Beer-sheba.
14b   They shall fall
        and never rise again.

This passage is difficult to analyze and interpret. We recognize two basic elements that have been intertwined.

1. A description of the End Time ("on that day"), in which the young people, the fair virgins and the young warriors, are afflicted. The picture is in keeping with a number of others in this group, beginning with 2:16 and including 4:2, 8:3, and 8:9. In our passage this configuration includes both v 13 and v 14b, and forms an envelope around the second component, 14a.

2. The second component consists of a Woe directed against a special group who swear by different deities. They are represented by a goddess at the capital city of Samaria, and by gods in Dan at the northern limit of the northern kingdom and in Beer-sheba at the southern limit of the southern

kingdom. The statement in v 14a, which belongs to the long list of Woes in the book of Amos going back at least to 5:7 and perhaps including other participial forms used in different contexts earlier in the book, is the last of this kind in Amos. It epitomizes the group of those targeted by the Woes, those who resist the word and rebel against it, and who are guilty of violating the covenant obligating loyalty to Yahweh. Apostasy and idolatry are clearly involved in this description, though the prophet leaves the explicit inference to the hearer or reader. It is the group pilloried in 4:4–5, who are told to go to other shrines, and again in 6:4–6, where Beer-sheba is mentioned, but where the word is less sarcastic and more pleading. Now we can learn what the fundamental sin is: regardless of the name of the deity worshiped at Samaria, Dan, and Beer-sheba, the worship is apostate and the participants who do so willingly must be punished. We can connect this Woe with the subsequent statement of punishment, "And they will fall and they will not rise again." This fate would be generally suitable for idolaters and apostates, but the connection is weak and the fate does not fit firmly or singly with the presumed crime. The words in 14b fit better with v 13, for the picture there seems incomplete and we look for a parallel or complementary description of the destiny of the young warriors in comparison with that of the fair virgins. It seems clear that it is the young women who are fainting from thirst, but what about the chosen men of military age? It seems both reasonable and probable to link them with 14b or vice versa and to see the *bḥwrym* as the principal subject of the verbs *wnplw* and *yqwmw*. They will fall in battle never to arise again (cf. the occurrence of the same roots in 5:2, where Israel is symbolized as a virgin). It is perfectly feasible for the young women to be included in the m. pl. verbs in 14b (because *yqwmw* is m. pl. we infer that *nplw* should be constructed the same way, though the form is common to both genders), but it is questionable whether the young men can be included with the virgins in the 3d f. pl. verb in v 13, *ttʿlpnh*. Normally the verb agrees in gender, number, and person with the first subject and the others are included. This pattern is common with initial masculine subjects but rare in cases like this one. It is more likely that the men fall in battle, while the women suffer the consequences of siege and defeat, namely, starvation and attendant ills. But because the actions are concurrent or closely associated and the verbs hardly exclusive, we should probably conclude that both groups participate in relative proportions in the disastrous consequences. The structure is both enveloping and dramatic, with the verbs at the beginning of the couplet (v 13, *ttʿlpnh*) and the end (v 14b, *wnplw wlʾ-yqwmw*) and the subjects in the middle (*hbtwlt . . . hbḥwrym*, v 13). Thus the first verb is f. pl. and emphasizes the role of the women, while the last verb is m. pl. (*yqwmw*) and emphasizes the role of the men. The intervening verb is neutral (*wnplw*) and reflects the possibility of inclusion and joint participation. The women faint from starvation and the men fall (in battle) not to rise again; but men can starve as well as women and women can fall (in battle, though probably not as fighters but as victims in the mid-course or immediate aftermath) not to rise (cf. 5:2, where the subject is the virgin Israel). The primary reference in each case is indicated by the gender of the verbs, and the description is structured in such a way as to provide both comprehensive coverage of a broad section of the population (young men and young women) and reciprocity, so that all participate in consequences while emphasizing particular roles or experiences. It is all very cleverly and skillfully handled, and we owe the author-editor an additional vote of appreciation for winding into this piece his last Woe against those who swear by other, false deities and so bring down judgment and destruction upon themselves and the others. Obviously he wishes to tie the tragic fate of the young men and young women in the flower of their youth to the sins and transgressions of the leadership—the false swearers, those who take oaths by other gods. These people too will fall, never to rise again.

The False Gods of Samaria from Dan to Beer-sheba

In the woe of v 14, the subjects are accused of invoking various gods in their oaths. Three specifications are made:

1. They swear by the Ashmat of Samaria, no doubt invoking the name of this goddess in oath formulas. Just who she is, and whether the title or name given is authentic or a corruption, say, of the name Asherah, will be considered shortly. The formula itself is not given, so the statement is indirect.

2. In this and the following statement the oath takers are quoted directly. What they say is the oath itself, so we can expect it to conform to the standard oath formulas, the difference, and it is a reprehensible one, being that they are using the name of another deity in swearing solemn oaths. In this case, apparently, one or more deities recognized and worshiped at the sanctuary at Dan is in mind.

3. Another formula is provided in this case, referring to one or more deities at Beer-sheba, where another important shrine was located. The meaning of the critical term *derek* is much disputed, and we will return to it later.

To sum up, a Woe is pronounced on a certain group of people identified with a particular activity, which in general would include most people at one time or another. That activity is oath taking, a solemn and serious business in life and for some important purpose or other. In this case, however, a special group is identified: those who, in taking oaths and in swearing to do or refrain from doing something, to confirm a promise or the like, are invoking not the name of Yahweh the God of Israel but some other deity. There are two ways in which the deity in each instance is identified: in the first case, a name or title is offered, while it is less clear in other cases. But in every case the name of a city is added, a city in which there was at least one shrine. Because the three named cover the full length of both countries or greater Israel, they seem to be representative rather than exhaustive. The major omission is the temple city par excellence, Jerusalem, but no doubt the reason is that the temple there was dedicated to Yahweh, and oaths taken in the name of Yahweh of Jerusalem would be acceptable and not under prophetic attack. The oath is taken in the name of the deity, and the deity is often identified with a particular city or shrine. We know, for example, that at Quntillet ʿAjrud, the principal deity is called "Yahweh of Shomeron" (*yhwh šmrn*), though apparently invoked by name far away from that location. So here the author (or prophet) is not telling us where the invocation is taking place, but rather where the god is customarily located, that is, where his statue or representative symbol is. While the syntax in the second and third parts is not clear we can begin with the goddess, who is called *ʾašmat šōměrôn*. It now appears that this designation of a female deity is not a derogatory or scurrilous substitute for Asherah (the construct perhaps *ʾašrat*), though it may be an epithet of that goddess. As she is located at Samaria and Yahweh also is associated with Samaria in a contemporary inscription (about 800 B.C.E.), this deity may be his consort, and perhaps is invoked by these people along with Yahweh on the common understanding that gods come in pairs, male and female, and it is better to invoke them together when it comes to guarantees, assurances, and, of course, curses. There is a god named *ʾăšîmāʾ* in 2 Kgs 17:30, associated with Hamath, who may be the male version of the deity mentioned here. In any case there is no reason to doubt and every reason to believe that a particular goddess is intended, and because presumably her statue and shrine were located in Samaria, she may well have been associated with Yahweh at this time, though earlier with Baal, whose temple in Samaria was well known (cf. the story of Jehu's bloody massacre at the temple of Baal in Samaria, 2 Kgs 10:18–27; see vv 12–17 for the location). We think it is possible that the same or another goddess is referred to in Amos 2:7, a new explanation of an old *crux interpretum*. Other goddesses may be referred to in Ezek 8:3, 5 and Zech 5:8; but of course these passages reflect later periods and different places.

When it comes to the next deity and oath formula, there are additional difficulties. The standard formula adapted for use here would be, "By the life of the god(s) of Dan." We would not expect what we have, namely, a 2d m. s. pronominal suffix and a vocative case for the city or shrine. The oath would not be addressed to the city or shrine or to the deity but rather to another party in the exchange, in which case the second person is not inappropriate in the formula itself. That problem raises the question whether the *k* in the sequence *'lhyk dn* is really the suffix or merely a particle trapped in the middle of a construct chain, similar to the now familiar enclitic *mem,* which is occasionally found in the same situation but is often mistaken for the absolute m. pl. ending (cf. Deut 33:11 where, for MT *motnayim qāmāyw,* which does not make sense, we should recognize the phenomenon and read instead *motnê-m qāmāyw,* "The loins of those who stand against him"; the Samaritan Pentateuch has the correct reading, but it has been reached by eliminating the archaic enclitic *mem: mtny qmyw.* So here we suggest the following reading: *ḥê 'ĕlōhê-k dān,* "By the life of the god(s) of Dan." Just which god or gods are meant is not clear. We know that Yahweh was worshiped at Dan, albeit in connection with a bull image. Presumably other gods were also worshiped there; if so, then they could be female as well as male. Does the form *'elōhê* refer to more than one? Normally when the plural form *'elōhîm* or one of its combining forms is used, such as the construct or stem with suffixes, it refers either to the true God and thus is regarded as singular or to other gods, in which case it is taken to be a numerical plural. But it is also the case that in the outside world or in Israel, where idolatry was practiced, the term in the plural could also be used of a single deity, not Yahweh. While more than one god was often invoked in the course of an oath, they are either invoked separately by name or, at the end of the list, a number will be lumped together as the other or rest of the gods of this or that state. So here the initial formula would invoke a particular god by name. Because the text does not read that way, we may see it as a generic usage, reflecting the summation at the end, the gods of Dan. In conclusion, we would say that the formula is an open one, not specific but applicable to any particular deity or several or all of them together, "By the life of . . . the god of Dan," or "By the life of the God of Dan." It could also reflect the closing formula, "By the life of the gods of Dan." But the last may be less likely.

When it comes to the next and last formula, we have several observations to make. The formula is almost precisely parallel to the preceding one, and we note especially the references to Dan and Beer-sheba—one of the best-known pairs of names in the Bible. Everyone knows that they mark the boundaries of the double kingdom, so their use here in Amos, which is unique for him, has something to contribute to the picture. They form a powerful combination, a kind of merism encompassing the whole country; and we must therefore interpret the oath taking as a universal practice and problem for the prophet. In other words, we suggest that the prophet is not necessarily talking about local cults at the two shrine cities mentioned but rather that the other alien god or gods mentioned in connection with oath taking are worshiped and invoked everywhere in the country. One god has been identified in the first clause, *'ašmat šōmĕrôn;* the other—or is it another?—is referred to in the second clause, namely, "the god of Dan." The third clause apparently gives us yet another divine name or title, *drk,* vocalized as the familiar Hebrew word *derek.* There are several other possibilities, however. First there is another root *drk,* which refers to power and dominion and is attested in Ugaritic and other West Semitic dialects. It has also been identified in a number of biblical passages and may be present here as a title or epithet of a deity: the dominant or ruling one (cf. the Phoenician goddess Derketo, whose name derives from the same root; here we would have the male equivalent). Another possibility is that we should read the word *dōr,* for circle or company of gods, and see the oath formula here as an invocation of the pantheon at Beer-sheba. That reading leaves a suffixed *kaph* that, as we have already seen, poses problems in the second colon. We may be grateful that the Masoretes did not recognize a 2d m. s. suffix here, and if they did not recognize the personal name here at least they thought it was a noun.

We are now ready to put together the miscellaneous findings about these two parallel clauses introduced by the verb *wĕʾāmĕrû.* Just what is it that they, the oath takers who swear by the *Ašmat* of Samaria, actually say? They say, "By the life of your god!" which is the standard formula for invoking the deity of the person for whom you are taking an oath or for sealing some agreement. There are a few cases in which we read *ḥay yhwh ʾĕlōheykā,* "By the life of Yahweh your God." What we have here is the abbreviated version, without the name of the deity, which is to be provided. Compare, for example, *ḥy-yhwh ʾlhy yśrʾl* (1 Sam 25:34; 1 Kgs 17:1); and *ḥy-yhwh ʾlhyk* (1 Kgs 17:12, 18:10). In the third clause we have the name of a god or another title—*drk*—which probably stands for Baal (Jeremiah accuses the people in his day of swearing by Baal, 12:16) or some other male deity. So the second oath is "By the life of *drk.*" We can combine them in the formula, "By the life of *Drk* your god"—an oath formula used by these people everywhere from Dan to Beer-sheba, not only in temples and shrines but wherever oaths are sworn and for whatever purpose. It is a scathing indictment. They swear by the goddess of Samaria and no doubt by the other god there as well, her consort, and they use the formula "By the life of ——, your god" everywhere. Thus we can complete the final combination; the general statement at the beginning is made explicit by the quotations of the formula that follows. To convey the full force and meaning of this indictment, we suggest the following paraphrase:

> Woe to those who take oaths by the Ašmat of Samaria and her consort Drk (perhaps actually Asherah and Baal), and who use this formula, "By the life of DN [whether Ašmat or Drk] your God." Furthermore they do this—committing apostasy—all over the combined kingdoms from Dan to Beer-sheba, which are representative of the two kingdoms [combinatory because they make

a traditional coupling, and merismatic because they include the whole territory].

A few words about the oath formula may be in order. The most common form of the legal and normative oath in Israel was simply *ḥay yhwh,* which we find numerous times in the Bible, and also in the Lachish Letters. In a few cases we find an expanded and more formal expression, *ḥay yhwh ʾĕlōhê yiśrāʾēl* (1 Sam 25:34; 1 Kgs 17:1). In two instances we have the form that we take to be the standard or model for the usage in Amos, *ḥay yhwh ʾĕlōheykā* (1 Kgs 17:12, 18:10). In both cases the words are addressed to Elijah the prophet, once by the widow of Sidon and once by Obadiah the prime minister. In the woman's case, identifying Yahweh as "Elijah's God" makes sense because the woman is a Gentile and not even a formal convert. But Obadiah is an Israelite himself and a faithful worshiper of Yahweh, so the identification of Yahweh as "your God" is part of the formula and has no particular significance except to affirm that the God being invoked is as much the God of the hearer as of the speaker. The implication for our passage is that those who make the oaths in the name of one or another of the gods mentioned identify the god (or gods) as the god of the hearer(s) as well, thus compounding the defection from Yahweh.

In some instances also we have double oaths, in which the life of the deity and the life of the person are invoked side by side. The formula goes as follows: *ḥay yhwh wĕḥê napšekâ* (1 Sam 20:3 [David speaking to Jonathan]; 1 Sam 25:26 [Abigail speaking to David]; 2 Kgs 2:2, 4, 6 [Elisha speaking to Elijah]; etc.). We may reconstruct the formula used by the apostates roughly as follows, *ḥê drk wĕḥê <ʾšmh> ʾĕlōheykā,* "by the life of *DRK* and by the life of *ʾŠMH* your gods!" (In the case of both divine names, the Masoretes vocalized as though the words were common nouns, *ʾašmâ* and *derek;* at present we cannot record the original forms.) As noted previously, the word *ʾlhym* in its various forms is construed as singular when it refers to Yahweh or El, the God of Israel, but as plural when referring to other gods. We interpret *ʾlhyk* here as a reference to both foreign deities mentioned in the text; but it could be taken as a singular and be referred to *DRK* in the parallel passage.

As previously noted, the woe against those who swear by false gods is embedded in a futuristic depiction associated with defeat in battle and the dreadful consequences that ensue. The association may seem somewhat tenuous, but it should be noted that the Woe is the last in a long series and sums up all of the others. The fundamental sin or transgression is apostasy, abandonment of Yahweh for other gods, demonstrated in the invocation of the other deities in oath taking, a basic function and feature of the conduct of social, political, and economic existence and central to religious observance and practice. As we have also shown, the practice just described is widespread, extending through the length and breadth of the land, a culmination of the indictment against all classes and groups of society who are targeted by the woes. At the same time, the collapse and death of the young people is itself a culmination of the tragedies of the End Time, announced already in 2:16 and repeated with increasing frequency and power in the following chapters. The description here fills out the picture of devastation and ruin following on defeat in battle, plunder and violence in the city, forced exile of the people, slaughter and starvation everywhere. For the prophet, in any case, the dual message conveyed in the series of Woes and in the cycle of futurist or eschatological oracles comes to a fitting close.

SUMMATION

We can now examine the whole section, 8:4–14, in the light of its position in The Book of Visions (7:1–9:6) and in particular of its insertion between the fourth and fifth visions. Just as the story of the confrontation between Amos and Amaziah is placed between the third and fourth visions for a discernible purpose, namely, to show that the message of the visions has been confirmed by the prophet's experience in delivering or trying to deliver his message, so too we must consider whether a similar objective is served by the placement of the oracles in 8:4–14 between the fourth and fifth visions.

According to our hypothesis there ought to be some correlation or point of contact between the message of the visions and the content of the oracles, and perhaps an indication that they belong to the period between these two visions or, more strictly, between the phases of the future that are portrayed and explained to the prophet. Thus we have identified the first pair of visions with Phase One of the prophet's message about Israel, while the second pair of visions delineates Phase Two of the forecast. With these visions the decision to destroy the nation has been reaffirmed and made irreversible. Both Visions 3 and 4 affirm the same conclusion and lock in the confrontation scene to that period of certain doom and irreversible judgment. So logically, all of the material after the second pair of visions should reflect that point in the forecast of the future, and should point ahead to Vision 5 and its expression of the culmination of the prophetic message. The last vision presents Phase Three, a kind of aftershock of the preceding Phase Two. If Phase Two assures the end of the nation and the dreadful consequences that go with such a disaster, then Phase Three is a further elaboration with even more dreadful effects, tightening the screws on an already decimated and defeated people. If a hundred survive from a thousand, only ten will survive from the hundred, and even those ten will finally perish. We have interpreted Phase Three to mean that the leadership, especially those indicated in the Woes, will be exterminated. Because they are the most guilty of crimes against God and their fellows, they will pay the penalty to the utmost. None of them will escape, as the fifth vision makes clear—no matter how far they go and how inaccessible the refuges to which they flee, they will be overtaken, recaptured, and brought back for final judgment (actually the judgment has already been rendered, so no further proceedings are necessary) and for summary execution by divine agents available at the scene. In our opinion, the apparently miscellaneous and heterogeneous items in 8:4–14 fit the prescription offered and form a coherent unit filling the space between the fourth and fifth visions. Because the body of the book proper comes to an end with the fifth vision, except for a closing apostrophe (9:5–6) and the Epilogue of the work (9:7–15), the transition between Visions 4 and 5 has to be complete in itself and offer whatever commentary there is going to be on both the transition and the final state of affairs depicted in the last vision.

We note that the first unit, 8:4–6, belongs to the proclamation pattern established in chaps. 3, 4, and 5 (*šimʿû* [*ʾet-*] *haddābār hazzeh*) with a slight variation (*šimʿû-zōʾt*). But it also contains a Woe formula, or at least it is aimed at a group who constitute the proper subject for the Woes: the plural participle with the definite article. Here it is the *šōʾăpîm* of 8:4 (i.e., those who crush the poor) whose crimes are spelled out in a bill of particular charges. With this indictment we must then associate the final Woe and its group of violators, the *nišbāʿîm* of 8:14 at the end of the unit, thus forming an envelope around the whole. The wicked merchants are matched with those who swear falsely, each group representative of all who have betrayed the trust placed in them as they violate their obligations and who fail to fulfill their responsibilities. The merchants fail in the area of human relations and obligations, a major theme in the book of Amos, while the others are guilty at the foundation level of religious commitment—the first and ultimate violation. We see both sets of criminals as active throughout the larger area of Jacob//Israel, and the crimes as being committed everywhere (from Dan to Beer-sheba). This circumstance will help to explain further the divine response in 8:7–8. The relation between the oath takers in v 14, along with the merchants of 8:4–6, and the oath taking of Yahweh has not been noted hitherto, and it should be. False oaths by false gods may be futile and meaningless, though the effect is to undermine the survival of the society with the breakdown of its contractual system. By contrast, Yahweh's oath is sure and certain, its consequences unavoidable and inevitable; "I will never forget any of their misdeeds." This is the third oath attributed to Yahweh, all of them negative and menacing, all affirming a judgment against the leadership of the country (4:2; 6:8). The consequence is described in vivid terms in v 8, where the land trembles and rises and falls like the great river of Egypt. The action and its effects can be clarified by reference to 9:5, the last three cola of which are almost identical with the last three of 8:8. What causes the earth to melt in 9:5 and tremble in 8:8 is the hard blow from Yahweh in his role as "the Striker" (*hannôgēaʿ* [9:5]). The sequence can be described in the following manner: Yahweh has sworn that he will never forget "any of their misdeeds." This oath refers back to the behavior of the shopkeepers and merchants of 8:4–6 but does not exclude the swearers by false gods in 8:14, if indeed they are not the same people or mutually interactive and overlapping groups. We need to ask one more question of those people in 8:14. We have been told that they swear by false gods and have an idea that they take their oaths in the presence of somebody they call "you" (*ʾlhyk*); but what is it they swore to? Clearly they must have affirmed the truth of some assertion and backed it up by an oath, which was quite appropriate for merchants, among others, and entirely so if they were affirming the legitimacy of their role in some transaction, especially if defending themselves against charges. False dealing confirmed by false swearing by false gods makes a suitable climax and conclusion of the whole sorry list of misdeeds in the prophet's catalog and explains why Yahweh has sworn an entirely different kind of oath in his own name, and why he then acts on that oath by striking the land so that it shakes or trembles.

The shaking of the land is violent enough to threaten life and safety. We are warned about such a shaking in the first verse of the book, and now in the last part of the record there seems to be a reference to this event, though the specific word *raʿaš* (earthquake) is not used here (but cf. 9:1, *wyrʿšw*). Now that the blow falls, it will be accompanied by universal mourning (the singular form *yôšēb* [8:8] has the same meaning as the plural *yôšĕbê* [9:5]), which leads to the next unit, vv 9–10, a fuller description of such mourning.

The word *zōʾt* in v 8 echoes the same word in 8:4, where it is the object of the verb *šimʿû*. But if we ask just what it is the prophet wants them to hear, the answer is not so clear. It should be a direct quotation of words addressed to them. What follows the identification of his audience ("the oppressors") is a series of qualifying remarks about what they say and what they do (vv 4b–6). No doubt the prophet would like them to know what he thinks of both their words and their deeds, but those verses are simply an elaboration of the identification of the audience:

8:4a Hear this, you who trample upon the poor,
  4b   and put an end to the wretched of the land;
  5a   who say:
            "When will the new moon pass,
            so that we may sell our grain;

and the sabbath,
so that we may open our stores of grain?"—
5b   who reduce the quantity (*ephah*),
while raising the price (*shekel*);
and cheat with crooked scales;
6a   who buy the needy for money,
and the poor for a pair of sandals
6b   —"and that we may sell the husks of grain."

The direct address, the body of the speech, can only begin in v 7 with the solemn statement,

8:7a   Yahweh has sworn by the pride of Jacob:
7b   "I will never forget any of their misdeeds."

Then the prophet adds the comment in v 8 (here paraphrased):

For this reason—that is, the oath sworn by Yahweh that he will never forget what they have done—should not the earth tremble, and everyone who dwells in it mourn?

We believe there is an ellipsis here. The word "this" refers to the same "this" in v 4, namely, the speech to "the crushers of the poor" and more particularly to the oath of Yahweh, quoted directly, "I shall never forget." The mourning on the part of the inhabitants to follow is a consequence of the trembling of the land. In this case the trembling is meant literally, as the final bicolon shows (the reference to the rising and falling of the Nile is a comment on the trembling of the land, not on the mourning of the inhabitants), and the mourning follows the destruction caused by that upheaval. An earthquake that produces the rippling effect described and makes the land rise and fall like a body of water must be one of major proportions, with heavy damage to life and property in settled areas. The cause is Yahweh's striking the earth (9:5), an action that should be presupposed in 8:8. It completes the picture of the section, which is a unity and extends from 8:4 through 8:8.

We find a similar structure in vv 9–14, in which the parts are welded together by common elements or woven together by threads that run through the separate sections. As we now observe the entire unit 8:4–14, the parallel key words that provide the basic subject and the common point of reference are the two m. pl. participles, *hš'pym* and *hnšb'ym,* both with the definite article and deriving from the Woe formula familiar to us especially from 6:1–6, but used frequently in the book. The word "Woe" is found only twice altogether (5:18 and 6:1), but the theme is clearly present in the context in which the word appears, so that all such participles in the vicinity are extensions of the same Woe. Even where a different formula or framing device is used, the appearance of the participle designating a particular group (or rather ultimately the same group, but different parts of it, or the same people engaged in different activities or seen under different categories) itself evokes the Woe theme. That evocation certainly seems to be present here. The *š'pym* are addressed in the second person, while the *nšb'ym* are described in the third person; but, as noted everywhere in the prophetic literature, there is frequent shifting back and forth as the stance of the speaker and the direction of the message change. Thus the *š'pym* are addressed directly in 8:4, but the quotation of the divine speech, relayed by the prophet, has Yahweh speaking about them in the third person. In vv 9–10, however, we are back to direct address, and 2d m. pl. pronominal suffixes are used (*ḥgykm* and *šyrykm*). Then in vv 11–12 the subject of the verbs (*wn'w, yšwṭṭw, ymṣ'w*) is 3d m. pl., but we believe it is the same group throughout, basically the *š'pym//nšb'ym*, the oppressors of the poor, among whose besetting sins and perhaps at the root of the whole problem is their predilection for swearing (falsely) by false gods. It is to be noted that these plural pronominal elements permeate the whole unit, and the only available and viable subjects are the ones mentioned, which are strategically located at the beginning and at the end of our piece (vv 4–14). Theoretically an alternate subject could be *hbḥwrym* in v 13, but it is clear that the young men are not being charged with any crimes; their demise in the disaster that is coming is being lamented. The fault lies with the others.

If we now look at vv 9–10, we note here a continuation and elaboration of the theme of mourning already adumbrated in familiar passages previously discussed: the dirge in 5:2 and the more elaborate development in 5:16–17. This passage is more elaborate still and completes the series. Reference must also be made to the persons addressed, "I will turn your festivals into mourning, and all your songs into a dirge" (v 10). We have suggested that the "you" addressed here are the same 2d m. pl. people addressed in v 4, but not excluding the same group identified in another fashion in v 14. Now we point to another linkage with Amos 5:21–24, where the same nouns occur, *ḥgykm* (v 21) and *šyryk* (v 23). The people being condemned in those verses belong to the same general group, while the moment in the timetable of doom is somewhat earlier than what we have in 8:9–10. In the former passage they are still celebrating their feasts with songs of joy, but it will not be for long; Yahweh has rejected them and their feasts. In 8:9–10 the feasts and songs will be changed into an unceasing period of mourning, with only songs of lamentation to accompany it. The people in chap. 5 are condemned for failure to practice justice and righteousness and urged to do those things instead of celebrating their own piety (5:24). The particular shortcomings of the people in 8:4–6 are spelled out in some detail, but they are prime examples of the same failing, namely, to practice elementary honesty and fairness in the marketplace.

Proceeding then to vv 11–12, we note here the 3d m. pl. verbs and ask who the subjects are. The nearest candidates are the m. pl. nouns in vv 13–14, and both the *ḥbwrym* and the *nšb'ym* might be included (and the latter bring along with them the *š'pym,* v 4). Of the two the latter are more likely, because the evident irony in the description implies that those who are now seeking futilely for "the word of Yahweh" are the ones who rejected it when it was available and who were responsible for the famine that followed, because they shut the mouths of the prophets who were entrusted with it. That observation fits squarely around those who swear by false gods. As already noted, the passage here takes us back to the beginning of the book and Amos' mordant and self-reflective statements on the subject. One of the first charges leveled against the leadership was that they not only refused to listen to the prophets but actually forbade them to speak (2:12). In 3:7–8 there is a brief discussion of the point at issue: prophets are commissioned to bring the word of Yahweh and are under divine compulsion to do so. But the people in authority not only fail to heed the words, they refuse even to hear them. It is not enough to have the words of former prophets or the traditions about them and their teaching. What is needed is the current and contemporary words of the deity mediated by a chosen servant, a living messenger with a living word. The climax is reached in the confrontation between Amos and Amaziah in which, after Amos delivers the word, he is warned by the high priest at Bethel never to speak there again, a perfect example of the general charge leveled by the prophet in chap. 2. The consequence is inevitable. If this is the way prophets, duly commissioned and entrusted by God with his word, are to be treated, then Yahweh will stop sending them. There will be no prophets to bear the word, and without them no word will be available to the leaders or the nation. That dearth, which is more serious and potentially worse than a famine of food and a thirst for water, will usher in the age of ultimate doom, because without access to the word of Yahweh, the nation will be irretrievably lost.

The remaining verses, 13–14, have been discussed at some length, and we will only summarize here. The ominous message "on that day" of the fainting and dying of the beautiful young maidens and the choice young men is wound around the last of the Woes, against those who swear by false gods. The latter are the perpetrators of the evils described in the section beginning at 8:4, while the former are the victims whose demise is to be mourned so bitterly (vv 8–10). The section is brought to its proper conclusion at this point and leads directly to the fifth and final vision in 9:1–5. The unit 8:4–14 provides the information necessary to an understanding and appreciation of the fifth vision, which in turn spells out the fate of those described in the lead-in material. While the destruction of the temple and the slaughter of the population imply a different group, mainly priests and civil leaders, from the one in 8:4–14 (mainly thieving and blasphemous merchants), the separation may not be as wide or deep as it seems. The linkage is to be seen in such passages as 5:21–24 and 2:6–8, where commercial lying and cheating are associated with the celebration of religious feasts and worship generally. The same classes and families are involved, and the crimes and sins, while listed separately, are charged to the same people. If the primary indictment in the book of Amos turns on the issue of justice and righteousness (*mišpāṭ ûṣĕdāqâ;* cf. 5:7, 24; 6:12; also 5:15), then whether those charged with disregarding or contemptuously violating the basic charter of Israel's existence are acting in the commercial, political, or religious spheres, they are equally guilty. Behind these gross violations is the basic, primary sin, abandonment of Yahweh for other gods and different systems of belief and behavior.

Both series, of woes and of futuristic projections, culminate in the final vision, the destruction of the temple and the annihilation of the people in and around it, with provision for tracking down and executing any who might survive and attempt to escape. The means of destruction are heavenly or angelic (9:1), but the effects are earthly and catastrophic. The anticipated earthquake (*hrš* in 1:1 and *wyrʿšw* in 9:1) is described in its awesome violence corresponding to the prediction in 8:8, parallel to 9:5 (which together form a frame around the final oracles of disaster and doom, *whyh bywm hhwʾ* and *ymym bʾym* and the final vision).

We believe that the fifth vision ends with the closing formula at the very beginning of 9:5 (the first three words). The two-word formula *ʾdny yhwh* is used a number of times in the series of visions to make divisions and separate units. It occurs eight times in the first four visions, while its components occur several times separately. Because it occurs at the very beginning of the first vision, which opens this unit (7:1), we would expect something at the end, and we find a slightly expanded version, which contrary to the standard division of the text does not fit well with what follows, and which has its own pattern repeated in earlier versions of the same type of apostrophe to the deity. A *chart* of the occurrences of *ʾdny, yhwh,* and *ʾdny yhwh (ṣbʾwt)* in 7:1–9:5a follows on the next page.

The final apostrophe in 9:5–6 concludes The Book of Visions. In this respect it serves the same purpose as the apostrophe at the end of chap. 4 (v 13), which concludes the first major unit (chaps. 1–4) of the book of Amos. The remaining apostrophe to the deity occurs in chap. 5 (vv 8–9). Its function is similar in that it also offers a description of the deity along the same lines as the others. But its placement is somewhat more difficult to explain. It occurs in the middle section (chaps. 5–6), separate from the others, but if it had served the same structural purpose as the others, we would have expected to find it at the end of chap. 6 (or even 5) but hardly where it is, toward the beginning of the unit.

	yhwh	ʾdny	ʾdny yhwh (ṣbʾwt)
7:1			X
2			X
3	X		
3	X		
4			X
4			X
5			X
6	X		
6			X
7		X	
8	X		
8:1			X
2	X		
3			X
9:1	X		
5			X
	6	1	9

Elsewhere we have compared the three hymns, which share a number of features. In each there is a series of participles that describe or characterize significant attributes of the deity. The first hymn (4:13) has a formal symmetry and elegance that surpasses the others. It consists of five participial clauses, each brief, followed by the name of this unique deity, Yahweh, in an elaborate form. The second and third (5:8; 9:5–6) vary from this pattern having only three participles (unless we include 5:9 with 5:8 as part of the apostrophe, in which case that poem has four participles and three verbal clauses, making a total of seven. In 5:8 the three participles are complemented by two verbal clauses to make a total of five (or seven if we add the participle and verb in 5:9). In 9:5–6, we have three participles but as many as five verbal clauses, to make a total of eight. We have already observed that 9:5 overlaps heavily with 8:8, three of the four cola being nearly the same, while the fourth has similar elements. It is at this point that the principal expansion in the apostrophe has occurred in comparison with the other apostrophes in the book, for three additional verbal clauses accompany the first participle while in the other two examples the first participle is followed immediately by the second (4:13a and 5:8a). Nevertheless, there is no reason to suppose that 9:5 has been expanded by anyone except the author. The purpose is to tie this closing piece to the interior content of The

Book of Visions and thus show that the transcendental, universal deity is the same one involved in the daily and yearly affairs of the nations, that a stroke from the deity knocks the earth off balance and destroys the work of men. Thus the first participle in 9:5 has a more direct connection with the course of events than any of the others in the several apostrophes, and it signals the point of contact and its effects in dramatic fashion. Somewhat similar is the reference (also unduplicated) to Yahweh as the treader on the high places of the earth, a reference to the deity in his role as mighty all-conquering warrior in the first series (4:13). This reference is doubtless a reflection of the martial imagery that is so prominent in the early chapters of the book, especially the great indictment of chaps. 1–2 and its climax in the eschatological battle of 2:14–16.

The remaining items in v 6 are fairly standard, though the details are distinctive. In 6a the initial participle (*hbwnh*) is balanced by the perfect 3d m. s. form of the verb *ysd* in a chiastic position at the end of the second colon:

	Syllables	Stresses
habbôneh baššāmayim maʿălôtāw	$3 + 3 + 3 = 9$	3
waʾăguddātô ʿal-ʾereṣ yĕsādāh	$5 + 1 + 1 + 3 = 10$	3

Who built its upper stories in the sky,
    and its supports he founded upon the earth.

There is a slight difference in the text between the kethib (*mʿlwtw*) and qere (*maʿălôtāyw*), whether the noun is singular or plural before the 3d m. s. suffix; but it is possible that it simply preserves the *defective* older spelling of the plural without the *yod,* which is a characteristic marker of the plural form, m. and f. before pronominal suffixes. In any case we have a complex combinatory arrangement in v 6a, in which the parts interlock and interact in subtle ways. In our judgment a single structure or building is involved, one that Yahweh himself has erected (*hbwnh//ysdh*). This structure is in the heavens but has been founded upon the earth (or even the underworld); in other words, its foundations are deep (*bšmym//ʿl-ʾrṣ*). This building must be his great palace complex, the same one described as having been built with his own hands in Exod 15:17 and in Ps 78:69, where the same verbs are used while the parallel to *ʾrṣ* is *rmym,* no doubt a reference to heaven. The structure referred to in Ps 78:69 is not the temple in Jerusalem but the heavenly/earthly original of which the Jerusalem structure is intended to be the replica. (The verse must be read in the light of both of the other passages dealing with the same point, Exod 15:17 and Amos 9:6.) It has its upper stories (pl.) in the heavens, while its foundations are embedded in the earth, even the underworld. Exactly what *ʾgdtw* means in the Bible is not clear; it occurs only three other times and seems to mean "a bunch" or "a band" (Exod 12:22; 2 Sam 2:25; Isa 58:6). Here the suggested rendering is "vault" (something bonded or banded together), but that is little more than a guess. Taking all of the components together, we visualize a gigantic building (*hêkāl*) with upper stories in the heavens and with the basis or foundation in the earth or under it, established in the underworld. This structure is God's own handiwork and constitutes his dwelling place.

The passage in Exod 15:17 has been dealt with exhaustively by numerous scholars (Childs 1974:240; Cross 1973:112–44; Freedman 1981), but it seems clear to us that the sanctuary here is not an earthly temple made by human hands but the heavenly palace of Yahweh made by him with his own hands. This palace is located in conjunction with the special mountain of the deity: in Exodus 15 it must be Sinai, while in Psalm 78 it is just as clearly Mount Zion. No specific location is provided in the passage in Amos. Just how the mountain functions in relation to the heavenly temple is not clear, but we can guess that from the top of the holy mountain one could see the heavenly palace, for it is on the mountain that Moses is shown the *tabnît* of the heavenly palace, apparently a model of it, perhaps a circumlocution for the palace itself. In some fashion the heavenly palace is located near the site of the mountain, though its foundations are in the netherworld and its upper stories are in heaven. It is possible that the mountain itself, also a creation of the deity (cf. 4:13, "the Shaper of the mountains") is part of the temple, the link between foundations and superstructure. The text of Exod 15:17 reads as follows:

> You brought them in and you planted them
> > in the mountain of your inheritance,
> the fixed place of your throne which you made, Yahweh
> the sanctuary, my Lord, your hands created.

The parallel terms are combinatory; thus the *mkwn lšbtk* is probably the throne room in the sanctuary—the holy of holies. And the second verb and its subject make explicit that this sanctuary was made by Yahweh's own hands, not by someone else or by others at his direction. Just what it was that Yahweh made with his own hands and just where it is remain in doubt, but it is clearly quite vast, with its towers in the heavens and its foundations on or probably under the earth. Probably only certain parts of it are visible at any particular time from any single vantage point. A look at Isa 66:1 might provide a clue, though the reference there may be hyperbolic. While the images cannot be pinned down precisely, the heavenly temple probably encompassed a good part of both heaven and earth.

We may now return to Ps 78:69 and its context. We can begin at v 67 and
go through v 71:

> 67   *wayyim'as bě'ōhel yôsēp*
>   *ûběšēbeṭ 'eprayim lō' bāḥār*
> 68   *wayyibḥar 'et-šēbet yěhûdâ*
>   *'et-har ṣiyyôn 'ăšer 'āhēb*
> 69   *wayyiben kěmô-rāmîm miqdāšô*
>   *kě'ereṣ yěsādâh lě'ôlām*
> 70   *wayyibḥar bědāwīd 'abdô*
>   *wayyiqāḥēhû mimmiklě'ōt ṣō'n*
> 71   *mē'aḥar 'ālôt hěbî'ô*
>   *lir'ôt běya'ăqōb 'ammô*
>   *ûběyiśra'ēl naḥălātô*

> 67   He rejected the tent of Joseph,
>   he did not choose the tribe of Ephraim;
> 68   but he chose the tribe of Judah,
>   Mount Zion, which he loves.
> 69   He built his sanctuary like the high heavens,
>   like the earth, which he founded forever.
> 70   He chose David his servant,
>   and took him from the sheepfolds;
> 71   from tending the suckling ewes he brought him
>   to be the shepherd of Jacob his people,
>   of Israel his inheritance.

The main double theme of this section of the poem is Yahweh's rejection
of Joseph//Ephraim and the choice of the tribe of Judah and of David his
servant. There is also reference to Zion, which he loved, an allusion to the
establishment of Jerusalem as the capital of the kingdom, and at least a hint
that the sanctuary or temple will be erected there (on Mount Zion). But
v 69 should be seen as a retrospective view regarding the heavenly temple,
because its replica or representative building is now going to be built in
Jerusalem.

But first, what does v 69 say? "And he built like [the] heights [of heaven]
his sanctuary, like [the] earth he established it forever." It seems clear from
a comparison of this passage with Amos 9:6 that the author is not really
comparing the sanctuary with heaven and earth, though that interpretation
would be possible, but rather indicating the way the sanctuary is laid out.
We note two other points. (1) As the second colon stands, we are inclined to
read the words after *k'rṣ* as a relative clause, "like earth, which he founded

forever." But it is not necessary to do so. We would have to supply the missing relative pronoun, *ʾšr*. While the latter is rarely used in early poetry, it occurs frequently in this poem, such as in v 68 and elsewhere (vv 3, 4, 5, 11, 42, 43), so if it were intended or implied, it probably would have been in the text. (2) The word *lʿwlm* is not future but past, as often in Hebrew poetry (Dahood 1966:56, 180). The reference here is to the distant past, when Yahweh made his great palace. And referring to the other point, the parallelism of *bnh* and *ysd* shows that the same object is in mind, or that the objects belong to the same structure as in Amos 9:6.

The feminine suffix may be a puzzle in Ps 78:69, but the same suffix on the same verb is no problem in Amos 9:6 because the object there is feminine (and note also the resumptive suffix there). Ironically, Amos 9:6 could be read like the Psalm's, "upon the earth that he founded"; but we think that it is clear in both cases that the subject of the verse is not the earth but the sanctuary whose foundations are in the earth (or the netherworld). There are two explanations of the 3d f. s. suffix on the verb in Ps 78:69: (1) it may refer to an unexpressed noun such as *ʾgdh*, which designates the divine palace or some part of it, carried over from a traditional passage such as Amos 9:6; or (2) in pre-exilic times, assuming that the psalm was written down, m. and f. 3d s. suffixes would have been written with *h.* When it came time to revise the spelling and change most masculine suffixes from *he* to *waw*, the scribes left the *he*, thinking it was a feminine suffix; and subsequently it was vocalized that way. But it is actually masculine because it refers to the *miqdāš* earlier in the verse. The comparative *k* refers to the past when he did these things—the new temple on Mount Zion (or the tabernacle of David) will be like the one Yahweh built himself for himself in the dim past. The divine temple that was built in the ancient past extended from earth to heaven, its foundations on the former, its superstructure in the latter. So we must understand here the prepositions that are present and accounted for in the Amos passage. We would then read as follows:

> 69   As he built in the heavenly heights his sanctuary
> and as upon the earth, he founded it[!] in dim antiquity.

Even if we ultimately decide that *ysdh* is a relative clause modifying *ʾrṣ* in both places (it cannot be one way in one place and another in the other; but, perhaps regrettably, it can be a relative clause with retrospective suffix in both places) we do not think it would change the essential meaning of both passages, that he built his sanctuary with its upper stories in heaven and its foundation on earth. As for *lĕʿōlām*, it would refer to the past in any case: the earth was created "from eternity." The same is true of the heavenly palace, which was built a long time ago but which could well be "for eternity" too.

The last bicolon of 9:6 is identical with that of 5:8 except for a slight spelling difference in the opening participle: *haqqôrē'* (5:8) and *haqqōrē'* (9:6), in which the latter preserves the older form of the word while in 5:8 the spelling includes the *waw* for the long *ō* of the participle. In general, the spelling in Amos as in all of the minor prophets is quite late, among the latest in the canonical books; but in forms such as this one the spelling is not entirely consistent.

The passage has been examined previously, and it may suffice here to point out that this reference may not be simply an expression of praise and awe at the might and majesty of God. There is also a possible allusion to the specific occasion on which the combination of swelling seas and intense rainfall produced the Great Flood that wiped out most living things; it was understood to be not only a manifestation of irresistible divine power but also an expression of divine judgment. The wording is not the same and the description may be innocent, reflecting the idea that waters to fructify the earth well up from the great mythic freshwater ocean in the underworld. Nevertheless, the verb *špk* is used often of Yahweh pouring out his wrath upon his people or Jerusalem, and in a few cases it will be poured out "like water" (*kmym*), so the connection is one that could easily be made. On this note, The Book of Visions comes to a close.

REVIEW AND SUMMATION

As is clear even from a casual reading, the section of Amos from 7:1 through 9:6 is dominated by the series of visions. The series is interrupted twice, between the third and fourth visions and between the fourth and fifth visions, by the insertion or inclusion of materials not directly connected with the visions but which, as we have tried to show, belong to the structure of the unit. The material divides about equally into two parts, and these may again be subdivided into appropriate subsections. The first part consists of the first four visions or, better, the first two pairs of visions, including the first insertion within the second pair of visions. The insertion is approximately the same length as the report of the visions. The second part consists of the second insertion and closes with Vision 5. The second insertion is about twice as long as the account of the fifth vision, so in fact more space is devoted to the insertions than to the visions; but it is the latter that provide the framework and the essential meaning for the material in this part of the book. The word counts are as follows:

	Visions		Insertions
1.	41 (7:1–3)	1.	132 (7:10–17)
2.	39 (7:4–6)	2.	148 (8:4–14)
3.	43 (7:7–9)		280
4.	42 (8:1–3)		
5.	73 (9:1–5a)		
	238		

1.	Visions	238
2.	Insertions	280
3.	Closing	29
	Grand Total	547

We propose the following outline:

I. The first four visions	7:1–8:3	(297)
A. The first pair	7:1–6	(80)
1. First vision	7:1–3	(41)
2. Second vision	7:4–6	(39)
B. The second pair and insertion	7:7–8:3	(217)
3. Third vision	7:7–9	(43)
4. First insertion	7:10–17	(132)
5. Fourth vision	8:1–3	(42)
II. The second insertion and the fifth vision	8:4–9:6	(250)
1. The second insertion	8:4–14	(148)
2. The fifth vision	9:1–5aA	(73)
3. Concluding Apostrophe	9:5aB–6	(29)

In the following review we wish to consider first of all the visions and what they tell us about Amos, the prophet and the man, and about his relations with Yahweh and the nature and significance of the message received.

I. Amos

The visions provide an insight not only into Amos' calling and commission as a prophet but also into his grasp of the essentials of the Israelite faith and its meaning for him and for his people at a critical juncture in their history. The more strictly theological aspects of these experiences also deserve attention, because they reveal unusual details of the relation between God and prophet and important features of the divine personality. In addition, as we have tried to show, the visions provide an outline and a guide for both the course of Amos' ministry and the historical development of his message, as well as a mechanism for organizing and classifying the oracular and other materials preserved in the book.

At the same time we must not neglect the insertions. The first one provides us with practically all of the information (except for the heading in 1:1) we have about the historical figure of the man and the only specific incident in his career as a prophet. One need only compare that circumstance with the book of Jeremiah, which is replete with both autobiographical and biographical data about that prophet, to see at once how little we really know about the man from Tekoa, and at the same time how precious that little is. Without the account of the confrontation at Bethel we would know practically nothing and would have to guess practically everything about the way the prophet pursued his calling, and the circumstances under which at least some of his oracles were delivered. As it is we must still guess a great deal about many things, including when and where the oracles were delivered, how long he continued as a prophet, and what happened to him. But we would be much worse off without the information in the first insertion (compare, for example, books such as Joel or Zephaniah, Nahum or Habakkuk, where the only direct information we have about any of those prophets is in the heading, itself barely more than the name, and we must glean the rest from the content of the oracles, a chancy business at best).

The second insertion, about the same length as the first, also serves an important purpose, though it is not at all the same. It has material belonging to and continuing three series that begin much earlier in the book: the Woe series, which starts early but has its main content in chaps. 5–6, is here continued and effectively brought to a climax (there may be a straggler in the Epilogue, but it is only that); and the eschatological or futurist group using formulas such as *bywm hhw'* and *ymym b'ym* also reaches a critical point here. There is a dramatic reversal in the Epilogue, where this series plays a central and climactic role. But here the negative expectations are brought together, and a final picture of unrelieved disaster is presented. Just as the first insertion fits well into the framework of the second pair of visions, which form an envelope around it, and expresses in dialogue and drama the content of those visions and their conclusive, irreversible judgment, so the second insertion bridges the distance between the second pair of visions and the fifth and last one. This vision adds only a single main ingredient to the picture of doom, namely, the relentless pursuit of the temple personnel and presumably the leadership generally after the debacle already predicted earlier. A special and worse fate is held out for them, beyond the normal fate of those who inhabit the condemned nation. The third series consists of the oaths.

The Book of Visions is the heart of the book of Amos because it tells us how Amos became a prophet, what he saw and heard in the presence of his God, and the nature of the message he brought back with him from those experiences. When the visions are combined with the only story about Amos in action, then we have both sides of the biography: the personal inner experience and the public outer expression in the full glare of opposition from the highest authorities, along with most of the rest of the people (7:10b). But happily for future generations, and no doubt against the wishes of those who opposed him from the start, the record was made and preserved, and his experience was written down.

Thus the first of the great prophets of the eighth century, at an extraordinary time in the history of two tiny kingdoms and with implications reaching far beyond their borders, steps out of the anonymity of village life onto the stage. There were prophets before him, great ones, greater than he or his contemporaries would be; but their lives and work had been carried out under other conditions and auspices. Their work was central and their legacy was all-important. Without the tradition beginning with Moses and continuing with Samuel especially, but also with such men as Nathan and more recently—perhaps within living memory—those unmatched heroes of the faith, Elijah and Elisha, there could not have been prophets at all in the eighth or any other century. No matter how reluctant kings and priests may have been to listen to unpleasant words, especially by irascible prophets, the tradition made a firm place for such persons; whatever their fate as individuals and whatever impact or lack of it their words may have had, there were always those who heard and remembered, who saved and preserved the words delivered. Ultimately the best were vindicated and their work canonized. When the Babylonian exiles began to patch together their lives and their faith after the trauma of defeat and captivity, they put together an official record of their experience from the first day of creation to the present moment of their own existence, the thirty-seventh year of the exile of their king Jehoiachin. It was all there, but it was unthinkable that it could be published and sanctioned without a supplementary collection of the prophets, whose work and words made it possible for others to write their history, to be grateful for their survival, and to have a future to look forward to and celebrate.

In this massive collection, containing the bulk of the pre-exilic prophets including majors and minors, the book of Amos has a distinction, because he was the first and led the way. Others followed, and a new tradition was established. When the collection was put together it included the prophets who had foreseen and predicted the catastrophic experiences of the two kingdoms, beginning in the eighth century and ending with the destruction of first one and then the other of them. The prophets of the eighth century had spelled it all out before it happened and had explained in detail the whys and wherefores, so that when those terrible things happened, the victims had a realistic appraisal of their circumstances to ponder and serious instructions regarding what to do about them. Those who had predicted the worst could also promise a best, a future that would reverse the present. So if the great history was a textbook study of everything that had gone wrong, an unsparing analysis of a great tragedy, then the books of the prophets, while not less damning in their indictment of the nations and their population, nevertheless held out a hope for the future that made survival possible. The two collections were inseparable from the start. The one illuminated the shadows of the past and provided people who were deprived of home, king, and country with a history and an identity that was proof against the blandishments of pagan society and life in Babylon, as equally against threats of utter destruction. The other provided hope, promise, and assurance for the future. Without the latter there could have been no future. The heretics of the eighth century, the rejected voices of the years of the first commonwealth, were now the voices of authority and accepted wisdom.

Among them Amos and his book played an all-important part, because he was preeminent. Each prophet was distinctive and no man's lackey or imitator, but they had a great deal in common, and ultimately the cumulative force of their oracles won the day. However terrible the doom they proclaimed, and however certain the fate of the condemned, their words were preserved and lived on, along with the other words of survival and return. Alone among the nations, Israel and Judah had this tradition, and they alone had a chance to survive the onslaught of the great powers in those centuries.

There is a grim lesson in the fact that the larger, more powerful and wealthier peoples fell by the wayside and vanished along with countless other national groups, but one of the smaller, weaker, and less viable states survived. Judah fell, like Israel, but its people persevered, and in the end they were rescued. They had the story of the prophets and inherited the legacy of both north and south, and that finally was what counted. So even though Amos was sent to the north and probably uttered most of the preserved oracles there, and clearly had the great confrontation there as well, his message was for all of Israel and was preserved in the south along with those of the other prophets. He and his message came home to his own. The same is true of Hosea, a prophet of the north whose principal messages were for his own kingdom. Both the message and the experience of that prophet also belong to the south, and ultimately Judah inherited the whole tradition. Amos represents a turning point; he was the first of the new breed of prophets, who appeared on the scene after a gap and perhaps a break in the succession. He accuses the leadership of silencing the prophets, and we wonder what happened to the bands of prophets established and led by Elijah and Elisha, apparently gone by the time of Amos. There are prophets to be sure, but for the most part they merit neither respect nor title, hangers-on and hirelings of the court who merely give prophecy a bad name. It is no accident that Amos denies any connection with professional prophets of any kind. He insists on the distinction. He is a nonprophet who prophesies because he has been called from another way of life entirely to bring an urgent message. Yahweh searched outside the ranks of "the prophets" to seek someone to bear that message. Amos was the man.

The visions reflect the substance of this self-evaluation. Amos does not explain how he received visions. Clearly it is not a matter of training or instruction in the art of being a prophet! Visions can be described, even analyzed, but the experience still defies explanation. Practically everyone has dreams and many have visions, but only visions from the living God count, and Amos somehow knew that his were. He describes the visions rather matter-of-factly, but the crucial distinction is the presence of the deity in them, a presence that is both visual and audible. Seeing does not occur without hearing. True, the first vision conveys its own message; even for a neophyte the message is unmistakable. But then the words come; Amos speaks and Yahweh responds. The second vision follows the same pattern. With the second pair of visions, however, the positions are reversed, and Yahweh speaks first.

What is essential for understanding Amos as man and prophet is the absolute conviction of actual personal contact with the deity, Yahweh the God of Israel. Amos had been a worshiper of Yahweh all his life, no doubt, so Yahweh was not a stranger to him. He would know the traditions and the stories of earlier prophets. Knowing about God is one thing, but knowing him is quite another. They are not unrelated, however, and when Yahweh appears in a vision and speaks, the man Amos is ready. He sees and he speaks. The first verbal contact is initiated by Amos, even before Yahweh can speak his message. Even before he hears it, Amos has a message for God. We assume this to be the first contact of a direct nature between Yahweh and prophet initiated by the former. Presumably Amos does not know yet that he has a mission, only that he has been shown a terrible vision of disaster in the form of a locust plague. He will see worse later, but we must not underestimate the dreadful implications and consequences. The book of Joel reflects the awesome nature of locust plagues and the incredible devastation that those insects can and do inflict up to the present time. Without knowing why he has been shown this vision; but, clearly recognizing its source, Amos flings himself into the breach as intercessor even before he is a prophet. That action is unique in the annals of Israel and of its prophets. The only other successful intercession of this kind recorded in the Bible is credited to Moses, who intervened in the crisis of the golden calf. But he was already a seasoned veteran of many intimate meetings with the deity and the successful leader of his people out of Egypt, when he attempted the extraordinary intervention. Between that time and

Amos no one managed to do it in a story still found in the Bible, though Samuel is credited with intercessory powers and made a strenuous if unsuccessful attempt to use them. No doubt there were others too. Even more remarkable than the intercession is the response. Amos reports that Yahweh repented and affirmed "It shall not happen."

Without going over this question again at length, we want to stress two things.

1. Amos' initial response to a vision of doom makes very clear his own feeling about his people and something of his character. He is a dedicated partisan of his people and will soon again intercede as he has just done. The message received from Yahweh is not one he would have adopted on his own. He resists the message and makes every effort to change it. That is his role in the first pair of visions. But he is finally overpowered by the deity and must deliver Yahweh's message to his people, not Amos' message. He can say what he pleases to Yahweh and he succeeds in changing the deity's mind. But that is only a reprieve. The threat remains.

2. Amos knows that the message is urgent and the time short. His intercession buys time, but no more than that. The threat of judgment is there, and only full-scale repentance will avert the threat of judgment. So the first phase of Amos' ministry begins with dire warnings and urgings to repent. These speeches reflect his successful intervention and show that Amos' message from the beginning was given in the shadow of a provisionally suspended conviction and condemnation. The divine repentance was real but could only be temporary. So Phase One of Amos' ministry must have been urgent and frantic. There was no time to lose.

In the book of Amos not much of this Phase survives, either because there was precious little time and he did not say much, or because those speeches were not remembered or recorded. It may be that he discarded them himself because they did not suit the later phases in which he was more heavily involved. It is also possible that Amos' attitudes changed with time and experience. The rebuffs received at the hands of those who should have known better doubtless convinced him, along with the later visions, that the cause was hopeless and that with the current generation the end of the nation would come. But it is unlikely that Amos would wash his hands of everybody in the nation. Anyone who spoke so eloquently about the mistreatment of the poor and helpless, whose defender and protagonist was Yahweh himself, could not have written everyone off together and at once. His heart might harden against the leadership, against those whose actions were bringing disaster and destruction on everyone, and who were inflicting pain and suffering on the innocent and righteous, but he would not add to the indignity heaped on the righteous by condemning them too. This distinction is the legacy of Phase One.

From the first set of visions we derive the initial impact on a man, doubtless steeped in the tradition and a faithful worshiper and servant of Yahweh, according to contemporary convention. But the visions were the first direct contact between God and this worshiper and must have had a profound impact on the man. We see it in his intervention, unique in the annals of Israel's religious history; we see it also in the report of Yahweh's repentance. We must ask about the second vision: when does it occur; what is its purpose and function? Is it just a literary flourish? The structure is carefully worked out so that the account is practically a duplicate. But there are both serious and subtle differences. Because the outcome is the same we may wonder whether it is a purely literary exercise designed to reinforce the first. But the logic (psychological and otherwise) is different. If the transaction is a real one, then the purpose of the second one could hardly have been to duplicate and reinforce the first. The same may well be true with the third and fourth, where Yahweh arranges matters in order to reveal a changed determination about "my people Israel" and then duplicates it in order to confirm the third. The message has been determined by Yahweh; in the first vision of the second pair he communicates that message to Amos, and in the second vision he repeats and thus confirms it. Together they leave no doubt about that decision. Amos plays no part in its formulation and does not affect the course of events in either of those visions, which might be regarded as the standard or normal pattern. In such circumstances the visions can come in direct and rapid sequence or can be separated by a period of time.

The first two visions are another matter altogether. While at first sight the order or literary pattern, with its repetition of almost identical language, seems to make it fall into the same classification as the second pair, the content is very different, as is the outcome. The central factor in each case is the prophet's intervention rather than compliance with an order or commission from God. The latter, in fact, was not issued or was issued in a different form, allowing Amos to deliver a message different from the one planned by the deity. It is difficult to know how to interpret the second vision in the light of the first. In some ways it would make better sense to interpret them as coming simultaneously, so that the interchange between prophet and deity was one and the same. But that possibility is clearly ruled out by the slight changes in language, which show that they are in sequence and the second presupposes the first. The other way would be to regard them as alternates, but that interpretation is ruled out also. The only way to read them is to see them as separate events, with the situation at the beginning of the second vision essentially the same as at the beginning of the first.

Yahweh's intention in the second vision is the same as in the first, or worse, because the vision is much more devastating in its implications: not just an agricultural disaster but a cosmic catastrophe of unlimited violence, consisting of the all-consuming fire from heaven that plays such a central role in the great opening oracle. We may guess therefore that it is really a test on God's part to see whether Amos really meant his intercession or whether it was a spontaneous response not seriously thought through. Looked at another way, it also becomes a test of the deity. What can Amos have thought, having just interceded successfully with Yahweh to spare Jacob, on seeing a vision from Yahweh in which a worse disaster was threatened? Clearly in the second vision we have a test of wills. Amos will not budge. His earlier intercession is now reinforced; it is both spontaneous and reasoned. He has had time to think about it. And Yahweh's response is not trivial either. The whole exercise is not merely a test of the prophet, though Yahweh is frequently if not constantly in the business of testing people (cf. Gen 22:1; Deut 8:3; Job 1–2).

The purpose was not just to find out how Amos felt and what his reaction would be, though clearly Yahweh would wish to know those things, and in particular the mettle of a man who is going to be entrusted with a critical message to be delivered under the most difficult of circumstances. But it is impossible to believe that Yahweh planned his own repentance or that it was a mere ploy used as part of the testing. We are not here speaking about ultimate theological issues but rather about human perception of the interaction, as part of the story. We must take the account of the vision and the decisions reached at face value. The intercession clearly was purposeful and intentional. Amos was not testing God. The same was true of the repentance; whatever other divine purposes it may have served, it was genuine. The second case, therefore, presupposes that God has changed his mind once again, and the second time his expectations may have been mixed. He must have been surprised by Amos' initial outburst, but could hardly have been the second time. His own second response could hardly have been spontaneous, as the first may have been; but he is known as the One who repents over the evil (hanniḥām ʿal-hārāʿâ; cf. Joel 2:13; Jonah 4:2), and he is true to his character. The dynamics of the second vision and dialogue are different from those of the first, and presumably both parties learn more about themselves and about each other in the process.

There may be a lurking suspicion that the first set of visions serves only to lead up to and enhance the second set, that the real purpose has nothing to do with divine repentance or a genuine opportunity for Israel to repent on its part but is only a dramatic literary prelude to the significant, operational visions in the second set. The purpose then would be only to provide Amos with some experience in receiving visions and responding to them. His spontaneous reaction only shows that he is naïve and does not understand his real role, which he learns thoroughly only with the second set of visions. Yahweh for his part is fully prepared for the novice's responses and reacts appropriately, reassuring the prophet that he is a kind and forgiving deity, in accordance with the tradition and Amos' expectations. But all of this prologue is designed to test and educate Amos so that he will be ready when the operational visions come and he is given his marching orders. In other words, the first two visions were preliminary tests designed to give Amos laboratory experience, using a simulation as it were. The device for terminating the rehearsal was the statement of divine repentance, which was far from Yahweh's real intention. All along that purpose was conveyed in the content of the first two visions, restated and confirmed by the second pair. That this analysis is a genuine possibility is supported by what Jeremiah says about Yahweh's dealings with him: the prophet claims to have been deceived and abused by the deity and manipulated into untenable situations all for ulterior reasons either concealed by God or misrepresented to the prophet (Jer 20:7–18). In Amos, however, we find no such complaint. If Amos was duped he remained so. We prefer to believe that he was not: that he was aware of different possibilities in his relations with Yahweh and that he assessed the circumstances correctly.

While in retrospect the intervention did not directly affect the course of history, and the visions proved to be accurate forecasts, Amos believed that the interchanges with Yahweh were genuine and that the latter's repentance was real. Amos was much closer to the situation than anyone else, and his judgment must prevail. The initial experiences with Yahweh provided a valuable lesson to the prophet. They confirmed that Yahweh reveals his plans to prophets and that prophets can influence divine decisions. Even after they are reversed—we noted a series of reversals in the sequence of visions—the fact about Yahweh remains: he is gracious and compassionate and above all the one who repents of the evil. In spite of the final irreversible judgment against greater Israel, and in spite of the terrible consequences, Yahweh did repent yet again, and Jerusalem and Judah were spared (Jer 26:19).

Jeremiah reports still another divine repentance after the fall of Jerusalem and the final destruction of the state (42:10). Amos was not misled or mistaken. Not only were the visions real, but the dialogue was also. It was the experience and knowledge of God gained from the first pair of visions that made it possible for Amos to accept the burdensome mission imposed on him in the second pair of visions. If Yahweh was engaged in training and testing Amos for his task as a prophet, and no doubt he was, Amos nevertheless was discovering the true nature of his God and confirming that knowledge in the give and take of dialogue and confrontation.

In the case of the second set of visions, we have noted that both are orchestrated entirely by the deity, and the purpose in them is to confirm the prophet in his mission and to ensure that there will be no modification of the message, deviation from it, or innovation on it. Having experienced the heady role of counselor and intercessor, the prophet now must accept his status as messenger and deliver the explicit word of Yahweh. In accordance with the assertion made in 3:7, Yahweh has consulted with his prophet, and now it is the prophet's duty to conform to the prescription in 3:8. So we see at least two sides to the prophet's character as he progresses through the visionary experiences. He accepts his role and defines his position vis-à-vis his mentor, and he prepares for his task.

The fact that the story of his encounter with Amaziah is sandwiched in the middle of the second pair of visions is important and instructive. The decision by the editor (or the prophet) was clearly deliberate. Ordinarily one might expect to find it between the two sets or after the second set, as is the case with the second insertion; but the curious location between two visions that belong together, one reinforcing the other, requires an explanation and one that does not merely state the obvious. The answer lies in the juxtaposition of the two confrontations: Amos as the receiver of the message from Yahweh, and Amos as prophet and messenger to Bethel and its priest. Whether the author/editor intended the reader to understand the order of events sequentially—that is, that Amos experienced Vision 3 first, then confronted Amaziah, and afterward had Vision 4—is possible but debatable. It has seemed more likely to us that the visions came in rapid succession, and that on the strength of them Amos proceeded to Bethel to deliver his fiery message.

It is possible that the fourth vision confirmed the third one after the meeting with Amaziah, though in view of Amaziah's haughty resistance to the prophet and his message, no further confirmation was really needed. We feel that in view of the experience of the first two visions and the several reversals of decisions, the prophet would have needed and wanted the assurance of the fourth confirming vision with its repetition of the final decisive message before setting out on such a hazardous mission. The reinforcement of the fourth vision was a necessary precursor to his trip to Bethel. So we explain the inclusion of the story between the two visions as an editorial effort to juxtapose the two blocks of material in the closest possible manner so that the reader experiences the two confrontations simultaneously, even though they happened in sequence. It is even possible that both the visions and the confrontation happened in the same place at approximately the same time. We are not told where Amos had the visions, and it is possible that they came to him while he was traveling and preaching the word of repentance following the altered decisions after the first and second visions. In any case, the two experiences are juxtaposed and are to be kept together in interpreting the material. What we have then is a split-screen presentation, with Amos conferring with Yahweh in one panel and confronting Amaziah in the other. Needless to say, it is the first that explains the behavior of the prophet in the second. The story of the event at Bethel is the prime illustration of what the commission and the message given to

Amos in the pair of visions meant in practice. The prophet learned his lesson well and delivered the message from God as a faithful, obedient servant. Precisely because of that he behaved the way he did and said what he said at Bethel. The encounter was not simply a violent argument between two headstrong men who differed on matters of local propriety and protocol. It was the irreconcilable conflict between opposing spokesmen for the one God: the primate of the leading sanctuary in the north and the undocumented visionary from the south. In fact, the one speaks for himself and the interests of those who share power and prestige ostensibly in the name of and for the sake of Yahweh, but not in actuality, while the other speaks for the same deity but out of a genuine experience in vision and dialogue. The editor could not have produced a more vivid contrast between manmade and divinely inspired religion.

The hardening process is also seen in the fifth vision, which—if we are right—reflects the circumstances growing out of the confrontation at Bethel. The transition to Phase Three, with its emphasis on condign and individual punishment of the leadership arises from the conviction that there can be no future for Israel if the leadership survives the disaster. They would only bring about another tragedy later on. If the victims and common people are to survive at all, then the leaders must be identified separately and eliminated. It is no accident that the fifth vision is located at the temple (which one is not specified, and any of several may be in view), because that is where the trouble is centered and where the apostasy began, all in the name of true religion. The primary reference would inevitably be to the high priest and his cohorts, but the slaughter will extend through the ranks of the leaders. Where or when Amos had this vision we cannot determine, but it should be related to the disastrous confrontation with Amaziah because it was on that occasion that the decision of doom was sealed. There is no longer a question of divine repentance or certainly of human repentance, only of putting the denunciations on record and waiting for the judgment to occur.

II. God

Equally in The Book of Visions we find a more sharply focused picture and presentation of the deity. The essential elements appear in various places, including the two dominant themes that turn up repeatedly: the broad depiction of Yahweh as the creator and controller of the universe (e.g., 4:13, 5:8) and as the redeemer who brought his people from Egypt (e.g., 2:10, 3:1, 5:25) to the promised land (2:9–10). Along with these classical attributions, there is the more personal aspect of his dealings, especially with the prophets and their role in the chain of communication between

God and the world of human beings, Israel in particular (cf. 2:11–12, 3:7–8, and 5:10–12 as well as perhaps v 13).

In chapters 7:1–9:6 the broad theme of the universal deity is presented in the closing apostrophe (9:6), while the God of the Exodus is not mentioned explicitly until we are in the Epilogue (9:7). The other aspect of the deity, as the one who speaks to and through the prophet, receives particular emphasis here, through the medium of the visions and the dialogues between Yahweh and Amos. There is further information in the interchange between Amos and Amaziah, in which Amos explains how he became a prophet and what kind of relations a true prophet can have and does have with the true God. It is here that we are given a private portrait of Yahweh the mentor, sponsor, and commander of the prophet, in balance with the portrait of the prophet as participant in the decision-making process, as intercessor, and as messenger of his Lord. As the prophet's personality emerges more fully from the description of the encounter with God, and from that of his confrontation with the high priest in a form of counterpoint, so the deity's personality is more sharply delineated in the course of the same encounter. He is a personal God, not less majestic or powerful, awe-inspiring and authoritative, but clearly the same God who described himself to Moses in that climactic revelation on the mountain as the all-gracious and compassionate One, merciful as well as just. For Amos the revelation of the deity through the visions is primarily in terms of his prophetic office and mission. The surprise, if any, comes with the clarification of his role. This God not only spoke the words for Amos to hear and then repeat, but he listened when Amos spoke. In fact, the latter came first —the listening God before the speaking God (*deus audiens*, not only *deus loquens*). And a God who could listen could also reflect and reconsider and change his mind, and did, not arbitrarily or capriciously but in response to human intercession. The interchange between Amos and Yahweh in chaps. 7–8, in the course of the first four visions, represents the theological high point of the book and reveals the deity's personality as do few other passages in the Bible. On the one side is the message from God to the prophet, the message that makes up the substance of the book of Amos, a compilation of representative and distinctive oracles. From what we know of the prophet, he faithfully performed his duty to deliver the message that he received. It was a sacred trust, and to discharge his responsibility he was willing to risk everything of value to him, up to and including his life. Above all, he was not disobedient to the heavenly vision.

On the other side, there is the prophet's message to the deity, which indeed came first. Even before he accepted his role as messenger, he claimed his role as counselor and intercessor, and imposed his will on the deity before the deity imposed his will on him. Yahweh is revealed as the One who consults: note that Amos makes the claim for prophets generally that they are members of the privy council who are consulted before decisions are made, not just told afterward (cf. 3:7). The status that Amos assumes is much disputed in later books, and we do not find any prophet afterward actively succeeding in this claim. Isaiah only asks questions politely and does not offer advice or instructions. Jeremiah struggles intermittently and sometimes vehemently, but he is clearly forbidden to disagree with decisions and is not allowed to help shape them or even intervene with the deity. If Jeremiah's God repents he does so by his own choice and without instruction or advice, least of all from the prophet. As for Ezekiel, he shows no disposition whatever to debate with the deity or to challenge his decisions. On the contrary, the God of Ezekiel does not repent at all.

It is perhaps curious but not less significant that at the heart—or chronologically (and logically) at the very beginning (7:1–6)—of Amos' ministry there should be a unique account of intercessions by a neophyte, who is not yet an active prophet in a book devoted largely to oracles of denunciation and damnation. The corresponding repentance of the deity, showing in a specific encounter that compassion and mercy are essential elements in his character, is in striking contrast to the attributes of justice, judgment, and drastic punishment that are the main content of the book. The mystery of the tension, even competition, between the attributes of retribution and mercy that combine to form divine equity is ultimately insoluble in human terms. It is said that before the Day of Atonement Yahweh himself prays that his attribute of mercy will outweigh his attribute of judgment as decisions must be rendered for the coming year.

What remains important for understanding the prophet and his book is that in his introductory experience with the deity Amos prevailed over the latter in securing a decision for mercy, nothing less, and in direct response to the prophet's direct plea. In spite of all reversals, a veritable kaleidoscope of reversals, that initial, basic impression could never have been erased. And if the deity was revealed as first of all the forgiver, the prophet was perceived as an intercessor like the great exemplar of all prophets, Moses himself. Ultimately (in our opinion) such a God and such a man could not consign the whole people and the whole nation to permanent perdition. There would be judgment and punishment in profusion, and a whole generation of leaders would be executed mercilessly; but there would also be mercy. Amos would have been derelict in his insight and his duty alike had he not foreseen such an outcome. After all, he had seen God close up and had heard him speak the words of remission; he knew. No matter how firm or secure the reversals, and they were very firm, the same God who repented once or twice could and would repent again. As Jeremiah reports, that is exactly what happened in the days of Hezekiah when, in spite of a firm decision to destroy (announced grimly by the good prophet Micah), Yahweh—on his own and in response to the repentance of Hezekiah and his people—reversed the decision and spared the city. Isaiah 36–37 (= 2 Kings 18–19) has a different account of the event, but the essential points are the same. The decision to save the city is made in response to Hezekiah's prayers and entreaties, but nothing is said of a prior judgment against the city, and the reason given for saving it is that Yahweh will do it for his own sake and for that of his servant David.

Jeremiah reports another act of repentance on Yahweh's part in his own time, after the capture of Jerusalem and the destruction of the temple by Nebuchadnezzar in 587. The God who repented in the wilderness at Moses' behest and again at the request of the prophet Amos could repent again, in spite of reversals. Amos knew that from the beginning, based on his private knowledge of the nature of God. That knowledge is expressed not only in the description of the visions but at critical points in the book, which refer to the possibilities of repentance by the people and later, we believe, the possibility of another final repentance on the part of Yahweh: a reversal of the judgment and a restoration of the people.

III. The Message and the Response

What remains to be discussed is the resultant message from God through the prophet to the people and the way it was received. We postulate that after the first two visions or even between them, Amos proclaimed the message hammered out in the exchange after the first and second visions. It was a message of warning and threat and an urgent appeal to repent. There are examples of this message in some parts of the book, notably 5:4–5 and 5:14, and traces elsewhere; but, as expected, there is nothing of this phase in The Book of Visions. The message there is the product of the second pair of visions, and there are also indications of Phase Three (based on the last vision). Much of the book contains examples of the Second Phase, and by and large what has been preserved comes out of the second pair of visions and belongs to Phase Two. The specific context in which that message is presented is the temple at Bethel and the confrontation with the priest there, Amaziah. What is of special interest is not so much the initial message, which is given at greater length and in greater depth elsewhere (the actual public address may well have been the architectonically magnificent oracles in chaps. 1–2, the speech against the eight nations), but the response on the part of the authorities and the rapid transition from Phase Two to Phase Three as Amos produces specific condemnations of the houses of the king and high priest. This set adds the specific sentence of dynastic destruction that may have been implied in Phase Two, but which is made explicit in Phase Three. What emerges in the confrontation is the fact that there is a total failure in comprehension on the part of the priest. He is completely unable to grasp the reality of Amos' message or even the possibility that

God could speak such a message through this man or at all. To us it is all very understandable and tragically regrettable. A high priest is often the last person to know the mind of his God. Consider the pathetic case of the old priest Eli having to ask the boy Samuel for information about God's plans for the house of Eli. Here too the prophet has unwelcome news for the high priest, the difference being that Eli recognized the truth when he heard it, while Amaziah had achieved a permanent state of obdurate impermeability.

The interaction between an irreversible decision of punitive judgment and an absolute resistance to the truth made further communication both impossible and absurd. The story of the confrontation provides us with a rare glimpse of the audience that heard the prophet and his awful message (cf. Jer 7 and 26, or 1 Kings 22). Elsewhere the words are only spoken, not heard; here they are heard and produce a response, a very negative one. The lesson is clear that Amos discharged his duty. He fulfilled the requirements of his office, delivering the message of his God. No response in fact was expected, and the one that was given was unsatisfactory. The people and especially their leaders had not only resisted the word, but rejected the messenger. There would be no further messages to them. Next would come the action of God.

The second insertion (8:4–14) provides confirmatory data. It is clear that the prophet expects no response and does not seem to get any. The targets of his attacks seem to be oblivious to his presence as they pursue their wicked idolatrous ways and works, and he seems like a recording angel compiling the roster and the dossier on each of them. As they rush along, unthinking, to a destiny they imagine to be quite different from what the prophet describes for them (cf. those who await impatiently the dawning Day of Yahweh in 5:18–20: they are all different elements in the group addressed in all of the Woes, but they are singled out by use of the word "Woe" itself as typical or representative of all), the oracles will end and a silence will engulf them, the silence in which there is no word from Yahweh (8:11–12). Thereafter, the final violent action will begin (8:8, 8:13–14, and 9:5), followed by endless unrelieved mourning (8:9–10). The people, especially here the leaders, have only themselves to blame for the outcome.

III.A. THE FIRST FOUR VISIONS
(7:1–8:2)
III.A.1. THE FIRST PAIR OF VISIONS
(7:1–6)
III.A.1.a. THE FIRST VISION (LOCUSTS)
(7:1–3)

7 ¹Thus my Lord Yahweh showed me: Indeed he was forming locusts, just when the latter growth was beginning to appear, that is, the latter growth after the king's mowings. ²When they were about to devour the vegetation of the land entirely, I said, "My Lord Yahweh, please forgive! How can Jacob survive, as he is so small?" ³Yahweh repented of this. "It shall not happen," Yahweh said.

NOTES

The Book of Visions contains the only narrative material in the book of the prophet Amos. There are six incidents: five visions, presented as autobiography, and the confrontation with Amaziah, related in the third person. The visions, at least the first four, have a stereotyped form; that is, they repeat certain formulas, like the eight oracles against the nations in the Great Set Speech and the plagues in 4:6–11. The formulas serve simply as a framework for the cycle of visions, and to present the first four as two similar pairs. The regularities have not been developed in the direction of poetry. It is only the oracular material in chaps. 8 and 9 that displays the marks of parallelistic poetry, and then only in Amos' peculiar manner. The narrative and accompanying dialogue have the form of prose. The narrative also uses the language of prose, as judged by the incidence of the "prose particles." It happens that *'ăšer* is never used, which shows that we do not have the flowing literary prose of standard Hebrew as used in the Primary History and especially Deuteronomy. Even so, there is no indication that *ha-* and *'et-* were avoided: *'et-'ēśeb hā'āreṣ* in 7:2 is typical, and it has the syntax usual in prose.

The narratives, and especially the visions, are not composed in the ample prose of classical Hebrew storytelling. The language is spare, sometimes almost opaque, and the dialogue is lean, almost abrupt. In the first two visions Amos addresses God by his full title "my Lord Yahweh," but his contribution to the dialogue in the third vision is one word, in the fourth vision a two-word phrase, in the fifth vision nothing! Yahweh's contribution to the dialogue shows a contrary development: two words in the first vision, four in the second, eleven in the third. The similar reply in the fourth vision (8:2b) is amplified in an oracle (8:3). The oracle that grows out of the fifth vision is even longer. Amos' intercessions dwindle and fail.

7:1. *my Lord Yahweh.* The title is characteristic of Amos and dominates The Book of Visions. The LXX does not agree entirely with the MT in such details, but the variations are innocuous and provide no firm grounds for adjustment of the Hebrew text.

	MT	*LXX*
7:1	*ʾădōnāy yhwh*	*kyrios*
2	*ʾădōnāy yhwh*	*kyrie kyrie*
3a	*yhwh*	*kyrie* (vocative!)
3b	*yhwh*	*kyrios*
4a	*ʾădōnāy yhwh*	*kyrios*
4b	*ʾădōnāy yhwh*	*kyrios*
5	*ʾădōnāy yhwh*	*kyrie kyrie*
6a	*yhwh*	*kyrie* (vocative!)
6b	*ʾădōnāy yhwh*	*kyrios*
7a	*ʾădōnāy*	*kyrios*
8a	*yhwh*	*kyrios*
8b	*ʾădōnāy*	*kyrios*
15a	*yhwh*	*kyrios*
15b	*yhwh*	*kyrios*
16	*dbr yhwh*	*logon kyriou*
17	*yhwh*	*kyrios*
8:1	*ʾădōnāy yhwh*	*kyrios*
8:2b	*yhwh*	*kyrios*
8:3	*ʾădōnāy yhwh*	*kyrios*

The LXX recognizes the double name only in Amos' two intercessory pleas. Otherwise it renders by *kyrios* either the double name or each name separately.

showed me. The same formula is used for the first four visions. The fifth has "I saw my Lord" (9:1).

indeed. Literally rendered, it would be "and behold." All four visions continue in this way.

forming. The participle *yôṣēr* lacks a preceding explicit subject, as normally used; *qōrēʾ* in v 4 has the same construction (its subject comes later). The formative verb (*ywṣr*) is also used in 4:13, where it is parallel to *brʾ* (used in the Creation story in Genesis 1). It states in the strongest possible way that an event such as a locust plague is directly caused by Yahweh. The insects are specially created for the occasion. The ancient versions already toned this down; the LXX has *epigonē akridōn*, "offspring of locusts." This shift has enticed modern interpreters and translators (e.g., NEB) to suppose that the Hebrew should read *yēṣer*. The salient meaning of this word in the OT is "thought," "imagination," "purpose"; only later does it acquire the psychological connotation of "impulse" or "drive." The meaning "object" or "artifact" (i.e., something formed) is found only in Isa 29:16 and Hab 2:18. The word *yēṣer* as the "form" of man (Ps 103:14) is related to Gen 2:7–8. As in Amos 4:13, the verb loses its metaphorical associations with the potter's craft and means "create."

locusts. Of the many terms available for describing the various species of orthopterous insects (Driver and Larchester 1915:89–93; Andersen 1961–62), the word used here probably means "swarm(s)." It is rare, being found again in the OT only at Nah 3:17.

latter growth. The pinpointing of the locust plague to an exact moment in the agricultural year gives actuality to the experience. It happened at a particular season in the real world; the infinitival construction modifies "he showed" as well as "creating." We can infer that the locusts also were real, that the essence of the vision was to reveal the fact that Yahweh was creating them. The term *leqeš* occurs only here in the OT. It has associations with *malqôš*, "spring rain" in March and April. The word *lqš* occurs in the Gezer Calendar, where it comes after the first season of sowing. Because that calendar is an almanac of farming tasks, *lqš* there probably means "late sowing" rather than "spring growth." The infinitive *ʿălôt* secures the idea of growth (Gen 40:10; 41:5, 22 [grain]; Deut 29:22 [grass]; Jonah 4:6 [gourd]; Isa 55:13; Ezek 47:12 [trees]). The LXX word, *heōthinē*, "[coming] early in the morning," seems to be off the track.

The agricultural year in the Gezer Calendar ends with *yrḥ qṣ* (same spelling as *qēṣ* in Amos 8:2b), the season of final fruit-gathering in late summer or early autumn. It is therefore possible that Amos' visions all took place in a single year, with the second one—cosmic fire—having as its real-world counterpart an excessively hot summer.

that is. The literal translation is "and behold." The syntax of v 1b is problematical. There is no predicator, and the use of *leqeš* after *hallāqeš* raises doubt that the two nouns have the same referent. It seems to be not part of the vision but a further definition of the time of the event in the real world. Again it is quite precise, a touch of authenticity.

The LXX reading, "and behold one locust, the king Gog," is wide of the mark and points to a *Vorlage* already corrupt or else to great freedom in interpreting an obscure text allegorically and apocalyptically.

LXX	Vorlage	MT
kai idou	=	*wĕhinnēh*
brouchos	*yeleq*(?)	*leqeš*
heis	*'eḥād*	*'aḥar*
Gōg	*gôg*	*gizzê*
ho basileus	=	*hammelek*

Neither the word-for-word correspondence, nor the intelligibility of the LXX, nor the consonantal matches can make the apparent *Vorlage* a competitor with the MT. The translator's tendentiousness and his late hermeneutic rule out the LXX as a viable variant here.

mowings. The verb *gzz* means "shear." It is only the agricultural context of Amos' first vision that suggests that here *gizzê* means "mowings," a time reference suitable for control by the preposition "after." The only other possible occurrence of this word is, significantly, in a royal psalm (72:6). The beneficence of the king is compared extravagantly with the rain showers, which, like the wise teaching of Moses (Deut 32:2), water the grass. The *gēz* could therefore refer to the royal pasture lands or fodder crops, or the crops that are taken as a kind of tax to supply the king's animals with fodder. The mention of "the king" is probably not incidental, referring merely to the time of year when the king's grass is mowed. It documents a threat to the king's own (and therefore the nation's) prosperity.

2. *When.* Literally, "and it was." The use of *wĕhāyâ* to continue the story is unaccountable, and most scholars have been content to accept Wellhausen's emendation to *wayĕhî.* Less drastic is Huesman's proposal to read the infinitive absolute, *wĕhāyōh* (1956b:433). These adjustments do not entirely solve the problem, for it is still necessary to take *'im* as temporal "when." The result is still not happy, for it makes the following verb indicative, "when they had finished eating the grass of the land" (RSV; cf. NJPS, NIV). The LXX's *kai estai* confirms the MT and correctly renders the following subordinate clause as subjunctive. The usage of *wĕhayâ* is modal, "and it would have been, it would have completely eaten the vegetation of the land."

It is important to recover the scenario, if at all possible, in order to make sense of Yahweh's remark, "It shall not happen." For if Amos sees that the locusts "had finished devouring the herbage in the land" (NJPS), and then God says, "It shall not happen," then the whole thing takes place in a vision and nothing happens at all in the real world. If, however, the vision is given in the context of a real plague, which, we suggest, is the very one described in 4:9 (note the scope and scale of what is reported there), then the visionary component is specifically the revelation that it is Yahweh who is creating these pests. The vision also discloses the meaning of Yahweh's act. It is directly against the people of Israel in terms of 3:2; it is intended to call them to repentance, as the refrain in 4:6–11 shows; and that intention can only be understood if the Lord's purpose is explained to the people in the context of the experience of the plague itself. We do not believe that the people were left to their unaided reflections, to work out for themselves, if they could, that the right way to respond to a plague of locusts is to repent toward God and specifically to repent by doing justice in the gate. They should have known, if they remembered covenant stipulations and sanctions. But the prophet's unique role, and Amos' personal involvement in the situation, make it clear to us that he would have supplied the needed commentary, interpretation, and exhortation to put the matter beyond doubt and to make the condemnation "yet you did not return to me [Yahweh]" (4:9) incontrovertible.

The beginning of v 2 thus reflects the desperate circumstance in which the plague has already reached its limit. Yet there is no sign of repentance. The events and dialogue reported in 7:1–3 could all transpire in thirty seconds. We are to suppose that this is the briefest possible report of the bare essentials of an experience and an encounter that could have taken quite some time to arrive at a resolution. Amos is not only appalled at what might happen; he is horrified at what has already happened. Because they have not repented, the only hope is that the prophet might intercede successfully. As a result of his intervention, there is a last-minute reprieve.

The prophet has to pay a high price in credibility for taking on responsibility for the people in this way. Next time it will be harder for him to make his point, "If you do not repent, you will certainly perish." "You said that last time, and it did not happen," they could retort.

vegetation. The term *ʿēśeb* is somewhat general, but when used specifically it refers to natural growth of grasses, rather than to cultivated crops.

forgive. The only subject of this verb in biblical usage is God. Its use by Amos in his supplication brings out a point that is not otherwise made in the report of the vision: the plague is due to sin. While the LXX's *hileōs genou,* "be merciful," catches the spirit of the prayer, it loses the objective reference of *slḥ* by appealing to God's mercy and grace.

How? The use of *mî* (normally "who?") requires careful study. "Jacob" is the subject of *yāqûm.* The meaning "how?" is makeshift, and alleged parallels (Isa 51:19; Ruth 3:16) are not really the same. The LXX has solved the problem by making Jacob the object ("Who will raise Jacob up?"); but this reading requires the *hipʿil* of the verb, and *ʾet* would also be necessary. In the context of earnest prayer, *mî* expresses intense desire, sometimes in the full expression *mî yittēn,* sometimes alone: for example, "Would that all the

Lord's people were prophets" (Num 11:29), "Oh that Jacob might survive!" This prayer is parallel to *sĕlaḥ-nāʾ*.

small. The basis of appeal is the fact that Jacob is small, not Yahweh's
compassion nor the people's contrition. Amos presents the nation as weak
and pitiable. It is a curious argument, and it is hard to find any basis for it
in the traditions. The description is all the more startling because in 6:8
Yahweh said, "I abhor the pride of Jacob." And "small" is not the way the
prosperous complacent nation saw itself.

The conjunction *kî* can be translated "because," and the subordinate
clause can be attached to either of the preceding ones: "Forgive [Jacob]
because he is small!" It is possible, indeed likely, in a clause of this kind,
that *kî* is an elative modifier of the adjective: "He is so small!" (cf. NIV).

3. *repented.* The language is strong and should not be softened in the
interest of theological scruples. In the context of the locust plague and
Amos' prayer, the meaning is objective. The point is not whether Amos
made Yahweh feel sorry. He forgave Jacob; Jacob survived; the plague
abated. It is worth emphasizing that the verb *niḥam* is mainly used to
describe Yahweh's change of mind or change of conduct. It describes a
human behavior modification only in a handful of cases, and only in one of
repentance for sin (Jer 8:6). In many instances Yahweh "repents" of the evil
(*rāʿâ*) he was planning to do (Jonah 3:9, 10; 4:2) or was actually doing, but
the same expression can be used when Yahweh changes his mind about
doing something good (Jer 18:10) or regrets creating humans (Gen 6:6–7).

The imperative of *nḥm* is used only twice in the OT; in Moses' somewhat
peremptory supplication in Exod 32:12 and in its reflex in Ps 90:13. Moses
commanded Yahweh to repent. The LXX translates *hinnāḥēm* by *hileōs
genou* ("be merciful" = *sĕlaḥ* of Amos 7:2) in Exod 32:12, and *paraklēthēti*
("be invoked," making it passive) in Ps 90:13, as if the literal meaning were
embarrassing. But the translator of Amos 7:3a had no such compunction,
rendering the verb as imperative, Yahweh as vocative: *metanoēson, kyrie,
epi toutō,* "Repent, O Lord, for this," as if it were parallel to v 2bA. Terms
such as "relent" or "regret" focus attention at the wrong point. It is a
change of conduct (in this case cancellation of the plague) that is needed,
not just a change of mind, and least of all a change of feeling (see the
Excursus, "When God Repents").

of this. The preposition *ʿal* with *nḥm* refers to the thing repented of.

It shall not happen. The assurance is simple and sounds final. In view of
subsequent developments, it cannot be taken as an unconditional commitment and promise. The parable of the potter (Jer 18:1–4) and the exposition
that goes with it (Jer 18:5–11—a sermon on repentance) leaves the situation
open for decisions either way, by either the divine or the human participant. But Yahweh's changes of plan and behavior are in response to human
change, which can be repentance or, failing that, prophetic intercession.

The fact that it happens all over again in the second vision supports this view of the case. And use of "it too" in the second vision shows that the similarity between the two is recognized and indeed important. Yet there is no indication that any need is felt to discuss and explain how the resumption of the plagues was able to override the assurances given in the first vision. It would be quibbling to argue that Yahweh had agreed not to destroy Jacob completely with locusts but still felt quite free to destroy him by some other means.

III.A.1.b. THE SECOND VISION (FIRE)
(7:4–6)

7 ⁴Thus my Lord Yahweh showed me: Indeed my Lord Yahweh was summoning showers of fire. When it had consumed the Great Deep, and was consuming the allotted land, ⁵I said, "My Lord Yahweh, please desist! How can Jacob survive, as he is so small?" ⁶Yahweh repented of this. "This also shall not happen," my Lord Yahweh said.

NOTES

7:4–6. The second vision is a twin of the first. Both use the same formulaic framework, and even the speeches are almost the same. Both have the curious detail of *wĕhinnēh* immediately followed by a participle, but here the subject is present and comes last (confirmed by the LXX, which, however, has simply *kyrios*). The use of *'et* and the definite article shows that it is composed in standard prose. The minor variations are:

1. the use of *ḥdl* rather than *slḥ* in the supplication;
2. the addition of *gam-hî'* to Yahweh's reply;
3. the use of the fuller title "my Lord Yahweh" in the final rubric.

The main difference, of course, lies in the content, the description of the destruction, this time by fire. The verb "eat" is common to the activities of the two destroyers. The second vision does not have anything corresponding to the elaborate time reference in v 1.

The activity of Fire is presented in two moments (v 4b), and the careful use of different verb forms in the narrative development places Amos' intervention at the decisive moment, when the fire has already devoured (*wattōʾkal*) the Great Deep and was about to devour (*wĕʾākĕlâ*) or was already devouring the *ḥēleq* (cf. the note on *wĕhāyâ* in v 2). The RSV, JPS, and JB translations preserve this all-important detail; but the NEB lost it by translating both verbs "to devour" as if the whole operation were still in prospect, and the NIV lost it by translating both as past tense, as if the whole operation were completed (cf. the LXX).

The second vision has the same mythic components and cosmic perspective as the first, only more so. While the locusts could be a natural phenomenon (and the time reference seems to frame their activity, not just the occasion of the vision), the Fire that can engulf the waters of the vast subterranean Ocean is beyond the capacity of the world with which we are familiar.

The similarity of this Fire to the one that destroys all of the major cities in the region in chaps. 1–2 and the unidentified cities in the last plague of 4:11 is important. Indeed we believe it is the same Fire throughout. The visions, the creation hymn, and the judgment oracles all have the same cosmic outlook, in which Yahweh is perceived as the Maker and Destroyer of the whole universe.

7:4 *summoning showers of fire* (*qrʾ lrb*, literally, "calling to contend"). The only serious textual difficulty in the second vision is presented by the word *lārîb*. The great similarity between the idiom used twice in the hymns —*hqrʾ lmy-hym*, "he who calls [to] the waters of the Sea" (5:8, 9:6)—and the one here invites a reading "calling [to] the . . . of Fire." The *defective* spelling of *rîb* attracts additional doubt, and the idiom *rb b-* is not suitable, for the preposition usually identifies the party accused (Gen 31:36; Judg 6:32; Hos 2:4). Two attractive emendations have been proposed. The first assumes a Heb *Vorlage lahab ʾēš* (Isa 29:6, 30:30; Joel 2:5) or *lhbt ʾēš* (Ps 29:7), which may be rendered "a flame of fire." This emendation is fairly drastic, for the two variants have only two consonants in common. This objection does not apply to the second emendation, proposed by M. Krenkel in 1866 and reactivated by D. R. Hillers (1964): *lrb(y)b ʾš*, "for a shower of fire." In consonantal orthography this one requires only a revision of word boundaries. The idea of fire from heaven associated with rain and hail is found in the Bible, but the expression needed does not occur elsewhere. Other objections to the proposal are as follows:

1. only the plural *rĕbîbîm* occurs in the OT;
2. the associations of *rĕbîbîm* are with gentle fructifying showers, not with cataclysmic storms;
3. in Ugaritic texts *rbb* is parallel to "dew," suggesting drizzle

(cf. Deut 32:2 and Mic 5:6). A downpour of fiery drops would not engulf the Deep;

4. the event is exactly like the one described in Deut 32:22; Fire goes out from Yahweh and devours everything; comparison with rain seems incongruent with this picture;

5. elsewhere in Amos it is simply Fire that does such things (cf. 5:6);

6. the idiom *lārîb bā'ēš* can be accepted as distinct from the usual "contend against," by comparing the use of fire to consume cities devoted to *ḥērem,* where *bā'ēš* is instrumental; and

7. the LXX's *kai idou ekalese tēn dikēn en pyri Kyrios,* "and behold, the Lord called for judgment by fire," supports the MT.

It is important to decide whether the word *rîb* is authentic. One thinks of the covenant *rîb* or dispute, which lies behind 2:9–12 and 3:2. Such a note is otherwise absent from the visions. But without it there is no indication of the reason or motivation for the horrendous destructions revealed or threatened in the visions. The word *rîb* connects the visions with the salient issues of the prophecy, the controversy over the people's rejection of *tôrâ* (2:4, Judah) and their perversion of justice and righteousness (5:7, 15, 24; 6:12b). Such a connection must be understood, but, apart from *rîb* in v 4, it would have to be taken for granted and read into the visions. The commentators are obliged to interpret the destructions in the visions as punishment; but the process of accusation and condemnation (*rîb*) is found in the visions themselves only in this word.

Great Deep. It is a fixed phrase (Gen 7:11; Isa 51:10), entirely archaic and mythic; hence the lack of the article. Compare "the *tĕhôm* that lies down in the netherworld" (Gen 49:25; Deut 33:13). If there is also a connection with the phenomenal world, it would correspond to the drought of 4:7–8 and to a stage in which even the wells and springs have dried up (1 Kgs 18:5).

allotted land. In the structure of the passage, *ḥēleq* must be something matching the Great Deep, though it is obviously not a synonym, but a complement. The word *ḥēleq* is usually patrimonial land (*ḥēleq wĕnaḥălâ;* hendiadys). Deuteronomy 32:9 identifies Jacob as Yahweh's *ḥēleq//ḥebel naḥălātô,* and that poem also contains the closest parallel we have to the imagery of Amos 7:4. Compare Deut 32:22:

> *kî-'ēš qādĕḥâ bĕ'appî*
> *wattîqad 'ad-šĕ'ôl taḥtît*
> *wattō'kal 'ereṣ wîbūlāh*
> *wattĕlahēṭ môsĕdê hārîm*

> For a fire was kindled by my anger,
>   and it burned to the depths of Sheol,
> and it devoured the earth and its increase,
>   and it set on fire the foundations
>   of the mountains.

The fire is the same in both passages, and the evidence of Deut 32:9 is important confirmation of our identification of the fire in Amos 7:4 (and right through Amos 1–2) as cosmic fire from Yahweh himself. The *tĕhôm rabbâ* is comparable to if not identical with "lowest Sheol" (Jonah was in Sheol and Tehom [2:3, 6] at the roots of the mountains [v 7]). It is tempting to complete the equations by identifying Amos' *ḥēleq* with Deuteronomy's "the earth and its yield." But Deut 32:22 has "earth" between Sheol and the foundations of the mountains, and in that sequence earth could have its mythic meaning of "Underworld." The word *yĕbûl,* however, normally means agricultural produce, and we think that this word gives "earth" its usual meaning. Deuteronomy 32:22 then describes the downward movement of the divine Fire twice. In verse 22a it goes from God's nostrils to the bottom of the Abyss; in v 22b it consumes the earth from surface to foundations. Of the three stories of the universe, only heaven is left. In Amos the action is, if anything, more mythological: Yahweh "calls" for judgment by fire, just as he calls for judgment by water (5:8, 9:6). In Amos 7:4 fire destroys the deep underground reservoir from which water comes into springs and wells, the mythic explanation of the failure of these sources, which only happens as a later consequence of extreme and prolonged drought. It would accordingly be the counterpart of the second plague (4:8). People would go from town to town looking for water because most towns were located at reliable springs. Connection of the cosmic Fire with the fifth disaster (4:11) is also implied, for the comparison with Sodom and Gomorrah is obvious, and actual fires in field and forest are inevitable after prolonged drought. The mythic terminology does not lose touch with familiar and "natural" catastrophes. The mythic language prevents them from being viewed as merely natural events. The vision makes certain to the prophet that the fire came from the Lord, just as the language of Amos 4:6–11, with the explicit and repeated pronoun "I," puts the matter beyond all doubt. Only the prophet has seen the fire of Yahweh at the base of the world, but all of the people know that the springs have failed and the wells are dry. The report of the vision supplies the people with the true explanation, if they are prepared to believe it. The burning of the *ḥēleq* is a threat to Jacob, so "the *ḥēleq*" means "his," namely, Yahweh's, domain (the LXX has *tēn merida kyriou* in some manuscripts). The picture would, however, be very lopsided if only the territory of Israel were the counterpart to the *tĕhôm rabbâ.*

In Amos' view, however, the land under Yahweh's supervision and in his gift, allocated equally to Aramaeans, Israelites, and Philistines, encompasses at least the territory claimed as his jurisdiction in chaps. 1–2. We are justified, accordingly, in identifying [Yahweh's] *ḥēleq* as consisting of all of the countries in which he shows an interest. And because that interest is grounded in ownership due to creation, we cannot set any geographical limits to the extent of the catastrophes itemized in 4:8–11. Israel is in the center of it all, to be sure; but as far as Amos knows, the troubles could be worldwide. If the visions do not make the extent altogether clear, the Hymns do; and together they place the matter beyond dispute.

5. *desist.* The effect of *-nā'* with the imperative, here and in v 2, makes the command peremptory rather than polite. Apart from the variation *slḥ/ḥdl,* Amos' plea is the same. The change registers a shift, as if forgiveness were no longer possible, not to be expected or requested. The forgiveness granted in the context of the first vision was the last time. All Amos can hope for now is that the severity of the punishment will be abated so that little Jacob might at least survive.

6. *This also.* The phrase *gam-hî'* (not in v 3) was interpreted by the Masoretes as the subject of the following verb. Otherwise it serves as a link back to the threat in the first vision.

Comment on the First Pair of Visions (7:1–6)

The first pair of visions correlates with the series of plagues described in 4:6–11. In particular, the first vision depicts a locust plague that is one of the features of the third plague (4:9). The second vision of a cosmic Fire corresponds to the fifth and last plague (4:11). This tie-in suggests that the visions were associated with actual events in recent history.

A possible account is as follows. A series of plagues comes to the country, as described in 4:6–11; whether in the sequence there described is not of immediate concern. There are the usual interpretations of divine punishment, as in the days of Elijah. But in the course of the plagues Amos has a vision and perceives the true message, that the nation is at risk and without repentance will be destroyed. We presume that Amos interceded immediately and there was a respite. Amos must then mount a campaign to preach repentance to the people. Nothing happens, and the other plagues come along. Finally the last plague, a terrible fire, reminiscent of the total destruction of Sodom and Gomorrah, wreaked fearful damage in the nation: "and you were like a brand plucked from what was burned." Again Amos has a vision and perceives that destruction of the nation is imminent. Again he intercedes and once again Yahweh relents, to give Amos a chance once more to preach repentance. And again the mission is a failure.

We cannot go farther in connecting the plagues of 4:6–11 with the visions. The match is only partial, and the subsequent visions do not invite a similar linkage. The first two visions are distinguished not only by Amos' successful intercession but also by the fact that they describe calamities as if they were actually happening, but were prevented from running their full course. The other visions do not have this kind of concreteness and immediacy.

The connection, if valid, gives Amos a direct involvement in the plagues, or at least two of them. But because all are presented on the same basis, we must suppose that his involvement was the same for all of them. Amos associates himself with Yahweh's disappointment and eventual exasperation over the people's failure to repent. There must have been oracles of repentance along with the plagues, and the result is coherent if Amos himself brought them. It can be further inferred that the first two visions led to an announcement that respite had been secured, while the second two visions would have been reported as a radical change in Yahweh's policy: no more postponements.

So we may now begin the historical account with the plagues and in particular the first plague. They provide the context in which Amos has his first pair of visions. It is very appropriate that they should do so, because whereas people generally—and the other prophets specifically—would interpret them as signs of divine displeasure and warnings about a further judgment to come, only Amos sees here the full import of the threat against the survival of the nation. He has a vision either before, during, or after the actual plague in question, but there is a correlation between them. We might then see Phase One as moving to a climax, even though the five plagues go round in the same way and the two visions are presented as similar in their outcome. We must ask if the explanation for mitigating the plagues *five* times, in spite of the fact that the people never repented under any of them, is that Amos made intercession five times, but only two of these interventions are reported as visions.

III.A.2. THE SECOND PAIR OF VISIONS AND INSERTION (7:7–8:3)

It will be seen that the heart of this unit, and hence of the book, is the section running from 7:7 through 8:3. Here, wrapped together, are the third and fourth visions, forming an envelope around the confrontation between Amos and Amaziah at Bethel. These two visions define the main phase of the message entrusted to the prophet, the certainty of doom and destruction, while the story reports the reaction when the message was delivered and points the way to the climax and conclusion in the final vision and Phase Three. Here we have in a single package the decisive confrontation between Yahweh and Amos, which determined the exact form and content of the prevailing message in the book, the prophet's role in delivering it, and the equally decisive but totally different confrontation between Amos and Amaziah, which settled the course of Israel's subsequent history. Brought together in a binocular tableau are God and prophet, prophet and priest, message and people in a dramatic and unforgettable juxtaposition: the book in brief.

The visions in the second pair are twins, like the first pair, but the presentation is different. The only biographical notice of Amos that we possess has been inserted between them. The contrast between the first-person autobiographical form of the visions and the third-person biographical form of the confrontation with Amaziah is enough to show that the canonical arrangement is editorial. But it is not casual or careless.

The introductory essay on The Book of Visions has shown how closely this incident has been woven into the visions. Here we need only remark the exact correspondence between Amaziah's prohibition—*lō' tôsîp 'ôd* (7:13)—and Yahweh's repeated decision—*lo' 'ôsîp 'ôd* (7:8, 8:2). There is clearly a close connection; but what is it?

If the confrontation had been placed between the first pair of visions and the second pair, the sequence would have suggested that Yahweh's decision in Visions 3 and 4 was a reaction to Amaziah's behavior. If the incident had followed the second pair of visions, the sequence would have suggested that Amaziah's rejection of Amos was his reaction to the messages of those visions. As it is, the decision of the editor to place that story right between the two visions of the second pair leaves the connection unresolved. It places that incident and those visions in the closest possible connection, but it does not indicate in which direction the connection (temporal or logical) goes. The contiguity of the first two visions suggests that the second pair were likewise originally adjacent. Indeed, there seems to have been an "autobiography" source consisting of those visions and nothing more. The formal differences between these four and the fifth (9:1), along with the detachment of the fifth from the others, throws some doubt on the fifth one (not enough, in our opinion, to warrant rejection of it) as part of that autobiography. But it is precisely the occurrence of the visions in pairs and the preservation of the first pair in contiguity that indicate that the editor's decision to override that original arrangement by inserting the story of the confrontation into the second pair must have been calculated with a view to achieving some quite specific effect.

When 7:7–8:3 is viewed as a compositional unit, its symmetry is evident. The two visions in the second set follow the same outline. In contrast to the global scope of the first two, in the second set Amos sees two everyday objects, a plumb line (if that is what it was) and a basket of summer fruit. Amos identifies these objects in response to a question. Yahweh then makes a comment on the names with an identical conclusion, "I shall never spare them again." There is no more interaction. Amos ventures no supplication.

In each case the immediate comment (7:8b, 8:2b) is elaborated into additional exposition (7:9, 8:3). These similarly positioned statements resemble each other in addition by targeting the cultus as the object of judgment, the sanctuaries (7:9) and their personnel (8:3). In addition, 7:9 names "Jeroboam's house" as marked down for direct personal attack by Yahweh "with my sword." Bethel has already been singled out for destruction (3:14, 5:5), but now for the first time (it is in fact the only time) the king is named and condemned.

It is very important to determine whether these verses are integral parts of the visions, for both 7:9 and 8:3 are the points at which the confrontation of 7:10–17 is firmly grasped. The setting of the confrontation in the cultus is framed by the judgments against the cultus in 7:9 and 8:3. If these verses are only editorial joins, made to carry the story of the confrontation, then the actual (i.e., historical, not just literary) connection of the confrontation with the visions is not demonstrated. But if these verses belong to the vision experiences (and are not just later expansions of them), then the connections between the visions and the confrontation are quite strong. The two predictions of what Yahweh is going to do now (7:9 and 8:3) are essential to the visions. Without such statements the meaning of the repeated "I will never again pass by them" is unclear and could be misunderstood. In the first two visions, Yahweh's replies (both virtually identical) explain or imply what he will not do. He will arrest the plague (if it is in progress already in the real world) or cancel it (if it is seen only as a threat in the vision), so that little Jacob will survive. "I will not pass by" could mean "I will not visit them again." But the connection of this affirmation with the Great Set Speech shows that it means "I will not spare them again, I will not remove the plagues again [as I have already done in the first two visions]." In the visions themselves the ambiguity of 7:8bB and 8:2bB is resolved by the judgment oracles that immediately follow.

The tokens of these close original connections remain in the themes of 7:7–8:3 and in the vocabulary used to present the material. As already observed, the focus throughout is on the cultus and its officials, including the king, in a manner different from the interest in other parts of the book (in 2:8 and in 5:5, 21–23 it is the worshipers who are attacked). The name "Isaac," with its peculiar spelling, is found in both components (7:9a, 7:16b), as is the name Jeroboam (7:9b, 10). Also, *bqrb ʿmy yśrʾl* (v 8) // *bqrb byt yśrʾl* (v 10).

These observations about the literary integrity of 7:7–8:3 and the inference that it arises from a single historical situation do not permit a more precise analysis of the logical connections (cause and effect) between visions and confrontation. In the essay on the phases in Amos' ministry and at other places throughout this study, we have explored this problem from many angles. The best reconstruction we can propose is to identify the failure of the people to repent (4:6–11) as the main reason for the transition from Phase One (first two visions and The Book of Woes) to Phase Two (The Book of Doom). The Book of Doom proclaims the now inevitable judgment, as does the second pair of visions.

The suitability of the Great Set Speech (chaps. 1–2) as the main part of Amos' discourse in the precincts of the shrine at Bethel is generally recognized by scholars. We go farther and suggest that all of chaps. 1–6 derives from the accumulation of Amos' preaching. The Book of Woes (or material of which it is a representative selection) was included to supply needed background from Phase One as *apologia* for Amos and as justification for Yahweh.

The severity of the confrontation with Amaziah, whatever its practical consequences, brings us very close to the end of Amos' career. With Amaziah's prohibition of further prophecy on the part of Amos, the situation deteriorates even more, and the last vision ushers in the third phase, with judgments even more severe than those in Phase Two.

Amaziah's intervention is, then, a last-minute attempt to silence Amos. The judgment has come too close to home. Amos' mention of the king (7:9 —he could, of course, have named him in other oracles, not now recorded, but speculation of this kind gives us little assistance in understanding the book that we now have) gave Amaziah the firm grounds he needed to accuse Amos of sedition. And this point suggests that a report of the third vision was part of his preaching at Bethel and up and down the country, because Amaziah declares that "the land cannot endure all his words" (v 10b). The two visions go together, and the judgment against the cultus (7:9, 8:3) was seen by Amaziah as an even more direct and personal threat to which he was bound to respond.

Finally, we should point out that the presentation of 7:7–8:3 is another instance of a pattern in which two blocks of material (here visions and confrontation) are joined tightly by sandwiching one inside the other.

III.A.2.a. THE THIRD VISION (7:7–9)

7 ⁷Thus he showed me: Indeed my Lord was standing beside a plastered wall (wall of *'ănāk*), with a lump of tin (*'ănāk*) in his hand. ⁸Yahweh said to me, "What do you see, Amos?" I said, "A lump of tin (*'ănāk*)." My Lord said, "Soon I will put grief (*'ănāk*) in the midst of my people Israel. I shall not spare them again."

9a   "The high places of Isaac will be devastated,
            and Israel's sanctuaries will be laid waste;
9b   and I shall attack Jeroboam's house with my sword."

NOTES

7:7–9. This vision is the most obscure of all. The difficulty arises because the meaning of the keyword *'ănāk* remains uncertain. It is difficult to exercise restraint in view of this unfortunate fact, because the traditional picture of Yahweh standing with a plumb bob in his hand, apparently testing the trueness of a wall (the wall being Israel) is one of the most familiar and best loved of all of the depictions in the book of Amos. The account is completed with the application of the vision to the people of Israel and the ominous words of judgment that parallel the similar treatment in the fourth vision, 8:2. The added pronouncement in v 9 serves as a bridge to the narrative in 7:10–17, while the corresponding comment at the end of the fourth vision (8:3) serves to conclude the presentation of the first four visions.

The oracle in v 9 has a certain poetic quality, though the last clause is indistinguishable from good literary prose.

		Syllables	Stresses
9aA	wĕnāšammû bāmôt yiśḥāq	8	3
9aB	ûmiqdĕšê yiśrāʾēl yeḥĕrābû	10	3
9b	wĕqamtî ʿal-bêt yārobʿām beḥāreb	10	4

The bicolon in v 9a is well formed, with close, if not synonymous parallelism between verbs and nouns and straightforward double chiasm. Note as well the balance between the perfect (wnšmw) and imperfect (yḥrbw) verbs. The terms yśḥq and yśrʾl here are synonymous, referring to the northern kingdom, while bmwt and mqdšy may be complementary descriptions of the sanctuaries at the high places of the country. Presumably the combination would include both temple buildings such as the one at Bethel and the open-air sanctuaries elsewhere in the land.

The last clause (v 9b) introduces the narrative concerning the confrontation between Amos and Amaziah at the Temple in Bethel and forms an envelope around the whole story with v 17bB, the last clause in that verse:

9b　　　and I shall attack Jeroboam's house with my sword

17bB　and Israel shall surely go into exile from its land.

That the two statements belong together and form a single statement, split for literary or rhetorical purposes, is shown by the partial paraphrase provided by Amaziah in citing this statement by Amos as part of the formal charge to the king. Thus in 7:11 we read:

For Amos has said the following:
　　"By the sword shall Jeroboam die,
　　and Israel shall surely go into exile from its land."

The two statements, which we take to be equivalent—though Amaziah's version is more provocative and probably designed to attract the king's attention if not stir him to vigorous action—form an axis that connects the beginning and end of the story and fixes a central point about which the narrative turns. In both versions, we are dealing with literary prose, hardly verse.

7:7. *Thus he showed me.* The verb is the same in the four paired visions, and in the other three has "my Lord Yahweh" as subject. The fact that an explicit subject is lacking here could be an original stylistic variation of no consequence or the result of a simple error. The presence of a subject "Lord" (= Yahweh) in the LXX and in the Vulgate has some value but is not decisive, considering their tendency to level things through. What makes the point worth discussing is the fact that the next clause also differs from the corresponding ones in Visions 1 and 2. There *hinnēh* is followed immediately by a participle; in Vision 1 there is no subject; in Vision 2 it comes later. Verse 7aB has normal syntax, and the subject *'ădōnāy* (alone, i.e., without the usual *yhwh;* cf. vv 7:8b, 9:1) is confirmed by the Vulgate's *Dominus.* It is lacking, however, in the LXX. An inner Greek variant supplies "a man" (cf. JB, NEB), patently interpretive, either to avoid the anthropomorphism or to make it easier to manage the four occurrences of *'ănāk* that are so hard to put into a single picture. The fifth vision also presents the Lord as standing (same participle) beside something, so that detail is unobjectionable.

standing. The use of the root *nṣb,* "station oneself," rather than, say, *'md,* does not permit fine distinctions to be made. It is worth remembering, however, that Yahweh usually sits enthroned as king in sessions of the heavenly council, so this vision experience is different from the usual involvement in the divine *sôd.* There is no need to suppose that anyone but Yahweh and Amos were involved.

beside. Compare *'al* in 9:1. Beginning with the LXX's *epi* the preposition has sometimes been interpreted as "upon" (JPS).

plastered wall. The interpretation of this word depends on the meaning of *'ănāk;* but the meaning of this word, which occurs nowhere else in the Bible, can only be inferred from its context. That context, unfortunately, yields little in the way of clues. We are in a vicious circle. The most plausible explanation is that putting the *'ănāk* "in the midst of my people Israel" is like putting a plumb-line against a wall to test the accuracy of the workmanship. The image is certainly colorful and is helpful in homilies; but there is no evidence to support it, and the several objections to it, in their accumulation, make the proposal doubtful. Unfortunately we have nothing better to suggest in its place; and solutions that resort to emendation, however ingenious, do not have the same claim as one that succeeds in making sense of the text.

From the text itself it may be inferred that an *'ănāk* is a visible object that may be held in the hand. It can be an attribute of a wall, and placing it "in the midst of" the people of a nation brings about (or symbolizes) devastation. The meaning "plumb-line" can be made to fit all of this if a wall of *'ănāk* is a wall built with the help of a plumb-line, and putting the plumb-line into the midst of Israel means testing the trueness (straightness, moral uprightness) of people. Taking the last point first: if Yahweh is about to put the plumb-line "against" the wall, why is the term "among" (*bqrb*) used? Does it have a different reference when it is used again in v 10? If it is what Amos is talking about, why does he not use the standard expression "line" (*qāw*) and "plummet" (*mišqōlet*)?

The scholars of antiquity did not know the meaning of the word *'ănāk:* Targum *dīn,* "judgment"; Vulgate "a wall of plaster"; the Greek versions variously "adamantine," "molten" (Theodotion), "shining" (Aquila), which at least indicate that it is some kind of metal. Jerome already knew the meaning "tin," which has support from comparative Semitic lexicography. Akkadian *anāku* means "tin" or "lead" (*AHW* 1:49), but the latter is debatable (Landsberger 1965:285ff.). The point is important, for if it means only "tin," it is less likely to refer to a specific implement made out of another metal (lead).

The fourth vision provides a possible control for this investigation. The two visions are very much alike in form, and presumably the interlocution works in the same way. The discussion of the two operational terms, *'ănāk* and *qāyiṣ*, proceeds along similar lines. Both begin with a two-word phrase (*ḥōmat 'ănāk*//*kĕlûb qayiṣ*) and then concentrate on the second term.

	VISION 3	VISION 4
Amos sees	ḥōmat 'ănāk	kĕlûb qāyiṣ
	'ănāk	
He answers	'ănāk	kĕlûb qāyiṣ
Yahweh says	'ănāk	haqqēṣ

The switch from *qāyiṣ* to *qēṣ* in the fourth vision shows that a play on two similar words is involved. They could even be homonyms in the northern dialect, in which the diphthong would contract so that *qêṣ < *qayṣ* is like *qēṣ <*qiṣṣ*. The word "basket" was accordingly added to secure the meaning of "summer fruit" and to prepare the way for the wordplay that follows. The movement is from something concrete and visible, "a basket of summer fruit," to something abstract, "the end." A similar play on words takes place in the visions of Jeremiah (chap. 1). There is a palpable wisdom ingredient in this kind of jump from one thought to another with no more connection than a superficial (purely phonological) similarity between words (punning; Lindblom 1955). Does the third vision resemble the fourth vision in this detail as well? If so, the *'ănāk* is an object that Amos sees in Yahweh's hand, but the *'ănāk* that Yahweh is going to put in the midst of Israel is something else, perhaps not an object at all. This analysis redefines the problem, but it does not solve it. In fact, it makes it worse, because now we need two meanings for *'ănāk* and we lack even one.

It is usually assumed that *'ănāk* has the same meaning in its three unmodified occurrences. It has even been possible to give it the same meaning in *ḥōmat 'ănāk* by paraphrasing, "a wall built with a plumb-line." As already mentioned, the phrase was understood differently in antiquity, *'ănāk* being identified as the material the wall was built of—presumably some metal (or plaster [Vulgate]). In the mythic realm, of course, the palaces of the gods are built of precious stones and metals, but such a detail seems extraneous in the present connection. The reference to the wall can be made more natural if the first *'ănāk* is either deleted (JB, NEB) or emended to *'eben* (Rudolph 1971a:234). Verse 7 then presents a single picture, "My Lord was standing beside a wall [the nature of the wall is not important] with an *'ănāk* in his hand."

The wall, as the starting point of the vision, has been explained as the initial stimulus for free association in reverie that passed into ecstasy. "Amos happened to be watching a workman testing a wall with a plumb-line. Soon the prophet's mind passed into fantasy. The workman became Jehovah himself; the wall, about to be broken up because of its faulty condition, was Israel" (Cripps 1969:97). If that explanation is correct, the symbolism is allegorical, and no play on the meaning of *'ănāk* is involved. The greatest difficulty in the way of this interpretation lies in verse 8b, especially if v 9 is its continuation. Wolff (1977:295) eludes this difficulty by insisting that v 9 was not part of the vision. If the third and fourth visions come out at the same point, then the sayings "never again" and "the end has come" are the same. But to put the plumb-line against the wall is not the end, but only the beginning of judgment. Yahweh is about to put an *'ănāk* "in the midst" of Israel, not "against" it (*'al*), as one would do with a wall. This action will bring about the devastation described in v 9. Hence the suspicion that the *'ănāk* to be placed in the midst of Israel is not a plumb-line, but a different implement, a crowbar or a chisel (Rudolph 1971a:234–35) or even a battering ram (as suggested by Marti, 1904), presumably also made out of *'ănāk*. More adventurous is Riedel's (1902) proposal to read *'ănakkeh,* "I shall smite"; but this emendation requires further adjustments in the text. Horst's (1929) reading *'ănāḥâ,* "groaning," recognizes the problem; but the solution is too drastic. Verse 8b implies an act of demolition, not just of measurement; hence the suggestion of the JPS footnote to read "pickax" throughout.

A remarkable feature of these visions is the fact that Amos shows no curious interest in the appearance of Yahweh himself—even less than Isaiah, who is reticent enough on this point and who tells more about the appearance of the seraphim than about Yahweh. In the fifth vision Amos saw Yahweh "standing beside *the* altar" (same idiom). There is no interlocution, no interest in the visual side of the experience. The oracle follows immediately. The definite article points to a specific object, and without further explanation it must be the main altar of the (Bethel) shrine. The destruction that follows is aimed at the same installation. A similar connection should be sought between the wall and the people of Israel in the third vision.

The first two visions are unified by the idea of devouring. There is no similar connection between Visions 3 and 4. Indeed, there is a formal similarity between Visions 3 and 5 (Yahweh standing beside something). In view of the identical pronouncement "I shall never spare them again" and the similarities between the two following judgment oracles (7:9, 8:3) the indications are that "the end is coming for my people Israel" and "Soon I will bring *'ănāk* among my people Israel" should be very close in meaning.

8. *I said, "A lump of tin."* Amos is referring to the *'ănāk* in Yahweh's hand, not to the "wall of *'ănāk*" just mentioned.

I will put. Perhaps the best solution of the problem of *'ănāk* in Amos 7:7–8 is to recognize the presence of three different roots or words in the four occurrences of *'nk*. In later Mishnaic and Talmudic Hebrew two different words are attested. Thus the *ḥômat 'ănāk* would be a glazed or plastered wall, so rendered in the Vulgate, indicating that Jerome was aware of this word in contemporary Hebrew and in the rabbinic tradition. For the second and third occurrences we would hold to the meaning "a lump of tin" held in the hand of Yahweh and seen by Amos. In the final occurrence we recognize still another word *'ănāk* with the meaning "grief, wrong, oppression"; cf. TB Baba Metsia, 59a, where the connection with Amos 7:8 is noted. Here we find the play on words needed for the ominous meaning of the vision and comparable to the punning in the fourth vision. Hence the rendering: "I will put grief in the midst of my people Israel."

spare. The exact meaning of *'ăbôr* in this context (and in 8:2) is hard to pin down, making it difficult to find out what it is Yahweh says he will never do for Israel again. It must be something that he has done previously, or has been doing up until this point. In the context of the Book of Visions, this action, now to be discontinued or not to be repeated, can only be the positive response to Amos' intercessions in the first two visions. At that time the Lord desisted from the destructive punishment; now he will not. There is an implication that it is useless for Amos to intercede.

The two pairs of visions and the ensuing dialogues develop in quite opposite ways. Indeed they were set up differently from the beginning. The first two visions are open and obvious; the destruction is well under way and there can be no mistaking the outcome. Amos immediately perceives what is going on and spontaneously intervenes. In complete contrast to this, the second pair of visions is obscure and enigmatic. The *'ănāk* and the basket are not transparent symbols, so Amos does not know how to respond to them. He has to be questioned, and cannot avoid pronouncing the words whose meaning he does not yet know, but whose meaning precludes intercession.

This helps us to fill out the implications of *'ăbôr* in 7:8 and 8:2. The Lord will never again mitigate or arrest or cancel the judgment. On the contrary, he will carry out the sentence, and the two following oracles (7:9; 8:3) give the details (because Wolff [1977:301] does not accept the connection of these oracles with the visions, he says that they "report no decision concerning the form of punishment"). Even so, it is curious that the core of these oracles is a statement of what Yahweh will not do, or will not continue to do, or will not do again. The verb 'br was not used to describe any previous action, now never to be repeated. We have to discover the reference of 'br entirely by study of the context. But does this inferred meaning for 'br agree with its use in other places? In Amos 5:17 Yahweh says "I will pass, 'e'ĕbōr, in your midst," causing weeping and wailing. An exactly opposite meaning is required in 7:8; 8:2, where not passing brings destruction. "Passing over" as the opposite of judging is met in the idiom 'br 'l-peša' (Mic 7:18; Prov 19:11), and lô in Amos 7:8; 8:2 matches lišᵊ'ērît naḥălātô in Mic 7:18. The meaning of the verb itself is so general that it requires an object to give it palpable context, and when the object is tôrâ, ḥōq or bĕrît it means "transgress," or "disregard," and can parallel "forget" (Deut 26:13), as noted by Waldman 1973.

With the meaning of "overlook," the object can be one's own duty, or another's failure. In the latter sense it means to "forgive" as in Mic 7:18. Amos 5:17 shows that 'br describes movement through physical space (Exod 17:5); but when forgiveness is described as the removal of sin, the hip'îl of 'br is used (Zec 3:4). Mic 7:18 remains the best clue, where 'ōbēr 'al-peša' is parallel to nōśē' 'āwōn with all its echoes of Exod 34:7. Furthermore, comparison with lišᵊ'ērît in Mic 7:18 shows that lô in Amos 7:8; 8:2 is not the direct object, as in most translations, but an ethical dative. Hence we can infer that peša' is the understood object of 'br, and provides another link between the second pair of visions and the oracles against the eight nations, where peša' is a key word.

9. This oracle is in two parts: v 9a is directed against the cultus, v 9b against the king. Verse 9a is a well-formed bicolon and reads as follows:

	Syllables	Stresses
wĕnāšammû bāmôt yiśḥāq	8	3
ûmiqdĕsê yiśrā'ēl yeḥĕrābû	10	3

The second line is a little long by classical norms. The standard line in much of Hebrew poetry is 8 : 8 = 16 syllables and 3 : 3 stresses or accents. The chiasmus is complete and perfectly balanced. The alternation of perfect with imperfect verb is not quite classical, for the waw-consecutive (with the perfect nšmw) is more at home in later poetry and prose. The parallelism of Isaac and Israel is unusual, but its occurrence again in v 16 suggests that it is deliberate and significant.

The third line has no immediate parallel, but its connections with v 9a show that we have a tricolon. The opening verb is like the one in v 9aA (also a perfect form with waw-consecutive), and the last word, beḥāreb, echoes the verb at the end of v 9aB (sharing three consonants). As shown by comparison with v 11, its literary connection is with the last clause in v 17, with which it forms a rhetorical envelope around the whole story

(7:9–17) of the confrontation between Amos and Amaziah. The point made here and repeated later is that the confrontation turned into conflagration because of the double pronouncements at the beginning and end, also in the middle: the end of the house of Jeroboam by the sword (9b) and the sending of Israel into exile (17b; cf. v 11).

Coote denies the statement to Amos as part of his argument for dating the prophet to about 722 B.C.E. According to Coote, a seventh-century Judean editor added the detail so as to bring Amos into conflict with the namesake of the founder of the Bethel shrine (1981:20–24).

9a. *Isaac*. The spelling with *ś* instead of the usual *ṣ* occurs twice here. Its occurrence again in Jer 33:26 and Ps 105:9 (= 1 Chr 16:16) shows that it is a legitimate variant. In those places Abraham//Isaac. The pairing of Isaac and Israel is unique and leads to the question of the contemporary connotation of the terms. When repeated in v 16 it is "the house of Isaac." The context suggests that here Isaac is a surrogate for the northern kingdom, for the following reasons:

1. The parallel "Israel" (unmodified) usually refers to the northern kingdom in Amos;
2. King Jeroboam is named;
3. the setting is the Bethel shrine.

Elsewhere in the Bible all of Isaac's connections are with the south, and specifically with Beer-sheba. In v 16 the LXX replaces Isaac with Jacob, an easier reading. But in v 9 it reads "high places of laughter," confirming the MT (perhaps *yṣ'q* instead of *yś'q*) but evading the word "Isaac."

9b. *Jeroboam*. For the first time Amos has openly criticized the royal family. "Jeroboam's house" could mean his realm; but the nation is usually called Israel or Joseph (or Isaac). It could also mean the dynasty or the present royal family, but in all cases the king himself would be included.

Judgment is given against the people of Israel (v 8). The particular targets are the cult installations (v 9a) and the royal family (v 9b). Verse 17 additionally threatens exile (included in Amaziah's report [v 11]). Up to this point the king has not been openly criticized in the messages for Israel. Most of the oracles in the first set against the nations include a threat against the ruler, his capital, or both, as well as exile for the nation (1:5) or for the king and his court (1:15). The oracle against Israel (2:6–8) does not include any punishment. Amos 7:9 supplies this lack.

The threat that emerges from the series of plagues (chap. 4) does not culminate in specific details either. Amos 4:12 does not go on to say what God "will do"; it is stated later in the book in connection with the visions.

In any case, the king cannot be excluded from the Woes and plagues set out in chaps. 4–6. The leadership is attacked at many points. In other stories it is the king who leads national repentance to avert the Lord's punishment (Jer 26:19; Jonah 3; 2 Chr 12:5–7). In the opening oracles punishment of the ruler and punishment of the nation are the same.

If Amos expected v 9 to be fulfilled literally, and soon, events proved otherwise. As far as we know Jeroboam died of natural causes; he certainly enjoyed a long reign of more than forty years, was immensely successful in the battlefield, and outlived Amos' prophecy for many years, if we are correct in placing the prophet's career early rather than late in that reign. Jeroboam's house came to an end with the assassination of his son Zechariah, and it was another twenty years at least before the sanctuaries were demolished.

III.A.2.b. FIRST INSERTION: THE CONFRONTATION (7:10–17)

7 ¹⁰Then Amaziah the priest of Bethel sent word to Jeroboam, the king of Israel: "Amos has conspired against you inside the house of Israel; the land cannot endure all his words.

11a   For Amos has said the following:
         'By the sword shall Jeroboam die,
11b   and Israel shall surely go into exile from its land.'"

¹²Then Amaziah said to Amos: "O seer, go, run away to the land of Judah. ¹³Eat your food there, and there do your prophesying. But at Bethel never prophesy again, because it is the king's chapel, it is a royal temple."

¹⁴Then Amos answered Amaziah: "I was no prophet, nor was I trained as a prophet, but I am a cattleman and a dresser of sycamores. ¹⁵And Yahweh took me from following the flock. And Yahweh said to me: 'Go prophesy to my people Israel.' ¹⁶Now hear Yahweh's word! You say,

         'Don't prophesy against Israel,
         and don't preach against Isaac's domain!'
17a   Yahweh, on the contrary, has said the following:
         'Your wife shall become a prostitute in the city,
         your sons and your daughters shall fall by the sword;

your land shall be parceled out by the measuring line;
17b   you yourself shall die in a polluted land;   .
and Israel shall surely go into exile from its land.' "

INTRODUCTION

In contrast to the autobiographical visions, this episode is biographical.
But its association with the visions is close and extensive, at least in literary
terms and as far as the final edition of the book is concerned. What the
original historical connections may have been is harder to say.

The episode now reads like a fragment of a story. The abrupt beginning,
"And Amaziah said . . ." with *waw*-consecutive, lacks the kind of lead-in
(usually a time reference) that is usual at the onset of a narrative in Hebrew
storytelling. Likewise, it does not end; it breaks off at its most dramatic
point, at the climax, when tension has reached its highest pitch. The confrontation leads to words of increasing violence, until Amos pronounces
judgment against Amaziah in the most direct and personal terms (v 17).
Something had to happen after that. Just as Amos did not follow Amaziah's orders meekly, so it is impossible to believe that Amaziah simply
listened to Amos' message and then allowed the prophet to go about his
business. Unfortunately we are told nothing. Speculation can suggest various dénouements, but nothing is known and nothing can be known. The
editor obviously told the story not to provide an account of Amos' life but
to present an oracle about Amaziah.

The story has been composed to fit the pair of visions into which it is
now inserted. In the visions, if nowhere else in the book, we reach the
closest possible point to original and authentic Amos compositions. In view
of the replicated forms of the two pairs and their autobiographical form, we
must conclude that in their first expression these visions made a solid,
continuous block (whether the fifth one was an immediate continuation of
the original series is a distinct question, not germane to the present issue).
The editor has managed to attach the confrontation episode to the second
pair of visions in a way that makes for smooth reading. It is a token of his
skill in making the joins that scholars are not sure whether the oracle in v 9
is part of the third vision or an editorial transition from that vision to the
confrontation. Because of the balance between 7:9 and 8:3 we think that
these two oracles are the outcome of their respective visions. More specifically, 7:9 is the starting point and chief provocation for Amaziah's outburst. It was clearly not the only provocation, albeit possibly the latest and
worst, for Amaziah refers to "all" of Amos' words, which have been spread
throughout the land (v 10b). The naming of the king in v 9 gave Amaziah a

most incriminating pretext for reporting Amos to Jeroboam and for ordering him to stop prophesying.

In spite of the immediate continuity secured by the words "Israel" and
"Jeroboam" repeated (in chiasmus) from v 9 to v 10, we must suppose a
sharp break at that point in the original occurrence. In vv 7–8 Amos is face
to face with Yahweh in a vision; in vv 10–17 he is face to face with Amaziah
in Bethel. This gap can be narrowed if we suppose that 7:1–9 represent the
actual words spoken by Amos in Bethel, reporting his visions. At the end of
the third vision Amaziah interrupts (v 12), having already sent a report to
the king (vv 10–11). If we look for the beginning of such a narrative, we
have to go back to 1:1–2. "And he said" in 1:2 introduces Amos' consolidated messages (in the NOTES on these words we left it open whether "he"
might refer to Yahweh, so that the whole verse is spoken by Amos; but the
more natural interpretation is to ascribe these words to the narrator). The
narrative structure of the complete book is then quite simple. There is a
heading or title (1:1) with a time reference ("two years before the earthquake"). "And he [Amos] said . . ." carries 1:2–7:9 as "the words of
Amos."

The narration then continues with 7:10, "Then Amaziah sent . . ." No
location is given. But the way the story is now told points to Bethel as the
final locale of Amos' total message in its accumulated form. This reading
indicates that the confrontation with Amaziah took place two years before
the earthquake.

The story of the confrontation itself (vv 10–17) shows considerable artistry. The narrative portions, as distinct from the dialogue, are composed in
standard prose, as might be expected. The message to the king (oral, but
possibly in the form of a letter) is itself a small narrative. It contains Amaziah's account and summary of Amos' activity (v 10b) along with a specimen of his oracles (v 11), the one Amaziah considered to be most incriminating. Amaziah's words to Jeroboam (v 10b) are virtually a bicolon, and
his words to Amos (vv 12–13) have considerable literary merit.

The narrative framework of the confrontation proper is quite simple:
"Then Amaziah said to Amos . . ." (v 12) "And Amos answered
Amaziah . . ." (v 14). There is not a word about time, place, circumstances, causes, or consequences. It is hardly a story at all, for there is no
buildup, no development, no dénouement—only an exchange of one speech
each; hardly a dialogue. By his parsimony, the narrator has avoided all
distractions and restricted the interest entirely to the spoken words. And
those words present the central issue of the book: the rejection of the word
of true prophecy by the highest representative of the nation's religious life,
and the prophet's refusal to desist.

Amos' reply consists of two parts. The first (vv 14–15) is a story within a
story. It reports his personal background (v 14) and his call (v 15). The

latter is reported with minimal essentials. The words of Yahweh's commission (v 15) are brief. The second part of Amos' reply moves on to declare another oracle, this time a direct rejoinder to what Amaziah has just said. The use of "therefore" twice gives the oracle two layers. First Yahweh said, "Prophesy!" *Therefore* Amos prophesies (v 16). Then Amaziah said, "Don't prophesy!" *Therefore* he and his family are doomed (v 17).

The themes and tensions of the confrontation are thus seen to be complex and closely interwoven. It is full of contrasts. Amaziah's report of Amos' activity as "conspiracy" (vv 10–11) contrasts with Amos' own account of his activity as compulsion (vv 14–15). Amaziah orders Amos to be silent (vv 12–13, 16b); Yahweh orders Amos to speak out (vv 14–15). Amos' reported prediction of the king's death and the people's exile (v 11b) is matched by a similar prediction of death for the priest and his children and the exile of the people (v 17b).

The story of the confrontation is pinned into the third vision by some verbal links: "in the midst of my people [the house of] Israel" (vv 8, 10); Jeroboam (vv 9, 10, 11); the sword (vv 9, 11); sanctuary (vv 9, 13). Earlier critics did not notice, or at least did not appreciate, these compositional details, which justify the retention of 7:10–17 where it is. Preferring a simple and neater presentation, in which the five visions come in unbroken succession, 7:10–17 was placed either before them (Baumann 1903:52) or after them (Löhr 1901:27). Instead of blaming its present unsuitable position on a thoughtless editor or scribe, we accept the features described above as evidence of deliberate artistry, so that we can proceed to ask what effect was intended by bringing the materials into that partly symmetrical, partly lopsided structure.

NOTES

7:10. *sent.* A messenger, possibly with a letter. But the usual epistolary formulas are lacking.

Amaziah. The shorter postexilic form of the name points to modernization either in transmission or, more likely, in the preparation of the final edition of the twelve Minor Prophets as a single collection. This adjustment can be associated with the introduction of a considerable number of "modern spellings," as found throughout the book. Cripps (1969:73) drew attention to the *plene* spellings *ypwl* (9:9), *dwyd* (9:11), *ḥwrš* (9:13), and *qwṣr* (9:13; but L is *defective* here) in the Epilogue, arguing from the greater proportion of them for a late date. But the concentration of *plene* spellings in the Epilogue is not disproportionate. They are found throughout the book, for example, in the Hymns—*ywṣr* (4:13), *qwr'* (5:8), *ybw'* (5:9), *nwg'*

(9:5), *tmwg* (9:5), *ywšby* (9:5), and *bwnh* (9:6). Even the visions, the originality of which no one doubts, have been touched up in this way—*ywṣr* (7:1), *lʾkwl* (7:2), and *ʿbwr* (7:8, 8:2). The name Uzziah also has its shorter postexilic form in 1:1 (cf. Hos 1:1; Mic 1:1; Zech 1:1; and contrast Isa 1:1; Jer 1:1). In view of the common editorial procedures reflected in these headings, the divergence of the Minor Prophets in this detail represents a scribal development in that group of spelling norms later than those in the major prophets.

the priest of Bethel. The title is unique. It points to a head priest of a specific shrine. No other Israelite priest is so named, not for any temple or city; the title "the priest of Yahweh" is used only once (1 Sam 14:3). The plural occurs in 1 Sam 22:17–21; Isa 61:6; and 2 Chr 13:9. Other priests are identified by their city—the priest of On (three times in Genesis 41–42)—by their country—Jethro of Midian (Exod 3:1, 18:1)—or by their god—Baal (2 Kgs 11:18 = 2 Chr 23:17), Dagon (1 Sam 5:5). Because he bore a Yahwistic name, Amaziah presumably belonged to a line of orthodox priests, attending to the legitimate interests of the most important cult installation of the northern kingdom. On precisely these grounds does he seek to eject Amos (v 13).

conspired. The root *qšr* has connotations of organizing a group for purposes of insurrection and revolution (2 Sam 15:12; 2 Kgs 11:14; 12:21; 14:19; and 15:15, 30, all involving an attempt on the life of the monarch), or treachery against a suzerain (2 Kgs 17:4) or against God (Jer 11:9). In 1 Sam 22:7–8 Saul complains that the Benjaminites are all conspiring with David against him (cf. vv 11–19). The verb describes Baasha's murder of Nadab (1 Kgs 15:27), Zimri's murder of Elah (1 Kgs 16:16), Jehu's murder of Joram (2 Kgs 9:14, 10:9), Shallum's murder of Zechariah (2 Kgs 15:10), Pekah's of Pekahiah (2 Kgs 15:25), Hoshea's of Pekah (2 Kgs 15:30), and the assassination of Amon (2 Kgs 21:24). Prophets, notably Elisha, were often behind such developments, and Amaziah evidently thought that Amos was up to something similar. At least he wanted to give Jeroboam that impression. In making his report, Amaziah also assures the king that Amos has no popular support; in fact, "the land cannot endure all his words."

Rosenbaum locates *qešer* in a semantic field that includes Hebrew words for subversion, rebellion, etc., and concludes that it means precisely "treason" rather than sedition. From this he deduces that Amos was a northerner. Yet he does not include *pešaʿ* in the discussion. His argument becomes more tenuous when he identifies 9:11–15 as Amos' treasonable message, "that hegemony in the divided kingdom would pass from Israel to Judah" (1977:132–34). But there is no hint of such a plot at the crucial point of confrontation with Amaziah. And we have shown that Amos' critique is aimed equally at both kingdoms.

Two things have to be considered in estimating the gravamen of Amaziah's charge: first, the accuracy of his quotation of Amos' words (v 11); second, his interpretation of Amos' preaching as "conspiracy." We do not have to quibble over the verbal differences between what Amos said in v 9 and what Amaziah said that Amos said in v 11. The only significant difference between the two statements is that in v 11 Jeroboam himself is singled out as the target of "the sword," while in v 9 it is "The house of Jeroboam." It has been proposed that v 9 reflects a revision of the original prophecy (quoted in v 11) to accommodate the historical fact that Jeroboam was not killed by the sword. Hence "The house of Jeroboam" in v 9 is interpreted as excluding Jeroboam and referring to the family or dynasty of Jeroboam, a reflection of the report that Jeroboam's son Zechariah was assassinated shortly after taking the throne (2 Kgs 15:8–11).

We do not think the argument is persuasive or convincing. We think that the two statements are essentially equivalent, with one emphasizing the attack on the king and the other including the dynasty, which would be normal in such cases. When a usurper assassinated the king, it was taken for granted that he would also make every effort to eliminate all possible heirs to the throne. In his prophecy about Amaziah, Amos includes his children in the sentence of death. With respect to Jeroboam, the statement in v 9 would include the king as head of his house, and v 11, by implication, would extend to the other members of the family, especially potential heirs. Had Amos or an editor wished to exclude the king from such a judgment, other language was available, as for example the prophecy uttered by Huldah about the kingdom of Judah during the reign of Josiah (2 Kgs 22:14–20). Huldah specifically exempts Josiah from the coming destruction of the kingdom and states that "you shall be gathered to your grave in peace" (v 20). Unlike Jeroboam, who died peacefully, Josiah died violently at Megiddo at the hands of Pharaoh Neco II of Egypt.

There is no indication that Amos was involved in political machinations to achieve the fulfillment of his own prophecies. Nevertheless, the menace of his words (v 9) could not be mistaken. Even if not anointed to the task, as Jehu and Hazael were, an adventurer like Shallum, murderer of Jeroboam's son, could claim that he was fulfilling the command of God and could have appealed to the words of the prophet for validation of his action.

endure. The word literally means "contain." Jeremiah 20:9 has the same idiom and must have the same sense:

> It was in my heart like a burning fire,
> bound up in my bones:
> and I was weary to contain it (*kalkēl*),
> and I was not able (*lō' 'ûkāl*).

The *hip'il* (as in Amos 7:10) is used literally in Jer 6:11 and figuratively in Jer 10:10 (the nations cannot contain Yahweh's wrath) and Joel 2:11 (no one can endure the Day of Yahweh). Compared with these passages, Amaziah's statement could express anxiety that Amos' words, if not suppressed, might prove to be more than the land can sustain, in other words, they will bring about the ruin of the country (along with that of the king). Certainly Amos' messages were directed against the whole nation, including its leadership.

11. *For Amos has said.* The introductory formula is a parody of the normal prophetic utterance: *kōh 'āmar yhwh.* Amaziah clearly rejects Amos' claim that the words are those of Yahweh and that he is only the messenger bearing them. He is eager to attribute the words to Amos, thereby convicting him of sedition out of his own mouth, while denying that the latter is a true prophet or that there is any link with Yahweh.

shall Jeroboam die. Amaziah's version of v 9bB is more explicit about Jeroboam, but it is not inconsistent with the latter.

exile. There is no previous report of Amos having said the exact words of 11b, but he does say them in v 17bB, and the same reinforced verb—*gālōh yigleh*—occurs in 5:5. Israel is threatened with exile in 5:27; 6:7. It is important to note how deeply embedded is the threat of exile in the authentic prophecies of Amos. Even if we give him the latest possible date, it has to be before the death of Jeroboam about 746 B.C.E., well before the beginning of Tiglath-pileser III's campaigns in the following decade. At that stage the seriousness of the threat would have become apparent to any thoughtful person. Even more, when these things began to happen in actuality, Amos' prophecies would at long last have attained a credibility that they did not achieve in his lifetime, at least not among the leaders.

There is also a sharp discrepancy between the two parts of Amaziah's version of Amos' message. They cannot be parts of the same scenario. A conspiracy against the king would be an internal movement, a plot by a usurper who removes the king and takes over the country. Such conspiracies had already occurred many times in Israel's history and once in Judah's (Athaliah). Then it would be business as usual, as on previous occasions. It would not make much difference to most of the people. The threat of wholesale removal of the population "from its land" is altogether different. It implies foreign conquest and means the end of the nation. If the two parts of v 11 are to be connected, it can only be in a causal sequence of some duration. A plausible scenario would begin with replacement of Jeroboam's dynasty by a usurper. The effect of this civil disruption would be to weaken the nation and expose it to attack by its enemies. The result of a subsequent foreign invasion and conquest would be exile of the population with its leaders. In fact, this sequence of events took place in Israel after the replacement of the house of Jeroboam, but only the first and last stages are indicated in the prophecy reported here. None of the intervening events and personalities is mentioned, and there is no reason to suppose that the prophecy was based on the later history. It would be reasonable to see the collapse of the nation and captivity of the population as the final consequence of the fall of the dynasty and its replacement by one or more usurpers in sequence. It is also possible that the first clause—the statement that Jeroboam would die by the sword—refers to death in battle, as happened to more than one king of Israel and of Judah. Then defeat in battle against a foreign enemy could lead directly to capture of the capital city and captivity of the people.

With respect to the two parts of v 11 (combining elements from vv 9b and 17bB), there are two ways of interpreting or explaining the connection. They may belong together as parts of a single scenario or program, in which the king is killed in battle against a powerful enemy, who then proceeds to conquer the land and its capital and carry the population, including its leadership, into captivity. Such an interpretation would suit v 11 as such but would fit less well with Amos' statement in v 9b—"I shall attack Jeroboam's house with my sword," which implies a domestic upheaval or internal revolution in which a usurper assassinates the king ("by the sword") and replaces him on the throne. Apparently, Amaziah understood the words in this way, for he accuses Amos of being part of such a conspiracy. Such a conspiracy and usurpation might have foreign connections, and it is not unheard of for foreign kings to have a hand in the murder of neighboring kings and the forcible change of dynasties. But such activities could hardly involve or result in capture or captivity unless the conspiracy were only a pretext for the ulterior designs of the alien king on the nation itself. In any case such a usurpation, with its attendant civil disruption, might well lead to a weakening of the nation and to its exposure to attack from outside. Such an invasion, if successful, would be followed by the siege, capture, and sack of the capital city and thus the captivity and exile of the people. So whatever picture of the preliminary stages was envisioned by the prophet and by the priest—and they may have been different —the end result was all too familiar; and both would have agreed that Amos was portraying the end of the kingdom.

7:12–13: AMAZIAH'S SPEECH

We cannot imagine that the exchange between Amaziah and Amos was restricted to the few words reported in vv 12–15. Only the briefest essentials are given. We do not know if the high quality of Amaziah's speech derives from his training and experience in oratory, or whether it represents a skillful reworking by a professional editor. It would be misleading to call his utterance a poem, but it exhibits literary artistry, including parallelism and chiasmus among other features of the best prose and poetic styles.

		Syllables
12aB	*ḥōzeh lēk bĕraḥ-lĕkā ᵓel-ᵓereṣ yĕhûdâ*	11/12

12b	*we³ĕkol-šām leḥem*	5 ⎫ 10
	wĕšām tinnābēᵓ	5 ⎭
13a	*ûbêt-ᵓēl lōᵓ-tôsîp ᶜôd lĕhinnābēᵓ*	11
13b	*kî miqdaš-melek hûᵓ*	5 ⎫ 11
	ûbêt mamlākâ hûᵓ	6 ⎭

The speech can be construed as four lines of ten to twelve syllables each, but the display above brings out the poetic character of the two pairs of short lines (12b, 13b). Modern translations all present the speech as prose, but the repetitions, the parallelism, the diction, and the unusual word sequences indicate that it is artfully composed.

The two longer lines (vv 12aB and 13a) juxtapose the two places with which Amos was most closely associated (in the book): the land of Judah, where he made his home and his livelihood, and Bethel (in the land of Israel), where he attempted to fulfill his role as prophet. Amaziah, not without malice, proposes that Amos concentrate and consolidate his activities in one place, the other place, not Bethel. Note their chiastic placement. Each verse spells out the significance of the two locations. The repetition of *šām* in v 12b (again chiasmus) balances the repetition of *hûᵓ* in v 13b (cf. *ᵓānōkî* in v 14). The verb *tinnābēᵓ* at the end of v 12 matches *hinnābēᵓ* in the first line of v 13, another chiasmus.

The speech does not proceed in logical steps. The first thing is to stop Amos from prophesying at Bethel (v 13a), for the reason given in v 13b. He must go back to Judah (v 12aB) and prophesy there (v 12bB), and so earn a living (v 12bA).

12. *seer.* The LXX version is *ho horōn* (vocative). Several nouns were used in biblical times to denote prophets (true or false), and several verbs were used to describe their activity. There was a turnover in usage, and some of the vocabulary acquired negative associations. The denominative *nipᶜal nibbāᵓ*, as used here, is the usual verb. It is neutral in connotation and covers a wide range of phenomena, including both genuine ecstasy and artificial frenzy. It does not take an object, but it does have various adverbs, "against *X*," "in the name of Yahweh." As the general term it can refer to true or false prophesying, just as a *nābîᵓ* can be a true or a false prophet. In the present passage Amos denies that he is a *nābîᵓ* but insists on acting like one, by prophesying. The *hitpaᶜel* describes more abnormal states and be-

haviors and is used more often to express disapproval. In 2 Kgs 9:11 it is parallel to *mĕšuggāʿ*, "crazy." In v 16 the *nipʿal* is paralleled by *taṭṭîp*, "drip," possibly but not necessarily pejorative. The range covered by *ḥōzeh* includes a royal consultant such as Gad (2 Sam 24:11); but this usage is otherwise found only in Chronicles (1 Chr 25:5; 2 Chr 29:25; 33:18; 35:15), which applies the term to scribes also (1 Chr 29:29; 2 Chr 2:15; 9:29; 19:2; 20:34). It is not sound method to include Amos automatically in one of these categories as though the word itself implied official status (Zevit 1975).

It is less clear whether Amaziah's use of the participle *ḥōzeh* to address Amos is a recognition of his role and status, or whether it was intended to be an insult and a rejection. In the book's title the verb is used in a positive way, and, although the root *ḥzh* is not used in the vision reports, there can be no doubt that Amos is presented as a genuine visionary. Nevertheless, he himself insists that he is only a herdsman and a tender of sycamore trees, and his editor identifies him as a shepherd.

The point at issue between Amaziah and Amos is not whether Amos is a genuine prophet, because we are not quite sure what Amaziah thought on that subject. He gives Amos a title, *ḥōzeh*, that could be an acknowledgment of his authenticity; he recognizes that his activity is described by the verb *nibbāʾ*. He is happy for Amos to keep on with that activity, as long as it is not in Bethel: "Flee to Judah and prophesy there!"

If Amaziah really believed that Amos was a "seer" who really did "prophesy," then he is guilty of the crime of Amos 2:12. In Amos' eyes he certainly was guilty, and the judgment of v 17 is precisely due to Amaziah's rejection of the prophet and prohibition of his activities. The story does not go into Amaziah's inner arguments and rationalizations. It is not clear whether he knew that the message was the true word of Yahweh, but rejected it nevertheless; or whether he sincerely believed that Amos was an upstart and an impostor, a political conspirator from another nation, using prophecy as the vehicle for his sedition. If only the latter, then Amaziah's obvious course and inescapable duty was to apprehend Amos. The king would expect nothing less.

In spite of the hostility, Amaziah's words are formal, hardly abusive, but nevertheless peremptory and menacing. They include no attempt to expose or denounce Amos as a fraud, though the tone and manner of rejection are present. They could amount to a recognition that he is a real seer who does prophesy. Amaziah's advice could then express a compromise, a caution and uncertainty in his own mind. He hesitates to take more drastic measures because, for all he knows, Amos might be a real prophet and therefore sacrosanct. But Amos is also a human being, and if he can take a hint that he is not wanted and leave voluntarily, Amaziah will avoid the danger of committing a profanation against one of Yahweh's agents. Although in his report Amaziah expresses concern for the king, he is also aware of Amos' effect on the population. His report that "the land cannot endure all his words" (v 10) could have been intended to reassure the king that Amos had not secured any significant following, that the people found his message unacceptable—which was probably quite true. Prophets rarely find honor in any country. But at least it makes the point that in Amaziah's opinion it was not in the public interest for Amos to remain at large in Israel.

The reason he gives to Amos himself (v 13) focuses on the place where Amos is to do his prophesying. As is often the case with state officials and public servants, who have no intrinsic authority grounded in personal gifts and qualifications, spiritual or intellectual, Amaziah falls back on jurisdiction, on rules and regulations. You cannot preach in his shrine without authorization, and ultimately the king's approval, for the latter supports and controls the administration there. Amos did not even have the minimum credential of citizenship. Amos' status and validation, in his own view, depended entirely on the intrinsic truth and power of his message; he had no official base, no institutional backing, no external certification.

run away. Balak used a similar command to get rid of Balaam when the latter did not prophesy what the king hoped to hear (Num 24:11). In each case it is the offended person who gives the advice, which implies escaping from danger, danger that would arise from the person giving the advice. It was equally within the power of Balak or Amaziah to dispose of the alien prophet. In each case it is possible that the person in authority was restrained by the fear of the consequences of doing violence to a holy person. This fear implies partial recognition of the prophet's privileged status; but at the same time it is somewhat superstitious, for it is the physical presence of the prophet himself they wish to get rid of, as if doing so would make any difference to the God who sent him.

The case of Balaam (Num 24:11) is enough to undermine Rosenbaum's argument that Amos was a northerner, and that "the person fleeing is a native or 'permanent resident' of the place *from which* [our emphasis] he departs" (1977:134). Rosenbaum also repeats the argument of Schmidt (1917) that if Amaziah was telling Amos to go back to where he came from, the verb *šwb* would have been more appropriate, adding the arguments that *qešer* is not the act of an outsider and that *brḥ* describes the flight of a resident (1977:135–36). If this were the case, it would not have been necessary for Amaziah to specify that Amos had done this "inside the territory of Israel." And it would make even more inexplicable Amaziah's encouraging Amos to depart.

We do not know what power Amaziah had to back up his hint, should Amos not cooperate, whether temple guards had police powers to detain or forcibly eject troublemakers. There must have been some kind of security service to regulate the good order of the sacred precincts. The elaborate rules against the intrusion of unqualified or disqualified persons (Leviticus) must have required coercion from time to time. But no such machinery is seen in operation here.

We cannot imagine that Amaziah was trying to be helpful to Amos. Amos did not thank him for the advice. He was stung into vehement reply. It seems as though Amaziah underestimated Amos' courage. The hireling flees because he is a hireling (John 10:13). He did not just want to get rid of him; he wanted to counteract his message by discrediting him. To imprison him or kill him on the spot would not have been effective. It would have given the movement (if Amos had any kind of following) a martyr. The words of a martyr would be remembered, not the words of a coward. Perhaps it was because the incident did end in martyrdom that it was remembered, along with the message of the prophet at that time. The prophet's *apologia* became his monument.

land of Judah. Here the rivalry and suspicion between the northern and southern kingdoms come out. But in no instance is it ever said of a prophet of Yahweh that he was sent to only one part of the nation, or that he was authorized to operate only in a restricted territory. It seems clear that Amos had more to say about the north than the south. Amaziah's command is more blunt. It is not an argument over whether Yahweh has sent Amos, where he sent him, or what he told him to say. He is simply told to go away to the land of Judah, presumably whence he came.

13. *there.* The repetition of *šām* is probably sarcastic and shows that it is all right with Amaziah if Amos does his prophesying somewhere else.

Eat your food. Taken at face value, the expression refers to the simplest essentials of life. If it means "earn your living," it is the only place in the Bible in which this expression is so used. Many inferences have been made from this interpretation. Samuel divined for a fee; at least Saul's servant thought so (1 Sam 9:8; cf. 1 Kgs 14:3; 2 Kgs 8:8). Micah considered extortionate demands for pay to be characteristic of false prophets (Mic 3:11). The female prophets of Ezekiel 13, who sound more like sorceresses, provided their sinister skills "for handfuls of barley and for pieces of bread" (Ezek 13:19). Although we do not know how Amos secured his livelihood after his call, there is no indication that he received any remuneration for his work as a prophet. He is identified by his old profession, but v 15 may indicate a clean break with the old life.

If Amos continued to derive support from his hometown or used his personal means, then Amaziah's point could be that only there should he ply his trade. The emphasis on Bethel as a royal establishment then secures the point that they have their own staff, and outsiders without official status are neither needed nor wanted. Amaziah's description of Amos is tantalizingly incomplete. The idea that Amaziah considered him to be (or simply represented him as) an *agent provocateur* in the pay of the king of Judah (Winckler 1895) goes far beyond the evidence. In fact it goes against the evidence of Amos' own words. In spite of his unremitting attacks on the power elite and bureaucratic establishment in every aspect—commercial, military, judicial, ecclesiastical—Amos never addresses the proletariat (whose just causes he has so much at heart), inciting them to secure for themselves the justice of which they have been deprived. Throughout the entire book the only agent of retribution is Yahweh. In the one recorded statement that supplied Amaziah with evidence that Amos was guilty of sedition against Jeroboam, it was Yahweh who threatened to rise up against the king's house with a sword. Doubtless, if the matter had been probed further, it might have come out that the sword in question would be wielded by some human agent (the leader of a coup from within or of an invasion from outside). The mere fact that Amos never bothers to go into such details (the farthest he gets into that is the *gôy* of 6:14) shows that for him the secondary agencies are quite unimportant and need not be used at all.

Although the evidence in the oracles does not corroborate such an interpretation of Amaziah's charge in v 10 or of the insinuation in v 12 that Amos is a paid undercover agent for a plot, there is no question that Amaziah believed or wanted others to believe that Amos was engaged in illegal political activity and that it was the real reason for Amos' journey to Bethel. But if this allegation was true, we are back once more to the unsolved question: why, in that case, did he merely report to the king and let the suspect go?

Bethel. Amaziah looks after the precinct for which he is personally responsible; but because he orders Amos back to Judah, he tacitly places all of (northern) Israel out of bounds. Note the omission of the preposition *b-*, as often before nouns beginning with *b-*.

king's chapel//royal temple. The Heb is *mqdš mlk//wbyt mmlkh.* The terminology poses a number of problems. First, we note the absence of the article in both of the similar phrases in parallel. The JPS makes both indefinite, "a king's sanctuary and a royal palace." Others make both definite, "the royal sanctuary . . . the state temple" (Wolff 1977; NIV; JB). Some take one as definite and the other indefinite: "the . . . a" (RV, RSV, NEB). As the ban applies only to Bethel, it gives the impression that the reason is its unique status. The omission of the article with definite nouns reflects poetic usage.

Second, translators' decisions seem to have been influenced by conclusions about what is referred to—the city of Bethel itself or one or two special buildings in it. If the city as such is intended, why are the pronouns in v 13b masculine? Perhaps the reason is that *byt* is masculine or that the pronouns should agree with the predicates of those clauses.

Third, do the parallel statements about Bethel in v 13b point to two distinct buildings in the city, a palace and a temple, or do they describe two aspects of the shrine (or shrine-city), which is significant for both king and kingdom?

A palace and a shrine are likely to be found together in a capital city or acropolis. In Jerusalem the temple was a chapel adjunct to the palace in the first place, and a national center only in a secondary sense, dependent on the king as chief patron and representative of all people in the cult. Amaziah could be underscoring Jeroboam's personal interest in what happened there, without suggesting that it was a private chapel. It was clearly a center of national pilgrimage with important patriarchal associations, all the more reason for kings to combine religious and political interests there. In view of the latter connection, Amaziah may not have been free to exercise his own authority in a case of possible sedition. Under the circumstances, a report to the king as the chief executive of the country would be appropriate and necessary.

Did Jeroboam II have a palace in Bethel? There is no record of it. The collocation of the four words is puzzling. The "royal palace" is customarily *byt hmlk*. In Esther the palace is *byt mlkwt*. The *byt* of a king can be the whole realm (country) or dynasty (2 Sam 7:16).

Although Bethel was an ancient cult center, going back to the patriarchs, notably Jacob, Jeroboam I had established there (also at Dan) the cult of the golden calf, "the sin of Jeroboam ben-Nebat with which he made Israel to sin." This tradition could account for Amaziah's description of Bethel as *miqdaš melek*. The phrase *byt mmlkh,* "house of kingdom," probably does not describe the royal palace (JPS), but the "state temple" (Wolff 1977), another designation of Bethel (or of its cult building) as both a national and a royal shrine.

Amos (v 9) had combined his attacks on the royal house (*byt*) with those on the sanctuaries (*mqdš*). So here Amaziah associates royalty with the temple at Bethel.

7:14–17: AMOS' REPLY

The prophet's reply is in two parts. First, he denies the priest's insinuation and rejects his demand that he should go back to Judah and never prophesy in Bethel again (vv 14–15). This part is Amos' *apologia,* and it is a succinct account of what we can only identify as his call (v 15). It is very brief. The only autobiographical detail it supplies is that he was actually engaged in his work as a shepherd when it happened. The main point,

almost the only point, is that he is under inescapable obligation to deliver
the prophetic word to Israel.

The confrontation goes beyond this standoff, however. Amos has something more to say, an additional prophecy. It sounds as though it were
generated spontaneously, but it is presented as an oracle from Yahweh with
the usual formulas (vv 16aA, 17aA). Amaziah's attempt to muzzle Amos is
given as the reason for the pronouncement of judgment (v 17). It is directed
largely against Amaziah himself, his family, and his property, but the nation is not excluded (v 17bB).

The dialogue in this section is as poetic as most of the oracular material
in the rest of the book, but this is only partially recognized in translations.
Both JPS and NEB versions present it all as prose, while the RSV and the
NIV present the prophecy in vv 16–17 as verse. The narrative portion of
Amos' *apologia* in vv 14–15 is too brief to permit the development of epic
sequences, "And Yahweh took me, and Yahweh said to me. . . ."
Yahweh's speech in v 15bB consists of two simple commands.

Amos' statement about himself in v 14 can be construed in four lines:

$$lo^{\circ}\text{-}n\bar{a}b\hat{\imath} \qquad \qquad {}^{\circ}\bar{a}n\bar{o}k\hat{\imath}$$
$$w\breve{e}lo^{\circ}\ ben\text{-}n\bar{a}b\hat{\imath} \qquad {}^{\circ}\bar{a}n\bar{o}k\hat{\imath}$$
$$k\hat{\imath}\text{-}b\hat{o}q\bar{e}r \qquad \qquad {}^{\circ}\bar{a}n\bar{o}k\hat{\imath}$$
$$\hat{u}b\hat{o}l\bar{e}s\check{s}iqm\hat{\imath}m$$

The repetition of *'ānōkî* in the first bicolon mimics Amaziah's repetition of
hû' in v 13b. The passage is hardly poetry, but it is not simple prose either.
It gains much of its impressiveness from the threefold repetition of *'ānōkî*.

Amos' report of Amaziah's speech in v 16 is a single bicolon with simple
parallelism:

	Syllables
lō' tinnābē''al-yiśrā'ēl	8
wĕ lō' taṭṭîp 'al-bêt yisḥāq	8

"Don't prophesy against Israel,
don't preach against Isaac's domain!"

The prophecy against Amaziah in v 17 is more detailed:

17a	*'ištĕkā bā'îr tizneh*
	ûbāneykā ûbĕnōteykā baḥereb yippōlû
	wĕ'admātĕkā baḥebel tĕḥullāq
17b	*wĕ'attâ 'al-'ădāmâ ṭĕmē'â tāmût*
	wĕyiśrā'ēl gālōh yigleh mē'al 'admātô

17a　"Your wife shall become a prostitute in the city,
　　　　and your sons and your daughters shall fall by the sword;
　　　　and your land shall be parceled out by the measuring line;
17b　and you yourself shall die in a polluted land;
　　　　and Israel shall surely go into exile from its land."

This verse is scarcely poetry; it lacks parallelism, and it does not scan very well. The lines are unusually long. Yet it is not ordinary prose. The most conspicuous rhetorical feature is the syntax of the first four lines, with the unusual placement of the verb last. Each clause has three elements, and all have the same sequence: Subject + Prepositional Phrase + Verb. The last clause likewise has three elements, but here the sequence is Subject + Verb + Prepositional Phrase. The effect is powerful. The placement of the subject first in each case gives an inventory of the five things of which Amos predicts the fate. The placement of the verb last in each of four successive clauses creates suspense. The disclosure of degradation, death, loss, death, and exile is shocking. Moreover, the order of the clauses is unusual, beginning with the wife and ending with Amaziah, the person directly addressed. We would expect the central figure to be listed first and then the sons, to be followed by the women (cf. Gen 7:7). The reversal here is intended to build to the climactic identification of Amaziah as the principal target of the prophetic denunciation, which is made all the more emphatic by the use of the independent personal pronoun (weʾattâ . . . tāmût, "And as for you . . . you shall die," v 17bA). Compare a similar and familiar rhetorical climax in 2 Sam 12:7: ʾattâ hāʾîš, "You are the man!"

14. *prophet.* There can be no question that Amos functioned as a prophet. The Lord told him to prophesy, and he did. Here he disclaims the title nābîʾ or even ben-nābîʾ, as a member of a class whose status in society was recognized. Amaziah had not called him by this title. He does not disown the title hōzeh, neither does he claim to be a hōzeh.

The fact that he denies the title nābîʾ but asserts the activity of the denominative verb has made v 14 one of the best-known cruxes in the book. Just what did Amos mean when he said "I am not a prophet," when he obviously was one? The discussion continues unabated and without resolution. (Besides the inevitable discussion in every commentary, the following have given special attention to the verse: van Hoonacker 1941, Rowley 1947, Danell 1951, MacCormack 1955–56, G. R. Driver 1955, Ackroyd 1956–57, Vogt 1956–57, Gunneweg 1960, Cohen 1961, Smend 1963, Schmid 1967.)

In the immediate context he could be refuting Amaziah's insinuation. "I am not the kind of prophet you think I am." This reading would be all right for the part of Amaziah's speech that hints that Amos was a hireling. But Amaziah had called him hōzeh, as if he were a true seer.

The parallel *ben-nābîʾ* could mean "a member of a prophetic community," of the kind known from the earlier days of Samuel and Elijah/Elisha but not attested in the eighth century. More likely the term would apply to an apprentice ("disciple" [JPS]) than a successor in hereditary office. As Amos disowns any such traditional or institutional affiliation, we must assume that that kind of prophet was now in disrepute, at least in Amos' estimation. Perhaps they had degenerated into soothsayers and diviners, prophesying for pay (cf. Mic 3:5–7).

Another approach is to make all of the verbless clauses in v 14 dependent on the subsequent narrative clause for their (past) time reference: I [was] not a prophet . . . ; on the contrary (*kî*) I was a herdsman. And [then] Yahweh took me . . . [and then I did become a prophet]. In other words, Amos is making the point that he is not the kind of prophet that Amaziah considers him to be. He is only a prophet because Yahweh took him and ordered him to prophesy. Although he does not use the term "raised up," his account of his call (or, rather, his being taken) places him in the succession of 2:11, and his steadfastness places him under the compulsion of 3:8.

cattleman. The Heb is *bôqēr*, literally, "herdsman." Although *bāqār* is the collective name for a herd of cattle, in contrast to *ṣōʾn*, sheep and goats, the additional information that Amos used to be "following the flock" has influenced the Greek translation as *aipolos,* goatherd (a *hapax legomenon* in the LXX). It remains possible that Amos was a kind of jack-of-all-trades: cowboy, shepherd, seasonal farm worker; but not a prophet. See the discussion of *nôqēd* in 1:1.

The alleged contrast and hostility between agricultural farmer and stockman is found more in books than in real life, as far as this country was concerned. A well-to-do person like Nabal, who lived in Maon, some twelve kilometers south of Hebron, could boast of large flocks of sheep and goats (1 Sam 25:2) as well as ample supplies of produce from field and orchard (1 Sam 25:18).

a dresser of sycamores. Both participles describe professions. Earlier versions took *bôlēs* to mean a fruit picker: KJV, "gatherer"; Douay, "plucking." The sycamore fig—sometimes called "fig-mulberry"—can attain a majestic height in a land in which tall trees do not easily grow and produces luxuriant foliage and abundant fruit. But the fruit was small and was generally left to be eaten by poorer people. The cultivation of this fruit required expert attention and time-consuming care. If the fig matured naturally, it generally spoiled on the tree. To prevent this outcome each fig was prepared for harvest by either peeling some of the skin or making a small incision a few days before it was gathered.

In 1 Chr 27:28 sycamores are located in the Shephelah. They were susceptible to frost (Ps 78:47). Hence it is not likely that Amos did this work around his native Tekoa. It is too tenuous an inference to make from this information that sycamore tending was Amos' native trade and that Tekoa was not his original home (Budde 1925:81). It is not so easy to contradict Amos 1:1, and Amos 7:12 makes it clear that Amos was at least a Judean whose ministry in the north was resented as an intrusion and rejected as unauthorized.

15. *took.* It can mean to remove someone by death (Job 1:21) or to translate to heaven (Gen 5:24). In the latter sense it could describe (temporary) admission to the divine assembly. But it need not mean more than transference to another vocation. While we cannot reconstruct Amos' personal or prophetic career completely, we must connect the visions with the "call," just as in the cases of Isaiah, Jeremiah, and Ezekiel. They are not explicitly mentioned by Amos here, but the normative tradition in the Bible associates prophetic calls with visions, and it is unlikely that the vision associated with Amos' call would be omitted when others were included. No doubt his call to prophesy is to be associated with the first vision, though he assumed the role of intermediary before embarking on his mission as a prophet.

the flock. Like Moses he was called from behind the flock (Exod 3:1). As in the call of Moses, the provocation was the oppression of Israel by an unjust and tyrannical ruler. Like Moses he had a vision of fire (Exod 3:2; the language of Amos 7:4 is close to that of Deut 32:22). Also like that of Moses his mission was accompanied by a series of plagues. After the plagues are ineffective, more drastic measures are set in motion.

16. What part of Amaziah's speech goaded Amos the most? The title *ḥōzeh?* The command to leave? The insinuation that he was a hireling? The argument that it was the king's shrine? None of the above. It was the command not to prophesy.

Amos' account of Amaziah's ban does not match the words reported in v 13. In Ezek 21:2, 7 *haṭṭēp//hinnābēʾ* appears in a good sense. In the *qal* the verb means "drip" (intransitive), with water, wine, or myrrh as subject. The *hipʿil* is causative, and Amos uses it in 9:13, where the mountains drip new wine, and the connotation is good. The verb is used in Mic 2:6 to describe prophecy that attempts to stifle prophecy: *ʾal-taṭṭîpû yaṭṭîpû,* "They preach, 'Don't preach!'" When it appears again in Mic 2:11, the word is used to discredit false prophets who work under the influence of wine or for the sake of receiving wine in return for their services.

With a neutral or positive meaning in Ezekiel and a derogatory use in Micah, the flavor of the word in Amos 7:16 is indeterminate. It could be no more than a poetic parallel and synonym for "prophesy." But if used in Micah's sense, it is branding Amos as a mere driveler, or as a rent-a-prophet.

The LXX author evidently felt a pejorative sense, using *ochlagōgēsēs,* "[mis] lead the crowd."

17. It is interesting that Amos does not repeat or reinforce his message about Jeroboam. He concentrates on Amaziah. The sword is prominent in the prophecies of The Book of Visions (7:9, 11, 17; 9:1, 4, 10). The latter verses extend the threat to all of the people, including exiles. Analysis of v 17a–bA suggests that there is an envelope construction, with the first and fourth lines forming a pair, while the second and third lines also belong together (note the parallelism of *ḥereb* and *ḥebel*). The second line might seem to present a slight discrepancy, because falling by the sword suggests death in combat and both daughters and wives are more likely to become victims of rape and captivity. There are numerous exceptions and variations, but basically the men can expect the sword while women are forced into slavery and degradation. But as Amos himself tells us, war is no respecter of persons or gender, and women along with men are victims of the sword (cf. 1:13). The picture in the first line, however, suggests destitution. That a priest's wife should be forced into prostitution would be the worst kind of disgrace.

COMMENT

The discrepancy between Amos' utterance (v 9) and Amaziah's version is never clarified, and it is possible that Amaziah interpreted Amos' words as a direct threat to the royal house, including the king. It is also possible that Amaziah sharpened the charge so as to elicit a stronger response from the king. It is curious that with such a serious charge, conspiracy against the life of the king and the royal house, the only action taken was to banish Amos or, even less, simply to advise him to leave town. Can it be that they did not take prophets very seriously in these days and especially in the north? Or that they distinguished between prophets and prophets, with the official prophets being accorded status while itinerant seers without adequate credentials were merely ignored, unless there was an indication that people were responding? Apparently the priest here had come to a different opinion of this prophet—that he was very dangerous and his words seditious. Presumably Amaziah was asking for and expecting some executive response from Jeroboam. In the meantime, however, he simply tells Amos to go away to the land of Judah. This fact is curious, for if he wanted the king to take an active interest in what Amos was saying and presumably planning to do, would he invite the prophet to leave? Would he not detain the man until the matter could be investigated by the king? The similar case with Jeremiah in the temple area (Jeremiah 7 and 26) shows what could and would be done when a prophet was considered disruptive and seditious (and no one accused Jeremiah of conspiracy against the king, only of saying terrible things about the temple). Later, when Jeremiah was accused of treason, he was again arrested and put in prison (Jer 37:11–38:6). But on this occasion, Jeremiah was arrested and almost put to death; whereas, as far as we can tell, Amos was free to go his way. Maybe the priest was only interested in impressing the king with his diligence and his loyalty in protecting the latter's name from defamation. Amaziah certainly does not appear to be afraid of Amos because he is a prophet or superstitious about a prophet's powers. But why does he send him away when he is charging him with sedition, treason, and conspiracy to assassinate the king? One might say that all he had was Amos' own words as evidence and that the conspiracy charge was obviously false and would not stand up in court. But such a claim applies modern standards to ancient legal practice. At the least one would expect Amos to be detained and perhaps sent to the king for further examination.

Amos in turn responds spiritedly to Amaziah, in a pointed rebuttal. He does not reply to the charge of conspiracy, however, and does not repeat the threat to the king and his house. Instead he insists that he is on the Lord's business and has no other choice about prophesying. He gives no indication at all about whether he will comply with Amaziah's order to leave. In fact he attacks the priest directly, spelling out what the destruction of the shrine and sanctuary at Bethel will mean for Amaziah as chief priest there. As the chief priest of the major shrine of the northern kingdom, Amaziah is deeply implicated in all of the crimes against God and man charged by the prophet; hence the message of doom is both institutional and personal. Amaziah as high priest will be taken captive, and his family will be slain except for his wife, who will become a harlot in the city. We have no way of knowing the outcome of the confrontation and altercation. Ultimately Amos may have left, but whether on his terms (or those of the Lord) or Amaziah's is not clear; or he may have been incarcerated and later released or executed. Neither do we know anything of the king's reception of the message from the priest or any response to it.

With regard to "conspiracy," the standard and frequent expression is that so-and-so conspired against the king and killed him. So the use of the term here is a strong indication that Amaziah believed that Amos came north in order to organize a conspiracy to kill the king and thus carry out the word of Yahweh. This belief would be the reason for sending word to the king about Amos. But it might also explain why Amaziah does not seem to take the threat very seriously. People conspiring to kill the king hardly advertise those things. On the contrary, they act secretively (compare the stories of Ahijah and Jeroboam and especially the secret anointing of Jehu by Elisha's agent). Conspiracies are typically secret affairs; so a public announcement would almost certainly mean that the speaker was not involved in such a conspiracy. One existed or would exist later on, perhaps inspired by the prophet's words; but it followed after and was not related to the present circumstances.

Amaziah states two things: that Amos has conspired against the king in the midst of the house of Israel, and that the land cannot contain all his words. He then goes on to quote Amos' words on the subject: first, that Jeroboam will die by the sword, apparently a reference to the conspiracy; and second, that Israel will surely go captive from its land (a reference to the consequence of the king's death). While Amaziah could be charged with altering the words to suit his own purposes, neither at this point nor in the sequel, when Amos quotes Amaziah, is anything said either to or about the other challenging the quotation as inaccurate. While both Amos and Amaziah are furious about what the other has said or is quoted as saying, neither charges the other with tampering with the words. As there is a difference between what is offered as a quotation and what was actually reported earlier (cf. vv 9 and 11 or 16 and 12), the question is what the writer or editor intended by these rather loose paraphrases, for it is obvious that, as in most stories, he could have cited and quoted verbatim or nearly so.

The answer seems to lie in the complex structure of this little story and in the author's ultimate design. Instead of quoting and repeating, as in most stories with dialogue, the author here is compressing and not repeating when Amaziah quotes Amos or vice versa (and this balanced pattern is a significant part of the intricate structure). We suggest that what seems like a paraphrase of an earlier statement is actually a quotation of something said in the dialogue but not recorded at the point at which the remark was made. In this fashion the author produces a curious pair of monologues, in which the speakers in effect carry both sides of the conversation independently of each other. Thus in vv 10–13 Amaziah carries the burden of the story, while in vv 14–17 Amos does. Amaziah sends word to the king and, in the process, quotes Amos. Then he turns to Amos to finish the altercation, as though he were responding to what Amos had just said, while in fact he is responding to information that is provided both later (vv 15–16) and earlier (v 9).

Amos, for his part, first speaks to an issue not clearly raised but implied by Amaziah, then quotes Amaziah (a statement that Amaziah probably made in response to the oracle recorded in v 9) instead of echoing the statement by Amaziah in v 13, before making a final response in v 17. Just as v 16 reflects a statement by Amos in v 9, so v 17 repeats in part the quotation offered by Amaziah in v 11. In short, we have a complex, compressed structure in this story with the climactic elements in the middle (Amaziah's remark in vv 12–13 and Amos' declaration in vv 15–16) while the beginning (v 9) and end (v 17) form a sequence that envelops the narrative. This analysis of the structure and the envelope around the story is confirmed by the direct quotation by Amaziah in v 11, which combines a variant of 9b with 17bB. That there is not much to choose between 9b and 11aB is shown by the similarity in theme and the repetition of keywords, *yrbʿm* and *ḥrb;* the chiasm simply illustrates the possibilities. Both positions, first and last, are emphatic and point to the violent nature of the death of Jeroboam alone or of his whole house. While possible interpretations may vary, the passages should interpret each other, especially if both are regarded as authentic oracles of Amos, for "Jeroboam's house" would include Jeroboam, while the particular reference to Jeroboam would not necessarily exclude his dynasty. As matters turned out it was not Jeroboam but his son Zechariah who died by the sword, and with him the dynasty ended. The prophecy may have been understood as fulfilled by this action, but it probably was not the intended meaning. The exile came later and was not directly related to the demise of Jeroboam's dynasty. Five more kings came and went before the end of the kingdom and the captivity of the people, so that prediction was hardly fulfilled in the sense intended by combining the prophecy of exile with the death of the reigning king. All of this evidence serves to confirm the authenticity of the oracle as coming from Amos himself (correctly quoted by Amaziah, though the charge of conspiracy was undoubtedly false, and it is precisely the latter charge that Amos denies by his expostulation about his real status and calling). Within a generation or so the real outcome was known, and if the prophecies were created *post factum* then they would have been compounded more carefully and constituted a more accurate prediction by the prophet. The prophet himself would have been least likely to alter a prophecy, as the case in Ezekiel 29 shows (cf. the prophet's own revision of an earlier prediction that was not fulfilled, 29:17–20 and 26:7–14).

Why was Amos told not to preach or prophesy at Bethel? Twin simultaneous accusations and predictions were proclaimed by him. The sanctuaries would be destroyed and the house of Jeroboam would be punished. In connection with the latter, the prophet also announced the certainty of exile from the land. Because these are very serious threats, the charge against Amos for making them (essentially the same as that made against Naboth in the celebrated case of his vineyard, that he cursed God and king [1 Kgs 21:10, 13]) is also very serious. We surmise that the message Amaziah sent to Jeroboam is the conclusion of the story, not the beginning. As in journalistic reports, the main point or summary is given first and then the preceding details are filled in. Thus we believe that the altercations that are described in vv 12–17 led up to Amaziah's decision to report a dangerous matter to the king and seek a response regarding how to deal with it. Thus vv 10–11 serve as a recapitulation of the episode emphasizing its conclusion. As previously noted, it hardly makes sense for Amaziah to report this dangerous threat to the state and to the person of the king, and then encourage the suspected seditionist to escape. On the one hand, if Amaziah believed that the threat to the crown was real and imminent (as the statement shows) then he was duty bound and it was also in his own best interest to arrest the suspect and hold him at the king's pleasure. We call attention to somewhat analogous circumstances in the cases of Micaiah ben-Imlah, who was held in custody pending a final determination by the king (1 Kgs 22:27–28); and of Jeremiah, who was detained at the temple after making a speech similar to the one given here by Amos (Jer 7:1–15; 26:1–19). In other words, without having to decide the merits of the case, the authorities would hold the suspect while the matter was being investigated and until the king could make an informed decision. As the charges were very serious—conspiracy against the king and his house—and the penalty on conviction was death, it would have amounted to an act of complicity with the accused to allow him to depart. We recall the episode at Nob in which David had dealings with the high priest, Ahimelech, who unwittingly abetted the former in his escape from Saul (1 Sam 21:1–9). Just the fact that the priest was involved with a declared outlaw was sufficient in Saul's eyes to make the former equally guilty and subject to dire retribution (1 Sam 22:11–19). In other words, we are dealing with the most serious possible charges, and the reported statement that Amaziah encouraged Amos to depart and, in fact, to go to another country outside the jurisdiction of the king of Israel would be indefensible and incomprehensible. At the very least Amaziah would place the man under arrest and hold him at the king's pleasure. It is to be expected that on receipt of a message, especially one coming from an official of Amaziah's rank and in his position, concerning conspiracy and a named conspirator, the king would take immediate action to investigate the matter. In view of the prima facie case against the prophet (namely, his own words, reported by others and clearly not denied by him) he would be brought to the king for a final determination of the case. We are reminded here of the fate of Uriah, another prophet, who said things similar to Jeremiah's words and understandably was deemed by the authorities to be seditious, treasonous, and probably blasphemous (Jer 26:20–23). Thus any threat to the sanctuary could be so regarded in the light of Deuteronomic and Priestly theology, which understood the temple to be the place of divine presence, whether symbolized by God's name or by his glory. The essential ingredients of this theology certainly did not begin with D and P but were part of the basic Israelite view of sanctuaries all over the country, especially those central shrines such as Bethel and Jerusalem, where the divine presence was emphasized for both political and theological reasons.

In view of this serious discrepancy in the statements, attitudes, and actions of the priest at Bethel, we must ask whether the story is told in simple chronological order or, rather, what would have been a realistic sequence of events in the light of the report. We also must ask what the author, compiler, or editor may have intended. In other words, how can we interpret the data to reflect a plausible picture and explain the apparent discrepancies? Taking the story at face value, the elements in the sequence in which they are recorded present an anomaly that can hardly be resolved. It should be recognized that the reporter has organized the pericope in artistic fashion, with its envelope construction and the vertical and horizontal focus on the key charges.

If we suppose, then, that vv 10–11 constitute the summary of the episode reported to the king by Amaziah at its conclusion, then the pieces fall into place without difficulty. After Amos' words in chaps. 1–2 (the Great Set Speech) and perhaps other elements found in chaps. 1–6 (closing with the provocative words in 7:9a) were heard by or reported to Amaziah, it was clear that the priest must do something about such a person. His immediate reaction, on the basis of information gleaned on the spot or known before, was to tell the "seer" to go away, to stop speaking such things and to leave decent people alone. This reaction, recorded in vv 12–13, was no doubt based on previous responses to itinerant prophets, some of whom had found their way to Bethel in earlier times. No doubt it was a customary and important forum for such men of God. (The priest's comments on the royal character of the sanctuary serve as a warning to Amos that he is treading on dangerous ground by specifically mentioning the royal house and the nation over which it exercised authority and for which it had responsibility.) Amaziah seems to overlook, or not take seriously into account, the threat to the sanctuaries, perhaps for two reasons. The threat is more general and less easily made the subject of a formal charge, and in the report to the king requesting action the emphasis would be on the political threat and the provable charge (namely, that Amos had uttered a threat against king and nation). The more strictly religious or theological issue might also be clouded by the prophet's clear claim to speak not only in the name of Yahweh, but Yahweh's own words.

We conclude, then, that Amaziah's initial verdict on Amos was that the latter was a typical itinerant seer or prophet (no significant difference here), a professional who carried out his obligations to his deity and made his living by his proclamations and other divinatory services, and one who could be frightened off by peremptory commands and thinly veiled threats of more serious action if the prophet did not leave the premises immediately and permanently. Presumably the priest was an experienced administrator and an authority figure accustomed to handling matters in his own city and at his sanctuary. At that stage of the episode the best judgment was that in spite of the inflammatory talk there was no serious threat to anyone, not to Israel, not to the king, and not to the sanctuary and priesthood. But there were good grounds for preventing any further oracles: the prophet might be a troublemaker, and the best procedure was to get rid of him.

Now we must go back and refine the approach somewhat, or reconstruct the episode as a sequence of interchanges between prophet and priest in the light of the clues and hints given by the compiler. We begin with the general framework, chaps. 7:1–8:3. Here we have four visions, given in pairs, with the Amaziah story embedded in the second pair. The theory is that Amos went to Bethel after seeing the two pairs of visions, and reported them with brief comments at the sanctuary. The provocative statement that sets off the altercation with Amaziah is found in v 9a, which, if the third and fourth visions were described together (as we think), must be combined with 8:3 to produce the full but limited exposition of what the divine pronouncement means: I shall never spare them again—on the contrary, the following will happen:

7:9   The high places (open-air shrines) of Isaac will be devastated,
          and Israel's sanctuaries will be laid waste;

8:3   The palace singers shall howl in that day
              —Oracle of my Lord Yahweh!—
       many are the corpses that will be cast away everywhere.
       Silence!

The final word is "Silence!" in the presence of death and corruption (cf. 6:10, where the silence is specified in relation to mentioning the name of the Lord). In any case, if we assume that Amos' address on the occasion of his visit to Bethel included a brief description of the two pairs of visions, the latter accompanied by an equally brief statement about the "end" and what it would consist of, then we can isolate the particular contents of the address as follows: first 7:1–6, 7:7–8, and 8:1–2 to include the four visions. Then the words of condemnation would follow, including 7:9a and 8:3 roughly as they stand. The closing words, especially 7:9a but also the references to the palace singers and the mounds of corpses, provoked a response from Amaziah either because he had come out to hear the "seer" from the south or because he had heard a report about the prophet's utterances and come out to investigate.

We can then construct the priest's response to Amos' threat to the sanctuaries and high places of Israel out of the quotation of Amaziah's words by Amos (v 16). Whether 8:3 belonged to Amos' original remarks or was appended to the whole in order to serve as a literary conclusion is not clear, and the question can be left open. The response in any case reflects the oracle in 7:9a, for it shares the unusual pairing *yiśḥāq//yiśrā'ēl* (and in chiastic form). The statement in 7:16 is perfectly plausible and suits the circumstance:

> Don't prophesy against [or about] Israel,
> don't preach against [or about] Isaac's domain!

In view of the dangerous character of Amos' remarks specifically aimed at Israel//Isaac, Amaziah warns the prophet not to preach on such a subject, or to say anything against the country to which he has come. This warning seems to be enough for the first round.

Amos, however, is not about to be silenced even by a well-meaning priest, so he offers an elaboration on the original oracle in v 17, which is the direct sequel to Amos' quotation of an earlier remark made by Amaziah. While the earlier speech is quoted by Amos, we assume that it is authentic and that the author intended us to understand that the words had been uttered earlier, only he does not wish to repeat them in separate contexts. It is enough to have them once.

Amos directly challenges the priestly prohibition by adding some new thoughts on the subject of the destruction of high places and sanctuaries. This time he zeroes in on the local shrine where Amaziah is the incumbent high priest, so he speaks as follows (logically—and metrically—rendered) in v 17:

> Therefore, thus has Yahweh said,
> "Your wife shall become prostitute in the city,
> and your sons and your daughters shall fall by the sword;
> and your land shall be parceled out by the measuring line;
> and you yourself shall die in a polluted land."

The description here reflects the consequences of invasion and conquest: the allocation of conquered land to those who shared in the victory, while those whose land it was are taken captive to die on foreign soil (unclean land), a somber fate especially for a priest. The use of the independent pronoun focuses attention on Amaziah and his personal destiny to die in exile in an unclean land, also on those close to him, the members of his family and the land that belongs to him, on which he and his family live. It may simply be a description of the land as a whole but also as the land in which he lives and to which he belongs. Four times the 2d m. s. suffix is used in addition to the pronoun itself to stress repeatedly that it is Amaziah's fate that is the subject of the oracles: your wife, your sons, your daughters, and your land will all share the fate of the defeated, the desecrated, and the overwhelmed—as will you.

Amos escalates the stakes in this second utterance, now clearly implying the necessary and expected consequence of conquest and filling in the details of the immediate context and location, namely, what will happen at Bethel itself. Moreover, he is now aiming his shot directly at the leader of this sanctuary by attacking Amaziah head on with words of doom and disaster. It is no wonder that the priest, thoroughly exasperated though hardly intimidated, responds in kind by denigrating Amos and commanding him to depart the premises. He has heard quite enough to wish to hear no more, ever. Previously he had instructed Amos to stop prophesying about or against the northern kingdom. Now he commands him to stop prophesying at Bethel permanently, never again to prophesy at all at this sanctuary. On the contrary, if he wishes to speak as a prophet then he must do so elsewhere, in his home country, where presumably he has the necessary standing and credentials. Calling Amos a "seer" is not a derogatory expression in itself. Amaziah's designation of Amos as *ḥōzeh* reflects Amos' report of the visions that constituted his call and commission. The problem is not in the designation or title, but in the characterization of the position. In effect, Amaziah accuses Amos of being a professional prophet, one who earns his living by his utterances. He makes it clear that there is no place for such a person at the sanctuary at Bethel and that he should go to the land of Judah, restricting his professional activities to his homeland, where he can presumably earn a living. The command never again to prophesy at Bethel carries with it the warning and instruction not to speak against the sanctuary there as Amos has been doing. Bethel surely is included in the general condemnation of v 9a and the denunciations of v 17, which are aimed at Amaziah himself but nevertheless must include or presuppose the destruction of Bethel and its sanctuary. The forced prostitution of his wife and the death of his children can only be consequences of a successful conquest of the place, not to speak of his own exile. Finally, the parceling out of the land may refer specifically to the city and its district, not only to any private property of the priest's household. It may be speaking of the land in terms of his authority over and responsibility for the sanctuary and its grounds, or even the city and its district, with which he had a unique relationship of supervisory authority if not ownership.

With respect to Bethel and its sanctuary, there is an added point. The whole city, very likely—including the sanctuary and a palace if there was one there—were under the special protection of the king. As Amaziah says, it is a royal chapel (= a sanctuary of the king) and it is a royal house (= house of the kingdom). It is not clear whether one establishment or two is intended, or whether there are two components in one enclave or complex. The important thing here is the emphasis on king and kingdom—Bethel is a national shrine, a holy place with explicit and direct ties to the throne. The linkage of the sanctuary at Bethel with the northern kingdom and monarchy is attested from the very beginning, with the founding of the rival kingdom of Israel by Jeroboam I in the tenth century. Its tradition as an especially significant shrine goes back to patriarchal times. The implication for Amos is a warning that he is treading on even more dangerous ground than he may have imagined. He is in a royal sanctuary, and anything he says or does there may bring him into conflict with the civil administration, as it already has with the ecclesiastical authorities. There is at least the hint now that further activity around or in Bethel will bring Amos to the attention of people who have both the tradition and the authority to deal summarily with troublemakers.

This warning may be the last one that does not carry with it the threat of police action. Amaziah may still have felt that the best way to handle a prickly and troublesome person such as Amos was to frighten him off rather than to take more drastic measures, particularly because Amos came to prophesy, and dealing with prophets was a difficult matter; there was always the outside chance that he might be a true prophet. Better not to shoulder too much responsibility for a stranger like this; if no harm were done and he were merely dismissed then probably no harm would come to Bethel and Amaziah. But there were limits, and Amos was dangerously close to trespassing on them, if he had not already done so. The words had been uttered, and their effect was yet to be gauged. They had also been heard and might be believed, with unpredictable effects. Worse, they might reach persons with no love for the priest at Bethel, and he might ultimately be blamed for not doing more than he had so far done. If the matter were not closed quickly, then it might develop in unforeseen and highly dangerous ways.

But Amos had no desire to cooperate with this priest, having once decided on his course of action, namely, to be responsive to the heavenly vision and to act as a true prophet in delivering the message at the central shrine of his God in the north. There was no turning back. In response to the priest's strongly worded invitation to leave the sanctuary and the country quickly (compare Elijah's instantaneous departure from the same country in response to Jezebel's peremptory threat in 1 Kgs 19:2 after the debacle at Mount Carmel for her prophets and retainers), he sets forth his credentials as a prophet, his priorities and necessities. They include coming to Bethel and delivering his message at the sanctuary, regardless of consequences. To accept the priest's order and to leave in such a way as to negate what he had already done, failing to complete those elements of the mission which had not yet been carried out, would falsify his mandate to prophesy.

First he defends himself from the implied charge that he is a professional prophet, and probably a false or mercenary one at that. Emphatically, and in a style that reflects the manner of the priest, Amos affirms that he is neither a prophet nor a member of the prophetic guild. This claim no doubt surprised Amaziah, who was beginning to realize that Amos was not the person he thought he was dealing with and hence probably not amenable to the techniques and devices used by authorities to control dissidents. It left a gap in the chain of information that had to be filled—to provide the necessary data to justify Amos' presence. If he was not a prophet, then who was he and what was he doing here at Bethel? The ominous implications could only reinforce the uneasiness of any bureaucrat in trying to cope with unknown quantities and qualities, and would reinforce Amaziah's decision to take a different tack entirely with this man.

Amos was, as anyone who bothered to ask would find out, a rancher and a farmer, a man of the country, in other words, like anyone else. By distancing himself from professional prophets and prophetic guilds Amos reveals himself as a lone figure, one who is unclassifiable, but with a unitary focus and guided by a personal vision. His mandate came from God himself, who took him from following the flock—a cliché out of Israel's past but one that was packed with tradition and power. Israel's history was largely shaped by ex-shepherds: Moses, who was caring for a flock when summoned directly to service by the God of the holy mountain; and David, the archetypal shepherd boy, who was called to be the Lord's anointed from his duties to the flock to serve a larger flock as ruler and king. Amos was called by Yahweh the God of Israel and the world to prophesy to that same people, so he had come and would deliver the message he had been given, obviously in disregard of all other factors. What might happen afterwards as a result of his preaching was not for him to determine or decide, but it would be very much the concern and business of those who had heard or could hear that message. Once he delivered the message and had discharged his duty, what happened to him was hardly important. His words would count, however, and a heavy responsibility weighed upon those who heard them and who had the chance to let others hear them. Interruption of or interference with the word of God could and would have the most dire consequences, so in a sense Amaziah was being warned at least as much as he was giving warning. He was on trial as much as he was putting Amos on trial.

Now we come to Amos' closing words in this dialogue. While the reconstruction is hypothetical, the overall picture is not. We know that finally Amaziah resolved the issue for himself by sending word to the king about this obstreperous, oracular nonprophet with the credentials and words of a true prophet. In order to initiate and justify as serious a charge as sedition and treason it was necessary for Amos to say something that fitted the specifications and would enable Amaziah to take definite action. Those words, repeated in substance by Amos and Amaziah (quoting Amos), provide the structural axes on which the whole story rides and form both the envelope for the story and its central content. We refer to the divided bicolon in vv 9b and 17bB, a statement that is given in substantially the same form in v 11, only here the two parts are given consecutively, confirming our analysis that associates the two separated parts:

9b   and I shall attack Jeroboam's house with my sword.

11   By the sword shall Jeroboam die,
       and Israel shall surely go into exile from its land.

17bB   and Israel shall surely go into exile from its land.

Amos' statement and Amaziah's paraphrase of it provide the basis for Amaziah's action in notifying the king. While much has been made of the difference between Amos' statement about the house of Jeroboam and Amaziah's adaptation of it, they probably amounted to the same thing at the time. It is possible that Amaziah was quoting a different version of the prophecy made by Amos earlier or that he interpreted Amos' statement to foreshadow a direct attempt on the king's life. It is possible that he sharpened the language to ensure an immediate and concerned response from the king, though it is difficult to imagine that the king would have been less or differently concerned by the two messages, or that he might have responded differently if he had received the messages in 9b and 17bB rather than the ones in v 11. Any message containing the words "sword" and "Jeroboam" and delivered in the name of Yahweh would be bound to receive serious attention. The difference between the messages only becomes important to those who are concerned about the fulfillment of prophecy, when one looks back to see how predictions and historical events match. The prediction attributed to Amos by Amaziah was not literally fulfilled, and if we choose we can blame Amaziah for the discrepancy and protect Amos' reputation for prophetic accuracy. It is recorded that Jeroboam's son, Zechariah, reigned as king for only six months before he was assassinated by a man named Shallum, who then assumed the kingship, thus bringing to an end the house of Jeroboam II. This chain of events clearly fulfilled the version of the prediction given in v 9b as Amos' own words. There can be little doubt that Amos was right about the fate in store for the dynasty of Jehu, the house of Jeroboam.

Once Amos has uttered fateful words about the royal house, then the picture changes and Amaziah no longer has options. Now he must report the affair to the king and transfer Amos to royal jurisdiction. Until this point he is not only free to deal with Amos in terms of sanctuary privileges and responsibility but, because the question of prophetic credentials, claims, and rights is involved, as the chief ecclesiastical authority he must do so. While there are political and civil implications in what Amos has said, and the attack on the sanctuaries of Israel is legitimate cause for concern—especially because Bethel is a royal foundation—the area of jurisdiction might be disputable, and a cautious priest might hesitate in summoning the civil authorities to intervene. It might still seem best to send the prophet away, banishing him from sanctuary and country.

Once Amos speaks in menacing terms about the royal house and mentions the conquest of the kingdom, however, there is no longer a choice. On the face of it Amos is guilty of "sedition," and now to let him go, much less encourage him to depart, would be a criminal act of its own, aiding and abetting a conspirator against the state. So while Amaziah's earlier decision could be justified on the grounds that Amos had not yet said anything of a directly political and revolutionary nature, now Amaziah must report to the king, explaining precisely the words that lie at the heart of the charge, namely, that Amos has conspired against the king. Once such a charge is made against Amos it would be absurd to let him go, much less encourage him to do so. He must be held in custody until the king decides what to do. One would speculate that the king would wish to investigate the matter and perhaps seek an interview with this prophet. It is hard to imagine that Amos would want or seek any other outcome. He has already rejected the priest's advice to leave under his own power. He certainly has jeopardized his position by making explicit threats against the king's house and cannot be unaware of the probable (or almost certain) consequences. Just as he sought, or certainly did not try to avoid, a confrontation with the priest at Bethel, he probably would have welcomed a meeting with the king, whether at Bethel or at Samaria. We do not know what may have happened after word was sent to the king, but it is most unlikely that Amos merely returned to Tekoa to tell his disciples about his adventures or to write his memoirs. Whether he survived the encounter with priest and (probably) king in Israel we do not know and may never know, but that there was more to Amos' venture to the north we may be sure. Just as we do not know and may never know what finally happened to St. Paul in his trial before Caesar (Nero) in Rome (Acts 28:17–21), we do not know what happened to Amos; but in both cases we may be sure that the biblical figure welcomed that opportunity to present his case even to the highest authority, because each felt himself to be commanded by a still higher authority and under a compulsion that could not be resisted.

It is to be noted that in other instances of a similar nature, the ecclesiastical authorities, when confronted with cases of possible civil disobedience, regularly turned to the civil authorities for assistance; often as a matter of policy they handed over people who might be guilty of criminal offenses to the royal administration. So in this case, as soon as Amaziah is aware that Amos is uttering threats against the reigning dynasty, he properly notifies the king. He interprets Amos' role as that of conspirator and active participant in an attempt to overthrow the government. Amaziah was almost certainly wrong about Amos, though finally we cannot tell whether Amos' writings may have had something to do with the successful assassination attempt against Jeroboam's son (or with any that may have failed). This connection may not be entirely farfetched, as kings had reason to be concerned (cf. the involvement of Elijah and Elisha in the change of government not only in Israel but also in Aram, in both cases by encouraging tacitly or actively the assassination of the reigning monarch and his replacement by the assassin). Prophets in the eleventh to ninth centuries wielded considerable power and exercised it in making and unmaking kings —from Samuel to Elijah and Elisha and including people like Nathan, Ahijah, and doubtless others. To a part of this charge Amos would have to plead guilty, the difference being that there was no conspiracy, or at most a conspiracy of two. Amos had no confederates that we know of or can imagine, and only one sponsor, God himself. It seems clear that the latter was the chief conspirator, whose purpose was just as clearly to destabilize the situation in the north, to lead to the overthrow of the government, and to destroy the nation. Amaziah was entirely right to warn the king of a conspiracy, but it was not of the kind in response to which either Amaziah or the king was likely to do what was needful: namely, repent. Amaziah goes on to say that the land cannot bear or contain all of Amos' words, a statement that, along with the quotation from Amos, is calculated to stir the king to action. At least there must be no more words; but what can be done about the words already said? Here, as elsewhere in the structure of the passage, we see the hand of the author, who is interested not only in telling a good story but in presenting a message of his own, or rather one from Amos and from his God. Amaziah, like another priest who conveyed truth he was not clearly aware of (John 12:49–52), is uttering a profound truth the force of which he would resent and resist. Amos' words have already penetrated the defenses of Bethel and Israel, and it is already too late to do anything about them. The leaders may silence Amos now and forever, but the damage has begun and will increase. The words cannot be neutralized or contained; they burst the bonds and restraints, and work in the city and the state, bringing about the reality of which they speak. They are self-fulfilling because they have the power to produce results in conformity with their contents. Once said they have a life of their own, and the outcome is already inherent in their contents.

While the outcomes for Amaziah, Amos, Jeroboam, and his house are of great interest to us as students and historians, they were not so important to the author, and he leaves us dangling just as the story reaches a climactic point. We have a few hints about later political developments but not about Amos and Amaziah. The chances are we never will. But for the author the real story has been told. The word was spoken—directly and explicitly— and is at large in Israel, in the ears and minds and hearts of those who heard it. Amos has fulfilled his mission, and Amaziah and even the king will play their appropriate roles. Somehow—and the author hardly gives us any information on this point—the words and the tradition have been preserved so that others can hear and respond. Thus the word continues to do its work in the world (cf. Isa 55:10–11).

III.A.2.c. THE FOURTH VISION (RIPE FRUIT) (8:1–3)

8: [1a]Thus my Lord Yahweh showed me: [1b]Indeed there was a basket of summer fruit (*qāyiṣ*). [2a]He said, "What do you see, Amos?" I said, "A basket of summer fruit (*qāyiṣ*)." [2b]Yahweh said to me, "The end (*qēṣ*) is coming for my people Israel; I shall never spare them again."

8:3a   The palace singers shall howl in that day
           —Oracle of my Lord Yahweh!—
3b   many are the corpses which will be cast away everywhere.
           Silence!

INTRODUCTION

This is the simplest and clearest of the visions. In form and development it matches the third vision, and the identical core statement (v 2bB) shows that they are twin revelations of the same moment in Amos' career and in Yahweh's treatment of Israel.

We have already used the similarities between the third and fourth visions in an attempt to unravel the meaning of the word *'ǎnāk* in the former. The meaning of the word pair *qāyiṣ/qēṣ* in the latter presents no such difficulties. Comparison of the second pair of visions (as a set) with the first pair (as a set) has given us the footings on which the whole structure of the book has been erected. The first vision contains the word "beginning"; the fourth contains the word "end." Both are references to seasons in the agricultural year. It is therefore conceivable that the entire development, and thus the entire public activity of Amos, took place in less than one calendar year; but we do not think that this frame allows time for all that happens.

More time is needed for the series of plagues reviewed in 4:6–11, especially if Amos was personally involved in bringing his message of repentance to the people as disaster followed disaster.

By comparing 7:7–9 with 8:1–3 we have argued that the oracles of judgment that emerge from the third and fourth visions are integral to them, or at least not demonstrably extraneous and merely editorial. Harper (1905:181) linked 8:3 to 8:9 to make a strophe. This connection is not needed; in fact, it does harm, for it dismantles the structure of the third and fourth visions as they embrace the story in 7:10–17. But the observation is useful all the same, for it shows that there are also thematic links between the fourth vision and the oracles that follow in chap. 8. And finally we have argued from the various links between the second pair of visions and Amos' encounter with Amaziah, that the latter incident is closely connected with the visions in which it is now embedded, at least thematically. The chronological connections within 7:7–8:3 are harder to work out. The nearest we can get to a solution is to blame the hardening of Yahweh's attitude in the shift from Visions 1 and 2 (when he is still susceptible to the prophet's intercession) to Visions 3 and 4 (when no more reprieves will be granted) to the refusal of the people to repent (4:6–11). The even greater intransigence shown by Amaziah in forbidding prophecy altogether at Bethel and, by inference, in all of Jeroboam's domains, then leads to the even more drastic messages of the fifth vision and its accompanying oracles (9:1–6). The intervening collection (8:4–14) contains Woes and judgments that continue the series begun earlier in the book. Their connections with the visions are more indeterminate. The fresh beginning in 8:4 ("Hear this") suggests a supplementary Book of Woes, or a continuation of The Book of Woes (chaps. 5–6), with the main Book of Visions (7:1–8:3) embedded in it. Or, seen another way, The Book of Woes (5:1–6:14; 8:4–14) and The Book of Visions (7:1–8:3; 9:1–6) have been interdigitated. As a result the fifth vision (9:1–2—its end is not cleanly marked) is embedded in oracular material (8:4–14; 9:3–6). This arrangement is somewhat miscellaneous, almost fragmentary, and could be no more than a supplementary addition of Amos traditions that could not be worked into the better-organized body of the book. The latter explanation is not satisfactory either, for no clear ending can be found for any original unsupplemented edition.

The form in which the interpretation of the fourth vision has reached us in the MT has been traditionally understood as resting on play with the sound of words, not with the symbolic meaning of the visual objects. It is quite different from the first two visions in this respect. In those two, the actions of locusts and of fire are similar, and are presented in a manner that brings out their similarity. The use of the verb "eat" in each case also provides a firm link with both the opening oracles of the Great Set Speech (chaps. 1–2), where the same verb occurs in each of the first seven, and with the plagues (4:7). The meaning of these visions is obvious and requires no comment or exposition. Amos speaks first, in order to expostulate and intercede.

The third and fourth visions proceed quite differently. The scene in each case is static, in contrast to the action in the first two, which causes Amos to cry "Halt!" Now the Lord speaks first, asking Amos what he sees. He replies as briefly as possible, with one word, *'ănāk* (7:8), and with one phrase, *kĕlûb qāyiṣ*.

NOTES

8:1b. *summer fruit.* The word *qāyiṣ* means summertime in contrast to winter (Gen 8:22; Amos 3:15; Zech 14:8; Ps 74:17). It follows the grain harvest (*qāṣîr;* Jer 8:20). While early fruits may ripen before summer (Isa 28:4), the word *qāyiṣ* alone can denote fruit. The species are not designated, but *qāyiṣ* fruits are distinguished from "vintage" (*bāṣîr;* Jer 48:32; Mic 7:1) and raisins (2 Sam 16:1-2). Along with wine, *qāyiṣ* can be stored for future use (Jer 40:10-12) or used to provision an army (2 Sam 16:1-2). Presumably such fruits are dried. In the Gezer Calendar the month of *qṣ* comes at the end of the agricultural year, after the vintage. The *defective* spelling of that word, which must be absolute, suggests that *qyṣ* in the MT might be due to a Judahite or even later scribe correcting the spelling to standard pronunciation. It could have been Amos' own pronunciation, if we assume that the country districts of Judah used the same dialect as the standard Hebrew of Jerusalem, which is not necessarily the case, and might be considered unlikely when we think of the usual patterns of dialectal geography. Although Gezer belonged to Ephraim it is close to Judah, and the pronunciation of **qayṣ* as *qêṣ* could represent a rural versus urban contrast in the south. On the face of it Amos would have said *qayṣ,* but because *haqqēṣ* is the only vocable uttered by Yahweh, we do not know which side of the isogloss *qayṣ/qêṣ* he preferred for "summer." The attestation of the word in Ugaritic (*qṭ = qêṭu < *qayṭu*) and at Byblos (*gi-e-zi = qêṣi*) isolates the Judahite (or Jerusalem) pronunciation, *qayṣ,* within Canaanite, with the possibility that the pronunciation of both words was originally *qēṣ* in Amos' presentation. That is, the comment in v 2bA does not solve the conundrum by resolving the ambiguity, because *qēṣ* could mean either "summer[-fruit]" or "end" for most Israelites.

For the intriguing suggestion (hardly demonstrable) that the last word of Gezer Calendar involves the same sound play, and that Amos might even have known the mnemonic, see B. D. Rahtjen 1964.

2b. *end.* The most common associations of this word (*qēṣ*) are with time, especially when the verb is "come" (Ezek 7:2–6). The former is made explicit in *ʿēt qēṣ* (Dan 8:17; 11:35, 40; 12:4, 9), and *qēṣ* can be identified as an abbreviation of this phrase in many of its occurrences, such as Gen 6:13 and Ezek 7:2a, which need not be emended. Ezekiel 7 plays on the theme:

7:2a	*qēṣ* "[the] end [-time]"
2b	*bāʾ haqqēṣ*
3	*ʿattâ haqqēṣ*
5	*rāʿâ hinnēh bāʾâ*
6	*qēṣ bāʾ*
	bāʾ haqqēṣ
	hinnēh bāʾâ—
7	*bāʾâ haṣṣĕpîrâ*
	bāʾ hāʿēt
	qārôb hayyôm
10	*hinnēh hayyôm*
	hinnēh bāʾâ
12	*bāʾ hāʿēt*
	higgîaʿ hayyôm
25	*qĕpādâ-bāʾ*

The whole passage is too intricate to analyze in detail here. It elaborates on the theme of final punishment, in other words, punishment that will bring the nation to an end. While *qēṣ* could indicate the end of a probationary period or time of grace (secured by Amos' intercessions in the first two visions in Amos), which is indicated by the accompanying explanation that he would never again pass by them, at this stage the end of the reprieve means the end of everything.

The word "and" at the beginning of the next verse shows that it is a continuation and explication of the pronouncement in v 2; and the eschatological time reference "in that day" confirms that "the end" has acquired that connotation.

8:3. With the rubric omitted, this verse, which could be a distinct oracle or oracle fragment, consists of two lines:

	Syllables
wĕhêlîlû šîrôt hêkāl bayyôm hahûʾ	12
rab happeger bĕkol-māqôm hišlîk hās	10

The construction of the second line is problematic; the last two verbs could be separate exclamations or even fragments that do not belong here at all. The lack of "and" before v 3b leaves the connection between the two lines indeterminate. They are connected thematically, and the wailing in v 3a is due to the heavy casualties in v 3b. But the formal, logical, and syntactic connections among the various parts have been differently perceived by different translators and interpreters.

The length of the first line has been eased by assigning "in that day" to the next clause. This move also supplies the next clause with a needed component: on that day . . . the corpses [will be] many. Rudolph strikes out "on that day," along with the rubric, as a later eschatologizing insertion. The use of the same rubric in 8:9 suggests that "on that day" is part of it; but in each case only "oracle of my Lord Yahweh" is parenthetical. The phrase *rab happeger* makes a good clause, with or without "on that day," whether *rab* is taken as a predicate adjective or as a perfect verb (Wolff 1977:318 n.g.). The former is preferable, for the verbs cannot all be "perfect" if the first one is given its usual future meaning with *waw*-consecutive. The verbless clause can then be future (RV). This parsing also lessens the strain that is created if *šîrôt hêkāl* and *rab happeger* are both taken as construct phrases. Even so, no solution is entirely satisfactory. "The corpses are many" would follow on best from v 3a as a circumstantial clause *wĕhappeger rab*. Hence some take v 3b as three incoherent exclamations (NJPS, NEB, NIV). But this reading implies an attributive phrase "many, many bodies" (NIV).

3a. *singers* (or "songs"). The structure of v 3 is the same as 7:9a, so *šyrwt* should be the subject of the verb *hylylw*. The problem is that *šyrwt*, which is a *hapax legomenon*, should mean "singers" but apparently means "songs." It may be a figure of speech or a by-form, but the latter is doubtful. The usage is generally clear, and we seem to be stuck with an anomaly. The chief difficulty is the presence of the *yod* as a vowel letter, if the word was originally and correctly *šārôt*. Still, the best we can do is: the singers of the palace/temple will howl. Anything else seems clumsy and awkward. Curiously, 5:23 has *šryk*, which could be *šāreykā*. In 8:10 *šîrêkem* are songs in contrast with a dirge, so they are either for rejoicing in the cult or for merrymaking in secular feasts.

palace (or "temple"). As both king and priest are the objects of judgment in chap. 7, either meaning of *hêkāl* fits the context. The female singers point to the palace rather than the temple, but other language points to the sacred precincts. We had the same problem in The Book of Woes, where the music in the cult is rejected (5:23), and the "idle songs" of 6:5 could be cultic but most likely belong with palace revels and debauchery.

howl. The verb always has a subject, never an object, except in Ezek 30:2, where the wail cry is "Alas the day!" There can be an additional modifier: "for Moab" (Jer 48:31; cf. 51:8); "upon their beds" (Hos 7:14); "because of a broken spirit" (Isa 65:14).

3b. *corpses.* The wailing in v 3a is clearly connected with the scale of the casualties: cf. *rōb ḥālāl wĕkōbed pāger*, "hosts of slain and heaps of corpses" (Nah 3:3). The word *peger* is collective (1 Sam 17:46).

The ingredients of v 3b could be disjointed cries, and grammatical connections need not be sought among them. The JB makes v 3b a subordinate clause giving the reason for v 3a. But the fragments in v 3b could be the actual sobs of the mourners. "Everywhere" could go with *rab happeger*, but it is more often connected with *hišlîk*. The picture of dead bodies lying around everywhere because there is no one to bury them (Ps 79:3) is the final stage of defeat and devastation. An element of desecration could also be involved if the enemy exposes the bodies and forbids their removal (cf. 7:9a).

cast away. See the note on the similar use of this verb in 4:3. Elsewhere the verb describes the disposal of corpses. It has two aspects. One is the use of dead bodies to defile a sacred place (1 Kgs 13:24–28), even taking bones out of graves for that purpose (Jer 8:2; Lev 26:28–33; 2 Kgs 23:15–20; Ps 79:1–4; Amos 2:1). So Isa 14:19 has the curse, "And you are cast out [*hošlaktā*, passive, which would be appropriate in Amos 8:3b] from your grave like a loathed *nēṣer* [not "branch" but "carrion" (NJPS)], slain, stabbed by the sword." The other is the profanation of the body by leaving it on the battlefield or setting it out for scavengers (Jer 9:21, 16:4). The use of *hišlîk* here points to the latter.

A literal rendering would be: "the multitude of corpses in every place [everywhere] he has cast forth." Because the subject has not been identified, the impersonal active may be the equivalent of a passive form: the multitude of corpses have been cast forth everywhere.

Silence! The same word is used in 6:10 in a similar context.

III.B. THE FIFTH VISION (8:4–9:6)

III.B.1. SECOND INSERTION: WOES (8:4–14)

III.B.1.a. WOES (8:4–6)

8:4a Hear this, you who trample upon the poor,
4b   and put an end to the wretched of the land;
5a   who say:
                    "When will the new moon pass,
                        so that we may sell our grain;
                    and the sabbath,

so that we may open our stores of grain?"—

5b   who reduce the quantity (*ephah*),
                while raising the price (*shekel*);
            and cheat with crooked scales;

6a   who buy the needy for money,
                and the poor for a pair of sandals

6b   —"and that we may sell the husks of the grain."

III.B.1.b. OATH (8:7–8)

8:7a   Yahweh has sworn by the pride of Jacob:
7b   "I will never forget any of their misdeeds."
8a   For this reason, should not the earth tremble,
8b   and everyone who dwells in it mourn?
        Shall it not all rise like the Nile,
            and be tossed about,
                then sink like the Nile of Egypt?

INTRODUCTION

When we look at the inserts, we note their organic connections with the sequence of visions. We have discussed the dynamic linkage between the story of the incident at Bethel and the visions that surround it. The same is true of the second insert, though the bonds are less close between Visions 4 and 5. As we have noted, the materials, while superficially unrelated, are tied together by two threads leading from earlier material in the book, the Woes and the futurist predictions, combining concern about the leading classes with portrayals of the ultimate doom. They fit well between Phase Two, in which the irreversible decision of doom is pronounced, and Phase Three, in which the relentless pursuit of surviving leaders will be carried out. While this group of oracles is generally regarded as a heterogeneous collection deriving from a variety of times and circumstances, most of them much later than Amos, we think they are an integral part of The Book of Visions and constitute a striking example of the prophet's message aimed at a particular group of the population. Here the prophet's famed social criticism is focused on those who buy and sell in the marketplace, who combine unseemly greed and avarice with all of the well-known forms of cheating, culminating in unscrupulous, flagrantly illegal, and immoral dealing in human beings. Note should be taken of the extraordinary echoing pattern that resonates between this passage and 2:6, where these miscreants are first identified, the only group in the entire list to be specified twice. Among all of those singled out in the Woes they are listed first and are mentioned again toward the end: the crushers and grinders of the poor (*hš'pym*, 2:7 and 8:4). In 2:6 they are accused of selling the righteous for silver and the poor for a pair of sandals, while in 8:6 they are accused of buying the destitute for silver and the poor for the same pair of sandals (the identical phrase).

The circumstances of this nefarious and strictly illegal practice of buying and selling debtors into slavery is what the prophet is talking about, for what he has in mind is not the price of the slave (which was normally much higher) but rather the amount of money for which the righteous poor are being sold to satisfy the debt. The regulations governing this practice are scattered in the Torah, but note Lev 25:39–46, where a distinction is made between brother Israelites and foreigners. The latter may be enslaved permanently, but not the former. The people under attack are dealers in the debt-slave trade. They are marked out early in the book and brought up for judgment and sentence at the end. The crimes mentioned in various places in the book (especially 5:10–12, but cf. 4:1), besides these passages, are spelled out in greater detail in 8:4–6 than elsewhere. A major theme of social justice—or the lack of it—comes to a head here. Amos, as messenger of God, deals in a representative fashion with the ethical side of covenant obligation. Such obligations are not more independent of or separate from the essential responsibility of citizenship in the kingdom of God than more formal obligations of worship and service, and violations in this sector are subject to the same stern judgment. It is revealing that the theme of justice in the marketplace, in all of its aspects, occupies Amos' attention; perhaps it is a reflection of his experience as a rancher and orchard keeper but also of his keen observation of the practice of true and false religion on the horizontal plane, at eye level as it were, person to person.

Parallel to and joined with this concern is another representative group, with its characteristic and glaring sin. They are mentioned in 8:14 and, together with those in 8:4, wrap up the unit:

> 8:4 *haššō'ăpîm*
> 8:14 *hannišbā'îm*

The latter are those who swear falsely, that is, by false gods; but it is the combination of the two that counts. This particular violation of the covenant code is both primal (i.e., the first of all commandments, the

Hauptgebot) and ultimate. It is difficult to believe that people all over the country were swearing by the *'šmh* of Samaria or the *drk,* but such seems to be the case, and there is ample evidence of polytheism and idolatry in Israel and Judah during these centuries. Whether the groups are identical or only overlap and interlock is immaterial, though one may easily imagine that cheating merchants will swear to their honesty by false gods, and that those who worship those gods would deal treacherously with their fellow human beings. Each group symbolizes the corrupt leadership or entrepreneurial class in the country, and together they combine the ethical and the theological aspects of covenant violation.

Along with the indictment of the ruling class distributed through the branches of government and hierarchy goes the sentence, also detailed in a group of sketches of the classic features of divine judgment. So in the second insertion various threads of indictment and punishment, already presented in different ways in earlier parts of the book, are brought to a head. Amos' intense devotion to the practice of equity and right dealing is expressed equally in the denunciation of the oppressors and in his protective concern for the poor. At the same time his dedication to the great tradition of Israel's one God, the unique distinction of this otherwise insignificant people, finds expression in his proclamation of the true God and his mighty deeds and the condemnation of false religion and its adherents. The second insertion reflects the escalation of Yahweh's campaign against his people, but especially the corrupt and idolatrous leadership, and proceeds directly into the climactic vision in 9:1–4, with its picture of final historical judgment and the execution of the guilty.

NOTES

8:4–8. The oath that begins with v 7 and continues into the threat of v 8 could be regarded as a distinct unit. But in spite of the mixture of *Gattungen,* the references to "their deeds" (v 7) and "on account of this" (v 8) are best managed if they connect back to the indictment implicit in the Woe of vv 4–6. That piece also is not pure and simple by form-critical tests. The opening call, "Hear this," which has ties with 3:1, 4:1, and 5:1, begins an exhortation or accusation. But the context, vocabulary, and participial constructions link vv 4–6 to 2:7 and other statements throughout the book that we have identified as "Woes." The movement from second to third person corresponds to the shift to a more objective assessment of the situation when the Woe changes to an oath. Including v 8 brings the question asked by Yahweh into juxtaposition with the question asked by the oppressors in v 5. The analysis resembles that in 5:18–20, where the people are looking forward to the future; but it will turn out to be quite different from what they hope for and expect.

As part of the series of Woes, vv 4–8 have connections with the other Woes. In particular, v 6a is almost a repetition of 2:6b. The oath in v 7 balances the one in 6:8 (there the oath opens the unit, vv 8–14; here it closes it). The judgment in v 8 takes us back into vision, with cosmic-mythic imagery that prepares for the final Hymn in 9:5–6. It also provides an eschatological interface for v 9, which opens out into v 10. And v 10 (mourning) harks back to v 3 as well as to v 8, so that vv 1–3 and vv 9–10 could be viewed as a solid frame around vv 4–8, making a large, coherent unit. Our isolation of vv 4–8 is thus for convenience only.

Taking vv 4–8 as a composite unit, vv 4 and 7 go together and form an envelope around vv 5–6. Verses 5–6 have a similar introverted structure, with vv 5a and 6b serving as an envelope around vv 5b and 6a. Note the chiasmus *našbîrâ* . . . *bar//bar našbîr*. Verse 4 announces the themes of the woe, which are developed and expanded in vv 5–6. Verse 4a is picked up by vv 5a and 6b, and v 4b is explicated in vv 5b and 6a.

Unlike previous Woes, which denounce each fault briefly with a single bicolon in which a participle is usually followed by a finite verb, in this Woe the lead participle (v 4a) is followed by a series of construct infinitives. Another feature is the report of the actual speech of the evildoers.

Amos condemns his contemporaries for both their words and their works. For just as his speech (the divine utterance) is an event and an action, so their words are deeds. He accuses them of saying:

2:12 You shall not prophesy
4:1   Bring, that we may drink
5:14 The Lord will be with (us)
6:13 Have we not by our own strength taken Qarnaim for our-selves?
8:14 By the life of your God, [from] Dan, etc.
9:10 Evil shall not overtake and meet us

Compare also 5:18. Amos 8:5–6 reports the longest of these speeches, attributed by Amos to the objects of his Woes. It brings out in more detail the commercial side of their oppression.

In spite of the mixed character of the unit from the form-critical point of view, the material has been strung together by means of various series of similar expressions, which run like threads across the fabric, and by means of wordplay (sound and meaning).

The technique is compositional rather than poetic, if parallelism is the main criterion. Verses 4 and 6a are the best formed bicola, and together they constitute a tetracolon with its own elaborate structure. The keyword '*ebyôn* occurs in the first and last lines of the four. It has different parallels in each bicolon, standing in chiasmus with *dallîm* in v 6. The line lengths (9 : 7 :: 6 : 8) also balance, chiastically. The complementary 2:6–7 likewise has four statements, and 8:4 and 6a are chiastic in relation to 2:6–7.

2:6a	ṣaddîq	'ebyôn		6b
6b	'ebyôn	dallîm		8:6a
2:7a	dallîm	'ăniwwê-'āreṣ		4b
7b	'ănāwîm	'ebyôn		8:4a

The series in 8:4–6 begins and ends with *'ebyôn*, with plural nouns as parallels, and in chiasmus.

Verse 6aB is an exact repetition of 2:6bB. Their parallels have complementary verbs: "sell" in 2:6, "buy" in 8:6. These matching infinitives have been plugged into their contexts by means of different prepositions: *'al* in 2:6b repeats the preposition of the opening formula (v 6a); *l-* of 8:6 ties into the series of infinitives in the rest of the Woe: *lĕhaqṭîn* . . . *lĕhagdîl* . . . *lĕ'awwēt* . . . *liqnôt*. This series unifies vv 5b and 6a. A balancing series of first-person verbs makes vv 5a and 6b an envelope around the rest: "we will sell," "we will open," "we will sell" (grain in each case). It is a mistake to bring these clearly related materials closer together by transposing v 6b into v 5 (Wolff 1977:322, n. h). The effect is powerful. It shows that these people regarded cereals and human beings equally as stock for sale. Their practices were both dishonest and inhumane.

The theme of selling grain, presented as the speech, audible or tacit, of the merchants themselves (vv 5, 6b), comes in very short lines (mostly four or five syllables), in contrast to the longer lines (mostly eight or nine syllables) in the rest of the unit.

In spite of this wide variation in line length and minimal use of parallelism, the poetic character of the piece is shown by the vocabulary. There is no occasion to use the relative pronoun (relative clauses are rare in poetry, as long clauses are avoided; but, if used, *'ăšer* would be understood). The most striking thing is the many nouns clearly definite in meaning (as translations recognize) but lacking the definite article. Apart from the opening participle, where the *he* is vocative, it occurs only in *haḥōdeš* and *haššabât*, where it is demonstrative—"this new moon," "this sabbath,"—because they make their remarks (or think these thoughts) while the festival is actually in progress. The verbal art is found more in wordplay or sound play:

> wĕlašbît . . . našbîrâ šeber
> wĕšabbāt; šeber . . . bar;
> našbîr nišba‘

8:4a. *trample.* See notes on 2:7a.

4b. *put an end.* The form is *wĕlašbît,* and it is difficult in three respects:

1. An infinitive rather than a finite verb is used to follow the participle of a Woe; but this usage ties into the whole series of infinitives that register intention.

2. The omission of *-h-* of *hip‘il* throws some doubt on the form, because it is preserved in *lhqtyn* and *lhgdyl,* which follow. The resulting chiastic pattern, *lšbyt, lhqṭyn, lhgdyl, l‘wt,* suggests that the first and last match. But changes to bring them even closer (e.g., *lšḥt*) would be going too far.

3. The root itself seems to have been chosen in anticipation of a play on the word *šabbāt.* It is also climactic, for it takes the activity with which the whole series of woes began (2:6–7) to the point of eliminating the destitute from society altogether. They are first impoverished, then sold off, perhaps to foreign slavers (2:6, 9). See our discussion of *hišbattî* in Hos 1:4 (Andersen and Freedman 1980:182–83). The LXX could not cope with the infinitive; it has *katadynsteuontes,* which (in feminine form) translates *hāʿōšĕqôt* in 4:1. Reading a similar participle here certainly makes it easier, but to explain the MT version as an error due to *šbt* in v 5 misses the point that the verb was chosen precisely to achieve wordplay.

wretched. A common idiom for *hišbît* is "cause to cease from . . ." often *min-hāʾāreṣ* (Lev 26:6; Ezek 34:25), meaning "to destroy completely." The phrase *ʿaniwwê-ʾāreṣ* is thus elliptical for "the poor [from] the land." While most construct phrases realize a simple genitive relationship, with no intervening material permitted between the two related nouns, a preposition is sometimes found at this point. The opposite would be the use of a construct relationship instead of modification by means of a preposition.

5a. *When.* The question *ʿad mātay,* "how long?" expresses impatience at a waiting period that never seems to end. The note of resolution struck in the following two cohortative verbs shows that the merchants are looking ahead and making plans. If they are thinking about nothing else during the festivals, then Amos' analysis penetrates to their inmost value system, behind the facade of religiosity. These people were scrupulous in observing the religious holidays, but their hearts were not in it. Because they were unable to conduct their business at such times, the question may be asked whether they were actually officers of the cult (even such a person as Amaziah) who at other times were active in the market. At the very least we can infer that the priests and profiteers were hand in glove, just as we have seen from 5:10–12 that merchants and magistrates were collaborators in fraud and cover-up.

new moon. The status of the new-moon festivals in Israel is not as prominent in the records as that of the festivals attached to the agricultural year.
To judge from 1 Sam 20:5, 34 it was mainly a family celebration in the early
days. It receives scanty notice in the Pentateuch (Num 10:10, 28:11–15).
This passage, along with Ezek 46:2–3, indicates that it resembled the sabbath in banning work. Amos does not express disapproval of the festival as
such. His criticism has more point if the people condemned are not giving
their minds to a legitimate claim of God on their devotion. Isaiah (1:13–14)
and Hosea (2:13) adopt a more negative attitude.

sabbath. (See Tsevat 1972 and Hallo 1977.) Hosea 2:13 confirms the
association of *ḥōdeš* and *šabbāt.* In view of the enormous importance that
the sabbath gained in postexilic times and the dominance it enjoys until this
day in Jewish religious life, it is surprising that it receives so little attention
in pre-exilic records. Yet the Decalogue guarantees its antiquity; it also
certifies its humane purpose (Exod 23:12; Deut 5:14) and highest possible
motivation in imitating the example of God himself (Exod 20:11).
Nehemiah's problem was different (13:15–22); the people of his day were
doing business on the sabbath.

The LXX has the plural, and Targum identifies it as the interval before a
sabbatical year. The implication would be that in the off-season only those
who had grain stores could engage in commerce and inflate the price. But
v 5b shows that their gains came from fraud, not just profiteering.

sell . . . grain. a. With the exception of the Joseph story, where it occurs many times, *šeber* occurs again only in Neh 10:32. The verbs (*qal* for
"buy," *hipʿil* for "sell") are denominative, but it is not clear why a special
and exclusive verb should be needed to describe commercial transactions
involving this commodity. The LXX uses a neutral "traffic," "gain." Its
lack of an object reflects the redundancy of the cognate. The proposal to
follow suit by omitting *šbr* from the MT (BHS) overlooks this simple factor
(Rudolph 1971a:261).

grain. b. There is no indication of a difference between *šeber* and *bar;*
they are synonyms.

open. The verb has been found difficult. It has been interpreted as "display" (Cripps 1969) or simply "market" (NIV) or "offer" (JPS). The NEB
adds "again" as if it had been shut up for the holiday; but "wheat" is not a
suitable object for "open." The collocation of verbs is justified by Gen
41:56, *wayyiptaḥ . . . wayyišbōr,* "and Joseph opened all that was in them
and sold [grain] to Egypt." The Samaritan Pentateuch adds *br* after *wyšbr,*
which may be the original reading, *br* having been lost by haplography.
Either *wyšbr [šbr]* or *wyšbr [br]* would be suitable, as both combinations
occur here: *wnšbyrh šbr* (5a) and *br nšbyr* (6b, in reverse order). The LXX
has the object *pantas tous sitobolōnas* and the Peshitta, *ʾwṣrʾ.* Compare with
the latter the object that the LXX supplies, for "open," *thēsaurous.*

These versions are interpretive. They do not warrant the "restoration" of *'ôṣār* (or plural) in Gen 41:56 or Amos 8:5. The interpretation is probably correct; "open" is elliptical, or *bar* is elliptical for "grain [-stores]." In any case both nouns go with both objects.

5b. *reduce the quantity.* The next three infinitives explain three techniques for fraud, one involving the measure of dry volume (*'êpâ*), one the measure of currency (*šeqel*), one the scales. Commentators are not quite sure how they worked.

The problem of honesty in the marketplace was universal in antiquity and even in more recent times. Compare the following quotation:

> I have neither increased nor diminished the grain measure.
> I have not added to the weight of the balance.
> I have not weakened the plummet of the scales.
> (*ANET* 34, 388; Lambert 1960:133; cf. also Lambert 1957–58).

These age-old rackets called forth frequent legislation in the ancient world, with definitions of standard weights and measures as well as efforts at price control.

The NJPS translation correctly recognizes the *hip'îl*s as comparative, "too small" (not just "small" [RSV]). "Skimping the measure" (NIV) could mean using a true vessel, but not filling it (putting wax in the bottom to reduce capacity is an old trick).

raising the price. This expression refers to using false weight when it comes to payment. They make the *shekel* great, meaning that the marked weights used to balance the silver or gold made in payment are doctored so that the actual weight of the stones or metal pieces is higher than the marked weight. Hence the unwitting customer pays more than he should for his goods. Either this procedure or the preceding one will give an unfair advantage and an unmerited profit to the seller. Combined they could double the effect and threaten the survival of unwary customers.

crooked. "Scales of deceit" are the opposite of "correct or true balance" (*ṣedeq*). The verb is used in Job 8:3 with the words *mišpāṭ* and *ṣedeq* as objects; and cf. Job 34:12, where Elihu denies that "El declares [the righteous] to be wicked or that Shadday twists justice." In Amos 8:5 the equipment has been tampered with, perhaps by shifting the fulcrum from the middle of the beam. "Cheat" is not quite the meaning of *l'wt*, which is nearer to "bend" or "twist." The verb is used with a person as object (Ps 119:78; Job 19:6; Lam 3:36), meaning "to defraud them of justice." In Lam 3:36 the use of the adverbial phrase *brybw* with *l'wt* suggests that here fraud is perpetrated with the false scales. In the setting of Amos 8:5, between vv 4 and 6, we may suppose that the poor are the victims of the frauds in v 5, being cheated *by means of* a false balance and by defective weights and measures.

6a. See the NOTES on 2:6b.

6b. *husks of the grain*. Selling these husks is the final insult and outrage. Not only is the quantity too small and the price too high; the product itself is inferior. The exact meaning of the word *mappāl*, which occurs only here in the OT, is not clear. The LXX read it as *mkl*, "from every product." Deriving *mappāl* from *npl*, "fall," leads to the idea of "sweepings."

7a. *pride*. In 6:8 Yahweh swore "by himself" that he hates "the pride of Jacob." In the NOTES on that verse we pointed out that *g'wn* can be legitimate pride or detestable arrogance. "The pride of Jacob" could even be a title for God. If so, the *b-* here could be *essentiae*. He swore by himself in his character as the Pride of Jacob. If "Jacob's Pride" means Jacob's god, perhaps it is polar and can mean either a false god or the true God, just as *gā'ôn* is ambivalent. It may be, too, that the expression here is an abbreviated form of the longer sentence in 6:8 and that the meaning is essentially the same, "Yahweh has sworn [by himself . . .] against the arrogance of Jacob."

7b. *forget*. In the full form of an oath there is a conditional protasis—"*if* I should do thus-and-so"—followed by an apodosis—"*then* let thus-and-so happen." The apodosis can be a self-curse: "let me be cursed or punished [in some fitting manner] if I ever do what I say I will not do, or fail to do what I say I will do." The oath used then serves as a renunciation, a vow not to do what is stated. Often the consequences are not explicitly stated, as if the content of the curse were provided by the ritual act, such as killing the animal victim, or as if the curse were too horrible to mention, and the person left it to the gods or guardians of the oath to determine a suitable punishment. In this form the conditional conjunction "if" is virtually a negation—"I will never forget. . . ." It is a more powerful way of saying "I will remember."

The biblical writers for the most part were not interested in the abstract, theoretical question of how an omniscient God could forget anything. As with all descriptions of mental and emotional states—to know, love, hate, remember, forget—there is always a behavioral component. When Yahweh says of Israel in Hos 2:15, "She went off after her lover(s) / and forgot me," the first action defines the second. It does not mean that all knowledge and recollection of Yahweh was lost, but he was not kept in mind. Similarly, when Yahweh says in Jer 31:34, "I will forgive their iniquity, / and I will remember their sin no more," the first action defines the second. The sin will not be brought to mind; it will no longer be a factor in their relationship and in Yahweh's interaction with Israel. It is the same in Amos 8:7. This oath matches the double response to Amos' plea in the first two visions, where Yahweh was prepared to forget their misdeeds, and the double and opposite response in the second pair of visions, where he resolves "never again" to pass over them.

misdeeds. The word can be neutral in moral connotation (Prov 20:11), and can even be used for acts of God (Mic 2:7; Pss 77:12, 78:7). But it is mainly used of human deeds, and even without the attribute "bad" (which is frequently used) it means "evil deeds."

After the implied negative of the oath, an adversative statement is needed, "but, on the contrary, I will remember and punish." A judgment oracle naturally follows.

8. This verse is almost the same as 9:5. There are subtle differences, however; so we have to ask if they are original and intentional or represent textual divergence in transmission due to error committed by scribes in copying the manuscripts.

8:8aA	*ha'al zō't lō'-tirgaz hā'āreṣ*
9:5aA	*hannôgēa' bā'āreṣ wattāmôg*
8:8aB	*we'ābal kol-yôšēb bāh*
9:5aB	*we'ābelû kol-yôšebê bāh*
8:8bA	*we'ālĕtâ kā'ōr kullāh*
9:5bA	*we'ālĕtâ kay'ōr kullāh*
8:8bB	*wĕnigrĕšâ wĕnišqâ kî'ôr miṣrāyim*
9:5bB	*wĕšāqĕ'â kî'ōr miṣrāyim*

Changes in closely similar texts can take place in either direction, diverging or converging; but the main trends in doublets are toward leveling and normalization (Andersen 1960). The treatment of Amos 8:8//9:5 in the Targum Jonathan illustrates the process. On the one hand, Targum Pseudo-Jonathan preserves some of the differences between 8:8 and 9:5 of the MT, such as the singular/plural of 8:8aB and 9:5aB (the LXX does this too, but the Peshitta does not). The LXX does not have anything corresponding to *wĕnigrĕšâ* (in MT 8:8; it does not occur in MT 9:5), but the Peshitta has a good translation, *wndḥwq*, while the Targum has a paraphrase *wytryk yt ytbh'*, "and he will destroy the inhabitants." This clause is a continuation of its interpretation in which a king is brought into the act. Apart from the mixed treatment of *wngršh*, all of the versions have brought 8:8 and 9:5b into line, a process partly reflected in the qere of 8:8—(kethib) *wnšqh* > (qere) *wnšq'h*. The Peshitta translates *trgz* and *tmwg* by the same verb, *zw'*, used by the Targum in 9:5 but not in 8:8, where it prefers *ṭḥrwb*, in keeping with its naturalizing tendencies. The LXX preserves a distinction between these two verbs, though *saleuōn* is somewhat interpretive, because it makes the earth the object and is not accurate ("shake" rather than "melt"). In the MT "the earth" is the obvious subject of the feminine verbs that follow, and it is a notable difference between 8:8aA and 9:5aB that the earth is described in varying terms (it shakes in 8:8 and melts in 9:5), but behaves in the same way in the sequels (8:8aB and 9:5aC): all of it rises and falls like the Nile. The versions have found different subjects for these verbs. In the Targum it is a king who comes up and seizes the land (cf. Jer 46:7–8). The LXX and the Peshitta take *klh* as the subject, identifying it as "its completion" (Peshitta's *qṣh* is an echo of 8:1–2). The methodological moral of this excursion into textual criticism is that each version has simplified, leveled, and interpreted the parallel passages in its own way (sometimes in the same way). But neither any one of them nor any combination offers a feasible, let alone viable, alternative to the MT. The MT in 8:8 is the more difficult and untidy; that in 9:5 is more symmetrical and poetic. The Hymn is probably the more original, being traditional; and, being a quotation wrenched from its background, its meaning remains obscure to us, though it would have been clear enough to Amos and to his original listeners and subsequent readers who knew where it came from. So it seems that 8:8 is a different adaptation of a part of the same Hymn for use in an oath *cum* judgment oracle, and that it was used in anticipation of and preparation for the Hymn that was coming up later. We conclude that 8:8 was not originally the same as 9:5, and therefore we hesitate to emend either in the direction of the other, while allowing that doublets and errors may have crept into the text.

The close similarity between 8:8 and 9:5 has important consequences for form-critical studies of Amos. If both are authentic and original with Amos (or at least an integral part of the first edition prepared by a disciple of the prophet, presumably someone who knew his mind), then the formal differences among oath (8:7), judgment speech (8:8), and cosmic Hymn (9:5) are slight. In the present and larger context of finished literary composition, these items have thematic functions that are true to their original oral use in various contexts, but which are also appropriate in their present *literary* context. The even earlier and traditional theophanic setting of an epiphany Hymn such as 9:5 is not lost either; but it is now projected into a future in which historical judgment dissolves into a mythic eschaton.

If 9:5 is eliminated as not only secondary but extraneous, its similarities to 8:8 can be seen as mere imitation, and 8:8 could still be retained as original. We could even ask if 9:5, with its more conspicuous mythic opening line (9:5aB is clearly mythic [cf. Mic 1:4], while 8:8 can be interpreted more naturalistically), has moved too far in that direction and taken 8:8 with it. An opposite inference—that because 9:5 is a gloss, 8:8 must be one also from the same hand—is going too far the other way.

8a. *should not.* The normal *hălōʾ* has been split into component parts;

that we must read it as the negative question requiring a positive answer is clear: "For this reason, should not the earth tremble?" The arrangement probably results from the desire to put the interrogative first but also to have the phrase *ʿl-zʾt* near the beginning. Actually it seems just to be a stylistic device that calls attention to the terms but does not affect the meaning. That the result is the same as if *hlʾ* were written together is seen from a literal rendering, "Is it because of this that the land does not tremble?" But that version is opposite to the intended meaning, as shown by the subsequent comparison with the rise and fall of the Nile. The normal rendering presumably would have been *hălōʾ ʿal-zōʾt*, "Is it not because of this?" which is the way it must be rendered in English. What it shows is that compound expressions, even very short ones, can be split up and other elements inserted between the parts, as we have argued concerning construct chains and other bound constructions.

tremble. The subject, *hāʾāreṣ*, is ambiguous. If the parallel in v 8aB is synonymous, the word *hʾrṣ* could mean the land of Israel here and in v 8aB its inhabitants. The verb can describe the agitation of people (Jer 33:9), equivalent to *ḥrd* (Isa 32:11; cf. Amos 3:6). In view of v 8b, and especially in the light of the connections of v 8b with 9:5, more cosmic convulsions could be in mind, affecting all of the world's inhabitants.

mourn. This verb has connections with the cognate noun in v 10. Note also the link between the same verb in 1:2 and the earthquake in 1:1.

8b. *Nile.* The parallelism is climactic, emphasizing the reference to the Nile by repetition. There are three different spellings of this word in four occurrences. The standard spelling *kyʾr* is used in 9:5 (twice), as befits its traditional character. The *plene kyʾwr* (8:8bB) is rare. It occurs only here and five times in Isaiah (19:7–8, 23:3). The fourth spelling, *kʾr* (8:8bA), is defective and may be suspect. The Masoretes vocalized it as "like the light," perhaps under the influence of the next verse (*ʾôr*). Normally the Hebrew word is spelled *plene: ʾwr*.

tossed. In the second colon of 8b we have two verbs, one of which is a mystery while the other does not fit well in the context. In this respect 9:5 seems superior, with the reading *šqʿh*, which balances the verb in the first colon, *ʿlth*, and suits the context: "It [the earth] rises and sinks like the Nile of Egypt." The cola balance beautifully, and the sense is entirely acceptable. The earth has melted like a river under the touch of Yahweh. The sensation of feeling the land move, rise and fall, is usefully associated with earthquakes, and the feeling of those who experience the phenomenon is akin to being seasick. The melting of the earth as a result of direct divine contact is more or less appropriate, though the associated imagery in a comparable passage in Micah describes the melting and flowing of the mountains while here it is rather the earth's heaving up and down that is portrayed in the comparison with the Nile.

What is the picture: inundation or undulation? The comparison with the Nile suggests inundation. It rises and falls; but it is not a cataclysm and does not generate gigantic, destructive waves. The shock waves of an earthquake are more like the waves of the sea, and we should note that in both 8:8 and 9:5 it is the earth that is referred to; it is not water coming up over the earth like the Nile, it is the earth reduced to liquid and flowing like the Nile. Amos 9:5 and Mic 1:4 are essentially the same once it is noted that "mountains" represent "earth" in many cosmological schemes, in both creation and eschatological mythic imagery (Isa 40:12; Ps 90:2[E3]).

In creation (Job 38:11) the sea was expelled from the land,

> And I prescribed bounds for it,
> and set bars and doors to keep it out.

The dashing of the waves on the shore is a perpetual assault of this monster, trying to return to his original domain. The Flood was a temporary reversion to this primal status, and Amos 5:8b (= 9:6b) anticipates a similar cataclysm in the final judgment. Psalm 46:3–4 describes this ultimate reversion of cosmos to chaos in similar terms:

> 'al-kēn lō'-nîrā' bĕhāmîr 'āreṣ
> ûbĕmôṭ hārîm bĕlēb yammîm
> yehĕmû yeḥmĕrû mêmāyw
> yir'ăšû-hārîm bĕga'ăwātô

Therefore we will not be afraid when earth is changed
and when mountains topple into the heart of The Sea,
Its waters rage they foam
Mountains convulse in its surging.

In the end the land is liquefied once more (at a touch [9:5]) and flows away to merge with the sea as it was in the beginning. Amos seems to be using glimpses of both of these scenarios: creation of the present arrangement either by removing the water from the earth's surface or by solidifying land out of the primal water, with the reversal of these processes in the ending of the world.

Earthquake vocabulary is reflected in 8:8 more explicitly. Thus the earth is said to tremble in 8a, and this theme is picked up in 8b with *ngrš*, which here is rendered "tossed," "driven about"; literally, "and she will be driven out." The normal meaning of the active forms, mainly *pi'el*, is "to drive out," and they are used regularly with people as objects in a wide variety of circumstances. There is perhaps sufficient evidence to support that interpretation here. The *nipʿal* occurs only three times: here, Jonah 2:5 (which is normal usage and not pertinent to the issue here), and Isa 57:20:

> *wĕhārĕšāʿîm kayyām nigrāš*
> *kî hašqēṭ lōʾ yûkāl*
> *wayyigrĕšû mêmâyw repeš wāṭîṭ*

> But the wicked are like the tossing sea
> [the sea that has been driven out];
> For it cannot be quiet,
> And its waters tossed up mire and dirt.

If we ask how the wicked are like the sea, the answer is given by the two verbs, they are expelled and they expel. The sea was expelled from the land, and it retaliated by expelling muck and mud onto the land.

sink. With respect to the second verb in the colon, *wnšqh,* very little can be said. The qere for this word is *nišqĕʿâ,* a presumed *nipʿal* perfect 3d f. s. of *šqʿ* in conformity with the verbal root in 9:5. The kethib would then be regarded as an error in which the ʿ was inadvertently dropped. A difficulty with this view, apart from its apparent ease in avoiding questions concerning the text of v 8, is that no other occurrence of the *nipʿal* of this root is known in the Hebrew Bible, which enhances the possibility that *qere* simply is an ad hoc solution to the difficulty. Other possibilities do not commend themselves. The *qal* form of the root *nšq* would hardly make sense, though the form would fit that of the parallel colon (as in 9:5). A supposed *nipʿal* of *šqh* with the meaning "watered" might suit the effect of the Nile on the surrounding land but would not be in keeping with the rest of the verse. It looks as though the best reading is in 9:5 and that we have a pair of inferior variants in 8:8. Of the two, *ngrš* is probably more original and more viable, because it is comparable to *trgz* in 8aA and can be used in connection with bodies of water. The other one, *wnqš,* seems to be beyond recovery or defense. It seems vaguely to be the result of influence from the preceding verb, and from the reading in 9:5, a true conflation.

COMMENT

Compare v 6 with 2:6, where the same material is found but with a significant change of the verb from *mikrām* to *liqnôt*—namely, from selling to buying. What does that charge signify? Here we seem to have the reverse procedure; now they are purchasing poor people who are presumably being sold to satisfy trivial debts. At least this is the supposition, based on the analysis of the passage in chap. 2. It is also instructive that in chap. 2 the parallel (or explicative) terms are ṣdyq and ʾbwyn, while here they are synonymous, dlym and ʾbwyn, but the general idea is the same. The practice is reprehensible not primarily in legal terms but in terms of justice and equity and above all concern for the well-being of people in dire circumstances. The merchants, along with others of the entrepreneurial class, are accused of heartlessly cruel behavior in dealings with customers and especially the poor, whether in buying or selling or here in the case of debt settlement.

Verse 4a denounces those who crush or trample the poor. Their behavior is described in vv 5a–6b: they cannot wait to transact business and deplore the restrictions on commercial activity on the new moon and the sabbath, an indication that such rules were in force and had some effect in those days. So-called blue laws based on the old codes are referred to in a way that indicates that in pre-exilic times they were observed or at least imposed by the authorities. It is clear that in the Decalogue the sabbath was a day of rest. The observance of the new moon is less well attested in the literature, but there is enough evidence to show that it was already part of the religious calendar. The chief source of information is 1 Samuel 20, where repeated references make clear that the observance of the new moon had an important place in Israelite life. Confirmation comes from Isaiah and Hosea in the eighth century (Isa 1:13–14; Hos 2:13, 5:7). In Isaiah it is included in a long list of celebrations, observances, sacrificial procedures, and the like that reflect the liturgical practice at the Jerusalem temple, but no doubt also at other shrines in both north and south. For a later period we have references in Ezekiel (45:17 and 46:3) and exilic Isaiah (47:13). A passing reference in 2 Kgs 4:23 shows that the observance of the new moon, as of the sabbath, was taken for granted. The reference can be dated to the time of Elisha (mid-ninth century) and confirms that the tradition is old and continuous. The passage in Amos shows that these observances were deeply rooted in the nation's life and practice. Even overt pressures from the business community failed to dislodge the observance of these days as religious occasions, on which ordinary work and business could not be conducted. There is testimony here, perhaps inadvertent, from Amos to the strength of a religious establishment in enforcing restraints on the business group in spite of resistance from that influential sector. Amos acknowledges the commitment of the priesthood and laity to religious festivals and religious occasions of all kinds, and their assiduous devotion in the offering of sacrifices and other ritual requirements. Yet observance of the sabbath would reflect not only a fundamental commitment to the religion of Israel, but also one that ran counter to the economic interests of the group who were a principal target of the prophet's denunciations. Nevertheless, it is not their observance of the sabbath and new moon but their desire to violate the restrictions of those days that holds his attention, in addition to the repression that they inflict on their fellow human beings the rest of the time.

The people targeted in this unit are merchants dealing in grain, which is brought from the countryside to the city market and sold there. The sharp practices of the merchant, which are not only exploitative but crooked, are the subject of still another tirade. The connection is that the merchants would like to extend the days and hours for marketing the produce that they have presumably bought from the farmers. But the prophet says that the purpose of all of this activity is to fleece the consumers in a variety of ways, which are combined here to produce an ugly picture of corruption. The prophet identifies three malefactions practiced by the merchants: false measures, false weights, and deceptive balances. Any one would be enough to insure a high illicit profit, but all combined reflect the cold, cruel, calculated exploitation and greed that devour the people.

The three together constitute a catalog of charges against unscrupulous merchants who are accused of attempting to maximize profits first by trying to infringe on the restrictive laws governing the holy days, typically the new moon and the sabbath, and second by actively manipulating measures, weights, and scales. It is to be pointed out that such activities cannot exist without the passive acquiescence and ultimately the connivance of the authorities. While the immediate target of the charges is the business community, there are implications for the civil and ecclesiastical authorities. A just measure, a just weight, and balanced scales are required by the covenant between Yahweh and his people in its most elemental form, and violation of the covenant at this level is simply intolerable.

The message pronounced in v 4—"Hear this"—is delivered in v 7: "Yahweh has sworn," a pronouncement that echoes 4:2 and 6:8. The formula requires the translation "Yahweh has sworn by the pride [or citadels —cf. 6:8] of Jacob," but identifying the *g'wn y'qb* is a serious problem. On the basis of the other formulas in 4:2 and 6:8 we would expect a self-identification, and it is possible to analyze "pride of Jacob" as a designation of Yahweh, in other words, that Yahweh has sworn by himself as the Pride of Jacob. The idiom *nšb' b-* is well established and is used this way regularly. One difficulty is that the expression *g'wn y'qb* occurs a number of times with a different meaning, in the sense of Jacob's pride or arrogance for which Jacob is condemned, and it never clearly means anything else, though in one or two passages it has been proposed that we have a designation of God (cf. Hos 5:5 and 7:10). While such a possibility exists, it is exceedingly hard to adopt such an interpretation in the face of the usage in Amos 6:8, where in a similar example of oath taking (in this case it is *bnpšw* —by his life) Yahweh is quoted as saying, "I abhor the pride (= towers) of Jacob, and his citadels I hate." Is it likely that the prophet would use the identical expression to mean two completely different things, as "Jacob's pride [or arrogance]"—or the heathen gods in which he takes pride—and as a designation of Yahweh himself as the true "Pride of Jacob"? It is hard to believe. In addition, the combination of oath and detestation of the pride of Jacob in 6:8 suggests that the reading in 8:7 is elliptical and that what we should expect is a statement similar to 6:8—Yahweh has sworn (by himself), "I hate the pride of Jacob [or proud ones in Jacob] and will never forget their misdeeds." That wording would be fine, but there is no evidence that anything has been lost. On the contrary, v 7 matches its mate or counterpart v 4 almost exactly and probably is complete as it stands. Furthermore, the correct antecedent of the 3d m. pl. suffix on *m'śyhm* ("their doings") is the participle at the beginning of v 4—*hś'pym*—certainly not *g'wn y'qb*, which is singular to begin with and not descriptive of the people who are charged with false and malicious dealings.

It might be possible to understand the *b-* here as adversative and read, "Yahweh has sworn against the pride of Jacob." That course is a desperate one because the usage is uniform and the evidence for an adversative formula is nonexistent for *b-* and virtually so for any other preposition with this verb. It does not seem to be a viable option. Finally, one may read "Pride of Jacob" not as a self-designation of Yahweh but as an ironic denigration of Israel. Because Israel has this *g'wn* and may even swear to it or by it, Yahweh himself will swear by it. While there is always the possibility of irony in the Bible and among the prophets, it is hard to see what is gained by such an analysis. A literal translation may be the best procedure in the circumstances: "Yahweh has sworn by the pride of Jacob." Whether or not it is a self-designation of Yahweh, or serves some other undefinable purpose cannot finally be decided; but the first requirement is to render the passage as it stands and try to fit it into its context. The anomaly of the relation with 6:8 and the divergent meanings of the same phrase remain.

The oath itself is solemn indeed and commits the deity to an unremitting remembrance—I will never forget—of all "their misdeeds." The latter are exemplified by the catalog of wicked attitudes and evil works given in the preceding parenthesis and in all of the "Woes." It fittingly comes at the end of the whole series. The implied threat of punishment is spelled out elsewhere; the wrongdoers will surely receive the just recompense of their misdeeds.

The actual punishment is not specified here but rather at the end of the chapter, where we pick up another participle with the definite article (*hn-šb'ym*, v 14) to go with *hś'pym* in v 4. The fate of those who oppress the poor (vv 4–6) and those who swear by false gods will be to "fall and never rise again" (v 14). Compare 5:2 about Israel, the virgin, which will fall to rise no more.

This connection implies that the unit extends from 8:4 through 8:14, and it is possible that we must go beyond this point to 9:5–6 to include the parallel passages 8:8 and 9:5 or even to 9:10, where we seem to have the last of the Woes and participles with the definite article. This last group is probably not the same as the others, and the construction is somewhat different.

Amos 8:8 hardly belongs with what follows and probably should be regarded as a closure for the oracle in vv 4–7. Because the latter is a self-enclosed unit, it may be more precise to see v 8 as a divider with a connection to the corresponding lines in 9:5. The latter, in turn, form part of the liturgical apostrophe that separates the last vision from the closing oracles of the book.

INTRODUCTION TO AMOS 8:9–14

At first sight this additional material reads like a miscellaneous assortment of prophetic speeches belonging to form-critical categories found elsewhere in the book. They give the impression that pieces in the collection of Amos' sayings left over from the editorial work that produced the book so far were added at the end with less attention to order and structure. This possibility has to be considered both here and again when we come to examine chap. 9, especially the material in the Epilogue (9:7–15), where there may be pieces that do not come from Amos at all.

The remainder of chap. 8 can at least be described as echoing and completing elements or themes already encountered in the earlier parts of the book:

> Lamentation (8:9–10; cf. 5:1–3; 5:23, 6:6, 8:3)
> Famine (8:11–12; cf. 4:6, 6:4, 7:12–13)
> Woe (8:13–14; cf. other Woes, also oaths in 6:8, 8:7; with v 13, cf. 4:7–8)

Moreover, the eschatological note, which comes increasingly to the fore in the transition from Phase One to Phase Two, is struck even louder in 8:9–14, and it reaches a crescendo in chap. 9. The traditional formulas, along with the content, achieve that effect and have links with earlier occurrences in The Book of Doom (2:16 and 4:2) and later ones in the Epilogue (9:11, 13):

I. The Book of Doom
        2:16   *bywm hhw'*
        4:2   *hnh ymym b'ym*

II. The Book of Visions
        8:3   *bywm hhw'*
        8:9   *whyh bywm hhw'*
        8:11   *hnh ymym b'ym*
        8:13   *bywm hhw'*

III. Epilogue
        9:11   *bywm hhw'*
        9:13   *hnh ymym b'ym*

When we examine the usage and placement of these formulas in the book of Amos, we note that there is a symmetrical structure in the distribution and arrangement of the eight instances: five using the expression *bywm hhw'* and three with the corresponding formula, *hnh ymym b'ym.* The middle one, in 8:9, has the expanded formula with the precedent *whyh,* no doubt a deliberate deviation from the established pattern in order to call attention to this important central section.

The formulas occur in pairs (always in the order [*whyh*] *bywm hhw'* followed by *hnh ymym b'ym*) in each of three major units, The Book of Doom, The Book of Visions, and the Epilogue. They are conspicuously absent from The Book of Woes (chaps. 5–6), which, as we have pointed out, for the most part reflects the concerns and contains the oracles pertaining to phase one of the ministry of Amos, and in which we would least expect to find the eschatological note struck by these formulas.

Interspersed among the three pairs of formulas noted are single instances of the phrase *bywm hhw'* producing a symmetrical pattern, as shown in the following table. At the same time, these two balancing examples are grouped around the middle section in chap. 8, producing a concentration that matches the opening or closing pairs:

	Number	*(whyh) bywm hha'*		*hnh ymym b'ym*
I. The Book of Doom	2	1		1
II. The Book of Visions	4	3		1
III. Epilogue	2	1		1
Totals	8 =	5	+	3

III.B.1.c. LAMENTATION (8:9–10)

8:9a　And it shall happen on that day
　　　　　　　　—Oracle of my Lord Yahweh—
　　　　that I shall make the sun set at noon
9b　　　　　　and I shall make the earth dark in broad daylight.
10a　　　　I will turn your festivals into mourning,
　　　　　　and all your songs into a dirge.
　　　　I will put sackcloth on every pair of thighs,
　　　　　　and baldness on every head.
10b　　　　I will make it like the mourning for an only son,
　　　　　　and its climax like the bitter day.

NOTES

8:9–10. This passage is one of the most poetic, or at least one of the most regular, of Amos' compositions. The time frame is the future, and five perfect verbs, with *waw*-consecutive, are used in succession. The result is perhaps a little monotonous, and in classical poetry imperfects can be used as parallels. It creates an atmosphere of relentless achievement, producing a great disaster. The eight lines are arranged in four bicola. Each bicolon begins with a *waw*-consecutive, and the first bicolon has this construction in both lines. The other three have only one verb each; that is, the parallelism is incomplete. The first four verbs begin with *h*- (three are *hip'il*), and the fifth (*qal*) has -*h* as suffix. "All" is used in three successive lines (10a), and the key word *'ēbel* (twice in v 10) has links with v 8. The word "songs" is another link to earlier material (v 3—there feminine [a problem, see the NOTES], here masculine). The word *'aḥărît* (v 10b) was used in 4:2 (a problem in both places).

We may regard this unit as a solid example of standard poetry of the First Temple Period, presumably of the eighth century B.C.E. It is composed in the common meter of the bulk of the poetry of the Hebrew Bible, sixteen-syllable lines divided roughly in the middle, with three stresses in each half-line or colon. Thus the meter of the quatrain of bicola may be summarized as follows:

	Syllables	*Stresses*
9aB–b:	$9 + 9 = 18$	$3 + 4$ (or 3) $= 6/7$
10aA:	$9 + 8 = 17$	$3 + 3 \quad = 6$
aB:	$9 + 6 = 15$	$4 + 3 \quad = 7$
b:	$7/8 + 7 = 14/15$	$3 + 3$ (or 2) $= 5/6$
	$34/35 + 30 = 64/65$	$13 + 11/13 = 24/26$

The norm for a poem of this structure would be sixty-four syllables and twenty-four stresses. It will be seen that the poem conforms closely to the posited pattern. With respect to the prose particle count, while the sample is small, there is only one, a definite article (*h-*) in twenty-eight words for a percentage of 3.6, well within the norm for classical poetry.

It is not always easy to determine the number of stresses or accents in colons or bicola, but on the basis of comparative data, especially from similar material in the book of Lamentations, we can suggest the following rules of the road. Content and action words—verbs and nouns—should be counted, prepositions generally not unless they are compounded and more than one syllable. Pronouns, when independent, are to be counted, but not pronominal suffixes or prefixes.

In counting stresses we expect a total of twenty-four for the poem and therefore six in each bicolon or three in each colon. The only deviations or possible variations from the norm are in cola 2, 4, 5, 6, and 8. In cola 2 and 8 we have parallel constructions: *bywm ʾwr* and *kywm mr.* While we would normally give these phrases two accents, the fact that there is a total of only three syllables each suggests that one accent will suffice. That would give colon 2 three accents and colon 8 two accents. In nos. 4, 5, and 6, we give the combinations *wkl, ʿl-kl,* and *wʿl-kl* each an accent, making the totals for colon 4 three, colon 5 four, and colon 6 three.

Looking at the chart, we see that the syllable count is sixty-four or sixty-five, depending on whether we count *wśmtyh* as three syllables or four, because the MT is ambiguous. The underlying spelling shows three syllables, while the vocalization points to four. Because sixty-four is the norm we opt for the lower count. The balance between cola is tipped slightly in favor of first cola against second cola, the totals being thirty-four and thirty, thus giving a slight flavor of the qinah or falling rhythm. This imbalance has also affected the stress count, which will come out $13 + 11/13 = 24/26$, with a slightly greater emphasis on the first cola over the second group. The structure as a whole is much closer to that of Lamentations 5 (also sixteen-syllable lines divided in the middle but with a bias toward first cola over second cola) rather than Lamentations 1–4, where we have typical qinah rhythm, $3 + 2 = 5$ stresses and $8 + 5$ (or $7 + 6$) $= 13$ syllables overall, at least throughout chaps. 1–3 (chap. 4 is slightly different, with a higher syllable count, but the same 3 : 2 in stresses).

The repeated use of *waw* at the beginning of all eight cola and especially before perfect verbs is characteristic of later rather than earlier poetry, but exactly when the shift took place is not certain. This little poem in our opinion should be dated not earlier than the eighth century, but as far as form is concerned it could be somewhat later.

The pronoun "your" in v 10aA can also be applied to the nouns ("thighs," "head") in v 10aB. The only obscure point in the poem is the reference of "her" in v 10b.

The poem is remarkable for the full use of prepositions:

9a–b	*b-*	(*l-*)	*b-*
10aA	*l-*		*l-*
10aB	*ʿal-*		*ʿal-*
10b	*k-*		*k-*

8:9a. *I shall make the sun set.* The reiterated *waw*-consecutives sound like the threats in the old cursing texts of covenant renewal, particularly "and I shall send" (*piʿel* in chaps. 1–2, *hipʿil* in 8:11; cf. Lev 26:22; Ezek 14:13). The idiom for sunset is normally *bāʾ haššemeš.* Here the *hipʿil* highlights its supernatural cause.

The verse should be linked with the Hymns in 4:13 and 5:8, just as 8:9b has links with 9:5. It might be a prediction of a solar eclipse. Its fulfillment, like that of the earthquake (see NOTES on 1:1), would have established or enhanced Amos' reputation. Micah 3:6 speaks about an opposite effect, the confounding and discrediting of the prophets, possibly of false ones, who, along the lines of Amos 5:18, contradicted Amos' message and forecast instead the coming of Yahweh as light.

9b. *broad daylight.* The phrase is unique, and the LXX took each noun separately—*en hēmera to phōs.* The exact denotation is not clear, but the opposite is *yôm hōšek* (Joel 2:2; Zeph 1:15). In view of the parallelism, *ʾôr* could mean "sun," as it does in a few other places (Hab 3:4; Isa 9:1, 60:3; Judg 19:26). Another possibility, in view of the mythic background everywhere in the book, especially when cosmic elements are discussed, is that here *ʾrṣ* is the netherworld to which the sun goes when it sets.

the earth. Difficulty has been found in this phrase because of the preposition. There is no reason not to identify it as the object, and there is no need to call it an Aramaism on that account (cf. *lywm* in 6:3), let alone to delete it for that reason or to improve the meter (Cripps 1969:248). The LXX translates *epi tēs gēs,* implying that its *Vorlage* had a preposition with the word *ʾrṣ.*

10a. *mourning.* Harper makes the connection with v 3 closer by reconstructing vv 9 and 3 as the original strophe (1905).

10b. *only son.* The noun *'ēbel* is modified in its third occurrence (cf. Jer 6:26). It constitutes the most intense grief (Zech 12:10). This mourning would be expressed most plaintively by the bereaved mother. Compare Naomi's use of the word "bitter" to describe her desolation (Ruth 1:20). This is the simplest explanation of the otherwise unrelated pronoun, "her" (cf. Jer 6:26). There is a long-range connection with "virgin Israel" in 5:1–2. Here it is the people or the land (v 8; cf. Hos 4:3) personified as a woman mourning the loss of children (4:10, 8:13). The LXX translator felt the difficulty and changed the pronoun to masculine, which would not have been necessary if they had thought it referred to "day," which is feminine in Greek. Cripps (1969:249), Rudolph (1971a:265), and Wolff (1977:322, n. n) are content to fall back on the idea that the feminine is "neuter" or "indefinite," referring to the whole situation in a general way (*GKC* §135p).

III.B.1.d. FAMINE OF THE WORDS (8:11–12)

8:11a   Behold! The time is coming
       —Oracle of my Lord Yahweh—
   when I will send famine throughout the earth:
  11b   not a hunger for food,
         nor a thirst for water,
      but a famine of hearing Yahweh's words.
  12a They shall wander from sea to sea,
      and from north to east,
  12b they will run back and forth,
      seeking the word of Yahweh—
        but they shall not find it.

NOTES

8:11–12. We follow the general opinion that vv 11–12 and 13–14 are identified as distinct oracles (RSV, JB, NIV, JPS) with interlocking connections. Thus the motif of drought connects v 13 with v 11. The cause, "thirst," is a link between v 13 and v 11, so that "hunger" and "thirst" occur twice each, indicating that there is a double hunger and thirst, natural drought and famine along with hunger and thirst for the words of Yahweh. The fifth vision (9:1) is clearly a new beginning; it is not connected with 8:14 (the altar of 9:1 is very likely the one at Bethel). The eschatological label in v 13 connects it with v 9, so it could be the last of the oracles that follow the fourth vision, even though v 13 itself reads like a fragment, for it has no internal development and is somewhat prosaic. By a similar argument, 8:14 is the counterfoil to 8:8 (see the COMMENT on 8:14), so it is connected with the preceding material, even though not directly linked to v 13.

Identifying the participle as a sign that v 14 is a Woe denunciation, we link it in other ways with the many similarly constructed Woes found throughout the book. In addition, this final mention of Samaria and Beersheba completes the series of references to the cities of Israel and Judah (3:9, 14; 4:1, 4; 5:5, 6; 6:1, 14). Another detail in v 14 connects it with 5:2a, as if v 14b were another ending for The Book of Woes:

> 5:2a   *nāpĕlâ lōʾ-tôsîp qûm*
> she has fallen, she will never stand up again

> 8:14b   *wĕnāpĕlû wĕlōʾ yāqûmû ʿôd*
> they shall fall, and never rise again.

The difficulties in vv 11–12 were solved by earlier scholars by deleting portions that they found troublesome. Duhm discarded all of v 11 except the first line (1911). Proksch deleted the problematical middle line of v 12 (1910). Wolff rejects the last part of v 12 (1977). Löhr rejected vv 11–12 as obvious interpolations (1901:13).

11a. *I will send.* Here *hipʿil; piʿel* in the Great Set Speech. The former is rarer and perhaps stronger (Exod 8:17 [flies]; Ezek 14:13 [famine]).

famine. The result of drought, so there is a shortage of both bread and water.

11b. *hearing.* The word is used in the sense of "obeying" (cf. Ezek 33:30–33).

Yahweh's words. The usual expression is singular. The same phrase in 2 Chr 29:15 is not clear (the LXX is singular). In 2 Chr 11:4 it is prophecy, as in Exod 4:28, Num 11:24, and Josh 3:9 (versions are singular). The phrase occurs seven times in Jeremiah; cf. Ezek 11:25. The difference in meaning is slight, and variants can occur either way, by dittography of *dbr yhwh* or by haplography of *dbry yhwh*. Compare the MT and the LXX at Num 15:31, Deut 5:5, and 1 Sam 15:1; but the change is more likely to take place from the less common plural to the more common singular expression (Josh 3:9; 1 Sam 8:10; 2 Chr 11:4). Where a distinction can be perceived, the plural refers to the written form of prophetic messages, as in Jer 36:4, 6, 8, and 11, all referring to the scroll that Jeremiah dictated (37:2; cf. the reference in narrative in Jer 43:1). Ezekiel 11:25 is in the same tradition. The plural in Exod 24:3–4 is equated with the Book of the Covenant (cf. Exod 34:27–28, where the words of the covenant are called "the ten words"). Before the seventh century the *dibrê yhwh* seem to describe the written code centered on the Decalogue. The term in Deut 5:5 may be plural too and is directly connected with the Decalogue.

The equivalent expression, "the words of the covenant," seems to have the same basic meaning. So in Amos a famine or dearth of hearing the words of Yahweh seems to mean a failure to abide by the Decalogue as explicitly asserted in Hosea 4 (cf. Jeremiah 7). In other words, it is not a famine of words from Yahweh, but a famine of hearing as obeying (cf. Isaiah 6 on how the prophet's message is to be given and received; the formula for obedience to the covenant includes hearing and doing; and Ezek 33:30–33, where people come to hear the prophet but do not act according to what they hear).

The usage may be described as follows: *dbry yhwh* is used exclusively in narratives about the delivery of divine words to people through prophets. It is not used for oracular utterances. The first clear case is Moses, who speaks words and then writes some of them down. The phrase is then attached to the Decalogue and the Book of the Covenant. The usage in Jeremiah mainly refers to the scroll on which the collected words were written. In Amos 8:11 we are justified in seeing a special usage: the plural is unusual but to be preserved here in Amos, in an essentially narrative context. The connections with the Sinai pericopes, especially in Exod 24:3–4, are sufficiently strong to warrant the interpretation suggested.

There is inevitably some contamination between *dbry yhwh* and *dbr yhwh,* but the distinction is maintained with consistency. The plural form is used only in narratives (as here), never as the designation of a prophetic oracle. The words are available in written form but people refuse to listen to them. When they seek the word of Yahweh they will not find it because God will stop sending prophets to deliver his word. In short, if the people will not listen to the words that are available, they will be denied access to his word. At that time in the future, when they finally stop listening to the written code, the Mosaic tradition, and they seek the word, they will not find it because the oracle has to be delivered by a prophet and there will be none. Behind this pronouncement is the terrible tension between authorities and prophets, the unwillingness to accept prophets who have hard messages. Jeremiah was brought down to Egypt (Jeremiah 43) because they wanted a prophet along but refused to pay attention to him or to Ezekiel, who was brought to Babylon with the exiles but was treated as an entertainer, not as a messenger of God (Ezek 33:30–33). It all adds up to the conclusion that God will not send prophets to those who refuse to listen and obey.

The first stage of the future scene, when "days are coming," will involve a famine of hearing and obeying the words of Yahweh (the written code given by Moses at Sinai). There is no famine of the words, which are well known, established, and conveniently forgotten. The contrast with Moses and Sinai seems deliberate: at that time Moses fasted while receiving the words and the people listened and promised to obey. Now or in the future there will be no famine of food and drink, rather of listening and obeying, and that dearth will bring judgment.

12a. *wander.* The verb *nāʿû* implies aimless and unsteady movement, cf. 4:8. The next verb ("rove") implies random unplanned movement.

north . . . east. Four directions are set for these movements, and the prepositions suggest that they are explored to their farthest limits, in other words, to the ends of the earth. It would be simple if they were the four cardinal points, but the unusual movement from north to east leaves the connections and identities of the two seas unclear. Emendation of the first to "south to west" (JPS) secures the four points, but no biblical listing begins with south (see below). Paraphrase into our conventional terms (north–south–east–west—NEB) evades the issue.

Often *yām* refers to the Mediterranean, the only ocean in Israel's immediate experience; and it can mean "west" without any specific reference to this "sea," *miyyām l-* (Josh 8:9, 12, 13). The references to north and east are clear enough, which leaves "south" as the meaning of the second sea. The result (WSNE) is unique in the Bible. "From sea to sea" is the extent of the messiah's dominion (Zech 9:10; Ps 72:8). Here there are four reference points, but the fourth ("the ends of the earth") seems general, not a cardinal direction.

Our familiar NSEW is found only in Gen 13:14. Other combinations are:

NWSE   (1 Kgs 7:25 = 2 Chr 4:4; incomplete in Isa 49:12)
EWNS   (1 Chr 9:24; Isa 43:5–6; Ps 107:3)
ESWN   (Numbers 2; 35:5)
ENSW   (1 Chr 26:17)
WENS   (Gen 28:14)
WNSE   (Deut 3:27)

In Amos 8:12 the second sea fills the slot for south. In realistic terms it could be the Dead Sea (in that case the search is restricted to the northern kingdom) or to the southern outlet to sea lanes in the Gulf of Aqaba.

There does not seem to be any special significance in the order; the purpose is simply to indicate that the search is in all directions and covers the whole land, possibly the whole earth. The place of sunrise takes us to the mythic land at (or beyond) the sunrise (where Gilgamesh found Utna-pishtim). In addition, *ṣāpôn* is a legendary place, not just a compass point. Another way to secure the divine secrets is to infiltrate heaven itself and take the documents. Such a proposal is scotched in Deut 30:12, and Deut 30:13 likewise discounts the suggestion: "who will go over the sea for us, and bring it [the word] to us, that we may hear it and do it?" Moses' argument was that no such journey was needed, because "the word is very near you; it is in your mouth and in your heart" (30:14). That propinquity is now denied by Amos.

12b. *seeking.* There is balance between *lišmōaʿ ʾēt dibrê yhwh* (v 11bB) and *lĕbaqqēš ʾet-dĕbar-yhwh* (v 12b). Note, however, the difference in number.

they shall not find it. Poetic justice is involved here. When the word was given, it was not received; when it is desired it will be withheld. This outcome follows from the sin of 2:12, particularly as committed against Amos himself (7:10–17). The implication is that at that time Amos was the only authentic mouthpiece of the deity; and if he was not heeded, but rather silenced, no other channel was available.

III.B.1.e. WOES (8:13–14)

8:13 On that day
      the loveliest virgins will faint
      and the choicest youths from thirst.
14a (Woe to) those who swear by the Guilt of Samaria,
      who say:
        "By the life of your god!"
        [from] Dan—
    and:
        "By the life of your pantheon!"
        —[to] Beer-sheba.
14b They shall fall
      and never rise again.

NOTES

8:13–14. This passage is an unusual interlude in the book of Amos, especially to be introduced by an eschatological formula, "On that day," which appears frequently in Jeremiah and sparsely elsewhere.

Verse 13 is an excellent specimen of Amos' rhetoric. It can be read as one long clause; it is one of the few verses that the Masoretes did not punctuate with *'atnaḥ*. While "youths" is a stock parallel for "virgins," the feminine is rarely first (Jer 31:13; Lam 1:18, 2:21); in addition, only "virgins" has an adjective, so the pattern is unbalanced. As the sentence stands, both nouns are connected with the feminine verb, and the adverb "with thirst" goes with both. It may be that *hbḥwrym,* "the youths," should be construed with the verbs in 14b—"and they shall fall and never rise again"—where the verbs are 3d pl. and one of them is certainly masculine while the other may be either gender.

Initially it reads like a replay of the plagues either in the Egypt of the time of the Exodus or in the series reported earlier in Amos. But there is an immediate shift from famine of food and lack of water, which was the critical problem in the wilderness wanderings, to a developed analogy with the word or words of Yahweh. The theme is not unknown elsewhere in the Bible, and certainly the prophets (and especially the book of Deuteronomy) emphasize the central importance of the word(s) of God. The passage may even be regarded as a commentary on the message in Deuteronomy 8, that man does not live by bread alone but by every word that proceeds from the mouth of God. Probably the immediate reference in Deut 8:3 is to the miraculous feeding and watering accomplished by the word of God as a demonstration of Israel's total dependence for sustenance on its covenant with God. But the passage in Deuteronomy could easily be read as emphasizing the greater value of the divine word in nourishing the spiritual life in contrast to ordinary food and drink, which sustain the body.

Elsewhere, especially in Proverbs and other wisdom literature, the great, supreme value of divine wisdom in sustaining and enriching life is stressed in contrast to more mundane sustenance. Here a famine is contemplated in time to come, a famine of hearing the word of Yahweh—presumably a time in which there will no longer be prophets or at least true prophets, authentic hearers and deliverers of the word of Yahweh, because that is their primary responsibility. Only at such a time will people wander all over the land seeking the revelation of God, but it will be denied to them. It is difficult to fit these sentiments and observations, which are true enough, into the picture we have of eighth-century prophecy and the book of Amos in particular; but there is so much we do not know about Amos and his times that it is difficult to make a judgment in this as in other matters about a specific text. There is implied throughout this book, and the eighth-century prophets generally, a view that is reinforced by the later prophets, that unless people listen to the prophets whom Yahweh has commissioned and sent the day will come in which there will be no prophets to deliver the word of Yahweh, and there will be a famine, a dearth of these lifesaving and life-giving words without which Israel cannot survive. Then, in this somber view of the End Time, people will feel the loss and the absence of the word keenly, and will search throughout the length and breadth of the land, but will find nothing—no word from Yahweh. This outcome is somewhat different from the scenes of violence and destruction that are typical of the book of Amos and other prophetic works, but it fits the general picture nonetheless. It would be futile to try to point to a time or setting in which words such as these would fit better than another, but at least we can argue that the sentiments expressed are consistent with the general outlook among the eighth-century prophets and Amos in particular.

Reasons have already been given for distinguishing v 14b from v 14a. While not unsuitable as a judgment against the apostates of v 14a, v 14b applies to all of those denounced in the woes in chaps. 2–8, and has a linkage with 5:2. Verse 14a is one of the few places in which Amos attacks pagan worship in Israel. But see H. M. Barstad, who finds much more such polemic in the book (1984).

8:13. *thirst.* Verse 13 could be an aspect of the desolation described in vv 11–12. The imagery of v 12 suggests a simultaneous search for water (as in 4:8—the opening verb, *wĕnāʿû,* is an important link) and for the word of Yahweh (as in 4:4 and 5:5) over a wide area. Verse 13 reminds us more of the scenes in the book of Lamentations, a city under siege. The fate of young people is a recurring theme in prophetic laments (Isa 23:4; Jer 31:13; 51:22; Ps 78:63; Lam 1:15, 18; 2:21).

14. See the NOTES on 2:8. Two of the gods mentioned here may be consorts, though each would have his or her own cult and shrine. Each has a more famous center, *ʾšmh* in Samaria, *drk* in Beer-sheba, with both together at Dan. Another analysis identifies a third individual, an unnamed god at Dan. A third interpretation locates a female god at Samaria, a male at Dan, with *dr(k)* interpreted as the pantheon in Beer-sheba.

14a. *Guilt of Samaria* (or *Ashmat of Samaria*). The reference is to a female deity named for the city. Because "Ashmah" means "shame," this might not have been her real name, but an insulting substitute used by opponents of the cult—rhyming perhaps with Asherah. But compare *ʾašîmāʾ* (2 Kgs 17:30). She is associated with a god of Dan and a god of Beer-sheba, the latter apparently called *Drk.* In this region it was usual for gods to occur as a pair of consorts, called generally *Baʿlu* and *Baʿlatu,*

"Lord and Lady": Baʿlu (Hadad) and Anat at Ugarit, Hadad and Sala at Gozan (Tell Fekheryeh), Chemosh and Ashtar in Moab, Yahweh and Asherah at Quntillet ʿAjrud, Yahweh and Anat at Elephantine. It is practically certain that the sexuality of such divine couples was celebrated in their cults, and the usual ritual procedure involved a performance by human surrogates. Hosea 4:10–19 shows that females of priests' families were assigned to such duties. Amos 2:7b–8 suggests that this ritual had been democratized; any male worshiper could couple with the goddess through her surrogate. If 8:13 is linked with 8:14, then the shrines enabled the young men and women of Israel to be promiscuous under the blessing of religion.

COMMENT

Comparison of 8:14 with 8:7 shows that these verses work together to form a larger inclusion (cf. 5:7 and 18, where the two participles with the definite article form a pair, as do the ones here as well as the ones in 6:13–14). While the unit in vv 4–7 is not strictly a Woe—as the opening words, *šimʿû zōʾt*, show—the form otherwise is comparable with v 14, and there can be little question that there is a connection between vv 4–7 and 14. While v 14 is abbreviated in comparison with 4–7, it shares several of the same elements and the contents combine with those of 4–7 to form a single entity. Thus the two participles match each other: *hšʾpym*, "those who trample," and *hnšbʿym*, "those who swear." In both cases a brief description of the group is followed by a form of *ʾmr* to provide a direct quotation, a self-convicting statement expressing the quality or characteristic that makes them a target of divine anger. And v 14b supplies the punishment or consequence that will overtake all of the guilty parties—"They shall fall and never rise again." This statement applies not only to the "swearers" but also to the "tramplers." Similarly, the divine oath in which Yahweh promises never to forget their deeds, which leads to the judgment in 14b, would apply equally to those who swear by the Ashmat of Samaria. The conflict and contrast of oaths are an essential element in this literary structure. Therefore the last line of the former unit is to be linked with the first line of the latter, and the oath-taking God juxtaposed with the oath-taking apostates.

Thus Yahweh swears by the pride of Jacob while his opponents swear by the "Guilt of Samaria," a goddess. The pattern is the same:

8:7a   *nišbaʿ yhwh bigʾôn yaʿăqōb*
       Yahweh has sworn by the pride of Jacob

8:14a   *hannišbā'îm bĕ'ašmat šōmĕrôn*
those who swear by the Guilt of Samaria.

The precise contrast or association may elude us, but the link between the
ambiguous expression in v 7 and the blasphemous one in v 14 may help to
explain its usage in the divine oath. One would expect Yahweh to swear by
himself or a suitable surrogate, as elsewhere in Amos (4:2, his holiness; 6:8,
himself), and perhaps that is what the *g'wn y'qb* signifies. The choice may
be influenced by the contrasting identification of the deity with whom the
false swearers of v 14 are associated: *'šmt šmrwn*. It may even be that the
designation *g'wn y'qb* was used as an epithet of the ancient God of the
Fathers, of the league and nation, and was variously regarded as the chief
god of the Amorite/Canaanite pantheon (ultimately El but with possible
pagan associations perhaps as consort of Asherah, possibly even Baal) or as
the unique God of the Mosaic Covenant, Yahweh. Here the latter is intended, but the association of *g'wn y'qb* and *'šmt šōmĕrôn* may involve more
than mere juxtaposition.

The oath taken by the swearers in v 14 in the name of the goddess of
Samaria is then extended and expanded in the following citations. Thus
they say: "By the life of your gods, O Dan!" which can also be rendered
"your god," for *'lhyk* could be read as singular. But why should Dan (and
Beer-sheba) be addressed? It is not normal to do so. The use of the place-
name is to identify or localize the god—so it must be the "gods of Dan"
and the "divine circle at Beer-sheba"; or, taking them together, "the pantheon" or "the circle of gods" at Dan and Beer-sheba; or more likely the
traditional phrase, "from Dan to Beer-sheba," a merismus for the entire
land of Israel (compare v 12a, where the whole country is described by the
four points of the compass). Thus we are actually talking about a typical or
standardized oath formula for the roster of gods or pantheon available to
the people in the entire country. The Woe therefore is aimed at all of those
who swear by the Guilt of Samaria, presumably the chief goddess, and who
use the ordinary oath formula "by the life of." What follows, then, is a
summary statement including the whole circle of gods, whether taken together or in groups or separately, all of the gods identified with sanctuaries
at Dan and Beer-sheba and everywhere between those limits. These major
shrines were well known, but that fact should not obscure the point that
they stood at opposite ends of the country (reflecting the traditional borders
of ancient and ideal Israel) and represented not only the borders but everything between. So we can speak of the whole circle of gods worshiped
everywhere in Israel (and Judah), from Dan to Beer-sheba. The reference is
not only to the gods and goddesses worshiped in Israel but to all people
within those borders who swear by the same gods. Thus we have an inclusive indictment of the practice and the practitioners. The passage reflects a

condition in the country similar to what the Deuteronomic History says about the worship of Israel and Judah during the reigns of most of the kings, that pagan polytheistic worship was carried on in all of the high places, not just in the sanctuaries from Dan to Beer-sheba. We would have to render the oath formulas as follows:

And they say:
> By the life of your gods at Dan
> and by the life of your circle of gods [pantheon] at Beer-sheba.

or, paraphrasing:

> By the life of your pantheon [circle of gods] from Dan to Beer-sheba: all the gods worshiped in the Holy Land, at all the shrines, and by all the people.

Neither Dan nor Beer-sheba is in the vocative but must be treated the way Samaria is in *šmt šmrwn;* these are the gods whose statues and cults are located in shrines at Dan and Beer-sheba or anywhere between. The worshipers who swear by the life of their gods naturally are residents in the same territory.

Here we are clearly dealing with the same class as in v 4: the business people who go merrily about their trade fleecing their unfortunate customers and doing so under the authority of religion. Every act of oppression and injustice is confirmed and defined by oath.

The response of the one true God, who swears an oath by himself and in his own name, is that "I will never forget any of their misdeeds." This is the counterstroke to all of these false oaths confirming and legalizing criminal acts. Yahweh will never forget those transactions, those deeds, and those confirmatory oaths. Such oaths were standard practice in business and politics, as shown in business documents dealing with inheritance in Sippar (Old Babylonian: Hammurapi). At the end of a document there is a fixed form. They swear by the life of the god of the city and his consort:

> Shamash and Aja his consort [in Sippar]
> Marduk
> and Hammurapi [the king]
> Names of witnesses and date.
> (Numerous specimens in Harris 1975)

In the vassal treaties of Esarhaddon, the many gods invoked are specified by their cities (*ANET* 534–35). In fact the list includes all gods and all countries.

The second-person suffix is used with the oath formula to identify the other party in a dialogue. Thus we find the expression, "By your life, by the life of your soul," showing that the oath is used in a transaction or treaty. Here the dealings are personal and commercial and the formula is conventional and typical. This information only adds weight to the argument that the two groups described in vv 4 and 14 overlap heavily, if they are not entirely congruent. Similarly, the crimes committed in vv 4–6 and confirmed and validated by the abominable oaths in v 14 are marked out by God in v 7 for judgment, a promise confirmed by his own oath (v 7). The judgment itself is pronounced in v 14b.

The connections between vv 7 and 14 are thus close and integral. The reason for invoking the gods in oaths was so that they could remember and be invoked again in the future as custodians of the agreement, monitors of its observance, and punishers of any breach. The only one who can act effectually is Yahweh himself, the only deity they have left out of their comprehensive lists. (It would not have made any difference if he *had* been included along with the rest, or even if his name had been used exclusively to validate untruthful depositions [Exod 20:7].)

The irony is that even if they ignore him, he notes and remembers all of their misdeeds. Just as v 7a is parallel to v 14a, so v 7b matches v 14b to make a good bicolon from otherwise single lines:

> 7b I will never forget any of their misdeeds.

> 14b They shall fall and never rise again.

Note the similar function of the odd line in 9:4b.

III.B.2. THE FIFTH VISION (9:1–6)
III.B.2.a. TEMPLE AND EARTHQUAKE (9:1–4)

9:1a I saw my Lord standing beside the altar.
  He said:
> "Strike the capitals
>   so that the thresholds shake!
> and smite them on the head—all of them;
> and their remainder I will slay with the sword;

1b	no fugitive among them shall make good his flight, no survivor among them shall escape.
2a	If they dig down to Sheol, from there my hand shall fetch them.
2b	If they climb up to Heaven, from there I will bring them down.
3a	If they hide themselves on the top of Carmel, I will seek them out from there at once, and seize them.

3b	If they conceal themselves from my eyes on the bottom of the Sea,
	    I will command the Serpent from there at once,
	        and he shall bite them.

4a	If they go into captivity before their enemies,
	    I will command the Sword from there at once,
	        and she shall slay them.

4b	For I shall set my eye upon them to do them harm and not good."

NOTES

9:1–4. The fifth vision and associated materials (oracle [vv 2–4], Hymn [vv 5–6]) complete The Book of Visions. The prophecies of vv 7–10 could be included as well, but they lead into the eschatological epilogue (vv 11–15). The vision passes into the oracle without a break (cf. 7:9 and 8:3), but this time the prophecy is more elaborate.

There are two phases: (1) the demolition of the shrine (v 1aA); (2) the decimation and extermination of the people (1aB–4), which begins in the shrine itself. Verse 4b is a general description of God's attitude throughout, not just his final action:

> For I shall set my eyes upon them
> to do them harm and not good.

Verse 1aB anticipates the outcome if "their *'aḥărît*" means "what is left of them." Thus there is an inversion: a remark suitable for the beginning comes last (v 4b), and a remark suitable for the end comes first (v 1aB).

The five possibilities listed in vv 2–4 are presented as a series of "if" clauses followed by statements of what Yahweh will do in each case. Each such statement begins with *miššām*, even though *min* cannot mean "from" in the last two. As with the series of five verbs in 8:9–10 the repetition creates an impression of relentlessness. These statements become longer

and longer. The two in v 2 are short (fourteen and twelve syllables); those
in vv 3–4 longer (twenty, twenty-eight, twenty-seven). The greater length is
partly due to the use of two verbs to describe the actions predicted in
vv 3–4. They use *waw*-consecutive futures as in 8:9–10, in other words,
prose syntax. The use of *'et* and *ha-* likewise points to prose. Apart from the
use of the same interclause syntax in all five conditional sentences, there is
no development of poetic parallelism.

The six possibilities are related in various ways. The first pair deal with
Sheol and *Shamayim,* the second with the highest mountain and deepest
sea. The first two havens are reached by strenuous effort—"dig," "climb"
—and the second pair are places to "hide." The verb "take" describes
God's capture or seizure of such escapees in the first and third cases. In the
last two he "commands" an agent (Serpent and Sword) to complete their
destruction. The net result is to expand the view from the altar to the
cosmos.

Why is there only one vision in the third set, while the previous ones
came in pairs? There is not much point in saying that they must have come
in pairs and that the sixth vision, matching the fifth, must have been lost; or
to say that, because the fifth one does not have a mate like the others, it is
not authentic (it differs also in other details—*rā'îtî* instead of *hir'anî,* etc.).
But an established pattern is easy to replicate, so the fact that it is different
from the others tells against its being a later imitation. Even in a series of
three it is possible to apply the rule that one in a set will have a major
variation from the others. The pattern already established for the first four
visions (or two double visions) builds up an expectation that the next experience will likewise consist of twin visions. The absence of a sixth vision
may give the impression that the sequence ended abruptly. There were no
more words or visions from Yahweh: 8:11–12 predicts the consequences.
The famine of hearing the words of the Lord (v 11) results not simply from
a ban imposed on Amos, or even from his imprisonment or banishment.
There are no more visions or oracles for anyone.

The vision and its associated oracles present the same combination of
realism and fantasy that is met in the other visions and indeed throughout
the whole book. The altar, capitals, and thresholds are real, while the Lord
and his agents of destruction are seen only in vision. The prospects of
escape in v 1b or of captivity in v 4aA are real, but the other destinations
are fantastic—the mythic Carmel, an ultimate refuge, and a mythic Snake,
perhaps the primal dragon now restrained and entirely under Yahweh's
command.

9:1a. *I saw.* The wording here differs from "he showed me" of the first
four visions.

beside. The word could mean "upon"; compare the same problem in 7:7.
In the latter the iconography could be that of the deity standing on the

back of its typical cult animal, as Yahweh might have been imagined to be stationed on the back of the golden calf. But standing on an altar is not the same, and "beside" is better. Yahweh's presence in the sanctuary, where normally the priest would be standing or officiating, would indicate that something out of the ordinary, something ominous, was about to happen.

the altar. With the article it points to the great altar at Bethel. Amos could have been within viewing distance of this structure when he had his vision, the appearance of Yahweh being an exclusive feature for the prophet. The visionary experience might have occurred after the clash with Amaziah, but without specific data we are reduced to speculation.

He said. The expectation that this report, like the other four, would continue with more details of what Amos saw, and not go on immediately to state what Yahweh said, has led some scholars to delete or transpose this word (Wolff 1977:334, n. a). This move in turn requires further changes: the imperative and jussive verbs must be indicative. But the vision does not report what Yahweh has done, rather what he sets in motion. A. Weiser sees the present text as a retreat from anthropomorphic language, by making Yahweh operate indirectly by issuing commands (1929:42). Nevertheless, Yahweh appears in person, and the language draws on the mythic world for its figures and descriptions. The question arises as to who is commanded to smite the capital: surely not the prophet, rather a member of the heavenly court, as commentators have recognized from early times to the present.

Strike. Compare 2 Sam 24:15–17, where God restrains the destroying angel from wreaking further havoc among the people.

capitals. The word is often taken as collective, to match the plural "thresholds," because complete demolition is in view. Zephaniah 2:14 has the opposite pattern, with the plural "capitals" followed by singular *sap.* If a single pillar was intended here, it would be a central support for a roof structure (Judges 16).

thresholds. Because the solid doorsills were part of the lower structure, their shaking shows that the whole building was disturbed (Isa 6:4). Assuming that v 1aB describes the collapse of the roof on the people inside, A. van Hoonacker (1908) read *sippûn,* "ceiling" (1 Kgs 6:15); cf. JB.

smite. The root *bṣʿ* in Hebrew means "acquire gain by violence." This line has been connected with the preceding, the suffix on *bṣʿm,* in spite of the strange pointing, referring to the capital(s). The "head," then, would signify the top of the column; or it may be connected with the following, and then either "the heads of all the people" (RSV) or, matching it with *ʾaḥărît,* "the first of them . . . the last of them" (NJPS). The decision depends very much on the meaning of *wbṣʿm,* which has been rewritten in many different ways to alleviate perceived or imagined difficulties. Wolff (1977) and Rudolph (1971a) between them gather half a dozen suggestions.

It is to Wellhausen's credit that he gave up on this problem, which indicates how difficult it is, for he was generally able to produce a solution both ingenious and appealing, and with relatively moderate recourse to emendation, considering the practices of his time.

head. We did not succeed entirely in explaining *bĕrōš* in 2:7; neither can we do so here. The four lines in vv 1aB–1b make a quatrain that shifts the scene suddenly from the shrine to the battlefield. The vocabulary of 2:14–16 appears once more. It is characteristic of an engagement of armies in the open, not of people in a city, whether besieged or demolished by an act of God such as an earthquake. Falling, never to rise again (8:14b) also describes battle casualties. The idiom "by the sword" is implied, and the usage in 9:1aB confirms the expectation. There does not seem to be any direct connection between v 1aA and its context. Edghill and Cooke find the rest of this fragment in 3:14b (1926:87).

all of them. No antecedent is immediately available for the pronominal suffix. The pronoun occurs in all four cola: *-ām//-ām; lāhem//lāhem,* and continues through v 4. This piece (vv 1aB–4) can be linked to 8:14 and 9:10, the latter two making a good tetracolon with chiasmus:

> 8:14a   those who swear . . . and say . . .
> 14b   They shall fall . . .
>
> 9:10a   [they] shall die by the sword . . .
> 10b   those who say . . .

We can then identify "all the sinners of my people" (v 10) as the referent throughout.

remainder. The word *'aḥărît* is problematic in all of its occurrences in Amos (4:2, 8:10, and 9:1). In each case the pronominal suffix causes difficulty. Amos 9:1 offers the best hope of clarification, for it shows that "their *'aḥărît*" can be killed with the sword. In 4:2 "your *'aḥărît*" are carried off with fishhooks; in 8:10 "her *'aḥărît*" is mourned bitterly. The simplest common factor is a "remnant," killed in battle (9:1), taken captive (4:2), or exiled and then killed. It involves total loss in that the mourning is like that for an only child (8:10). In view of the affinities between Amos 9:1–4 and Ps 139:7–12, we may compare Ps 139:9 *'aḥărît yām,* "the remotest limit of the west," with the usage here: *'aḥărîtām* might mean "every last one of them."

slay. The inclusion in v 4b identifies the agent as "the [angel of the] Sword."

2. *dig . . . climb.* They go to Sheol or Heaven to get away from God, who is in between—that is, in this world. He brings them back to where he is by dragging them down from heaven and hauling them up from the

underworld. This activity of scaling heaven is thus different from the motif in many ancient stories in which a hero tries to storm the home of the gods themselves for various presumptuous or arrogant purposes (Prometheus, Etana, and many more). Compare Jer 51:53.

The developments traced in vv 1–4 are a pseudo-sorites in which the stages are:

1. There is a catastrophe in the temple of Bethel, whose pillars fall on "all of them" (v 1aB).

2. But if anyone is left (ʾaḥărîtām) God will slay them. There will be a battle from which no one will escape (v 1b).

3. Even if they do escape from that (or at least survive) and go into captivity before their enemies (v 4a), God will command the Sword to slay them.

The same tragic outcome, death in battle or in exile, encompasses four other possibilities, which take us into mythic places: Sheol, Heaven, Carmel, Sea. The fact that this Sea is the abode of the Serpent shows that we have moved into myth, but not out of this world, for these places are theoretically accessible to refugees. The fact that Carmel is included with the rest shows that it too is a legendary, not an ordinary place.

The overall pattern is as follows:

$$
\text{Real}\begin{bmatrix} 1 & \text{Battle} \\ \text{Down}\begin{bmatrix} 2 & \text{Sheol} \\ \text{Up}\begin{bmatrix} 3 & \text{Heaven} \\ 4 & \text{Carmel} \end{bmatrix} \end{bmatrix}\text{Mythic} \\ 5 & \text{Sea} \\ 6 & \text{Exile} \end{bmatrix}
$$

The pseudo-sorites continues through these additional possibilities, even though each stage would seem to be final. The series begins with the places most difficult of access—Sheol and Heaven; the five "if" possibilities are of decreasing difficulty.

there. All commentators are struck by the similarities between Amos 9:1–4 and Ps 139:7–10. In formal terms the similarity is closest in the use of *šām* in Ps 139:8(E9):

ʾim-ʾessaq šāmayim	If I scale heaven
šām ʾattâ	thou art there.

Note also *gam-šām* in v 10.

Heaven and Sheol are the vertical extremes in the Psalm (order reversed in Amos), matching "dawn" (*šḥr;* cf. *mzrḥ* of Amos 8:12) and "sea" as horizontal limits. Not only is the cosmic map different in Amos; the theological perspectives contrast even more. Although both passages deal with the question of hiding from God, the Psalm has a more clearly formulated theory of divine ubiquity, as perceived and conceived by a wondering worshiper; whereas Amos affirms the divine mobility and universal potency, from God's point of view.

3b. *Serpent.* The one in 5:19 is familiar, the one in 9:3 mythic. The verb "to bite" (*nšk*) is the same. Even in 5:19, where the act seems accidental, it is implied that attempts to escape divine retribution prove futile and fatal. Amos 9:3 makes it clear that Yahweh controls and commands all creatures.

4a. *captivity.* The idiom *hlk bšby* is common (Deut 28:41; Isa 46:2; Jer 22:22; 30:16; Ezek 12:11; 30:17, 18; Lam 1:5 [without the preposition], 18; and Nah 3:10).

COMMENT

The vision begins with the Lord standing beside the altar at the temple, presumably the one at Bethel, where the confrontation between Amos and Amaziah (described in chap. 7) took place. This, the fifth and final vision, is a member of the series but set apart from the others both in form and in content. The vision itself is brief, as are the others, but the comment is more extended and sums up the significance of all of them in an abrupt action. The extended series of *'im* clauses and their consequences remind us of the initial series of oracles in chaps. 1–2, while the number five has correlations in various places: the plagues in chap. 4 and of course the visions in chaps. 7–9. The final statement, with its ominous warning about the "eye" of God, is in keeping with other concluding remarks, but the decisive word concerning the outcome of this last, terrifying debacle is to be found in the series of comments leading up to the command to "the Sword" (perhaps the name of a heavenly agent who is the sword wielder par excellence or the personified weapon of choice both for gods and men) to slay "them." It is further reinforced by the statement in the introduction (v 1a) that closes the matter succinctly and definitely: "and their remainder [presumably anyone surviving all of the other disasters] I shall slay with the sword."

The unit is carefully constructed; it is literature of a high order, but prosaic more than poetic. It uses a series of formulas to repeat and enhance the central ideas, and a certain balance and symmetry are achieved. But they are not of a poetic or metrical nature, and care should be taken not to force the unit into some artificial metrical scheme by random or systematic emendation. The closing line (v 4b) sums up the unit and in fact brings the vision material to a close. It links with other statements of a similar nature —for example, it echoes 8:7, "I will never forget any of their misdeeds" with its complement, "They shall fall and never rise again" (8:14b). It may also be tied to the comment on the first group of visions that we find in 7:9 and 17b, and probably 8:3 as well. In fact, the link should more appropriately be forged with the vision comment, for this one is the last of the series; but grammatically and syntactically it may be closer to the framing comments in 8:7 and 8:14. In any event, the concluding line in 9:4 is connected to material in the same unit, in the earlier part before the major section consisting of the five 'im clauses. The last three cola of v 1, with their emphasis on the killing of the people and the closing off of all escape routes, spell out what is meant by the baleful eye of the deity as he determines harm and injury for his people rather than success.

It is indeed the emphasis on the closing off of possible avenues of escape that characterizes the whole piece. The disaster itself is accomplished in a moment. Yahweh gives the command, and an unnamed (angelic) agent presumably carries it out. It is not necessary to dwell on that detail because it is essential to the understanding of the message from God that his word is immediately self-effectuating. The command is the deed, and ultimately in the OT the word is itself its fulfilling event, the agent by which verbal statement becomes physical and historical event: substantive, real. The mythic character of the unit needs to be noted, if only because it is usually overlooked. The initial command to smite the temple is issued to an unnamed agent but one who is able and equipped to carry it out. Because later the Serpent and the Sword are also commanded to carry out the wishes of the Warrior God there is no doubt that another (or the same) agent here wields his weapon too. Different elements in the destructive process are mentioned: the shaking of the temple, presumably an earthquake (the verbal root here, $r\check{s}$, is the commonly used one; cf. the cognate noun in 1:1), the destruction of the temple, and the death of the surviving population centered around the temple, beginning with the priests and their families and extending throughout the country. The rest of the material deals with the impossibility of escape and the confident assurance that no matter where they flee or whatever escape they try, they will be caught and will be subject to summary judgment and execution with all others. The preoccupation with this theme, that all will be caught and that no one will escape, dominates the whole passage and is especially marked in the 'im clauses. The examples extend from the natural and historical to the mythical and fantastic, in reverse order, but the theme is the same: no one can escape and no refuge will prove secure against the search and seizure of Yahweh and his agents.

The series of "if" clauses begins with the mythic pair, *Sheol* and *Shamayim*. Even if one could escape to those regions, one would not find haven in either place. The long arm of Yahweh would reach out and seize the culprit, bringing him out of Sheol and down from Heaven. Here the agent is described as the hand of Yahweh. Just as there is no hiding place in Sheol, so there is none in Heaven. It seems curious to begin the list in such remote places, both in terms of locale and in terms of the realities being discussed and threatened. The logic, however, is allowable: the outermost limits are described first, and gradually the boundaries are drawn in, from heaven and hell—which are at the outermost bounds of the three-tiered universe of biblical and general Near Eastern antiquity—to the second pair, which extends from the top of Carmel to the bottom of the Sea. Now we are in the realm of geographic reality, and in fact the contrast between the top of Carmel and the bottom of the Sea can be drawn on the same map. It is only a step from Carmel into the Mediterranean. In the middle realm of earth there are also limits: from top to bottom here, in contrast with the first pairs, in which the span was from bottom to top. Just as there is no escape within the limits of the universe (Sheol and Shamayim), so there is none within the limits of the middle level, where earth is.

The third group consists of only one item and is properly in the middle of the others, neither on the mountaintop nor under the sea but on roughly level ground: the march of the captives over the land to their dismal destination. The exile, which is a basic ingredient of the prophet's threats throughout, now takes on a new dimension, that of possible refuge or escape from the wrath of God. Elsewhere exile is a final blow, the end result of divine anger and punishment; but here it constitutes a potential escape route. Such a conception lies beyond the thinking of most OT writers, and the horrors and agonies of forced exile and ultimate captivity are a sufficient doom for prophets to pronounce. But here Amos goes beyond the others in arguing that even in exile or on the road thereto Yahweh will pursue his unhappy former (and present) subjects and through his agent the Sword will finish them off. It is as though those forced to leave by their conquerors and captors were trying by this means to escape the judgment of their God; and the prophet assures them they will not and cannot escape by these devious and questionable means.

Such a view seems to be in conflict with practically everything else we read about the exile in the Bible. It was intended as judgment and punishment, but one that would allow for survivors and provide a basis from which the return and restoration could be launched (cf. Jeremiah and Ezekiel on the subject of the exiles and the idea that they were to be the nucleus of the new community to be restored by Yahweh). In fact, both prophets make clear that the future for Israel lies with its exiles in Babylon rather than with the local inhabitants in Jerusalem. But in the grim statement here, exile is considered only as a mechanism of possible escape that will prove ineffective. No one will escape the just recompense for his/her misdeeds. In practice, exiles were hardly favored people, and the forcible uprooting of people from their native soil must have been one of the enduring tragedies of human experience. Purely in terms of survival the death rate among the victims must have been appalling. Innocent and guilty alike could hardly have escaped or even survived the agonies of forced exile and captivity. But to turn matters around and imply that exile is not merely insufficient as punishment but is actually an escape hatch for the truly guilty, so much so that it is singled out as a possible evasion of just punishment, turns matters on their head. Furthermore, in the reverse logic of the prophet's thinking, this view represents the climax and culmination of the vengeance of God, who pursues those whom he judges throughout the limits of his domain, from hell to heaven, from mountaintop to sea bottom, and along all the roads that lead captives away from his own land of Israel. It is difficult to find a doctrine of a saved and saving remnant in this climactic oracle coming out of the fifth vision reported by the prophet, or even of a survival from which to build a new and restored kingdom. This word on exile and escape in effect caps and supersedes the dismal pronouncement in the context of the third and fourth visions—7:17, repeated in 7:11. The threatened exile is not the worst that will happen, but those who survive that experience will be pursued and overtaken by the Sword of Yahweh, whoever the particular agent may be.

The general interpretation of the fifth vision and its oracle holds that the focus is on Bethel, its temple and personnel. It is a follow-up on chap. 7 with its devastating attack on the sanctuaries and more particularly on the high priest. Here the vision is of the destruction of the temple at Bethel, commanded by Yahweh and to be carried out by the angelic agent who strikes the capitals and the thresholds. On the one hand it is a vision of God commanding one of his agents to strike the temple, and on the other it is a realistic picture of the damage that an earthquake (also an act of God) will do to a structure with pillars. The violence of the earthquake will destroy even the foundations, that is, the floor plan including thresholds and entryways, which usually survive when everything else has disappeared. Archaeologists reconstruct on the basis of foundations and trenches even when the structures have been completely demolished. Here the destruction, divinely authorized and commanded, is complete (cf. Ps 137:7). It is a vision with material consequences, but it does not provide a historical or entirely realistic account of the way in which the destruction will be carried out, whether by foreign armies or by violent natural catastrophe. In fact, both seem to be involved, because the prophet insists that there will be no survivors. Any who survive the initial disaster will be tracked down and dispatched. The view, then, is that the Bethel sanctuary and its personnel were the direct target of this unparalleled onslaught and that both the sanctuary and its priests would be obliterated, regardless of attempts to escape. We believe that the description of annihilation here is centered on and limited to the sanctuary and its people (perhaps the whole city), but does not necessarily include the nation and certainly not the world. In other words, it is selective destruction but, within its limits, total.

The extreme measures aimed at Bethel need to be understood in the context of its traditional status and importance in the history of Israelite religion. From patriarchal times it was a sacred center and is especially associated with Jacob. Even though it never was a national capital it retained its status as a central shrine through all of the vicissitudes of nationhood. While eclipsed by Jerusalem with the rise of David and Solomon, it was restored to prominence by Jeroboam I, who intended it to be a rival to the southern capital. The rivalry between the two shrines must have been very bitter, and the degree of hostility can be documented in the story of Josiah's destruction of the sanctuary at Bethel and the sacrificial slaughter of its priests and other temple personnel (cf. 2 Kgs 23:15–20—in particular vv 19–20, which indicate that the priests were sacrificed and the bones burned on the altars to desecrate them permanently). The use of the word *zbḥ* for the slaughter of the priests shows that the action was understood as a ritual of sacrifice and was intended to end the history of the shrine and its priesthood forever. It is of interest that excavations at Bethel have never uncovered the remains of the sanctuary, or even its location. While it may be found some day, it is clear that little if anything survived the destruction and desecration.

Amos' fury against the sanctuary can hardly be explained in terms of the rivalry between Jerusalem and Bethel or in the light of the latter actions of Josiah, except as they may reflect the intense hatred of the heterodox sanctuary. There is the tradition in the Deuteronomic History of prophetic denunciation of Bethel and its works in the long episode described in 1 Kings 13 (cf. 12:25–33). This story contains a condemnation of Bethel and of Jeroboam as well as the only clear case of prophecy after the event in this material, an explicit forecast of the destructive cleansing of the place by Josiah, thus anticipating the latter's invasion of the area about three hundred years later.

Amos' tirade fits in well with this viewpoint and shows that among prophets such as Amos Bethel symbolized the worst aspects of official religion in the north, extending from the time of Jeroboam I, with further corruption and contamination contributed by later kings and the local priesthood.

Behind the current denunciation lies an earlier history of conflict and dissension. Somehow the story of the golden calf in Exodus cannot be separated from the cult of the golden bulls at Bethel and Dan inaugurated by Jeroboam I. It is hard to believe that Jeroboam was initiating something new or that this cult was not based on some version of the episode in the wilderness. It may well be that the association of the bull figure with the God of Israel goes back to patriarchal times and was revived by Jeroboam in order to compete successfully against the more recent rival, Jerusalem. The patriarchal God was El Shadday, and the association with Bethel confirms both the name and primary location of the deity, who may be Amorite El or Canaanite El but in any case El the dominant figure in many versions of northwestern Semitic religion. We may postulate a direct link with the bull figure, a title applicable to El (also Baal). The conflict between this god, at home in Canaan and among the patriarchs, and Yahweh, the desert-mountain deity from the southland, introduced by Moses to Israel after his contact with the priest and people of Midian and settlement among them, is complex and far from one-sided or clear-cut. According to the prevailing tradition, the bull figure associated with El is destroyed and its followers annihilated by Moses, the representative of Yahweh and his faithful Levites. Aaron's role is of interest because he apparently represents the older, patriarchal El religion and presumably was the archetypal priest for Bethel, as Moses was for the sanctuary at Dan. It may be that the original conflict, reflected in the golden calf episode in the wilderness and revived in the story of Jeroboam and the sanctuaries at Bethel and Dan, was between adherents of Aaron—representing the old patriarchal El, with their base in Canaan—and those of Moses—representing Yahweh, the God of Sinai and the Decalogue, of deliverance from Egyptian bondage and the wilderness sojourn. The triumph of Yahweh in the wilderness was later softened and smoothed over in the settlement in Canaan, and the shrines, centers, and territories pertaining to El the patriarchal deity were consolidated under the leadership of Yahweh and his representatives. But in the process the two gods, Yahweh and El, were equated, and the terminology of each was applied to the other. The old rivalries and conflicts remained, however, in spite of the recognition that Yahweh indeed was El under certain aspects, or that El was the all-inclusive father figure in whom all other gods, even Yahweh, would find their niche.

The revival of the bull cult at its most important center, Bethel, was a sure sign of the corruption of Mosaic religion and the reintroduction of pagan factors and features from which Yahwism could recover only with difficulty, if at all. The extirpation of the bull cult and the extermination of the priests there were the necessary strategy to eliminate once and for all the threat of polytheism and idolatry. Thus was the ancient conflict finally resolved, with the forcible elimination of the sanctuary and its priesthood and the abolition of its cult, while the role and epithets, the attributes and characteristics of El as chief of the gods, as covenant designer and fulfiller, could be transferred to Yahweh to enhance the authority and status of the desert warrior from Sinai.

III.B.2.b. HYMN (9:5-6)

9:5a My Lord Yahweh of hosts:
         who strikes the earth so that it melts,
            and all who dwell in it mourn;
5b   it all rises like the Nile,
            and subsides like the Nile of Egypt;
6a   who built its upper stories in the sky,
            and its supports that he founded upon the earth;
6b   who summoned the waters of the sea,
            and poured them over the surface of the earth—
               His name is Yahweh!

NOTES

The relation of this third Hymn (or apostrophe) to the ones in 4:13 and 5:8–9 has been discussed in the NOTES and COMMENTS at those places.

9:5a. *My Lord Yahweh.* This is Amos' favorite name for God, and here it combines with *haṣṣĕbā'ôt* to make a unique expression. It is also unusual for the name to come at the beginning of such an apostrophe. The ending in v 6bB is standard. The combination completes a pattern that embraces the three hymns:

4:13	*yhwh*	*'lhy ṣb'wt*	*šmw*
5:8	*yhwh*		*šmw*
5:27		*'lhy ṣb'wt*	*šmw*
9:5	*'dny yhwh*	*hṣb'wt*	
9:6	*yhwh*		*šmw*

Compare Hos 12:6 for *'lhy ṣb'wt*. The title *yhwh ṣb'wt* is usual.

The basic structure of this Hymn is supplied by three participles, each with the article. They celebrate three distinct moments or events in Yahweh's relationship with his creation, but no narrative thread is apparent. It is neither a mini–creation story nor an apocalypse, though it has elements of both. Verse 5 largely repeats 8:8 (though the two passages start differently) and describes a destructive theophany. The continuation of the opening participle by means of three *waw*-consecutive future verbs makes this one the most prophetic (apocalyptic-eschatological) of the three. Verse 6a describes cosmic creation (heaven and earth). Verse 6b, which has already been used in 5:8b, is a miniature flood story. The perfect verb in chiastic parallelism with the participle in v 6a is in epic style; the *waw*-consecutive past in sequence with the participle in v 6b is more like classical narrative.

its upper stories . . . and its supports. The reference would be to the heavenly *miqdāš* or to the whole cosmos as a vast residence for God (Exod 15:17). Together they make up the edifice that Yahweh has built or will build. But what is it? Its upper stories reach into the skies, while its lower levels rest upon the earth. The description of the Tower of Babel is similar, for the top extended to the sky; but it was manmade, while the building in this passage was erected by Yahweh. While Yahweh is creator of the mountains, his own mountain included, here we are speaking of a building, itself related to the sacred mountain and symbolic of it, but which functions as a palace for the deity and his entourage. Just as the temple tower of Babylonia linked heaven and earth and was shaped like the sacred mountains that did so—its upper story or stories were called heaven and its base was on earth—so here the palace of God, which he himself builds, is described in the same terms as the temple that is reflective of the sacred mountains that link heaven and earth.

The basic picture is that there are two kinds of sanctuary: one heavenly, made by God himself, that is located in heaven, commonly on top of or above a mountain sacred to the god (Sinai or Horeb to Yahweh, Ṣaphon to Baal, etc.); the other, an earthly shrine, that is a replica of the heavenly palace, usually at the foot of the same mountain or at some distance from it. Yahweh is present in both but in different ways. Here the reference is to his building activity. This activity apparently involves both structures, the heavenly temple that he builds himself (with his own hands, but it could actually be carried out by heavenly agents, just as Baal's house is built by the artificer god and his cohorts) and the earthly counterpart that is built at his direction, according to the plan of the original in heaven and under his sponsorship and protection. Hence the upper structure in heaven and the lower structure on earth together represent the abiding place of the Most High. Apparently this combination is what Amos or his editor had in mind.

supports (or *vault*). The Heb word *'ăguddâ* occurs four times in the Bible and is given four distinct meanings in the lexicons:

1. Exod 12:22, a bunch of hyssop used for sprinkling;
2. 2 Sam 2:25, a band of soldiers;

3. Isa 58:6, the thongs of a yoke; and
4. Amos 9:6, a vault (of the sky).

Numbers 1 and 2, and perhaps no. 3 as well, have the idea of a set of items held together in some way. See Isa 58:6:

ḥarṣubbôt rešaʿ//ʾăguddôt môṭâ
bands of wickedness//thongs of a yoke.

The only other occurrence of ḥarṣubbôt (Ps 73:4) does not assist in sharpening the meaning.

The equation of ʾăguddâ with "vault" in Amos 9:6 rests on two arguments. (1) It is parallel to maʿălōtāw, which are assumed to be the upper parts of a building, with ʾăguddâ as an approximate synonym. But the connection with "earth" and ysd suggests foundation structures. (2) There is an alleged Arabic cognate, ʾijādun. The Heb ʾăguddâ would seem to be the same as Akk agiddû (agittû), a Sumerian loanword meaning "bandage" or "turbanlike headgear" (CAD 1.1.151). The Akkadian synonym list Malku VI (143) has agittû equivalent to ṣimdu or ṣindu (Heb ṣemed), which occupies the same semantic field; e.g., ṣimittu is the crosspiece of a yoke (CAD 1.151). The word ṣimdu has the following meanings (ṣimdu A, CAD 16.196f.):

1. bandage;
2. team of draft animals;
3. brickwork; and
4. architectural arrangement.

In the first two it resembles both Heb ʾăguddâ and Heb ṣemed. The semantic connection between the first two meanings ("band") and the last two ("structure") is not evident. It may be only a coincidence that ʾăguddâ likewise has architectural associations: ṣimdu means brickwork in the lower portions of a building. Even without this hint, the balance of Amos 9:6 suggests that maʿălôt refers to an upper structure and ʾăguddâ refers to a lower structure.

The text of Amos 9:6 can be translated in two ways:

	Syllables	Stresses
habbôneh baššāmayim maʿălôtāw	$3 + 3 + 3 = 9$	3
waʾăguddātô ʿal-ʾereṣ yĕsādāh	$5 + 1 + 1 + 3 = 10$	3

The one who built in the skies [heavens] his upper stories and his assemblage [a bound structure] upon the earth, which he founded or

and its assemblage on earth—he founded it.

Because both *'gdtw* and *'rṣ* are feminine nouns, the suffix on *ysdh* could refer to either; hence the variant renderings. The parallel passage in Ps 78:69, however, offers only one grammatical possibility, *'rṣ*, because the other possible referent in that verse is a masculine noun:

	Syllables	Stresses
wayyiben kĕmô-rāmîm miqdāšô	$2 + 2 + 2 + 3 = 9$	4
kĕʾereṣ yĕsādāh lĕʿôlām	$2 + 3 + 3 = 8$	3

And he built like the heights his sanctuary
   like the earth that he founded from of old.

We think that the 3d m. s. suffixes in Amos 9:6 refer to the sanctuary rather than to Yahweh. The other observation is that we should interpret the clause *'rṣ ysdh* the same way in both passages (Amos 9:6 and Ps 78:69). In Amos 9:6 we have a perfect chiasm, with the verbs at the ends and the prepositional phrases in the middle. The implication is that the verbs match and balance and hence ought to refer to comparable things. There is no grammatical hindrance to reading the 3d f. s. suffix on *ysd[h]* as referring to *'gdtw*, though it is redundant and affects the symmetry. Grammatically it works better with *'rṣ* as a retrospective suffix in what would normally be a relative clause with *'šr*. But this is a fossil poetic expression that occurs often enough to make it clear that *'šr* is unnecessary. One could exercise either option; we note that the RSV reads the suffix as referring to *'gdtw:*

   Who builds his upper chambers in the heavens
   and founds his vault upon the earth.

The RSV ignores the redundant suffix, but note how it renders Ps 78:69:

   He built his sanctuary like the high heaven,
   like the earth, which he has founded forever.

We think the two clauses must be rendered in the same way, and that grammatically Ps 78:69 should be rendered as RSV does, though we lose the parallelism of the verbs. In that verse we have a partial chiasm, which suggests that *l'wlm* refers to *mqdšw* rather than to *'rṣ*. So we would render the passage as follows:

   And he built like the heights his sanctuary
   And like earth, which he founded, from of old.

(That is, "he built his sanctuary . . . from of old.") Furthermore, *mqdšw* describes the heavenly sanctuary, not the earthly one to be built on Mount Zion. With regard to the prepositions *kĕmô* and *kĕ*, they compare the sanctuary with the (heavenly) heights and the earth (below), indicating the vast dimensions of the divine palace. It was as high as the sky and as low as the earth—it extended from one to the other. Essentially the same idea is expressed in Amos 9:6, but the prepositions are different, more explicit.

The main reason why it is difficult to disconnect the verb *ysd* from the noun *'rṣ* is that they are bound together in a great variety of passages. A partial list follows.

> 1. Ps 24:1–2
> *layhwh* **hā'āreṣ ûmĕlô'āh**
> **tēbēl** *wĕyōšĕbê* **bāh**
> *kî-hû' 'al-yammîm yĕsādāh*
> *wĕ'al-nĕhārôt yĕkônĕnehā*

> To Yahweh belong *the earth* and its fullness,
> the world and those dwelling in it;
> for it is he who *founded it* upon the seas,
> and upon the rivers he set it firmly.

> 2. Ps 89:12
> *lĕkā šāmayim*
> > *'ap-lĕkā 'āreṣ*
> > *tēbēl ûmĕlô'āh*
> > *'attâ yĕsadtām*

> To you belong the heavens,
> > also [indeed] to you is *the earth*
> > the world and its fullness,
> > as for you, *you founded them.*

> 3. Ps 102:26
> *lĕpānîm hā'āreṣ yāsadtā*
> *ûma'ăśeh yādeykā šāmāyim*

> In olden times *you founded the earth,*
> and the heavens are the work of your hands.

> Probably there is a combination here, with the verb taking both objects and the phrase also applying to both:

You founded the earth and the heavens,
which are the work of your hands.

The sense is clear, and the reference is to creation: *lpnym*, literally, "formerly," that is to say, "in ancient times."

> 4. Ps 104:5
> *yāsad-ʾereṣ ʿal-mĕkôneyhā*
> *bal-timmôṭ ʿôlām wāʿed*
>
> *He founded the earth* upon its bases,
> so that it should not be shaken for ever and eternity.

Here the time frame is future; but note the absence of any preposition with *ʿwlm wʿd*.

> 5. Prov 3:19
> *yhwh bĕḥokmâ yāsad-ʾereṣ*
> *kônēn šāmayim bitbûnâ*
>
> Yahweh by Wisdom *founded the earth,*
> he established the heavens by understanding.

Here we have three combinations: He founded/established the earth/heavens by wisdom/understanding. There is also a partial chiasm (two-way, not three-way).

> 6. Job 38:4
> *ʾêpōh hāyîtā bĕyosdî-ʾāreṣ*
>
> Where were you when *I founded the earth?*

> 7. Isa 48:13
> *ʾap-yādî yāsĕdâ ʾereṣ*
> *wîmînî ṭippĕḥâ šāmāyim*
>
> Indeed my [left?] hand *founded the earth*
> and my right hand spread out the heavens.

> 8. Isa 51:13
> *wattiškaḥ yhwh ʿōśekā*

> *nôṭeh šāmayim*
> *wĕyōsēd ʾāreṣ*
> *wattĕpaḥēd tāmîd kol-hayyôm*

And you have forgotten Yahweh your maker,
who stretched out the heavens,
and who *founded the earth,*
and you have feared continually at all times.

9. Isa 51:16b
lintōaʿ šāmayim
wĕlîsōd ʾāreṣ

To stretch out the heavens
      and to *found the earth*

10. Zech 12:1
nōṭeh šāmayim
wĕyōsēd ʾāreṣ

Who stretched out the heavens
      and who founded the earth.

The association of *ysd* and *ʾrṣ* in all of these passages is unmistakable and certain. But in no case do we have a parallel usage with *bnh* such as we have in Ps 78:69 and Amos 9:6. We would say that the odds are in favor of the relative clause interpretation: higher for Ps 78:69 but likely in both cases. The other, making the object of the verb the *ʾgdh* or some equivalent feminine noun, seems a little farfetched, more so in the psalm where the only other referent is *mqdšw*, which is masculine. But even in Amos the connection with *ʾgdtw* is awkward because of the redundancy. The only thing to consider is the balancing of the verbs, *bnh//ysd*. But it is instructive that this logical parallelism does not occur in any of our passages. It does, however, occur elsewhere. There is a good example in Isa 44:28:

> *wĕlēʾmōr lîrûšālayim tibbāneh*
> *wĕhêkāl tiwwāsēd*

Saying to Jerusalem, "It shall be built,"
      and of the temple, "Its foundation shall be laid."

The parallelism is clear, and it seems equally clear that both verbs refer to the temple in Jerusalem, in spite of the apparent disagreement in gender between the noun *hykl* (usually taken to be masculine) and the verbs, which are parsed as 3d f. s. Whether the verbs have been attracted to the noun *yrwšlm*, which is feminine, or to the word *hykl*, which is construed as feminine (cf. *hyklwt*, Hos 8:14), the point is that both verbs are linked to the same subject. Also 1 Kgs 16:34:

> *bĕyāmāyw bānâ ḥî̂ʾēl bêt haʾĕli ʾet-yĕrîḥōh*
> *baʿăbîrām bĕkōrô yissĕdāh*
> *ûbisgûb ṣĕʿîrô hiṣṣîb dĕlāteyhā*

> In his days Hiel of Bethel built Jericho;
> He laid its foundation at the cost of Abiram
> 　　　his first-born,
> and set up its gates at the cost of his
> 　　　younger son Segub.

Here *bnh* and *ysd* are in the same context but not used strictly in parallel construction (cf. Josh 6:26, where the same grouping occurs).

Zech 8:9

> *bĕyôm yussad bêt-yhwh ṣĕbāʾôt*
> *hahêkāl lĕhibbānôt*

> On the day when the house of Yahweh of hosts was founded,
> The temple was to be built.

The parallelism in Zech 8:9 is solid, but the rendering is difficult. The word *ysd* is used for founding the different temples, and perhaps that is the proper model instead of founding the earth (cf. 1 Kgs 5:31–32; 6:37; 7:10; Hag 2:18; Zech 4:9; 8:9; Ezra 3:6, 10, 11, 12; 2 Chr 3:3 [*ysd*//*bnh?*]).

The whole matter must now be reconsidered in the light of the evidence available. We have the following facts to contend with.

1. There is a close association between the verb *ysd* and the noun *ʾrṣ*. They go together a number of times, with God as the actual or implied subject and earth as the object; the reference is always to the founding or creation of the earth. Where a parallel noun is used, we generally have either *tēbēl*, which is a synonym, or *šāmayim*, which is a complement (going all the way back to Gen 1:1 or 2:4). In general, parallel verbs are used with *kwn* (in the *pôlel-kônēn*) as a synonym, or various verbs used with *šmym*, such as *nṭh*, to complete the balance.

2. It is noteworthy that the verb *bnh* is never used with *ʾrṣ* or its parallel in any of the passages in which *ysd* is used with *ʾrṣ* The root *bnh* does not

seem to be used for the creation of heaven or earth or any of their synonyms. It is used for building almost everything else.

3. When the verbs *bnh* and *ysd* occur in close association, the reference is always to a building or other structure, including especially a temple. In all of these cases, the verbs occur in parallel construction and have the same or synonymous objects (or subjects if the verbs are passive).

4. The root *ysd* is used in both ways: to describe the creation or founding of the earth, and to describe the founding or making of a building such as a temple. When it is used in association with the former, the parallel verbs are *kwn* or *nṭh,* among others. When it is parallel to *bnh* it is associated not with founding the earth but with founding a building.

5. The only apparent exceptions are in the two passages under discussion, in which all of these ingredients are present: the verbs are *bnh* and *ysd;* the nouns are *šmym* or *rmym* (probably a synonym or a reference to something in heaven) and *ʾrṣ;* and there is reference to a structure as well, *mqdš* in Ps 78:69 and *mʿlwt*//*ʾgdh* in Amos 9:6. It looks like and is a mixture; but how is the verb *ysd* to be understood? Is it basically a description of the creation of heaven and earth with a passing reference to a sanctuary; or is it a depiction of the founding and building of a temple with a reference to heaven and earth; or is it split in half, one part going one way and the other the other way?

We can now draw some conclusions. It is clear that we do not have the first pattern in either passage. While the heavens are mentioned (or a synonym) they are not connected with any of the verbs used to describe the way they came into being (*nṭh, kwn, ṭpḥ*). The verb used is *bnh,* and in both cases the object is a building or part of one (the sanctuary in Psalm 78 and its upper parts in Amos 9:6). We can therefore rule out the first pattern.

A second possibility is that the first part of each line (or first colon) refers to the building of the heavenly temple, while the second nevertheless refers to the founding of the earth. From the point of view of grammar and structure that solution may seem the most credible but also the least satisfying with respect to overall intention and effectiveness as a piece of poetry. The passage in Amos 9:6 is clearly focused on a great structure that Yahweh has built with its upper part in the heavens and its lower part on the earth. That subject takes care of the first six words, leaving only the last for reconsideration. On the basis of the evidence assembled it could with equal correctness refer to the founding of the temple (or whatever part of it *ʾgdh* refers to) or to the founding of the earth. The decisive question concerns the poet's intention. Was the last word, *ysdh,* added simply to expand the reference to "earth," or was it used in order to fill out and balance an integrated and unified bicolon dealing with a single main theme, thus forming a complete chiasm?

hbwnh bšmym mʿlwtw
wˀgdtw ˀ-ˀrṣ ysdh

The verbs are at the ends, the direct objects are in the middle, and the prepositional phrases lie between: ABC//C'B'A'

habbôneh//yĕsādāh
baššāmayim//ʿal-ˀereṣ
maʿălôtā[y]w// waˀăguddātô

Needless to say, if in fact the verbs were not actually complementary, the chiasm would be defective. In the case of the other pairs the complementary character is quite clear: the *mʿlwt* and the *ˀgdh* are different parts of the same structure, namely, the great divine *miqdāš*, as we know from the parallel passage in Ps 78:69. The terms "heaven and earth" constitute a standard combination in ancient poetry. Not only do they complement each other, they also form a merism. So it seems likely that the verbs also complement each other, and, just as *mʿlwtyw* is the object of *hbwnh*, *ˀgdtw* will be the real object of *ysdh* (with its retrospective suffix). In this respect we come out with the majority of scholars and the RSV, among other translations.

But this analysis and conclusion will affect our evaluation of the parallel phenomenon in Ps 78:69. Here the temptation to go with the second or split solution will be even greater because of the grammatical factors involved. The only visible antecedent for the 3d f. s. suffix on *ysdh* is *ˀrṣ*, the immediately preceding word, and it may be that intentionally or not the poet fell victim to the prevailing word combination and associated the verbal root *ysd* with the noun *ˀrṣ*. But the arguments used in connection with Amos 9:6 are also applicable here. The primary focus of the verse is on the temple that Yahweh has built. The direct object of the first verb is *mqdš*, and we would expect the second verb, it if is parallel to the first, to deal with the same, a similar or complementary object, instead of qualifying an indirect object such as *ˀrṣ*, which is parallel to a word that has no qualifier. Structurally the sentence is similar to Amos 9:6 in the sense that the parallel terms *rmym* and *ˀrṣ* are both preceded by prepositions, *kmw//k*. We may also note that the final word has adverbial force (*leʿôlām*) and could be associated with either *ˀrṣ//rmym* or *mqdšw*. In either case the phrase must be rendered as referring to past time, because the bicolon describes a shrine already built, one that is cosmic in dimensions and eternal in its durability, hence, "from of old." While the same could be said of either "earth" or "the heavenly sanctuary," in this verse the reference should more properly be to the *mqdš* and is entirely appropriate. The parallel construction is also partly chiastic, as we note:

wayyiben	*lĕʿôlām*
kĕmô-rāmîm	*yĕsādāh*
miqdāšô	*kĕʾereṣ*

or

wybn kmw-rwym	*mqdšw*
kʾrṣ ysdh	*lʿwlm*

Just as the verbs and prepositional phrases form a chiastic pattern and should be construed in interlocking fashion, so the two remaining terms belong together, and *mqdšw* . . . *lʿwlm* make a solid combination: "his sanctuary . . . from of old" (or, paraphrasing, "his eternal sanctuary").

From the foregoing we conclude that *ysdh* belongs to the same complex of ideas and should therefore refer primarily to the building rather than to the earth. The only serious problem is the 3d f. s. suffix in *ysdh*, and we must try to explain its presence. There are several possibilities. (1) The poet may have been influenced by the other passages in which *ysd* is used with *ʾrṣ* and inadvertently used the 3d f. s. suffix when a 3d m. s. suffix was called for. (2) It may be even more likely that when the poem was originally written no distinction was made in the spelling of the suffix; before the exile (and perhaps through the sixth century) both the 3d m. s. and the 3d f. s. suffix would have been spelled with a *he*, as *ysdh*. When the revised spelling was introduced and *waw* substituted for *he* as the 3d m. s. suffix with singular nouns (but not as the 3d f. s. suffix, which preserved the *he*), the editor or scribe who made the change overlooked this one because he assumed (on the basis of numerous examples) that the suffix referred to the nearest antecedent, *ʾrṣ*, which was feminine, instead of the preceding word, *mqdšw*, which was masculine. So the *he* was left and was henceforth construed as feminine.

On balance we prefer the second explanation. In any case, the interpretation of Ps 78:69 should be essentially the same as that of Amos 9:6, allowing for slight shifts and changes in wording and emphasis. Both describe the great heavenly temple built by Yahweh with its top in the heavens and its infrastructure on earth—a building built from of old. In the Psalm there is a connection, probably a comparison with the temple (or tabernacle) to be erected on Mount Zion. But the temple in v 69 is cosmic and from eternity, not earthly and temporal.

CONCLUDING COMMENT ON THE BOOK OF VISIONS

The major components of this section are the visions, and they reflect the broader range of the prophet's call and concerns. On the basis of the names mentioned and the other details we have concluded that the visions reflect the divine judgment against both nations (it is even possible that they go beyond them to the sins of the others listed in chaps. 1–2, but we have no clear information on that point) and that it was either Amos' own conclusion or a divine decision that the northern kingdom, Israel, should be the prime target both of judgment and of prophesying. So Amos 7:1–8:3 at any rate focus on the northern kingdom as the particular center of attention for the general message derived from the visions. The third and fourth visions stipulate emphatically that Yahweh will not forgive "my people Israel" (7:8, 8:2), which we take to include both kingdoms. Amos may confirm this broader application when he tells Amaziah that "Yahweh said to me, 'Go prophesy to my people Israel' " (7:15). These are the only three places in which the expression ʿmy yśrʾl is used, and we think it shows clearly that Amos went to Bethel as a consequence of seeing the third vision, if not both the third and the fourth visions. It is hard to decide what the envelope (7:7–8 and 8:1–2) around the narrative really signifies, but we would judge that Amos had already seen both visions and was firmly placed in Phase Two when he went up there. He may well have delivered the Great Set Speech on that occasion, because it is the classic Phase Two speech (strictly judgmental and the same statement in slightly different language that we find in Visions 3 and 4: I will not forgive him and I will not reverse it. The mood and tone are the same. And that speech is proof that all of Israel is included in the two visions. So if the connection is correct, then our conclusions based on other considerations are confirmed. The visions point to the speech and the speech reflects the visions. The connection also shows us how Amos made a speech out of a vision. He took Yahweh's two speeches of eleven words (7:8) and ten words (8:2) and, without using the same words, nevertheless translated them into an extended oracle embodying the same ideas. Amos no doubt would say for several reasons that every word came from Yahweh, which is probably true; but we recognize that it was filtered through the responsive and creative mind of the prophet.

While the message is general it is also specific. Just as the opening speech both distinguishes between and includes both kingdoms (Judah, 2:4–5; Israel, 2:6–8; their common source in 2:9–13; and perhaps both together in the denouement in 2:14–16), so the narrative in 7:10–17 does the same. Immediately following 7:15 (which refers to the larger entity), Amos quotes Amaziah about not prophesying against Israel (just the north), so Amos is able to shift the focus back to the northern kingdom. That focus does not mean that Judah and the other kingdoms are safe, far from it; but Amos is in the north, speaking to the north, and thus his primary focus is on the north. When he tells Amaziah what is going to happen to him (Amaziah) and his family, he is talking about the north and specifies that the north (Israel) will go into exile. So we have essentially the same picture in the second set of visions and the story encased between them that we have in The Book of Doom: northern Israel among the nations, or something like that. In that speech (chaps. 1–2), Judah is placed ambivalently. It is treated like the other six, because Israel is treated somewhat differently. But it is joined to Israel as soon as Amos goes back to the Exodus (3:1).

There are two points of particular interest. First, in 7:15 Amos says that Yahweh told him to prophesy to "my people Israel." When did he do so? Is that prophesying connected with the visions or separate from them? We think the answer is clear. All of these matters are interlocking, just as when Amos and Amaziah quote each other it is for stylistic reasons, and we can take it that the quotations are reliable. Here too the writer does not want to write it down twice, so he has Amos quote Yahweh and we must find where the quote came from. The reference to ʿmy yśrʾl is probably an intentional giveaway and indicates that after Yahweh explained the vision, he then told Amos exactly what Amos quoted him as saying. So that phrase binds the second set of visions even more tightly to the episode at Bethel, and thus we have a larger nucleus for reconstructing the prophet's mission.

The other point goes back to the first pair of visions. It would be difficult to prove anything about the scope of the first vision, but the second one gives us a clue when it speaks of haḥēleq (7:4). The LXX apparently translated ḥēleq yhwh, which would only make explicit what could be inferred from the MT, that the whole of Yahweh's sacred territory is involved, which would not be restricted to the northern kingdom.

We can say with some confidence that the visions are broad enough to include both kingdoms. But the specific application, especially of the second set, brought Amos north to speak about eight kingdoms, even though the focus of particular attention was Israel, with its capital at Samaria and its major shrine at Bethel.

We must now consider the second half of The Book of Visions. Here we are dealing with the transition to Phase Three, which is depicted in the fifth vision. The key to this transition is 8:3, which serves to close the description of the fourth vision and at the same time to open the way to the fifth vision in 9:1–4. There may be an important connection between the vision of the destruction of the temple (9:1) and the violent massacre in the palace described in 8:3. The latter also contains the formula *bayyôm hahû*', which links it with the subsequent material, where *bywm hhw*' occurs twice more (8:9, 13). We recall as well that the only other occurrence of *bywm hhw*' (except for 9:11, which has a different orientation but is also linked to the others) is at 2:16, and this fact gives us a clue as to the place of 8:3 in the development.

At the end of the first insertion (7:10–17), Amos is at the edge between Phases Two and Three. He has obviously come to the end of his patience in trying to deal with both Amaziah and Jeroboam and is talking about the doom that hangs over the heads of the leadership. He says that Amaziah will die in an unclean land among the exiles. Amos seems to be letting Amaziah die of natural causes, disgraced, exiled and with his family dead or equally humiliated; but in fact he is threatening the priest with the same death that Amaziah quoted him as predicting for Jeroboam. How will Amaziah die?—by the sword, in all likelihood. The implication that Amaziah will share in the king's fate is to be found in the reference to Jeroboam (7:11), where the same verb is used (*yamût* in v 11, *tāmût* in v 17), or even in v 9, where "the sword" plays a prominent role. So this linkage would mean that Amos has targeted both Jeroboam and Amaziah for execution, which is the precise method of judgment for Phase Three, as we will see. But maybe these statements are just the tip of the iceberg, and the full force of Phase Three will only be realized later, namely, that everyone included in the woes is also going to be punished that way. For clear Phase-Three references to execution by the sword look at 9:4, which reflects the judicial power, while 9:3 is its mythic equivalent. But the decisive passage is the climax and culmination of Phase Three in 9:10, where precisely the same language is used as in the confrontation scene, except that the whole class is sentenced to execution:

bahereb yāmûtû kōl ḥaṭṭā'*ê* '*ammî*
All the sinners of my people shall die by the sword.

That line concludes the judgment of the people of the Woes (indeed it is the last Woe—so it is clear that everyone mentioned in a Woe is finally sentenced to death). The two main phases can be classified and described as follows.

1. Phase Two is defined by the second pair of visions and is filled out in The Book of Doom, especially the great opening speech. The message is, briefly, that the eight kingdoms will be destroyed and there will be some exiles. The specific fate of Israel is destruction and exile of its population, a threat repeated frequently.

2. Phase Three is represented by the last vision. It specifies that the leadership will not be spared even in exile. They will all be summarily

executed (just dying is too good for them). Amos 9:1–4 is absolutely with-out pity or kindness. No one will escape, and they will all be executed. If any escape the Sword they will be bitten by the Serpent instead. Phase Three, for reasons given, has to be tied to the Woes, so The Book of Woes belongs here as well. Amos' strategy (or his editor's) in including the last of the Woes in the second insertion into The Book of Visions can now be appreciated. It achieves a more nuanced effect.

The Woes dominate Phase One and, at that stage and in that setting, they can serve as accusation and indictment; but the implied sentence and judg-ment are not yet final. Indeed it is still possible to mix the Woes with urgent exhortations to repent.

When all of this material is subsequently incorporated into the great sanctuary address at Bethel (which should have included practically every-thing we now have in 1:2–8:3, and possibly much more that was not pre-served), the Woes take on a different character, for they are now back-ground and basis for the judgments of Phase Two. In one more step, all Phase-Two material, which already incorporates Phase One, is retained in the final comprehensive statement, all of the materials being wound tightly together.

The author has thus achieved several effects at once. The Book of Woes can be studied as a distinct unit, which still documents Phase One. The Woes, found mainly there, are pinned into the other two "books" by an opening and a closing Woe. These two Woes are partly identical, partly complementary, and together they bring the other Woes into a connection with Phases Two and Three. Amos 2:7, the first of the series, plugs them all into the oracle against Israel in the Great Set Speech. Amos 8:4 (all but the last—8:14, which is related to 8:4, is still to come) plugs them all into Phase Three. In other words, Amos has been pursuing the same group all the time, with 9:10 as the very last summary, so that "all the sinners" are all of the people targeted in all of the Woes.

We do not mean that everything in those sections belongs to the Phase or vision that is dominant. We have to account for Phase One material that arises from the first pair of visions. The only real Phase-One oracles left in the book are in The Book of Woes, especially 5:4–5, 14, and 5:24, but there is very little. Otherwise it is basically Phase Three, along with that snippet in 5:15 which points beyond to a Phase Four. The plagues represent the failure of Phase One and end it.

Phase Four is the easiest of all to identify and isolate, mainly the last two oracles (9:11–15) in that order, 4A (IV.B.1) and 4B (IV.B.2). They repre-sent, respectively, the culmination of the *bywm hhw'* and the *ymym b'ym* series. In 4A (*bywm hhw'*) we have the first aspect of the restoration, and it involves the end of the judgment, by applying Phase Three to Edom, no doubt something the remaining Israelites and Judahites would have been happy to help with. The phrase *bywm hhw'* refers to Phase Three. We have it in 8:3, which has to be linked with the last vision and everything between (8:4–14). The latter is clearly a Woe section and properly belongs with Phase Three, not least because with the exception of *g'wn y'qb* in 8:7 there are no national references: we have the internal division between those who are condemned and those who might survive. The other *bywm hhw'* passage in 8:13–14 belongs here too, not only because of the Woe people but also because of the battle scene in which the young men fall. The vision in 9:1–4 involves both methods of destruction. The earthquake is clear enough, but there is also Yahweh with his sword in 9:1. It is his battle sword, while the sword in 9:4 is the judicial sword. Now we must come back to 2:14–16, where we have *bywm hhw'* and the insistence that no one will escape: compare the words in 2:14–16 with 9:1:

9:1	**lō'-yānûs** *lāhem* **nās**
	wĕlō'-yimmālēṭ lāhem pālîṭ
2:14	*wĕ'*ābad **mānôs** *miqqāl*
	. . .
	wĕgibbôr **lō'-yĕmallēṭ** *napšô*
	. . .
2:15	*wĕqal bĕraglāyw* **lō'** **yĕmallēṭ**
	wĕrōkēb hassûs **lō'** **yĕmalleṭ** *napšô*
2:16	*wĕ'ammîṣ libbô baggibbôrîm*
	'ārôm **yānûs** *bayyôm-hahû'*

In 2:16 the subject may flee, but neither he nor anyone else will escape. From this point it follows that *bywm hhw'* basically reflects Phase Three situations and that 2:14–16 belongs to that phase. The affinities with Vision 5 and the other *bywm hhw'* passages show that Phase Three is in mind and explain why it did not quite fit into the other materials in The Book of Doom.

The complementary example of *bywm hhw'* material is 8:9–10, a dreadful dirge, clearly Phase Three, because this is when the tragedy comes home with all its brutality. It could fit Phase Two also, but the bulk of the mourning passages are in The Book of Woes. Thus we can now put 5:16–17 in place and see it as a combination with 5:18–20, also with the dirge in 5:2 and the curious material in 5:3, with its correlates in 6:9–10.

We also think we can sort out the use of the special names: Joseph would be Phase Three, while Isaac belongs more likely to Phase Two. The *g'wn yʿqb* is Phase Three (cf. Woes), *yʿqb* alone is Phase One, *byt yʿqb* is Phase Three, 3:13 is right for Phase Two, but 9:8 looks like Phase Three.

If we look at the other eschatological expression, *ymym bʾym,* there are only three instances in Amos, and they seem to be heterogeneous. They are obviously important because the closing oracle uses the phrase and clearly depicts the final stage of Phase Four.

One other occurrence is in 8:11–12, which describes the famine of the word. According to our analysis it might be placed with other Phase-Three material because it is in the section 8:4–14. But it hardly fits with the theme of the extirpation of the sinners. This material ties into the theme of prophecy and the absence of the word of Yahweh. It should be connected with the comments about the prophets in 2:11–12, 3:3–8, and especially 7:10–17; it seems to go better with Phase-Two material. This passage also refers to the period of the end of Phase One, when the people fail to repent, and when prophets attempt to speak but the leaders shut them up. So it really is an aspect of Phase Two. It is the waiting period between the end of prophetic utterances and the actual disaster.

The first occurrence of *ymym bʾym* is in 4:2, which is a classic example of Phase Two. It is true that these people qualify for the Woes and are a distinctive group, but in Phase Two they share the general fate. In any case, no clear distinction is made between the population generally and the elite, though the leaders are identified and condemned, but we do not hear of them being sentenced to execution. That fate befalls them in Phase Three.

We can make a distinction in Phase Two, but it is horizontal, not vertical. There is the general destruction forecast in the Great Set Speech, which includes all of the nations. Then there is the special material on the fate of the northern kingdom, which is singled out in several passages such as this one (8:11–12). So it looks as though *ymym bʾym* splits around Phase Three and functions in Phases Two and Four, which is not surprising, because Four reverses Two, while Three is a special refinement of Phase Two, which has no future: it is an execution. The one point at which *bywm hhwʾ* functions in Phase Four is to indicate the transition from the final annihilation of Edom to the golden age.

If we try to apply the new insights to the name "Israel," we would point out the following: *ʿmy yśrʾl* is used in Phase Two and again in Phase Four (the third and fourth visions, the confrontation in Amos 7, and the last oracle, which reverses Phase Two). *ʿAmmî* alone in 9:10 belongs to Phase Three. The phrase *byt yśrʾl* belongs substantially in Phase One (The Book of Woes) but is also found elsewhere. In 9:9 we are in Phase Three. It looks as though the divisions in the book of Amos can be organized in a variety of ways and that on the whole they tend to reinforce one another in terms of both subject matter and Phases, and in some cases terminology.

PART IV

Epilogue

(9:7–15)

Introduction to the Epilogue

Two completely opposite notes are struck at the end of the book. A final statement is made about Yahweh's evenhanded jurisdiction over all of the nations (9:7), which results in judgment against them all (chaps. 1–2). That judgment will bring about total destruction (vv 9:8–10). Yet, right to the end, that threat is issued in paradoxical language: destruction will be complete—"I shall destroy it from the surface of the earth" (v 8aB); "All the sinners of my people shall die" (v 10aB)—and yet, "I shall not utterly destroy the house of Jacob" (v 8b). The parable of the sieve (v 9) sets forth this enigma.

How can there be any future after the total destruction described and predicted so many times in the earlier part of the book? The closing verses (11–15) contradict this complete annihilation so absolutely that many scholars have been unable to fit them into the rest of the book. It would have been quite impossible for Amos himself to turn around so completely at the end of his career and to reaffirm the old hopes of security and prosperity that he had denounced as fallacious and obsolete. Therefore these verses must have been added much later by an editor, who wished to soften the severity of the prophet's word and who wished to bring a message of hope to the survivors of the catastrophe. This addition represents a later triumph of an optimistic world view over the prophet's message, a contradiction and cancellation of Amos' true words, carried out right in his own book!

What an irony if Amos, having defied Amaziah, and having stood firmly by his principles, finally fell into the hands of an editor who was able to turn his words into their exact opposite! It would require a very audacious person to do such a thing; and he would have to have a fairly low estimate of the authority and finality of the prophet's genuine words. He would also have to foist his revised version on a community that would be just as jarred and puzzled by the sudden change at the end as we are; but who, unlike ourselves, could make inquiries (if the previous version had enjoyed any degree of public recognition or circulation) and expose such tampering.

Such a reviser would also have to have a high regard for his own better understanding of the matter. But if he had a contrary message, why cobble it onto the end of such a solid and sustained presentation of views the opposite of his own? Why not simply ignore or suppress the book of Amos altogether?

Later editorial additions and revisions have been detected at many places throughout the book of Amos, mainly of an eschatological character, like the Epilogue. Most of them, notably the three Hymns, heighten the theme of total destruction that will take place in the End Time. We have already argued that none of these passages can be convincingly denied to Amos, admitting all along that little or nothing in the book can be *proved* to come directly from Amos himself either.

The status of this Epilogue as integral to the whole book will be discussed in detail in the concluding comment. Here we will make only two preliminary points. The first is: Why bother at all? The intensity of Yahweh's rage against "all the sinners of my people" does not arise from a detached and disinterested commitment to abstract principles of justice that are met when just penalties are fully applied, and when the total elimination of evil brings everything to a satisfactory conclusion. The simple solution, now that creation has been so hopelessly corrupted, is to annihilate the lot and revert once more to self-existent deity as the only reality, as it once was before God had the idea of creating a world distinct from himself. That simple but drastic remedy was tried once in the great Flood, though even then there was an exception; it was not tried again, and it is not contemplated as a possibility in the Bible. The driving will of God is to have a creation and to be related to his creatures. The intensity of his anger is a measure of that commitment.

His concern and care are shown even more profoundly at the high points of the book: the visions, especially the first two. Here Yahweh allows himself to be persuaded by the plea of one man, so responsive is he to his creatures. And the argument that reaches into the depths of God, beyond justice and equity, is a simple command not to destroy the creation completely. Amos has often been presented as a single-minded champion of justice, and therefore as a prophet of unmitigated doom. He does not behave this way when he is alone with God. Here he has moved onto ground different from justice, and he has found Yahweh on that same ground. On the ground of justice, crime brings punishment. That is all there is to be said. If Yahweh were no more than a God of justice, the story would be quite simple. On the grounds of mercy, justice can be met by compensation or atonement, and forgiveness can be secured on the basis of repentance and reparation. In the early stages of Amos' career every effort was made to arrest Israel's headlong flight into doom by minatory plagues and preaching, calling the people to repentance. Yet even when they fail to repent, there is a call to meet God (4:12). This summons sounds threatening, but what immediately follows is not a prediction of disaster, rather a celebration of God's spectacular power in the original creation and continual management of the world (4:13).

So one must ask if Yahweh's clear preference, to sustain and secure his world and his people, at any cost and on any pretext, is ever totally abandoned and replaced by disillusionment, despair, and destruction. Does God ever lose hope or give up?

The second general point to be made about the Epilogue as a reaffirmation of divine hope at the end of the book is its primitive this-worldly character. It is not at all like the elaborate and fantastic otherworldly apocalypses that came to the fore in the last stages of OT times. It is no more than a restoration of the old way of life for Israel and Edom(!) and of the old monarchy with all of the best features of city and country life. This depiction can hardly be called apocalyptic. Its affinities lie with the old covenant promises. We can outline the whole section as follows:

	Words	
Introduction (v 7aA)	7	7
Divider (7aB): *n'm yhwh*	2	31
I. (vv 7b–8bA)	29	
Divider (8bB): *n'm yhwh*	2	30
II. (vv 9–10)	28	
III. (vv 11–12a)	26	30
Divider (12b): *n'm yhwh 'śh z't*	4	
IV. (vv 13–15bA)	48	51
Ending (15bB): *'mr yhwh 'lhyk*	3	
		149

Just as the first Hymn fragment (4:13) closes The Book of Doom (chaps. 1–4), so the third Hymn fragment (9:5–6) closes The Book of Visions (7:1–9:6). The remaining nine verses strike two antithetical notes, one sounding the end of the nation (9:7–10), the other its future restoration (9:11–15). The two units are themselves very complex, with numerous themes and images all woven together. They are also closely linked, in spite of their contrasting messages. The entire passage (vv 7–15) has many connections with all preceding units of the book of Amos and thus serves as a climactic and final statement.

In what follows we shall discuss these matters in detail. To introduce the subject, we suggest for this unit the following structural analysis.

1. Verse 7 forms a double introduction, each part of which (7a and 7b)

opens with a positive question (formulated negatively but requiring a positive answer, and rhetorical in any case). The order is reversed, for 7a introduces the second part and 7b the first part.

2. The unit as a whole divides into three parts, the first two forming an interlocking larger component, while the last forms a coda or epilogue to the Epilogue. The entire section is bounded by second-person forms, though the opening used the 2d m. pl. form (v 7a) and the closing uses the 2d m. s. suffix (v 15b).

A. 9:7b–10   First or interior ring
   1. v 7b   Introduction
   2. vv 8a, 10 The destruction of the sinful kingdom
   3. vv 8b–9 The survival of the house of Jacob/Israel scattered among the nations

B. 9:7a, 11–12 Second or outer ring
   1. v 7a   Introduction
   2. v 11   The restoration of the *skt dwyd*
   3. v 12   The final battle against Edom

C. 9:13–15   The epilogue of the Epilogue = coda
   1. v 13   The superabundance of the New Age
   2. v 14   The restoration of the people and renewal of the land
   3. v 15   The permanent planting

What is described here is nothing less than the whole history of Israel among the nations, from the time of the Exodus until that day (*bywm hhw'*) on which the nation will be rebuilt and its people replanted forever on its land, never to be disturbed again.

The unit under consideration summarizes the essential content of the preceding eight-plus chapters, including especially the judgment and punishment to be meted out to the eight nations of chaps. 1–2. Regarding these nations, emphasis is placed on the fate of the two Yahwist kingdoms, their obliteration and removal from the political scene. The survival of a remnant in exile results in a further judgment against the leadership ("the sinners of my people" in v 10, who are identified with the targets addressed by the Woes), who are to be executed.

The surviving remnant will return to witness the revival of the kingdom of David, which will be joined by all of the nations who bear the name of Yahweh in a war to the death against the remnant of Edom. Only when full victory has been achieved will the final act of the great drama of return and revival take place. This act is described in hyperbolic language of superabundance and satiation, the rebuilding of cities, the replanting of vineyards and gardens, and the enjoyment of their fruits. Finally the solemn affirmation is made that "I will plant them [=my people Israel] upon their land, and they shall never be rooted out of the land that I have given them."

IV.A. THE END OF THE NATION (9:7–10)
IV.A.1. THE WICKED NATION (9:7–8)

9 ⁷ᵃAren't you like Cushites to me, O Israelites?—Oracle of Yahweh—⁷ᵇDidn't I bring Israel up from the land of Egypt, the Philistines from Caphtor, and Aram from Qir? ⁸ᵃIndeed, the eyes of my Lord Yahweh are upon the sinful kingdom; I shall destroy it from the surface of the earth. ⁸ᵇNevertheless, I shall not utterly destroy the house of Jacob—Oracle of Yahweh!

NOTES

9:7–8. This unit is bounded by the words "oracle of Yahweh," which occur near the beginning (v 7) and at the end (v 8). The famous question in v 7 is in two parts, each beginning *hălô*. Such a rhetorical question expects a positive answer. Why the Cushites are selected to lead the comparison (v 7a) is not clear. The second question lines Israel up with the Philistines and Aramaeans and ties the Epilogue firmly to the Great Set Speech. Apart from the rhythmic composition, the double question, and the series of three origins—Egypt, Caphtor, Qir—the oracle has no other poetic features.

The next verse brings out the other side of Yahweh's evenhanded treatment of all of the nations of the region. Just as they have been dealt with favorably and generously, so they will be judged. But v 8 concentrates on "the sinful kingdom," which is unnamed. It must at least include Israel. If generic, it could be any and all of the eight nations listed in chaps. 1–2.

The threat is immediately qualified; in fact, v 8b almost contradicts v 8a: "I shall destroy . . . nevertheless I shall not utterly destroy the house of Jacob." The discourse switches abruptly from third to first person, which continues right to the end of the book. Yet v 8aA cannot be bracketed out from the rest, for it contains the noun ("the sinful kingdom") needed as antecedent for the pronoun "it" in v 8aB. Verse 8 is clearly prosaic in structure and style.

7. Does the repeated question *hălô*'show that vv 7a and 7b are twins, or does the different terminology keep them apart? In v 7a "Cushites"//"Israelites"; in v 7b "Israel"//"Philistines"//"Aram."

7a. *Cushites.* Cush has many distinct biblical associations, which change from time to time:

> 1. It is rarely used alone, and then of a fabulous land (Gen 2:13) in the most remote parts (Zeph 3:10; Ezek 29:10) where rare jewels are to be found (Job 28:19).
>
> 2. In the time of Isaiah it is mentioned in parallel with or as equivalent to Egypt (Isa 18:1). This usage reflects the political facts of the time (2 Kgs 19:9 = Isa 20:3–5).
>
> 3. Later it occurs in lists, some quite long, reflecting a different political situation and other geographical horizons (Nah 3:9; Jer 46:9; Ezek 30:4, 5, 9 and 38:5). Compare Isa 11:11.
>
> 4. This terminology can be projected back into the Exodus story (Isa 43:3, 45:14). This usage is perhaps a reflex of no. 2, but Ps 68:32 suggests it could be older.

The lists in Ps 87:4 and Amos 9:7 could reflect an early view of the god Elyon as suzerain over this whole region (cf. Deut 32:8).

The country *kûš* is always spelled *plene* (30 times); the gentilic, in its various forms, also has the full spelling (with *waw*), but there are exceptions (4 times out of 27) as here with *kšyym*. The spellings in v 7, *kšyym* and *plštyym,* are unique in the Hebrew Bible; only here are the two words spelled out in full. Elsewhere only one *yod* is used. The question is whether this full spelling reflects the real pronunciation, which is then to be read even when only one *yod* is used in the spelling. In other words, the spelling with one *yod* is *defective,* and we must read the *yod* as consonantal, as one of them must be in the current cases (Andersen and Forbes 1986:168). Alternatively, we may suppose an artificial hypercorrection here on the basis of other gentilics such as Kittiyîm (Kittites), reflected here in the full spelling, whereas the shorter spelling reflects the real-life situation and actual pronunciation (perhaps reduced from the longer form), resulting in a correspondence of short spelling and short pronunciation. It may be noted that much of the spelling in the Minor Prophets reflects late practice (i.e., full spelling with vowel letters), which is true across the board, whether the particular prophetic book be early or late. Late postexilic spelling has been normalized throughout the Book of the Twelve; the case here, while unusual because there are no other examples elsewhere, is nevertheless instructive.

As far as its geographical location can be defined in relation to Egypt and to Put and Lud, Cush has been identified with Nubia or Ethiopia. Amos' solitary mention of this people leaves them without associations to guide us to his thought and intention. In what way is he trying to say that the Israelites are just like the Cushites, as far as Yahweh is concerned? No stories are told of Yahweh's dealing with this nation, which seems to be the remotest of all known peoples. The following question, if a parallel and an explication, lines the Cushites up with the nearer and better-known Philistines and Aramaeans, all of whom have been moved around and settled into their lands by the same God and on the same basis.

The opposite is said of Israel in contrast to other nations in 3:1–2, also in connection with the Exodus. The distinction does not lie in a unique historical experience. Other peoples have likewise been given a land, though there is no hint that Philistines and Aramaeans were rescued from slavery in Caphtor and Qir.

The dialectic of v 7 could be, "Aren't you like the Cushites, just another enslaved and exploited people under the Egyptians?" Answer: "No! There is a difference. You [Yahweh] delivered us [Israel] from bondage in Egypt." The response is, "But I also did the same for other peoples—the Philistines and Aramaeans (to name but the two most familiar to Israel)."

7b. *bring . . . up.* The same idiom is used in 2:10 and 3:1.

Caphtor. The identity of this place has been subject of discussion in three recent monographs—Hellbing 1979, McCaslin 1980, and Strange 1980. See also Knapp 1985. On the ethnic identity of the Philistines see Dothan 1982:21–23.

8a. *eyes.* Compare "my eyes" in v 4b.

the sinful kingdom. The phrase is unique and undefined. The reference to "kingdom" could be an oblique attack on some specific monarchical regime. In the wake of chap. 7, it could only be that of Jeroboam. If this is the reference, the definite adjective could be superlative, with Israel, the last of the eight, seen as the most sinful.

destroy. Compare the original treatment of the Amorites in 2:9.

8b. *Nevertheless.* The word *'epes* is variously classified as a noun ("nothing," Amos 6:10); as a modifier, either privative (Job 7:6; Prov 14:28, 26:20), or negative (e.g., Isa 54:15—"not from me"), or existential (= *'ên*); or as an adverb ("nothing but"). In BDB a pseudo-preposition *bĕ'epes,* "without," is identified. Joined to *kî* it reinforces the adversative meaning of the latter and introduces a contrasting fact, or a significant modification of a statement already made (Judg 4:9; 2 Sam 12:14). Verse 8 thus becomes paradoxical: "I shall destroy the sinful kingdom from the surface of the land. But in spite of all that, I shall not completely destroy the house of Jacob." The unusual position of the negative *lō'* before the infinitive absolute emphasizes the negation of the intensification, not of the action itself.

Not: "I shall not destroy the house of Jacob *at all,*" but "I shall not *completely* wipe out the house of Jacob." If the house of Jacob is the same as the sinful kingdom, the statements are contradictory. If the two are quite distinct, v 8b is a *non sequitur.*

As we have observed, *byt yʿqb* in all likelihood refers to all of Israel, the predecessor of the divided kingdoms, and to the two together; so the survival of one of them would meet the requirements of the verse or the survival of remnants and captives, because a full end is nowhere affirmed.

IV.A.2. THE SIEVE (9:9–10)

9:9a Indeed I will command:
    I will shake the house of Israel among all the nations
 9b   just as the grain is shaken in a sieve,
       but no kernel falls to the ground.
 10a   All the sinners of my people shall die by the sword,
 10b   those who say:
      "Calamity shall not even come close,
       much less confront us, during our lifetime."

NOTES

9:9a. *I will command.* This word was already used twice (vv 3, 4).

shake. The form is *qal,* already used in 4:8 and 8:12.

all the nations. The same wording recurs in v 12. He does not have only one nation (Assyria) in mind; he expects Israel to be scattered everywhere (cf. Hos 9:17). Failure to recognize that most of the Epilogue is prose has led to foolish attempts to turn it into regular verse by drastic rewriting. Here, however, the deletion of "among all the nations" is supported by its omission in some LXX manuscripts; but the evidence is hardly persuasive.

9b. *is shaken.* The *nipʿal* has no subject and could be general. "Grain" is often supplied, but this emendation sets up a problem for the word "pebble" in the next verse.

sieve. This Heb word, *kĕbārâ,* occurs only here in the OT, but its use in later Hebrew makes the meaning certain. The LXX interprets it as a winnowing fan.

grain. The word *ṣĕrôr,* when it does not mean "bundle," occurs again in the Bible only in 2 Sam 17:13, where the LXX renders *lithos,* "stone," as the Targum did here; likewise Aquila (*poēphion*) and Jerome (*lapillus*). But the LXX has the curious reading *syntrimma* as if from *šeber,* which could have been translated "grain" and might have stood in the LXX's *Vorlage* as a result of trying to account for the preserved text (MT) by interpretation. Because the meaning "pebble" is the most likely, the *kĕbārâ* has been interpreted as a sand sieve (NJPS). Recovery of the true picture requires more than the determination of the words' meaning. Is the sieving an act of judgment or of conservation, when something is prevented from falling to the ground (cf. 1 Sam 3:19)? Hence the interpretation of *ṣĕrôr* as "grain" or even "ear" (NIV). The grain is retained in the sieve, fine dust and fragments falling through. If, however, the pebble is the bad ingredient, then the good grain (or fine sand) passes through the fine mesh. In any case, the purpose of sifting is to separate the good from the bad. But how is this process like the wandering of the house of Israel in all the nations? There is no clear teaching in Amos of a righteous or faithful remnant to be spared the disaster and remain in the land or to survive in exile. This point makes v 9 all the more important; for it is one of the few places, however obscure, that makes a distinction between those marked for total extermination (vv 1–4, 8a, 10) and those to be excepted. It confirms the qualification given in v 8b.

10a. *sinners.* Only here and in Isa 13:9 is this noun modified by a genitive. In Amos "my people" is always an object of positive regard, usually "my people Israel" (7:8, 15; 8:2; 9:14). The construct is not appositive; the qualification suggests that not the whole people, but only the sinners "of" (among) the people will be killed. It is possible that the *nomen rectum* is the deep-structure object, "those who sin against my people," distinguishing the ruling and exploiting the classes, enumerated in the participles of the Woes, from the righteous, their victims. We suggest that "the sinful kingdom" (v 8a) is similarly selective. The LXX reads *tēn basileian tōn hamartōlōn,* as if it read *hḥṭ'ym.*

10b. *who say.* The definite article with the participle could be the vocative particle (*h-*), making this line the last of the series of Woes that extend through the book. Note especially 6:13. It probably sums up the indictment of the whole group and applies to them all. It also defines the phrase "the sinners of my people," which does not include everyone. In the other Woes very clear identifications are given of these sinners and their sins, and clear distinctions are made between those who are culpable and answerable, and those who are their victims. It is inconceivable that the distinctions made in the indictments would not also hold up in the punishments.

come close. The *hipʿils* are internal. There is no need to read *qal* (BDB 621a, cf. v 13) or *nipʿal* (Wolff 1977) or to make "the evil" the object

(NEB). In comparable cases (Isa 41:21–22) the meaning is similar to *qal*, but intensive or elative, "it won't come close to us." The same applies to "confront." The *hip'il* of *qdm* occurs only here and in Job 41:3, where it is transitive (but where emendation is widely advised). Two specimens are better than one, whether the two cases of *hiqdîm* or the two *hip'ils* in sequence here. The LXX has the same syntax, with intransitive verbs. But this fact is not a warrant for retroverting to *qals*: "It won't affect us in the least."

These are the people who are not sick over the crash of Joseph; who are callous, cold, self-indulgent, and avaricious; who oppress the needy; and who welcome the Day of Yahweh, convinced that for them it will be a day of light and not darkness (contrary to what the prophet has said) and in any case that finally no disaster will touch them at all. They are impervious to warning, threat, or plea, and they and all their crew will be swept away. That is the last word of the prophet on "the sinful kingdom" and the "sinners of my people."

us. The compound preposition is peculiar. It combines *b-* (normal with *qdm*) with *'d* (normal with *ngš*), but in reverse order. But *b'dynw* ("because of us") is not spelled with *-y-* anywhere else, while it is usual with *'d* in suffixation. Emendation of three words in a row (BHS) is far too drastic (Hammershaimb 1970:140).

calamity. The definite article points to a specific disaster, already mentioned. It refers to the "evil time" (5:13), the "dark day" (5:18), the "bitter day" (8:10).

The doctrine of Prov 13:21 is that *rā'â* pursues sinners but *tôb* rewards the righteous. The creed of v 10b was based on a false belief that God was with these people (5:14).

COMMENT

The theme of vv 7–10 seems to be similar to that of chaps. 1–2 on the one hand and 3:1–2 on the other. The Israelites are like the Cushites to Yahweh, meaning that he exercises equal control over both. It shows not a lack of interest in Israel but an equal one in Cush, which may be regarded as a distant land, at the edge of the world and with little or nothing in common with Israel. All that can be suggested as a bond is the common experience of servitude to Egypt, which not only oppressed Israel but also exercised domination over Cush.

The other comparison seems to make more sense and is in reverse order. The basic, central event in Israel's history was the Exodus, redemption from slavery in Egypt. If the Israelites make the point that is also made in

3:1–2, there is an answer for it: First, Yahweh has also brought other peoples from distant places to their present location, thus exercising equal sovereignty and thus expressing equal interest in their destiny and status. This fact does not diminish his concern for Israel, but that special interest belongs with others to make up Yahweh's rule, both in principle and in practice, in his true domain, the world. Second, any special or unique concern about Israel is expressed in moral and ethical terms. Israel's distinction is that Yahweh will judge it all the more severely because of the connection. This view, which is explicit in 3:2, is implied in 9:7 because of what follows in v 8.

Admittedly, Yahweh brought Israel out of Egypt, but he did the equivalent for Philistines and Aramaeans, neither of whom even acknowledge his rule and authority. Nevertheless, they belong to him and their destiny is in his hands, just as Israel's is. This explanation of equal special interest then allows Amos to repeat what was said earlier, that the special nature of Yahweh's relations with Israel requires him to be just, and he will punish the sinful kingdom precisely because he has been involved from the beginning with its history. The implication is that the same general rules apply to the other peoples and that each will have to answer for its behavior to the supreme judge, a matter spelled out in detail in the oracles against the nations in chaps. 1–2. Here, however, as in 3:1–2, the focus and emphasis are on Israel. The other nations are being brought in for purposes of comparison and to make the point in a different way, not only that Yahweh is God of the whole world, concerned about specific nations and peoples and their destinies, but also that Yahweh expresses his special interests in this or that nation in comparable ways, and that for Israel the comparisons mean two things: Israel may be special in its relationship but that relationship does not exclude other special relationships that are cataloged in terms of peoples and treatments. Furthermore, to the extent that in the special relationship the emphasis will continue to be ethically informed and the meaning of the relationship will be spelled out in terms of moral principle and practice, Israel along with the others will be held strictly accountable to God for its behavior. In fact, the more special and unusual the relationship the more severe the judgment.

The comparison with the Cushites is curious. For the period of Amos we are just too early for the rise of the Cushite Dynasty that took over Egypt, only to surrender its power to the Assyrian invaders in the course of the ensuing century. There does not seem to be any indication of the enhanced status of the Cushites in Amos, a circumstance reflected and documented in First Isaiah. Cushite success and conquest of Egypt do not seem to be in the picture here, or certainly not the collapse of their hegemony over Egypt and reversion to the southern territory of Nubia after the early part of the seventh century B.C.E. The references in Jeremiah and Ezekiel seem to reflect an entirely different picture, one that does not concern us here. There is an older tradition that mentions Cushites in the period of the wilderness wandering, in particular Moses' marriage to a Cushite woman. Whether these are the same people or nation is much debated, and clearly we cannot build a thesis on this point. There are also references in early Psalms such as 68, perhaps 87; but these references are not easily explicated and the internal relationships remain obscure.

With regard to the set of three comparisons in v 7b, it may be speculated that there is a connected thread apart from the obvious use of the same verb to define the actions, namely, that Yahweh brought them all from one place to another. The comparison with Israel is explicit and deliberate. So the various implications and overtones that we associate with the Exodus must be present with regard to the Philistines and the Aramaeans, though the details will differ. The association of the three groups in the Syro-Phoenician or Palestinian region is obvious enough, and the same three—Israel, Philistia, and Aram—turn up as part of the series in chaps. 1 and 2. For better or worse, and especially in the eighth century, the experiences and fates of the several nations were bound up with one another, as chaps. 1–2 make clear. Here we find the suggestion that their origins were as well.

While the dates of all three movements resulting in the later presumably permanent settlement in the current tradition are debatable, it is plausible to suggest that these movements occurred during the same period of time. We can date the Philistine migration in the period of upheaval and movement that characterized the transition from the Late Bronze to the Early Iron Age in the Near East. It was a period of collapse for the great empires and of the emergence of the Sea Peoples, among whom we reckon the Philistines, as well as of the movement and settlement of many Semitic groups, including Israelites and Aramaeans. We can date the settlement of the Philistines on the southwest coast of Canaan during the reign of Rameses III, who repelled a major invasion of the Sea Peoples (which included the Philistines, who are mentioned for the first time in Egyptian sources).

The date of the Exodus is still much debated, but a consensus is emerging for a date in the 20th Dynasty, at the end of the Late Bronze Age. A corresponding date for the settlement in Canaan in the twelfth century would seem appropriate, perhaps a little later than that of the Philistines rather than before it (ca. 1150 B.C.E.), because of the reference to *plšt* "Philistia" in the Song of Moses (Exod 15:14) as already in place at the time of the Exodus (Freedman 1975:9–10). If we put the Exodus and Settlement at roughly the same time or a bit later than the Philistine appearance in the same region we will not be far off the mark, say, twelfth century for both.

With respect to the Aramaeans, they are mentioned as early as the twelfth century in Assyrian inscriptions and are well documented from the eleventh century on in the region of modern Syria. Biblical references begin with the Patriarchs (cf. Genesis 10 and the Table of Nations), but these may be regarded as anachronistic in some measure. The reference to Aram in the oracles of Balaam may be historical, however, and in any case that Balaam's home territory was Aram and Syria rather than Edom, as suggested by some scholars, is now widely accepted. Whether there were organized kingdoms in the region as early as the twelfth century is not clear, but certainly they were in being by the eleventh century and perhaps before. The references to David's wars and other relations with the Aramaeans, along with the appearance of royal Aramaean inscriptions as early as the tenth–ninth centuries, offer general confirmation of an early date for the emergence of Aramaean city-states. Just where and what Qir was have not been determined, but there is no reason to doubt that there was such a place in the days of Amos (cf. 1:5) or that the Aramaeans had come from that region centuries before. The common view is that it lay to the east of the classic territory of Aram, and there seems to be no good reason to doubt this claim, but how far and in what particular region seems beyond recovery at the present time, especially because the place-name has so far not appeared in cuneiform or alphabetic sources.

Now we must turn to 9:8b to resolve the matter of the survival of a remnant. As there is an apparent contradiction between this statement and the preceding one, it is important to explain the difference and justify it in terms of the book of Amos, the prophecies of Amos and other prophets of his time, and the background or setting in which the problem of divine justice is worked out in historical and natural events. The justice and mercy of God are at stake here, and the issues need to be spelled out, analyzed, explained, and finally resolved.

In our judgment there is no necessary contradiction between the two statements, requiring separation and assignment to different speakers, authors, and editors. Neither is it feasible to regard the second statement as a later qualification of the first, namely, that there will be a destruction but it will not be total. That reading is possible, but on the basis of v 8a and other statements elsewhere in Amos, it is clear that a devastating but not necessarily total destruction was in his mind and expressed in his message. From the statements made about the royal and ecclesiastical establishment and the categories of wicked, heartless, and thoughtless people listed in various woes throughout the book, we know that they will be pursued to the ends of the earth and finally obliterated from it. But it is our view that the "sinful kingdom" is not to be equated fully with the "house of Jacob" but rather with "the sinners of my people." Broadly speaking, there are two groups in Israel, the sinners and the sinned against. There are both righteous and unrighteous, and while they will participate in the common destiny of the nation (the invasion, conquest, and exile are clearly adumbrated by the prophet), the ultimate fate of the different groups will not be the same. While the group of leaders and oppressors will be tracked down to the last person, the other group will survive, in part at least, and its fate will be different from that of the others. The mercy of God requires that some special consideration be given even to the worst of sinners, but Amos has long since concluded that the time and opportunity and finally the possibility of mercy for the evildoers, beginning with priest and king, have run out, and that judgment and punishment are determined.

But justice itself, not mercy, is required for the just along with the unjust, and it would strike at the very heart of Israelite religion and self-awareness to say that all will fall together, that in the promised destructions moral and ethical distinctions will be erased and that no difference in destiny will be seen between the righteous and unrighteous. The charge that God indeed is indifferent to these factors, as in the skeptical/cynical philosophy of Ecclesiastes, or that he is hostile and malicious, as in the bitter analysis by Job of God's way with the world, simply shows that thinkers and theologians in Israel were sensitive to the overriding issue of divine justice. It also indicates that theodicy was not a postexilic invention but an issue that bothered and engaged Israelites from earliest times, especially with their concentration of powers and attributes in the person of a single God. However much real experience of the cataclysms and catastrophes of nature and history may have supported the view that human beings share a common fate regardless of individual merit or desert, biblical speakers and writers are unanimous in the view that God is just and righteous first of all, that he makes moral distinctions, and that historical experience ultimately must vindicate his justice and their view. So, if for no other reason, there must be a place in the thinking of prophets like Amos to vindicate the justice of God and his moral stance. The same argument that justifies, even necessitates, the condemnation and punishment of the nation because of the sins of omission and commission on the part of its leaders and power elite also requires that those who are themselves victims or those whose lives and behavior conform to the divine requirements be spared the same fate. To some degree, it is clear that they will share equally because the nation itself is doomed (that doom is inevitable and follows from the elementary fact of the social aspect of life). Nevertheless, there is also a necessary separation of groups on the basis of morality and behavior. It is to this problem and its resolution that the words of 9:8–10 are addressed.

The paradigm for this solution to an intricate and difficult problem is the story of Sodom and Gomorrah and the other cities of the plain. Three of the four eighth-century prophets mention one or more of these cities explicitly (only Micah does not; Amos mentions Sodom and Gomorrah [4:11], as does Isaiah [1:9–10, 3:9, 13:19]; Hosea refers to Admah and Zeboiim instead [11:8; cf. Genesis 14, where all five cities of the plain are described]) and specifically compares those cities and their fate with their counterparts in contemporary Israel and Judah, namely, Samaria and Jerusalem. In other words, it is clear from the usage that the story of the destruction of Sodom and Gomorrah is well known and has already become a standard benchmark in discussions of divine justice and mercy, and that it is applied theologically and homiletically to the contemporary scene by these prophets. The lesson is a permanent fixture in prophetic literature, and later prophets have at least as much or greater interest in the matter. The comments, interpretations, and inferences are expanded to cover many other related points in the ongoing debate and discussion of God's righteousness and the destiny of nations (cf. especially Zeph 2:9; Jer 23:14; and extensively in Ezekiel 16, esp. vv 46–56; we may cautiously use later citations and comments to illustrate the ongoing discussion).

The story presupposed by the prophets may not be identical with the one preserved in Genesis 18–19, but the outline and essential elements are comparable. Here was a prime example of divine judgment and punishment of a sinful city (or several, but Sodom will serve). Also involved in the question of divine justice and punishment of the guilty is that of the disposition of the case of the innocent. In the discussion over the issue, Abraham emphasizes that a just God must deal justly with all of the people in the cities of the plain. There is no quarrel about this principle, but Abraham interprets it to mean that God should spare the whole city with all of its wickedness, or rather with its wicked and guilty people, for the sake of the righteous people there on the basis of some numerical ratio. Such an outcome would really fall under the heading of divine mercy because it involves a relaxation of strictly retributive principles; but such modification in the direction of mercy and kindness is considered a natural and essential ingredient in the divine administration of the orders of justice. The practical issue of the exact ratio of good to bad is not entirely resolved, but in the case of Sodom and Gomorrah the issue of mercy and the possibility of saving the city (or cities) on the basis of the presence of a few good people in it are explored. The redemptive and salvific power of the righteous is limited, however, and the case cannot be resolved in those terms. At the same time, Abraham's initial argument that it would not be just to sweep away the righteous with the wicked is not contested either. In fact, this idea is unthinkable in the divine governance of the universe. Everyone must receive his or her just deserts: the wicked must be punished, not rewarded, and the righteous must not be punished along with the wicked as though there were no difference. So neither principle of extension, of extending the righteousness of the righteous to protect the guilty or of extending the guilt of the wicked to inflict punishment on the righteous, is appropriate. In the end the cities are destroyed with their wicked inhabitants, while the only righteous person identified in Sodom—Lot—is spared and removed from the city along with those covered by his righteousness; or perhaps all of them are rescued because of Abraham's righteousness (cf. Gen 19:29).

The incident gave rise to much scholarly and sometimes casuistic discussion over "merit" (zĕkût) as a kind of commodity that might be accumulated in greater quantity than a person needed, so that the excess could be transferred to the account of others who without it would not reach the necessary minimum (Marmorstein 1920). Abraham did not lower the number below ten, and this figure was taken as the limit. Without this minimum there cannot be a nucleus of righteous persons (minyān) in a town (m. Sanh. 1:6), and the rabbis even advised the rest to leave when the number fell below that level.

It has never been clear why ten should have been the cutoff point. Abraham's argument—"Why should you destroy the city over a short-fall of five?" (Gen 18:28)—could have been continued by decrements of one so that eventually the destruction of a community with only one just person in it would have been declared unjust. A willingness to go to this limit lies behind Yahweh's instructions to Jeremiah to see if he can find even one person who does justice in Jerusalem, "so that I may pardon her" (Jer 5:1-2).

Abraham began with fifty, reduced the number by five in two steps to forty, and then by tens to ten. At this point he stops, having become increasingly hesitant and worried that his persistence will provoke Yahweh. When proposing ten, Abraham speaks as if it is the last chance (Gen 18:32). Homilists have chided him for giving up at this point instead of pressing through beyond the threshold at which God would say, "That [say, four] is not enough." Perhaps the intention of the storyteller was to leave the minimum number of righteous persons that immunizes a city undefined. In any case, it would not have made any difference to the outcome, as far as Sodom was concerned, even if Abraham had proceeded to the limit of one. Abraham had extracted a promise that God would "spare the whole place" for the sake of a mere handful of righteous, and he went back home believing that he had achieved his aim. Yet the Lord destroyed the city all the same, not so much because the minimum number of just persons was not there but because all of the righteous persons were first removed. The angel explained that he could not move against Sodom until the righteous had been moved out of range. In fact, their transfer to Zoar is enough to save that city from the fate of the rest.

The same principle is at work in the story of Noah and the Flood. It underlies the great ongoing narrative of the Bible and the oracles of the prophets. The basic principle is that God is just in all of his dealings with the world of human beings, and that in spite of appearances to the contrary no one can ever have just cause for complaint. We hold that this principle informs the teachings of the eighth-century prophets, and explains the oracles of Amos on matters involving judgment against nations and particularly against Israel and involving the destiny of other peoples and individuals in the Near East in those days.

As applied to his contemporary situation, it means that the nation (Israel certainly and Judah along with many other nations) will shortly come to the end of its corporate history. Responsibility for this disaster belongs to the leadership, which has brought condemnation on the state, the collective entity to which all Israelites belong, also upon itself as the guilty party. The leadership will be exterminated, and all others will share in the fate of the nation. But there will be survivors, and for them there will be a new and different kind of future, with ultimate revival and restoration of the kingdom.

In practice it would be hard to argue that the distinction between good and bad and the separation of the two camps were observed and the division carried out in history. All we can say is that there was a conquest, there were survivors, and many of them went into exile. Among the latter were those marked for destruction, and they would be pursued relentlessly by the Sword, appointed by God for that purpose. But there would be others, marked for preservation and survival, and ultimately for return and renewal of the kingdom.

What is new and distinctive in Amos here is the proposal that the exilic group will be divided by some procedure, with the wicked leaders meeting death by the Sword as the final judgment in their case, while others will constitute the nucleus of a new community to be restored some day. The process is described by reference to a sieve (mentioned only here in the Hebrew Bible) that is used to separate wheat from chaff. The imagery may be drawn from the practice of sieving grain so that the kernels remain in the sieves and the smaller particles of dust and dirt fall through onto the ground. The statement that "no pebble [= kernel] will fall to the ground" indicates that in this operation it is what remains in the sieve that is of value, while what falls to the ground will be discarded or destroyed. The effect of exile among the nations will be like shaking grain in a sieve. The purpose is not to punish but to separate the two groups. What remains in the sieve will be saved for future use, while what falls through the holes to the ground will be destroyed. This image would cover the case in hand, with the "sinners of my people" falling to the ground while the remnant of Jacob will be saved in the sieve.

The words at the beginning of v 9, "Indeed I will command," echo the statements in 9:3–4, where Yahweh is said to command the Serpent and the Sword to pursue and destroy the people marked out for destruction. While a loose connection between 9aA and the rest of v 9 may be posited, it is more likely that the orders and actions are separate: that Yahweh orders the agents mentioned in 9:3–4, but only implied here, to carry out their mission and destroy the sinners of the people by the sword. It is the conclusion of the search and destroy directive applied to the group responsible for the "breach of Joseph" and the imminent downfall of the nation.

The argument about the justice and mercy of God reaches a climax in the discussion in the late seventh and early sixth centuries B.C.E., especially as reflected in the books of Jeremiah and Ezekiel. A question is raised in these books about another aspect of the problem of justice and punishment in the form of a proverb: "The fathers ate sour grapes and the children's teeth are set on edge" (Jer 31:29; Ezek 18:2). Both prophets agree that the proverb is bad and theologically untrue. Obviously they must concede that there is a measure of truth in its reflection on human experience. It can look as though a later generation suffers for the sins of an earlier one, contrary to one of the basic principles of criminal law in the Bible: only the guilty should suffer for their crimes, not the innocent (cf. 2 Kgs 14:5–6; Deut 24:16 with Jer 31:30; Ezek 18:4, 20). Jeremiah contends that in the new age no one will be able to repeat the proverb because it will have lost its validity. Ezekiel argues that it never was true and that everyone gets what he or she deserves, and there is no transfer of merit or demerit, of rewards or deserts.

An illustration of this principle is to be found in the elaborate parable involving the three ancient heroes of righteousness: Noah, Job, and Daniel (i.e., the Dn'il [probably pronounced the same as in the Bible] of Canaanite tradition and of the Aqhat legend in the Ugaritic tablets). Ezekiel argues that if these three righteous men were living in Jerusalem, their righteousness could not save the city and its inhabitants (Ezek 14:12–20). They alone would be saved because they are righteous, and the rest would be destroyed. Under these strict rules their righteousness would not even serve to protect their families (contrary to the stories told about them in the tradition, in which Noah and Job are able to save or intercede on behalf of their families, and presumably also in the case of Daniel). But in conformity with the principle of divine justice, they themselves would be spared while the city and its inhabitants perished. God does not punish the righteous and innocent. He may on occasion spare the guilty or mitigate and postpone their punishment, but it would be untrue to his nature and violate the fundamental principles of divine justice to inflict punishment on the innocent and righteous. That is the basis of the prophetic message, and it provides the key to understanding it as it deals with the destiny of Israel and the fate of the people.

The issue of collective versus individual personality in the view or conception of Israel is not involved here. The distinction between collective and individual views of Israel is too sharply drawn by many scholars, and the distinction is hardly one of chronology or evolution. Admittedly, there are shifts in emphasis and nuances, but both elements are present in Israelite religion and self-consciousness from earliest times. The notion that the idea of religion as an individual matter only emerges or becomes dominant after the collapse of the state, or that from the exile on the collective view of Israel vanishes or declines in importance, is more a caricature than a portrayal of the biblical picture of these components. From the start they were interwoven in the description of Yahweh's relations with his people. Each individual is a member of the larger community of faith, but the community consists of individuals who have distinct responsibilities and obligations as members of the community. For example, the commandments are clearly addressed to individuals and serve to regulate the attitudes and activities of individuals in relation to God, to the community, and to each other. Each individual has a dual responsibility: he or she is answerable for personal and familial behavior under the rule of the commandments, and is also responsible for the way in which the commandments are observed by other individuals and the community as a whole. In a similar fashion the destiny of the individual is bound up with that of the community, but at the same time it is affected by the individual's decisions and behavior. The relative weight given to the individual and to the community may vary from circumstance to circumstance, and there may be a general trend to emphasize the role and status of the individual in the course of time. But to speak of purely collective thinking (i.e., in terms of corporate personality) in pre-exilic times and of individual consciousness in exilic and postexilic times is overly simplistic and falsifies the evidence in the Bible for a continually varying mixture of factors and the interaction of these principles in the history of Israel's religion.

The statement of the issue in terms of an individualistic versus communal view of human personality and accountability in very general terms also overlooks the fact that responsibility is weighted in the direction of the leadership. They may be relatively few in number, yet the well-being of the masses depends on their commitment to righteousness in both their public duties and their private lives. Amos is not so theoretical or unrealistic in his assessment of the situation as to ignore the pragmatic fact that the failure of the few at the top can bring more harm than the failure of the many at the bottom. In the end it reaches up to the king himself: the single person at the top of the pyramid is the most responsible for the fate of the whole kingdom.

Perhaps the most important clue to the meaning of the unit 9:7–10 is the reference to the "sinful kingdom." Because of the associations and analogies with 9:1–4 and 7:10–17 it seems clear that the focus of attention is on the leaders of the kingdom—the priest and his associates and the king and royal house—and correspondingly on those described by the participles— the people who think, speak, and do all of the wrong things and who constitute the same establishment and aristocracy, but viewed in different categories. In the end these people constitute the sinful kingdom, the real kingdom or kingdom within a kingdom, and it is they and their realm that will be destroyed, ultimately without a survivor. As an example, Amaziah will witness the destruction of the temple, the priesthood, and his own family and will then go into exile, where he will die in an unclean land (7:10–17). Compare 2 Kgs 25:5–7, containing the description of King Zedekiah's fate, which was to witness the execution of his children and then have his eyes put out, knowing that with his death his line would be cut off.

As for the Bethel sanctuary and its personnel, the destruction will be complete with any survivors not surviving, any escapees not escaping (9:1), and those going into exile being pursued there by the Sword (9:4; cf. vv 8, 10).

The sinful kingdom is matched by "the sinners of my people" in v 10; all of them will die by the sword, just like those who seek to escape (9:4). The sons and daughters of Amaziah will die by the sword, and Jeroboam and his house as well. The links seem secure, and we can conclude that the judgment and slaughter are intended to be total, but for a specified and limited group: the leadership. As for the rest, there may be some recourse for them, not because this idea cropped up later with the survival of the southern kingdom and the ultimate return of exiles, but because the same justice by which God destroys the sinful nation requires that there be some provision for those who are not sinful. There must be some distinction even if catastrophic events, whether historical or natural, tend not to make such distinctions, and wars and earthquakes seem to kill indiscriminately. In the end, the God who controls both nature and history and who is both just and kind must make distinctions and provisions for moral differences. If all share the same fate and if everything ends the same way, as the Preacher contends, then much or most of the Bible is beside the point. The prophets were not prepared to concede this view and persisted in believing and insisting that history and nature work for God's purposes and that the basic moral lessons of righteousness and justice are borne out by history.

In our analysis, therefore, we link vv 8a and 10 (along with 9aA) as the prediction and pronouncement of doom on the "sinful kingdom"—"the sinners of my people"—those already singled out as the architects and builders of disaster. Those who led the nation astray must now pay the price of their folly, their apostasy, and their sinfulness in administering the country. The country itself will suffer as a consequence, more terribly than its people really deserve; nevertheless, God will not make a full end because that would not be an act of divine justice, quite apart from his *ḥesed* (kindness) and *ḥēn* (grace). So we believe that vv 8b, 9aB, and 9b apply to the nation as a whole. Aside from the leadership (the aristocracy, those who have authority and bear responsibility, who will be utterly rooted out and destroyed, even in exile) the rest of the nation will suffer, but will not become totally extinct.

Verse 7 provides the background for the statements to follow. It is a comment on the doctrine of election. The order in v 7a is opposite to that in 7b. Verse 7a begins with Cushites and ends with the Israelites—"Aren't you like Cushites to me, O Israelites?" This remark would imply that the Israelites are like everyone else, which is true; but it can also mean that the Cushites are like Israel. Each has a special relationship with Yahweh. Just because Israel makes that claim, the claims of others are not thereby ruled out. In any case, election is not exclusive. Each is different, but the implication certainly is that the degree of chosenness is qualified by a comparable degree of responsibility, with corresponding consequences.

The second part of 7b starts with Israel and ends with Philistines and Aramaeans. Just as God has brought Israel up out of Egypt—an act of grace and kindness that not only sets Israel apart but imposes a heavy responsibility commensurate with the act of deliverance—so in like manner and degree has he done for the Philistines and Aramaeans. They too are singular objects of divine intervention on their behalf, and they too are correspondingly responsible to the God who is their Lord. This verse not only sums up the meaning of the message in chaps. 1–2 and 3:1–2, but provides the framework and ideological structure for the statements to follow. While the remarks are limited to Jacob//Israel, they could apply equally or proportionately to any and all other national groups, including specifically the ones mentioned. And it applies particularly to Philistines and Aramaeans, who have been the subject of the same sort of judgment in chap. 1. Note that the Philistines and Aramaeans are in that order in 9:7 and in exactly the reverse order in chap. 1, where they are the first two nations mentioned. So we have a very long-range chiasm here, but one that is plausible, showing that there is a deliberate link between the passages. A further proof is that the place-name Qir occurs in both passages (1:5 and 9:7—the readings are almost identical, *ʾrm qyrh*//*ʾrm mqyr*). The place-name *qyr* occurs only four times in the Bible, and two of them are in Amos, which can hardly be an accident (compare the usage of Jeshurun as a special name of Jacob//Israel, which occurs only four times in the Bible, two of them in Deuteronomy 33, where they have a similar structural function). The other instances of Qir occur in 2 Kgs 16:9 and Isa 22:6. In the latter, Qir is parallel to Elam, which may give some idea of its location. If Qir is in the vicinity of Elam then it is a long distance from Syria. In 2 Kgs 16:9 we have the statement that Tiglath-pileser III, in response to a request by Ahaz king of Judah (about 734 B.C.E.), attacked Damascus, captured it, "and took it (its population) captive to Qir." The wording is almost identical with that of Amos 1:5, but there is no reason to think that either passage is dependent on the other. No doubt the practice was not initiated by Tiglath-pileser, and it was well known that Aramaeans were transported to Qir by the Assyrians when they rebelled and proved obstreperous about paying regular tribute. The policy of transferring populations was a long-established one in Assyria, but whether they deliberately returned people to their original homeland is not certain; and in fact it would seem to be contrary to their intention, which was to uproot people and displace them so that the ties to their homeland would be broken and the only identification and nationality they would have would be as members and part of the Assyrian Empire. At the same time, if we are right and the migration from Qir occurred centuries before, and the only real link with the ancient homeland was that of memory and tradition, the transfer would not in fact be inconsistent with the stated policy.

In the other case, the Philistines are duly mentioned in both passages but not Caphtor, because in this instance there is no suggestion of a return to an ancient homeland. The Assyrians could hardly oblige in that respect, and besides they seem not to have applied the procedure to coastal towns and naval powers. Caphtor is mentioned only twice more in the Bible: Deut 2:23 and Jer 47:4 (where the island of Caphtor is linked with the Philistines).

Here we have the basis for the argument that Amos uses to justify the condemnation of Israel. God had rescued these people from bondage in Egypt and had the right to make demands of them and to punish them for failure to live up to the standards he had imposed and they had accepted. According to 9:7 God had the same right to judge the Philistines and Aramaeans, and for the same reason. He was their God as well, who had brought them from distant places to a new land on which they could settle. Therefore he had the right to make demands and to punish them for failure to live up to the standards imposed. Presumably comparable claims could be made concerning the other peoples listed in the first two chapters, thus explaining the nature and purpose of the judgments pronounced in chaps. 1–2.

Beginning in v 8a we have the judgment against "the sinful kingdom," in particular the heads and executors of the administration, ecclesiastical and civil. As explained, this group includes those singled out for extermination, the targets of the Woes, and in particular the royal and priestly establishments. The judgment that has been given in numerous places is summarized yet again in v 8aB: "I shall destroy it from the surface of the earth." This claim is equivalent to the statements in 5:27 and 7:17 (cf. 7:11) about the exile, and we can understand "the land" here as specifically "her land" (= "his land" in 7:17). The pronominal suffix refers to the kingdom or, in this case, the authorities who exercise rule in the land. The corresponding terms are to be found in v 10a, where "the sinners of my people," who are to be identified with the same establishment, are consigned to the sword, exactly as in the case of the royal entourage in 7:11 and 7:9, 17, where Jeroboam and his house are targeted for death by the sword. The same imagery is used of the priest's children (7:17) and finally of any survivors of the slaughter who may go off into exile (9:4). It may be noted that the order of the parts, vv 8aB and 10a, is just the reverse of the corresponding statement in 7:11, as follows:

9:8aB   *wĕhišmadtî ʾōtāh mēʿal pĕnê hāʾădāmâ*
  10a   *baḥereb yāmûtû kōl ḥaṭṭāʾê ʿammî*

        I shall destroy it from the surface of the earth
        All the sinners of my people shall die by the sword

7:11   *baḥereb yāmût yārobʿām*
        wĕyiśrāʾēl gālōh yigleh mēʿal ʾadmātô

        By the sword shall Jeroboam die,
        and Israel shall surely go into exile from its land
        [cf. 7:9b and 17bB].

For the group mentioned in 8a and 10aB there is no recourse, no hope, no escape. Slaughter is the destiny in store for them, those who are mentioned in 7:9–17 and 9:1 especially, and those who are identified in all of the Woes expressed in chaps. 5–9. The latter group is specified in this last of the participial forms:

        those who say:
            "Calamity shall not even come close,
                much less confront us, during our lifetime."

IV.B. THE RESTORATION (9:11–15)
IV.B.1. THE BOOTH OF DAVID (9:11–12)

9:11a   On that day I will set up David's booth that has fallen,
  11b   I will repair their breaches,
            and I will restore his ruins;
        I will rebuild it as in the days of old—

12a   so that they may dispossess the remnant of Edom,
                    even all the nations over whom my name was
                                                                pronounced—
12b   Oracle of Yahweh, who will do this.

IV.B.2. THE CALENDAR:
SUPERABUNDANCE (9:13–15)

9:13a   Indeed the time is at hand
                —Oracle of Yahweh!—
            when the plowman will overtake the reaper,
            and the treader of grapes the sower of seed;
13b   the mountains will drip with sweet wine,
                and all the hills will flow with it.
14a   Then I will restore the fortunes of my people Israel;
            they shall build the ruined cities, and inhabit them;
            they shall plant vineyards, and drink their wine;
14b   they shall cultivate gardens,
                and eat their fruit.
15a   I will plant them upon their land,
15b   and they shall never be rooted out of the land
                that I have given them—
                    Yahweh your God has spoken!

INTRODUCTION

The conclusion to the book of Amos divides into two parts: vv 11–12,
which opens with *bayyōm hahû'*, and vv 13–15, which opens with *hinnēh
yāmîm bā'îm*. Each unit also ends with an oracular colophon.

The opening formulas occur in reverse order in 8:11–14, with *hnh ymym
b'ym* in 8:11 and *bywm hhw'* in v 8:13. (See earlier treatment of these
formulas.) It is also to be noted that the fuller form of the first formula
occurs in 8:9: *whyh bywm hhw'*. As the book draws to a close, we recognize
a process of tying up threads and winding down the action, with 9:11–15
echoing and ending what was started in 8:9–13, especially because 8:4–7
and 8:14 constitute still another envelope. In 8:9–13 we found a combina-

tion of two units: (1) vv 9–10, referring to the Day of Yahweh and its disastrous effects, ending with unrelieved mourning; (2) vv 11–13, speaking of the famine of hearing the words of the Lord and the failure to find his word. These disasters are reversed and rectified in the closing scenes of the book. The two units speak in turn of the restoration of the booth or hut of David (vv 11–12) and the restoration of the well-being of the people of Israel (vv 13–15).

The composition can scarcely be called a poem, and the language is that of prose at many points, at least to judge by the use of "prose particles," *'et* (six times), *ha-* (six times), and *'ăšer* (twice). The parallelisms between adjacent lines are obvious, but the connections between more distant units are equally important. The whole is unified by a series of predictions or promises in the first person, mostly using the *waw*-consecutive future, which are interspersed with third-person statements:

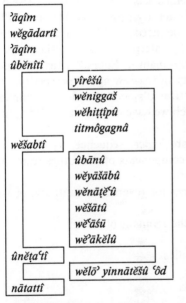

'āqîm	I will set up
wĕgādartî	and I will repair [the wall]
'āqîm	I will restore [raise]
ûbĕnîtî	and I will rebuild
yîrĕšû	they may (dis)possess
wĕniggaš	and [he] will overtake
wĕhiṭṭîpû	and [they] will drip
titmôgagnâ	[they] will flow
wĕšabtî	then I will restore
ûbānû	and they shall build
wĕyāšābû	and [they will] inhabit
wĕnāṭĕʿû	and they shall plant
wĕšātû	and [they will] drink
wĕʿāśû	and they shall cultivate [make]
wĕʾākĕlû	and [they will] eat
ûnĕṭaʿtî	and I will plant
wĕlōʾ yinnātĕšû ʿôd	and they shall never be rooted out
nātattî	I have given

In this manner several themes are interwoven and combined. A block of four statements of what God will do (v 11) is balanced by a block of six statements of what they will do (v 14), which sits between two more statements of what God will do (vv 14aA, 15a).

These two series have in common the important verbs "build" and "plant." This connection shows in the first place that the future restoration will be a combined effort of God and man. Second, it reverses the judgment of 5:11. Note that "build" ends one series and begins the other.

The negated statement in verse 15b is climactic and final, and the repetition of "their land" closes out one of the major themes of the book, in which they have been threatened repeatedly with removal from the land.

Recognizing v 15 as a distinct unit that combines the first-person and third-person participants, we analyze the structure of the rest as interlocking: "they may (dis)possess" follows the first-person block; "I will restore" leads the third-person block. All of these descriptions of rebuilding and replanting are natural enough; but in the center (v 13) is a more utopian passage, which is the true climax of the unit.

These positive prophecies at the end of the book reverse the negative oracles in the body of the book—9:14a reverses 4:6–11; 9:14b reverses 5:11; 9:15 reverses 7:11, 17. In other respects the developments predicted here are a recapitulation of the original conquest. Compare v 12 with 2:10. Most importantly, the clause šabtî ʾet-šĕbût (v 14) reverses the repeated lōʾ-ʾăšîbennû of the Great Set Speech.

Who are the objects of these marvelous acts, the receivers of these blessings? Two groups are mentioned: "Israel my people" (v 14), and "all the nations over whom my name was pronounced" (v 12). The latter phrase is unusual and difficult; and it is usually interpreted as the other object of "they will possess," along with "the remnant of Edom." Thus, "Israel my people" ends up as the sole beneficiary of the new age of prosperity. Other specific components of this unit are "David's booth" and "the remnant of Edom," both strange expressions which we have not yet succeeded in fitting into the drama.

Rearranging the contents into more logical sequence, we propose the following chronological order of the components of the future restoration:

14aA Then I will restore the fortunes [or reverse the captivity] of Israel my people,

12a so that they may dispossess the remnant of Edom
    and all the nations.

14aB They shall build the ruined cities
    and inhabit them;
    they shall plant vineyards
    and drink their wine.

14b They shall work/cultivate gardens
    and eat their fruit.

15 I will plant them upon their land
    and they shall never be rooted out of the land
    that I have given them.

11 On that day I will raise up the fallen booth of David,
    I will repair their breaches,
    and I will restore his ruins;
    I will rebuild it [the booth] as in the days of old.

NOTES

11. This verse is framed by two time references: "On that day" and "as in the days of old." Between these phrases are four clauses, which constitute two pairs in an intricate envelope construction with chiasm. The clue to the arrangement is to be found in the curious sequence of pronominal suffixes after the first clause: "their [3d f. pl.] breaches"; "his [3d m. s.] ruins"; "and I will rebuild it [3d f. s.]." The last suffix evidently refers back to "the booth (*sukkat*) of David" and shows that the first and fourth clauses form an envelope around the middle clauses. In similar fashion the second and third clauses are linked by the f. pl. forms: the 3d f. pl. suffix in *pirṣêhen* and the only f. pl. noun in the verse, *hărīsōtāyw*. The 3d m. s. suffix with *hrstyw* refers back to David in the first clause. Thus the repeated verb *ʾāqîm* serves to open the clauses that constitute the envelope and to close the middle pair, as may be seen in the following arrangement:

> 9:11a   *bayyôm hahû'*
> 11b   *ʾāqîm ʾet-sukkat dāwîd hannōpelet*
>   **wĕgādartî** *ʾet-pirṣêhen*
>   *wahărīsōtāyw ʾāqîm*
>   **ûbĕnîtîhā** *kîmê ʿôlām*

> 9:11a   On that day
> 11b   I will set up David's booth that has fallen,
>   and I will repair their breaches,
>   and I will restore his ruins;
>   I will rebuild it as in the days of old.

The first and last clauses make good sense together, though we may be uncertain about just what the clause "David's booth that has fallen" signifies. With respect to the middle pair, we interpret the breaches and the ruins as references to David's kingdom or more particularly his city (Jerusalem). Its walls have been breached and its buildings, public and private, lie in ruins.

11a. *David's booth.* The meaning and significance of this curious expression are much debated: for example, whether it means the realm or the dynasty of David, and why it was used here. The fact that the booth has "fallen" has been declared to prove that this verse (and all of vv 11–15 along with it) could only have been composed after the fall of Jerusalem and the house of David in the sixth century. The reference to the remnant

of Edom has likewise been understood as reflecting these later developments. In the history of interpretation it was unavoidable that such expressions would be attached to such well-known events and seen as remarkable
predictions of events long after Amos' time. From that position, it is only a
short step to labeling these utterances as simulated prophecies after those
events. Similar difficulties attach to the oracles against Edom and Judah in
chaps. 1–2, which have been linked to the references to David and Edom in
chap. 9.

The LXX's *skēnēn* confirms the singular *sukkat,* but it levels both the
pronouns and the verbs, translating both *gdrty* and *bnyty* by *anoikodomēsō.*

12. The reversal of Israel's fortunes in the future is sometimes described
in the Bible in extravagant terms as a conquest of the whole world and
subjugation of all nations, including those that had previously conquered
and subjugated Israel. Verse 12 is often interpreted along similar lines. Both
"the remnant of Edom" and "all the nations over whom my name was
pronounced" are taken as the object of this possession, or rather dispossession. In the context of the reference to the booth of David, these nations are
identified as those over whom that king had ruled, bringing them into
subjection under the name of Yahweh. The region involved would then be
identical with David's empire and would coincide with the region covered
in the Great Set Speech (chaps. 1–2).

There are problems with this analysis. The coordination of "all the nations . . ." with "the remnant of Edom" as equivalent objects of "they
may dispossess" is lopsided and awkward. The omission of *'et* before the
second component is against normal syntax, and attracts suspicion. This
problem can be resolved by recognizing "Edom and all the nations" as the
coordination phrase, the *nomen rectum* of "remnants," hence the single use
of *'et*—"the remnant of Edom-and-all-the-nations. Another solution is to
identify the "and" as resumptive, so that "all the nations" is the subject of
the verb, "they may dispossess." This phrase could also be the antecedent
of the plural pronouns in vv 14–15. When Israel is exiled from its land, the
expression is *'admātô* (7:11–17). So here *'admātām* means the land(s) of all
of the nations. The booth of David and the remnant of Edom are in the
center of the stage, but the stage is as wide as that in chaps. 1–2 and in
keeping with the spirit of 9:7.

The LXX has *ekzētēsōsin* for the first verb, as if from *yidrĕšû.* It has also
made "the remnant of Edom" more compatible with "all the nations" by
translating the former *hoi kataloipoi tōn anthrōpōn,* as if it read *'dm (defective)* = *'ādām.* Defective spelling of Edom is unknown in the MT (except
for the gentilic form), but it is possible that *'dm* survived to the time of the
LXX alongside of *'dwm.*

12a. *my name.* The statement that Yahweh's name is pronounced over
all of the nations is unprecedented. Elsewhere, Yahweh's name is called

over the temple, or Israel (2 Chr 7:14). Isaiah 63:19 categorically denies that the divine name is used with any other peoples. If Amos 9:12 is to be harmonized with such texts, then "all the nations" cannot be the antecedent of the relative clause. The relative clause must be seen as the subject— "Those over whom my name is pronounced [i.e., my people Israel] will possess the remnant of Edom and all the nations."

12b. *do this.* Compare 4:12. The use of *'lhyk* in 4:12 and 9:15 is another link.

13. Here the fertility of the land is described in hyperbolic terms. The cycle of agricultural activities traced represents roughly the normal procedures in the calendar, one major activity in each season or quarter:

1. Plowing—autumn (October, before the early rain);
2. Sowing—winter (after the first rains);
3. Reaping—spring (after the late rain); and
4. Grape treading—summer (late).

The arrangement links the beginning and ending of the planting cycle (plowing and reaping) in immediate succession, as if spring followed hard on autumn. There is so much to be reaped that the task will hardly be completed before it is time to plow once more, scarcely a normal state of affairs. The other activities are not causally linked, but the idea seems to be that grape treading would continue from summer to winter, when sowing would begin. The implication is that the crops of grain and grapes are so great that it takes all of the intervening time to complete one task before the other begins.

The order is not sequential in time or in the normal procedures; rather, the activities are paired in an alternating fashion. In addition, the order of plowing and planting in combination with reaping and treading is reversed: plowing naturally precedes reaping, but treading precedes sowing in a sort of chiasm. Perhaps the purpose is impressionistic: to speed up the cycle and point to the happy result caused by superabundant produce. Leviticus 26:4–5 gives a somewhat more orderly picture of the same eschatological picture of plenty: the whole year is filled by the cycle of agricultural activity. The time is hardly enough to bring in the crops; work is continuous, as are the reward and the satisfaction. The end effect in Amos is the picture of mountains dripping wine, hills melting under the endless flow of the delectable beverage.

In the first bicolon the same verb serves for both units; in the second line two participles balance the two in the first line. But whereas the opening pair are unmodified, the second pair have objects. The second colon overbalances the first, and the effect is cumulative and climactic. In the second bicolon the verbs are in a chiastic pattern. This time there is only one object, the parallel and synonymous subjects being a common and conventional pair (masculine//feminine). The difference is compensated for in the second line by addition of the climactic "all" (which has a double-duty function) and by the use of the intensive-reflexive form of the verb.

13a. *sower.* In BDB 604b Amos 9:13 is listed as the only case of *mšk* meaning "trail seed (draw along in sowing)." In Judg 4:6 and 5:14, *mšk* means "march." Compare Ps 126:6, *nōśēʾ mešek-hazzāraʿ*, "carrying the trail of seed." Rudolph (1971a:279) thinks *mešek* means "(seed-)bag," the verb being denominative.

14. In a logical structure, the two related acts of God, reversing their fortune and planting them once more in the land, would precede the reconstruction by God (v 11) and by man (v 14). And all of it comes before the abundance of v 13.

14a. *restore.* The idiom *šabtî šĕbût* can refer to return from captivity, but the case of Job (42:10) shows that it describes the reversal of fortunes, and restoration to a previous prosperous state (cf. Zeph 2:7, 3:20). The concluding statement (v 15a), reversing the threats of expulsion from their lands directed at Israel (7:11, 17) and other nations (1:5, 15) shows that return from exile is part of the program. Furthermore, because the booth of David is to be erected once more, "my people Israel" must cover both kingdoms. The prophecy shows no awareness that the exile would take place in two distinct stages, different for the two kingdoms, and no awareness that the return would involve mainly Judahites in an unsymmetrical way.

build. God and man both engage in the work of rebuilding and replanting. Compare Ezek 36:36 (God does it); Ezek 28:25–26 (they do it). The prominence of this expectation in later prophets, when the ruin of cities and devastation of farms had taken place (Jer 33:10; Isa 54:3, 65:21), gives weight to the argument that the similar passage in Amos 9:14 is an exilic or postexilic addition.

drink . . . eat. The sequence is abnormal and arresting. It can be explained as a flashback to 6:4–6 or as an inclusion that reverses the circumstances, turning the curse into a blessing. The sequence is chiastic with the normal one in 6:4–6, also with the harvesting described in 9:13.

15b. *Yahweh your God has spoken!* This is the expanded form of the colophon used regularly in the book of Amos, beginning with the Great Set Speech. More impressive is the connection with the words with which the Speech begins and which are repeated at the beginning of each of the pronouncements: *kh ʾmr yhwh,* which is balanced and closed by the overlapping *ʾmr yhwh ʾlhyk,* a striking inclusion and fitting conclusion to the book.

COMMENT

The basic question concerns the date of this final unit. Is it from Amos and the eighth century, or does it belong to the exilic or postexilic edition of the minor prophets? It must be granted that the oracle seems to presuppose the collapse of the Davidic monarchy and dynasty along with the exile of the population. But the terms are general, and the picture of restoration hardly reflects the reality of the postexilic return. It seems to belong to the general predictions of restoration that we find scattered through the Primary History and the major prophets, especially Jeremiah and Ezekiel. The restoration requires a united Israel under the rule of its long-standing dynasty (that of David). The returned people is called Israel, and the land includes not only the traditional territory of Israel but areas that belonged to Israel in the days of the united monarchy (the remnant of Edom and all of the other nations). The language varies from the realistic to the hyperbolic, and the climactic vision is that of a land flowing with milk and honey (to borrow an image from a similar context), one in which the mountains drip with wine and the hills flow with the blood of the grape. The new age will be what the old age was intended to be.

The picture is much the same as what we find elsewhere in the basic Bible of the sixth century, but there is little if anything that can be pinned to that century. There is no suggestion of the Babylonian captivity or the Persian restoration. Except for the reference to the fallen booth of David, the oracle on restoration, return, and revival could have come from almost any period from the middle of the eighth century on, when the reality of invasion, conquest, and exile was thrust on the consciousness of Israel and Judah by prophets from both north and south. If we had a clearer idea of what this unique expression in the Bible meant, we might be in a better position to judge just when the oracle was uttered and the context in which it was issued. The reference to David seems to indicate that his dynasty has fallen from power and that his descendants no longer rule over the land. In any event, the booth of David has fallen and needs to be rebuilt. That prospect becomes a legitimate and lively hope only when king and kingship, nation and people have reached an end, a point of decision and conclusion, something that occurred in Judah shortly after the beginning of the sixth century B.C.E.

Summary of 9:7–15

THE EPILOGUE AND THE PROBLEM OF UNITY

Ostensibly there are five discrete and somewhat disjointed or discon-
nected parts in the Epilogue of the book of Amos (9:7; 9:8; 9:9–10; 9:11–12;
and 9:13–15), and in general all or most of the material is denied to Amos
and more particularly to the eighth century or any period near it. Opinions
vary about individual items, and some elements are regarded as reflecting
the insights of the prophet. While we recognize that a final word on questions of authorship is impossible, it is our opinion that the material is
carefully integrated and well organized, and that it belongs to the book of
Amos, if not in its original formulation, then in one composed shortly
thereafter and well within the lifetime of people who knew the prophet and
had heard his words.

In support of these views we have pointed to a number of links between
the experiences and sentiments found in the Epilogue and those in different
parts of the book. Some of them are fleeting echoes, others are substantive
links that require and attest to a mastermind or general editor. And some of
these points of contact will be noted as we proceed with the analysis, but
the main purpose of this essay will be to analyze the structure of the whole
and the way the parts fit into it. As in earlier analyses we will study the
various devices used by the author/editor to define and separate the units
and to link and unite them, in particular the distribution and arrangement
of the divine name and formulas, and of the name "Israel" and its associates. There are introductory formulas, concluding formulas, and other elements that mark divisions and point to links at some distance.

We find the following major and minor divisions, some of which have
been recognized for a long time. Thus the major division is found at the end
of v 12 (note the *Patuaḥ* divider in the MT). The closing unit, vv 13–15,
stands apart from the rest, so the first separation is between vv 7–12 and
vv 13–15. The larger of these sections also breaks down into smaller parts,
but we wish to observe that both sections are futurist in character. That
focus is evident in the case of the last unit, which is really the epilogue of
the Epilogue, but it is also true of the first section, which serves as the
prologue or lead-in to the other. The last unit has the characteristic formula
hinnēh yāmîm bāʾîm, which we have already encountered in earlier parts of
the book (cf. 4:2–3 and 8:11–12). But the coming days at the end of the

book are very different from and in marked contrast to those other days. What is obvious in vv 13–15 is less evident in vv 7–12 chiefly because the futurist formula is tucked away well along in the unit—v 11 to be exact—still, it not only describes or prescribes a future very different from those introduced by the same formula in the body of the book (cf. 2:16; 8:3, 9, 13), but also introduces the unit in spite of its belated appearance. The formula is somewhat displaced, but there are important links between the unit vv 11–12 and the opening verse (v 7). For various good reasons the composer preferred to begin with a series of sharp rhetorical questions and then move to the thematic formula, varying from standard usage. So the first large part is characterized by the futurist formula *bywm hhw²*, while the second or concluding part is introduced by *hnh ymym b²ym*.

Taking the larger section first, we note the following subsections or units:

1. v 7, consisting of two rhetorical questions introduced by *hlw²;*
2. v 8, introduced by *hnh;*
3. vv 9–10, introduced by the almost identical *ky-hnh;* and
4. vv 11–12, introduced by *bywm hhw².*

It seems to us that the parts line up in a double ring or envelope fashion: thus parts 1 and 4 are closely associated, and the same is true of parts 2 and 3. Let us look at the central section first. We have already noted that parts 2 and 3 each begin with *hnh* (there is a slight variation in v 9—*ky hnh*—but *hnh* is the more important term). Then we observe that the phrase *byt y²qb* toward the end of v 8 is matched by *byt yśr²l* in v 9, which evokes the similar proximity of the terms *bny yśr²l* and *byt y²qb* in 3:12–13, except that they are in reverse order. We note too the presence of the divine name, *²dny yhwh,* in v 8, and the balancing formula, *n²m yhwh,* at the end of the same verse (for our purposes it might have been more useful to have it at the end of v 9). We note also the linkage between "the sinful kingdom" (*mmlkh hḥṭ²h*) in v 8 and the "sinners of my people" (*ḥṭ²y ²my*) in v 10, which we take to be basically equivalent expressions.

When it comes to parts 1 and 4, the outer ring or envelope, we suggest that the opening formula in v 11 (*ywm hhw²*) serves as the introduction to the whole piece, not just to part 4, because the first part (v 7) has no introductory formula. We also note the presence of a multipurpose formula in v 7 (*n²m yhwh*) and its correspondent at the end of v 12 (*n²m yhwh ²śh z²t*), an unusual elaboration, but not out of keeping with the practice of varying routine and repeated terms at strategic points. At the end of v 12 we have a strongly marked closing and at the beginning of v 13 we have an opening formula. Together they define the major division in the whole Epilogue.

As it turns out, the formulas for the center section are both in v 8, while the opening and closing formulas for the outer ring are both in vv 11–12. We still think we are justified in proposing the divisions and combinations as indicated and for the reasons given. The main question about linkage is how 9:7 fits with anything else in the Epilogue. It certainly has strong ties with the Great Set Speech of chaps. 1–2 and provides an important clue if not a key to understanding the theological substructure in that speech, namely, the nature and dynamics of the relationship of Yahweh with the eight nations. Here in 9:7 an important clue is provided in the listing of the three nations, all of whom are mentioned in the earlier oracle.

But aside from tying threads together from various parts of the books, which is no small function for a conclusion, what connection or function does 9:7 have in the Epilogue, especially the larger first section? The answer may lie in a connection between the nations in v 7 and the nations in v 12. The latter speaks in a very curious way about "all the nations over whom my name was pronounced." The phrase *kl-hgwym* is the subject rather than one of the apparent objects of the verb *yyršw* (the construction of the object with a single construct and a peculiar compound absolute defies most of the rules of grammar governing such cases, and in this instance also good sense). But who are these nations who even in a distant future will dispossess the remnant of Edom? Only two nations, historically, bore the name of Yahweh or were reckoned as his clients and worshipers; but in the future— according to most prophetic and other biblical passages—the future kingdom would be a united one, not a divided one, so there would not be even two to fill the larger capacity of a word like *kōl*. Other nations must be included; we are assured even in these verses that there will be an Israel bearing Yahweh's name, but will there be others? Certainly there are indications in a number of places in the Bible that the day would come on which other peoples and nations would worship the one true God (cf. the well-known passage in Isa 2:2–4 = Mic 4:1–3), and in v 7 an explanation is given of why some of them should. Equally with Israel they have been recipients of the grace of God, who brought them from other places and put them in the lands they possess. In the new age they may come to recognize the God who is responsible for their existence, survival, and ultimate restoration. What will be true for Israel, namely, a survival and then a restoration of fortunes, will be true for them equally. And we suppose that while the list in 9:7 is limited to three members it is intended to include others as well, those listed in Amos 1–2. How many and which ones are not clear, but between vv 7 and 11–12, four are listed and more may be included, some on one side of the great battle and victory, some on the other. The reference to David, however difficult it may be to interpret the *sukkat* that is associated with him, is also significant, because it could be said that in his day Yahweh's name and authority were known among the nations, at least the eight that constituted his empire and sphere of influence. The restoration of the kingdom of Israel and its allies is perhaps in view here, and the nations mentioned in v 7 along with others from the list in Amos 1–2 are probably intended. All of these nations owe their existence to Yahweh's gracious actions, and in the future they will acknowledge that basic fact.

It may be argued that on the basis of the oracle in chaps. 1–2 none of these nations would survive the judgment and destruction announced and that therefore in Amos' view such a future as contemplated here would be impossible. We have suggested that he believed that there would be a future for Israel and therefore for other peoples as well, though in what shape or form and by what names and territories are not clearly indicated. If Edom is to be plundered in some future struggle, there must be nations to achieve it. The nations indicated here would include some of Israel's neighbors, perhaps those at one time part of the Davidic kingdom, possibly those who acknowledge Yahweh as their creator and protector. It remains a difficult question.

The Name Israel

We have already discussed the variety and distribution of the name "Israel" in the book of Amos including the Epilogue. There are four occurrences of the name in the Epilogue plus one occurrence of Jacob. It is of interest to note that each of the four different ways in which the name "Israel" occurs in Amos is used here:

1. *yśrʾl*   (v 7)
2. *byt yśrʾl*   (v 9)
3. *bny yśrʾl*   (v 7)
4. *ʿmy yśrʾl*   (v 14)

This arrangement looks like the result of a deliberate plan to recapitulate the usage in the book itself. We have noted that Israel by itself is used for the northern kingdom only, while the other three designations are interchangeable and stand for all of Israel at some point in its history, past, present, or future. In the Epilogue, however, we believe that all of the references are to Israel the totality, that none of the uses (including *byt yʿqb*, "the house of Jacob," in v 8) refers to the northern kingdom alone. There seems to be no difficulty with the compound expressions in this regard, but the use of Israel alone is a notable exception. It is used in a context in which the obvious meaning of the passage requires all of Israel, for it is a statement about the Exodus and Yahweh's deliverance of Israel from bondage in Egypt. It is almost as though the writer solved his problem by contradiction. He used Israel alone because it was required, but he also put it in a

well-known and frequently repeated statement, and in which the true
meaning could not be in doubt. (This is the one clear exception to the rules
derived from a study of all forty-five instances of the use of Israel and other
names for the people of God.) The context should probably have been
enough, but the author/editor did one thing more in order to meet all
requirements. He actually split one of the compound expressions so that he
could use Israel by itself to satisfy the requirement of completeness in his
group, but he put the other element elsewhere in the passage so that the
reader could find it and make the connection, thus interpreting the use of
the term correctly. The word "Israel" stands alone in v 7, and the word
ʿammî stands alone in v 10. Thus we have a second instance of this phrase
in the Epilogue (cf. v 14). It has been broken up and is in reverse order, but
it is still quite recognizable. Thus the author achieved both objectives. We
can add in support of this analysis that it is the only place in the book of
Amos in which the word ʿammî stands alone. In the other four cases it
precedes "Israel" immediately, and in every case the meaning embraces the
whole of Israel. In addition, this is the only place in which the name
"Israel" alone clearly refers to the same entity. The answer is that the two
words belong together and are meant to be read and understood that way,
but were separated by the writer to fulfill other purposes. Technically it is
the breakup of a stereotyped expression.

GENERAL ANALYSIS OF 9:7–12

Two principal actions are contemplated and discussed in this unit: one
deals in destruction and the other in restoration. The first phase is the
completion of the action warned about and threatened throughout the
book, while the second phase of restoration and renewal will develop out of
the earlier one. The second phase is concentrated largely in vv 11–12,
signaled by the phrase *bayyôm hahûʾ;* but the great restoration is anticipated in v 7a, and thus we have an envelope construction. Each ring begins
with the same word of interrogation: 7a introduces the second phase, while
7b introduces the first phase, which is the phase of judgment and devastation widely advertised in the earlier chapters, and especially in the classic
condemnation of chaps. 1–2.

Thus vv 7b through 10 constitute the phase of destruction, interwined,
however, with the rescue of the remnant of the house of Jacob//house of
Israel in vv 8–9. The second phase, constituting 7a and 11–12, deals with
the reconstruction of the kingdom of God in which all of the nations bearing Yahweh's name will have a place of honor; but there is a feature left

over from the first phase, namely, that the remnant of Edom will be evicted from their land.

Why Edom alone? Its sole mention here as the only nation explicitly excluded from the final restoration matches its prominence in the Great Set Speech. The sentiment expressed here agrees also with the special animus against Edom, of all nations, in other parts of the Bible (Ob, Jer, Ps 137). Even in the ultimate redemption, issues of justice will not be left behind.

Briefly put, we may say that vv 7b–10 evoke the vivid description of destruction in chaps. 1–2. Three of the nations listed in chaps. 1–2 are grouped here in reverse order from that in the early chapters, which shows that the linking is quite deliberate. Here an adequate explanation is given for the threatened judgment in the earlier chapters. The case against Israel has been spelled out in detail through the book and the same point has been made, namely, that Yahweh brought the Israelites out of Egypt and gave them a land to live in. He has every right to demand worship and service from his people and every right to judge and condemn them if they fail to meet minimum standards of behavior in public and private life, in the whole sphere of religious and secular activity. The point here is that the same principle applies to the others because each owes its existence to the gracious activity of Yahweh and its allegiance to the same God. Because they are not clearly aware of the relationship they will not be judged as strictly, but they fall so far short of even minimum requirements that they too will be destroyed, which is precisely what follows in v 8a. Then v 7b is the protasis to which 8a is the apodosis. Because Yahweh has acted graciously to each of the nations listed, and they have failed to respond, therefore he will judge them and destroy them. We know it is true for Israel, for that is the brunt of the book's message; but the statement in 9:7b is not mere repetition of what has already been said. It extends the range of Yahweh's gracious action on behalf of the other nations. (The idea is already hinted at in 7a, but there the meaning is quite different.)

Thus in 8a we must ask who or what is meant by "the sinful kingdom," which is threatened with destruction "from the face of the earth." The immediate response would be "Israel" in the sense of the "northern kingdom," because there can be little doubt that that is a central feature of the prophet's message. But if only that kingdom were intended, why should the prophet mention two other nations in 7b? As we have argued, he is evoking chaps. 1–2, and the most obvious thing about those chapters is that the same general destruction (with some variations in the added details) is threatened and assured for all eight nations listed there. So if we say that "the sinful kingdom" in 8a is Israel, the statement may be true but insufficient. Why limit ourselves to Israel? Each nation in the list according to Amos is equally guilty and equally under judgment. We must never think about what actually happened in the next fifty or two hundred years and draw up a scorecard of who fell and who survived and what percentage of successes and failures the prophet had, in other words, what his batting average was. From his perspective each is exactly like the others (but not in the usual ways we imagine). Here it is because each has received divine favor and owes God obedience, and is under judgment for failing. Strictly speaking, one might limit the list to which the term "sinful kingdom" is applicable to those mentioned in 7b, but it is more likely that the list is comprehensive and intended to include the eight in chaps. 1–2. We note that Edom is mentioned in v 12 and is placed on the receiving end of disaster, so it is clear that the nations mentioned in chaps. 1–2 will all receive their due.

Put into the language of grammar and syntax, we would say that the phrase "against the sinful kingdom" (*bmmlkh hht'h*) is distributive, representative, and exemplary. To make our point we would render "against [or on] each sinful kingdom" (those named in v 7b and the rest listed in chaps. 1–2) and that each of them will be destroyed from the face of the earth (cf. "the remnant of Edom" in v 12). It will be noted that Judah is included along with Israel and those named and not named here.

But there is a radical and essential exception, stated immediately following in v 8b, in the case of "the house of Jacob," which includes both Israel and Judah. The nations will be destroyed (there is no doubt that Amos, like Hosea and Micah, believed that Judah would be overrun and trampled underfoot in the same way that Israel would be), but a remnant of Israel (in the larger sense) will survive. There is no contradiction between 8a and 8b, but the difference is not that Israel the northern kingdom will be destroyed and Judah the southern kingdom will be spared. That would be reading too much history into the material and is not what the passage means. As we have noted, the prophet develops the view near the end of the book that in the destruction of the nation some will be spared, but the leadership will be annihilated. Here he affirms the point that there will be survivors, but there will be no mercy for the nation and the leaders who represent it. Whether the same possibility existed in his mind for other nations is not clear. In some cases he speaks of everyone perishing, for example, the Philistines in 1:8 (cf. *š'ryt plštym*) and probably the Edomites (cf. *š'ryt 'dwm* in 9:12), while there is a hopeful word for the other remnant: *š'ryt ywsp* (5:15). But the question remains open for the others.

We would also argue that the citations of *byt y'qb* in 8b and of the parallel *byt yśr'l* in 9a strengthen our point about "the sinful kingdom." Had the prophet meant only Israel, the northern kingdom, by that reference, he could have provided the necessary specification and, in any case, had he meant that Judah would survive while Israel would fall, he would have used other terms for the survival. What will survive and be restored can only be all of Israel, whatever the particular political makeup of the actual survivors. The symbolism of the twelve tribes and the desert league remains intact in all futurist visions. So out of the debacle to engulf the eight nations identified, listed, condemned, and promised destruction from the earth, a remnant of larger Israel will survive.

Just what will divide those who survive from those who perish is explained in a very difficult and obscure figure of speech in the following verses. In vv 9–10 those who survive and those who perish in Israel are clearly identified. It is stated in v 10 that "the sinners of my people" will perish. The others will survive. Although the survivors and their survival are dealt with first in v 9, it will be easier to deal with the others first. In v 10 we have an inverted Woe, the last in the book; the fate of these people is spelled out clearly: they will perish by the sword, a terminology well known in the book of Amos and used of persons and groups who are quite familiar to us: the house of Jeroboam (7:9, and Jeroboam himself if Amaziah is quoting Amos accurately in 7:11) and the whole group connected with the fallen temple in 9:1–4. Because it is a Woe we are reminded of all of the different groups who make up the class as a whole, the sinners of my people, and their behavior. The term "my people," as already noted, is always used in direct association with "Israel" elsewhere in the book of Amos and should be construed the same way here (we have argued that it is part of the same pair with "Israel" in v 7b, only the author has separated the parts, a variation called "breakup of a stereotyped expression" for which he is noted). The reference is not restricted to the northern kingdom, because as we have shown the Woes are addressed to southerners and northerners alike, especially in the main section of Woes in chap. 6 (vv 1–6), where Zion and Samaria are in parallel cola. The Woe is against those who say (h'mrym) that evil will not overtake them. The juxtaposition of what they say and what will happen to them is decisive.

Now we must look for the survivors. The passage, v 9, is difficult, although the comparison is clear enough: "I will shake the house of Israel among all the nations, just as the grain[?] is shaken in a sieve." The problem relates to the outcome. Just what is it that does not fall to the ground? Normally when a sieve is shaken something falls. That idea is expressed quite plainly in Nah 3:12, where we read "all your fortresses are [like] fig trees with ripe [first] fruits; if they are shaken, then they will fall upon the mouth of the eater." The meaning is that if the trees are shaken, then the fruit will fall. But in Amos 9:9 we are lacking a few elements. First, we do not seem to have a conclusion about the shaking of Israel, though we can infer that those who are shaken out of the sieve will perish and those who do not fall to the ground will be saved. The simile of the sieve is not complete either. We are not told just what is being shaken in the sieve. Then instead of being told what falls through the holes in the sieve we are told what does not fall, namely, the ṣrwr ("pebble" or "bundle" but perhaps "kernels" or the like). Of course, in the imagery of a sieve it is usually but not always what is left in the sieve that is important and valuable, while what falls through is discarded; but perhaps with grain the purpose of the sieve, after the usual waving to remove the chaff, is to remove impurities such as rocks and other items. As Yahweh says that he is commanding or ordering a certain action or agent, one suspects that the normal procedure is being reversed here, and that the purpose of the sieving operation is not to save but to catch people: v 10 implies that the people who do not fall through the sieve, namely, the leaders, will be judged and executed (as we interpreted 9:4, a passage that is very similar to 9:8a–10a, only in reverse order). So we suggest that, contrary to common usage, the simile of the sieve ties the action to the result in v 10: those who fall through the sieve are safe in exile, while those snared in the sieve are selected for execution. The bundle or pebble in v 9b, what remains in the sieve and does not fall through, belongs to the bundle of death rather than of life (cf. 1 Sam 25:29). Thus v 9aA, "Indeed, I will command" does not go well with what follows immediately, "I will shake . . ." but rather with what follows farther on: "All the sinners of my people shall die by the sword." Between these lines we have the complicated simile, the essential meaning of which seems to be: the shaking of the people among the nations will result in a separation between two groups, just as sieving anything will result in a separation between what falls through the holes and what remains in the sieve. In this case, Yahweh is clearly interested in what does not fall but is preserved in the sieve. While it could be argued either way, the interest here seems to be minatory and negative. The people left in the sieve, namely, the prominent ones, are the ones destined for the sword, bringing vv 9–10 into line with v 8a and with the procedure described in 9:4, where the same group is in mind. The people under the judgment of the sword are those identified by the Woes scattered throughout the book but also concentrated in The Book of Woes (chaps. 5–6). Note especially that the word used here for the Woe, *h'mrym*, otherwise colorless ("Woe to those who say") is actually used in one other place, 6:13, at the end of The Book of Woes. The two statements (in 6:13 and 9:10) attributed to those people dovetail nicely and confirm that the writer has the same group in mind: in 9:10 they are identified in the broadest possible terms, clearly intended to include all of those described in the Woe formulas.

Having settled the first phase with the judgment on the nation and the sinful leaders of Israel (including Judah), we must turn our attention to the survivors and what is going to happen to them. In v 9 it is said that they will be scattered "among all the nations (*bkl hgwym*)." The latter expression will turn up again in v 12, only there it is qualified by the relative clause "over whom my name was pronounced." Just who are these nations? We have both negative and positive indications to guide us. First we say who they are not. They are not any of the eight nations under judgment in chaps. 1–2. They will all be eliminated (including the remnant of Edom, which manages to get a call in the same v 12), including Israel and Judah. But as we have seen the remnant of all of Israel will be scattered among the nations, and it looks as though there will also be exiles and survivors from some of the other nations. There seem to be some from Aram (who will go into exile) and Ammon, but not from the Philistines or Edomites; not enough is said about the others to make a judgment. It seems quite possible that some of those people may have a future, but if so it will be as a part of "all of the nations."

The positive note is struck by the mention of the Cushites (*bny kšyym*) in v 7a, and now we must ask why they are mentioned. They are clearly distinguished from the group in vv 7b and 12, who are part of the doomed eight. There is no word of judgment against the Cushites, and they are mentioned here as representative of the nations, among the most distant of all from Israel. The notion that they will be among the nations who will be called by Yahweh's name is not as farfetched as it may seem. We are not talking about actual history but about prophetic visions of the future. Amos has picked one name out of many possibilities, but we think that his purpose was to select a neutral entity as representative of the whole group who would one day become part of the international kingdom of Yahweh. We need only look at the classic statement on Cush by Isaiah (not far away in time) to see that he expected Cush to bring gifts to Yahweh at his temple in Jerusalem (Isa 18:1–8, esp. 7–8). So they are symbolic of the larger list of nations.

What, then, does v 7a mean? Yahweh says to the Israelites: "Are you not to me like the sons of the Cushites?" The parallel use of *bny kšyym* and *bny yśr'l* is designed to show that the comparison is both precise and serious. The obvious point is that Yahweh treats all nations impartially and that Israel receives the same attention as the Cushites and vice versa. The usual view is that because Cush is far away and Yahweh has never shown great interest in its people, Israel can expect the same kind of treatment, that is, it should expect no favors or special attention. Then the text proceeds to the judgment against the sinful nation and the death of "the sinners of my people." But we think the meaning is the opposite. A new day is coming, when the nations that survive will all worship Yahweh, and the Israelites in their midst will come back home to their own land and will worship their God as do the others. In short, the Israelites who survive the drastic purge will be joined by the survivors in other nations in a glorious restoration. So v 7a leads us to the closing unit of this section of the Epilogue, vv 11–12.

On that day (*bywm hhw'*) Yahweh will raise up the fallen booth of David and rebuild it as in the days of old. There is an envelope construction in v 11, for the interior details refer to slightly different objects: the repairing of their (3d f. pl.) breaches refers to the walls, and the rebuilding of its (3d m. s.) ruins refers to the citadel or fortified center. The language is symbolic and not intended to refer to a specific structure that has fallen down. The scene is clearly eschatological, with "all the nations" again in the picture, only here they are characterized as worshipers of Yahweh. That indication immediately evokes the passages about the End Time, when the nations will come to Jerusalem to pay homage and tribute to the one true God (cf. Isa 2:2–4 and Mic 4:1–3). So we should not expect to apply historical literalism to a passage like this one. The expressions in v 11 refer, in our judgment, to the whole restored Davidic kingdom. The great state of Israel will be reconstituted as it was in the days of David and Solomon. The difference now will be that everything will work as it ought. And the other nations that lie outside the Davidic realm will worship the same God and bring their offerings to Jerusalem. The picture would seem to be very close to that of the visions and views of Isaiah, not only in chap. 2, but especially chap. 19:23–25, in which Egypt and Assyria share equally with Israel (= all of Israel) in the golden age (cf. also Isa 11:10–11 and even 12–16 for another glimpse of the same future as in Amos 9). The destruction of the remnant of Edom is given as part of this picture (9:12), an indication that the ancient imperium of David and Solomon is to be restored. It is to be noted that Amos or the prophet of the Epilogue is not merely indulging in nationalistic pride. The worst judgment and the most terrible purges are to be inflicted on Israel (and Judah). Only when all judgments have been carried out against the eight nations will there be a restoration and restitution. The great nations will be left intact, but they will worship Yahweh along with many other peoples. The restoration of Israel and its renewal, on the land promised to the fathers and settled under Moses and Joshua, are part of the fabric of biblical belief. It would be very strange if Amos had any other view of the ultimate future. Most of the prophets shared it, with significant variations in detail. What distinguished them and their views from their nationalistic compatriots and counterparts was the insistence on ethical responsibility, submission to the will of Yahweh, and the balanced view of election as not an excuse for self-indulgence and self-righteousness but a call to service and an acceptance of hard duty and heavy responsibility.

The unit closes with the oracular formula *nᵊʾm yhwh,* which we expect, and the added participial phrase *ʿōśeh zōʾt,* a faint echo of the hymnic passages in strategic points in the book, especially at 4:13 and 9:5–6. It speaks of the God who "does this" or "has done" or "will do." All of the tenses may be involved. What is "this" in this context? Clearly it includes everything adumbrated and specified in the verses, both the judgment and the restoration. God here is not only a *deus loquens* but above all a *deus faciens.* The use of the root *ʿśh* echoes its basic meaning "creates" when used of God in two of the three apostrophes in which the same *qal* participial form occurs: 4:13 and 5:8. Another verb is used in 9:6, but it is synonymous—*habbôneh.*

STRUCTURAL ORGANIZATION OF 9:7–12

Verse 7a is set off by the formula *n'm yhwh* and serves as an introduction to the whole unit. It is followed by three roughly equal units:

1. 7b–8, set off by *n'm yhwh* at the end of v 8 (29 words);
2. vv 9–10 (28 words); and
3. vv 11–12, set off by the formula *bywm hhw'* at the beginning and by *n'm yhwh 'sh z't* at the end (26 + 4 = 30 words).

Let us examine the arrangement more in detail. Although vv 7a and 7b begin with the same word (*hlw'*) and each asks a question expecting a positive answer, they nevertheless move in different directions, with the first question having closer connections with the last unit (vv 11–12), but also with the second unit (v 9), and the second question leading directly into the first major unit, but also having connections with the second, where the two principal themes come together:

> *hălō' kibnê kušiyyîm 'attem lî běnê yiśrā'ēl*
> Aren't you like Cushites to me, O Israelites?

The parallelism is precise and unique between the *bny kšyym* and the *bny yśr'l.* This is the only place in the Bible that the Israelites are compared directly with the Cushites, and the only place that the form *bny kšyym* is used, clearly paralleling the expression *bny yśr'l.*

We translate the expression neutrally to avoid the notion that the statement is derogatory in any sense. In itself the statement affirms what is clearly implied throughout the book, that is, the universal authority and sovereignty of Yahweh, who is the God of Israel but also the God of the Cushites. This affirmation is very important because its converse, namely, that the Cushites are one of the peoples of God, or will be, is equally affirmed in the eschatological passage in vv 11–12. The Cushites are one of "all the nations over whom my name has been pronounced" in v 12. They are used in v 7a to represent "all the nations" mentioned in v 9a and again in v 12. Their remoteness and current noninvolvement in the scene of most of the activity in the book of Amos establishes their function here. They have not been mentioned in the book so far and for good reason. They have nothing in common with the nations mentioned in 7b, the Philistines and the Aramaeans, who represent the group of eight peoples condemned and doomed to destruction in the opening oracle (chaps. 1–2), with which our piece has many important connections. The Cushites belong rather to the other group of nations (*kl-hgwym*) mentioned later as the ones among whom Israel will be scattered, also as the ones who will bear Yahweh's name just as Israel does. All of these ideas are expressed or hinted at in the equal-treatment clause of v 7a. It means not that Yahweh has no special interest in Israelites and that they are like Cushites to him, that is, remote and unimportant, but rather that just as there is a special relation between Yahweh and Israel there will be a comparable relation with the Cushites, who also belong to him and who represent a whole group of nations who also belong to him and will become his publicly and formally.

It is important to note that the world is divided diplomatically into camps by v 7a and 7b: 7a compares Israel to the Cushites, one of the noninvolved nations (i.e., most of the nations or all of the other nations), while 7b identifies Israel with the Philistines and Aramaeans, who represent the eight nations condemned in the major oracle of chaps. 1–2. The Israelites belong in a strange way to both groups as the story of the last days unfolds. Composite Israel (consisting of Israel and Judah) will be destroyed along with their six neighbors, as explained in vv 8–10 and reflecting the major proclamation of the book of Amos. Nevertheless there will be survivors who will be scattered among the nations (v 9), and ultimately (*bywm hhw'*) the booth of David will be restored and they along with the rest of the nations, by then converted to the worship of the true God, will join in driving out the last of the eight nations remaining in the territory (= the remnant of Edom). Then the golden age will ensue. The end result, the restoration of Israel to its land, is elaborated in the final section vv 13–15. We may further observe that v 7a constitutes direct address, using the 2d m. pl. pronoun, while elsewhere in the verse we have the third person, indirect address.

The placement of the oracle formula *n'm yhwh* (*'šh z't*) as a marker at the end of units or between units is the key to the organization of the material. Its use as a divider between 7a and 7b is deliberate; we must begin Part I with 7b, whereas 7a stands by itself as a somewhat enigmatic statement directed to Israel by Yahweh. The next occurrence of the formula at the end of v 8b clearly divides Part I from Part II. We might have expected the same formula at the end of v 10 to separate Part II from Part III, but there is none. The more elaborate form appears at the end of Part III and serves as a divider between it and Part IV. The final occurrence is near the beginning of Part IV (v 13). It seems to have been displaced from its expected place at the end of Part IV and of the whole piece by the use of a more elaborate ending to the book: *'āmar yhwh 'ĕlōheykā* (which is the only occurrence of this formula in the book, although *'mr yhwh* is common and there are some variants with *'dny*).

Part I. 9:7b–8

[7b]*hălô' 'et-yiśrā'ēl he'ĕlêtî mē'ereṣ miṣrayim ûpĕlištiyyîm mikkaptôr wa'ărām miqqîr*

Didn't I bring Israel up from the land of Egypt, the Philistines from Caphtor, and Aram from Qir?

The assertion here has much in common with the previous one, namely, that the relationship of other nations with God is comparable to that of God and Israel. The reference to the Exodus from Egypt makes it clear that the basis for the divine judgment against Israel is being reasserted. The same point has been made twice before: in chap. 2, as the reason that Yahweh can make claims and hence judgments against his people; and then even more emphatically in chap. 3:1–2. In a general inversion, Yahweh begins here with the case established against Israel at the end of the list in chaps. 1–2, and now proceeds to fill in the same basis for the other nations but in reverse order and skipping to the first two listed in chap. 1. Thus we have the judgments in chaps. 1–2 beginning with Aram and Philistia and ending with Israel; here the order is reversed in giving the basis for the divine claim to allegiance and the justification for punishing breach of contract.

	Judgment	*Basis*
1. Aram	1:3–5	9:7b (3)
2. Philistia	1:6–8	9:7b (2)
3. Israel	2:6–8, 14–16	9:7b (1)

What is affirmed here is that Yahweh will treat these nations alike because he always has. The same basic argument applies. The underlying reason is that he chose each of them, delivered each of them, and gave each of them the land on which they live. Each has been guilty of violation of the implied or explicit covenant between them, and hence they will all share the same fate, which is national destruction. We take the group here to be representative of all eight. Three are mentioned in this verse and a fourth, also destined for disaster, is named in v 12; the destruction of the remnant of Edom is presumably the last phase of the end of the eight nations and paves the way for the establishment of the new order. It is difficult to imagine that the omission of the remaining four nations means that they will escape the fate of the others. As in the case of the Cushites, the names used are meant to be exemplary or representative. The threat of chaps. 1–2 will be carried out.

8a *hinnēh ʿênê ʾădōnāy yhwh bammamlākâ haḥaṭṭāʾâ wĕhišmadtî
ʾōtāh mēʿal pĕnê hāʾădāmâ*
Indeed, the eyes of my Lord Yahweh are upon the sinful kingdom; I shall destroy it from the surface of the earth.

8b *ʾepes kî lōʾ hašmêd ʾašmîd ʾet-bêt yaʿăqōb*
Nevertheless, I shall not utterly destroy the house of Jacob.

The way in which we resolve the apparent contradiction between the two statements of v 8 is to say that the kingdoms of Israel and Judah will be destroyed from the face of the earth, but there will be survivors who can be identified with the house of Jacob, that is, with the combined entity. We assume that the prophet believed that one kingdom would not outlast the other by more than a few years and that the cataclysm that would engulf them would also sweep over the remaining six. In certain instances he speaks of the survival of a remnant or an exile, while in others there may be total destruction. We have argued that Amos makes clear his expectation that the nations(!) will fall but there will be identifiable survivors. These are the people meant in this passage, and their destiny is further spelled out in the following verse. We do not believe that v 8 should be interpreted to mean that Israel (the wicked kingdom) will be destroyed but Judah will be spared. There is no basis for that view. Both kingdoms will be destroyed, but there will be survivors of the debacle. They will also meet different fates, but in the end a remnant will not only be saved but also renewed and restored. If the broken pair *yśrʾl* (v 7) . . . *ʿmy* (v 10) represents the disastrous fate that awaits both nations and most of its population, the combined or reunited phrase *ʿmy yśrʾl* in v 14 represents the restoration of the people, their return, and the renewal of land and people, again representing "all of Israel."

Part II. 9:9–10

⁹ᵃ*kî-hinnēh ʾānōkî mĕṣawweh wahăniʿôtî bĕkol-haggôyîm ʾet-bêt
yiśrāʾēl* ⁹ᵇ*kaʾăšer yinnôaʿ bakkĕbārâ wĕlōʾ-yippôl ṣĕrôr ʾāreṣ*

10a   *baḥereb yāmûtû kōl ḥaṭṭāʾê ʿammî*
10b   *hāʾōmĕrîm lōʾ-taggîš wĕtaqdîm baʿădēnû hārāʿâ*

^{9a}Indeed I will command: I will shake the house of Israel among
all the nations ^{9b}just as the grain is shaken in a sieve, but no
kernel falls to the ground.

10a   All the sinners of my people shall die by the sword,
10b   those who say:
   "Calamity shall not even come close, much less confront us,
    during our lifetime."

Note the similar phrases in 6:11 and 9:9:

   6:11 *kî-hinnēh yhwh měṣawweh*
   9:9 *kî-hinnēh ʾānōkî měṣawweh*

In 9:9 as in 6:11 the direct quotation is separated by some digressive material and the speech begins in v 10. The continuation of 6:11aA is probably
6:12–14. As we have already suggested, the opening clause (9:9), "Indeed I
will command," does not fit well with the next word, "I will shake," but
rather forms an envelope with v 10 around the extended simile in what
remains of v 9 (aB–b). Thus we read as follows:

   Indeed I will command:
    "All the sinners of my people
    shall die by the sword."

Compare this with 9:4aB: "I will command the Sword at once, and she
shall slay them."

   9:9a, 10a: *kî-hinnēh* **ʾānōkî měṣawweh** . . .
       baḥereb yāmûtû kōl ḥaṭṭāʾê ʿammî

   9:4aB **ʾăṣawweh ʾet-haḥereb**
       waharāgātam

Not only is the idea the same but so is the target. Essentially the same
group is in mind in the visions in 9:1–4 as in the denunciation in 9:7b–10.
The picture in both places, in our opinion, is the retrieval or capture of
exiles, their presentation before the high court, and their summary judgment and execution by "the Sword" of Yahweh.

The phrase *ḥṭʾy ʿmy* ("the sinners of my people") is at the same time the
subject of the following participle: *hāʾōměrîm*, "those who say." Here we
have the last of the Woes. The main group of Woes is found in what we call
The Book of Woes (chaps. 5–6), but they are scattered throughout the

whole book, beginning in 2:7 and continuing all the way to 8:14, where we have identified those who swear by false gods as the target of the Woes. What we have here in 9:10 is an overall designation for the same group, "the sinners of my people." All of those who belong to the many interlocking and overlapping groups identified by their attitude and activities in the series of Woes are here brought together under a single rubric. The participle h'mrym is also found in 6:13, the last in the main block of Woes (chaps. 5–6. See the discussion *ad loc*).

These people can also be compared with the fatuous optimists of 5:18–20 who eagerly await or even seek the Day of Yahweh. Here too the contrast between expectation and interpretation and what will actually happen is absolute: they look for light and they will have darkness. So those who say that no evil will come near them, that there will be great distance between disaster and them, are equally and totally mistaken. In 9:10 the contrast is emphasized brutally. The ultimate tragedy will overtake and confront them: execution by the sword of judgment. The same destiny is prescribed in 9:4b, again with an absolute distinction and contrast, "For I shall set my eyes upon them to do them harm and not good" (*lĕrāʿâ wĕlōʾ lĕṭôbâ*).

Several other Woes could be adduced, but perhaps enough has been shown to indicate that the final Woe gathers up the basic drive and force of the others in the book, and uses language familiar from the book but organized in a fresh and interesting fashion. Thus the two verbs in 9:10b should be analyzed and understood in the following manner: both are *hipʿil* forms, but neither is causative; rather they are elatives or so-called internal or intensive forms. In the positive sense they would mean (1) *taggîš* = it will draw very near; it will come very close, so close as to overtake; and (2) *wĕtaqdîm* = it will confront violently; it will meet head on. The normal meaning in the *piʿel* means to meet or confront, but the *hipʿil* intensifies the meaning here. In this passage, however, we have a negative particle, *lōʾ*, which clearly applies to both verbs (cf. Hos 1:6b–7a for a similar phenomenon, discussed at tedious length by Andersen and Freedman 1980:188–92). The effect is to reverse the meaning emphatically. It would not be correct simply to negate the renderings we have given. The meaning is not, "It shall not come very close, and it shall not confront us violently." The meaning has to be at the opposite end of the scale: "The calamity will not come anywhere near us," in other words, it will be at the furthermost possible remove. The other verb should be translated, "It will not confront us at all"—that is, there will not be any confrontation of any kind.

In short, the people speaking are boasting, like the others mentioned in 5:18 and 6:13. They are making an absolute statement conveyed by the use of two verbs where one would do and by using the *hipʿil* or elative when something less forceful would have been appropriate. They reinforce each other through the device of a single negative particle, as though the two verbs were really one double verb expressing the total confidence that the speakers and calamity would remain as far apart as conceivable. This mood is also reflected in the sentence construction, with the subject of the verbs at the very end of the sentence, as far away from the speakers as the sentence allows. That our interpretation is no pure fancy or embroidery is shown by the placement of the subject after the prepositional phrase. It is optional, of course, where the words are placed, but the speakers (*h'mrym*) have put "the evil" (*hr'h*) as far away as possible. That the word *hr'h* is the last word of the unit that began with v 7b conveys succinctly what is in the prophet's mind. It is here that the Woes come to an end.

Before going on to the last two units of the book we will examine once more the structure of this section (vv 7b–10). We now see the two major components, each further subdivided into two parts, as follows:

A. vv. 7b–8	*Words*	*Syllables*
1. v 7b	10 ⎫	26 ⎫
	⎬ 29	⎬ 68
2. v 8	19 ⎭	42 ⎭
Divider: *n'm yhwh*		
B. vv 9–10		
1. v 9	17 ⎫	40 ⎫
	⎬ 28	⎬ 67
2. v 10	11 ⎭	27 ⎭
Totals	57	135

Not only is the structure basically balanced and symmetrical, it is also inverted or chiastic. The inner sections, A2 (v 8) and B1 (v 9), are introduced respectively by *hinnēh* (v 8) and *kî-hinnēh* (v 9); the terms *byt y'qb* and *byt yśr'l* in vv 8 and 9 respectively balance each other (they have the same scope or reference and include both nations). Note also the corresponding verb forms, *wĕhišmadtî* (v 8) and *wahănî'ôtî* (v 9), each of which has an echo in its own unit, *hšmyd 'šmyd* (v 8) and *ynw'* (v 9).

Turning to the outer ring or shell (vv 7b and 10), we find the following points of contact. The principal bond linking v 7b with v 10 is the breakup of the standard phrase "my people Israel," which occurs regularly (four times) in the book (the nearest or relevant example is in 9:14; the others are all in the vision sequence, 7:7, 15, and 8:2). Here the phrase is divided between vv 7b and 10, with "Israel" in v 7b and "my people" in v 10, the only instance of *'my* apart from *yśr'l* in the whole book. And each term helps define the other, so that the meaning is the same as that for the whole expression in both places. "My people Israel" in our opinion always designates the whole people, whether as in 7b the ancient group who came up from Egypt, or the contemporary double state (7:7, 15, and 8:2), or as in 9:14 the future united people.

Furthermore, the two passages in 7b and 10 together are a restatement in similar and striking language of the central and provocative message of 3:1–2. The same two points are made in both places: (1) "I brought you up from the land of Egypt; therefore . . ." and (2) "I will punish you for your iniquities" corresponds to "all the sinners of my people will perish by the sword." In 3:1–2 the connection between the divine deliverance and divine punishment is made directly, and no doubt in direct conflict with the established creed, while in 9:7b, 10 the connection is remote and used to bind the outer elements, but the intention is much the same. It is precisely because Yahweh redeemed them from slavery in Egypt and gave them a land to live in that he can make claims on them and pronounce judgments against them. In both instances the second clause follows inexorably from the first.

> 3:1–2   Hear this word that Yahweh has spoken about you, O Israelites, about the whole family that I brought up from the land of Egypt:
> 'Only you have I known of all the families of the earth; therefore I will punish you for all your iniquities."

> 9:7b, 10a   Didn't I bring *Israel* up from the land of Egypt?
>
>   . . .
>
> All the sinners of *my people* shall die by the sword.

In both cases, the whole of Israel is in the view of the speaker, all those who came up from the land of Egypt, those who claim descent from the Israelites of old. The reasoning is the same and the conclusion is too, more general in 3:2 and more specific in 9:10a.

At the same time, there are also cross-links binding all of the parts together. Thus the opening words of v 9, *ky hnh 'nky mṣwh,* clearly introduce and are linked with the statement in v 10 rather than the remainder of v 9, which is a parenthetic remark (cf. also 9:4, which explicates the situation presupposed in 9:9–10). Similarly, "the sinful kingdom" (v 8) must be connected with the "sinners of my people" in v 10, which in turn establishes the necessary link with "Israel" in v 7b.

Part III. 9:11–12

The next unit, vv 11–12, is linked with the very beginning of the Epilogue, v 7a, and provides continuity for the rhetorical question asked there, which is how the Israelites and Cushites are alike. The answer is given piecemeal, partly in passing in v 9 and more completely in vv 11–12. Our position is that the Cushites stand for and represent the rest of the nations —those beyond the territory of the eight nations under divine judgment. The Cushites clearly are not one of the eight, but they are one of the nations among whom the Israelites will be scattered (v 9, *bkl-hgwym*). They well qualify for membership in the group specified in v 12 (all the nations over whom my name was pronounced), as suggested by references in the book of Isaiah (cf. 11:11 for exiles in Cush; 18:1–7 for Cush as worshipers or tribute bearers to Yahweh in Jerusalem).

The place of this passage (vv 11–12) in the general sequence and the events described in it have been discussed. It follows the scene of judgment described in vv 7b–10. In the earlier passage, the judgment against the eight kingdoms is affirmed but details are given only for Israel (and Judah). The sinful kingdom is to be destroyed from the face of the earth and the population scattered among the nations. The sinners (including all of those designated in different categories) will be executed, but a remnant will survive. In the new section, the nations now converted to the true religion will complete the judgment of God against the eight nations by eliminating the last of them, Edom (v 12), and then the way will be clear for the reestablishment of the Davidic imperium, depicted under the figure of a booth in the field (a military image). The order of events is not entirely clear, but it appears that the military action on the part of the nations occurs first and only then is the restoration and rebuilding of the Davidic realm undertaken. This development leads naturally to the final picture of supernatural prosperity and abundance in the land, with guarantees of everlasting security and peace (vv 13–15).

Closer examination of the text turns it the other way around, making it necessary to place the elimination of Edom after the refounding of the Davidic realm, so that once the latter is reestablished the campaign against Edom is a joint effort by all of the nations gathered under the banner of Yahweh, including united Israel and its many allies. (Among them presumably are the Cushites and no doubt many others.) The reason is that v 12 begins with *lĕmaʿan,* which clearly suggests either purpose or result, but in either case the dispossession of the Edomites would come after the rebuilding of "the booth of David" (v 11). It might be possible to go back to the clause *ʾnky mṣwh* in v 9 for a lead-in to the clause beginning with v 12, but the formula at the beginning of v 11 poses a significant barrier to crossing over for this link. It seems that the two actions proceed side by side, with the rebuilding of Israel progressing while the judgment against the nations is completed with the campaign against Edom.

We can set up the passage as follows:

> 9:11a   *bayyôm hahû>*
>   *>āqîm >et-sukkat dāwîd hannōpelet*
> 11b   *wĕgādartî >et-pirṣêhen*
>   *wahărīsōtāyw >āqîm*
>   *ûbĕnîtîhā kîmê <ôlām*

> 9:11a   On that day I will set up David's booth that has fallen,
> 11b   and I will repair their breaches,
>   and I will restore his ruins;
>   I will rebuild it as in the days of old—

We have here an envelope construction in which the outer ring forms the basic message. What ties the units together is the 3d f. s. suffix on *bnytyh*, which goes back to the noun *skt* in the first colon; the suffixes on the nouns in the middle two cola show that they have a different orientation (they also form a clear-cut chiastic structure) about the "booth of David." The internal ring, consisting of the second and third cola, has a slightly different focus, though that combination also contributes to the total picture. There are other ways to combine the verbs, but the essential framework and internal structure are unaffected. The primary emphasis is on the reconstruction and restoration of "the booth of David," which is to be raised up from a fallen state and rebuilt as in the days of old (note that *<wlm* here refers to the distant past, namely, the time of David).

As the expression *skt dwyd* is unique in the Bible, its exact reference may never be recovered, but the general sense probably can be. That it serves here as a symbol of the days of David seems clear, and that there is an emphasis on the bright side of that reign seems equally clear. For many biblical writers, including a number of prophets, the halcyon era of David (and Solomon) was not only the Golden Age past but a promise and pattern for the Golden Age future. It could stand for one or more of the buildings of the capital city that had symbolic importance: the Davidic tabernacle, or the royal palace, or something called "the tower of David" (Cant 4:4), which may have been different. It is more likely to be the tabernacle than the others because that is the one structure presumably erected by David for which we do not have a name. It is possible that the dynasty is meant, although this sense is not likely because the normal term for it (along with other meanings or entities) is *byt*, and Amos shows no aversion to its use in this sense (cf. *byt yr<bm*, "the house of Jeroboam," in 7:9).

There are also possible military connections, both in the word *sukkâ* and in the other terms mentioned in this verse: the *pĕrāṣîm* and the *hărīsôt*. The word *skh* is used in 2 Sam 11:11 to describe battlefield conditions, and the statement is made by Uriah that "the ark and Israel and Judah are dwelling in *booths,* while Joab and the servants of my lord are camping on the ground." The association of the ark with the armies of Israel and Judah is understandable because apparently the ark was still brought to the battlefield. The reference here to booths may make sense with regard to the ark, but hardly for Israel and Judah, and especially if Joab's army is in the field. Perhaps it refers to the main force and the reserves, but it remains doubtful, and probably a better proposal is to see them encamped at Sukkoth, a city and military base in Transjordan with a long history of occupation by and association with Israel. In any case, the reference here probably will not help us, for it is not likely that the passage in Amos 9:11 has in mind the restoration and rebuilding of Sukkoth, unless it is understood symbolically for the imperium of David (which seems rather farfetched). Besides, we take seriously the spelling and vocalization, which are different.

It may be more helpful to look at 1 Kgs 20:12, 16, where there is another reference to "booths." It is possible, however, that here too the reference is to Sukkoth, though the location is not specified. It may be that temporary structures like pavilions were put up for use by kings and military commanders, but the passages are sufficiently vague that we cannot be sure. Perhaps the military connection is no more than a possibility, but it is more likely than any association in Amos 9:11 with the place-name Sukkoth. Because the terminology has possible military associations and a military campaign is mentioned in v 12, it is equally possible that the *sukkat dāwîd* refers to David's military campaigns and implies a correlation between his series of victories throughout the same area that has been placed under divine judgment. The last stage in the new series of campaigns is the defeat and elimination of the remnant of Edom, thus allowing the full restoration of the Davidic kingdom. It is at least interesting and may be significant that in the description of David's campaigns in 2 Samuel 8, the list of conquests and subjugations begins with the Philistines (v 1) and ends with Edom (vv 13–14) just as we have in Amos 9:7b–12. There can be no doubt that the nations listed in Amos 9:7b–12 are scheduled for judgment and destruction. The order is the same in the two places, except for the omission of Moab in Amos 9; it is found in 2 Samuel 8:

	2 Sam 8		*Amos 9*	
1.	Philistines	(1)	Philistines	(7)
2.	Moabites	(2)		
3.	Aram	(3–8)	Aram	(7)
4.	Edomites	(13–14)	Edom	(12)

Compare these partial lists with the full list in Amos 1–2:

1. Aram (1:3–5)	5. Ammon (1:13–15)
2. Philistines (1:6–8)	6. Moab (2:1–3)
3. Tyre (1:9–10)	7. Judah (2:4–5)
4. Edom (1:11–12)	8. Israel (2:6–8)

We are told in 2 Sam 8:15 that "David reigned over all Israel and David administered justice and equity to all of his people." This statement reflects the ideal set forth by the prophet repeatedly in his book: as we have shown, the keywords used in this verse, *mišpāṭ ûṣĕdāqâ,* are central to Amos' thought. Apparently the restoration of such a realm as David ruled over with justice and righteousness is what the prophet had in mind. And the subjugation of Edom was the last of David's campaigns leading to the full establishment of justice and equity for all people in all of Israel. So here the same pattern is envisaged, with a brief reference to the last campaign. It does not make a great deal of difference whether the account in 2 Samuel 8 is historically accurate on this score, for it is more a matter of tradition, especially recorded tradition, than of fact. The order of submissions and payments is different in 2 Sam 8:12, where we have Edom first, followed by Moab, Ammon, Philistia, Amalek, and finally Zobah.

Coming back to Amos 9:11–12, we see here a picture of the revival of the Davidic kingdom, whose ruler would be a descendant of that king. The *sukkat dāwîd* would be a symbol of the realm and the rule just mentioned. Why would it be described as fallen and in need of raising and rebuilding? One obvious answer, given by most scholars, is that when this passage was written, there was no national entity called Israel or Judah, no Davidic dynasty, nothing. In other words, it is a postexilic prophecy. But this one has little or nothing in common with such prophecies, not least being the unique expression *skt dwyd.* In our view what had fallen was the empire, and that had happened a long time ago. The little country of Judah and the somewhat larger nation of Israel hardly constituted even together (and as often as not they were divided and at war with each other) much of a match for the ancient realm, so nostalgia for the great days of the united kingdom and the Golden Age of David and Solomon must have started early and increased steadily over the years. When we consider the numerous, often ill-advised efforts of kings both north and south, but especially in the south, to restore the ancient borders and reclaim the glory of the past, we must affirm that these were not just the daydreams of postexilic pseudepigraphers, but that kings and priests, prophets and people shared them during the years after the death of Solomon right down to the Exile and beyond. The *sukkat dāwîd* had fallen a long time before, and efforts to raise and rebuild it often failed, with disastrous results. After all, it was in the lifetime of the father of the current king of Judah, Uzziah, that he (Amaziah) had suffered a disastrous defeat at the hands of Jehoash, king of Israel (2 Kgs 14:8–14). So when Uzziah came to the throne (2 Kgs 14:21 and 15:1–7), the state of his kingdom could well have corresponded to the picture presented here in Amos 9—the kingdom of Judah had been crushed and the only resemblance to the mighty empire of David and Solomon was in the name of the country (Judah) and that its capital was the city of Jerusalem. Later on both contemporary kings, Jeroboam and Uzziah, would make valiant and successful efforts to build up their kingdoms, but at the time that we suppose Amos to have exercised his ministry little if anything had been achieved, and Judah especially was in a perilous state. It is not unlikely that the assassination of Amaziah resulted from his disastrous mismanagement of affairs of state, resulting in an unnecessary but catastrophic defeat. There is a gap of at least fifteen years between the one and the other event, but the shame of Amaziah's defeat; the loss of Jerusalem, which was seized; and his personal captivity could hardly have endeared him to his subjects. So the restoration of the days of old, the Davidic kingdom, was a lively theme for people and prophets alike long before the Exile and the end of the Davidic dynasty. What Jeroboam and Uzziah actually accomplished was not what the prophet had in mind, but it is likely that the oracles were all composed and delivered long before those developments occurred.

What seems clear is that the prophet has in view the raising and rebuilding of "the booth of David," which in some significant way is emblematic of the kingdom that he ruled; we have discussed briefly "their breaches" (probably in the walls) and "his ruins" (perhaps of the tower or citadel) as other emblematic features of the realm. Admittedly, the picture is one of ruin, but that view is accounted for by the repeated references to and descriptions of the devastation and destruction that are about to overtake all eight of the nations listed in chaps. 1–2 and in particular those which constituted or formed part of the realm of David. The renewing and rebuilding will begin before the end of the destructive phase, because the renewed kingdom will be involved with "all the nations" in the final campaign against Edom (v 12):

> *lĕma'an yîrĕšû 'et-šĕ'ērît 'ĕdôm*
> *wĕkol-haggôyīm 'ăšer-niqrā'šĕmî 'ălêhem.*

so that they may dispossess the remnant of Edom,
> even all the nations over whom my name was pronounced.

We interpret the passage to mean that the remnant of the Edomites will be dispossessed by a coalition of nations bearing the name of Yahweh. Thus we take the construct chain *kl-hgwym* ("all the nations") to be the subject of the verb *yyršw,* not some unnamed subject "they." The difficulty with this interpretation is the presence of the conjunction "and" (*wĕ*) before the chain. As a result it looks as if "all of the nations" are part of the object, as if we should translate, "That they will dispossess the remnant of Edom and all the nations who are called by my name" (cf. the RSV, which renders it thus). That reading makes for a strange alliance. There is no hint of the subject, though it would appear to be the people who are also the beneficiaries of the divine initiative in restoring "David's booth." To suppose, however, that the action against Edom will also be against "all the nations over whom my name was pronounced" does not make very good sense. Why should Yahweh or anyone else engaged in the restoration of a traditional Davidic realm at the same time embark on the dispossession of the remnant of "all peoples called by the name of Yahweh"? It is much easier to explain the *waw* before *kl* as epexegetic or emphatic and as marking the divisions in the sentence, though *kl-hgwym* remains the subject for the verb. As already indicated, the nations mentioned here are selected out of "all the nations" in v 9, among whom the survivors of "the house of Israel" will be exiled. The nations are those that are converted to the true faith and that will participate with the rebuilt Davidic kingdom in driving out or destroying (literally, *exterminare,* which originally meant to drive out of a certain territory, not to exterminate). In our judgment these nations include and are typified by the Cushites (v 7a), who are not named among the eight destined for destruction and who are expected to become a Yahwist people (cf. Isa 18:1–7, esp. v 7). They are the only nation listed, but they are simply an example, and no doubt the expression *kl-hgwym ʾšr-nqrʾ šmy ʿlyhm* is intended to include many others, perhaps (if we can follow the book of Isaiah once again) Egypt and Assyria (cf. Isa 19:23–24). With the final defeat of the Edomites the prophecy of chaps. 1–2 will have been fulfilled, the period of judgment will have ended, and the era of renewal or rebuilding, already begun (v 11), can now reach full maturity.

We have already discussed the closing formula at the end of v 12. It is the standard *nʾm yhwh* plus a qualifying phrase, *ʿśh zʾt,* which is a deviation from the norm, itself a frequent practice of the author/editor. It marks a major division in the Epilogue, just as the simple formula *nʾm yhwh* does at the division between v 7a and 7b and between vv 8 and 9. After this pause, the author will take us into the new age of renewal and restoration, of fulfillment, endless peace, and prosperity.

Part IV. The Epilogue of the Epilogue (9:13–15)

13aA *hinnēh yāmîm bāʾîm*
      nĕʾūm-yahweh

Indeed the time is at hand
—Oracle of Yahweh!—

Here we have the formal opening of the last unit of the last section, and it is set off by the standard formula, no doubt to give due weight and attention first to the time—the indefinite but eschatological future, when the final state of things will be established, after which no material changes will ever occur, certainly no calamitous or destructive events.

		Syllables	*Stresses*
13aB	*wĕniggaš hôrēš baqqōṣēr*	$3 + 2 + 3 = 8$	3
	wĕdōrēk ʿănābîm	$3 + 3 = 6$	2
	bĕmōšēk hazzāraʿ	$3 + 2 = 5$	2

when the plowman will overtake the reaper,
   and the treader of grapes
   the sower of seed.

The four participles define four different agricultural activities or four different roles for the Israelite farmer. Each of them not only describes an activity but also indicates the season, and the order can be established on the basis of experience both past and current. From the beginning to the end of the agricultural year we can list them as follows:

		Season
1.	Plowing (*ḥwrš*) (1)	Autumn
2.	Sowing (*mšk hzrʿ*) (4)	Winter
3.	Reaping (*qṣr*) (2)	Spring
4.	Treading (*drk ʿnbym*) (3)	Summer

We may ask why the author did not keep to the normal order but has juggled the components, thus producing some confusion. A number of factors have entered into the picture, which have complicated matters. Nevertheless, there is a logic in the procedure, and we will try to untangle the elements. But just a look at a relatively uncomplicated arrangement will be appropriate. In Gen 8:22 we read about the basic, standard sequence of the seasons, as ordained by Yahweh:

> 'ōd kol-yĕmê hā'āreṣ
> zera' wĕqāṣîr
> wĕqōr wāḥōm
> wĕqayiṣ wāḥōrep
> wĕyôm wālaylâ
> lō' yišbōtû

During all the days of the earth
    Seedtime and harvest
    and cold and heat
    and Summer and Fall
    and Day and Night
        shall not cease.

We note the seasons as follows:

1. *zera'* = winter
2. *qāṣîr* = spring
3. *qayiṣ* = summer
4. *ḥōrep* = autumn

The arrangement is clear, simple, and direct, though it does not follow the conventional calendars by beginning either in the autumn or in the spring. Two of the roots are the same as in Amos, but two are not. It is clear that this text provides no model for the more complex system adopted in Amos. In Amos 9:13 we must deal with the forms, the verbs, and the sequence. The general idea commonly perceived here is that the agricultural processes have been accelerated in order to produce more crops per year, hence greater abundance and prosperity. The following points should be noted.

1. The plowman is listed first, which is appropriate because the agricultural season properly starts with plowing, an exercise undertaken in the autumn, after the beginning of the civil year.

2. He is said to come close to or follow closely on the reaper, whose work is normally done in the spring. In effect, the time has been compressed because normally the land lies fallow during the summer months after the harvest and before the first rains in the autumn. But no particular activity with respect to the land has been omitted. Once the crop has been harvested, the next step is plowing to start the agricultural year. The only compression is time, for normally there is a gap between harvesting and plowing.

3. Turning to the next pair, we find the grape treader close on the heels of the seed sower. The grape treading is a summer activity following the harvest, while seed sowing is naturally done in winter after the plowing.

Associated with sowing is pruning (cf. the Gezer Calendar), and we assume that the activity symbolizes the season and includes other associated activities. What the writer is saying is that the treader of the grapes is following hard on the sower of the seed (or we might say the pruner of the vine). It is perfectly appropriate because the summer activity naturally follows that done the previous winter. The only unusual point is that there is a speedup of the season, with summer activity placed immediately after winter activity. But we have suggested all along that this propinquity is the chief feature of the new prosperity, the acceleration of the agricultural year, speeding up production by compressing the seasons. When we combine this statement with the next one, which describes the new abundance in equally hyperbolic terms, we can say that in the new age there will be double (or multiple) production in exactly half the time. Activities normally separated by half a year have been compressed into adjoining seasons, and the two six-month cycles represented here are compressed so that single seasons are adequate for the rapid transitions. Regarding the pairings and the order, we recognize that a pair of single-word items, ḥwrš and qṣr, is followed by two-word items, drk ʿnbym and mšk hzrʿ (cf. the list of warriors in Amos 2:14–16, where the three one-word classifications are followed by three two-word classifications, while the seventh and final one consists of three words). Then we note that in the agricultural cycle there is one normal sequence and one inversion: plowing properly begins the year, so it should not follow something but should be followed. Because in this arrangement what follows logically or chronologically is put first and what precedes is put second, and because the author wanted to begin with the proper first activity, he had to put a later activity (reaping) earlier, that is, borrowed from the previous year. The inversion is balanced by the normal sequence in the second. Within the normal agricultural year, grape picking and treading comes in the summer long after sowing (and pruning), properly a winter activity.

So the writer has managed to give a catalog of the agricultural year covering the four basic seasons and their corresponding activities. By juggling the routine or normal order he has also managed to accelerate the pace and give a picture of vigorous if not turbulent activity, reflecting the abundance of the new age, and without violating logic even though he substitutes his own instead of a more normal or regular procedure. The next passage, v 13b, complements and extends the preceding one:

	Syllables	Stresses
wehiṭṭîpû hehārîm ʿāsîs	$4 + 3 + 2 = 9$	3
wĕkol-haggĕbāʿôt titmôgagnâ	$2 + 4 + 4 = 10$	3

> the mountains will drip with sweet wine,
> and all the hills will flow with it.

This passage is a classic bicolon with verbal chiasm (i.e., the verbs are at
the ends and the noun subjects are in the middle). The placement of the
subject of the second verb *kl-hgbʿwt* before the verb is for the sake of the
chiasm, as otherwise we would expect it after the verb. We also have the
alternation of perfect and imperfect forms, though technically the use of
waw-conversive before the perfect form makes the sequence acceptable according to prose rules. But in poetic structures this device is independent of
the use of *waw* to affect the force of the verb. In addition, we note the
double-duty use of the particle *kl,* which for the sake of balance and symmetry should apply equally to "the mountains" as to "the hills." It is also
known as backward gapping, often considered either unacceptable, un-
demonstrable, or too rare to consider. There are, in fact, numerous cases,
many like this one, barely noticed and generally ignored. Strictly speaking,
ʿāsîs is the pressed-out juice of the grapes, hardly fermented at that stage.
The imagery here is hyperbolic, and there is an implied metaphor for abundance and wealth. The imagery is found elsewhere in the prophetic literature; compare a particularly close parallel near the end of Joel (4:18):

	Syllables	Stresses
wĕhāyâ bayyôm hahûʾ		
yiṭṭĕpû hehārîm ʿāsîs	$3 + 3 + 2 = 8$	3
wĕhaggĕbāʿôt tēlaknâ ḥālāb	$5 + 3 + 2 = 10$	3

> And it shall come to pass in that day:
> The mountains will drip with new wine,
> and the hills will run with milk.

This passage has the same chiasm, but the verbs and verb forms are different, and there is a second object in the second colon. The objects in both
cola seem to be indirect, but the assumed prepositions are omitted. We
should interpret Amos 9:13 in the same manner and see the *hipʿil* of *ntp* not
as causative but as intensive. In Amos the mountains send cascades of new
wine down their sides, while in Joel they drip; there is no direct dependence
either way, but both formulations stem from the same tradition, the tradition of the futurist visions. To introduce the passage in Amos one formula
is used (*hnh ymym bʾym*), while another one is used in Joel (*bywm hhwʾ*).
The latter also occurs in Amos, but the former (*hnh ymym bʾym*) does not
turn up in Joel.

What is especially intriguing about the usage in Joel is that these similar
statements come near the end of the respective books. Not far away, in

Joel 4:16, we have a bicolon that is identical with one in Amos, only in Amos it is the opening statement in the book (after the heading). Amos 1:2 and 9:13b correspond to Joel 4:16 and 18 so closely as to preclude some accidental or coincidental concurrence. Whatever it may show about the relationship of the books and about the editing and arranging of the Book of the Twelve Prophets, it seems to show that the opening and closing of the book of Amos are related. The further item, namely, that the next colon in Joel 4:16—wĕrā'ăšû šāmayim wā'āreṣ, "and heaven and earth will shake" —speaks of an earthquake or actually a cosmic shaking involving the whole universe, may urge us to look at the possible linkage between Amos 1:2 and 9:1–5, where the earthquake in the vision may correspond to Joel's vision. Any connection with Amos 1:1 would be speculative, although no doubt it was the earthquake in 1:1 that was regarded as the actualization of the vision in 9:1–4(5).

The *hipʿil* form *htypw* in Amos is unique when used in the physical sense of dripping dew or mist. The comparison with Joel 4:18 shows that it is intensive or elative in Amos 9:13. The other verb in Amos is similarly hyperbolic: the hills melt into a mighty cascade of new wine, somewhat more dramatic than Joel, though with the contrast between red wine and white milk, Joel's usage does not lack in color and imagination.

We now approach the last part of the last part, the epilogue of the epilogue of the Epilogue, 9:14–15, which is the final reversal of the fortunes of Israel and the coda of the book. All of the language is familiar, made familiar to us especially by Deuteronomy and Deuteronomic literature. It belongs to the book, but whether this or any other part of the Epilogue comes from the mouth or hand of Amos would be difficult if not impossible to prove and difficult to defend. The material can be organized in the following way:

> 14a   *wĕšabtî 'et-šĕbût ʿammî yiśrā'ēl*
>   *ûbānû ʿārîm nĕšammôt wĕyāšābû*
>   *wĕnāṭĕʿû kĕrāmîm wĕšātû 'et-yênām*
> 14b   *wĕʿāśû gannôt wĕ'ākĕlû 'et-pĕrîhem*

> 14a   Then I will restore the fortunes of Israel my people;
>   they shall build the ruined cities, and inhabit them;
>   they shall plant vineyards, and drink their wine;
> 14b   they shall cultivate gardens, and eat their fruit.

The restoration of Israel is couched in familiar terms. The language is traditional and has wide usage, so it can refer to a return from exile or a restoration of captives to their homeland or, more generally, as in Job 42, to a restoration of fortunes, a reversal of misfortunes. Here it probably has the wider, more general meaning, though the specific sense of return from captivity could hardly be excluded in view of Amos' expectations about the Exile, at least of the north and almost certainly also of the south. Here, however, the emphasis is certainly on the reversal of fortunes, for the opening words of v 14 make use of the same root (*šwb*), which appears so frequently in the opening chapters and the Great Set Speech (*P-'šybnw* repeated eight times, and with recurrences of the root elsewhere, as for example *wl'-šbtm* repeated five times in chap. 4, in response to the plagues). The story throughout that chapter is a tragedy of reversed decisions and missed opportunities: because Israel failed to repent in spite of all the chances given (cf. *lō'-šabtem 'āday;* 4:6, 8, 9, 10, 11), Yahweh reversed his repentance and made an irreversible decision (cf. *lō-'ăšîbennû*, 2:4, 6) to condemn and destroy his people. Now, at the end, the final reversal will take place, reversing all of the negatives of the past and restoring people and land together.

The opening words of v 14 and the equivalent expressions are found verbatim in Jer 30:3 and a number of times in both Jeremiah and Ezekiel. They are also used with other nations in the same prophets (e.g., Moab, Jer 48:47; Ammon, 49:2; Egypt, Ezek 29:14). The usage also occurs in Hosea, Joel, and Zephaniah. Curiously enough, although it is widely regarded as "Deuteronomic," it occurs only once in the Deuteronomic corpus, at Deut 30:3. The usual interpretation is that the expression is late and its usage is focused on the period of the exile, and that occurrences in the earlier prophets are secondary. We studied the question in connection with Hosea, and come here to a similar conclusion. About the affinities there is no question, but can literary dependence and its direction be established? We think not in either instance and suggest rather that the expression was a common one, or at least known, that it is not restricted to exilic or captivity contexts, and that the case remains unproved. Admittedly, the usage is concentrated in the exilic prophets, Jeremiah and Ezekiel; but is that the period in which it began? It is difficult to say.

Except for a missing prepositional phrase after *wyšbw*, which we might have expected (*wĕyašābû bāhen*) but which is hardly necessary, the passage flows smoothly. The second colon is reminiscent of other late passages, some of which are to be found in exilic and postexilic Isaiah: 58:12 and 61:4; cf. Ezek 36:36. But it is not exactly the same as any of them, and we do not think there is any direct borrowing (cf. Isa 54:3, where we have *'rym nšmwt;* also Ezek 36:35).

When it comes to the remaining clauses, these too are reminiscent of exilic writings, such as Jer 31:5, Ezek 28:26, and Isa 65:21. Typically Deuteronomic language is different, emphasizing either the opposite circumstances as part of a curse—Deut 28:30, 39 ("you will plant vineyards and not drink the wine," cf. Amos 5:11)—or the reverse of the curse—how the Israelites occupied cities they had not built and enjoyed the fruit of vineyards they had not planted (Deut 6:11 and Jer 24:13). Here the reversal of Amos 5:11 is notable: instead of being deprived of the fruits of their labor they will now enjoy them.

The last of these passages is less common, but there are parallels in Jer 29:5, 28; note, however, the reversal of Amos 4:11, where blight and pest have attacked and destroyed the gardens along with the vineyards and orchards. So we may say that while the whole passage evokes similar passages of renewal, restoration, and rebuilding, none are exactly the same, and much of the imagery derives from or is similar to treaty blessings or, in reverse, curses. While we may well think of the exilic period as the best context for such a passage, direct borrowing is not demonstrated or demonstrable, and the experience of exile or knowledge of its details did not begin with Judah in the sixth century or with Israel and Judah in the eighth. Briefly, if the prophet foresaw the great tragedy of destruction and exile described so vividly in the book, he would know what was required to reverse those circumstances and restore the country. None of what we read was beyond his scope or his capability. Comparison with the well-known future age of universal prosperity and peace found in Isa 2:2–4 (= Mic 4:1–3) would be appropriate.

The point could be made, to assist the view that Amos 9:14–15 is based on a vision, that Isa 2:2–4 (= Mic 4:1–3) is a contemporary (or near-contemporary) piece (there are always those who say it must be later *because* it is an eschatological vision, but opinions are more divided on this passage than on Amos 9:14–15). Isaiah 2:2–4, which explicitly uses the term "he had a vision," *ḥāzâ,* has the same melding of the realistic and the mythic that is derived from prime moments of the past (creation and the best aspects of Israel's early history). It also mingles nationalism with universalism. And, contrariwise, there is no awareness of a specifically Assyrian or Babylonian conquest, exile, or return. The cosmology is primal and mythic, derived from old creation stories, not the sophisticated otherworld cosmology of late apocalypses. In other words, these are good specimens of eighth-century eschatology, and there are other points of connection with Amos, such as the "house of Jacob," to which reference could be made.

In v 15 we have literary prose, even rhythmic and oratorical prose, but hardly poetry:

> 15a   *ûneṭaʿtîm ʿal-ʾadmātām*
> 15bA *wĕlōʾ yinnātĕšû ʿôd mēʿal ʾadmātām*
>   *ʾăšer nātattî lāhem*

> 15a   I will plant them upon their land,
> 15bA and they shall never be rooted out of the land
>   that I have given them.

The language here is more traditional. The theme of planting the people in their land goes all the way back to the Song of the Sea (Exod 15:17, where, however, the land is the original sacred territory around Mount Sinai) and is used elsewhere. It is quite frequent in Jeremiah (cf. 24:6, 32:41, 42:10, parallel to *ntš* as here; also Jer 1:10, 18:9, 31:28; Ezek 36:36). Again the theme is the same as in Amos but not the language. The parallel terms, *nṭˁ//lˀ ntš,* are also found in Jeremiah; in fact, they are used to characterize his ministry, in other words, to pluck up and tear down, also to plant and to build. Here Amos emphasizes the positive side and affirms the final reversal: they will never be plucked up from the land on which they will be planted once more; the land promised of old is now to be given once more in perpetuity. The repetition of *ˀdmtm* is clearly for emphasis, and the relative clause *ˀšr ntty lhm* evokes the classic statement of Yahweh's initial intervention on their behalf, 2:9–10. Now everything will be restored and fulfilled as originally intended.

The book of Amos ends with 9:15bB:

> *ˀamar yhwh ˀĕloheykā*
> Yahweh your God has spoken!

The presence of the second-person suffix (*ˀlhyk*) carries us back to v 7a, the last place the second person was used. There has been a shift from plural (for *bny yśrˀl*) to singular (for *ˁmy yśrˀl* perhaps, though it need not be the actual antecedent). The other two instances of *ˀlhyk* in Amos do not seem to be of much help in identifying the pronominal suffix here—8:14, where the addressee is not identified; and 4:12, where it is Israel, the northern kingdom.

INDEX

INDEX OF AUTHORS

INDEX OF WORDS

INDEX OF SCRIPTURAL
REFERENCES

2 Samuel

1 Kings

Job